DEATH & DYING, LIFE & LIVING

eighth edition

Charles A. Corr   Donna M. Corr   Kenneth J. Doka

CENGAGE

Australia • Brazil • Mexico • Singapore • United Kingdom • United States

CENGAGE

Death & Dying, Life & Living,
Eighth Edition
Charles A. Corr, Donna M. Corr,
Kenneth J. Doka

Product Director: Marta Lee-Perriard

Product Manager: Nedah Rose

Project Manager: Seth Schwartz

Content Developer: Kassi Radomski, LD

Marketing Manager: Heather
Thompson

Digital Content Specialist: Jackie
Hermesmeyer

Digital Project Manager/Media
Producer: Jayne Stein

Manufacturing Planner: Karen Hunt

Intellectual Property Analyst: Deanna
Ettinger

Intellectual Property Project Manager:
Betsy Hathaway

Sr. Art Director: Vernon Boes

Cover Image Credit: Courtesy of Clyde
M. Nabe

Art and Cover Direction, Production
Management, and Composition:
Lumina Datamatics, Inc.

For product information and technology assistance, contact us at
Cengage Customer & Sales Support, 1-800-354-9706.

For permission to use material from this text or product,
submit all requests online at **www.cengage.com/permissions**.
Further permissions questions can be e-mailed to
permissionrequest@cengage.com.

Library of Congress Control Number: 2017948769

ISBN: 978-1-337-56389-5

Cengage
20 Channel Center Street
Boston, MA 02210
USA

Cengage is a leading provider of customized learning solutions with employees residing in nearly 40 different countries and sales in more than 125 countries around the world. Find your local representative at **www.cengage.com**.

Cengage products are represented in Canada by Nelson Education, Ltd.

To learn more about Cengage platforms and services, visit **www.cengage.com**. To register or access your online learning solution or purchase materials for your course, visit **www.cengagebrain.com**.

Printed in the United States of America
Print Number: 01   Print Year: 2017

We dedicate this eighth edition of *Death & Dying, Life & Living* to our colleagues in the Association for Death Education and Counseling and in the International Work Group on Death, Dying, and Bereavement, as a small token of our thanks for the insights and support they have shared with us over many years

The days of our lives, for all of us, are numbered. We know that. And yes, there are certainly times when we aren't able to muster as much strength and patience as we would like. It's called being human. But I have found that in the simple act of living with hope, and in the daily effort to have a positive impact in the world, the days I do have are made all the more meaningful and precious. And for that I am grateful.

—Elizabeth Edwards (1949–2010)

Death is no enemy of life; it restores our sense of the value of living. Illness restores the sense of proportion that is lost when we take life for granted. To learn about value and proportion, we need to honor illness, and ultimately to honor death.

—A. W. Frank, *At the Will of the Body* (1991, p. 120)

Kenneth J. Doka   Donna M. Corr   Charles A. Corr

Courtesy of Susan Marie Ramsey

CHARLES A. CORR, PhD, is a long-time member of the Association for Death Education and Counseling (ADEC; Board of Directors, 1980–1983), the National Hospice and Palliative Care Organization (NHPCO), and the International Work Group on Death, Dying, and Bereavement (IWG; Chairperson, 1989–1993). Currently, he is Senior Editor of a quarterly e-journal for NHPCO's Children's Project on Palliative/Hospice Services (ChiPPS). His publications include 35 books and booklets, such as *Helping Children Cope with Death: Guidelines and Resources* (1982; 2nd ed., 1984), *Childhood and Death* (1984), *Adolescence and Death* (1986), *Handbook of Adolescent Death and Bereavement* (1996), *Adolescent Encounters with Death, Bereavement, and Coping* (2009), and *Children's Encounters with Death, Bereavement, and Coping* (2010), as well as 5 books coedited with Donna Corr and 135 book chapters and articles in professional journals. Dr. Corr has received awards from ADEC, Children's Hospice International (CHI), the Center for Death Education and Bioethics at the University of Wisconsin–La Crosse, the Musculoskeletal Transplant Foundation, and Southern Illinois University Edwardsville. In 2016, he received IWG's Herman Feifel Award for Outstanding Achievement in Thanatology.

DONNA M. CORR, RN, MS in Nursing, has experience in open heart, kidney transplant, oncology, and hospice nursing. For 17 years, she was a faculty member (rising from Instructor to Professor) in the Nursing Faculty of St. Louis Community College at Forest Park in Missouri, and then a Lecturer for two semesters at Southern Illinois University Edwardsville. Her publications include five books coedited with Charles Corr: *Hospice Care: Principles and Practice* (1983), *Hospice Approaches to Pediatric Care* (1985), *Nursing Care in an Aging Society* (1990), *Sudden Infant Death Syndrome: Who Can Help and How* (1991), and *Handbook of Childhood Death and Bereavement* (1996), as well as two dozen book chapters and articles in professional journals. Books edited by Donna and/or Charles Corr have received five Book of the Year Awards from the *American Journal of Nursing*.

KENNETH J. DOKA, PhD, FT, is a Professor of Counseling at the Graduate School of The College of New Rochelle, an ordained Lutheran minister, a licensed mental health counselor, and Senior Consultant to The Hospice Foundation of America, for whom he hosts annual teleconferences and edits the monthly *Journeys: A Newsletter to Help in Bereavement*. Dr. Doka introduced the groundbreaking concepts of *disenfranchised grief* and *adaptive grieving styles*. His publications include over 100 chapters and articles in professional journals, as well as 35 books, the most recent of which are *Disenfranchised Grief: New Directions, Challenges, and Strategies for Practice* (2002), *Counseling Individuals with Life-Threatening Illness* (2009), *Grieving beyond Gender: Understanding the Ways Men and Women Mourn* (2010), and *Grief Is a Journey* (2016). A long-time member of both ADEC (President, 1993–1994) and IWG (Chairperson, 1997–1999), Dr. Doka is editor of *Omega, Journal of Death and Dying*, one of the major professional journals in this field. His awards include a *Special Contributions to the Field Award* from ADEC and he was the recipient of the *Distinguished Alumni Award* from his alma mater, Concordia College. Additional awards came from the Scott and White Medical System, the Billy Esposito Foundation, and the Center for Death Education and Bioethics at the University of Wisconsin-LaCrosse.

Brief Contents

Contents

3   Changing Attitudes toward Death   45

4   Death-Related Practices and the American Death System   65

10   Coping with Loss and Grief: How Individuals Can Help   256

11   Coping with Loss and Grief: Funeral Practices and Other Ways Communities Can Help   283

PART FIVE **Developmental Perspectives 319**

12 Children 322

18   Aided Death: Assisted Suicide, Euthanasia, and Aid in Dying   514

Preface

In his allegory, "The Horse on the Dining-Room Table" (our Prologue in this book), Richard Kalish wrote that we cannot magically make death disappear from our lives nor can we erase completely the anxiety and other forms of distress often associated with death-related issues. However, we can talk about encounters and attitudes, share insights and practices, learn from each other, and strive together to cope more effectively with dying, death, and bereavement. It is in that spirit that we offer the eighth edition of *Death & Dying, Life & Living* as a new contribution to ongoing conversations about dying, death, and bereavement. Our hope is that constructive interactions related to these subjects will help all of us lead richer and more productive lives. We are particularly pleased that Professor Kenneth J. Doka, one of the best known and most productive workers in this field, has agreed to join us as coauthor of this new edition and as a contributor to the discussions undertaken here.

It has sometimes been suggested that there really is nothing new to teach about in this field. In fact, in the interval since the seventh edition of this book was published, new encounters with death have occurred, new issues have come to the fore, new insights and attitudes have emerged, and much that is of enduring value has evolved and matured. We have worked diligently to incorporate these and other death-related developments as will be seen in the text itself and in the section of this Preface that identifies new materials in this eighth edition.

FEATURES

This book can be used as a primary textbook for undergraduate and graduate courses in death, dying, and bereavement; as a supplementary text in related courses; and as a general resource in this field. Individual instructors and other readers can easily adapt the contents of this book to their own needs and preferences. In particular, different Parts of the book can be studied in any order, and most chapters within a specific Part can be read on their own. On this book's Instructor Resource Center, instructors can download the following supplementary materials to support teaching and learning:

- Instructor's Manual, which provides suggestions about how to use this book, educational resources (from organizations, printed materials, guest speakers, and audiovisuals), and detailed guides with extensive activities for each chapter.
- Test bank questions, including LMS-ready versions, for each chapter.
- A complete and updated set of PowerPoint lecture slides

For any or all of these materials, instructors can go to **login.cengage.com** to create an account and log in to it, or contact their local Cengage sales representative.

Each of the seven Parts in this book opens with a short introduction, and every chapter begins with a bulleted list of Objectives and a representative vignette or case study. Each chapter closes with a brief Summary, a Glossary, some Questions for Review and Discussion, a list of Suggested Readings, and Selected Web Resources, which include some useful search terms along with organizational and Internet sites. In addition to the text, three Appendices identify and provide annotated descriptions of books on death-related topics for children and adolescents.

The following features distinguish our work in this book:

1. A careful exploration of the main features of *death-related experiences* in our society examined in terms of *changing encounters with death*, *changing attitudes toward death*, and *changing practices associated with death* within the *American death system*

2. An emphasis on *coping with death-related experiences*—instead of merely reporting how individuals *react* to death-related encounters, we highlight *responses* that individuals make in the form of *efforts to manage* those encounters and to integrate their implications into ongoing living

3. The use of a *task-based approach* to explain coping—by individuals and by communities—with life-threatening illness and dying, with loss and grief, with funeral and memorial rituals, and as bereaved children, adolescents, or adults of different ages

4. Sensitivity to a *developmental perspective,* which considers death-related issues in ways that emphasize experiences of individuals within four different eras in the human life course: as children; as adolescents; as young and middle-aged adults; and as older adults

5. An emphasis on *cultural patterns within American society* that recognizes distinctive modes of death-related encounters, attitudes, and practices typically found in Americans of Hispanic, African, Asian or Pacific Island, and American-Indian or Alaskan Native backgrounds, as well as *other examples of diversity in our society*

6. A practical orientation that highlights *helping with death-related experiences*—helping others; helping oneself; and helping through families, social groups, institutions, and communities

7. An appreciation of *moral, ethical, legal, religious, and spiritual values* not only in debates about controversial issues such as aided death or in accounts of organ and tissue donation, but also throughout the book as an essential framework for such topics as care of the dying, support for the bereaved, and helping children and adolescents

8. Recognition of *important lessons about life and living*—lessons about limitation and control, individuality and community, vulnerability and resilience, and quality in living and the search for meaning—that can be learned from the study of death, dying, and bereavement

NEW TO THIS EDITION

Several instructors who have used this book as a basis for classroom or distance learning courses have asked us not to change its fundamental structure. We have accepted that advice and have retained the basic organizational structure and substance of the book for this edition. However, as appropriate, we have thoroughly revised the internal contents of the text. For example, in Chapter 1 there is a new vignette on the Death Cafe movement, an expanded account of the endings of the Little Red Riding Hood story, and an example of a personal death-related encounter involving one of the coauthors of this book.

In Part Two, Chapter 2 offers new information on how lifestyle factors impact encounters with death and an updated comparison of mortality data between the United States and Canada, noting how death-related encounters differ in significant ways between these two countries and asking why those differences appear to be generally more favorable to Canadians. Chapter 3 includes a new section on Terror Management Theory, Chapter 4 adds information on the Ebola epidemic in West Africa and new examples of mass murders in the United States, and Chapter 5 sharpens our efforts to challenge ethnocentrism, avoid cultural and racial stereotyping, and appreciate the value of cultural conscientiousness in understanding and helping others

Concerning coping with dying in Part Three, Chapters 6–8 add information on the primary regrets of the dying; a new box on active listening techniques; reflections on differences between being a pastor and a chaplain (with implications for all who seek to help dying persons); and additional research studies evaluating hospice care. As well, the section on pediatric palliative and hospice care is significantly rewritten, and the World Health Organization's definition of palliative care is added.

In Part Four, the structure of Chapter 9 is completely revised to reflect Doka's schema of new understandings of bereavement, grief, and mourning. In addition, there are new sections on attachments, absent grief, and Catherine Sanders' theory of six phases in mourning, plus new comments on the DSM-5 in the section on complicated grief reactions. In Chapter 11, a new figure graphically illustrates roles of digital and social media in coping with loss and achieving digital immortality.

In Part Five, we devote four full chapters to developmental perspectives, more than any other comparable book in our field. Here, Chapters 12–15 are enriched with new statistical data and supported by three Appendices that identify and briefly describe an updated selection of books on death-related topics for young readers. We believe these Appendices are the most thorough and helpful sources of information about death-related literature for young readers available from any textbook (and perhaps from any other book-length source) in our field. Further, Chapter 12 adds information on The Conversation Project, while Chapter 13 includes an updated account of adolescent involvements in the digital universe, a new description of an adolescent girl's bereavement after the death of her father, and a report on the death of an adolescent who was "skitching."

In Part Six, Chapter 16 now includes a new section on conversations about death-related matters, new information about Physician Orders for Life-Sustaining Treatment (POLST), and revised data on recent numbers of transplant candidates, organ transplants, and organ donors (both living and deceased). Chapter 17 adds new information on firearm laws and suicide, while Chapter 18 is reframed to focus on aided death, a new perspective that permits a better account of aid in dying, new information on the Death with Dignity Act in Oregon, and reports on aided death developments elsewhere in the United States and in other countries. A section in Chapter 19 sharpens our account of violence and security.

In Part Seven, Chapter 20 stands alone to clarify that its goal is to use one specific disease context to illustrate the basic themes and underlying structural features of this book. To that end, the descriptions of Alzheimer's disease and related disorders are refined to incorporate new data on encounters with these diseases, their staging, and the dying trajectories and deaths that follow from them. There also are a new section on communicating diagnoses and new examples from the lives and deaths of Robin Williams and Glen Campbell.

Attention to the digital universe appears throughout this new edition, but especially among the Questions for Review and Discussion at the end of each chapter, where Selected Web Resources and greatly updated and expanded Suggested Readings can also be found.

Throughout this eighth edition we report the most recent statistical data currently available from the National Center for Health Statistics (NCHS) and other sources. This includes final data for 2014 on numbers of deaths, death rates, and causes of death for the population as a whole in Chapter 2; for four selected cultural and racial subgroups in Chapter 5; for children, adolescents, young and middle-aged adults, and older adults in Chapters 12–15; and for Alzheimer's disease and related disorders in Chapter 20. We also provide the most recent NCHS data available on average life expectancy and place of death in Chapter 2, as well as on accidental deaths and homicide in Chapter 4. In addition, in Chapter 2 we include a newly updated figure on cancer-related deaths from the American Cancer Society.

Beyond that, we draw on the most recent data available from the U.S. Census Bureau concerning selected cultural and racial groups in Chapter 5, and concerning hospitals, long-term care facilities, and home health care programs in Chapter 8. Chapter 8 also reports the most recent data available on hospice programs from the National Hospice and Palliative Care Organization—including the striking fact that hospice programs cared for more than 1.6 million Americans in 2014. Chapters 8 and 12 also describe recent developments in pediatric palliative/hospice care.

Further, we provide recent data from: the Centers for Disease Control and Prevention in Chapter 2 concerning HIV and AIDS in the United States; UNAIDS concerning experiences with HIV and AIDS around the world; Statistics Canada concerning mortality data in Canada; the American Association of Suicidology in Chapters 13 (concerning adolescents), 15 (concerning older adults), and 17 (concerning the American population as a whole); the United Network for Organ Sharing in Chapter 16 concerning organ and tissue donation and transplantation; the Oregon Department of Human Services in Chapter 18 on aided death under the Oregon Death with Dignity Act; and the Alzheimer's Association in Chapter 20.

Among many other distinctive features in this eighth edition of *Death & Dying, Life & Living* there are new or significantly revised boxes, figures, tables, photos, and drawings, plus approximately 600 new references in a total of nearly 2,600 entries. Once again, most boxes have been divided into two primary types: "PERSONAL INSIGHTS" that report significant perspectives from individuals and "FOCUS ON" pieces that explore a specific subject or set of resources. Other boxes, in a distinctive format, appear as "ISSUES FOR CRITICAL REFLECTION," designed to stimulate discussion on 17 critical topics. We have also again worked diligently to simplify and clarify the text of this eighth edition, to make its tone even more personal, and to update its factual base.

ACKNOWLEDGMENTS

We are grateful to all who shared personal and/or professional life experiences with us, including our students and colleagues, thereby teaching us many of the important lessons about death, dying, and bereavement that are described in this book. We thank all who helped in the preparation of this eighth edition, in particular those who are credited in the text for the boxes, photos, and images that they helped us obtain and that are such important features of this book. Professors Mary Alice Varga of West Georgia University and Carla Sofka of Sienna College offered important guidance about the digital universe.

We are indebted to all of the many reviewers who helped us on previous editions of this book. For this new edition, we owe a particular debt of gratitude to seven experienced classroom instructors who took part anonymously in early review processes. It is extremely helpful to receive insightful and constructive comments from knowledgeable educators who teach courses in this field in a variety of institutions and contexts. We greatly appreciate their willingness to share insights and ideas to help strengthen this new edition. At our publisher, we appreciate the help and guidance we have received from Kassi Radomski, Nedah Rose, and their colleagues.

Although we have worked diligently to provide accurate, up-to-date knowledge about death, dying, and bereavement, neither we nor anyone else could claim to have completely covered every aspect of this extraordinarily broad field of study. For that reason, we encourage readers to pursue additional opportunities available to them for further study and research on these subjects. We welcome comments and suggestions for improvements that might be made in this book, because we know that imperfections are inevitable in as large and sweeping an enterprise as this project and in a field that changes rapidly and has many ramifications. Such comments or suggestions—along with outlines or syllabi for courses in which this book has been used, as well as references and other supplementary materials—can be sent to us by e-mail at **ccorr32@tampabay.rr.com**.

Charles A. Corr
Donna M. Corr
Kenneth J. Doka

Prologue

The Horse on the Dining-Room Table

by Richard A. Kalish

I struggled up the slope of Mount Evmandu to meet the famous guru of Nepsim, an ancient sage whose name I was forbidden to place in print. I was much younger then, but the long and arduous hike exhausted me, and, despite the cold, I was perspiring heavily when I reached the plateau where he made his home. He viewed me with a patient, almost amused, look, and I smiled wanly at him between attempts to gulp the thin air into my lungs. I made my way across the remaining hundred meters and slowly sat down on the ground—propping myself up against a large rock just outside his abode. We were both silent for several minutes, and I felt the tension in me rise, then subside until I was calm. Perspiration prickled my skin, but the slight breeze was pleasantly cool, and soon I was relaxed. Finally I turned my head to look directly into the clear brown eyes, which were bright within his lined face. I realized that I would need to speak.

"Father," I said, "I need to understand something about what it means to die, before I can continue my studies." He continued to gaze at me with his open, bemused expression. "Father," I went on, "I want to know what a dying person feels when no one will speak with him, nor be open enough to permit him to speak, about his dying."

He was silent for three, perhaps four, minutes. I felt at peace because I knew he would answer. Finally, as though in the middle of a sentence, he said, "It is the horse on the dining-room table." We continued to gaze at each other for several minutes. I began to feel sleepy after my long journey, and I must have dozed off. When I woke up, he was gone, and the only activity was my own breathing.

I retraced my steps down the mountain—still feeling calm, knowing that his answer made me feel good, but not knowing why. I returned to my studies and gave no further thought to the event, not wishing to dwell upon it, yet secure that someday I should understand.

Many years later I was invited to the home of a casual friend for dinner. It was a modest house in a typical California development. The eight or ten other guests, people I did not know well, and I sat in the living room—drinking Safeway Scotch and bourbon and dipping celery sticks and raw cauliflower into a watery cheese dip. The conversation, initially halting, became more animated as we got to know each other and developed points of contact. The drinks undoubtedly also affected us.

Eventually the hostess appeared and invited us into the dining room for a buffet dinner. As I entered the room, I noticed with astonishment that a brown horse was sitting quietly on the dining-room table. Although it was small for a horse, it filled

much of the large table. I caught my breath, but did[...]
one to enter, so I was able to turn to watch the other[...]
I did—they entered, saw the horse, gasped or stared[...]

The host was the last to enter. He let out a sil[...]
the horse to each of his guests with a wild stare. H[...]
Then in a voice choked with confusion he invited u[...]
His wife, equally disconcerted by what was clearly an unexpec[...]
the name cards, which indicated where each of us was to sit.

The hostess led me to the buffet and handed me a plate. Others lined up behind
me—each of us quiet. I filled my plate with rice and chicken and sat in my place. The
others followed suit.

It was cramped, sitting there, trying to avoid getting too close to the horse,
while pretending that no horse was there. My dish overlapped the edge of the table.
Others found other ways to avoid physical contact with the horse. The host and
hostess seemed as ill at ease as the rest of us. The conversation lagged. Every once in
a while, someone would say something in an attempt to revive the earlier pleasant
and innocuous discussion, but the overwhelming presence of the horse so filled our
thoughts that talk of taxes or politics or the lack of rain seemed inconsequential.

Dinner ended, and the hostess brought coffee. I can recall everything on my plate
and yet have no memory of having eaten. We drank in silence—all of us trying not to
look at the horse, yet unable to keep our eyes or thoughts anywhere else.

I thought several times of saying, "Hey, there's a horse on the dining-room
table." But I hardly knew the host, and I didn't wish to embarrass him by mentioning
something that obviously discomforted him at least as much as it discomforted me.
After all, it was his house. And what do you say to a man with a horse on his dining-
room table? I could have said that I did not mind, but that was not true—its presence
upset me so much that I enjoyed neither the dinner nor the company. I could have
said that I knew how difficult it was to have a horse on one's dining-room table, but
that wasn't true either; I had no idea. I could have said something like, "How do you
feel about having a horse on your dining-room table?", but I didn't want to sound
like a psychologist. Perhaps, I thought, if I ignore it, it will go away. Of course I knew
that it wouldn't. It didn't.

I later learned that the host and hostess were hoping the dinner would be a success
in spite of the horse. They felt that to mention it would make us so uncomfortable
that we wouldn't enjoy our visit—of course we didn't enjoy the evening anyway.
They were fearful that we would try to offer them sympathy, which they didn't want,
or understanding, which they needed but could not accept. They wanted the party to
be a success, so they decided to try to make the evening as enjoyable as possible. But
it was apparent that they—like their guests—could think of little else than the horse.

I excused myself shortly after dinner and went home. The evening had been
terrible. I never wanted to see the host and hostess again, although I was eager to
seek out the other guests and learn what they felt about the occasion. I felt confused
about what had happened and extremely tense. The evening had been grotesque. I
was careful to avoid the host and hostess after that, and I did my best to stay away
altogether from the neighborhood.

Recently I visited Nepsim again. I decided to seek out the guru once more. He
was still alive, although nearing death, and he would speak only to a few. I repeated
my journey and eventually found myself sitting across from him.

Once again I asked, "Father, I want to know what a dying person feels when no one will speak with him, nor be open enough to permit him to speak, about his dying."

The old man was quiet, and we sat without speaking for nearly an hour. Since he did not bid me leave, I remained. Although I was content, I feared he would not share his wisdom, but he finally spoke. The words came slowly.

"My son, it is the horse on the dining-room table. It is a horse that visits every house and sits on every dining-room table—the tables of the rich and of the poor, of the simple and of the wise. This horse just sits there, but its presence makes you wish to leave without speaking of it. If you leave, you will always fear the presence of the horse. When it sits on your table, you will wish to speak of it, but you may not be able to.

"However, if you speak about the horse, then you will find that others can also speak about the horse—most others, at least, if you are gentle and kind as you speak. The horse will remain on the dining-room table, but you will not be so distraught. You will enjoy your repast, and you will enjoy the company of the host and hostess. Or, if it is your table, you will enjoy the presence of your guests. You cannot make magic to have the horse disappear, but you can speak of the horse and thereby render it less powerful."

The old man then rose and, motioning me to follow, walked slowly to his hut. "Now we shall eat," he said quietly. I entered the hut and had difficulty adjusting to the dark. The guru walked to a cupboard in the corner and took out some bread and some cheese, which he placed on a mat. He motioned to me to sit and share his food. I saw a small horse sitting quietly in the center of the mat. He noticed this and said, "That horse need not disturb us." I thoroughly enjoyed the meal. Our discussion lasted far into the night, while the horse sat there quietly throughout our time together.

PART One

LEARNING ABOUT DEATH, DYING, AND BEREAVEMENT

Life and death are two aspects of the same reality. To see this fact represented in graphic form, look at the image on page 2 of this book. You can decipher its meaning by rotating the image one-quarter turn clockwise and then one-quarter turn counterclockwise from its original position. Clearly, one could not properly understand one aspect of this image ("life") without also grasping something about its second aspect ("death"). In other words, we believe that learning about death, dying, and bereavement is an important way of learning about life and living. Just as every human being is inevitably involved in learning about life and living, we suggest that each person is also engaged in a process of learning about death, dying, and bereavement. In this book, we pursue that process in a deliberate and explicit way.

Our Prologue, Richard Kalish's allegory, "The Horse on the Dining-Room Table," teaches us that it is desirable to talk about death together, to share insights and attitudes, to try to learn from each other, and to strive to cope more effectively in the face of death (see Corr, 2015d). But how do we begin?

One good place to start is with some preliminary remarks about education in the field of death, dying, and bereavement. Thus, in Chapter 1 we examine some concerns that lead people to study death-related subjects, how this type of education is conducted, its four principal dimensions, its six central goals, and some things we can learn about life and living by engaging in these studies. These introductory remarks are a kind of warm-up for the main event that follows in the remainder of this book. Some readers might prefer to bypass this warm-up by jumping directly to the central work of this book and returning later to Chapter 1. Others will benefit from these preparatory comments about certain aspects of the project ahead.

Education about Death, Dying, and Bereavement

Objectives of this **Chapter**

▶ To explore the *nature* and *role* of education about death, dying, and bereavement (often called "*death education*")

▶ To examine *concerns* that lead people to discuss and study death-related subjects

▶ To look briefly at *how education about death, dying, and bereavement is conducted*

▶ To describe *four dimensions* of education *about death, dying, and bereavement*

▶ To identify *six main goals* of education *about death, dying, and bereavement*

▶ To indicate *lessons we can learn about four central themes in life and living* by studying death, dying, and bereavement

Death and life: two dimensions of the same reality. To interpret the meaning of this drawing, rotate the image one-quarter turn clockwise, then one-quarter turn counterclockwise from its original position.

DEATH CAFE

The phrase **Death Cafe** identifies both a movement and the individual gatherings that occur as part of that movement. The movement began in Switzerland when Bernard Crettaz held his first Café Mortel on March 23, 2004. Later, a review of a book by Crettaz (2010) led a British web designer, Jon Underwood, to host a Death Cafe gathering at his home in London in September, 2011 and to establish a website for the movement. The website stipulates that Death Cafe events are always offered on a not-for-profit basis; in an accessible, respectful, and confidential space; with no intention of leading people to any conclusion, product, or course of action; and alongside refreshing drinks and nourishing food. The overall objective of Death Cafe gatherings is "to increase awareness of death with a view to helping people make the most of their (finite) lives."

The Death Cafe movement was brought to the United States by Lizzy Miles and Maria Johnson, who hosted the first gathering in a suburb of Columbus, Ohio, on July 19, 2012. Their promotion for this gathering described it as "a pop-up event where people get together to talk about death and have tea and delicious cake" (Miles, 2013). The phrase "pop-up event" indicated that this was to be a gathering, not a physical space like a restaurant, and signified that these events are not planned or scheduled on a regular basis. The word "people" suggested that attendees may come with friends or be unknown to each other before joining the gathering. Mention of "tea and delicious cake" signified that these events are warm and inviting, with no preset agenda.

According to the website, as of August 3, 2017, there have been 4954 Death Cafe gatherings in 51 countries around the world. Death Cafe gatherings are not intended to be grief support groups, lecture or educational sessions, or avenues for promoting a business or cause. Both hosts and other attendees have typically commented that the gatherings are "safe" and "interesting" forums in which people can talk about whatever is on their minds related to death, dying, and bereavement. Karen Van Dyke, who hosts Death Cafe gatherings in San Diego, has been quoted as saying, "When you talk about sex you don't get pregnant, when you talk about death you do not die" (Accomando & McVicker, 2014).

People choose to take part in Death Cafe gatherings for many different reasons, but it is worth noting that the Death Cafe movement and its gatherings have arisen spontaneously, appear to be meeting a felt need, and demonstrate that at least some people in our society and elsewhere are willing and able to talk openly about death-related subjects (Miles & Corr, 2017). (Note: What seems to be a more directive approach is offered by Death Over Dinner.)

A TABOO TOPIC? A DEATH-DENYING SOCIETY?

In times past, it was often said that death was a *taboo topic* in American society, a subject that was somehow not acceptable for scholarly research, education, or public discussion (Feifel, 1963a, 1963b). If that was true, it was as if death needed to be quarantined in order not to infect the way in which people wished to think about and live out their lives. That has led some people to claim, even today, that ours is a "death-denying society." But although some people do not want to talk about death-related subjects and may comment that a course on death and dying must be depressing or "morbid," how can it be claimed that there is complete denial here? After all, isn't there evidence to the contrary in the very existence of multiple courses across North America on various aspects of death, dying, and bereavement, the reality of this book you are reading, and the people who take part in Death Cafe gatherings? (Since you are reading a book about death, dying, and bereavement, and discussing education in this field, these topics must no longer seem to you to be taboo or forbidden. If so, see Issues for Critical Reflection #1).

Many years ago, Dumont and Foss (1972) analyzed conflicting claims about acceptance and denial of death. They concluded that: (1) "[A]vailable evidence strongly suggests that it is quite untenable to assume that there exists *an* 'American' attitude toward death" (p. 85) and (2) "[T]here is substantial evidence to indicate that the culture of the United States and the individuals in this society *both* accept *and* deny death, simultaneously" (p. 95). Earlier, Talcott Parsons (1963), an American sociologist, suggested Americans have an active orientation toward death. Parsons meant that Americans value efforts to control death by strongly trying to regulate to prevent accidental ("unnecessary") and "out of order" deaths (such as that of a child), minimizing pain in dying, and curtailing the toll of death by preparing the bodies of the deceased at funerals so they look as life-like as possible. Parsons felt that Americans choose to avoid aspects of death that cannot be controlled.

The argument for acknowledging the role of death in our society has been supported over many years by pioneers like Herman Feifel (1959, 1977a), Cicely Saunders (1967), and Elisabeth Kübler-Ross (1969), who encouraged behavioral scientists, clinicians, and humanists to pay attention to death-related topics. As a

---

ISSUES FOR CRITICAL REFLECTION
#1 Teaching about Death, Dying, and Bereavement

Before you read the rest of this chapter, you might ask yourself what you would do if you were asked to take part in teaching about these subjects. How would you respond to questions like the following?

- **Who** should be taught about these subjects? Children, adolescents, adults of various ages?
- **Who** should be involved along with you in teaching about these subjects? Individuals who have had death-related experiences, persons who are formally trained or certified in these subjects, parents or religious leaders, anyone at all?
- **What** topics should be part of this teaching program? Loss and grief, life-threatening illnesses and dying, suicide, aided death, how to cope effectively with death-related challenges, and views about life, death, and the possibility of an afterlife?

- **Where** should this teaching take place? In the home, in religious institutions, in public or private schools, in colleges or universities, in programs of professional education?
- **When** should this teaching be offered? Before people are forced to confront a death-related encounter? After a public tragedy, such as a suicide, mass death, or natural disaster? As part of general preparation for living? As an element in vocational training programs?
- **How** should this type of education be offered? Informally as part of education about life? As a formal component of some other subject like biology, nursing, philosophy, psychology, religious studies, or sociology? As a separate subject in its own right?
- **Why**, if at all, should we engage in this type of education in the first place?

result, in recent years, new programs have been developed on care of the dying, support for the bereaved, and research about death-related attitudes. These developments are part of what has been called the *death-awareness* movement or *thanatology* (from *thanatos*, the Greek word for *death*, + *ology* = a science or organized body of knowledge) (Doka, 2003; see also Stillion & Attig, 2015). As indicated in the title of this book and the calligraphy on page 2, we believe that death and life are so intertwined that the body of knowledge in this book is focused on life and living considered from the perspective of death and dying. In this, we follow Kastenbaum (2012, p. xv) who defined "thanatology" as "the study of life—with death left in" and the guru's advice in the last three paragraphs of the Prologue to this book (on p. xxviii).

CONCERNS LEADING PEOPLE TO STUDY DEATH-RELATED SUBJECTS

Let's think about this subject in more specific ways. Why did instructors begin to offer courses on what has come to be called **death education** (a popular phrase in this field, but one that may not be a very good name for the study of life and living from the standpoint of death and dying; see Corr & Corr, 2003c)? And why did people want to talk about and study death-related issues (Bucklea, 2013)? We think that *some of the concerns that help this type of education thrive* include the following:

- Some people become interested in these subjects because of *work they are already doing or are preparing to do in a profession or vocation in which they expect to be asked to help people who are coping with death-related issues.* These include students or those working in fields like counseling, education, funeral service, medicine, the ministry, nursing, and social work, as well as individuals who volunteer in hospice organizations.
- Many people have pressing personal concerns because they want *to learn how to cope more effectively with a current encounter with someone who is dying or with their own grief and mourning after their significant other has died.*
- Others say they want *to prepare for personal experiences that might or could be expected to arise in the future.* For example, some say: "No important person in my life has yet died, but I know it can't continue this way as my grandparents are getting pretty old." These people don't want to wait until events demand a response under pressure; they prefer to be proactive by preparing themselves and others (as much as possible) to cope with death-related challenges.
- Finally, some people are simply *curious about some death-related topic or issue in this field,* such as debates about assisted suicide or how one might talk to children about death and loss.

Do any of the above apply to you? If so, death-related education programs should try to help you meet your interests by developing a special sensitivity to and compassion for your concerns. That is especially true if participants in these educational programs include people who have experienced the death of a loved one in the recent past, whose close relative or friend is presently trying to meet the challenges of a terminal illness, or who may themselves be living with a life-threatening condition.

Of course, education is different from counseling, and a classroom or an online course is not really an appropriate context for individual therapy. So, we need to offer this caution: Education alone may not be sufficient to address your needs if you are unable to cope with difficult personal experiences by yourself. If you are in such a situation, it may be desirable to seek personal counseling or therapy. Also, if you have recently experienced a major loss in your life and are not comfortable with a dispassionate, educational approach to death-related topics, you might choose to postpone enrolling in a course in this field until some later time. In short, a formal course may not meet all needs at all times.

HOW IS EDUCATION ABOUT DEATH, DYING, AND BEREAVEMENT CONDUCTED?

This type of education may be conducted formally or informally. *Formal* or *planned education* about death, dying, and bereavement is usually associated with organized instructional programs of the type found in schools, colleges and universities, graduate education, professional workshops, and volunteer training programs (Berman, 2011; Corr, 2015a; Dickinson, 2012; Hayasaki, 2014; Loerzel & Conner, 2016; Noppe, 2007). These formal programs can be of many types. Some are taught in traditional classrooms, but lately many are taught online, whether as credit-bearing offerings for degrees in various fields or thanatology-related programs, or as part of continuing education or certification programs.

One imaginative example designed to be used as a basis for formal education in the community is *Lessons from Lions: Using Children's Media to Teach about Grief and Mourning* (Adams, 2006), a resource that can be used to teach children (and adults) about grief and mourning in primary school classrooms or grief support groups. This slim booklet provides an outline and ten slides from the Disney movie, *The Lion King*, to encourage discussion about three common but unhelpful reactions following a loss: (1) running away from the problem, the pain, and those who know and love you best; (2) pretending the bad thing never happened; and (3) never telling anyone about your grief reactions.

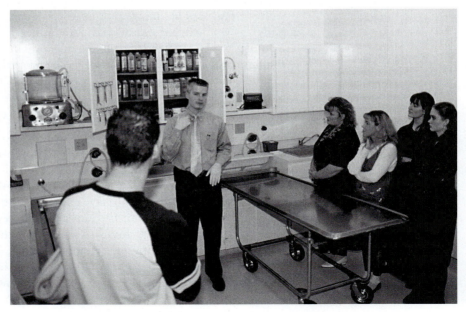

Students learn during a planned visit to a funeral home.

Chastin Brinkley

Early examples of **formal education about death, dying, and bereavement** in secondary schools typically focused directly on death, dying, and bereavement (Stevenson, 2004). Examples of such courses can still be found (e.g., Campbell, 2016), although many recent courses are more likely to emphasize topics like: coping with loss (including bereavement and grief, but in which "death" is a secondary element); suicide and suicide prevention (aimed more directly at students than earlier programs developed for faculty, staff, and parents); violence and violence prevention (in which loss and grief are typically addressed as factors contributing to violence); or crisis counseling courses for school counselors and teachers, as well as agency-based counselors (R. W. Stevenson, personal communication, February 9, 2007). One of the main goals of this book is to support formal educational programs however they may be organized.

Informal or *unplanned education* about death, dying, and bereavement is more typical and more widespread, although it may not always be recognized for what it truly is. Most human beings first learn about loss, sadness, and coping from a parent or guardian and through interactions within a family or similar social group (Gilbert & Murray, 2007). They also learn about these topics from their own experiences, the people they meet in their lives, and events in which they take part. The media (notably television and videos) and many other sources contribute raw materials and insights to a lifelong process of informal education that may take place almost without one's notice. Also, Death Cafe gatherings, the Internet, and various self-education activities (e.g., Straub, 2015) can contribute to this type of informal education. (For an example of how death has been (mis)treated in one well-known children's story, see Issues for Critical Reflection #2.)

ISSUES FOR CRITICAL REFLECTION

#2 Do You Know What Really Happened to Little Red Riding Hood?

Which, if any, of the following excerpts from the Little Red Riding Hood story is familiar to you?

Example 1

The Wolf, seeing her come in, said to her, hiding himself under the bedclothes:

"Put the custard and the little pot of butter upon the stool, and come and lie down with me."

Little Red Riding Hood undressed herself and went into bed, where, being greatly amazed to see how her grandmother looked in her night-clothes, she said to her:

"Grandmamma, what great arms you have got!"

"That is the better to hug thee, my dear."

"Grandmamma, what great teeth you have got!"

"That is to eat thee up."

And, saying these words, this wicked wolf fell upon Little Red Riding Hood, and ate her up.

Source: From Lang, 1904, p. 66.

Example 2

"The better to EAT you with," said the wolf. And he sprang from the bed and ate Little Red Riding Hood up.

A passing woodsman stepped into the house to see how Little Red Riding Hood's grandmother was feeling. And when he saw the wolf, he said, "Ah ha! I've found you at last, you wicked old rascal!" He lifted his ax, and with one blow, killed him. Then he cut the wolf open and out stepped Little Red Riding Hood and her grandmother.

(continues)

They thanked the woodsman for what he had done. Then all three sat down and ate the cake and the butter and drank of the grape juice, which Little Red Riding Hood had brought.

Source: From Jones, 1948.

Example 3

"THE BETTER TO EAT YOU WITH, MY DEAR," cried the wolf. He pushed back the covers, and jumped out of the bed. Then Little Red Riding Hood saw that it was the big wolf pretending to be her grandmother!

At that moment a hunter passed the house. He heard the wolf's wicked voice and Little Red Riding Hood's frightened scream. He burst open the door. Before the wolf could reach Little Red Riding Hood, the hunter lifted his gun to his shoulder and killed the wicked wolf. Little Red Riding Hood was very happy and she thanked the kind hunter.

Grandmother unlocked the door and came out of the closet, where she had been hiding. She kissed Little Red Riding Hood again and again. And she thanked the hunter for saving them both from the big wolf. They were all so happy that they decided to have a party right then and there. … And they all lived happily ever after.

Source: From Anonymous, 1957.

Example 4

"All the better to EAT you with!" cried the wolf.

With that, Little Red Riding Hood let out a scream and ran from the room. The wolf gave chase with hunger in his eyes.

"Stop!" cried a loud voice.

Little Red Riding Hood looked up to see a woodcutter holding his ax in the air. He reached for the wolf and grabbed him by the tail. Then the woodcutter carried the wolf into the forest.

Grandmother came running up to Little Red Riding Hood. She had been hiding in the garden shed. [After she had run out of the front door when frightened by the first sight of the wolf.]

"Grandmother! I am so glad you are safe!" cried Little Red Riding Hood. "I was worried that the wolf had eaten you."

Grandmother gave Little Red Riding Hood a great big hug as the woodcutter came out of the woods.

"I do not think that wolf will trouble you again," he said, adjusting his cap.

Source: From Anonymous, 2013, pp. 35–37.

Note the changes from Example 1 in which both Grandmother and Little Red are eaten by the wolf and presumably they die—which reinforces the basic moral of the original story; to Example 2 in which they are eaten but then experience a type of instant reappearance (resurrection?) when the woodsman cuts the wolf's stomach open (and apparently the wolf dies); to Example 3 in which a hunter kills the wolf *before* he can eat Little Red and Grandmother emerges from a closet where she had been hiding; to Example 4 in which both Little Red and Grandmother escape from the wolf, no one is eaten, and even the assumed death of the wolf occurs offstage.

Why do you think people made these changes to the end of this beloved story?

Opportunities for informal education also emerge naturally from **teachable moments.** These are the unanticipated events in life that offer important occasions for developing useful educational insights and lessons, as well as for personal growth (see Personal Insights 1.1 for an unexpected encounter on the part of one of our co-authors that was for him also a teachable moment). For example, a natural disaster, an act of violence like the horrific events of September 11, 2001, barely avoiding an auto accident, the death of a pet, the funeral of a loved one, or a visit to a cemetery are only a few of the many instances in which teachable moments thrust themselves into the middle of life and offer important opportunities for **informal education about death, dying, and bereavement** for both children and adults.

Visiting a cemetery with a child can provide a "teachable moment."

Courtesy of Kevin A. Corr

PERSONAL INSIGHTS 1.1

A Personal Vignette and a Teachable Moment

For several years, an elderly couple in their 80s (let's call them Mike and Maggie) came to Florida from Michigan to rent the house next door to us during the months of January and February. Although they were not married, they had known each other since grade school and had been together for 14 years after each was widowed earlier.

Late one evening immediately after they had arrived, Mike had a massive heart attack. I was in bed, but was woken by the sound of loud engines, which turned out to be several fire rescue and ambulance vehicles parked along the street with lights flashing. Fearing that bad things were happening, I threw on some clothes and went outside to join two neighbors standing across the street.

Soon, Mike was taken out on a gurney into an ambulance and driven away. Some minutes later, Maggie was escorted from the house by a police officer and also driven away.

I wish I had reached out to her at that point, but I soon realized she would be alone in the emergency department of our local hospital with no other family or friends in this area. I thought someone should go to be with her and one of our neighbors (a nurse who did not know this couple) encouraged me to do so.

When I arrived at the emergency department, I found Maggie sitting in an exterior waiting area. She said she was pleased I had come. Soon, a staff person invited her to come in to an interior family waiting area and Maggie asked me to accompany her. She said she was glad to have some company so that she

(continues)

would not just be sitting there alone thinking about what might be happening with Mike. Between her attempts to telephone relatives up north (especially Mike's son), she talked in brief bursts about many different topics. I mostly listened and offered occasional comments.

After a short wait, a physician and a nurse came into the room. The doctor asked who we were and how each of us was related to Mike. He also asked what had happened before Maggie had called 911 and emergency responders had arrived at the house. Finally, he told us that efforts on the scene and in the hospital to revive Mike had not been successful. Maggie said, "Is he gone?" The doctor said, "Yes."

The nurse and doctor then explained that what would now happen would depend on the medical examiner (presumably because the death had occurred suddenly to someone who was not under the care of a local physician). They said they would keep Mike's body until that determination and other arrangements had been made. Maggie said they were not married and did not have advance directives, so legal decisions would have to be made by Mike's son who was finally contacted by telephone and spoke with a hospital staffer.

After Maggie was given an opportunity to view Mike's body, she commented that he looked better than he had appeared at the house. I drove her home, offered her a cup of coffee or tea and a bed for the night in our house (which she declined), and promised to drive her to the airport the next morning to meet her son who had already arranged to fly in from a nearby state.

By morning Maggie had decided to leave immediately to go back home. She had arranged all of their possessions to be packed into Mike's car and driven back up north by her son. We met her son at the airport, they spoke for a few moments, she flew out, I drove her son back to the house, we packed the car, and he left.

There seem to me to be at least two lessons here. Perhaps you will think of others?

1. Even after a long career teaching courses on death and dying, I was initially slow and unsure how to respond to this unexpected, death-related event. My nurse neighbor deserves credit for urging me to actually do what I dimly sensed should be done—just to make myself available to Maggie, be present, listen actively, and provide practical assistance as needed. Supporting a person in crisis or immediately after a death didn't take heroic action, just being a good neighbor.

2. There was nothing I could have done to help Mike. However, helping Maggie in this situation involved offering support to a living person. In this book, I hope you will come to appreciate that much of what we teach and learn about death, dying, and bereavement is really about life and living. In fact, life and death are inevitably intertwined as shown in the story about the horse in our Prologue and in the calligraphy on page 2. As you read though this book, I invite you to reflect on how much each subject we address is really about life and living.

Source: Charles A. Corr.

FOUR DIMENSIONS OF EDUCATION ABOUT DEATH, DYING, AND BEREAVEMENT

We believe there are four **dimensions of education about death, dying, and bereavement**. These four dimensions relate to what people know, how they feel, how they behave, and what they value. In other words, these are the cognitive, affective, behavioral, and valuational dimensions of this education, distinguished here for the sake of clarity but interrelated as aspects of the overall educational process.

First, this type of education is obviously a *cognitive* or intellectual enterprise because it provides factual information about death-related experiences and tries to help us understand or interpret those events. For example, this education offers facts about death-related encounters (see Chapter 2), insights into society's death system (see Chapter 4), descriptions of cultural patterns among different groups of Americans (see Chapter 5), and information about topics like suicide (see Chapter 17). Also, this type of education identifies new ways of organizing or interpreting the data of human experience, such as the one that took place in the early 1980s when some physicians observed relatively rare forms of skin cancer (Kaposi's sarcoma) and pneumonia (Pneumocystis carinii) in an unusually high number of young, otherwise healthy, homosexual males. These observations helped to identify a new disease and cause of death, acquired immunodeficiency syndrome (AIDS) and human immunodeficiency virus (HIV) (see Focus On 2.1 on pp. 29–30 in Chapter 2 in this book).

Second, the *affective* dimension of education about death, dying, and bereavement has to do with feelings, emotions, and attitudes (see Chapter 3). For example, this type of education tries to sensitize those who are not bereaved to the depth, intensity, duration, and complexities of grief and mourning following a death. In this regard, many bereaved persons have told us that it appears insensitive and arrogant to them when someone who is not bereaved says, "I know how you feel." How could that be true of someone who has not experienced their losses? To the bereaved, such statements (however well intentioned they may be) seem to diminish the uniqueness and poignancy of their losses. Also, in our society many people still seem to think—wrongly—that a few days or weeks may be more than adequate to "forget" or "get over" the death of an important person in one's life. In fact, mourning a significant death in one's life is far more like an ongoing process of learning to live with one's losses than it is like solving a problem once and for all (see Chapter 9). Sharing and discussing grief reactions and mourning responses are important parts of the affective dimension of education in the field of death, dying, and bereavement.

Third, education about death, dying, and bereavement has a *behavioral* dimension when it explores why people act as they do in death-related situations, which of their behaviors are helpful or unhelpful, and how they could or should act in such situations. Much individual and social behavior, both public and private, appears to try to avoid death-related encounters. Often, that occurs because people do not know what to say or what to do in such situations. They pull back from the dying and the bereaved, leaving people alone in very stressful circumstances, without support or companionship at a time when sharing and solace may be most needed. In fact, a better understanding of the needs of those who are coping with dying and/or bereavement (see Chapters 6 and 9) demonstrates that there is much that individuals and social organizations can do to be helpful in such situations (see Chapters 7–8 and 10–11). Above all, this behavioral education points out the great value embodied in the *simple presence* of a caring person, someone who does not so much talk to those who are coping with death and loss, but who *actively listens* to them. This type of education can help us develop skills in interacting with such persons.

Fourth, in its *valuational* dimension, education about death, dying, and bereavement can help to identify, articulate, and affirm the basic values that govern human lives. Life as we know it is inextricably bound up with death. *We would not have this life as we know it if death were not one of its essential parts.* Life and death, living and dying, attachments and loss, happiness and sadness—neither alternative in these and many other similar pairings stands alone in human experience. Death provides an essential (and inescapable) perspective from which humans can try to achieve an adequate understanding of their own lives (see Chapter 19).

Reflecting on values is closely related to many of the death-related challenges that confront us as we move forward in the 21st century: terrorism and the threat of nuclear warfare, epidemics and their prevention, famine and malnutrition, dislocation of populations and ethnic cleansing, capital punishment, abortion, assisted suicide, euthanasia, and many of the quandaries posed by modern medicine and its complex technologies. Values also come sharply into focus when adults are asked what they will tell children about death. Education in this field shows that death should not be hidden from children, and that life should not be portrayed as an unending journey without shadows or tears (see Chapter 12). Hiding death from children, even if we really could do that, will not prepare them to cope effectively with future losses, a common part of human life. It is far better to introduce children proactively to the realities of life and death in ways that are appropriate to their developmental level and capacities, together with the support of values that will enable them to live wisely and cope with death constructively.

SIX GOALS OF EDUCATION ABOUT DEATH, DYING, AND BEREAVEMENT

Education that is well planned always has in mind some general goals and specific objectives that it hopes to accomplish for and with its participants. For example, college courses are commonly designed to encourage critical thinking in order to help individuals judge for themselves the value, meaning, and validity of subjects they address. Education about death, dying, and bereavement incorporates these broad aims and typically links them to more limited purposes (Wass, 2004).

We were challenged to think about our own goals when we were teaching our first course on death and dying. With no advance notice, we received the letter reproduced in Personal Insights 1.2 from a person who had not been in our course and whom we did not know. We appreciated Mrs. Koerner's comments about our course, but we were also a bit perplexed: How should we evaluate her remarks? Should we really take credit for teaching people how to die, as Mrs. Koerner seemed to think we were doing? That letter challenged us to think about what we want or hope to accomplish in our courses. As a result, we have come to recognize six basic goals in this type of education.

PERSONAL INSIGHTS 1.2

A Letter to a Teacher in a Course on Death and Dying

October 16, 1975

Dear Dr. Corr,

Want to thank you for your course "Death and Dying."

Not having been in your classroom, you might wonder what prompts me to write this letter.

My mother was one of the most dedicated Christians we in our lives have ever known.

She became very ill and it took 54 days, in and out of an Intensive Care Unit, for her to die.

Doc and I spent as much time as humanly possible at her side.

One day she looked at me with her beautiful soft brown eyes and said, "Why didn't anyone teach me how to die? We are taught at our mother's knee how to live but not how to die."

Hope your course will help people through this experience because we will all have a turn unless the Rapture comes first.

God bless you,

Dr. and Mrs. S. Koerner

The first goal of education about death, dying, and bereavement is *to enrich the personal lives* of those to whom it is directed. In the end, as the ancient Greek philosopher Socrates is reported to have said, "The really important thing is not to live, but to live well" (Plato, 1948 [*Crito*, 48b]). Death-related education contributes to this goal by helping individuals to understand themselves more fully and to appreciate both their strengths and their limitations as finite human beings.

A second goal of this type of education is *to inform and guide individuals in their personal transactions with society*. It does this by making them aware of services and options they have to choose from in such matters as end-of-life care or funeral practices and memorial rituals.

A third goal is *to help prepare individuals for their public roles as citizens*. Here, education helps to clarify important social issues that face society and its representatives, such as advance directives in health care, assisted suicide, euthanasia, and organ and tissue donation (see Chapters 16 and 18).

A fourth goal is *to help prepare and support individuals in their professional and vocational roles*. Those whose work involves teaching about death, caring for the dying, or counseling the bereaved can benefit from the insights offered by a well-grounded education about death, dying, and bereavement.

A fifth goal is *to enhance the ability of individuals to communicate effectively about death-related topics*. Good communication is essential when discussing topics that appear difficult for many people.

A sixth goal is *to assist individuals in appreciating how development across the human life course interacts with death-related issues*. Children and adolescents, as well as young, middle-aged, and older adults, face issues that are both similar and dissimilar in many ways, and they cope with them differently when they confront death, dying, and bereavement (see Chapters 12–15).

WHAT ARE SOME OF THE THINGS WE CAN LEARN ABOUT LIFE AND LIVING BY STUDYING DEATH, DYING, AND BEREAVEMENT?

As you read this book, we suggest you ask yourself what you are learning about death, dying, and bereavement, as well as what that is teaching you about life and living. For ourselves, as we noted near the beginning of this chapter, we have come to see that life and death, living and dying, are inexorably intertwined. That explains the title of this book and our basic conviction that the study of death-related topics inevitably and simultaneously teaches us about life and living (Corr, 2015c).

For example, studying death, dying, and bereavement reminds us that we humans are finite, limited beings. From this realization, we learn our first lesson, namely, that while there are many things in life that we can *control*, there also are many *limitations* that make our control less than complete.

Further, when studying death-related topics, we recognize that ultimately it is always an individual person who must deal with these particularized experiences: no one else can die our death or experience our grief. These events are marked by their unique individuality. However, studying death, dying, and bereavement also reveals to us that being human means being involved in a community and being inescapably linked to other persons. Thus, a second lesson about life and living that emerges from the study of death, dying, and bereavement is that life and death involve both *individuals* and *communities*.

Again, although we often prefer to ignore our mortality, both life and death make our vulnerability to pain and suffering all too obvious. Still, education about death, dying, and bereavement helps us realize that this vulnerability is not the same as helplessness. We learn that most human beings have powerful coping capacities and are amazingly resilient. In fact, some persons respond to death-related challenges in ways that can be ennobling and even awesome. Thus, a third lesson from our studies of death, dying, and bereavement is that human beings find themselves located between *vulnerability* and *resilience*.

Beyond this, the fourth lesson is that our studies of death-related topics reveal the importance of *quality in living* and *the human search for meaning*. One man who was facing his own imminent death founded an organization called "Make Today Count" (Kelly, 1975). In so doing, he implicitly recommended that *we all should try to make every day in our lives count* by striving to maximize the quality of our own lives right now and by appreciating that life can be good even though it is transient. When death challenges the value of life, this type of education shows that humans work hard to find sources of inspiration and religious or philosophical frameworks within which enduring meaning can be established. Thus, *quality in living* and the *search for meaning* are significant issues for those who are coping with death as well as for those who are simply living their day-to-day lives.

We believe you will find these four lessons appearing and reappearing throughout this book, sometimes in obvious ways, but often a little below the surface of our explorations. In that sense, these four lessons or themes (control/limitation;

individuality/community; vulnerability/resilience; and quality in living/the search for meaning) are subtexts throughout this book. You can enrich your studies of the subjects in this book if you will occasionally *stop to dig below the surface of the text*, take time to reflect on what you are reading, and bring to the surface themes like these—as well as any others you may find.

Summary

In this chapter, we examined education about death, dying, and bereavement. We considered some reasons why individuals have or might become interested in this type of education. We mentioned formal education of the type represented by this book, as well as informal modes of education that are most evident in what we called *teachable moments* and the Death Cafe movement. We explored four central dimensions of this type of education (cognitive, affective, behavioral, and valuational). We looked at six goals for death-related education, and we asked what we could learn about life and living through the study of death, dying, and bereavement. All of this reminds us of the main lesson from the teachings of the guru in Prologue to this book: human beings cannot magically make death, loss, and grief disappear from their lives, but they can profitably study these subjects and discuss or share insights with each other as ways of making death less powerful by learning to live richer, fuller, and more realistic lives.

Glossary

Death Cafe: both a social movement and a series of individual events or informal, pop-up gatherings in which people (mostly strangers) are invited to come together without a pre-set agenda for a discussion of death-related topics while sharing food and drink

Death education: teaching and learning about death-related subjects, such as dying and bereavement

Dimensions of education about death, dying, and bereavement: *cognitive*, *affective*, *behavioral*, and *valuational*

Formal education about death, dying, and bereavement: planned and organized instruction involving death-related topics

Informal education about death, dying, and bereavement: death-related education emerging from everyday experiences and exchanges

Teachable moments: unanticipated life events that offer important occasions for developing educational insights and lessons, as well as for personal growth

Questions for Review and Discussion

1. Would you be willing to join or host a Death Cafe gathering in your home area? Why or why not?
2. This book is part of an effort to improve education about death, dying, and bereavement. Would you recommend this type of education to a friend or relative? Why or why not?
3. What is it in your own life that brought you to the study of death, dying, and bereavement?
4. Have you had any previous online or face-to-face experiences with formal or informal education about death, dying, or bereavement? If so, what were those experiences like and what did they teach you?

5. What do you think you might learn about death, dying, and bereavement and/or about life and living from reading this book?
6. What do you think you might learn from sharing what you are studying with others? (If you wish to share what you learn from such exchanges with the authors of this book, please e-mail us at: ccorr32@tampabay.rr.com; KnDoka@aol.com.)
7. Have you ever sought to learn about the subjects covered in this chapter by searching the Internet or exploring social media? Did that help you? Why or why not?
8. The Prologue to this book is "The Horse on the Dining-Room Table" by Richard A. Kalish. The Epilogue is "Calendar Date Gives Mom Reason to Contemplate Life" by Elizabeth Vega-Fowler. Read these pieces now if you have not already done so. What did you learn from each of them? What similarities and differences do you see in the lessons that these authors want to teach us?

Suggested Readings

This list and those at the end of each chapter in this book focus almost exclusively on book-length publications. Among these, general resources in the field of death, dying, and bereavement include the following:

Bryant, C. D. (Ed.). (2003). *Handbook of Death and Dying* (2 vols.)

Bryant, C. D., & Peck, D. L. (Eds.). (2009). *Encyclopedia of Death and the Human Experience* (2 vols.)

Doka, K. J. (Ed.). (2007c). *Death, Dying and Bereavement* (4 vols.)

Howarth, G., & Leaman, O. (Eds.). (2001). *Encyclopedia of Death and Dying*

Kastenbaum, R. (Ed.). (2003). *Macmillan Encyclopedia of Death and Dying* (2 vols.)

Morgan, J. D., Laungani, P., & Palmer, S. (Eds.). (2003–2009). *Death and Bereavement around the World* (5 vols.)

Stillion, J., & Attig, T. (Eds.). (2015). *Death, Dying, and Bereavement: Contemporary Perspectives, Institutions, and Practices*

Full bibliographical data for these publications are in the References at the end of this book. Journal articles and other literature can be located via the Internet, using search terms at the end of each chapter.

Selected Web Resources

Some useful search terms include: DEATH CAFE; DEATH EDUCATION; FORMAL EDUCATION; INFORMAL EDUCATION; TEACHABLE MOMENTS.

You can also visit the following *organizational and other Internet sites*:

Association for Death Education and Counseling (ADEC)

Center for Death Education and Bioethics, University of Wisconsin–La Crosse

Death Café

Death Over Dinner

King's University College Centre for Education about Death and Bereavement

PART Two

DEATH

Gordon Allport once said that in some ways each of us is like *every other* human being, in other ways each of us is only like *some* other human beings, and in still other ways each of us is like *no* other human being (J. W. Worden, personal communication, April 22, 2001). In studying death, dying, and bereavement, it helps to sort out these various aspects: the universal, the particular, and the uniquely individual. Part Two examines the particular: contemporary experiences with death in the United States.

Human beings always live within particular *social and cultural frameworks*. Of course, not every individual or group shares every aspect of the experiences that characterize a society as a whole. Thus, specific individuals and members of distinct groups within the United States and any other country are likely to have their own unique experiences with life and death. This leads us, in the chapters that follow, to describe both the broad context of American society and representative examples of diversity in death-related experiences within and outside that general framework.

Human beings also live within particular *historical frameworks*. Thus, the patterns of experience with death within contemporary American society differ from the experiences of individuals who lived in earlier periods in the United States. (And, of course, the death-related experiences of people living in other countries may be either similar or very different from those of most Americans, now or in the past.)

In the four chapters that follow, we examine three key components of *death-related experiences*:

- *encounters with death*
- *attitudes toward death*
- *death-related practices*

These three components are specific aspects of *the totality of human experience*, each shaping the others and each being shaped by the others. In everyday human experiences, encounters, attitudes, and practices are so closely intertwined as to be almost impossible to tell apart. We discuss them in this book in separate chapters to facilitate individual analysis. Think of it like a triangle with the points representing the three elements of death-related experiences and the sides representing the possibility of interactions between the points (see Figure II.1).

Thus, in Chapter 2 we explore *death-related encounters* and therefore would put *encounters* at the top of the triangle, with *attitudes* at the bottom left and *practices* at the bottom right. Then, in Chapter 3, we explore *death-related attitudes* and thus would rotate our triangle in a clockwise direction to put *attitudes* at the top, with *practices* at the bottom left and *encounters* at the bottom right. Finally, in Chapter 4, as we explore *death-related practices*, we would again rotate our triangle in a clockwise direction to put *practices* at the top, with *encounters* at the bottom left and *attitudes* at the bottom right.

To enrich our account of death-related experiences, in Chapter 5 we explore issues of diversity and distinctive cultural patterns in death-related encounters, attitudes, and practices. By contrast with the earlier portrait of mainstream American society in Chapters 2–4, this profile in Chapter 5 helps make us more sensitive to cultural, racial, ethnic, social, and other differences between individuals and groups in the United States as they relate to experiences involving death, dying, and bereavement.

Figure II.1   Death-related Experiences

Death-related experiences

Jack Dagley Photography/Shutterstock.com

CHANGING ENCOUNTERS WITH DEATH

Objectives of this **Chapter**

▷ To identify and explain *death-related encounters* as a component of *death-related experiences*

▷ To identify the following principal features of current death-related encounters in the United States:

1. Death rates (and differences related to gender, class, infant mortality, and maternal mortality)

2. Average life expectancy

3. Causes of death (communicable versus degenerative diseases)

4. Dying trajectories, their duration and shape

5. Place of death

▷ To indicate some ways in which these features of death-related encounters have changed over time

▷ To describe six factors associated with these changes:

1. Industrialization (including transportation and communication)

2. Public health measures

3. Preventive health care

4. Cure-oriented medicine

5. The nature of contemporary families

6. Lifestyle

BRYAN LEE CURTIS SHARES HIS ENCOUNTER WITH DEATH

Bryan Lee Curtis asked a local newspaper to publish his story along with two photographs. One photo, taken just before his 34th birthday, shows Curtis with his two-year-old son when both seemed to be in excellent good health; the second, *taken just nine weeks later* and reprinted here, shows him less than three hours before his death with his wife and son at his bedside (Landry, 1999a). Curtis wanted his story and photographs to inform people about the dangers of smoking and to encourage changes in attitudes, behaviors, and values related to smoking. (NOTE: Permission has only been granted to reproduce one of these photos here; both can be viewed via an Internet search using Brian's full name.)

Curtis died from advanced lung cancer as a result of his 20-year habit of smoking that had spread to his liver. He began smoking at age 13, eventually building up to a habit of more than two packs of cigarettes a day. His addiction was so strong that he was unable to quit smoking until just a week before his death when he could no longer do so because of the ravages of his illness.

The newspaper was concerned that readers would respond negatively to Brian's story and its accompanying photos. In fact, readers' comments were overwhelmingly positive; they understood very well the message that Curtis was trying to communicate. As a result, Bryan Lee Curtis' story and pictures appeared on websites around the world and were widely reprinted (Landry, 1999b; Noack, 1999).

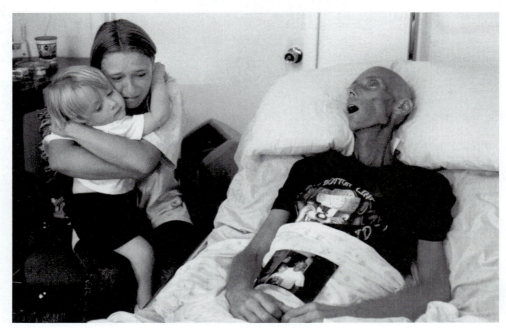

Bryan Lee Curtis on the day of his death, about nine weeks after he was diagnosed with advanced lung cancer.

ENCOUNTERING DEATH IN AMERICA TODAY

As indicated in the introduction to Part Two, death-related experiences include three components: death-related encounters, attitudes, and practices. In this chapter, we examine *death-related encounters* by considering some typical ways in which Americans *encounter or meet up with death* early in the 21st century. Significant features of these encounters are not always obvious, nor are they the only ways in which humans have interacted or might interact with mortality. Earlier people did not encounter death as we do now, nor do many people in other parts of the world today. So, we indicate throughout some of the ways in which these encounters have changed over time in the United States.

Demographic statistics can teach us a lot about contemporary encounters with death. For example, the National Center for Health Statistics (NCHS) reported that there were 2,626,418 deaths in the United States in 2014 (the year for which most recent final data are available as this chapter is written; see Table 2.1). These encounters with death occurred in a resident population that the U.S. Census Bureau estimated was approximately 318.6 million. Such encounters help to shape our present and future attitudes toward death, our death-related practices, and our broader experiences with life and living. However, it is difficult to grasp a number as large as 2.6 million deaths, and we cannot study all of their aspects simultaneously. So, we concentrate in this chapter on outlining five central features within the broad patterns of death-related encounters in U.S. society.

Death Rates

The first important factor in understanding death-related encounters is **death rates**, which are typically determined by choosing some specific group of people and dividing the number of those in the group who die during a particular time period by the total population of the group. For instance, the overall death rate for males of all races in the United States in 2014 was determined by dividing the number of deaths among these males by the total number of males in the entire population. Usually, a death rate is expressed as some number of deaths per 1,000 or 100,000 persons. Crude or unadjusted death rates per 100,000 persons for 2014 are shown in Table 2.1 for the entire population of the United States, as well as for males and females separately, all of which round out roughly to 8.0 per 1,000. By contrast, "The age-adjusted death rate [which takes into account the aging of the population] was 724.6 deaths per 100,000 U.S. standard population, a decrease of 1% from the 2013 rate and a record low figure" (Kochanek, Murphy, Xu, & Tejada-Vera, 2016, p. 1). In general, age-adjusted death rates are more accurate in comparing subgroups in the population.

Death rates can only be determined with accuracy on the basis of extensive demographic data drawing on birth, death, and census records. Such data are typically available in modern societies; without them, as in the past or in many poor and not well-organized societies today, statistical accuracy gives way to more or less imprecise estimates. Even in a society like the United States, it takes quite some time to assemble, organize, and make available detailed mortality data. The broad patterns in these data show only slow changes over time in encounters with death in the

Table 2.1 **Number of Deaths and Unadjusted Death Rates (per 100,000 Population) by Age and Gender: United States, 2014**

Age	All Races, Both Sexes		All Races, Male		All Races, Female	
	Number	Rate	Number	Rate	Number	Rate
All ages	2,626,418	823.7	1,328,241	846.4	1,298,177	801.7
Under 1	23,215	588.0[a]	12,866	638.6[a]	10,329	535.0[a]
1–4	3,830	24.0	2,172	26.7	1,658	21.3
5–9	2,357	11.5	1,357	13.0	1,000	10.0
10–14	2,893	14.0	1,771	16.8	1,122	11.1
15–19	9,586	45.5	6,828	63.3	2,758	26.8
20–24	19,205	83.8	14,289	121.7	4,916	44.0
25–29	21,925	99.7	15,619	139.9	6,306	58.2
30–34	25,252	117.3	17,078	158.0	8,174	76.3
35–39	29,325	147.2	18,500	186.1	10,825	108.4
40–44	41,671	202.4	25,193	246.5	16,478	158.9
45–49	65,016	311.3	39,281	379.6	25,735	244.2
50–54	110,901	491.3	67,096	605.7	43,805	381.1
55–59	157,170	730.6	95,992	919.1	61,178	552.8
60–64	191,638	1,032.2	116,206	1,308.9	75,432	778.6
65–69	222,834	1,454.0	129,802	1,790.6	93,032	1,151.9
70–74	248,707	2,246.1	138,846	2,722.5	109,861	1,839.3
75–79	282,072	3,560.5	149,259	4,250.5	132,813	3,011.1
80–84	342,432	5,944.6	167,171	7,018.6	175,261	5,187.5
85 yrs and over	826,226	13,407.9	308,785	14,642.2	517,441	12,765.7
Not stated	163	—	110	—	53	—

[a] Death rates for "Under 1" (based on population estimates) differ from infant mortality rates (based on live births).
Source: Kochanek et al., 2016.

form of slight gains in overall numbers of deaths and average life expectancy (ALE), and slight declines in nearly all forms of death rates.

Changing Death Rates in the United States

Studies of international data on death rates have long shown that Americans—and those who reside in many other developed societies around the world—have many advantages in their encounters with death. Notable advantages for those living in

American society in the 21st century can be shown by comparing current U.S. death rates with those at the beginning of the 20th century.

In 1900, death rates were much higher than they are today in the United States and in most industrialized nations of the world (see Table 2.2). In 1900, the death rate for the entire American population of approximately 76 million people was 17.2 deaths per 1,000. By 1954, that rate had dropped to 9.2 per 1,000 (U.S. Bureau of the Census, 1975). That was a decline of nearly 47% in just over a half century—a stunning change unparalleled in any other period in human history. Still, as Table 2.2 shows, by 2014, the overall unadjusted American death rate had dropped even lower to approximately 8.2 per 1,000. (See also, Jin, 2016, & Ma et al., 2015, which point to a 40% drop in U.S. death rates from 1969 to 2014.)

As overall death rates get lower and lower, it is increasingly difficult to reduce them further. Contrast a decline of nearly 47% from 1900 to 1954 with a decline of about 11% in the 59 years from 1954 to 2014. Thus, recent declines in overall death rates in the United States have slowed and may be approaching a minimum level below which they are not likely to fall. Unfortunately, research by Shiels and colleagues (2017) suggests that death rates among some segments of the American population may actually be rising in ways that are "extremely unusual in high-income countries" (p. 1043).

Reductions in overall death rates significantly impact encounters with death. Above all, they mean that most living Americans are likely to have fewer encounters

Table 2.2 Unadjusted Death Rates by Gender and Age, All Races, per 1,000 Population: United States, 1900 and 2014

	1900			2014		
	Both Sexes	Males	Females	Both Sexes	Males	Females
All ages	17.2	17.9	16.5	8.2	8.5	8.0
Under 1	162.4	179.1	145.4	6.0	6.4	5.4
1–4	19.8	20.5	19.1	0.2	0.3	0.2
5–14	3.9	3.8	3.9	0.1	0.2	0.1
15–24	5.9	5.9	5.8	0.7	0.9	0.4
25–34	8.2	8.2	8.2	1.1	1.5	0.7
35–44	10.2	10.7	9.8	1.8	2.2	1.3
45–54	15.0	15.7	14.2	4.0	5.0	3.1
55–64	27.2	28.7	25.8	8.7	11.0	6.6
65–74	56.4	59.3	53.6	17.9	21.8	14.4
75–84	123.3	128.3	118.8	45.6	53.7	39.6
85+	260.9	268.8	255.2	134.1	146.4	127.7

Source: U.S. Bureau of the Census (1975) and Kochanek et al. (2016).

with natural death than did our great-grandparents. The typical American alive today will have lived through fewer deaths of family, friends, and neighbors than did his or her ancestors at the same time of life. Nowadays, death is less likely to occur at home; instead, notification of that event is likely to take place via a telephone call from a hospital or a knock on a door by a police officer (Post, 2017). But, however it occurs, death in our society often appears as a stranger, an alien figure that has no natural or appropriate place in human life.

Differences in Changing Death Rates: Gender and Class

Substantial declines in death rates throughout the 20th century were found in nearly every segment of the population in the United States. But this is not the whole story. The most prominent variables that affect death rates are gender, race, and social class (Field, Hockey, & Small, 1997; Rogers, Hummer, & Nam, 1999; Stillion, 1985). Weaver and Rivello (2007) have also argued that "social capital," defined as a situation involving "a community…where a spirit of trust prevails, where crime and violence are low, where resources are accessible to support healthy lives and lifestyles, and where the sick receive needed care" (p. 33), has a strong, inverse effect on mortality rates. We will consider racial and cultural differences in Chapter 5. Here, we focus on gender and class differences.

In terms of gender, death rates for males in the United States in 1900 were somewhat higher than those for females (see Table 2.2). By 2014, however, while crude death rates for males and females in our society were nearly equal at about 8.5 versus 8.0 per 1,000, age-adjusted death rates show a marked contrast of approximately 8.6 versus 6.2 per 1,000. There may be many reasons why males die earlier. Some hypothesize that males are genetically weaker. Since the male XY chromosome lacks some of the genetic material of the female XX chromosomal structure, females may have a genetic advantage. This is evident in several genetic diseases such as muscular dystrophy or hemophilia that are sex-linked, so males inherit the condition while females will be carriers. A second hypothesis is that male roles are associated with more risk-taking behaviors. Finally, males may tend to have more dangerous or stressful jobs that shorten life span. All of these claims have some support; note, however, that as women's opportunities in the work force have increased, the gap between male and female deaths has narrowed.

In terms of class or societal differences, it has long been known that a "social inequality of death" exists whereby members of the least advantaged socioeconomic classes tend on average to have higher death rates than members of middle and upper socioeconomic classes within the same society. That is, those who are better off economically are likely to have advantages of better housing, nutrition, access to health care, education, and financial resources (Barr, 2014; Davidson, 2015; Marmot, 2015). However, there still may be some more subtle differences within and between members of various socioeconomic classes. One key variable in the United States is that an estimated 14.2% of the U.S. population lacked health insurance coverage in 2014 (Smith & Medalia, 2015). In fact, compared with other industrial nations, the United States is the only country that does not provide health insurance to all of its citizens (Davis et al., 2014). In recent years, the Patient Protection and Affordable Care Act (often called "Obamacare") enacted in 2010 has helped an estimated 20 million people obtain health insurance and has dropped the uninsured rate from 16% to 9% (Blumenthal & Collins, 2014; Frean et al., 2016).

Differences in Changing Death Rates: Infant and Maternal Mortality

The United States was the richest country in the world at the beginning of the 20th century and remains so in the 21st century. During that period, overall death rates for infants—newborns and children under one year of age—were 28 times lower in 2014 than in 1900 (5.82 infant deaths per 1,000 live births versus 162.4 infant deaths (Kochanek et al., 2016). That is a major reduction in infant death rates in just over 100 years.

However, Osterman and colleagues (2015, p. 1122) estimated that: "Twenty-six countries with at least 40 000 births had lower IMRs [infant mortality rates] than the United States in 2012. Eight countries had an IMR less than half the US rate in 2012, and only 1 country [the Slovak Republic] besides the United States reported an IMR >5 infant deaths per 1000 live births." While some of these countries have distinctive features, such as relatively homogeneous populations, clearly the United States with its relatively high percentage of preterm births ranks poorly here. (For additional information on infant deaths and death rates for children under one year of age, see Chapter 12 and Table 12.2.)

Decreases in infant death rates directly affect not only infants who would have died if past conditions had continued to prevail but also other members of society. For example, parents in 1900 were far more likely to encounter the death of one of their children than are parents in the 21st century (Rosenblatt, 1983). Much the same is true for siblings of a child who dies.

Further, pregnancy and birth are not only life-threatening for babies; they can also be life-threatening for their mothers. Maternal death is defined as "the death of a woman while pregnant or within 42 days of termination of pregnancy, irrespective of the duration and site of the pregnancy, from any cause related to or aggravated by the pregnancy or its management but not from accidental or incidental causes" (WHO, 2015, p. 53). In the United States, one estimate is that there were 1063 maternal deaths in 2015 for a rate of 26.4 maternal deaths per 100,000 live births (Kassebaum et al., 2016). This figure is very high and significantly exceeds the goal of not more than 3.3 maternal deaths per 100,000 live births that the United States had hoped to reach by the year 2000. Moreover, experts estimate that more than half of all maternal deaths in the United States are preventable. Especially, young mothers and those who view pregnancy as risk free or whose pregnancy is unintended or unwanted may fail to seek proper care that might prevent or treat complications leading to death.

Of course, death is always a greater threat to vulnerable populations than to those who are healthy and well off. Death rates shortly after the beginning of the 20th century were high for the sick, the weak, and the aged, and they continue to be high for similar groups today. Currently, death rates for nearly every vulnerable group are much lower than they were in times past. Those who are most vulnerable to death today are not as fortunate as their less vulnerable contemporaries, but as a group they are far better off than their counterparts were in 1900. Many deaths are now avoided that would have taken place in our society in the past or that might still take place in other societies today.

AVERAGE LIFE EXPECTANCY

A second important factor in understanding changing patterns of encounters with death is **average life expectancy** (ALE), a factor closely related to death rates. Note that *life span* (the maximum length of life for individuals or the biological limit on length of life in a species) should not be confused with *life expectancy* (an estimate of the average number of years a group of people will live). Here, we speak only of life expectancy (not life span), and we express that as an average figure.

Thorson (1995, p. 34) dramatized the fact that life expectancy figures are averages by imagining "a sample of ten people, six of whom died by age 1 and the rest of whom lived full lives of eighty years." In this group, the six infants lived less than a total of 6 years, whereas the other four people lived a total of 320 years. To say that 32.6 years (6 + 320 ÷ 10) was the ALE for all ten individuals in this odd group would misrepresent both the whole cohort and each of its subgroups.

Projected ALE for all individuals born in the United States in 2014 rose to a record high of 78.8 years (Kochanek et al., 2016). ALE in 2014 for all males was 76.4 years versus 81.2 years for all females. For all Caucasian Americans, ALE was 79.0 years versus 75.6 years for all African Americans. In the same year, record high projected average life expectancies were reached for Caucasian-American and African-American males (76.7 years and 72.5 years, respectively), as well as for Caucasian-American and African-American females (81.4 years and 78.4 years, respectively). Also, the gender gap in ALE for the population as a whole narrowed from 6.4 years in 1995 to 4.8 years in 2014, while the racial differential between Caucasian-American and African-American populations narrowed from 6.9 years to 3.4 years.

ALE identifies the average remaining length of life that can be expected for individuals of a specific age. For example, an American who was 20 years of age in 2014 could expect to live an additional 59.6 years on average, a 40-year-old person could expect to live an average of 40.7 additional years, a 60-year-old person could expect to live an average of 23.3 additional years, and an 80-year-old person could expect to live an average of 9.2 additional years.

From the early 20th century through the second decade of the 21st century, overall ALE in the United States increased from fewer than 50 years to 78.8 years. That is a gain of more than 50% in a little over 100 years! In other words, it was not until the latter portion of the 20th century in the United States and in some other industrialized countries that the ALE exceeded the biblical promise of "three score and ten" (i.e., 70) years. Of course, some individuals have always lived beyond estimated averages; that is the whole point of averages: many individuals in a group exceed the average figure and while others do not reach it.

In general, ALE increased rapidly in the United States during the 20th century because of a major decrease in the number of deaths occurring during the early years of life. When more individuals survive birth, infancy, and childhood, ALE for the population as a whole rises. Over time, however, it becomes more and more difficult to reduce death rates (especially during infancy and childhood) and to extend ALE. When lowering death rates among the young is more difficult, improvements in death rates among adults and the elderly have a more modest impact on increases in overall ALE. Most of the early and relatively easy victories have already been won in the campaign to lower death rates and increase ALE. The battles that lie ahead will be much more difficult. Perhaps that is why the rate of increase in ALE in the United States has slowed in recent years. Also, as Dong, Milholland, and Vijg (2016) argue, "Our results strongly suggest that the maximum lifespan of humans is fixed and subject to natural constraints."

One last point to note is that as ALE increases, it is the elderly who are more and more perceived by individuals in our society as the dying—so much so that in our society, death is exclusively associated in many people's minds with the aged. Table 2.1 shows that approximately 73% of all deaths in the United States in 2014 involved those who were 65 years of age or older.

CAUSES OF DEATH: COMMUNICABLE VERSUS DEGENERATIVE DISEASES

A third important factor in understanding death-related encounters has to do with *causes of death*. Around 1900 in the United States, the largest number of deaths resulted from infectious or **communicable diseases** (see Table 2.3). These are acute diseases that can be transmitted or spread from person to person (Van Panhuis et al., 2013). Earlier cultures experienced sporadic waves of communicable diseases, such as epidemics of influenza, cholera, scarlet fever, measles, smallpox, and tuberculosis that would run through human communities. Perhaps the most famous of these epidemics, at least for Europeans, was the black (bubonic) plague of the 14th century that killed nearly 25 million people in a total European population much smaller than that of today (Gottfried, 1983).

Table 2.3 **The Ten Leading Causes of Death, in Rank Order, All Races, Both Genders: United States, 1900 and 2014**

Rank	Cause of Death	Crude Unadjusted Death Rates per 100,000 Population	Percentage of All Deaths
1900			
	All causes	1,719.1	100.0
1	Influenza and pneumonia	202.2	11.8
2	Tuberculosis (all forms)	194.4	11.3
3	Gastritis, duodenitis, enteritis, etc.	142.7	8.3
4	Diseases of the heart	137.4	8.0
5	Vascular lesions affecting the central nervous system	106.9	6.2
6	Chronic nephritis	81.0	4.7
7	All accidents	72.3	4.2
8	Cancer (malignant neoplasms)	64.0	3.7
9	Certain diseases of early infancy	62.6	3.6
10	Diphtheria	40.3	2.3
2014			
	All causes	823.7	100.0
1	Diseases of the heart	192.7	23.4
2	Cancer (malignant neoplasms)	185.6	22.5

(continues)

Table 2.3   **The Ten Leading Causes of Death, in Rank Order, All Races, Both Genders: United States, 1900 and 2014 (*continued*)**

Rank	Cause of Death	Crude Unadjusted Death Rates per 100,000 Population	Percentage of All Deaths
3	Chronic lower respiratory diseases	46.1	5.6
4	Accidents (unintentional injuries)	42.6	5.2
5	Cerebrovascular diseases (stroke)	41.7	5.1
6	Alzheimer's disease	29.3	3.6
7	Diabetes mellitus (diabetes)	24.0	2.9
8	Influenza and pneumonia	17.3	2.1
9	Nephritis, nephrotic syndrome, and nephrosis (kidney disease)	15.1	1.8
10	Intentional self-harm (suicide)	13.4	1.6

Sources: U.S. Bureau of the Census (1975), Kochanek et al. (2016), and Heron (2016).

Communicable diseases are often accompanied by observable symptoms like diarrhea, nausea, vomiting, headache, fever, and muscle ache. In cultures where vaccines and/or antibiotics were not or are not available—and in many undeveloped or poverty-stricken portions of the world today—those providing physical care for people with communicable diseases mainly dealt (or still deal) with these symptoms rather than with their underlying causes. They tried to isolate the ill person to minimize the likelihood of spreading the disease. They also offered or continue to offer such things as shelter from the elements, a warm fire, a place to rest, hydration, hot food (chicken soup!), and a cool cloth to wipe a feverish brow.

Today, relatively few people in developed countries die of communicable diseases—with the notable exception of deaths associated with influenza and pneumonia, septicemia, and infection by the human immunodeficiency virus (HIV) and acquired immunodeficiency syndrome (AIDS) (for encounters with HIV/AIDS, see Focus On 2.1). Still, recently there has been growing concern about potential threats from other communicable diseases such as bird flu, meningitis, and the West Nile virus (Garrett, 1995; Wolfe, 2011) (see Issues for Critical Reflection #3). Another prominent example is large numbers of deaths caused by the Ebola virus mainly in West Africa in 2014. On a broader scale, special interest has been directed to a possible resurgence in the lethal potential of drug-resistant communicable diseases such as tuberculosis, which might become particularly dangerous in environments like hospitals and nursing homes where ill and potentially vulnerable people live together in close quarters. There also has been much concern about the possibility that some people might use biological agents in terrorist acts (Cordesman, 2005; Miller, Engelberg, & Broad, 2001; Tucker, 2001). Nevertheless, Hunter and Reddy (2013, p. 1343) concluded that "Noncommunicable diseases will be the predominant global public health challenge of the 21st century."

FOCUS ON 2.1

Encounters with AIDS and HIV

In 1981, two unusual disease entities (*Pneumocystis carinii* pneumonia and *Kaposi's sarcoma*) were reported in otherwise healthy men in Los Angeles and New York City (Centers for Disease Control [CDC], 1981a, 1981b, 1981c). These early reports all involved homosexual males who were rapidly dying at a relatively young age (15–52 years old) of infectious diseases that were otherwise seldom fatal in America.

Further study found similar occurrences of unusual life-threatening conditions and deaths among hemophiliacs, Haitian immigrants, intravenous drug users, children in families in which one or both parents had the disease, and heterosexual partners of persons with the disease. These people all shared three characteristics: (1) *a common syndrome*—a clinical entity or recognizable pattern of manifestations arising from an as-yet-unknown underlying cause; (2) an apparent *deficiency in the immune systems* of those experiencing this syndrome; and (3) no evident genetic or natural basis for the syndrome. Together, this suggested that these individuals had somehow developed an *acquired immune deficiency syndrome* (AIDS), a condition in which an individual's immune system has become so dysfunctional that the person falls victim to *opportunistic infections* or unusual diseases and is therefore at heightened risk of dying.

Because the underlying cause of AIDS remained unknown, it was not clear why such diverse individuals were experiencing immune dysfunction. Eventually, however, the CDC (1992a, 2008) was able to go beyond clinical findings to establish a biological marker that defined AIDS as a situation in which individuals had a CD4+ T-lymphocyte (often called *T cells* for short) count of less than 200 per microliter (normal count is around 1,000 per microliter). Now, individuals could be diagnosed with AIDS even if they displayed no overt symptoms linked to the syndrome. Diagnoses could be made much earlier so that understandings of average length of survival of people with the disease changed as persons living with AIDS were seen to live much longer than previously expected. Also, more cases of AIDS were identified, especially among women and children whose disease had not been recognized when AIDS was viewed primarily through clinical manifestations most often found in adult males.

Because AIDS appeared in many individuals with *hemophilia*, it seemed that the transfusions of blood or blood products they received to combat their bleeding problems might be contaminated with an unknown agent causing AIDS. Even though blood donors were screened and the blood itself was filtered to remove potential contaminants, only *sterilization* would kill a microscopic virus. This indicated that *AIDS was caused by a virus*, one identified by researchers in 1983 that came to be called the human immunodeficiency virus (HIV; Grmek, 1990). In short, AIDS is the advanced state of HIV infection, a virus later shown to have come to North America from Africa via the Caribbean in the 1970s (Worobey et al., 2016).

Identification of a viral infection led to tests for *antibodies* manufactured by human immune systems in their fight to repel this foreign agent. However, persons who are unaware of their HIV status or whose bodies have not yet

(continues)

Encounters with AIDS and HIV

developed antibodies identifiable by a test might still be infected with the virus and be capable of transmitting it to others.

In the mid-1990s, additional research led to the development of new therapeutic regimes designed to limit or slow down the destruction of the immune system, improve the health of people living with HIV, and possibly reduce their ability to transmit HIV. As a result, since 1977 HIV/AIDS have no longer been among the 15 leading causes of deaths in the United States. However, 6,721 individuals died from this cause in 2014 (Kochanek et al., 2016). As of June 2016, the CDC estimates that 1.2 million people were living with HIV disease in the United States and 1 in 8 did not know it (CDC, 2016).

This means that HIV infection begins as a communicable disease and remains lethal for many people. Those who avoid death may to find themselves living with a chronic condition requiring them to follow strict treatment regimens for the rest of their lives, to submit to careful monitoring, and to cope with significant costs and potential side effects.

Currently, HIV infection is most likely among men who have sex with men, those who engage in high-risk (e.g., unprotected) heterosexual encounters, and injection drug users. Increasingly, HIV disease is becoming an experience of women, persons of color, and members of younger generations who may not remember the deadlier, early days of the epidemic (Fauci & Marston, 2015; Strathdee & Beyrer, 2015).

The risk of acquiring HIV can be minimized by not sharing blood or bodily fluids, for example, by not having vaginal, oral, or anal sex with an infected person and by not sharing needles or syringes for any reason. Just a single exposure can result in infection, even if it does not always do so (Fauci & Marston, 2015).

ASDF_MEDIA/Shutterstock.com

Here are some of the men, women, and children who might be at risk of becoming infected with HIV and developing AIDS.

ISSUES FOR CRITICAL REFLECTION
#3 Threats of Epidemics in the 21st Century

The initial appearance of HIV and AIDS alerted people that an infectious disease could once again become a significant factor in human mortality, even in the developed world. In fact, HIV disease rapidly turned into an epidemic affecting a large number of individuals within a specific locale or population group during a specific period of time, and then a pandemic affecting large numbers of persons over a larger geographical area during a specific period of time. Here are just four examples of other important epidemic or pandemic threats in the 21st century.

First, in 2003 a strain of influenza virus first found among birds in Asia began to spread and was reported in England in 2007 (Cowell, 2007). Since that time, the number of persons infected with this strain has continued to increase. While the actual number of persons infected so far has remained small, the high mortality rate for this group is worrisome (Eckert, 2007). Some estimates suggest that were the virus to mutate further, allowing human-to-human transmission, millions of persons could become infected within months. In the 1918–1920 flu pandemic, half a million people died from the disease in the United States. According to one report, "if a 1918–1920 pandemic hits the US today, nearly two million people would die and 30% of the country's 300-million people would be infected" (Zaheer, 2007). Meltzer, Cox, and Fukuda (1999) estimated that a pandemic of this size would cost from $71 to $166 billion, 80% of which would be due to deaths resulting from the disease. Such a pandemic would also put a severe strain on health care resources, making treatment that much more difficult (Fineberg, 2014).

Second, tuberculosis is another infectious disease that threatens to reach epidemic proportions. Since 1985, the number of cases of tuberculosis in the United States has risen by 14%. In particular, a strain of the bacillus causing tuberculosis has developed that is resistant to several of the drugs typically used to treat the disease. New York City experienced an epidemic of this multidrug-resistant strain in the 1990s. It cost nearly $1 billion to control that epidemic (National Institute of Allergy and Infectious Diseases [NIAID], 2005). The World Health Organization has labeled multidrug-resistant tuberculosis a global emergency since 2–3 million people die every year from

it. Persons with weakened immune systems, those suffering from poor nutrition, and those who are advanced in age are most vulnerable to the disease, but worldwide, tuberculosis is the leading cause of death among young adults and women of childbearing age (NIAID, 2005). The mortality rate associated with multidrug-resistant tuberculosis is high, nearly 70% (Simone & Dooley, 1994).

Third, another possible source of an epidemic is the *Staphylococcus aureus* bacterium. It also has evolved a strain resistant to many of the drugs long used to control it. *Staphylococcus aureus* infections typically have been found in health care institutions. Recently, however, new strains of the bacterium (community-acquired strains) have appeared outside these institutions with more serious effects and some deaths. While less virulent forms of the community-acquired bacillus cause blisters and cellulitis, which are not difficult to treat, the newer strains attack internal organs and infect the blood stream. These infections can overwhelm the heart or destroy lung tissue, leading to death (Voyich et al., 2005). As a result, it has been reported that "Invasive MRSA [methicillin-resistant *Staphylococcus aureus*] infection affects certain populations disproportionately. It is a major public health problem primarily related to health care but no longer confined to intensive care units, acute care hospitals, or any health care institution" (Klevins et al., 2007, p. 1763).

Fourth, in 2014, a particular strain of the Ebola virus killed over 11,000 people in three countries in West Africa (Mullan, 2015). One man infected with the virus flew to the United States where his disease came into full flower and he eventually died. A few other individuals, mostly health care workers, became infected in Africa, were repatriated to the United States, treated, and survived.

Each of these situations demonstrates that there are infectious diseases that threaten human communities, even those with well-developed health care systems. New forms of treatment will have to be developed in the face of the ever-evolving environments of infectious agents if epidemics and pandemics are to be prevented or controlled. This will require heavy investments, both monetary and creative.

In North America today, the largest numbers of death result from the long-term wearing out of body organs, a deterioration associated with aging, lifestyle, and environment. That is, people in our society mostly die from a set of chronic conditions or causes called **degenerative diseases**. In fact, the four leading causes of death in the United States (diseases of the heart, malignant neoplasms [cancers], chronic lower respiratory diseases [formerly called chronic obstructive pulmonary diseases or COPD], and cerebrovascular diseases) all fall into the category of degenerative diseases. Two of these degenerative diseases (heart disease and cancer) alone have accounted for more than half of all deaths in North America in recent years, despite the fact that death rates from both of these causes have been in gradual decline for many years (Kochanek et al., 2016). For a visual representation of when and how people died in the United States in 2013, by gender, consult Marczak, O'Rourke, and Shepard (2016). (Interestingly, Makary and Daniel [2016] have argued that medical errors—not usually included on death certificates—are actually the third leading cause of death in the United States; for additional information on leading causes of death around the world, consult Global Burden of Disease Study 2013 [2014].) Deaths from degenerative diseases have their own typical characteristics. For example, vascular diseases (e.g., coronary attacks, strokes, embolisms, aneurysms) sometimes cause quick, unanticipated deaths. Nevertheless, although the exposure of the underlying condition may be sudden (as is suggested by the term *stroke*), these diseases themselves usually develop slowly over time and generally produce a gradual (but often unnoticed) debilitation. When such debilitation does not occur or is not recognized, the first symptom may be a dramatic, unexpected, almost instantaneous death. Such a death may be relatively painless—in one's sleep or after a rapid onset of unconsciousness. However, deaths resulting from degenerative diseases are more often slow and may be quite painful—even heart attacks do not necessarily lead to "easy" or "quick" deaths (Jones, Podosky, & Greene, 2012; Singer et al., 2015).

Many people know something about leading causes of death in our society. Still, it is surprising to discover inadequacies in what they think they know (Largo, 2006). Consider the example of cancer, currently the second leading cause of death in our society. In fact, cancer is really a collection of diseases, each of which involves malignant cells that reproduce aggressively and each with its own distinctive characteristics and mortality rate (Mukherjee, 2010). When we have asked students to identify the leading cancer cause of death for males and for females, they most often reply that it is prostate or colon cancer for males and breast cancer for females. In fact, since the early 1950s for males and the mid-1980s for females, the leading cancer cause of death for members of both genders has been lung cancer (see Figure 2.1). Thus, in 2014, in the United States, 84,910 males died of cancer of the lung, bronchus, and trachea by comparison with 28,344 males who died of prostate cancer, while 70,701 females died of cancer of the lung, bronchus, and trachea by comparison with 41,213 who died of breast cancer (Kochanek et al., 2016). High numbers of deaths from lung cancer are a particularly ironic outcome for women who were told by cigarette advertising, "You've come a long way, baby." ("And, if so, why are they still calling us 'baby'?" one female student once asked.)

Figure 2.1   Cancer Death Rates by Gender and Site, United States, 1930–2014.

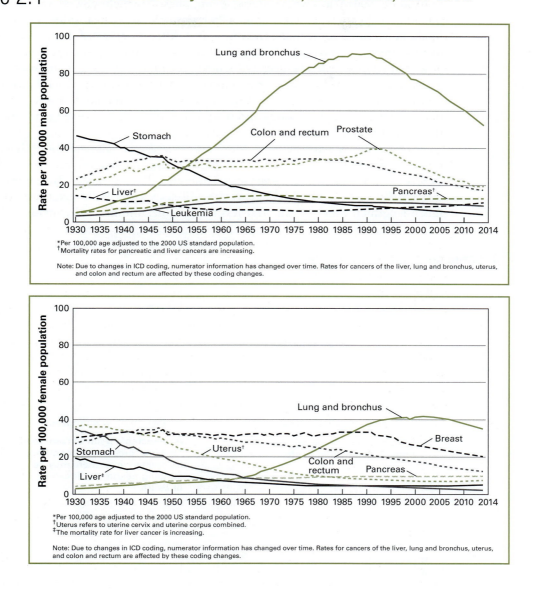

*Per 100,000 age adjusted to the 2000 US standard population.
†Mortality rates for pancreatic and liver cancers are increasing.

Note: Due to changes in ICD coding, numerator information has changed over time. Rates for cancers of the liver, lung and bronchus, uterus, and colon and rectum are affected by these coding changes.

*Per 100,000 age adjusted to the 2000 US standard population.
†Uterus refers to uterine cervix and uterine corpus combined.
‡The mortality rate for liver cancer is increasing.

Note: Due to changes in ICD coding, numerator information has changed over time. Rates for cancers of the liver, lung and bronchus, uterus, and colon and rectum are affected by these coding changes.

DYING TRAJECTORIES

Different causes of death are typically associated with distinct patterns of dying called **dying trajectories,** a fourth important factor in understanding death-related encounters (Glaser & Strauss, 1968). Differences in these trajectories are distinguished primarily by duration and shape. *Duration* in the dying trajectory refers to the time involved between the onset of dying and the arrival of death. This is the so-called **living–dying interval** that Pattison (1977) described as including an "acute crisis phase" (one that often involves rising anxiety generated by the critical awareness of impending death), a "chronic living–dying phase" (which may contain a variety of potential fears and challenges), and a "terminal phase" (which is likely to emphasize issues concerning hope and concerns about different types of death). *Shape* in the dying trajectory designates the course of the dying process, whether one can predict how that process will advance, and whether death is expected or unexpected. Some dying trajectories involve a swift or almost instantaneous onset of death, while others last a long time; some can be anticipated, others are ambiguous or unclear (perhaps involving a series of remissions and relapses), and still others give no advance warning at all (see Figure 2.2).

Most communicable diseases are characterized by a relatively brief dying trajectory. The period from the onset of the infection until its resolution, either in death or in recovery, is usually short—measured in hours, days, or weeks. By contrast, dying trajectories associated with degenerative diseases are usually lengthier, sometimes much lengthier; they are often far less predictable; and they may involve long-term

Figure 2.2 **Some Contrasting Dying Trajectories.**

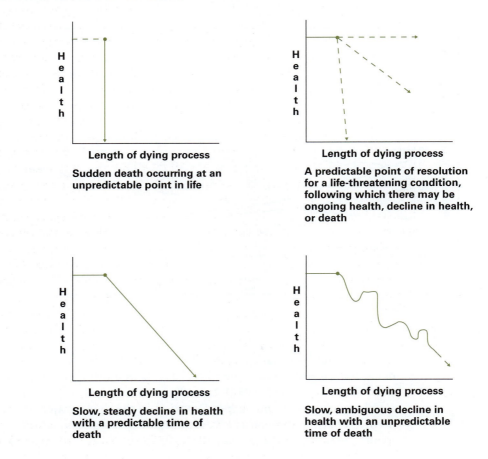

Sudden death occurring at an unpredictable point in life

A predictable point of resolution for a life-threatening condition, following which there may be ongoing health, decline in health, or death

Slow, steady decline in health with a predictable time of death

Slow, ambiguous decline in health with an unpredictable time of death

• Onset of disease

pain and suffering, loss of physical control over one's body, and/or loss of one's mental faculties. Diseases with dying trajectories of this latter type include Parkinson's disease, motor neuron disease (e.g., amyotrophic lateral sclerosis, often called "ALS" or "Lou Gehrig's disease"), muscular dystrophy, multiple sclerosis, and especially Alzheimer's disease (see Chapter 20 in this book).

Consider cancer as an example of a degenerative disease often displaying a complicated dying trajectory. Cancer is one of the most dreaded diseases in our culture, despite the fact that it is much less often a fatal diagnosis and much less typically a disease with a prognosis of imminent death than it was 25 years ago (Mukherjee, 2010). Perhaps much of the fear of cancer has to do with the dying processes that we associate with this disease. Familiar images of cancer usually involve discomfort, pain, and suffering for a long period. These images have been reinforced by the popular media and by the personal stories of a number of prominent individuals (see Focus On 6.1 in Chapter 6). Nevertheless, this is not an entirely appropriate depiction of cancer. Not all cancers are fatal, some do not involve much pain or discomfort, some can be "cured" either outright or at least in the sense that intervention leads to survival for five years or more, and much depends on family history and individual circumstances (Corr, 2010).

The effects of therapeutic interventions that are available to treat some degenerative diseases may complicate differences in the duration and predictability of their dying trajectories. When interventions are successful, they may restore quality and long life to persons with such diseases. Alternatively, an intervention may halt the advance of the disease and leave affected individuals to live out the balance of their lives in a partially debilitated or handicapped condition. Other interventions may only be able to slow (not halt or bring to a stop) the progress of a degenerative disease or prolong the dying of people with the disease. This prolongation of living/dying may be measured in terms of weeks, months, or even years.

The relative prominence of degenerative diseases in the United States today alters experiences with dying and death. Although death is less frequently encountered in our society, when it does occur it is often associated with a protracted and ambiguous or unpredictable dying trajectory (Gill et al., 2010). Thus, Gawande (2010, p. 39) has written: "For all but our most recent history, dying was typically a brief process...the interval between recognizing that you had a life-threatening ailment and death was often just a matter of days or weeks. ...people usually experienced life-threatening illness the way they experienced bad weather—as something that struck with little warning—and you either got through it or you didn't." On one hand, degenerative disease and the lengthier, more ambiguous dying trajectories often associated with them may provide more time for individuals to say their good-byes, get their affairs in order, and prepare for death. On the other hand, experiences with dying from these more typical causes of death in our society often drain physical, emotional, social, spiritual, and financial resources.

PLACE OF DEATH

A fifth factor in understanding death-related encounters is where people die or the **place of death** (Hamano et al., 2016). Imagine that it is the year 1900. You are at the bedside of a loved one who is dying. You are *in that person's home*, because that is where perhaps as many as 80% of all people in the United States die in 1900: in their own beds (Lerner, 1970). You and your loved one are surrounded by sights, sounds, smells, and people that are familiar. Hospitals or other sorts of health care institutions are not the places where most people living in 1900 encounter death. (This is also true of many encounters with death in most developing countries around the world in the 21st century). In 1900, only people who have no personal resources or no family and friends to care for them are likely to be found in public hospitals as they approach death (see the section on hospitals in Chapter 8 in this book). In 1900, those who have the personal or economic resources certainly would not want to leave the comforts of home—their own bed, their own friends and family—to go somewhere else to die. By contrast, more than 64% of people in 2014 in the United States died *in a public institution* of some sort (a hospital, long-term care facility, or a hospice facility)—in a strange place, in a strange bed, and surrounded mostly by strangers (see Table 2.4).

In 1900, you and other members of the family would have been the primary health care providers. What you provide to the dying person is largely palliative care—that is, care for distressing symptoms. If there is fever, you apply a cool cloth along with frequent washings. If the dying person is hungry, you prepare familiar, favorite foods. If the dying person grows frightened, you hold his or her hand, sit with him or her, read or recite words of comfort, pray together, and share your love.

When death is near, you also are near, in the same or a nearby room. After death, you clean and clothe the body—the last act of love in a lifelong drama. The body might well be left in the bed while friends and neighbors "visit." Or perhaps the

Table 2.4 Place of Death: United States, 2014

	Number	Percentage
Total	2,626,418[a]	100.0
	Number	**Percentage**
Medical facility		
Inpatient	793,434	80.98
Outpatient	173,422	17.70
Dead on arrival	12,958	1.32
Total	979,814	37.31
Hospice facility	187,099	7.12
Nursing home/long-term care	523,075	19.92
Decedent's home	773,609	29.45
Other place	160,330	6.10
Place unknown	2,491	0.09

[a]Data include deaths of nonresidents of the United States.

Source: Centers for Disease Control and Prevention, National Center for Health Statistics. Underlying Cause of Death 1999-2015 on CDC WONDER Online Database, released December, 2016. Data are from the Multiple Cause of Death Files, 1999-2015, as compiled from data provided by the 57 vital statistics jurisdictions through the Vital Statistics Cooperative Program. Accessed at http://wonder.cdc.gov/ucd-icd10.html on May 10, 2017 4:29:21 PM

body is placed in a coffin (sometimes handmade by you and other family members—another last action for the deceased) and laid out in the parlor for a wake or visitation. After the funeral, the body is lowered by the family into a grave that you have helped to dig in a nearby family plot or churchyard. As a mark of special honor, the family fills in the grave. The struggles of one family to do this are well depicted in William Faulkner's novel *As I Lay Dying* (1930).

In this situation, death is familiar. Most people have seen, heard, and been touched by the death of a family member. Children are included; if grandmother is dying in her bed at home, children participate by sitting and talking with her or helping with small chores. Children are present during the wake (since it is held in the home) and the funeral. Death is not a stranger to these children.

All these customs have changed for most (but not all) Americans. In 1949, 49.5% of all deaths in our society occurred in some sort of health care institution (mainly in a hospital). Subsequently, increasing numbers of deaths took place in a public institution. In recent years, however, partly as a result of the development of the hospice movement, there has been a modest shift away from hospitals and nursing homes into private residences and hospice facilities, but the majority of deaths in our society now still occur in traditional public institutions. This has occurred despite the fact that, "When surveyed about their preferences for dealing with a terminal illness, most people (86%) indicated that they would prefer to be at home in their final days" (Groff et al., 2016, p. 1610).

In general, since the last half of the 20th century death has gradually moved out of the mainstream of life for many people and families have more and more become spectators at a family member's death, rather than participants or primary caregivers. When many Americans die today, they are away from the people they know best and with whom they have shared personal, long-term histories. This is not a criticism of professional caregivers; our point is only to note that they are not the same people who would have provided care in the past. When there is an absence of long-term relationships with the person who is dying, those who are providing care may be unaware of his or her personal interests, values, needs, and preferences. This is one reason why many contemporary Americans report that they fear dying more than death. It is also one reason why there has been so much recent interest in advance directives as an effort to ensure that one's voice will be heard and respected when critical decisions are made in end-of-life care (see Chapter 16).

Because dying now often occurs outside the home, death is unknown, or at least not well known, to many of us. In these circumstances, family members may not be present at the moment of death in our society. Except among certain groups (e.g., some Mormons, Orthodox Jews, and Amish), the last loving actions—cleaning and dressing the body—for most persons who die in our society are performed by strangers: nurses, nurses' aides, and funeral directors. The body is most likely taken from the place where death occurred to a funeral home. There, after preparation, the family may see the body dressed, arranged, made up. In many ways, the actual event of death is hidden or removed from the lives of most people. Also, at many cemeteries today, families are taken from the gravesite before the casket is lowered into the grave, or the last separation may take place at a chapel near the cemetery entrance and at a distance from the actual gravesite. All of these customs can force family members into the helpless, empty inertia of mere observers.

In short, direct, personal encounters with many facets of natural human death have been diminished in our society. Care for the dying and of the dead has been moved away from the family and out of the home for many in our society (although this situation is changing somewhat with the support of programs like hospice). Thus, few may experience the moments immediately before, at the time of, or directly after the death of someone they love. For all others, death is increasingly distanced—some would say estranged or made alien—from the mainstream of life's events (Erickson, 2013).

One other way to take note of the importance of the place of death has recently emerged from some international and national comparisons. For example, The Economist Intelligence Unit has published a Quality of Death Index (2015) that ranks palliative care in many countries around the globe in terms of four factors: basic end-of-life health care environment, together with availability, quality, and cost of end-of-life

---

ISSUES FOR CRITICAL REFLECTION
#4 Why Do Death-Related Encounters Differ in North America?

The United States and Canada are similar in many ways; still, as shown in the following table, their typical death-related encounters in 2013 differed in many obvious respects.

Why do you think that is the case? Why does Canada appear to fare better in several of the following comparisons?

	The United States of America[1]	Canada[2]
Overall population	308,745,538	35,155,451
Numbers of deaths	2,596,993	252,338
Unadjusted death rates (per 1,000 population)	8.2	7.2
Age-adjusted death rates (per 1,000 population)	7.3	4.8
Infant mortality rates (per 1,000 live births)	5.96	4.9
Average life expectancy		
overall	78.8 years	81.5 years
males	76.4 years	79.4 years
females	81.2 years	83.6 years
Place of death		
in hospital	37.8%	62.8%[3]
nonhospital	61.6%	37.0%
unknown	0.6%	0.2%

Leading causes of death in the two countries were quite similar, except cancer (malignant neoplasms) was the #1 cause of death in Canada in 2013, diabetes mellitus (6th) and influenza/ pneumonia (7th) outranked Alzheimer's disease (8th) as leading causes of death, and suicide (intentional self-harm) was the 9th leading cause of death in Canada.

Sources: [1]National Center for Health Statistics (www.cdc.gov/nchs); figures from Xu et al., 2016.

[2]Statistics Canada (http://www.statcan.gc.ca/), figures retrieved on 3-9-17.

[3]In Quebec, Canada's second largest province, deaths in residential and long-term care centers are. included in "hospital" category.

care. The United States was ranked #8 on the resulting index (the United Kingdom was ranked #1). Although Canada was only ranked #11, some available data suggest that Canada has a more favorable set of death-related encounters than those in the United States (see Issues for Critical Reflection #4). Finally, reports from both the Canadian Hospice Palliative Care Association (2015) and the Dartmouth Health Atlas point out significant variations in end-of-life care within both Canada and the United States. In short, where you live can make a great difference in how you die.

WHAT FACTORS HELPED BRING ABOUT THESE CHANGING ENCOUNTERS WITH DEATH?

Six factors are closely related to changing encounters with death. They help explain why and how death rates began to decrease in a noticeable way in the 19th century and have continued to decline thereafter. (NOTE: Search the Internet for "Blue Zones" or read Buettner (2012, 2015) to learn about geographical or demographical areas of the world in which people lead measurably longer lives.)

The earliest and most important factor in changing encounters with death was **industrialization** in the late 18th and 19th centuries. Industrialization had bad aspects, such as child labor, but it also brought about increased food production, better clothing, and better housing, thereby supporting a healthier population. In short, industrialization led to improvements in the environment and in the general standard of living that, in turn, meant death became a less familiar visitor in human lives.

Industrialization also helped develop more effective means of communication (e.g., telegraph and telephone) and more effective means of transportation (e.g., rail systems, better highways, more efficient trucking) that, in turn, changed patterns of encounters with death. For instance, when crops failed in one place surpluses from elsewhere could be moved to that place, and malnutrition and starvation could be alleviated or eliminated. By contrast, when food shipments are blocked by inadequate port or distribution facilities (and at times by corruption) many deaths from hunger and malnutrition can result.

The second major factor in reducing death rates involved **public health measures** that first achieved significance in the 19th and early 20th centuries. For example, threats posed by many communicable diseases (such as cholera, typhoid, encephalitis, and malaria) were reduced by a better understanding of how they were transmitted (e.g., by mosquitoes or rats) and subsequent control of those means of transmission. Also, Pasteur's discovery in the late 19th century that many communicable diseases are caused by microbial agents led to isolation or quarantine of those with such diseases, separation of drinking water sources from sewage, and other improvements in basic sanitation. These actions helped prevent morbidity and mortality in society as a whole. This reduced overall death rates, but young people—infants in particular—continued to die at high rates. Nutrition and preventive health measures for individuals had to be better understood before overall death rates, and especially deaths in infancy, could be reduced further. When such measures were pursued in increasingly effective ways, there were significant gains in ALE during the late 1930s and 1940s.

The third major factor working to reduce death rates is **preventive health care** for individuals. For example, vaccination permits an individual's own immune system to build up defenses by inoculating or infecting the person in a controlled way with an infectious agent (Allen, 2007; Mello, Studdert, & Parmet, 2015; Yang & Silverman,

2015). Preventive measures like this originated with Jenner's introduction in 1798 of a vaccination for smallpox (Riedel, 2005), but it took nearly a century for another such advance: Pasteur's introduction in 1881 of a vaccination for anthrax (Wehrle & Top, 1981). From that time, the number of available vaccines increased rapidly, although at irregular intervals. These vaccines protected more and more persons from deadly—often childhood—diseases, thus quickly helping to increase average length of life. Other forms of preventive health care for individuals include the use of media to circulate advice on healthy diet and exercise, warnings against the health-related dangers of tobacco use, and efforts to persuade pregnant women not to drink alcoholic beverages or use illegal drugs.

All of these factors influenced changing encounters with death before the fourth major variable, the rise of modern **cure-oriented medicine**, first became significant early in the 20th century (Warraich, 2017). Then hospitals began to be major contributors to health care. The biomedical model of disease became dominant, emphasizing cure over prevention. Physicians became important in providing health care and interventions became curative in many key ways. Special technologies were developed to provide this type of care. Because they often are quite expensive, these technologies are located in particular places, mainly hospitals and specialized outpatient clinics. Thus, health care is usually not delivered to where the sick person is (no more or only rare medical home visits); rather, the person with a disease is delivered to the place where health care is provided.

Medicine had now become an important factor in reducing death rates and accelerating changes begun much earlier. Especially since the introduction of successful antibiotics (i.e., antimicrobial agents such as penicillin)—largely a post–World War II (after 1945) phenomenon—modern medicine contributed to improvements in death rates and ALE, at least in industrialized nations. Along with earlier factors, modern cure-oriented medicine has affected both overall death rates and infant death rates, although the latter have not declined as quickly as the former and only approached their current levels in the late 1950s and 1960s. Still, the Commonwealth Fund concluded from a comparison with 10 other countries that, "The United States health care system is the most expensive in the world, but comparative analyses consistently show the U.S. underperforms relative to other countries on most dimensions of performance" (Davis et al., 2014, p. 3).

A fifth significant factor in how death is experienced has to do with the **nature of contemporary families**. When families were large, extended social groups who usually lived near each other and had members (especially women) who stayed at home, many members could be counted on to take part in caring for the ill, the dying, the bodies of the dead, and the bereaved. Encounters with dying, death, and bereavement occur in quite different ways when the population in most developed countries is rapidly aging and families are smaller, more are obliged to have all of their adult members work out of the home, more are scattered throughout the country or the world, and with members who are generally less connected to each other (Seale, 2000). This is especially true when family and other kinship groups are shattered or nonexistent, as is the case for many single and homeless individuals. Religious communities and friendly neighbors might have taken up some of the slack, but for many in our mobile, secular, and impersonal societies those ties are also less typical, less strong, and less available.

A sixth factor influencing how death is encountered is **lifestyle**. How we live our lives often has a direct bearing on when and how we die. Thus, research has shown that *nearly half of all deaths in the United States arise from or are associated* *with underlying causes that are, in principle, preventable* (McGinnis & Foege, 1993; Mokdad et al., 2004). Tobacco use, poor diet, and limited physical activity, are the actual underlying causes of the largest number of preventable deaths in our society. For example, the story of Bryan Lee Curtis near the beginning of this chapter plainly demonstrates the harmful effects of using tobacco products. Research is clear and convincing that smoking is the major factor that has led to lung and bronchial cancers becoming the leading cancer causes of death among both men and women in our society (see Figure 2.1). In addition, research on low-intensity smoking confirmed that "there is no risk-free level of exposure to tobacco smoke" (Inoue-Choi et al., 2016). Thus, a study of active cigarette smokers and those who have quit smoking in three time periods over a 50-year period from 1959 to 2010 (Thun et al., 2013, pp. 361–363) showed that:

> the relative and absolute risks of death from smoking continue to increase among female smokers; the relative risks of death from lung cancer, COPD, ischemic heart disease, any type of stroke, and all causes are now nearly identical for female and male smokers.... [F]or men 55 to 74 years of age and for women 60 to 74 years of age, the rate of death from all causes combined is now at least three times as high among current smokers as among those who have never smoked.... [Further] quitting smoking at any age dramatically lowers mortality from all major smoking-related diseases.... Quitting smoking is much more effective than reducing the number of cigarettes smoked....

Additional studies have shown that many deaths are caused by a variety of cancers and other diseases not previously associated with smoking (Carter et al., 2015; Jha et al., 2013; Siegel et al., 2015). Also, Öberg and colleagues (2011) demonstrated that secondhand smoke is the underlying cause of death for more than 600,000 people worldwide every year with a special impact on children and nonsmoking adults. In the light of these and other reports, it is no wonder that the U.S. Department of Health and Human Services (2014, 2016) has issued numerous reports from 1964 through 2016 on the dangers of smoking and other addictive behaviors, pointing out lives that have been saved by quitting smoking. Also, the U.S. National Cancer Institute and the World Health Organization (2016, p. 4) reported that, "Tobacco use remains one of the world's leading causes of preventable premature death" and research by Kasza and colleagues (2017) has identified dangers in the recent proliferation and popularity of non-cigarette tobacco products. As a result of these and multiple other efforts to reduce smoking, "The steady decline in smoking rates among U.S. adults that began in the early 1960s has accelerated substantially during the 7 years of the Barack Obama presidency.... If the current rate of decline were to continue, the prevalence of smoking among U.S. adults would fall from its current level of 15.3% to zero by around 2035" (Fiore, 2016, p. 1410).

Similarly, eating high-cholesterol foods predisposes to heart and circulatory problems (Kessler, 2009). Also, ingesting large amounts of alcohol and sweetened beverages, along with consumption of other high-sugar foods and lack of regular exercise, helps explain the increasing rates of obesity and diabetes among Americans (Stahre et al., 2014). Further, practicing safe driving techniques affects the prevalence of deaths from motor vehicle accidents. In addition, lack of exercise, misuse of firearms, certain forms of risky sexual behavior such as engaging in unprotected sex, and illicit drug use all contribute to early and avoidable deaths.

Concerning obesity, data from the 2011–2012 National Health and Nutrition Examination Survey (Ogden et al., 2014; The GBD 2015 Obesity Collaborators, 2017) has shown that 34.9% of adults 20 years of age and over in the United States have a body mass index (BMI) of 30 or greater and thus are classified as obese. (BMI = weight in pounds divided by height in inches, and again divided by height in inches, then multiplied by 703; many BMI calculators are available on the Internet.) In addition, 16.9% of all children and teens aged 2–19 years are classified as obese. Obesity and being overweight are both dangerous in themselves and can slow the long-term trend toward increases in ALE (e.g., Institute of Medicine, 2012; U.S. Department of Health and Human Services, 2010). Moreover, a group of over 100 retired senior military leaders called for action in a report entitled, "Too Fat to Fight" (Mission: Readiness, 2010) in order to change the situation in which 27% of young adults are too overweight to serve in the military, a circumstance that can impact military readiness and national security. Deleterious effects on health of obesity and overweight have also been shown in a study of countries around the world (The GBD 2015 Obesity Collaborators, 2017).

The six factors outlined in this section—industrialization, improved public health measures, preventive health care for individuals, the rise of modern cure-oriented medicine, the nature of contemporary families, and lifestyle—seem to be the most prominent variables that influence overall encounters with death in our society. Some of these factors go back centuries; others have only become prominent in recent years. Taken together, the overall influence of these factors has been to reduce encounters with death, thereby removing death in many key ways from the home and from the mainstream of modern living. Also, death is all too often encountered without some of the community supports that might have been in place in the informal family and other social networks of times past. Of course, this does not mean that death no longer comes into our world in any way; the issue is *the form death takes* when it does present itself. For example, when death rates (especially those associated with birth and infants) are as low as they now are in the United States, potential parents can decide to have fewer offspring and to delay first pregnancies since they are less fearful than parents in earlier times that death will disrupt their plans. Other individuals may be too complacent about their use of tobacco and alcohol products, their poor diet, their lack of physical exercise, or the importance of having their children vaccinated. The form death takes depends on certain variables, such as the leading causes of death, the dying trajectories we encounter, the place where death occurs, and how our family, our ethnic group, and our local community are or are not able to rally to support individuals experiencing dying, death, and bereavement.

We will all die, sooner or later. And we will all have encounters with dying, death, and bereavement during our lives. What this chapter has shown is that those encounters will typically be different for us as members of contemporary society than in times past in our own country or currently in many other parts of the world. Encounters with death in the United States today are an important component in a special set of experiences. In many ways, these death-related experiences represent desirable improvements over the lot of other human beings; in other ways, they have less favorable implications. We will explore further aspects of those changing experiences with death in subsequent chapters.

Summary

In this chapter, we learned about *contemporary encounters with death*, especially those found in the United States and in other developed countries. We examined those encounters both in themselves and as they differ from mortality patterns in our society in the past or in developing countries in other parts of the world at present. In the United States today, death rates are lower overall, ALE is longer, people die most often from degenerative rather than communicable diseases, typical dying trajectories are more prolonged and more ambiguous, and more people die in public institutions than at home. In addition, we examined six variables or principal factors that are correlated with these changes in death-related encounters: industrialization, public health measures, preventive health care for individuals, modern cure-oriented medicine, the nature of contemporary families, and lifestyle.

Glossary

Average life expectancy (ALE): an estimate of the average number of years members of a group of people are projected to live

Communicable diseases: diseases that can be transmitted or spread from person to person

Cure-oriented medicine: medical science and health care practice primarily designed to cure, reverse the course, or halt/slow the advance of diseases or other life-threatening conditions

Death rates: numbers of deaths among members of a given population group divided by the total number of those in the group; usually expressed as some number of deaths per 1,000 or 100,000 individuals

Degenerative diseases: diseases that usually result from long-term wearing out of body organs, typically associated with aging, lifestyle, and environment

Dying trajectories: patterns of dying or the ways in which dying plays out, typically distinguished by *duration* (the time between the onset of dying and the arrival of death) and *shape* (the course of the dying, its predictability, and whether death is expected or unexpected)

Encounters with death, dying, and bereavement: ways in which we confront or meet up with death-related events

Extended family: a large kinship group whose members often live near each other

Industrialization: the organization of the means of production, especially manufacturing, into industries; often involving mechanization versus hand labor

Living–dying interval: the period between the onset of dying and the arrival of death

Place of death: the physical place in which death occurs, for example, in a home or public institution

Preventive health care: medical and health care primarily designed to prevent or minimize the likelihood of acquiring disease or putting one's life at risk

Public health measures: community actions to protect or improve the health of society's members, for example, to provide safe drinking water and to dispose of sewage, garbage, and other contaminants

Questions for Review and Discussion

1. Changes in encounters with death in contemporary society can be seen in death rates and ALE. How have these sets of data changed over the last hundred or so years in the United States? How have these changes affected your encounters with death, dying, and bereavement?

2. How do we distinguish communicable diseases from degenerative diseases as causes of death, and what are the typical patterns of dying associated with each of

them like? How might these different causes of death affect your encounters with death, dying, and bereavement?

3. This chapter noted changes in the place where people typically die. How are encounters with death likely to be different when a person dies at home versus away from home (e.g., in an institution like a hospital or long-term care facility)? How do changes in place affect your encounters with the death of a person who is dying and with those who are his or her survivors?

4. Have you ever used online resources to learn more about encounters with dying, death, and bereavement? Were they helpful? Why or why not?

Suggested Readings

The basic materials for demographic studies of mortality are found in:

Centers for Disease Control and Prevention (CDC). *Morbidity and Mortality Weekly Report.* Provides current information and statistics about disease.

National Center for Health Statistics (NCHS). This CDC agency offers various publications; among these, the *National Vital Statistics Reports* summarize mortality data.

National Safety Council. *Injury Facts.* Published annually.

U.S. Bureau of the Census. (1975). *Historical Statistics of the United States, Colonial Times to 1970, Bicentennial Edition.*

U.S. Census Bureau. *Statistical Abstract of the United States.*

Selected Web Resources

Some useful search terms include: AVERAGE LIFE EXPECTANCY; COMMUNICABLE DISEASES; CURE-ORIENTED MEDICINE (OR CURATIVE CARE); DEATH ENCOUNTERS (OR DEATH-RELATED ENCOUNTERS OR ENCOUNTERS WITH DEATH); DEATH RATES (OR MORTALITY RATES); DEGENERATIVE DISEASES; DYING TRAJECTORIES; FAMILY (SIZE/STRUCTURE); INDUSTRIALIZATION; INFANT MORTALITY RATES; LIFESTYLE; LIVING-DYING INTERVAL; MATERNAL DEATH OR MATERNAL MORTALITY RATES; PLACE OR LOCATION OF DEATH; PREVENTIVE HEALTH CARE; PUBLIC HEALTH.

You can also visit the following *organizational and other Internet sites:*

Centers for Disease Control and Prevention (CDC)

Epidemiology of Dying and End-of-Life Experiences

National Center for Health Statistics (NCHS)

National Safety Council

U.S. Census Bureau

World Health Organization

TIMOTHY A. CLARY/AFP/Getty Images

Changing Attitudes toward Death

Objectives of this **Chapter**

▷ To explain the concept of an "attitude" and to identify **death-related attitudes** as a component of death-related *experiences*

▷ To describe the meaning of "death anxiety" and to explore interest in understanding that concept

▷ To examine terror management theory

▷ To identify four basic categories of death-related concerns and responses found in individuals

▷ To sketch a theory of five dominant social patterns in Western attitudes toward death

▷ To illustrate the role that attitudes play in death-related experiences through examples taken from contemporary Amish life in North America and from the New England Puritans of the 17th century

AMISH ATTITUDES TOWARD DEATH

John Stolzfus bore one of the most common names in the Old Order Amish community in eastern Pennsylvania where he had lived all of his life. The Stolzfus family traced its roots through 18th-century immigrants from Alsace and then back to Swiss origins in the 16th-century Anabaptist movement. The Anabaptists were persecuted in Europe for their rejection of infant baptism (on the grounds that children come into the world without a knowledge of good and evil and thus do not need to be baptized as infants to remove sin) (Kraybill, 2003). No Amish (whose name comes from their founder, Jacob Ammann) remain in Europe today, but an estimated 250,000 live in various parts of the United States (especially in Ohio, Pennsylvania, and Indiana) and in the Canadian province of Ontario (Hostetler, 1993, 2013; Kraybill, 2001; Kraybill, Johnson-Weiner, & Nolt, 2013; Kraybill, Nolt, & Weaver-Zercher, 2010; Nolt, 2003; Nolt & Meyers, 2007; Weaver-Zercher, 2001; Zielinski, 1997).

As a member of a close-knit Amish community, John Stolzfus centered his life on religious beliefs and practice, a large extended family, and work on a farm. The Old Order Amish are known for their distinctive dress. Men wear plain, dark clothes fastened with hooks and eyes, broad-brimmed hats, and full beards without mustaches; women dress in bonnets and long, full dresses. Members of this community use horse-drawn buggies instead of automobiles, espouse pacifism, and reject many modern devices (such as high-line electricity and tractors with pneumatic tires).

These are the outward expressions of a slow-changing culture that is determined to follow its understanding of biblical injunctions. Its central guidelines include separation from the world: "Be not conformed to this world" (Rom. 12:2) and "Be ye not unequally yoked together with unbelievers" (2 Cor. 6:14). Amish society turns inward to community to worship God and follow the example of the life of Jesus, to moderate the influences of humanity's evil circumstances, and to preserve values in ethical relationships through obedience and conformity. As Kraybill has written (2001, p. 28), "Amish faith has not been separated from daily living; it penetrates their entire way of life." The Amish blend together an emphasis on oral tradition, shared practical knowledge, closeness to nature, respect for elders, striving for self-sufficiency, and smallness in social scale. Usually, 25–40 households in geographical proximity form a congregation or church district and take turns in hosting biweekly religious services in their homes.

The Stolzfus family rose with the sun and went to bed shortly after nightfall. As a child, John was assigned chores that helped meet his family's needs. This type of work continued during his school years, with responsibilities appropriate to his age, growth, and maturity. John's schooling did not extend beyond the eighth grade because the Amish find that sufficient for the lives they have chosen to lead. They are wary that additional formal education might only tend to subvert their traditional beliefs and values. Like most of his peers, at the age of 16, John experienced *rumspringa*, a "running around" coming-of-age ritual in which the strict rules of Amish community life are temporarily lifted while the individual ponders a voluntary decision to be baptized (Shachtman, 2006; Stevick, 2007). After that, he was baptized at the age of 18 into his local church district, thereby making a formal, lifelong commitment to the church. One day soon after, he married a young woman from the same community.

The young couple initially lived with John's family and he continued to work on their farm (although these days many Amish "work away," i.e., off a farm in a factory or small business). Eventually, through a small inheritance from a relative and with financial help from their families, John and his wife bought a small piece of land for their own farm. The birth of their first three children, building their own house, and the great communal activity of raising a barn on their farm all marked a productive period in John's life.

Shortly after the birth of their fifth child, John's wife died. Relatives helped to care for the children and with work on the expanding farm until one of his wife's unmarried cousins was willing to marry John and take on the role of mother for his existing children and for the additional children they would have together. After that, life went on for many years in a quiet and steady way. In time, the offspring from both of John's marriages grew up and were themselves married. John and his second wife became respected members of their community, he as a deacon or minister to the poor in the church, and she for her work in church groups and for her quiet presence at community gatherings.

In due course, after what he thought of as a good life, John began to decline in vigor and in his ability to get around. In accordance with Amish customs, a small house (called a "grandfather house") was built next to the main farmhouse, and John retired there. After his retirement, John concentrated on reading his beloved Bible, whittling simple wooden toys, and spending time with his second wife, their children, and their grandchildren. When he could no longer get out of bed, both John and other members of his community realized that his death was not far off. Gradually, Amish neighbors of all ages began to come by to pray together and say good-bye one last time. John spoke openly of his coming death and used these visits to encourage others to prepare for and calmly accept their own deaths. At the age of 82, John Stolzfus died peacefully one night in his own bed, as one of his daughters sat quietly in a nearby rocking chair and two of his grandchildren slept in their own beds in the same room.

John's body was embalmed by a non-Amish funeral director and then returned to the home where male family members dressed his body in traditional white garments (Bryer, 1979). The body was placed in a six-sided wooden coffin that had been made ready a few weeks before, and the coffin was laid out in the central room of the house on top of two sawhorses and several planks covered by a plain sheet. Friends helped with many of these arrangements and made sure that those who had known John were notified of his death. That evening, the next day, and the following evening, other members of the community came to the house to bring gifts of food and to offer practical, emotional, and spiritual support to John's family. Several people took turns sitting with the body throughout the night until the grave could be dug and other preparations made for the funeral. In keeping with the whole of his life, John Stolzfus' funeral was a simple event, a familiar ritual that involved members of the community in the services, the burial, a communal meal afterward, and a recognized pattern of consolation activities during the following weeks and months. No one was shocked or surprised by this death or by its related events. Experience, tradition, and shared attitudes had prepared individuals and the community as a whole to support each other and to contend with the cycles of life and death in their midst. (For a real-life example of Amish mourning after traumatic deaths, see Focus On 3.1.)

FOCUS ON 3.1

Amish Mourning after Traumatic Deaths

On October 2, 2006, Charles Carl Roberts IV invaded the one-room West Nickel Mines Amish School in southeastern Pennsylvania. After freeing all the adult women and boys, Roberts shot ten girls, killing five of them and wounding the others before he took his own life (Ruth, 2011; Yoder, 2007).

Many outsiders found the response of the Amish community to this horrific event to be remarkable. The community responded by shunning publicity and asking the media to refrain from "close-up gawking and picture taking" (Levin, 2006, p. 4A). Instead, they released a statement that said in part, "We don't know or understand why this happened, but we do believe that God allowed this to happen" (Levin & Hall, 2006, p. 3A). Most notable was the lack of anger on the part of the Amish, together with their powerful support system for the primary mourners and the community itself in the face of such tragedy.

Four qualities of Amish life were prominent in the ways in which the people of this community coped with these events (Hampson, 2006, p. 3A):

- Believing that the world is basically evil, they accepted God's plan, however mysterious or painful it may be and trusted that the dead children were now in heaven.
- Acting on the Christian injunction to turn the other cheek and to love one's enemies, the Amish bowed to their suffering and made efforts to console bewildered members of Roberts' family.
- Following a general practice of not acting in ways that emphasize one's individuality, the Amish did not rush to speak to the media or show much emotion publicly.
- Working closely together and helping each other, the Amish acted *as a community* to prepare the series of wakes, funerals, and burials for the five dead children and to provide meals for those who would attend. They also cared for surviving victims, demolished the school building in which the shootings occurred, and built a new school on nearby land owned by a member of the community.

In all of this, the Amish provided distinctive examples of acting out a specific form of religious faith, a willingness to forgive those who had done them harm, and a painstaking effort at reconciliation (Kraybill, Nolt, & Weaver-Zercher, 2007). Religious faith and the community itself provided the needed support.

WHAT IS AN ATTITUDE AND HOW DO ATTITUDES INFLUENCE ENCOUNTERS?

In Chapter 2, we examined *death-related encounters* as one central component of our death-related experiences. In this chapter, we explore a second central component: our *death-related attitudes*. According to the *Oxford English Dictionary* (1989), the term *attitude* arose in art. Originally, it meant the disposition or posture of a figure in statuary or painting. That led to the notion that a posture of the body could be related to a particular mental state. From there, the term *attitude* came to be associated with some "settled behaviour or manner of acting, as representative of feeling or opinion" (vol. 1, p. 771).

In other words, an attitude is a way of presenting oneself to or being in the world. If one's bodily posture (one's attitude) includes an upraised fist, a general tenseness, and a facial grimace as one leans toward another person, that posture will affect how the particular encounter develops. Compare such an attitude with one that includes open arms, a smile, and a generally relaxed body. Examples of attitudes expressed in everyday behavior include offering to shake hands when one meets another person or spreading one's arms wide and hugging or kissing the cheek of an individual as a form of greeting. Both of these behavioral patterns indicate friendliness, lack of hostility, and the absence of a weapon in one's grasp. Attitudes like these influence one's encounters by predisposing the person who is being greeted to a friendly or cordial response. Thus, one's way of being in the world, or how one meets the world, often influences the kinds of encounters one has and how those encounters are likely to develop. It also works the other way around; one's encounters influence one's own bodily postures and habits of mind.

This means that we human beings *contribute* to our experiences. We are not merely passive receivers of information. We shape and form our knowledge of what is happening, depending on our prior beliefs and feelings. We meet the world from a particular stance, in specific ways. The Amish do this in their special ways, and the Puritans (whom we discuss at the end of this chapter) did it in theirs; everyone does it in some way or other. Thus, a central issue relating to attitudes concerns the ways in which patterns of belief and feeling enter into what we think and do, especially as our attitudes become dispositions or habitual ways of thinking about and acting in the world.

This is true both for attitudes in general and for those that are specifically related to death. That is, death-related attitudes are both products and determinants of many of our encounters with the world. They dispose us favorably to some types of death-related encounters, while leaving us not so favorably disposed—or even negatively disposed and actively hostile—to others. At the same time, events around us help in their own ways to shape our knowledge and understanding of the world. Death-related encounters certainly play an important role in shaping death-related attitudes as shown in Focus On 3.2.

FOCUS ON 3.2

Death-Related Attitudes Concerning HIV and AIDS

Less than ten years elapsed between the first reports of a new disease and its emergence as a leading cause of death. Such a rapid rise of a deadly syndrome with (at first) no known cause is unprecedented (Centers for Disease Control and Prevention [CDC, 1992b]). Not surprisingly, many became frightened by

(continues)

Death-Related Attitudes Concerning HIV and AIDS

these changes occurring so quickly around them. Their early responses of ignorance and fear all too often led to social stigma and outright discrimination (Sontag, 1978, 1989). Many persons infected with HIV were treated badly by former friends, in the workplace, in schools, in matters of housing, and even by some health care personnel (e.g., Liu et al., 2012). Some infected persons internalized a sense of stigma, hiding their HIV status, or even isolating themselves socially. Critics argued that the government's attitude seemed to be one of indifference to what was developing into a major public health tragedy (Shilts, 1987).

Even after the HIV was identified and the cause of AIDS became known, many were disturbed that the disease was most often directly associated with sexual behavior or sharing needles for illicit drug use. Some found it easy to make moral judgments about individuals they thought were engaged in immoral

(continues)

Death-Related Attitudes Concerning HIV and AIDS

behaviors. Here, attitudes inserted themselves in hurtful ways. For example, Ryan White became a symbol for many who were denied the right to attend school because some thought he was a danger to his classmates (White & Cunningham, 1991). In fact, as a hemophiliac who had contracted AIDS from tainted blood products that were required to sustain his life, Ryan's compromised immune system was actually at much greater risk of acquiring opportunistic infections from his peers. Similar negative attitudes arose when the family of Clifford and Louise Ray discovered their three hemophiliac sons had been infected with HIV. Although they had expected support from their community in Arcadia, Florida, when they tried to enroll their sons in regular school classes, they experienced ugly protests, death threats, and had their house burned down by unknown persons (Buckley, 2001). Clearly, the attitudes involved in these situations most harmed those who had been sickened by the newly discovered viral agent.

From a global perspective, attitudes have had significant impact on encounters with HIV and AIDS. Local attitudes and behaviors influenced by specific cultures have led to many individuals in certain countries becoming infected by HIV. Most often, these attitudes and behaviors involve sexual behavior. In heterosexual transmission, this typically reflects lack of access to condoms; religious, cultural, or psychological influences that work against their use; sexual coercion and violence experienced by women and girls; and situations in which females are unable to control the terms on which they have sex (all of which are found in Sub-Saharan Africa and elsewhere). Among men who have sex with men, HIV infection is facilitated in some regions (such as Latin America) by religious and cultural prohibitions against acknowledging homosexual behavior and against taking appropriate precautions. In other regions (including Western Europe and North America), because "few young gay men have seen friends die of AIDS, and some mistakenly view antiretrovirals as a cure, there is growing complacency about the HIV risk" (UNAIDS, 2001, p. 9). In all forms of sexual transmission, multiple sexual partnerships and large sexual networks facilitate HIV infection. Such infection can also spread to the general population through prostitution, the partners of infected persons, and the sexual partners of injecting drug users.

At one point, the CDC (2006, p. 587) noted "the widespread belief that AIDS is no longer a problem or a severe disease in the United States." In fact, the CDC continued, "HIV/AIDS remains a potentially deadly chronic disease" (p. 588). The difficulty is that "Complacency, stigma, and discrimination persist and all decrease motivation among persons and communities to adopt risk-reduction behaviors, get tested for HIV, and access prevention and treatment services" (p. 587). In part as a result of attitudes like these, the CDC (2016) reported that in the United States in 2015, an estimated 39,513 person were

(continues)

FOCUS ON 3.2 *(continued)*

Death-Related Attitudes Concerning HIV and AIDS

diagnosed with HIV and 18,303 were diagnosed with AIDS. Approximately 1.2 million Americans are HIV positive, but because a significant portion of them do not know their infection status, many are only diagnosed shortly before they develop AIDS, making early treatment impossible. Clearly, early HIV testing would reduce the spread of disease, extend life expectancy, and reduce costs of care. Such testing is especially important for persons at higher risk and in high-prevalence populations (Frieden, Foti, & Mermin, 2015).

Consider what we learned in Chapter 2: unlike John Stolzfus, most people in the United States today die in a hospital or other institution. As a result, their deaths may be physically removed from the presence of family members and friends. That makes such deaths remote from their survivors. Most Americans today do not often confront death directly, a circumstance that can contribute to and support a belief that death is, or should be, invisible. To put this another way, if one's habitual way of behaving in the face of someone else's stress is to withdraw because it creates discomfort, then one is likely to stay away from the hospital where someone is dying. In this way, *attitudes* toward death (e.g., "death is stressful—stay away from stressful situations") influence encounters. The attitudes that one holds may tend to encourage one to withdraw or become remote from encounters with death. To show this, we next examine the following four topics: death anxiety; terror management theory; death-related concerns and responses; and some implications of death-related attitudes.

DEATH ANXIETY

Much research on death-related attitudes has had to do with matters related to **death anxiety** (e.g., Neimeyer, 1994; Neimeyer & Van Brunt, 1995; Neimeyer, Wittkowski, & Moser, 2004). Results of these studies are interesting, especially when repeated reports confirm the plausibility of their conclusions. For example, in many studies, women report higher death anxiety than men (e.g., Lester, Templer, & Abdel-Khalek, 2006). It is not clear precisely whether women really are more anxious than men about death or whether women are simply more open than men in discussing their attitudes toward emotionally intense subjects. Many studies also note that older adults appear to report somewhat less death anxiety than some younger persons (e.g., Russac et al., 2007). Also, it seems that individuals who firmly believe or firmly disbelieve in religion and an afterlife seem to have less death anxiety than those who do not share such a value framework (e.g., Wink & Scott, 2005). Death anxiety has also been examined in terms of other demographic (e.g., occupation, health status, and experience with death) and personality (e.g., psychopathology) factors, but results are more mixed. Tomer and Eliason (1996) argued that death anxiety may not be linear (i.e., increasing or decreasing steadily as life goes on) but may vary with life accomplishments and past or future regrets.

Death anxiety remains a complex and not fully understood subject (Kastenbaum, 2000). Moreover, the efforts of researchers to measure various forms of death anxiety, to determine the variables that do or do not influence such anxiety, and to compare different population groups in terms of their death anxieties face several difficulties. For example, many of these studies seem to have assumed that: (1) death anxiety does exist (in all humans and all respects, or just in some?); (2) individuals will be both willing and able to disclose their death anxieties; and (3) adequate instruments and methodologies are available to identify and measure death anxieties. Further, however much or little an individual may be anxious about death, most of the research on this subject depends upon self-reports (in response to questionnaires, interviews, projective tests), usually taken on a one-time basis (and, therefore, cross-sectional, with little additional background or follow up) from conveniently accessible groups like college students. Those conducting these studies make efforts to be sensitive to questions of interpretation, such as: How valid or reliable are such reports? Are they representative or taken out of context? In particular, if one's score on a death anxiety scale is low, does that indicate low death anxiety or high denial and active repression of scary feelings? Note that the familiar distinction between *fears* (attitudes or concerns directed to some specific focus) and *anxieties* (attitudes that are more generalized and diffuse or less particularized in their objects) is set aside in most of this research.

Still, instruments for studying death anxiety have improved since the early Death Anxiety Scale (Templer, 1970; see also Lonetto & Templer, 1986) involving 15 short statements that one endorses as true or false to a number of other measures such as those described in the *Death Anxiety Handbook* (Neimeyer, 1994). There also have been efforts (e.g., Neimeyer & Van Brunt, 1995) to encourage greater sophistication and effectiveness in this field.

TERROR MANAGEMENT THEORY

Ernst Becker argued in *The Denial of Death* (1973) that the unique ability of humans to be aware of their individual mortality and inevitable death creates anxiety. Consequently, efforts are made to deny that terrifying fact. As a conceptual model in social psychology, **terror management theory** (TMT; e.g., Greenberg, Pyszcynski, & Solomon, 1986) extends this view by arguing that fear of death and annihilation leads to a condition of anxiety and terror that underlies much individual and social behavior. In particular, TMT draws on the ideas like the following from Becker:

> Man has a symbolic identity that brings him sharply out of nature…. He is a creator with a mind that soars out to speculate about atoms and infinity, who can place himself imaginatively at a point in space and contemplate bemusedly his own planet. This immense expansion, this dexterity, this ethereality, this self-consciousness gives to man literally the status of a small god in nature….Yet, at the same time…man is a worm and food for worms. This is the paradox: he is out of nature and hopelessly in it…housed in a heat-pumping, breath-grasping body that once belonged to a fish…it aches and bloods and will decay and die. (p. 26)

Kastenbaum (2009, p. 276) interpreted Becker to mean that:

> Human existence … is a terrifying dilemma. We do not want to face the creature facts of our being, and so we don't. As individuals we distract ourselves within the flurry of daily

life; as a society we pretend to be powerful, protective, and enduring....The desperate mission of individual behavior patterns and societal institutions is to disguise, blunt, or transform the experience of what Becker might have called *primal terror* ...

If this view is correct, individuals' quest for positive self-esteem leads them to both seek and need society's illusions to overcome their death-related terror. That is, terror management is the primary goal of human motives. Research inspired by TMT has sought to confirm this and to explore ways in which the interplay between cultural symbolic systems and individual self-esteem work to avoid, reduce, buffer, or otherwise manage death-related terror (there is a YouTube video entitled "Flight from Death: The Quest for Immortality" that offers a visual exploration of the ideas involved in TMT). Neimeyer (2009, p. 298) described results of such research as having been "consistently provocative, demonstrating that confrontation with death can drive a wide range of social attitudes and behaviors."

TMT has been criticized for being unable to explain why older adults who are more closely approaching deaths than their younger counterparts are often reported to have less death anxiety than their juniors, and why human creativity and growth are not compatible with genuine acceptance of death. Such criticisms have led to modifications or amplifications of TMT (Solomon, Greenberg, & Pyszcynski, 2004). For our purposes, this may suggest two points. First, perhaps everyone is not as terrified by the thought of his or her personal death as TMT has proposed. Thus, Freud (1959c, p. 289) suggested that individuals are not really so anxious about their own deaths because "It is indeed impossible to imagine our own death...at bottom nobody believes in his own death, or...in the unconscious every one of us is convinced of his own immortality." Also societal death systems (see Chapter 4) offer more than illusions; in supporting the dying and the bereaved such systems try not just to reduce fear or terror, but to encourage constructive coping with imminent death and/or the aftermath of the death of a love one, and thereby allow individuals to achieve authenticity and realize their human potential. A second, related point is that in the bereavements of many people, it is often the death of a significant other that seems to be most important to them. Such bereavements are most often characterized by sadness, sorrow, and grief, rather than terror. More generally, how universal, how persistent, and how salient is most people's focus on death-related terror? What, exactly, are people anxious, fearful, or even terrified about in relation to death? We consider some answers to this last question in the next section.

DEATH-RELATED CONCERNS AND RESPONSES

One way to move forward in our thinking about death-related attitudes might be to pay attention not merely to aversive attitudes (such as anxiety, distancing, fear, denial) but to more accepting attitudes as well. It is also useful to sort out death-related attitudes in terms of the specific focus of their concern. For example, the word *death* is often used to designate, not the situation or state of being dead, but the *process of dying* or coming to be dead. Thus, when we say, "John had a very difficult death," we are likely referring not to the actual fact of his death but to the manner of his dying. Alternatively, the word *death* sometimes refers primarily to the *aftermath of a death*. Thus, one might say, "Mary is finding John's death to be quite hard." These different ways of speaking reveal that death-related attitudes can center on one or more of the following: (1) attitudes about *my own dying;* (2) attitudes about *my own death;* (3) attitudes about *what will happen to me after my death;* and (4) attitudes related to *the dying, death, or bereavement of someone else.*

My Own Dying

Attitudes (which include beliefs, feelings, postures, and dispositions to action) are frequently directed to *my own dying.* Such attitudes among people in North America commonly reflect fears and anxiety about the possibility of experiencing a long, difficult, painful, or undignified dying process, especially in an alien institution under the care of strangers who might not respect one's personal needs or wishes. People who hold these attitudes often express a preference that their dying might occur without any form of distress, without prior knowledge, and in their sleep. Some even try hard not to think about their death, whereas others set out in proactive ways to prepare an advance directive (see Chapter 16) to try to ensure that their dying process will not be unduly prolonged and painful.

In other societies or among individuals who are guided by a different set of concerns, many people hold attitudes that lead them to fear a sudden, unanticipated death. For such individuals, it is important to have time to address what some have called "unfinished business" by expressing to their loved ones such sentiments as "Thank you," "I love you," "I am sorry for anything I might have done to hurt you," "I forgive you for anything you might have done to hurt me," or simply, "Good-bye"—a contraction for "God be with you" (Byock, 2004). Others may wish to have enough time and awareness to "get ready to meet their Maker" or otherwise prepare themselves for death through meditation and a special positioning of the body. Many want to satisfy personal concerns about how their goods will be distributed after their deaths. Some individuals who value setting an example for others or bearing suffering for some altruistic or religious motive may even look forward to their dying with courage and some degree of anticipation. Attitudes toward my own dying are at the heart of each of these examples (see Issues for Critical Reflection #5).

ISSUES FOR CRITICAL REFLECTION

#5 My Own Personal Death-Related Attitudes

In this chapter, we discuss death-related attitudes from a variety of perspectives. One way to bring this home more personally is to ask you to reflect on your own individual attitudes. Many years ago, instructors in courses and books like this one asked participants to write their own eulogies or to fill out a personal death certificate. They called this exercise the "Do-It-Yourself Death Certificate" (see Sabatini & Kastenbaum, 1973). You can do such an exercise by drafting a personal eulogy or by drawing on the Standard Certificate of Death reproduced as Figure 16.1 on p. 458 in this book.

In general, however, exercises of those types did not work very well. In part, that was because the underlying premise was not realistic. That is, in the ordinary course of events none of us will be present to fill out our own death certificate or to write our own eulogy. These exercises also fell prey to fantasizing when individuals did not approach them seriously, for example, "I died at the age of 143 after having made billions of dollars and having changed the entire world for all humankind by inventing…"

One way to heighten the sense of realism in an exploration of personal attitudes is to ask you to describe what it might be

(continues)

like to encounter the death of someone you love. After all, each of us may well be present when someone we love dies. The point is not so much to confront the imagined reality of your loved one's death, but to reflect on the attitudes that imagining this possibility arouses in you as you engage in this exercise. What are those attitudes and why do you think you have them?

Another, perhaps simpler, approach is to ask you not how you might LIKE to die, but how you would NOT WANT TO DIE. For example, NOT by drowning or in a fire, NOT in a motor vehicle accident or at the hands of terrorists. The point then is to ask yourself "WHY NOT THAT WAY?" and to ask what factors entered into your choices.

These types of exercises can be undertaken privately to enhance self-awareness. They can also be subjects for discussion in a class or other group, or individually with close friends or family members.

If you have undertaken one of these types of exercises, what did you learn about yourself (or others) as a result?

My Own Death

A second category of death-related attitudes is primarily concerned with death itself, specifically *my own death*. Here the main issue is how the prospect of my imminent death impacts what I am experiencing right now. For example, those who find life difficult or filled with hardships might look forward to its ending, to the simple cessation of the tribulations they are now experiencing—whatever happens after death. Such persons might reject difficult, painful, or expensive interventions along with those perceived as likely to be ineffective. Alternatively, those that value life very highly—including relationships with those they love—might resist their own deaths with all possible means at their disposal because death will result in their losing what is so important to them. In either of these cases, the main focus of concern is on my own death itself and its immediate implications for me (not on what happens after death or on what is happening or may happen to others).

What Will Happen to Me after My Death?

A third category of death-related attitudes concerns *what will happen to me after my death*. Here, the central concerns have to do with what the consequences or aftereffects of death will mean for me. For some people, that might involve anxiety about the unknown. For other people, it might include a fear of judgment or punishment after death. For still others, it might depend on anticipation of or hope for a heavenly reward for a lifetime of hard work, upright living, or faithfulness. In a similar way, many see death itself as merely a bridge or passage to another life in which the conditions of their existence might be improved over this present life or in which a reunion might be achieved with a loved person who had died earlier. All of these attitudes have primarily to do with some outcome or result for the self that is thought to follow after my own death.

The Dying, Death, or Bereavement of Someone Else

The death-related attitudes examined thus far in this section all involve attitudes held by an individual about his or her experiences in relationship to what will or may happen prior to, at the time of, or after his or her own death. A fourth set of death-related attitudes is principally concerned with the *dying, death, or bereavement of someone else*. For example, I might be mainly concerned about the implications of someone else's dying or death. I might worry that I will not be sufficiently strong and resourceful to see an ill or dying person whom I love through the challenges and losses that he or she faces. Or perhaps I look forward to taking care of someone who so frequently cared for me in the past. If so, I might make arrangements to keep that person at home with me, rather than permitting him or her to enter some institutional care setting. Equally, I might be concerned about impending separation from someone whom I love. I might be fearful about how I will be able to go on with living after someone else to whom I am close and upon whom I depend is gone. By contrast, if the dying individual is a disagreeable person or is experiencing great difficulty in his or her struggles, I might anticipate the relief that will be associated with that person's death.

Alternatively, it might be the implications for someone else of my dying or death that are of primary concern to me. For example, I might be concerned about the burdens that my illness and dying are placing upon those whom I love. Or I might be worried about what will happen to loved ones after I am gone or how my death will affect plans and projects that I had previously pursued. With these concerns in mind, some individuals strive to remain alert as long as they can so that they can spend more time with those they love. Others make provisions to support their survivors-to-be. Still others redouble efforts to complete their prized projects or at least to take them as far as they can.

SOME IMPLICATIONS OF DEATH-RELATED ATTITUDES

Two major implications of our discussion of death-related attitudes follow. First, such attitudes vary greatly and, second, humans can exert some influence over their own death-related attitudes. In terms of *variation in death-related attitudes*, it is common to hear talk of fears and anxieties in attitudes about death. These are familiar elements or aspects of death-related attitudes, perhaps because dying, death, and bereavement represent something sharply different from or even opposed to the everyday life we now know. So, if we ask ourselves what most bothers or frightens us about the implications of death, or what are some ways in which we would *most not like to die*, it is not surprising that fears and anxieties quickly rise to the surface. However, death-related attitudes need not always center on fear or anxiety. In general, humans may adopt a broad range of attitudes, feelings, and emotions concerning death and its implications, just as they can have many different attitudes about various aspects of life and living.

In terms of the *influence that humans can exert over death-related attitudes*, humans are able to reflect upon their own and other possible attitudes, select with some degree of freedom the attitudes they wish to hold, and change their attitudes in light of new encounters or additional reflection on matters related to death. That is why many epitaphs, such as this one from an 1830 grave marker in Connecticut, encourage individuals to develop what are thought to be appropriate attitudes toward death and life:

> Remember me as you draw nigh,
> As you are now, so once was I.

As I am now, so must you be,
Prepare for death and follow me. (Jones, 1967, p. 148)

Another point of view was offered by a man who survived the extraordinary challenges of the Nazi concentration camps in World War II who wrote: "Everything can be taken from a man but one thing: the last of the human freedoms—to choose one's attitude in any given set of circumstances, to choose one's own way" (Frankl, 1984, p. 86). Our attitudes are basic to human life and behavior, but they can be changed—even though such changes may not be easy to make.

FIVE DOMINANT PATTERNS IN WESTERN ATTITUDES TOWARD DEATH

Historians, sociologists, and anthropologists also have contributed to our understanding of the richness and complexity of death-related attitudes. Philippe Ariès (1974b, 1981, 1985), a French cultural historian, developed an insightful and instructive account of Western attitudes toward death over a period of several centuries up to modern times. He found five dominant patterns of these attitudes and linked them more or less to specific historical time frames. His historical analysis may or may not be convincing; in any event, it is not important for our purposes here. Instead, in this section, we briefly describe some of the central components of Ariès' five patterns. What comes out of this work is a greater awareness of the richness and complexity of death-related attitudes we mentioned previously. Here, the focus is mainly on large-scale social and cultural attitudes, but many similar themes can be found in the attitudes of individuals.

Ariès named his five patterns of attitudes toward death *tame death, death of the self, remote and imminent death, death of the other*, and *death denied* (some others have called this last pattern *forbidden death*). They can be briefly described as follows:

- *Tame death*: Here, death is familiar and simple; it is regarded as inevitable and no attempt is made to evade it. Persons who are dying typically calmly await their deaths. As well, death is a public or social event. The dying are usually surrounded by loved ones and members of the community, all of whom wait peacefully for the end. Attention is focused on a community deeply affected by the loss of one of its participants. (Compare the death of John Stolzfus in the vignette near the start of this chapter.) Finally, the afterlife is not threatening because death is seen as a sort of sleep; either one will ultimately be woken to eternal bliss or one remains forever asleep.
- *Death of the self*: Attention is focused on the person who dies, now seen as a separate individual distinct from other members of society in both life and in what follows death. Death produces great anxiety in that person because it is believed one is either rewarded or punished in a future state. (For this, see the example of the New England Puritans described in the next section.) Death of the self involves a final testing period; what one does at this moment determines what will happen to one after death (and indeed the meaning of one's whole life). Just before death, there may be a struggle between a patron saint and the devil, followed by a final judgment. Several religious traditions have similar beliefs. For instance, some Jews believe it is important at the moment of

death to recite the Shema ("Hear, O Israel: the LORD is our God, the LORD alone, You shall love the LORD your God with all your heart, and with all your soul, and with all your might"—Deuteronomy 6:4, 5). Muslims are taught that invoking the Divine Name at the moment of death can be salvific (Jonker, 1997; Kassis, 1997). And some Buddhists hold that chanting the name of Amitabha Buddha at this point in one's life will ensure that one will end up in the Pure Land after death (Yeung, 1995). In the West, anxiety about the moment of death once led to the development of a formal **ars moriendi** or an art of dying well (Kastenbaum, 1989a).

- *Remote and imminent death*: One's attitude toward death is basically highly ambivalent. Death is viewed as a wholly natural event (not a supernatural one), but still great effort is made to keep it at a distance. Death is now viewed as untamed and invasive. Because it is natural, it is imminent; because it is dangerous and frightening, it is remote. In short, death is both inviting and repelling, beautiful and to be feared—and thus, attitudes toward death are of two minds.

- *Death of the other*: Here, the main focus of attention is on the survivors. Death primarily involves a breaking of relationships. For survivors, death results in an intolerable separation from the one who dies. Feelings and behaviors may go nearly out of control (wailing, keening, throwing oneself in the grave, etc.). This romanticized view of death led survivors to try to communicate with the dead or somehow maintain closeness to them. For the one who dies, death is primarily a period of waiting for some type of reunion or way of being rejoined with loved ones in some other state.

- *Death denied/forbidden death*: With increasing reliance on institutional care, dying persons are typically more or less isolated from others in the community. The very fact that the person is dying is often denied, both to that person and to those around her or him. Also, with the medicalization of Western society, death is no longer seen as entirely natural. Some individuals pursue extraordinary intervention measures designed to forestall death—which may also prolong their dying. The focus is on other people's responses to the person's death and on how it makes them feel uncomfortable. Except for a brief funeral period that typically involves only the closest associates of the dead person, when a death does occur, society does not pause in its ongoing rhythms of work and play (just the opposite of what Ariès described in "tame death"). Emotions, both before and after the death, are to be suppressed or concealed and thus channeled in "safe" ways. Mourning itself may be seen as morbid or even pathological (Ariès, 1974a). In all of these ways, death has come to be hidden from ordinary view, to be seen as unnatural, forbidden, indecent, and, as Gorer (1965a) argued, even **pornographic**.

It can be instructive to look at these five patterns as independent categories or snapshots of social attitudes. In fact, however, as Ariès admitted, they overlap each other, both within cultural/historical periods and even within individual persons. Further, when one studies the basic components of each of these patterns, it becomes apparent that these are not just Western patterns. Rather, some components of each of them can be found in almost all cultures (for examples demonstrating this, see Chapter 5).

THE PURITANS OF 17TH-CENTURY NEW ENGLAND

The critical role of attitudes in shaping the character of experiences with death can be illustrated in one final example: that of the Puritans of 17th-century New England. We selected this example because it draws upon a historical group in the United States and because their views differ in so many ways from some prominent contemporary death-related attitudes. Also, although both the Amish and the Puritans are Christian communities, their lives display quite different attitudes. In addition, these examples remind us that the patterns Ariès has described are not strictly sequential; one pattern does not simply replace another; different groups may emphasize different attitudinal patterns (or different aspects of a pattern).

The Puritans originated as a reformist group within the Church of England. Those Puritans who came to America searched for a new land in which they would be free to uphold their beliefs and practice their religion as they wished. The New England Puritans established thriving settlements in various colonies, but their presence was particularly notable in Massachusetts during the middle and latter portions of the 17th century. Here, they emphasized the importance of preaching and conversion through an intense personal experience.

For the Puritans, everything that existed or happened was part of a divine purpose. At the same time, they viewed human history since Adam and Eve as one long descent into ever-deepening depravity. In this situation, no human being could be truly worthy of salvation nor could any good works earn the favor of God's grace. Nevertheless, the Puritans believed that God, in His infinite mercy and love, had chosen a select and predetermined few for salvation.

The great question for each individual Puritan was whether he or she was a member of God's holy elect. No one could ever have confident knowledge concerning the answer to that question. To think that one did have such knowledge would be to think that one understood the all-knowing mind of God. More likely, to believe that one was assured of salvation was good evidence that one had actually succumbed to the seductive falsehoods of Satan. Confidence in the "sure and certain hope of resurrection to eternal life" was simply not open to the Puritans.

Nevertheless, fear of death and the question of personal salvation preoccupied individual Puritans in ways not found among the Amish. Each Puritan struggled continuously with his or her conscience to discern, in the midst of innumerable signs of personal depravity, at least some indicators or "marks" that he or she might be among the chosen few. Thus, Puritanism was "a faith marked by a never-ending, excruciating uncertainty…[in which] the Puritans were gripped individually and collectively by an intense and unremitting fear of death, while simultaneously clinging to the traditional Christian rhetoric of viewing death as a release and relief for the earth-bound soul" (Stannard, 1977, pp. 75, 79). For the Puritans, one must constantly recognize one's own utter and total depravity, while at the same time praying earnestly for a salvation that one is helpless to secure.

Puritan preachers dwelt vividly on the contrast between the potential terrors and bliss of the afterlife. Those who were not among the elect would be subject to the eternal torment of the damned. Those who actually were among the elect were still troubled by lack of certainty even up to the very moment of death. Thus, as Stannard (1977, p. 89) argued, "The New England Puritans, despite their traditional optimistic rhetoric, were possessed of an intense, overt fear of death—the natural consequence of what to them were three patently true and quite rational beliefs: that of their own utter and unalterable depravity; that of the omnipotence, justness, and inscrutability of God; and that of the unspeakable terrors of Hell."

These attitudes toward death among the New England Puritans had implications not only for individual adults but also for children and for society as a whole. The Puritan worldview combined a deep love of children with a strong sense of their depravity and sinful pollution (so different, in this latter regard, from the Amish). Also, the era of the Puritans in New England was a time when infants and children actually were at great risk of dying and when parents gave birth to many children hoping that at least some would remain alive to care for them in the hour of their own deaths. Perhaps for both these reasons, in their personal relationships with their children, Puritan parents were advised to maintain an attitude of "restraint and even aloofness, mixed with...an intense parental effort to impose discipline and encourage spiritual precocity" (Stannard, 1977, p. 57).

Puritan children were constantly reminded of the likelihood that they might die at any moment. They were threatened with the dangers of personal judgment and damnation in which even their own parents might testify against them. They could not expect to reunite with parents after death and they were reminded of the guilt they would bear if through sinfulness they should bring harm to their parents. In this vein, books for children, including even the *New England Primer* (1727/1962) from which they learned the alphabet, were designed to remind young readers of the imminence and possible consequences of death. All of this differs from most 21st century attitudes, or even from 19th-century emphases, such as those expressed in the famous McGuffey's readers (1866), which stressed the eternal reunion of children and parents after death for a new life in heaven (Minnich, 1936a, 1936b; Westerhoff, 1978).

Burial practices are a particularly good indicator of death-related attitudes among the New England Puritans. At first, absence of ceremony and restraint of emotion reflected the Puritan reaction to the excesses of "papist" practices. That is, the corpse was regarded as a meaningless husk, burial was swift and simple, and excessive displays of sadness or grief were discouraged. Funeral sermons were not delivered at the time of burial and were not very different from other forms of preaching.

In the latter half of the 17th century, however, Puritan society in New England underwent many changes that threatened the prospects for its holy mission. Several important early leaders died (e.g., John Winthrop, Thomas Shepard, John Cotton, and Thomas Hooker), while a civil war in England and an ensuing official doctrine of religious toleration isolated the New England Puritans in their emphasis on doctrinal righteousness. Also, growing immigration and mercantilism in America produced an increasingly complex society in which the Puritan community declined in numbers and significance.

In reaction, the embattled New England Puritans developed increasingly elaborate funeral practices. Church bells were rung on the day of the funeral, a funeral procession conducted the coffin to the burial ground, and those who returned to the home of the deceased after the burial were given food and distinctively designed, costly funeral rings as tokens of attendance. As the deaths of Puritan leaders and community pillars were experienced, prayer was conducted at the funeral, and funeral sermons took on the form of eulogies. Gravestones carved with elaborate verses praising the moral and religious character of the deceased began to mark the sites of burial. Clearly, a special set of attitudes toward death existed in Puritan New England, shaped by deeply held beliefs and implemented in earnest practice.

Summary

In this chapter, we examined attitudes toward death—involving clusters of beliefs, feelings, habits of thought, behaviors, and underlying values. We learned that individuals can have a variety of concerns and responses to death—including those that focus on one's own dying, the death of oneself, what will happen to the self after death, and the dying, death, or bereavement of another—and that they can have some influence over those personal attitudes. We also saw different sets of social attitudes toward death in Ariès' account of five dominant patterns across Western history (tame death, death of the self, remote and imminent death, death of the other, and death denied) and in two specific examples (the Amish in North America today and the New England Puritans of the 17th century). Patterns of death-related attitudes, both in society and among individuals, can be strikingly different and diverse. Such patterns have changed before; they can, and will, change again. None is the eternal essence of how human beings everywhere and throughout all time think about, feel about, or behave in the face of death.

Glossary

Ars moriendi: literally, the "art of dying," a practice that focused on what one should do to die well

Death anxiety: concerns or worries related in some way to death

Death-related attitude: a more or less settled way of being in the world, presenting oneself to the world, behaving or acting that reflects some belief, opinion, or feeling related to death

Forbidden death: a death-related attitude that views death as offensive and unacceptable, something to be denied and hidden from public view; a phrase from Ariès

Pornography of death: a death-related attitude much like forbidden death, implying that death is dirty and indecent, and yet somehow titillating and intriguing; a phrase from Gorer

Tame death: a death-related attitude that views death as familiar and simple, a public event mainly affecting the community; a phrase from Ariès

Terror management theory: a theory in social psychology arguing that the unique ability of humans to become aware of the inevitability of their deaths produces anxiety, denial, and terror; efforts to manage such terror are seen in individual behaviors and the symbolic cultural systems that seek to provide life with meaning and value.

Questions for Review and Discussion

1. Think about how this chapter described attitudes toward death, dying, and bereavement. How do attitudes differ from encounters (as discussed in Chapter 2)? How were your attitudes affected by your encounters (either directly or through the media) with a specific death-related event?

2. This chapter described two specific sets of attitudes regarding death taken from the present-day Amish and the Puritans in 17th-century New England. How are

the attitudes of these two groups similar or different and how did they affect their encounters with death, dying, and bereavement?

3. Think about the four categories of death-related concerns and responses described in this chapter: attitudes about your own dying, your death, what will happen to you after death, and the dying, death, or bereavement of someone you love. Which of these is most important to you at this point in your life and why? What are your chief concerns about these matters?

4. Ariès described five patterns of societal attitudes toward death. Which of the five patterns seems most familiar to you? Which aspects of each of the five patterns can you find in your own experience?

5. Have you ever used online resources to learn more about death-related attitudes? Why or why not? If you did use such resources, were they helpful to you? Why or why not?

Suggested Readings

For depictions of various attitudes toward death in America, as well as in Western art, literature, and popular culture, see:

Bertman, S. L. (1991). *Facing Death: Images, Insights, and Interventions*

Crissman, J. K. (1994). *Death and Dying in Central Appalachia: Changing Attitudes and Practices*

Enright, D. J. (Ed.). (1983). *The Oxford Book of Death*

Farrell, J. J. (1980). *Inventing the American Way of Death: 1830–1920*

Geddes, G. E. (1981). *Welcome Joy: Death in Puritan New England*

Hostetler, J. A. (1993). *Amish Society* (4th ed.)

Isenberg, N., & Burstein, A. (Eds.). (2003). *Mortal Remains: Death in Early America*

Jackson, C. O. (Ed.). (1977). *Passing: The Vision of Death in America*

Kastenbaum, R. (2000). *The Psychology of Death*

Kraybill, D. B. (2001). *The Riddle of Amish Culture* (Rev ed.)

Kraybill, D. B., Johnson-Weiner, K. M., & Nolt, S. M. (2013). *The Amish*

Mack, A. (Ed.). (1974). *Death in American Experience*

Shachtman, T. (2006). *Rumspringa: To Be or Not to Be Amish*

Siegel, B. (Ed.). (1997). *The Last Word: The New York Times Book of Obituaries and Farewells—A Celebration of Unusual Lives*

Stannard, D. E. (1977). *The Puritan Way of Death: A Study in Religion, Culture, and Social Change*

Weir, R. F. (Ed.). (1980). *Death in Literature*

Zielinski, J. M. (1997). *The Amish across America* (4th ed.)

Selected Web Resources

Some useful search terms include: ARS MORIENDI; DEATH ANXIETY; DEATH ATTITUDES (OR DEATH-RELATED ATTITUDES); DEATH DENIAL; FORBIDDEN DEATH; PORNOGRAPHY OF DEATH; TAME DEATH; TERROR MANAGEMENT THEORY.

You can also visit the following *organizational and other Internet sites:*

American Anthropological Association

American Psychological Association

American Sociological Association

BELIEVE: Religious Information Source website (multiple topics)

Death Studies **(published by Taylor & Francis)**

Illness, Crisis & Loss **(published by Sage Publications)**

Mortality **(published by Taylor & Francis)**

OMEGA, *Journal of Death and Dying* **(published by Sage Publications)**

Courtesy of Ron Olshwanger

Death-Related Practices and the American Death System

Objectives of this Chapter

- To identify death-related *practices* as a component of death-related *experiences*
- To explain the concept of a "death system" in every society, including its functions and components
- To describe selected examples of death-related practices in the United States:
  1. Human-induced death associated with accidents; homicide; terrorism; war; genocide; and ethnic cleansing; the Holocaust; and the nuclear era

2. Death and language the phrase as illustrated in contrasts between language about death and death-related language
3. Death in media news reports (vicarious death experiences) and entertainment (fantasized death and violence)

SEPTEMBER 11, 2001

September 11, 2001, was a clear, fall day on the East Coast of the United States. It was also a day that was to be filled with horror, large-scale death and injury, and massive destruction of property.

On that Tuesday morning, people went to work at the 110-story towers of the World Trade Center in New York City and at the Pentagon in Arlington, Virginia. About the same time, crews and passengers boarded commercial airliners in Boston, suburban Washington, D.C., and Newark.

Shortly after takeoff, hijackers commandeered four commercial airliners, each with a full load of fuel for a transcontinental flight to California. The hijackers took over these flights, removed their pilots, and diverted the planes to their own ends. At 8:46 A.M., one plane was flown into the north tower of the World Trade Center about 20 stories below the top of the building. Eighteen minutes later, a second plane crashed into the south tower in a similar way. Shortly thereafter, at 9:37 A.M., a third plane crashed into the southwest side of the Pentagon. On the fourth plane, some passengers joined together to resist the terrorists, fought with them, and prevented them from carrying out their plan to crash into the Capitol or White House in Washington, D.C. As a result of that struggle, this last plane crashed near the small town of Shanksville in southwestern Pennsylvania, shortly after 10:00 A.M. (Kashurba, 2006; Morgan, 2006).

Just before 10:00 A.M., the south tower of the World Trade Center collapsed as a result of the structural damage suffered from being hit by the airliner and especially from the intensity of the subsequent fire fed by jet fuel. Approximately 29 minutes later, the north tower also collapsed. Later, other buildings in the World Trade Center complex and a nearby Marriott hotel collapsed.

Some 246 passengers and crew members aboard the four airliners (plus 19 terrorists) died in these events. In addition, 2,752 people died at the scene of the World Trade Center plus an additional 125 at the Pentagon. At the World Trade Center, one of the most horrifying sights was seeing people jump to their deaths from high towers to escape intense fire. Those who died at this site included workers at the offices, shops, and restaurants in the complex, visitors, and 414 firefighters, police officers, and emergency medical responders who rushed into the buildings or set up nearby command posts in their efforts to save lives. In New York City, many bodies were consumed by the fires or buried under massive rubble that was only gradually removed from the scene. Some bodies were identified through DNA testing; many other families were never able to recover the bodies of their loved ones.

THE DEATH SYSTEM IN EVERY SOCIETY

In this chapter, we turn to **death-related practices** as the third key element in our general portrait of *experiences with death in our society*. Our goal is to supplement what we have already learned about *death-related encounters* in Chapter 2 and *death-related attitudes* in Chapter 3 and to show how encounters and attitudes affect practices. To do this, we began with the events of September 11, 2001, an encounter with death that could hardly have been imagined before it took place, one that has drastically affected American attitudes and practices. Of course, there are a bewildering variety of death-related practices in the United States, too many to explore adequately in a single chapter. We also cannot fully separate practices from encounters and attitudes. For that reason, we use the concept of a **death system** to organize and provide context for the death-related practices selected for discussion here.

Kastenbaum (1972, p. 310) originally defined a death system as the "sociophysical network by which we mediate and express our relationship to mortality." Later (in 2012), he described the death system as "The interpersonal, sociophysical, and symbolic network through which society mediates the individual's relationship to mortality" (p. 105), and he noted that "We face death alone in one sense, but in another and equally valid sense, we face death as part of a society whose expectations, rules, motives, and symbols influence our individual encounters" (p. 77; see also Corr, 2014). The presence of death systems, which are easily recognizable by most members of a society when attention is drawn to them, reflects the existence and importance of social infrastructures and processes of socialization in human interactions with death, dying, and bereavement (Parsons, 1951). According to Kastenbaum, each societal death system has its own characteristic functions and components (see Focus On 4.1).

FOCUS ON 4.1

Functions and Components of a Societal Death System

Functions of a death system include:

- *To give warnings and predictions*, as with sirens or flashing lights on emergency vehicles or media alerts concerning the likelihood of violent weather, an earthquake, or a terrorist act
- *To prevent death*, as in the work of police or security officers and emergency medical care systems
- *To care for the dying*, as in modern hospice programs and some aspects of hospital services
- *To dispose of the dead*, as in the work of the funeral industry, cemeteries, and crematories
- *To work toward social consolidation after death*, as in funeral rituals and bereavement support groups
- *To help make sense of death*, as in the case of many religious or philosophical systems
- *To bring about socially sanctioned killing* of either humans or animals, as in training for war, capital punishment, and the slaughtering of livestock for food

Components of a death system include:

- *People*—individuals whose social roles are more or less directly related to death, such as funeral directors, medical examiners and coroners, life insurance agents, lawyers, and florists

(continues)

Functions and Components of a Societal Death System

- *Places*—specific locations that can have a death-related character, such as cemeteries, funeral homes, health care institutions, and the "hallowed ground" of a battlefield or disaster
- *Times*—occasions associated with death, such as Memorial Day or the anniversary of a death
- *Objects*—things linked to death, such as death certificates, hearses, obituaries and death notices in newspapers, tombstones, and a hangman's gallows or electric chair
- *Symbols and images*—items that signify death, such as a black armband, a skull and cross-bones, certain organ music, and selected words or phrases ("Ashes to ashes, dust to dust …")

Source: Based on Kastenbaum (1972, 2012; see also Corr, 2014).

Some type of death system is found *in every society*. It may be formal, explicit, and widely acknowledged in some of its aspects, even while it is largely hidden and often unspoken in other aspects. As Blauner (1966) has shown, many small, primitive, tribal societies must organize many of their activities around death's recurrent presence. In large, modern, impersonal societies, such as in the developed countries of North America and Western Europe, the social implications of death are often less disruptive, less prominent, and more contained—at least until shocking events occur. An example of such a stunning event occurred on April 20, 2010, when an explosion on the Deepwater Horizon drilling rig operated by BP (formerly British Petroleum) killed 11 crew members and injured 17 more. Subsequently, oil flowing from the damaged well did extensive damage to marine and wildlife, as well as to fishing and tourism industries along the coast of the Gulf of Mexico. Natural disasters, such as those highlighted in Focus On 4.2, offer other examples of extensive loss of life and inadequacies in local death systems.

Four Disasters and Death Systems

Natural disasters can present major challenges to societal death systems, especially when combined with human and societal deficiencies. Here are four of many notable examples of disasters that at least temporarily overwhelmed local death systems.

Hurricane Katrina formed over the Bahamas, crossed south Florida as a Category 1 hurricane, strengthened to Category 5 status as it moved northward over the Gulf of Mexico, and came ashore on August 29, 2005, over southeast Louisiana as a Category 3 storm with sustained winds of 100–140 miles per hour. The effects of the storm stretched some 400 miles across the Gulf coast.

(continues)

FOCUS ON 4.2 *(continued)*

Four Disasters and Death Systems

Some portions of the American death system functioned very well in response to this hurricane. For example, the National Hurricane Center gave advance warnings of the storm's likely track and Coast Guard helicopters rescued many stranded people. Regrettably, Katrina exposed deficiencies in the levee system intended to protect New Orleans. When some levees failed or were overtopped, 80% of the city was flooded. Also, overall efforts of local, state, and federal officials were severely criticized for lack of leadership and mismanagement in failing to evacuate the populace or to provide them with shelter, food, and drinkable water for many days. Ultimately, this storm caused more than 1,800 deaths and over $150 billion worth of damage across the Gulf coast, making it the costliest natural disaster in U.S. history.

On January 12, 2010, an underground earthquake with an estimated magnitude of 7.0 struck Haiti, the poorest country in the Western hemisphere, with an epicenter 16 miles WSW of the capital of Port-au-Prince. The most reliable estimate is that this earthquake killed 160,000 people and injured many more, while doing massive damage to homes, public buildings, and infrastructure. Government services were overwhelmed. Some international aid did help, but

New Orleans skyline and areas of the city flooded after Hurricane Katrina.

(continues)

Four Disasters and Death Systems

recovery has been slow and many people were still living in tent camps and temporary shelters years later. All of this was compounded by an outbreak of cholera in October of 2010 that killed over 8,200 Haitians and hospitalized hundreds of thousands more by August 2013. Unfortunately, in October 2016, Haiti was struck by Hurricane Matthew, which killed hundreds of people and caused massive property damage. Sadly, it was again followed by a cholera outbreak. Here, death systems did not exist or functioned poorly.

On March 11, 2011, a three-part series of events created a crisis in Japan. First, the strongest earthquake ever to hit Japan—measuring 9.0 on the Richter scale—occurred off the northeastern coast. Second, an ensuing tsunami sent a massive wave of water onto the shore overtopping protective sea walls. By March 2015, official estimates confirmed nearly 16,000 deaths, over 6,000 injured, more than 2,500 people missing, and well over 225,000 people displaced from their former homes. Third, although power plants at several nuclear reactors in the area automatically shut down, they still required water to cool their reactor cores and pools of stored fuel rods. With diesel generators destroyed and electrical power unavailable, engineers tried (with only partial success) to prevent leakage of radioactive materials and avoid or minimize meltdowns of nuclear fuel by venting steam into the air (causing small explosions) and pumping seawater into the reactors (which effectively rendered them unusable in the future).

Prior to these events, Japan had an extensive system in place to respond to natural disasters. Rescue efforts involving hundreds of thousands of troops and police began immediately; many lives were saved that would otherwise have been lost. Also, many countries promptly sent search and rescue teams and other forms of assistance to help. Even with these advantages in the Japanese death system, the prime minister called this the worst crisis the country faced since World War II; the World Bank estimated this was the costliest natural disaster in world history.

In December 2013, an outbreak of Ebola virus disease began in Guinea, West Africa, which then spread to Liberia and Sierra Leone. Ebola outbreaks had occurred earlier, but this one reached epidemic proportions. Many factors contributed: conditions of extreme poverty; years of armed conflict in the area; mistrust of government officials; local burial customs involving washing of bodies after death (which helped spread the virus); and disease in densely populated cities (Gates, 2015). By mid-May, 2015, an estimated 27,000 people had been infected and over 11,000 had died (Mullan, 2015). One man travelled to the United States where his disease flared up; after he died, two U.S. nurses developed symptoms and were successfully treated. In West Africa, some foreign health care workers became infected; most were sent home, treated, and survived. Clearly, health care systems and infrastructures in these West African countries were not up to this challenge. In the United States, public misunderstandings and distorted attitudes, fed by media reports led to unwarranted fears of Ebola (SteelFisher, Blendon, & Lasala-Blanco, 2015).

As it actually operates, the death system in contemporary American society appears to act in many important ways to remove death from the mainstream of life, to minimize its presence, and to gloss over many of its harsh aspects. That is, our death system often acts to support distancing or denial of death. The problem with this is that we may have "created systems which protect us in the aggregate from facing up to the very things that as individuals we most need to know" (Evans, 1971, p. 83). Still, other aspects of our death system draw attention to death and respond to its appearances. And death systems can change when they are confronted by new situations involving novel encounters with death.

The key point here is that every society needs to have some system for coping with the fundamental challenges that death presents to human existence. Thus, it is helpful to the study of death, dying, and bereavement to examine the nature of a society's death system and the ways in which it functions. Given the subject of this book, we consider in this chapter many examples of death systems that were not always working at their best. But it is important to note that death systems frequently are helpful for many individuals within the societies in which they operate. We will see many examples of the effective operation of death systems in the remainder of this book.

THE AMERICAN DEATH SYSTEM AND THE EVENTS OF SEPTEMBER 11, 2001

The September 11, 2001 attack occurred within the continental United States and struck at some of the most prominent symbols of American economic and military power: the World Trade Center towers and the Pentagon. Like terrorist attacks throughout the world with which many people have had to learn to cope with for a long time, this one killed and injured innocent men, women, and children. This attack also raised homicidal terrorism to a new level within the United States, exceeding in its scope other terrorist incidents affecting Americans at home or abroad. Included among victims of the attack were individuals of many ethnic cultures, races, religions, and backgrounds. For example, the Council on American-Islamic Relations has reported that at least 32 Muslims (excluding hijackers) were among the victims. Citizens from 90 countries as diverse as Australia, Germany, India, Israel, Mexico, Pakistan, South Korea, and the United Kingdom were also among the victims. As well, 24 Canadians have been identified as dead or missing and presumed dead, most of whom lived in New York and worked in or were visiting the World Trade Center; two were passengers in the aircraft that hit the buildings.

On September 11, many Americans seemed surprised that terrorists would or could attack the United States directly. In fact, for some time, knowledgeable observers had expected some type of terrorist action on American soil. Unfortunately, components of the American death system did not provide specific *warnings and predictions* that might have prevented any or all of these events. For example, it would have been important to know that some suspicious individuals had gained entry into the United States, that some of them were taking flying lessons (but not expressing interest in takeoff and landing procedures), and that some terrorist circles had been showing interest in using commercial airliners as weapons. For many reasons, this very important function of sounding warnings, making specific predictions, communicating information effectively, and acting on that information to protect the country was not successful. The National Commission on Terrorist Attacks

(2004; see also Kean & Hamilton, 2006) identified many failures of intelligence and coordination, as did former Senator Bob Graham (2004) through his work as cochair of the House/Senate Joint Inquiry into Intelligence Community Activities Before and After the Terrorist Attacks of September 11, 2001.

Still, on September 11 itself, other individuals and aspects of the American death system almost immediately sprang into action. Having learned from mobile phones about earlier crashes, some passengers on one flight joined together to try to overcome their hijackers and frustrate the terrorists' goals, causing the plane to crash in Pennsylvania (see Beamer, 2002). Others used phones to try to warn outsiders about what was happening. Still others who could do so left messages on answering machines like the one Brian Sweeney left for his wife, Julie:

> Hey, Jules, it's Brian. I'm on a plane and it's hijacked and it doesn't look good. I just wanted to let you know that I love you and I hope to see you again. If I don't, please have fun in life and live your life the best you can. Know that I love you and no matter what, I'll see you again. (*St. Petersburg Times*, 2001)

Our death system was evident in its more formal aspects when many firefighters, police officers, and others rushed to the scenes of the tragedy and ran into burning buildings in an attempt to *prevent death* and save lives—only to lose their own lives when the buildings collapsed. In addition, the Federal Aviation Administration immediately grounded all airplanes in the United States to forestall a further attack from the air and to make it difficult for coconspirators to leave the country. This action created problems for United States and other aviators, as well as for Canada and its social systems (see Focus On 4.3).

Further examples of the American death system in operation after the September 11 attack include the work of the FBI, which began to scrutinize selected telephone conversations for congratulatory calls, to seek out material witnesses and others who might have been involved in this terrorist conspiracy, and to trace the sources of funding that the attack required. In addition, hospitals and rescue workers prepared to *care for the injured and the dying*, while pathologists and funeral directors set out to *dispose of the dead* in appropriate ways by removing bodies from the scene, identifying them, and preparing them for final disposition. Unfortunately, disposing of the dead was a very long and difficult process that ultimately was only partly successful in recovering and identifying the dead (Kastenbaum, 2004).

In the days after September 11, there was powerful support for *social consolidation*, along with long-drawn-out stress and uneven government response. Mayor Rudy Giuliani of New York and other political and religious leaders moved to extend and coordinate many of these efforts. Individuals and communities faced significant challenges in trying to *help make sense of death* in these circumstances. Many Americans came together in memorial services and around rallying symbols, such as the phrase "United We Stand" or the song "God Bless America." Counselors advised how adults should speak to children about these events, and President George W. Bush spoke to the nation and to the world about American perceptions of these events as an attack not only on the United States but also on the civilized world. The Congress approved a new cabinet-level Department of Homeland Security.

Finally, Americans quickly shifted from perceiving themselves as victims of killing to outraged warriors. The president mobilized American military power and the

FOCUS ON 4.3

Canadians and the September 11, 2001 Attack

When the United States grounded all aircraft at 9:42 A.M. shortly after the initial September 11 attacks and closed its entire airspace, serious challenges were posed to inbound aircraft over the Atlantic and Pacific oceans. Many have not realized that Canadians and their social systems responded in extraordinarily helpful ways. All aircraft eastbound to North America across the Pacific Ocean from Asia that could not easily return to their point of origin were diverted to airports in Western Canada, primarily Vancouver. An even larger number of aircraft westbound across the Atlantic Ocean were diverted to alternate airports in Eastern Canada. All landed safely in Canada without incident and were on the ground by 6:00 p.m. EDT.

Just one example of the Canadian response to this crisis can be seen in the small town (pop. c. 10,000) of Gander, Newfoundland (DeFede, 2002). Gander boasted an unusually long runway as a result of its role as a refueling stop during World War II before jet engines became standard on airliners. In addition, Gander offered the easternmost commercial airport in Canada. Its geographical location and runway facilities made Gander especially appropriate to receive large airliners and the people they carried.

As a result, on September 11, 2001, the people of Gander (and other nearby small towns) were most generous in welcoming into their homes and public facilities almost 6,600 passengers and crew from 38 diverted flights. All of those visitors were cared for in remarkably kind ways until the last plane departed on September 16.

international political community in an attempt to root out and bring to justice those who were behind the conspiracy that culminated on September 11. These events also led to some **socially sanctioned killing**—for instance, through the U.S. invasion of Afghanistan and the overthrow of its Taliban leaders because they supported al-Qaeda. Subsequently, the United States also mounted an invasion of Iraq as a result of the belief—subsequently shown to be unfounded (e.g., Mueller, 2006)—that the then-leader of that country, Saddam Hussein, was a supporter of Islamist terrorism and a threat to the world.

The September 11 attack resulted in many challenges to personal safety and security for Americans at home and abroad. These challenges impacted the American death system in significant ways, but did not overwhelm it. Above all, these events mobilized American society in many ways and at many different levels. In 2004, the National Commission on Terrorist Attacks issued a report describing systemic deficiencies that contributed to the September 11 attack and offered recommendations to improve U.S. intelligence and homeland security operations. After much debate, the Congress passed legislation signed by the president to implement many of the National Commission's recommendations.

HUMAN-INDUCED DEATH

The World Health Organization (2014) has provided extensive data on violence and its prevention around the world in recent years, showing an enormous increase in the suffering and numbers of deaths that human beings have visited upon themselves and others. In part, this is the result of an increase in the number of people who are alive. A population explosion, such as that occurring in the last century, inevitably results in more deaths no matter what else happens. However, it may also lead to more tension and stress that may then increase interpersonal violence and premature deaths. In this section, we examine **human-induced deaths** associated with accidents; homicide; terrorism; war, genocide, and ethnic cleansing; the Holocaust; and the nuclear era. (Other examples of human-induced death, such as suicide, assisted suicide, and euthanasia, will be examined in Chapters 17 and 18.)

Accidents

Accidents or *unintentional injuries* became the fourth leading cause of death in the United States in 2014, accounting for 135,928 deaths, an age-adjusted death rate of 40.5 per 100,000, and approximately 5% of all deaths that year (Kochanek et al., 2016). These deaths may involve causes such as falls, transport accidents, poisoning, drowning, and deaths involving fires. Assuming that each accidental death affects an average of just ten survivors, well over 1 million persons were affected by such deaths in the United States in 2014 and many other millions suffered disabling injuries.

Death rates for accidents declined by more than one-quarter during the period 1979–1992; however, those rates have been gradually increasing since 2000. The declines seem to have resulted from educational efforts that urged Americans to become more safety conscious in their driving practices—for example, by driving more carefully, wearing seatbelts, not driving after consuming alcoholic beverages, and not using cell phones or sending text messages while driving. In recent years, increases in overall accidental deaths appear to be related to an expanding population, increasing numbers of fragile older adults, and an upsurge in fast-paced, stress-filled lifestyles in our highly developed technological society.

The National Safety Council (NSC) reviews all forms of accidental injuries and deaths, along with many other types of human-induced injuries and deaths in its annual report booklet, *Injury Facts* (2016). The NSC also offers on its Web site a chart listing the odds of dying from various causes and a graphic image of such odds.

Motor vehicle accidents were among the most significant causes of deaths in our society in 2014, they accounted for 35,398 deaths or approximately 26% of all accidental deaths. By contrast with deaths from such causes as homicide (15,872) or HIV (6,721) that are prominent in the public mind, the much larger number of deaths from automobile accidents every year seems to have little impact on American attitudes. Vehicle accidents affect members of every age, gender, racial, and cultural group. They are most common among teens, young adults, and older adults, and they are historically much higher for males than for females.

Accidental deaths are most often sudden and unexpected; those involving motor vehicles may also be violent. The person killed may be disfigured in the accident, perhaps even burned. The scenario may go like this: a knock on the door by a police officer or a telephone call from a hospital announces that someone is dead (Iserson & Iserson, 1999). Disbelief and denial may follow: "He (or she) had just driven to

A wrecked car mounted on a pole to urge motorists to drive carefully.

a movie! How could he (or she) have died?" If the body is mutilated, survivors may never see it again. If not, and if the person is delivered to a hospital for stabilization, attempts at emergency intervention or determination of death—sometimes followed by requests to authorize organ, tissue, or eye donation—may pose unexpected challenges to shocked family members. Everything may seem unreal. Losses, grief, and mourning following such a death are often complicated and take many forms as illustrated in a video entitled "Your Distracted Driving Killed Me."

Homicide

Homicide (now termed "assault" in the new international system of classifying and coding causes of death) is an act by one human being that is intended to or actually does kill another human being. In the United States in 2014, there were 15,872 homicide deaths with an overall death rate of 5.0 per 100,000 (Kochanek et al., 2016). The good news is that homicide dropped from among the 15 leading cause of death for the population as a whole in 2010 to 16th and then to 17th in 2014. The bad news is that homicide "is still a major issue for some age groups. In 2014, homicide remained among the 15 leading causes of death for age groups 1–4 (3rd), 5–14 (5th), 15–24 (3rd), 25–34 (3rd), 35–44 (5th), and 45–54 (13th)" (Kochanek et al., 2016, p. 10). Also, modern-day American society has long had the dubious distinction of leading the industrial West in both the number and rates of homicide.

The distribution of homicide deaths varies widely across the population. In addition to its prominence as a cause of death among children, adolescents, and young adults, perhaps the most disturbing features of the demography of homicide are gender and racial differences. Homicide was the cause of nearly 3.8 male deaths versus females in 2014. Homicide was also a leading cause of death among African Americans who die from this cause at an overall rate of 17.8 per 100,000 (32.1 for males alone).

Two noticeable features in American homicide deaths can lead to better understanding of this subject. First, for many years, approximately 50% of all homicides have occurred between family members or acquaintances. A corollary of this is that in 90% of all homicides the victims and the assailants are of the same race. A second prominent feature of homicide in our society is that it is heavily correlated with the use (or misuse) of firearms, which were involved in 11,008 homicide deaths in 2014. As Siegel, Ross, and King (2013, p. 2098) reported "We observed a robust correlation between higher levels of gun ownership and higher firearm homicide rates....states with higher rates of gun ownership had disproportionately large numbers of deaths from firearm-related homicides." In a separate study, Kalesan and colleagues (2016) concluded that "Projected federal-level implementation of universal background checks for firearm purchase could reduce national firearm mortality from 10.35 to 4.46 deaths per 100 000 people, background checks for ammunition purchase could reduce it to 1.99 per 100 000, and firearm identification to 1.81 per 100 000" (see also Gostin, 2016).

What we learn from the data on homicide is that it is a significant component in American encounters with death. Increasingly, homicide is the cause of deaths in groups that have not typically been thought of as otherwise vulnerable to death—notably, children, adolescents, and young adults. In addition, some homicide deaths appear utterly capricious and meaningless, as when a stray bullet from a drive-by shooting or carjacking strikes someone uninvolved in that activity. All of these factors help to explain why homicide is a prominent factor in how many contemporary Americans think about death.

Nevertheless, in a sense, homicidal behavior is overplayed in its significance in discussions of the American death system. For example, popular media have tended to seize on and give disproportionate attention to selected examples of violence and homicide, such as those involving homicide in schools and other everyday situations (Cullen, 2009; Kass, 2014; Langman, 2010; Lysiak, 2014; Newman, 2004; see also Issues for Critical Reflection #6 in this chapter and #17 in Chapter 19. While much is known about these incidents, there is much yet to learn about them and much to do to minimize their likelihood.

ISSUES FOR CRITICAL REFLECTION
#6 Mass Murders

Although rare, a number of mass murders occurring in contexts that appear to most Americans to be safe environments have taken place in the United States during the last two decades. For example:

- On April 20, 1999, 2 students at Columbine High School in Littleton, Colorado, used multiple weapons to kill 12 students, one teacher, and themselves, while also wounding 21 others.

- On October 2, 2006, Charles Carl Roberts IV invaded the one-room West Nickel Mines School in southeastern Pennsylvania and eventually shot 10 girls, killing 5 of them and wounding the others before he took his own life.

- On April 16, 2007, a disgruntled student, Cho Seung-Hui, killed 32 people and himself, while also wounding 17 others on the campus of Virginia Tech University in Blacksburg, Virginia.

(continues)

ISSUES FOR CRITICAL REFLECTION *(continued)*
#6 Mass Murders

- On January 8, 2011, outside a supermarket in Tucson, Arizona, Jared Lee Loughner killed 6 people and wounded 13 more, including U.S. Representative Gabrielle Giffords.
- On July 20, 2012, in a movie theater in Aurora, Colorado, James Eagan Holmes used a shotgun, a semiautomatic rifle, and a handgun to kill 12 people and injure 70 others.
- On December 14, 2012, 20-year-old Adam Lanza fatally shot 20 children and 6 adult staff members at Sandy Hook Elementary School in Newtown, Connecticut, before killing himself.
- On June 17, 2015, Dylan Roof killed the church pastor and 8 others at an evening Bible study meeting at Emanuel African Methodist Episcopal Church in Charleston, South Carolina.
- On December 2, 2015, Syed Rizwan Farook and Tashfeen Malik, killed 14 people and seriously injured 22 others in San Bernardino, California; both were killed by police later that day.
- On June 12, 2016, Omar Mateen killed 49 people and wounded 53 others attending Latin Night at Pulse, a gay nightclub in Orlando, Florida, before he was killed by police officers after a three-hour standoff. This was the deadliest mass shooting by a single gunman in U.S. history, the deadliest incident of violence against LGBT people in U.S. history, and the deadliest terrorist attack in the United States since the 9/11 attacks.
- On July 7, 2016, Micah Johnson killed 5 police officers and injured 7 other officers and 2 civilians in Dallas, Texas; after a standoff, he died when police detonated an explosive delivered by a remote-controlled robot. This was the deadliest attack on law enforcement officers since 9/11.

Commenting on one of these events, President Obama said: "At some point we as a country will have to reckon with the fact that this type of mass violence does not happen in other developed countries."

Earlier, Fox (2007; see also Fox & Levin, 2005, 2006) commented that "Seven of the eight largest mass shootings in modern U.S. history have occurred in the last 25 years." He also pointed out that these shootings are a subset of mass murders, defined as events "in which four or more people are killed in the same episode" to distinguish them from serial killings that occur over time. Fox suggested that several changes in our society may have contributed to the rise of these tragic events.

- We are a more mobile and rootless society, often living in locations where we have no friends or extended family to fall back on.
- More of us live in urban areas where we may not even know our nearest neighbors.
- Many of us have lost access to once-familiar features of traditional communities, such as stable marriages or partnerships, extended families, and religious institutions that might previously have provided support and acted as moderating influences on our behavior.
- We are an open, democratic society, vulnerable in many ways, while at the same time, we stress individual rights, aggressive competition, and immediate gratification, with little compassion for those who do not succeed (however, that is to be defined).
- More of us have easier access to firearms, especially to powerful, semiautomatic weapons, along with knowledge and training in how to use them.

Fox also described typical characteristics of the (mainly male) perpetrators of these mass shootings as the following:

- They often have a long history of frustration and failure and a diminished ability to cope with life's disappointments.
- They externalize blame, frequently complaining that others didn't give them a chance or are not fairly treating their ethnic, racial, or gender group.
- They commonly lack emotional support from friends or family and are often described as "loners."
- They generally suffer a precipitating event or major disappointment they view as catastrophic.
- They have access to weapons that are powerful enough to satisfy their need for revenge.

One point to keep in mind about homicides in schools is that they are very atypical experiences. In fact, the annual report from the U.S. Departments of Education and Justice, *Indicators of School Crime and Safety: 2014* (Robers et al., 2015, p. 6), reported that, based on preliminary data, "Between July 1, 2011 and June 30, 2012, there were a total of 45 school-associated violent deaths in elementary and secondary schools in the United States.... Of the 45 student, staff, and nonstudent school-associated violent deaths occurring during this time span, there were 26 homicides, 14 suicides, and 5 legal interventions." Despite this, the report added that "Over all available survey years, the percentage of youth homicides occurring at school remained at less than 2 percent of the total number of youth homicides, and the percentage of youth suicides occurring at school remained at less than 1 percent of the total number of youth suicides." Comments like this last one have led researchers like Fox and Levin (2006, p. 131) to observe that "Despite the school violence hype and panic, schools actually are the safest place for our kids to be." We may have a distorted picture of school violence in general and homicide in particular because, as one commentator (Twomey, 2001, p. 14A) noted: "the news media report crime, particularly violent crime, far out of proportion to its actual occurrence."

The basic facts to keep in mind about homicide in the American death system are that since 1992 it has been declining in relative importance as a leading cause of death in the overall American population. However, homicide is far too often a cause of death in the United States for its present levels to be tolerated. Americans must strive to prevent or minimize instances of homicidal violence in our society. To do so, we need to set aside erroneous and misleading perceptions of homicide in the United States and come to understand this important death-related phenomenon and its causes in accurate, factual terms.

Nearly all homicides result in sudden and unexpected death with a brief transition from the act of violence to the death. As such, this type of death presents special problems for survivors: as secondary victims, they are faced with an unexpected death in circumstances that may be unclear, traumatic, and often involves some social stigma, and each may cope in unique ways (Dyregrov et al., 2016; Englebrecht et al., 2016). Even if the agent is identified, it may not help. Survivors' grief may be further complicated when the agent is a family member, friend, or peer, and when the homicide has been deliberately perpetrated on innocent people (Klebold, 2016). Also, legal proceedings against the agent may be complex, and families of victims are often deliberately shut out of or kept at a distance from such proceedings. A sense of outrage, fed by impressions of injustice and lack of control, may complicate their mourning (Bucholz, 2002).

Terrorism

For many reasons there is no single, universally recognized definition of the word **terrorism**. Still, Hoffman's (2006, p. 43) description of terrorism as "the deliberate creation and exploitation of fear through violence or the threat of violence in the pursuit of political change" seems helpful. Richardson (2006) added that terrorists seek three things: (1) *revenge* for perceived or actual hurts to themselves or to some community with which they identify and to redress a perceived sense of humiliation; (2) *renown* in the form of publicity, attention, and glory for the individual and the cause, a kind of notoriety basically conferred on them by their community and their adversaries; and (3) *reaction*, which might involve their opponents' surrendering or engaging in widespread repression since either demonstrates the terrorists' strength and communicates their message.

Terrorism is not a new phenomenon. What has changed recently is the frequency and magnitude of terrorist acts. In earlier times, no single act could destroy thousands of lives and millions of dollars' worth of property in a few seconds. As a result, this is still a new death-related reality with which people in the 21st century will have to cope for the foreseeable future. We explore terrorism here by reflecting on its perpetrators and their goals, the means used, and the implications for death, dying, and bereavement.

Perpetrators of Terrorism and Their Goals   Three broad categories of terrorism can be identified by distinguishing between terrorist acts carried out by individuals, groups, or states. In examples of *individual terrorism*, one person characteristically engages in an act that harms or kills others and destroys property, often acting as a lone agent or perhaps with the support of one or two other individuals. Frequently, this is done to express anger or frustration with those who are targeted or in an effort to mobilize the larger society to rectify some perceived wrong or to act in some other desired way. For example, two brothers, Tamerlan and Dzhokhar Tsarnaev, placed pressure cooker bombs near the finish line of the Boston Marathon on April 15, 2013. When the bombs exploded, they killed three people and injured an estimated 264 others. In the aftermath of the bombing, the brothers killed an MIT policeman and the older brother (Tamerlan) was killed after a shootout with police before the younger brother was captured. On April 8, 2015, Dzhokhar Tsarnaev, a naturalized U.S. citizen, was found guilty on all charges and later was sentenced to death. See other examples, especially those perpetrated by "homegrown violent extremists," in Issues for Critical Reflection #6 in this chapter.

Group terrorism is practiced when a formally or informally organized group of people attempts to do harm for religious, political, or ideological reasons to those whom it perceives as its opponents. For example, in the United States after the Civil War the Ku Klux Klan (KKK) engaged in threats, beatings, lynching, and other terrorist acts supposedly to protect the familiar way of life of Southern whites and to keep freed African Americans "in their place." Other well-known recent examples of group terrorism are seen in the actions of the so-called Islamic State group (ISIS or ISLS), an organization seeking to establish an Islamic caliphate in Iraq and Syria (see Stern & Berger, 2015; Warrick, 2015), and in the activities of Boko Haram in northern Nigeria. These groups have killed many civilians and others who do not share their specific religious beliefs or goals. In general, group terrorism can have many different goals, for example, to force outsiders to leave the country, to overthrow what is perceived as a puppet regime, to lay claim to political power, or to try to set up a separate state.

State-supported terrorism is a strategy most often employed by a political administration against its own or a neighboring population. Terrorism of this type may be explicitly undertaken or only tacitly supported by a government. This sort of terrorism is generally employed by a stronger side against a weaker group in an effort to coerce them into certain behaviors or to remove them from the society by either forced emigration or extermination. For example, Saddam Hussein employed terrorist tactics (in the form of poison gas) against some Kurdish communities in Iraq in 1988, and the Nazis in Germany in the late 1930s and early 1940s acted to eliminate

Jews and members of other groups they blamed for various problems or believed to be hostile to their goals.

Means Employed by Terrorists   Terrorists employ a wide variety of violent means that may or may not put the terrorists themselves at risk. For example, Timothy McVeigh and the Tsarnaev brothers engaged in a form of terrorism that involved *acting at a distance*. McVeigh used a truck bomb to destroy the Alfred P. Murrah Federal Building in Oklahoma City on April 19, 1995, killing 169 people and injuring more than 500 others (Linenthal, 2001; Michel & Herbeck, 2001), while the Tsarnaev brothers were no longer actually present at the scene when their bombs exploded.

In Iraq and Afghanistan in recent years, roadside bombs ("improvised explosive devices" or so-called IEDs) exemplify similar *acts-at-a-distance*. Two other examples of this type of terrorism, both of which failed, include an attempt to detonate a car bomb on May 1, 2010, in New York City's Times Square and a plan to set off a bomb at a Christmas tree lighting ceremony in Portland, Oregon, on November 26, 2010. The New York perpetrator, Faisal Shahzad, a Pakistani-born, naturalized American citizen, pled guilty and is currently serving a sentence of life imprisonment without possibility of parole; the Portland perpetrator, Mohamed Osman Mohamud, a naturalized U.S. citizen born in Somalia, was the subject of an FBI sting operation. He was charged with attempted use of a weapon of mass destruction, tried, found guilty, and sentenced to 30 years in prison plus lifetime supervision upon release.

By contrast, some terrorist acts require *the direct presence of the perpetrator*. These include the behavior of snipers or kidnappings with the aim of achieving some political (rather than merely economic) goal. These acts frequently are planned to allow for the possibility of escape from immediate retribution, even though they may put the life of the individual terrorist at risk. Examples of this type of terrorism include mass shootings in San Bernardino, California (December 2, 2015), and in Orlando, Florida (June 12, 2016), as well as an incident on July 17, 2015, in Chattanooga, Tennessee, when Mohammad Youssuf Abdulazeez, a Kuwaiti-born, naturalized U.S. citizen, killed four Marines, and injured three others (including a Navy petty officer who died the next day) before he was killed in a shootout with police.

In addition, individuals and groups have engaged in acts of *terrorism through self-destruction* in which the death and devastation they seek to cause is achieved through the sacrifice of the terrorists' own lives (Gambetta, 2006). Best known in examples of *suicide bombings*, this has been a familiar form of terrorism in the Middle East over many years. The most spectacular example of this form of terrorism occurred in the September 11, 2001, attacks. One additional suicide bombing attempt failed on December 25, 2009, when a young Nigerian, Umar Farouk Abdulmutallab, attempted without success to detonate plastic explosives hidden in his underwear on a flight from Amsterdam to Detroit. He was convicted of attempting to use a weapon of mass destruction and attempted murder of 289 people and sentenced on February 16, 2012, to four life terms plus 50 years without parole.

Implications of Terrorism for Death, Dying, and Bereavement   Acts of terrorism most often employ violent means that result in traumatic losses. Typically, they cause sudden deaths, injuries that may lead to subsequent death or disability, and damage to property. Death, disability, and destruction may be primarily aimed at official representatives of the perceived opponent but often are indiscriminate or heedless of harm

The World Trade Center burning on September 11, 2001.

Dan Howell/Shutterstock.com

visited on others. In addition to causing multiple deaths and mutilation, bereavement and grief associated with such acts is usually complicated. Individuals have no time to prepare for such deaths and bodies may be destroyed, leaving survivors little or nothing to bury. Their grief is increased by knowing that other human beings were the deliberate agents of these deaths. They agonize over why the terrorist act was not prevented or what could have been done to mitigate its consequences. They are grimly aware that the terrorists acted with indifference both to those who would be harmed by their acts and to other innocent people who might become involved. Personal security and safety are challenged, as are common assumptions about life and the world. In addition, survivors may feel abandoned by a social system that often is unable to either find or prosecute the perpetrators.

With all of this said about terrorism, it is useful to keep in mind Kurzman's comment (2011, pp. 14–15) that "terrorism is not a leading cause of death in the world. If we want to save lives, far more lives would be saved by diverting a small portion of the world's counterterrorism budgets to mosquito netting." This bears on our discussion of selectivity in media reporting later in this chapter.

War, Genocide, and Ethnic Cleansing

War, genocide, and ethnic cleansing are all terms that apply to attempts at *socially sanctioned death* involving large numbers of people both as perpetrators and as victims. Although war, genocide, and ethnic cleansing all involve violence, they differ in that the goal in *war* is typically to overcome another society or group (or to repel aggressive action), **genocide** refers to violent crimes committed against groups with the intent to destroy the very existence of the group, and **ethnic cleansing** ostensibly involves the relocation of population groups but often in fact becomes a form of genocide. International groups like the United Nations have sought to regulate the conduct of war (think of the Geneva Convention); by contrast, such groups have defined genocide as a crime and have often treated ethnic cleansing in similar ways as a criminal activity. In each case, arranging for and bringing about large numbers of deaths requires extensive and systematic organization.

In cases of outright *war*, the number of deaths arising is astonishing. Take just four examples from the 20th century: (1) World War I (1914–1918) produced an estimated 37 million deaths; (2) World War II (1939–1945) led to an estimated 22–25 million military deaths and 40–52 million civilian deaths; (3) the Korean War (1950–1953) produced well over 3 million combatant and civilian deaths; and (4) the Vietnam War (1955–1975) resulted in more than 4 million deaths. In the 21st century, wars in Iraq, Afghanistan, and Syria have killed thousands of American military service personnel, plus many coalition personnel, numerous indigenous civilians, and people from other countries.

Numbers of people killed in wars often do not include civilian deaths that are notoriously difficult to identify. Generals count dead combatants on both sides because that is important for them to know or at least to estimate accurately. The number of civilians killed (sometimes downplayed or dismissed as "collateral damage") is of lesser interest from such perspectives—unless, of course, one is among or somehow connected to those civilians. Also, figures on civilian deaths may even be hidden for a variety of reasons—for instance, to avoid evidence of war crimes.

Examples of *genocide* are equally easy to identify. The German massacre of the Herero peoples in Southwest Africa is often considered the first genocide of the 20th century and a precursor to the Holocaust (Olusoga & Erichsen, 2010). Subsequently, the Ottoman Empire is accused of causing 800,000 to 1.5 million deaths of Armenians during World War I (Dadrian, 2003); Josef Stalin in the 1930s is estimated to have ordered the deaths of 10 million kulaks (a group of relatively affluent peasants or independent farmers thought of as class enemies); Mao Ze Dong's orders are estimated to have led to the deaths of 30 million Chinese during his "Great Leap Forward" in 1959–1961; the Chinese have killed more than 1 million Tibetans since 1950 (Ingram, 1992); and the communist Khmer Rouge killed an estimated 1–2 million Cambodians during the latter half of the 1970s in their attempt to create a so-called classless society (Skidelsky, 2004).

More recently, in 1994, the Rwandan government called on its Hutu majority population to murder everyone in the Tutsi minority (Gourevitch, 1998). Similarly, in 2003, the Sudanese government began an ongoing genocide in the western Darfur region of the country. Best estimates are that 300,000 people have been killed and over 3 million displaced, or made homeless. As a result, the International Criminal Court has issued warrants for the arrest of Sudanese President Omar al-Bashir and other Sudanese officials on charges of war crimes, crimes against humanity, and genocide.

With regard to *ethnic cleansing*, although the activities it represents can be seen in many contexts across history, the phrase seems to have been popularized by the media during the 1990s especially in relationship to conflicts in certain regions of the former Yugoslavia involving Serbs, Croats, and Bosnians. The phrase itself has no fixed or legal definition, but it is often characterized in ways like the following:

> Despite its recurrence, ethnic cleansing nonetheless defies easy definition. At one end it is virtually indistinguishable from forced emigration and population exchange while at the other it merges with deportation and genocide. At the most general level, however, ethnic

cleansing can be understood as the expulsion of an "undesirable" population from a given territory due to religious or ethnic discrimination, political, strategic or ideological considerations, or a combination of these. (Bell-Fialkoff, 1993, p. 110)

While some aspects of this definition may make ethnic cleansing sound relatively benign, in fact means employed in these processes have included murder, torture, arbitrary arrest and detention, extrajudicial executions, rape and sexual assaults, confinement of civilian population in ghetto areas, forcible removal, displacement and deportation of civilian population, deliberate military attacks or threats of attacks on civilians and civilian areas, and wanton destruction of property. Thus, as a consequence of ethnic cleaning and the killing of 8,000 Bosnian Muslim men and boys in the city of Srebrenica in 1995 and the expulsion of thousands of others, on March 24, 2016, the former Bosnian Serb leader Radovan Karadžic and the first president of the *Republika Srpska* was found guilty of genocide in Srebrenica, war crimes, and crimes against humanity, and sentenced to 40 years' imprisonment.

Bell-Fialkoff (1993, p. 110) described ethnic cleansing in the United States in a way that challenges Americans to reflect on their own history whether we agree with him:

Under this definition, then, the slow dispersal and annihilation of North America's indigenous population was indeed ethnic cleansing. In their efforts to gain and secure the frontier, American settlers "cleansed" most Indians from their lands, even though the process was slow and, until the nineteenth century, carried out mainly under private initiative. On the other hand, the removal of thousands of Africans from their home continent, however harsh and despite the fact that it denuded many regions of their original inhabitants, would not be considered ethnic cleansing. The aim was to import a desired slave population, not to expel any particular group.

There are two general points to note about war, genocide, and ethnic cleansing: (1) they produce social disruption leading both directly and indirectly to suffering and death and (2) it is often difficult to grasp or make sense of these events and resulting deaths. For the first point: the United Nations High Commissioner for Refugees reported that in 2016, there were 65.3 million forcibly displaced people worldwide, over half of whom were children. This is the highest number ever of such displaced people and a problem likely to worsen in the immediate future.

Several thousand refugees are blocked at the Slovenia town of Dobova from travelling onward to Germany.

Janossy Gergely/Shutterstock.com

For the second point, even if we could obtain accurate figures for deaths associated with war, genocide, and ethnic cleansing in the many different contexts in which they have appeared (something often very difficult to do), how could we possibly make sense of such terrible events? How can we grasp the deaths of huge numbers of people, often (but not always) in far-off locations? Many have found the death of a single beloved person to be incomprehensible. How to make sense of the deaths of thousands or millions may well elude our imaginations (Elliot, 1972). A danger here is that we may become inured to these activities and desensitized to the numbers of deaths they involve. Both the activities and the deaths may seem so unimaginable that we may stop trying to comprehend them. But that may make us even more vulnerable to accepting them as tolerable.

The Holocaust

During World War II, what became under the Nazis a systematic program to eliminate whole classes of people from the face of the earth is still regarded as unique for its scope and political or ideological basis (Dawidowicz, 1975; Friedländer, 1995, 2007; Hilberg, 2003; Pawelczynska, 1979; Reitlinger, 1968). The Nazis slaughtered 6 million European Jews and millions of others during the late 1930s and early 1940s.

The Nazi program of genocide was fueled by a particular ideology (not merely politics or economics or even military considerations). According to the Nazis' perverted philosophy, members of the Jewish "race"—along with whole categories of other people, such as gypsies (Roma), severely mentally and physically handicapped people, Jehovah's Witnesses, and homosexuals—were classed as *Untermensch* or subhuman. At first, this led to outbursts of anti-Semitism, loss of civil and human rights, relocation and ghettoization, and shipment to "concentration camps." Inhabitants in many of these camps soon became a slave labor force working on behalf of the German war effort, although this did not protect them from extremely harsh living and working conditions, inadequate rations, and brutal pressures of all sorts that led to large numbers of deaths. At the same time, random violence, terror, and crude forms of systematic killing were implemented both within and outside the camps in areas that fell under Nazi control. Ample and adequate documentation of these horrors is available from both firsthand witnesses (e.g., Kulka, 1986; Langbein, 1994; Levi, 1986) and later historians (Gilbert, 1993).

In 1941, a decision was made to achieve the "final solution of the Jewish question" by "a program aimed at murdering every last Jew in the German grasp" (Browning, 2004, p. 424; see also Roseman, 2002). In search of efficiency, relatively crude methods of killing—bludgeoning, hanging, and shooting people to death; machine gunning and burying them in mass graves; and using engine exhaust gases to suffocate those who were being transported in closed vans to locations where their bodies were burned or interred—were replaced by the infamous gas chambers and crematories of the "extermination camps" (*Vernichtungslager*). The term itself is significant: one kills a human being, but one exterminates a less-than-human pest.

This final stage of **the Holocaust** occurred mainly in occupied Poland, especially at a former military barracks on the edge of the city of Auschwitz (Oswiecim)—whose gate still today proclaims the infamous and cruelly ironic motto, "*Arbeit macht frei*" ("Work makes one free")—and its newly constructed satellite about two miles away in the countryside at Birkenau (Brzezinka). Here, in the words of the camp commander (Hoess, 1959, p. 160) "the greatest human extermination center of all time" was developed. And here (but elsewhere also), cruel and hideous experiments were undertaken under the guise of medical research (Lifton, 1986; Michalczyk, 1994).

According to authoritative calculations, at Auschwitz/Birkenau alone, "the number of victims was at least 1.1 million, about 90% of whom were Jews from almost every country in Europe," although with slightly different data and assumptions, "the number of Jewish victims killed in the camp would rise to about 1.35 million, with the total number of Auschwitz victims reaching about 1.5 million" (Piper, 1994, pp. 62, 72). All of these deaths took place from the time when the first prisoners arrived (June 14, 1940)—and especially after September 1941, when the use of cyanide gas was first tested—until January 27, 1945, when the Soviet army liberated the camp and freed some 7,000 remaining prisoners. Toward the end, it is reported that some 80% of the mainly women, children, and elderly who arrived in the daily transports at Auschwitz/Birkenau (which tied up railroad equipment desperately needed by the German military for the war effort) went directly to their deaths from the notorious "selections" held at rail side. Children were particular targets because the Nazis viewed them as "useless eaters" and expected they would grow up into undesirable adults (Heberer, 2011; Stargardt, 2006).

Nothing like this had been seen in the world previously. To visit Auschwitz many years after the Holocaust is to confront an enormous incongruity between what is in many ways an ordinary, even banal, setting and innumerable images of horror that endure as a reminder of the dark side of human capacity (Corr, 1993b; Czarnecki, 1989). As Günter Grass once wrote: "Even if surrounded with explanations, Auschwitz can never be grasped" (1990, p. 96). Perhaps that is why some writers (such as Czech, 1990; Gilbert, 1993; Harran & Roth, 2000) have employed the techniques of chronology and cartography to depict the horrors of the Holocaust in impersonal, dispassionate ways, whereas others (such as MacMillan, 1991; Wiesel, 1960) have used literary forms to convey in imaginative and evocative ways messages about the Holocaust that are not effectively transmitted in other genre. And there have been impressive accounts of what was involved in survival and resistance within the death camps of the Holocaust (Des Pres, 1976; Langbein, 1994).

Two U.S. soldiers look at dead prisoners on a railroad car at an unidentified concentration camp, April to May, 1945.

Everett Historical/Shutterstock.com

The basic lesson for all to draw from these horrible events—like many fundamental morals—is simple: "We have the choice between the Holocaust as a warning and the Holocaust as a precedent" (Bauer, 1986, p. xvii). Although some have sought to deny the facts of the Holocaust (Lipstadt, 1993), its reality and implications continue to resonate within the North American death system (Novick, 1999). For example, the book *Schindler's List* (Keneally, 1982; see also Crowe, 2004) and the Oscar-winning movie (1993) of the same title; the dedication in 1993 of the U.S. Holocaust Memorial Museum in Washington, D.C.; the founding in 1994 of the Survivors of the Shoah Visual History Foundation in Los Angeles; and the December 10, 2010, report from the National Archives on the recruitment after World War II of ex-Nazis by American intelligence agents (Breitman & Goda, 2010).

The Nuclear Era

From its outset, the **nuclear era** introduced a form of socially sanctioned death and an ongoing death-related threat for which there is no adequate historical precedent. Nuclear power was first unleashed on July 16, 1945, at the Trinity test site in New Mexico. It became a new force for death at Hiroshima on August 6, 1945, when an estimated 100,000 people died in a single flash of light and, again, three days later at Nagasaki, when 50,000 more died in the second atomic bombing. In both Japanese cities, mass death from the blast and the heat of the bomb was joined for the first time to the lingering effects of radiation, secondary effects believed to have caused deaths equal in number to those killed outright.

What was unique at Hiroshima was the instantaneous quality of the first large-scale wave of deaths and the fact that they resulted from a single nuclear "device." Also distinctive were the lingering effects of radiation and the unparalleled destructive potential of nuclear weapons. The scope and character of this new way of encountering death have challenged the best efforts of reporters (such as Hersey, 1948; Lustig, 1977) and scholars (such as Lifton, 1964, 1967) to articulate their implications. For example, to Lifton, the horror of nuclear weapons was that they seemed to demolish many of the ways that individuals looked to attain symbolic immortality by destroying all descendants, creations, and nature itself (see Chapter 19 in this book for the concept of "symbolic immortality"). The use of nuclear power at Hiroshima and Nagasaki has also led to debates about the moral, political, and other aspects of using such weapons (e.g., Alperovitz, 1995; Lifton, 1982; Lifton & Mitchell, 1995; Maddox, 1995).

In both the Holocaust and Hiroshima, as well as in various terrorist assaults, women, children, and the elderly were killed as readily as men in the military. During World War II in particular, saturation bombing and other methods of waging war intentionally blurred the distinction between combatants and noncombatants (Grayling, 2006). These techniques were employed as much to destroy civilian morale as to damage specific military targets. At Hiroshima and Nagasaki, that strategy was carried further in such a way that life itself seemed to come under a threat against which there was no adequate defense.

Since 1945, the lethal potential of nuclear weapons has been magnified many times over, along with their accuracy and modes of delivery (Arkin & Fieldhouse, 1985). Death and destruction can now be brought down on humankind in a degree and form far beyond the wildest dreams—or nightmares—of human beings over nearly the whole of recorded history.

The level of tension associated with nuclear weapons declined somewhat with the dissolution of the Soviet Union in 1991 and subsequent efforts to destroy some warheads and their delivery systems. However, there are still worries that economic difficulties in Russia and elsewhere may lead to problems with remaining nuclear weapons. Furthermore, many are now concerned about nuclear threats from terrorist groups or rogue governments who might construct so-called "suitcase bombs" or crash planes into nuclear reactors (Allison, 2004). And since 2001, the international community has struggled with how to contain or discourage nations (notably, North Korea and Iran) who either have or seek to develop their own nuclear weapons. In 1947, the *Bulletin of the Atomic Scientists* established a "doomsday clock" to reflect what were perceived as extraordinary dangers faced by the world from the threat of nuclear weapons (and later also from climate change). As of June 2017, the clock stands at just two-and-a half minutes before midnight as a result of "unchecked climate change, global nuclear weapons modernizations, and outsized nuclear weapons arsenals."

The nuclear era has also revealed another face as nuclear power has become a source of much-needed energy supplies. Here, the initial appearance is benign and welcome; and in many ways it has remained so. However, accidents in nuclear reactors at Three Mile Island in Pennsylvania in 1979 (Walker, 2004), at Chernobyl in Ukraine in 1986, and the results of a natural disaster in Japan in 2011 (see Focus On 4.2) showed that even a peaceful source of nuclear energy can pose a real threat to humankind. Explosion, fire, and local irradiation, however lethal they may be to the surrounding territory, are nothing compared to the airborne radiation and long-term contamination of land, water, food supplies, and people of the type that followed the events at Chernobyl and in Japan.

How are the dangers associated with nuclear weaponry and nuclear power to be kept in check? How should they be balanced against legitimate needs for self-defense and sources of energy to sustain quality in living? More broadly, what does it mean to live under the nuclear shadow? For some, it seems the subject does not bear thinking about; they simply put it out of their minds through techniques of dissociation and denial. For others, the power of the threat and the difficulty of doing anything about it diminish their joy in living and their sense of promise for the future. For all, it is a new and unprecedented dimension of death-related experiences in the 21st century.

Looking back, Lifton and Mitchell (1995, p. xi) wrote, "You cannot understand the twentieth century without Hiroshima." We would say that death-related experiences in the 21st century cannot be understood without considering the various forms of human-induced death examined in this section. In particular, terrorism, war, genocide, and ethnic cleansing, the Holocaust, and the nuclear era must be taken into account. All of these involve mass death. Terrorism, war, genocide, and ethnic cleansing most often have to do with ideological, religious, and political conflict. The Holocaust resulted from a perverted ideology, and the nuclear era reflected a new technology. In each case, the results have involved what Leviton (1991a, 1991b) called "horrendous death," a transformation in both the quantity and the quality of human encounters with death that remains momentous and without parallel even now in the 21st century.

DEATH AND LANGUAGE

One way in which a society and its death system try to control and influence how death is experienced is evident in language patterns and practices. Both **language about death** and **death-related language**—which may seem to be the same thing, but are in fact quite distinct—reflect strong social messages concerning appropriate emotions and behaviors regarding death.

Language about Death

In the death systems of many societies around the world, as Smith and Kelly (2012) found when they initiated a blog about global attempts to avoid talking directly about death and dying, many people often go to great lengths to avoid saying words like *dead* and *dying*. In place of this direct language, individuals commonly employ **euphemisms**—that is, they substitute a word or expression with comparatively pleasant or inoffensive associations for language that they view as harsher or more offensive, even though the latter ways of speaking might more precisely designate what is intended. As Keyes (2010, pp. 7–8) wrote, euphemisms are "words or phrases substituted for ones that make us uneasy." Thus, people don't die; they merely "pass away." In principle, euphemisms are pleasing ways of speaking; in practice, they usually involve underlying attitudes that seek to "prettify" language, to make it appear more delicate, "nice," or socially acceptable, and to avoid seeming disagreeable, impolite, or nasty. Using euphemisms is not necessarily undesirable in itself, but it can become so when it is excessive or when it reflects an unwillingness to confront the realities of life and death directly. A brief survey of "sympathy cards" ("She's not dead, she's just sleeping") can illustrate this point.

Euphemisms that relate to death are and have long been familiar to most users and students of language (Neaman & Silver, 1983; Rawson, 1981). They arise in many contexts. Well before recent interest in "thanatology" (itself a euphemism for death-related studies), these figures of speech were recognized by scholars (e.g., Pound, 1936). Terms like "kicked the bucket" (originally a graphic description of one way of committing suicide by hanging) or "bought the farm" are euphemistic descriptions of death. The "dearly departed" have been "called home," "laid to rest," or "gone to their reward." Much the same is true for those who "conk out," who are "cut down," "turned up their toes," or whose "number is up." Anyone who is "on his last legs" has "run the good race," "is down for the long count," and "it's curtains." The precise status of those who are "no longer with us" is not nearly as clear as those "who have been put to bed with a shovel."

Professional caregivers sometimes say that they "lost" a patient or that the individual "expired." Such language always has some original foundation. One has lost the company of a spouse or friend who has died; the spirit or last breath has gone out of the person who expired. But those who use such expressions today are usually not thinking of such linguistic justifications. They are most often simply unwilling to speak directly. Hence, the hyperbole of bureaucratic health care, which twists death into the contortions of "negative patient care outcome" or the ways in which counterespionage agencies talk about "terminating with extreme prejudice" instead of speaking about killing.

The change in labels from "undertaker" (a word that the *Oxford English Dictionary* traces back to 1698 in England) to "mortician" (a term originating in America in 1895 with roots in the Latin word *mors* or death) to "funeral director" or "funeral services practitioner" reflects both a euphemistic tendency and a broadened vocational scope.

Language may be more effective as a vehicle for accurate communication when people speak directly in ways that are neither excessively camouflaged nor brutal. Consider the state to which our society has come in trying to express in ordinary language what veterinarians do to very sick or infirm pets. Among many people to whom we speak, such animals are not simply "killed" or "euthanized." Rather, they are "put to sleep." What does that convey to young children who may then be urged to stop asking annoying questions and take a nap? It is challenging to try to express the same point in some other way in colloquial but effective English. Some say that animals are "put out of their misery" or "put down." Does that help explain things?

Euphemisms are not solely linked to death. On the contrary, they are ways to stand back from or cover over all sorts of taboo topics. Consider, for example, common expressions for genital organs or excretory functions. Both the New England Puritans of the 17th century and adherents of the Romantic Movement in the United States during the 19th century firmly censored talk about sexuality even as they readily spoke of death (usually for moral or religious purposes). In the 21st century, it often seems that people have simply inverted these attitudes and practices so as to be tongue-tied about death but all too unrestrained in talking about sex.

Direct speech and candor are not always desirable. Frankness can be admirable or out of place; the same is true for avoidance. Both overemphasis and underemphasis, whether on sexuality or on death, are equally unbalanced postures. Both distort and demean central realities of life. Still, as Neaman and Silver (1983, pp. 144–145) argued many years ago, contemporary American society is special:

> At no other time in history has a culture created a more elaborate system of words and customs to disguise death so pleasantly that it seems a consummation devoutly to be wished....
>
> The motives for euphemizing death are in many ways similar to those for disguising our references to pregnancy and birth. Great superstition surrounded these events, as did great distaste and a sense of social impropriety. Propelled by these feelings, we have attempted to strip death of both its sting and its pride—in fact to kill death by robbing it of its direct and threatening name. The terms change and the euphemisms grow, but the evasion of the word "death" survives.

Linguistic attempts to avoid talking about death are more than detours around the unpleasant. Euphemisms become problematic whenever they are not held in check or counterbalanced by personal experience. Most euphemisms originated in a rich soil of experiential contact with death. As death-related encounters have become increasingly less frequent and more limited in much of modern society (see Chapter 2), these essential roots of language have dried up. The problem with an overabundance of euphemisms in recent talk about death is that they reveal and themselves contribute to a kind of distancing or dissociation from important and fundamental events of life itself.

Death-Related Language

One might conclude from the preceding section that death-related language is simply absent from most ordinary speech. Such a conclusion would be "dead wrong." In talk about actual events pertaining to death and dying, it is quite common for language about death to be avoided. But in a curious and paradoxical reversal, *death-related language* is frequently used in talk about events that have nothing to do with actual death and dying (Partridge, 1966; Wentworth & Flexner, 1967; Weseen, 1934).

Most people in contemporary American society speak quite openly about dead batteries, dead letters, a deadpan expression, a dead giveaway, deadlines, and being dead drunk. Everyone knows people who are dead tired, dead on their feet, dead certain, deadbeats or dead broke, deadly dull, deadlocked, dead to the world in sleep, or scared to death. Marksmen who hit the target dead center have a dead eye or are dead shots. Gamblers recognize a "dead man's hand" (aces and eights, all black cards; the hand that Wild Bill Hickok was holding when he was shot dead), while truckers "deadhead" back home with an empty vehicle. Parents may be "worried to death" about children who "will be the death" of them. Those who are embarrassed may "wish they were dead" or that they "could just die." Orville Kelly (1977, p. 186), a man with a life-threatening illness, reported encountering a friend who said, "I'm just dying to see you again."

Similarly, in today's society when one has nothing else to do, one may be said to be killing time. There is quite a difference between a lady-killer who is dressed "fit to kill" and a killjoy. And most contemporary people know what it means to "die on base," "flog a dead horse," or "kill the lights." To "kill a bottle of whiskey" leaves us with a "dead soldier." To be "dead as a doornail" is to be as hammered into insensitivity as was the nail head driven into the center of doors against which knockers were once struck before doorbells came into prominence. Good comedians "slay" their audiences who "die of laughter"; poor comedians "die on their feet."

In these and many, many other similar phrases, death-related language emphasizes and exaggerates what is said. To be dead right is to be very right, completely or absolutely right, the most right one can be. Death-related language dramatizes or intensifies a word or phrase that might have seemed too weak on its own to convey the intended meaning or depth of feeling. It trades on the ultimacy and finality of death to try to heighten or intensify whatever is being said.

Placing this familiar use of death-related language alongside common euphemisms teaches interesting lessons about linguistic practices in the contemporary American death system. Death language is frequently avoided when people speak of death itself, but it is often employed (sometimes with enthusiasm) when they are not speaking directly about death. In fact, language is powerful; naming can influence the reality we experience. Perhaps that is why death-related language is easily employed in "relatively safe situations" that have nothing to do with death itself, but just the reverse is the case when one uses euphemisms that seek to soften death or allude to it obliquely.

DEATH AND THE MEDIA

The media play an important role in the contemporary American death system, as is evident in news reports and entertainment programs. As we saw in Chapter 2, many Americans have limited personal experience with natural human death. However, most people in the United States have experienced in a vicarious or secondhand way thousands of violent or traumatic deaths. One estimate is that "by the time the average child graduates from elementary school, she or he will have witnessed at least 8,000 murders and more than 100,000 other assorted acts of violence. Depending on the amount of television viewed, our youngsters could see more than 200,000 violent acts before they hit the schools and streets of our nation as teenagers" (Huston et al., 1992, pp. 53–54). These vicarious experiences come to us through news and entertainment services provided by newspapers and magazines or on the radio, but it is television and other electronic media that appear to be most influential.

Vicarious Death Experiences: News Reports in the Media

On September 11, 2001, and in the days immediately following, television and the Internet perhaps were at their best in informing the American public about a horrific, death-related event. They had hard news to report and graphic images to share. However, that was a high point not always typical of the media in general or television in particular. For example, human-induced deaths are pervasive on televised evening news reports in scenes of death and destruction from the ongoing conflicts in Afghanistan, Iraq, and Syria or from various natural disasters. In these and other media reports, homicide, accidents, war, and other forms of traumatic death and violence are staple "newsworthy" events. Hence the slogan, "If it bleeds, it leads" (Kerbel, 2000).

In fact, routine accounts of violence and war on television or the Internet often generate a kind of psychological immunity in the general public to the impact of death. Experiencing violent death in these vicarious ways often does not seem to have the same impact as being there in person. Watching someone being shot to death on a smaller-than-life-sized television or computer screen is quite different from direct participation in the event. These media deaths are distant or remote for most people; actual death often remains outside our direct experience despite many vicarious encounters with its surrogates.

A flip side of this issue arises when government and the media actually hide some deaths from view. As part of an official policy, the remains of persons killed in the wars in Iraq and Afghanistan were for many years forbidden to be shown arriving back in the United States. Attempting to hide war deaths from the public by limiting in this way what the media can show can lead to a failure to grasp the full reality of those military actions. (Two counterexamples occurred when the "PBS News Hour" showed pictures of service members when their deaths were made official and pictures had become available, and when Canadians lined overpasses on the now-renamed "Highway of Heroes" to honor fallen members of their military on their journey from a military airbase to the coroner's office in Toronto.)

One reason for the remote or distanced quality of most these newsworthy events is that they are *a highly selective portrait of death and life* in today's society and around the world. Anything "newsworthy" is by definition out of the ordinary. We know this and can recognize the truth in the words of one commentator (Krugman, 2001, p. 16A) who observed that "the media, and especially news channels that have to keep people watching all day, thrive on hype." As a result, the news media are preoccupied with the deaths of special persons or special sorts of death. They depict death in a selective, distorted, and sensationalized way to individuals in a society that has less and less contact with natural human death. Ordinary people who die in ordinary ways are not newsworthy; they are tucked away in death announcements on the back pages of a newspaper or silently omitted from television news programs. Television in particular is heavily focused on stories that can be accompanied by dramatic visual images.

A striking example of the problem of selectivity in media reports is given in Kurzman's comments (2011, p. 15) about terrorism and the media:

> [T]errorism dominates the headlines far out of proportion to its death toll. Terrorists are grimly successful at attracting public attention. Of the thousands of violent incidents that occur around the globe each day, the world media efficiently sifts for hints of terrorist motivations, then feeds these incidents over the wire services and satellite networks to news consumers who may not realize how rare terrorism really is. In this way the media are accomplices to terrorism. They bring the perpetrators' message to vast audiences; without these audiences, the terror would only be felt locally. Indeed, if a terrorist act occurred and nobody heard about it, it would be a failure. The media is just doing its job in reporting terrorist violence—if a terrorist act occurred and journalists didn't cover it, we would consider the media to have failed. But the result is that media consumers, ordinary folks who try to keep up with world affairs, get a skewed picture of the prevalence of terrorism.

One exception to the rules of newsworthiness are brief notices reporting the fact of an individual's death, names of survivors, and plans (if any) for funeral or burial services (Johnson, 2006). Typically, these *death announcements* (sometimes called *obituaries*) appear in small type (a source of complaint among some elderly or visually impaired readers), in alphabetized columns, near the classified ad section in newspapers. This location is not surprising, since death announcements are essentially public notices often paid for by survivors and usually arranged through funeral directors. Like the classified ads, which they resemble, death announcements record ordinary events of everyday life. They differ greatly from news stories that the media run without charge to mark the deaths of prominent persons.

The selectivity implicit in what is thought to be newsworthy carries with it an odd kind of reassurance. It encourages people to comfort themselves with thoughts like these: because I am not a very special person and because I do not expect to die in a very special way, I can distance myself from the staple fare of death in newspapers and on television and thus from unpleasant associations with death.

The specialized and highly selective drama of death in media news reports is insubstantial and abstract; it lacks the definite shape, texture, and concreteness of one's own life. Having been shocked by so many out-of-the-ordinary newsworthy events, people often become thick-skinned, passive spectators, hardened against the personal import of death. It becomes just one more among many distant and unusual phenomena paraded before us in a regular, unending, and not always very interesting series.

Sometimes, however, the unusual modes of death reported so selectively in the media may themselves come to be seen as ordinary or typical. For example, extensive and highly dramatized coverage of tragic school shootings in our society has led many to believe that death is common in our high schools when, in fact, schools are among the safest places for children in America (Robers et al., 2015). By contrast with these dreadful events in which a small number of deaths have been blown out of proportion, one's own death—which is not perceived as anything like these second-hand events—may come to appear less likely and less proximate.

Fantasized Death and Violence: Entertainment in the Media

The distortion of death in news reports is compounded in many entertainment programs in the media. Death and violence are ever present in such media—on television and in movies, video games, and music lyrics (Wass, 2003). But this is typically a very unrealistic presence. Think of cowboy, war, or gangster movies, police or military shows, and science fiction fantasies on television or videos, battles with alien invaders in video games, and the language of much "gangsta rap."

What is most remarkable about the typical portrayal of death in these media is that it is usually very unrealistic or **fantasized**. Those who die are unimportant people or "bad guys." Heroes and heroines repeatedly survive extreme peril, whereas actors die one week only to reappear unharmed the next. Violent fantasies of a very graphic nature are acted out, but suffering, grief, and other consequences of this violence and death are mostly noticeable for their absence. Murders take place, but audiences are chiefly interested in whether their perpetrator can be identified. Killings occur, but they usually satisfy a sense of poetic justice, and their consequences are not of much interest. The realities of death, dying, and bereavement are rarely apparent. Thus, Schultz and Huet (2000, p. 137) concluded: "In American film, death is distorted into a sensational stream of violent attacks by males, with fear, injury, further aggression, and the absence of normal grief reactions as the most common responses."

A committee of the American Academy of Pediatrics (AAP) (1995) studied this subject and concluded that "American media are the most violent in the world, and American society is now paying a high price in terms of real-life violence" (p. 949). Some reject a cause-effect link between media and real-life violence, but the AAP has noted that a majority of researchers in the field (e.g., Comstock & Paik, 1991; Eron, 1993; Strasburger, 1993) are convinced that such a link has been firmly established. Thus, the AAP (1995, p. 949) concluded that "although media violence is not the only cause of violence in American society, it is the single most easily remediable contributing factor."

Children's cartoons on television illustrate this very special vision of death, although they may often be more benign than many of the examples just cited. These cartoons simplify the complexities of other entertainment forms. Since children's attention spans are assumed to be short and distraction is always likely, the plot must be gripping and must continually reassert its hold over viewers (Minow & LaMay, 1995). Thus, television cartoons frequently emphasize lively action, as in cats chasing mice or dogs chasing cats. Many of these action cartoons may incorrectly reinforce a perception in some children that death is temporary. For example, in the well-known *Road Runner* cartoon series, Wile E. Coyote relentlessly pursues the flightless bird only to be caught repeatedly in his own traps. He is constantly the apparent victim of horrible death experiences, but he always enjoys an instant resurrection and each time survives in the end. In other words, *he never dies; he just keeps getting killed*. Destruction is followed so rapidly by delight, joy, and renewed activity that there is no time for grief. The cartoon is about the ongoing action of an endless chase. It is not really about death, although inevitably it communicates many messages about that subject.

In the latter part of the 20th century, death became an even more vivid presence in adult entertainment. Earlier, no one ever bled when shot or stabbed in a movie. Fistfights erupted in saloons, six-guns blazed away, actors staggered against walls and crumpled in death—but all the while their clothes were clean and their hats usually remained firmly on their heads. By contrast, the movie *Saving Private Ryan* (1988) was widely praised as portraying the real horrors of war because it showed lost limbs and ghastly wounds. Nowadays, shock and horror in the media are often excessive, and graphic depictions of blood, gore, and crashing automobiles are standard fare in much that passes for modern entertainment. So much artificial blood and apparent mayhem can make today's movie and television viewers jaded. It is no longer easy to surprise or impress them or even to catch and hold their attention.

More recently, many video games designed for children and adults have traded on various forms of violence and death involving fantasy figures or replicas of real human beings to capture the interest of their audiences. In 2004, a new video game that could be downloaded from the Internet (for a suitable fee) even allowed the player to assume the role of Lee Harvey Oswald in the act of assassinating President John F. Kennedy! His brother, Senator Edward Kennedy, is reported to have described this video as "despicable." It is certainly an extraordinary example of its genre, but not at all unique in contributing to a widespread desensitization to the realities of violence and death. Again, death has been distorted through a process of selectivity and fantasization.

The Internet, particularly in its social media forms, is another aspect of death-related practices influencing our death system. Although the number of death notifications via social media is unknown, it is likely to be quite high, since a growing number of people are getting their news via online and social media (American Press Institute, 2014). We also know that more and more people are turning to online and social media sites for avenues of grief resources and support (Sofka, Cupit, & Gilbert, 2012), a phenomenon termed **thanatechnology** (Sofka, 1997, p. 553).

Selectivity is unavoidable in reporting the news or telling a story and fantasy is neither unhealthy nor undesirable in itself. The games, songs, and fairy tales of childhood have long been full of fantasy and death, and children have coped without major difficulty. Two factors have been central: (1) the way in which the violence and death—and their real-life consequences—are (or are not) presented and (2) a firm grasp by the audience on the essential distinction between fantasy and reality. The problem in our society is a looser grip on the realities of life and death, coupled with increasing violence and gore. Selectivity, distortion, and fantasy become dangerous in media depictions of death when they substitute for or supplant a balanced appreciation of life.

Summary

In this chapter, we explored selected examples of *death-related practices* in the United States and throughout the world in order to complement our discussions of death-related encounters and attitudes in Chapters 2 and 3. We introduced the concept of a societal "death system" and the example of the terrorist attacks in the United States on September 11, 2001, to show how the American death system mobilized itself in response to a particularly difficult challenge. We then examined a series of examples that showed the contemporary American death system in operation. Subsequently, we offered an account of various forms of human-induced deaths, including deaths associated with accidents, homicide, terrorism, war, genocide, ethnic cleansing, the Holocaust, and the nuclear era. Throughout, we indicated how these events changed human encounters with death and have had important ongoing implications up to the present time. Next, we considered American linguistic practices, noting that many individuals use euphemistic language to avoid talking about death as such, even as they use death-related language to discuss topics that are not at all related to death. Finally, we identified highly selective and fantasized portraits of death and violence in the media (in both news reports and entertainment).

These death-related practices, along with many others that we explore throughout this book, show that we should not conclude as some (such as Gorer, 1965a; Kübler-Ross, 1969) have done that ours is merely a "death-denying society," one from which death has largely been exiled as a social or public presence. The evidence presented in this chapter suggests that it is more defensible to argue (as do Dumont & Foss, 1972; Weisman, 1972) that death-related practices in the United States are neither simply death denying nor death accepting. These practices and the American death system express both types of attitudes—sometimes separately, sometimes simultaneously—along with other attitudes as well.

Glossary

Accidents: unintentional injuries

Death-related language: speech that employs language about death to describe or intensify talk about subjects that have nothing to do with death

Death-related practices: familiar routines, procedures, and actions that follow from or are related to death-related encounters and actions

Death system: the formal or informal structure that every society employs to mediate between death and its members; composed of specific components designed to perform particular functions

Ethnic cleansing: using force or threats to make an area ethnically homogeneous by removing from that area persons of another ethnic or religious group

Euphemism: language that substitutes a word or expression that is thought to be less distasteful or offensive for one more exactly descriptive of what is intended

Fantasized death: unrealistic portraits of death (in the media)

Genocide: the annihilation or attempted annihilation of an entire race of people

The Holocaust: a genocidal attempt by the Nazis during the late 1930s and early 1940s to completely destroy or annihilate the Jewish people

Homicide: the action of one human being that kills another human being (sometimes called "assault")

Human-induced death: death resulting from the actions or inactions of human beings

Language about death: speech about topics like death, dying, and bereavement

Nuclear era: the period from July 1945 to the present during which the splitting of the atom unleashed a new form of power that can be used for weapons or as a source of energy

Socially sanctioned killing: societal actions intended to bring about killing and/or death among their own members or among members of other societies, for example, war or genocide

Terrorism: violent acts or threats designed to intimidate or create fear on behalf of some religious, political, or ideological goal while deliberately targeting or disregarding the safety of noncombatant civilians

Thanatechnology: technology-related resources about grief and loss, such as videos and computer programs

Questions for Review and Discussion

1. This chapter described selected examples of death-related practices in the United States in recent years. Do you see how death-related *practices* join with death-related *encounters* and *attitudes* to make up a mosaic of death-related *experiences* in our society? Are our descriptions of death-related practices in our society representative of your experiences within that society?

2. This chapter introduced the concept of a *death system* and its five components: people, places, times, objects, and symbols. Think about the death system you live within. What components (i.e., what people, places, etc.) of this system have you encountered?

3. In the 20th century, violence has become an ever-larger factor in encounters with death. What role (if any) have accidents, homicide, or terrorism played in your encounters with death? Think about a specific example of an accidental death, a homicide, or a terrorist assault. How, if at all, did that event affect your attitudes and behaviors?

4. Can you think of additional examples of pertinent speech patterns as you read or discussed the sections on language about death and death-related language in this chapter?

5. A great deal of information about the subjects explored in this chapter and death-related practices in general can be obtained from searching the Internet. Have you ever done such online searching? If so, what did you learn? If not, why not?

Suggested Readings

On terrorism and violence, consult:

Allison, G. (2004). *Nuclear Terrorism: The Ultimate Preventable Catastrophe*
Combs, C. C., & Slann, M. (2002). *Encyclopedia of Terrorism*
Hoffman, B. (2006). *Inside Terrorism* (2nd ed.)
Krueger, A. B. (2007). *What Makes a Terrorist: Economics and the Roots of Terrorism*
Kurzman, C. (2011). *The Missing Martyrs: Why There Are So Few Muslim Terrorists*
Lankford, A. (2013). *The Myth of Martyrdom: What Really Drives Suicide Bombers, Rampage Shooters, and Other Self-Destructive Killers*
Martin, G. (2003). *Understanding Terrorism: Challenges, Perspectives, and Issues*
National Commission on Terrorist Attacks. (2004). *The 9/11 Commission Report: Final Report of the National Commission on Terrorist Attacks upon the United States*
Pape, R. A. (2005). *Dying to Win: The Strategic Logic of Suicide Terrorism*
Richardson, L. (2006). *What Terrorists Want: Understanding the Enemy, Containing the Threat.*
Sageman, M. (2004). *Understanding Terror Networks*

Schmid, A. P. (Ed.). (2011). *The Routledge Handbook of Terrorism Research*

Stern, J., & Berger, J. M. (2015). *ISIS: The State of Terror*

U.S. Department of State, Bureau of Counterterrorism. (2015). *Country Reports on Terrorism 2014*

Warrick, J. (2015). *Black Flags: The Rise of ISIS*

Wright, L. (2006). *The Looming Tower: Al-Qaeda and the Road to 9/11*

Among the many historical, biographical, and literary accounts related to the Holocaust, see:

Bauer, Y. (1982). *A History of the Holocaust*

Czarnecki, J. P. (1989). *Last Traces: The Lost Art of Auschwitz*

Czech, D. (1990). *Auschwitz Chronicle, 1939–1945*

Dawidowicz, L. S. (1975). *The War against the Jews l933–1945*

Friedlander, H. (1995). *The Origins of Nazi Genocide: From Euthanasia to the Final Solution*

Gutman, I., & Berenbaum, M. (Eds.). (1994). *Anatomy of the Auschwitz Death Camp*

Harran, M.J., & Roth, J. (2000). *The Holocaust Chronicle: A History in Words and Pictures*

Helm, S. (2014). *Ravensbrück: Life and Death in Hitler's Concentration Camp for Women*

Hilberg, R. (2003). *The Destruction of the European Jews*

Pawelczynska, A. (1979). *Values and Violence in Auschwitz: A Sociological Analysis*

Reitlinger, G. (1968). *The Final Solution: The Attempt to Exterminate the Jews of Europe 1939–1945* (2nd rev. ed.).

Wiesel, E (1960). *Night*

On the beginning of the nuclear era and some of its implications, see:

Arkin, W., & Fieldhouse, R. (1985). *Nuclear Battlefields*

Hersey, J. (1948). *Hiroshima*

Lifton, R. J. (1967). *Death in Life: Survivors of Hiroshima*

Lifton, R. J. (1979). *The Broken Connection*

For euphemisms and death-related language, consult:

Keyes, R. (2010). *Euphemania: Our Love Affair with Euphemisms*

Neaman, J. S., & Silver, C. G. (1983). *Kind Words: A Thesaurus of Euphemisms*

Selected Web Resources

Some useful search terms include: ACCIDENTS; ASSAULT; DEATH PRACTICES (OR DEATH-RELATED PRACTICES); DEATH-RELATED LANGUAGE; DEATH SYSTEM; ETHNIC CLEANSING; EUPHEMISMS; FANTASIZED DEATH; GENOCIDE; HOLOCAUST; HOMICIDE; LANGUAGE ABOUT DEATH; MEDIA AND DEATH; NUCLEAR ERA (ALSO CHERNOBYL, HIROSHIMA, NAGASAKI, THREE MILE ISLAND); SOCIALLY SANCTIONED DEATH; TERRORISM; WAR.

You can also visit the following *organizational and other Internet sites:*

Association of Holocaust Organizations

Concerns of Police Survivors (COPS)

Doomsday Clock

Federal Bureau of Investigation, Uniform Crime Reports

Mothers Against Drunk Driving (MADD)

National Organization for Victim Assistance (NOVA)

National Organization of Parents of Murdered Children, Inc. (POMC)

Survivors of the Shoah Visual History Foundation

Tragedy Assistance Program for Survivors (TAPS)

U.S. Department of Homeland Security

U.S. Holocaust Memorial Museum (Washington, D.C.)

washington1775/Shutterstock.com

Cultural Patterns and Death

In the previous edition of this book, this chapter was coauthored by Tashel C. Bordere, PhD

Objectives of this **Chapter**

Chapters 2–4 describe death-related encounters, attitudes, and practices, along with prominent features of the modern American death system. Everyone in our society shares this broad background. We all live and interact, to one degree or another, within our society's overall death system. For example, some societally designated official must pronounce a person as dead—no matter who that person may be.

But this story is incomplete. In fact, the United States is not a single, homogeneous entity with only one universal cultural death system and a single set of death-related encounters, attitudes, and practices. In fact, there is a kaleidoscope of rich cultural heritages among groups from varied social backgrounds (e.g., familial, social, cultural, racial, ethnic, and religious groupings), each of which may display unique patterns in some aspects of its death-related experiences. Thomas (2001, p. 40) described culture as "a unified set of values, ideas, beliefs, and standards of behavior shared by a group of people; it is the way a person accepts, orders, interprets, and understands experiences throughout the life course." This chapter has the following objectives as we explore cultural patterns in some subgroups within American society:

▶ To demonstrate *how racial, cultural, and other factors interact with death-related experiences*

▶ To describe some specific patterns of death-related *encounters* in four selected racial/ethnic groups in the United States: Hispanic Americans, African Americans, Americans who trace their backgrounds to Asian countries or the Pacific Islands, and American Indians and Native Alaskans

▶ To explore some death-related *attitudes* within these four groups

▶ To illustrate some death-related *practices* within these four groups

▶ To resist tendencies to ethnocentrism in our analyses whereby some individuals and groups, consciously or unconsciously, take their encounters, attitudes, and practices as the standard by which other individuals and groups should be measured and judged

▶ To suggest some of the many lessons we all can learn as we seek culturally conscientious ways of understanding and helping each other

A HAPPY FUNERAL

A charming picture book for young readers entitled *The Happy Funeral* (Bunting, 1982) describes two young Chinese-American sisters who are preparing to take part in their Grandfather's funeral. When their mother tells May-May and Laura about Grandfather's death, she says he will have a happy funeral. The girls are puzzled by that concept. "It's like saying a sad party. Or hot snow. It doesn't make sense" (p. 1).

The girls are perplexed and unclear about many of the events that follow. Although they loved their Grandfather and are clearly expected to be participants in this community event, the girls have not had much experience with death and funerals. They are insiders to the community, but outsiders in many ways to what is about to happen. Above all, they do not expect to be happy at their Grandfather's funeral.

At the funeral home, bunches of flowers are everywhere and incense sticks burn in front of Grandfather's casket. There are many gifts for Grandfather's "journey to the other side," such as a map of the spirit world, some food, and half a comb (Grandmother keeps the other half, to be rejoined when she is reunited with her husband after her own death). A cardboard house, play money, and pictures of various objects (e.g., a drawing of Chang, the black dog that Grandfather had when he was a boy, and a picture of a red car with a silver stripe of the kind that Grandfather was never able to have in this life) are burned, with the idea that they will become real when they turn into smoke and rise to the spirit world.

At the funeral service in the Chinese Gospel Church, there are more flowers and a big photograph of Grandfather framed in roses. The adults talk about Grandfather's fine qualities and the many good things he did. Some of the adults cry, and Laura feels a big lump in her throat when she realizes how tiny Grandmother is and that she is even older than Grandfather. After the ceremony, a woman gives a small candy to each of the mourners "to sweeten your sorrow" (p. 22). Then Grandfather's casket is put in a glass-sided car, and his photograph is propped on the roof of one of the two flower cars. With a marching band playing spirited music, the cars parade throughout the streets of Chinatown.

At the cemetery, Grandfather's casket is placed on a wooden table next to a big hole in the ground. The minister says that Grandfather is going to his spiritual reward, but Laura tries to think of him flying the wonderful kites that he used to make. During all of these events, Laura alternates between warm memories and feelings of sadness, between smiles and tears. Eventually, she realizes that although she and May-May were not happy to have their Grandfather die, his funeral really was a happy one because he was ready for his death and he left a good legacy through his well-lived life and everyone's fond memories of him. Mom "never said it was happy for us to have him go" (p. 38).

THE SIGNIFICANCE OF STUDYING CULTURAL PATTERNS

As we noted in the introduction to this chapter, thus far we have explored general patterns surrounding death and grief in American society. Although such patterns undoubtedly exist, unique beliefs and practices, grounded in specific social and historical contexts, coexist among the many subgroups within the larger society. These beliefs and practices have important implications for understanding and working collaboratively in effective ways with bereaved individuals and families. That is, every member of American society does not approach events in their lives from exactly the same cultural background and stance. In this chapter, we highlight common patterns in the beliefs and practices of four racial/ethnic groups within American society in order to help us:

- *To appreciate the rich diversity within and between groups in American society*
- *To develop greater sensitivity and a richer understanding of encounters, attitudes, and practices surrounding death and grief within a context (e.g., historical, familial, spiritual)*
- *To empower ourselves to provide more effective care for others in our communities*
- *To learn more about ourselves by comparing and contrasting our experiences with those described in this chapter*

A common reaction when learning about customs that differ from our own, particularly with death-related beliefs and practices, is to view them as "weird" and often as deficient. In other words, "practices that are difficult to understand are usually interpreted as indicators of psychopathology by the dominant society" (Hanson, 1978, p. 20). Actually, they might simply represent another culture's way of conducting its affairs; that is, practices that are unfamiliar to people from one group might be viewed as wholly appropriate and valuable to individuals from another group. To fail to appreciate this is to adopt a judgmental approach that is characteristic of "ethnocentrism" (Anderson & Taylor, 2007).

An illustration of ethnocentrism is seen in a story about two men who were visiting the gravesites of their deceased loved ones with items to memorialize their loved ones. One man looked at the other and said, "I would love to see your loved one eat that rice." The other man said in reply, "My loved one will eat this rice when your loved one smells those flowers." What may be weird to one person may make perfect sense to another and might simply represent a different culture's perspective on life. As Albert Einstein once said, the world as we see it is only the world as we see it; others may see it differently. One benefit of achieving a better understanding and appreciation of others and of ourselves is that it puts us in a position to provide more sensitive and appropriate care (as professionals, volunteers, or fellow human beings) to those who are coping with dying, death, and bereavement.

It is important to be educated about the rich diversity and complexities that exist within and between groups while not limiting ourselves to such information, but rather using it to increase our awareness. Maintaining limited views leads to false assumptions, generalizations, and oversimplifications of what otherwise are likely to be sophisticated beliefs and practices surrounding death and grief for families. Cultures are not stagnant; they are constantly in flux, changing based on political, economic, educational, and other factors. Hence, we increase our effectiveness in understanding and working with dying and bereaved families when we commit ourselves to *culturally conscientious practice* or an openness to evolving knowledge about diverse groups within their diverse contexts (Bordere, 2009a). Assuming this perspective aligns us with the continuous evolution of cultural death customs.

Following the structure of Chapters 2–4 in this book and the way in which U.S. government sources identify and organize statistical data, we describe in this chapter encounters with death, attitudes toward death, and death-related practices in *four prominent American racial and ethnic groups*: Hispanic Americans, African Americans, Asian and Pacific Island Americans, and American Indians and Native Alaskans. We chose these four groups because it is their members whom readers are most likely to meet and those for whom the largest fund of research data is available.

We appreciate that the great diversity of people in the United States goes well beyond these four examples, but no single chapter could do justice to so many potential populations. And it is important to note that diverse people, such as lesbians, gays, and people with disabilities, are found within the four subgroups considered here and each of whom may have their own distinctive issues to consider (e.g., see Bristowe, Marshall, & Harding, 2016). In fact, all of us are complex, multifaceted individuals, so much so that in any given group, death-related encounters, attitudes, and practices are likely to be influenced by our sexuality, civilian or military status, (dis)abilities, gender, racial, cultural, ethnic, or religious backgrounds, and many other factors. As someone once pointed out to us, an African-American gay male enlisted in the military may have a vastly different grief experience than a married heterosexual Black male both within African-American subcultures and the larger culture. In short, this chapter offers an initial exploration of a very large subject area; many who might wish to go beyond its constraints can do so by drawing on other resources, including the Suggested Readings at the end of this chapter.

In general, descriptions of *encounters* with death within the four groups examined in this chapter are the most reliable because they draw on demographic data from the National Center for Health Statistics. By contrast, research on death-related *attitudes* and *practices* typically depends on a sample of selected members of a specific group. Such studies usually warn that the population sample is limited in size or makeup and thus does not support broad generalizations about the group as a whole. Thus, this chapter basically offers a series of snapshots of attitudes and practices within these groups. There is much room for you, as a reader of this book, to supplement this chapter (see Issues for Critical Reflection #7).

HISPANIC-AMERICANS

According to data from the U.S. Census Bureau (2016), in 2014, Hispanics were the largest minority group in the United States, making up approximately 17.4% of the total population (see Table 5.1). This is more than a doubling of the total population for this group since the 1990 census count. However, this needs careful qualification.

ISSUES FOR CRITICAL REFLECTION
#7 How Can a Reader Supplement Descriptions of Death-Related Experiences Given in This Chapter?

Because research on experiences with dying, death, and bereavement in many racial, cultural, and ethnic groups is limited, we can only present brief profiles of death-related encounters, attitudes, and practices within the four minority groups examined in this chapter. The strength of this approach is the ways it acts to counter ethnocentrism. The limitation of this approach may mean that a reader who is a member of one of these cultures (or of some other cultural group) may or may not recognize his or her own experiences in these accounts. One way to enrich your own and others' understanding of the patterns within these and other cultures' death-related encounters, attitudes, and practices would be for you to take time to note which of these descriptions are compatible with your own experiences and which are not. In addition, thinking about and discussing with others your own cultural and family experiences can fill out and supplement the profiles we have provided, thereby educating all of us more fully about these issues.

Throughout this chapter, we note that none of the cultures we study here is itself monolithic or homogeneous. As a result, when specific populations are studied, the participants in the study may not be representative of the whole minority culture; often, they are mostly representative of some subgroup within the minority culture. Thus, among Americans of Hispanic/Latino origin, there are Puerto Ricans, Mexican Americans, Cuban Americans, and persons with backgrounds from Central and South American countries. Obviously, these are quite different cultures; their lack of homogeneity is seen in the debate among persons from these cultures as to whether and for whom terms like *Hispanic, Latino*, and *Chicano* are the best descriptors. (We recognize that some members of this broad group prefer one descriptor over the others, but we feel obliged throughout this chapter to follow the ways in which the National Center for Health Statistics categorizes subgroups in the U.S. population.) In addition, among African Americans, there are persons born in America, the Caribbean, and Africa. Also, Asian Americans trace their ancestries to very different societies, including China, Japan, Kampuchea (Cambodia), Korea, Thailand, and Vietnam, or to the Pacific Islands (e.g., Hawaii and Samoa). Finally, among American Indians and Alaska Natives (sometimes called Native Americans or "First Nations Peoples"), there are hundreds of distinct groupings (e.g., Navajo, Zuni, Dakota, Seminole, and Crow, as well as Aleuts and Eskimos). Individual American Indians can trace their ancestral homes to nearly every part of the North American continent. It is naive and prejudicial to think of these many subgroups within our four primary ones as essentially interchangeable or wholly like the others within the primary group.

Thus, readers should keep in mind *the need to avoid the danger of stereotypes*. Everyone discussed in this chapter is simultaneously an American, a member of some particular cultural group (or subgroup), and an individual person. No one of them in his or her death-related experiences is completely identical to any other individual—even to other members of his or her own cultural group, because like all human beings, each is a *unique individual*.

Census estimates describe the resident population of the 50 United States. Residents of the Commonwealth of Puerto Rico and the U.S. Island Areas (the U.S. Virgin Islands, Guam, American Samoa, and the Commonwealth of the Northern Mariana Islands) are counted separately and are not included in totals given in Table 5.1. Still, the totals in Table 5.1 reflect real increases in this population, as well as significant revisions in the census process. Real changes in the Hispanic-American population during recent years resulted from high immigration (especially from Mexico and Central America) and high birth rates. Revisions in the census process involved census coverage and the census questionnaire itself (e.g., the new questionnaire asked, "Is this person Spanish/Hispanic/Latino?"). Perhaps more importantly, there is a growing number of multiracial people in the United States (Pew Research Center, 2015) and individuals responding to recent census surveys were permitted to classify

Table 5.1 Resident Population: United States, 1900 and 2014

	1900[a]		2014[b]	
	Number	Percentage	**Number**	**Percentage**
Total population	75,994,000	100.0	318,857,056	100.0
Male	38,816,000	51.1	156,936,487	49.2
Female	37,178,000	48.9	161,920,569	50.8
Hispanic[c]	(NA)		55,387,539	17.4
Not Hispanic	(NA)		263,469,517	82.6
One race only:	(NA)		308,388,111	96.7
Caucasian Americans	66,809,000	87.9	246,660,710	77.4
African Americans	8,834,000	11.6	42,158,238	13.2
Asian Americans and Pacific Islanders	(NA)		18,080,654	5.7
American-Indians and Alaska Natives	(NA)		3,960,971	1.2
Two or more races	(NA)		7,996,483	2.5

[a]Excludes Alaska and Hawaii.

[b]Excludes individuals living in the Commonwealth of Puerto Rico and the U.S. Island Areas who are counted separately. Note also that in the 2010 census, individuals could report more than one race, as well as "Hispanic"; as a result, numbers within categories for 2014 may add to more or less than the total population given above.

[c]Persons of Hispanic origin may be of any race; not included in data for the total population.

Source: U.S. Census Bureau, 2016.

themselves in more than one racial or cultural category—reflecting the so-called "Tiger Woods description," whereby this famous golfer describes himself as "Caublinasian" to reflect the ethnic blend in his ancestry of Caucasian, Black, American-Indian, and Asian. Further, to speak of a "Hispanic" American is to point to a cultural category, not a racial one. In fact, Hispanic Americans may be of any race. Therefore, in recent census reports some individuals (e.g., those with parents of different races), who were formerly classified in just one racial category (solely as Caucasian Americans, African Americans, etc.), may have chosen to add a second such category or also to classify themselves as Hispanic. All of this reinforces our concerns about conceptual and methodological problems in carrying out research on Hispanic Americans, problems that have led some (e.g., Duarté-Vélez & Bernal, 2007) to recommend focusing on narrower groups within this diverse population, defined perhaps by social, cultural, and contextual factors, as well as more traditional gender and developmental variables.

Nevertheless, although the present figures may be in part an artifact of the new processes and the classification system used in recent census surveys, the Hispanic portion of the American population has clearly been growing lately. Some people of Hispanic origin are recent immigrants, others have lived in the continental United States for generations, and all Puerto Ricans have been U.S. citizens since 1917.

Table 5.2 **Deaths and Age-Adjusted Death Rates (per 100,000 U.S. standard population) by Specified Race or Hispanic Origin and Gender: United States, 2014**

	Both Sexes	Age-Adjusted Death Rates[a]	Male	Age-Adjusted Death Rates[a]	Female	Age-Adjusted Death Rates[a]
All origins[b]	2,626,418	724.6	1,328,241	855.1	1,298,177	616.7
Caucasian Americans, total	2,237,880	725.4	1,128,993	853.4	1,108,887	617.6
Non-Hispanic Caucasian Americans	2,066,949	742.8	1,035,345	872.3	1,031,604	633.8
Hispanic origin[c]	169,387	523.3	92,474	626.8	76,913	437.5
African Americans	308,960	849.3	157,733	1,034.0	151,228	713.3
Asian and Pacific Island Americans	61,570	388.3	31,686	462.0	29,884	331.1
American-Indians and Alaska Natives	18,008	594.1	9,829	685.4	8,179	514.1

[a]"Age-adjusted death rates are constructs that show what the level of mortality would be if no changes occurred in the age composition of the population from year to year.... Age-adjusted death rates also are better indicators of relative risk when comparing mortality between...sex or race subgroups of the population that have different age distributions" (Murphy et al., 2015, p. 3).

[b]Figures for origin not stated are included in "All origins" but are not distributed among specified origins.

[c]Persons of Hispanic origin may be of any race; these data should be interpreted with caution since race and Hispanic origin are reported separately on death certificates and because of inconsistencies between reporting Hispanic origin on death certificates and on censuses and surveys.

Source: Kochanek et al., 2016.

Hispanic-American Encounters with Death, Dying, and Bereavement

Efforts to study numbers of deaths and death rates among Hispanic Americans face special difficulties. In the United States, most data collected on death rates come from records in county offices. Such records depend upon death certificates, which provide separate spaces to record the race and the specific Hispanic origin of the individual who died (see Figure 16.1). Much depends, therefore, on the accuracy of the person who fills out the death certificate and on reliable information from his or her sources. Nevertheless, these are the best data available and the foundation for all that follows here.

Within the United States, data on *numbers of deaths* and *age-adjusted death rates* for Hispanic Americans in 2014 are given in Table 5.2. These numbers of deaths are strikingly low, amounting to approximately 6.5% of all deaths in the United States within a group that represents 17.4% of the total population. As a result overall average life expectancy for Hispanic Americans is high at an estimated 81.8 years.

Several factors contribute to relatively low numbers of deaths and death rates among Hispanic Americans: many in this community are young persons; Hispanic-American immigrants may have been (self) selected for their general good health; and some Hispanic Americans may return to their country of origin to die or when they are seriously ill. This picture likely will change as the Hispanic-American population ages, as more of its members are born within the United States, and as it increasingly integrates itself into the mainstream society. Also, like many in other cultural groups, especially those dominated by immigrants, as Hispanic Americans adjust to their surrounding culture in the United States, they often take on many of the characteristics of the larger culture, further confounding claims about that which is distinctive in Hispanic-American death-related experiences. Among *causes of death*, Hispanic Americans as a group have relatively high age-adjusted death rates for diabetes mellitus, diseases of the heart, chronic liver disease and cirrhosis, and homicide (Heron, 2016; Kochanek et al., 2016). The first three of these are chronic conditions reflecting various underlying causes; homicide is more typically a cause of death for young Hispanic-American males. Variances in homicide rates among different Hispanic-American communities suggest that additional factors are also at work, such as poverty and other socioeconomic variables.

Hispanic-American Attitudes toward Death

When we turn to attitudes associated with death-related experiences, it quickly becomes apparent that there is much less information available for study. Thus, what we present in this chapter are snapshots of four minority cultures, beginning with those describing Hispanic-American attitudes.

■ *Importance of family*: Beginning with work by Kalish and Reynolds (1981) and continuing through the present, research shows that family plays an influential role in shaping Hispanic-American attitudes and in serving a protective function (Umaña-Taylor & Yazedjian, 2006). Kalish and Reynolds described Mexican-American families in their study as tightly knit and as striving to maintain a strong locus of emotional support in the family unit. This assertion was reinforced by Thomas (2001), who reported that Hispanic Americans place high value on being cared for by family members (see also Delgado & Tennstedt, 1997a). In fact, Thomas reported that Hispanic elders stress that the family should be involved extensively in both planning and providing care. Not to do so may be seen as not fulfilling one's responsibilities. And in a study of Puerto Rican sons providing care for ill parents, Delgado and Tennstedt (1997b) reported that these men took on this role out of a "sense of responsibility."

■ *The role of religion*: Religion is another significant influence shaping Hispanic-American attitudes. In their study of Mexican Americans in Los Angeles, Kalish and Reynolds (1981) found that 90% of their participants were Roman Catholic and Catholicism remains the dominant religion among all Hispanics in the United States. This church's teaching about an afterlife and rituals, such as funeral masses, sacramental anointing of the sick, and prayers for the dead, likely play significant roles in how Hispanic Americans think about, approach, and cope with dying and death. In a case study of Mexican-American families following the death of a child, Doran and Hansen (2006) found that beliefs about being reunited in the afterlife helped families maintain a sense of connection to the deceased, which helped with coping.

■ *Relationship between life and death*: One belief shared by many Hispanic Americans is the continuous relationship between life and death (Clements et al., 2003; Munet-Vilaró, 1998). Death is seen as a complement to life and as part of an ongoing cycle in which the living both anticipate reunification in the afterlife while also valuing maintaining a connection in the present life. This connection

A young Hispanic couple stands at a gravesite.

is apparent among Mexican-American families experiencing the death of a child who viewed death as transformative and life changing as opposed to a single event (Doran & Hansen, 2006). Such deaths were described as "life-long, ever-present processes that intermittently required more intense negotiation" or more concerted efforts at maintaining the connection in the present life between the surviving families and the deceased children (p. 209).

■ *Fatalism and anticipatory grief*: Munet-Vilaró (1998) reported that Puerto Rican parents of children with leukemia tended to see the disease as a "death-sentence" and were "fatalistic" about its outcome, even in the face of countervailing evidence. She believed this attitude helped the parents and children prepare for an eventual death. Also, Grabowski and Frantz (1993) suggested that this attitude helped to ease the intensity of grief for those adopting it (for more on "anticipatory grief," see Chapter 9).

Death-Related Practices among Hispanic Americans

■ *Care of the dying*: As in many other cultures, caregivers for relatives among Hispanic Americans are most often female (Gelfand et al., 2001). Although such care can be stressful for the person providing it, Cox and Monk (1993) found that most of these caregivers did not seek formal assistance for their stress. They concluded that "reluctance to use such programs may be attributed to a cultural resistance to sharing familial problems with outsiders or to admitting that caring for a parent or spouse is too demanding" (p. 98). This leads to the typical expectation in a Hispanic-American culture that family members are required to provide such care; not to do so is seen as failing in one's responsibilities to the family. Such reasoning may also help to explain why Hispanic Americans are unlikely to use nursing homes for family members. Of course, as Hispanic Americans become more acculturated to the dominant culture (more women working, for instance), the ability of family members to provide such care may be undermined.

- *Presence at death*: Some studies have suggested that some Hispanic Americans find value in being with a dying relative so that any unresolved conflicts can be worked on. However, Iwashyna and Chang (2002) found that fewer Mexican Americans now die at home. In such circumstances, care amid institutional constraints may make it more difficult to realize this value.

- *Mourning practices*: Hispanic-American mourning practices usually include an open expression of grief, but this typically differs by gender. "Although it is not unusual to hear women wailing loudly, calling out the name of the deceased, and fainting, machismo...plays a significant part in the lack of emotional response of adult Latino men. Latino men are expected to 'be strong' for the family and usually do not grieve openly" (Clements et al., 2003, p. 21).

- *After-death rituals*: Rituals focused around death can take a variety of forms among Hispanic Americans. Some are much like those of the dominant culture, including open caskets, a requiem mass in the church, and a procession to the burial site. One challenge for some Hispanic families relates to decision-making surrounding the burial site. Because of the significance of family and connectedness, some families struggle with the issue of burying the deceased in one location (e.g., Mexico) and then living in a different place (compare the Hispanic-American death-related events and practices described in three children's books in Focus On 5.1).

FOCUS ON 5.1

Three Children's Books with Hispanic Themes or Spanish Texts

No Tenremos Un Nuevo Bebé. A young child describes her reactions when the anticipated birth of a new sibling does not happen. Grandma picks up a young bud off the ground and uses it to explain that while most buds keep growing and become flowers, some don't—like this one. The girl realizes that something like this happened to their baby. Grandma says no one is to blame and we do not always have answers. [In English as *No New Baby: For Siblings Who Have a Brother or Sister Die before Birth*.]

Since My Brother Died/Desde Que Murió Mi Hermano is a wistful book that describes a child who wonders if a brother's death was only a dream or if something could have kept him from dying. The child reports the sadness in the family as well as his (her?) own physical reactions like headaches and stomachaches. Afraid of forgetting this brother, the child begins to paint, and a series of colorful illustrations gradually turn into rainbows and the trust that life can go forward.

A Mural for Mamita/Un Mural Para Mamita is a book about a young girl, her family, and their entire neighborhood as they plan a memorial service, a fiesta in tribute to the girl's grandmother who had recently died after a long

(continues)

illness. As the proprietor of the local *bodega*, Mamita was well known and greatly loved in the neighborhood. The girl's special contribution to this event is a brilliant mural painted on the side of Mamita's store. Hispanic-American traditions are affirmed as the family and the extended community join in this tribute to a central figure in their lives. Also notable are the ways in which the adults emphasize that this event is a celebration of Mamita's life, freely include the young girl in these events, and allow her to give full reign to her creative expression of love for her grandmother. [The texts in these last two books appear in both English and Spanish.]

- *Ongoing connections and presence of the deceased*: The desire to maintain an ongoing connection between survivors and the deceased is apparent in the practices (e.g., dreams, pictorial remembrances, storytelling, keepsakes, faith-based connections) of many Hispanic-American families at death. A consistent theme regarding these ongoing connections is that they are often welcomed and serve an important function in the grief process for individuals across ages, sexes, classes, and generations in this cultural group. Note also that the connection is often interactive whereby the deceased appear to maintain life-like qualities and abilities that allow for such connections in various encounters between survivors and the deceased. For example, Doran and Hansen (2006) reported that one family greeted their deceased loved one as if he was physically present during their cemetery visits. We also see the life-like qualities of the deceased related to the belief that the survivor's adjustment to the death could impact the deceased in the afterlife, that the deceased would not "be at peace" or be able to "sleep comfortably" if, for example, the survivor experienced too much sorrow or preoccupation.

    > In this connection, Shapiro (1995) provided a lengthy description of the mourning of a Puerto Rican woman ("Carmen") in Boston who reported dreams in which her deceased mother appeared and spoke to her. She was both comforted and disturbed by these visits. Two younger children also reported that their mother "continued to be a physical presence in the household," although they found such experiences frightening. Older siblings, too, reported that they experienced spiritual visitations by their mother, but they found these to be understandable manifestations of their mother's spirit. Thus, although different family members responded to such experiences in a variety of ways, Shapiro concluded that "Puerto Rican culture is more comfortable than the secular American culture with the idea that the deceased continues to exist in the family as a spiritual presence" (p. 169). To be unaware of or insensitive to these beliefs and practices may significantly interfere with the open communication necessary to understand and provide good care to members of this culture.

    Note that individuals across many cultures describe and benefit from various experiences with the deceased (e.g., talking to the deceased in dreams). Hispanic Americans may simply be more likely to report on their experiences than individuals in some other cultures.

An altar display at a Day of the Dead Festival at the Hollywood Forever Cemetery.

- *Religion and practices*: In addition to Hispanic-American religious beliefs and practices noted above, Roman Catholics may have a novena (usually in the home) including a nine-day period after the funeral in which the rosary (a specific series of prayers) is said in the deceased person's name. During the time of the novena, the house may be kept closed, allowing the family an undisturbed period for mourning (Grabowski & Frantz, 1993; Munet-Vilaró, 1998).
- *Day of the Dead*: Another ritual specifically found in Mexican-American communities is the *Day of the Dead* (Brandes, 2006; Garciagodoy, 2000; Moss, 2010). This ritual traces its ancestry both to Roman Catholic tradition (it occurs on November 2, Roman Catholicism's Feast of All Souls) and to pre-Hispanic Mexican traditions. Traditional practices surrounding the Day of the Dead in Mexico often involve the cleaning and displaying of items at various altars, offering food to spirits of the dead, and family visits to the cemetery to put flowers on the grave of the deceased. As cultures evolve, however, so do their accompanying rituals. Thus, Mexican families living in the United States may or may not celebrate *the Day of the Dead* and those that do, while embracing the overarching values of the ritual (i.e., ongoing connection), may observe it in other ways. For example, reflecting the value of connectedness, Doran and Hansen (2006) found that one family ate sandwiches, the deceased child's favorite food, on *the Day of the Dead* (as opposed to offering food to spirits in a traditional sense in the Mexican context). In doing so, the family found both comfort and a sense presence of the deceased—"you think you're eating with [him]."

AFRICAN AMERICANS

African Americans are the second largest minority group among residents of the United States, making up 13.2% of the total population (see Table 5.1). In many ways, African Americans are linked by origins on the African continent, the history of slavery and slave trading, and experiences of discrimination. Slavery itself was a practice with many death-related implications. These included the killings involved in taking individuals prisoner, removing them from their tribal homes, suffering and death during transport to the New World, harsh living and working conditions on this side of the Atlantic, and all that is entailed in being treated as objects who could become the property of others. That background influences many aspects of contemporary African-American experiences with death in America. As Kalish and Reynolds (1981) once wrote, "To be Black in America is to be part of a history told in terms of contact with death and coping with death" (p. 103).

African-American Encounters with Death, Dying, and Bereavement

In terms of *numbers of deaths*, African Americans experienced 12.2% of all deaths in the United States in 2014 (see Table 5.2). These deaths result in *age-adjusted death rates* of 8.5 per 1,000, higher than those for the U.S. population as a whole and for all of the subgroups listed in Table 5.2.

Nevertheless, relative disadvantages in death rates for African Americans may not have resulted simply from ethnicity. Many minority groups in American society are disadvantaged in their socioeconomic standing, and such disadvantages almost always reveal themselves in higher death rates. One decade-long study of 530,000 individuals confirmed that employment status, income, education, occupation, and marital status—as well as race—all have "substantial net associations with mortality" (Sorlie, Backlund, & Keller, 1995, p. 949). Poverty, inadequate access to health care, and higher incidences of life-threatening behavior have direct implications for death rates. Because racial, cultural, and socioeconomic factors of this sort are so complex and closely intertwined, it is difficult to identify or rank causal factors that influence death rates for African Americans as a group. Still, correlations between membership in some subgroups within this population and the statistical likelihood of dying at an earlier age than many members of other subgroups or the population as a whole are evident.

Research by Umberson and colleagues (2017) developed this point and identified some of its implications. According to this research, "Results indicate that blacks are significantly more likely than whites to have experienced the death of a mother, a father, and a sibling from childhood through midlife. From young adulthood through later life, blacks are also more likely than whites to have experienced the death of a child and of a spouse " (p. 915). That leads these authors to note that, "These results reveal an underappreciated layer of racial inequality in the United States, one that could contribute to the intergenerational transmission of health disadvantage" and they conclude that, "Our findings highlight the spiraling damage of racial disparities in life expectancy and point to the need for interventions and policies that address bereavement and loss in high-risk populations."

One can, therefore, describe the situation facing African Americans today in various ways. For example, estimated *average life expectancy* for an African-American infant born recently is 75.6 years (Harper, Rushani, & Kaufman, 2012; Kochanek et al., 2016). Among some African-American subgroups, however, things may be different. For example, at one point in time, McCord and Freeman (1990) demonstrated that African-American males living in Harlem, an area of New York City, were less likely to reach the age of 65 years than men living in Bangladesh, one of the poorest countries in the world. As these authors wrote, the "situation in Harlem is extreme, but it is not an isolated phenomenon. Similar pockets of high mortality have been described in other U.S. cities" (p. 176).

Death rates do not themselves directly reveal the underlying factors from which they result. Still, in studies in which other factors were held constant, some aspects of these death rates and average life expectancies were found to be more directly related to education and socioeconomic status than to race or ethnicity. This finding is not surprising. For instance, Powell-Griner (1988) reported that higher risks of infant mortality are associated with illegitimacy, blue-collar families, inadequate prenatal care, and low birth weight. Quite often these factors are not unrelated to each other; where they are added together, they are likely to converge in a way that puts infants and others at higher risk of premature death (Plepys & Klein, 1995).

In terms of *causes of death*, the greatest disparity for African Americans is the large numbers of homicides for this population as a whole (Heron, 2016; Kochanek et al., 2016). Thus, in 2014, there were more deaths of African Americans from homicide (8,059) than among Caucasian Americans (7,523)—yielding age-adjusted death rates of 17.8 versus 3.1 per 100,000—even though the Caucasian-American population is 6 times larger than the African-American population. The disparity is even sharper for males in these groups: 7,903 homicide deaths among African Americans versus 7,397 among Caucasian Americans, yielding age-adjusted death rates of 17.2 versus 3.0 per 100,000. Further, homicide is the leading cause of death among African-American males between the ages of 15 and 24. To be young, African American, and male in our society is to find oneself at unusual risk for death by homicide. By contrast, age-adjusted death rates from suicide are much lower among African Americans than among Caucasian Americans (5.5 to 14.7 per 100,000), although deaths from suicide appear to be increasing among young, African-American males. Clearly, further study of cultural variables that appear to mitigate suicide risk in this population is desirable.

In addition, there is a disproportionately high percentage of deaths from HIV disease among African Americans in the United States. In 2014, there were 3,014 deaths from HIV (and an age-adjusted death rate of 1.1 per 100,000) among Caucasian Americans versus 3,591 deaths (and a death rate of 8.3) among the much smaller African-American population. For African-American males, the HIV age-adjusted death rate contrast is 1.8 to 11.9; for African-American females, the contrast is 0.4 versus 5.4. Plainly, deaths associated with HIV infection represent major inequalities for and among African Americans.

African-American Attitudes toward Death

- *Importance of family*: Systematic study of attitudes associated with death, dying, and bereavement among African Americans is not extensive, but major themes relating to attitudes toward care of the dying among African Americans have remained consistent. As with many other collectivist cultures that value interdependence, the literature describes a pattern in which family support is a key element for African Americans in coping with both life and death-related situations (Clements et al., 2003). This focus on sustaining family members within the family is apparent in the care of aging individuals who are rarely placed in nursing facilities (Thomas, 2001). Similarly, among African Americans, there is a strong emphasis on family support in providing end-of-life care within the home. For instance, in their study comparing African-American to Caucasian-American caregivers of persons with Alzheimer's disease, Owen, Goode, and Haley (2001) found that 53% of the African-American patients died at home, whereas only 38% of the Caucasia-American patients did so. Other common sources of support include a reliance on friends, church associates, and neighbors when dealing with these issues.

Hayslip and Preveto (2005) showed that for African Americans and other minority cultural groups in the United States, there has been an increased focus on family and relationships, a shift toward more interest in being informed about one's own terminal prognosis, and a more personal approach to funeral and mourning observances.

■ *Suspicion of the medical community*: Several researchers have reported that some African Americans exhibit a long-standing mistrust of the medical community (e.g., Jenkins et al., 2005; Taxis, 2006). Waters (2001) found that the African Americans in her study believed they received less health care than did Caucasian Americans, and they believed they would not receive all of the appropriate health care they needed if they wrote a living will. Such concerns are not unwarranted as racial and ethnic disparities, whether intentional or not, have been found in both the provision and quality of health care for underrepresented groups (Freeman & Payne, 2000; Geiger, 2002; Mosby, 2013; Payne, Medina, & Hampton, 2003). Some researchers believe that distrust of the medical community among many African Americans can be traced back to what has been called "medical apartheid," that is, historical experiences with medical neglect or mistreatment, such as those found in the Tuskegee syphilis experiment (see Focus On 5.2).

An elderly man with a life-threatening illness being supported at home by his extended family.

Courtesy Suncoast Hospice

What Was the Tuskegee Syphilis Study?

The Tuskegee syphilis study was conducted by the U.S. Public Health Service, beginning in 1932. It was intended to study the consequences of syphilis infection in African Americans as compared to that same infection in Caucasian Americans. Researchers recruited 399 poor African-American sharecroppers in Alabama for the study. Participants were not informed of the nature of their disease; they were simply told they had "bad blood" and they initially received the only known treatments for the infection. However, since the results of the study at that point were unimpressive, treatment was halted in order to study the progress of the disease until the participants died. Even after penicillin became available in the mid-1940s and was shown to be effective in treating the disease, the men were left untreated. The study was not halted until 1972 after it was exposed in the press. Approximately 100 of the men died of the disease over the course of the study. (For more information on the Tuskegee study, see Jones, 1992).

Nevertheless, in her book on what she calls "medical apartheid" Washington (2006, pp. 180–181) offers the following observation:

> But it is important to look beyond this one study in examining African Americans' aversion to the health-care system. By focusing upon the single event of the Tuskegee Syphilis Study rather than examining a centuries-old pattern of experimental abuse, recent investigations tend to distort the problem, casting African Americans' wariness as an overreaction to a single event rather than an understandable, reasonable reaction to the persistent experimental abuse that has characterized American medicine's interaction with African Americans.

Death-Related Practices among African Americans

- *Advance directives and termination of life support*: Several researchers (e.g., Owen, Goode, & Haley, 2001; Tschann, Kaufmann, & Micco, 2003; Waters, 2001) have reported that doubts among African Americans about their treatment by the health care system may account, at least in part, for resistance to making advance plans, either for treatment at the end of life or for after death. Similar concerns may also bear on reluctance to terminate life support.
- *Hospice services and organ donation*: Many researchers have also reported that African Americans are less likely to use hospice services or to donate organs after death (e.g., Barrett, 2006; Greiner, Perera, & Ahluwalia, 2003; Minniefield, Yang, & Muti, 2001; Yancu, Farmer, & Leahman, 2010). It may be that some of these decisions are less related to mistrust and more related to cultural values (e.g., religious or spiritual beliefs ["it's God's will"]), unmet needs (e.g., lack of diversity of hospice staff), or misinformation (e.g., lack of understanding of the purposes of hospice or of the need for organ donation and what it involves).

In each of these last points, our study of attitudes and practices in minority cultures sheds light on what is needed for the provision of culturally conscientious care. As Thomas (2001, p. 42) has written: "Communication about end-of-life issues is the key to understanding and making rational decisions." Anything that gets in the way of good communication can impede both rational decision making and the provision of good care (Mazanec & Tyler, 2003).

More broadly, as health care providers improve their contextual understandings of the beliefs and accompanying behaviors of some African Americans regarding health care, more efforts are being made toward understanding culturally appropriate end-of-life care (West, 2004) and overcoming barriers that affect access and use of hospice and palliative care (Winston et al., 2005). To this end, Kagawa-Singer and Blackhall (2001) offered a list of culturally informed suggestions for communicating with families about end-of-life care.

- *Coping with violent and nonviolent deaths*: Research involving one group of African Americans showed that despite differences in the violent versus nonviolent death of a family member or friend, survivors "were able to successfully cope with their grief using coping mechanisms that emphasize social bonds and religious faith" (Henderson et al., 2015, p. 18). To be more specific, "religious coping was important for nonviolent death events, while social support and emotion (e.g., crying) were themes that emerged for violent death events" (p. 1). The authors concluded that their research "highlights the varied coping methods that may minimize negative emotions and promote resilient individuals" among this bereaved population (p. 18).

- *Mourning practices*: In times of grief, African Americans often utilize the funeral service, which frequently takes place in a church, as the primary forum for catharsis or open expressiveness. Counseling services are infrequently sought among this population. The service is often intentionally designed (e.g., music, such as "I'll Fly Away," eulogy, reopening of the casket at the end of the service) to evoke such emotional expressiveness. The funeral also serves to provide a dignified and often celebratory "send off" or "home-going" (e.g., as is apparent in the appearance of the casket and the number of people in attendance) to individuals who may not otherwise have achieved such social status in their lifetime (Holloway, 2003).

  In one study of Black adolescent males' perceptions of their participation in New Orleans Jazz or "Second line" funeral processions (rooted in ceremonies dating back to slavery), Bordere (2009b) found that the youth understood the ritual as designed to facilitate a view of death as a cause for celebration (i.e., deceased is headed to a "better place…better than down here"), remembrance, and unification. Focus On 5.3 offers examples taken from four books about life, death, and mourning in the lives of African-American children.

- *Funeral directors*: In the African-American community, funeral directors are typically held in unusually high regard. Their status as representatives of an industry that is one of the most profitable enterprises in the African-American community in large part grew out of a necessity to properly lay to rest individuals in the community. As such, funeral directors help to provide social recognition that is typically important in African-American mourning practices.

Four Children's Books with African-American Themes

The following books explore themes of loss and death in situations involving young African Americans. *Kate, the Ghost Dog: Coping with the Death of a Pet* describes an African-American girl who finds her dog has died. Aleta is angry and tries to claim that Kate has come back as a ghost. With the help of family and friends, she is eventually able to remember Kate as "a memory worth cherishing."

An unusual depiction of *Psalm Twenty-Three* is given in a book by that title. The author/illustrator depicts a world of love and fear faced by an urban, African-American family. Still, the whole is framed in a positive way through the text of the familiar psalm that compares God to a loving shepherd who will guide and safeguard us in our tribulations.

What might be seen as another profession of faith appears in *Sweet, Sweet Memory*. After Grandpa dies, a young African-American girl named Sarah and her grandmother come together to find support and comfort. As they reflect on Grandpa's life, they find consolation in stories and sweet memories of him. In particular, they recall that he always said, "The earth changes. …Like us it lives, it grows. Like us…a part of it never dies. Everything and everyone goes on and on."

Solace is found in a different way in another book after a father dies suddenly. Tia is a 10-year-old African-American girl in *Sunflowers and Rainbows for Tia: Saying Goodbye to Daddy*. She describes how she, her seven-year-old twin brothers, her mother, and her grandparents feel after this unexpected loss. Tia tells about her sadness and grief, along with her fears that Mama might also die and leave the children alone. She also relates how people came over to the house to express their love for Daddy, support her family, and bring food to share. Being involved in many of the preparations and taking part in Daddy's funeral helps Tia, especially when she was allowed to bring Daddy's favorite sunflowers to the ceremony and a big rainbow shone through the clouds on the way to the cemetery.

■ *The importance of storytelling*: Rodgers (2004) studied the mourning practices of several African-American widows in the Northwest. She emphasized the central importance of storytelling in these women's handling of their grief. Tracing this emphasis back to the oral traditions of their African heritage, Rodgers suggested that "storytelling was at the heart of every widow's description of her lived bereavement experience" (p. 12). In telling their stories, Rodgers found that the women took on the roles of the various people in the story, using different tones and accents in their voices, as well as hand and body gestures and facial expressions to make the story live. Such vivid enactments of their stories were helpful to them in their mourning processes. Beyond this, Rosenblatt and Wallace (2005a, 2005b) have shown how often narratives of grieving African Americans feature themes of racism in the lives of deceased family members.

ASIAN AND PACIFIC ISLAND AMERICANS

Asian and Pacific Island Americans are individuals who trace their origins back to various countries in Asia or to the Pacific Islands. Together, they are the third largest minority group among residents of the United States, making up 5.7% of the total population (see Table 5.1). The largest of these communities are Chinese Americans, followed by Filipino Americans, Asian Americans from India, Vietnamese Americans, and Korean Americans. Differences between Asian and Pacific Island communities complicate research on many death-related topics.

Asian and Pacific Island American Encounters with Death, Dying, and Bereavement

Numbers of deaths: Among Asian Americans and Pacific Islanders, numbers of deaths in 2014 are given in Table 5.2. Taken together, these constitute about 2.3% of all deaths in the country for that year.

Age-adjusted death rates: In the Asian-American and Pacific Island American community as a whole, age-adjusted death rates were approximately 3.9 per 1,000, lower than similar rates for all of the subgroups in the U.S. population listed in Table 5.2. Among Asian Americans as a whole, cancer and diseases of the heart are the leading *causes of death*. Among human-induced causes of death in this population, age-adjusted death rates in 2014 for suicide (6.0 per 100,000) and homicide (1.5 per 100,000) were noticeably low (Heron, 2016; Kochanek et al., 2016). Highest rates of suicide among indigenous Hawaiians and other Pacific Islanders have been seen among males aged 15–25.

Lauderdale and Kestenbaum (2002) reviewed mortality statistics in the United States between 1990 and 1999 for persons 65 and older among six Asian-American groups: Chinese, Indian, Japanese, Korean, Filipino, and Vietnamese. Because this study was based on enrollees in Medicare Part B, it had a large sample size (varying from 116,000 for Indian males to 737,000 for Chinese females)—unlike many other studies on cultural issues. Results revealed that Asian-American men and women 65 years of age and older consistently have lower mortality rates than the comparable Caucasian population. This disparity could not be linked to socioeconomic status, the relation within each subgroup of immigrant to U.S.-born persons, or the mortality levels in the countries of origin. Even the Vietnamese, who of all the subpopulations studied had more persons with incomes below the poverty level, not only upheld the advantage of the other groups in mortality rates but also proved to have the greatest advantage.

Asian and Pacific Island American Attitudes toward Death

■ *Communication issues*: Kalish and Reynolds (1981) found members of the Japanese community in Los Angeles to insist on maintaining control over communication. Thus, even when members of this community were dying and in distress, they were often quite restrained in communicating what they were feeling to health care providers. This sort of restraint is influenced by another attitude found among many Asian Americans: the belief that talking about bad things may actually produce them (Braun, Tanji, & Heck, 2001). This belief may help explain why death is something of a taboo subject among some Chinese

Americans (Eisenbruch, 1984; Tanner, 1995). It also likely is influential in results from studies among Japanese Americans (Hirayama, 1990), Cambodian Americans (Lang, 1990), and Chinese Canadians (Tong & Spicer, 1994): family members may prefer that dying persons not be told that they are dying (e.g., see the children's book described in Focus On 19.1 in Chapter 19).

■ *Decision making*: Many Asian-American cultures are patriarchal and hierarchical (McQuay, 1995). In our context, this means that there is some specific person, usually the oldest male or at least an older member of the family (Blackhall et al., 1995; Crowder, 2000), who is expected to make any decisions about the care of family members.

■ *Physician-assisted suicide*: Braun and colleagues (2001) studied attitudes toward physician-assisted suicide among several Asian-American groups in Hawaii. Attitudes of these groups tended to be linked to religious factors and their acculturation to the dominant culture. Thus, first-generation Filipinos, who were primarily Roman Catholic, saw euthanasia and suicide as prohibited acts, while Filipinos who worked in health care held that withholding futile treatment and providing pain medication, even when that suppressed respiration, were acceptable.

Of the five groups studied, Filipinos and native Hawaiians were most resistant to physician-assisted suicide. Thus, Braun and colleagues (2001) reported that native Hawaiians (who had the worst health status and the shortest life expectancy of the groups studied) distrusted the health care system, fearing that they did not receive appropriate care from it. Chinese-American and Japanese-American participants in the study approved of physician-assisted suicide by large numbers (in fact, by larger numbers than the Caucasians in the study).

■ *Attitudes toward funerals*: Crowder's (2000) study of Chinese funerals in San Francisco described disagreements within the community about the appropriateness of various traditional customs. These disagreements tended to occur between those who were more acculturated to the dominant culture and those who were more recent immigrants to the United States. Still, most Asian Americans believe funeral rituals to be very important to help maintain healthy relationships between the living and the dead (Hirayama, 1990). Crowder wrote: "For the Chinese, funerals are major life passage rituals. ... Ancestor worship...is the cornerstone of Chinese cultural belief, social structure, and religious practice. With death, a family member can be a beneficial ancestor, and funerals are the ritual means of accomplishing this transition" (p. 452). [Two children's books containing Asian-American perspectives are described in the vignette near the beginning of this chapter and in Focus On 19.1 in Chapter 19 in this book.]

Death-Related Practices among Asian and Pacific Island Americans

■ *Mourning practices*: Kalish and Reynolds (1981) described mourning customs of Japanese Americans in Los Angeles as quite conservative. For instance, they found that few members of this group believed that remarriage, or even dating after the death of a spouse, was appropriate.

■ *Blending Western and non-Western elements in Asian-American funeral rituals*: Crowder's (2000) description of Chinese funerals in San Francisco (a large

The Green Street Mortuary Band leads a funeral procession in San Francisco's Chinatown.

enclave of Chinese Americans in the midst of a big U.S. city) reported that people living there had to adapt their traditional customs to the expectations and legal boundaries for behavior set by the larger community. Therefore, Chinese funerals in this context are often a melding of rituals that can be traced to non-Western settings (usually from the country of origin) with Western settings. This blending of traditions can also be found in Samoan-American funerals, which bring together Samoan tradition, elaborate Christian ceremony, and the realities of a new environment, which usually include the giving of gifts in the form of both money and fine Samoan mats (King, 1990).

■ *One description of a Chinese-American funeral*: Crowder (2000) identified five components in a Chinese-American funeral she observed (compare this description with the vignette near the beginning of this chapter). First, there was a visit to the mortuary where the family lined up in hierarchical order (oldest son first, and so on) to receive visitors. The casket was placed among other items: food offerings and a paper house, paper people ("servants"), and paper money. Second, on the next day, the funeral proper occurred at the mortuary, with a Methodist minister conducting the service. Then everyone "paid their last respects" and attendees lined up in order for the procession. Third, a Western band began to play as the procession left the mortuary and moved through Chinatown. During the procession, "spirit" money (plain paper) was thrown from the hearse, in part, it is believed, to ward off spirits who might interfere with the corpse. Fourth, at the gravesite, after the casket had been lowered into the grave, flowers were thrown into the grave and the paper house, "servants," and money were burned. Fifth, the funeral party then retired to a "longevity" banquet to provide support and reintegration for the mourners.

■ *Gravesite visits*: Since many Asian-American communities believe in a continued interaction between the living and the deceased, and that the well-being of living descendents is at least partly related to the care taken on behalf of deceased ancestors, many members of such groups visit gravesites on a frequent basis and care for such sites to express their ongoing concern and care for their ancestors (Hirayama, 1990).

AMERICAN INDIANS AND NATIVE ALASKANS

Readily available information about death-related experiences among American Indians and Native Alaskans is limited, not always reliable and not easily subject to generalization. There are hundreds of American-Indian tribal groups in the United States and Canada, varying in size from fewer than 100 members (e.g., Picuris Pueblo in New Mexico) to the Cherokee and Navajo, with over 200,000 and 300,000 members, respectively (U.S. Census Bureau, 2016). Each American-Indian group has its own set of patterns of death-related encounters, attitudes, and practices (Cox, 2010).

Official estimates place the total population of American-Indians residing in the United States at nearly 4 million persons, or 1.2% of the total population (see Table 5.1). However, not all American Indians live within a tribal group or on tribal lands where data about their death-related experiences can easily be identified. Many American Indians live in urban areas where they may be invisible in many ways to an external observer. Also, many additional individuals claim partial American-Indian ancestry. For all of these reasons, generalizations about death, dying, and bereavement may be particularly hazardous for this relatively small but very heterogeneous portion of American society.

American-Indian and Native Alaskan Encounters with Death, Dying, and Bereavement

In terms of *numbers of deaths*, American Indians and Native Alaskans experienced less than 0.7% of all deaths in the United States in 2014 (see Table 5.2), yielding an *age-adjusted death rate* of 5.9 per 1,000. Still, these are aggregate figures, subject to all the limitations just noted. Death is likely to be encountered in quite different ways in different American-Indian and Native Alaskan groups.

Historically, *causes of death* among American Indians and Native Alaskans have most often involved communicable diseases, diabetes mellitus, and chronic liver disease and cirrhosis, as well as accidents and suicide (Heron, 2016). As some of these causes have become less prominent overall and the average life expectancy of most American Indians has increased, heart disease and cancer have become leading causes of death in these groups. Still, alcohol abuse, leading to high death rates from alcohol-related cirrhosis of the liver, and homicide remain prominent in some American-Indian groups, suggesting that additional and more specific research is needed.

Homicide and suicide among American Indians and Native Alaskans have been the subject of competing reports and deserve careful study in specific native populations (Alcántara & Gone, 2007, 2008; Olson & Wahab, 2006). In 2014, homicide in this overall population involved 264 deaths for an age-adjusted death rate of 5.8 per 100,000, while suicide was reported as the cause of 489 deaths, yielding an age-adjusted death rate of 10.8 per 100,000 (Kochanek et al., 2016).

For homicide, Bachman (1992) argued that what appear to be high death rates in some American-Indian communities are influenced by such factors as the historical experience of a kind of internal colonialism, social disorganization, cultural conflicts, a subculture of violence, economic deprivation, and abuse of alcohol and drugs. In fact, when socioeconomic status and other cultural factors are controlled, it appears that "racial differences in homicide rates decrease substantially" (Holinger et al., 1994, p. 20).

By contrast with an apparent overemphasis on suicide among American-Indian and Native Alaskan youth in particular, *cultural continuity* is an important protective factor in reducing such suicide rates (Chandler & Lalonde, 1998; Chandler et al., 2003). Cultural facilities, educational experiences, land claims, and self-government serve to preserve the culture and contribute to a reduction in suicide rates in these youth groups. Other protective factors include strong family relationships, connectedness to tribal leaders, and social support (Borowsky et al., 1999).

Finally, in many specific American-Indian groups, several researchers have reported that automobile accidents are a significant factor in high death rates (e.g., Carr & Lee, 1978; Mahoney, 1991). However, high vehicular death rates among American-Indian populations may in part be attributed to their living in areas where people live far apart from one another and where roads are often in poor condition. In these conditions, increased motor vehicle use is necessary but can also be dangerous. This is compounded when poverty and alcoholism are additional contributing factors.

American-Indian and Native Alaskan Attitudes toward Death

- *Role of nature and cycles of life*: General belief systems surrounding death among American Indians include a view of death as normative, part of the natural and ongoing life cycle, and transformative as opposed to permanent (Van Winkle, 2000). There is a valuing of nature and balance occurring cyclically or, more specifically, in "fours" (i.e., four elements, four seasons, four phases of the moon) (Chaudhuri, 2001). Walker (2008) found among a Muscogee Creek tribe that death is perceived as essential to ensuring balance in nature and the life cycle by allowing the earth to produce new life. The Muscogee Creeks also share a belief in life after death whereby they will be reunited with deceased loved ones at death. These beliefs contribute to a largely optimistic view of death among the Creeks that allows for celebratory rituals at death.

  Nevertheless, death-related attitudes of specific American-Indian groups may range from acceptance with limited or no anxiety, as is found among many Creeks (Walker, 2008; Walker & Balk, 2007) to high levels of fear, often found among Hopi Indians (Mandelbaum, 1959) and to death avoidance found among many Navajos (McCabe, 1994), who maintain taboos that "favor bringing the sick into the hospital to die rather than permitting them to die at home" (Carr & Lee, 1978, p. 280) so that the home will not be polluted by the encounter with death. These differences show that each American-Indian group and even each individual American Indian may have a distinctive set of attitudes toward death—to which others must be sensitive and respectful.

- *Relationship between life and death*: Several observers (e.g., Brown, 1987; Walker & Thompson, 2009) have noted that a common theme among many American-Indian groups is a tendency to view life and death not in a linear but in a circular or interwoven fashion in which death is viewed as part of life. This belief is illustrated both in some American-Indian legends (e.g., see Personal Insights 5.1) and in four children's books with American-Indian perspectives (see Focus On 5.4).

PERSONAL INSIGHTS 5.1

Why Do People Die? A Navajo Legend

When they [the Navajo people as the "Origin Legend" describes early events in their emergence into this world] reached the mainland, they sought to divine their fate. To do this someone threw a hide-scraper into the water, saying: "If it sinks we perish, if it floats, we live." It floated and all rejoiced. But Coyote said: "Let me divine your fate." He picked up a stone, and saying, "If it sinks we perish; if it floats we live," he threw it into the water. It sank, of course, and all were angry with him and reviled him; but he answered them saying: "If we all live, and continue to increase as we have done, the earth will soon be too small to hold us, and there will be no room for the cornfields. It is better that each of us should live but a time on this earth and then leave and make room for our children." They saw the wisdom of his words and were silent.

Source: From Matthews (1897, p. 77).

FOCUS ON 5.4

Four Children's Books with American-Indian Perspectives

These books emphasize American-Indian beliefs about the intertwining of life and death across time and generations. *The Great Change* and *Beyond the Ridge* each describe death as a moment of transition from life on earth to life in the spirit world. In *The Great Change*, an American-Indian grandmother explains to her nine-year-old granddaughter that death is not the end, but the Great Change. As she says, "We need death in order to have life." Death is part of the unbreakable Circle of Life in which our bodies become one with Mother Earth while our souls or spirits endure. Similarly, *Beyond the Ridge* depicts an elderly Plains Indian woman who experiences the afterlife believed in by her people. At her death and as her body is prepared according to their customs, the woman makes the long climb up a difficult slope to see the Spirit World beyond the ridge.

Annie and the Old One reinforces the need to accept death as part of life. Her grandmother (the Old One) tells a ten-year-old Navajo girl, "When the new rug [that the girl's mother is weaving] is taken from the loom, I will go to Mother Earth." Annie tries to forestall that outcome by misbehaving in school, hoping that her mother will have to stop weaving to talk with her teacher. At night, she releases the goat and the sheep from their pen so the adults will have to spend time rounding them up. Annie even tries to unravel the weaving in secret. When the adults realize what is going on, grandmother explains that we are all part of a natural cycle, one that includes both death and life. Finally, Annie recognizes she cannot hold back time and she is ready herself to take part in the weaving.

(continues)

FOCUS ON 5.4 *(continued)*

Four Children's Books with American-Indian Perspectives

My Grandmother's Cookie Jar describes a special cookie jar shaped like an Indian head. Although the jar is a little scary to her granddaughter, anxieties fall away when Grandma removes its headdress, reaches inside, and takes out a cookie. As they share cookies each evening, Grandma tells stories of her Indian people of long ago. The stories make Indian ways, Indian pride, and Indian honor come alive for the girl. After Grandma's death, Grandfather gives the jar to the girl. He tells her it is full, not of cookies but of Grandma's love and her Indian spirit heritage. He says someday the girl will have children of her own and she'll put cookies in the jar. And the girl knows that when she tells Grandma's stories with each cookie, she will be keeping Grandma's spirit alive and the spirit of those who went before her.

- *Communication patterns*: Death-related attitudes can be noticed in communication patterns found among American Indians both at the end of life and after death. For example, Thomas (2001) reported that some American Indians believe that talking about dying and death may cause it to happen. This often results in little discussion about advance directives. Among the Navajos, in particular, conversations about death are avoided as is speaking the name of the deceased (McCabe, 1994). This contrast with communication patterns among the Creeks, who value talking about, laughing, and sharing happy memories of the deceased within the family context as central to the grief and coping process (Walker, 2008; Walker & Balk, 2007).
- *Survivor actions and the postdeath journey*: Clements and colleagues (2003) reported that some Navajos believe that what survivors do after the death of the person can affect the deceased person's journey into the next world. Postdeath rituals are very important for these persons.

Death-Related Practices among American Indians and Native Alaskans

- *Caring for the dying*: In Canada, people from remote areas who have acute life-threatening or long-term chronic illnesses are normally referred for treatment in urban tertiary-care hospitals. For First Nations peoples, this practice removes them from their home communities and often means the death occurs in the alien cultural environment of an urban hospital. One report (Kaufert & O'Neil, 1991) described ways in which trained native interpreters acted as mediators for Cree, Ojibway, and Inuit patients who were terminally ill: (1) as language translators; (2) as cultural informants who could describe native health practices, community health issues, and cultural perspectives on terminal illness and postmortem rituals to clinical staff; (3) as interpreters of biomedical concepts to native peoples; and (4) as patient and community advocates, for instance, by enabling patients to return to their communities to spend their final days with their families.
- *Mourning practices*: In terms of grief and its expression, consistent with the valuing of collectivism or family support in many underrepresented groups, a concern for others may take precedence over support for self. This pattern is

evident within Muscogee Creek society, where emphasis is often placed on support for family (i.e., by family members, other clans, community) or on being "the strong one," with high emotional expressions of grief, or in particular sadness, happening to a great extent in isolation or alone (Walker, 2008). Grief or feelings of sorrow are expected but should be followed by positive adjustment and should not be prolonged. In fact, among the Creek a *Micco* or expert in Indian medicine intervenes in cases of prolonged grief or depression (Walker & Balk, 2007). This view of how grief should and should not be expressed matches reports from other Native-American groups. For example, Preston and Preston (1991) found among the Cree that support should be "followed by a return to outward self-reliance and composure, though the inward, private feelings may still be strong" (p. 155). Similarly, in Crow culture, Long (1983) found that this emphasis on inward expressions of grief contributed to a flattening of many children's emotional grief responses and an avoidance of sharing or acknowledging what they were feeling.

■ *Postdeath rituals*: Many American-Indian groups have distinctive bereavement rituals, as shown in this account of Navajo postdeath rituals: "The deceased's relatives and friends have 4 days after the death [to complete] cleansing and preparation of the body, burial, mourning, and disposing of the deceased's belongings by giving them away to others or by destroying them (often by burning)....The body is washed, and the face is painted with *chei* (i.e., a war paint made of soft red rock...mixed with sheep fat) and white corn to protect the deceased on the journey [to the next world]. The deceased is clothed in his or her best clothing and blessed with corn pollen. The deceased's hair is tied with an eagle feather to symbolize a return home. Traditionally, the deceased was buried in the family's hogan...and then the hogan was abandoned....On the morning of the fourth day...the deceased's relatives and friends wash themselves

Grave sites of Native Americans at the Carmel Mission in Carmel by the Sea, California, are marked with stone circles and wooden crosses with abalone shells.

as a symbol of cleansing themselves of the event of the burial" (Clements et al., 2003, p. 23).

Tanacross Athabaskans of east central Alaska include a funeral and a *memorial potlatch* among their after-death rituals. The funeral involves preparing the corpse, building a coffin and grave fence, and conducting a Christian religious service. Non-relatives assume the work of preparing the body and building the funeral structures because the spirit of the dead person is thought to be dangerous to relatives. However, relatives prepare a three-day ceremony involving feasting, dancing, singing, oratory, and a distribution of gifts (such as guns, beads, and blankets) on the last night to those who have fulfilled their obligations. This ceremony is the memorial potlatch, which "marks the separation of the deceased from society and is the last public expression of grief" (Simeone, 1991, p. 159). One reason to distribute gifts is to objectify and personalize the grief of the hosts. Through the whole potlatch ceremony, social support is provided and strong emotions of grief are given legitimate expression in the community, but the larger social context contains grief in a culture that values emotional reserve.

Summary

In this chapter, we examined death-related encounters, attitudes, and practices among Hispanic Americans, African Americans, Americans who trace their backgrounds to Asian countries or the Pacific Islands, and American Indians and Native Alaskans. In so doing, we tried to be careful to respect both differences and similarities between and within these groups. We also tried to reflect the present state of our imperfect knowledge about these groups and to avoid stereotypes. Without going beyond the four groups selected for analysis in this chapter, we noticed the rich diversity of death-related experiences within American society. Each of these groups is both a part of the larger society in which we all share and a distinct entity with its own unique death system. Normally, membership in such a cultural group is a matter of birth and socialization; individuals are not usually able to choose such membership. Also, it can be difficult to overcome ethnocentric tendencies in which one is inclined to draw on long-standing experiences of one's own group as the norm and treat other groups as outsiders who vary from that norm. However, everyone can learn from the various cultural groups that exist in the United States. Taking part in the death-related practices of such groups (when outsiders are permitted to do so), reading about their attitudes and rituals, and sharing personal experiences (e.g., through discussions in an academic course) can enrich all of us, both as individuals and as citizens in a multicultural society. In the list of suggested readings that follows, we identify some resources for additional cultural research in the field of death, dying, and bereavement both within and beyond North America, and we occasionally cite examples of such work throughout this book.

Glossary

African Americans: Americans whose cultural origins trace back to the Black cultures of the African continent (especially West African nations)

American Indians (sometimes called Native Americans or "First Nations Peoples"; for statistical purposes, this group often includes Native Alaskans): Americans whose cultural origins trace back to the indigenous populations of North America

Asian Americans: Americans whose cultural origins trace back to the Asian continent

Cultural patterns: distinctive features arising from a unified set of values, ideas, beliefs, and standards of behavior shared by a group of people

Hispanic Americans: Americans whose cultural origins trace back to countries in which the dominant language is Spanish (e.g., Cuba, Mexico, and Puerto Rico, as well as Central and South American countries)

Pacific Island Americans: Americans whose cultural origins trace back to the Pacific Islands (e.g., Hawaii and Samoa)

Questions for Review and Discussion

1. This chapter explored four different, specific death systems within the overall American death system. What major factors did you note as similar among or unique to each of the four groups described?

2. What do you view as key relationships between death-related encounters and attitudes, on one hand, and death-related practices, on the other, in any one or more of the four groups discussed here?

3. Focusing on your own ethnic, religious, familial, or economic background, can you identify a particular death-related encounter, attitude, or practice that you have had to explain or defend to someone who does not share your background? Why did that topic seem unusual to the other person? How did you explain the origins and significance of that topic?

4. Did you ever search online for information about death-related encounters, attitudes, or practices in different cultural or racial groups? If so, what did you learn? If not, why not?

Suggested Readings

Books on cultural diversity and different cultural experiences with death within American society include the following:

Andrews, M. M., & Boyle, J. S. (Eds.). (2016). *Transcultural Concepts in Nursing Care* (7th ed.)

Barr, D. A. (2014). *Health Disparities in the United States: Social Class, Race, Ethnicity, and Health* (2nd ed.)

Braun, K., Pietsch, J., & Blanchette, P. (Eds.). (2004). *Cultural Issues in End-of-Life Decision Making*

Chase, S. (2012). *Surviving HIV/AIDS in the Inner City: How Resourceful Latinas Beat the Odds*

Churn, A. (2003). *The End is Just the Beginning: Lessons in Grieving for African Americans*

Cox, G. (2010). *Death and the American-Indian*

Doka, K. J., & Tucci, A. S. (Eds.). (2009). *Diversity and End-of-Life Care*

Fadiman, A. (1997). *The Spirit Catches You and You Fall Down: A Hmong Child, Her American Doctors, and the Collision of Two Cultures*

Giger, J. N. (2017). *Transcultural Nursing: Assessment and Intervention* (7th ed.)

Hayslip, B., & Preveto, C. A. (2005). *Cultural Changes in Attitudes toward Death, Dying, and Bereavement*

Irish, D. P., Lundquist, K. F., & Nelson, V. J. (Eds.). (1993). *Ethnic Variations in Dying, Death, and Grief: Diversity in Universality*

JanMohamed, A. B. (2004). *The Death-Bound-Subject: Richard Wright's Archaeology of Death*

Kolb, P. (Ed.). (2014). *Understanding Aging and Diversity: Theories and Concepts*

LaVeist, T. A., & Isaac, L. A. (Eds.). (2012). *Race, Ethnicity, and Health: A Public Health Reader* (2nd ed.)

Leach, M. M. (2006). *Cultural Diversity and Suicide: Ethnic, Religious, Gender, and Sexual Orientation Perspectives*

Lee, C. C. (Ed.). (2013). *Multicultural Issues in Counseling: New Approaches to Diversity* (4th ed.)

Leong, F. T. L., & Leach, M. M. (Eds.). (2008). *Suicide among Racial and Ethnic Groups: Theory, Research, and Practice*

McGoldrick, M., Giordano, J., & Garcia-Preto, N. (Eds.). (2005). *Ethnicity and Family Therapy* (3rd ed.)

Moller, D. W. (2012). *Dancing with Broken Bones: Poverty, Race, and Spirit-Filled Dying in the Inner City* (rev. & expanded ed.)

Oliviere, D., Monroe, B., & Payne, S. (Eds.). (2012). *Death, Dying, and Social Differences* (2nd ed.)

Parry, J. K. (Ed.). (2001). *Social Work Theory and Practice with the Terminally Ill* (2nd ed.)

Parry, J. K., & Ryan, A. S. (Eds.). (2003). *A Cross-Cultural Look at Death, Dying, and Religion*

Pedersen, P. B., Lonner, W. J., Draguns, J. G., Trimble, J. E., & Scharron-del Rio, M. R. (Eds.). (2016). *Counseling across Cultures* (7th ed.)

Purnell, L. D. (2014). *Guide to Culturally Competent Health Care* (3rd ed.)

Purnell, L. D. (Ed.). (2013). *Transcultural Health Care: A Culturally Competent Approach* (4th ed.)

Robben, A. (Ed.). (2005). *Death, Mourning, and Burial: A Cross-Cultural Reader*

Rosenblatt, P. C., & Wallace, B. R. (2005b). *African-American Grief*

Smedley, B. D., Stith, A. Y., & Nelson, A. R. (Eds.). (2004). *Unequal Treatment: Confronting Racial and Ethnic Disparities in Healthcare*

Smith, H. I., & Johnson, J. (2008). Partnered Grief: When Gay and Lesbian Partners Grieve

Spector, R. E. (2012). *Cultural Diversity in Health and Illness* (8th ed.)

Suarez, R. (2013). *Latino Americans: The 500-Year Legacy That Shaped a Nation*

Sue, D. W., & Sue, D. (2015). *Counseling the Culturally Diverse: Theory and Practice* (7th ed.)

Tomer, A., Wong, P. T., & Eliason, G. T. (Eds.). (2007). *Existential and Spiritual Issues in Death Attitudes*

Trask, B. S., & Hamon, R. R. (Eds.). (2007). *Cultural Diversity and Families: Expanding Perspectives*

Washington, H. A. (2006). *Medical Apartheid: The Dark History of Medical Experimentation on Black Americans from Colonial Times to the Present*

Whipple, V. (2014). *Lesbian Widows: Invisible Grief*

Wright, R. H., Mindel, C. H., Tran, T. V., & Habenstein, R. W. (2012). *Ethnic Families in America: Patterns and Variations* (5th ed.)

For examples of reports on death-related experiences outside North American society, see the following:

Abrahamson, H. (1977). *The Origin of Death: Studies in African Mythology*

Brandes, S. (2006). *Skulls to the Living, Bread to the Dead: The Day of the Dead in Mexico and Beyond*

Brodman, B. (2011). *The Mexican Cult of Death in Myth, Art and Literature*

Counts, D. R., & Counts, D. A. (Eds.). (1991). *Coping with the Final Tragedy: Cultural Variation in Dying and Grieving*

Danforth, L. M. (1982). *The Death Rituals of Rural Greece*

Field, D., Hockey, J., & Small, N. (Eds.). (1997). *Death, Gender and Ethnicity*

Garciagodoy, J. (2000). *Digging the Days of the Dead: A Reading of Mexico's Dias de Muertos*

Goody, J. (1962). *Death, Property, and the Ancestors: A Study of the Mortuary Customs of the LoDagaa of West Africa*

Hockey, J., Katz, J., & Small, N. (Eds.). (2001). *Grief, Mourning and Death Ritual*

Kalish, R. A. (Ed.). (1980). *Death and Dying: Views from Many Cultures*

Lewis, O. (1972). *A Death in the Sanchez Family*

Morgan, J. D., Laungani, P., & Palmer, S. (Eds.). (2003–2009). *Death and Bereavement around the World* (5 vols.)

Moss, J. (2010). *The Day of the Dead: A Pictorial Archive of Dia de los Muertos*

Parkes, C. M., Laungani, P., & Young, W. (Eds.). (2015). *Death and Bereavement across Cultures* (2nd ed.)

Robben, A. C. (Ed.). (2004). *Death, Mourning, and Burial: A Cross-Cultural Reader*

Rosenblatt, P. C., Walsh, P. R., & Jackson, D. A. (1976). *Grief and Mourning in Cross-Cultural Perspective*

Scheper-Hughes, N. (1992). *Death without Weeping: The Violence of Everyday Life in Brazil*

Selected Web Resources

Some useful search terms include: AFRICAN AMERICANS AND DEATH; ALASKA NATIVES AND DEATH; AMERICAN-INDIANS AND DEATH; ASIAN AMERICANS AND DEATH; CULTURAL PATTERNS; ETHNICITY AND DEATH; HISPANIC-AMERICANS AND DEATH; NATIVE AMERICANS AND DEATH; PACIFIC ISLAND AMERICANS AND DEATH.

You can also visit the following *organizational and other Internet sites:*

Association of Asian Pacific Community Health Organizations

Ethnic Elders Care

National Alliance for Hispanic Health

National Black Women's Health Imperative

National Minority AIDS Council

National Native American AIDS Prevention Center

PART Three

DYING

In an extended sense of the word, every living thing can be said to be *dying* or moving toward death from the moment of its conception. However, that would stretch the meaning of the word *dying* so far as to make it useless for most customary purposes. Even if we are all dying in some broad sense, some of us are more actively dying than others. In Chapters 6–8, we examine the special situation of those living persons who are closely approaching death—the situation more properly designated as *dying*.

Some people act as if individuals who are dying are already dead or are as good as dead. That is incorrect, unhelpful, and often hurtful. As Northcott and Wilson (2017, p. xv) have written: "Dying is a process; death is an event." If that is so, then *dying persons are living human beings*; they remain living persons as long as they are dying. Thus, we emphasize two points here: (1) dying is not the whole of life, but it is a special situation in living and (2) death is the outcome of dying, not its equivalent.

Some ask, when does dying begin? When a fatal condition develops, when that condition is recognized by a physician, when knowledge of that condition is communicated to the person involved, when that person realizes and accepts the facts of his or her condition, or when nothing more can be done to reverse the condition and preserve life? It is not clear whether any or all of these elements are sufficient to define the state of dying. The situation is reminiscent of a remark attributed to the English statesman Edmund Burke (1729–1797) that it is difficult to determine the precise point at which afternoon becomes evening, even though everyone can easily distinguish between day and night.

For that reason, it is more helpful to focus not on *when dying begins*, but on *what is involved in dying*. Thus, in Chapter 6, we explore *coping with dying*, together with two types of theoretical models designed to help us understand such coping. In Chapter 7, we investigate *ways in which individuals can help persons who are coping with dying*. And in Chapter 8, we look at *how society has tried to respond to the needs of dying persons*, including the ways in which society has organized formal programs to care for those who are coping with dying. Here we give special attention to hospice programs and what they offer for end-of-life care.

Courtesy of Ann Fitzsimmons

Coping with Dying

Objectives of this **Chapter**

An individual with a life-threatening illness or someone who is in the process of dying is first of all *a person, a living human being*. This fact is fundamental to all that follows: *people who are dying are living human beings*. There may be much that is distinctive or special about individuals with life-limiting conditions or life-threatening illnesses, and particularly about those who are actively dying. That is because the *pressures of dying* often underscore the *preciousness of living*. However, like all other living persons, those who are dying have a broad range of needs and desires, plans and projects, joys and sufferings, hopes, fears, and anxieties.

Dying is a part (but only one part) of our experiences of life and living; the event of death has not yet taken place until life, living, and dying have ended. One cannot already be dead and yet still be dying. To be dead is to be through with the processes of dying; to be dying is still to be alive.

Dying persons are not merely individuals within whom biochemical systems are malfunctioning. That may be important, but it is not the whole story. Dying is a human experience, and human beings are more than mere objects of anatomy and physiology. If they were merely those sorts of objects, we would not need to pay any attention to the other dimensions of dying persons.

In fact, each person who is dying is a complex and unique entity, intermixing physical, psychological, social, and spiritual dimensions. Psychological difficulties, social discomfort, and spiritual suffering may be just as pressing and significant for a dying person as physical distress. To focus on any one of these dimensions alone is to be in danger of ignoring the totality of the person and overlooking what matters most to him or her. To avoid that danger, in this chapter, we investigate a series of issues that relate to dying persons and those who are involved with such persons in pursuit of the following objectives:

▶ To define *coping* and explain some of its key elements

▶ To describe *coping with dying*, recognizing that such coping typically involves more than one person

▶ To explain the concepts of *dying trajectories* and *awareness contexts*

▶ To explore two types of models—one based on *stages*, the other on *tasks*—that have been proposed to explain what is involved in coping with dying

▶ To examine an account of *five phases of living with a life-threatening illness*

ONE FAMILY COPING WITH LIFE-THREATENING ILLNESS AND DYING

Josephina Ryan was 63 when she first felt a small lump in her right breast. Until that awful moment in the shower, Jo thought she had been very fortunate in her life. She had met Matt when he was stationed in her native Philippines. After their marriage and return to the States, the Ryans had five sons and a daughter, now all well established in their own lives and careers. Three of the boys and Christy were married, and they had given their parents six grandchildren between them. Jo had enjoyed raising her children and then returning to her career as a third-grade teacher. Matt was coming up to retirement as a high school principal. He had been very fortunate five years ago when an early diagnosis and surgery had cured him of prostate cancer. After Matt's retirement, they were anticipating traveling around the country in an RV and spending more time visiting their children and grandchildren.

When Matt was diagnosed with prostate cancer, it was as if he had been hit over the head with a club. He was stunned and just didn't seem to know what to do. Jo was the strong one throughout that ordeal. She took a brief leave of absence from teaching, coordinated Matt's medical care, kept in touch with all the kids, and was a gentle rock on whom Matt could lean. It helped that the testing and the surgery went by pretty fast, and Matt experienced no postoperative complications.

Jo had feared breast cancer, because it had caused the death of her mother and her aunt several years ago. So Jo had been relieved when her family physician had given her a clean bill of health after her annual physical exam six months ago. But now it seemed like maybe it really was her turn.

Still, her first thoughts were about Matt and the kids, not herself. Christy was a strong person, but Jake and Patrick still turned to Mom when they encountered tough times. And, except for Tom and his wife, they all lived far away. There were just so many things to think about!

Jo's biopsy shocked the Ryans. They had to decide quickly about treatment. A partial mastectomy and what the physicians called a "prophylactic" combination of radiation and chemotherapy seemed to kill all the malignant cells, but the nausea, hair loss, and other side effects were really hard to bear. Matt looked like a lost child during this time, as if he were wandering through life but not recognizing any familiar landmarks.

Afterward, Jo and Matt did have some good times together. They sincerely hoped "the terrors" (as they called them) were all gone. But not many months later (or so it seemed), it looked as if the cancer had only gone into hiding temporarily and was roaring back with a vengeance. Jo's physicians were unsure whether this was a new disease or a recurrence of the old one. In any event, it must have lurked silently for a while to account for its rapid development and spread. There were more tests, new diagnoses, and several rounds of treatment, but the cancer kept spreading.

Toward the end, Jo could hardly leave her bed. Prayer was comforting for the Ryan family, but it was truly a difficult time for Jo and Matt and all those who loved them.

COPING

The American humorist Josh Billings (1818–1885) is said to have observed that "life consists not in holding good cards but in playing those you do hold well." How we play our cards, particularly in response to life's major challenges, is a metaphor for how we cope, as Matt and Jo Ryan learned during their own struggles. In order to understand issues related to coping with dying, it will help first to clarify what coping means and what it involves.

A Definition of Coping and Its Central Elements

The term **coping** has been defined as "constantly changing cognitive and behavioral efforts to manage specific external and/or internal demands that are appraised as taxing or exceeding the resources of the person" (Lazarus & Folkman, 1984, p. 141; see also Monat & Lazarus, 1991).

This definition can help us understand both coping with living and coping with dying by:

- focusing on *processes* of coping, with special reference to their changing character—thus emphasizing that coping involves activity and is not static
- directing attention to *efforts* that are central to coping, whatever one is thinking or doing to cope—not only as affective traits that characterize internal feeling states—and reminding us that these efforts may take many forms (cognitive, behavioral, social, spiritual, and others).
- underlining attempts *to manage or adapt to* a situation, to live or get along with it as best one can.
- linking coping to efforts addressing *specific demands* (wherever or however they originate) *that are perceived as stressful*. (Note two corollaries: unperceived demands are usually not stressful; also, because perceptions may change, coping processes may adjust to new perceptions.)
- referring to efforts undertaken in response to *demands that are appraised as taxing or exceeding the resources of the person*, and thus distinguishing coping from routine automatized behaviors that do not involve an effortful response.
- taking care *not to confuse coping processes with their outcomes*.

In short, coping includes any efforts to manage stressful demands, however successful or unsuccessful such efforts might be. Coping does not necessarily seek to *master* stressful

Table 6.1 Coping: Three Focal Domains and Nine Types of Skills

Appraisal-Focused Coping

1. *Logical analysis and mental preparation*: Paying attention to one aspect of the crisis at a time, breaking a seemingly overwhelming problem into small, potentially manageable bits, drawing on past experiences, and mentally rehearsing alternative actions and their probable consequences
2. *Cognitive redefinition*: Using cognitive strategies to accept the basic reality of a situation but restructure it to find something favorable
3. *Cognitive avoidance or denial*: Denying or minimizing the seriousness of a crisis

Problem-Focused Coping

4. *Seeking information and support*: Obtaining information about the crisis and alternate courses of action and their probable outcome
5. *Taking problem-solving action*: Taking concrete action to deal directly with a crisis or its aftermath
6. *Identifying alternative rewards*: Attempting to replace the losses involved in certain transitions and crises by changing one's activities and creating new sources of satisfaction

Emotion-Focused Coping

7. *Affective regulation*: Trying to maintain hope and control one's emotions when dealing with a distressing situation
8. *Emotional discharge*: Openly venting one's feelings and using jokes and gallows humor to help allay constant strain
9. *Resigned acceptance*: Coming to terms with a situation and accepting it as it is, deciding that the basic circumstances cannot be altered and submitting to "certain" fate

Source: From "Life Transitions and Crises: A Conceptual Overview," by R. H. Moos and J. A. Schaefer. In R. H. Moos and J. A. Schaefer (Eds.), *Coping with Life Crises: An Integrated Approach*, pp. 3–28. Copyright 1986 Plenum Publishing Corporation. Reprinted with permission of Springer Science and Business Media.

demands. A coping person may try—more or less successfully—to master a particular situation but often is content to accept, endure, minimize, or avoid stressful demands.

Moos and Schaefer (1986) extended our understanding of coping by grouping coping skills into three separate categories (see Table 6.1): (1) *appraisal-focused coping* centers on how one understands or appraises a stressful situation; (2) *problem-focused coping* relates to what one does about the problem or stressor itself; and (3) *emotion-focused coping* involves what one does about one's reactions to the perceived problem. We prefer to call this last type of coping *reaction-focused coping* so as not to limit it to feelings alone (see Chapter 9, pp. 219–221). In any event, a person's coping may emphasize any one or all of these focal perspectives, and, as Moos and Schaefer (1986, p. 13) observed, "the word *skill* underscores the positive aspects of coping and depicts coping as an ability that can be taught and used flexibly as the situation requires."

Coping as Learned and Dynamic Behavior

Coping is central to the response one makes to any situation that is perceived as stressful. Such situations might involve almost any aspect of life or death: a death or a significant loss of any type (the ending of a relationship, failing to succeed in some endeavor, being fired from a job, a divorce, and so forth), as well as happier events, such as winning the lottery, taking up a new challenge in life, getting married, or having a baby. Any situation like this might be perceived as stressful. How it is perceived depends upon the individual. How the individual responds to such situations will have much to do with how he or she has learned to respond (Corr & Corr, 2007a).

In thinking about coping, Davidson (1975, p. 28) wrote: "We are born with the *ability* to adapt to change, but we all must *learn* how to cope with loss." As individuals move through life, they observe how others around them cope with separation, loss, and endings—the "necessary losses" (Viorst, 1986) that none of us can avoid, such as a child's discovery that his or her parents are not superhuman or an adult's observations of elderly parents who are becoming less able to care for themselves. Often, we try out in our own lives strategies we have watched others use in coping, or we simply rely on methods that have proved satisfactory to us in the past. Some of us have little choice in the ways in which we are able to cope: the situation may not present us with many alternatives. Sometimes we can do little about the source of the stress and must focus mainly on our reactions to that situation. In any case, each individual tries to acquire a repertoire of skills that facilitate coping with challenges in life, responding to needs, and helping that person adapt in satisfactory ways.

In seeking to understand coping, it is important to know *how individuals who are coping perceive their situation and what they are actually thinking or doing in specific contexts of stressful demands* (Hinton, 1984; Silver & Wortman, 1980). One must ask what this particular person is actually thinking or doing as the stressful encounter unfolds, not what people in general do in similar situations, and not even what that individual might do, should do, or usually does in such circumstances. As we observed in the vignette near the beginning of this chapter, Matt and Jo Ryan each reacted to and coped with their spouse's life-threatening illness in different ways. Also, because coping involves shifting processes as the relationship between the person and his or her environment changes, different forms of coping may be undertaken at different times. For example, defensive responses may give way to problem-solving strategies. Thus, what is critical is the actual focus of the individual's coping at any given time.

All of the ways in which one learns to cope are not likely to be of equal value. Some ways of coping are useful in most situations. Some have value in certain situations but not in others. Some merely seem to be effective even though they actually are counterproductive. Some ways of coping may be satisfactory to one person but hurtful to others. The better we learn to cope with past and present losses, the more likely we will be able to cope effectively with future losses.

In each particular situation, we can ask: What does the individual perceive as stressful? How is the individual coping with that stress? Why is he or she coping in this particular way? These questions apply to coping with dying as well as to coping with all other challenges in living. For that reason, although there are significant differences between death and other sorts of stressors or losses, how one copes with the "little deaths" (Purtillo, 1976) and other stressful challenges throughout life may be indicative of how one is likely to cope with the large crises associated with dying and death.

Coping with Dying: Who Is Coping?

Coping with dying typically involves more than a single individual. In reflecting on coping with dying, we typically focus on the ill person, the principal actor at the center of the coping challenge. That is where we should always begin, but we should not end there because coping with dying is not solely confined to ill and dying persons. Coping with dying is also a challenge for others who are drawn into such situations.

These include the family members and friends of the dying person, as well as volunteer and professional caregivers who attend to the dying person and must face that person's death (Grollman, 1995).

Confronting coping with dying and imminent death are experiences that resonate deeply within the personal sense of mortality and limitations of all who are drawn into these processes. A family member who says to a dying person, "Don't die on me," may be conveying anguish at the pending loss of a loved one. A caregiver who says, "I hope we won't lose Mr. Smith tonight," may be expressing frustration at his or her inability to prevent the coming of death or concern with the consequences that Mr. Smith's death will bring for the caregiver. In the case of families, it is especially important to note that people who are coping with dying do so not only as particular, unique individuals but also as members of a family system, and as members of society—all of which influence their coping (Rosen, 1998). For example, a conflicted relationship between a parent and a child or between two siblings who have fought for years may generate special issues that need to be addressed in the context of coping with dying.

Coping with dying is usually multifaceted. It involves more than one person, and thus involves more than one set of perceptions of what is going on, more than one set of motivations, and more than one way of coping. Those who wish to understand coping with dying need to identify *each person* who is involved in that activity and listen carefully to what his or her coping reveals (Kessler, 2000). Only by active and empathetic listening can we hope to understand what the coping means for each individual in each particular situation. Only by striving to understand each individual's coping efforts can we hope to appreciate how he or she is interacting in the shared dynamic of the situation. Sensitivity to outward behaviors, to underlying feelings, and to key variables is essential in such listening. (See Focus On 6.1 for examples of what individuals have written about coping with dying.)

FOCUS ON 6.1

Selected Descriptions of Coping with Life-Threatening Illness

Albom, M. (1997). *Tuesdays with Morrie: An Old Man, A Young Man, and Life's Greatest Lesson*

Barnard, D., Towers, A., Boston, P., & Lambrinidou, Y. (2000). *Crossing Over: Narratives of Palliative Care*

Brokaw, T. (2015). *A Lucky Life Interrupted: A Memoir of Hope*

Buchwald, A. (2006). *Too Soon to Say Goodbye*

Chen, P. W. (2006). *Final Exam: A Surgeon's Reflections on Mortality*

Cousins, N. (1979). *Anatomy of an Illness as Perceived by the Patient: Reflections on Healing and Regeneration*

Fanestil, J. (2006). *Mrs. Hunter's Happy Death: Lessons on Living from People Preparing to Die*

Fazakerley, J., Butlin-Battler, H., & Bradish, G. (2012). *Just Stay: A Couple's Last Journey Together*

Frank, A. W. (2002). *At the Will of the Body: Reflections on Illness* (new Afterword)

(continues)

FOCUS ON 6.1 *(continued)*

Selected Descriptions of Coping with Life-Threatening Illness

Gelfand, D. E., Raspa, R., Briller, S. H., & Schim, S. M. (Eds.). (2005). *End-of-Life Stores: Crossing Disciplinary Boundaries*

Gunther, J. (1949). *Death Be Not Proud*

Hanlan, A. (1979). *Autobiography of Dying*

Jury, M., & Jury, D. (1978). *Gramps: A Man Ages and Dies*

Kalanithi, P. (2016). *When Breath Becomes Air*

MacPherson, M. (1999). *She Came to Live Out Loud: An Inspiring Family Journey through Illness, Loss, and Grief*

Mandell, H., & Spiro, H. (Eds.). (1987). *When Doctors Get Sick*

Pausch, R., with Zaslow, J. (2008). *The Last Lecture*

Quindlen, A. (1994). *One True Thing*

Romm, R. (2009). *The Mercy Papers: A Memoir of Three Weeks*

Rosenthal, T. (1973). *How Could I Not Be Among You?*

Schwartz, M. (1999). *Morrie: In His Own Words*

Solomon, A. (1994). *A Stone Boat*

Tolstoy, L. (1884/1960). *The Death of Ivan Ilych and Other Stories*

DYING TRAJECTORIES AND AWARENESS CONTEXTS

Glaser and Strauss (1965, 1968) described two key variables in coping with dying: the nature of the dying trajectory and the degree to which those who are involved are aware of and share information about dying. These variables describe both the individual situation and the social context within which coping with dying takes place.

Dying persons do not move toward death at the same rates of speed or in the same ways. Processes of dying or coming to be dead have their own distinctive characteristics in each individual case. As we saw in Chapter 2, Glaser and Strauss (1968) suggested that we should understand **dying trajectories** in terms of two principal characteristics: the time or duration between the onset of dying and the arrival of death, and the certainty or predictability of the course of the dying process (see Figure 2.2).

Some dying trajectories involve an up-and-down history of remission, relapse, remission, and so on—often in a rather unpredictable way. Other dying trajectories make relatively steady progress toward death. In some cases, the dying trajectory may be completed very briefly, even instantaneously; in other cases, it may be slow, extending over a period of weeks, months, or even years as in Alzheimer's disease and other end-of-life situations involving dementia (see Chapter 20 in this book).

Obviously, there are variations on these simple patterns. For example, the time when death will occur or the moment when the process will resolve itself so that its ultimate outcome becomes clear may or may not be predictable. We may know that the person will die, when the death will occur, and how it will take place, or we may be unclear about one or more of these points.

Awareness contexts involve social interactions among those who are coping with dying. Glaser and Strauss (1965) argued that once a person is known to be dying, the relationships between that person and his or her close associates and health care providers can take at least four basic forms:

- *Closed awareness* is a context in which the person who is dying does not realize that fact. The staff, and perhaps also the family, may know that the person is dying, but that information has not been conveyed to the dying person—nor does he or she even suspect it. Many have thought (and some still do, especially in certain cultural groups) that it is desirable not to convey diagnostic and prognostic information to dying persons. In fact, this knowledge usually cannot be hidden for long. Communication is achieved in complex, subtle, and sometimes unconscious ways, and awareness is likely to develop at several levels. For example, changes in one's own body linked to progression of the disease, along with alterations in the behaviors of others or changes in their physical appearance, often lead at least to gradual or partial recognition that all is not well.

- *Suspected awareness* identifies a context in which the ill person may begin to suspect that he or she has not been given all of the information that is relevant to his or her situation. For a variety of reasons—for example, tests, treatments, or other behaviors that do not seem to correspond with the supposed problem—the person who is ill may begin to suspect that more is going on than is being said. This may undermine trust and complicate future communications.

- *Mutual pretense* describes a context that was once (and may still be) quite common, in which the relevant information is held by all the individual parties in the situation but is not shared between them. In other words, mutual pretense involves a kind of communal drama in which everyone involved acts out a role intended to say that things are not as they know them to be. Think how people reacted to the horse on the dining-room table in the Prologue to this book. As mutual pretense is lived out, it may even be conducted so as to cover over awkward moments when the strategy of dissembling or evading the truth fails temporarily. This is a fragile situation; one slip can cause the entire structure to collapse. Mutual pretense requires constant vigilance and a great deal of effort. Consequently, it is extremely demanding for everyone involved.

- *Open awareness* describes a context in which the dying person and everyone else realizes and is willing to discuss the fact that death is near. Those who share an open awareness context may or may not actually spend much time discussing the fact that the person is dying. Sometimes one or the other person may not want to talk about it right then. After all, as has aptly been said, "No one is dying 24 hours a day." But there is no pretense; when persons are ready and willing to discuss the realities of the situation, they are able to do so.

These are four different types of awareness contexts, not steps in a linear progression from silence or inhibition to openness. The point is that social interactions and coping with dying are likely to be affected by awareness contexts. Every awareness context brings with it some potential costs and some potential benefits. For example, sometimes the anxiety and grief of the family member (or staff person) raised by the oncoming death of a loved one may make discussion of that event too difficult to endure. Avoidance of reality can get some people through a difficult moment and thus, in certain circumstances, may be a productive way of coping—at least temporarily.

However, open awareness usually allows for honest communication if participants are ready for such interactions. It permits each involved person to participate in the shared grief of an impending loss. Vital words of concern and affection can be spoken. Ancient wounds can be healed. Unfinished business—between the dying person and his or her family members, friends, or God—can be addressed. These benefits come at the cost of having to admit and face powerful feelings (e.g., anger, sadness, and perhaps guilt) and recognized facts (e.g., tasks not completed, choices unmade, and paths not taken). This can be difficult and painful. Still, for many persons these costs are preferable to those associated with lack of openness. Always, one balances costs against benefits in both the short and long run.

With these understandings of coping, dying trajectories, and awareness contexts in mind, we turn next to two types of models that have been proposed to explain coping with dying.

COPING WITH DYING: A STAGE-BASED APPROACH

The best-known model of coping with dying is the **stage-based model** put forward by Dr. Elisabeth Kübler-Ross. In her book *On Death and Dying* (1969), Kübler-Ross reported that her interviews with adults who were coping with dying led to a theoretical model of five psychosocial stages (see Table 6.2). She interpreted these stages as "defense mechanisms" that "will last for different periods of time and will replace each other or exist at times side by side" (p. 138). She also maintained that "the one thing that usually persists through all these stages is *hope*" (p. 138).

In other words, Kübler-Ross saw dying persons as people in stressful situations. Because they are living persons, like people in other stressful situations, they employ or develop different ways of reacting to their situations. So dying persons may cope by withdrawing, or by becoming angry, or by finding what has occurred in their lives up to now that might make death acceptable. One major point she underlined is that *different people cope in different ways at different times and in different contexts*.

Kübler-Ross's stages appealed to many who read about or heard of this model. Her work helped to bring dying persons and issues involved in coping with dying to

Table 6.2 Kübler-Ross's Five Stages in Coping with Dying

Stage	Typical Expression
Denial	"Not me!"
Anger	"Why me?"
Bargaining	"Yes me, but…"
Depression	
Reactive	Responding to past and present losses
Preparatory	Anticipating and responding to losses yet to come
Acceptance	Described as a stage "almost void of feelings"

Source: Based on Kübler-Ross (1969).

public and professional attention. In general, her model identified common patterns of familiar psychosocial reactions to difficult situations. Also, she drew attention to the human aspects of living with dying, to the strong feelings experienced by those who are coping with dying, and to what she called the "unfinished business" that many want to address. Kübler-Ross said that her book is "simply an account of a new and challenging opportunity to refocus on the patient as a human being, to include him in dialogues, to learn from him the strengths and weaknesses of our hospital management of the patient. We have asked him to be our teacher so that we may learn more about the final stages of life with all its anxieties, fears, and hopes" (p. xi).

However, there are major difficulties in accepting Kübler-Ross's model as it was presented. Early research by others (e.g., Metzger, 1980; Schulz & Aderman, 1974) did not support this model. Also, since its initial appearance in 1969, there has been no independent confirmation of its validity or reliability, and Kübler-Ross advanced no further evidence on its behalf before her death in August 2004. On the contrary, many clinicians who work with the dying have found this model to be inadequate, superficial, and misleading (e.g., Pattison, 1977; Shneidman, 1980/1995; Weisman, 1977). Widespread acclaim in the popular arena contrasts with sharp criticism from scholars and many who work with dying persons (Klass, 1982; Klass & Hutch, 1986; see also Issues for Critical Reflection #8).

ISSUES FOR CRITICAL REFLECTION
#8 What Can We Learn from the Legacy of Elisabeth Kübler-Ross?

After the death of Elisabeth Kübler-Ross (on August 24, 2004; see Kessler, 2004), it is appropriate to reflect on the legacies of her life and work (Kramer, 2005). Some see her theoretical framework of five "stages" experienced by dying persons as set forth in her book, *On Death and Dying* (1969), as her main bequest, but also notable are her lectures, presentations, and other publications that captured the attention of a broad range of audiences. Her workshops in which she taught about the skills involved in being a good care provider for oneself and for others are another significant part of her legacy. And there are many who have been interested in her thoughts about out-of-body experiences and the afterlife.

In general, though, perhaps the most enduring lessons from the work of Kübler-Ross are found in the brief Preface (p. xi) to her famous book (Corr, 1993a, 2011). For first lesson, Kübler-Ross asked her readers to "refocus on the patient as a human being." She meant by this to point out that those who are coping with dying are *still alive* and often have, as she said, "unfinished business" that they want and need to address. They are not (yet) dead, and they deserve to be acknowledged as vital and still active.

For the second lesson, Kübler-Ross called upon her readers to "include [the patient] in dialogues, to learn from

[that person] the strengths and weaknesses of our…management of" his or her illness and interests. This lesson is not just about patients, but includes anyone who is coping with dying. Its main application, however, is to all of the individuals—professionals, volunteers, family members, and friends—who set out to help anyone engaged in such coping. In this lesson, Kübler-Ross drew attention to the fact that none of us can be an effective care provider unless we *listen actively* to those we seek to serve and identify with them in their own tasks and needs.

For the third lesson, Kübler-Ross highlighted our need to ask those who are coping with dying "to be our teacher so that *we* may learn more about the final stages of life with all its anxieties, fears, and hopes." This lesson emphasizes *our need to learn from* those who are coping with dying *in order to come to know ourselves better*—as limited, vulnerable, finite, and mortal, but also as resilient, adaptable, interdependent, and lovable (see also advice from a dying physician: Bone, 1997).

These three lessons are: (1) about all who are dying and coping with dying; (2) about becoming and being a provider of care; and (3) about what we all need to live our own lives in the most authentic ways.

One detailed evaluation of this stage-based model raised the following points: (1) the existence of these stages as such has not been demonstrated; (2) no evidence has been presented that people actually do move from stage 1 through stage 5; (3) the limitations of the method have not been acknowledged; (4) the line is blurred between description and prescription; (5) the totality of the person's life is neglected in favor of the supposed stages of dying; and (6) the resources, pressures, and characteristics of the immediate environment, which can make a tremendous difference, are not taken into account (Kastenbaum, 2012). These last two points mean that we cannot describe the ways in which humans respond to the stresses of dying, independently of personal, social, and cultural influences. In fact, our history and environments are essential components influencing how we respond to stress. In Chapter 5, we learned that different cultures have different expectations, values, and practices that influence how their members will respond to stress. To leave these out of one's theory is to provide an inadequate account of actual human experience.

Think for a moment about the traits that Kübler-Ross described as stages: clearly, they are so broadly formulated that they actually designate a variety of reactions. For example, "denial" can describe the following range of responses: (1) I am not ill; (2) I am ill, but it is not serious; (3) I am seriously ill, but not dying; (4) I am dying, but death will not come for a long time; or (5) I am dying and death will come shortly (Weisman, 1972). Similarly, "acceptance" may take the form of an enthusiastic welcoming, a grudging resignation, or a variety of other responses. Weisman also pointed out that denial may have positive value when it permits ill persons to take part in therapy and sustain hope. Further, Weisman offered another way to look at denial and acceptance by proposing the concept of "*middle knowledge*," according to which individuals may sometimes affirm and at other times deny the closeness of death all throughout the illness. If so, then the important question is not "Does the patient accept or deny death?" But rather "When, with whom, and under what circumstances does the patient discuss the possibility of death?"

In addition, Kübler-Ross elsewhere made clear that by "depression" she meant sadness, not clinical depression, which is a psychiatric diagnosis of illness and not a normative coping process. Further, we know that there are many ways, not just five, in which to react to dying or any other important event in life.

Moreover, there is no reason to think that the particular five ways identified by Kübler-Ross are linked together as *stages* in a larger process (Corr, 1993a, 2011). This is the most important point to which Kübler-Ross partly agreed when she argued for fluidity, give-and-take, the possibility of experiencing two of these responses simultaneously, or an ability to jump around from one stage to another. This suggests that the language of "stages," with its associated implications of linear progression/regression, is not really appropriate for a cluster of disconnected coping strategies. Stage theories are attractive because they describe a relatively simple, straight-lined, predictable course of behavior, one culminating in a clear end—but that does not mean such theories are valid or reliable.

Another problem with this model—for which its author is not wholly responsible—is that many people have misused it. This is ironic because Kübler-Ross set out to argue that dying persons are mistreated when they are objectified—when they are treated as a "liver case" or as a "cardiac case." Unfortunately, since the publication of *On Death and Dying*, some people have come to treat dying persons as a "case of anger" or a "case of depression"; others have told ill persons that they have

already been angry and should now "move on" to bargaining or depression; and still others have become frustrated by those whom they view as "stuck" in the dying process. (But if I am stuck in the dying process, does that mean I cannot die?) Misusing the Kübler-Ross stage model in ways like these forces those who are coping with dying into a preestablished framework that reduces their individuality to little more than an instance of one of five categories (anger, or depression, or…) in a schematic process. That is why Rosenthal (1973, p. 39), when he was coping with his own dying, wrote, "Being invisible I invite only generalizations."

All these points suggest that the language of stages and the metaphor of a linear theory (*first* one denies, *then* one is angry, *then* one bargains, etc.) are simply not adequate as a basis for explaining coping with dying. As an alternative, it might be better simply to speak of a broad range of responses to the experience of dying. Essentially, this is what Shneidman (1973a, p. 7) meant by what he called a "hive of affect," a busy, buzzing, active set of feelings, attitudes, and other reactions, to which a person returns from time to time, now expressing one posture (e.g., anger), now another (e.g., denial). The person may return to the hive and experience the same feelings again and again, sometimes simultaneously, sometimes one day after another, sometimes with long intervals in between.

COPING WITH DYING: A TASK-BASED APPROACH

We consider a **task-based model of coping with dying** because it avoids metaphors that emphasize a passive or merely reactive way of understanding such coping. As Weisman (1984) noted, coping involves more than an automatic, defensive response. Also, a posture of defense is largely a *negative* one; it channels energy into avoiding problems, rather than achieving some kind of adaptive accommodation. That may be useful initially and sometimes on later occasions—for example, denial can be a way of providing time to mobilize personal or social resources. Still, *coping is, or at least can be, an active process, a doing with a positive orientation that seeks to resolve problems or adapt to challenges in living.*

Tasks point to work that can be undertaken in coping with dying. Like all other work, one can always choose not to take on a particular task. One can proceed with a task, leave it for another time, or work on it for a while and then set it aside. In the face of a series of tasks, one can choose to undertake all or none of them, to attempt this one or that one. Choice in task work implies empowerment.

Tasks are not merely *needs*. They cannot be reduced to and may include more than needs, even if needs often underlie the task work that one undertakes. The term *task* identifies what a person is trying to do in his or her coping, the specific effort that he or she is making to achieve what is required or desired. Focusing on the language of "needs" often shifts the focus to what others might do to help. Assistance from others in support of an individual's coping tasks can be important and may even be necessary, but it usually ought to take second place to the person's own coping efforts.

We explore a task-based model to show that individuals who are coping with life-threatening illness and dying are actors, not just reactors. They can decide to cope with their experiences in various ways. This emphasizes the active efforts that are, at least in principle, open to the person coping with dying. Even when such efforts are not possible in practice (e.g., when an individual is unconscious), a task-based model encourages others to see things from the individual's point of view and to arrange or modify their efforts accordingly. That is critical to appreciate the complexity, richness, and variability of the human experiences of living with life-threatening illness and coping with dying.

A Task-Based Model for Coping with Dying

Corr (1992a) proposed that four primary areas of task work can be identified in coping with dying based on the four basic dimensions in the life of a human being: the physical, the psychological, the social, and the spiritual. Table 6.3 lists these four areas of task work along with some suggestions about the central types of tasks in coping with dying that might be linked to each area. Still, coping involves individualized responses to concrete situations such that our understanding of coping with dying must reflect the specific tasks undertaken by each individual who is coping.

Physical Tasks   Physical tasks are associated with bodily needs (such as hydration and nutrition) and physical distress (such as pain, nausea, or constipation). *Bodily needs* are fundamental to maintaining biological life and functioning. As Maslow (1971) argued, satisfaction of fundamental bodily needs is usually the indispensable foundation on which the work of meeting other needs can be built. In addition, *physical distress* cries out for relief both for its own sake and in order that the rest of

TABLE 6.3 Four Areas of Task Work in Coping with Dying

Areas of Task Work	Basic Types of Tasks in Coping with Dying
Physical	To satisfy *bodily needs* and to minimize *physical distress* in ways that are consistent with other values
Psychological	To maximize *psychological security, autonomy,* and *richness* in living
Social	To sustain and enhance those *interpersonal attachments* that are significant to the person concerned and to maintain selected *interactions with social groups within society or with society itself*
Spiritual	To address issues of *meaningfulness, connectedness,* and *transcendence* and, in so doing, to foster *hope*

Source: Based on Corr (1992a).

life can be appreciated and lived well. For example, individuals who are experiencing intense pain, severe nausea, or active vomiting are unlikely simultaneously to be capable of rich psychosocial or spiritual interactions.

Note, however, that people can and sometimes do choose to subordinate bodily needs and physical distress to other values. For example, martyrs have endured torture for the sake of spiritual values and some individuals have sacrificed their own lives for the sake of protecting those whom they love. More simply, individuals who are dying may choose to accept a slightly higher degree of pain or discomfort to be able to stay at home, rather than entering an institution in which constant supervision by skilled professionals might manage their distressing physical symptoms better. Others offered the support of in-home services may prefer to be in an institution, where they have less fear of being alone, falling, and lying unattended for hours.

Psychological Tasks A second area of task work in coping with dying concerns psychological security, autonomy, and richness. Like the rest of us, individuals who are coping with dying seek a sense of *security* even in a situation that in many ways may not be safe. For example, if they are dependent on others to provide needed services, they may need to be assured that those providers are reliable.

Also, most individuals who are coping with dying wish to retain their *autonomy*, insofar as that is possible. Autonomy is the ability to be in charge of one's own life (*auto* = self + *nomous* = regulating). In fact, no one has complete control over the whole of one's life; each person is limited and all of us are interdependent in a host of ways. Autonomy designates the shifting degrees and kinds of influence that individuals are able to exercise within everyday constraints. Still, for most persons, it is important to retain some degree of self-government. Some wish to make the big decisions in their lives on their own; others simply wish to designate who should make decisions on their behalf. Some turn over much of the management of their own bodies to professionals, even while they retain authority over some symbolic decisions. An outsider cannot say in advance how autonomy will or should be exercised; that would undercut the very notion of *self*-regulation (Gaylin & Jennings, 2003).

For many people, achieving a sense of security and autonomy contributes to a *psychological richness in living*. Many who are near the end of life still appreciate opportunities for a regular shave and haircut, to have their hair washed and set, to use a special bath powder, or to dress in a comfortable and attractive way. Some dying persons may find it important to their psychological well-being to have a taste of a favorite food or to continue a lifelong habit of drinking a glass of wine with meals. The issues involved here refer to *personal dignity and quality in living.*

Social Tasks   A third area of task work in coping with dying concerns two interrelated aspects of social living. Each of us is involved in attachments to other individual persons as well as in relationships to society itself and to its subordinate groups.

One set of social tasks has to do with sustaining and enhancing the *interpersonal attachments* valued by the coping person. Dying individuals often narrow the scope of their interests. They may no longer care about international politics, their former duties at work, professional sports, or a large circle of friends. Instead, they may increasingly focus on issues and attachments that involve a progressively smaller number of individuals (and perhaps a pet) now perceived as most important in their lives. In this way, they gain freedom from responsibilities now judged to be less compelling or more burdensome than before. The scope of their social interests and concerns has shifted to fit their new priorities.

There is no obvious set of interpersonal tasks on which each person *must* focus. Only the individual can decide which attachments he or she values, and these decisions may alter as one lives through the process of coping with dying. However, autonomy is restricted in a fundamental way if the significance of each attachment is not a matter of the individual's own decision making.

A consequence of this interpersonal dimension of coping with dying is that each person involved will have at least two sets of tasks: one conducted on his or her own behalf and another conducted in relation to the interests of others who are involved. For example, a dying person may face some tasks related to his or her own concerns and others related to the concerns of family members or caregivers. The person may choose to decline further efforts at cure because they are too burdensome and offer too little promise of help; in so doing, that person may be obliged to help family members or caregivers accept this decision and become reconciled to its implications for how soon death will arrive. Similarly, family members may have tasks related to their own concerns, as well as tasks related to their responsibilities to assist the dying person. For themselves, they may seek rest or relief from the burdens of caregiving; for the ill person, it may be important for them to be available to provide companionship and a sense of security. Although only the individual can decide the relative importance of these often-conflicting tasks, it is usually helpful if the dying person and his or her support persons can discuss these matters openly.

A second set of social tasks has to do with *maintaining interactions with social groups within society or with society itself*. Society seeks to protect its citizens from harm, to prohibit certain types of behavior, to ensure that property is correctly handed over to legitimate heirs, and to offer certain sorts of assistance and benefit. Social groups may have their own religious and cultural rituals, expectations, and prohibitions. Like all events in living, dying implicates people in social systems. These systems are constructed and implemented by individuals, but they represent the interests of the group. Social tasks in coping with dying include interacting with social systems as may seem desirable or necessary, responding to demands that society and its organizations continue to make (e.g., hospital bills and income taxes may still need to be paid), and drawing on social resources as needed (e.g., to obtain hospital equipment, transportation, or "Meals on Wheels" services from charitable organizations).

Spiritual Tasks   The spiritual area of task work in coping with dying is more difficult to describe than the other three areas, for several reasons. First, for many, there is little agreement about just what is meant by "spiritual" (Klass, 2006; Stanworth, 2003), but most would agree that "spiritual" concerns are not merely limited to or identified with "religious" concerns. Even individuals without religious connections can have spiritual tasks to work on; others need to pay attention to and respect such spiritual tasks.

Second, modern societies are increasingly made up of many subcultures, and this is true spiritually, too. Roman Catholics and Muslims, Baptists and Hindus, Buddhists and Unitarians, Dakota and Zuni Native Americans, atheists and agnostics— these and many others (and variations on all of these) may be found among those whose spiritual tasks we are trying to understand. Although we cannot be expected to know and to understand all of these traditions and positions on spiritual issues ahead of time, we can be sensitive to and respect them as part of an individual's coping with dying.

One helpful way to approach the spiritual concerns of dying persons (and those around them) is to identify common themes running through this area of task work (Doka, 1993b; HealthCare Chaplaincy Network, 2016; Lattanzi-Licht, 2007). Spiritual issues typically involve one or more of the following concerns, which are thus significant components of spiritual task work in coping with dying:

Praying or meditating with someone who is coping with dying can be spiritually valuable.

Courtesy Suncoast Hospice

Meaningfulness: People who are coping with dying may seek to identify, recognize, or formulate meaning for their lives, for death, for suffering, and for being human. Several types of questions may be pressing in these circumstances: Is my life meaning-full (and often this means worth-full)? If I must die, what does that mean for the value of my having lived? Why is there so much suffering associated with my dying or with my loved one's dying? What does it mean to be human (and when, if ever, does one stop being human, even if life is still present in some form)? These questions are thrusts toward wholeness and integration, and away from fragmentation (Nabe, 1987).

Connectedness: Illness, and especially life-threatening illness, threatens to break the connections that lend coherence to one's life. For example, one can feel disconnected from one's body (why won't it do what I want it to do?), from other persons (why can't they understand how much pain I am in?), and from whatever one holds the transcendent to be (where is God in all this?). It is often important for a person in this situation to reestablish broken connections or to maintain and deepen existing connections. There are psychological and social components to this work, but the spiritual aspect goes deeper or underlies these other dimensions because (again) it is tied to the search for meaning and integrity.

Transcendence: People working on spiritual tasks are often looking toward a transcendent level or source of meaning and connection. "Transcendence" refers to that which goes beyond (though it may also be found in) the ordinary, and especially to that which is of ultimate, surpassing worth. This concern is often tied to issues of **hope** (Groopman, 2004). Religious people may work to enrich and deepen their connections with God or some basic reality (the Atman or the Tao) and may seek to realize some religious hope (to be absolved of sin, or to overcome metaphysical ignorance, or to achieve eternal bliss). Nonreligious people may also focus on transcendent hopes—for example, to find their place in a reality that is more than just the individual's moment in the life of the universe, to become one with the elements, to continue to contribute to the life of the society through one's creations, students, and descendants even after one has died.

The focus of hope may change over time, and how one acts on one's hopes depends on the individual and his or her culture, history, environment, and condition. One person may be focused primarily on personal aspirations (will I realize nirvana, will I meet God face to face?), whereas another person may be more concerned about the welfare of the group (will my descendants continue to contribute to the ongoing life of the group?).

Spiritual task work is as varied and multiform as is task work in the other three areas. And spiritual tasks are irreducibly individual; one Protestant Christian's spiritual tasks are not necessarily (indeed, are seldom) the same as another Protestant Christian's spiritual tasks. Recognizing this is critical both for properly understanding spiritual task work and for helping persons cope with their spiritual tasks.

An Observation on This Task-Based Model This outline of four areas of task work in coping with dying describes areas of potential task work. These are general categories of tasks for everyone who is coping with dying (not just the dying person). Tasks may or may not be undertaken; some may be more or less necessary or desirable. Individuals need not take up any specific task or set of tasks. On the contrary, a task-based model is intended precisely to foster empowerment and participation in coping with dying. This means each individual person will and should be allowed to decide which tasks and sets of tasks are important *to that person*. As a result, in any given situation, one person's tasks might very well be in disagreement or conflict with another person's tasks, thereby creating a challenge to either or both of them to find some way to work through that conflict. Moreover, although individual tasks of this sort may be completed, it is never possible to finish all of the task work that confronts an individual. For the dying person, work with tasks ends with death; for those who live on, these and other tasks may arise in coping with bereavement. These areas of task work may also serve as guidelines for helping those who are coping with dying, as we will see in Chapter 7. When they help identify regrets in the life one has lived, they can help to reshape the last portions of one's life and the lives of others who learn from them (see Focus On 6.2).

LIVING WITH LIFE-THREATENING ILLNESS

Doka (1993a, 2009) situated coping with dying in a larger context of living with life-threatening illness. He thereby drew attention not only to coping at the very end of life, but also to unique stressors that typically arise: prior to a diagnosis; during what is often a relatively lengthy period of living with a chronic life-threatening illness; and even when one does not die but must still face challenges in recovering from the illness. In all of this, Doka observed that human life is always temporal and sequential. There are befores, nows, and laters in all of our experiences. Accordingly, a good model of coping with dying ought to throw light on challenges that arise from

---

FOCUS ON 6.2

The Top Five Regrets of the Dying

As a result of working in palliative care for many years, Bronnie Ware wrote a blog, later expanded into a book, in which she reported what she had learned from dying persons about the principal regrets they had or anything they would do differently. Here are five most common things these persons taught her:

1. *I wish I'd had the courage to live a life true to myself, not the life others expected of me.*

2. *I wish I didn't work so hard.*

3. *I wish I'd had the courage to express my feelings.*

4. *I wish I had stayed in touch with my friends.*

5. *I wish that I had let myself be happier.*

If, as we have argued throughout this book, the study of death and dying can teach us valuable lessons about life and living, perhaps attention to these regrets can help us live richer and more meaningful lives.

Source: Based on Ware (2012).

what has already happened in living with a life-threatening illness, what is in the process of taking place, and what is yet to come. Doka addressed this by describing how coping tasks might differ across **five phases in living with a life-threatening illness:**

■ The *prediagnostic phase* is associated with initial indicators of illness or disease: will I ignore these indicators (by hoping that things will get better and "it" will go away on its own), try to minimize my responses to their presence, decide to investigate their significance (and, if so, how)? Will I ask family members or friends to tell me what to do, turn to a traditional healer, seek out medical or other professional sources of advice for investigation or diagnosis of the potential problem? All of this involves tasks of recognizing possible danger or risk, trying to manage anxiety or uncertainty, and developing and following through on a health-seeking strategy.

■ The *acute phase* of a life-threatening illness is that period in which one might try to understand the disease, maximize health and lifestyle, foster coping strengths and limit weaknesses, develop strategies to deal with issues created by the disease, arrange for cure-oriented interventions, explore the effects of the diagnosis on one's sense of self and others, ventilate feelings and fears, and/or incorporate the reality of the diagnosis into one's sense of past and future.

■ The *chronic phase* of living with a life-threatening illness involves tasks like managing symptoms and side effects, carrying out health regimens, preventing and managing health crises, managing stress and examining coping, maximizing social support and minimizing isolation, normalizing life in the face of disease, dealing with financial concerns, preserving one's self-concept, redefining relationships with others throughout the course of the disease, continuing to ventilate feelings and fears, and finding meaning in suffering, chronicity, uncertainty, and decline.

■ If death does not occur, the *recovery phase* still does not free the person from a need to cope. As Doka (1993a, p. 116) noted, task work is ongoing even here because "recovery does not mean that one simply returns to the life led before. Any encounter with a crisis changes us. We are no longer the people we once were." Tasks in the recovery phase include dealing with the aftereffects of illness and anxieties about recurrence, reconstructing or reformulating one's lifestyle, and redefining relationships with caregivers (think of Matt Ryan after the successful treatment of his prostate cancer in the vignette near the beginning of this chapter).

■ The *terminal phase* is the time in which an individual is faced with a new set of tasks, such as coping with ongoing challenges arising from the disease, its side effects, and treatments; dealing with caregivers and (perhaps) deciding to discontinue cure-oriented interventions or turning to interventions designed to minimize discomforting symptoms; preparing for death and saying good-bye; preserving self-concept and appropriate social relationships; and finding meaning in life and death (this was Jo Ryan's situation after the recurrence of her cancer in the vignette near the beginning of this chapter).

Doka's exploration of changing phases and tasks is sensitive to the many human—physical, psychological, social, and spiritual—aspects of coping with life-threatening illness. It also highlights three critical factors that influence all coping activities: (1) the wide variety of social and psychological variables (cultural, social, and personal) that enter into processes of coping with life-threatening illness and dying; (2) the developmental context within which the individual confronts this challenge (which we explore in Part Five); and (3) the nature of the disease, its trajectory and effects, and its treatment.

HOW DO THESE THEORIES ABOUT COPING WITH DYING HELP US?

Kastenbaum and Thuell (1995, p. 176) observed that "strictly speaking, there are no scientific theories of dying, if by 'theory' we mean a coherent set of explicit propositions that have predictive power and are subject to empirical verification. There are distinctive theoretical approaches, however, each of which emphasizes a particular range of experience and behavior." The three approaches that Kastenbaum and Thuell examined (and that have been explored elsewhere; see Corr, Doka, & Kastenbaum, 1999) are Glaser and Strauss's account of dying trajectories and awareness contexts, the stage-based schema advanced by Kübler-Ross, and the task-based model proposed by Corr.

Nevertheless, we should not assume that if we do not currently have everything we might want from a theoretical standpoint we do not have anything at all. For that, we should keep in mind these remarks from Carl Jung (1954, p. 7): "Theories in psychology are the very devil. It is true that we need certain points of view for their orienting and heuristic value; but they should always be regarded as mere auxiliary concepts that can be laid aside at any time." These comments have two related aspects: (1) theories should never stand as barriers that come between us and those we are trying to understand or help, but at the same time (2) we depend upon theories to guide us and point us in good directions, as well as to help us listen carefully and draw out of individuals and their situations important things that we need to learn. Thus, while each of the theoretical frameworks described in this chapter has limits, they also each have strengths of their own and they each contribute in their own distinctive ways to our understandings of coping with dying. In so doing, these theories represent the major contributions to this field that are currently available, and they define the present state of our knowledge about coping with dying.

Summary

In this chapter, we explored coping with dying by describing coping processes in ways that respect their many elements and the many individuals involved in such coping. Coping with dying is a part of coping with living, even though dying presents special issues and challenges. We considered dying trajectories and awareness contexts, stage-based and task-based models for explaining coping with dying, and five phases in living with a life-threatening illness. Also, we insisted that any adequate account of coping with dying must refer to the whole human being, to each individual human being, and to all who are involved.

Glossary

Awareness contexts: social interactions among those who are coping with dying arising from the types of communication about the facts of the situation

Coping: changing efforts made to manage perceived stressors

Dying trajectories: patterns of dying or the ways in which dying plays out, typically distinguished by *duration* (the time between the onset of dying and the arrival of death) and *shape* (the course of the dying, its predictability, and whether death is expected or unexpected)

Five phases in living with a life-threatening illness: according to Doka, these are the prediagnostic, acute, chronic, recovery, and terminal phases

Hope: expectations that one looks forward to based on faith and trust; here, related to coping with dying

Stage-based model of coping with dying: Kübler-Ross named five "stages" (denial, anger, bargaining, depression, and acceptance) in how persons coping react to and attempt to manage their stressors

Task-based model of coping with dying: Corr identified four areas of task work in coping with dying: physical, psychological, social, and spiritual

Questions for Review and Discussion

1. Think about some moment in your life when you were quite ill. What was most stressful for you at that time? If you felt fear, what were the sources of your greatest fears? What did you want other people to do for or with you at that time? Did you engage in online searching to learn more about your illness and how you could best cope with it? Now try to imagine yourself in a similar situation, only adding that the illness is a life-threatening one. What would be similar or different in these two situations?

2. One central notion in this chapter is the concept of coping. In what ways in the past have you coped with stressful situations? Did you turn to friends, books, social media, or the Internet for help? Now choose someone you know well and reflect on how he or she copes with stress. What strengths and limitations do you note in your own ways of coping and in this other person's methods of coping?

3. In our analysis of dying trajectories, awareness contexts, a stage-based model, and a task-based model, which seemed to you to be most (or least) innovative, interesting, and helpful?

4. If you think about the coping processes of dying persons as involving tasks, how might this model affect your understanding of a dying person? How might it affect your interactions with such persons?

5. Have you ever turned to social media or the Internet to learn more about coping with dying and the other subjects in this chapter? Did it help you? Why or why not?

Suggested Readings

Researchers, scholars, and clinicians have written about various aspects of coping with dying in:

Ahronheim, J., & Weber, D. (1992). *Final Passages: Positive Choices for the Dying and Their Loved Ones*

Byock, I. (2004). *The Four Things That Matter Most: A Book about Living*

Cheatham, C. (2014). *Hospice Whispers: Stories of Life*

Doka, K. J. (1993a). *Living with Life-Threatening Illness: A Guide for Patients, Families, and Caregivers*

Doka, K. J., & Tucci, A. S. (Eds.). (2011). *Beyond Kübler-Ross: New Perspectives on Dying, Death, and Grief*

Egan, K. (2016). *On Living*

Hawkins, B. (2011). *Transitions: A Nurse's Education about Life & Death* (2nd ed.)

Kaplan, K. B. (2014). *Encountering the Edge: What People Told Me before They Died*

Kellehear, A. (2014). *The Inner Life of the Dying Person*

Kessler, D. (2007). *The Needs of the Dying: A Guide for Bringing Hope, Comfort, and Love to Life's Final Chapter*

Kübler-Ross, E. (1969). *On Death and Dying*

Linder, E. (2013). *Hospice Voices: Lessons for Living at the End of Life*

Lynn, J., Harrold, J., & Schuster, J. L. (2011). *Handbook for Mortals: Guidance for People Facing Serious Illness* (2nd ed.)

Morhaim, D. (2011). *The Better End: Surviving (and Dying) on Your Own Terms in Today's Modern Medical World*

Staton, J., Shuy, R., & Byock, I. (2001). *A Few Months to Live: Different Paths to Life's End*

Tobin, D. (1999). *Peaceful Dying: The Step-by-Step Guide to Preserving Your Dignity, Your Choice, and Your Inner Peace at the End of Life*

Ware, B. (2012). *The Top Five Regrets of the Dying: A Life Transformed by the Dearly Departing*

Wehr, J. (2015). *Peaceful Passages: A Hospice Nurse's Stories of Dying Well*

Wyatt, K. M. (2011). *What Really Matters: 7 Lessons for Living from the Stories of the Dying*

Selected Web Resources

Some useful search terms include: AWARENESS CONTEXTS; COPING; DYING TRAJECTORIES; HOPE; STAGES IN DYING; TASKS IN COPING WITH DYING.

You can also visit the following *organizational and other Internet sites:*

American Psychological Association

Cleveland Clinic, Center for Continuing Education

ehospice

Harvard Health

Healthfinder.gov

Healthline

I Can Cope Online

Mayo Clinic

MedlinePlus

WebMD

Claudio Rossol/Shutterstock.com

Coping with Dying: How Individuals Can Help

Objectives of this **Chapter**

▷ To show that helping persons who are coping with dying requires both the specialized expertise of professionals AND the human presence of family members, friends, and volunteers

▷ To explore four primary dimensions of care: physical, psychological, social, and spiritual

▷ To make clear how coping tasks, when properly understood, can become guidelines for helpers

▷ To consider the importance of effective communication

▷ To examine stress, compassion fatigue, and burnout among helpers and to explain how helpers can and should take care of themselves

▷ To focus, once again, on the centrality of hope

INDIVIDUALS WHO HELPED ONE FAMILY COPE WITH LIFE-THREATENING ILLNESS AND DYING

Just as Josephina Ryan helped her husband Matt when he had prostate cancer, Matt tried to be there for Jo when she experienced a new bout with the cancer that would eventually take her life. But Matt admitted right away that he just didn't know how to be very helpful. He struggled to keep up with practical matters like putting food on the table, cleaning the house, and doing laundry, but he wasn't good at such chores, and his spirits had suffered a hard blow. Jo knew that Matt meant well and she tried to pitch in whenever she could, but her energy level was declining. It was hard to watch Matt wander around the house aimlessly, and she worried about what would happen to him after she was gone.

The Ryans' children tried to help as much as they could. Most of the burden fell on the oldest son, Tom, and his wife, since they lived in town. They helped with some household chores and took Matt to shop and do other errands. Matt was happy to get out of the house and to see Tom's children, but he always worried about Jo back home. In fact, at first Jo wasn't very good at accepting help from Tom and his wife or from the Ryans' other children when they would fly into town for short visits. She had always been the capable, competent mother doing for others. Her cultural background and personality didn't make it easy for her to let others take over that role, and the children complained that she was pushing them away just when they knew she must need help most.

Even if Jo had been more open to accepting help, many friends and neighbors to whom they might have turned also didn't really know how to help in useful ways. Some offered unhelpful advice or empty clichés, while others just withdrew in confusion. The Ryans were fortunate, however, in their long-standing friendship with Sharon and Bill Applegate. Both Applegates were retired: Sharon from her work as a nurse's aide and Bill as assistant principal at Matt's high school. Sharon pitched in to help Jo with basic, practical care. She knew helping to wash and bathe people made them feel better, while also preventing bedsores and other complications associated with confinement in bed. Before Jo became bed-bound, Sharon showed Matt and Tom how to help her get around to exercise stiff muscles and how to transfer her to a wheelchair. Later, she offered advice on moving and positioning Jo in bed. Sharon also devised little jobs for the grandchildren and suggested activities they could undertake as "junior helpers."

Bill helped just by spending time with Matt and taking over some practical chores like cutting the lawn that now overwhelmed Matt. Bill and Matt didn't actually talk very much, especially about Jo, but Matt seemed to appreciate Bill's presence, and Bill made sure to let Matt know they could discuss whatever he wanted to talk about. This whole illness thing and the prospect of Jo's dying made Matt feel very isolated and overwhelmed. Bill's presence helped make things seem a bit less awful. Sometimes Bill could tell Sharon or others in the family what was on Matt's mind and suggest things they could also do to help.

Jo's death was very sad for Matt, the whole Ryan family, and the Applegates. But Sharon and Bill were gratified at the funeral when Matt told them that Jo's last wish had been to be at home as long as possible before her death. He knew that wouldn't have been possible without their help, and he wanted them to know how much he appreciated their support in helping him do everything that he could do for his wife and his family. "You made a very bad time just a little bit better," he said, "I'll always be grateful."

CARING FOR PERSONS WHO ARE COPING WITH DYING: HUMAN AND PROFESSIONAL TASKS

Caring for persons who are coping with dying is not an activity to be carried out only by people who are specially trained to do so (Goldman, 2002; Golubow, 2001; Wolfelt & Yoder, 2005). Certainly, dying persons and others who are coping with dying are people with special needs, some of which can best or perhaps only be met by individuals with special expertise. For example, a dying person may need a physician's prescription for narcotic analgesics or a sacramental act by a member of the ordained clergy. However, much of the required care is not related to special needs; it involves fundamental concerns common to all living human beings, even though they are concerns that may take on a special intensity under the pressures of coping with dying.

For example, dying persons need to eat, they need to exercise their bodies, minds, and spirits, and they need above all to be *cared about, not just cared for*. For most of the 24 hours in each day, the care that dying persons need is not specialized care. This care can be provided by any of us. A hand held, a grief or joy shared, and a question listened to and responded to: these are human moments of caring that can be offered by anyone who is willing and able to do so. In short, "the secret of the care of patients is still caring" (Ingles, 1974, p. 763; see also Peabody, 1927).

Frank (2002, pp. 45–49) offered the following comment:

> The common diagnostic categories into which medicine places its patients are relevant to disease, not to illness. They are useful for treatment, but they only get in the way of care. … Caring has nothing to do with categories; it shows the person that her life is valued because it recognizes what makes her experience particular. One person has no right to categorize another, but we do have the privilege of coming to understand how each of us is unique. … Terms like pain or loss have no reality until they are filled in with an ill person's own experience. Witnessing the particulars of that experience, and recognizing all its differences, is care.

Dame Cicely Saunders, initiator of the modern hospice movement, is reported (Shephard, 1977) to have said that dying persons ask three things of those who care for them: (1) "*Help me*" (minimize my distress); (2) "*Listen to me*" (let me direct things or at least be heard); and (3) "*Don't leave me*" (stay with me; give me your presence).

It is important to recognize the many ways in which we can help those who are coping with dying. Sometimes, what helpers can do is simple and obvious, not dramatic and world-shaking (see Personal Insights 7.1). But even when we cannot do something specific to help, all of us—professionals and nonprofessionals alike—can offer an **empathetic presence** by actively listening to and staying with dying persons and their significant others. This is the lesson that Sharon and Bill Applegate learned as they helped Jo and Matt Ryan.

To provide adequate care for the dying, we must address the many fears, anxieties, desires, and tasks of dying persons. The same applies to family members and friends of the dying person—those significant others who are also coping with dying. We may be more or less successful in meeting these responsibilities because of pressures of limited time, energy, information, or resources. But if we are serious about providing good care, we ought not to fail to address these needs because of lack of understanding or attention to what is needed by those who are coping with dying. In this chapter, we provide information about and draw attention to ways we can help those who are coping with dying.

PERSONAL INSIGHTS 7.1

The Tale of the Stranded Starfish

As a man walked a desolate beach one cold, gray morning, he began to see another figure, far in the distance. Slowly the two approached each other, and he could make out a local native who kept leaning down, picking something up, and throwing it out into the water. Time and again he hurled things into the ocean. As the distance between them continued to narrow, the man could see that the native was picking up starfish that had been washed upon the beach and, one at a time, was throwing them back into the water. Puzzled, the man approached the native and asked what he was doing.

"I'm throwing these starfish back into the ocean. You see, it's low tide right now and all of these starfish have been washed up onto the shore. If I don't throw them back into the sea, they'll die up here from lack of oxygen."

"But there must be thousands of starfish on this beach," the man replied. "You can't possibly get to all of them. There are just too many. And this same thing is probably happening on hundreds of beaches all up and down this coast. Can't you see that you can't possibly make a difference?"

The local native smiled, bent down, and picked up another starfish, and as he threw it back into the sea he replied, "Made a difference to that one!"

Source: Author unknown.

DIMENSIONS OF CARE

There are *four primary dimensions of care* for those who are coping with dying: physical, psychological, social, and spiritual (Saunders, 1967). Here, we consider each of these in turn with special attention to their application to dying persons. These dimensions are also relevant to others coping with dying: family members and friends of the dying person as well as professional and volunteer helpers/caregivers.

Physical Dimensions

For many dying persons, one of the most pressing needs has to do with **physical dimensions**, that is, the control of *physical pain or distress*. When pain is present, it must be properly studied and carefully understood (Kessler, 2007; Melzack & Wall, 1991; Wall, 2002; Wall & Melzack, 1994). In addition, there is a well-established distinction between two basic types of pain: acute pain and chronic pain (Portenoy & Payne, 1992).

Acute pain is a form of pain that is essential to human life. Those who do not feel acute pain—for example, when they touch a hot stove—are in danger of serious harm. When individuals are ill, physicians often obtain the information they need to make an accurate diagnosis by eliciting careful, specific descriptions of pain or distress. For instance, acute pain associated with kidney stones guides both diagnosis and treatment. Thus, acute pain is not always or completely undesirable. In fact, it may help to enhance both the quality and the quantity of our lives. Of course, dying persons may experience acute pain, too. They may develop symptoms—including physical pain—that may or may not be directly related to the illness that threatens their lives. Thus, Saunders reminded caregivers that a toothache hurts just as much when you are dying.

Chronic pain, however, does not serve any of these constructive functions. Chronic pain does not assist in diagnosis because the diagnosis has already been made. Nor does chronic pain protect the person from dangers in the environment. It is just there, always there. Sharp or dull, constant or intermittent, chronic pain forms the backdrop of whatever the person is doing at the moment. When it is intense, it can become the whole focus of attention of those experiencing such pain (LeShan, 1964).

In life-threatening illness, chronic pain is often associated with a disease that will lead to death. Proper care of the dying person must involve efforts to manage or at least to diminish distress arising from chronic pain—whatever its origin. It may not always be possible to eradicate chronic pain totally, but even to reduce such pain from agony to ache is a notable achievement. Care of the dying has shown that chronic pain can be controlled or at least greatly diminished in most cases (Cherny, Fallon, Kaasa, Portenoy, & Currow, 2015; Institute of Medicine, 2011; McCartney, 2014; Twycross & Wilcock, 2002, 2008). Needless pain in end-of-life care is a tragedy when good research has taught so much about the nature of pain and the role of analgesics and other therapeutic modalities in its management (Melzack, 1990). Appropriate medications and supportive therapy can see to it that chronic pain need not so fill the consciousness of dying persons that they can pay attention to nothing else but their pain.

The challenge for therapeutic interventions is to select just the right medication(s) to meet the need(s) of the individual, to achieve just the right balance of responses (without under- or overmedication), and to employ an appropriate route of administration. The philosophy of pain management in end-of-life care has often emphasized administration of medications via oral routes (in liquid, tablet, or capsule form) to avoid the pain of injections. However, both injections and suppositories have been recognized as appropriate in certain cases (for instance, when rapid results achievable by injections are required or when individuals are nauseated and cannot swallow). These routes have been supplemented by slow-release analgesic tablets, long-term continuous infusion devices (similar to those used for insulin by some diabetics), transdermal patches and specially formulated creams, and patient-controlled analgesia (whereby individuals have some measure of control and autonomy in administering their own medications, often resulting in less overall medication than might otherwise have been employed).

Drug therapy is not the *only* method of controlling chronic pain. As research leads to a better understanding of the nature of disease, it is evident that most pain has a psychological component. Thus, McCaffery and Beebe (1989, p. 7) wrote, "Pain is whatever the experiencing person says it is, existing whenever the experiencing person says it does." That is, *pain is distress as an individual perceives it.* Pain management may seek to alter the threshold or the nature of that perception, just as it may block the pathways or the effects of a noxious stimulant. Biofeedback, guided imagery, meditation, therapeutic touch, and techniques of self-hypnosis may also assist persons to control their pain or to manage its effects. Also, constructive psychological support and physical therapy may encourage individuals to relax and keep muscles and joints active, thereby lessening the physical pain that occurs when a person remains immobile. These therapies can work alongside medications and other interventions.

When drug therapies are used, long-standing research has demonstrated that many dying persons, including long-term patients with far-advanced cancer, can tolerate large doses of strong narcotics without becoming "doped up" or "knocked out" (Twycross, 1979b, 1982). The goal is not total anesthesia (unconsciousness), but rather analgesia (an insensibility to pain). This goal can be achieved in most cases by choosing the correct medication(s) for the situation and by carefully titrating or balancing dosages against the nature and level of pain (Quill et al., 2014; Twycross & Lack, 1997). (In extreme cases, medications can also be used to achieve what has been called "palliative sedation" or "terminal sedation," but these instances are rare, they require very careful assessment, they involve critical ethical decision making as a therapy of last resort, and they are not uncontroversial [National Ethics Committee, Veterans Health Administration, 2007; Quill, Lo, & Brock, 1997].)

If the right drug is used and the dose is calibrated to the precise level needed to control pain and *no further*, then the pain is well managed. The right drug is crucial (Twycross & Wilcock, 2008). Pain may arise from a variety of sources—for example, direct damage to tissue, inflammation, or pressure. Each source of pain and each route of transmission may require its own appropriate medication. Also, each drug must be selected in terms of the needs of an individual patient, its method of administration, the time intervals at which it will be given, and potential problems with side effects or interactions with other drugs the person may be taking. For example, some drugs like the narcotic Demerol are quick-acting and potent, which makes them useful for dealing with episodes of acute pain. However, such a drug may not retain its efficacy long enough to suit someone with chronic pain. If so, a dying person for whom it is prescribed may be in pain again in two or three hours, well before the next dose is administered. This is *not* effective pain control. Morphine and some other strong narcotics have proven their effectiveness in end-of-life care because their effects last long enough to manage chronic pain until the next dose.

Well-established research (e.g., Twycross, 1976) has shown that **addiction** *does not occur*, even when strong narcotics are prescribed in high doses for dying persons. This should now be well known. The psychological "high" and subsequent cravings for steadily escalating doses that characterize addiction are not found. This may have to do with ways in which medications are administered and absorbed in the body: they can be given by mouth in single doses or as a timed-release medication. If necessary, intravenous injections or infusions can be used.

Dying persons may become *physically dependent* on strong narcotics, but that also occurs in other situations—for example, in the use of steroids. Here, **dependence** means only that one cannot withdraw the drug abruptly or while it is still required without harmful side effects. Such physical dependence without underlying emotional disorder is easily terminated and has long been recognized not to constitute an additional problem (Anonymous, 1963). Otherwise, it is as if the body uses the drug to deal with the pain it is experiencing, and it signals when the drug or dose is not correct. Too small or too weak a dose allows pain to return; too large or too powerful a dose induces drowsiness.

Once individuals learn that their pain really can and will be well managed, the dose provided can often be reduced because they no longer are fearful and tense in the face of *expected* pain (Twycross, 1994). Effective drug therapeutics provide a sense of security that reduces anxiety. Addressing such psychosocial components of pain can lower the threshold of analgesia and may make it easier to manage discomfort.

Relaxation may actually allow individuals to tolerate more pain and accept a lower drug dose.

Dying persons may also experience other physical symptoms that can be just as distressing as or even more distressing than physical pain (Saunders & Sykes, 1993). These symptoms include constipation (a common side effect of narcotics), diarrhea, nausea, and vomiting. Sometimes there is weakness or reduction in available energy, loss of appetite, or shortness of breath. Similarly, loss of hair, dark circles around the eyes, and changes in skin color may also be matters of concern to those who place high value on self-image and how they look to others. Also, if someone lies in bed for long periods, skin ulcers or pressure sores can become a potential source of added discomfort and risk for infection. Reducing this source of distress has always been a concern of effective care for the dying (Kemp, 1999).

Dehydration illustrates another issue frequently encountered in dying persons (Zerwekh, 1983; see also Gallagher-Allred & Amenta, 1993). An intravenous infusion might be used, but that method may add another source of pain to the burdens of ill persons near end of life. Also, it may overload with fluid a body that is weak and whose organ systems may no longer be functioning effectively. Often, small sips of juice or other fluids, ice chips, or flavored mouth swabs may be enough to maintain quality of life. This shows that effective care for dying persons must address all of their distressing physical symptoms and must do so in ways suited to their current situation. Such care may require intervention on the part of physicians, nurses, and other professional caregivers, but family caregivers and significant others can also play important roles in these situations, especially when they are shown how to be most helpful to the ill person and their own physical needs (e.g., exhaustion) are met.

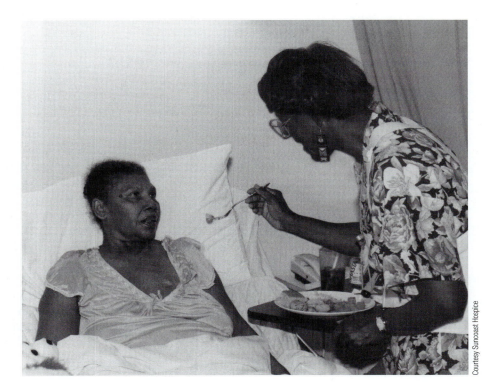

Enjoying a meal has both physical and psychological benefits.

Courtesy Suncoast Hospice

Psychological Dimensions

Another set of concerns revolves around **psychological dimensions** and tasks in coping with dying. Care providers may be even more uncomfortable working with these issues than with those having to do with physical dimensions in dying persons. It is difficult to be with someone in physical pain, but we may be even more uneasy in the face of so-called negative feelings. However, someone who is dying is likely to express these sorts of feelings at one time or another. Such a person may experience anger, sadness, anxiety, and fear. In the face of such feelings, people often wonder what is the right thing to say or to do.

Frequently, there is no specific or universal right thing to say or to do, but that does not mean there is *nothing* to say or to do. In fact, one can say and do many things to be helpful. Often, the most helpful thing is simply to *be present and listen*, making sure that whatever one does say is true, reliable, supportive, and caring (Zerwekh, 1994). To hunt for some way to make all fear, anger, or sadness disappear is to begin a hopeless search. These feelings are real, and they must be lived through.

A student once told us that she believed someone informed of a prognosis of impending death would become sad, an emotion she thought of as undesirable. She said she would seek any means to prevent it from occurring, or, if it did occur, to end it. This is unrealistic. If someone is given unhappy news—of any sort—sadness is a likely and *appropriate* response. Furthermore, some people—including many professional caregivers—too quickly identify sadness with depression. But to realize that one is going to die is to be faced with a loss (perhaps many losses)—and in the face of loss, human beings grieve.

Anger is another feeling that may be particularly discomforting. Anger is often viewed as a destructive emotion rather than an understandable reaction when one's needs are frustrated or one is hurt, a reaction that can be expressed constructively or destructively. Those who are coping with dying often feel lots of anger. They may be angry because of the losses they are experiencing and because others—apparently for no good reason—are enjoying happy, healthy, and satisfying lives. Further, because of physical or other restrictions, a dying person's anger may be limited in the ways in which it can be expressed; strong feelings may be projected onto others—whatever or whoever is most readily available, whether or not that is appropriate.

This sort of anger needs to be identified, acknowledged, and expressed. Feelings like this cannot simply be made to go away. Feelings are real; one cannot just stop feeling what one is feeling. Nor is it reasonable to expect that strong feelings should always be suppressed. For example, anger and an outpouring of adrenaline go together; the anger must be worked off, much like the physical rush of adrenaline. When a helper is the object of growls, complaints, or screaming, it may not be very consoling to realize there is usually nothing personal in such expressions of anger and other strong feelings—but that is often the case.

In such situations, the lesson to learn is *to be comfortable with one's own discomfort*. That is, our task as helpers is not to discover the magical "right" thing to say to make dying persons no longer have such feelings. Letting them talk about why they feel as they do and giving them "permission" to do so through bodily or verbal cues—*really listening to them*—may be the most helpful thing one can do (Nichols, 1995).

In addition, many dying persons have reported that it is *not* helpful for someone to say to them "I know how you feel." For one thing, this is almost certainly not true. Most individuals have not really been in the situation of the other person to whom such a remark is made, and no one can really experience the feelings of another individual. Also, such a remark is often perceived (rightly or wrongly) as an attempt to minimize or trivialize the feelings of the person to whom it is addressed.

How can people who are experiencing "negative" feelings be helped? If this question means how can someone make them stop having those feelings, the question may say more about our discomfort with their feelings and our need to end that discomfort than it does about the needs of those who are coping with dying. Keep in mind two things. First, *outsiders cannot make anyone feel different or better.* Second, *that may often be an inappropriate goal.* Dying people must live with and through their feelings, just as they must live with and through all of the rest of their life experiences. They can be helped to do that by assistance in identifying their feelings, by acknowledgment of their feelings as appropriate to their particular situations (if that is, in fact, the case), and by permission for them to vent or share their feelings.

There are no magic formulas here, no cookbooks for the right behaviors or statements. Nevertheless, what does seem to help people who are coping with dying is for someone to listen to them and to take seriously what they are feeling. Helpers can *be present* to such persons (physically, emotionally, existentially) and can *listen actively* to what they say (see Focus On 7.1). If helpers turn off their own internal monologues, if they stop hunting around for the "right" response, and if they just *listen empathetically*, that can help. As Nouwen (1986, pp. 34–35) explained:

> [W]hen we honestly ask ourselves which persons in our lives mean the most to us, we often find that it is those who, instead of giving much advice, solutions, or cures, have chosen rather to share our pain and touch our wounds with a gentle and tender hand. The friend who can be silent with us in a moment of despair or confusion, who can stay with us in an hour of grief and bereavement, who can tolerate not-knowing, not-curing, not-healing and face with us the reality of our powerlessness, that is the friend who cares.

Similarly, one hospice chaplain reported that in his work he learned that "the biggest problem with those who are seriously ill, especially with a terminal condition, is isolation and loneliness. People avoid contact because they don't know what to say due to feelings of inadequacy and helplessness. If they only realized that they possess the greatest gift that the people need, and that is their presence" (Fitts, 2015).

In offering their presence, helpers can engage in a process of reminiscence with the persons they seek to serve. Reminiscence affirms that he or she was and is a vital person, that his or her life had and has meaning, and that he or she leaves legacies. Life review activities such as making audiotapes or videotapes or simply sharing one's thoughts in conversation or writing help because they say to the dying person, loudly and clearly, "You matter; you and your feelings are real and important to me" (Pelaez & Rothman, 1994). If family helpers or visitors can do so honestly, it is important to share how that person who is now dying helped or influenced each of them. Also, we can always speak about common interests such as shared activities, politics, or sports. Still, it is important to be sensitive about a dying person's responses because it is not uncommon for such persons to disengage from activities and interests once held. It also helps to hear what the dying person needs, rather than what others think the person needs. **Compassion** or *empathy*, which reaches out to understand and feel

FOCUS ON 7.1

Active Listening Techniques

Statement	Purpose	To do this…	Examples
Encouraging	■ To convey interest. ■ To encourage the other person to express themselves however they need to. ■ To share more.	■ Don't agree or disagree. No opinions. ■ Use neutral words. ■ Use varying voice intonations. ■ Show genuine interest.	■ Help me understand what you mean. ■ Can you please tell me more about…? ■ Uh-huh… ■ Yes… ■ I see…
Clarifying	■ To help clarify what is being said. ■ To get more information. ■ To help the speaker see other points of view.	■ Ask open ended questions. ■ Take a guess at the speaker's meaning and ask if you understood them correctly.	■ What do you think of that? ■ How do you feel now? ■ When did this happen? ■ So you mean that… ■ If I've got this straight, you feel/mean… ■ What I'm hearing you say is…
Restating (…what you've heard as-is without interpretation)	■ To show you are listening and understanding what is being said. ■ To review progress. ■ To pull together important ideas and facts.	■ Restate basic ideas and facts. ■ Repeat 2 or 3 words of what you are hearing. ■ Raise the pitch of your voice at the end of your restatement (like a question) so that the speaker can correct your guess if needed.	■ So you would like your parents to trust you more, is that right? ■ I'm hearing you say that you are not prepared for this next procedure? ■ You're not finding me being very helpful right now? ■ You'd like to be alone?
Reflecting (…back feelings and emotions)	■ To show that you understand how the person feels. ■ To help the person evaluate his/her own feelings after hearing them expressed by someone else.	■ Take a guess about how the speaker feels. ■ Reflect feelings, emotions or body sensations.	■ You seem very upset. ■ You sound very low today. ■ I'm guessing that made you very angry. ■ How shocking. ■ How frustrating. ■ How comforting. ■ What a surprise!
Validating (What meaning does this have for the person?)	■ To acknowledge the worthiness of the person and their experiences. ■ To link the person's feelings to what matters to them and what needs were met or unmet for them. ■ To hear and understand how important/unimportant something is for a person. ■ To check your interpretation.	■ Acknowledge the value of their issues and feelings. ■ Show appreciation for their efforts and actions. ■ To let the speaker know that what he/she is saying or feeling makes sense to you. ■ To acknowledge a person's diversity.	■ Did you find that hard? … fun? … tough? … exciting? … frustrating? … something to be proud of? ■ Ouch. That must have really hurt. ■ It's tough doing that alone. ■ It sounds like you are very proud. You did it anyway! ■ Even though it was a tough divorce, you managed to stay in touch with your kids. ■ Making things right is important to you, huh?

Source: Developed and reprinted by permission from the training staff and volunteers at Hospice Wellington, in Guelph, Ontario. Copyright 2016.

along with the other person, is quite different from *pity*, which commiserates with the other individual from a hierarchical and distant standpoint (Halifax, 2011). As Garfield (1976, p. 181) wrote years ago, "The largest single impediment to providing effective psychosocial support to the terminal patient is the powerful professional staff distinction between 'US' and 'THEM.'"

Something else that can be done to help, at least in many instances, is to *touch the person*. Some people are uncomfortable with physical touch. Such people keep a fairly large personal space around themselves; they may resent and resist intrusion by others into that space. However, sickness may break down some of these barriers. For example, a body massage may be *psychologically* helpful. Often, it is helpful for a friend or concerned person to touch one's wrist or arm, hold one's hand, or give a hug. Not everyone responds favorably to this; each person is an individual with personal expectations and values. Helpers must respect the dying person's values on this point. Seeking permission might be desirable. But for many persons who are coping with dying, gentle touch is psychologically healing.

Many of the psychological tasks of dying persons can be helped by anybody, whether that person is a professional caregiver or not, although some preparation and training may help (Doka, 2014b; Parkes, Relf, & Couldrick, 1996). If there are psychological dimensions of coping with dying that run deeper and that interfere with the individual's quality in living, a professional counselor or therapist may be helpful. Similarly, those who are especially competent to assist with psychological tasks might be called on for help when coping with dying is accompanied by clinical depression, confusional states, or specific forms of mental illness (Stedeford, 1978, 1984). After all, if the goal is to provide whatever care is needed to make this time of life as good as possible, the lesson must be that no particular expertise or mode of care should be looked on as irrelevant just because the person happens to be dying.

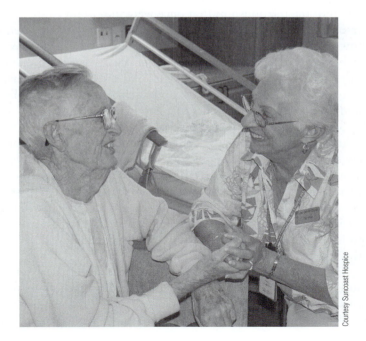

A parish visitor greets a hospice patient.

Courtesy Suncoast Hospice

There is no evidence that coping with dying on its own is associated with psychiatric problems, such as suicidal tendencies (Brown, Henteleff, Barakat, & Rowe, 1986). Thus, Stedeford (1979, pp. 13–14) suggested that, as a general rule in caring for those who are coping with dying, "sophisticated psychotherapy is not as necessary as are sensitivity, a willingness to follow the patient rather than lead him, some knowledge of the psychology of dying, and the ability to accept the inevitability of death." In the end, we are best able to help a dying person or anyone coping with dying when we are able to begin to cope with the reality of our own mortality and our prior experiences with profound losses. Not to do so often complicates our ability to help because it may fail to appreciate whose needs are being addressed. The fundamental criterion for all aspects of caring for dying persons and their family members is that *caring must be made relevant and must be seen to be relevant to the needs and tasks of the person whom one is trying to help.* Caregivers must always ask, "What is the relative value of the various available methods of treatment *in this particular patient?*" (Cade, 1963, p. 3).

Social Dimensions

Social dimensions in coping with dying are often just as urgent as physical and psychological dimensions. These social dimensions are expressed, first, in the special relationships that most individuals form with one or more people who occupy cherished roles in their lives. It is to these special people that one brings one's intimate achievements and tribulations. Within these relationships, individuals seek safety and security. In their shelter, one makes plans, works through problems, and defines that which is meaningful. Here love is expressed most basically in the sharing of two or more lives. Often, it is sufficient merely to be in the company of such special persons to feel a bit better and less beset by the problems of living.

Persons coping with dying can be helped when the relationships they value are fostered and encouraged. When energy levels are low, they may not be able to sustain all of the relationships that once were important to them. Because their circle of personal involvements may change its shape, size, or character, they may want to be shown how to uphold their most significant relationships. They will want to continue to give care to and to receive care from the special people in their lives. Sensitivity to the identities of these special people, to the nature of their attachments with the person coping with dying, and to how such relationships can be maintained and nurtured is an important part of caring and helping.

Social dimensions also include concerns about one's role and place in the family, in the workforce, and in the community at large. For example, economic concerns may be very important. In our society, many people worry about how their families will survive economically, given the costs of health care and the disappearance of the income the dying person had formerly provided. There are other concerns, too: Will that project I started at work be completed? What will happen to my business (clients, customers, stockholders, employees, students, parishioners)? How will my spouse be able to cope with being a single parent of young children? Who will take care of my aged parents or aging spouse?

Questions like these arise for many who are dying. Helpful responses to such concerns include allowing those who are coping with dying to talk about their concerns and advocating for such persons. That is, one can listen and try to help these people find resources that may be of assistance with their specific (or not so specific)

Reading to a patient from sources that interest that individual is a form of social caring.

problems. This type of advocacy involves acting on behalf of or in place of others to try to serve their needs. Another type of advocacy involves enabling or empowering individuals to act for themselves in seeking to satisfy their requirements. Note that it can be disempowering to take over the work of coping from the other person; it may be sufficient to help that person recognize his or her options and think about ways to go about accomplishing personal tasks. Social roles offer an excellent opportunity for people to assert and maintain autonomy. Social workers, family therapists, counselors, and lawyers are often able to help in areas of social tasks.

Spiritual Dimensions

Dying persons often face a variety of *spiritual tasks*. Many of these tasks concern a search for meaning, for establishing, reestablishing, and maintaining connectedness with oneself, other persons, and with what the person perceives as the transcendent (Longaker, 1998; see also Chapter 6 in this book). It is important to note that the **spiritual dimensions** of a person's life are not separate from but rather often underlie and run through physical, psychological, and social dimensions.

Caregivers cannot *provide* meaning or connectedness for another individual, nor can they *give* to such individuals an experience or understanding of the transcendent. When asked, one may share one's convictions with others. But when dying persons ask spiritual questions, they may not be interested in our responses. Instead, they are often trying to "tell their own stories" or "sing their own songs" (Brady, 1979).

When we first sat with people who raised spiritual issues, we guardedly began to answer them. Sometimes these persons just looked at us and appeared to listen to us; sometimes they went on talking right over our replies. When we stopped talking, they continued with their own thoughts on these matters. Eventually, we learned that

A chaplain visiting
a patient at home.

Courtesy Suncoast Hospice

individuals often ask questions about what matters to them spiritually as a way of
articulating these issues in their own minds. Talking was a way of developing their
own thinking, and perhaps they were attempting to determine whether we would
allow them to spin out their own answers. Again, what is usually being asked for is
for someone to be present, to be empathic, to listen, and to *travel with them on their
journey* (Ley & Corless, 1988).

Helpers can assist in this process. People find meaning, connectedness, and an
experience of the transcendent in a variety of ways (Binkewicz, 2005). Among these
are objects (sacred books, a volume of poetry, photographs, icons, sculptures); places
(a mosque, a cabin in the woods, one's own home); ritual actions (having a text read,
receiving a sacrament, praying, having others lay their hands on you); communities
or specific groups of people (a church choir or a support group); particular times (the
month of Ramadan, Yom Kippur, Christmas, one's own or a loved one's birthday, an
important anniversary in the person's life); teachings and ideas (including perhaps a
statement of faith, such as the Apostles' Creed for Christians, the Shahada for Muslims, or the Shema for some Jews); and specific persons (a shaman, rabbi, imam, or
family member—perhaps one's child). By attentively asking and listening, caregivers
can explore what an individual judges to be helpful. With that in mind, caregivers can
bring the person to the source of help or bring the helpful resource to the person. In
this way, a caregiver can hold his or her own beliefs in his or her heart while helping
to support the dying person on his or her (*not the caregiver's*) spiritual journey. Spiritual quests are rarely if ever completed, even up to the moment of death. Seeking out
meaning, fostering connectedness, and grounding hope can be enriched and deepened
throughout the entirety of a person's life. A caregiver's role is to support and sustain
this ongoing process.

In one of his thoughtful "Grace Drops" essays (reproduced here as Personal
Insights 7.2), Chaplain John Fitts reflects on what he learned about the role of a

chaplain, a person who must meet and try to be of assistance to many different people who may hold diverse beliefs and attitudes about what they are experiencing in coping with dying. Notice his emphasis on presence and active listening.

An important avenue of support for the dying person struggling with spiritual issues may be to enhance that individual's opportunities for creativity (Bertman, 1999; Bolton, 2007; Romanoff & Thompson, 2006). For example, creative opportunities

---

PERSONAL INSIGHTS 7.2

What's the Difference?

People often ask me, "What's the difference between a pastor and a chaplain?" I know what they mean since it is a question that I asked at one time. I soon discovered the difference when I enrolled in a Clinical Pastoral Education program. My ministry was never the same.

As a pastor I went through seminary learning the Bible and theology and left after five years convinced that I either had the answers to people's problems or at least access to them. When my parishioners came to me for counseling, I was thinking of the solution and a verse to back it up as they were talking. I was quick to point out just the answer they needed, and it was generally received with appreciation before we closed in prayer. All too often, however, it wasn't long before I heard either directly or indirectly that the problem persisted and discouragement had set in.

The hardest lesson I learned as a novice chaplain was the importance of listening. Our group sessions with my peers helped me learn this. They were ruthless in their critique of my methods and mentality. "But," I protested, "the answer is so clear."

"Of course it's clear to you. But it has to be clear to them. They have to find their own solution. All you have to do is listen and be there with them. In some ways your training gets in your way," they pointed out.

Three principles were the essence of my learning about listening, and it was not easy.

1. Stop thinking up solutions and really listen to what this person is telling me. Pay close attention. Notice the tone of voice, the body language, the facial expressions. Are they sad, angry, defensive. These things may tell you more than their words.
2. If someone says, "What should I do?" Be careful. Say something like, "Tell me what you have tried. How did that work out? Perhaps we can brainstorm some possible solutions."
3. Sometimes people don't want a solution, they just want someone to listen. We are so quick to solve the problem we forget the person. Sometimes we need to just "shut up and do nothing."

So to me, this is the difference. Learning to listen opened a door of ministry that was rewarding and has not completely closed yet.

Source: John C. Fitts. Used by permission.

can be found in massage, music, literature, drama, and the visual arts, some of which are stock in trade for occupational and other therapists (Dain, Bradley, Hurzeler, & Aldridge, 2015). Creative endeavors of all types reflect specifically human qualities in coping with living and dying. They can be undertaken in diverse settings (in institutions or in homes) where helpers can work together with those who are coping with dying to foster meaning and connectedness.

One last word really has to do with all of the dimensions in which one might seek to help a person who is coping with dying. Because the person has dealt with an issue once does not mean the issue is now settled. The issue may arise again. Questions like "Who is going to see to it that my child gets a good education?" or "What does my dying at age 26 mean?" are likely to be revisited again and again. Helpers need to be ready to listen to the person, wherever he or she is today, *at this moment*. There is no fixed goal at which the dying person or anyone who is coping with dying—along with those who are listening to that person—has to arrive. Although it may be unwise to put off a question or request—death is always an unexpected visitor—one can rest assured that as long as there is life there will always be more questions, needs, desires, and concerns. No one ever finishes *all* of the business of life, if for no other reason than that each moment lived brings *new* business.

TASKS AS GUIDELINES FOR HELPING

One reason why we emphasize a task-based approach to coping with dying in this book is to identify guidelines for helping those who are coping with dying. We can develop such guidelines by focusing on specific tasks the dying person or other persons affected by the dying person (a family member, partner, lover, friend, or caregiver) are pursuing. A helper (whether a professional or layperson) can facilitate and assist any of these persons with their task work. Of course, a person may not wish to have this sort of assistance. Or it may be that the individual is attempting to carry out his or her perceived tasks through some behavior (e.g., suicide) that is ethically or legally unacceptable to the one who is asked to help. One person's choices of how to live out his or her life do not necessarily always impose obligations on others.

Careful attention to how the individual who is coping with dying perceives and responds to potential tasks can shape specific approaches in helping (see Focus On 7.2). For example, a dying person may express a need to get in contact with an estranged relative. That might lead a helper to assist in making a telephone call, sending an e-mail or text message, writing a letter, or it might be appropriate (if the dying person so wishes) for the helper to make the first contact as an liaison with the estranged relative.

Family members are often the persons most likely to provide much of the care needed by one of their dying relatives and to want to do so. (An extensive report on unpaid family caregiving in the United States is available from the National Alliance for Caregiving [NAC] & AARP Public Policy Institute, 2015.) Family members form part of the natural, informal networks surrounding a dying person. As such, it is important to encourage them in this work, to draw upon their strengths, to urge them to recognize their limitations, and to assist them in anticipating the challenges they may be facing as a disease progresses (Doka, 2008; Family Caregiver Alliance, 2015; Hospice Foundation of America, 2007; National Institute on Aging, 2015). Above all, it is critical to be aware of the needs of family caregivers and to support them so they

FOCUS ON 7.2

Five Themes for Caring and Some Practical Suggestions

THEMES	PRACTICAL SUGGESTIONS
1. **Remember** that you are a different person than the other individual.	Be cautious in supplying answers that you find meaningful; each person has unique experiences and must find his or her own meanings. If asked for your perspectives, do not speak as one who has and intends to give absolute truth, but rather as one who has found some perspectives meaningful in light of your life experiences.
2. **Recognize** that to be facing one's death or the death of a loved one is a profound experience that to some degree involves tasks that each individual must carry out for himself or herself.	Be authentically present: this means to be with the person in that particular moment, paying attention to his or her tasks. Listen to what the person who is coping with dying has to say about his or her particular, individual life experiences, including his or her successes, struggles, and failures as well as his or her search for meaning; allow that person a safe space in which to come to understand those life experiences and that search for meaning. Try to understand the experiences of the other person by carefully listening and then imagining what it is to be that other person at this particular moment. Be attentive to the clues—subtle or obvious—as to what that person wants from you at this particular moment, for example, whether he or she wants to be alone or accompanied by you or by someone else. Accept silence as a form of presence, too; recognize your discomfort with that silence and resist the impulse to fill it with chatter or teaching.
3. **Respect** the meaning and values of those for whom you are providing care.	Avoid making judgments about the other person's meanings and values. Keep in mind that none of us can fully comprehend what the other's life experiences are and have been and that none of us is infallible in our own knowledge or understanding.
4. **Reinforce** the person's decision-making capacity and support his or her actual decisions.	Ask questions that help the individual clarify his or her preferences, desires, values, and needs, and help the person make choices based on his or her responses to your questions. Be an advocate for the person with other care providers in seeking to realize his or her decisions.
5. **Reminisce** with the person about his or her life and meaning.	Elicit stories from the person about his or her life experiences. Allow the person to reminisce and support the person as he or she remembers and repeats these stories. Record these stories so that they may be shared. Make available to the person (and significant others) poems, songs, readings, rituals, or prayers that are important to the individual and that help in the process of remembrance—thus supporting the development of meaning.

Source: Adapted from Colorado Collaboration on End-of-Life Care (no date).

do not exhaust themselves in overly heroic efforts. (In this regard, a survey conducted by the Human Resources Professionals Association in Canada [Staff, 2014] showed that "compassionate care leave policies in the workplace increase engagement and retention among Canadian employees caring for terminally ill loved ones.")

Professionals and other helpers from outside the family can play important roles in enabling and monitoring family caregivers as they assist their dying relatives and each other. For a family member caring for a dying person at home, a helper might provide some temporary relief from the physical burdens of care or some time off for psychological or social rejuvenation. The helper might offer to take over some of the physical care to provide the family caregiver with some time for uninterrupted sleep or rest. Or the helper might just sit with the dying person so that the family caregiver can leave the confines of the house to shop, see a movie, or seek some other form of reinvigoration. A perceptive helper might offer to take young children out for a day in the park so that a dying person and his or her spouse might have time alone together. Helpers who are aware of a particular family's structure, history, and relationships will be most useful because they will be sensitive to the interpersonal dynamics within the family, attentive to its cultural or ethnic background, and able to mobilize its internal resources.

The principle underlying all of the examples given here is that *coping tasks can become guidelines for helpers if these tasks always are appreciated by everyone involved in their concrete, specific, and individual circumstances*. For example, as they talk together, a dying person and a helper might agree upon several coping tasks that could be undertaken. An astute helper will then make it possible for the dying person to determine which (if any) task(s) should be undertaken first and when, and even to change those decisions as time passes. This enhances the autonomy and security of the dying person while accepting the measure of control he or she still retains at a time when so much may be out of control.

Individuals who are coping with dying may surprise us as they choose tasks that are important to them at any given moment. They may be more concerned to have a beloved pet with them than to permit visits from some humans who are not very close friends. They may still be preoccupied with how they appear to others or with pursuing a planned diet. They may find more comfort in talking to a hospital janitor than to a psychiatrist. They may be more grateful to someone who cleans their eyeglasses, gives them a back rub, or trims their ingrown toenails than to the chaplain who offers spiritual advice. They may be more interested in one last taste of a fast-food hamburger—what the British describe as "a little of what you fancy" (Willans, 1980)—than in carefully planned nutritional meals from the dietary department.

This range of reactions reminds us once again that dying persons are living human beings. They need to sing their own songs and not be "killed softly" by somebody else's song, to live out their own lives in ways they find appropriate. This does not imply that helpers should be merely passive; they can offer options, suggest things to do, and create opportunities. Sometimes it is important to urge people rather strongly to do something they do not want to do but would serve them in ways they may not yet have realized. Experienced caregivers learn when to be a bit insistent in matters like this and when to back off. Finally, however, decision making must rest primarily with the person being helped, not with the helper.

Helpers of all types need to listen to and be guided by the dying person; otherwise, helpers are merely imposing their own agenda on the dying person. When one learns that someone is coping with dying, strong feelings well up, and one's urge may be to try to make everything right again. While that is frequently not possible, one should not conclude that nothing is possible. As long as an individual is alive, it is always possible to do something to improve the quality of his or her life. For this, we must move toward (not away from) the person who is coping with dying.

What one does is not always or even mainly of primary importance. What counts is that one's actions show that one cares. Often, the action can be something simple and concrete. The gesture may not be accepted; it may not even be acknowledged. Dying persons (like everyone else) can be grumpy or exhausted. For those who care, that will not matter too much, because the gesture is made for the sake of the other person, not for one's own sake.

Just as one should begin with the person to be helped wherever he or she is, not where the helper thinks that person should be, so too helpers should begin with themselves wherever they are, with their own talents, strengths, and limitations. Sharing honest emotions or feelings of uncertainty can be a good way to start. Laughing, listening in an interested and nonjudgmental way, and just silently being present are often appreciated. Avoiding insensitive clichés is a good idea (Linn, 1986). Offering help in specific and practical ways is desirable. Conveying one's own sense of hope, fostering opportunities for growth (Byock, 1997, 2012), and sharing (often in nonverbal ways) one's conviction that the life of the other person is and has been meaningful in one's own life can be eloquent forms of caring. Holding a dying person's hand and crying with that person speak volumes when words are not really possible.

EFFECTIVE COMMUNICATION

In the past, our death system often advised us not to speak frankly to dying persons about their diagnoses and prognoses (e.g., Oken, 1961; recall our discussion of closed awareness contexts in Chapter 6). It was thought that candor would undercut hope and the will to live or even encourage people to end their own lives prematurely. There is, in fact, no evidence that this did or does take place. Even so, the key issue in **effective communication** is whether specific acts of communication are responsive to the needs of dying persons and are carried out in a thoughtful and caring way. The content of the communication may not be as important as the ways in which it is expressed and understood. One can brutalize a vulnerable person with the truth, just as one can harm with falsehood. Buckman (2001, p. 1002) highlighted the importance of effective communication by quoting a family member who said, "Doctors doing this job badly will never be forgiven; doctors doing it well will never be forgotten."

For the most part, our death system now encourages speaking with greater candor to dying persons about their diagnoses and prognoses (Novack et al., 1979). In part, this came about because people realized that "communication about end-of-life issues is the key to understanding and making rational decisions" (Thomas, 2001, p. 42). Accordingly, anything that gets in the way of such communication can impede both rational decision making and, in turn, the provision of good care (Fallowfield, Jenkins, & Beveridge, 2002). Also, society began to place increased emphasis on informed consent and patients' rights (Annas, 2004; President's Commission, 1982; Rozovsky, 2015). Consent to professional intervention or any sort of supportive treatment cannot be freely given unless it is based on information that is needed to understand the current situation, the nature of the proposed intervention, and its

Differences in age need not be a barrier to effective communication.

likely outcome(s). Even in the direst of situations, the necessary information can be provided in a caring manner, and consent can be obtained in ways that foster the dignity of all who are involved.

Yet, there is also a danger here because blunt truth-telling can be brutal. Doka (2014b) suggests *open communication*, a process in which one never lies but always answers questions truthfully—once it is clear what the person is really asking. A person who asks whether he or she is dying may be asking for information or for reassurance that he or she is not near death. Open communication also stresses that one should answer in a way that allows continuing dialog. For example, if someone asks "Am I dying?" and we answer "yes," there is little more to say. However, if we ask why the person thinks he or she is dying, or what he or she wishes, we can continue a conversation. One patient in hospice—bedbound and in the final stages of cancer—asked, "When will I be able to drive again?" His nurse was shocked by the question and told him he would never drive again. A better response would be something like "It must be hard to just lie in bed" or "Where would you wish to go if you could drive?"

Two good examples of how to enhance effective communication in coping with dying are available. Buckman (1992b) offered a set of suggestions about how to break bad news (see Table 7.1). Never an easy task, it is essential both for the person who needs to know about his or her own situation and for the helper who needs to convey information and confirm that he or she can be relied on. The steps proposed in Table 7.1 are not necessarily a universal scenario, but they do point to a larger literature on preparing helpers to communicate effectively (e.g., Buckman, 1992a, 2010; Cassell, 1985).

A second example is found in what is called **nearing death awareness** (Callanan & Kelley, 2012; see also Sanders, 2007). This concept recognizes that

Table 7.1 How to Break Bad News: A Six-Step Protocol

Step 1	Start carefully: Get the physical context right; if humanly possible, speak face-to-face, in an appropriate setting, and with attention to who should be present.
Step 2	Find out how much the person already knows: Listen for intellectual understanding, communicative style, and emotional content.
Step 3	Find out how much the person wants to know: Determine at what level the person wants to know what is going on; offer willingness to explore matters further in the future.
Step 4	Share the information: Start from the person's point of view; have an agenda with desired objectives; share information in small chunks, in plain, nontechnical language; check reception frequently; reinforce and clarify information frequently; check communication levels; listen for the person's concerns; blend your agenda with that of the person.
Step 5	Respond to the person's feelings: Identify and acknowledge the person's reactions.
Step 6	Plan for the future and follow through.

Source: Based on Buckman, 1992a.

communications from dying persons are too often dismissed as empty or enigmatic expressions of confusion. Instead, Callanan and Kelley argue that such communications may actually reflect either (1) special awareness of the imminence of death and efforts to describe what dying is like as it is being experienced by the individual or (2) expressions of final requests about what is needed before the individual can experience a peaceful death. These alternatives draw attention to efforts dying persons are making to communicate and, once more, stress the indispensable role of **active listening**.

Effective communication is an important part of fostering hope and quality in living when individuals are coping with dying. It is also important in self-care and in obtaining assistance in meeting the needs of helpers themselves. How one communicates with those one is trying to help can become a model for all helping interactions. The challenge in helping others appears on two basic levels: (1) to keep company with the dying and with others who are coping with dying—even when that requires one to be comfortable with one's own discomfort and to do nothing more than sit quietly together in silence; and (2) to learn how to identify and respond effectively to the particular physical, psychological, social, and spiritual tasks that are part of a specific individual's coping with dying. The challenge in helping oneself lies in learning to use effective communication to find greater satisfaction in the helping role and to seek from others the professional and personal support that all helpers need.

HELPING HELPERS: STRESS, COMPASSION FATIGUE, BURNOUT, AND SELF-CARE

A task-based approach to coping with dying reminds helpers that they also have their own coping to consider. Self-care is essential in effective coping with stress and preventing development of compassion fatigue or caregiver burnout. **Stress** can arise when helpers experience intense or long-term involvement in situations that are emotionally demanding perhaps because of witnessing people in crises or feeling moral distress about what one is asked to do. The stress generated by such situations can come to be perceived as oppressive and a hardship that can no longer be borne. If that happens, helpers may experience **compassion fatigue** when they feel emotionally drained (Figley, 2015; Todaro-Franceschi, 2012). It is only natural then to try to withdraw and distance oneself from the sources of stress. **Burnout** is an extreme form of compassion fatigue when helpers become physically, emotionally, and mentally exhausted, especially because of long-term involvement in emotionally demanding situations coupled with a sense of powerlessness and an inability to achieve their goals as providers of care.

Whether they are family members, volunteers, or professionals, helpers are also human beings with needs and limitations. As such, helpers must find effective ways to cope with stress and not overburden their own resources (Funk, Waskiewich, & Stajduhar, 2013; Mathieu, 2011; Teater & Ludgate, 2014). Otherwise, they may become unable to continue to help in productive ways. The best helpers are those who operate from a foundation in a rich and satisfying life of their own, rather than from a sense that they are overwhelmed by stressors and problems of their own (Larson, 1993). They practice what Renzenbrink (2004) has called "relentless self-care." Good helpers also have interpersonal and organizational support that bears witness to the fact that one does not have to be dying to be important (Papadatou, 2009).

Helpers cannot operate solely from their own need to be needed. They must care about those whom they are helping, but their love must also include themselves. The best helpers are those who can also take care of themselves and who take time to meet their own needs. In other words, helpers must strive for a balance between too much involvement and too much distance in their interactions with the needs of others (International Work Group on Death, Dying, and Bereavement, 2006; Papadatou, 2000; Vachon, 2007). The desired balance, often called **detached concern** (Larson, 1993), **detached compassion** (Pattison, 1977), or **trauma stewardship** (Lipsky, 2009), involves entering into the situation of the person being helped in a way that enables the helper to continue to function effectively in the helping role. Such a posture must be achieved in individual ways by each helper and certainly requires considerable self-awareness. As Nouwen (1972) indicated, caregivers must recognize that they are "wounded healers."

Stress and burnout in helpers have long been the subject of much study (e.g., Selye, 1978b). Research has shown that stress more often arises from the situation within which one is working and the colleagues with whom one works than from the fact that one is working with dying persons and others who are coping with dying (Vachon, 1987, 1997). In each case, then, one must carefully examine the specific sources of stress and the mediators that may modify that stress in various ways (Friel & Tehan, 1980). Thoughtful programs to address stress within members of organizations that provide care include such elements as careful staff selection, training, team building, supervision, and the provision of both formal and informal methods support (Papadatou, 2009). When such a program is coupled with the development of an individual philosophy of care and attention to one's own needs for care (whether self-care or care from others), helping those who are coping with dying need not be more stressful than many other activities in our society (Harper, 1994; LaGrand, 1980; Lattanzi, 1983, 1985).

Many of the basic elements in an effective program of managing stress and taking care of oneself are found in a series of suggestions set forth in Table 7.2 and in what Selye (1978a, p. 70) called "a kind of recipe for the best antidote to the stresses of life":

> The first ingredient ... is to seek your own stress level, to decide whether you're a race-horse or a turtle and to live your life accordingly. The second is to choose your goals and make sure they're really your own, and not imposed on you. ... And the third ingredient to this recipe is altruistic egoism—looking out for oneself by being necessary to others, and thus earning their goodwill.

Good helpers need to evaluate their own strengths and weaknesses (see Personal Insights 7.3) as well as being open to suggestions and support from other persons—even from the dying person or the family they are helping. Indeed, when dying persons are freed from the burden of distressing symptoms and made to feel secure, they can often be very thoughtful and sensitive in caring for those around them. In short, none of us is without needs in coping with someone else's mortality or with our own mortality. We all can benefit from help as we look to our own tasks in coping.

Table 7.2   Suggestions for Stress Management and Self-Care

- Be proactive: *Effective intervention begins with good prevention.*
- Take charge: *Adopt an active strategy of coping focused on one or more of the following: your appraisal of the stressful situation and its sources, what you can do about the situation, or what you can do about your own reactions to the situation.*
- Set limits: *Seek a dynamic balance between demands and resources; limit time and involvements with those you are helping.*
- Compartmentalize: *Put some physical and psychological distance between your home life and your work life.*
- Develop a stress-hardy outlook:
  Strive to view potentially stressful situations as challenges, that is, as opportunities for growth rather than as threats.
  Strive to balance your commitments to work, family, and friendships.
  Strive to develop the conviction that life's experiences are—within limits—within your control (and a sense of humor that helps to keep stress and striving in perspective).
- Practice the art of the possible: *Do what you can even though there is always much that you cannot do; be patient and creative.*
- Improve your communication and conflict resolution skills: *Stress often arises when you are caring and compassionate, but do not know what to say or what to do.*
- Rejuvenate yourself: *Employ techniques of exercise, relaxation, and meditation in self-care because stress is unavoidable.*
- Know yourself: *Befriend yourself; be gentle with your inner discomforts.*
- Maintain and enhance your self-esteem: *Develop a positive view of your skills and yourself; doing good can help you to feel good; recognizing your commitment to meaningful work can help you feel better about yourself.*
- Strengthen your social support: *Encouragement, support, and feedback can enhance self-esteem and your sense of self-efficacy.*

Source: Based on Larson, 1993.

PERSONAL INSIGHTS 7.3

On Facing and Understanding One's Limitations

Once you face and understand your limitations,
you can work with *them instead of having them*
work against you and get in your way,
which is what they do when you ignore them,
whether you realize it or not.
And then you will find that, in many cases,
your limitations can be your strengths.

Source: Hoff, 1983, pp. 48–49.

HOPE

It is sometimes said that there can be no more hope for dying persons, that they are hopeless cases, and that working with the dying must be a hopeless endeavor. Such assertions reveal a narrow understanding of the role that **hope** plays in human lives (Corr, 1981; Cousins, 1989). We hope for all sorts of things. I hope that someone will (continue to) love me. He hopes that he can have his favorite food for dinner tonight. She hopes to be able to see her sister again. Many of us hope to live as long as we possibly can. Some dying persons hope to live until a special birthday, a holiday, or the birth of a new grandchild. Many hope for an outcome grounded in their spiritual convictions. Perhaps we all hope that our own situation and the situations of those we love will be at least a little bit better while we are dying and after our deaths. Here, hope for a cure may give way to hope for a good dying process and death (Webb, 1997). Helpers hope that their interventions will make a difference even in a life that may soon be over. Until death comes, most of us hope that whatever it is that is making us uncomfortable will be reduced or removed from our lives. This last hope—like many other hopes that we may entertain—cannot always be realized. Still, it is only one hope among many.

Few situations in life are ever completely hopeless. So when someone says, "This situation is hopeless," it may just signify a failure of imagination. Often, it represents the point of view of an outsider (e.g., a care provider) and his or her judgment that there is no likelihood of cure for the person in this situation. Usually, this type of statement indicates that the speaker has focused exclusively on a single hope or a narrow range of hopes that cannot be realized in a specific set of circumstances. It would be far better to appreciate the therapeutic potential of hope. This is a serious point, but it has also been suggested in a lighthearted way: "After all, hope contains no mono or polyunsaturated fats, cholesterol, sugars, artificial sweeteners, flavors or colors; it's classified as 'generally recognized as safe' by the FDA and is a known anti-carcinogen" (Munson, 1993, p. 24).

In fact, "hope, which centers on fulfilling expectations, may focus on getting well, but more often focuses on what yet can be done" (Davidson, 1975, p. 49). Hope is a typically human phenomenon (Veninga, 1985). But it is fluid, often altering its focus to adapt to changes in the actual situations within which we find ourselves. So we must listen carefully to each individual—including to those who are trying to help people cope with dying—to determine the object of his or her hope. We must also distinguish between hope, which is founded in reality, and unrealistic wishes, which merely express fanciful desires.

Summary

In this chapter, we explored ways individuals—professionals or laypeople—can contribute to helping persons coping with dying. We examined four primary dimensions in such care (physical, psychological, social, and spiritual), and we used a task-based model to suggest guidelines for helping both others and oneself. We ended with comments on effective communication, helping helpers, and hope.

Glossary

Active listening: making oneself available to another without interference from one's own concerns; being fully attentive to the needs and concerns of the other

Acute pain: distress in any dimension of an individual's life that is characteristically time limited, although it may recur; may be mild, moderate, or intense

Addiction: a form of habitual dependence upon analgesics (e.g., narcotic drugs) characterized by psychological "highs" and a subsequent craving for steadily escalating doses

Burnout: an extreme form of compassion fatigue when helpers become physically, emotionally, and mentally exhausted, especially because of long-term involvement with emotionally taxing situations coupled with a sense of powerlessness and an inability to achieve their goals as providers of care

Chronic pain: distress in any dimension of an individual's life that is characteristically ongoing and not time limited; may be mild, moderate, or intense

Compassion: "feeling with" another person, involving presence, active listening, and empathy; to be contrasted with "pity" that always implies a "looking down upon"

Compassion fatigue: a condition in which helpers feel emotionally drained as a result of intense or long-term involvement in emotionally demanding situations

Dependence: reliance upon drugs or other supports that does not necessarily imply the features of addiction; requires that the drug or other support can be terminated or withdrawn in a phased fashion (not "cold turkey") to avoid undesirable side effects

Detached concern or detached compassion: a way of entering into the situation of the person being helped that enables the helper to continue to function effectively in the helping role

Effective communication: interactions whose specific acts are responsive to the needs of the other and are carried out in a thoughtful and caring way; both the content of the exchange and the ways in which it is expressed and understood are important

Empathetic presence: making oneself available to a person in distress; characterized by active listening, empathy, and compassion

Four dimensions of care for individuals who are coping with dying:

   Physical dimensions: designed to address bodily pain or other sources of corporeal distress

   Psychological dimensions: designed to address emotional or cognitive distress

   Social dimensions: designed to address interpersonal tensions or difficulties as well as interactions with social groups or organizations

Spiritual dimensions: designed to assist individuals in their search for meaning, for establishing, reestablishing, and maintaining connectedness with oneself, other persons, and with what the person perceives as the transcendent

Hope: expectations that one looks forward to based on faith and trust; may involve different prospects

Nearing death awareness: communications from a dying person that reflect either (1) special awareness of the imminence of death and efforts to describe what dying is like as it is being experienced by the individual or (2) expressions of final requests about what is needed before the individual can experience a peaceful death

Stress: hardship or adversity that imposes pressure or strain; here associated with death-related issues

Trauma stewardship: caring for others and responding to their suffering in a thoughtful, intentional way by developing a quality of compassionate presence

Questions for Review and Discussion

1. Think about some time in your life when someone you loved was quite ill or dying. What was most stressful for you at that time? What did you do or what might you have done that you now think was helpful or unhelpful to the person who was ill or dying?

2. There are extensive resources available on the Internet or through social media about how one can help oneself or others who are coping with dying. Have you ever accessed such resources? If so, did they help you? If not, why not?

3. This chapter described four dimensions of care for the dying: physical, psychological, social, and spiritual. Think about someone you know who was or is dying. How did these four dimensions or aspects of care show up in that situation?

4. In this chapter, we pointed out that effective communication is or can be important both for dying persons and for those who are helping such persons. Why is communication important for the dying and their helpers? What promotes effective communication among such people? What is an example from your own experience of poor communication? Of good communication?

5. In this chapter, we suggested that hope is or can be important both for dying persons and for those helping such persons. How can hope be important for those who know they or the person for whom they are caring will soon be dead? What does hope mean to you?

Suggested Readings

The lives, viewpoints, and legacies of two women who have been pioneers in care of the dying appear in:

Clark, D. (Ed). (2002). *Cicely Saunders—Founder of the Hospice Movement. Selected Letters 1959–1999*

DuBoulay, S. (1984). *Cicely Saunders: The Founder of the Modern Hospice Movement*

Gill, D. L. (1980). *Quest: The Life of Elisabeth Kübler-Ross*

Kübler-Ross, E. (1997). *The Wheel of Life: A Memoir of Living and Dying*

Saunders, C. (2003). *Watch with Me: Inspiration for a Life in Hospice Care*

Welch, F. S., Winters, R., & Ross, K. (Eds.). (2009). *Tea with Elisabeth: Tributes to Hospice Pioneer Dr. Elisabeth Kübler-Ross*

For guidance on ways to help persons who are coping with life-threatening illness and/or dying, see:

Abrahm, J. L. (2014). *A Physician's Guide to Pain and Symptom Management in Cancer Patients* (3rd ed.)

Berzoff, J., & Silverman, P. (Eds.). (2004). *Living with Dying: A Comprehensive Resource for Health Care Professionals*

Buckman, R. (1992a). *How to Break Bad News: A Guide for Health Care Professionals*

Buckman, R. (1992b). *I Don't Know What to Say: How to Help and Support Someone Who Is Dying*

Buckman, R. (2010). *Practical Plans for Difficult Conversations in Medicine: Strategies that Work in Breaking Bad News*

Byock, I. (1997). *Dying Well: The Prospect for Growth at the End of Life*

Byock, I. (2012). *The Best Care Possible: A Physician's Quest to Transform Care through the End of Life*

Callanan, M. (2009). *Final Journeys: A Practical Guide for Bringing Care and Comfort at the End of Life*

Callanan, M., & Kelley, P. (2012). *Final Gifts: Understanding the Special Awareness, Needs, and Communications of the Dying*

Cassell, E. J. (1985). *Talking with Patients: Vol. 1, The Theory of Doctor-Patient Communication; Vol. 2, Clinical Technique*

Cassell, E. J. (1991). *The Nature of Suffering and the Goals of Medicine*

Chochinov, H. M. (2011). *Dignity Therapy: Final Words for Final Days*

Davies, B., Reimer, J. C., Brown, P., & Martens, N. (1995). *Fading Away: The Experience of Transition in Families with Terminal Illness*

Davison, A., & Evans, S. (2014). *Care for the Dying: A Practical and Pastoral Guide*

Doka, K. J. (2014b). *Counseling Individuals with Life-Threatening Illness*

Gawande, A. (2014). *Being Mortal: Medicine and What Matters in the End*

Gordon, P. S. (2016). *Psychosocial Interventions in End-of-Life Care: The Hope for a "Good Death"*

Hammes, B. J. (Ed.). (2012). *Having Your Own Say: Getting the Right Care When It Matters Most*

Institute of Medicine. (2011). *Relieving Pain in America: A Blueprint for Transforming Prevention, Care, Education, and Research*

Institute of Medicine. (2014). *Dying in America: Improving Quality and Honoring Individual Preferences near the End of Life*

Kemp, C. (1999). *Terminal Illness: A Guide to Nursing Care* (2nd ed.)

Kuhl, D. (2002). *What Dying People Want: Practical Wisdom for the End of Life*

Kuhl, D. (2006). Facing Death, Embracing Life: Understanding What Dying People Want

Landay, D. S. (1998). *Be Prepared: The Complete Financial, Legal, and Practical Guide for Living with a Life-Threatening Condition*

Lipman, A. G. (Ed.). (2004). *Pain Management for Primary Care Clinicians*

Nouwen, H. (1994). *Our Greatest Gift: A Meditation on Dying and Caring*

Parkes, C. M., Relf, M., & Couldrick, A. (1996). *Counseling in Terminal Care and Bereavement*

Quill, T. (1996). *A Midwife through the Dying Process: Stories of Healing and Hard Choices at the End of Life*

Rosen, E. J. (1998). *Families Facing Death: A Guide for Health Care Professionals and Volunteers* (Rev. ed.)

Sanders, M. A. (Ed.). (2007). *Nearing Death Awareness: A Guide to the Language, Visions, and Dreams of the Dying*

Saunders, C. M., & Sykes, N. (Eds.). (1993). *The Management of Terminal Malignant Disease* (3rd ed.)

Twycross, R. G. (1994). *Pain Relief in Advanced Cancer*

Twycross, R. G., & Wilcock, A. (2002). *Symptom Management in Advanced Cancer* (3rd ed.)

Wall, P. (2002). *Pain: The Science of Suffering*

Werth, J. L., & Blevins, D. (Eds.). (2006). *Psychosocial Issues near the End of Life: A Resource for Professional Care Providers*

Wooten-Green, R. (2001). *When the Dying Speak: How to Listen to and Learn from Those Facing Death*

Zitter, J. N. (2017). *Extreme Measures: Finding a Better Path to the End of Life*

Support for family caregivers and other helpers is discussed in:

Figley, C. R. (Ed.). (1995). *Compassion Fatigue: Coping with Secondary Traumatic Stress Disorder in Those Who Treat the Traumatized*

Katz, R. S., & Johnson, T. A. (Eds.). (2016). *When Professionals Weep: Emotional and Countertransference Responses in Palliative and End-of-Life Care* (2nd ed.)

Larson, D. G. (1993). *The Helper's Journey: Working with People Facing Grief, Loss, and Life-Threatening Illness*

Lipsky, L. (with Burk, C.). (2009). *Trauma Stewardship: An Everyday Guide to Caring for Self while Caring for Others*

Mathieu, F. (2011). *The Compassion Fatigue Workbook: Creative Tools for Transforming Compassion Fatigue and Vicarious Traumatization*

Papadatou, D. (2009). *In the Face of Death: Professionals Who Care for the Dying and the Bereaved*

Renzenbrink, I. (Ed.). (2011). *Caregiver Stress and Staff Support in Illness, Dying, and Bereavement*

Teater, M., & Ludgate, J. (2014). *Overcoming Compassion Fatigue: A Practical Resilience Workbook*

Selected Web Resources

Some useful search terms include: ADDICTION; BURNOUT; COMPASSION; COMPASSION FATIGUE; DEPENDENCE; DIMENSIONS OF CARE; EFFECTIVE COMMUNICATION; EMPATHY; HOPE; PAIN (ACUTE AND CHRONIC); STRESS.

You can also visit the following *organizational and other Internet sites*:

Americans for Better Care of the Dying

Association for Clinical Pastoral Education

Association for Professional Chaplains

The Caregiver Resource Center

Caring Connections

Family Caregiver Alliance

National Alliance for Caregiving

National Family Caregivers Association (NFCA)

Pain.com

Coping with Dying: How Communities Can Help

Objectives of this **Chapter**

▸ To explore *formal programs of care* that seek to help individuals who are coping with dying

▸ To emphasize *the importance of recognizing and responding to the needs of persons who are coping with dying* and *growing awareness of the need for better end-of-life care*

▸ To describe the *hospice philosophy* through ten principles or desirable elements in an institutional program of care for those who are coping with dying

▸ To outline the historical development and current roles of four social institutions that care for persons coping with dying: *hospitals*, focusing on *acute care*; *long-term care facilities*, focusing on *chronic care*; *home health programs*, focusing on *home care*; and *hospice programs*, focusing on *end-of-life care*

▸ To explain the central characteristics of *pediatric palliative and hospice care*

▸ To clarify similarities and differences between *hospice care* and *palliative care*

SOCIAL INSTITUTIONS THAT HELPED ONE FAMILY COPE WITH LIFE-THREATENING ILLNESS AND DYING

A local hospital provided some of the care that Matt and Jo Ryan needed. Each was diagnosed and received initial treatment there, and both were seen for a time in the hospital's outpatient clinics after their initial surgeries. Fortunately, Matt needed no further care other than regular follow-up observations. Jo's situation was more complicated, especially when she faced the demands of her advanced illness.

For a while a community home health care program helped by providing regular nurse visits during daytime and weekday hours. Nevertheless, Jo's needs grew as her health declined, and she could no longer remain at home. At that point, the security of a local nursing home that had previously cared for her mother seemed to offer Jo a good alternative.

Jo liked the relaxed pace of the nursing home and even made some friends there. However, over time, she found that many of the residents were older than she was, and some seemed confused and unable to sustain a relationship. Matt had always been unsure about whether it was a good idea to have Jo stay in any type of facility, and he very much missed her at home. The last straw came when one of the residents unwittingly frightened the children of their son, Tom. His family then visited less often.

Jo felt very much alone and overwhelmed by her problems until someone suggested that she talk with a representative of a local hospice program. That led to a transfer to the hospice inpatient unit. The support of the hospice team for Jo and her family helped minimize sources of distress and improved their quality of life. Jo's pain and other symptoms were now managed effectively; both her physical condition and her spirits improved greatly. Jo felt that she had almost miraculously regained control of her life.

With support from the hospice home care team, Jo was even able to go home to be with Matt and her family for several months. In the end, with help from the hospice team, she died in her own bed at home.

RECOGNIZING AND RESPONDING TO THE NEEDS OF PERSONS WHO ARE COPING WITH DYING

"What people need most when they are dying is relief from distressing symptoms of disease, the security of a caring environment, sustained expert care, and assurance that they and their families will not be abandoned" (Craven & Wald, 1975, p. 1816). This single sentence itemizes many of the concerns of those who are dying and what they need from social organizations and programs of care.

During the 1960s and 1970s, some professionals began to wonder whether care provided to those who were dying was properly recognizing and responding to their needs. Studies conducted in Great Britain (e.g., Hinton, 1963; Rees, 1972), Canada (e.g., Mount, Jones, & Patterson, 1974), and the United States (e.g., Marks & Sachar, 1973) confirmed that the answer was no. Three points seemed to be central: (1) caregivers did not always realize or acknowledge the level of pain and other forms of distress being experienced by individuals who were dying; (2) caregivers did not always have or believe they had at their disposal effective resources to respond to the needs of those who were dying; and (3) individuals who were dying often worried that

Stefan Verwey

their wishes might be ignored. In practice, this meant that those who were dying were frequently told: "Your pain cannot be as bad as you say it is"; "You can't really be feeling like that"; "We cannot offer stronger dosages of narcotics or you will risk becoming addicted"; "We have to save really strong medications until they are truly needed"; "There is nothing more that we can do."

It is unfortunate when caregivers who want to help do not have the resources to do so. Thus, many were grateful when new forms of narcotic analgesics became available to help dying persons. But it is tragic when the needs of those who are dying are not recognized and when that is compounded by too little understanding or misguided fears about whether or how to mobilize available resources to meet those needs.

New perspectives were required on several key points, including the following:

- The situation of those who are coping with dying (Noyes & Clancy, 1977; Pattison, 1977)
- The nature of and prevalence of pain when one is dying (LeShan, 1964; Melzack & Wall, 1991; Smith et al., 2010; Wall & Melzack, 1994)
- Appropriate therapeutic regimes for those who are dying, which involve carefully selected narcotics, other medications, and complementary therapeutic

interventions (Melzack, Mount, & Gordon, 1979; Melzack, Ofiesh, & Mount, 1976; Twycross, 1976, 1979a)

- The value of holistic, person-centered care and interdisciplinary teamwork (Corr & Corr, 1983; Saunders & Sykes, 1993)
- The importance of end-of-life conversations about decision making that involve dying persons, their family members, and the professionals caring for them (Larson & Tobin, 2000)
- Ways in which the social organization of programs serving those who are coping with dying affect the care provided (Saunders, 1990; Sudnow, 1967)

These new elements are all embodied in the hospice philosophy and are implemented in most hospice programs. Some of these elements are also incorporated in palliative care and other programs of care for those who are coping with dying.

During the 1990s, there was increasing interest in **end-of-life care**, even while research identified ongoing deficiencies in such care (e.g., Field & Cassel, 1997; Webb, 1997). One key study provided quantitative data from controlled, clinical research conducted in five teaching hospitals in the United States (SUPPORT Principal Investigators, 1995). The SUPPORT (Study to Understand Prognoses and Preferences for Outcomes and Risks of Treatments) project examined end-of-life preferences, decision making, and interventions in a total of 9,105 adults hospitalized with one or more of nine life-threatening diagnoses. The two-year first phase of the study observed 4,301 patients and documented substantial shortcomings in communication, overuse of aggressive, cure-oriented treatment at the very end of life, and undue pain preceding death. The two-year second phase of the study compared the situations of 4,804 patients randomly assigned to intervention and control groups with each other and with baseline data from Phase 1. Physicians with the intervention group received improved, computer-based, prognostic information on their patients' status, while a specially trained nurse was assigned to the intervention group in each hospital to carry out multiple contacts with patients, families, physicians, and hospital staff in order to elicit preferences, improve understanding of outcomes, encourage better attention to pain control, facilitate advance care planning, and enhance patient–physician communication.

The SUPPORT study evaluated outcomes using the following criteria: the timing of written "Do not resuscitate" (DNR) orders; patient and physician agreement (based on their first shared interview) on whether to withhold resuscitation; the number of days before death spent in an intensive care unit either comatose or receiving mechanical ventilation; the frequency and severity of pain; and the use of hospital resources. Results were discouraging. Phase 2 intervention "failed to improve care or patient outcomes" (p. 1591) and led investigators to conclude that "we are left with a troubling situation. The picture we describe of the care of seriously ill or dying persons is not attractive" (p. 1597). This is disheartening in light of the scope of the study, its capacity to measure targeted outcomes, the careful design of its interventions, the existence of a well-established, professional knowledge base and models within our health system for this type of care, and the degree of ethical, legal, public, and policy-making attention recently directed to issues related to end-of-life decision making and quality of care. Unfortunately, similar results have been confirmed by other studies drawing on data from the SUPPORT project and from other research (e.g., Curtis et al., 2011; Krumholz et al., 1998; Supportive Care of the

Dying: A Coalition for Compassionate Care, 1997). Further, a study by Singer and colleagues (2015) concluded that "despite national efforts to improve end-of-life care, proxy reports of pain and other alarming symptoms in the last year of life increased from 1998 to 2010" (p. 175). Another study concluded that "chemotherapy use among patients with chemotherapy-refractory metastatic cancer is of questionable benefit to patients' QOL [Quality of Life] in their final week. Not only did chemotherapy not benefit patients regardless of performance status, it appeared most harmful to those patients with good performance status" (Prigerson et al., 2015). Clearly, there is much for individuals, professionals, communities, health care systems, and other organizations to do to improve end-of-life care in our society (Wolf, Berlinger, & Jennings, 2015).

HOSPICE PHILOSOPHY AND PRINCIPLES

In response to the concerns described in the previous section, the development of a new philosophy or way of caring for dying persons and their families was needed. We can summarize the central principles of the new **hospice philosophy** in the following ten points. When properly understood and correctly applied, these principles can become the key elements in guiding any practical program of care for individuals who are coping with dying.

1. *Hospice is a philosophy, not a facility—one whose primary focus is on end-of-life care.* In England, the hospice movement began by building its own facilities. This reflected the social situation and health care system in a particular country at a specific time. Going outside existing structures is one classic route for innovation. However, it is not the facility in which hospice care is delivered that is essential; the main factors are the principles that animate services and the quality of the care itself. That philosophy or outlook on care is the central point, along with a focus on persons who are coping with dying.

2. *The hospice philosophy affirms life, not death.* Dying is a self-limiting condition. Individuals can and will die by themselves, without assistance from others. The challenge is to support life, not allowing people to die or bringing about death. Helping a person to live may be difficult when that person is close to death and is experiencing distress in dying. Processes of dying often impose special pressures on quality in living. The key point is to affirm life, to care for and about persons who are coping with dying because they are living and struggling with these special pressures.

3. *The hospice philosophy strives to maximize present quality in living.* Hospice is a form of palliative or symptom-oriented care that tries to minimize discomfort. Without abandoning interest in cure, the hospice philosophy is focused on other forms of caring when cure is no longer a reasonable expectation. In this way, hospice epitomizes the historical medical adage: "To cure sometimes, to relieve often, to comfort always." This is not merely the opposite of "active treatment" (an inaccurate phrase that usually is used to mean cure-oriented treatment), for that would make it merely some passive mode of care. As Feudtner and Morrison (2012, p. 694) have written, "Intensive care is composed of both invasive care and intensive caring, and even if the former is failing, the latter can continue unabated." In other words, "the care of the dying patient is an active

treatment peculiar to the dying patient" (Liegner, 1975, p. 1048; reprinted 2000, p. 2426). Thus, hospice and other desirable programs of care for those coping with dying embody an active and aggressive mode of care whose focus is on the alleviation of distressing symptoms as well as on prospects for personal growth at the end of life, even when the underlying condition from which distress arises cannot be halted or reversed (Byock, 1996). As Saunders (1976, p. 674) observed, this is "the unique period in the patient's illness when the long defeat of living can be gradually converted into *a positive achievement in dying*" (our italics).

4. *The hospice approach offers care to the patient-and-family unit.* This means that both the dying person and those whom he or she regards as "family" form the unit receiving care and helping to give care (see Figure 8.1). Hospice care seeks to provide a sense of security and the support of a caring environment for all who are involved in coping with dying—ill persons together with their families, friends, and other involved persons (Stedeford, 1987). The principle here is the importance of family-centered care for those who are coping with dying.

5. *Hospice is holistic care.* Recognizing that the people being served are persons, whole human beings, hospice care assists them in working with their physical, psychological, social, and spiritual tasks. It seeks to listen to these concerns and to enhance quality in living in each of these dimensions. Good end-of-life care is holistic in nature (Lloyd-Williams, 2008).

6. *Hospice offers continuing care and ongoing support to family members coping with dying, death, and loss both before and after the death of someone they love.* Care for family members and friends is relevant both before and after the

Figure 8.1 **A Hospice Interdisciplinary Team**

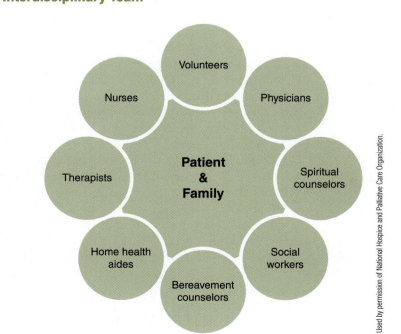

Used by permission of National Hospice and Palliative Care Organization.

death of the person they love. Good end-of-life care is intended to have a positive impact on these individuals (Christakis & Iwashyna, 2003). (We will return to this topic in Chapters 10 and 11 when we discuss how to help the bereaved.)

7. *The hospice approach combines professional skills and human presence through interdisciplinary teamwork.* Special expertise in end-of-life care and in the management of distressing symptoms is essential. Expert medical and nursing care are critical. However, the availability of human companionship is equally important. Professional caregivers can offer human presence, but it is often a special gift of hospice volunteers. Appropriate use of one's expertise and one's presence is dependent upon being available and actively listening to understand correctly the needs of dying persons and their family members. Everyone on the team can pay attention to the needs and wishes of those being served and can report those concerns back to other members of the team. Interdisciplinary teamwork demands respect for the special skills and abilities of others, time to exchange information and insights, and a certain amount of "role blurring" in assisting all whom the hospice program is serving. Interdisciplinary—not merely multidisciplinary—teamwork is essential to good end-of-life care in any programmatic setting.

8. *Hospice programs make services available on a 24-hour-a-day, 7-day-a-week basis.* Hospice seeks to recreate caring communities to help dying persons and their families. Wherever such communities already exist naturally and whenever dying persons and their families are not experiencing significant distress, there may be no need for formal hospice programs. When and where a need does exist, these programs must be available around the clock, just as a caring community is—perhaps through phone contacts or the ability to have a caregiver come to the dying person's bedside wherever that person may be. Good end-of-life care does not take holidays or go off duty.

9. *Participants in hospice programs give special attention to supporting each other.* Caring for those who are coping with dying or bereavement and working within the structure of an interdisciplinary team can be stressful. Thus, hospice programs offer both formal and informal programs of support for their own staff members and volunteers. This is important in any program that seeks to offer effective end-of-life care.

10. *The hospice philosophy can be applied to a variety of individuals and their family members who are coping with a life-threatening illness, dying, death, or bereavement.* In its modern usage, at first hospice care was mainly concerned with illnesses like cancer and their implications, chiefly for older adults. But the hospice philosophy need not be restricted to these conditions or to specific settings and institutions. To benefit from the hospice philosophy, there must be time and opportunity to allow services to help the tasks of the patient-and-family unit. Thus, hospice and other forms of optimal end-of-life care require some advance notice that dying has begun and death is imminent, willingness to accept the benefits and restrictions of the hospice philosophy, and an opportunity to mobilize services in particular circumstances. Given these conditions, the hospice philosophy has been applied in recent years to a broad range of diseases at the end of life (such as dementia and Alzheimer's disease, end-stage heart, kidney, and lung diseases, and HIV/AIDS) and to situations involving children and adolescents.

These principles have been implemented in sets of standards for hospice care established by both the Canadian Hospice Palliative Care Association (Ferris et al., 2002) and the National Hospice and Palliative Care Organization (NHPCO; 2010b) in the United States.

FOUR PROGRAMS OF CARE FOR PERSONS WHO ARE COPING WITH DYING

Near the beginning of this chapter, we described the experiences of Jo Ryan and her family. We can understand those experiences more fully and come to appreciate better ways in which hospice principles can be put into practice in any setting by examining the development, role, and principal functions of the caregiving programs that Jo encountered, especially during the last, difficult parts of her life. Programs of this sort are typically associated with an institution and are always based in some physical facility, but it is the services they offer to persons who are coping with dying that are really critical. Relevant institutions here are hospitals or medical centers, long-term care facilities (often called nursing homes), home health care programs, and hospice programs. Each of these institutions specializes in a particular type of care, but all can play some role in caring for individuals who are coping with dying and in addressing the many challenges currently found in attempts to improve end-of-life care (Jennings, Kaebnick, & Murray, 2005).

Acute Care: Hospitals

In the United States and other developed countries today, most people receive most of their acute medical care in hospitals, and a large portion of deaths occur there. As a result, **hospitals** play a major role in shaping the end of life in American society (Kaufman, 2006).

The word *hospital* is derived from the Medieval Latin *hospitale*, meaning a place of "reception and entertainment of pilgrims, travellers, and strangers" (*Oxford English Dictionary*, 1989, vol. 7, p. 414). In the ancient world, the first hospitals took in pilgrims, travelers, the needy, the destitute, the infirm, the aged, and the sick or wounded. Such institutions were usually associated with some type of religious fraternity or community.

As Western culture became more urbanized, hospitals began to change. A division of labor began to characterize Western society. Specialization in carrying out tasks became the normal method of operation. No longer did one institution perform many basically different functions; instead, separate institutions now undertook separate functions.

In the United States up to the 19th century, care of the sick and dying occurred mainly at home and was mostly provided by family members. Hospitals played virtually no role in such care. In fact, in 1800 there were only two private hospitals in the United States, one in New York and one in Philadelphia (Rosenberg, 1987).

Of course, even in that society, there were persons who were too sick to be cared for at home or who had no home or no one at home to take care of them. If such persons were also poor and could not afford to hire someone to take care of them, they ended up in an *almshouse*. Almshouses were charitable public institutions that housed the insane, the blind, the crippled, the aged, the alcoholic, travelers, and ordinary working people with rheumatism, bronchitis, or pleurisy. These diverse types of people were freely mixed together in large, crowded wards in dark, stuffy, unpleasant places. Without adequate funding, sometimes more than one person had to sleep in a single bed. Few people entered almshouses voluntarily.

Around the beginning of the 19th century, modern hospitals were advocated mainly as having an *educational* function for physicians; they were not seen as being primary agents of medical care. These early hospitals had little to offer and were avoided by anyone who could do so; they were often viewed as "unnatural" and demoralizing. Thus, the physician V. M. Francis wrote in 1859 (pp. 145–146) that

> the people who repair to hospitals are mostly very poor, and seldom go into them until driven to do so from a severe stress of circumstances. When they cross the threshold, they are found not only suffering from disease, but in a half-starved condition, poor, broken-down wrecks of humanity, stranded on the cold bleak shores of that most forbidding of all coasts, charity.

Until the middle of the 19th century, care provided in a hospital was usually no better than what could be obtained elsewhere. Hospital care mainly involved patients reporting of symptoms and "treatment" of such symptoms (usually without much ability to affect underlying causes) as well as that could be done. This mostly meant allowing the body to heal itself and, above all, not interfering in that process.

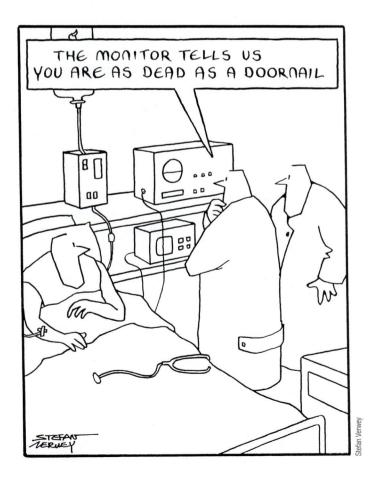

Basically, what a good hospital provided was a place to rest, shelter from the elements, and decent food.

Major changes occurred during the Civil War in the 1860s. First, understanding of disease changed. Formerly, the body was seen as "a system of ever-changing interactions with its environment. … Every part of the body was related inevitably and inextricably to every other" (Rosenberg, 1987, pp. 71–72). Health and disease were seen "as general states of the total organism … The idea of specific disease entities played a relatively small role in this system of ideas and behavior." Now disease began to be seen as involving specific entities and predictable causes. In the 1860s, Pasteur and Lister contributed to the germ theory of disease. This dramatically changed Western culture's understanding of what caused disease and what could be done to treat disease. Henceforth, science with its theories and technology would change the face of modern medicine. Human bodies were seen as complex machines, disease was thought of as a breakdown in the body's machinery, and therapy involved "fixing" the "malfunctioning part"—or, as in many cases in recent years, replacing that part. "This new way of understanding illness necessarily underlined the hospital's importance" (Rosenberg, 1987, p. 85).

The Civil War itself also taught that cleanliness, order, and ventilation were of great help in bringing about a return to health. For the first time in American history, people (mostly soldiers) of all social classes experienced care in (military) hospitals. Hospital care and associated attitudes were changing.

Immediately after the Civil War, many new hospitals were built, resulting in health care—and thus, dying—moving more and more into hospitals. (As an aside, note that according to Rosenberg [1987, p. 31], one almshouse surgeon complained in 1859 that "dead bodies were often left in the wards and placed directly in coffins while the surviving patients looked on." Some people believed this was hard on surviving patients and recommended that such happenings should be hidden from public view. Here is a germ of what Ariès [see Chapter 3] called in our time: the denial of death.) After the Civil War, people increasingly died in hospitals.

As a result, "prospective patients were influenced not only by the hope of healing, but by the image of a new kind of medicine—precise, scientific, and effective" (Rosenberg, 1987, p. 150). So, hospitals were now expected to be places for curing specific diseases. The body's malfunctioning part was to be worked on and made functional again so that the person could get on with his or her life. In this context, death is an unhappy reminder that "scientific" medicine is not always effective—if *effective* means capable of producing a cure. In this sort of hospital and according to this medical outlook, death is an anomaly, something abnormal. For health care providers, an inability to "fix" the problematic part of the body may suggest personal ineffectiveness, that is, a kind of failure. (Contrast this with Ungerleider's comment [2015] that "I no longer see death as a failure but as a place we are all headed at some point—and if I can help someone live the fullest to the very end, I have practiced the best medicine.")

By the end of the 19th century, "moribund patients were systematically transferred to special rooms" (Rosenberg, 1987, p. 292). In some places, whole wards or units were set aside for those who were not expected to recover—out of sight and, to the degree possible, out of mind.

In the 1960s, specific criticisms began to arise about hospital care (or lack of effective care) for dying persons. Hospitals in modern culture are largely **acute care,** short-term facilities whose purpose is mainly to treat specific diseases and to return people to society with more or less the same functional capacity they had before they became ill. Put simply, hospitals are dominated by medical professionals who see themselves as involved in curing people (Starr, 1982). This is why many hospitals are now called "medical centers" or "health centers." Thus, Chapple (2010) argued that the very organizational structure of these institutions and their ideology of rescuing people from death make them unsatisfactory places for care of the dying. Perhaps that is one reason why in recent years the proportion of persons dying in acute care hospitals has declined (Teno et al., 2013).

Providing acute care is an expensive business. Diagnostic tools become ever more precise—and costly. Stethoscopes are inexpensive diagnostic tools; CAT scanners are not. An appendectomy is a relatively inexpensive procedure; a kidney or heart/lung transplant is not. To permit someone to spend time in a hospital, when no therapy leading to a cure is available, may seem to waste bed space and the time and energy of busy caregivers who have been specially trained in the techniques of cure-oriented intervention. In its historical context, this claim seems to make sense. No wonder economists and health planners have become involved since the 1980s in attempts to make the use of expensive hospital services more economically efficient (Stevens, 1989). However, economic efficiency ought not and must not be the sole criterion for acute care institutions. In particular, humane care of dying persons may require bringing additional values into consideration, as Jo Ryan learned when she was in the hospital, and there have been some recent efforts made in this direction (e.g., Blinderman & Billings, 2015; Loggers et al., 2013).

Long-Term or Chronic Care: Long-Term Care Facilities

Another type of institution that Jo Ryan and her family experienced and in which many people die these days is the long-term care facility, often called a **nursing home**. Before the 1930s, there were no **long-term care facilities** in this country (Moroney & Kurtz, 1975). **Chronic care** facilities arose as hospitals became more and more acute care facilities and as urbanization helped change the nature of the family from an extended model or group of relatives living in the same community to a nuclear model usually restricted to husband, wife, and minor child or children who often lived at a distance from other kin. Also, as average life expectancy increased, many Americans no longer expected to work until just days or hours before death. They were either unable to work or, for various reasons, decided to retire from work well before their deaths. Many of these people required assistance in caring for themselves and in activities of daily living as they lived out the remainder of their lives. In this, they joined a group of *younger people with chronic diseases or other handicapping conditions* who also experienced problems in taking care of themselves.

These factors led to a situation in which long-term, chronic disability and illness increased while care for people with these conditions became less available. Long-term care facilities fill this gap. In general, they provide a place to live, assistance with routine activities of everyday living, and some level of help or skilled nursing care. Long-term care facilities usually do not provide intensive physician care.

Developing mechanisms to offer financial assistance to those who become ill toward the end of their lives played an important part in the expansion of long-term care facilities, especially after the passage of the Social Security Act of 1935 in the

United States. With funding available from the personal savings of individuals, their relatives, the government, health insurance, and a retirement package (most often provided as a non-salary benefit by employers), potential providers of care began to think about offering services to this newly defined population. Primary sources of payment for services to residents of long-term care facilities who are 65 years of age and older now include Medicaid and Medicare, plus private insurance, the resident's own income, family support, Social Security benefits, and retirement funds.

Until the 1980s, most hospitals did not think of themselves as profit-seeking enterprises. By contrast, many long-term care facilities have sought both to provide a service and to be a profitable business. This puts some pressure on long-term care facilities, because the sort of care they provide—labor-intensive, round-the-clock care—is expensive. In practice, this has meant that most of those who work in long-term care facilities are nurse aides, thus controlling costs and increasing profits by reducing costs of labor. Since long-term care facilities often experience a high staff turnover, even when training of new persons is minimal, it must be constantly repeated. For both care providers and person being cared for, this often means that new faces and personalities must be met. Thus, care can feel discontinuous and uncertain.

There are many different types of long-term care facilities, and they may be described differently in different places. Most are primarily funded by Medicare, Medicaid, private insurance, and/or out-of-pocket payments. The best-known long-term care facilities and the ones most relevant to our concerns are *skilled nursing facilities* in which professional nurses provide 24-hour care following orders from a physician and guiding bedside care delivered by nursing assistants and aides. These facilities primarily serve individuals with chronic health conditions rendering them unable to care for themselves or perform activities of daily living. For example, individuals with advanced dementia may exhibit disorientation, memory loss, wandering, and combativeness—all of which require constant supervision. Some skilled nursing care facilities serve special populations, such as ventilator-dependent patients.

Individuals in long-term care facilities can generally be divided into two groups: "short stayers," who mostly come from hospitals and who are either rehabilitated and return home or who die within a relatively short period of time, and "long stayers," who are in the facility for months or years until they die. The importance of the rehabilitative role is shown by the fact that many long-term care facilities discharge approximately 30% of their residents each year. In most long-term care facilities, occupancy rates are quite high. Residents in many facilities may be very dependent; many are quite elderly, chronically ill, confused, and even emotionally disturbed. Such individuals most often lack an available caregiver at home; they may be single, widowed, childless, and, in general, less well-off economically than the rest of the population. Although long-term care facilities provide services to persons needing different sorts of care—from those needing brief, intensive rehabilitation to those who are incontinent, mentally impaired, seriously disabled, or very old and very frail—it is the long-term, chronically disabled persons who more and more often occupy beds in long-term care facilities.

In 2014, almost 1.4 million persons were estimated to be residents in long-term care facilities in the United States (Harris-Kojetin et al., 2016). These residents were overwhelmingly Caucasian American and two-thirds female. However, taken together they represented less than 3% of all individuals 65 years of age or older. Thus, the notion that to be old in the United States means to be in a nursing home is a misperception; most older adults (over 97% of the nearly 48 million Americans who are 65 years of age or older) do not live in long-term care facilities. Still, as the population ages and hospitals stays become shorter, the pressure on long-term care facilities and on family caregivers is likely to grow.

Society seems content with relatively low overall levels of staff education and compensation in many long-term care facilities, perhaps indicating that the increasing importance of such facilities is not valued properly. However, many residents and people who work in long-term care prefer the slower and more orderly routines of these facilities, along with opportunities to develop enduring personal relationships within them, by contrast with the more hectic pace and rapid patient turnover in acute care (although some of this may not be accurate when long-term care facilities are understaffed).

Many long-term care facilities operate with high standards and quality services for their residents. Still, there are periodic outcries in the media, in the public, and from legislative bodies about the quality of care provided in long-term care facilities, and we are all familiar with aged relatives who plead, "Don't send me to a nursing home."

Quality of living and dying in long-term care facilities can be measured in various ways. One indicator is found in the limited contacts between residents and those outside the institution, a situation in which some residents may have no visitors or only a few, perhaps on an irregular basis. For many, this suggests disengagement from or diminishment of external social networks. It has also been argued that there is too much isolation when one is dying in a long-term care facility and insufficient attention to bereavement needs of the institutional community, although that may be changing (Shield, 1988). Because of an acute illness or for other reasons, some individuals are transferred from long-term care facilities to acute care hospitals shortly

An aide has a close relationship with a resident in a long-term care facility.

Courtesy Suncoast Hospice

before they die (Bottrell, O'Sullivan, Robbins, Mitty, & Mezey, 2001; Travis, Loving, McClanahan, & Bernard, 2001). Nevertheless, approximately 20% of all deaths in the United States in 2014 took place in a long-term care facility.

Long-term care facilities provide services that Americans apparently want or need: someone (else) to take care of long-term, chronically disabled, and sometimes dying people. Thus, this sort of program was well suited at least for a time to the needs of Jo Ryan and her family. However, an institution designed for long-term care and chronic illness may not be well suited to the requirements of dying persons as is clear from one study (Oliver et al., 2014, p. 744) that conducted interviews with family members to establish that "a multitude of barriers to quality end-of-life care [exist] in the nursing home setting, and demonstrate that support for family members is an essential part of quality end-of-life care for residents. This study suggests that nursing homes should embrace the opportunity to demonstrate the value of family participation in the care-planning process."

Jo Ryan eventually needed a level and type of service that her nursing home was not able to provide. Thus arises a stereotype often associated with dying persons: alone, afraid, seriously disabled, in unrelieved distress, uncared for, and perhaps uncared about. This stereotype is probably unfair in terms of the actual care provided in many long-term care facilities, but it looms large in the minds of many who may or may not have experienced these institutions with family members or friends. In other words, like hospitals, long-term care facilities do not always provide a comfortable institutional model for dying in our society. Still, long-term care facilities have improved their responses to dying persons in recent years and in many cases have associated themselves with hospice principles or programs of care (Gozalo, Plotzke, Mor, Miller, & Teno, 2015; Miller, Lima, Gozalo, & Mor, 2010; Unroe et al., 2014).

Home Care: Home Health Care Programs

Home health care programs have a long history as part of the health care systems in many societies, such as the district nurse structure in England and the Victorian Order of Nurses (VON) in Canada. In the United States, many city and county public health departments, the Visiting Nurse Association (VNA), and private home care agencies provide home care services.

The rapid growth of **home health care programs** in the United States during recent decades has responded to new needs, together with changes in society and in its health care system. For example, a growing number of frail or confused elders created new demands for **home care**. Also, in the 1980s, a large number of mental health patients were relocated from psychiatric and other institutions to the community. More recently, federal and other third-party payers placed limitations on inpatient funding (in the form, for example, of "diagnostic-related groups" that capped payment for specific health conditions at a fixed amount), which pressured acute care institutions to discharge patients earlier (often much earlier) than had been previous practice. This desire to limit rising costs in health care by keeping individuals out of expensive institutions as much as possible is a key factor in the expansion of home health care in many forms, whether it is provided by traditional home health agencies, new home care agencies in the private sector, newly developed home care departments of hospitals, or comprehensive hospice programs.

Unlike the other three institutions considered in this chapter, home health care programs are not distinguished by a specific kind of illness. All home health care is essentially a form of skilled nursing care (with supplementation in many cases from social workers, counselors, clergy, pharmacists, physical therapists, homemakers, personal care attendants, dieticians, physicians, occupational therapists, speech therapists, or audiologists). Also, all home health care can be addressed to problems arising from a wide variety of illnesses or conditions. The distinctive feature of this form of care is *the location in which it is provided*; home health care programs deliver their services *in the patient's own home*. For the most part, Medicare, Medicaid, and personal financial resources pay for home health care in our society.

Most home health care programs do offer care for dying persons, although they are not primarily or exclusively committed to providing that type of care. Indeed, some staff members in home health care programs have developed broad experience and expertise in caring for dying persons. As caregiving institutions, however, home health care programs usually do not claim specialized expertise in end-of-life care. Most home health care programs that offer skilled nursing care now make services available on a 24-hour-a-day, 7-day-a-week basis. Some home health care programs also offer a multidisciplinary team approach to care, but that may become problematic when third-party payers will not reimburse for some types of services, such as spiritual or emotional care. In those circumstances, the home health care program must either depend upon the expertise of its skilled nurses to assess and respond to general family and environmental concerns or leave additional needs to other community agencies. In short, much home health care is based on diagnostic categories and funding that relate to a desire to control costs, not necessarily to patient or family needs. Of course, these are broad generalizations.

In recent years, a variety of economic, organizational, and other factors have impacted home health care programs in our society. Although many new home health care programs have been started, some have gone out of business. Others have added a hospice component to their services or may have incorporated some aspects of the hospice philosophy of care in their work. In some settings, a hospice patient who shows improvement may be discharged to a home health care program until his or her condition worsens and he or she is readmitted to hospice care.

End-of-Life Care: Hospice Programs

Hospice programs of the type that Jo Ryan used near the end of her life have become an important way of caring for those who are coping with dying, offering essential services in a cost-effective manner. Such programs do this by operating out of a distinctive philosophy of care and by delivering most of the care they offer in the homes of those they serve. For this reason, the term *hospice* may be more appropriately used as an adjective to describe a type of care rather than as a noun to identify a place. Unfortunately, research has shown that "despite relatively high hospice awareness and favorability, myths and misperceptions about hospice still abound—and may drive ethnic disparities in end-of-life care" (Cagle et al., 2016, p. 27). (The Hospice Foundation of America offers an online Hospice Knowledge Quiz to help educate about hospice care.) Here, we review how hospice programs developed.

Hospice programs trace their roots back to medieval institutions offering rest and support for weary travelers (Stoddard, 1992). In their modern sense, hospice programs offer care for those who are in the final stages of the journey of life. Services are mainly designed to provide care for those who are dying, or who have no reasonable hope of benefit from cure-oriented intervention, along with their family members.

Whatever their origins, the great impetus for modern **hospice care** came from Dame Cicely Saunders, who founded St. Christopher's Hospice in London in 1967 (DuBoulay, 1984; Parkes, 2007b). Originally a nurse, Dame Cicely retrained as a social worker after injuring her back and then as a physician to pursue her goal of devising and offering better care to the incurably ill and dying. She worked out her views at St. Joseph's Hospice in London's East End during the 1950s, doing research on medications to manage chronic pain in dying persons. Later, she went outside the National Health Service (NHS) in England to found St. Christopher's as a privately owned inpatient facility to implement her theories of clinical practice, research, and education in care of the dying.

At first, it was thought that innovations of this sort could only be undertaken in independent, purpose-built, inpatient facilities. However, in England this original hospice model was later followed by inpatient facilities built with private money and then given to the NHS to operate, and eventually by inpatient units within some NHS hospitals (Ford, 1979; Wilkes et al., 1980). England has also seen the development of hospice home care teams designed to support the work of general practitioners and district nurses (Davies, 1999) as well as hospital support teams that advise on the care of the dying in acute care hospitals (Dunlop & Hockley, 1998) and programs of hospice day care (Corr & Corr, 1992a; Wilkes, Crowther, & Greaves, 1978). This history is both similar to and different from the growth of hospice care in North America and elsewhere around the world (Clark, 2007; Clark, Small, Wright, Winslow, & Hughes, 2005).

Canadian efforts in this field began in the mid-1970s with "palliative care services" at the Royal Victoria Hospital in Montreal and St. Boniface General Hospital in Winnipeg. Services included an inpatient unit in a large acute care teaching hospital, a consultation service, a home care service, and a bereavement follow-up program (e.g., Ajemian & Mount, 1980). At present, although "support for hospice palliative care is almost unanimous" among Canadians and there have been significant advances in funding and provision of services in recent years (Canadian Hospice Palliative Care Association, 2015, p. 1), there are still significant limitations on the availability of palliative and end-of-life care services, depending largely on where people live in the country.

Hospice Care in the United States   The first hospice program in the United States opened in September 1974 as a community-based home care program in New Haven, Connecticut (Corless & Foster, 1999; Foster, Wald, & Wald, 1978; Friedrich, 1999; Lack & Buckingham, 1978). By 2014, the National Hospice and Palliative Care Organization (NHPCO, 2015) estimated there were approximately 6,100 operational hospice programs in all 50 states, the District of Columbia, Puerto Rico, Guam, and the U.S. Virgin Islands. (For information about hospice services or links to a local hospice program, call the Hospice Helpline at 800-658-8898, or contact NHPCO at 703-837-1500, or consult the hospice directory provided by the Hospice Foundation of America.)

Hospice programs in the United States in 2014 showed a wide variety of organizational models. Most were independent freestanding agencies; others were hospital-based, divisions of home health agencies, or based in long-term care facilities and other institutions. About 28% of hospice programs in the United States were nonprofit in character, 68% were for-profit, and about 4% were run by government organizations, such as the Veterans Administration (cf., Wachterman, Marcantonio, Davis, & McCarthy, 2011). Approximately one-third of all American hospice programs have their own inpatient facility.

In 1982, funding for hospice care was approved as a Medicare benefit emphasizing home care for older adults who qualified for Medicare. Admission criteria typically require a diagnosis of terminal illness, with a prognosis of fewer than six months to live. Hospice services fall into four basic categories: routine home care (a category that reflects nearly 93.8% of all patient care days); general inpatient care (4.8%); continuous in-home care (providing for the presence of a trained hospice staff member in specified blocks of time [1%]); and short-term inpatient respite care (0.4%). Different reimbursement rates apply to each of these categories, with rates increasing over time and adjusted to take into account differential costs in different geographical areas.

In 2014, the Medicare hospice benefit covered over 85% of all hospice patients and paid for more than 90% of patient care days (other funding sources include managed care or private health insurance, Medicaid, and charitable donations). The Medicare benefit emphasizes home care and reimbursement on a prospective, flat-rate basis. Thus, the hospice program receives the amount specified in a given rate category for each day in which a person is enrolled in its care, regardless of the services it actually provides to that person on any given day. All monies provided under the Medicare hospice benefit (except for those paid to an attending primary physician) go directly to the hospice program, which is responsible for designing and implementing each individual plan of care. No service is reimbursed unless included in that plan of care and approved by the hospice interdisciplinary team. This gives the hospice program an incentive to hold down costs and only to provide care relevant to the needs of an individual patient-and-family unit. The **interdisciplinary team** is central, including both patients and their family members, professionals from many different disciplines, and trained volunteers (look again at Figure 8.1). The interdisciplinary team develops and implements the plan of care, by contrast with multidisciplinary teams in which specialized health care professionals work largely independently under the direction of a single person (usually a primary physician) with loose coordination.

Despite its challenges (e.g., Stevenson, 2012), the Medicare hospice benefit is a model for other forms of reimbursement for hospice services in the United States and is a desirable option for the individuals who qualify (U.S. Department of Health and Human Services, Centers for Medicare & Medicaid Services, 2016). The benefit is available in all U.S. hospice programs qualified for Medicare certification (92.8%). It can be changed by federal legislation, but it is presently broader than other Medicare benefits and is intended to cover all costs of the care provided. The benefit does have upper limits on reimbursement to a hospice program, but they are expressed in terms of program averages and total benefit days for which the program will be reimbursed, not in figures that apply to any particular individual. Once a person has been accepted into a Medicare-certified hospice program and continues to qualify for its services, the law prohibits involuntary discharge—whether or not reimbursement funds are still flowing. Voluntary disenrollment is possible, although research shows that terminal cancer patients who exercised that option subsequently experienced increased hospitalizations, greater likelihood of dying in the hospital (versus at home), and higher costs (Carlson et al., 2010).

Some believe hospice care in the United States is too closely identified with death. For example, under the Medicare guidelines, a patient who enters hospice care must accept the fact that he or she is dying and must agree to forego cure-oriented interventions (although that individual retains the right to withdraw from hospice care at any point). This may be one reason why some minority groups in the United States with strong sanctity-of-life values appear to underutilize opportunities for hospice care and why there has been a geographical disparity in hospice utilization (Connor, Elwert, Spence, & Christakis, 2007, 2008; Elk, 2016).

NHPCO estimates that in 2014, hospice programs served between 1.6 and 1.7 million patients. In that year, around 1.2 million Americans died while receiving hospice care—roughly 46% of all Americans who died that year—while more than 15% of hospice patients were discharged alive because they no longer needed or qualified for this type of care (cf. Teno, Plotzke, Gozalo, & Mor, 2014). In 2014, 58.9% of hospice patients were able to die in a place that they called home (a private residence, a nursing home, or other residential facility) and 31.8% died in a hospice facility. Only 9.3% of hospice patients died in an acute care medical facility, by contrast with the general population for whom nearly half die in such a facility. Average length of enrollment in hospice care in 2014 was 71.3 days; median length of service was 17.4 days.

NHPCO describes hospice patients in 2014 as follows:

- About 53.7% were female and 46.3% male.
- Approximately 84% of patients were 65 years of age or older.
- Approximately 76% were Caucasian Americans, 7.6% were African Americans, 3.1% were Asian Americans or Pacific Islanders, 0.3% were American Indians or Alaska Natives (0.3%), and 13.1% were individuals who identified themselves as multiracial or were otherwise classified.
- Leading diagnoses on admission were advanced cancer (36.6%); dementia including Alzheimer's disease (14.8%); end-stage heart disease (14.7%), lung disease (9.3%), and debility unspecified (5.4%); other significant diagnoses on hospice admission included stroke or coma, end-stage kidney or liver disease, motor neuron diseases, and HIV/AIDS.

Hospice care can be relevant for persons with many different diagnoses, but it is clearly most suitable when diseases impose a high burden on caregivers and when accurate prognoses can be obtained.

Some 430,000 volunteers contributed an estimated 19 million hours of service to hospice programs in 2014, whether in direct support to patients and family members, clinical support (e.g., administrative activities), or general support activities (e.g., fund-raising and as members of boards of directors). The work of these volunteers has been shown to be critical in family members' favorable evaluations of the care their loved ones received (Block et al., 2010). Moreover, because a significant portion of all Medicare costs go toward care of people in their last year of life and almost 50% of those costs are expended in the last two months of life, hospice care at home often substitutes for more expensive hospitalizations.

Finally, according to NHPCO statistics for 2014, hospice programs provided bereavement care for a minimum of one year to an average of two family members per hospice patient who died. In addition, 91.6% of all hospice programs provided some level of bereavement services to their communities with community members receiving approximately 12.3% of all hospice bereavement services in 2014.

Hospice care recognizes that many types of volunteers can play a part in good care—even animals!

Courtesy Suncoast Hospice

Efforts to Expand and Evaluate American Hospice Services   Hospice principles have been implemented in many different ways mainly having to do with the needs of particular communities and especially with the structure of local health care and social services systems. In the United States, the hospice emphasis on home care fits with efforts to minimize inpatient care and to encourage home care as more appropriate and more economical. In addition to encouraging physicians to refer (Obermeyer, Powers, Makar, Keating, & Cutler, 2015; Teno & Connor, 2009), the hospice movement has sought to reach out to underserved groups, to expand access to hospice services, and to emphasize the importance of cultural diversity (Varney, 2015), while also building alliances with academic institutions and other community organizations and reflecting on the heritage and future of the hospice movement.

Here are examples of research studies designed to evaluate aspects of hospice care in the United States:

- Connor, Pyenson, Fitch, Spence, and Iwasaki (2007) used a retrospective statistical analysis of 4,493 patients with five types of cancer and congestive heart failure, a sample of 5% of the entire Medicare beneficiary population for 1998–2002. They concluded that "the mean survival was 29 days longer for hospice patients than for nonhospice patients" (p. 238). In this cohort, medications and other aspects of hospice care intended to manage distressing symptoms and improve the quality of life not only did not hasten death, but they actually extended the length of life in ways that might be especially important to patients and their family members.
- Taylor, Ostermann, Van Houtven, Tulsky, & Steinhauser (2007; see also Tangeman, Rudra, Kerr, & Grant, 2014; Unroe et al., 2016; Zhang et al., 2009)

demonstrated that hospice care reduced Medicare costs by an average of $2309 per hospice patient and showed there would be further cost savings for seven out of ten patients if they had longer enrollments in hospice care. They concluded that "more effort should be put into increasing short stays as opposed to focusing on shortening long ones" (p. 1476).

■ Temel and colleagues (2010; see also Temel et al., 2017 and Zimmermann et al., 2014) reported that early palliative care for lung cancer patients achieved meaningful improvements in quality of life and mood. They also lived 23.3% longer than those who delayed palliative treatment as was currently the standard. Median survival for earlier palliative care patients was 2.7 months longer than those receiving standard care. The authors hypothesized that "with earlier referral to a hospice program, patients may receive care that results in better management of symptoms, leading to stabilization of their condition and prolonged survival."

■ Kelley, Deb, Du, Aldridge Carlson, and Morrison (2013) established that hospice enrollment saves money for Medicare and improves care quality not only for patients enrolled 53–105 days before death but also for those enrolled 1–7, 8–14, and 15–30 days prior to death. The authors concluded that "instead of attempting to limit Medicare hospice participation, the Centers for Medicare and Medicaid Services should focus on ensuring the timely enrollment of qualified patients who desire the benefit" (p. 552).

■ Obermeyer and colleagues (2014) studied a nationally representative 20% sample of Medicare fee-for-service beneficiaries with poor-prognosis cancer who died in 2011, comparing those receiving hospice care with matched control patients not receiving hospice care, and concluded that "those receiving hospice care vs not (control), had significantly lower rates of hospitalization, intensive care unit admission, and invasive procedures at the end of life, along with significantly lower health care expenditures during the last year of life" (p. 1888).

■ Lustbader and colleagues (2016) conducted a retrospective analysis of 651 decedents to evaluate the impact of a home-based palliative care (HBPC) program implemented within an Accountable Care Organization (ACO) on cost and resource utilization; results showed "significant cost savings, fewer hospitalizations, and increased hospice use in the final months of life."

■ Teno and colleagues (2004; see also El-Jawahri et al., 2016) examined evaluations by family members of care received by their loved ones, to conclude: "Family members of patients receiving hospice services were more satisfied with overall quality of care: 70.7% rated care as 'excellent' compared with less than 50% of those dying in an institutional setting [that is, in a hospital or nursing home] or with home health services" (p. 88).

■ Rhodes, Teno, and Connor (2007) examined bereaved African American family members who reported that what they perceived as disparities in care provided for their loved ones by contrast with care provided to other patient populations decreased when they enrolled in hospice programs.

Other research and personal testimony has complemented these studies by showing that morale is high among those who work in hospice care (Denny, 2016; Richardson, 2007).

PEDIATRIC PALLIATIVE AND HOSPICE CARE

The World Health Organization (1998) defines palliative care for children as:

> the active total care of the child's body, mind and spirit, and also involves giving support to the family. It begins when illness is diagnosed, and continues regardless of whether or not a child receives treatment directed at the disease. Health providers must evaluate and alleviate a child's physical, psychological, and social distress. Effective palliative care requires a broad multidisciplinary approach that includes the family and makes use of available community resources; it can be successfully implemented even if resources are limited. It can be provided in tertiary care facilities, in community health centers and even in children's homes.

More recently, NHPCO (2014, p. 2) has defined **pediatric palliative and hospice care** (PP/HC) as:

> … both a philosophy and an organized method for delivering competent, compassionate, and consistent care to children with chronic, complex, and/or life-threatening conditions, as well as their families. PP/HC is planned and delivered through the collaborative efforts of an interdisciplinary team with the child, family, and caregiver(s) as its center. PP/HC is provided along with concurrent disease-modifying therapy when disease-modifying therapy is appropriate, or as the main focus of care when disease modifying therapies are no longer effective and comfort is of utmost importance.
>
> Effective management of pain and other distressing symptoms, along with psychosocial care, spiritual care, and decision-making guidance, are critically important beginning at diagnosis and continuing throughout the course of a child's life and beyond. Therapies take a holistic approach, assisting children and families in fulfilling their unique physical, psychological, educational, social and spiritual goals while remaining sensitive to developmental, personal, cultural and religious values, beliefs and practices.

Almost every aspect of pediatric palliative and hospice care is complex from the relatively small number of appropriate children, their differing family situations and needs, their diverse chronic or life-threatening/life-limiting conditions, their varying illness trajectories, the multiple services they require, clinical models of delivering appropriate care, funding mechanisms, research paradigms, educational initiatives, ethical concerns, communication strategies, staffing ratios and management, and effective pain/symptom management interventions, along with perceptions of pediatric care providers (see also American Academy of Pediatrics, 2013; Davies et al., 2008). Two interesting aspects of this complexity are (1) "PPC [pediatric palliative care] teams currently serve a diverse cohort of children and young adults with life-threatening conditions. In contrast to the reported experience of adult-oriented palliative care teams, most PPC patients are alive for more than a year after initiating PPC" (Feudtner et al., 2011, p. 1094) and (2) "Pediatric palliative care teams may offer support for [other] providers when they experience staff distress" (Jonas & Bogetz, 2016, p. 683).

Children who are appropriate for pediatric palliative or hospice care may receive their care from hospital-based programs, freestanding pediatric hospice facilities, hospice-based programs, or community agency or long-term care facility-based programs, but the availability of some of these services is limited and careful attention needs to be paid to transitions between them or between them and home. Challenges are seen in a cross-sectional, national study of pediatric palliative care programs in children's hospitals, which noted that the growth of such programs has been coupled with "a marked variation in how these programs are staffed, the level of funding for staff effort to provide PPC, and the number of consultations performed annually" (Feudtner et al., 2013, p. 1063).

Pediatric palliative/hospice care is supported by NHPCO's ChiPPS program (Children's Project on Palliative/Hospice Services), which offers a free, quarterly e-journal and other materials. More resources are available from the End-of-Life Nursing Education Consortium, The Initiative for Pediatric Palliative Care, Together for Short Lives in the United Kingdom, and the International Children's Palliative Care Network. Also, The Children's Hospice and Palliative Care Coalition offers help in both English and Spanish for parents coping with challenges associated with a life-threatening illness in a child through diagnosis, treatment, death, and bereavement. Research has shown that there is a national and global need for family-centered, community-based, pediatric palliative care that can improve quality of lives for both children and their family members (eHospice, 2015; Gans et al., 2015).

Finally,

> Implementation of the concurrent care portion of the ACA [Affordable Care Act] is an immense milestone in the field. PP/HC teams no longer must wait for families to forgo curative treatment in order to become involved in care. This obviates the expectation that patients and families must fit the traditional Medicare hospice benefit. Earlier involvement allows the team to help the family better navigate both the health care system and the illness journey and make important decisions with accurate information and support. Though state-by-state adoption of the concurrent care provision is still spotty, a significant burden can also be lifted from families as they can pursue disease-directed therapies while also utilizing the extensive and crucial support structures that come with involvement of PP/HC services. (NHPCO, 2014, p. 10)

HOSPICE CARE AND PALLIATIVE CARE

Just as the word *hospice* (in its various forms) has its own history and meaning, so too do the words *palliative* and *palliation* (and related terms; *Oxford English Dictionary*, 1989, vol. 11, p. 101). In health care, "to palliate" means "to alleviate the symptoms of a disease without curing it." Thus, treatment of the common cold is a kind of palliative care because, while there is no cure for the common cold, when individuals have a cough or cold, aspirin, decongestants, antihistamines, antiexpectorants, medications to dry up unwanted secretions, and other interventions (including rest, hydration, and nutritious food) are often employed to improve quality of life. In short, symptoms are palliated until the virus that causes the cold works through its own biological trajectory and reaches its natural limits, while the body's own resources rally to repel the invader and restore the person's health. Meanwhile, even though cure is not offered, most people are grateful that their distress is at least partially relieved. In all its forms, palliative care means addressing symptoms rather than underlying causes (Quill et al., 2014; Twycross, 2011).

The World Health Organization (2002) has defined **palliative care** as:

> an approach that improves the quality of life of patients and their families facing the problems associated with life-threatening illness, through the prevention and relief of

suffering by means of early identification and impeccable assessment and treatment of pain and other problems, physical, psychosocial and spiritual. Palliative care: provides relief from pain and other distressing symptoms; affirms life and regards dying as a normal process; intends neither to hasten or postpone death; integrates the psychological and spiritual aspects of patient care; offers a support system to help patients live as actively as possible until death; offers a support system to help the family cope during the patient's illness and in their own bereavement; uses a team approach to address the needs of patients and their families, including bereavement counseling, if indicated; will enhance quality of life, and may also positively influence the course of illness; is applicable early in the course of illness, in conjunction with other therapies that are intended to prolong life, such as chemotherapy or radiation therapy, and includes those investigations needed to better understand and manage distressing clinical complications.

The *Global Atlas of Palliative Care at the End of Life* (Worldwide Palliative Care Alliance, 2014, p. 5) accepts this definition with the following qualifications: (1) palliative care is needed in chronic as well as life-threatening/life-limiting conditions; (2) there is no time or prognostic limit on the delivery of palliative care (palliative care is based on need and should be provided early in the course of the illness); (3) palliative care is needed at all levels of care, including not just specialist palliative care services but at primary and secondary levels of care as well; and (4) palliative care is not limited to any one care setting. On that basis, in January 2014, the World Health Organization approved a resolution on "strengthening of palliative care as a component of integrated treatment within the continuum of care."

On this basis, hospice care is a form of palliative care—one addressed primarily to distressing symptoms in dying persons or those with a life-threatening condition who are nearing the end of their lives—while palliative care has a broader scope not confined to end of life. In theory, palliative care can be seen as the application of principles many of which were first developed in hospice care. Thus, it may be difficult to distinguish these two modes of care and perhaps not critical to do so when they can work hand in hand (Aungst, 2009). Key goals in both hospice and palliative care include effective pain and symptom management; holistic care; and seamless linkages to relevant services however and wherever they are provided.

Still, many in the medical community have adopted the phrase *palliative care* and used it in ways that are both broader and narrower than the phrase *hospice care*. *Palliative care* or *palliative medicine* is now used mainly to designate a type of medical care that addresses the relief of distressing symptoms (e.g., Bruera, Higginson, von Gunten, & Morita, 2016; Cherny, Fallon, Kaasa, Portenoy, & Currow, 2015). However, in practice that need not necessarily imply the full scope of services and interdisciplinary team approach that typify hospice care, by contrast with traditional multidisciplinary teamwork in which members of specialized health care professions work largely independently under the direction of a single person (usually a primary physician) with loose coordination.

Without the centrality of the interdisciplinary team, in the narrower meaning of the term *palliative care*, primary emphasis is likely to be placed on the role of the physician, pain and symptom management, and on hospital-based care. Nevertheless, as Quill (2007, p. 1912) has noted: "The palliative care movement continues to grow dramatically in the United States. Most academic medical centers now have palliative care consultation services, and other hospitals are launching such programs at an increasing rate." Later, Quill and Abernethy (2013, p. 1175) argued that "there are far too many seriously ill patients with unaddressed palliative care needs to have specialized palliative care teams caring for all of them" and concluded with the hope "that every medical field will define a set of basic palliative skills for which they will be primarily responsible and distinguish them from palliative care challenges requiring formal consultation." Also, a survey of bereaved families whose loved ones died in a leading U.S. hospital led Morris and Block (2015, p. 915) to recommend that "all hospitals implement basic bereavement programs for families of all deceased patients as the standard of care."

Another study (Dumanovsky et al., 2015) also demonstrated steady growth in U.S. hospital palliative care programs, but added: "Nevertheless access to palliative care remains uneven and continues to depend on accidents of geography, hospital size, and hospital ownership." Also, a further study (Spetz et al., 2016) reported that few hospital palliative care programs meet national staffing recommendations. More broadly, research by Teno, Freedman, Kasper, Gozalo, & Mor (2015, p. 622) concluded that "substantial unmet needs in end-of-life care remain. Continued efforts are needed to improve the quality of end-of-life care" (see also Rubin, 2015). The future will depend on physician education, institutional structures, and reimbursement policies.

At the same time, this meaning of the phrase *palliative care* is broader than that of *hospice care* because the former is not necessarily limited to end-of-life care. In this sense, palliative care may apply to many physician-centered efforts to manage pain and other distressing symptoms with or without reference to their origin or their relationship to dying and death. In its richest sense, this meaning of palliative care can bring important resources of pain and symptom management to a broad range of patients; in its most superficial sense, this usage of palliative care may mean little more than traditional forms of physical and psychosocial care.

These are not merely arbitrary shifts in linguistic usage; they represent various competing forces. On the one hand, for example, some have chafed at the limits imposed by regulations governing hospice care and by what they perceive to be a "death sentence" that some associate with the word *hospice*. On the other hand, there has been a desire to introduce care of distressing symptoms early in the disease process ("to move hospice care upstream," as the saying goes) by introducing palliative care concurrently with cure-oriented care (Kelley & Morrison, 2015) as well as having an option available for patients and families who want to stop aggressive cure-oriented interventions.

AN INSTITUTIONAL RECAPITULATION

Within the American death system, as we have seen in this chapter, four institutions currently care for most persons who are coping with dying.

■ *Hospitals* of all sorts (general hospitals, specialized medical or psychiatric institutions, and tertiary-care trauma centers or teaching hospitals) provide *acute care*, emphasizing assessment and diagnosis of illness and disease together with cure-oriented interventions for reversible or correctable conditions. Most hospitals offer a wide variety of medical services through their own internal facilities, such as emergency departments, medical or surgical wards, and intensive care units, or through outpatient departments and clinics. Physicians also offer some types of care in their offices, in community clinics, and in various specialized centers. Most of these services are not primarily designed for dying persons. Still, a significant portion of hospital-based care is directed toward the last six months of life (Jacobs, Bonuck, Burton, & Mulvihill, 2002). Also, approximately 37% of all deaths in our society in 2014 occurred in hospitals or were brought to these institutions for confirmation and certification of death (see Table 2.4 in Chapter 2).

- *Long-term care facilities or nursing homes* offer *chronic care*—that is, custodial, nursing, and rehabilitative care for individuals with chronic illnesses and other disabling conditions. Such institutions do not merely serve the elderly, nor are more than a very small percentage of the elderly in our society residents of such institutions at any one time. Around 20% of all deaths in our society in 2014 occurred in long-term care facilities (see Table 2.4 in Chapter 2).

- *Home health care programs* of many types (services of county and municipal health departments, the VNA, private home health care agencies, and home care departments of hospitals) deliver *home care* chiefly in the form of skilled nursing and ancillary care. This care is provided to many different kinds of clients, some of whom may be dying.

- *Hospice programs* offer *end-of-life care* for dying persons and their families. That care is conducted under the supervision of a hospice interdisciplinary team. In our society, hospice services most often take place in the home, but they may also be delivered in a hospital, a long-term care facility, a hospice inpatient unit, or via a hospice day care program. Hospice programs in the United States originally offered care primarily to elderly cancer patients, but that is no longer the case. Currently, cancer diagnoses apply to less than half of U.S. hospice admissions. In fact, hospice principles are now being applied to care of persons with AIDS (O'Neill, Selwyn, & Schietinger, 2012), individuals with motor neuron diseases like amyotrophic lateral sclerosis (ALS or Lou Gehrig's disease; Thompson, Murphy, & Toms, 2009), persons with Alzheimer's disease and other forms of dementia (Corr, Corr, & Ramsey, 2004), and other adults who are coping with various life-threatening conditions, such as end-stage heart, lung, or kidney disease. In recent years, hospice programs and other agencies have also been leaders in sponsoring and developing programs of pediatric palliative and hospice care for children, adolescents, and their family members. As a result of these many developments, hospice programs currently care for roughly 46% of all people who die in our society and approximately 7% of all deaths in our society in 2014 occurred in a hospice facility.

Summary

In this chapter, we examined ways in which our society provides care for individuals who are coping with dying through formal programs and institutions. We did this by identifying ten principles in the hospice philosophy to serve as a model for such care. Also, we described the historical development of care and its current practice in hospitals, long-term care facilities, home care programs, and hospice programs, with special reference to the care of dying persons and their families. We also added some comments on pediatric palliative/hospice care and on the relationship between hospice care and palliative care.

Glossary

Acute care: cure-oriented services that diagnose and treat specific diseases with the goal of returning an individual to full health or at least to halting or slowing the progression of the disease

Chronic care: services for persons who need rehabilitation or who cannot perform activities of daily living

End-of-life care: services for persons who are nearing death and for their family members

Home care: nursing and other ancillary services delivered to individuals in their places of residence

Home health care programs: organizations that deliver home care services

Hospice care: services designed to implement the hospice philosophy; a form of palliative care offered near the end of life

Hospice philosophy: an outlook, attitude, or approach to care that affirms life and attempts to maximize present quality in living for patient and family units who are coping with dying

Hospice programs: organizations that deliver hospice services by offering holistic care to dying persons and their family members using an interdisciplinary team

Hospitals: organizations delivering acute care services; often called "medical centers" or "health centers"

Interdisciplinary team: an organized group of professional caregivers and volunteers working together to plan and implement care; typically involves a certain amount of "role blurring"; contrasted with multidisciplinary teamwork in which members of specialized health care professions work largely independently with loose coordination

Long-term care facilities: institutions that deliver chronic care services; may be residential care, intermediate care, or skilled nursing care facilities

Nursing homes: (see Long-term care facilities)

Palliative care: services designed to relieve distressing symptoms of a disease without curing their underlying causes

Pediatric palliative and hospice care: both a philosophy and an organized method for delivering competent, compassionate, and consistent care to children with chronic, complex, and/or life-threatening conditions as well as their families

Questions for Review and Discussion

1. Think about the situation of Jo Ryan as described in the vignette near the beginning of this chapter. Try to focus on her experiences at different points in time: when she first discovered the small lump in her right breast, when she was told that she needed a mastectomy, when she developed cancer again sometime later, when she received services from a community home health care program, when she was admitted to a nursing home, when she was transferred to a local hospice inpatient unit, when she went home to be with her family, and when she neared the end of her life. What types of care did Jo need at any or all of these different points in her life? What programs of care were best suited to her needs at these different points?

2. This chapter discussed care provided by hospitals, long-term care facilities, home health care programs, and hospice programs. Think about being a person with a life-threatening illness (perhaps you can think about someone you know, such as a relative or a friend). What might be the advantages and limitations of being cared for by each of these programs?

3. How would you describe the essential elements in the hospice philosophy of care? Why do you think those elements were originally implemented in different ways in England, Canada, and the United States? Could hospice-type principles be implemented in other institutions (e.g., in hospitals, long-term care facilities, or home health care programs) in the United States?

4. What experiences (if any) have you had with hospice programs or other forms of palliative care?

5. Ample information and guidance concerning all of the issues and institutions examined in this chapter are available on the Internet. Have you ever searched online for such information and/or guidance? If so, did you find the help you sought? If not, why not?

Suggested Readings

Hospice and palliative care principles are set forth in many books and other sources, such as:

Breitbart, W. S., & Alici, Y. (2014). *Psychosocial Palliative Care*

Bruera, E., Higginson, I., von Gunten, C. F., & Morita, T. (Eds.). (2016). *Textbook of Palliative Medicine and Supportive Care* (2nd ed.)

Cherny, N., Fallon, M., Kaasa, S., Portenoy, R. K., & Currow, D. C. (Eds.). (2015). *Oxford Textbook of Palliative Medicine* (5th ed.)

Connor, S. R. (2009). *Hospice and Palliative Care: The Essential Guide* (2nd ed.)

Cox, G. R., & Stevenson, R. G. (Eds.). (2013). *Final Acts: The End of Life, Hospice and Palliative Care*

Egan, K. (2016). *On Living*

Ellershaw, J., & Wilkinson, S. (Eds.). (2011). *Care of the Dying: A Pathway to Excellence* (2nd ed.)

Ferrell, B. R., Coyle, N., & Paice, J. (Eds.). (2015). *Oxford Textbook of Palliative Nursing* (4th ed.)

Field, M. J., & Cassel, C. K. (Eds.). (1997). *Approaching Death: Improving Care at the End of Life*

Fine, P., & Kestenbaum, M. (Eds.). (2012). *The Hospice Companion: Best Practices for Interdisciplinary Assessment and Care of Common Problems during the Last Phase of Life* (2nd ed.)

Keegan, L., & Drick, C. A. (2011). *End of Life: Nursing Solutions for Death with Dignity*

Kirk, T. W., & Jennings, B. (Eds.). (2014). *Hospice Ethics: Policy and Practice in Palliative Care*

Lipman, A. G., Jackson, K. C., & Tyler, L. S. (Eds.). (2000). *Evidence-based Symptom Control in Palliative Care: Systemic Reviews and Validated Clinical Practice Guidelines for 15 Common Problems in Patients with Life-limiting Disease*

Lynn, J., Schuster, J. L., Wilkinson, A., & Simon, L. N. (2008). *Improving Care for the End of Life: A Sourcebook for Health Care Managers and Clinicians* (2nd ed.)

Matzo, M., & Sherman, D. W. (Eds.). (2014). *Palliative Care Nursing: Quality Care to the End of Life* (4th ed.)

Meier, D. E., Isaacs, S. L., & Hughes, R. (Eds.). (2010). *Palliative Care: Transforming the Care of Serious Illness*

Quill, T. E., & Miller, F. G. (Eds.). (2014). *Palliative Care and Ethics*

Reese, D. J. (2013). *Hospice Social Work*

Reith, M., & Payne, M. (2009). *Social Work in End-of-Life and Palliative Care*

Saunders, C. M., Baines, M., & Dunlop, R. (1995). *Living with Dying: A Guide to Palliative Care* (3rd ed.)

Saunders, C. M., & Kastenbaum, R. (1997). *Hospice Care on the International Scene*

Smith, F., & Himmel, S. (2013). *Changing the Way We Die: Compassionate End of Life Care and the Hospice Movement*

Twycross, R. G. (2011). *Introducing Palliative Care* (4th ed.)

Watson, M., Lucas, C., Hoy, A., & Wells, J. (2009). *The Oxford Handbook of Palliative Care* (2nd ed.)

Webb, M. (1997). *The Good Death: The New American Search to Reshape the End of Life*

Worldwide Palliative Care Alliance. (2014). *Global Atlas of Palliative Care at the End of Life*

Worldwide Palliative Care Alliance. (2015). *Palliative Care and the Global Goal for Health*

Yennurajalingam, S., & Bruera, E. (Eds.). (2016). *Oxford American Handbook of Hospice and Palliative Medicine and Supportive Care* (2nd ed.)

Zitter, J. N. (2017). *Extreme Measures: Finding a Better Path to the End of Life*

Hospice and palliative care principles are applied to situations involving children in:

Armstrong-Dailey, A., & Zarbock, S. (Eds.). (2009). *Hospice Care for Children* (3rd ed.)

Brown, E. (with Warr, B.). (2007). *Supporting the Child and the Family in Paediatric Palliative Care*

Carter, B. S., Levetown, M., & Friebert, S. E. (Eds.). (2011). *Palliative Care for Infants, Children, and Adolescents: A Practical Handbook* (2nd ed.)

Center to Advance Palliative Care. (2017). *Pediatric Palliative Care Field Guide: A Catalog of Resources, Tools and Training to Promote Innovation, Development and Growth*

Field, M. J., & Berhman, R. E. (Eds.). (2003). *When Children Die: Improving Palliative and End-of-Life Care for Children and Their Families*

Goldman, A., Hain, R., & Lieben, S. (Eds.). (2012). *Oxford Textbook of Palliative Care for Children* (2nd ed.)

Grinyer, A. (2012). *Palliative and End of Life Care for Children and Young People: Home, Hospice, Hospital*

National Institute of Nursing Research. (2015). *Palliative Care for Children: Support for the Whole Family When Your Child Is Living with a Serious Illness*

Wolfe, J., Hinds, P., & Sourkes, B. (Eds.). (2011). *Textbook of Interdisciplinary Pediatric Palliative Care*

For developments in medicine, hospitals, home care, and long-term care facilities, consult:

Chapple, H. S. (2010). *No Place for Dying: Hospitals and the Ideology of Rescue*
Diamond, R. (1992). *Making Gray Gold: Narratives of Nursing Home Care*
Gubrium, J. F. (1997). *Living and Dying at Murray Manor*
Kaufman, S. R. (2006). *And a Time to Die: How American Hospitals Shape the End of Life*
Kellehear, A. (2007). *A Social History of Dying*
Kellehear, A. (Ed.). (2009). *The Study of Dying: From Autonomy to Transformation*
Matthews, J. L. (2016). *Long-Term Care: How to Plan & Pay for It* (11th ed.)
Morley, J., Tolson, D., Ouslander, J., & Vellas, B. (2013). *Nursing Home Care*
Rosenberg, C. E. (1987). *The Care of Strangers: The Rise of America's Hospital System*
Rowles, G. D., & Teaster, P. B. (Eds.). (2016). *Long-Term Care in an Aging Society: Theory and Practice*
Shield, R. R. (1988). *Uneasy Endings: Daily Life in an American Nursing Home*
Starr, P. (1982). *The Social Transformation of American Medicine*
Stevens, R. (1989). *In Sickness and in Wealth: American Hospitals in the Twentieth Century*

Selected Web Resources

Some useful search terms include: ACUTE CARE; ASSISTED LIVING FACILITIES; CHRONIC CARE; END-OF-LIFE CARE; HOME HEALTH CARE; HOME HEALTH PROGRAMS; HOSPICE CARE; HOSPICE PHILOSOPHY; HOSPICE PROGRAMS; HOSPITALS; INTERDISCIPLINARY TEAM; LONG-TERM CARE FACILITIES; NURSING HOMES; PALLIATIVE CARE.

You can also visit the following *organizational and other Internet sites*:

American Academy of Hospice and Palliative Medicine

American Association of Homes and Services for the Aging

American Health Care Association

American Hospice Foundation

American Hospital Association

Canadian Hospice Palliative Care Association

The Catholic Health Association of the United States

The Center to Advance Palliative Care

Children's Hospice and Palliative Care Coalition

Children's Project on Palliative/Hospice Services (ChiPPS)

End-of-Life Nursing Education Consortium

Hospice and Palliative Nurses Association

Hospice Association of America

HospiceDirectory.org

Hospice Foundation of America

National Association for Home Care

National Hospice and Palliative con Organization

Partnership for Parents/Padres Com padres

VA Hospice and Palliative Care (VAHPC) Initiative, U.S. Department of Veterans Affairs

BEREAVEMENT

"Two-sidedness is a fundamental feature of death ...There are always two parties to a death; the person who dies and the survivors who are bereaved" (Toynbee, 1968a, p. 267). In fact, as we saw in Part Three, the situation is even more complicated than this would suggest. Prior to death, issues in coping with dying concern not only the person who is dying but also his or her family members, friends, and care providers (whether professionals or volunteers). All of these individuals, except the person who dies, are survivors-to-be. For each of these individuals, "a person's death is not only an ending; it is also a beginning" (Shneidman, 1973a, p. 33).

In Part Four, we examine the experiences of these bereaved persons. Nearly everyone has encountered some sort of loss in his or her own life, so we all know something about these experiences. In that sense, loss in general is one of the really fundamental and very familiar experiences in human life. But loss is a very broad subject, including both death-related and non-death losses. Our special concern in this book is death-related losses; we seek to improve our understanding of the many aspects of these losses and their consequences. In Chapter 9, we explain key elements and variables in the *experiences of persons who are coping with loss and grief*. In Chapter 10, we offer practical guidance for *individuals who seek to help bereaved persons*. And in Chapter 11, we turn to *ways in which communities within our society can contribute to this work and have organized themselves to help the bereaved*.

CHAPTER

9

Alan C. Heison/Shutterstock.com

Coping with Loss and Grief

Objectives of this Chapter

▶ To explore the nature of death-related experiences of loss and grief, the language and concepts employed to understand those experiences, and efforts involved in coping with them

▶ To define the key concepts of *loss* and *bereavement*

▶ To clarify the concept of *grief* itself and *five critical variables* that influence an individual's grief

▶ To define the term *mourning* as it is used in this book

▶ To explain the phenomena of *anticipatory grief* and *anticipatory mourning*

▶ To briefly describe classical models of normal or uncomplicated grief and mourning, such as those involving phases or stages

▶ To show how new understandings of grief and mourning have replaced those classical theories

▶ To contrast accounts of mourning as involving fixed end points with opportunities for growth and transformation

▶ To clarify what is involved in complicated grief

▶ To describe grief and mourning in families

ONE WOMAN EXPERIENCING HER LOSSES

Stella Bridgman was 43 when her 18-year-old son took his own life. His death was the tragic ending to a troubled history starting with marijuana and beer, but escalating to hard liquor and cocaine, plus problems at home, in school, and with his part-time job.

Even though her son had a history of erratic and self-destructive behavior, it was a huge shock to Stella when she found his body. Her pain was very sharp. "It was like being punched in the stomach," she said later. Stella experienced a great sense of sadness in losing someone who had been a central part of her life for so many years and whose life had sprung from her own body. She was also hurt that her son could reject her (as she viewed it) in this brutal way and spurn the very life she had given him.

At the same time, Stella was furious at her son for doing this to her and to his 15-year-old sister. She also experienced guilt as she asked herself over and over again whether there was anything in addition to what she had already been doing that she might have done to prevent his death.

The death of her son was not the first loss that Stella had experienced. Her father had died in a distant war when she was a little child; she had not really known him. Her mother, a heavy smoker, had developed lung cancer at a relatively early age and died after a difficult illness a little more than 10 years ago. That was the first death that seemed to have real significance in her life.

The death of her husband in a fiery automobile accident five years later was another harsh event that left Stella with two young children, a small sum of money from insurance and savings, and no job. She had never anticipated that possibility. All the widows she had known were elderly women. Stella turned to her church, became very protective of her children, and rejoined the workforce.

Eventually, Stella did marry again, to a widower whom she met at a church social activity, but her son disliked his new stepfather and the three siblings who came with him into the new "blended" family.

Each of the major deaths in her life had a different impact on Stella. When her mother died, Stella felt as if she was experiencing the death of her past. She found it hard to go forward without the support of the parent who had always been with her. When her first husband died, Stella felt as if it was the death of her present life, a way of living with which she had become comfortable both before and after her mother's death. But the suicide of her son was like the death of her hopes for the future. Could she cope with this new blow on top of all the others? And could she pull all of her energies together one more time and once again find the strength to live on for herself and for her daughter?

Stella asked over and over: "What did I do?" "Why did this happen?" and "How can I go on?"

NEW UNDERSTANDINGS OF LOSS, BEREAVEMENT, GRIEF, AND MOURNING

One way of understanding Stella Bridgman's experiences of loss, bereavement, grief, and mourning is to employ an adapted version of Doka's (2011) outline of new understandings of these concepts that have recently emerged from scholarly research. There are seven primary headings in this schema:

1. A broader and more inclusive understanding of loss
2. An expanded appreciation of what is involved in grief

3. Cautions about classical accounts of universal phases or stages in grief
4. New accounts of personal pathways and possibilities for active coping in bereavement
5. Revising and renewing relationships versus relinquishing ties
6. Appreciations of possibilities for transformation and growth in grief
7. Recognition of more complicated variants and the necessity for careful assessment

A BROADER AND MORE INCLUSIVE UNDERSTANDING OF LOSS

To love is to give "hostages to fortune" (Bacon, 1625/1962, p. 22). Everyone who experiences love or who forms an attachment to another runs the risk of losing the loved person or object and suffering the consequences of loss. If so, then "to grieve is to pay ransom to love" (Shneidman, 1983, p. 29).

Attachments

Of course, it is in loving that a person shares with others and enriches his or her life. **Attachments** are those very special, enduring relationships through which individuals satisfy fundamental needs (Bowlby, 1969–1980; Parkes, Stevenson-Hinde, & Marris, 1993). Stella Bridgman loved the father she had never known, her mother, her two husbands, her own children, and her second husband's children. Several writers have warned that not to love in these ways would be to cut oneself off from the rewards of human attachment—to restrict and impoverish one's life. For example, Lewis (1960, p. 169) wrote:

> To love at all is to be vulnerable. Love anything, and your heart will certainly be wrung and probably be broken. If you want to make sure of keeping it intact, you must give your heart to no one, not even to an animal. Wrap it carefully round with hobbies and little luxuries; avoid all entanglements; lock it up safe in the casket or coffin of your selfishness. But in that casket—safe, dark, motionless, airless—it will change. It will not be broken; it will become unbreakable, impenetrable, irredeemable … The only place outside Heaven where you can be perfectly safe from all the dangers and perturbations of love is Hell.

Similarly, Kalish (1985b, p. 181) added, "Anything that you have you can lose; anything you are attached to, you can be separated from; anything you love can be taken away from you. Yet, if you really have nothing to lose, you have nothing." In other words, the only alternative to experiencing the pain of loss would be to have nothing in our lives that is worth losing. Or as Brantner (in Worden, 1982, p. xi) said so aptly: "Only people who avoid love can avoid grief. The point is to learn from it and remain vulnerable to love." To learn about grief and mourning, we begin with some thoughts about loss and bereavement.

Loss

There are *many types of losses* that occur throughout human lives (Harris & Gorman, 2011; Viorst, 1986). For example, I may break up with someone I love, be fired or laid off from my job, have to leave my home and relocate, misplace a prized possession, fail in some competition, have a body part amputated, or experience the death of someone close to me. What these and other significant losses all have in common is that the individual who loses something is separated from and deprived of the lost person, object, status, or relationship. This is the *primary loss*—the termination of the attachment or relationship; *secondary losses* are those that follow from a primary loss. John Irving described the complexities of primary and secondary losses in one of his novels (1989, p. 128):

> When someone you love dies, and you're not expecting it, you don't lose her all at once; you lose her in pieces over a long time—the way the mail stops coming, and her scent fades from the pillows and even from the clothes in her closet and drawers. Gradually, you accumulate the parts of her that are gone. Just when the day comes—when there's a particular missing part that overwhelms you with the feeling that she's gone, forever— there comes another day, and another specifically missing part.

Death-related losses inevitably involve endings, separations, and secondary losses, as seen in the example of Stella Bridgman. What any death will mean to those who live on depends on the losses it involves for those individuals and the ways in which they interpret those losses. For example, death may mean the end of the time I share with my spouse or partner, a separation from one of my parents, or the loss of my child. Death may involve a relief from an abusive relationship or from the suffering of a dying person (Elison, 2007; Elison & McGonigle, 2004). However, I interpret a death-related loss, it is likely to involve at least some challenges and pain for me because that loss will impact and alter my life in important ways. Even if I am able to view death in the framework of a possible afterlife and eventual reunion with the loved one or as a transition of the person who died into a realm of ancestors who continue to interact with us, I will still be a person who has been left behind and I am now no longer able to enjoy the direct, physical presence of the person who died. Moreover, losses through death may sometimes be complicated—for example, when attachments are problematical, when dying is long and difficult, or when death is sudden, unexpected, or traumatic.

Losses that are not related to death, often called *nonfinite losses*, can also be complicated in their own ways (Harris, 2011). Such losses may be as hurtful as those arising from death, perhaps even more hurtful in some cases. For example, about half of all marriages in the United States now end in divorce. When that happens, there is often one spouse who wishes to terminate the relationship, another who does not wish to do so or who is less determined on that outcome, and perhaps a third person (such as a child) who is involved in what is happening and directly affected by its implications but not immediately able to influence what is taking place. Each of these individuals will experience different types of losses in the divorce. As in death, there is always loss in divorce, but there may also be elements of deliberate choice, guilt, and blame that are not always associated with a death. Divorce may also be complicated by theoretical (if not practical) opportunities for reconciliation and the inevitable implications of subsequent life decisions by all who are involved in its aftermath. Note that divorce is only one example of nonfinite losses with ongoing, complex, and powerful implications that can have traumatic repercussions that challenge our assumptive worlds. Other examples include unemployment, infertility, loss of health, disability, or consequences of natural disasters.

Ambiguous losses are another important type of loss that may or may not directly involve a death and can overlap with nonfinite losses (Boss, 2000). They can be losses in which the person or object is physically absent but still psychologically present, as in examples when a family member disappears or a child has been put up for adoption. Alternatively, they can involve losses in which a person is psychologically absent but still physically present, as in cases of traumatic brain injury or advanced dementia. Ambiguous losses are relational disorders that can challenge a person's identity, complicate grieving or mourning processes, frustrate desires for closure, and even lead to disenfranchised grief (see Chapter 10). Promoting resilience in the face of ambiguous losses is a key goal (Boss, 2006).

Often, as we reflect on our lives, we can identify individuals or objects whose loss would mean a great deal to us. However, sometimes the meaning and value of the lost person or object is only fully appreciated after the loss has taken place. In any event, to understand the implications of any experience of loss, we must look back to the underlying relationships and attachments on which it is founded.

Traumatic Loss

A death or loss is properly termed *traumatic* when its circumstances include certain objective elements, such as "(a) suddenness and lack of anticipation; (b) violence, mutilation, and destruction; (c) preventability and/or randomness; (d) multiple death; and (e) the mourner's personal encounter with death, where there is either a significant threat to personal survival or a massive and/or shocking confrontation with the death and mutilation of others" (Rando, 1993, pp. 568–569). (Note that all of these elements apply to the losses experienced on September 11, 2001, as well as the natural disasters and mass shootings described in Focus On 4.2 and Issues for Critical Reflection #6 in Chapter 4).

The shocking effects of a traumatic loss or death often overwhelm a survivor's capacity to cope (Rando, 1996). There may be no opportunity to say good-bye or finish unfinished business. Because what has happened does not seem to make sense, there is often an obsessive effort to reconstruct events so as to comprehend and integrate them retrospectively. Also, traumatic events are often accompanied by intense emotional reactions (e.g., fear, anxiety, a sense of vulnerability, and loss of control),

A firestorm in the hills near Los Angeles, California.

increased physiological arousal (stimulation/excitement), and a sense of vulnerability, victimization, and powerlessness, as well as fantasies of grotesque dying and aggressive thoughts of revenge (Rynearson, 2001, 2006). Further, trauma is often followed by major secondary losses, such as those involved in not having a body available after the death that can be viewed to confirm the loss, a need to rescue others or attend to the wounded, and the demands of legal inquiries.

When traumatic deaths or losses are perceived as preventable, survivors often channel outrage into intense efforts to find their cause, fix responsibility, and impose punishment. When such traumatic losses are perceived as random, survivors may try to ward off their terror by assigning blame to others or even to themselves, so as to defend against the perception that such events are truly arbitrary and unpredictable, that they cannot be protected against. Traumatic events that involve multiple deaths or losses—especially when they occur simultaneously or in rapid succession—can produce a form of *bereavement overload* in which survivors find it difficult to sort out and work through their losses, grief reactions, and mourning processes for each individual tragedy. Traumatic events that involve an individual's personal encounter with death can involve a significant threat to personal survival or can follow a massive or shocking confrontation with the death and mutilation of others. All traumatic events involve losses or death that are outside the ordinary range of human experience and that are usually associated with intense fear, terror, and a sense of helplessness (Zinner & Williams, 1999). Such events may or may not lead an individual to experience posttraumatic stress disorder (PTSD), whose basic symptom categories include re-experiencing the traumatic event, avoiding stimuli associated with that event or numbing of general responsiveness, and increased psychological arousal.

Traumatic losses shatter the "strongly held set of assumptions about the world and the self which is confidently maintained and used as a means of recognizing, planning, and acting" (Parkes, 1975, p. 132). Janoff-Bulman (1992) defined an **assumptive world** as "a conceptual system, developed over time that provides us with expectations about the world and ourselves" (p. 5). She argued that the fundamental convictions in most people's assumptive worlds are: "The world is benevolent"; "The world is meaningful"; and "The self is worthy." She insisted that such beliefs are broad, but not foolhardy, because they "afford us the trust and confidence that are necessary to engage in new behaviors, to test our limits" (p. 23).

If we consider traumatic events in terms of their effect on our fundamental assumptions, "in the end, it is a rebuilding of this trust—the reconstruction of a viable, non-threatening assumptive world—that constitutes the core coping task of victims" (Janoff-Bulman, 1992, p. 69). This is the path from being merely a **victim** to becoming a **survivor** in the full sense of that word—someone who not only survives the death but also survives the bereavement by living in a healthy way after the loss (Corr, 2002b; O'Hara, 2006). This path to survivorship is challenging because it depends on coping with the traumatic aspects of the encounter, as well as the loss and grief found in all bereavement (Beder, 2005; Kauffman, 2002). Thus, Rosenbaum (2015, p. 799) wrote: "The need to seek meaning in tragedy is fundamentally human, and yet the impulse to find reasons where there are none is as dangerous as it is therapeutic ... when something bad happens, we assume there's a cause that can be remedied, that someone is accountable?"

Janoff-Bulman (1992) described those who have coped effectively with traumatic events and challenges to their fundamental convictions and assumptive worlds in the following way:

> These survivors recognize the possibility of tragedy, but do not allow it to pervade their self- and worldviews .... [For such survivors] the world is benevolent, but not absolutely; events that happen make sense, but not always; the self can be counted on to be decent and competent, but helplessness is at times a reality...There is disillusionment, yet it is generally not the disillusionment of despair. Rather, it is disillusionment tempered by hope .... [In the end, this view] involves an acknowledgment of real possibilities, both bad and good—of disaster in spite of human efforts, of triumph in spite of human limitations. (pp. 174–175)

There are two important points here. First, it is useful to distinguish a traumatic loss or death from a traumatic bereavement because the characteristics of the reactions and responses to the event may differ from those of the event itself. Also, some individuals may experience a traumatic bereavement in connection with an event that is not perceived by others as objectively traumatic. Second, without in any way minimizing the suffering involved in traumatic losses, Calhoun and Tedeschi (1999, 2006; see also Tedeschi & Calhoun, 1995, 2007; Tedeschi, Park, & Calhoun, 1998) have noted the possibility of posttraumatic growth, particularly when assisted by an "expert companion"—someone who possesses scholarly knowledge of bereavement, grief, and trauma, clinical training, and an awareness of limitations and ambiguity in the face of issues associated with traumatic losses.

Bereavement

The term **bereavement** refers to the state of being bereaved or deprived of something. That is, bereavement identifies the objective situation of individuals who have experienced a loss of some person or thing they valued. Three elements are essential in all bereavement: (1) a relationship or attachment with some person or thing that is valued; (2) the loss—ending, termination, separation—of that relationship; and (3) an individual who is deprived of the valued person or thing by the loss.

Both the noun *bereavement* and the adjective *bereaved* derive from an old verb, *reave*, which means "to despoil, rob, or forcibly deprive" (*Oxford English Dictionary*, 1989, vol. 13, p. 295). Thus, a bereaved person is one who has been deprived, robbed, plundered, or stripped of someone or something that he or she valued. In principle, the losses experienced by bereaved people could be of many kinds; in fact, this term is most often used to refer to the situation of those who have experienced a loss through death. In other words, our language tends to assume that bereavement is about death and that death always entails a more or less brutal loss of someone or something that is important to the bereaved person. The brutal and horrifying qualities of a death or other loss, such as a traumatic one, will clearly affect the nature of the subsequent bereavement.

AN EXPANDED APPRECIATION OF GRIEF

We address here six questions about grief: (1) What is grief? (2) How does grief relate to disease, depression, and guilt? (3) Is grief typically a normal and healthy reaction to loss? (4) What makes a difference in grief? (5) What is anticipatory grief? and (6) Can grief be absent?

Loneliness is a frequent companion to loss (an illustration from *Tear Soup*—see Personal Insights 10.2).

Illustrations © 1999 Taylor Bills, Publication © 1999 Grief Watch

What Is Grief?

Grief *is the term that indicates one's reactions to loss.* When one suffers a significant loss, one experiences grief. The word *grief* signifies one's reactions, both internally and externally, to the impact of the loss (see Personal Insights 9.1). The term arises from the grave or heavy weight that presses on bereaved persons (*Oxford English Dictionary*, 1989, vol. 6, pp. 834–835). Not to experience grief for a significant loss is an aberration. It would suggest that there was no real attachment prior to the loss, that the relationship was complicated in ways that set it apart from the ordinary, or that one is suppressing or hiding one's reactions to the loss.

The term *grief* is often defined as *the emotional reaction to loss.* One needs to be careful in speaking that way. As Elias (1991, p. 117) noted, "broadly speaking, emotions have three components, a somatic [i.e., bodily or physical], a behavioral and a feeling component." As a result, "the term *emotion,* even in professional discussions, is used with two different meanings. It is used in a wider and in a narrower sense at the same time. In the wider sense the term *emotion* is applied to a reaction pattern which involves the whole organism in its somatic, its feeling and its behavioral aspects. ... In its narrower sense the term *emotion* refers to the feeling component of the syndrome only" (p. 119).

PERSONAL INSIGHTS 9.1

Auden on Grief

Stop all the clocks, cut off the telephone,
Prevent the dog from barking with a juicy bone,
Silence the pianos and with muffled drum
Bring out the coffin, let the mourners come.
Let aeroplanes circle moaning overhead
Scribbling on the sky the message HE IS DEAD,
Put crêpe bows round the white necks of the public doves,
Let the traffic policeman wear black cotton gloves.
He was my North, my South, my East and West,
My working week and my Sunday rest,
My noon, my midnight, my talk, my song;
I thought that love would last for ever: I was wrong.
The stars are not wanted now: put out every one;
Pack up the moon and dismantle the sun;
Pour away the ocean and sweep up the wood;
For nothing now can ever come to any good.

Source: "Stop All The Clocks," copyright 1940 W. H. Auden and renewed 1968
by W. H. Auden, from *Collected Poems*, by W. H. Auden. Used by
permission of Random House, Inc.

Grief clearly does involve feelings, and it is certainly appropriate to think of the affective or feeling dimensions of grief. Anyone who has personally experienced grief or who has encountered a grieving person will be familiar with the outpouring of feelings that is a prominent element of most grief. However, it is also important to recognize that *one's reactions to loss are not merely a matter of feelings*. Grief is broader, more complex, and more deep-seated than this narrower understanding of emotions and emotional reactions to loss might imply (Doka, 2007b, 2011; Rando, 1993).

Grief can be experienced and expressed in numerous ways, including:

- *Physical sensations*, such as hollowness in the stomach, a lump in the throat, tightness in the chest, aching arms, oversensitivity to noise, shortness of breath, lack of energy, muscle weakness, dry mouth, or loss of coordination
- *Feelings*, such as sadness, anger, guilt and self-reproach, anxiety, loneliness, fatigue, helplessness, shock, yearning, emancipation, relief, numbness, or a sense of depersonalization
- *Thoughts or cognitions*, such as disbelief, confusion, preoccupation, a sense of the presence of the deceased, paranormal experiences, or dreams of the deceased
- *Behaviors*, such as sleep or appetite disturbances, absentmindedness, loss of interest in activities formerly enjoyed, crying, avoiding reminders of the deceased, calling out and searching, sighing, restless overactivity, or visiting places and cherishing objects that are evocative of the deceased

- *Social difficulties* in interpersonal relationships or problems in functioning within an organization or social group
- *Spiritual searching* for a sense of meaning, hostility toward God or a higher power, turning to one's value framework, or perhaps realizing that it is inadequate to cope with this particular loss

To think of grief solely as a matter of feelings is to risk misunderstanding and missing this full range of reactions to loss.

As we seek to grasp the full meaning of grief, we should also note reports that grief can be associated with increased risk of illness or morbidity in bereaved persons (Glick, Weiss, & Parkes, 1974). Grief may also be a contributing factor in leading to the death of some bereaved persons.

How Does Grief Relate to Disease, Depression, and Guilt?

We can learn more about grief by comparing and contrasting it with three other phenomena: disease, depression, and guilt.

First, some writers (such as Engel, 1961; see also Stroebe, 2015) have noted that there are many similarities between *grief* and *disease*. For example, a significant loss may affect a bereaved person's ability to function, at least temporarily. Also, metaphors of healing are commonly employed to describe the processes and time required to overcome this impaired functioning. However, there are important distinctions between grief and disease. Grief is a "dis-ease," a discomforting disturbance of everyday equilibrium, but it is not a "disease" in the sense of a sickness or morbid (unhealthy) condition of mind or body. In fact, most grief is an appropriate and healthy reaction to loss.

Second, sadness and other common manifestations of grief do resemble some of the symptoms associated with the diagnosis of *clinical depression* since both may involve an experience of being pressed down upon and a withdrawal from the world. However, in general, grief is a healthy reaction to loss, whereas clinical depression is a mental disorder or disease (Ferszt & Leveillee, 2009). That is, grief is typically characterized by sadness, despair, fatigue or low energy, tears, loss of appetite, poor sleep, poor concentration, happy and sad memories, and mild feelings of guilt, while major depression is typically characterized by feelings of worthlessness, exaggerated guilt, suicidal thoughts, low self-esteem, powerlessness, helplessness, agitation, loss of interest in pleasurable activities, and exaggerated fatigue (Schwartz, 2013). Thus, Freud (1959a) long ago recognized the difference between **mourning** or the normal processes associated with grief and what he called **melancholia**, which is his language for the illness state of depression. As Worden (2009, pp. 32) observed, "Even though grief and depression share similar objective and subjective features, they do seem to be different conditions. Depression overlaps with bereavement but is not the same .... Freud believed that in grief, the world looks poor and empty while in depression, the person feels poor and empty." Long-standing research (e.g., Clayton, Herjanic, Murphy, & Woodruff, 1974; Schneider, 1980; Zisook & DeVaul, 1983) confirms that grief and depression are different types of experiences. Thus, Stella Bridgman was beset by her loss and grief, but she was not clinically depressed.

Third, *guilt* may be part of the total grief reaction, but it is important to disentangle issues of guilt from the larger grief experience and address them separately. **Grief** is the broad term for reactions to loss; **guilt** refers to thoughts and feelings that assign blame (often self-blame), fault, or culpability for the loss. Guilt experienced by bereaved persons may be realistic or unrealistic. *Unrealistic guilt* is often part of a process of *reality testing* induced by a loss in which a temporary acceptance of blame may in the long run prove to be one way of confirming that there was, in fact, nothing the bereaved person could have done to prevent the death. By contrast with clinical depression, when guilt is experienced during bereavement, "it is usually guilt associated with some specific aspect of the loss rather than a general overall sense of culpability" (Worden, 2009, p. 32). Guilt may arise from one's role (e.g., as parent and protector) or from something that one believes he or she should or could have done or not done. For example, even though Stella Bridgman knew her son had brought on himself many of his own difficulties and finally his death, she agonized over whether she ought to have found some other ways to help him more. Eventually, she realized she had done all she could and her son was ultimately responsible for taking his own life.

Is Grief Typically a Normal and Healthy Reaction to Loss?

Ordinary, uncomplicated grief is a healthy, normal, and appropriate reaction to loss. As May (1992, p. 3) has written:

> Grief is neither a disorder nor a healing process; it is a sign of health itself, a whole and natural gesture of love. Nor must we see grief as a step towards something better. No matter how much it hurts—and it may be the greatest pain in life—grief can be an end in itself, a pure expression of love.

Similarly, Lindstrom (2002, p. 20) remarked: "To be able to think in terms of past, present, and future, to love and to grieve, is part of the human existential plight and dignity. Grief may add meaning and perspective to one's life just as shadows give depth to a landscape."

Bereaved persons may not be at ease with their situation or with themselves, but they are not, on that ground alone, diseased or depressed in any medical or psychiatric sense. Although encounters with death, grief, and bereavement may not be very frequent or ordinary experiences for many people, the fact that they are *unusual* does not mean that they are *abnormal* or alien in the way disease is foreign to health. Each death that Stella Bridgman experienced was difficult and demanding in its own way, but in each case she came to realize that her grief was normal and fully warranted by her encounter with loss. (Other people may turn to the Internet in an effort to determine whether or not their grief is "normal." In that medium they can share reactions online that they might be hesitant to speak about offline.)

For these reasons, in this book, we speak of *signs* or *manifestations* of grief, not *symptoms*. Symptoms are indicators of disease, but bereavement and grief simply are not states of disease from which symptoms would arise. Bereavement and grief may be unusual and daunting, but they are not in themselves abnormal, morbid, or unhealthy.

Some people say that, if they were to die, their friends should have a party and not be sad. This misrepresents the nature both of grief and of human attachments. It tells people that they ought not to be experiencing what they actually are experiencing or what they may need to experience. Honest reactions to loss are real; they cannot be turned on and off at will. All human beings react to significant losses; few have much control over what those reactions will be right after an important loss.

In addition, loss always has social implications for those who go on living. When I love someone, I experience joyful feelings and other reactions that I usually need and want to express. When I lose someone I have loved, I also have feelings and other grief reactions, and I usually need to express or give vent to those reactions, too.

Moreover, after a death only part of our grief is for the person who died. In large measure, our grief is for ourselves as people who have been left behind:

> When someone you love has died, you tend to recall best those few moments and incidents that helped to clarify your sense, not of the person who has died, but of your own self. And if you loved the person a great deal … your sense of who you are will have been clarified many times, and so you will have many such moments to remember. (Banks, 1991, p. 43)

That is why we experience grief even after a slow, lingering, or painful death when we believe that the dying person has been released from distress and is at last at rest. It is also why we encounter grief even when our religious beliefs and theology assure us that the dead person has gone on to a new and better life. Whatever else has happened, as bereaved persons we have experienced a real loss. It is not selfish or improper to react to that loss with grief; it is simply a realistic human reaction.

We have already noted that experiences of bereavement and grief may be more and more unusual or infrequent in a society in which average life expectancies have been greatly extended and death seems less often to enter our lives. However, these changes in our encounters with death should not lead us to view bereavement and grief as *abnormal* parts of life. Loss, death, and grief are normal and natural parts of human life. Because they may be unusual in our experience and are typically associated with a sense of being out of control, it often appears to bereaved persons that they are losing their minds. This is rarely true. *Reacting and responding to loss is in itself a healthful process, not a morbid one*. It may take courage to face one's grief and to permit oneself to experience one's reactions to significant losses, but ultimately we do that in the interests of our own welfare (Tatelbaum, 1980).

In recent years, many bereaved persons have turned to the Internet as part of an effort to determine the normality of their grief. Often, that can be helpful, partly because the anonymity and wide variation of online accounts of grief allows people to say things online that they might be reluctant to say offline or face-to-face. Sometimes, grievers merely need to unload their strong feelings, which may prompt others to recommend personal grief counseling or support (Paulus & Varga, 2015; Varga & Paulus, 2014). Social media sites such as "the burgeoning phenomenon of Facebook memorial pages" (Irwin, 2015, p. 119) can provide an alternative to traditional memorialization rituals.

Of course, loss and grief can befall individuals who already have a psychiatric or physical illness, as well as those who are in good health. Thus, the appropriateness of one's grief must always be assessed on an individual basis. *Grief is very much an individualized phenomenon*, unique in many ways to each particular loss and griever. The same griever is likely to react in different ways to different losses; different grievers are likely to react in different ways to the same loss. *Because there is no universal reaction following any given loss, one person's grief should not be construed as a standard by which others should evaluate themselves*. To remember this is to be sensitive and open to the very broad range of manifestations associated with loss, and not confuse normal reactions with the abnormalities of disease.

Finally, loss can sometimes lead to complicated grief reactions; if so, therapeutic intervention is warranted. We return to the subject of complicated grief reactions later in this chapter.

What Makes a Difference in Bereavement and Grief?

Five critical variables influence experiences of bereavement and grief:

1. The *nature of the prior attachment* or the *perceived value* that the lost person or thing has for the bereaved individual
2. The *way in which the loss occurred* and the *concurrent circumstances* of the bereaved person
3. The *coping strategies* that the bereaved individual has learned to use in managing prior losses
4. The *developmental situation of the bereaved person*—that is, how one's being a child, adolescent, adult, or elderly person influences one's grief and mourning (Corr, 1998a)
5. The *nature of the support that is available to the bereaved person after the loss* from family members, friends, other individuals, and social institutions (Parkes, 1976)

We explore the first three of these factors in this chapter, along with the family context for grief. We will discuss social support in Chapters 10 and 11, and we will consider developmental issues in Part Five.

Prior attachments are not always what they seem to be. The full import of a relationship may not be appreciated until it is over. Some relationships are dependent, abusive, ambivalent, distorted, or complicated in many ways. Almost all relationships are multidimensional. A person whom I love is likely to be significant in my life in many ways—for example, as spouse or partner, helpmate, homemaker, sometime antagonist, lover, competitor, parent of my children, guide in difficult times, breadwinner, critic, comforter. Each of these dimensions influences my grief experience and may represent a loss that will need to be mourned. Special difficulties may be associated with the death of a person when the relationship with that person involved abuse, mistreatment, violence, or ambivalent feelings.

The way in which the loss takes place and the circumstances of the bereaved person are also critical to how we experience grief. For the way in which a loss takes place, some losses (like the suicide of Stella Bridgman's son and losses associated with violence or unexpected natural disasters) occur in sudden, shocking, or traumatic ways (Doka, 1996b). Some losses can be foreseen or predicted; others cannot. Some losses occur gradually and allow time for anticipation and preparation; others are drawn out and difficult. Some losses are untimely and contrary to what we expect in the natural order of things; others fit more easily into our sense of the overall patterns of life. Thus, Shakespeare (*Hamlet*, IV, v: 78) wrote that "when sorrows come, they come not like single spies, but in battalions" and a popular saying reports "it never rains but it pours." What these quotations mean is that losses often do (or at least seem to) compound each other by their frequency, altering what might otherwise have been a brief, gentle shower into an extended torrential onslaught. In general, deaths that are "off time"—that occur well before or long after our expectations might have prepared us for them—are likely to be among those we find most difficult (Rando, 1984).

An American soldier is overwhelmed by grief and exhaustion.

NEstudio/Shutterstock.com

In addition to the characteristics of the loss itself, *the circumstances that surround the bereaved person at the time of the loss* also influence the overall bereavement experience. For example, a person who is physically healthy, mentally in top form, and generally at ease with life may be in better condition to cope with loss than someone who is simultaneously beset with a variety of physical, mental, and other challenges in living. Some losses take place at a time in one's life when other burdens or challenges are heavy. Others are complicated because they are part of a series of losses following rapidly one after another that impact a single individual. Still other losses involve many deaths at the same time, as in the deaths of several members of an extended family in a single fatal accident. And the events of September 11, 2001, uncovered complications arising from multiple deaths in a large-scale disaster. For example, many of the men killed at the World Trade Center in New York City were married and relatively young or in mid-life. A significant number of their wives were pregnant at the time. As a result, when their husbands died these women were left on their own to face the challenges of pregnancy and giving birth.

In Chapter 6, we pointed out that throughout their lives *different individuals are likely to develop different types of coping strategies*. These are our constantly changing efforts to manage perceived stressors. Each of these coping strategies may be more or less effective. Once a significant loss or death occurs, we are likely to try to cope by employing coping strategies and skills that we previously acquired (Folkman, 2001). Thus, despite the many differences between death and other losses, it is often a good rule of thumb to ask how someone has coped with other losses earlier in his or her life to expect how that person is likely to cope with death and bereavement (Shneidman, 1980/1995). In understanding and assessing an individual's coping strategies, it is important to keep in mind not only that person in isolation but also the cultural and spiritual environments and values that have surrounded and influenced that person. We are all individuals, but the persons we become are inevitably affected by these and many other factors that help shape us. Developing new and more effective coping skills usually requires more time and energy than are likely available in the immediate aftermath of a death or other significant loss. Thus, Stella Bridgman initially did not believe her coping skills were adequate to enable her to cope with the loss and grief arising from the suicide of her son.

What Is Anticipatory Grief?

The concept of *anticipatory grief* was first introduced by Lindemann (1944) and has since been the subject of numerous inquiries (e.g., Fulton & Fulton, 1971; Fulton & Gottesman, 1980; Rando, 2000; Siegel & Weinstein, 1983). Broadly speaking, anticipatory grief refers to grief experiences that take place prior to but in connection with a significant loss that is expected to take place but has not yet occurred—for example, grief that occurs in advance of, but somehow still in relation to impending death. A forewarning of death is a necessary condition for anticipatory grief, but the heart of the matter is the grief reaction to the anticipated, but not yet actually realized, loss. Edgar Allan Poe provided a clear example of **anticipatory grief and mourning** in describing his reactions (on more than one occasion) to his wife's anticipated death (see Personal Insights 9.2) and similar examples of anticipatory grief have been reported in children who are facing death (Sourkes, 1996).

PERSONAL INSIGHTS 9.2

An Extract from a Letter by Edgar Allan Poe on January 4, 1848

"You say—'Can you *hint* to me what was the terrible evil' which caused the irregularities so profoundly lamented?' Yes; I can do more than hint. This 'evil' was the greatest which can befall a man. Six years ago, a wife, whom I loved as no man ever loved before, ruptured a blood-vessel in singing. Her life was despaired of. I took leave of her forever & underwent all the agonies of her death. She recovered partially and I again hoped. At the end of a year the vessel broke again—I went through precisely the same scene. Again in about a year afterward. Then again—again—again & even once again at varying intervals. Each time I felt all the agonies of her death—and at each accession of the disorder I loved her more dearly & clung to her life with more desperate pertinacity. But I am constitutionally sensitive—nervous in a very unusual degree. I became insane, with long intervals of horrible sanity. During these fits of absolute unconsciousness I drank, God only knows how often or how much. As a matter of course, my enemies referred the insanity to the drink rather than the drink to the insanity. I had indeed, nearly abandoned all hope of a permanent cure when I found one in the death of my wife. This I can & do endure as becomes a man—it was the horrible never-ending oscillation between hope & despair which I could not longer have endured without the total loss of reason. In the death of what was my life, then, I receive a new but—God! how melancholy an existence."

Source: Poe (1948), vol. 2, p. 356.

Rando (1986c, p. 24) originally defined anticipatory grief as "the phenomenon encompassing the processes of mourning, coping, interaction, planning, and psychosocial reorganization that are stimulated and begun in part in response to the awareness of the impending loss of a loved one and the recognition of associated losses in the past, present, and future." This very broad definition includes both grief reactions and mourning processes; refers equally to past, present, and future losses; incorporates a shifting time frame as the dying person moves toward death; and encompasses the perspectives of both the dying person and his or her survivors-to-be.

One problem with this definition is that the adjective *anticipatory* seems to be inappropriate since the grief in question is not limited solely to future or expected losses. A second problem is that the noun *grief* is inexact since the definition includes both grief and mourning. For those reasons, Rando (1988) first argued that although the phenomenon of anticipatory grief is real, the term itself is a misnomer. Subsequently, she shifted to the phrase *anticipatory mourning* in the title of a later book (Rando, 2000).

In any event, it seems clear, for example, that when a husband is dying, a wife may realize that she has already lost the help he used to give her around the house (a past loss), that she is currently losing the vigorous ways in which he used to express his love for her (a present or ongoing loss), and that she will soon lose the comfort of his presence and the shared retirement they had planned together (an expected or anticipated loss). Each of these losses may generate its own grief reaction, and each may stimulate a mourning process in which one tries to cope with that loss and its associated grief reaction. However, these experiences need not be inconsistent with maintaining the loving ties that characterize an attachment between two living people. After all, partners often experience other losses—a job, a beloved home, a loved parent or friend—but continue to love each other through the loss.

Some criticisms of the concept of anticipatory grief (e.g., Fulton, 2003) led to recommendations to distinguish between anticipatory grief and anticipatory mourning (Corr, 2007a). If so, anticipatory grief would be understood more narrowly as including only reactions to losses that have not yet occurred and are not yet in process—losses that are expected but have not yet become actualized. Anticipatory mourning would then designate efforts to cope with those anticipated losses and their related grief. Losses that have already been realized would be subject to familiar accounts of grief and mourning, although they take place prior to a death and do not involve anticipation. As such, all of these predeath experiences are components of a larger context of reacting to and coping with dying (Corr & Corr, 2000); they influence what happens afterwards but do not take the place of postdeath grieving and mourning.

Can Grief Be Absent?

This question was first asked by Helene Deutsch in 1937. Her conclusion was that if there was a real loss of a loved individual, the absence of any emotion was clearly problematic. In recent years, that conclusion has been called into question. Bonanno (2004, 2009) has emphasized that humans have a natural resilience toward adapting to loss—that for many individuals, grief reactions to loss are relatively mild and persons are soon able to effectively function at work, school, or home (Bonanno et al., 2002; Bonanno, Wortman, & Nesse, 2004). Resilient grievers tended to be generally optimistic, were in good psychological health, had an intrinsic sense of spirituality, focused on positive memories, enjoyed facing challenges, and had a belief that even in the worst situations they could learn and grow. Bonanno found that many of these individuals felt that as a result of the loss, they now experienced deeper personal connections and a renewed spirituality and sense of meaning in life. Resilience was facilitated when these grievers tended to experience fewer stresses or losses at the time, the death was not sudden, and they had an opportunity to say goodbye.

CAUTIONS ABOUT CLASSICAL MODELS OF GRIEF AND MOURNING INVOLVING UNIVERSAL PHASES OR STAGES

Recalling Stella Bridgman's experiences in the vignette near the beginning of this chapter allows us to describe and raise cautions about classical accounts of grief as involving universal stages, while also alerting us to important distinctions between grief and mourning. In so doing, we can keep in mind how she was impacted in a variety of ways by the death of her son. Her initial grief reactions were intense, but she had not at that time moved very far forward with her mourning.

Language about Mourning

We think of mourning in this book as an essential process for those who are trying to cope with loss and grief, one that is equally important in helping such persons find ways to go forward with healthful living and adapt to the new world in which they find themselves. As such, mourning has two complementary forms or aspects. It is both an *internal, private, or intrapersonal process*—our inward struggles to cope with or try to manage both the loss and our grief reactions to that loss; and an *outward, public, or interpersonal process*—the overt, visible, and shared expression of grief, together with efforts to obtain social support. Some authors (such as Neimeyer and Attig who are discussed later in this chapter) who prefer to emphasize the distinction between these two aspects use terms like **grieving** for the intrapersonal dimension of coping with loss and reserve the term **mourning** for the interpersonal aspects or social expression of grief. We prefer a single term to designate both aspects of mourning, and we use that term to refer to the interactions of the personal and social dimensions of human beings. In this chapter, we concentrate on intrapersonal or intrapsychic dimensions of mourning; we will examine public or interpersonal aspects of mourning more closely in Chapters 10 and 11.

Another way to grasp the meaning of the term *mourning* is to consider the words of Jesus in the Sermon on the Mount: "Blessed are those that mourn, for they shall be comforted." But bereavement, loss, and grief are all burdens; how can they be a blessing? The blessing can only be in the capacity to mourn and grow through the loss. As Shneidman (1980/1995, p. 179) wrote: "Mourning is one of the most profound human experiences that it is possible to have. … The deep capacity to weep for the loss of a loved one and to continue to treasure the memory of that loss is one of our noblest human traits."

Classical Models of Grief and Mourning

We know that human reactions and responses to loss are complex, personal, and culturally influenced. Historically, what might be called a "standard model" of grief and mourning was developed to describe what was going on when people struggled with loss. Doka (2007b) traced this model back to an article by Freud (1959a) in which he argued that people responding to loss have to "work through" their grief. From this, the dominant model for what is going on in managing loss is that there is a certain amount of **grief work** that must be lived through, acted out, and expressed if mourning is to be "completed" in some acceptable manner; and that grief work mainly has to do with the emotions associated with loss. However, this whole model has been questioned, both in terms of its basic assumptions and in terms of its adequacy (Granek, 2010; Harris, 2010; Jordan & Neimeyer, 2007; Konigsberg, 2011; Wortman & Silver, 1989, 2001).

This attempt to organize the human experience of mourning into a fairly straight-forward picture led in early studies to a theoretical framework or model that began from assumptions like these: (1) that there is some universal human pattern to how human beings respond to loss and (2) that pattern can be best understood as a series of normative **stages or phases** that successful mourners work through toward some goal of completion. These assumptions led to a dominant way of thinking about mourning by trying to uncover and describe these stages or phases in a manner that will clarify how grief work is lived through (Corr & Corr, 2007b). Some examples of such models follow. (Note that space limitations limit the theoretical models we can describe here; prominent theorists like Rando [1993] and Rubin [1999; Rubin, Malkinson, & Witztum, 2003] have offered other models.)

Parkes on Four Phases in Mourning   Drawing on work by Bowlby (1961, 1969–1980), Parkes (1970b, 1996) proposed *a phase-based theory* that described *four phases in mourning*: (1) shock and numbness, (2) yearning and searching, (3) disorganization and despair, and (4) reorganization. These phases are said to be elements in an overall process of **realization**—making real in one's inner, psychic world what is already real in the outer, objective world.

Shock and numbness are typical features of almost every account of initial reactions to loss although they may recur at a later date or in different circumstances. Feeling dazed, stunned, or detached reflects the impact of the loss. For some, the effect is like being encircled by an invisible protective shield, a kind of "psychic closing off." Those who are shocked often find it difficult to take care of basic needs like nutrition, hydration, or making decisions. This is a natural defense against bad news and unwanted pain. It is almost always a passing or transitory condition, although it may reappear from time to time.

Yearning and searching reflect an effort to return to things as they once were. As the pain of grief penetrates the dissolving barriers of shock and one realizes the magnitude of one's loss, many may be unwilling to acknowledge the loss. Instead, one may *yearn* or pine for a time that is now gone and may search for what has been lost. *Searching* may be triggered by a glimpse of someone who resembles him, by a whiff of her perfume, by the strains of "our" song (Parkes, 1970b). In fact, yearning and searching are doomed to failure after a death as the title of the novel, *You Can't Go Home Again* (Wolfe, 1940), indicates. Grasping that fact is to realize the depth, extent, and finality of the bereaved person's loss.

Disorganization and despair react to the inability to bring the past back to life. If the past is truly gone, then who am I now and how can I live my life (see Personal Insights 9.3)? It is hard to answer questions like these, tough to concentrate on multiple new challenges, and easy to become distracted or bewildered in the face of new demands. Much that was previously taken for granted has been called into question.

Getting through just a few moments, an hour, or one day at a time may be very demanding. Those who are disorganized and disoriented struggle to find ways to go forward.

Reorganization occurs when one can begin to pick up the pieces of one's life again and start to shape them into "new normals" for future living. One has to find a new way of living as someone no longer attached in ways he or she once was. Most bereaved persons do achieve some reorganization in their lives. It is a heroic accomplishment in the struggle to develop and define a new mode of living.

Some writers offer five (Weizman, 2005), seven (Kavanaugh, 1972), or ten (Westberg, 1971, 2010) phases in their models of mourning. Others combine yearning/searching and disorientation into a three-phase model: (1) shock; (2) a period of intense or active grieving; and (3) reestablishment of physical and mental balance (Gorer, 1965b; Tatelbaum, 1980). Similarly, Rando (1993) described three broad phases in mourning: avoidance, confrontation, and accommodation. The number of phases in these models is not as important as whether they are useful in helping us to understand the experiences of mourning.

Sanders on Six Phases in Mourning   Sanders (1989) drew on her research to suggest that most people followed a common sequence of phases in the process of grieving, describing in each phase the psychological, cognitive, and physical manifestations of grief. To Sanders—a psychologist who began studying grief after the accidental death of her adolescent son—the first phase was *shock* as individuals begin to feel the impact of the death. In this phase, physical reactions can include weeping, tremors, or loss of appetite; psychological reactions may involve distancing, egocentric phenomena, or preoccupation with thoughts of the deceased; and cognitive manifestations can include disbelief, restlessness, a heightened state of alarm, or a sense of unreality or helplessness. Sanders' research recognized both the individuality and multiplicity of grief reactions—a significant advance over stage theory.

For Sanders, shock acted as a buffer leading to a second phase, *awareness of loss*. As the shock recedes, funeral rituals end, and friends withdraw, primary grievers experience the full force of their loss. Here is an intense period of high emotional and cognitive arousal as separation anxiety is intense and stress is prolonged. Now, grief is both raw and deeply painful. Crying, anger, frustration, guilt, yearning, anxieties, and shame are common. Bereaved individuals often experience sleep disturbances in this phase creating fatigue. Psychologically, bereaved individuals may still experience denial and disbelief.

Conservation-withdrawal is the third phase in Sanders' account of bereavement. This is a long, sometimes never ending, phase of grief. Grieving people now seem to be functioning, but they have little energy for anything else. Pain is now more chronic than acute. Often, grievers feel physically weak and helpless—going through the motions rather than actively living life. Bereaved individuals may express a belief that they are in state of "hibernation"—a sort of holding pattern as they struggle to adapt to the loss.

To Sanders, bereaved persons face three choices in this phase. This is an important contribution. In the face of physical and psychological stress, with an immune system overburdened by chronic stress, some may consciously or unconsciously seek their own death rather than live without the person who died. Others may assume that the energy for major life adjustments requires more strength and power than they currently possess. They may choose to live their remaining lives in a diminished state of chronic grief. Still others may make a conscious decision to move forward— to move on and adjust to their loss.

Individuals who choose to move forward experience a fourth phase: *healing—the turning point*. In Sanders' research, many bereaved individuals could actually point to a moment where they consciously decided that their lives needed to change. For example, an older widow heard her young granddaughter ask her mother, the widow's adult daughter, "why grandma always cries?" The widow resolved that she had to do something lest she be remembered as the "grandma who always cried." Along with many others in this phase, she chose to reconstruct her identity and live with a sense of restored physical health, increased energy, and psychological vigor.

Individuals like this move to a fifth phase of bereavement that Sanders called *renewal*. While such people still have occasional bad days and episodic moments of grief, such as at the anniversary of the death and other significant events, they now experience a new level of functioning characterized by enhanced self-awareness, increased levels of energy, personal revitalization, and renewal of social ties. These bereaved individuals have learned to live without the physical presence of the deceased even as they retain an internal sense of that person's presence. For Sanders, bereaved persons in this phase could even sometimes enjoy memories of the deceased without the high emotional arousal often experienced earlier in the grieving process.

Late in her life, Sanders suggested a sixth phase that some individuals may experience—*fulfillment*. Here the loss is so integrated in one's life that it is difficult, even as the individual still grieves, to perceive a life without the loss. Here one believes that one has done well not only despite the loss but in a very real way *because of* the loss (Doka, 2006).

Sanders' phase theory represents significant advances over the stage theory of Kübler-Ross (1969). First, Sanders offered a research-based sequence of mourning, rather than a set of clinical observations of the types of reactions that bereaved person's experience. Second, Sanders' work emphasized that bereaved individuals had many different types of reactions including physical, psychological, social, and cognitive—emphasizing both the individuality of the grief process and expanding the range of reactions associated with grief. Her work on mitigating factors showed how the characteristics of the bereaved individual, the context of the death, and the social support available influenced the process of grief.

Above all, Sanders was one of the first theorists to affirm that individuals had choices *within* grief. She stressed that bereaved individuals were active participants in the mourning process, rather than simply passively coping with a process they could not control. Sanders' phase of renewal, and later, fulfillment, resonates well with current trends in contemporary bereavement theory such as posttraumatic growth (Calhoun & Tedeschi, 2006), affirming that a loss can lead to significant personal development. In addition, her work emphasized that grieving persons maintain a conscious attachment to the deceased that foreshadowed work on continuing bonds (Klass, Silverman, & Nickman, 1996).

Kübler-Ross, Kessler, and Others on Stages in Mourning   In Chapter 9, we learned that Kübler-Ross proposed a theory of five stages in coping with dying (denial, anger, bargaining, depression, and acceptance). In a book published shortly after her death, the same stage-based theory is applied to bereavement without offering any additional evidence for doing so (Kübler-Ross & Kessler, 2005). Nevertheless, at the same time, we are told:

> The stages have evolved since their introduction, and they have been very misunderstood over the past three decades. … They are responses to loss that many people have, but there is not a typical response to loss, as there is no typical loss. Our grief is as individual as our lives.
>
> The five stages … are tools to help us frame and identify what we may be feeling. But they are not stops on some linear timeline in grief. Not everyone goes through all of them or goes in a prescribed order. (p. 7)

This is puzzling. If grief is an individual experience, then there are not just five typical or normative responses to loss; and if there is no prescribed order, then there really is no justification for continuing to speak of "stages" (see Corr, 2015b).

Despite these caveats, Maciejewski, Zhang, Block, and Prigerson (2007) offered an empirical justification for another, slightly different stage theory of grief that identified four sets of sequential responses to loss by death—disbelief, yearning, anger, and depression—plus acceptance, which was the dominant *initial* reaction. According to these authors, "[D]isbelief decreased from an initial high at 1 month postloss, yearning peaked at 4 months postloss, anger peaked at 5 months postloss, and depression peaked at 6 months postloss. Acceptance increased throughout the study observation period" (p. 297). Because the maximum values for all five grief indicators occurred within a six-month period, the authors concluded that these "stages" and this period of time describe the "normal" course of grief.

These stage-based models of grief and mourning have been criticized for methodological limitations, such as drawing on particular population groups (adults living with life-threatening illnesses for Kübler-Ross and Kessler; older, adult, white females following the death of a spouse for Maciejewski and colleagues). In fact, all phase- and stage-based models, such as those initially proposed by Parkes and later by Sanders, are essentially broad generalizations about common elements in (some? most?) grief and mourning. However, models based on particular populations may not apply very well beyond the group(s) from which they originated. Also, a study of an ethnically diverse sample of young adults who had been bereaved by either natural or violent causes found only limited support for any stage theory by contrast with individualized processes of meaning making that do not depend on time since the loss (Holland & Neimeyer, 2010). Clearly, one must be quite cautious in applying stage/phase models to individuals experiencing grief and mourning. That is why Stroebe, Schut, and Boerner (2017) have sought to caution health care professionals that bereaved persons are misguided through the stages of grief.

In addition, these phase- and stage-based models all seem to describe a rigid, linear schema in which one phase or stage is said to follow another in sequence (Hall, 2014). That leads to talk about how much time is appropriate for mourning and to suggestions that mourners will "go through" these phases almost in a passive way, without doing anything else. This is like thinking of mourning as an experience in which a dirty automobile is hooked up to an automatic car wash machine, dragged through the process passively, and turned out "clean" at the end. An obvious question here—especially because we know that grief and mourning tend to increase and decrease at different times (e.g., anniversaries) in a person's bereavement journey—is why many so people seem to be so attracted to linear theories that appear to move in a relatively straight line from the initial crisis (death) through a series of steps to a relatively "satisfactory" conclusion (acceptance)? Holland and Neimeyer (2010, p. 116) suggested "that human beings are inveterate seekers of patterns to organize the flux of experience in a fashion that enhances their sense of prediction and control"; if so, a sequential plotting of grief reactions and responses "may correspond to the fundamentally narrative structure of much of human thought." Perhaps we are inclined to create a heroic narrative of a journey from tragedy to triumph in our theories of bereavement? Some of these are criticisms and questions are like those we saw of the stage-based theory of coping with dying in Chapter 6 (see also Personal Insights 9.4).

PERSONAL INSIGHTS 9.4

The Five Stages of Grief

The night I lost you
someone pointed me towards
the Five Stages of Grief.
Go that way, they said,
it's easy, like learning to climb
stairs after the amputation.
And so I climbed.
Denial was first.
I sat down at breakfast

(continues)

The Five Stages of Grief

carefully setting the table
for two. I passed you the toast—
you sat there. I passed
you the paper—you hid
behind it.
Anger seemed more familiar.
I burned the toast, snatched
the paper and read the headlines myself.
But they mentioned your departure,
and so I moved on to
Bargaining. What could I exchange
for you? The silence
after storms? My typing fingers?
Before I could decide, *Depression*
came puffing up, a poor relation
its suitcase tied together
with string. In the suitcase
were bandages for the eyes
and bottles of sleep. I slid
all the way down the stairs
feeling nothing.
And all the time *Hope*
flashed on and off
in defective neon.
Hope was a signpost pointing
straight in the air.
Hope was my uncle's middle name,
he died of it.
After a year I am still climbing,
though my feet slip
on your stone face.
The treeline
has long since disappeared;
green is a color
I have forgotten.
But now I see what I am climbing
towards: *Acceptance*
written in capital letters,
a special headline:
Acceptance,
its name is in lights.
I struggle on,
waving and shouting.
Below, my whole life spreads its surf,

(continues)

PERSONAL INSIGHTS 9.4 *(continued)*

The Five Stages of Grief

all the landscapes I've ever known
or dreamed of. Below
a fish jumps: the pulse
in your neck.
Acceptance. I finally
reach it.
But something is wrong.
Grief is a circular staircase.
I have lost you.

Source: Pastan (1978), pp. 61–62.

NEW MODELS OF ACTIVE COPING AND PERSONAL PATHWAYS

New models of active coping and personal pathways in bereavement can be illustrated by theories of **processes in mourning**, for example, tasks in mourning; the dual process model; adaptive grieving styles; and meaning reconstruction.

Tasks in Mourning

Worden broke new ground in 1982 by recommending that we think of mourning in terms of *tasks*, rather than stages or phases. His account of *a task-based theory* has been refined over the years and is now expressed in the following four **tasks in mourning**: (1) to accept the reality of the loss; (2) to process the pain of grief; (3) to adjust to a world without the deceased; and (4) to find an enduring connection with the deceased in the midst of embarking on a new life (Worden, 2009). A task-based model of this sort has the important advantage of emphasizing that mourning is an active process (Attig, 1991, 2011), which is similar in some ways to the description of task-based models for coping with dying that we discussed in Chapter 6. Here, examining each of these four tasks in mourning provides a valuable new way of understanding some of the basic dynamics of mourning and their complexities.

Worden's first task involves efforts *to accept the reality of the loss*. These efforts may not be apparent in initial grief reactions, but they underlie all of the long-term work of mourning. When confronted by the death of someone loved, people often feel an immediate sense of unreality. "It can't be true," they say. As a temporary or transitional reaction to a significant change in our lives, this is wholly understandable. Nevertheless, making one's loss real and coping with one's grief involve acknowledging and accepting the reality of the death.

To fail to accept the reality of the loss is to move toward delusion and the bizarre. For example, Queen Victoria of England had the clothes and shaving gear of her dead husband (Prince Albert) laid out every day long after his death. Efforts like this are really extreme attempts to suspend living at the precise moment of death so as not to face its harsh implications. They also represent attempts to stay connected to that person without changing one's life. However, wishing that life could resume at some future moment—unchanged from the way it was in the past—is at best unrealistic.

According to Worden, bereaved persons also face a second task in mourning *to process the pain of grief*. As Parkes (1996, p. 191) has written, "Anything that continually allows a person to avoid or suppress this pain can be expected to prolong the course of mourning." Productive mourning acknowledges that the pain encountered during bereavement is essential and appropriate. The challenge is to find ways of experiencing this pain that are not overwhelming for the particular individual. Often, the intensity of a bereaved person's pain and its tendency to consume the whole of his or her universe decline gradually as healthy mourning proceeds. One mother said: "It had to. You simply couldn't live with that level of pain." Other bereaved persons say they have learned to live with the pain of their grief.

Pain is hurtful, both to individuals and to those around them. Not surprisingly, many try to avoid the pain of grief. Some turn to drugs or alcohol to shroud their distress, but that may only drive it underground in their bodies and psyches. Some people, like young Simba after the death of his father in the Disney movie, *Lion King*, literally try to run away from their grief by fleeing the place where the loss occurred (Adams, 2006). Others attempt to wipe out all memory and traces of the deceased in order to be relieved of the task of facing the pain of grief after a loss. Ultimately, this strategy of coping through flight is futile. "Sooner or later some at least of those who avoid all conscious grieving break down—usually with some form of depression" (Bowlby, 1969–1980, vol. 3, p. 158).

A society that is uncomfortable with expressions of grief may encourage bereaved persons to flee from grief's pain by distracting them from their loss or assuring them that the loss was really not all that significant. The wrongheaded message here is that people should not "give in" to grief, an experience that people giving this message may see as morbid and unhealthy. Sometimes, society reluctantly acknowledges that individuals may need to mourn, but then tells them—for example, by commenting that they have "broken down" with grief—that they should only do so alone and in private. Prohibiting people from tasks they need to accomplish—and may need help to learn to accomplish—is often hurtful to the individuals in question and to society itself. Mourning is in principle a healthy and healthful process.

The third of Worden's mourning tasks is *to adjust to a world without the deceased*. Parkes wrote, "In any bereavement it is seldom clear exactly what is lost" (1987, p. 27). Bereaved individuals often need to engage in a voyage of discovery to determine the significance of the now-severed relationship, to identify each of the various roles that the deceased played in the relationship, and to adjust to the fact that the deceased is no longer available to fill such roles. This is difficult; a bereaved person might try to ignore this task or withdraw from its requirements. But life calls us forward. Young children need to be fed, changed, and bathed whether or not a spouse has died. Someone must put food on the table and wash the dishes. Avoiding the secondary losses and new challenges by adhering to a posture of helplessness is usually not a constructive coping technique—especially not as a long-term or permanent stance. For many bereaved persons, developing new skills and taking on roles formerly satisfied by the deceased are productive ways of adjusting to loss and growing after a death.

Worden describes the fourth task of mourning as one that asks the bereaved person *to find an enduring connection with the deceased in the midst of embarking on a new life*. This involves two interrelated challenges. Finding an enduring connection means that those who are bereaved should not "forget" the deceased person and erase his or her memory. That is neither possible nor desirable. Similarly, embarking on a new life means working out some healthful way to live one's life without the physical presence of the person who died. That does not necessarily involve investing in another relationship—for example, through remarriage or deciding to have another child. Options of this sort are not open to all bereaved persons. Even when a bereaved person enters into a new relationship, it is important to recognize that no two relationships are ever the same. No new relationship, whatever it may be, will ever be identical to or play the exact same role in the person's life as the one that has now ended.

Clearly, death changes relationships. To think that is not true is to delude oneself. Thus, Worden's fourth task of mourning calls upon the bereaved person to modify or restructure the relationship with the deceased in ways that remain satisfying but that also reflect the changed circumstances of life and death. Perhaps for this reason, Worden (1996, pp. 15–16) once observed that, "The task facing the bereaved is not to give up the relationship with the deceased, but to find a new and appropriate place for the dead in their emotional lives—one that enables them to go on living effectively in the world." In that context he described his fourth task in a slightly different way: "To relocate the dead person within one's life and find ways to memorialize the person."

Satisfying Worden's fourth task would lead a bereaved person to reconceive his or her own personal identity, to restructure his or her relationship with the deceased person in light of the loss that has taken place, to avoid becoming neurotically encumbered by the past in ways that diminish future quality in living, and to remain open to new attachments and other relationships. Symbols and symbolic gestures can be important in this fourth task (see Personal Insights 9.5).

Worden's theory offers an interpretation of coping (here, mourning) as, in principle, a proactive way of striving to manage one's loss and grief. The task efforts he describes can enable bereaved persons to regain some measure of control over their lives. Worden (2009, p. 39) wrote that the tasks of mourning "do not need to be addressed in a specific order," even though "there is some ordering suggested in their definitions." And he added: "Tasks can be revisited and worked through again and again over time. Various tasks can also be worked on *at the same time*. Grieving is a fluid process ..." (p. 53).

The Dual Process Model

The dual process model (Stroebe & Schut, 1999, 2010; see also Richardson, 2010) argues for an *oscillation* or alternation between two complementary sets of coping processes: (1) one that is *loss oriented* or concerned primarily in coping with loss and (2) the other that is *restoration oriented* or concerned primarily in coping with "restoration" (see Figure 9.1). *Loss-oriented processes* involve the intrusion of grief into the life of the bereaved, grief work, the breaking of ties to the deceased, and overcoming resistance to change. *Restoration-oriented processes* include attending to life changes, doing new things, and avoiding or distracting oneself from grief. Note that "restoration" in this model is not about trying to make real once again the mourner's former world of lived experiences (which no longer exists) or the old assumptive world (which has also been shattered or at least rudely shaken by the loss). Rather, it concerns efforts to adapt to the new world in which bereaved persons find themselves. What is restored is not a past mode of living, but the ability to live productively in the present and future.

PERSONAL INSIGHTS 9.5

Four Widows on Finding an Enduring Connection with Their Deceased Husbands and Moving on with Life

Each one of four widows dealt with her wedding ring in a different way after her husband died. One removed her ring and put it away in her jewelry box. "We were married until death parted us," she said. "Now I am no longer married to him." She did not mean that she no longer loved her former husband, but she wanted to emphasize through her actions that death had separated them and that the separation was a permanent one.

A second widow continued to wear her wedding ring on the third finger of her left hand. She knew her husband was dead, but she wanted to emphasize that she still felt connected to him. She felt very content with the legacy of her long, happy, and fulfilling marriage, and she did not intend to look for another husband or a new relationship with another man.

A third widow moved her wedding ring from the third finger of her left hand to her right hand. She did not want to take it off completely or hide it away because it was an important heirloom from her grandmother. Also, she sought an outward sign both to show that she thought of herself as no longer married while also maintaining some tangible indicator of a continuing bond with her deceased husband.

A fourth widow removed her husband's wedding ring before his body was buried. She had a jeweler refashion it, along with her own wedding ring, into a new piece of jewelry, a pendant that she wore around her neck every day. She said, "Now I have a new relationship with my deceased husband, and my lovely pendant symbolizes that new relationship."

Source: Based on Corr (2001).

The key point is that the dual process model posits an interaction or interplay between two sets of dynamic and interrelated processes in coping with bereavement. "Working through" one's loss and the grief reactions to the primary loss represents only one side of this duality; addressing secondary losses and new challenges in moving forward with healthy living is the other side of things. The dual process model insists that bereaved persons will shift back and forth from focusing on loss to focusing on the future. The model also observes that emphases in coping with bereavement may differ from: (1) one cultural group to another; (2) one individual to another; and (3) one moment to another. Overall, this model emphasizes the effort coping requires of bereaved persons, the potentially active nature of mourning, the complexity of the processes involved, and an oscillation between those processes.

In a supplement to their earlier work, the authors of the dual process model argue that all of this may be affected when the bereaved person faces an overload and finds it difficult to continue working in this oscillating way (Stroebe & Schut, 2016).

Figure 9.1 A Dual-Process Model of Coping with Bereavement.

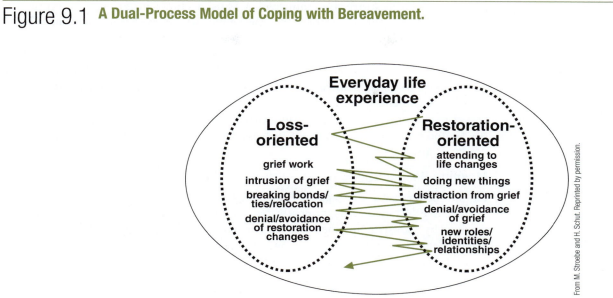

From M. Stroebe and H. Schut. Reprinted by permission.

Adaptive Grieving Styles

Another way of appreciating active coping and personal pathways can be seen in the account of *adaptive grieving styles* proposed by Doka and Martin (2010). This model distinguishes between **intuitive grievers** who emphasize experiencing and expressing emotion, by contrast with **instrumental grievers** who focus on practical matters and problem solving. These two grieving styles are described not as exclusive alternatives, but as poles on a spectrum, in which mixed or *blended* styles occupy the broad middle.

A key advantage of this model lies in its insistence that mourning *is not primarily about gender, but about style*. Thus, this model overthrows claims that there are exclusively "feminine" or "masculine" ways of coping with or adapting to loss. For example, Staudacher (1991, p. 3) maintained that "there is only one way to grieve. That way is to go through the core of grief. Only by experiencing the necessary emotional effects of your loved one's death is it possible for you to eventually resolve the loss." She described this as the "conventional" model characteristic of women from which men should learn. By contrast, Golden (1996, 2013) and others (e.g., Lund, 2000) have proposed a theory of "masculine grief" in which (all?) bereaved men are said to focus on feelings of anger and guilt, suppress other emotional responses and hide vulnerability, emphasize thinking about the loss (versus feeling), favor a desire for solitude, be reluctant to share grief or seek help, value self-reliance, assume the role of protector, seek to solve practical problems or engage in physical actions, and immerse themselves in work.

It is surely true, that women and men often express their reactions to loss and cope with their grief in different ways because they have been socialized to perceive themselves and their roles in different ways. However, not all women have been socialized in a single, rigid way and not all men have been socialized in a single, contrasting way. Individuals of both genders have different backgrounds, personalities, and ways of living out their lives. As a result, some women are instrumental grievers, and some men are intuitive grievers. (Note that the characters of the cold, distant mother and the warm, supportive father in the novel and film *Ordinary People*

[Guest, 1976] illustrate this point well.) Thus, a man who grieves by expressing rather than repressing his emotions is not being "effeminate," nor is a woman being "masculine" or not being feminine if she does not share her grief. Such judgments by others merely add another layer of stress to the many difficulties with which bereaved persons are already trying to cope. In fact, many men and many women may adopt mixed or blended grieving styles, which are neither wholly intuitive nor wholly instrumental, in different situations. Thus, individuality in coping with loss and grief is legitimized and even emphasized, although it may still be possible to identify shared patterns among groups of bereaved persons whose members may or may not be of a specific gender.

Meaning Reconstruction

Human beings naturally seek to "make sense out of" many of the events that occur in their lives. They do this, typically, by "finding meaning" in some existing framework or by "constructing meaning" in new ways. The challenge to existing meanings often becomes a particularly pressing concern when one has suffered a significant loss (Davis & Nolen-Hoeksema, 2001). The phrase **meaning reconstruction** covers both "meaning making" and "meaning finding" and is another way of thinking about what is involved in mourning. It reflects the natural desire of humans to impose some structure or coherence on disorder and the chaotic elements of their lives (see the example in Personal Insights 9.6). For example, Neimeyer (1998, 2000, 2001, 2007) has argued that bereaved persons need to engage in a process of reconstructing meaning in their lives and has even asserted that "meaning reconstruction in response to a loss is the central process in grieving" (1998, p. 110). (Note that Neimeyer and some others prefer to speak of grieving and grievers, rather than mourning and mourners.)

According to Neimeyer (2000) meaning, reconstruction includes the attempt to find or create new meaning for the life of the survivor, as well as for the death of the loved one. This involves both a process of working out the meaning of the loss as the individual sees it and the integration of the results of that process into the life of the bereaved person. Two prominent ways in which one might seek to reconstruct meaning after an important loss include: (1) developing a benign or favorable account of the significance of the loss, often achieved through religious, philosophical, or spiritual frameworks ("He's with his God now"; "She's no longer suffering and is finally at peace") or (2) focusing on some positive benefits that apply to those left behind ("I'm now a more sensitive and caring person"; "We're closer together and more focused on family"). These are just two examples of how bereaved persons might seek to reconstruct meaning in their lives; each individual may do so in his or her own ways and at his or her own pace. As a result, advocates of this approach to interpreting mourning argue that it "challenges the notion that grief unfolds in predictable patterns over time" (Holland, Currier, & Neimeyer, 2006, p. 183).

According to Neimeyer (2007, pp. 195, 199, 203), three principles at the heart of processes of meaning reconstruction are: (1) "Grieving entails reaffirming or reconstructing a world of meaning that has been challenged by loss"; (2) "Adaptation to bereavement typically involves redefining, rather than relinquishing, a continued

PERSONAL INSIGHTS 9.6

The Good Samaritan and the Wounded Man

Humans often undertake efforts to try to make sense out of or construct meaning for events that happen in their lives. Such efforts are, of course, not limited to postdeath bereavement situations. For example, a patient at St. Christopher's Hospice in London who was dying of a progressive paralysis once reflected on her situation shortly before her death. As someone who had already lost control of most of the muscles in her body and who was likely, in the near future, to lose the ability both to speak and to swallow food, it is not difficult to understand that she would ask why these terrible afflictions were happening to her.

In this case, Enid Henke (1972, p. 163) wondered what the purpose was for her life at that particular time and how what was happening to her at this moment fit into her overall life story. The conclusion she eventually reached was that "my present purpose is simply to receive other people's prayers and kindness and to link together all those who are lovingly concerned about me, many of whom are unknown to one another."

Her friend, with whom she was sharing these reflections, said: "It must be hard to be the wounded Jew when by nature you would rather be the Good Samaritan," referring to the familiar parable in the Gospel of Luke (10:25–37).

Henke replied: "In reflecting on the parable I am particularly interested in the fact that we are not told the wounded man recovered. I have always assumed that he did, but it now occurs to me that even if he did not recover the story would still stand as a perfect example of true neighborliness."

All parables have an open-ended quality that leaves them open to interpretation. Here, Henke draws on the parable of the Good Samaritan to make sense out of her own situation in which she does not expect to recover from her progressive illness.

---

bond with the deceased"; and (3) "Narrative methods can play a role in restoring or re-storying a sense of autobiographical coherence that has been disrupted by loss." Creating narratives or stories about what has happened often provides opportunities for catharsis or release of emotional tension for the narrator and can help to keep memories alive by producing "an account that condenses a complicated set of events and perceptions into a single comprehensive unit" (Bosticco & Thompson, 2005, p. 10). Other writers agree that narratives or "the drive to story" offer ways for mourners to create order in disorder or find meaning in the meaningless (e.g., Frank, 2010; Gilbert, 2002). The presence of supportive and empathetic listeners can help persons who create such stories.

Attig (2000) also emphasizes narratives in his view that bereaved persons are challenged to move from "loving in presence" to "loving in separation." For Attig (2011), this challenge has to do with "relearning the world," which he describes as "a multi-dimensional process of learning *how* to live meaningfully again after loss" (p. xxxix), and he adds: "By no means easy at first, we can reach past the pain of separation and affirm the abiding meanings and continuing presence of our loved one in memory and legacy" (p. liii). Processes involved in relearning the world include grieving individually, within our families, and within our communities and cultures, in ways that "engage with several of the great mysteries of life in the human tradition" and that allow us to "make a multifaceted transition from loving in presence to loving in absence" (Attig, 2001, p. 34).

Individual grievers engage in meaning reconstruction at different times, in different ways, and in different connections with their cultures and communities. Some may be able to move on with their lives without doing much beyond dealing with their feelings and practical matters, perhaps because their losses fit into already-existing meaning frameworks such as those found in religious or philosophical convictions (Braun & Berg, 1994). Other bereaved persons may not feel a strong need to make sense out of the loss of an attachment in which they had not been very invested. By contrast, still other persons, especially those who have experienced violent or traumatic losses, may find it quite difficult to engage in reconstructing meaning in their lives. However, Davis, Wortman, Lehman, and Silver (2000) offered evidence to suggest that at least some persons bereaved after a sudden, unexpected death do not attempt to seek meaning in their losses and may be no worse off for that.

REVISING AND RENEWING RELATIONSHIPS: CONTINUING BONDS

Historical accounts of grief and mourning often argued that bereaved persons must sever ties with the deceased by withdrawing emotional energy from the person who has died in order to go forward with a healthy life. In contrast to this view, Klass, Silverman, and Nickman (1996; see also Field, 2006; Klass, 2006) drew on research with bereaved children, spouses, and parents to demonstrate the importance for many bereaved persons of efforts to maintain an ongoing connection to the individual who has died. These connections involve **continuing bonds** with an internal representation of that individual. Such bonds are dynamic, not static. They involve negotiating and renegotiating the meaning of the loss over time. Continuing bonds develop in ways that allow the deceased to remain a transformed or changed but ongoing presence in the inner lives of the bereaved. Connections of this type "provided solace, comfort and support, and eased the transition from the past to the future" (p. xviii).

According to these authors, "the continuing bond has been overlooked or undervalued in most scholarly and clinical work" (p. xvii), and there has been "little social validation for the relationship people reported with the deceased or absent person" (p. xviii). Nevertheless, they believe continuing bonds involve new and altered relationships that reflect "the reality of how people experience and live their lives" (p. xix). They are aspects of normal mourning processes and do not represent psychopathology. Stroebe and Schut (2005) have suggested that the key issue is whether continuing or relinquishing bonds to the deceased is helpful or harmful, in what ways or under what circumstances, and for whom. Doka (2011) added that continuing bonds can contribute in positive ways if these connections allow bereaved persons to acknowledge their losses while also making possible continuing growth.

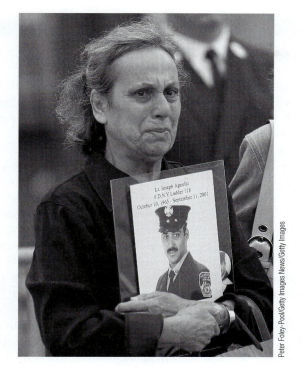

A picture of a deceased family member, here a firefighter/son who died on 9/11/2001, is an important memento for a bereaved parent.

Anderson (1968, p. 5) touched on continuing bonds in a different way when he observed that "death ends a life, but it does not end a relationship." If this is true, then mourning also involves "enriched remembrance" (Cantor, 1978; see Personal Insights 9.7, which contains many interesting insights even though we might not wish to speak of outcomes of mourning in terms of healing and completion). The concept of **enriched remembrance** involves efforts to restructure the relationship so as to carry its legacy forward with the bereaved person into his or her new modes of living. If so, effective mourning frees the bereaved to live meaningful lives in their new situation—without wholly abandoning what they have lost.

Other reports have come from some bereaved persons who have sensed the continued presence of the deceased in their lives or have from time to time received after-death communications. Most often, these individuals have found comfort in these extraordinary or paranormal experiences (see LaGrand, 1997, 1999, 2001, 2006). One challenge in mourning is to decide what such experiences might mean and to find ways to integrate them into healthful, ongoing living.

Finally, increasing numbers of bereaved persons have been using the Internet and social media, particularly Facebook, to provide death notifications and to continue ongoing relationships with the deceased (see Figure 11.1 in Chapter 11 in this book for an illustration of the many ways online sources can be used to aid in bereavement). They visit the Facebook page of the person who died, commenting there on pictures, posting memories, and talking directly with the deceased (Pennington, 2013; Williams & Merten, 2009). Some have undertaken to "keep alive" the digital identity and/or the Facebook page of a deceased person (McEwen & Scheaffer, 2013). Clinicians may want to be aware of these practices when working with bereaved clients to help with tasks of mourning (Falconer, Sachsenweger, Gibson, & Norman, 2011).

When Is Mourning Complete?

The emotional pain caused by loss suffered does not move toward forgetfulness. It moves, rather, in the direction of enriched remembrance; the memory becomes an integral part of the mourner's personality. The work of mourning has been completed when the person (or cherished thing) no longer appears as an absence in a barren world but has come to reside securely within one's heart. Each of us must grieve in his or her own manner and at his or her own pace. For many people, one year seems to bring completion. Others require much more or much less time. Periodic waves of grief are often felt for the remainder of one's life. The mourning process must be given the freedom to find its own depth and rhythm; it cannot be artificially accelerated. A loss, like a physical wound, cannot heal overnight. There is no way to hurry the stages of tissue growth and there is no way to speed up the healing process of mourning. But, when mourning has been completed, the mourner comes to feel the inner presence of the loved one, no longer an idealized hero or a maligned villain, but a presence with human dimensions. Lost irreversibly in objective time, the person is present in a new form within one's mind and heart, tenderly present in inner time without the pain and bitterness of death. And once the loved one has been accepted in this way he or she can never again be forcefully removed.

Source: From *And a Time to Live: Toward Emotional Well-Being during the Crisis of Cancer*, by R. C. Cantor, pp. 66–67 (with minor adaptations). Copyright © 1978 by Harper & Row, New York. Reprinted by permission of the author.

POSSIBILITIES FOR GROWTH AND TRANSFORMATION IN GRIEF AND MOURNING

Our analyses of grief and mourning lead to two important questions about **outcomes of mourning**: Are there *fixed end points* in grief and mourning? and Are there *opportunities for growth and transformation* in these experiences?

Fixed End Points

However grief and mourning are interpreted, their goal has often been described as leading to *recovery, completion,* or *resolution* (Osterweis, Solomon, & Green, 1984; Parkes & Weiss, 1983). However, these terms have fallen into disfavor among contemporary scholars and writers (e.g., Berns, 2011; Boss & Carnes, 2012). For example, to *recover* from one's grief seems to suggest that grief is an unhealthy situation like an illness or disease. It also seems to imply that once one is recovered or "healed," one could be essentially unchanged by the experience. Also, *recovery, completion,* and *resolution* all seem to suggest *a fixed end point for mourning*, a once-and-for-all closure after which there is or should be no more mourning. If that were true, mourning would have an identifiable and preset outcome in both principle and time.

Fixed end points as a goal of mourning are often linked to the views of Freud (1959a)—although that has been questioned by some (e.g., Rando, 1993;

Siggins, 1966)—or at least with much psychoanalytic theory, which stresses detachment or withdrawal (decathexis) of emotional attachment from the deceased. Paying attention to continuing bonds in bereavement rejects the view that mourning should involve little more than detachment, "letting go of," or "forgetting" the deceased.

Fixed end points in bereavement may be assumed without question, because they seem to match with phase- or stage-based theories of mourning and because of our desire to assign a specified time period—for example, several weeks or months, one year—as being necessary or sufficient for mourning. "Time heals," we are frequently told. (This adage fits nicely with comparisons between bereavement and physical wounds.) However, this is really not accurate. Time alone does not heal (Smith, 2004b). We have to do more than just "wait it out." What really counts is how an individual uses the time on his or her individual mourning journey. The central issue is the nature of the activities that constitute productive mourning and where they actually lead those who are bereaved. Thus, Fleming (personal communication, 9/28/95) observed, "It is not the time we have to use, but the use we make of the time we have."

Previously, we criticized views of grief and mourning as disease states. Here, talk about "recovery" seems equally unsuitable unless one uses that term to mean not a return to a former, predeath way of living, but a forward movement to a new way of living in the aftermath of loss (Balk, 2004). If mourning really is an individual journey, then it need not have a single, fixed outcome for all bereaved persons. Instead, for at least many bereaved individuals, mourning will involve coping with loss and its aftermath, addressing the urgent demands of acute grief, carrying forward the legacy of the relationship in an appropriate way into the new postdeath life, and learning to develop and live with "new normals" throughout the rest of the person's life.

Worden (2009, p. 76) wrote: "Asking when mourning is finished is a little like asking, 'How high is up?' There is no ready answer." He continued: "There is a sense in which mourning can be finished, when people regain an interest in life, feel more hopeful, experience gratification again, and adapt to new roles. There is also a sense in which mourning is never finished" (p. 77). Bereaved persons who are asked "When did your grief end?" or "When was your mourning over?" often respond: "Never." A bereaved person may rebound from the initial impact of loss and acute grief, while still experiencing subsequent eruptions of renewed grief and never getting fully done with all that mourning involves in learning to live with their losses and grief (see Personal Insights 9.8). On this point, Freud (1960, p. 386) wrote in the following way to a friend whose son had died: "Although we know that after such a loss the acute stage of mourning will subside, we also know that we shall remain inconsolable and will never find a substitute. No matter what may fill the gap, even if it be filled completely, it nevertheless remains something else."

Opportunities for Growth and Transformation

The possibility of becoming a better person through mourning is analogous to the possibility of growing through coping with dying. For example, we are told that in the Chinese language, the term for "crisis" is represented by two symbols, one for "danger" and the other for "opportunity." Whether this is accurate linguistically, the point to grasp is that bereavement involves both loss and restoration as described by the dual process model. However, one should not think of "opportunity" here as a lucky chance to seek benefits or advantages; rather, the sense is that of a crucial

PERSONAL INSIGHTS 9.8

Small, Sharp Jagged Stones

When I was about eight years old my family moved to Birmingham, Alabama. Mom and Dad bought a house on the side of one of the mountains surrounding the city. My father wanted a little room, so he bought the lot next to us, insuring no close neighbors. The problem was that the lot was slanted deeply away from the house. So, my Dad, a salesman and always on the lookout for a deal, bought truckloads of fill dirt and soon we had a level side yard. We put up a basketball goal and had a large yard to play sports.

The problem with the fill dirt was that it was filled with small, sharp, jagged stones that were a nuisance. They hurt our feet and were painful when we fell on them. My Dad came to my brother and me and offered us ten cents a bucket to pick up the small stones. That was big money back in 1953. So we picked up stones for hours on end. We seemed to have removed every rock there was in the yard. We weren't especially wealthy, but certainly proud. Then it rained. The next morning we went out into our freshly picked yard and there were thousands of small, sharp, jagged stones. It was as if we had never worked at all.

I thought of this when I was doing grief work with Logan, a widow of a minister whose 35-year-old daughter had died of a brain tumor. We spent months dealing with her feelings and the myriad of memories that brought her pain and sadness. After several months, it seemed we had made real progress. Then she told me about little things she found that brought her pain, small things that she had forgotten. Some of these were white gloves, feeding ducks at the lake, Applebee's Restaurant, the Tampa Bay Buccaneers football team, and other seemingly innocuous things. There were more things for the two of us to discuss and deal with. Each one was a painful reminder of the unfulfilled hopes and dreams of an energetic and bright light suddenly extinguished.

We plodded on, taking them one at a time.

Source: John Fitts, used by permission.

point at which new (perhaps dangerous) things may begin. In this way, dying and bereavement both involve dangerous opportunities. They are, or can be, transformative experiences whose outcomes may leave us better or worse off (Schneider, 2012). But note that even for positive growth in a bereaved person after a death, the price that one pays may be heavy. Thus, after the death of his son Rabbi Harold Kushner (1981, pp. 133–134) wrote:

> I am a more sensitive person, a more effective pastor, a more sympathetic counselor because of Aaron's life and death than I would ever have been without it. And I would give up all of those gains in a second if I could have my son back. If I could choose, I would forgo all the spiritual growth and depth which has come my way because of our experiences, and be what I was fifteen years ago, an average rabbi, an indifferent counselor, helping some people and unable to help others, and the father of a bright happy boy. But I cannot choose.

As a rough guideline, we might say mourning is advancing satisfactorily when the bereaved person is able to think of the deceased person without the same intensity of pain that was previously experienced. Evidence of this ability is usually apparent when the bereaved person can once again take up tasks of daily living and can invest in life. For most people, this takes much more time than our society is usually willing to concede, although for some it may not take as long. Certainly, the first year of bereavement—with all of its anniversaries, special days, and moments that remind the bereaved person again and again of the absence of the deceased and the loss that has been experienced—is a time of special challenge, a period when "anniversary reactions" may be especially prominent. But there is nothing magic in a single year; a second year of bereavement may be even more difficult as it drives home the finality of the first year's experiences (Clayton, 1973, 1974; Glick, Weiss, & Parkes, 1974; Parkes, 1970a).

Mourning is about more than coming back from a bad time; it is also about learning to go forward (Stearns, 1988). Many, if not most, mourners are resilient and find that their lives do improve even after difficult bereavements, but they also can and likely will re-mourn their losses as they find themselves in different places in their future lives (Bonanno, 2004, 2009; Dutton & Zisook, 2005; Gorman, 2011a; Rynearson, 2006). Bereaved persons who are successful in their mourning processes become **survivors** in the full sense of that word (Corr, 2003). As Ernest Hemingway once wrote, "The world breaks everyone and afterward many are strong at the broken places." They have not only lived on after the death of someone they loved, but beyond that they have coped with their losses and their grief reactions in constructive ways, and they have managed to adapt their lives to fit the new world into which their loved one's death rudely thrust them. This is a heroic and awesome achievement.

COMPLICATED GRIEF REACTIONS

Thus far in this chapter, we have taken the view that the human experiences of grief and mourning are—at least for the most part—normal and healthy. Still, all human processes can become distorted and unhealthy. We examine the subject of complicated grief here because we want to contrast it with previous discussions of healthy, **uncomplicated grief reactions** and because complicated grief is important in itself for the relatively small group of people who experience it. These people experience an excessive and hurtful form of grief that can overwhelm them in a persistent way and trap them in unproductive, maladaptive behavior. Originally, this had been called "pathological grief" (discarded as too judgmental in tone; see Volkan, 1970). Later, some advocated for what they termed "prolonged grief disorder" (Prigerson, Vander-werker, & Maciejewski, 2008), but the phrase "complicated grief," defined by Shear (2015, p. 153) as "intense grief after the death of a loved one that lasts longer than expected according to social norms and causes functional impairment," seems to have prevailed. In short, **complicated grief** refers to grief reactions or mourning processes that are not only unusual but also abnormal in the sense of being deviant and unhealthy. (Note that many, but not all, discussions of this topic in the literature do not make the distinction between grief and mourning that we have used throughout this book.)

Complicated grief reactions have long been recognized in a general way (e.g., Demi & Miles, 1987). Like many other writers, Worden (2009) identified four types of complicated grief reactions:

- *Chronic grief reactions*, which are excessive in duration and never come to a satisfactory conclusion; often individuals realize they are not making progress in getting back into living again
- *Delayed grief reactions*, in which grief at the time of the loss is inhibited, suppressed, or postponed, not surfacing again until later, when it most often appears as an excessive reaction to a subsequent loss or other triggering event
- *Exaggerated grief reactions*, which are excessive and disabling in ways that may lead to the development of a phobia or irrational fear, to physical or psychiatric symptoms, or to aberrant or maladaptive behavior
- *Masked grief reactions*, in which individuals experience symptoms or behaviors—including the complete absence of grief (Deutsch, 1937)—that cause them difficulty but they do not recognize it as related to the loss

In general, complicated grief reactions seem to develop as a result of difficulties in the relationship with the deceased (e.g., ambivalent, dependent, or narcissistic relationships); the circumstances of the death (e.g., uncertainty about or unwillingness to accept the fact of death, or a situation of multiple or traumatic losses); the bereaved person's own history or personality (such as a history of depressive illness, a personality that employs withdrawal to defend against extremes of emotional distress or does not tolerate dependency feelings well, or a self-concept that includes being the "strong" one in the family); or the social factors that surround the experience (e.g., when a loss is disenfranchised as socially unspeakable or socially negated, or when a social support network is absent).

Parkes (2006b, p. 2) argued that "numerous clinical studies have supported the existence of complicated grief, which is usually seen as taking two forms: an inhibited or delayed form and a chronic or persistent form." He added that, "Of the two, the chronic form is the most frequent."

Despite a general recognition that some individuals have complicated reactions to loss, The American Psychiatric Association had been hesitant in the *Diagnostic and Statistical Manual of Mental Disorders (DSM)* to acknowledge complicated grief as a disorder. Still, prior to the publication of the fifth edition of the *Diagnostic and Statistical Manual of Mental Disorders* (DSM-5; 2013), there were extensive discussions and controversies about how to acknowledge a small group of people who seem to have complicated reactions to grief that disable their ability to function at home, work, or school (e.g., Shear, Boelen, & Neimeyer, 2011; Parkes, 2006a, 2007a; Prigerson & Maciejewski, 2006).

Ultimately, the DSM-5 did recognize complications to grief in a number of ways. The most prominent of these was removal of the "bereavement exclusion" for *Major Depressive Disorders*. That exclusion had previously barred diagnoses of a *Major Depressive Disorder* (except in certain specified circumstances) until a full year after a death—to avoid, it was thought, confusing normal grief with depression—a period later reduced to two months, and now eliminated in DSM-5. Some (e.g., Attig et al., 2013) argued that this will lead to harmful effects: (1) normal reactions to the death of a loved one will now be easily misclassified as the mental disorder depression; (2) antidepressants prescribed for depression, but which have not been shown to be helpful for grief-related issues, may now be commonly ordered for bereaved people; and (3) the vast majority of prescriptions for antidepressants are written by primary care physicians, not psychiatrists, who may have little professional training in responding to the bereaved.

Other changes in the *DSM-5* are: complicated grief is included as a subtype of Adjustment Disorders (*Adjustment Disorder in Relation to Bereavement*); adults are now allowed to be diagnosed with *Separation Anxiety Disorder*—a condition once only diagnosable with children—recognizing that while grief involves yearning for the deceased, fear of separation from other attachment figures is the central factor in *Separation Anxiety Disorder*; and *Persistent Complex Bereavement-Related Disorder* is identified as a condition that merits further study, one that may be included as a diagnosis in future editions of the *DSM* if continuing research offers support. Some have suggested that there may be other forms of complicated grief that should be added to subsequent editions of the *DSM* (Rando et al., 2012).

Critics of the construct of "complicated grief," such as Bonanno (2006) and some contributors to a symposium on complicated grief (Parkes, 2006a), argue that it risks stigmatizing, pathologizing, and medicalizing a normal if difficult bereavement experience, thereby turning familiar supportive work on the part of family members and friends over to secularly trained professionals, and that complicated grief rather than being an internal reality is an externally imposed social role with cultural and historical origins. Efforts to define and defend the concept of complicated grief will need to take account of such criticisms, clarify its relationship to traumatic grief and post-traumatic stress disorder (see Ehlers, 2006), and find its place within existing understandings of grief and mourning (see Stroebe, Schut, & van den Bout, 2013).

It is important for helpers to be alert to potential complications in grief and mourning, and to obtain appropriate assistance that would help to untangle complications in grief reactions. However, because of the inevitable individuality of grief reactions, professional assessment is often required both to distinguish idiosyncratic but healthy grief reactions from complicated and unhealthy grief reactions and to intervene in useful therapeutic ways (Figley, 1999; Jacobs, 1999; Naparstek, 2005; Rando, 1993; Shear, 2015).

GRIEF, MOURNING, AND FAMILIES

Grief has most often been understood in everyday life and studied in the professional literature as an individual reaction to loss. Until recently, not much attention had been given to the role(s) of **families** or other similar social groups in bereavement (Brabant, 1996; Shapiro, 1994). In this section, we ask four questions: (1) How are families significant in their members' bereavements? (2) How do families differ in the ways in which they affect their members' bereavements? (3) Do families grieve as a unit? and (4) Do families as a unit cope with loss and grief?

The answer to our first question is that, at a minimum, grief within a family "consists of the interplay of individual family members grieving in the social and relational context of the family, with each member affecting and being affected by the others" (Gilbert, 1996, p. 271). This means that a family system (whatever one may identify as one's "family" and however it may be constituted) almost always provides a context that will influence its members' experiences of loss, grief, and mourning.

Carolyn Cole-Pool/Getty Images News/Getty Images

At the 10th anniversary commemorating the 9/11 terrorist attacks in New York City, grief in a family member remains very intense.

Second, families are different in the ways in which they affect their members' bereavement. To the degree that they are able or try to, families socialize or exert influences that prepare their members to value relationships, acknowledge losses, express grief, and mourn in their own specific ways. Each family also forms relationships within its unit in its own way. For example, extremely enmeshed families will entangle their members very closely with each other, whereas disengaged families offer more autonomy and may not provide much support to their members. Some families allow their members considerable freedom in how they express grief and mourning; other families expect all members to express grief and mourning in the same way. For example, in Chapter 5, we noted that some Hispanic-American families encourage women to express grief freely, but expect men to be stoic and impassive. Other family characteristics that may be relevant to the grief of members include whether the family system engages in secrecy or open communication, the availability of extended family, the family's social and economic resources, the prior role and functioning of the deceased member in the family system, and the existence of conflicted or estranged relationships at the time of death (Walsh & McGoldrick, 2004b). In short, families may be permissive or restrictive and supportive or unsupportive in how they expect and tolerate expressions of grief and mourning by their members.

Families also differ in their place in a family developmental life cycle (McGoldrick & Walsh, 2004). Losses may occur at different points in what systems theorists portray as a three-generational family life cycle (Carter & McGoldrick, 1988; McGoldrick, Carter, & Garcia-Preto, 2010; Walsh & McGoldrick, 1988): to unattached young adults who are between families; to young couples who are joining together and creating new family units through marriage; to families with young children; to families with adolescents; to families who are launching children and moving on; or to families in later life.

Each of these family types is likely to be coping with different developmental challenges. For example, a new couple may be struggling with issues of commitment to their developing family system, whereas an established couple who are launching children and moving on may be coping with unfamiliar issues of personal and family identity. For a new couple, questions that arise might include: "Can each of us accommodate our previous independence to make a go of our new family unit?" or "Can we work together to become parents and bring children into the world?" By contrast, a couple that is moving on after launching children might ask: "Can we readjust ourselves to take advantage of the opportunities of our new empty nest?" or "Do we still have parental roles to fulfill now that our children have moved away?" In short, families at different points in their life cycle may have different strengths and limitations to make available to their bereaved members. Such families may be affected in different ways by bereavement and by different sorts of losses.

A third question is whether families grieve as a unit. This goes beyond thinking of families only as the context for each of their members' individual grief and mourning. Shapiro (1994) has argued that grief is a family process, but Montgomery and Fewer (1988) contend that this confuses individual- and family-level properties. For Montgomery and Fewer, responses to loss are found in families and families engage in the public or interpersonal processes of mourning, but families do not engage in the intrapersonal processes of experiencing loss and grief—perhaps for the simple reason that families are not persons. That is why one can often observe significant differences in the grief and mourning of individual family members. Gilbert (1996, p. 273) agrees with this view when she writes: "Families do not grieve. Only individuals grieve. This is done in a variety of contexts, one of which is the family."

Still, it is clear that major losses, such as death, do bring disorder into **family systems,** and families must cope with that disruption. Thus, the answer to our fourth question is that bereaved families do engage in a type of systemic coping with loss and grief. Death affects the often-unspoken set of assumptions in a family about how life ought to be, well-established roles and relationships, and everyday responsibilities and routines. These and other aspects of family life must be reconsidered and reconstructed (Lamberti & Detmer, 1993). In addition, since loss and grief can "have an effect across the boundaries separating one generation from the next," there may be a "multigenerational ripple effect" from a significant death (Detmer & Lamberti, 1991, p. 366).

Following a death, Walsh and McGoldrick (2004b) have argued that two major tasks confront family members and family units: (1) to share acknowledgment of the reality of death and to share the experience of loss and (2) to reorganize the family system and to reinvest in other relationships and life pursuits. (Note that each of these broadly combines two of the mourning tasks for individuals described by Worden and restates them in family systems terminology.) The first set of these tasks involves recognition of the loss and its implications, sharing grief reactions, and tolerating individual differences within the family system. The second set of tasks requires family members to reconstruct what the family means to them and their sense of identity as a family, reapportioning or abandoning activities and roles formerly assigned to the deceased, and restructuring or transforming relationships with the deceased so as to allow family members to maintain a sense of connection with that person and with their past even as they move toward the future. Open, honest, and supportive communication within the family system is essential to all of these tasks. Family rituals or shared ways of dealing with issues that bring members together, such as memorialization practices, commemorative activities, or prayer, are often useful (Kissane & Bloch, 2002; Nadeau, 1998).

Summary

In this chapter, we began by exploring a broad account of different types of losses, including attachments, traumatic losses, and bereavement. Next, we took up an extended examination of the meaning of grief, including anticipatory grief. Then we described and raised cautions about three classical models of mourning based on phases or stages. That led to an explanation of newer models of active coping and personal pathways in mourning, including tasks, the dual process model, adaptive grieving styles, and meaning reconstruction. We then explored continuing bonds with the deceased, fixed end points in mourning, and opportunities for growth and transformation. The chapter concluded with comments on complicated grief reactions and issues related to grief, mourning, and families.

Glossary

Anticipatory grief and mourning: experiences of grief and mourning occurring prior to but in connection with a significant loss that is expected to take place

Assumptive world: a conceptual system that provides individuals with expectations about the world and themselves to guide planning and acting

Attachments: relationships through which individuals satisfy fundamental needs

Bereavement: the objective situation of individuals who have experienced a loss of some person or object they valued; three key elements: a *relationship or attachment with* some person/object that is valued, the *loss* of that relationship, and an *individual* deprived of the valued person/object by the loss

Complicated grief reactions or complicated mourning: grief reactions or mourning processes that are abnormal in the sense of being deviant and unhealthy, thereby overwhelming bereaved persons, leading to maladaptive behavior, and inhibiting progress toward satisfactory outcomes in mourning;

Continuing bonds: ongoing connections with a representation of the deceased that can enable the deceased individual to remain a transformed but constant presence in the inner lives of the bereaved

Enriched remembrance: Cantor's phrase for mourning efforts to restructure the relationship with the lost person/object so as to carry its positive legacies forward into the bereaved individual's new life

Families or family systems: typically, a key context that influences their members' experiences of loss, grief, and mourning; may take many forms

Five critical variables influence experiences of bereavement and grief: the nature of the prior attachment; the way in which the loss occurred and the concurrent circumstances of the bereaved person; coping strategies used by the bereaved person; the developmental situation of the bereaved person; the nature of the support available to the bereaved person

Grief: the term that indicates one's reactions to loss; may include *physical, psychological* (emotional, cognitive), *behavioral, social, or spiritual* reactions

Grief work: processes of coping with loss and grief; similar to *mourning* as that term is used in this book

Grieving: a term used by some to designate the internal or intrapsychic aspects of what we identify in this book as *mourning*; we prefer to think of *grieving* as "processes of experiencing and expressing grief"

Guilt: thoughts and feelings that assign blame (often self-blame), fault, or culpability for a loss or death

Intuitive versus instrumental grieving: terms used to contrast two extremes in a spectrum of adaptive grieving styles; *intuitive* grievers emphasize experiencing and expressing emotion, *instrumental* grievers focus on practical matters and problem solving

Loss: to be separated from and deprived of a valued person, object, or status by death or in other ways; *primary losses* involve the ending of a basic attachment; *secondary losses* follow from a primary loss

Meaning reconstruction: efforts to make sense of loss by finding or creating new meaning in the death of the loved one and in the new life of the bereaved person

Melancholia: Freud's term for clinical depression

Mourning: responses to loss and grief involving efforts to cope with those experiences and learn to live with them by incorporating them into ongoing living; some writers confine mourning to external or social expressions of grief and rituals used in coping with bereavement

Outcomes of mourning: many laypeople and theoreticians speak of fixed end points like *recovery, completion, or resolution*; we prefer to think of mourning as an open-ended set of processes that offer opportunities for growth and transformation

Phases in mourning: describes mourning as a series of phases, for example, shock and numbness; yearning and searching; disorganization and despair; reorganization

Processes in mourning: describes mourning as involving processes; for example, the dual process model, adaptive grieving styles, and meaning reconstruction

Realization: Parkes's term to describe what is involved in "making real" all of the implications of loss; "making real" in one's inner, subjective world that which is already real in the outer, objective world

Stages in mourning: describes mourning as a series of stages, for example, denial, anger, bargaining depression, and acceptance

Survivors (of bereavement): individuals who have found their way to healthy living after a death

Tasks in mourning: describes mourning as involving a series of tasks, such as to accept the reality of the loss; to process the pain of grief; to adjust to a world without the deceased; to find an enduring connection with the deceased in the midst of embarking on a new life

Traumatic losses: shocking losses whose objective elements shatter assumptive worlds

Uncomplicated grief reactions: healthy, normal, and appropriate reactions to loss

Victims (of bereavement or trauma): individuals who have been hurt, harmed, "reaved" by loss

Questions for Review and Discussion

1. Think of a time when you experienced the loss of some person or thing that was important in your life. What made this an important loss for you? How might it have been different if you had lost a different person or thing, or if the loss had occurred in a different way?
2. How did you react to that loss? Try to be as complete as possible in developing this description of your reactions to the loss, including thoughts, feelings, behaviors (actions), and beliefs.
3. How did you cope with that loss? What helped you or did not help you to cope with the loss or to integrate it into your ongoing living? Did you draw on social media or the Internet? Was that helpful or not? Why?

Suggested Readings

Introductory descriptions of loss, grief, and mourning appear in:

Davidson, G. W. (1984). *Understanding Mourning: A Guide for Those Who Grieve*

Doka, K. J. (2016). *Grief Is a Journey: Finding Your Path through Loss*

Freeman, S. J. (2005). *Grief and Loss: Understanding the Journey*

Harris, D. L. (Ed.). (2011). *Counting Our Losses: Reflecting on Change, Loss, and Transition in Everyday Life*

Viorst, J. (1986). *Necessary Losses*

Westberg, G. (2010). *Good Grief*

Additional analyses of bereavement appear in the following:

Attig, T. (2011). *How We Grieve: Relearning the World* (rev. ed.)

Bonanno, G. A. (2009). *The Other Side of Sadness: What the New Science of Bereavement Tells Us about Life after Loss*

Boss, P. (2000). *Ambiguous Loss: Learning to Live with Unresolved Grief*

Calhoun, L. G., & Tedeschi, R. G. (Eds.). (2006). *The Handbook of Posttraumatic Growth: Research and Practice*

Center for the Advancement of Health. (2004). Report on Bereavement and Grief Research [Special issue.] *Death Studies, 28(6)*

Doka, K. J. (Ed.). (2007). *Living with Grief: Before and after the Death*

Doka, K. J., & Martin, T. L. (2010). *Grieving Beyond Gender: Understanding the Ways Men and Women Mourn* (rev. ed.)

Doka, K. J., & Tucci, A. S. (Eds.). (2017). *When Grief is Complicated*

Greitens, E. (2015). *Resilience: Hard-Won Wisdom for Living a Better Life*

Klass, D., Silverman, P. R., & Nickman, S. L. (Eds.). (1996). *Continuing Bonds: New Understandings of Grief*

Nadeau, J. (1998). *Families Make Sense of Death*

Neimeyer, R. A. (Ed.). (2001). *Meaning Reconstruction and the Experience of Loss*

Okun, B., & Nowinski, J. (2011). *Saying Goodbye: How Families Can Find Renewal through Loss*

Osterweis, M., Solomon, F., & Green, M. (Eds.). (1984). *Bereavement: Reactions, Consequences, and Care*

Parkes, C. M., & Prigerson, H. G. (2010). *Bereavement: Studies of Grief in Adult Life* (4th ed.)

Parkes, C. M. (2006). *Love and Loss: The Roots of Grief and Its Complications*

Rando, T. A. (Ed.). (2000). *Clinical Dimensions of Anticipatory Mourning: Theory and Practice in Working with the Dying, Their Loved Ones, and Their Caregivers*

Raphael, B. (1983). *The Anatomy of Bereavement*

Sanders, C. M. (1989). *Grief: The Mourning After*

Stroebe, M. S., Hansson, R. O., Stroebe, W., & Schut, H. (Eds.). (2001). *Handbook of Bereavement Research: Consequences, Coping, and Care*

Stroebe, M. S., Hansson, R. O., Schut, H. A., & Stroebe, W. (Eds.). (2008). *Handbook of Bereavement Research and Practice: Advances in Theory and Intervention*

Thompson, N. (2012). Grief and Its Challenges

Thompson, N., Cox, G. R., & Stevenson, R. G. (Eds.). (2017). *Handbook of Traumatic Loss: A Guide to Theory and Practice*

McCoyd, J.L.M., & Walter, C. A. (2016). *Grief and Loss across the Lifespan: A Biopsychosocial Perspective* (2nd ed.)

Selected Web Resources

Some useful search terms include: ANTICIPATORY GRIEF AND MOURNING; ASSUMPTIVE WORLDS; ATTACHMENTS; BEREAVEMENT; COMPLICATED GRIEF OR COMPLICATED MOURNING (CHRONIC, DELAYED, EXAGGERATED, MASKED); CONTINUING BONDS; DEPRESSION; ENRICHED REMEMBRANCE; GRIEF; GRIEF WORK; GRIEVING; GUILT; LOSS; MEANING RECONSTRUCTION; MELANCHOLIA; MOURNING; OUTCOMES OF MOURNING; SURVIVORS; TRAUMATIC LOSS, UNCOMPLICATED GRIEF REACTIONS.

You can also visit the following *organizational and other Internet sites*:

AARP (formerly, American Association of Retired Persons)

Australian Centre for Grief and Bereavement

Genesis Bereavement Resources

Grief Digest Magazine (published by the Centering Corporation)

GriefNet, Rivendell Resources

Living with Loss: Hope and Healing for the Body, Mind and Spirit (published by Bereavement Publishing, Inc.)

Living with Loss Foundation

MedlinePlus (multiple topics)

National Grief Support Services, Inc.

U.S. National Institute of Mental Health, National Institutes of Health

CHAPTER 10

Coping with Loss and Grief: How Individuals Can Help

Objectives of this Chapter

▌ To identify *five fundamental needs* of bereaved persons

▌ To describe *some unhelpful messages* often directed to bereaved persons

▌ To explain the concept of *disenfranchised grief and mourning*

▌ To discuss some implications of *pet loss and deaths of companion animals*

▌ To offer some *constructive suggestions for helping* the bereaved

▌ To point out *ways individuals can help bereaved persons with cognitive, affective, behavioral, and valuational tasks in mourning*

▌ To identify and explain *ten principles for facilitating uncomplicated grief*

INDIVIDUALS WHO HELPED ONE WOMAN DURING HER MOURNING

When her mother died after a long, lingering illness, Stella Bridgman (see the vignette at the beginning of Chapter 9) turned for consolation to her husband, to some relatives and friends who lived nearby, and to her church. They provided enough help to enable her to resume a normal life.

But then her first husband died and it got much worse after her teenage son took his own life. Many of her friends withdrew from her and were not helpful. They felt uncomfortable in the presence of her intense distress, and she felt she was being badly treated and even stigmatized by how some people regarded her because she was now associated with a death by suicide.

Some people tried to tell Stella they knew what she was feeling, but she did not find that helpful—she knew none of them had experienced her losses and what they said seemed to minimize what she was experiencing. Many people would not mention her son's name because they thought that would only make Stella feel bad. They found it especially difficult to talk about the way he had ended his life. Mostly, people tried to avoid Stella and steered clear of any reminders of her loss.

When others withdrew from her, Stella felt isolated and lonely. When others tried not to mention her son's name, Stella perceived this as compounding her initial loss. By not even talking about her son, she feared people were erasing all mention and memory of his life. Above all, Stella felt hurt by these actions of people from whom she had expected assistance and support.

Stella did find one or two people who really helped her. Each of these people simply gave her a hug, lent her an ear in person or by telephone, and just remained available to Stella. In their presence, Stella knew she didn't have to be careful about what she said or the feelings she expressed. They did not behave as if they needed to have Stella "get over" her grief. One good friend occasionally brought food or came over to cook nutritious meals. Another encouraged Stella to talk about her losses and suggested going out for walks together.

Stella knew the story of Job from the Bible. So she was sensitive to the differences between the very proper church elder who reminded her of the slogan, "God never gives us burdens heavier than we can bear," and the young clergyperson who was wise enough to be silent when Stella needed to express her anger at God for letting these tragedies befall her.

FUNDAMENTAL NEEDS OF BEREAVED PERSONS

Davidson (1984) wrote that bereaved persons have **five fundamental needs:** social support, nutrition, hydration, exercise, and rest. Among these, social support is most frequently mentioned and it is often a major post-death variable in coping with grief. In Chapter 9, we saw that the factors that make a difference in bereavement and grief include: the nature of the prior attachment; the way in which the loss occurred and the concurrent circumstances of the bereaved person; the coping strategies that the individual has learned to use in dealing with previous losses; the developmental situation of the bereaved person; and the nature and availability of support for the bereaved person after the loss. Only the last of these—social support—can be changed after a death has occurred. It is the main subject of this and the next chapter.

Illustrations © 1999 Taylor Bills. Publication © 1999 Grief Watch

Friends can help grieving persons by encouraging them to exercise (an illustration from *Tear Soup*—see Personal Insights 10.2).

An experienced hospice bereavement volunteer once said that the single thing that can most help a bereaved person is the "presence of a caring person." It is not as important what a person says or does—although there are better and worse things that one might say or do—as that the person does cares and is available (Donnelley, 1987). Being present and actively listening is a way of giving oneself to the other, of putting aside one's own concerns to let the other talk about his or her concerns (see Personal Insights 10.1).

The other factors mentioned by Davidson are often ignored in advice about bereavement. People who are bereaved may experience a disinterest in food and a general loss of appetite. They also may lack energy or the ability to concentrate on the tasks required to prepare nourishing meals. That is why many communities have traditions in which friends and neighbors bring food and drink to the bereaved. In addition to not nourishing themselves properly, bereaved persons sometimes add to their own poor nutrition and dehydration by consuming empty calories or drinking alcohol, which dehydrates them. Also, bereaved persons need exercise and rest. Some bereaved persons experience insomnia or other sleep disruptions, whereas others sleep continually without ever feeling really rested. Healthy exercise and a good night's sleep can contribute to a productive mourning process. Those who seek to help bereaved persons can do much to see that they obtain adequate nutrition, hydration, exercise, and rest.

> ### PERSONAL INSIGHTS 10.1
>
> ### Listen
>
> *When I ask you to listen to me,*
> *And you start giving me advice,*
> *You have not done what I asked.*
> *When I ask that you listen to me,*
> *And you begin to tell me why I shouldn't feel that way,*
> *You are trampling on my feelings.*
> *When I ask you to listen to me,*
> *And you feel you have to do something to solve my problems,*
> *You have failed me, strange as that may seem.*
> *Listen: All that I ask is that you listen,*
> *Not talk or do—just hear me.*
> *When you do something for me*
> *That I need to do for myself,*
> *You contribute to my fear and feelings of inadequacy.*
> *But when you accept as a simple fact*
> *That I do feel what I feel, no matter how irrational,*
> *Then I can quit trying to convince you*
> *And go about the business*
> *Of understanding what's behind my feelings.*
> *So, please listen and just hear me*
> *And, if you want to talk*
> *Wait a minute for your turn—and I'll listen to you.*
>
> *Source:* By an anonymous author, as appeared in the
> *St. Louis Post-Dispatch*, September 19, 1998, p. D3.

UNHELPFUL MESSAGES

All too often, our society conveys **unhelpful messages to bereaved persons.** Typically, these are clustered around: (1) attempts to minimize the loss that has been experienced; (2) admonitions not to feel (or, at least, not to express in public) the strong grief reactions that one is experiencing; and (3) suggestions to get back to living promptly and refrain from disturbing others with one's grief and mourning.

The first of these clusters of messages may involve statements like the following:

- "Now that your baby has died, you have a little angel in heaven." (But my pregnancy was not intended as a way of making heavenly angels.)
- "You can always have another baby," or "You already have other children." (But neither of these will replace the child who died.)
- "You're still young, you can get married again." (But that will not bring back my first spouse or lessen the hurt of my loss.)

- "You had a good, long marriage." (But that only makes me feel more keenly the pain of what I have lost.)
- "After all, your grandfather was a very old man." (But that made him all the more dear to me.)

From the standpoint of the bereaved, these messages seem to suggest that their losses were really not all that important or that the deceased person was not truly irreplaceable. Some messages suggest that survivors should stop thinking about those who have died. One related implication is that individuals should not perceive their bereavement as so very difficult. Another implication is that friends and relatives of the bereaved person, or society as a whole, need not permit the grief-related needs of the bereaved persons to change their daily routines very much.

Isadora Duncan (1927) experienced some of these unhelpful messages after the accidental death of her two small children, but she contrasted those messages with the following account of how one friend helped her:

> She used to rock me in her arms, consoling my pain, but not only consoling, for she seemed to take my sorrow to her own breast, and I realized that if I had not been able to bear the society of other people, it was because they all played the comedy of trying to cheer me with forgetfulness. Whereas Eleanora said: "Tell me about Deidre and Patrick," and made me repeat to her all their little sayings and ways, and show her their photos, which she kissed and cried over. She never said, "Cease to grieve," but she grieved with me, and, for the first time since their death, I felt I was not alone. (p. 292)

The second cluster of unhelpful messages to bereaved persons seeks to suppress the depth or intensity of the grief they are experiencing. For example, such individuals will be told:

- "Be strong," or "Keep a stiff upper lip."
- "You'll be fine," "Don't be upset," "Put a smile on your face."
- "You're the big man or woman of the family now."
- "Why are you still upset? It's been … [4 weeks, 6 months, a year]."
- "What you need to do is to keep busy, get back to work, forget her."

In fact, no one can simply stop experiencing what he or she is experiencing. Feelings and all of the other reactions to a significant loss are real. These grief reactions need to be lived with and lived through. Such reactions only change in their own ways and at their own pace. The underlying theme of this second cluster of messages is that it is not good for bereaved persons to experience some feelings or other grief reactions. Even when grief reactions are acknowledged in principle, it will often be suggested to bereaved persons that they should not experience their reactions in certain (especially public or powerful) ways. The principal theme in such messages is that these ways of experiencing one's grief are unacceptable to those around the bereaved person. In other words, the real message is that your grief is making others uncomfortable, and that is inappropriate.

The third set of messages is really a variant of the first two. It arises from the common practice in American society of what has been called "oppressive toleration." That is the view that people can do or say whatever they wish (or, in this case, experience and express grief in any way they might want to), as long as they do not disturb others. Accordingly, it is often made clear to bereaved persons in more or less subtle ways—and often in ways that are not very subtle at all—that if they insist, they can grieve as they wish, but in so doing they must take care not to bother those around them or disrupt the tranquility or happiness of society in general. As Garber (2016) has written, "Grief, in the popular imagination, is a sadness to be experienced and carried and borne as silently and as stoically as possible." This leads to what Garber called "grief policing," in which some criticize the bereaved for grieving wrongly, for example, by "crying crocodile tears." It may also be reflected in business practices that permit a bereaved person to take 1 or 2 days off work but then expect that individual to come back to work ready to function as if nothing had happened (Fitzgerald, 1999; Tehan & Thompson, 2013).

Thus, when people in our society speak of the "acceptability" of grief, they usually mean whether it is tolerable to the group, not to the bereaved person. When President Kennedy was assassinated and when President Reagan died from Alzheimer's disease, American society applauded their widows for the way they dealt with their bereavement in public—not least because they presented a stoic facade to society and to the media, which we could admire but not be disturbed by. It was widely ignored that the examples of these two widows may not have been relevant to or workable for most bereaved people and may have been particularly unhelpful for those having trouble expressing reactions to their losses.

Linn (1986) suggested that individuals who are grieving and hear unhelpful messages such as those described in this section should ask themselves three questions. The first is: *Why did it hurt?* The answer usually is that the comment invalidates an individual's loss or grief reactions. The answer to the second question—*What made them say it?*—often is that the other person was trying to be supportive—even if poorly so. The last question—*What can you say?*—is empowering. It reminds bereaved individuals that they can respond to such questions in constructive ways. Such efforts combat "grief policing" and are supported by public mourning rituals and many Internet venues in which grief is and can be expressed.

DISENFRANCHISED GRIEF AND MOURNING

Often, the unhelpful messages described here are not merely examples in which individuals have failed in the ways in which they tried (or did not try) to help bereaved persons. Usually, these deficiencies reflect specific cultural contexts in which a societal death system conveys to its members—whether in formal and explicit ways or through more informal and subtle messages—its views about what is thought to be socially acceptable or appropriate in bereavement. Social norms of this sort are often hurtful to bereaved individuals when the society and its members *disenfranchise* their grief and bereavement experiences.

Disenfranchised grief is "the grief that persons experience when they incur a loss that is not or cannot be openly acknowledged, publicly mourned, or socially supported" (Doka, 1989b, p. 4). To disenfranchise grief is to indicate that a particular individual does not have a right to be perceived or to function as a bereaved person. The important point here is that disenfranchised grief is not merely unnoticed, forgotten, or hidden; it is socially disallowed and unsupported.

Originally, Doka (1989b) explained that grief can be disenfranchised in three primary ways: either the relationship or the loss or the griever is not recognized. Doka also added that some types of deaths, such as those involving suicide or AIDS, may be "disenfranchising deaths" in the sense that they either are not well recognized or are associated with a high degree of social stigma. We witnessed that happening in the aftermath of Stella Bridgman's son's suicide in the vignette near the beginning of this chapter.

Relationships are disenfranchised when they are not granted social approval. For example, some unsuspected, past, or secret relationships might not be publicly recognized or socially sanctioned. These could include relationships between friends, coworkers, in-laws, or ex-spouses (Sapphire, 2012; Scott, 2000)—all of which might be recognized in principle but not in connection with bereavement—as well as relationships that are often not recognized by others as significant, such as extramarital affairs or same-sex relationships. Folta and Deck (1976, p. 235) argued that "The underlying assumption is that the 'closeness of relationship' exists only among spouses and/or immediate kin." This assumption is incorrect. Thus, Folta and Deck concluded "rates of morbidity and mortality as a result of unresolved grief may be in fact higher for friends than for kin" (p. 239).

Losses are disenfranchised when their significance is not recognized by society. These might include perinatal deaths, losses associated with elective abortion, or the loss of body parts. Such losses are often dismissed or minimized, as when one is simply told, "Be glad that you are still alive." Similarly, those outside the relationship may not appreciate the death of a pet even though it may be an important source of grief for anyone, regardless of age—child, adolescent, adult, or elder (see the next section in this chapter). Also, society often fails to recognize losses that occur when dementia blots out an individual's personality in such a way that significant others perceive the person they loved to be psychosocially dead, even though biological life continues (see Chapter 20 in this book).

Grievers are disenfranchised when they are not recognized by society as persons who are entitled to experience grief or who have a need to mourn. Young children and the very old are often disenfranchised in this way, as are mentally disabled persons (Kauffman, 2004; Lipsky, 2013).

In his later work, Doka (2002a) suggested two other situations that might disenfranchise grief. Sometimes the very nature or circumstances of the death might

Sadness is part of the lives of many children.

Courtesy Suncoast Hospice

constrain support. For example, deaths that carry stigma or public notoriety such as a suicide, homicide, or AIDS may make survivors reluctant to seek support. In other cases, such as a death by execution—support may be withheld.

In addition to the *structural elements of bereavement* (relationships, losses, and grievers), the *dynamic or functional elements of bereavement* (grief and mourning) may also be disenfranchised (Corr, 1998b, 2002a). For example, bereaved persons might be told by society that the way they are experiencing or expressing grief is inappropriate or that their ways of coping with the loss and the grief reactions are unacceptable. Some grief reactions and some ways of mourning are rejected because they are unfamiliar to folks in a particular cultural group or make others uncomfortable.

However, it occurs, "the problem of disenfranchised grief can be expressed in a paradox. The very nature of disenfranchised grief creates additional problems for grief, while removing or minimizing sources of support" (Doka, 1989b, p. 7). Many situations of disenfranchised grief involve intensified emotional reactions (e.g., anger, guilt, or powerlessness), ambivalent relationships (as in cases of abortion or between persons who once were lovers but no longer are), and concurrent crises (such as those involving legal and financial problems). **Disenfranchisement** may remove the very factors that would otherwise facilitate mourning (such as a role in planning and participating in funeral rituals) or make it possible to obtain social support (e.g., through time off from work, speaking about the loss, receiving expressions of sympathy, or finding solace within some religious tradition).

DEATHS OF PETS AND COMPANION ANIMALS

Deaths of pets and companion animals provide examples of losses that are often not well appreciated and may be disenfranchised. As Carmack (2003, p. 3) stated: "With great love comes great grief." That is true for all deeply felt attachments and is equally valid for losses involving pets and companion animals. In fact, research has shown that, "The death of a beloved companion animal induces a grief reaction of comparable severity to the loss of a significant human relationship" (Packman, Carmack, & Ronen, 2012, p. 335–336). Reflecting on attachments and losses associated with pets and companion animals reinforces previous lessons about bereavement while also leading to useful insights for helpers and preparing us to help bereaved persons with their tasks in mourning.

Children often have their first encounters with death in cases involving wild or domestic animals. Pets may give unconditional love to a child who finds the world to be sometimes harsh and scary. Since most pets have shorter life expectancies than do humans, animals often provide opportunities for children and others to learn about loss, sadness, and death (Kaufman & Kaufman, 2006). As a result, **pet loss** is a familiar subject in death-related books for children (Corr, 2004b; see Focus On 10.1). Pets can also help children, adolescents, and other humans learn about the responsibilities of caring for another living creature and thereby enhance their self-esteem (Rynearson, 1978).

Some people fail to appreciate or even dismiss the importance of attachments between children and animals. This attitude can lead to often well-intentioned actions that make the bereavement experience more difficult. For example, adults may try to hide the death of a companion animal, bury or dispose of it quickly in order to "protect" (as they think) a child from the need to share in this important ritual, or too hastily offer to get a new animal to "substitute for" or "replace" (as they think) the one that has died.

FOCUS ON 10.1

Deaths of Pets in Books for Children

There are so many books about the deaths of pets or companion animals that only a few examples can be cited here (see Appendix A for additional titles and full bibliographical information for those mentioned here). Two books describe adults who are initially not very sensitive to this type of death, even though they show that things can be made better. In *Not Just a Fish* Marybeth is shocked to find her pet goldfish floating upside down in his bowl. Although people say they are sorry Puffer died, they anger her by saying he was "just a fish." Then her father flushes Puffer down the toilet before Marybeth can bury him! Still, Aunt Lizzie understands Marybeth's loss and helps by arranging a memorial service and giving Marybeth a heart-shaped pin with a fish painted on it. A child's needs also go unappreciated in *The Accident* after Christopher's dog is hit and killed by a truck. His parents quickly bury the dog the next morning before Christopher can take part, but anger dissolves into tears when he and his father join together to erect a marker at Bodger's grave.

Several books like *Goodbye Mitch* and *Ocho Loved Flowers* describe the death of a cat from natural causes. After the death of another elderly cat, Alex and his father donate *Mustard*'s dishes and some money to an animal shelter. Because he is preoccupied with grief, Alex declines (for now) a well-meaning offer of a new pet. Similarly, after the death of his dog in *Growing Time*, Jamie is not ready at first for the new puppy his father brings home. But after Jamie can express his grief, he is able to accept the new relationship. And after the death of their dog, when family members regret not telling Elfie that they loved her, a boy says he did so every night. He realizes that his love for Elfie will continue even after her death and says to himself, *I'll Always Love You*. He doesn't want a new puppy right away, even though he knows Elfie will not come back and a time will come when he will be ready for a new pet.

Grunt, *Jasper's Day*, and *Remembering Oakley* are three tender stories about the need to euthanize elderly dogs with serious health problems. In each case, a child and parents take the dog to the veterinarian and join in the events, the deaths are quick and gentle, and time is spent focusing on shared memories of their lives together.

For memorial activities, *When Violet Died* describes a funeral conducted by some children after the death of their pet bird. The children are sad to think nothing lasts forever, but Eva recognizes that life can go on in another way through an ever-changing chain of life involving the family cat, who is pregnant, and her kittens. The story concludes that "maybe nothing lasts forever, but she knew a way to make it last a long, long time!" In another book, when a pet cat dies, a boy's mother suggests that he try to think of ten good things about Barney to say at the funeral. At first, he can only think of nine, but in the garden, the boy realizes that *The Tenth Good Thing About Barney* is that "Barney is in the ground and he's helping grow flowers … that's a pretty nice job for a cat" (p. 24).

There are also two activity books described in Appendix C that are designed to help children express their feelings and cope with the loss or death of a pet: *Remember Rafferty: A Book About the Death of a Pet … For Children of All Ages* and *Saying Goodbye to Your Pet: Children Can Learn to Cope With Grief*.

Source: © 2013 Cengage

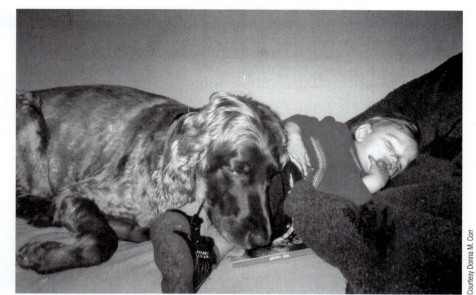

The attachment between a child and her dog provides security to both of them.

Courtesy Donna M. Corr

In addition to children, companion animals can play important roles for adults. These animals may comfort those who are lonely and isolated, and bring a spark of joy to residents in long-term care facilities who may otherwise have only limited social contacts outside the institution. Thus, one study (Banks & Banks, 2002, p. M432) concluded that "A single, 30-minute session of AAT [Animal-Assisted Therapy] per week for 6 weeks significantly reduced loneliness." Animals also help guard individuals in dangerous circumstances, and perform important duties in law enforcement and the military. Also, many persons who have various types of disabilities develop long-term attachments with the service dogs who provide guidance to them and help with various activities (see Focus On 10.2). When relationships like these are important in one's life, the death or loss of an animal can have a powerful impact on the humans involved (Planchon, Templer, Stokes, & Keller, 2002; Reisbig, Hafen, Drake, Girard, & Breunig, 2017; Ross & Baron-Sorenson, 2007).

Loss and grief may also be felt deeply in situations such as when a human being is no longer able to care for an animal and must turn it over to someone else, cannot pay for expensive veterinary services that it would need, must give it up entirely when relocating to new living quarters, or faces difficult choices when a sick or feeble animal must be euthanized (Stewart, 1999). The problem is that this type of grief may be intense, even though there are few, if any, well-recognized and widely accepted structures to assist in coping with such loss and grief (Carmack, 2003; Sife, 2014; Toray, 2004; Wrobel & Dye, 2003).

The importance of death-related losses involving pets and companion animals is evident in the existence of the Association for Pet Loss and Bereavement (www.aplb.org), Pet Peace of Mind (http://petpeaceofmind.org), which is "dedicated to helping hospice and palliative care patients care for their pets," and the website www.petloss.com. Also significant is the growing number of pet cemeteries in the United States (see the International Association of Pet Cemeteries & Crematories, www.iaopc.com), many of which are increasingly receiving and accepting requests for human remains (usually after cremation) to be buried alongside their deceased animal companions (Associated Press, 2011).

Service Dog Owners and Bereavement

Service dogs provide assistance for thousands of individuals who are visually or hearing impaired, as well as those who have cognitive, developmental, physical, or emotional disabilities. Typically, the person with the disability and the service dog develop a strong and unique bond. The many roles they share and the relationships they develop intensify their attachment, making it robust and interdependent. The partnership offers love, acceptance, care, friendship, and practical assistance with daily activities.

Canine Companions for Independence

Persons with disabilities often develop close bonds with the service dogs that promote their independence.

When death severs this relationship, the owner may be left with various losses and grief reactions. In addition to the loss of the devoted relationship with the animal, there are also important secondary losses. For example, support in areas of developing independence, security, safety, courage, and social networking is now compromised. Each of these and other losses will be grieved by the owner. Feelings of anxiety may lead owners to question whether they were somehow responsible for or contributed to the death. Owners may feel guilty because they could not save their beloved dog from illness, disability, and death. They may feel angry at their veterinarian, family, or friends for saying the wrong things.

(continues)

> **FOCUS ON 10.2** *(continued)*
>
> ## Service Dog Owners and Bereavement
>
> When persons with a mobility impairment no longer have a service dog by their side, it may be both physically and emotionally extremely challenging for them to seek support in the community. Reactions related to "fear of the future" and "how to carry on" may be a dominant theme in the early phases of grieving. How will I continue on without my beloved companion? Everyday issues, such as getting in and out of bed, getting dressed, and tending to daily activities, may become challenges even though they are hardly given a second thought by most people. The safety that was once experienced and is now lost may lead to isolation and withdrawal.
>
> To compound these grief reactions, we live in a world where few understand the complexity of emotions and challenges that the bereaved service dog owner faces and the deep sense of loss that is experienced. Comments such as "It was only a dog" or "You can get another one" tend to disenfranchise the grief of the bereaved service dog owner and leave that person feeling even more alone in his or her grief. Saying "I am sorry" or "How can I help" are usually welcome and an important step in offering understanding and support.
>
> *Source:* Rickie Robinson and Katherine Schneider. Used by permission.

We can learn from these comments on pet loss and deaths of companion animals several lessons that apply to all losses: (1) it is the relationship that is really central to appreciating the loss, not the object of the relationship (in this case, the animal in question); (2) the nature of the death or loss and the way it occurred will affect the bereavement; and (3) the circumstances of the bereaved person—both developmental (child, adolescent, adult, or elder) and situational (e.g., living alone, in a supportive family, or in an institution; having prior bereavement experiences or not; functioning with disabilities)—are also critical. As for helpers, individuals confronted by the loss of a pet or the death of a companion animal can be aided and supported, if others will take time to recognize the value of the relationships they have enjoyed with these animals, acknowledge the intensity of their losses, appreciate the challenges they now face, and explore with them their resulting needs (Butler & Lagoni, 1996; Cordaro, 2012; Katz, 2011; Lagoni, Butler, & Hetts, 1994; Packman et al., 2014; Straub, 2004).

SOME CONSTRUCTIVE SUGGESTIONS FOR HELPING

We are not as individuals condemned to fail to help or actually to hurt bereaved persons. We can avoid disenfranchising their grief and bereavement, and we can assist them in many ways. For example, after the sudden and unexpected death of his 10-year-old daughter, one father drew the following lessons for bereaved persons from his experiences (Smith, 1974, pp. 35–40):

1. Don't blame yourself for what has happened
2. Don't be brave and strong
3. Don't try to run away

4. Don't feel that you owe it to the dead child to spend the rest of your life tied to the place where he or she lived

5. Don't feel sorry for yourself

For helpers, Smith (1974, pp. 47–52) had the following advice:

1. Immediately after a death, *do something specific to help* (e.g., notify those who need to be told on the family's behalf, answer the telephone or free family members from other chores that may appear meaningless to them), or make known in other practical ways your willingness to help

2. Respect preferences the family may have to be alone

3. Assist in practical ways through the time of the funeral (e.g., help with meals, cleaning, driving)

4. In the difficult time after the funeral, do not avoid contact with the bereaved

5. Act normally and mention the name of the deceased person in ways that would have been natural before the death

6. Permit the bereaved to determine how or when they do or do not wish to talk about the deceased person

7. Don't try to answer unanswerable questions or to force your religious or philosophical beliefs upon vulnerable bereaved persons

8. Don't say, "I know how you feel"—no matter how much it may seem to be so—that is never true unless you have actually walked in the same path

9. Be available, but allow the bereaved to find their own individual ways through their mourning

Friends are often hesitant and may feel inadequate in approaching someone who is grieving a significant loss (see Personal Insights 1.1 in Chapter 1 in this book). Still, it is better to try to help than to do nothing. In making an effort to help, it is usually a good idea to try to avoid clichés or empty platitudes (Linn, 1986). Sometimes it may be enough to tell the bereaved person: "I don't know what to say to you," or "I don't know what to do to help," but also "What can I do for you right now?" And it can often be most helpful just to sit with or even cry with the bereaved person (see Personal Insights 10.2).

Henri Nouwen (1986, pp. 34–35) commented on guidance for helpers in the following way:

> [W]hen we honestly ask ourselves which persons in our lives mean the most to us, we often find that it is those who, instead of giving much advice, solutions, or cures, have chosen rather to share our pain and touch our wounds with a gentle and tender hand. The friend who can be silent with us in a moment of despair or confusion, who can stay with us in an hour of grief and bereavement, who can tolerate not-knowing, not-curing, not-healing and face with us the reality of our powerlessness, that is the friend who cares.

HELPING BEREAVED PERSONS WITH TASKS IN MOURNING

"For all bereaved, the central issue in any helping encounter is to learn to build a life without the deceased" (Silverman, 1978, p. 40). One value of Worden's (2009) account of tasks in mourning that we discussed in Chapter 9 is that those tasks can be adopted by individuals who are helping the bereaved as ways of determining how their assistance might most usefully be offered. Because Worden's tasks are

Tear Soup

A book called *Tear Soup: A Recipe for Healing after Loss* (Schwiebert & DeKlyen, 1999) tells the story of "an old and somewhat wise woman whom everyone called Grandy" (p. 1) who has just suffered a big loss in her life. Grandy faces her loss by making "tear soup," filling a pot over and over again with her tears, feelings, memories, and misgivings. She knows that the work of making tear soup must be done alone, is typically messy, and "always takes longer … than anyone wants it to" (p. 6). The resulting broth is bitter and making it is difficult work, but it has to be done.

Tear Soup affirms all of the feelings and experiences that bereaved people encounter, including their anger at God because they do not understand why this terrible loss has occurred and do not know where God is when they are feeling so all alone. The book rejects misguided advice like telling bereaved persons that if only they had true faith they would be spared their deep sadness, anger, and loneliness. Instead, Grandy continued to trust God, and she "kept reminding herself to be grateful for ALL the emotions that God had given her" (p. 29).

Tear Soup notes that people in our society are often not very helpful to the bereaved. They are eager to fix things and feel helpless when they cannot do that—so they want to know when this will all be over. Sometimes those who one might have thought were one's friends just drop out of sight and stay away. Even worse are individuals who take it on themselves to show the bereaved person how to make tear soup the "correct" way! Grandy teaches us that real help only comes from those special people who can be present and just listen. Their caring presence does not require the bereaved person to be careful about what is said and does not try to talk that person out of whatever he or she is feeling.

Tear Soup also speaks favorably of "special soup gatherings" in which bereaved persons can share stories that lead to both laughter and additional tears, and "where it's not bad manners to cry in your soup or have second helpings" (p. 37). Finally, *Tear Soup* holds out the hope of a day when one can eventually find it okay to eat something other than tear soup all the time. This does not mean Grandy is completely finished with her tear soup, but the hard work of making it is done and she knows she will survive—even as she keeps a portion of the soup in the freezer to taste a little from time to time.

Source: Based on Schwiebert and DeKlyen (1999). (Note: Images from *Tear Soup* are reproduced in this book on pp. 219, 258, and 312.)

specifically formulated as projects for the bereaved, they need to be adapted to serve as guidelines for helpers. We do that here by exploring ways to help bereaved persons with tasks that involve what they know or believe (cognitive tasks), their emotions or how they feel about their loss (affective tasks), how they act (behavioral tasks), and what they value (valuational tasks).

Throughout this process, helpers need to keep one important caution in mind. At a time when so much in a bereaved person's life is out of control and when he or she is so vulnerable to strong feelings, reactions, and pain, outsiders need to be careful not to take over the bereaved person's tasks of mourning and subtly (or not so subtly) shape them in their own ways (Wolfelt, 2005). Barring outright pathology—which might be identified as involving direct harm that a person is doing to himself or to others—bereaved persons must be permitted to lead the way in their mourning (read Personal Insights 10.1 again). This is what the title of the book *Don't Take My Grief Away from Me* means (Manning, 1979).

Helping with Cognitive Tasks

Everyone who is bereaved asks questions about what happened. All bereaved persons have a *need for information*. Knowing the facts about what happened is an essential step in making the event real in one's inner world. That is why many bereaved persons go over and over the details of the circumstances in which a death occurred. Outsiders often become impatient with this process. They ask: "What difference does it make if the car that hit her was blue or red? Isn't she still dead?" But that misses the point. Only when a bereaved person can fill in details like this in a personal intellectual mosaic can he or she grasp the reality of its pattern. Until then, the loss seems blank, devoid of color, unlike life, unreal, and untrue. Cognitive and other tasks may be especially important (and sometimes difficult) for bereaved persons who are used to exercising a high degree of control over their environment or whose social roles (e.g., as clergyperson, counselor, physician) make it hard for them to seek information and assistance from others.

Providing prompt, accurate, and reliable information is a key role for helpers. One day, when Arthur Smith (1974) was 600 miles away from home at a clergy conference, he was called to the telephone. His wife's voice simply said, "Rachel died this morning." Smith later wrote, "There is no other way to tell someone that a loved person has died" (p. 8). But in the circumstances, Smith's first reaction was to scan in his mind the list of sick and elderly persons in his parish who might have died. Failing to identify anyone with that name, he asked, "Rachel who?" The deep silence that followed signaled the moment in which Smith began to face the almost inconceivable fact of his daughter Rachel's death and his great loss.

Information is particularly important when the death is unexpected, untimely, traumatic, or self-inflicted (De Leo, Cimitan, Dyregrov, Grad, & Andriessen, 2014). Anything that adds to the shocking qualities of a loss contributes to a sense of unreality. Protests quickly arise: "This sort of thing doesn't happen here"; "This must be some kind of bad dream." Information is often urgently requested: about the cause of the loss, recovery of bodies, possible survivors, and so on. Sometimes requests for more information really cannot be answered and are not meant to be answered. Often, they actually are efforts to test reality, to obtain confirmation over and over again that the death has in fact occurred, and perhaps also to confront the hard truth that it will not or may not ever be adequately explained. Testing reality is one way in which bereaved persons move from shock and confusion to other processes of coping constructively with their loss(es) and grief.

For example, even though the ultimate cause of death remains unknown in cases of sudden infant death syndrome (SIDS), it is important that a "syndrome" or pattern of events can be identified. The postmortem examination and the associated investigation on which an appropriate diagnosis of the syndrome rests are critical as a basis for assuring bereaved parents that they did not bring about or in any way cause the death of their child and that nothing could have been done by anyone to prevent the death (see Focus On 12.1 in Chapter 12).

Helping with Affective Tasks

Helpers can also assist bereaved persons with affective or emotional reactions to the loss. These reactions typically include both feeling and somatic (bodily) components. Most bereaved persons have a *need to express their reactions to a loss or death.* To do this, they may require assistance in identifying and articulating feelings and other reactions that are strange and unfamiliar to them (Zeitlin & Harlow, 2001). Some bereaved persons find it difficult to acknowledge or explain their grief reactions. They ask questions of themselves and of others like: "What is happening to me?"; "Why am I experiencing such odd emotions or such a roller coaster of feelings?" Informed and sensitive helpers can give names to affective reactions that the bereaved are experiencing. Helpers can also assist in finding appropriate ways to express strong feelings and other reactions, ways that are safe for both the bereaved person and for others who may become involved.

Often, what is most needed is the company of a caring person who can acknowledge the expression and validate the appropriateness of the emotional reactions. For example, many bereaved persons have found comfort in reading *A Grief Observed,* the published version of the notebooks in which Lewis (1976) wrote out his feelings and the kaleidoscope of reactions he experienced after the death of

Survivors may mark the site of a death in personally meaningful ways.

Courtesy Clyde M. Nabe

his wife. He originally wrote only for himself as a way of venting his grief, but his description has rung so true with other bereaved persons that his little book provides the normalization and reassurance many desperately need. This model of writing out one's thoughts, feelings, and other reactions to loss has been followed with good results by many bereaved persons who keep a journal or other record of their bereavement experiences (Hodgson, 2008; Lattanzi & Hale, 1985). There is an extensive body of writings by bereaved persons (see Focus On 14.1 in Chapter 14), together with books intended to help the bereaved in these matters (e.g., Grollman, 1977; Rando, 1994; Sanders, 1992).

Helping with Behavioral Tasks

Bereaved persons very often need to act out their reactions to a loss. This behavioral aspect of grief frequently takes the form of activities that reflect a need to *mark or take notice of the death through some external event or action.* For example, nowadays we often see flowers, candles, or messages at the place of a public tragedy, "ghost bikes" where a cyclist has been killed, or impromptu roadside markers at the sites of motor vehicle accidents (Clark & Cheshire, 2004; Clark & Franzmann, 2006; Everett, 2002; Reid & Reid, 2001; we discuss this subject more fully in Chapter 11). Another type of behavioral task in bereavement can be observed in *commemorative activities that are designed to remember the life of the deceased or the legacy that he or she has left behind.* One widow described the value of commemorative activities in her comments about letters of condolence that she received from others who had known her deceased husband, even from individuals who were strangers to her (see Personal Insights 10.3; see also Haley, 2001). The goal of these commemorative activities is to preserve at least in some small measure the memory of the person or thing that has been lost. This may be realized in more or less formal or public ways, but it always involves some act or outward behavior. For example, one might plant a

---

PERSONAL INSIGHTS 10.3

Condolence Letters

People dread writing letters of condolence, fearing the inadequacy of their words, the pain they must address, death itself. And few people realize, until the death of someone close, what a benediction those letters are.

The arrival of letters about George was a luminous moment of each day. They made me cry. They made me feel close to him. They gave me the sense that the love he inspired in others embraced me. The best were the longer, more specific ones, the ones that mentioned something the writer cherished in George, or recounted some tale from his past that I was unaware of. Others were inexpressibly poignant. At one time I would have avoided writing any such letter, thinking it unkind to dwell on a subject that was the source of such pain, that I would be rubbing salt into a wound. But now I know that it is not unkind. There is so much joy mixed in with the pain of remembering.

Source: Reprinted from *Rebuilding the House,* by Laurie Graham (Viking Penguin, 1990), copyright Laurie Graham, 1990. Reprinted with permission.

tree in memory of one who has died. This seems to be particularly appropriate because it involves the nurturing of new life in a way that can be revisited from time to time.

Simpler forms of commemoration include attending a wake or funeral, since a prominent part of funeral ritual (see Chapter 11) has to do with commemoration and memorialization of the deceased. Other commemorative gestures might involve putting together a scrapbook of pictures and memories, designing and assembling a collage that symbolizes the life of the deceased, writing a poem about the person who has died, or tracing his or her place in a family tree. The point is not so much how the commemoration is accomplished as that something is done to take note of the life that has now ended and to celebrate its meaning or impact beyond itself.

Helping with Valuational Tasks

A fourth area for helping the bereaved has to do with *a need to make sense out of the loss*. The process of finding or making meaning is often central in bereavement, as explained in Chapter 9 (see also Cox, Bendiksen, & Stevenson, 2004b; Lamm, 2004). In death and loss, that which was a basis for meaning in one's life may have been severely challenged. Mourning initiates the processes of reinvigorating old value frameworks or seeking to construct new ones to take account of the changed realities in our lives.

An example of a parent struggling to find meaning in a difficult loss is found in book, *When Bad Things Happen to Good People* (Kushner, 1981), in which the author describes challenges involved in coping with his son's unusual, progressive illness (progeria) and death at a young age. Rabbi Kushner also focused on the task of finding or making meaning out of the events in his family's life. The conclusions he adopted—mainly that God is not responsible for the bad things that happen to us—have been a source of consolation to many bereaved people.

Some people have such faith or trust in their basic values that they can incorporate a loss directly or at least be patient until meanings begin to clarify themselves. Others must ask repeatedly the ultimate question—Why?—although there may come a time when that question is no longer helpful. Some ways of making meaning are idiosyncratic; many are widely shared among human beings. Some bereaved persons find consolation in the beliefs they share with a religious community; others turn to a personal philosophy or set of spiritual convictions. Sometimes answers from any or all of these sources are not readily available. Almost all human beings need some faith that life truly is worth living even when death has taken someone who is loved.

FACILITATING UNCOMPLICATED GRIEF: GRIEF COUNSELING

Thus far, we have been describing suggestions for "walking alongside" the bereaved person as a fellow human being or fellow griever (see Personal Insights 10.4). This reflects our view that grief and mourning are most often normal and uncomplicated. They are adequately served by caring and thoughtful helpers, whether trained or not. Professional intervention is not normally required although it may be helpful.

When professional intervention is indicated, Worden (2009) has proposed an important distinction between **grief counseling** and **grief therapy**. The former has to do with helping or facilitating the work of bereaved persons who are coping with normal or uncomplicated grief and mourning; the latter designates more specialized techniques used to help people with abnormal or complicated grief reactions.

> ### PERSONAL INSIGHTS 10.4
>
> ## For a Time of Sorrow
>
> *I share with you the agony of your grief,*
> > *The anguish of your heart finds echo in my own.*
> > *I know I cannot enter all you feel*
> > *Nor bear with you the burden of your pain;*
> *I can but offer what my love does give:*
> > *The strength of caring,*
> > *The warmth of one who seeks to understand*
> > *The silent storm-swept barrenness of so great a loss.*
> *This I do in quiet ways,*
> > *That on your lonely path*
> > *You may not walk alone.*
>
> *Source:* From *Meditations of the Heart,* by Howard Thurman.
> Copyright © 1953, 1981 by Anne Thurman. Boston: Beacon Press.

In helping bereaved persons, one must remain alert for manifestations of complicated grief reactions (Cox, Bendiksen, & Stevenson, 2004a). When those appear, individuals should be referred to appropriate resources for grief therapy (Neimeyer, 2012, 2016; Rando, 1993). However, one must not misinterpret normal grief reactions as abnormal or pathological reactions; that would be to misunderstand bereaved persons and to over-professionalize the help they need.

Most often, grief counseling takes the form of a one-to-one intervention with bereaved persons. As such, it can be offered by anyone who is properly prepared and qualified for this work. As a professional intervention to help persons who are coping with uncomplicated grief and mourning, grief counseling might be offered by psychologists, social workers, clergy, nurses, physicians, counselors, and funeral directors. Note, however, that not all professionals are equally competent as grief counselors. Also, there has been some controversy about whether formal grief counseling is actually effective and, if so, for whom (Allumbaugh & Hoyt, 1999; Currier, Holland, & Neimeyer, 2007; Forte, Hill, Pazder, & Feudtner, 2004; Jordan & Neimeyer, 2003; Larson & Hoyt, 2007a, 2007b; Neimeyer, 2000). Productive grief counseling grows out of caring communities, to which it adds formal understanding of experiences in bereavement, grief, and mourning as well as skill in helping individuals with their own coping or problem-solving processes. For such counseling, Worden (2009) identified the following ten principles as guidelines. Many of these principles are also relevant to nonprofessional ways of helping the bereaved.

1. *Help the Survivor Actualize the Loss.* In contrast to the sense of unreality that often accompanies bereavement, this principle recommends an effort "to come to a more complete awareness that the loss actually has occurred and that the person is dead and will not return" (Worden, 2009, p. 90). This is one reason why it is so important to identify the bodies of those killed in plane crashes, natural disasters, war, or terrorist attacks, as was demonstrated so vividly after

the collapse of the World Trade Center towers on September 11, 2001. Also, one can simply assist those who are bereaved to talk about their losses. Active listening and open-ended questions encourage a repeated review of the circumstances of the loss, as do visits to the gravesite. Immediate family members may be familiar with these details and can often become impatient with their repetition. However, as Shakespeare wrote in *Macbeth* (IV, iii: 209), bereaved persons need to "give sorrow words." A caring helper can aid this important process of growing in awareness of loss and in appreciation of its impact. Still, one must not push the bereaved too forcefully or too quickly to grasp the reality of a death if it appears they are not yet ready to deal with it. One must follow his or her own cues (see Personal Insights 10.5; but note how even this very sensitive expression of grief and mourning assumes a framework in "the stages of grief").

2. *Help the Survivor to Identify and Experience Feelings.* Many bereaved individuals may not recognize unpleasant feelings like guilt, anxiety, fear, helplessness, or sadness, or they may be unable to express their feelings and other reactions to loss in ways that facilitate constructive mourning. A helper can aid bereaved persons to be aware of their reactions to loss and then enable those reactions to find an appropriate focus. For example, some persons may find themselves blaming caregivers who were unable to prevent the death. Some may be angry

---

PERSONAL INSIGHTS 10.5

A Letter to My Family and Friends

Thank you for not expecting too much from me this holiday season.

It will be our first Christmas without our child and I have all I can do coping with the "spirit" of the holiday on the radio, TV, in the newspapers and stores. We do not feel joyous, and trying to pretend this Christmas is going to be like the last one will be impossible because we are missing one.

Please allow me to talk about my child if I feel the need. Don't be uncomfortable with my tears. My heart is breaking and the tears are a way of letting out my sadness.

I plan to do something special in memory of my child. Please recognize my need to do this in order to keep our memories alive. My fear is not that I'll forget, but that you will.

Please don't criticize me if I do something that you don't think is normal. I'm a different person now and it may take a long time before this different person reaches an acceptance of my child's death.

As I survive the stages of grief, I will need your patience and support, especially during these holiday times and the "special" days throughout the year.

Thank you for not expecting too much from me this holiday season.

Love,

A bereaved parent

Source: From "A Letter to My Family and Friends" in M. Cleckley, E. Estes, and P. Norton (Eds.), *We Need Not Walk Alone: After the Death of a Child,* Second Edition, p. 180. Copyright © 1992 The Compassionate Friends. Reprinted with permission.

at others who are also bereaved but who appear not to be very affected by the death. Still others are angry at themselves for what they have or have not done. Finally, some people are angry (and this is often difficult to admit) at the deceased for dying and leaving the bereaved person behind to face many problems. Thus, Caine (1975) berated her deceased husband for leaving her unprepared (as she felt) to cope with many challenges in life and to raise their children alone.

Questions like "What do you miss about him?" and "What don't you miss about him?" may help the person find some balance between positive and negative feelings. Unrealistic guilt that may be experienced as part of the overall grief reaction may respond to reality testing and lead to the realization that "We did everything we could have done." Many (but not all) bereaved persons may need to be gently encouraged to express, rather than repress, their sadness and crying. Recognizing strong feelings like anger and blame may help grievers begin to put them into perspective and move on. Similarly, it can be comforting to acknowledge that one did do some positive things prior to the death and may still be able to act in some effective ways even at a time when other things are unsettled or out of control. However, grievers must find their own comfort and forgiveness; helpers only facilitate the process and must try to do so with sensitivity and care.

3. *Assist Living Without the Deceased.* Helpers can assist bereaved persons to address problems or make their own decisions. Because it may be difficult to exercise good judgment during acute grief, bereaved persons are often advised

Talking to a counselor can help children, adolescents, and others cope with their losses and grief.

Courtesy Suncoast Hospice

not to make major life-changing decisions at such times, such as those involved in selling property, changing jobs, or relocating. Thus, a central lesson in Judy Blume's novel for young readers, *Tiger Eyes* (1981), is the realization that moving from Atlantic City, New Jersey (where her father was killed in the holdup of his 7-Eleven store), to live with her aunt in Los Alamos, New Mexico, was ultimately not a productive way for a teenage girl, her mother, and her younger brother to cope with their grief and with each other.

However, the role of the helper is not to take over problems and decision making for the bereaved. So, when issues arise concerning the making of independent decisions (such as how to deal with sexual needs in bereavement that may range from needs to be held or hugged to problems in attaining intimacy with a new person), a helper's main role is only to assist the person in the process of making decisions (DeFord & Gilbert, 2013). This is often best accomplished in a validating and nonjudgmental way. Enabling the bereaved to acquire new and effective coping skills empowers those who may perceive themselves to be powerless in their bereavement.

4. *Help Find Meaning in the Loss*. Finding meaning in the death of a loved one or in any other important loss in one's life is very much an individual project for a bereaved person, as we noted in Chapter 9. Helpers cannot simply assign meanings to a significant loss or determine what that loss will mean for the individual. Nevertheless, helpers can assist individuals as they search for a meaning they can live with or reassign meanings to the changed world in which they now live. One person recommended that helpers hold their own beliefs in their hearts, while allowing those they are helping to work out their beliefs. Some bereaved persons find comfort in religious or spiritual convictions that assure them in particular terms or in a general way that some meaning does exist. Others explain why a loss occurred in terms of the way the deceased person had behaved. Still others view losses as events from which they themselves can learn something. Even when a satisfactory reason cannot be assigned to a loss, many find meaning in activities related to the manner of the death that took the loved one away from them. For example, many establish a memorial or a scholarship in the deceased person's name, whereas others lobby to minimize handgun violence or impaired driving so their loved one's death will not have been in vain and hoping to prevent in the future similar deaths that seem so senseless and unnecessary.

5. *Facilitate Emotional Relocation of the Deceased*. This principle is not only or not always about encouraging the bereaved to form new relationships (see Personal Insights 9.5 in Chapter 9). As time passes, that may be appropriate. However, it is important not to do so too quickly in ways that inhibit adequate mourning. The central point of this principle is to "help the survivor find a new place in his or her life for the lost loved one, a place that will allow the survivor to move forward with life and form new relationships" (Worden, 2009, p. 99). This principle (along with others in this list) is illustrated by "linking objects" that facilitate recognition of loss, expression of grief, restructuring of relationships, and ongoing connectedness. Thus, for one son, attending a final game at a baseball stadium (Comiskey Park) in Chicago that was about to be closed revived important recollections of good times with his father, helped him experience and express his grief in ways he had previously avoided, and gave him precious memories to take with him into the future (Krizek, 1992). Restructuring

relationships with the deceased does not overthrow, supplant, or dishonor the dead; it encourages bereaved persons to live as well as possible in the future and to live as any deceased person who loved and cared for them would have wanted them to live.

6. *Provide Time to Grieve.* It takes time in a rich, multifaceted relationship to restructure attachments and close doors on aspects of the past that are now over. Intimate relationships develop on many levels and have many ramifications. Mourning, if it is to be adequate to the loss, can be no less complex. Some people rapidly regain equilibrium in their lives and quickly return to familiar routines. They may be impatient with a bereaved person who is moving more slowly or finding it more difficult to deal with his or her loss and grief. They may not appreciate how arduous it is to deal with critical anniversaries or the time around three to six months after the death, when so much support offered during the funeral and the early days of bereavement is no longer readily available. Effective helpers may need to be available over a longer period of time than many people expect, although actual contacts need not always be very frequent.

7. *Interpret "Normal" Behavior.* Many bereaved persons feel that they are "going crazy" or "losing their minds" because they may be experiencing things they usually do not experience, and they may, for a while, be unable to function as well as they have in the past. Help in normalizing grief reactions can be provided by others who are knowledgeable about or experienced with bereavement. Reassurance will be welcomed that extraordinary experiences or a preoccupation with the deceased are common in bereavement and do not usually indicate that one is actually going crazy. Encouragement of this sort guides and heartens the bereaved in their time of travail.

8. *Allow for Individual Differences.* This is a critical principle for helpers. The death of any one person affects each of his or her loved ones in different ways. Each bereaved person is a unique individual with his or her own relationships to the deceased and his or her own personality and coping skills. Each person travels his or her own journey in bereavement and mourns in his or her own ways. Help in appreciating the individuality of grief reactions and mourning processes is especially important for families or other groups who lose a member. It is even more critical when two parents try to understand the ways in which each of them may be reacting differently to the death of their child. Just as helpers need to respect the uniqueness of each bereaved person whom they seek to assist, so too bereaved persons should respect the individuality of grief and mourning in other persons who have been impacted by the same loss.

9. *Examine Defenses and Coping Styles.* By drawing the attention of bereaved persons in a gentle and trusting way to their own patterns of coping, helpers may enable the bereaved to recognize, evaluate, and (where necessary) modify their behaviors. This is the sensitive work of suggesting different ways of coping, not so much directly as by enabling the bereaved person (sometimes through a joint effort) to assess his or her own thoughts and behaviors. Questions such as "What seems to help get you through the day?" or "What is the most difficult thing for you to deal with?" may assist the bereaved person to understand how he or she is coping.

10. *Identify Pathology and Refer.* Most people who engage in helping the bereaved are not prepared to deal with complicated grief reactions on their own because most of us do not possess the specialized skills and expertise of a qualified grief therapist (Rando, 1993; Sanders, 1989; Sprang & McNeil, 1995). However, helpers and counselors can remain alert for manifestations of complicated grief and can play an important role in referring those who need them to appropriate resources. This referral is not a failure; it is a responsible recognition of one's own limitations.

Summary

In this chapter, we reviewed some of the many ways in which individuals can help those who are coping with loss and grief. We noted and explained examples of unhelpful messages to the bereaved, introduced and clarified the concept of disenfranchised grief, and suggested that losses involving companion animals and pets are often not well appreciated and may be disenfranchised. We also identified helpful ways in which to assist bereaved persons with tasks in mourning. This sort of assistance essentially constitutes a program for "befriending" the bereaved. Further, because the principles underlying professional grief counseling are similar to those that guide everyone who tries to help bereaved persons cope with uncomplicated grief and mourning, we explained ten principles for facilitating uncomplicated grieving.

Glossary

Disenfranchised grief: grief or mourning that persons experience when they incur a loss that is not or cannot be openly acknowledged, publicly mourned, or socially supported

Disenfranchisement: may apply to relationships, losses, grievers, grieving styles, or mourning processes

Five fundamental needs of bereaved persons: social support, nutrition, hydration, exercise, and rest

Grief counseling: helping bereaved persons who are coping with uncomplicated grief and mourning

Grief therapy: helping bereaved persons who are coping with complicated grief reactions

Helping bereaved persons with:
   Affective tasks: assisting with efforts to express emotions and feelings associated with a loss or death in a constructive way
   Behavioral tasks: assisting with efforts to mark or take notice of a death through some external event or deed, as well as with commemorative activities designed to celebrate and remember the life of the deceased or the legacies of that life
   Cognitive tasks: assisting with efforts to obtain information about the loss or death
   Valuational tasks: assisting with efforts to find meaning or to make sense out of the loss

Pet loss: death, loss, or ending of a relationship with a pet or companion animal

Unhelpful messages to bereaved persons: typically, these involve attempts to minimize the loss, admonitions not to feel or express strong grief reactions in public, and suggestions to get back to living promptly and not disturb others with one's grief and mourning

Questions for Review and Discussion

1. Think of a time when you experienced the death of someone you loved or the loss of something important in your life. What did you want others to do with or for you at that time? Who or what was helpful or unhelpful to you? Can you explain why that was so?
2. Think of losses that you experienced or that you observed (either directly or through the media) others experience in connection with any major public tragedy. What types of losses did you notice, and what were the main characteristics of those losses?
3. Have you ever drawn on social media or the Internet to find ways to help a bereaved person? Was that useful? If so, how or why? If not, why not?

Suggested Readings

For advice about helping oneself or others in grief, see:

Adams, C. A. (2003). *The ABC's of Grief: A Handbook for Survivors*

Attig, T. (2000). *The Heart of Grief: Death and the Search for Lasting Love*

Attig, T. (2012). *Catching Your Breath in Grief ... and Grace Will Lead You Home*

Baugher, B. (2013). *A Guide for the Bereaved Survivor*

Bowering, G., & Baird, J. (Eds.). (2011). *The Heart Does Break: Canadian Writers on Grief and Mourning*

Fitzgerald, H. (1995). *The Mourning Handbook: A Complete Guide for the Bereaved*

Grollman, E. A. (Ed.). (1981). *What Helped Me When My Loved One Died*

Kauffmann, J. C., & Jordan, M. (2013). *The Essential Guide to Life After Bereavement: Beyond Tomorrow*

Kushner, H. S. (1981). *When Bad Things Happen to Good People*

Lewis, C. S. (1976). *A Grief Observed*

Moffat, M. J. (1992). *In the Midst of Winter: Selections from the Literature of Mourning*

Neimeyer, R. A. (1998). *Lessons of Loss: A Guide to Coping*

Rando, T. A. (1994). *How to Go on Living When Someone You Love Dies*

Schwiebert, P., & DeKlyen, C. (1999). *Tear Soup: A Recipe for Healing after Loss*

Smith, H. I. (1999). *A Decembered Grief: Living with Loss When Others Are Celebrating*

Smith, H. I. (2004a). *Grievers Ask: Answers to Questions about Death and Loss*

Smith, H. I., & Jeffers, S. L. (2001). *ABC's of Healthy Grieving: Light for a Dark Journey*

Guidance for professional helpers is provided in the following:

Becvar, D. S. (2003). *In the Presence of Grief: Helping Family Members Resolve Death, Dying, and Bereavement Issues*

Boss, P. (2006). Loss, Trauma, and Resilience: Therapeutic Work with Ambiguous Loss

Cook, A. S., & Dworkin, D. S. (1992). *Helping the Bereaved: Therapeutic Interventions for Children, Adolescents, and Adults*

Crenshaw, D. A. (2002). *Bereavement: Counseling the Grieving throughout the Life Cycle*

De Leo, D., Cimitan, A., Dyregrov, K., Grad, O., & Andriessen, K. (Ed.). (2014). *Bereavement after Traumatic Death: Helping the Survivors*

Doka, K. J. (Ed.). (2002a). *Disenfranchised Grief: New Directions, Strategies, and Challenges for Practice*

Hanson, J. C., & Frantz, T. T. (Eds.). (1984). *Death and Grief in the Family*

Harris, D. L., & Bordere, R. C. (Eds.). (2016). *Handbook of Social Justice in Loss and Grief: Exploring Diversity, Equity, and Inclusion*

Harris, D. L., & Winokuer, H. R. (2016). *Principles and Practice of Grief Counseling* (2nd ed.)

Hooyman, N. R., & Kramer, B. J. (2006). *Living through Loss: Interventions across the Life Span*

Jeffreys, J. S. (2011). *Helping Grieving People—When Tears Are Not Enough: A Handbook for Care Providers* (2nd ed.)

Kosminsky, P. S., & Jordan, J. R. (2016). *Attachment-Informed Grief Therapy: The Clinician's Guide to Foundations and Applications*

Neimeyer, R. A. (Ed.). (2012). *Techniques of Grief Therapy: Creative Practices for Counseling the Bereaved*

Neimeyer, R. A. (Ed.). (2016). *Techniques of Grief Therapy: Assessment and Intervention*

Rando, T. A. (1984). *Grief, Dying, and Death: Clinical Interventions for Caregivers*

Rando, T. A. (1993). *Treatment of Complicated Mourning*

Rubin, S. S., Malkinson, R., & Witztum, E. (2012). *Working with the Bereaved: Multiple Lenses on Loss and Mourning*

Sanders, C. M. (1992). *Surviving Grief … and Learning to Live Again*

Sprang, G., & McNeil, J. (1995). *The Many Faces of Bereavement: The Nature and Treatment of Natural, Traumatic, and Stigmatized Grief*

Stewart, M. F. (1999). Companion *Animal Death: A Practical and Comprehensive Guide for Veterinary Practice*

Stroebe, M., Schut, H., & van den Bout (Eds.). (2013). *Complicated Grief: Scientific Foundations for Health Care Professionals*

Thompson, N. (Ed.). (2002). *Loss and Grief: A Guide for Human Service Practitioners*

Walsh, F., & McGoldrick, M. (Eds.). (2004a). *Living beyond Loss: Death in the Family* (2nd ed.)

Walsh, K. (2012). *Grief and Loss: Theories and Skills for the Helping Professions* (2nd ed.)

Walter, T. (1999). *On Bereavement: The Culture of Grief*

Webb, N. B. (Ed.). (2004). *Mass Trauma and Violence: Helping Families and Children Cope*

Weizman, S. G. (2005). *About Mourning: Support and Guidance for the Bereaved*

Worden, J. W. (2009). *Grief Counseling and Grief Therapy: A Handbook for the Mental Health Practitioner* (4th ed.)

Selected Web Resources

Some useful search terms include: DISENFRANCHISED GRIEF; GRIEF COUNSELING; GRIEF THERAPY; PET LOSS; TASKS IN MOURNING; WIDOW-TO-WIDOW PROGRAMS.

You can also visit the following *organizational and other Internet sites:*

American Counseling Association

Association for Clinical Pastoral Education

Association for Pet Loss and Bereavement

Association for Professional Chaplains

International Association of Pet Cemeteries & Crematories

National Mental Health Association

Petloss.com

Samaritans International

Stephen Ministries

Widowed Persons Service (WPS), AARP (American Association of Retired Persons)

Yossi Manor/Shutterstock.com

Coping with Loss and Grief: Funeral Practices and Other Ways Communities Can Help

Objectives of this Chapter

▶ To explain the role of ritual and community support in helping individuals cope with life crises

▶ To describe four types of community programs designed to help persons who are coping with loss and grief, including:

   1. Funeral practices and memorial rituals

   2. Aftercare programs in the funeral industry

   3. Hospice bereavement follow-up programs

   4. Support groups for the bereaved

SOCIAL INSTITUTIONS THAT PROVIDED SUPPORT DURING ONE WOMAN'S MOURNING

Stella Bridgman (see the vignettes at the beginning of Chapters 9 and 10) found consolation at her son's funeral. Although his life in recent years had seemed so troubled, she was surprised when so many of his friends, schoolmates, and coworkers came to the visitation. They told her about what he had meant to them and about their memories of helpful things he had done. When her son was buried next to his father, Stella believed he was finally at peace.

At the funeral and for many months afterward, the aftercare specialist at the funeral home checked in with Stella from time to time, gave her short pamphlets on loss and grief, suggested some books that she could read, and was available whenever she had questions. Although her son had not been in hospice care, the aftercare specialist referred her to the community bereavement program at a local hospice so that she might also draw on the resources it had to offer.

Four months after her son's death, Stella felt that she was only now experiencing the full impact of her loss. With the encouragement of the aftercare specialist, a friend took her to a meeting of a local chapter of The Compassionate Friends, an international organization of support groups for bereaved parents. Stella had heard about this group, but she had thought it would be too intimidating to go to a meeting on her own. She wondered: Will the group be welcoming or alien? Will it be helpful or not? What if my reactions overwhelm me or I just cannot tolerate the group experience? What if I am physically or emotionally unable to drive home? The presence and support of her friend helped calm these anxieties.

The group did not draw back when Stella expressed her pain, anger, guilt, and other strong feelings. Members of the group permitted her to give vent to such feelings, and they acknowledged the normalcy of her reactions. Group members also recognized the appropriateness of her questions and validated her experiences as a bereaved parent.

At one meeting, Stella said she felt like she was going crazy. Members of the group agreed that they had often felt that way, too. Stella expressed amazement that other bereaved parents could speak of their dead children without collapsing in tears. How could they go forward with their lives, get through the holidays, and even find it possible to laugh once in a while? Stella tried to tell herself that if these people had also walked "in the valley of the shadow of death" and were now able to find some way to live on, perhaps she could, too. But she could not see how to do that yet.

Over time, just by being themselves, these other bereaved parents showed Stella that one can survive horrendous losses and cope effectively with grief reactions, that life can once again become livable. Also, without needing to offer her any advice, the members of the group served as role models and provided Stella with options from which she might choose in determining how to live her own life.

LIFE CRISES AND RITUALS

Rituals play important roles in the lives of most human beings. Anthropologists and others have studied ritual for many years using various definitions of the key term. For example, Mitchell (1977, p. xi) described **ritual** as "a general word for corporate symbolic activity." The corporate or communal symbolic activity involved in ritual generally has two components: it involves *external (bodily) actions,* such as gestures, postures, and movements that symbolize interior realities; and it is *social*—that is, the community is usually involved in ritual activity (Douglas, 1970).

One can identify ritual practices of this sort in all human societies. Van Gennep (1961) emphasized the links between ritual and *life crises* or important turning points in human life, such as childbirth, initiation into adulthood, marriage, and death. Because crises involve a significant change or disruption in human life, they threaten the invasion of chaos. As a result, crises are "dangerous opportunities," as we noted in Chapter 9. Ritual can contribute some degree of ordering or orientation to such events. To the extent that ritual achieves that goal, it helps make the unfamiliar more familiar by providing guidance as to how one should act in these unusual (but not always unanticipated) circumstances. In other words, ritual seeks to "tame" strange or unusual experiences in human life to some degree.

Since death is one of the most imposing invasions of disorder and chaos in human life, it is not surprising that throughout history humans have made efforts to bring order into lives that have been affected by death (Bendann, 1930; Puckle, 1926). Archaeologists and anthropologists believe that some of the most ancient artifacts they have discovered had something to do with rituals associated with death and burial. Also, as one moves forward from prehistoric to more recent times, rituals associated with death are found in every societal death system. As Margaret Mead (1973, pp. 89–90) wrote: "I know of no people for whom the fact of death is not critical, and who have no ritual by which to deal with it."

Nevertheless, many individuals these days make efforts to avoid ritualized practices and appear to act as if they have no need for ritual. They do not come to graduation ceremonies, for example, or they try to avoid attending funerals. As a result, some have suggested that modern societies are making an effort to do away with all ritualized behavior. That is hardly accurate. In fact, evidence of the felt need for ritual at key moments in our lives can be found in the actions of numerous individuals and communities. Consider the spontaneous memorials that spring up where a public tragedy has occurred. Similarly, think about the informal roadside memorials that family members or friends use to mark the spot at which a loved one or close friend was killed in a motor vehicle accident (Clark & Cheshire, 2004; Clark & Franzmann,

A child holds a folded American flag at a funeral.

2006; Everett, 2002; Haney, Leimer, & Lowery, 1997; Reid & Reid, 2001) or the white-painted "ghost bikes" that mark the site of a cyclist's death in some places. In more formal ways, upon receiving news of the death of a person serving in the armed forces, the military appoints casualty or notification officers to convey the news in an official and sensitive way to the person's family and to try to provide any support family members may need (Sheeler, 2008). Elaborate funeral, burial, and memorial activities often follow the death of a member of the military, a police officer, or a firefighter. Officers attend the funeral in full-dress uniforms, flags are folded in precise ways and presented to surviving family members, buglers may play "Taps," and a firing squad may fire a volley into the air. Similarly, sports teams often wear black armbands after the death of a teammate, and a jersey may be "retired" in honor of that individual. In some communities, the death of a prominent or specially admired member may lead to flags being flown at half-staff and a moment of silence being observed at a social activity. In these and numerous other examples, we find that many bereaved people do not suffer alone and in silence. Instead, they take action to give vent to their loss and grief, to draw attention to what has happened, and to engage the community in their mourning—whether the community always approves of these actions (Doss, 2010; also see Issues for Critical Reflection #9). Mourning is a necessary and transformative experience (Ashenburg, 2003).

ISSUES FOR CRITICAL REFLECTION
#9 Some Criticisms of Roadside Memorials and Responses

Roadside memorials are seen throughout North America and elsewhere (Petersson, 2009). Usually they appear at the site of a traffic fatality, but they also can be found where drownings, homicides, or suicides have occurred (Collins & Rhine, 2003). Typically, these memorials appear on public or private land after a sudden and violent death. Because roadside memorials are spontaneously placed by the bereaved near where the death occurred, they mark the site as "sacred" to them in some sense. This is especially clear when some religious symbol (usually a cross) is used as part of the marker. However, other objects have also been used, such as "flowers, notes, poems, photos, music tapes, CDs, scarves, pinwheels, balloons" and "teddy bears, dolls, toys, or sports equipment" for young children (pp. 230–231).

Roadside memorials are not uncontroversial; here are four main types of criticisms. First, because these memorials may interfere with maintenance of the right-of-way along the road, some states remove them, while other states replace spontaneous memorials with state-sanctioned ones that are often plainer and less personal than the ones erected by bereaved individuals.

Second, some claim that roadside memorials are distracting to drivers and thus are a danger at the very site where the marker indicates a death has occurred. (Note: Collins and Rhine found that most people who erect roadside memorials do not intend their markers to serve as a warning to other persons.) However, these memorials are usually small and easily overlooked; as potential distractions they are less significant compared with the number and size of the advertisements commonly met alongside roadways.

Third, some people find roadside memorials to be a form of visual pollution or aesthetically offensive. However, Collins and Rhine found that most people were inclined to be sensitive to the grief of the bereaved and willing to accept some visual "blight" for their sake.

Fourth, some argue that these memorials violate the separation of church and state because they often use religious symbols as part of the marker and are frequently located in public spaces and on public property. Those opposing roadside memorials erected by private individuals suggest that any such marker should be placed there by the state, without religious symbols. But such state-approved markers can seem sterile and not very empathetic to the grief of those who have been bereaved by a death.

What do you think about roadside memorials?

A private roadside memorial . . . replaced by a standardized state memorial sign.

Courtesy Clyde M. Nabe

However, not every instance of ritual is equally valuable or effective for all bereaved persons or for all communities. Many ethnic and cultural groups have their own rituals (see Chapter 5 for some examples). Persons who are not members of those groups may not find comfort in such rituals, partly because they may not be familiar with the rituals or do not understand the meaning of their various components. Even members of such a group may find little solace in the ritual because it may represent views they do not personally hold or fail to address what they are experiencing individually.

In the next four sections of this chapter, we offer:

- A description of typical elements in contemporary American funeral practices
- Brief comments on contrasting views concerning the value of these practices
- An analysis of three central tasks associated with such rituals
- An account of the roles of cemeteries and selected memorial activities in helping bereaved persons

TYPICAL ELEMENTS IN CONTEMPORARY AMERICAN FUNERAL PRACTICES

Funeral practices in the American death system can take many forms. In this section, we describe these practices in a general way, while remaining aware that they may differ depending on local customs and religious, cultural, and ethnic perspectives. Typical elements usually found in many contemporary American **funeral practices** are:

- Removal of the body from the place of death
- Preparation of the body for viewing or final disposition
- A viewing of the body
- A funeral service
- Delivery of the body for final disposition
- In-ground burial or aboveground entombment in a mausoleum or crypt

As we learned in Chapter 2, most people in the United States today die in some type of public institution. When that occurs, staff members typically notify the family if they are not already present, help make arrangements to clean and care for the body until family members can arrive, assist in making contact with a local funeral director, and organize the removal of the body from the place of death. Members of a hospice or home care team often do much the same when a death occurs at home.

Although many Americans are not very familiar with the work of funeral service personnel, their roles are actually fairly straightforward (Michaelson, 2010). To begin with, they usually transport the body to a funeral home, while arranging for a death certificate to be properly completed and exchanged for a permit to bury the body or otherwise dispose of it. In some cases involving "direct disposition," the funeral director may simply transport the body to a crematorium or to another appropriate destination (such as the anatomy department of a local medical school) for a donation to medical education and research. In all of these cases, efforts will be made to show respect for the body as the remains of someone valued as a human being and to act in accordance with the religious or philosophical beliefs that an individual and his or her social group hold about life and death (Habenstein & Lamers, 1974).

Most bodies in the American death system are washed, embalmed, dressed, and prepared by funeral service personnel for a "viewing," "visitation," or "wake," as it may variously be described. In some cultural groups, family members or group representatives may carry out or take part in this work. **Embalming** grew in popularity in the United States after the Civil War as a practice that made it possible to ship dead bodies back home for burial from distant battlefields (Mayer, 2011). The most celebrated early example of embalming occurred following the death of Abraham Lincoln when his body, after lying in state in the U.S. Capitol rotunda and following a funeral service, was carried by rail on an extended journey from Washington, D.C., where he was assassinated, to Springfield, Illinois, for burial. The funeral train made many stops along its winding journey to serve the needs of grief-stricken Americans. If normal biological processes of decomposition had not been delayed, Mr. Lincoln's body would have become an object of social repugnance long before the train reached its destination.

Embalming today involves the removal of blood and other bodily fluids from a corpse and their replacement with artificial preservatives that are intended to help retard decomposition and color the skin. Embalming may or may not be accompanied by efforts to restore the cosmetic appearance of the corpse. No state law or federal regulation requires embalming to be done, unless certain conditions are present as when the body is to be transported on a common carrier, such as a train or airplane.

In the contemporary American death system, embalming is mainly practiced to permit viewing of the body during a wake or visitation in some public gathering (e.g., at a funeral home) or in cases of a funeral with an open casket (Iserson, 2001; Raether, 1989). Advocates argue that embalming prevents the spread of disease by disinfecting the corpse and neutralizing contaminants in discarded blood and bodily fluids. Actually, direct cremation, immediate burial in a sealed container, or refrigerating the body could achieve similar results. In fact, embalming is most often used to slow decay in the bodily tissues of the corpse. This provides time for relatives and friends of the deceased to gather from a distance in a large and dispersed society, and it makes possible viewing of the body once they have come together.

During a *visitation* or *viewing*, the casket containing the body is often open, either fully or at least to reveal the upper half of the body. On occasion, the casket may be closed—sometimes as a matter of preference, at other times because of the condition of the corpse. Typically, mourners approach the casket, sometimes to say a brief prayer or for a moment of reflection. Often, they return again and again to the casket to stare at, touch, or kiss the dead body. They seem to be saying final farewells and impressing a last image into their minds, even as the cold, rigid, and non-life-like features of the corpse convey to them in a silent but forceful way the realities of its differences from a living body. As they come together for a visitation or funeral, participants often find themselves sharing stories about the deceased or reminiscing in ways that help locate and secure that person (and themselves) in the history and memory of the community of those who were touched by the life of the deceased person.

Following a funeral or religious service, *disposition or disposal of bodies* is typically carried out in one of the following ways: burial in the ground; entombment in some sort of crypt, vault, or mausoleum above the ground; cremation and subsequent disposition of the remains of that process; or donation to a medical or other institution for purposes such as scientific research or professional education (Habenstein & Lamers, 1962; Iserson, 2001).

Mourners at a funeral in a cemetery.

RubberBall Productions/Brand X Pictures/Getty Images

In-ground burial is the most common form of body disposal in the United States. Generally, the body is buried within several days of the death, although some groups, such as Orthodox Jews and Muslims, seek to bury prior to sundown on the day of the death or at least within 24 hours. The period between death and burial in our society usually depends on the time needed to prepare the body, make necessary arrangements, and—above all—gather together family members and other key persons from distant locations. **Entombment** in some type of aboveground structure is essentially a variant on in-ground burial.

In the case of burial, historically there would be a formal procession of vehicles from a funeral home or place of worship to a cemetery, followed by a gathering of mourners around the casket at the burial site, brief prayers or last words about the deceased, lowering of the casket into a grave, individual tossing of symbolic shovelfuls of dirt over the casket, and filling in of the grave. In recent years, formal processions of vehicles have diminished, mourners are likely to be encouraged to leave the gravesite before the casket is lowered into a vault or grave liner (a concrete form placed within the grave that is designed to protect the casket and prevent settling of the ground), the vault is sealed closed, and the grave is filled in with dirt and covered with grass. Some cemeteries have built chapels and prefer that last rites be performed there, rather than at the gravesite. These practices mainly have to do with the workload of the cemetery's personnel and a desire not to risk upsetting mourners as workers lower the casket into the grave, enclose it within a vault or grave liner, and refill the grave.

Cremation is often popularly thought of as an alternative to embalming, viewing, and a funeral, but it may also follow those activities as a step between them and final disposition. The process typically involves placing the body in some sort of container and reducing its size through the application of intense heat (Doughty, 2014; Jupp, 2006; Prothero, 2001). The container need not be a casket; crematories usually only require that the body be turned over to them in an enclosed, rigid, combustible container that can be handled easily and safely. The body and its container are then heated to 1,600–1,800 °F for a period of two to three hours. Because most of a human body is water, the water evaporates. At the high temperatures reached during cremation, the rest of the soft tissues are consumed by spontaneous combustion. This process rapidly reduces the size of bodily remains to a residue that is primarily ash and those fragments of dense bone that have not been vaporized by heat. When these remains have cooled, they are collected and then usually ground up or pulverized into a coarse powder.

An alternative form of cremation available to the general public in some places is called **flameless cremation** (alkaline hydrolysis or chemical cremation). According to one report (Valentine, 2011), it

> works by placing a body in a pressurized drum that holds up to 400 gallons of water. A chemical [potassium hydroxide] is added and heated to 350 degrees. The heated mixture is recirculated through the drum for two to four hours. When the cycle is complete, soft tissue is dissolved into a soapy, murky liquid, which eventually makes its way into the city's wastewater system.

Proponents argue that this process is an environmentally friendly, "green alternative," involving an accelerated form of natural breakdown in which the ash remains returned to the family are lighter in color because they are clean and without carbon discoloration.

Following either form of cremation, the person responsible for the cremated remains or **cremains** may choose what to do with this residue. For example, the cremains may be scattered over water or enclosed in an urn or another permanent container. The urn may then be kept by the bereaved, buried in the ground, or placed in a niche (a small compartment) in a mausoleum-like columbarium. In recent years, some have arranged for a portion of the cremains to be flown into space, permanently entombed under water as part of artificial reef structures (Eternal Reefs), sealed in glass pendants or similar objects (Solstice Glass; Artful Ashes), or turned into diamond jewelry (LifeGems).

"The most remarkable changes in the American cemetery industry in the last forty years have been the resurgence of entombment as an important method of disposal and the steady, recently spectacular, rise of cremation" (Sloane, 1991, p. 220). Entombment in an aboveground space may reflect such variables as soil conditions (e.g., a high water table as in some parts of New Orleans), that make in-ground burial difficult or impossible, a desire to save land space, or a preference for final disposition in a structure that is enclosed, dry, heated, and air conditioned.

The Cremation Association of North America (CANA, 2016) reports that cremations were performed for 48.6 percent of all deaths in the United States in 2015 (68.8 percent in Canada). In recent years, the proportion of deaths involving cremation has been steadily increasing by 1–2 percent per year in both countries. CANA attributes growing interest in cremation to factors like lower costs, a wider range of disposition options, concerns about the environmental impact of traditional burials, the ability to transport cremated remains wherever one might relocate, and greater tolerance for cremation among many religions.

Some contemporary Americans prefer to *donate their bodies for teaching or research purposes*. If so, arrangements usually must be made well ahead of time with the receiving institution because there does not seem to have been a shortage of such donations in recent years. Also, careful preservation of the body is important for this purpose, and the techniques required to prevent decay are considerably more stringent than those used in a typical embalming procedure. Thus, the receiving institution will usually have a formal protocol for body donation and will typically require access to the body shortly after death. Following the use of a body for scientific or educational purposes, the elements that remain may be cremated or buried by the institution or returned to next of kin for similar disposition.

An alternative to a traditional funeral is a **memorial service**. Essentially, memorial services incorporate many of the practices that have already been described, but without the presence of a body. Memorial services might be held when a body has been lost at sea or is otherwise unavailable, when the body has been immediately cremated and the cremains scattered, when the body has been donated for medical research or education, or simply as a matter of preference. The focus in memorial services is typically on celebrating and commemorating the life of the deceased through music, poetry, readings, and personal testimonials (Hickey, 2006; Moore, 2009). *Memorial societies* in North America encourage memorial services as a way to reduce costs and to turn away from what they regard as an inappropriate emphasis on the corpse (Morgan, 2010; Slocum & Carlson, 2011). They do not favor embalming, caskets, and other efforts to prepare a body for viewing.

Two relatively new advocacy groups in this area are the National Home Funeral Alliance and the Green Burial Council. The former provides advice and guidance showing how individuals can provide safe and legal care for the body of a love one at home or in a prepared space through to disposition. The latter educates about and advocates for **green or natural burial**, that is, chemical-free, ecofriendly burial in a shroud or biodegradable container in a shallow grave that does not inhibit decomposition and allows the body to recycle naturally (Blakemore, 2016; Harris, 2008; Kelly, 2015).

For traditional funeral services, it is not possible to provide a single list of prices because costs for services and associated merchandise vary greatly across regions and by individual funeral home. The simplest way to determine costs is to ask a local funeral home for its general price list or draw up with a funeral director a "pre-need" plan (Bern-Klug, DeViney, & Ekerdt, 2000). Preplanning is offered by almost all funeral homes as a way to design a specific arrangement that suits an individual and to determine what it will cost. In Focus On 11.1, we identify some of the main cost elements that enter into the price of funeral services in the United States. Note that most funeral homes offer package arrangements that usually represent a savings from their itemized price lists. More information on funeral services in North America can be obtained from local sources (such as funeral homes, memorial societies, cemeteries, crematories) and from the national organizations listed in Focus On 11.2.

FOCUS ON 11.1

Typical Cost Items for Funeral Services and Merchandise

SERVICE	INCLUDES
Basic services of funeral director and staff, plus overhead costs	Having personnel available 24 hours a day, 365 days a year to respond to initial call; conducting arrangements conference; planning the funeral; consulting with family and clergy; shelter of the remains; preparing and filing necessary notices; securing and recording the death certificate and disposition permit, as necessary; coordinating with cemetery, crematory, and/or other third parties involved in final disposition; access to services of bereavement coordinator; plus a proportionate share of basic overhead costs (e.g., facility maintenance, equipment and inventory costs, insurance and administration expenses)
Additional services of funeral director and staff	Coordination and direction of funeral or memorial services at another facility, graveside services, or inurnment at place of final disposition; added charges for evening, Sunday, holiday or other special services

(continues)

FOCUS ON 11.1 *(continued)*

Typical Cost Items for Funeral Services and Merchandise

Embalming	Usually not required by law, but may be necessary if certain funeral arrangements (e.g., viewing, delay before funeral, transportation of the body over a long distance, and/or with certain diseases) are selected
Other preparation of the body	For example, restoration, cosmetology, washing and disinfection, manicuring, dressing
Transfer of deceased to the funeral home	Usually based on a stipulated distance, with added charges beyond that distance
Use of facilities and staff for viewing	At the funeral home first day; each added day
Use of facilities and staff for autopsy, funeral ceremony, memorial service, reception	At the funeral home; at another location or facility
Use of vehicles	Hearse; service/utility car; limousine
Pastoral services; music	
Cemetery plot and/or other charges	
Forwarding/receiving of remains to/from another funeral home	

MERCHANDISE	INCLUDES
	Items such as casket, outer burial container (vault or grave liner), cremation container/urn, guest register books, acknowledgment cards, memorial folders, flowers, clothing

SOME ALTERNATIVES

Direct cremation (basic services of funeral director and staff, proportionate share of overhead costs, removal of remains, transportation to crematory if required, necessary authorizations, and cremation). Also, alternative containers made of materials like fiberboard or composition materials.

Immediate burial plus casket (basic services of funeral director and staff, proportionate share of overhead costs, removal of remains, transportation to cemetery). With or without casket provided by purchaser.

Source: Based on Canine (1999), and general price lists from local funeral homes.

Selected National Resources for Information on Funerals and Related Matters

Catholic Cemetery Conference
www.catholiccemetergyconference.org
708-202-1242; 888-850-8131

Cremation Association of North America
www.cremationassociation.org
312-245-1077

Funeral Consumers Alliance
www.funerals.org
802-865-8300; 800-765-0107

Green Burial Council
www.greenburialcouncil.org
888-966-3330

International Association of Pet Cemeteries & Crematories
www.iaopc.com
800-952-5541

International Cemetery, Cremation, and Funeral Association
www.iccfa.org
703-391-8400; 800-645-7700

International Order of the Golden Rule
www.ogr.org
512-334-5504; 800-637-8030

Jewish Funeral Directors of America
www.jfda.org
703-391-8400; 800-645-7700

Monument Builders of North America
www.monumentbuilders.org
847-803-8800; 800-233-4472

National Funeral Directors and Morticians Assn.
www.nfdma.org
770-965-0064; 800-434-0958

National Funeral Directors Association
www.nfda.org
262-789-1880; 800-228-6332

National Home Funeral Alliance
www.homefuneralalliance.org
603-236-9495

Neptune Society
www.neptunesociety.com
954-556-9400; 855-646-3228

Selected Independent Funeral Homes
www.selectedfuneralhomes.org
847-236-9401; 800-323-4219

One last point: some American funeral directors have assumed roles in responding to mass disasters as members of a Disaster Mortuary Operational Response Team (DMORT, 1998). As temporary federal employees in this capacity, DMORT team members establish temporary morgue facilities; assist with victim identification using latent fingerprints, forensic dental pathology, or forensic anthropology methods; and conduct the processing, preparation, and disposition of human remains. The importance of this work was evident in the efforts of a DMORT team following the events of September 11, 2001 (Hazell, 2001).

CONTRASTING VIEWS CONCERNING THE VALUE OF CONTEMPORARY AMERICAN FUNERAL PRACTICES

There is a long and diverse history of comments on the value of contemporary American funeral practices. Three basic viewpoints seem to dominate:

■ Abolish these postdeath rituals: This view argues that American funeral and memorial practices represent a kind of fantasized flight from reality

(Mitford, 1963, 1998); such rituals should be abandoned; time, energy, and money invested in funerals should be used in some other way.

- Modify these rituals: One version of this view holds that typical American funeral practices are overly lavish and expensive; they should be replaced by other social rituals after death, such as less ostentatious *memorial services* conducted without the presence of the body and often held two or three weeks after the death (Morgan, 2010; Slocum & Carlson, 2011); this viewpoint would substitute one form of ritual for another but is not opposed to all death-related rituals. A different perspective arguing for modifying funeral rituals has been proposed (V. Pine, personal communication, 4/18/15) noting that most of our funeral rituals come from a previous century when death rates were relatively high as a result of accidents and acute diseases, and many who died in these ways were working and active in their communities or were children. Today, death rates are highest among the elderly. As a result, many people who attend funerals are primarily there to support the adult children of the deceased—their relationship with the deceased is indirect. Pine suggests that funeral rituals need to take into account this new demographic reality.

- Continue traditional rituals with minor alterations: This view maintains that these rituals help people make sense of, and bring order out of, what is potentially a disruptive, stressful, chaotic encounter with death (Long & Lynch, 2013; Manning, 2001; Raether, 1989), and they serve a constructive role in grief work (Howarth, 1996; Hoy, 2013); they can be modified or adapted to serve individual needs or desires.

Interestingly, long-standing research reports both criticisms of the funeral industry from clergy (e.g., Fulton, 1961; Kalish & Goldberg, 1978), together with much satisfaction among the general public (Bolton & Camp, 1987; Fulton, 1978; Kalish & Goldberg, 1980; Marks & Calder, 1982). Hyland and Morse (1995) noted that widespread public regard for the comfort offered by funeral service personnel is a striking achievement when one realizes that most of these services are provided by strangers in circumstances of great stress for the bereaved and during what is usually a relatively short period of contact. Also, research by Canine (1999) concluded that the vast majority of respondents who work in the funeral industry put "service to families" as their first priority. On the basis of this evidence, it cannot be maintained that there is widespread social dissatisfaction with funeral rituals within the American death system or that funeral service practitioners do not act without having the interests of society in mind. Of course, specific individuals and groups must decide about their own participation in funeral rituals and their assessments of these rituals' value. Clearly, opinions may differ in this sensitive area, both on the role of funeral rituals in general and on whether a particular funeral ritual provided a useful service in a specific instance.

In the following section, we offer an analysis of three basic tasks that ought to inform constructive funeral rituals. Our goal is to come to a better understanding of the nature and purposes of funeral rituals and other commemorative activities. We also want to help readers determine for themselves whether these rituals are effective in serving significant needs in their lives. To that end, note that in planning or taking part in a funeral or other memorial ritual of any kind, it is always appropriate to ask: what do these gestures, these actions, or these words mean or suggest? This question may be difficult to pose when a person is stricken with grief. A better time to think through the rationale for what might be desired in any postdeath ritual is before the ritual is needed. Preplanning that takes account of the individual and social tasks to which funeral and memorial rituals can contribute can be helpful in providing a funeral that successfully meets individual, familial, and societal needs.

THREE TASKS ASSOCIATED WITH FUNERAL RITUALS

Scholarly work by anthropologists and sociologists (Durkheim, 1954; Fulton, 1995; Goody, 1962; Malinowski, 1954; Mandelbaum, 1959) uses the language of *functions* to explain funeral rituals. In this book, we encourage proactive approaches in which bereaved and other vulnerable individuals can work to regain control over lives impacted by death. Thus, we prefer to interpret funeral and other memorial rituals through a *task-based approach*, one directing bereaved persons and society to focus on three key tasks: (1) to dispose of the body of the deceased in appropriate ways; (2) to contribute to making real the implications of the death; and (3) to assist in reintegration and meaningful ongoing living (Corr, Nabe, & Corr, 1994). We use these tasks here to explain and evaluate elements of funeral and memorial rituals.

Disposition of the Body

The first task to which funeral rituals should contribute is *to dispose of the body of the deceased in appropriate ways*. To fail in this task is to risk violating both social attitudes and community health—not to mention doing harm to oneself. As Staples (1994, p. 255) wrote: "The rituals of grief and burial bear the dead away. Cheat those rituals and you risk keeping the dead with you always in forms that you mightn't like. Choose carefully the funerals you miss." In all societies, ritualized **disposition of the body** requires respect for the body as the remains of someone valued as a human being. Thus, most humans are uncomfortable with allowing a corpse simply to be discarded or left lying around (Iserson, 2001). Also, dealing with a dead body requires behavior in accordance with the religious or philosophical beliefs that an individual and his or her society hold about life and death. Disrespect for either of these can result in serious conflict, as dramatized in Sophocles' *Antigone* when Antigone insists that her dead brother's body must be buried, while King Creon is concerned that such a burial would improperly show respect for a rebellious subject.

In society today, the question of how to properly dispose of a human body is remarkably complex. In any large and diverse society, there is a wide range of religious or philosophical beliefs about the nature of the person, the universe, or any afterlife. Together with or apart from such beliefs, custom is often the guiding force in many people's views about disposition of dead bodies. For example, decisions about embalming, a "visitation" (with or without a "viewing" of the body), whether to have a religious or nonreligious funeral or memorial service, cremation, and committal of the body or its cremains to earth burial are often made largely on the basis of the beliefs to which one adheres or the customary practices with which one is familiar. In all of these decisions what is important is the felt need to dispose of human bodies in what is viewed as a respectful and appropriate manner.

Making Real the Implications of Death

A second task addressed by funeral and memorial rituals is to contribute to **making real the implications of death**. Sometimes this is described as seeking "realization" or

PERSONAL INSIGHTS 11.1

Gordon Parks: The Funeral

After many snows I was home again.
Time had whittled down to mere hills
The great mountains of my childhood.
Raging rivers I once swam trickled now
                    like gentle streams.
And the wide road curving on to China or
              Kansas City or perhaps Calcutta,
Had withered to a crooked path of dust
Ending abruptly at the country burying ground.
Only the giant who was my father
                    remained the same.
A hundred strong men strained beneath his coffin
When they bore him to his grave.

Source: "The Funeral," from *Whispers of Intimate Things,*
by Gordon Parks, copyright © 1971 by Gordon Parks. Used by
permission of Viking Penguin, a division of Penguin Group (USA), Inc.

achieving "separation" from the deceased. This task may not be as easy as it might seem to someone who is not personally involved in the process. In fact, disentangling realistic and unrealistic or symbolic and literal elements in bereavement shortly after a death is difficult for many persons (see Personal Insights 11.1).

That is why it is so important to identify any part of the remains of a deceased person, as was made clear in the strenuous efforts to recover body parts from the rubble of the World Trade Center towers after September 11, 2001. That also explains comments from some bereaved persons in New York City who described others as lucky because at least they had a body to bury. If a bereaved individual is unable to accomplish this task of making real the implications of death, that person's life may be disrupted in some serious ways. Thus, it may be useful to engage in actions that help in the process of recognizing the permanent separation of the dead from the living (in this life, at least).

Funeral ritual is intended to be of assistance in this process of psychological separation of the bereaved from the deceased. Some argue that seeing the dead body may help make the death real. They bolster this argument with comments to the effect that bereaved persons often face special challenges in realization when there is no body—for example, when it has been lost at sea, never returned from combat, or consumed in a horrific explosion or fire. Even the presence of some token remains in a closed casket, so it seems, can be helpful to the bereaved (see Personal Insights 11.2).

If in fact funeral ritual is to help with making real the implications of death, then presumably some of the actions and events associated with it should point to the permanence of the separation of the dead from the living. Some have criticized contemporary American funeral practices as failing to support this separation from the deceased, arguing that the use of cosmetics and the expensive linings of caskets

PERSONAL INSIGHTS 11.2

A Wife's Description of What Was Recovered after the Death of Her Husband

My most enduring memory of my husband, Ronald Breitweiser, will be his final words to me, "Sweets, I'm fine, I don't want you to worry, I love you." Ron uttered those words while he was watching men and women jump to their deaths from the top of Tower One. Four minutes later, his Tower was hit by United Flight 175. I never spoke to my husband, Ron, again.

I don't really know what happened to him. I don't know whether he jumped or he choked to death on smoke. I don't know whether he sat curled up in a corner watching the carpet melt in front of him, knowing that his own death was soon to come, or if he was alive long enough to be crushed by the buildings when they collapsed. These are the images that haunt me at night when I put my head to rest on his pillow.

I do know that the dream I had envisioned, that I so desperately needed to believe—that he was immediately turned to ash and floated up to the heavens—was simply not his fate. I know this because his wedding band was recovered from ground zero with a part of his left arm. The wedding band is charred and scratched, but still perfectly round and fully intact. I wear it on my right hand, and it will remain there until I die.

Source: Kristen Breitweiser, Co-chairperson of the September 11 Advocates, Testimony on September 18, 2002, before the House/Senate Joint Inquiry into Intelligence Community Activities before and after the Terrorist Attacks of September 11, 2001 (as cited in Graham, 2004, p. 171).

both seem to promote an image of life rather than of death (Harmer, 1963, 1971; Mitford, 1963, 1998). If it is important to help the bereaved make the death real for themselves, then contributing to the appearance that the dead person is "asleep," head on a pillow, lying on a mattress, surrounded by beautiful bed linens, may be counterproductive—or so we are told. Another development concerns life-like poses that some have chosen for the deceased (see, e.g., Newcomb, 2014). The tension operating here seems to be between the task of making real the implications of a death and the desire to accommodate individual preferences and/or offer the bereaved a final, comforting "memory image" of the body of their loved one. Perhaps the challenge is to achieve all of these goals in satisfactory ways.

Some critics (e.g., Slocum & Carlson, 2011) argue that many aspects of contemporary American funeral practices draw too much attention to the *body* itself. On this view, making real the implications of death is concerned primarily with taking leave of the *person* as part of an overall process of restructuring relationships with the deceased. In other words, it is the loss of the person, not his or her body, that is the primary concern. In this sense, the gathering of family and friends is a social validation of significant relationships and the reality of the death.

Issues involved in realization and separation also arise at the place of burial. Sometimes mourners are encouraged to leave the gravesite before the body is lowered into the grave. In other cases, some cemeteries have encouraged mourners to perform any last rites and take leave of the body at a chapel on their grounds, rather than at the gravesite. One can understand some of the motivations behind these practices, such as to allow the cemetery employees to complete their work at their own pace and out of sight of tense mourners, but sending mourners away also distances them from the realities of the death and may thus run counter to the desired work of making real the implications of the death.

A second set of criticisms has been directed toward costs involved in much contemporary funeral practice (Arvio, 1974; Bowman, 1959). Airtight or watertight metal caskets are expensive objects. Critics have asked: what real purposes are served by such elaborate merchandise? Even if they prevent the body from decaying—and they surely do not when one considers that they could only inhibit the work of aerobic, not anaerobic, bacteria—why is that important?

Answers to these questions seem to reside at the psychological rather than the economic level of mourning. Some persons argue that spending money for a funeral and burial allows mourners to feel satisfaction in having shown respect and love for the person who has died. After all, expenditures involved in buying a casket and paying the associated costs of a funeral and burial are said to be one of the most substantial financial outlays that most people will make during their lives, exceeded only by the purchase of a house or an automobile. In this sense, expenses associated with a funeral can be seen as a kind of "going-away" present or final gesture of love toward the deceased. At least indirectly, this expenditure may support the realization that the dead person has in fact left the community of the living.

Purchases associated with funerals also represent to some people the last gift or service they can make to the person who has died. In addition, the conviction that the body will be "protected from the elements" may provide some psychological satisfaction to the bereaved. This may be true whether the merchandise or services actually do accomplish what the buyer thinks they will accomplish. After all, much of what is going on here—especially in its psychological components—is really designed to serve the needs of the living (Jackson, 1963). As one funeral director wrote, "Unlike the fast food restaurant, where value is determined solely by cost, the value of death rituals should be determined by the comfort and consolation they provide to the bereaved" (Weeks, 2001, p. 188).

Reintegration and Ongoing Living

The death of someone we love leads to *disintegration*, a breaking apart of the world as it has been known and understood. Thus, there is a third task facing the bereaved: *to achieve a new integration and thereby to promote meaningful ongoing living*. For many persons, funeral practices and other activities after a death can play important roles in beginning this process.

The *disintegration* experienced by bereaved persons may occur at one or more of four levels. First, people who experience the death of an important person in their lives often experience various kinds of *disintegration at the individual level*. They may feel a loss of integrity or wholeness within themselves. They may ask, "Am I going crazy?" Sleep patterns, eating patterns, and health concerns all may be disrupted by the death of a loved person. In short, customary ways in which individuals live in the world and their familiar sense of their own identity can be shredded by a death. The individual then faces the task of pulling himself or herself back together, usually with a somewhat altered if not wholly new identity.

Second, the impact of death may also be evident in *disintegration at the family level*. The death of a person has many meanings for those closest to that person. It may have economic repercussions for the family as a whole, such as the loss of the deceased's income, the loss of an owner of property, and the loss of the person who typically handled certain financial transactions. Death also has consequences for the ways in which those closest to the deceased person relate to each other and to the rest of the world. Members of the family may experience disruptions in their relationships with one another. They may have to renegotiate how they stand in their relationships to each other (How will siblings relate to each other now that the parent has died?) and to the family unit (Who will be responsible for which tasks?). Some bereaved individuals may lose part of their social identity as the relative (spouse, child, or parent) of the person who died. Death can exacerbate old tensions within a family, just as it may create new tensions. All of these effects are forms of family disintegration associated with death. They impose on members the task of reintegrating the family unit.

Third, almost all deaths also have implications for *disintegration at the social level*. This is most obvious when a public figure or someone of great social standing dies, such as a president or a celebrity, but the death of any person is likely to cause some measure of social disintegration. Who will make the decisions that person used to make? Who will take over the work associated with that person's job? Who will have to drive more often in the carpool? The structures of society—the whole civic or national society in some cases, but some level of society (the business or school or church) in most cases—will have to be reworked so that society can once again function as an integrated unit.

Fourth, *disintegration at the spiritual level* can involve tasks that are intellectual and perhaps most pressingly emotional. How does one make sense of a world in which this person is no longer present? As a residue of the dying period, there may be anger, frustration, and even despair. For many, this includes an anxiety about or a sense of being alienated from whatever the person holds to be transcendent (e.g., God). If the person has certain religious beliefs, those beliefs may be severely challenged ("How could God allow her to die such a painful death?"). Other beliefs may also produce uncertainty and anxiety: What has happened to the loved person now that she is dead? The tasks here concern reconfiguring one's understanding of how the world operates and also renegotiating one's relationship to whatever the person conceived the transcendent to be.

Funeral and related rituals can help to begin the process of **reintegration** or achieving new integration at each of the levels of disintegration noted here. For *reintegration at the individual level* funeral rituals can help mourners recognize that they need not see themselves as simply alone. The tasks they need to perform can be accomplished, in part through the aid of persons drawn to their sides by the funeral. Though mourners may feel overwhelmed by the grief and disorientation they are experiencing, they are not simply powerless or adrift on wholly uncharted seas. They cannot change the fact that a death has occurred, but they can, with the assistance of relatives, friends, and others, decide how to respond to that fact and how to regain some measure of control over the course of their lives.

The most obvious sign of *renewed integration at the family level* is often seen in the physical or geographical drawing together of persons who ordinarily see little of each other in their everyday lives. When families are scattered across the country or even beyond, a funeral is one moment when they are reintegrated physically, but also often psychologically and emotionally. Sometimes family members remark, half-jokingly, that they only seem to get together at funerals.

In some cultural groups, the funeral and other rituals associated with a death go on for months or even years (at different levels of activity during those periods). A good example of this is the Jewish tradition of rending or tearing one's clothes (*Keriah*) to symbolize a disruption in one's life, reciting the prayer for the dead (*Kaddish*), and organizing activities in specified ways for particular periods (Lamm, 2000). As Gordon (1974, p. 101) has written: "Judaism recognizes that there are levels and stages of grief and so it organizes the year of mourning into three days of deep grief, seven days of mourning [*shivah*], thirty days of gradual readjustment [*Sh-loshim*], and eleven months of remembrance and healing." Here, the support system assists the bereaved, again and again, in finding their way through the period of crisis and into the new world that they are entering—a world without the dead person in it.

By contrast, for many individuals in our society, the funeral takes place only a matter of days after the death. After that, participants scatter again, and for many people there is no agreed-upon or designated path through the wilderness of grief and mourning. Integration may be hard to achieve under such circumstances. (Awareness of the limitations of traditional funeral practices may have helped motivate many funeral directors to develop "aftercare" programs of support for the bereaved, which we discuss later in this chapter.) In any event, the most important considerations in this situation are how individuals make use of funeral ritual and how they follow up on the beginnings represented by that ritual.

For *reintegration at the social level,* funeral and memorial rituals can help to provide a sense that society is not going to fall apart because of a death. This has been seen in the funerals of many national leaders, like Presidents Kennedy (1963), Reagan (2004), and Ford (2006), but also in the ways in which the funeral and other postdeath activities associated with the death of Diana, Princess of Wales, in 1997, brought people around the world together. These and other public rituals (e.g., of celebrities) allow expression of grief, give testimony to the ongoing viability of the community, and provide opportunities for individuals to rededicate themselves to working on behalf of a better society in the future.

Mourners share their grief at a candlelight vigil.

Alan C. Heison/Shutterstock.com

Reintegration at the spiritual level is accomplished for those who hold certain spiritual or religious beliefs if the funeral can help bereaved individuals begin to answer their questions about the meaning of the death. Funeral rituals can also help firmly locate the bereaved in a supportive faith community. Most religious traditions have well-established rituals to help the bereaved in these ways. These rituals offer many believers reassurance about the continued support of God or some value framework in this life and even after it. Whether persons have those types of beliefs, the deceased person can be located and secured in the history and memory of the community of those who were touched by that individual through the sharing of stories about the person at a funeral or memorial service.

A funeral, then, can help bereaved persons begin to overcome the individual, family, social, or spiritual disintegration experienced after a death. Achieving a full measure of this type of integration may take much effort and a long time. Contemporary funeral rituals may not go very far toward accomplishing this task, but they can be a beginning as is seen in a personal comment by Deirdre Sullivan (2005), whose father had repeatedly told her from childhood onward "always go to the funeral." After he died quietly from cancer "on a cold April night three years ago," she reported,

> His funeral was on a Wednesday, middle of the workweek. I had been numb for days when, for some reason, during the funeral, I turned and looked back at the folks in the church. The memory of it still takes my breath away. The most human, powerful and humbling thing I've ever seen was a church at 3:00 on a Wednesday full of inconvenienced people who believe in going to the funeral.

CEMETERIES AND SELECTED MEMORIAL ACTIVITIES

Funeral rituals are not the only formal ways in which communities in today's death system try to support and assist persons who are coping with loss and grief. In addition to a visitation, the funeral, and burial or some other form of disposition of the remains, other typical **memorial activities** are found in cemeteries, memorial sculpture, memorial photography, and the use of the World Wide Web in mourning.

Activities following a death in America have gradually evolved into what has been called a distinctively American way of death (Farrell, 1980). To begin with, *cemeteries* serving many groups in American society have developed over time:

- From frontier graves, domestic homestead graveyards, churchyards, potter's fields, and town or city cemeteries (such as the New Haven Burying Ground in Connecticut) especially typical of the 17th and 18th centuries
- Through what were originally 19th-century rural cemeteries (like Mount Auburn in the Boston area) and lawn-park cemeteries (like Spring Grove in Cincinnati)
- To memorial parks in the 20th century (like Forest Lawn in the Los Angeles area) (Sloane, 1991)

A similar history, marked in its particulars by the unique character of the African-American community, has been documented for African-American burial sites (Holloway, 2003; Wright & Hughes, 1996).

Many American cemeteries are privately owned, whereas others have national (such as those for veterans), public (municipal or county), or religious owners. In the last 150 years, many cemeteries have stressed an esthetic layout, even a picturesque or pastoral landscape. Some have become major tourist attractions—for example, Forest Lawn Memorial Park in Glendale, California, which has been the object of both literary satire (Huxley, 1939; Waugh, 1948) and scholarly study (Rubin, Carlton, & Rubin, 1979). Recently, American society has also witnessed rapid growth in the number of cemeteries for pets or companion animals. The diversity and changing character of all these cemeteries reflect different attitudes associated with death and bereavement. Still, all cemeteries provide an exclusive place for disposing of a body or other remains, a unique location to which bereaved persons can return to acknowledge the reality of the death, and a special context in which they can maintain a connection with the individual who died (Bachelor, 2004).

A second dimension of memorial activities can be observed in the history of *memorial sculpture.* That history is linked to the evolution of cemeteries, in which wooden or stone markers have given way to marble, granite, and bronze. Some of these markers have been quite plain (providing, for example, only the name and dates of birth/death for the deceased). Others have included artistic icons and three-dimensional sculpture. In times past, grave markers often displayed elaborate and interesting epitaphs (see Personal Insights 11.3 for one example; also, Coffin, 1976; Mann & Greene, 1962, 1968; Meyer, 1992; Reder, 1969; Wallis, 1954). Recently, for esthetic reasons and to keep down maintenance costs, grave markers have largely taken the form of flush-to-the-ground plaques. Whatever their form, however, these markers commemorate a life and take note of its ending. Another type of memorial sculpture in American cemeteries is found in religious or abstract objects of art as centerpieces in the landscape, together with mausoleums, tombs, and other aboveground structures (Keister, 2004).

A third area of memorialization, *memorial photography,* developed with the invention and increasingly widespread use of photographic technology from the 19th century onward. Memorial photographs enable those who are bereaved to retain a tangible memento of the person and the funeral of the deceased (Burns, 1990). They include photos taken by relatives, as well as images created and preserved by professional photographers. More recently, some people have used cameras, smartphones, and other devices to take photos and make videos as a way to memorialize a life at the moment of its ending and to establish commemorative links to the past. Further advances in technology have led to the development of ways to share images

---

PERSONAL INSIGHTS 11.3

Benjamin Franklin's Epitaph

The body of Benjamin Franklin, Printer
(like the cover of an old book,
Its contents torn out
And stripped of its lettering and gilding)
Lies here, food for the worms.
Yet the work shall not be lost,
For it shall (as he believed) appear once more
In a new and most beautiful edition
Corrected and Revised
By the Author.

and memories associated with those who have died through social media and other digital media venues (De Vries & Roberts, 2004).

Some are uneasy with the idea of memorial photography (e.g., Lesy, 1973). However, the extent of this practice and its many variations—such as those depicted in *The Harlem Book of the Dead* (Van der Zee, Dodson, & Billops, 1978)—testify that it serves the needs of many individuals. In fact, memorial photography can help many bereaved persons simultaneously to distance themselves from the dead, acknowledge the implications of their loss, and carry with them an image of the deceased as they move on in their own lives (Ruby 1995). This directly parallels the three tasks for funeral ritual described in this chapter. Contrasting attitudes toward memorial photography illustrate tensions between practices that individuals perceive as helpful in their mourning and some public lack of understanding or discomfort with such practices. Efforts to achieve a new understanding of funeral and memorial ritual may help to ease these social tensions.

A fourth area of contemporary mourning rituals has developed recently as a result of the possibilities arising from the social media and the Internet. For example, some individuals have posted tributes to their loved ones who have died (De Vries & Rutherford, 2004). Others have used their online skills to find new ways to express or share their grief reactions and to make connections that might enable them to find some measure of solace. GriefNet is one of the best-known websites serving this last purpose, along with some of the other resources listed at the ends of the three chapters in this Part. Figure 11.1 illustrates some of the many ways in which individuals can and have called on the digital universe to help in their mourning activities.

Figure 11.1 Roles of Digital and Social Media in Coping with Loss and Achieving Digital Immortality

Developed by Professor Carla J. Sofka and reprinted by permission

AFTERCARE PROGRAMS IN THE FUNERAL INDUSTRY

The title of the book, *When All the Friends Have Gone* (Weeks & Johnson, 2001), reflects the need for *aftercare* that many funeral service organizations now provide. Such "aftercare" mainly includes any assistance and support offered to the bereaved after the funeral is over and the family members and friends have returned to the familiar patterns of their own lives. Although strictly speaking the term is not limited to the work of funeral services practitioners, "aftercare" has come to have a specific meaning within the funeral services industry. As Johnson and Weeks (2001, p. 5) observed: "Funeral home aftercare may be defined as an organized way to maintain a helpful and caring relationship with clients, offer continuing services to client families beyond the expected body disposition and accompanying rituals, and provide death, loss, and grief education to both clients and the community."

Aftercare programs in the funeral industry are rooted in the ongoing concern of some funeral directors for the welfare of the bereaved family members of their clients who prior to their deaths had been friends and neighbors in local communities. Such funeral directors were attuned to the bereavement needs of these people and were willing to offer their empathic presence to them. Defined by Johnson and Weeks as an informal or *"casual" level of aftercare*, this is the first of what they regard as four possible levels of aftercare (see Table 11.1). It involves simply listening while bereaved persons tell their stories, helping them complete paperwork for various bureaucracies and entitlements, and providing basic literature (often in pamphlet form) on grief and bereavement. No extra staff is required and costs are minimal.

As aftercare programs have become more formalized within the funeral industry, their design and implementation has varied greatly in keeping with the needs of the communities being served and the resources they commanded. Thus, Table 11.1 distinguishes three additional formal levels of aftercare based largely on the personnel involved; their training, personal qualities, and professional skills; the materials

Table 11.1   Levels and Characteristics of Funeral Home Aftercare Programs

Program Level	Staff	Activities	Cost
Casual (informal)	No extra staff	Visiting, chance meetings, sharing book lists, brochures	Minimal
Fundamental (formal)	Extra staff but no extensive training	Telephone calls, newsletters, socials, dinners, travel	Moderate
Standard (formal)	Extra staff with specific training in bereavement issues	Support group sponsorship/facilitation, lending library, special holiday programs, community education, cards on special days	Substantial
Premier (formal)	Extra staff: master's degree or higher with concentration on counseling and grief/loss issues	Individual counseling, children's programs, in-service training, community advisory boards, spokesperson for media	Substantial to unlimited

Source: From *When All the Friends Have Gone* by O. D. Weeks and C. Johnson (Eds.), p. 9. Copyright © 2001. Baywood Publishing Co. Reprinted with permission.

they use; the funding they require; and the activities in which they become engaged. (Note that when aftercare programs include community education and other services to the public at large, they are no longer confined to activities following a specific death and thus go beyond care *after* death.)

Funeral homes need to be alert to liability issues and to the professional qualifications and licensure of staff involved in aftercare. Nevertheless, it has been estimated that a majority of all funeral homes in North America are currently offering some form of aftercare. As we saw in the vignette near the beginning of this chapter, after the death of her son, Stella Bridgman benefited from the services of an aftercare coordinator. Thus, funeral industry aftercare is a growing reality in contemporary death systems as an aspect of community support and assistance for persons who are coping with loss and grief.

BEREAVEMENT FOLLOW-UP IN HOSPICE PROGRAMS

Hospice programs in the United States are required to provide support and counseling for the family members of those whom they serve. This service arises directly out of the hospice philosophy of holistic care that requires it to address the needs of both the dying person and his or her family members (see Chapter 8 in this book). This care begins not at the moment of death but at the moment of admission to a hospice program. That is, care is offered to family members to try to meet their needs both prior to and after the death of their loved one. Consequently, *bereavement follow-up services* are an essential component of hospice work, typically provided to two family members for each patient death.

Not all families need or accept bereavement follow-up from a hospice program. Some may have resources of their own that are adequate to cope with their bereavement, whether those same resources were sufficient to cope with dying. Moreover, hospice programs do not wish to disable surviving families by making them dependent on hospice services for the remainder of their lives (and no hospice program would have the resources to do that). Thus, **hospice bereavement follow-up programs** are a transitional service designed to assist those family members who desire help in coping with loss and bereavement, usually offered during the first 12–18 months after the death of a loved one. Issues that go beyond that support, either in their character or duration, would ordinarily require specific evaluation and would likely be referred to professional counseling or therapy.

Programs of bereavement follow-up in hospice care are commonly organized around a detailed and individualized plan of care for those who have been identified through careful assessment as key persons in bereavement (Caserta, Lund, Utz, & Tabler, 2016). This plan of care is initiated prior to a patient's death, although it will usually be reassessed when death occurs. The plan of care typically encourages participation by family members and staff in meaningful funeral services and rituals. Afterward, the follow-up program is most often conducted through mail, telephone, or personal contacts at regular intervals. Care is addressed to specific needs of the bereaved, such as information about typical patterns or problems in bereavement, grief, and mourning; recognition and validation of feelings and other grief reactions; guidelines for self-care; suggestions about ways to undertake or to join in commemorative and memorialization activities; referrals to bereavement support groups; and a shared conviction that life remains worth living.

Newsletters, cards or letters, individual counseling, annual memorial services, and other social activities are familiar components of hospice bereavement follow-up. Hospice programs also frequently establish support groups for the bereaved or work cooperatively with community organizations that provide such services. In addition, hospice programs typically offer bereavement services to all members of the community—whether they cared for the person who died—as we saw in the case of Stella Bridgman. Over 12 percent of all individuals served by hospice bereavement care in 2014 were community members who did not otherwise receive hospice care (NHPCO, 2015). Many of the direct services in hospice bereavement follow-up are carried out by experienced volunteers who have been selected and trained for such work and who are supported by professionals in this field. This is especially true when fiscal and staffing pressures impose limitations on hospice bereavement services.

SUPPORT GROUPS FOR THE BEREAVED

Support groups for the bereaved take many forms (Wasserman & Danforth, 1988). One type of support group helps bereaved persons mainly through talks and lectures by experts on a variety of practical problems. These groups show their members how to cook nourishing meals when they are alone, do small repairs around the home, complete income tax returns, invest their money, and so on. One group of funeral homes has called this type of group their LIFT program, which stands for "Living Information for Today." Another type of support group focuses on entertainment and social activities, such as holiday parties, visits to restaurants, or bus tours to nearby attractions. Both of these types of groups can be and are meaningful for many bereaved persons. However, they are not mainly concerned with addressing the central issues of grief and mourning.

The primary benefits of support groups whose main concern is to help individuals cope with loss and grief come from the assistance that members of the group give to each other (mutual aid) and from the opportunities that these groups provide for bereaved individuals to help themselves with grief work and tasks of mourning (self-help). As Silverman (1986, p. 210) noted, "mutual help generally has an advantage over professional help since it does not treat a person as ill and has an image-enhancing emphasis on learning from peers."

Recently, **online grief support groups** have become another popular option among grieving persons. Many of these groups are moderated by certified counselors and closely monitored. They provide an option for individuals who cannot access face-to-face support, are uncomfortable verbally communicating their grief, are experiencing disenfranchised grief, and are seeking other grieving individuals with similar experiences. This type of support is beneficial for bereaved persons who lack adequate social support in their offline world, seek legitimization of their grief, need to unload feelings in a safe space, and want to know that they are not alone in their grief (Hartig & Viola, 2016; Varga & Paulus, 2014). The depiction of mutual aid in Figure 11.2 offered by Parents of Murdered Children (POMC), a national organization with local chapters throughout the country, is broadly representative of the goals of many different types of offline and online bereavement support groups.

Because online grief support groups vary widely and because they often draw on principles and practices characteristic of more traditional offline or face-to-face

Figure 11.2 How POMC Helps

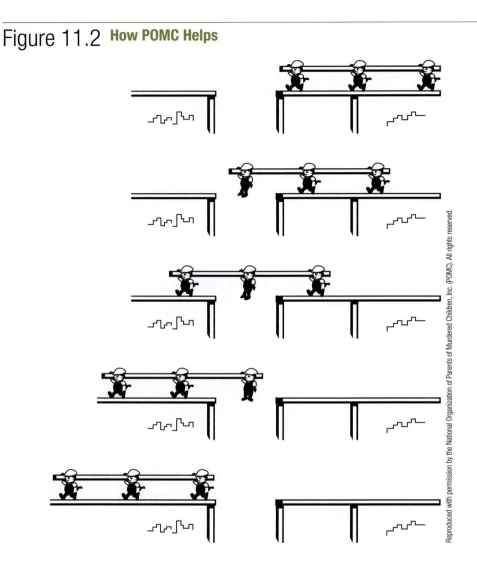

groups, we focus on the latter in the remainder of this section. These groups have arisen in response to a wide variety of loss experiences (see Focus On 11.3; also, Hoy, 2016). Their efforts may be local or not restricted to geographical boundaries, projects of a community agency, chapters of a national organization, or groups sponsored by an aftercare or hospice program. As noted, Stella Bridgman found help from a face-to-face support group.

Principles and Practices in Bereavement Support Groups

The very existence and rapid increase in numbers of different types of **bereavement support groups** shows that many bereaved persons need or seek assistance beyond what is readily available to them in their own family or everyday community. Mainly, what they seek is not professional counseling or therapy—it is help from others who have shared similar loss experiences. Thus, the main purpose of these groups is "to

Selected Examples of Bereavement Support Organizations

ORGANIZATION	DESCRIPTION
American Association of Suicidology www.suicidology.org 202-237-2280	Provides resources about suicide & local referrals to those bereaved by suicide; not a crisis center, but links to National Suicide Intervention Lifeline: 800-279-8255
Association for Pet Loss and Bereavement www.aplb.org 718-382-0690;	An organization of trained volunteers specializing in pet loss & bereavement; offers a quarterly newsletter, chat rooms, an Internet memorial site, & other services
Bereaved Parents of the USA www.bereavedparentsusa.org 845-402-2825	A national support group with a quarterly newsletter & local chapters serving bereaved parents, grandparents, & siblings
The Compassionate Friends (TCF) www.compassionatefriends.org 877-969-0010; 630-990-0010	An international support group serving bereaved parents & siblings; numerous U.S. chapters plus at least two in Canada
Concerns of Police Survivors (C.O.P.S.) www.nationalcops.org 800-784-COPS (2677); 573-346-4911	A support group for law enforcement officers & their family members affected by death & bereavement
First Candle www.firstcandle.org 800-221-7437; 443-640-1040	An organizations providing research & services about stillbirth, sudden infant death syndrome, & sudden unexplained infant death
Mothers Against Drunk Driving (MADD) www.madd.org; www.madd.ca 800-MADD-HELLP; 877-275-6233	Support and advocacy on behalf of people victimized by drunken or drugged driving offenses
National Donor Family Council (NDFC) www.donorfamily.org 800-622-9010; 212-809-2210	A national resource for information, support, advocacy, & education about organ/tissue donation & transplantation
National Hospice and Palliative Care Organization www.nhpco.org 800-658-8898; 703-837-1500	Advocates for hospice/palliative care programs & professionals to improve end-of-life care; sponsors the Hospice Helpline (800-658-8898) to help locate a local hospice program
National Organization for Victim Assistance www.trynova.org 800-TRY-NOVA (879-6682); 703-535-6682	Champions those harmed by crime or crisis through counseling and victim assistance services
National Widowers' Organization, Inc. www.nationalwidowers.org 800-309-3658	Educates the public about the special needs of men who have lost a spouse or life partner; promotes support groups for such men & research into their needs
Parents of Murdered Children (POMC) www.pomc.com 888-818-POMC (7662); 513-721-5683	Provides support & advocacy for those bereaved by homicide
Parents Without Partners, Inc. www.parentswithoutpartners.org 800-637-7974; 301-568-9354	An international organization with members & chapters throughout the United States and Canada offering services for single parents & their children

(continues)

FOCUS ON 11.3 *(continued)*

Selected Examples of Bereavement Support Organizations

ORGANIZATION	DESCRIPTION
SHARE—Pregnancy and Infant Loss Support who www.nationalshare.org 800-821-6819; 636-947-6164	A national mutual-help group for parents & siblings have experienced miscarriage, stillbirth, or early infant death
Tragedy Assistance Program for Survivors www.taps.org 800-959-TAPS (8277); 202-588-8277	Offers support & assistance to all members of the armed services & their family members who are impacted by death & bereavement

provide people in similar circumstances with an opportunity to share their experiences and to help teach one another how to cope with their problems" (Silverman, 1980, p. 40).

Groups of this sort take a variety of forms. They may be time-limited or ongoing. They may admit new members at any time or close themselves to additional members once the group has been formed. They may focus their work on all sorts of bereavement or organize themselves around a specific type of loss. They may be led by a bereaved person serving as an experienced volunteer or by a professional facilitator (Hoy, 2016; McNurlen, 1991).

The question of *leadership* is important, and it highlights the profound differences between grief support groups and therapy groups. These differences arise from the fact that support groups are designed to help otherwise healthy individuals cope with uncomplicated grief reactions, whereas therapy groups are intended to correct psychosocial disorders in individuals who need to restructure their lives in some important way. Members of grief support groups come together voluntarily because they are facing difficulties in coping with a shared life experience. Prior to their encounter with loss, such individuals were generally functioning normally. They do not seek to be changed in that, but they do want help in coping with losses that have taxed (often, overtaxed) their capacities.

Some bereavement groups do not permit nonbereaved persons to hold leadership posts; others assign leadership functions to a professional facilitator (Hoy, 2007; Klass & Shinners, 1983). Always, however, real, substantive expertise in bereavement groups is not perceived as hierarchical; it is found in the members themselves. Thus, members are encouraged to become involved with each other outside the group, and topics for discussion within the group are those that members bring up and choose to share. The focus in the group is not on offering solutions or giving advice but on the process of helping itself—talking about problems, exploring situations, and sharing experiences. This process is often guided by principles such as those in the "Serenity Prayer" (see Personal Insights 11.4), which is a frequent component of group ritual. Support groups for the bereaved combine elements of both self-help and mutual aid; one must help oneself, but one does so with the support of others in the group.

PERSONAL INSIGHTS 11.4

The Serenity Prayer

God, give us grace
to accept with serenity
the things that cannot be changed,
courage to change the things
that should be changed,
and the wisdom to distinguish
the one from the other.

Source: Sifton, 2003, p. 7.

Support groups for the bereaved usually have more or less explicit rules or values, such as that confidentiality and a nonjudgmental attitude are to be maintained, advice is not to be given, opportunities are made available for all to speak, side conversations are prohibited, everyone has the right to pass or remain silent, members respect each other's experiences and viewpoints, and meetings start and end on time. Safety issues are a matter of particular concern in groups for vulnerable people. Support groups usually prohibit "putdowns" or evangelization; they are also sensitive to the need to refer for individual counseling or therapy any persons who disrupt the work of the group or who might endanger themselves (Dyregrov, Dyregrov, & Johnsen, 2013).

Helping Factors in Bereavement Support Groups

Most bereavement support groups are organized around eight helping factors (McNurlen, 1991). Explaining these factors recalls the characteristics of The Compassionate Friends group that helped Stella Bridgman after her son's death.

- *Helping factor 1: Identification.* Bereavement support groups are founded on the shared experience of their members (Borkman, 1976). This is the basis for a bond through which group members can find *identification* with one another. In the group, bereaved individuals find that they no longer are or need to be alone. Although they may feel stigmatized or marked out by their loss experiences from so many others in the world, within the group they discover that others share similar experiences and that members of the group can learn from each other.

- *Helping factor 2: Universality.* Despite all of the individuality of the experiences of loss, there is a degree of *universality* found in support groups. In the group, individuals can recognize that they are not unique in their experiences and reactions. Those whom society views as different, shuns, or even stigmatizes because of what has happened to them can be helped by knowing that members of the group do not view them as "bad" or "wrong."

- *Helping factor 3: Catharsis.* Within the group, long-repressed, pent-up feelings can be let out for as long as necessary. Some people come to bereavement support groups shortly after their loss experience; others join many years later. Whatever the timing, new and old members typically are grateful to the group

Sharing experiences of loss and grief are one important role for a bereavement support group (an illustration from *Tear Soup*—see Personal Insights 10.2).

for permitting them to vent and share their feelings. They need *catharsis* and find opportunity for it in the group.

- *Helping factor 4: Guidance.* Individuals meet other bereaved people within the group from whom they can obtain *guidance* on how they might conduct their own lives after their loss. The group offers such guidance, not primarily through lectures, presentations, or advice, but by providing a forum in which members can describe, exemplify, and live out their experiences with loss and grief. These self-descriptions may or may not validate an individual's personal experiences, but as experiences are shared, important information, guidance, and reassurance are conveyed. For example, most bereaved persons welcome information about grief and mourning processes. Many need to know more about the specific types of losses they have experienced and those losses may define the nature of the group—for example, a group about parental bereavement, homicide and its implications, or sudden infant death syndrome. Some may need guidance about the social stigma associated with certain kinds of death, such as suicide or AIDS.
- *Helping factor 5: Instillation of hope.* For many bereaved persons, the interaction between new members and those who have been participants for some time is especially significant. Coming to know people who are further along in their grief journey permits newer members to witness ways in which their more experienced colleagues are managing both their grief and the rest of their lives. As this demonstrates that things can get better and have gotten better for others, hope is renewed that one's own life might also get better. This *instillation of hope* must be drawn from the group processes by the individual; it cannot simply be imposed from outside.
- *Helping factor 6: Existential issues.* Bereavement support groups often address *existential issues* involving questions, such as those concerned with the fairness of life, the benevolence of God, or the basic goodness of the universe. These are

questions involved in meaning making and meaning reconstruction that we discussed in Chapter 9. Answers to such profound questions can seldom be given to a person from someone else. More likely, one discovers that one must work out one's own answers or ways of living with such issues or even with an incompleteness or absence of answers. What a support group can provide in response to these questions is a safe place to recognize that the existential issues raised by loss, grief, and bereavement are legitimate and real, and that different people respond to them in different ways.

■ *Helping factor 7: Cohesiveness.* The bonding among members in a bereavement support group creates a safe, caring environment in a world that may appear in so many ways to be unsafe and uncaring after a significant personal loss. *Cohesiveness* or basic trust develops among members in most support groups, arising from two key features: the experiences that members share as bereaved persons and the discovery by hurt and vulnerable people that they can help each other simply by sharing their own great losses and pain. "Sharing of experience is the fundamental concept that distinguishes the mutual help experience from other helping exchanges...The essence of the process is mutuality and reciprocity" (Silverman, 1980, p. 10).

■ *Helping factor 8: Altruism.* Another sort of empowerment is related to *altruism* or giving to others, which is often a special experience of those who remain in a bereavement support group for an extended period. As they move into leadership roles or find different ways to share with others what they have obtained from their own experiences both in bereavement and within the group, senior members also may find new rewards for themselves. Klass (1985b, 1988) called this the great secret of bereavement support groups: in giving to others, one receives for oneself. Giving and receiving help reciprocally can enhance one's self-esteem. Those who make the transition from intense vulnerability in an early meeting to shared ownership of the group at a later point often interpret their newfound ability to help others as an important element in finding meaning in the life and death of their loved one (Klass, 1985a).

Help Outside the Group

Although the main work of support groups for the bereaved occurs within meetings, that is not the whole of what they have to offer. This point is often neglected. Established, ongoing bereavement support groups like The Compassionate Friends usually set up a network of referral sources for identifying potential new members. Mail or telephone contacts with such individuals may be among the earliest expressions of support to reach a bereaved person.

Sometimes it is enough for the bereaved to know that a support group is available "in case I really need one." That knowledge may be supplemented by regular mailings of a newsletter, which is another mode of support and reassurance that additional help is within reach. Groups may also generate announcements about their activities or reports about loss and grief in the local media. Together with annual memorial events, educational conferences, and public service endeavors, these are other forms of support that reach beyond the boundaries of the group itself.

Summary

In this chapter, we examined ways in which communities in the American death system have organized specific social programs to offer support and assistance to persons coping with loss and grief. This supplements our discussion in Chapter 10 of how individuals can help bereaved persons. In this chapter, we began with an analysis of life crises and rituals. Next, we described typical funeral practices in our society today, together with some alternative views of the value of those practices. After that, we offered an analysis of three tasks that organized funeral rituals should provide to help bereaved persons and the community: to dispose of the body in socially approved ways, to make real the implications of a death, and to begin to move toward reintegration and meaningful ongoing living. Individuals and communities who know the options available to them among funeral rituals can decide for themselves whether (and, if so, how) any specific funeral practice or associated ritual helps them accomplish these tasks. We added to this analysis a brief exploration of American cemeteries, memorial sculpture, memorial photography, and memorial activities involving social media or the Internet. Then we considered three other social programs for helping the bereaved within our contemporary death system: aftercare programs in the funeral industry, hospice bereavement follow-up programs, and support groups for the bereaved.

Glossary

Aftercare programs: informal and formal programs of support for the bereaved, usually offered by funeral service personnel after the funeral and disposition are completed; may include providing death education to the community

Bereavement support groups: organized efforts to help bereaved persons by combining elements of self-help and mutual aid

Burial (in-ground burial): disposition of the body (or of its "cremains") by placing it in a casket and then in the ground, usually in a cemetery and often within a vault or grave liner designed to protect the casket and prevent settling of land

Cremains: cremated remains, that is, ash and bone resulting from cremating a body

Cremation: a process of reducing the size of the body typically by subjecting it to intense heat, resulting in ashes and some bone fragments (which may then be ground up or pulverized)

Disposition of the body: removing the body of the deceased from the society of the living

Embalming: removal of blood and bodily fluids from a corpse, together with their replacement with artificial preservatives intended to retard decomposition and color the skin

Entombment: disposition of the body or its remains by placing them in a mausoleum, crypt, or other aboveground, tomblike structure

Flameless cremation: the use of chemicals and heat to dissolve soft tissues of the body

Funerals or funeral practices: formal services to mark a death and celebrate a life with the body present in a casket

Green or natural burial: interment of the body of a dead person in the soil in a manner that does not inhibit decomposition but allows the body to recycle naturally

Hospice bereavement follow-up programs: services offered to family members both before and after the death of a hospice patient or to community members experiencing loss

Making real the implications of death: helping the bereaved to grasp the import of the death; often implemented through formal activities of separation from the deceased

Memorial activities: activities intended to commemorate the life or legacy of someone who has died

Memorial services: formal services to mark a death and celebrate a life without the presence of a body

Online grief support groups: online groups to help bereaved persons seeking support in place of or in addition to offline support

Reintegration: pulling (back) together the bereaved individuals, family, or society disintegrated by a death

Ritual: corporate or communal symbolic activity, usually involving external (bodily) actions and social participation; designed to contribute order or orientation when crises disrupt life

Support groups for the bereaved: these take many forms, ranging from groups that emphasize assistance with practical problems or whose concerns are primarily social to groups that seek to help individuals cope with loss and grief through mutual aid and self-help

Questions for Review and Discussion

1. Think about rituals that you have experienced either in your own private life or in various public events. What purpose(s) do you think those rituals were intended to serve? Why did the persons involved choose to engage in those specific ritual actions?

2. Suppose someone you love has died. What types of activities would you want to include in a funeral or memorial service? What might or might not be helpful for you at such a moment? Compare your answers to an actual funeral or memorial service you have attended or have heard about.

3. Many bereaved persons report that they found help in their grief from funeral home aftercare programs, hospice bereavement follow-up programs, or bereavement support groups (online or offline). Why do you think those programs helped? What could we learn from such programs to improve our individual efforts to help the bereaved? Have you had any contact with such programs?

4. Many people have used social media and the Internet to get information or make choice about funeral rituals and community bereavement support resources. Have you done that? Why or why not?

Suggested Readings

Information about what happens to human bodies after death is provided by:

Iserson, K. V. (2001). *Death to Dust: What Happens to Dead Bodies?* (2nd ed.)
Roach, M. (2003). *Stiff: The Curious Lives of Human Cadavers*

Various aspects of funeral and mourning practices are examined in:

Ashenburg, K. (2003). *The Mourner's Dance: What We Do When People Die*
Canine, J. D. (1999). *What Am I Going to Do with Myself When I Die?*
Doughty, C. (2014). *Smoke Gets in Your Eyes: And Other Lessons from the Crematory*

Holloway, K.F.C. (2003). *Passed On: African American Mourning Stories, a Memorial*

Jupp, P. C. (2006). *From Ashes to Dust: The History of Cremation in Britain*

Laderman, G. (2005). *Rest in Peace: A Cultural History of Death and the Funeral Home in Twentieth Century America*

Long, T. G. (2013). *Accompany Them with Singing: The Christian Funeral*

Long, T. G., & Lynch, T. (2013). *The Good Funeral: Death, Grief, and the Community of Care*

Lynch, T. (2009). *The Undertaking: Life Studies from the Dismal Trade*

Manning, D. (2001). *The Funeral: A Chance to Teach, a Chance to Serve, a Chance to Heal*

Mayer, R. G. (2011). *Embalming: History, Theory, and Practice* (5th ed.)

McKenzie, K. M., & Harra, T. (2014). *Over Our Dead Bodies: Undertakers Lift the Lid*

Morgan, E. (2010). *Dealing Creatively with Death: A Manual of Death Education and Simple Burial* (14th rev. ed.)

Prothero, S. (2001). *Purified by Fire: A History of Cremation in America*

Slocum, J., & Carlson, L. (2011). *Final Rights: Reclaiming the American Way of Death*

Cemeteries, memorial photography, and other memorial practices are explored in:

Bachelor, P. (2004). *Sorrow and Solace: The Social World of the Cemetery*

Doss, E. L. (2010). *Memorial Mania: Public Feeling in America*

Everett, H. (2002). *Roadside Crosses in Contemporary Memorial Culture*

Francis, D., Kellaher, L., & Neophytou, G. (2005). *The Secret Cemetery*

Harris, M. (2008). *Grave Matters: A Journey through the Modern Funeral Industry to a Natural Way of Burial*

Keister, D. (2004). *Stories in Stone: A Field Guide to Cemetery Symbolism and Iconography*

Sloane, D. C. (1995). *The Last Great Necessity: Cemeteries in American History*

Wright, R. H., & Hughes, W. B. (1996). *Lay Down Body: Living History in African-American Cemeteries*

Yalom, M. (2008). *The American Resting Place: 400 Years of History through Our Cemeteries and Burial Grounds*

Concerning aftercare, hospice bereavement support, and self-help groups, see:

Ginsburg, G. D. (2004). *Widow to Widow: Thoughtful, Practical Ideas for Rebuilding Your Life* (rev. ed.)

Hoy, W. G. (2007). *Guiding People through Grief: How to Start and Lead Bereavement Support Groups*

Hoy, W. G. (2013). *Do Funerals Matter? The Purposes and Practices of Death Rituals in Global Perspective*

Hoy, W. G. (2016). *Bereavement Groups and the Role of Social Support: Integrating Theory, Research, and Practice*

Silverman, P. R. (2004). *Widow to Widow: How the Bereaved Help One Another* (2nd ed.)

Weeks, O. D., & Johnson, C. (Eds.) (2001). *When All the Friends Have Gone: A Guide for Aftercare Providers*

Wolfelt, A. (2004a). *The Understanding Your Grief Support Group Guide: Starting and Leading a Bereavement Support Group*

Selected Web Resources

Some useful search terms include: AFTERCARE PROGRAMS; BEREAVEMENT FOLLOW-UP; BEREAVEMENT HELPING FACTORS; BEREAVEMENT SUPPORT GROUPS; BURIAL; CREMAINS; CREMATION; DEATH RITUALS; DISPOSITION OF THE BODY; EMBALMING; ENTOMBMENT; FUNERALS; HOSPICE BEREAVEMENT FOLLOW-UP PROGRAMS; MEMORIAL SERVICES; MEMORIALIZATION; RITUAL; SUPPORT GROUPS FOR THE BEREAVED.

For self-help, body disposition, and funeral resources, see Focus On 11.2 and/or the following:

American Cryonics Society

Thefuneraldirectory.com (multiple topics)

Funeralplan.com

For bereavement support resources, see Focus On 11.3.

PART Five

DEVELOPMENTAL PERSPECTIVES

In much of this book, we describe what is common to all people or is at least widespread in contemporary American experiences of death. These common factors include death-related encounters, attitudes, and practices that involve and affect nearly everyone in our society, as well as experiences of coping with dying or bereavement in which many or all of us share, regardless of age or other descriptive factors. However, in addition to sharing in a common human community, each human being is also a member of a distinctive developmental subgroup. In the four chapters that follow, we consider death-related subjects from this latter perspective: *development across the life course*.

The merits of a developmental perspective first became evident in studies of childhood. Later, it was recognized that developmental processes can be identified throughout the human life course. However, more is known about some eras and some aspects of human development than about others.

Many thinkers, such as Freud (1959b), Jung (1970), Havighurst (1953), Bühler (1968), and Neugarten and Datan (1973), have contributed to our understanding of human development. Among such thinkers, Erikson (1963, 1968) is especially well known for describing eight distinguishable eras (sometimes called ages, periods, or stages) in human development (see Table V.1 on p. 320).

According to Erikson, a predominant psychosocial issue or central conflict characterizes each era in the development of an individual ego. These developmental conflicts involve a struggle between a pair of alternative orientations, opposed tendencies, or attitudes toward life, the self, and other people. The successful resolution of each of these developmental struggles results in a leading virtue, a particular strength or quality of ego functioning.

Table V.1 Principal Eras in Human Development

Era	Approximate Age	Predominant Issue	Virtue
Infancy	Birth through 12–18 months	Basic trust vs. mistrust	Hope
Toddlerhood	Infancy to 3 years	Autonomy vs. shame and doubt	Will or self-control
Early childhood; sometimes called play age or the preschool period	3–6 years	Initiative vs. guilt	Purpose or direction
Middle childhood; sometimes called school age or the latency period	6 years to puberty	Industry vs. inferiority	Competency
Adolescence	Puberty to about 21 or 22 years	Identity vs. role confusion	Fidelity
Young adulthood	21 or 22 to 45 years	Intimacy vs. isolation	Love
Middle adulthood or middle age	45 to 65 years	Generativity vs. stagnation and self-absorption	Production and care
Older adulthood; sometimes called maturity, old age, or the era of the elderly	65 years and older	Ego integrity vs. despair	Renunciation and wisdom

Note: All chronological ages given here are approximate
Source: Based on Erikson, 1963, 1968.

Developmental theorists argue that each normative conflict has a time of special prominence in a life course. Because this timing is controlled by development, not chronology, it only roughly correlates with age. According to developmental theory, failure to resolve the tasks of one era leaves unfinished work for subsequent eras. In other words, a developmental perspective asserts that: (1) developing individuals strive to integrate aspects of their inner lives and their relationships with the social world; (2) the integrative tasks undertaken in this effort depend on the different crises or turning points that unfold as development proceeds; and (3) the way in which the integration is or is not managed determines the individual's present quality of life, potential for future growth, and residual or unresolved work that remains to be achieved.

Erikson's model is not the only developmental framework that might enrich our study of death, dying, and bereavement, and many have noted some of its limitations or added to its details (e.g., Kail & Cavanaugh, 2015; Newman & Newman, 2014; Papalia & Martorell, 2014). The model is limited in its application to different cultural groups, it may apply equally to both sexes only in societies that give equal options to men and women (Gilligan, 1982/1993; Levinson, 1996), and it tends to describe individuals independently of familial or other systemic contexts (McGoldrick, 1988). Still, a developmental perspective does provide an important frame of reference from which to investigate death-related experiences.

In Chapters 12–15, we adopt a developmental perspective to appreciate the fact that "death is one of the central themes in human development throughout the life span. Death is not just our destination; it is a part of our 'getting there' as well" (Kastenbaum, 1977, p. 43). Our question here is: How or in what ways are death-related experiences distinctive during the principal eras of human development? Chapters 12–15 organize answers to that question around four developmental cohorts: children, adolescents, young and middle-aged adults, and older adults. We emphasize the chapters on childhood and adolescence because: (1) many subjects in other parts of this book are already closely associated with young, middle, and older adults; (2) there is so much that is distinctive in children's interactions with death; and (3) death-related issues in adolescence (which are also distinctive in many ways) are often overlooked or obscured by being merged into discussions of childhood, on the one hand, or adulthood, on the other hand.

Children

Objectives of This Chapter

▸ To enhance our discussion of children and their distinctive developmental tasks

▸ To describe typical encounters with death in the United States during childhood

▸ To explore research on the development of death-related concepts and attitudes during childhood

▸ To identify key issues for children who are coping with life-threatening illness and dying

▸ To survey central issues for children who are coping with bereavement and grief

▸ To establish principles for helping children cope with death, dying, and bereavement

Much still remains to be learned about children and issues related to death, dying, and bereavement. In the current state of our knowledge, we cannot always draw distinctions in death-related matters that parallel divisions between the various developmental eras in childhood. Moreover, the National Center for Health Statistics (NCHS) provides mortality data in age-related categories and formats that do not always match developmental theorists' distinctions among the various eras within childhood. Thus, in this chapter, we address childhood as a whole, emphasizing throughout what is unique and distinctive about this period and drawing finer developmental distinctions whenever we can.

ONE CHILD AND DEATH

In the film, *And We Were Sad, Remember?* (1979), the sound of a ringing telephone wakens a young girl named Allison during the night. Her father is calling her mother from a hospital in another town to report that his mother just died. After the call, Allison's mother explains that Grammie's heart had stopped and she is dead. Allison's mother says she will drive to Grammie's home tomorrow and asks whether Allison and her younger brother, Christopher, would like to go with her to Grammie's funeral. She explains what a funeral is, and Allison says she wants to attend. When Christopher wakes up, Allison asks if he would like to go with her to the "fumeral."

A day or two later, Allison's father tells her that he has arranged for her and Christopher to stay with an adult friend during the funeral and to have a fun adventure. Allison replies that her mother had told her she could go to the funeral. She insists she wants to attend and urges him to let her do so. He is quite reluctant, finally agreeing only that he will think about it and decide later. Allison says that whenever he says he will think about things, it usually means "no."

When the family and friends are all gathered at Grammie's home, Allison and her cousin get into an argument while they are playing with their dolls and acting out a scene involving illness and death. Allison wants to cover the doll that has "died" with a blanket. Her cousin says she has been told that dying is like going to sleep. If so, the doll will still need to breathe and it won't be able to do so if the blanket covers its face. The children take their dispute to Allison's father, who only tells them to stop fighting, put the dolls away, and get ready for bed. When Allison insists that he settle their dispute, he replies in exasperation: "Little girl, you don't have to worry about that for a hundred years!"

CHILDREN, DEVELOPMENTAL TASKS, AND DEATH

At one time in Western society, children were essentially thought of as miniature adults (Ariès, 1962). After infancy, when they became able to move about more or less independently, their clothing and much of their behavior were modeled along adult lines. As sensitivity to developmental differences grew, that viewpoint was abandoned in most Western societies, although the Amish (whom we met in the vignette near the beginning of Chapter 3) still follow some of these practices. Nevertheless, most researchers view childhood as different from other eras in human development and make distinctions between different eras within childhood.

In general, *childhood* is the period from birth to puberty or the beginning of adolescence (*Oxford English Dictionary*, 1989)—roughly, the first 10–12 years of life. Within this period, most developmental theorists (like Erikson, 1963, 1968) divide childhood itself into four distinguishable **developmental eras**: infancy, toddlerhood, early childhood (also called the play age or preschool period), and middle childhood (also called the school age or latency period). (Note that the term *child* can also include the unborn fetus; thus, some writers (e.g., Martorell, Papalia, & Feldman, 2014; Newman & Newman, 2014;) view the prenatal period extending from conception to birth as the very first era in the human life course.) For Erikson, **normative developmental tasks** within childhood are to develop *trust* versus mistrust in infancy, *autonomy* versus shame and doubt in toddlerhood, *initiative* versus guilt in early childhood, and *industry* versus inferiority in middle childhood (see Table V.1).

According to this account, infants who develop a sense of basic trust will become *confident and hopeful* because they will believe they can rely on people and the world to fulfill their needs and satisfy their desires. Toddlers—often depicted as willful agents in the "terrible twos"—who develop their own legitimate autonomy and independence will learn *self-control* and establish a balance between self-regulation and external dictates. In early childhood, the developmental conflict between initiative and guilt will appear in the form of a challenge to cultivate one's own initiative or desire to take action and pursue goals, but to balance that with the moral reservations that one has about one's plans. Combining spontaneity and responsibility in this way promotes a sense of *purpose or direction* in a child's life. In middle childhood, the developmental conflict between industry and inferiority involves developing one's capacities to do productive work, thereby achieving a sense of *competence* and self-esteem rooted in a view of the self as able to master skills and carry out tasks.

Of course, normative development varies within specific groups of children. Some youngsters advance in these developmental processes more rapidly than others. Some are delayed in their development by various physical or psychosocial factors, such as congenital anomalies, mental or emotional disabilities, or extreme external conditions involving starvation or war. Some are influenced more than others by the social, cultural, economic, or historical contexts in which they find themselves. In short, human development is not an absolutely uniform, lockstep process. In particular, although chronological or age markers (which are relatively easy to determine and appear to be objective) are often used to mark out and evaluate a child's development, in fact development is not primarily a matter of chronology but one of physical, psychosocial, and spiritual maturation. Thus, some persons who are adult in age and body remain at the developmental level of a young child and must, in many ways, be appreciated and treated primarily with the latter perspective in mind. Still, broad normative patterns in childhood development are influential in typical types of death-related encounters, understandings, and attitudes during childhood.

ENCOUNTERS WITH DEATH DURING CHILDHOOD

"'The kingdom where nobody dies,' as Edna St. Vincent Millay once described childhood, is the fantasy of grown-ups" (Kastenbaum, 1972, p. 37). In fact, the realities of life during childhood include both deaths of children and deaths of others that are experienced by children.

Deaths of Children

Children between birth and nine years of age made up approximately 12.7% of the total U.S. population in 2014. In that year, this group experienced 29,402 deaths (see Table 12.1), representing less than 1.1% of the more than 2.6 million deaths in the United States.

Infant Deaths More children die during infancy than throughout the remainder of childhood despite a slow but steady decline in the numbers of infant deaths over many years. In 2014, 23,215 infants died during their first year of life in the United States (see Table 12.1). About half of all infant deaths in 2014 were the result of five principal causes: congenital malformations, disorders related to short gestation and low birth weight, newborns affected by maternal complications of pregnancy, sudden

Table 12.1 **Number of Deaths during Childhood by Age, Race or Hispanic Origin,[a] and Sex: United States, 2014**

	Under 1 Year			1 to 4 Year			5 to 9 Year		
	Both sexes	Males	Females	Both sexes	Males	Females	Both sexes	Males	Females
All origins[b]	23,215	12,886	10,329	3,830	2,172	1,658	2,357	1,357	1,000
Caucasian Americans, total	14,883	8,297	6,586	2,592	1,452	1,140	1,683	965	718
Non-Hispanic Caucasian Americans	10,341	5,801	4,540	1,876	1,060	816	1,176	680	496
Hispanic[c]	4,772	2,627	2,145	769	421	348	531	301	230
African Americans	7,076	3,900	3,176	1,009	583	426	537	314	223
Asian and Pacific Island Americans	896	487	409	134	73	61	95	53	42
American Indians and Alaska Natives	360	202	158	95	64	31	42	25	17

[a]Data for specified groups other than Caucasian Americans and African Americans should be interpreted with caution because of inconsistencies between reporting race and/or Hispanic origin on death certificates and on censuses and surveys.

[b]Figures for origin not stated are included in "All origins" but not distributed among specified origins.

[c]Includes all persons of Hispanic origin of any race.

Source: Kochanek et al., 2016.

infant death syndrome (SIDS), and accidents (Kochanek, Murphy, Xu, & Tejada-Vera, 2016). These have been the leading causes of infant deaths for many years, despite the huge reduction in deaths from SIDS since the 1990s (see Focus On 12.1).

Overall death rates for all children under one year of age in the United States in 2014, along with those for members of selected subgroups in the population, are shown in Table 12.2. The more precise overall infant mortality rate (based on live births) was 5.82 per 1,000 in 2014. Although, as we noted in Chapter 2, this is a record low for the United States, according to The World Factbook (Central Intelligence Agency, 2016) this infant mortality rate is still higher than that of two dozen other industrialized countries in the world.

Deaths of Children after Infancy   Table 12.1 also shows number of deaths in the United States in 2014 among children between one and four years of age and between five and nine years of age. In both cases, accidents, congenital malformations, malignant neoplasms (cancer), and homicide (assault) were the leading causes of these deaths. In fact, accidents are the leading cause of death throughout all of childhood after infancy, with motor vehicle accidents becoming proportionately more prominent in later childhood. Throughout childhood, congenital malformations decline in relative significance as leading causes of death, while cancer and homicide increase in relative significance.

Among children who die, there are significant differences between Caucasian Americans and members of other American racial and cultural groups, as well as between males and females (see Tables 12.1 and 12.2). For example, the *number of*

Sudden Infant Death Syndrome

Sudden infant death syndrome, or SIDS, has long been the leading cause of death in infants from one month to one year of age (Corr & Corr, 2003b). Formally, SIDS is "the sudden death of an infant under one year of age which remains unexplained after a thorough case investigation, including performance of a complete autopsy, examination of the death scene, and review of the clinical history" (Willinger, James, & Catz, 1991, p. 681). Typically, an apparently healthy baby dies suddenly with no advance warning. Such a death is shocking because it involves a very young child and because it runs counter to the general pattern of our encounters with death.

Identification of this entity as a syndrome and its recognition by the World Health Organization as an official cause of death is significant in many ways. A *syndrome* is a recognizable pattern of events whose underlying cause is unknown. Whenever the SIDS pattern is identified, we know the infant's death did not result from child abuse or neglect; nothing could have been done to prevent the death, and there are ways to distinguish SIDS deaths from those caused by child abuse (AAP, 2006).

Since there is no way to screen for an unknown cause of death, SIDS deaths have been thought to be unpreventable. Thus, it has been said that the first symptom of SIDS is a dead infant. SIDS strikes across all economic, ethnic, and cultural boundaries and is not distinguishable from risk factors that put all babies in danger. The single demographic variable that appears to be critical for SIDS is the fact that it occurs only in infancy—with a noticeable peak in incidence around two to four months of age and during colder months of the year in different parts of the world. This suggests some association with infant development and environment, but does not explain SIDS.

In the early 1990s, new research (e.g., Dwyer, Ponsonby, Blizzard, Newman, & Cochrane, 1995) suggested that infants might be at less risk for SIDS if they were placed on their backs (supine) or sides for sleep, rather than on their stomachs (prone). This recommendation ran contrary to familiar advice that favored sleeping prone to reduce the risk that an infant might regurgitate or spit up fluids, aspirate them into an airway, and suffocate. It is now believed that any risk of suffocating in this way is far less likely than that of SIDS. Accordingly, as early as 1992, the American Academy of Pediatrics (AAP) concluded it was likely that infants who sleep on their backs and sides are at less risk for SIDS when all other circumstances are favorable (e.g., sleeping on firm mattresses and without soft toys nearby).

Even though the reasons for that are still not yet fully understood, the AAP (1992, p. 1120) recommended that "healthy infants, when being put down for sleep be positioned on their side or back." Subsequently, in June 1994, the federal government initiated the "Back to Sleep" campaign (Willinger, 1995). Dramatic and sustained reductions in SIDS deaths followed. The numbers of these deaths fell from approximately 5,400 deaths in 1990 to 1,545 in 2014, a reduction of more than 70%.

(continues)

FOCUS ON 12.1 *(continued)*

Sudden Infant Death Syndrome

As a result of huge declines in numbers of SIDS deaths, another AAP task force (2005, p. 1245) withdrew approval for sleeping on an infant's side, noting that "the AAP no longer recognizes side sleeping as a reasonable alternative to fully supine [on back] sleeping." Recognizing that a change in sleep position alone will not settle all problems, in 2011, an AAP task force announced a new policy statement in which the AAP,

> is expanding its recommendations from focusing only on SIDS to focusing on a safe sleep environment that can reduce the risk of all sleep-related infant deaths, including SIDS. The recommendations described in this policy statement include supine positioning, use of a firm sleep surface, breastfeeding, room-sharing without bed-sharing, routine immunizations, consideration of using a pacifier, and avoidance of soft bedding, overheating, and exposure to tobacco smoke, alcohol, and illicit drugs. (p. e1341)

In 2012, the name of the Back to Sleep campaign was changed to "Safe to Sleep" to encompass both SIDS and other sleep-related causes of infant death, such as "Sudden Undetermined Death Syndrome" (SUDS). Although the ultimate cause(s) of SIDS/SUDS remain unknown, many believe they result from the convergence of three risk factors: a vulnerable infant, a critical developmental period, and outside stressor(s). Nevertheless, much has been learned about risk factors and their reduction. Thus, parents and professionals are advised to place infants on their backs for sleeping on a firm mattress in a "naked" bed (one without loose blankets, quilts, pillows, or other objects), while avoiding overheating, maternal smoking during pregnancy, exposure to smoke in the infant's environment, and bed sharing (as a potential cause of suffocation) (see Moon & Hauck, 2015; Shapiro-Mendoza et al., 2014; Trachtenberg, Haas, Kinney, Stanley, & Krous, 2012). Use of a pacifier seems to be helpful.

Recently, Baby Boxes have come into vogue to support the Safe to Sleep campaign by providing non-toxic, chemical-free, and environmentally safe sleep spaces for infants. Baby Boxes derive from a 75-year-old tradition in Finland of giving safe-certified boxes filled with childcare supplies and educational materials to expecting and new parents, but perhaps their most important feature is the use of the Baby Box as a bassinet in which the infant can sleep on his or her back in an environment without dangerous elements.

Information for parents and providers, researchers, and health care professionals about SIDS and similar forms of infant death, risk reduction, and the Safe to Sleep campaign can be obtained from the National Institute of Child Health and Human Development and the Centers for Disease Control and Prevention.

deaths in children between one and four years of age and between five and nine years of age is much larger among Caucasian Americans than among all other groups in these tables. However, *death rates* in these age groups are especially high among African-American and American-Indian and Native Alaska children. Moreover, in general, the number of deaths and death rates are typically higher for male children than they are for females. Further, after infancy, deaths resulting from homicide and HIV infection

Table 12.2   **Death Rates (per 100,000 in the Specified Population Group) during Childhood by Age, Race or Hispanic Origin,[a] and Sex: United States, 2014**

	Under 1 Year[b]			1 to 4 Year			5 to 9 Year		
	Both sexes	Males	Females	Both sexes	Males	Females	Both sexes	Males	Females
All origins[c]	588.0	638.6	535.0	24.0	26.7	21.3	11.5	13.0	10.0
Caucasian Americans, total	505.5	551.3	457.6	21.8	23.8	19.6	10.9	12.2	9.5
Non-Hispanic Caucasian Americans	501.6	549.9	451.0	22.6	24.9	20.2	10.8	12.2	9.4
Hispanic[d]	471.0	508.3	432.1	18.7	20.1	17.2	10.2	11.4	9.1
African Americans	1,042.7	1,125.4	956.3	37.1	42.2	31.9	15.6	18.0	13.2
Asian and Pacific Island Americans	362.0	384.3	338.6	13.4	14.3	12.5	7.6	8.3	6.8
American Indians and Alaska Natives	461.9	509.7	412.5	30.8	41.0	20.4	10.7	12.6	*

[a]Data for specified groups other than Caucasian Americans and African Americans should be interpreted with caution because of inconsistencies between reporting race and/or Hispanic origin on death certificates and on censuses and surveys.

[b]Death rates for "Under 1 Year" (based on population estimates) differ from infant mortality rates (based on live births).

[c]Figures for origin not stated are included in "All origins" but not distributed among specified origins.

[d]Includes all persons of Hispanic origin of any race.

*Figure does not meet standards of reliability or precision.

Source: Based on Kochanek et al., 2016.

are disproportionately prevalent among African-American children. All these statistics clearly illustrate social inequalities of death within the contemporary American death system. It is especially hazardous to be an infant, a male child, and an African-American child in our society—and those hazards are compounded when poverty is included as an additional variable.

Deaths of Others Experienced by Children

Children also experience the deaths of other persons. No reliable data are available concerning the frequency or patterns of these death-related encounters, and it seems that many American adults often undervalue the prevalence and importance of these encounters for children. In fact, children may encounter the deaths of a grandparent, parent, sibling, another relative or primary caregiver, a classmate, friend, neighbor, teacher, pet, or wild animal. Encountering the death of a significant other in any of these ways can be an important experience for a child, with special meaning for his or her subsequent development.

Loss experiences differ for individual children. For example, a deceased grandparent or biological parent might not have lived with or spent much time with a particular child. As a result, a child might not perceive the death of that individual as a very important loss. By contrast, the death of a cherished pet, a childhood friend, or a caring neighbor might be a significant event in a child's life.

In addition, children within different cultural, ethnic, and socioeconomic communities are likely to encounter death in different ways. For example, all too many American children are direct or indirect casualties, the "silent victims" of familial and community violence (Groves, Zuckerman, Marans, & Cohen, 1993), either as immediate victims or as witnesses of violence that may involve multiple losses and traumatic deaths.

Moreover, although few American children directly experience deaths from starvation, civil disruption, or war, they may witness graphic reports of such deaths on television. Think of how children were exposed to extensive television coverage of death and destruction in: the terrorist attacks on the World Trade Center in New York City and the Pentagon in the Washington, DC, area on September, 11, 2001; ongoing conflicts in Afghanistan, Iraq, and Syria; mass shootings; the shooting of a young African-American man in Ferguson, Missouri, and subsequent violence in the community (Stiles et al., 2015); and devastation associated with various natural disasters.

Further, many years ago Diamant (1994) drew on a study by the American Psychological Association to show that children in the United States who watch two to four hours of television per day will have witnessed fantasized versions of 8,000 murders and 100,000 acts of violence by the time they finish elementary school. Such exposures have likely increased recently, along with participation in violent-themed video games. Because such fantasized depictions of death and violence are not real, adults often dismiss them as unimportant. However, they may be quite significant in the minds of children, especially youngsters who have little direct experience with natural human death that would enable them to put into perspective these surrogate deaths in the media. Criticisms of the messages inherent in the media and video games are consistent with claims that some are changing in positive ways (Robertson, 2014; Strasburger, Jordan, & Donnerstein, 2012).

The point is that children are exposed to these and other death-related events, whether adults or society recognize that fact (Slaughter & Griffiths, 2007; Slaughter & Lyons, 2003). Curious children are unlikely to ignore such events completely. What is more likely is that the ways in which a child acknowledges and deals with death-related events may not be obvious to adults in their environment. This was evident in the vignette near the beginning of this chapter, when Allison's father failed to understand and respond in helpful ways to her needs. Those who wish to help children in our society need to be sensitive to the many implications of encounters with death during childhood.

To appreciate ways in which children experience death, we next examine two additional topics associated with children's encounters with death: the development of death-related concepts and the development of death-related attitudes in childhood.

THE DEVELOPMENT OF DEATH-RELATED CONCEPTS IN CHILDHOOD

Systematic study of the development of children's understandings of death began in the 1930s (Anthony, 1939, 1940; see also Anthony, 1972; Schilder & Wechsler, 1934). Since then, numerous research reports on this subject have been published. We focus here on a classic report that is typical of these studies (Nagy, 1948/1959), as well as subsequent work by Speece and Brent (1996).

The Work of Maria Nagy

To learn about children's understandings of the concept of death, Maria Nagy (1948, 1959) examined 378 children living in Budapest just before World War II. The children were three to ten years of age, 51% boys and 49% girls, ranging from dull normal to superior in intelligence level (with most falling in the "normal" range). Nagy asked children ranging from *seven to ten years in age* to "write down everything that comes into your mind about death" (1948, p. 4); children ranging from *six to ten years in age* were asked to make drawings about death (many of the older children also wrote explanations of their creations); and discussions were held with *all of the children,* either about their compositions and drawings, or (in the case of three- to five-year-olds) to get them to talk about their ideas and feelings about death. Because of World War II, Nagy's results were not published until 1948; they appeared again in 1959 in a somewhat revised form.

Nagy's results (1948, p. 7) suggested **three major developmental stages:** (1) "The child of less than five years does not recognize death as an irreversible fact. In death it sees life"; (2) "Between the ages of five and nine, death is most often personified and thought of as a contingency"; and (3) "In general only after the age of nine is it recognized that death is a process happening in us according to certain laws." Nagy wrote that because "the different sorts of answers can be found only at certain ages, one can speak of stages of development" (1948, p. 7), although she later added that "it should be kept in mind that neither the stages nor the above-mentioned ages at which they occur are watertight compartments as it were. Overlapping does exist" (1959, p. 81). Brief descriptions of each of these stages, using Nagy's own characterizations, illustrate her results.

Stage 1: There Is No Definitive Death   In the first stage of children's conceptual development, Nagy believed that "the child does not know death as such" (1948, p. 7). Either the concept of death has not been fully distinguished from other concepts or its full implications have not yet been grasped. For this reason, *death is not seen as final*; life and consciousness are attributed to the dead. One way in which this occurs is when death is understood either as a departure or a sleep—that is, in terms of continued life elsewhere (departure) or as a diminished form of life (sleep). In Nagy's view, this denies death as a clear and unambiguous concept.

A second way in which the finality of death is not fully grasped is when children "no longer deny death, but … are still unable to accept it as a definitive fact" (p. 13). Such children cannot completely separate death from life; they view death as a gradual, transitional process (between dying and being buried or arriving in heaven) or as a temporary situation in which links with life have not yet been completely severed. In short, although death exists, it is not absolutely final or definitive.

Note that Nagy's description of children who have not grasped the finality or definitiveness of death does not necessarily imply blissful ignorance. Even when death is interpreted as a kind of ongoing living somewhere else, separation from someone who is loved and consequent changes in the child's life may still be painful. A child does not have to grasp fully the finality of death or the complete cessation of bodily activities to react to separation from the dead person.

Stage 2: Death = A Person   According to Nagy, in this second stage, *death is imagined as a separate person* (such as a grim reaper, skeleton, ghost, or death angel) or else *death is identified with the dead themselves* so that the children did not distinguish between death and dead persons. Nagy interpreted this concept as a *personification of death,* which means that the existence and definitiveness of death have been accepted, although, because of children's strong aversion to the idea of death, death is depicted as a person or reality that is outside of or remote from them. Those caught by the external force do die; those who escape or get away from the clutches of that force do not die. In this way, death is conceived of as final, but avoidable—not inevitable and not universal. Later researchers (e.g., Gartley & Bernasconi, 1967; Kane, 1979; Koocher, 1973, 1974) emphasized the theme of death's *avoidability* in this stage rather than its personification (which may only be a child's way of representing the avoidability of death through the device of an external figure). Nagy's results also may reflect some of the historical and cultural context of Hungary between the first and second world wars, a tumultuous time with street battles between fascists and communists, and a time during which images of the grim reaper and other such personifications were not uncommon in that country. Later children who focused on avoiding death made comments like the following when they were asked what they think of death and dying: "You have to get sick before you die, so I am never going to get sick and I'll never have to die" (Adler, 1979, p. 46).

Other children have made clear that they are not satisfied with the simple fact of death as disappearance. They want to know where and how the deceased person continues to live; some speculate about the nature of life in the grave. Because these theories are based on a child's limited life experiences, they may combine keen insight and misinterpretations, as well as feelings of anxiety and fear about what is going on.

Stage 3: The Cessation of Corporal Life   In this third stage, Nagy believed children recognize that death is a process operating within us. Such children view death as both *final and universal,* an aspect of life that is inevitable and not avoidable. Nagy thought this reflects a realistic view of both death and the world.

The Work of Mark Speece and Sandor Brent

After reviewing the literature and conducting their own research on children's understandings of death, Mark Speece and Sandor Brent (1984, 1992, 1996) concluded that the concept of death is not a simple, uncomplicated notion. It embraces a number of distinguishable sub-concepts, each of which is a central aspect in children's concepts of death. Speece and Brent identified **five principal sub-concepts involved in children's concepts of death**, some with subordinate components or elements (see Table 12.3).

Universality as a component in the concept of death involves the recognition that *all living things must eventually die.* This is complex, challenging children to bring together three closely related notions: all-inclusiveness, inevitability, and unpredictability. *All-inclusiveness* concerns whether the concept of death applies to *every* living thing ("Does everyone die?"); is no living thing exempt from death? *Inevitability* involves the *necessity* with which death applies to living things ("Does everyone have to die?") and indicates that death is ultimately unavoidable for all living things, regardless of its specific causes. *Unpredictability* relates to the *timing* of death. If death is all-inclusive and inevitable, it might seem that its timing would be certain and predictable—but that is not the case. In fact, anyone might perhaps die at any time. Children and others often try to avoid acknowledging the personal implications of this aspect of the universality of death.

Table 12.3	Sub-concepts Embraced by the Concept of Death

Universality
   All-inclusiveness
   Inevitability
   Unpredictability
Irreversibility
Nonfunctionality
Causality
Noncorporeal continuation

Source: Based on Speece & Brent (1996).

Two additional sub-concepts, irreversibility and nonfunctionality, are both aspects of the finality of death. **Irreversibility** has to do with the transition from being alive to being dead and to the state that results from death. So, once the physical body of a living thing is dead, it can never be alive again—barring miraculous or magical events and explanations. Medical resuscitation can apply only to a kind of boundary region between being alive and being dead, not to the state of death in which life in a physical body is irreversibly absent. **Nonfunctionality** means that death involves the complete and final cessation of all life-defining capabilities or functional capacities (whether external and observable or internal and inferred) typically attributed to a living physical body (Barrett & Behne, 2005).

In addition to universality, irreversibility, and nonfunctionality, Speece and Brent drew attention to two additional sub-concepts: causality and noncorporeal continuation. The sub-concept of **causality** involves comprehending the events or conditions that really do or can bring about the death of a living thing. This sub-concept responds to questions like "Why do living things die?" and "What makes living things die?" It asks children to achieve a realistic understanding of the external and internal events or forces that might bring about death—as opposed to magical thinking suggesting that bad behavior or merely wishing could cause someone to die.

The final component in the concept of death—which Speece and Brent term **noncorporeal continuation**—is reflected in children's efforts to grasp or articulate their understanding of some type of continued life apart from the physical body that has died. This is seen when children ask: "What happens after death?" or "Where does your soul or spirit go when you die?" Another example appears in the reflections of an 11-year-old girl whose experiences of living with HIV infection prompted her to write, "If only I could talk to someone in Heaven, then they could tell me how it is there, what things there are to do there, and what I should bring" (Wiener, Best, & Pizzo, 1994, p. 12). Research by Brent and Speece (1993) showed that children and adults commonly say that some type of continued life form—often, though perhaps not always, a mode of personal continuation—exists after the death of the physical body. This continuation may take many forms, such as the ongoing life of a soul in heaven without the body or the reincarnation of a soul in a new and different body.

Speece and Brent insisted that many researchers have been scornful of children's "beliefs in an afterlife" or systematically unwilling to enter into nonnaturalistic aspects of the concept of death.

After reviewing the literature on children's concepts of death, Speece and Brent concluded, "most studies have found that *by seven years of age* most children understand each of the key bioscientific components—Universality, Irreversibility, Non-functionality, and Causality" (1996, p. 43; emphasis added). Nevertheless, Speece and Brent cautioned that "age by itself explains nothing. It is rather a convenient general, omnibus index of a wide range of loosely correlated biological and environmental variables." Further, although some researchers (e.g., Lonetto, 1980) have maintained that children recognize death is possible for all other people before they apply it to themselves, Speece and Brent thought it more likely that most children understand their own personal mortality before they understand that all other people die.

Some Comments on Children's Understandings of Death

The work of Nagy and other researchers who have studied the development of death-related concepts in childhood exposes key elements in the concept of death, such as finality, avoidability versus inevitability, external versus internal forces, and universality. Much of this work has had the great advantage of fitting easily within larger theories or models of developmental psychology, such as those of Jean Piaget (1998; see also Piaget & Inhelder, 1958; Table 12.4). For example, Nagy's characterization of the earliest stages in her account of children's concepts of death agreed with Piaget's observations about an egocentric orientation and several other characteristics of what he calls preoperational thought—such as **magical thinking** (in which all events are explained by the causal influence of various commands, intentions, and forces; see Fogarty, 2000), **animism** (in which life and consciousness are attributed to objects that others think of as inanimate), and **artificialism** (in which it is believed that all objects and events in the world have been manufactured to serve people, a belief that Wass [1984] described as directly opposed to animism). Similarly, the universality and inevitability that characterize Nagy's final stage conform to Piaget's account of objectivity, generality, and propositional thinking in what he called the period of formal operations. This finding suggests that children's understandings involve a development or maturation in their capacity to form more and more abstract concepts of subjects like death.

However, research in this field has been plagued by methodological problems, such as a lack of precision and agreement in the terms and definitions used for various components of the concept of death, as well as a lack of reliable and valid standardized measures for these components. The ensuing literature has not unfairly been characterized as consisting of a "confusing array of results" (Stambrook & Parker, 1987, p. 154). Often, commentators have oversimplified their results, made them more rigid than originally suggested, or applied them uncritically. Many commentators have generalized from studies of particular groups of children (such as Nagy's Hungarian children, who were examined before World War II and before the advent of new cultural forces like television and the Internet) to other groups of children without taking into account historical or cultural variables in different populations. Speece and Brent (1996; as well as Kenyon, 2001; Lazar & Torney-Purta, 1991) advised that better research and a more nuanced grasp of results could follow from recommendations to distinguish, standardize, and operationalize key sub-concepts within the concept of death.

Table 12.4   Piaget's System of Cognitive Development

Period and Stage[a]	Life Period[b]	Some Major Characteristics
I. Period of sensorimotor intelligence	Infancy (0–2)	"Intelligence" consists of sensory and motor actions. No conscious thinking. Limited language.[c] No concept of reality.
II. Period of preparation and organization of concrete operations		
1. Stage of preoperational thought	Early childhood (2–7)	Egocentric orientation. Magical, animistic, & artificialistic thinking. Thinking is irreversible. Reality is subjective.
2. Stage of concrete operations	Middle childhood/preadolescence (7–11 or 12)	Orientation ego-decentered. Thinking is bound to concrete. Naturalistic thinking. Recognizes laws of conservation and reversibility.
III. Period of formal operations	Adolescence and adulthood (12+)	Propositional and hypodeductive thinking. Generality of thinking. Reality is objective.

[a]Each stage includes an initial period of preparation and a final period of attainment; thus, whatever characterizes a stage is in the process of formation.

[b]There are individual differences in chronological ages.

[c]By the end of age 2, children, on average, have attained a vocabulary of approximately 250–300 words.

Source: From "Concepts of Death: A Developmental Perspective" by H. Wass. In H. Wass & C. A. Corr (Eds.), *Childhood and Death*, p. 4. Copyright © 1984 Hemisphere Publishing Corporation. Reprinted with permission.

Adults striving to gain insight into children's understandings of death, to teach children about death, or to provide empathic support to children who are coping with death, must attend to at least four principal variables: developmental level, life experiences, individual personality, and patterns of communication and support (Hunter & Smith, 2008; Kastenbaum, 1977). With respect to *development*, cognitive development is not the only relevant variable; maturation is a multidimensional process that applies to all aspects of a child's life—physical, psychological, social, and spiritual. *Life experiences* are a critical but not yet well-studied factor, even though the quantity and quality of a child's encounters with death are likely to be influential in his or her understanding of death. Each child's *individual personality* will be a powerful variable in the ways he or she can and does think about death. And the death-related thoughts that a child shares with others will depend on his or her ability and willingness to *communicate,* together with the *support* and comfort he or she receives from those others.

A good example of all this is seen in quite different challenges that are presented to a child when he or she is asked to explain two simple sentences: "You are dead" and "I will die" (Kastenbaum, 2000). The first sentence applies to another person at the present time; the second refers back to the speaker but at some unspecified time in the future. The issues involved in grasping these two sentences are partly conceptual, but they also relate to the potential threat implied in the second sentence and the child's ability to grasp a future possibility. When children try to understand the concept of death and its various sub-concepts, those who are likely to do best will be children who have experienced a healthy development, who are able to draw on a fund of constructive personal experiences, whose self-concept is stable and well formed, who communicate openly, and who have adequate support from the adults around them.

Clearly, children do not always think of death as adults do. However, that does not mean they have no concept of death. For example, children who think of death as sleep have *an understanding of death* through which they try to make sense of their experiences—however undifferentiated that understanding may be from other concepts and however inadequate it may seem in the light of some adult standard. As Kastenbaum and Aisenberg (1972, p. 9) noted, "Between the extremes of 'no understanding' and explicit, integrated abstract thought there are many ways by which the young mind can enter into relationship with death." A good way to gain insight into children's understandings of death is to listen actively and carefully to the many questions they ask about this subject (Corr, 1996; Gabb, Owens, & MacLeod, 2013).

The basic lesson from research by Nagy and others is that children do make an active effort to grasp or understand death. Nagy (1948, p. 27) added an important corollary: "To conceal death from the child is not possible and is also not permissible. Natural behavior in the child's surroundings can greatly diminish the shock of its acquaintance with death." Allison's father in the vignette near the beginning of this chapter had not learned this lesson.

THE DEVELOPMENT OF DEATH-RELATED ATTITUDES IN CHILDHOOD

Children living in North America today receive many messages about death. These messages come from: the societal death system that surrounds the children, particularly as expressed through the media; the children's parents, family members, and other persons with whom they come into contact; and their own life experiences. Messages such as these often tell children that death is not an acceptable topic for discussion and that children are not permitted to take part in death-related events. Not all societies have transmitted this kind of message to children. For example, as we learned in Chapter 3, in contemporary Amish society and among the New England Puritans in colonial America, children are or were expected to take part in both happy and sad events in a family's life. Any other alternative would have seemed or would still seem undesirable and impracticable.

Death-related situations and experiences may be new to many children, but new experiences need not be overwhelming unless children have been led to view them that way. Nor are such experiences out of bounds from the inquiring mind of a child. The claim that "the child is so recently of the quick that there is little need in his spring-green world for an understanding of the dead" (Ross, 1967, p. 250) does not describe the authentic lives of contemporary children. In fact, there is ample evidence in everyday interactions with children and in long-standing scholarly literature (e.g., Childers & Wimmer, 1971; Koocher, O'Malley, Foster, & Gogan, 1976) that *normal, healthy children do have thoughts and feelings about death; they are curious about this subject.*

The specific form of any individual child's attitudes toward death, as toward any other significant subject, will relate to the nature of the child's encounters with death and to the developmental, personal, and societal forces that help to shape the child's interpretation and response to a given experience. Even young infants who have little experience or conceptual capacity give clear evidence of separation anxiety. Older children who had no role in a parent's death may nevertheless blame themselves if they believe that something they said or did was somehow magically related to the death. In short, attitudes toward death are complex, even in childhood, and may derive from many sources (Wass & Cason, 1984). To show this, we describe here two arenas in which death-related attitudes are apparent during childhood.

Death-Related Games

Long-standing research has demonstrated that death themes are pervasive in children's play in many societies throughout history (e.g., Opie & Opie, 1969). For example, Maurer (1966) suggested that peek-a-boo is a classic death-related game. From the child's egocentric perspective, what happens in this game is that the external world vanishes and then suddenly reappears. As a child focuses on the (apparent) disappearance of the world, he or she may become fearful; its reappearance will often produce delight. From a young child's perspective, many experiences like this involve attitudes that are (at least) quite similar to those associated with death.

Further, Rochlin (1967) studied children's play activities, demonstrating that "at a very early age well-developed mental faculties are functioning to defend oneself against the realization that life may end" (p. 61). Children appear to recognize that their lives might be changed in important ways by death, and they act on that recognition in the fantasy world of their play. Rochlin's research focused especially on children's games concerned with action, violence, and at least the potential for death. He concluded that "death is a matter of deep consideration to the very young child … thoughts of dying are commonplace … behavior is influenced by such thoughts" (p. 54). It is likely that this is even more significant in our modern era of digital games, videos, and the Internet. This is an important point, since play is the main work of a child's life.

The great importance of play in the lives of children is amply illustrated in evidence to show that play continued for many children even in the horrific conditions of the Holocaust (Eisen, 1988).

> Children's games incorporated the harrowing reality of the camp or ghetto environment. This kind of play was not an escape into fantasy or imagination but a way of assimilating the dangerous world that surrounded youngsters during the Holocaust. Role-playing in particular represented a creative means of accommodating and coping with the tremendous challenges youngsters confronted (Heberer, 2011, p. 300).

Death-Related Themes in Children's Rhymes, Songs, Humor, and Fairy Tales

Death-related themes appear frequently in children's rhymes and humor. For example, many have sung a little ditty in which "the worms crawl in, the worms crawl out." Others will be familiar with "Ring around the Rosie," but may not have realized that it is a song arising from an English plague and describing the roseate skin pustules of disease, as a result of which "we all fall down." Even lullabies, like "Rock-a-Bye Baby," are filled with falling cradle themes (Achté, Fagerström, Pentikäinen, & Farberow, 1990), and the child's prayer, "Now I lay me down to sleep," is a petition for safekeeping against death and other nighttime hazards.

Children's fairy tales, whether oral or written, are also chock-full of references to death (Lamers, 1995). Little Red Riding Hood and her grandmother are eaten by the wicked wolf in the original version of the story; they do not avoid death in various ways as later versions would have it (see Issues for Critical Reflection #2 in Chapter 1 in this book). The Big Bad Wolf who pursues the three little pigs with threats to huff and puff and blow their houses down dies in a scalding pot of hot water when he falls down the last chimney. Hansel and Gretel (who were left to die in the forest by their parents because there was not enough food) trick the wicked witch and shut her up in the hot oven where she planned to cook them. The wicked stepmother orders the death of Snow White and demands her heart as proof. A gentle kiss may awaken Sleeping Beauty from a state of coma, but the false bride in "The Goose Girl" is put into a barrel lined with sharp nails and rolled until she is dead.

Death-related humor and stories of this sort are not necessarily morbid or unhealthful for children. Bettelheim (1977) argued that they actually are wholesome experiences in which children can work through fears and anxieties related to death in safe and distanced ways. *Death is not absent from the fantasy world of childhood*. Its familiar presence debunks the view that children are simply unfamiliar with death-related thoughts and feelings. Indeed, many of today's television entertainment programs repeatedly, but incorrectly, suggest that people usually come to be dead by being killed, that only "bad" guys really die, and that death itself is not permanent (see Chapter 4 in this book). By contrast, even in the Nazi concentration camps children produced drawings and poetry (e.g., Volavková, 1993).

CHILDREN WHO ARE COPING WITH LIFE-THREATENING ILLNESS AND DYING

Children coping with life-threatening illness and dying frequently experience anxiety. As they acquire information about their condition, their self-concept is likely to change in discernible ways, and they are apt to share an identifiable set of specific concerns associated with dying.

Anxiety in Ill and Dying Children

Vernick and Karon's (1965) answer to the question, "Who's afraid of death on a leukemia ward?" was *everyone*—children, family members, and professional caregivers. This finding suggests that adults can come together and share with children. However, when Waechter (1971, 1984) studied ill and dying children, she found many parents and caregivers who did not share with children accurate information about their diagnoses and prognoses. Waechter investigated the attitudes of these children by creating four matched groups of six- to ten-year-olds: children with chronic disease for which death was predicted; children with chronic disease with a good prognosis; children with brief illness; and nonhospitalized, well children. During an interview, each child was given a projective test (a set of pictures for each of which the child was to develop a story) and a test to measure general anxiety.

A pediatric patient with a tracheotomy tube.

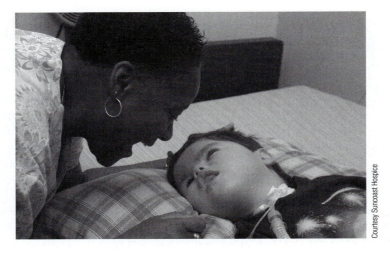

Courtesy Suncoast Hospice

Waechter demonstrated that anxiety levels in fatally-ill children were much higher than those in either of the other two groups of hospitalized children or in the well children. Also, the fatally-ill children expressed significantly more anxiety specifically related to death, mutilation, and loneliness than did other ill children. This was true even though the fatally-ill children had not been formally informed of their prognosis. Other studies of ill and dying children have reported similar findings (e.g., Lee, Lieh-Mak, Hung, & Luk, 1984; Spinetta & Maloney, 1975; Spinetta, Rigler, & Karon, 1973).

Acquiring Information and Changing Concepts of Self

A different approach was taken by Bluebond-Langner (1977, 1978), who used methods of cultural anthropology to identify keen awareness of their situation in hospitalized, terminally-ill children with leukemia. Bluebond-Langner identified five stages in the children's process of acquiring information (see the left-hand column in Table 12.5). The sobering—and really not very surprising—lesson from this portion of Bluebond-Langner's study is that children pay attention to important experiences in their lives and acquire information from people and events that impact closely on them.

Bluebond-Langner's research went one step further. She noted that acquisition of information was coordinated with parallel shifts in self-concept. As the children obtained information, they applied it to a changing understanding of themselves (see the right-hand column in Table 12.5). According to Bluebond-Langner, changes in self-concept were associated with events in the illness process and the information available to the children. Critical points here are the timing of these changes in relation to external events and the children's ability to integrate and synthesize information arising from their experiences to form new self-concepts.

Children learn from their experiences, from other children, and from the ways adults treat them. How could it be otherwise? What they learn is not only abstract information; it has meaning and significance for them. Alexander and Adlerstein (1958) suggested that the central point may be not so much the content of death conceptions as their significance for the individuals in question. We pursue this point

Table 12.5   The Private Worlds of Dying Children

Stages in the Process of Acquiring Information	Changes in Self-Concept
1. I have a serious illness.	1. From diagnosis (prior to which I had thought of myself as well) to awareness that I am seriously ill.
2. I know the drugs I am receiving, when and how they are being used, and their side effects.	2. At the first remission, to the view that I am seriously ill—but will get better.
3. I know the purposes of treatments and procedures.	3. At the first relapse, to the view that I am always ill— but will get better.
4. I understand that these treatments, procedures, and symptoms fit together to identify a disease in which there is a cycle of relapses and remissions (i.e., the medicines do not always last as long or work as well as they are supposed to) (does not include death).	4. After several more remissions and relapses, to the view that I am always ill—but will never get better.
5. I understand that the cycle of disease is finite, has an end, and that end is death— there is only a limited number of drugs, and when they stop working, I will die soon.	5. After the death of a leukemic peer, to the realization that I am dying.

Source: Adapted from *The Private Worlds of Dying Children,* by M. Bluebond-Langner, pp. 166, 169. Copyright © 1978 Princeton University Press.

in Chapter 13. Here we need only to observe that children's concepts of death are intimately associated with ways they feel about and interpret both themselves and the world around them.

Issues for Ill and Dying Children

Many advances have taken place in recent years in understanding pain and other distressing symptoms and in their management in different types of life-threatening childhood illnesses (see, e.g., Goldman, Hain, & Lieben, 2012). This increased understanding has led to official policy statements on care for children with life-threatening illnesses from the International Work Group on Death, Dying, and Bereavement (1993), Together for Short Lives in Britain, the World Health Organization (1998), and the American Academy of Pediatrics (AAP) (2000a). Nevertheless, many studies have confirmed deficiencies in the management of pain and other distressing symptoms in many children who are dying, even as they have offered guidelines for better care (e.g., Hurwitz, Duncan, & Wolfe, 2004; McCallum, Byrne, & Bruera, 2000).

Ill and dying children often have psychosocial needs focused around the importance of love and security with freedom from pain, freedom from deep-seated feelings of anxiety or guilt, a sense of belonging, a feeling of self-respect, and understanding of self (Masera et al., 1999). Many preschool children with a life-threatening illness have principal concerns about the causality of their illness, threats to body image, treatment procedures, and fears of dying, whereas school-age children most often have concerns about the future, education and social relationships, body image, and issues related to hospitalization and procedures. Much of the anxiety in ill children focuses on safety (from pain or other forms of distress, intervention procedures, bodily assault) and security (both within themselves and in relationship to family members, peers, and other important persons) (Attig, 1996; Sourkes, 1995). Stevens (1998) put much of this simply by proposing that the emotional needs of dying children will be: (1) those of all children regardless of health; (2) those arising from the child's reaction to illness and admission to a hospital; and (3) those arising from the child's concept of death.

Many of the concerns of dying children emphasize quality in living and the immediate or present-tense implications of various threats to quality in living. These issues fit with the tendency of many children to live in the moment. Moreover, it is important to recognize that cure rates for many illnesses that were once highly lethal for children have changed so dramatically in recent years that for many children the challenge has changed from coping with dying to living with a serious or life-threatening illness (Adams & Deveau, 1993; Doka, 1996a; Koocher & O'Malley, 1981; Spinetta & Deasy-Spinetta, 1981). Thus, it has been argued that the work of contemporary pediatric oncologists is guided by the motto "Cure is not enough" and by an emphasis on quality in living among survivors of childhood cancer (Schwartz, Hobbie, Constine, & Ruccione, 1994). Issues that are often central for survivors—or, as some prefer to say, "graduates"—of a life-threatening illness in childhood are: (1) normalization or incorporating the disease experience into one's life history; (2) learning to live with uncertainty that may lead to a heightened sense of vulnerability, overprotectiveness by adults, or a transformation of personal priorities, values, and goals; (3) learning to live with compromise and the ongoing repercussions of disease; and (4) overcoming stigma in social contexts (Ruccione, 1994). It is important also to assess and respond appropriately to the spiritual needs of children (Davies, Brenner, Orloff, Sumner, & Worden, 2002).

Similar concerns are found in children with chronic conditions, such as cystic fibrosis (e.g., Bluebond-Langner, 1996; Bluebond-Langner, Lask, & Angst, 2001) or HIV/AIDS. For example, one 12-year-old girl described coping with uncertainties posed by her illness in this way: "Living with HIV and knowing that you can die from it is scary.... I think it is hardest in this order: Not knowing when this will happen ... Not knowing where it will happen ... Worrying about my family ... What will happen to my stuff and my room?...Thinking about what my friends will think" (Wiener, Best, & Pizzo, 1994, p. 24).

CHILDREN WHO ARE COPING WITH BEREAVEMENT AND GRIEF

There once was a debate about whether children are able to mourn after a death (see, e.g., Furman, 1973; Wolfenstein, 1966). This debate rests on a failure to distinguish between grief and mourning, together with an absence of adequate models for childhood mourning. Children certainly experience grief (i.e., reactions to loss). They may cry, get angry, become depressed, have trouble sleeping, regress in their behavior, or react in other ways to loss. However, children may not respond to loss or express their reactions as adults do; they may not display their feelings as openly as many adults do and they may immerse themselves in everyday activities, such as play and school, instead of withdrawing into preoccupation with thoughts of the deceased person. Thus, children's grief reactions may be *more intermittent in character* than those of many adults and thus *longer in duration* (Worden, 1996). These children may be "dosing" themselves with their grief and mourning by allowing themselves to experience their grief reactions and their efforts to cope for a while,

Squib, a young owl, has lost his piece (peace) and is sad.

Lawrence Sfiles

but then turning away when that overwhelms them or when other concerns attract their attention. For bereaved children, it is also important to ask how normative developmental tasks influence encounters with loss, and vice versa: Can children feel secure when coping with loss and grief? Does healthy development help them in such coping?

The real issue for bereaved children is not so much whether they are able to mourn, but the nature of their reactions and responses to loss. That is, what are the central concerns that preoccupy bereaved children? And what are the tasks of mourning children face in coping with loss and grief?

Issues for Bereaved Children

Three central issues are likely to be prominent in the grief experiences of bereaved children and may apply to the perceived or real termination of any relationship for children: (1) Did I cause it (a death or some other form of loss) to happen?; (2) Is it going to happen to me?; and (3) Who is going to take care of me? The egocentricity of these issues is obvious. When a child does not rightly understand the causality involved in a loss, perhaps because of ignorance or magical thinking, it is not surprising that issues of origin and endangerment should present themselves.

The death of a parent or another caring adult may especially evoke the first and third of these issues. For example, if Mommy says in exasperation one day, "You'll be the death of me," and happens shortly after to be killed in a car accident, a child may be anxious about whether the latter event fulfilled the promise of the former. Similarly, when there is widespread discussion of a large-scale trauma, such as happened on September 11, 2001, or nightly media reports about deaths in some war or conflict, children may wonder about potential threats to themselves. And when children's welfare depends in so many ways on parents and other adults, the death of an important person might lead a child to be anxious about who will now provide the care that he or she needs (Silverman, 2000). As a result, many children who have experienced the death of a parent strive to maintain an emotional connection with the deceased parent by talking to that individual or holding on to symbolic linking objects, such as pictures or gifts (Silverman, Nickman, & Worden, 1992).

If someone dies in a family and a child perceives that Daddy (or the doctor or others) did not or could not prevent that sad event, the child may become concerned that he or she could experience the same unhappy fate. The death of a sibling or another child may be especially difficult since it strikes so close to the child's own self and may rob the bereaved child of emotional support from caregivers (Davies, 1999; Marshall & Winokuer, 2017; Toray & Oltjenbruns, 1996). A sibling or playmate is equally a companion, competitor, and alter ego. Experiencing such a person's death during childhood may have short-term outcomes in aggressive and attention-seeking behaviors (McCown & Davies, 1995), as well as long-term effects throughout the individual's childhood and later life (Schuurman, 2003).

The Harvard Child Bereavement Study established a detailed list of children's bereavement needs (Worden, 1996). These include:

- Adequate information—clear and comprehensible information about an impending death (whenever that is possible) and certainly after a death has occurred
- Fears and anxieties addressed—to know that they will be cared for and to experience consistent discipline
- Reassurance that they are not to blame
- Careful listening—by someone who will hear them out and not minimize their concerns
- Validation of their feelings—including respect for and safe ways to express individual reactions in their own ways
- Help with overwhelming feelings—especially when sadness, anger, anxiety, and guilt are intense
- Involvement and inclusion—both before and after a death, with preparation and without being forced to join in
- Continued routine activities—in the form of age-appropriate activities, such as play and school
- Modeled grief behaviors—through adults who can share their own grief and mourning and show how to experience and express grief and mourning in constructive ways
- Opportunities to remember—both after a death and throughout life

Children respond to bereavement experiences in ways that suit their particular developmental situation (Fleming, 1985; Silverman & Worden, 1992a). For example, children who do not appreciate the finality of death may wonder what the deceased person is now doing if he or she is thought to be somehow alive in a different way or in a different place. By contrast, children who appreciate that death involves irreversibility and nonfunctionality may ask very concrete questions about what happens to a dead body when it stops working.

Some bereaved children may delay beginning their grief work or revealing it to others. They may appear to turn away from death from time to time—for example, to play games, watch television, or go off to school. To adults, this may seem to display a lack of awareness, comprehension, or feeling. More likely, it simply involves a short attention span, a failure to realize that the loss is permanent, or a temporary defense against being overwhelmed by the implications of the loss. Strong feelings of anger and fears of abandonment or death are usually evident in the behaviors of bereaved children. Also, as we noted earlier, children often play death games as a way to work out their feelings and anxieties in a relatively safe setting. Such games are a familiar part of the lives of children; in them, a child can stand safely aside from the harm that comes to the toys or imaginary figures.

Worden (1996) also noted a "late effect" of bereavement in which a significant minority (though not all) of the school-age children in the Harvard Child Bereavement Study were encountering more difficulties at two years after the death of a parent than they were at earlier times (four months and one year after the death). This finding is closely correlated with the family context of the child and especially with the functioning of the surviving parent (Zucker, 2009). The lesson here seems to be the importance of being sensitive to the possibility of both ongoing issues for a bereaved child and those that may only arise at a later point in the child's bereavement. The death of a significant person in a child's life does not necessarily lead to complicated grief and mourning, but it can have a long-term impact through a sense of emptiness and the ongoing "presence" of the absent person.

Another distinguishing feature of childhood bereavement is seen in children who may talk to those around them, even to strangers, as a way of watching for reactions and seeking clues to guide their own responses. By contrast with adults who may withdraw into themselves and limit communication when they are mourning, children often ask questions over and over again—"I know that Grandpa died, but when will he come home?"—as a way of testing reality and confirming that what they have been told has not changed. Some questions from children baffle adults: "Where is dead?"; "When you die and go to heaven, what do you do there all day?"; "If Grandpa died and went up to heaven, why is he buried down in the ground?" When viewed from the developmental and experiential perspective of a child, these are quite logical efforts to interpret the meaning of what has happened.

Tasks in Mourning for Bereaved Children

Ill children, dying children, and children who are bereaved may all experience grief. They are all children who are reacting to the events and the losses that have occurred or are occurring in their lives. Mourning is the task work involved in attempting to cope with, adapt, and learn to live with loss and grief. In a bereaved child, the work of mourning will be superimposed on basic developmental tasks. Throughout childhood, mourning tasks may need to be addressed again and again in appropriate ways at different developmental levels and in different contexts. Thus, an individual child may mourn the death of his or her mother, her absence in the months and years that follow, what that then means for being different from schoolmates who have a living mother, and his or her inability to draw on the absent mother's support or to share achievements with her in later years. Reworking losses and grief responses in this way is quite consistent with developmental processes. Healthy mourning integrates losses in ways that shake off unhealthy obstacles and facilitate ongoing living (Furman, 1974). Worden (1996) identified four tasks of mourning that apply to bereaved children, although he noted that these tasks "can only be understood in terms of the cognitive, emotional, and social development of the child" (p. 12). According to Worden, these tasks are:

1. To accept the reality of the loss
2. To experience the pain or emotional aspects of the loss
3. To adjust to an environment in which the deceased is missing
4. To relocate the dead person within one's life and find ways to memorialize the person

This task-based account of mourning is quite similar to the adult model from Worden (2009) that we examined in Chapter 9. In particular, it reflects the great importance of maintaining some sense of the presence of the now-dead person in the child's life.

HELPING CHILDREN COPE WITH DEATH, DYING, AND BEREAVEMENT

In this section, we organize guidelines for helping children cope with death, dying, and bereavement in four clusters: some general suggestions; a proactive program of education, communication, and validation; helping ill or dying children; and helping bereaved children.

Some General Suggestions

The basic principle in helping children cope with death is more a matter of attitude than one of technique or easily definable skills. As Erikson (1963, p. 269) wrote: "Healthy children will not fear life if their elders have integrity enough not to fear death." Unfortunately, adults often adopt tactics that attempt to insulate children from death-related events, avoid such topics, and deny the finality of death. In so doing, they block children's efforts to acquire information, express their feelings, obtain support, and learn to cope with sadness and loss.

At the very least, children deserve assistance from their elders in dealing with challenges presented by death. Katzenbach (1986, p. 322) explained why this is so when he wrote:

> Do you know the sensation of being a child and being alone? Children can adapt wonderfully to specific fears, like a pain, a sickness, or a death. It is the unknown which is truly terrifying for them. They have no fund of knowledge in how the world operates, and so they feel completely vulnerable.

Death-related challenges, including those associated with the unknown and a child's sense of vulnerability, *will* arise, and children *will* attempt to deal with them. The only responsible option open to adults is to make available their knowledge, experience, insights, and coping resources to children (McCue & Bonn, 1996). As LeShan (1976, p. 3) has written: "A child can live through *anything,* so long as he or she is told the truth and is allowed to share with loved ones the natural feelings people have when they are suffering" (see Issues for Critical Reflection #10)

Adults cannot face death for their children or live on their behalf, but adults can prepare children to do this for themselves and can often walk alongside, at least part of the way. "Part of each child's adventure into life is his discovery of loss, separation,

#10 Should Adults Talk to Children about Death?

Adults often wonder if they should talk to children about death, what they should say, and how they should act with children in death-related situations. These questions arise in many ways: Should we discuss death with children or teach them about loss and grief even before a death takes place? What should we say to children after a death occurs? Should we take children to funeral services? Perhaps the most difficult of all questions of this type arise in situations in which adults (parents, family members, or care providers) are challenged by a child who has a life-threatening illness and who is facing his or her imminent death.

Researchers studied Swedish parents whose child had died from cancer between 1992 and 1997 (Kreicbergs, Valdimarsdóttir, Onelöv, Henter, & Steineck, 2004; see also Valdimarsdóttir et al., 2007). Among the 561 eligible parents, 429 stated whether they had talked about death with their child. More than a quarter of those who did not talk with their child about death regretted that they had not done so. Similar regrets were reported by nearly half of the parents who had sensed that their child was aware of his or her imminent death. By contrast, among the parents who had talked with their child about death, "No parent in this cohort later regretted having talked with his or her child about death" (p. 1175).

Despite all of the challenges involved in talking to a child about death and even in the very demanding circumstances of a child facing his or her imminent death, this study suggests that it is most often better to go ahead with such conversations. The main reason for this is that, as Rabbi Earl Grollman has often said, "Anything that is mentionable is manageable." Opening a line of communication with children is preferable to allowing them to try to cope on their own with incomplete or improperly understood information and the demons of their own imaginations. Moreover, a child who is able to have his or her concerns addressed in a thoughtful and loving way is a child who knows he or she has access to a trustworthy adult when there is a need to look for a source of support. As Beale, Baile, and Aaron (2005, p. 3631) wrote many years ago, "Avoiding discussion of dying for fear of depressing or frightening a child is a counterproductive strategy, which is not born out by data."

Note that The Conversation Project offers a free, downloadable *Pediatric Starter Kit: Having the Conversation with Your Seriously Ill Child* (see http://theconversationproject.org/wp-content/uploads/2014/10/TCP_PediatricSK_Forms_rev7.pdf) with advice from parents and palliative care specialists to help with these conversations based on the personality and cognitive level of the child. See also The Dougy Center and healthychildren.org.

non-being, death. No one can have this adventure for him, nor can death be locked in another room until a child comes of age" (Kastenbaum, 1973, p. 37).

Helping children cope with death is an ongoing process, not a unique event occurring only at one specific point in time. Children often return over and over to issues that concern them. Such issues need to be readdressed as children confront different developmental and situational challenges. It is part of their continuing maturation and socialization, which is carried out in a natural and effective manner when it draws on ordinary events in living and teachable moments, together with children's own questions and initiatives. Adults can also create opportunities for constructive dialogue with and between children. For example, summer camps for children who share an illness (such as cancer) have been shown to have value in expressing grief, helping to establish relationships that last well beyond the camp sessions, and supplementing in constructive ways relationships with healthy peers.

Adults may need to make special efforts to help children cope with death in a society that has limited experience with natural human death and whose death system all too often inhibits constructive interactions between children and death. This entails accepting certain related responsibilities (Corr, 1984a), such as:

- Undertaking preparation—by initiating a reflective analysis (which no person ever fully completes) of one's own thoughts and feelings about death, and by becoming familiar with basic principles in the body of knowledge that has been developed in this area
- Responding to real needs in children (rather than those adults project on them)
- Communicating effectively
- Working cooperatively—with children, with other adults, and with relevant institutions in society, such as educational and religious organizations

Cooperative work with and by children is well illustrated by one child (Gaes, 1987) who wrote *My Book for Kids with Cansur.* Helping can flow from children to adults as well as from adults to children.

A Proactive Program of Prior Preparation

Whenever possible, one helps children best by preparing them ahead of time to cope with issues associated with sadness and loss (Metzgar & Zick, 1996). The key elements in a proactive program of prior preparation are education, effective communication, and validation. In terms of *education,* adults can explore with children a relatively safe encounter with death, such as a dead bird found in the woods or a dead fish from the school aquarium (Stevenson & Stevenson, 1996b). "Teachable moments" that are not highly charged with personal feelings can represent good beginnings for adult–child dialogue (Carson, 1984). Children can also "try out" adult rituals by acting out various sorts of memorializing practices, as in one story about classmates who planted a tree in memory of their teacher's dead son (Simon, 1979). (Note that a child's beloved pet may present quite a different and much less "safe" situation than one arising from a strange, wild animal; see Butler & Lagoni, 1996; Tuzeo-Jarolmen, 2006; see also Focus On 10.1.)

An extensive body of death-related literature is now available to be read with or by children at all developmental and reading levels (see Appendix A and Appendix C; Arruda-Colli, Weaver, & Wiener, 2017; also Clement & Jamali, 2015; Corr, 2004a). For literature for parents, educators, and others who are helping children cope with death see Focus On 12.2, and in some areas, there may be workshops or college courses on issues related to children and death (Corr, 1984b, 1992b, 2002c). Ideas on how to use these resources are offered in Focus On 12.3. The underlying principle is that "any subject can be taught effectively in some intellectually honest form to any child at any stage of development" (Bruner, 1962, p. 33).

Effective education and prior preparation of all types depends on *effective communication.* Here, the central guideline is "take your cues from the children, answer what they want to know, what they are asking about, in their terms" (Bluebond-Langner, 1977, p. 64). Doka (1996a) suggested organizing one's approach around three questions: What does a child need to know?; What does a child want to know?; and What can a child understand? Each of these requires active listening, a process through which adults strive to grasp the real concerns of a child and to avoid responding with unnecessary, misleading, or unhelpful information. By employing language that is meaningful to children, one can minimize confusion of the sort generated by a priest in Agee's *A Death in the Family* (1969), who tried to

FOCUS ON 12.2

Selected Literature for Adults about Children and Death

Two wide-ranging resources for understanding and helping children in their encounters with death and bereavement are:

Corr, C. A., & Balk, D. C. (Eds.). (2010). *Children's Encounters with Death, Bereavement, and Coping*

Corr, C. A., & Corr, D. M. (Eds.). (1996). *Handbook of Childhood Death and Bereavement*

Books by six expert authors guide professionals in understanding and helping bereaved children are:

Christ, G. H. (2000). *Healing Children's Grief: Surviving a Parent's Death from Cancer*

Davies, B. (1999). *Shadows in the Sun: The Experiences of Sibling Bereavement in Childhood*

Silverman, P. R. (2000). *Never Too Young to Know: Death in Children's Lives*

Stokes, J. A. (2004). *Then, Now and Always—Supporting Children as They Journey through Grief: A Guide for Practitioners*

Webb, N. B. (Ed.). (2010). *Helping Bereaved Children: A Handbook for Practitioners (3rd ed.)*

Worden, J. W. (1996). *Children and Grief: When a Parent Dies*

Principles for helping children, a passage to be read with a child, and guidelines for responding to questions are offered in:

Grollman, E. A. (2011). *Talking About Death: A Dialogue Between Parent and Child (4th ed.)*

Five practical books offer useful advice for parents and other helpers:

Goldman, L. (2009). *Great Answers to Difficult Questions: What Children Need to Know*

Johnson, J. (2006). *Keys: To Helping Children Deal with Death and Grief*

Schaefer, D., & Lyons, C. (2010). *How Do We Tell The Children? A Step-by-Step Guide for Helping Children Two to Teen Cope When Someone Dies (4th ed.)*

Silverman, P. R., & Kelly, M. (2009). *A Parent's Guide to Raising Grieving Children: Rebuilding Your Family after the Death of a Loved One*

Trozzi, M., & Massimini, K. (1999). *Talking With Children about Loss: Words, Strategies, and Wisdom to Help Children Cope with Death, Divorce, and other Difficult Times*

Two useful booklets and four books address school-related issues:

Burns, D. M. (2014). *When Kids Are Grieving: Addressing Grief and Loss in School*

The Dougy Center. (1998). *Helping the Grieving Student: A Guide for Teachers*

The Dougy Center. (2003). *When Death Impacts Your School: A Guide for School Administrators*

Lerner, M. D., Volpe, J. S., & Lindell, B. (2003). *A Practical Guide for Crisis Response in Our Schools: A Comprehensive School Crisis Response Plan (5th ed.)*

Schonfeld, D. J., & Quackenbush, M. (2010). *The Grieving Student: A Teacher's Guide*

Stevenson, R. G. (Ed.). (2002). *What Will We Do? Preparing a School Community to Cope with Crises (2nd ed.)*

FOCUS ON 12.3

Some Guidelines for Adults in Using Death-Related Resources with Children

1. *Evaluate the book or other resource yourself before attempting to use it with a child.* No resource suits every reader, every child, or every purpose.

2. *Select resources, topics, and approaches that suit the needs of the individual child.* To be useful, any resource must meet the needs of a particular child.

3. *Be prepared to cope with limitations.* Every resource is likely to have both strengths and limitations. Adapt existing resources to individual purposes.

4. *Match materials to the capacities of the individual child.* Stories, pictures, music, play, drawing, and other options must suit the child's abilities. For example, in using literature, determine the child's reading or interest level. Direct a precocious child to more advanced materials; direct some older children to less challenging titles or invite them to join in partnership with an adult to assess the suitability of simpler materials for younger readers (Lamers, 1986, 1995) so that their abilities are not directly challenged by materials that are too difficult for them.

5. *Read or work along with children.* Seize opportunities for rewarding interactions and valuable "teachable moments" from which all can profit (Carson, 1984). Show interest in the child, provide interpretations as needed, and learn from the child.

explain that God had taken the children's father because he had had an "accident." The priest used this word to identify a fatal automobile mishap, but the children understood it to mean a loss of bladder control, and the adults never realized how foolish and perhaps frightening their message about God's responses to wetting your pants seemed to the children. Clear guidelines for notifying children of a death are important and helpful (Servaty-Seib, Peterson, & Spang, 2003).

Effective communication avoids euphemisms and inaccurate or inconsistent answers because they so easily lead children into misunderstandings that may be more disturbing than the real facts. Help in choosing the right words is provided by *What Does Dead Mean?: A Book for Young Children to Help Explain Death and Dying* (Jay & Thomas, 2012) and by *What Does that Mean? A Dictionary of Death, Dying and Grief Terms for Grieving Children and Those Who Love Them* (Smith & Johnson, 2006). Effective communication is also dependable: the child must be able to rely on what is said, even if it is not the whole of the available truth. Honesty encourages trust, the basis of all comforting relationships. Thus, it is better to admit what one does not know than to make up explanations that one really does not believe. After all, even good communication can be limited, fallible, and subject to error, as in the case of the children who were eager to attend a funeral to see the "polar bears" who would, so they thought they had heard, carry the casket (Corley, 1973; see also Brent, 1978). Although this piece of miscommunication is delightful in

some ways, it reminds us that children may not always correctly grasp what they are told. To minimize misunderstandings about death, adults should try to communicate effectively, and they should check to determine what a child has grasped by asking the child to explain what he or she understood from the message.

Adults must also consider that children communicate in many ways and at many levels (Kübler-Ross, 1983). They use: (1) symbolic nonverbal communication—which might take place through artwork of various types; (2) symbolic verbal communication—in which indirect comments about imaginary friends or anthropomorphized figures may really have to do with the child's own concerns; and (3) nonsymbolic verbal communication—which most resembles literal interchanges between adults. For example, during the last months before she died, one six-year-old child left notes hidden in various places acknowledging her awareness of the seriousness of her illness and expressing love for her parents and her sister (Desserich & Desserich, 2009). For children who lack many verbal skills, symbolic communication through art or other media may be a particularly important way of sharing deep-seated or emotionally charged concerns (Bonoti, Leondari, & Mastora, 2013; Furth, 1988). Thus, another six-year-old child drew a series of pictures of ships while he was dying—smaller and less colorful ships on a progressively darker background as the illness advanced (Grove, 1978).

Validation is a third important element of prior preparation, as well as of support for ill, dying, and bereaved children. This reflects an American-Indian belief that says: *If you give something a name and a shape, you can have power over it. However, if it remains nameless and shapeless, it will continue to have power over you.* Children who are trying to cope with death-related encounters need validation for their questions, concepts, language, and feelings. Adults can validate these and other aspects of children's death-related experiences by accepting them for what they are without judging them. Acknowledgment like this gives permission to explore what is confused and not yet well articulated. Such a process is empowering; correcting or "fixing" it is likely to be mistaken and harmful.

Helping Ill or Dying Children

The following principles for communication with ill or dying children provide a solid foundation for helping (Stevens, 1998):

1. First, determine the child's own perception of the situation, taking into account his or her developmental level and experience.
2. Understand the child's symbolic language.
3. Clarify reality and dispel fantasy.
4. Encourage expression of feelings.
5. Promote self-esteem through mastery of age-appropriate tasks and activities.
6. Make no assumptions about what the situation will entail; be open to what each encounter can teach; do not underestimate the child's ability to master life's challenges creatively and with humor and dignity.

Perhaps the best programs of care for ill and dying children (and their family members) are those that rely on *the principles of pediatric hospice or palliative care* as discussed in Chapter 8 in this book. The early impetus for the development of programs like these came from a project on home care for dying children and their families in Minnesota (Martinson, 1976) and the establishment of Helen House in Oxford, England (Worswick, 2000). In both cases, the emphasis was on a holistic program of child- and family-centered care (Davies & Howell, 1998). The Minnesota project demonstrated that for some children and families it was both feasible and desirable to take a child home to die. To do this, most families needed preparation for what they might expect to encounter, guidance on how to respond, and support to mobilize their own resources, as well as supplementary assistance to provide needed services. In a parallel way, Helen House confirmed the importance of skilled respite care for families facing the difficult challenges of one or more children with a chronic, life-limiting, or life-threatening illness. Each program involved recognition by parents of their need for pediatric palliative care, willingness to enter into such care, and evaluations of services received (Wolfe et al., 2000).

More recently, programs of **pediatric palliative and hospice care** have applied hospice principles to a wide variety of situations involving children with life-limiting or life-threatening conditions (Corr & Corr, 1985a, 1985b, 1985c, 1988, 1992b). This has been achieved in many different ways (e.g., at home, through respite care, or in a medical facility) and with various types of staffing (e.g., hospital, hospice, or home care personnel) (Davies, 1999; Himelstein, Hilden, Boldt, & Weissman, 2004). Applying these principles during pregnancy, at the time of birth (Sumner, Kavanaugh, & Moro, 2006) and in neonatal intensive care units (Siegel, 1982; Siegel et al.,

A hospice volunteer
visits an ill child.

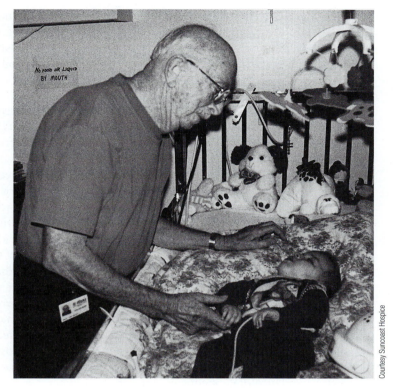

Courtesy Suncoast Hospice

1985; Whitfield et al., 1982), demonstrates that it is not the setting that is critical but the focus on holistic care for the ill child and on family-centered care for parents, siblings, and others who are involved.

The needs of children who are approaching the end of their lives and those of their families, have been well documented (e.g., American Academy of Pediatrics, 2000b; Field & Berhman, 2003). Children's Hospice International (Armstrong-Dailey & Zarbock, 2009) and NHPCO's ChiPPS project (Children's Project on Palliative/Hospice Services) have acted as advocates on behalf of these children and families. Training curricula have been published to prepare professionals for this work (Education Development Center, 2003; End-of-Life Nursing Education Consortium [ELNEC], 2003; NHPCO, 2003), along with a manual on how to develop a home-based support program for children and adolescents with life-threatening conditions (NHPCO, 2004). See also the Suggested Readings on this subject on p. 208 in Chapter 8 for some of the many books can guide both parents and professional providers in delivering this type of care. And many publications have focused on developing partnerships with ill children, good communication, attending to the preferences of children and their families, and the implementation of hospice-like principles in oncology and other forms of pediatric care (e.g., Hinds et al., 2005; Kaye, Friebert, & Baker, 2016; Solomon et al., 2005).

Ronald McDonald House programs in many communities offer a useful supplement to pediatric care services by providing economical, convenient, and hospitable lodgings for families while a child is receiving treatment in a pediatric medical facility. This service minimizes family disruption, reduces financial and logistical burdens (such as those involving travel, finding lodging, preparing food, and doing laundry), and permits constructive interactions (if not formal counseling) both within and among families who are facing difficult challenges in childhood illness.

Helping Bereaved Children

The task-based models described earlier for understanding bereaved children (Corr & Corr, 1998; Worden, 1996) provide a natural agenda for adults who are helping individual children. All bereaved children need information as a foundation for effective grief work (Goldman, 2006, 2014). They may need to know about death itself or about the facts surrounding a specific death, or they may need information about common reactions to loss or about coping with death and grief. Adults can provide such information and, in so doing, share their own grief and model good coping strategies (Zucker, 2009). Pediatricians, schools, religious institutions, and other community resources can also be helpful (e.g., AAP, 2000a; Fitzgerald, 2003; Schonfeld et al., 2016). Help is also available from the Coalition to Support Grieving Students. All who seek to help must—above all—try to view the loss from the child's perspective.

For example, adults often fail to appreciate the importance to a child of the death of a friend or pet, as discussed earlier in Chapter 10. Also, bereaved adults may all too easily overlook a child's grief on the death of a sibling. In each case, it is the relationship in all of its many dimensions—companion, buffer, protector, comforter—that is most important to a child. Adults do well to honor these losses rather than brush them aside as trivial. Respect for a child's experiences can be expressed in attention, honesty, avoidance of euphemisms, support, and (wherever possible) encouragement of the child's involvement in the death and subsequent memorialization.

In all deaths, good memories are as important to bereaved children as they are to adults (Christ, 2000). When possible, one should strive to lay down a fund of

A "teachable moment" can occur when a young child is allowed to take part in his grandmother's visitation.

Charles A. Corr

such memories before a loss or death occurs and help a child while someone else is dying (Smith, 2000). Even when that is not possible, as in cases of unanticipated death, an adult might work with a child after a death to develop and articulate the elements of a legacy that the child can carry forward into the future—for example, by examining a scrapbook or photo album depicting the life of the deceased or by sharing events from that life in which the child might not have participated. Helping bereaved children might also include assembling a memorial collage, donating to a worthy cause, or planting a living memorial.

In recent years, some have questioned whether children should take part in funeral and burial practices (Weller, Weller, Fristad, Cain, & Bowes, 1988). Comments like Grollman's (1967, p. 24) that "from approximately the age of seven, a child should be encouraged to attend a funeral" have wrongly led to views like those of Allison's father in the vignette near the beginning of this chapter that children under the age of seven should not be allowed to attend funerals. In fact, research (Fristad, Cerel, Goldman, Weller, & Weller, 2001; Silverman & Worden, 1992b; Søfting, Dyregrov, & Dyregrov, 2016) shows that taking part in bereavement rituals can help children cope more effectively with their losses and grief.

A basic rule is that no child should be forced to take part in any experience that will be harmful. However, harm need not occur when adults act on ideas suggested here: prior preparation, support during the event, and follow-up afterward. The child should be told ahead of time what will occur at the visitation, funeral, or burial; why we engage in these activities; and what his or her options are for participation. If the child chooses to take part in some or all of these activities, a caring adult should attend to his or her needs during the event. This adult must not be wholly absorbed in personal grief and must be free to accompany a child who might need to arrive late or leave early. After the event, adults should be available to discuss with the child his or her reactions or feelings, answer any questions that might arise, and share their own responses to what has taken place.

Concerns about disruptive behavior by children are no more unique to funerals and burials than they are to weddings. They can be addressed by providing a special time for children to come to the funeral home when adults are not present or by limiting the roles of the children at the event to those appropriate to their interest in and tolerance for public ritual. "The wise management of grief in children revolves around the encouragement and facilitation of the normal mourning process while preventing delayed and/or distorted grief responses" (Crase & Crase, 1976, p. 25).

Support groups for bereaved children can assist normal mourning processes after a death (Farber & Sabatino, 2007; Hughes, 1995). Two good models are: The Dougy Center: The National Center for Grieving Children and Families in the United States; and Winston's Wish in England. *The Dougy Center* (Chappell, 2001, 2008; Corr & the Staff of the Dougy Center, 1991), since 1982 has facilitated groups for children as young as ages 3–5 (Smith, 1991) and as old as 19, as well as programs for young adults, including groups focused on the death of a parent or caregiver; a brother, sister, or close friend; suicide; and homicide. It also offers concurrent groups for parents or other adult caregivers of the children being served. *Winston's Wish,* founded in 1992 (Stokes, 2004), offers a distinctive program of residential weekends (Stokes & Crossley, 1995), along with groups for families affected by suicide, services to schools, national training programs, an interactive website for adolescents, and a national helpline in England. Both programs offer helpful publications and other resources. (For additional activity books to help bereaved children, see Appendix C in this book.)

Allowing children to participate in a commemorative ritual—for instance, by releasing balloons in memory of someone who died (where that is allowed)—can assist them in their mourning.

Courtesy Suncoast Hospice

Both of these programs emphasize that grief is a natural reaction to loss—for children as well as for adults. Thus, both try not to stigmatize the bereaved children and adults whom they serve. Their goal is to offer supportive and preventive care. They honor the natural capacity to mourn in each individual and try to be available to each child and to trust his or her mourning process. Essentially, they walk alongside each child and uphold the vision that he or she will once again be able to find a way in life—even while remaining alert for signs of complicated grief and mourning processes.

Children may also be affected by traumatic death in the form of a homicide, suicide, or mass death caused by a natural disaster or some other form of violent or catastrophic event (Cohen, Mannarino, & Deblinger, 2006; Lareca, Silberman, Vernberg, & Roberts, 2002; Osofsky, 2004; Requarth, 2006). For example, the terrorist attacks on September 11, 2001, led professionals to observe the reactions of some very young children (Schechter, Coates, & First, 2002) and ways in which other children coped with their experiences through art (Goodman & Fahnestock, 2002).

When children are involved in traumatic events, it is often important to consider programs of **postvention**. This term, coined by Shneidman (1973b, 1981), was originally applied to interventions designed "to mollify the aftereffects of the event in a person who has attempted suicide, or to deal with the adverse effects on the survivor-victims of a person who has committed suicide" (1973b, p. 385). Postvention and other forms of assistance for children have since been expanded to apply to interventions before and after the fact that focus on children immediately or indirectly affected by a broad range of traumatic losses (Clements & Weisser, 2003; Goldman, 2001, 2004).

Principles for postvention with children include: (1) beginning the intervention as soon as possible; (2) implementing a comprehensive and coordinated plan involving affected persons and using relevant resources in the community; (3) providing supportive and caring assistance; (4) anticipating resistance or an unwillingness to cooperate from some persons; (5) expecting individual variations in the nature and timing of traumatic responses; (6) being alert for exaggerated responses that may place an individual's life or health in jeopardy; (7) identifying and changing potentially harmful aspects of the immediate environment; and (8) addressing long-term issues (Leenaars & Wenckstern, 1996). Ideally, postvention and all other programs of crisis intervention for children should be based on prior planning in schools and communities (Klicker, 2000; Lerner, Volpe, & Lindell, 2003; Rowling, 2003; Stevenson, 2002). Such programs should be led by a professional well-grounded in the principles of child development, in issues of coping with loss and grief, and in the special features of crises and trauma. Where group approaches are inappropriate or insufficient for a particular child, individual psychotherapy is indicated—even for a very young child (Lieberman, Compton, Van Horn, & Ippen, 2003; Webb, 2010).

Summary

In this chapter, we studied interactions between children and death in North American death systems. We described distinctive developmental tasks of childhood as background for exploring death-related experiences during childhood. In particular, we noted that death rates among infants and toddlers are high, while they are much lower in preschool and school-age children. We paid special attention to children's efforts to develop an understanding of the concept of death and its principal sub-concepts, as well as to the development of death-related attitudes in childhood. Next, we explored children's efforts to cope with life-threatening illness, dying, and bereavement. That led to describing both general suggestions and specific ideas about how to help children cope with death, dying, and bereavement. We also identified a number of useful resources for helping children cope with death.

Glossary

Animism: a view that attributes life and consciousness to objects usually thought of as inanimate

Artificialism: a view in which it is believed that all objects and events in the world have been manufactured to serve people

Causality: understanding events or conditions that do or can bring about the death of a living thing

Developmental eras in childhood: infancy, toddlerhood, early childhood (also called the play age or preschool period), and middle childhood (also called the school age or latency period)

Irreversibility: once a thing is dead, it cannot become alive again (barring miracles)

Magical thinking: a view in which all events are explained by the causal influence of various commands, intentions, and forces

Noncorporeal continuation: a view that some life form continues after the death of the physical body

Nonfunctionality: a dead body can no longer act in ways like a live body

Normative developmental tasks in childhood: to develop *trust* versus mistrust in infancy, *autonomy* versus shame and doubt in toddlerhood, *initiative* versus guilt in early childhood, and *industry* versus inferiority in middle childhood

Pediatric palliative and hospice care: the application of palliative and hospice principles to situations involving children and their family members

Postvention: after-the-fact interventions for individuals affected by traumatic loss

Stage-based theory of the development of children's understandings of death: according to Maria Nagy, in stage 1, there is no definitive death (i.e., death = a form of life = sleep or departure and living elsewhere); in stage 2, death is personified and contingent or avoidable; in stage 3, death is a process operating within us (i.e., the cessation of corporeal life = final and universal)

Sub-concepts involved in children's concepts of death: according to Mark Speece and Sandor Brent, these sub-concepts are universality (which itself encompasses all-inclusiveness, inevitability, and unpredictability), irreversibility, nonfunctionality, causality, and noncorporeal continuation

Universality: a sub-concept in which death is understood as applying to everyone, not to be avoided (all living things must eventually die), and nevertheless unable to be predicted as to its timing

Questions for Review and Discussion

1. The vignette near the beginning of this chapter depicted a father who did not respond in helpful ways to the death-related concerns of his daughter. How would you have responded or have wanted him to respond to those concerns?

2. Did you experience any death-related losses during your childhood? What did they mean to you?

3. Try to remember a time when you were a child and were seriously ill or experienced an important loss. What were your most significant concerns about that illness or loss? Or perhaps you know a child who has been in such a situation. If so, what were his or her most significant concerns?

4. If you were asked to suggest to adults how they could help children cope with death, what would you suggest? How would your recommendations differ (if at all) for different children or different losses?

5. Have you ever used social media or the Internet to learn more about helping children cope?

Suggested Readings

General resources on children and death include:

Adams, D. W., & Deveau, E. J. (Eds.). (1995). *Beyond the Innocence of Childhood* (3 vols.)

Corr, C. A., & Balk, D. C. (Eds.). (2010). *Children's Encounters with Death, Bereavement, and Coping*

Corr, C. A., & Corr, D. M. (Eds.). (1996). *Handbook of Childhood Death and Bereavement*

Concerning life-threatening illness in childhood, see the section on Pediatric Palliative and Hospice Care and the related Suggested Readings on that subject in Chapter 8, as well as:

Corr, C. A., & Corr, D. M. (Eds.). (1985a). *Hospice Approaches to Pediatric Care*

Sourkes, B. M. (1995). *Armfuls of Time: The Psychological Experience of the Child with a Life-Threatening Illness*

Zimmerman, J. (2005). *From the Heart of a Bear: True Stories of the Faith and Courage of Children Facing Life-Threatening Illness*

To understand bereavement and grief in childhood, consult:

Davies, B. (1999). *Shadows in the Sun: The Experiences of Sibling Bereavement in Childhood*

Doka, K. J. (Ed.). (1995). *Children Mourning, Mourning Children*

Doka, K. J. (Ed.). (2000). *Living with Grief: Children, Adolescents, and Loss*

Marshall, B. J., & Winokuer, H. R. (Eds.). (2017). *Sibling Loss across the Lifespan: Research, Practice and Personal Stories* (especially Part I)

McCoyd, J.L.M., & Walter, C. A. (2016). *Grief and Loss across the Lifespan: A Biopsychosocial Perspective* (2nd ed.; especially Chapters 3 & 4)

Rosengren, S., Miller, P. J., Gutierrez, I. T., Chow, P. I., Schein, S. S., & Anderson, K. N. (Eds.). (2014). *Children's Understanding of Death: Toward a Contextualized and Integrated Account*

Silverman, P. R. (2000). *Never Too Young to Know: Death in Children's Lives*

Sjöqvist, S. (Ed.). (2007). *Still Here with Me: Teenagers and Children on Losing a Parent*

Worden, J. W. (1996). *Children and Grief: When a Parent Dies.*

For helping children cope with loss and grief, see:

Christ, G. H. (2000). *Healing Children's Grief: Surviving a Parent's Death from Cancer*

Crenshaw, D. A. (Ed.). (2010). *Child and Adolescent Psychotherapy: Wounded Spirits and Healing Paths*

Emswiler, M. A., & Emswiler, J. P. (2000). *Guiding Your Child through Grief*

Fiorini, J. J., & Mullen, J. A. (2006). *Counseling Children and Adolescents through Grief and Loss*

Goldman, L. (2006). *Children Also Grieve: Talking about Death and Healing*

Goldman, L. (2009). *Great Answers to Difficult Questions: What Children Need to Know*

Goldman, L. (2014). *Life and Loss: A Guide to Help Grieving Children* (3rd ed.)

Grollman, E. A. (2011). *Talking about Death: A Dialogue between Parent and Child* (4th ed.)

Johnson, J. (2006). *Keys: To Helping Children Deal with Death and Grief*

Lowenstein, L. (2006). *Creative Interventions for Bereaved Children*

Marta, S. Y. (2003). *Healing the Hurt, Restoring the Hope: How to Guide Children and Teens through Times of Divorce, Death, and Crisis with the RAINBOWS Approach*

Monroe, B., & Kraus, F. (Eds.). (2010). *Brief Interventions with Bereaved Children* (2nd ed.)

Pomeroy, E. C., & Garcia, R. B. (2011). *Children and Loss: A Practical Handbook for Professionals*

Schaefer, D., & Lyons, C. (2010). *How Do We Tell the Children? A Step-by-Step Guide for Helping Children Two to Teen Cope When Someone Dies* (4th ed.)

Silverman, P. R., & Kelly, M. (2009). *A Parent's Guide to Raising Grieving Children: Rebuilding Your Family after the Death of a Loved One*

Smith, H. I. (2012). *When a Child You Love Is Grieving* (2nd ed.)

Stokes, J. A. (2004). *Then, Now and Always—Supporting Children as They Journey through Grief: A Guide for Practitioners*

Trozzi, M., & Massimini, K. (1999). *Talking with Children about Loss: Words, Strategies, and Wisdom to Help Children Cope with Death, Divorce, and Other Difficult Times*

Turner, M. (2006). *Talking with Children and Young People about Death and Dying* (2nd ed.)

Webb, N. B. (Ed.). (2015). *Play Therapy with Children in Crisis: Individual, Group, and Family Treatment* (4th ed.)

Webb, N. B. (Ed.). (2010). *Helping Bereaved Children: A Handbook for Practitioners* (3rd ed.)

For teaching children about death and other school-related issues, see:

Burns, D. M. (2014). When Kids Are Grieving: Addressing Grief and Loss in School

Clement, L. D., & Jamali, L. (Eds.). (2015). *Global Perspectives on Death in Children's Literature*

Deaton, R. L., & Berkan, W. A. (1995). *Planning and Managing Death Issues in the Schools: A Handbook*

The Dougy Center. (1998). *Helping the Grieving Student: A Guide for Teachers*

The Dougy Center. (2003). *When Death Impacts Your School: A Guide for School Administrators*

Gordon, A. K., & Klass, D. (1979). *They Need to Know: How to Teach Children about Death*

Klicker, R. L. (2000). *A Student Dies, A School Mourns: Dealing with Death and Loss in the School Community*

Lerner, M. D., Volpe, J. S., & Lindell, B. (2003). *A Practical Guide for Crisis Response in Our Schools: A Comprehensive School Crisis Response Plan* (5th ed.)

Schonfeld, D. J., & Quackenbush, M. (2010). *The Grieving Student: A Teacher's Guide*

Stevenson, R. G. (Ed.). (2002). *What Will We Do? Preparing a School Community to Cope with Crises* (2nd ed.)

Stevenson, R. G., & Stevenson, E. P. (Eds.). (1996b). *Teaching Students about Death: A Comprehensive Resource for Educators and Parents*

Selected Web Resources

Some useful search terms include: ANIMISM; ARTIFICIALISM; CAUSES OF DEATH IN CHILDHOOD; CHILDREN AND DEATH; COGNITIVE DEVELOPMENT; CONCEPTS OF DEATH; DEVELOPMENTAL ERAS OR TASKS IN CHILDHOOD; MAGICAL THINKING; NONCORPOREAL CONTINUATION; NONFUNCTIONALITY; PEDIATRIC HOSPICE OR PALLIATIVE CARE; POST-VENTION; TASKS IN MOURNING; UNDERSTANDINGS OF DEATH.

You can also visit the following organizational and other Internet sites:

American Academy of Pediatrics

American School Counselor Association

Association for the Care of Children's Health

Children's Hospice International

Children's Project on Palliative/Hospice Services (ChiPPS) of the National Hospice and Palliative Care Organization

Coalition to Support Grieving Students

National Alliance for Grieving Children

The Dougy Center: The National Center for Grieving Children and Families

The Initiative for Pediatric Palliative Care

Together for Short Lives

Winston's Wish

Ever Get A Pal Smashed?

TAKE THE KEYS.
CALL A CAB.
TAKE A STAND.

FRIENDS DON'T LET FRIENDS DRIVE DRUNK

U.S. Department of Transportation

Adolescents

Objectives of this Chapter

▸ To enhance our understanding of adolescents and their developmental tasks

▸ To describe typical encounters with death in the United States during adolescence

▸ To explore factors influencing death-related attitudes during adolescence

▸ To identify key issues for adolescents who are coping with life-threatening illness and dying

▸ To survey central issues for adolescents who are coping with bereavement and grief

▸ To examine issues concerning homicide and suicide among adolescents

▸ To establish principles for helping adolescents cope with death and bereavement

SOME HIGH SCHOOL STUDENTS ENCOUNTER DEATH AND GRIEF

That April was a tragic time at Central High School. On the third of the month, Tom Adkins and three other boys from Central were killed when a train hit their car at a railroad crossing. The engineer of the train reported that the car ignored the warning lights and drove around the crossing gates. Neither the train's whistle nor its emergency brakes had been able to prevent the high-speed crash. People said, "Isn't this awful! I can't believe this happened."

Two weeks later, two freshman girls at Central, Whitney Portman and Shawan Miller, were walking home when they found themselves in the middle of a gang fight. The territories of two youth gangs overlapped near the intersection where the two girls were crossing, and a dispute had developed over which group had "rights" to sell drugs on that corner. An exchange of insults led to some scuffling and a flare-up of tempers. Some members of one gang ran into a nearby house, got some weapons, and came out shooting. Whitney and Shawan were shot—two more victims of the neighborhood in which they lived. One girl died, the other was critically wounded. People said, "What can we do to stop this violence?"

Four days before the month ended, Anthony Ramirez, the senior cornerback on the football team, shot himself. Anthony was a good student who was well liked by his teachers and other students. He came from a close-knit, middle-class family, but that evening the rest of the family had gone to a basketball game in which Anthony's younger brother was playing. It was a bit unusual but not worrisome when Anthony chose to stay at home, saying that he had to study for a test. When the family came home they found Anthony in the garage lying in a pool of blood alongside his father's old shotgun, which he had used to end his life. There was no note.

The postmortem investigation revealed that many people were aware of some things that were going on in Anthony's life, but no one knew enough to grasp how badly he really felt. Some of Anthony's friends realized he would always laugh off inquiries about his feelings and keep people from getting to know the real person inside his popular image. Anthony's girlfriend admitted their relationship had recently ended, but said she had not realized how hard he had taken her rejection. Anthony's teachers and coaches talked about the pressures to excel that he always seemed to impose on himself; one recalled a long sullen period occasioned by what Anthony regarded as a bad grade. Anthony's parents and siblings spoke of their own recent preoccupations and wished they had realized how depressed he must have been. People said, "If only I had known."

THE DEFINITION AND INTERPRETATION OF ADOLESCENCE

In many societies, **adolescence** is an "in-between" or transitional period in human development between childhood and adulthood. At one time and perhaps still in some societies today, there was no such in-between period. Coming-of-age rituals marked a direct and relatively abrupt division between the era of childhood and the assumption of adult responsibilities (Ariès, 1962). By contrast, most modern societies have interposed a complex, evolving, and rather special developmental stage between the primary school years and full recognition of adult status.

The term *adolescence* derives a Latin root *(adolescentia)* that refers to the process or condition of growing up and designates a "youth" or person in the growing age (*Oxford English Dictionary*, 1989). In contemporary usage, an adolescent is someone who is no longer thought to be merely a child but who is not yet fully recognized as an adult. Thus, adolescents are normally expected to take on more advanced responsibilities than children and are usually accorded special privileges: educational programs for adolescents differ from those for children, and, as they mature, adolescents are ordinarily thought fit to take on work and wage-earning responsibilities, to qualify to drive a motor vehicle, to vote, to drink alcoholic beverages, and to get married (Arnett, 2000, 2007; Arnett & Tanner, 2006).

It is not accurate simply to equate adolescence with the teenage years. As we noted in Chapter 12, chronology on its own is not an accurate indicator of human developmental. In fact, most agree that the preteen phenomenon of puberty marks the beginning of the adolescent era. In adopting this marker, however, one must recognize three facts: individuals arrive at puberty at different times (with females typically becoming pubescent at an earlier age than males); puberty itself is more a series of related events than a single moment in time; and it is a historical reality that over the past 150 years the onset of puberty has come earlier in each generation (Kail & Cavanaugh, 2015; Newman & Newman, 2014).

The close of adolescence is less easily designated. In general, the principal developmental task of adolescence is the achievement of individuation and *the establishment of a more or less stable sense of personal identity* (see Table V.1). If so, then adolescence may end when an individual leaves home and his or her family of origin, takes up a career, or gets married. However, it is clear that some adolescents are deliberately choosing a slower path to adulthood for many reasons (Settersten & Ray, 2010). Also, the phenomena of leaving and returning home (perhaps repeatedly!) are now well known in our society and has led to what some call "boomerang kids in an accordion family" (Newman, 2012; see also Goldscheider & Goldscheider, 1999). These events clearly depend on a variety of individual, cultural, and economic factors, not development alone (Mortimer & Larson, 2002; Rathus, 2013). Thus, Conger and Peterson (1984, p. 82) aptly observed that adolescence is a physical, social, and emotional process that "begins in biology and ends in culture." Still, to speak too readily of the end of adolescence may be to focus solely on the negative or "closing off" side of the story without necessarily reflecting the positive development of *fidelity* or faithfulness—to self, to ideals, and to others—that Erikson (1963) proposed as the principal virtue to be achieved in adolescent development.

Apart from the definition of adolescence and despite the fact that it has been studied for many years (e.g., Hall, 1904), long-standing disagreements continue among scholars about how to interpret this era and how to characterize the adolescent experience (Bandura, 1980). For example, psychoanalytic perspectives have typically highlighted "storm and stress"—focusing on change, turbulence, and difficulties in adolescent life (see the right-hand image on p. 362). Anna Freud (1958, p. 275) even wrote, "To be normal during the adolescent period is by itself abnormal." By contrast, empirical research by Offer and his colleagues (e.g., Offer, 1969; Offer & Offer, 1975; Offer, Ostrov, & Howard, 1981; Offer, Ostrov, Howard, & Atkinson, 1988) has produced reports in which large numbers of adolescents from different cultures describe themselves as relatively untroubled, happy, and self-satisfied (see the left-hand image on p. 362). After reviewing available empirical research, Offer and Sabshin (1984, p. 101) observed that almost all researchers who have studied representative samples of adolescents "come to

Lawrence Shiles

To many adults, adolescents sometimes appear to be good "team players," but sometimes definitely not.

the conclusion that by and large good coping and a smooth transition into adulthood are much more typical than the opposite."

An evolving, transitional period in a life course such as adolescence clearly presents challenges to interpreters. Responses to these challenges color much that is said about the adolescent era. The danger is that adolescence is "the world's most perfect projective device for adults" (Offer et al., 1981, p. 121).

DEVELOPMENTAL TASKS IN EARLY, MIDDLE, AND LATE ADOLESCENCE

However one interprets adolescence as a whole, *three specific developmental subperiods* have been identified in this era: *early, middle,* and *late adolescence* (Blos, 1941, 1979; see Table 13.1). **Early adolescence** (beginning around age 10 or 11 for most individuals and lasting until around age 14) involves decreased identification with parents, increased affinity with peers, fascination with hero figures, and a growing interest in sexuality. Early adolescence usually centers on efforts to separate from dependency on parents in order to establish new personal ideals and interpersonal relationships.

Middle adolescence or "adolescence proper" (roughly ages 14–17) involves developing autonomy from parents, experimenting with "possible selves" or alternative self-concepts, and forging a distinctive, mature identity. Blos held that as middle adolescents strive to gain greater skill at being independent and self-governing, they experience a "second chance" or second individuation process. That is, middle adolescents can develop personal or individual resourcefulness by considerably reorganizing the values internalized from their parents, overcoming the egocentrism of childhood and early adolescence, and making choices about the roles and responsibilities they will assume in life.

Late adolescence (roughly ages 17–21 or 22) is ideally the era of stable character formation, achieved by meeting four distinct challenges: reaching closure in the

Table 13.1 Tasks and Conflicts for Adolescents by Maturational Phase

Phase I, Early Adolescence	Age	11–14
	Task	Emotional separation from parents
	Conflict	Separation (abandonment) vs. reunion (safety)
Phase II, Middle Adolescence	Age	14–17
	Task	Competency/mastery/control
	Conflict	Independence vs. dependence
Phase III, Late Adolescence	Age	17–21
	Task	Intimacy and commitment
	Conflict	Closeness vs. distance

Source: Based on Fleming and Adolph (1986, p. 103).

second individuation process, gaining personal strength by coping successfully with traumatic life events, forming historical continuity by accepting one's past and freeing oneself for growth and maturity, and resolving one's sexual identity.

This three-part framework can help us appreciate death-related experiences during adolescence.

ENCOUNTERS WITH DEATH DURING ADOLESCENCE

The National Center for Health Statistics (NCHS) publishes demographic data on numbers of deaths and death rates after early childhood in both 10-year age groupings (5–14 and 15–24 years of age) and 5-year age groupings (10–14, 15–19, and 20–24 years of age). Neither of these formats is consistent with our overall definition of adolescence or our understandings of its developmental sub-periods. Still, these data are all that we have available and they reveal many aspects of typical encounters with death during adolescence. In this chapter, we focus mostly on data related to individuals who are 10–14 and 15–19 years of age, but we also mention data for those who are 20–24 years of age.

Deaths and Death Rates among Adolescents

Adolescents between the ages of 10 and 19 made up approximately 13.1% of the total population of the United States in 2014; individuals between the ages of 20–24 years added just over 7.2% more. Numbers of *deaths of adolescents* in the same year are shown in Table 13.2. Together, these deaths represented a little over 1.2% of the more than 2.6 million deaths in the country that year. *Death rates* for these age groups in 2014 are given in Table 13.3. These rates are much lower than death rates for every other age group in the population except young children. In other words, as a group, adolescents die in fewer numbers and at lower rates than infants or adults in our society. Tables 13.2 and 13.3 also show

Table 13.2 Number of Deaths during Adolescence, by Age, Race or Hispanic Origin,[a] and Sex: United States, 2014

	10 to 14 Years			15 to 19 Years			20 to 24 Years		
	Both Sexes	Males	Females	Both Sexes	Males	Females	Both Sexes	Males	Females
All origins[b]	2,893	1,771	1,122	9,586	6,828	2,758	19,205	14,289	4,916
Caucasian Americans, total	2,070	1,266	804	6,954	4,867	2,087	13,806	10,174	3,632
Non-Hispanic Caucasian Americans	1,508	940	568	5,249	3,632	1,617	10,791	7,876	2,915
Hispanic Americans[c]	585	337	248	1,767	1,278	489	3,138	2,391	747
African Americans	667	411	256	2,165	1,668	497	4,437	3,390	1,047
Asian and Pacific Island Americans	109	71	38	282	172	110	561	436	125
American Indians and Alaska Natives	47	23	24	185	121	64	401	289	112

[a]Data for specified groups other than Caucasian Americans and African Americans should be interpreted with caution because of inconsistencies between reporting race and/or Hispanic origin on death certificates and on censuses and surveys.

[b]Figures for origin not stated are included in "All origins" but not distributed among specified origins.

[c]Includes all persons of Hispanic origin of any race.

Source: Kochanek et al., 2016.

that overall numbers of deaths and death rates increase with increasing age for all adolescents, regardless of gender, race, or ethnicity, especially as one moves beyond early adolescence to the middle and later years in this era.

Leading Causes of Death among Adolescents

The leading cause of death for all adolescent groupings in 2014 was accidents, as it has been for many years. Other leading causes of deaths included cancer, homicide, and suicide. Several things can be said about these leading causes of death during adolescence. First, the vast majority of all deaths among American adolescents between 10 and 24 years of age occurred from accidents, homicide, and suicide—and for that reason each played a role in the vignette near the beginning of this chapter.

Second, numbers of deaths from these three causes rose significantly in the transition from youngsters 10–14 years of age to those in the two older age groups. In fact, in both of these older age groups, accidents, homicide, and suicide led all other causes of death. The fact that human-induced causes should occupy all three leading positions in a ranking of causes of death is unique to these two age groups; for all other eras in human development, there is at least one disease-related or natural cause among the three leading causes of death.

Third, human-induced deaths, such as those involving accidents, homicide, and suicide, most often occur quickly and unexpectedly and are frequently associated with trauma or violence. Relatives and friends of adolescents who die in these ways

Table 13.3   Death Rates (per 100,000 in the specified population group) during Adolescence, by Age, Race or Hispanic Origin,[a] and Sex: United States, 2014

| | 10–14 Years | | | 15–19 Years | | | 20–24 Years | | |
	Both Sexes	Males	Females	Both Sexes	Males	Females	Both Sexes	Males	Females
All origins[b]	14.0	16.8	11.1	45.5	63.3	26.8	83.8	121.7	44.0
Caucasian Americans, total	13.2	15.8	10.5	43.5	59.3	26.8	80.4	115.3	43.6
Non-Hispanic Caucasian Americans	13.2	16.1	10.2	44.2	59.6	28.0	83.5	119.2	46.2
Hispanic Americans[c]	12.1	13.7	10.4	38.1	53.7	21.6	65.7	96.1	32.6
African Americans	19.8	24.0	15.4	62.3	94.4	29.1	114.1	172.3	54.5
Asian and Pacific Island Americans	8.8	11.4	6.2	23.1	27.9	18.3	38.4	58.8	17.4
American Indians and Alaska Natives	12.5	12.1	12.9	49.7	63.9	35.0	100.7	140.5	58.1

[a]Data for specified groups other than Caucasian Americans and African Americans should be interpreted with caution because of inconsistencies between reporting race and/or Hispanic origin on death certificates and on censuses and surveys.

[b]Figures for origin not stated are included in "All origins" but not distributed among specified origins.

[c]Includes all persons of Hispanic origin of any race.

Source: Kochanek et al., 2016.

are likely to perceive these deaths not only as untimely but also as shocking, like sudden and unanticipated disasters. Adolescents who encounter the death of a friend or classmate who dies suddenly will be affected in many ways as shown in a study of college nursing students when a classmate dies unexpectedly (Dorney, 2016). Some adolescents may encounter traumatic deaths or deaths that human beings cause or help to bring on themselves, which may have long-term implications for individuation and developmental tasks. For example, an adolescent's sense of competence and intimacy might be threatened by remorse arising from carelessness leading to an accidental death, anxiety from the homicidal death of a peer, or guilt from a perceived failure to save a friend from suicide.

Fourth, over two-thirds of all deaths from accidents among adolescents result from motor vehicle accidents. Such accidental deaths are typically perceived as preventable. For that reason, family members and friends often find themselves angry at the behaviors that led to such deaths and anguished over what might have been done to forestall such outcomes.

Fifth, in recent years, many deaths among late adolescents who are members of the military have taken place in connection with wars and conflicts as in Afghanistan, Iraq, and Syria. Often violent and sudden, deaths like these are difficult for their military peers, as well as for relatives and friends back home. Thus, on some evenings when *The PBS News Hour* shows photos in silence of these mostly young service people who have died, the experience for viewers is particularly poignant.

In summary, today adolescents in America and in many other developed societies are mostly healthy persons. Relative to other developmental groups, they enjoy very low death rates. The reason is that, as a group, adolescents have survived the hazards of birth, infancy, and early childhood, and they have not lived long enough to experience the degenerative diseases that are more characteristic of later adulthood.

Two Variables in Deaths of Adolescents: Gender and Race

Useful contrasts can be drawn among adolescents by gender and by race. Tables 13.2 and 13.3 show that adolescent males experienced more deaths and higher death rates than adolescent females in the United States for 2014. Essentially the same differences apply to accidental deaths, but the difference is significantly greater for deaths associated with either homicide or suicide.

When we compare adolescent deaths and death rates among various racial and cultural groups in our society, other important differences emerge (see Tables 13.2 and 13.3). For example, although there are many more deaths of Caucasian Americans in these age groups by contrast with deaths among African Americans, African-American adolescents died at far higher rates. Numbers of deaths in 2014 among younger adolescents (those 10–14 years of age) were much lower for American Indians and Alaska Natives, Asian and Pacific Island Americans, and Hispanic Americans. Death rates among younger adolescents were lowest for Asian and Pacific Island Americans, higher among American Indians and Alaska Natives, and for Caucasian Americans, but still not as high as those for African Americans. Caucasian-American adolescents are somewhat more likely to die in accidents or from suicide, whereas African-American adolescents are far more likely to die from homicide, diseases of the heart, and HIV infection.

Among all adolescents 15–19 years of age, males are over 2.5 times more likely to die than females (Table 13.2). Among non-Hispanic Caucasian Americans, this gender differential is less than 2:1, but it rises to over 3.5:1 among African Americans in this age group. Differences in death rates between Caucasian-American males and females are at ratios of nearly 3:1 for accidents, more than 4:1 for homicide, and almost 6:1 for suicide. By contrast, differences in death rates between African-American males and African-American females are at ratios of less than 2:1 for diseases of the heart, just over 2:1 for HIV infection, almost 4:1 for accidents, almost 8:1 for homicide, and more than 8:1 for suicide.

Deaths of Others Experienced by Adolescents

There are few reliable sources of data concerning *deaths of others that are experienced by adolescents*. One early study of more than 1,000 high school juniors and seniors reported that 90% of those students had experienced the death of someone they loved (Ewalt & Perkins, 1979). In nearly 40% of this sample, the loss involved the death of a friend or peer who was roughly their own age. The authors concluded that "adolescents have more experience with death and mourning than has been assumed" (p. 547). In 20% of the sample, the students had actually witnessed a death. A similar study found that when asked to identify their "most recent major loss," 1,139 late adolescent college and university students in New York State reported that the death of a loved one or a sudden death was the most common loss among a total of 46 different types of losses (LaGrand, 1981). In addition, Balk (1997, 2001, 2008) has shown that 22%–30% of all the college students he studied were grieving.

As well, Christ, Siegel, and Christ (2002) have pointed out that "In the United States, more than 2 million children and adolescents (3.4%) younger than 18 years have experienced the death of a parent." See, for example, the description one Canadian girl provides in Personal Insights 13.1 of her experiences after her father died when

---

PERSONAL INSIGHTS 13.1

Daddy's Girl

The year following my Dad's death was hard, but some things made it a little easier for me to handle. I started wearing his wedding ring on my neck. I thought that the kids at school would comment on it but they didn't. The stupid remarks I got were from adults: "Are you married?" or "You're too young to have a boyfriend!" It made me angry. It was obvious that none of those things were true and it was hurtful. I wanted to scream at them, to hurt them, but I kept my anger inside.

People who tried to relate to me because they thought they knew what I was going through were also difficult to deal with. "Oh, I know what you're going through." I didn't understand why they felt the need to relate to me. It hurt me more to keep bringing it up than not talking about it. I would have preferred a simple "I'm sorry about your Dad." I found myself appreciating and opening up more to the people who said things like that than the people who said stupid things.

I had some trouble at school in the month after it happened. A girl in my class accused me of lying to get attention when I told her my Dad had died. I tried to forget about it because I was so upset, but I just couldn't. It ended in a screaming match during a class when the teacher left the room and in the end, I got a very stiff and rehearsed apology. My friends noticed a change in me because I became quieter and kept to myself. I don't think they quite understood the magnitude of my experience, probably because I preferred to not share all of it with them. I found out who my true friends were during that first month: the ones that didn't question my behavior, were always willing to talk or just hang out if I wanted, or leave me alone, when I didn't.

I wouldn't say that I was depressed, just incredibly sad and grieved. Some days I would be happy, almost normal. Others I would just try to get through the day. Phrases like "What's wrong?" and "What do you want?" killed me. I wanted my Dad back and that was never going to happen.

There were also things that got me through this terrible time. I had great friends and family who were there for me to talk to anytime I wanted. At first, Mom and I had a hard time not fighting, because one of us would get upset about something, not say anything, and then explode about it days later. But we got better at it, became closer through all of this. I learned to cherish everything in life and not take friends or family for granted.

Grief is a journey. No matter how much time goes by, living in a world without Dad doesn't get any easier, the pain just gets easier to manage.

Source: Alexandra Hawkins. Used by permission.

she was 14. Clearly, it is not correct to think that modern adolescents have no experience with death and bereavement.

In addition, adolescents encounter deaths involving grandparents; neighbors, teachers, and other adults; siblings and friends; peers and slightly older youths in the military; pets and other animals; and celebrities and cultural heroes with whom they identify. Adolescence is also the first era in the human life course in which an individual can experience the death of his or her own offspring. Further, adolescents also report that they encounter a wide variety of painful loss-related experiences that do not involve death, such as the ending of friendships or loving relationships (LaGrand, 1981, 1986, 1988).

Many experiences with death and other losses may have special significance for an adolescent's developmental tasks. For example, early adolescents who are striving to achieve emotional emancipation from parents may experience complications in those efforts if a parent (or a grandparent to whom they are especially close or who is their surrogate parent) should suddenly die. Such an adolescent may feel abandoned by these adult deaths and may find it hard to attain a feeling of safety in these circumstances.

Similarly, middle adolescents who are seeking to achieve competency, mastery, and control at a time when they enjoy some sense of autonomy may experience a threat to their newfound independence if a friend or another member of their own generation should die (see Personal Insights 13.2). The likelihood that the death of another adolescent will be sudden, unexpected, traumatic, and often violent may enhance the threat to the surviving adolescent's own prospects and security. Adolescents who have carried over from childhood the "tattered cloak of immortality" (Gordon, 1986) or who maintain a "personal fable" (Elkind, 1967) of invulnerability may be shaken when confronted by the death of a person of their own age and similar circumstances (Noppe & Noppe, 2004).

Further, late adolescents who are working to reestablish intimacy and commitment with those who are significant in their lives may feel thwarted and frustrated when they encounter the death of a person of a younger generation—for example, a younger brother, sister, friend, or their own child. Dedicating themselves to a relationship with a person of this sort and achieving the closeness it can involve are stymied when the other person in the relationship dies. Such deaths may rebuff in a disturbing and disempowering way the older adolescent's efforts to reach out to others.

In addition, many adolescents were impacted by the events of September 11, 2001, and responded in their own unique ways (Noppe, Noppe, & Bartell, 2006). Also, adolescents are more likely than children to recognize and understand large-scale perils, such as global tensions: the threat or reality of war, and terrorism. As well, many adolescents are sensitive to: violence at home, in their schools and communities, and in the world at large; ongoing jeopardy associated with nuclear weapons; and problems involving the environment, such as acid rain, destruction of the world's rain forests, depletion of the ozone layer in the atmosphere, climatic warming, population growth, and waste disposal.

DEATH-RELATED ATTITUDES DURING ADOLESCENCE

Adolescents are diverse in many ways and death-related issues are also diverse. As a result, adolescents have many different death-related attitudes. Here are some key factors that influence those attitudes.

PERSONAL INSIGHTS 13.2

Who's Andrea?

The spring day dawned crisp and clear on the desert. A beautiful morning ... sun shining brightly, cheery children shouting and laughing as they bound toward school whilst slowly wakening commuters tap their fingers in rhythm to the FM beat, contemplating the successes of the impending day. It is February the third, a Wednesday, and a wonderful time to be alive.

It is also the anniversary of a devastating event in the life of Marsha, my wife, and I. An endless 2,192 days ago, we last hugged our daughter Virginia, an interminable 52,608 hours since we consoled her and swore that everything would be all right. A millennium since we felt her warm touch. When she died, a piece of us died with her. We will never forget her, even when it seems everyone else has.

On most occasions, when we seek to speak to her spirit, we visit the site of the accident that took her life. Today, however, our memories guide us to her resting-place, so that we may place a flower and reaffirm how much we still love and miss her. To speak through our hearts to a daughter who will forever remain 15 years old.

Her remains reside in a quiet, peaceful columbarium on church grounds that few others know about. It is the perfect foyer to heaven. But what is this? Another visitor has already been here, placed a flower, and left a note! Does someone else remember her? As we peer at the words on the tattered paper, authored by "Andrea," it seems as if God Himself has sensed our feelings of abandonment and sent the message.

As we journey home, one question continues to confound us; just who is Andrea? Neither of us can recall a friend of Virginia's named Andrea. Is Andrea really God incognito or simply a distraught young woman mourning the loss of her friend? One thing is for certain, Andrea, whoever she is, represents validation that Virginia made a difference while she lived on earth. She touched someone so deeply that even six years after her death she is remembered, mourned, missed and loved by someone other than her parents and family. It seems a fitting legacy to the days when she walked on the very ground that Andrea, the two of us, and the rest of humanity walk upon today.

Andrea's handwritten note:

Ginny,
I love-n-miss you very much and know someday we will see each other again.
Your always close in my mind-n-heart. With Love, Andrea.

Source: David Stanton (1999). Reprinted with permission.

Adolescent Understandings of Death

For *adolescent understandings of death*, researchers generally agree that, before or by the beginning of the adolescent era, individuals with normal cognitive development are capable of grasping the concept of death and its principal sub-concepts (see Chapter 12). Most adolescents in Western society are well into what Piaget and Inhelder (1958) called the period of formal operations, characterized by propositional and hypothetical-deductive thinking, generality of concepts, and an objective view of reality.

Still, it is not enough just to note that adolescents are *capable* of thinking in ways characteristic of adults. Noppe and Noppe (1991, 1996, 1997) suggested that **leading influences on adolescent understandings of death** may be ambiguities or tensions arising from biological, cognitive, social, and emotional factors. First, rapid *biological* maturation and sexual development is associated in many adolescents with an awareness of inevitable physical decline and ultimate death. This tension is represented in high-risk behaviors among many adolescents who seek to defy or "cheat" death. Although "the majority of adolescents engage in some risk-taking behavior but do not experience tragic consequences" (Gans, 1990, p. 17), this behavior is particularly hazardous in a world of high-powered automobiles, readily available drugs and firearms, eating disorders, binge drinking, and HIV. Adolescents conflicted by such challenges and possibilities may look fondly at what they seem to have lost in moving on from the more restricted, apparently simpler, world of childhood.

Second, as adolescents search for their own identity and reevaluate parental values, their newly developed *cognitive* capacities are challenged to take into account the inevitability of death. Thoughts about death in the abstract may or may not coexist with awareness of its personal significance for an individual adolescent. Looking bravely into what the future holds, adolescents may glimpse both positive and negative possibilities. In the end, they must come to appreciate that while there is much they can do to influence the shape of their futures, it is also true that many things are beyond their control.

Third, changing *social* relationships with family members and peers carry the potential for both enrichment and isolation. As their relationships enlarge in scope, especially by moving outside of their family of origin, adolescents seek to create a viable social life and to avoid a "social death." A new peer group offers a context in which an adolescent can find a new identity, but it also imposes scrutiny and its demands for conformity. This is further complicated when the chosen peer group is a gang that engages in violent behavior and strife with others. Also, in many adolescent peer groups, transient interpersonal difficulties can become sources of anguish and despair. For some, this may be compounded by moving into new academic and cultural settings and by specific ethnic influences that may encourage or inhibit certain kinds of public behaviors, such as the expression of grief and other reactions to loss.

Fourth, adolescent *feelings* about development and death are likely to be closely entwined. Achieving autonomy and individuation during the adolescent years is not only a matter of abandoning parent–child attachments begun in infancy. The real challenge for developing adolescents is to reformulate and make qualitative changes in such bonds, even as they develop new peer group attachments. This can involve threats to an adolescent's sense of self-esteem and purpose in life. Developmental feelings of loss and grief—the fear of losing oneself—coexist in many adolescents with feelings of being intensely alive.

Adolescent Involvements in the Digital World

The Internet is clearly a "significant aspect of the educational, social, and recreational experiences of adolescents" (Blais, Craig, Pepler, & Connolly, 2008, p. 535). Most adolescents are *digital natives*, by contrast with many of their parents and other

CREATISTA/Shutterstock.com

Adolescents are often more immersed in communications via the digital universe than in face-to-face contacts.

adults who are *digital immigrants* (Prensky, 2001). In ways not previously available, digital technologies shape adolescent attitudes by enabling them (and some younger children) to communicate with others, express and explore their own values and developing identities, and create new social communities.

Adolescent involvements in the digital world represent a very large and constantly evolving subject (Sofka, 2009; Sofka, Cupit, & Gilbert, 2012). At a minimum, the digital world gives access to a huge variety of information about death-related topics. More importantly, social media sites like Facebook make it possible for adolescents to share information about death-related events, express their grief, and seek grief support (Egnoto, Sirianni, Ortega, & Stefanone, 2014; Frost, 2014; Roberts, 2012; Williams & Merten, 2009). This is an important outlet, especially for adolescents and younger children who may not be ready to express their grief verbally in face-to-face interactions. Thus, one news report proclaimed "It's good for kids to tweet their grief" (Ridley, 2015; see also DeGroot, 2012).

Adolescents also use social media to stay connected to significant others who have died, often talking with them directly, and using this platform as an important tool in their coping (Williams & Merten, 2009). Too, online bereavement communities enable adolescents to offer condolences, share memories, and otherwise memorialize a person, friend, or pet who has died through grief-specific memorial sites or social networking sites. Online shrines and blogs can help to overcome the sense of isolation felt by many adolescents in their grief. (Look again at Figure 11.1 and note how its depiction of the use of digital and social media in bereavement is especially applicable to adolescents.)

However, not all Internet sites are benign. Some offer misinformation, others include hostile postings, some groups may encourage pathological behaviors, and cyber bullying is not unknown. Therefore, it is desirable to enter the digital world with some degree of prudence, to realize that privacy of personal information may not always be easy to achieve or maintain, and to monitor use of Internet resources. Some events or situations, like suicide, may call for special wariness against those who would post hurtful judgments and inflict pain. At the same time, when caring adolescents become aware of expressions of suicidal ideation and intent, as well as cries for help, they may be able to express empathy to individuals who need help, suggest referrals to suicide prevention hotlines, or direct peers to sites offering suicide prevention information and other helpful resources that can save lives. Various hand-held and other digital devices, like cell phones that allow both verbal communication and text messaging, and computers that enable e-mail and instant messaging, can also be used to share and in some cases obtain assistance in coping with death-related encounters and grief reactions.

Further, the entertainment media so prominent in the lives of many adolescents and preadolescents both influence and reflect their attitudes toward death (Strasburger, Jordan, & Donnerstein, 2012). For example, popular video games often involve animated simulations of violence and death. Historically, these depictions have largely been unrealistic, treating death "as both cheap and ephemeral," although some believe positive changes have occurred more recently (e.g., Robertson, 2014). Death-related themes are also prominent in movies and the fast-changing music scene familiar to most adolescents. For example, almost every adolescent can point to a song in one genre or another containing death-related themes and the website Songfacts has lists of songs about suicide and many other death-related topics. Death in many forms is widely present in the lyrics and other media directed to adolescents, even though some adolescents say they do not always listen to the lyrics so much as to the music itself.

Adolescents and the Personal Significance of Death

Another important point has to do with whether and how *the personal significance of death* is grasped by individual adolescents. This bears directly on an adolescent's sense of vulnerability or invulnerability. It particularly involves not merely surrogate experiences arising from various aspects of contemporary adolescent culture but also more critically *lessons learned—or not learned—by adolescents from their own life experiences* (Gutierrez & Park, 2015). The inability or unwillingness of many adolescents to recognize personal implications of mortality may have much to do with brain development during adolescence and implications for perception and judgment, the limits of adolescent life experiences, and the perspectives dominating much of adolescent life (Jensen & Nutt, 2015; Siegel, 2014). Thus, one analysis of driving patterns in middle and late adolescence identified two key factors: (1) adolescent drivers may simply not perceive risks inherent in their behaviors (such as the chance that an accident might occur or might result in serious consequences) and thus may inadvertently put themselves into situations fraught with danger and (2) adolescent drivers may perceive positive utility or value in taking certain risks, such as seizing control over one's life by acting independently, expressing opposition to adult authority and conventional society, coping with anxiety or frustration, or gaining acceptance from a peer group (Jonah, 1986; see also Carney, McGehee, Harland, Weiss, & Raby, 2015). Recall the vignette near the beginning of this chapter when Tom Adkins and his friends tried (unsuccessfully) to outrun a train with their car, and see Focus On 13.1.

Tolstoy captured the sense of invulnerability found in some adolescents in his classic novella *The Death of Ivan Ilych* (1884/1960, p. 131). As Ivan was dying in midlife, he thinks of his youth: "The syllogism he had learnt from Kiezewetter's Logic:

FOCUS ON 13.1

Skitching

A 15-year-old boy died on February 1, 2015. He was engaged in a practice called "skitching" (the word is a melding of "skating" + "hitching"). That is, he was holding onto the back of a car on a public street in order to pick up speed. An investigator later estimated the car was traveling between 20 and 25 mph.

The boy who died had apparently let go of the car before he lost control of his skateboard, wobbled, fell, and his head hit the pavement. He was not wearing a helmet. Bystanders performed CPR at the scene to no avail and the boy was pronounced dead at a local hospital within an hour.

The car, a Mercedes sedan owned by the driver's mother, was being driven by another 15-year-old who only had a learner's permit. That was illegal driving because state law only allowed anyone with a learner's permit to drive when accompanied by another licensed driver, 21 years or older, in the passenger seat. The two boys were apparently friends who had met earlier in the day at a nearby skate park. Police are consulting with the state attorney's office about potential charges against the driver and/or his parents.

The mother of the boy who died is reported to have said, "I never imagined him doing something like that. He was too bright for that. But he was 15, he was a teenager. He was adventurous.... One bad decision, one dumb decision, and it could take your life."

Grief counselors have been made available to students at the boy's high school, while his classmates and buddies have sought to share their memories and condolences with his mother.

Classmates said that because the city-owned skate park requires users to wear helmets, boarders will skate in the street instead, waiting for the "helmet guard" to leave at 5:30 p.m. so they can skate in the park helmet-free.

Based on: Sampson and Mettler (2015).

'Caius is a man, men are mortal, therefore Caius is mortal,' had always seemed to him correct as applied to Caius, but certainly not as applied to himself." In other words, mortality for the young Ivan Ilych was an abstraction, whose personal force and relevance to his own life became apparent to him only many years later as he was dying.

However, every adolescent is not indifferent to death-related threats. In one classic study (Alexander & Adlerstein, 1958), participants were asked to say the first word that came into their minds in response to a series of stimuli that included death-related words. Responses were measured in terms of the speed with which they were offered and by association with decreased galvanic skin resistance (increased perspiration or sweating). Participants aged 5–8 and 13–16 years had high death anxiety scores when compared with the scores of 9- to 12-year-olds. The researchers concluded that death has "a greater emotional significance for people with less stable ego self-pictures" (p. 175).

This suggests that death-related threats have greatest personal significance at times of transition in human development and, within adolescence, at times of decreased stability and self-confidence. That is consistent with a report that death anxiety is highest in teenagers and most closely associated with fears of loss of bodily integrity and decomposition (Thorson, Powell, & Samuel, 1998). Early adolescence for many is a time of little sense of futurity and a high degree of egocentrism (Elkind, 1967). Thus, a key variable in adolescent attitudes toward death may be the level of maturity the adolescent has achieved (Maurer, 1964); greater maturity being associated with "greater sophistication and acknowledgement of the inevitability of death as well as with enjoyment of life and altruistic concerns" (Raphael, 1983, p. 147).

In short, many adolescents tend to live in the moment and may not appreciate personal threats associated with death. The key issue for these adolescents may not simply be their capacity to think about death but rather ways in which the significance of death-related concepts is or is not related to their personal lives. This may not apply to adolescents who have broad and personal experiences with death, such as those who have learned important lessons from working as hospice volunteers (see Personal Insights 13.3). In general, however, most adolescents struggle to grasp the personal significance of death by confronting a paradox: they want to keep their feelings in perspective and distance themselves from intense death-related experiences, while at the same time they try to find meaning in abstract concepts of death by applying them in ways that have personal reference.

PERSONAL INSIGHTS 13.3

Two Experiences as a Teen Hospice Volunteer

In my first volunteer experience with hospice, I served as a teen mentor to a 12-year-old boy with a life-threatening illness. …This disease … limited his physical activity. As a teen mentor, I provided emotional support for this boy by helping him identify his other interests and by taking his mind off his illness. I visited him weekly and often assisted with homework, took him fishing, or simply talked with him about life. It was a truly incredible feeling to see him smile and to know that I made a difference in his life. Realizing that I contributed to the life of another, I gained a greater satisfaction with my own life, as well as a greater appreciation for its many gifts.…

One of the greatest challenges I encountered in my work with the terminally ill was through my unique friendship with a 107-year-old hospice patient named Joe and having that friendship come to an end in November 1998. It was indeed a challenge to grow close with Joe, knowing that our time together would be short. I overcame this challenge by focusing on Joe's life—a century of memories, history, and accomplishments. Each time I visited with Joe I was guaranteed to learn something new, whether it was a history lesson or a lesson on life. I felt that Joe, like all terminally ill patients, should live until he died, so I brought him lunch on occasion and shared pictures with him. When the time came for Joe to pass on, it was extremely difficult to focus on life amidst oxygen machines and tube feedings, yet I continued to hold his hand through it all. On one of Joe's last evenings, he told a friend and I that we were "the best gifts a man could ask for," and that he would never forget us. It was at that moment

(continues)

Two Experiences as a Teen Hospice Volunteer

that the familiar hospice message, "Every day is a gift," truly touched me. From Joe, I learned to cherish this gift of life and to help other hospice patients do the same by offering my compassion during the last stages of their lives.

Source: Copyright © 2000 by Education Development Center, Inc. Reprinted with permission. Corace, B., "End-of-Life Care: A Personal Reflection." In *Innovations in End-of-Life Care: Practical Strategies and International Perspectives*, Volume 2, M. Z. Solomon, A. L. Romer, K. S. Heller, and D. E. Weissman (Eds.). Larchmont, NY: Mary Ann Liebert Publishers, 2000, 81–82. This essay was originally published in Volume 2, Number 4, of the online version of *Innovations in End-of-Life Care* at www.edc.org/lastacts.

ADOLESCENTS WHO ARE COPING WITH LIFE-THREATENING ILLNESS AND DYING

Because dying and adolescence are both transitional experiences, Papadatou (1989, p. 28) wisely noted that "it could be argued that seriously ill adolescents experience a double crisis owing to their imminent death and their developmental age." Above all, dying adolescents need to live in the present, have the freedom to try out different ways of coping with illness-related challenges, and find meaning and purpose in both their lives and their deaths (Stevens & Dunsmore, 1996a). For most adolescents, effective coping with a life-threatening illness requires information about the disease, involvement in planning the treatment, and participation in decision making (Dunsmore & Quine, 1995; Freyer, 2004; Walter, Rosenberg, & Feudtner, 2013). A poignant example of what it is like when this does not happen appears in a study of attitudes and experiences of adolescents with HIV/AIDS, more than half of whom said that not being able to discuss their preferences was "a fate worse than death" (Garvie, He, Wang, D'Angelo, & Lyon, 2012), while in another study similar adolescents and family members found the experience of advance care planning to be "acceptable, worthwhile, and helpful with 99% attendance at all 3 sessions" (Dallas et al., 2016, p. 1).

The needs and reactions of adolescents with life-threatening illnesses have been summed up in a reminder that adolescents "are not so much afraid of death as of the dying" (Stevens & Dunsmore, 1996a, p. 109). Having a life-threatening illness challenges adolescents, leading to experiences of loss or alteration in such matters as: their sense of themselves as "pre-diagnosis persons"; body image; lifestyle (e.g., a perception of being in control and not unreasonably vulnerable may turn into one of vulnerability and being overprotected by others); everyday school activities; independence; relationships with parents, siblings, and friends; and a sense of certainty about the future.

In particular, Stevens and Dunsmore (1996a) observed that early adolescents with a life-threatening illness are likely to be especially concerned about physical appearance and mobility. They are also likely to rely on authority figures. Middle adolescents typically focus on what the illness will mean for their ability to attract a girlfriend or boyfriend, on emancipation from parents and authority figures, and on being rejected by peers. Late adolescents may be most concerned with how the illness will affect their lifestyle and their plans for a career and relationships.

Life-threatening diseases impact both the ill adolescent and others involved with that adolescent, as shown in a poem by an Australian adolescent who is reacting to

PERSONAL INSIGHTS 13.4

Only a Sibling

How do you tell someone you love
You don't want them to die
How can I try to be normal
I know I will cry

How do I cope with my anger
At life, at God and sometimes even at you
How can I put a smile on my face
While my insides are ripping in two

How can I tell you I'm frightened
Of the skeleton my brother's become
Tired and thin from your battle
A war that I'm scared cannot be won

How can I tell you I love you
When all our lives it's going unsaid
How do I stop you from drowning
When the water's already over my head

Every wince stabs me too, with pain
Why cannot I tell anyone how I feel
When I feel like I'm going insane

How can I think of my future
When it's possibly a future without you there
Why do I feel so damn helpless
And my problems too insignificant to share

How do I tell you, big brother
That I'm scared of what's happening to you
Why cannot anyone seem to understand
That your dying is killing me too.

Source: From "Only a Sibling," by Tammy McKenzie (nee McGowan),
CanTeen Newsletter. Copyright © 1992
CanTeen Australia Ltd. Reprinted with permission.

her brother's illness (Personal Insights 13.4). The challenge for both ill adolescents and those around them is to learn how to live with progressive, life-threatening diseases. This obligation places great demands on individual and familial resources and on communication processes within the family, especially when the dying trajectory is drawn out. Not surprisingly, adolescents often seek to play active roles in coping with the challenges they face (Dunsmore & Quine, 1995). Beyond good symptom management, adolescents need to be involved in their care and not be treated as younger children. For this, adolescents need to be given accurate information about their situation in a caring way and to be assured, in fact not just in words, that their views and concerns will be taken into account in deciding upon the interventions they are to receive and the ways in which those interventions will be delivered (Stevens & Dunsmore,

1996b). Most adolescents also need to live out their lives in their own ways and to maintain valued involvements with peers, school, and families—the ordinary milieu of adolescent life. Programs of pediatric palliative/hospice care for children and adolescents (see Chapters 8 and 12) can be very useful in this regard. Writing from that background, Rosenberg, Wolfe, Wiener, Lyon, and Feudtner (2016, p. E1; see also Lyon, Jacobs, Briggs, Yi, & Wang, 2013) argued that:

> In most cases, clinicians should gently but persistently engage adolescents directly in conversations about their disease prognosis and corresponding hopes, worries, and goals. These conversations need to occur multiple times, allowing significant time in each discussion for exploration of patient and family values. While truth-telling does not cause the types of harm that parents and clinicians may fear, discussing this kind of difficult news is almost always emotionally distressing....When done compassionately and respectfully, these conversations can have important implications for how patients live the end of their lives, how they die, and how their families and clinicians cope.

Papadatou (1989, p. 31) offered other advice for helpers in approaching adolescents and their families when they are coping with life-threatening illness: "We must also believe that we are not helpless or hopeless, but have something valuable to offer: an honest and meaningful relationship that provides the adolescent with a feeling that we are willing to share his journey through the remainder of his life."

ADOLESCENTS WHO ARE COPING WITH BEREAVEMENT AND GRIEF

As noted earlier, adolescents may experience bereavement through the deaths of many individuals whom they view as significant in their lives. In addition to family members, friends, and pets, almost every adolescent can identify a celebrity whom he or she idolizes and whose death would be a source of grief (Hall & Reid, 2009). Still, the most prominent feature in adolescent grief is reflected in the following article

Support from peers can often help adolescents when they are coping with loss and grief.

Meri Aaron Walker

title, "Adolescent grief: 'It never really hit me ... until it actually happened'" (Christ, Siegel, & Christ, 2002). Loss and grief are especially shocking within the vibrant, complex, and developing context of adolescence.

In the last three decades, a body of research has developed on adolescent bereavement (e.g., Balk, 1991a, 2014; Balk & Corr, 2001). Many studies have focused on adolescents who have encountered the deaths of a sibling or parent (e.g., Balk, 1991b; DeVita-Raeburn, 2004; Fleming & Balmer, 1996; Hyatt, 2015). Other research has considered the death of an adolescent's friend (Gootman, 2005; Oltjenbruns, 1996; Servaty-Seib, 2009; Servaty-Seib & Pistole, 2007) or pet, and experiences of bereaved adolescent parents (Barnickol, Fuller, & Shinners, 1986; Welch & Bergen, 2000), all of which can involve a close relationship and have a powerful impact on an adolescent.

Among the most prominent variables in adolescent bereavement are self-concept and developmental maturity. Thus, two studies of bereaved siblings reported that high *self-concept* scores correlated with lower intensity of grief, fear, loneliness, and confusion, while lower self-concept scores correlated with more of these difficulties (Balk, 1990; Hogan & Greenfield, 1991). An ongoing attachment to a deceased sibling was also identified in the lives of many bereaved adolescents (Hogan & DeSantis, 1992).

In terms of *developmental maturity*, a study of sibling bereavement among Canadian adolescents reported that while older bereaved adolescents experienced more psychological distress, younger bereaved adolescents experienced more physiological distress (Balmer, 1992). Increased psychological distress associated with greater developmental maturity was likely to be relatively transient, perhaps because these older adolescents (by contrast with their younger peers) were more likely to talk with friends about their bereavement and to find social support. Among other Canadian high school students, adolescents without religious beliefs and those with lower scores of perceived social support who experienced the death of a parent encountered more difficulties (Gray, 1987).

The important point to keep in mind is that "perhaps the most salient feature of adolescent adjustment following death is the *resiliency* evidenced by the bereaved participants in the face of traumatic loss" (Fleming & Balmer, 1996, p. 153; emphasis added). Similarly, research on bereaved college students showed that *hardiness* was inversely associated with grief misery, while closeness to the deceased was a significant predictor of *personal growth* because "the death loss of someone more central to one's life results in more introspection and more reorganization and/or restructuring of life values and priorities" (Mathews & Servaty-Seib, 2007, p. 199). In other words, bereavement during adolescence does not of itself predispose to ongoing psychological difficulties; it may actually help many adolescents to become more emotionally and interpersonally mature. However, bereavement may be problematic for vulnerable adolescents by reinforcing conditions they bring to their experience that predispose them to difficulties.

One special feature of adolescence is that "Adolescents are apt to think that they are the discoverers of deep and powerful feelings and that no one has ever loved as they love" (Jackson, 1984, p. 42). If so, adolescents may assume their grief is unique and incomprehensible—to themselves and to others. Thus, adolescents may only express their grief in short outbursts or may actively suppress it because they fear a loss of emotional control and do not want to be perceived by others as being out of control. Still, some bereaved adolescents can reach into themselves in powerful ways

A Hospice Teen Volunteer and the Death of Her Grandfather

My grandfather was diagnosed on January 13, 2000, with cancer of the colon, spleen, and lymph nodes. He died one month later on February 12. Needless to say, there was an extremely limited time period between his diagnosis and death in which we could prepare for the dreaded reality of the situation. However, since I have been trained as a hospice volunteer, I have learned that death can be approached as a celebration of life. I feel that I was able to celebrate my grandfather's life with him during the final moments that we did have together, and for that I am thankful. When I visited him two weeks before he died, Grandpa and I talked a lot, and I would simply sit by his bedside and hold his hand. Although it grew increasingly difficult for him to speak to us, he reminisced with me about a few of his early childhood memories and commented on the incredible change that has taken place in the morals and values from his generation to mine. He told me how proud he was of me and how he so hoped to know where Michael [her brother] and I would be going to college. Shortly after we had to go home ... he grew so weak that he could no longer talk on the phone with me. To make up for that lack of communication, I e-mailed my grandpa every day until he died. My grandma printed out each of the e-mails and read them to him in his bed. I told him how much I loved him, how proud I was to be his granddaughter, and how much he had taught me, growing up. Grandpa and I had been writing letters back and forth for the past ten years. I have kept each of his letters and put them into an album. I will forever cherish those precious letters, as they allow me to remember the special times and conversations I had with my grandfather.

Source: Copyright © 2000 by Education Development Center, Inc. Reprinted with permission. Tibbetts, E., "Learning to Value Every Moment." In *Innovations in End-of-Life Care: Practical Strategies and International Perspectives*, Volume 2, M. Z. Solomon, A. L. Romer, K. S. Heller, and D. E. Weissman (Eds.). Larchmont, NY: Mary Ann Liebert Publishers, 2001, 78–79. This essay was originally published in Volume 2, Number 4, of the online version of *Innovations in End-of-Life Care* at www.edc.org/lastacts.

to express their grief, as shown in the comments of one hospice teen volunteer about the death of her grandfather (see Personal Insights 13.5).

Bereaved adolescents can be helped in coping with their grief by activities that reduce stress (e.g., playing a musical instrument; see McFerran, Roberts, & O'Grady, 2010); their own personal belief systems; support from parents, other relatives, or friends; and professionals or mutual support groups who can normalize grief reactions (Balk, 1991c; Balk & Hogan, 1995; Hogan & DeSantis, 1994). Problems may arise as a result of ambivalent relationships with the deceased or with other survivors; a tendency of some adolescents to idealize the deceased, which may complicate mourning with guilt and self-blame; if society disenfranchises the relationship or the grief; the intense, if sometimes relatively transitory, quality of adolescent feelings; or the desire to fit in and not be different from peers.

As in coping with life-threatening illness and dying, adolescent bereavement involves a double crisis in which situational tasks overlay and in many respects parallel normal developmental tasks (Sugar, 1968). That is, for bereaved adolescents experiences involving protest or searching, disorganization, and reorganization (as described in Chapter 9) are often intertwined with normative developmental tasks of establishing emotional separation, achieving competency or mastery, and developing intimacy. According to Coleman's (1978) account of "focal theory"—which holds that most adolescents cope with stressors by concentrating on resolving one crisis at a time—the double crisis of adolescent bereavement (without further complications, such as a traumatic death, a suicide, or the death of one's own child) is especially challenging both for young copers and for their helpers, who may be trying to determine which aspects of adolescent coping emerge from development and which from bereavement (Corr, 2000).

Adolescent mourning is likely to be both continuous and intermittent, including, as it typically does, both grief that comes and goes and an overall mourning process that may involve an extended period of time (Hogan & DeSantis, 1992). As one adolescent whose father died when she was 14 titled her book, *Weird Is Normal When Teenagers Grieve* (Wheeler, 2010). Further, in personal relationships and in their social systems, adolescent bereavement is likely to involve secondary losses and incremental grief. Family dynamics and long-term consequences of death are important variables for adolescent development (Hogan & Balk, 1990; Lattanzi-Licht, 1996; Martinson, Davies, & McClowry, 1987).

ADOLESCENTS, HOMICIDE, AND SUICIDE

Two subjects that deserve special attention during the adolescent era are the human-induced deaths resulting from homicide and suicide.

Homicide and Adolescents

Following accidents, homicide is the second leading cause of death among adolescents in the United States, one that has been increasing in relative significance in recent years and shows significant gender and ethnic differences. In 2014, homicide was only the seventeenth leading cause of death for the population as a whole, but it remained the third leading cause of death for middle and late adolescents, resulting in 4,171 homicide deaths among individuals 15–24 years of age—almost 26% of all homicide deaths in the entire country that year in a group that represented only about 13.8% of the total population. The homicide death rate in this age group was 9.5 per 100,000.

From 1960 to 1990, the United States experienced a tripling or quadrupling of homicide rates among middle and late adolescents overall. Also, homicide rates were significantly higher for male adolescents as contrasted with females and for African-Americans as contrasted with Caucasian-Americans. Much of this was still true in 2014. Like suicide, *homicide deaths among adolescents are far more a male than a female phenomenon*—by a ratio of more than 8:1. Unlike suicide, *homicide death rates are far more an experience of African-Americans than Caucasian-Americans*, by a ratio of nearly 8:1 (Heron, 2016).

Since 1991, U.S. homicide deaths have declined for the population as a whole (see Chapter 4). Yet, in 2014, homicide remained the leading cause of death for

African-American males 15–24 years of age and the second leading cause of death for same-age African-American females. Youth homicide rates have long been higher in the United States than in any other country in the world (Fingerhut & Kleinman, 1989).

Homicide among adolescents is complex in both its implications and its origins (Busch, Zagar, Hughes, Arbit, & Bussell, 1990). It directly affects the people who are killed or injured, the *primary victims* like the two girls in the vignette near the beginning of this chapter, but it also can have negative effects on a broad range of *secondary victims*, such as relatives, friends, witnesses of such violence, and even those who perpetrate homicides. This may be especially significant for the individuation and developmental tasks of surviving adolescents.

In the United States, homicide typically involves firearms (Fingerhut, Kleinman, Godfrey, & Rosenberg, 1991) and is especially (although not exclusively) prevalent in urban settings, with most perpetrators and victims likely coming from the same ethnic or racial background (Ropp, Visintainer, Uman, & Treloar, 1992). In short, homicide involving adolescents is basically an extreme form of violence undertaken or experienced by adolescents in their own homes, schools, or communities (U.S. Department of Health and Human Services, 2001). Dysfunctional home environments along with violent communities beset by gang and drug-induced criminal activities are settings of real and chronic danger for many poor urban youth in American society. Declining rates of both homicide and suicide during a time when restrictive licensing of handguns was enforced in the District of Columbia revealed the interplay between homicide and social structure (Loftin, McDowall, Wiersema, & Cottey, 1991).

Adolescent homicide involving middle-class, socially advantaged, suburban, Caucasian-Americans (including females) has recently been brought to public attention by media coverage of school shootings in our society, especially through some widely publicized shootings at schools (Nader, 2011; see also Issues for Critical Reflection #6 in Chapter 4). In fact, events like these are relatively rare and do not negate the fact that schools are among the safest places for children in our society as shown by official U.S. government reports (e.g., Robers, Zhang, Morgan, & Musu-Gillette, 2015). However, the existence of school-related violence and death does point out that even in such settings, death can intrude in ugly ways.

In the end, it is urban, African-American and Hispanic-American males who are most at risk for becoming perpetrators or victims of adolescent homicide. Thus, "Youth homicide most often involves poverty and the apparently related interpersonal, domestic, and gang-related violence; victims and perpetrators share similar characteristics. Character disorders (e.g., impulse control, sociopathic problems) appear common to both victims and perpetrators of youth homicide" (Holinger, Offer, Barter, & Bell, 1994, p. 182). Above all, adolescent homicide typically occurs in contexts of peer and social influence (Barrett, 1996). Violent adults often act alone; violent adolescents usually act in groups. In some adolescent peer groups, violent behavior seems to be accepted, encouraged, and even regarded as a kind of rite of passage into the group (see Issues for Critical Reflection #11).

Some have argued that adolescent homicide should be regarded not principally as a criminal justice issue but rather as *a public health crisis* (e.g., Fingerhut & Kleinman, 1989). Explanations include the disputed claim that there is a subculture within some African-American ghetto communities that models and sanctions violence; "black rage" theories that violence results from an inadequate ability on the part of younger, nonwhite males to control impulses and cope with anger arising from

ISSUES FOR CRITICAL REFLECTION
#11 Youth Gangs

For some adolescents and young adults, youth gangs can represent a particularly lethal situation. However, many scholars suggest some degree of uncertainty as to just how significant the role of gangs is in the lives of most adolescents. Thus, although youth gangs get much media attention, there are some disagreements among different legal jurisdictions as to just what constitutes a "gang." Further, media report that some local law enforcement agencies and researchers are hesitant to use the "gang" label since it can so easily be applied to groups and individuals, can create bias and animosity, and is difficult to shed (Sullivan, 2015). Also, avoiding the label denies gangs the attention they seek. In any event, the National Gang Center provides information and resources for parents and communities, while the National Gang Intelligence Center (NGIC) integrates the intelligence assets of federal, state, and local law enforcement agencies to serve as a centralized resource for gang information and analysis. For example, the *2013 National Gang Report* from the NGIC distinguishes between: (1) street gangs—either neighborhood-based gangs or national street gangs, which together comprise 88% of all gang members; (2) prison gangs—9.5% of all gang members; and (3) outlaw motorcycle gangs—2.5% of all gang members, although this last group is thought to pose the greatest threat to society. Among these different types of gangs, there are female participants and members even within many male-dominant gangs, as well as some all-female gangs.

Gangs of different types typically rely on street-level drug distribution and gun trafficking as their primary sources of revenue, although many supplement their income with less risky crimes, such as prostitution and extortion. Some gangs commit violent crimes, including assaults, robberies, and intimidation. In recent years, most gangs have increasingly employed technology and social media to communicate covertly, conduct criminal operations with minimal risk of detection, intimidate others, and recruit new members. Gangs have also increasingly used firearms to achieve their goals.

Among different types of gangs, neighborhood-based gangs (NBGs) of the type that have been linked to crime in elementary, secondary, and high schools, and on select college campuses seem to be most significant for adolescents and young adults. Membership in NBGs waxes and wanes, with new members joining and existing members drifting away over time. Individuals appear to join NBGs for many different reasons, such as personal concerns or family and community issues. For example, scholars say that youth get "pulled" into a gang as a way of gaining gain money, power, recognition, or excitement, or because they believe gang membership is a good way to show family, neighborhood, or cultural pride. Conversely, some youth get "pushed" into a gang because of pressure from peers or fears for their safety thinking a gang will protect them from neighborhood crime and violence. Lack of protection, affirmation, and discipline from a stable family structure, as well as problems in school can also motivate a young person to join a gang. One consistent finding is that the largest numbers of gang members are found in poor, urban areas, many of which are African-American and Hispanic-American communities.

With these facts in mind, please reflect on questions like the following: Have you had contact with or been a member of a gang in your community? If so, what were those experiences like? Are NBGs prevalent in your community? If so, what do you think about the prevalence of gang activities in your community? What do you think might or should be done about gang activities in your community or in society at large by way of prevention or mitigation?

economic deprivation, poverty, and discrimination; the ready availability of alcohol, drugs, and cheap handguns in America; and the failures of many social institutions, often coupled with what appears to be a lack of interest in or a punitive attitude toward "difficult" adolescents (Barrett, 1996).

Clearly, American society and its death system need to reduce levels of violence among adolescents and to bring down both the number and rate of homicide deaths in this group. No simple solution is likely (Prothrow-Stith & Spivak, 2004), although Holinger and colleagues (1994) offered four recommendations: (1) gun control to limit the ready availability of firearms; (2) public education concerning the origins of these behaviors, together with what is already known about treatment and prevention strategies; (3) better training of professionals; and (4) more and better research on etiology and treatment.

Suicide and Adolescents

Suicidal behavior among adolescents has attracted long-standing attention (e.g., Lester, 1993; Peck, Farberow, & Litman, 1985; Stillion & McDowell, 1996) for two primary reasons: (1) to many, adolescence seems to be a healthy and productive era during which the individual evolves from child to adult and finds important openings to the future and (2) from 1960 to 1990, suicide rates among middle and late adolescents increased significantly—more rapidly than for any other age cohort (Maris, 1985).

In 2014, suicide was the cause of death of 1834 persons between 15 and 19 years of age and 3245 persons between 20 and 24 years of age (Heron, 2016). There also were 425 deaths during the same year that were identified as caused by suicide in early adolescents 10–14 years of age. In terms of death rates, there were increases from 2.1 per 100,000, to 8.7, to 14.2 from the youngest to the oldest of these three age groups (see Table 17.1). Clearly, there is ample reason for concern about youth suicide.

Adolescent suicidal behavior shows a major gender contrast in suicide attempts versus completions. Reliable estimates are that females attempt suicide at a ratio of about 3:1 by comparison with males, whereas males complete suicide at a ratio of more than 4.1 versus females. These and other disparities in adolescent suicidal behavior—for example, in middle versus late adolescents and in Caucasian-American versus African-American adolescents—suggest we have much to learn about their underlying dynamics.

It may seem paradoxical that self-inflicted death should be the second leading cause of death among middle and late adolescents during a developmental era often perceived by outsiders to be satisfying and promising. In fact, as we saw in the example of Anthony Ramirez in our vignette near the beginning of this chapter, suicide is often chosen by adolescents who do not share that rosy view of their situation, are overburdened by stresses, are unable to identify constructive options to resolve their problems, or are depressed that life is good and promising for others.

Suicidal behavior in adolescents and others often arises from many factors. Therefore, one should not oversimplify the situation of adolescents who attempt actions that may end their lives. Still, major variables in adolescents at risk for suicide include inadequacies or alterations in relationships between them and significant others; pressures to conform to peers; inexperience in coping with problems; and dysfunctional behavior. These factors are all associated with ineffective communication, inadequate coping skills, and the specific problems of developing adolescents. In addition, there is evidence to support the claim that gay and lesbian youth are at high risk for suicidal behavior for many reasons, including the attitudes of many members of our society toward homosexual persons (Gibson, 1994). Overall, adolescents "who experience a wide gulf between who they are and who they want to become are at risk for low self-concepts, self-hatred, depression, and suicidal behavior" (Stillion, McDowell, & May, 1989, p. 194). Such adolescents may be unable to express their needs, solve their personal problems, or obtain the assistance they require.

A depressed teen holds a handgun.

Sascha Burkard/Shutterstock.com

Adolescents who can neither resolve their problems nor put them into a larger perspective can become isolated, depressed, and may become desperate (Cobain, 2007). Self-destruction may appear to them to be their only available option. *Most often, this does not reflect a wish to be dead.* In fact, like others, many suicidal adolescents are ambivalent in their feelings about life and death and may be unclear about the personal finality of death. What may be most significant in such adolescents is their *overpowering urge to escape from a stressful life situation* (Berman, Jobes, & Silverman, 2006).

Adolescents who are ambivalent about ending their lives often attempt to communicate their need for help in some way or other, for example, by beginning to give away cherished possessions or speaking vaguely about how things would be better if they were no longer around. But these may not be very effective ways of getting across the desired message since the ability to communicate effectively is directly related to an ability to cope with problems. An adolescent who can describe his or her problems to others has usually made an important step toward managing them. Also, those to whom an adolescent tries to communicate his or her feelings may not recognize such messages as cries for help because the particular message may be obscure and many adolescent communications are exaggerated, or because those who are living healthful lives may be unable or unwilling to grasp the desperation associated with the message.

Even when outsiders cannot prevent adolescents from attempting or completing suicide, much can be done to minimize the likelihood of such behaviors. Efforts to increase self-esteem, foster the ability to make sound decisions, and enhance constructive coping skills in adolescents are all desirable. School-based education and intervention programs for teachers, counselors, parents, and adolescents are designed to teach about warning signs of suicide and practical strategies for offering help, such as peer counseling and crisis intervention (Leenaars & Wenckstern, 1991; Poland, 1989; Stevenson, 2002). The individuals to whom they are addressed are ideally positioned to identify and assist adolescents who might engage in suicidal behavior.

Some have been concerned that education about suicide may produce the very behaviors it is designed to minimize. This is one version of the so-called "contagion theory," whereby it is thought that mentioning suicide is likely to infect the hearer with a tendency to engage in this behavior. There is no clear evidence to support these views. However, in recent years, this concern has been associated with "cluster" or "copycat" suicides—that is, situations in which the example of others or reports in the media seem to have established models for troubled youth (Gould, Kleinman, Lake, Forman, & Midle, 2014). Thus, a large-scale Canadian study (Swanson & Colman, 2013) concluded that "Exposure to suicide [especially via a schoolmate's suicide or by personally knowing someone who died by suicide] predicts suicide ideation and attempt" (p. 870; see also Chapter 17 in this book).

What is dangerous for adolescents is not knowledge about suicide or about the suicidal behavior of others but anything they might perceive as giving approval to life-threatening behaviors (Berman, 1988; Davidson & Gould, 1989). This danger is not found in education that is frank about the negative consequences of suicidal behavior and which teaches adolescents that *suicide is a permanent solution to a temporary problem*. Effective education about suicide mobilizes resources for resolving problems in other ways and directs attention to the great pain that is a widespread legacy of adolescent suicide. Talking about suicide in a constructive educational format is far more likely to clear the air and minimize suicidal behavior than to suggest or encourage such behavior (Stillion & McDowell, 1996).

Crisis intervention programs offer a useful model of intervention to minimize suicidal behaviors in adolescents and others (Hatton & Valente, 1984). Such programs are directed precisely at those who are ambivalent about ending their lives. They encourage such persons to initiate telephone contact with the helping agency. Many of the volunteers who respond to such contacts are themselves adolescents who have been selected, trained, supervised, and supported in such work (Valente & Saunders, 1987). These volunteers offer a caring presence, an attentive companion during what is most often a limited period of crisis, a helper who can evaluate needs and aid in identifying alternative strategies for resolving problems, and a guide to additional resources for further assistance.

One area of adolescent suicide that is not well understood has to do with those who are left behind when someone completes a suicide. Grief following the suicide of an adolescent is likely to be intense. This applies to all who are so bereaved but especially to adolescent peers: "Adolescent suicide is a particularly toxic form of death for peers who are left behind" (Mauk & Weber, 1991, p. 115). Adolescent peer bereavement is frequently complicated by feelings of guilt, rejection, frustration, anger, and failure. It is also often overlaid by societal disapproval, labeling, and stigma—all of which add to the burdens of grief and mourning. Adolescents in such situations deserve sensitivity, care, and support in their bereavement. They should also be helped to celebrate and commemorate the life of their deceased friend. **Postvention** programs, designed to address the specific needs of early and middle adolescents (Hill & Foster, 1996) or later adolescents in college settings (Rickgarn, 1994, 1996), are useful both as interventions after a suicide or other traumatic death and as forward-looking preventive efforts designed to minimize self-destructive behavior in the future.

HELPING ADOLESCENTS COPE WITH DEATH AND BEREAVEMENT

Adolescents can be helped in their efforts to cope with death through education and preparation prior to the fact (both while they are adolescents and in their earlier childhood) and through support and constructive intervention at the time of and after a death.

Education and Prior Preparation

Parents and other adults influence adolescent coping with death by laying down solid foundations in childhood and by creating many of the social contexts in which adolescents live and function. Open lines of communication, sharing of thoughts and feelings, role modeling, and other constructive socialization processes enable adolescents to feel secure in themselves and find satisfaction in the rewards of living, even as they also take account of issues related to loss and death.

McNeil (1986) suggested six guidelines for adult communications with adolescents about death:

1. Take the lead in heightened awareness of an adolescent's concerns about death and in openness to discussing whatever he or she wishes to explore.
2. Listen actively and perceptively, with special attention to the feelings that appear to underlie what the adolescent is saying.
3. Accept the adolescent's feelings as real, important, and normal.
4. Use supportive responses that reflect acceptance and understanding of what the adolescent is trying to say.
5. Project a belief in the worth of the adolescent by resisting the temptation to solve his or her problems and by conveying an effort to help the adolescent find his or her own solutions.
6. Take time to enjoy the company of the adolescent and to provide frequent opportunities for talking together.

Communications of this sort can be supplemented by proactive programs of death education in secondary schools (e.g., Crase & Crase, 1984; Rosenthal, 1986; Stevenson & Stevenson, 1996a) and at the college level (e.g., Corr, 1978). An extensive body of death-related literature is designed for and can be helpful to middle school, high school, and other young readers (see Appendix B in this book; see also Lamers, 1986). Also, principles set forth in literature for adults about children and death (as suggested in Chapter 12) may be relevant to adolescents with suitable modifications. Moreover, there now is ample literature for professionals that deals directly with adolescents and death (e.g., Balk & Corr, 2009; Corr & Balk, 1996). All programs of education and support for adolescents must pay careful attention to the goals that one seeks to achieve and to the needs and experiences of adolescents. In designing a death-related course for adolescents, Rosenthal (1986) advised educators to make decisions about possible topics, objectives, materials, methods, and evaluation procedures in terms of three primary aspects: information, self-awareness, and skills for helping. The important thing is to reach out and make constructive contacts with vulnerable adolescents before they become isolated and alienated.

Support and Assistance after a Death

When a death occurs, something important has happened. The challenge to adults, then, is to initiate a constructive program that helps bereaved adolescents obtain accurate information about the loss and begin the process of interpreting and integrating that loss into their ongoing lives. Such a program should help bereaved adolescents identify emotional and other responses to a death, express their feelings in safe and manageable ways, find their own ways of coping, take active roles in funeral practices, commemorate losses in constructive ways, and find ways to go on with healthy and productive living (Fitzgerald, 2000). Activity workbooks and journaling projects may be useful, either as adjuncts to other interventions or for adolescents who are most comfortable addressing their grief in private ways (e.g., Barber, 2003; see also Appendix C in this book).

Counseling interventions with adolescents should be guided by two principles: (1) provide a safe environment in which the adolescent can explore difficulties and (2) assist with the process of addressing the developmental and situational tasks that are often closely interrelated in adolescent bereavement (Calvin & Smith, 1986). The second principle means that it must be the adolescent, not the counselor, who works out acceptable solutions to challenges in his or her own life. Educators can assist when they themselves understand the nature of bereavement, grief, and mourning. Research showing that "bereaved college students are at risk for decreased academic performance ... academic difficulties that may result in attrition" (Servaty-Seib & Hamilton, 2006, pp. 230 & 233) reinforces guidance for counselors offered by a number of authors (Balk, 1984; Cohen, Mannarino, & Deblinger, 2006; Fitzgerald, 2003; Zinner, 1985). Programs of *postvention* (described in Chapter 12 for children) have been developed for adolescents at both the secondary (Hill & Foster, 1996) and postsecondary (Lerner, Volpe, & Lindell, 2004; Rickgarn, 1994, 1996) levels.

Adolescents who are unwilling to talk to parents, counselors, or other adults may find it more congenial to address their death-related concerns in the context of a support group populated by peers with similar experiences (Tedeschi, 1996). By establishing a community of bereaved peers, groups of this sort dispel the stigma of being "different" or marked out by a death. This overcoming of isolation from others is important in all bereavement, but especially so in a developmental era like adolescence, in which struggles with identity and the need for peer validation is so characteristic. Support groups can provide important information to bereaved adolescents, offer help with tensions involving containing and expressing emotions, assist in confronting life's hard lessons, and confirm the fundamental message that it is only natural to experience grief in connection with a significant loss (see Personal Insights 13.6).

PERSONAL INSIGHTS 13.6

The Bill of Rights of Grieving Teens, by Teens at The Dougy Center

A grieving teen has the right....

... to know the truth about the death, the deceased, and the circumstances

... to have questions answered honestly

... to be heard with dignity and respect

... to be silent and not tell you her/his grief emotions and thoughts

... to not agree with your perceptions and conclusions

... to see the person who died and the place of the death

... to grieve any way she/he wants without hurting self or others

... to feel all the feelings and to think all the thoughts of his/her own unique grief

... to not have to follow the "Stages of Grief" as outlined in a high school health book

... to grieve in one's own unique, individual way without censorship

... to be angry at death, at the person who died, at God, at self, and at others

...to have his/her own theological and philosophical beliefs about life and death

... to be involved in the decisions about the rituals related to the death

... to not be taken advantage of in this vulnerable mourning condition and circumstances

... to have guilt about how he/she could have intervened to stop the death

Source: This Bill of Rights was developed by participating teens at The Dougy Center and does not represent "official" policies of the Center. Reprinted by permission.

Many adolescents recognize that there can be positive outcomes even in the wake of intense tragedy, such as a deeper appreciation of life, greater caring for and stronger emotional bonds with others, and greater emotional strength (Oltjenbruns, 1991). Adults can help to encourage such outcomes in adolescents and can learn important lessons from them in their own lives.

Summary

In this chapter, we explored interactions between adolescents and death within the contemporary American death system. We noted how the distinctive developmental tasks of early, middle, and late adolescence have a direct bearing on how adolescents relate to death. These tasks influence death-related encounters and attitudes among adolescents. In terms of encounters, we noted that adolescence is an era characterized by low death rates especially associated with human-induced deaths resulting from accidents, homicide, and suicide. In terms of attitudes, we saw that adolescents generally combine a strong emphasis on the present and a tendency to resist recognition of the personal significance of death. We also described issues confronting adolescents who are coping either with life-threatening illness or with bereavement and grief. We gave special attention to issues related to homicide and suicide in adolescent life. Lastly, we offered ways to help adolescents cope with death and bereavement.

Glossary

Adolescence: the era in human development occurring between childhood and adulthood; often characterized by the developmental task of achieving individuation and the establishment of a more or less stable sense of personal identity; not necessarily coextensive with the teenage years

Developmental eras in adolescence: early, middle, and late adolescence

Early adolescence: a period dominated by the goal of achieving emotional separation from parents and the conflict of separation versus reunion

Homicide among adolescents: currently the second leading cause of death (following accidents) in the United States among persons 15-24 years of age; especially notable as a cause of death among nonwhite males who are middle and late adolescents

Late adolescence: a period dominated by the goal of achieving intimacy and commitment and the conflict of closeness versus distance

Leading influences on adolescent understandings of death: ambiguities or tensions arising from biological, cognitive, social, and emotional factors, together with the digital era

Middle adolescence: a period dominated by the goal of achieving competency, mastery, or control and the conflict of independence versus dependence

Normative developmental tasks in adolescence: conceptualized by Erikson as involving a tension between "identity" vs. "role confusion"; successful resolution of this polarity leads to the virtue of "fidelity"

Postvention: after-the-fact interventions for individuals affected by traumatic loss

Suicide among adolescents: currently the third leading cause of death in the United States among persons 15-24 years of age; especially notable as a cause of death among white males who are middle and late adolescents

Questions for Review and Discussion

1. Have you had any experiences like those described in the vignette near the beginning of this chapter? If so, how did the administrators, teachers, parents, and other students at your school respond to those experiences? Did their responses help? Why or why not?

2. What sorts of death-related losses have you experienced in your own adolescence, and what did they mean to you? What helped you to cope with them? What help did you want or need but failed to find?

3. During your own adolescence, have you been seriously ill or have you had an important personal loss? Or perhaps you know an adolescent who has been in such a situation? If so, what were your/his/her most significant concerns about that illness or loss?

4. What would you recommend to adults as ways they could help adolescents cope with death-related challenges? How would your recommendations differ (if at all) for different adolescents or situations?

5. Today's adolescents are said to be constantly connected to social media and the Internet? Are you connected in those ways? Could they or did they help you in coping with the subjects of this chapter?

Suggested Readings

General resources on adolescents, their development, and death include:

Arnett, J., & Tanner, L. (Eds.). (2006). *Emerging Adults in America: Coming of Age in the 21st Century*

Balk, D. E. (2014). *Dealing with Dying, Death, and Grief during Adolescence*

Balk, D. E., & Corr, C. A. (Eds.). (2009). *Adolescent Encounters with Death, Bereavement, and Coping*

Corr, C. A., & Balk, D. E. (Eds.). (1996). *Handbook of Adolescent Death and Bereavement*

Corr, C. A., & McNeil, J. N. (Eds.). (1986). *Adolescence and Death*

Kalergis, M. M. (1998). *Seen and Heard: Teenagers Talk about Their Lives*

Milevsky, A. (2015). *Understanding Adolescents for Helping Professions*

Offer, D., Ostrov, E., & Howard, K. I. (1981). *The Adolescent: A Psychological Self-Portrait*

For life-threatening illness in adolescence, see the section on Pediatric Palliative and Hospice Care and the related Suggested Readings on that subject in Chapter 8, as well as:

Krementz, J. (1989). *How It Feels to Fight for Your Life*

Pendleton, E. (Comp.). (1980). *Too Old to Cry, Too Young to Die*

Bereavement and grief in adolescence are explored in the following:

Balk, D. E. (Ed.). (1991a). *Death and Adolescent Bereavement: Current research and future directions. Journal of Adolescent Research*, 6(1)

Balk, D. E. (2011). *Helping the Bereaved College Student*

Balk, D. E. (2014). *Dealing with Dying, Death, and Grief during Adolescence*

Crenshaw, D. A. (Ed.). (2010). *Child and Adolescent Psychotherapy: Wounded Spirits and Healing Paths*

Doka, K. J., & Tucci, A. S. (Eds.). (2014). *Living with Grief: Helping Adolescents Cope with Loss*

Fitzgerald, H. (2000). *The Grieving Teen: A Guide for Teenagers and Their Friends*

Gootman, M. E. (2005). *When a Friend Dies: A Book for Teens about Grieving & Healing*

Grollman, E. A. (1993). *Straight Talk about Death for Teenagers: How to Cope with Losing Someone You Love*

Hyatt, E. G. (2015). *Grieving for the Sibling You Lost: A Teen's Guide to Coping with Grief and Finding Meaning after Loss*

Marshall, B. J., & Winokuer, H. R. (Eds.). (2017). *Sibling Loss across the Lifespan: Research, Practice and Personal Stories* (especially Part II)

McCoyd, J.L.M., & Walter, C. A. (2016). *Grief and Loss across the Lifespan: A Biopsychosocial Perspective* (2nd ed.; especially Chapter 5)

Servaty-Seib, H. L., & Fajgenbaum, D. G. (2015). *We Get It: Voices of Grieving College Students and Young Adults (with contributions by 33 inspirational young adults)*

Servaty-Seib, H. L., & Taub, D. J. (Eds.). (2008). *Assisting Bereaved College Students*

Sjöqvist, S. (Ed.). (2007). *Still Here with Me: Teenagers and Children on Losing a Parent*

Wheeler, J. L. (2010). *Weird is Normal when Teenagers Grieve*

Teaching adolescents about death or helping them to cope with death-related issues is examined in:

Fiorini, J. J., & Mullen, J. A. (2006). *Counseling Children and Adolescents through Grief and Loss*

Fitzgerald, H. (1998). *Grief at School: A Guide for Teachers and Counselors*

Luxmoore, N. (2012). *Young People, Death and the Unfairness of Everything*

Malone, P. A. (2016). *Counseling Adolescents through Loss, Grief, and Trauma*

Stevenson, R. G. (Ed.). (2002). *What Will We Do? Preparing a School Community to Cope with Crises* (2nd ed.)

Stevenson, R. G., & Stevenson, E. P. (Eds.). (1996b). *Teaching Students about Death: A Comprehensive Resource for Educators and Parents*

Turner, M. (2006). *Talking with Children and Young People about Death and Dying* (2nd ed.)

Suicide and life-threatening behavior among adolescents and children are explored in:

Berman, A. L., Jobes, D. A., & Silverman, M. M. (2006). *Adolescent Suicide: Assessment and Intervention* (2nd ed.)

Cobain, B. (2007). *When Nothing Matters Anymore: A Survival Guide for Depressed Teens* (rev. & updated ed.)

The Dougy Center and the American Foundation for Suicide Prevention. (n.d.). *Children, Teens, and Suicide Loss*

King, C. A., Foster, C. E., & Rogalski, K. M. (2013). *Teen Suicide Risk: A Practitioner Guide to Screening, Assessment, and Management*

Klagsbrun, F. (1985). *Too Young to Die: Youth and Suicide*

Lester, D. (1993). *The Cruelest Death: The Enigma of Adolescent Suicide*

Losey, B. (2011). *Bullying, Suicide, and Homicide: Understanding, Assessing, and Preventing Threats to Self and Others for Victims of Bullying*

Miller, D. N. (2011). *Child and Adolescent Suicidal Behavior: School-based Prevention, Assessment, and Intervention*

Peck, M. L., Farberow, N. L., & Litman, R. E. (Eds.). (1985). *Youth Suicide.*

Stillion, J. M., & McDowell, E. E. (1996). *Suicide across the Life Span: Premature Exits* (2nd ed.)

Selected Web Resources

Some useful search terms include: ADOLESCENTS AND DEATH; CAUSES OF DEATH IN ADOLESCENCE; DEVELOPMENTAL TASKS IN ADOLESCENCE; HOMICIDE AND ADOLESCENTS; SUICIDE AND ADOLESCENTS.

You can also visit the following *organizational and other Internet sites:*

American School Counselors Association

Boulden Publishing

Centering Corporation

Children's Project on Palliative/Hospice Services (ChiPPS) of the National Hospice and Palliative Care Organization (NHPCO)

Coalition to Support Grieving Students

Compassion Books

The Dougy Center: The National Center for Grieving Children and Families

National Alliance for Grieving Children

YOUTH.ORG

Young and Middle-Aged Adults

Objectives of this **Chapter**

▌ To enhance our discussion of distinctive developmental tasks of young and middle-aged adults

▌ To describe typical encounters with death in the United States during young and middle adulthood

▌ To explore death-related attitudes during the adult years

▌ To identify central issues for young and middle-aged adults who are coping with life-threatening illness and dying

▌ To examine key issues for young and middle-aged adults who are coping with bereavement and grief

AN ORTHODOX ARCHBISHOP FACES HIS MOTHER'S DEATH

My mother died of cancer over a period of three years. She was operated on unsuccessfully. The doctor told me about it and then added: "But of course you will not say anything to your mother."

I said: "I will." And I did.

I remember how I came to her and said to her that her doctor had rung and that the operation was not successful. We kept silent for a moment and then my mother said: "And so I shall die."

I said: "Yes."

And then we stayed together in complete silence, communing without any words. I don't think that we thought thoughts. We faced something that had entered life and made all the difference to life. It was not a shadow. It was not an evil. It was not a terror. It was the ultimate. And we had to face this ultimate without yet knowing what this ultimate would unfold itself into. We stayed as long as we felt we had to stay. And then life continued.

But two things happened as a result. The one is that at no moment was either my mother or I walled up within a lie, forced into a comedy, deprived of any help. At no moment had I to come into my mother's room with a smile that was untrue, or say words that were untrue. At no moment were we to play a comedy of life conquering death, of illness waning, of things being better than they were, when we both knew they were not. At no moment were we deprived of one another's help. There were moments when my mother felt she needed help. She would then ring the bell and I would come and we would speak of her dying, of my bereavement.

She loved life. She loved it deeply. A few days before she died she said that she would be prepared to live 150 years in suffering, but to live. She loved us. She grieved over separation: "Oh, for the touch of a vanished hand and the sound of a voice that is still."

And then there were other moments when I felt the pain of it, and I would come and speak of it to my mother. And she would give me her support and help me face her death. This was a deep and true relationship. There was nothing of a lie in it....

There was another side.... Because death could come at any moment, and it would be too late to put right something that had gone wrong, all life has to be at every moment an expression, as perfect and complete as possible, of a relationship that is one of reverence and love. Only death can make things that seem to be small and insignificant into signs that are great and significant. The way you prepare a cup of tea on a tray, the way you put cushions behind the back of a sick person, the way your voice sounds, the way you move—all that can be an expression of all there is in a relationship.

If there is a false note, if there is a crack, if something has gone wrong, it must be repaired now, because there is the inevitable certainty that later it may be too late. Death confronts you with the truth of life, with a sharpness and a clarity that nothing else can convey. (Extract from A. Bloom [1999]. Used by permission of SPCK Publishing & Sheldon Press.)

YOUNG AND MIDDLE-AGED ADULTS, DEVELOPMENTAL TASKS, AND DEATH

Young and middle adulthood together fill a period of some 40 years in the human life course, extending from the end of adolescence in the early 20s to the beginning of older adulthood in the mid-60s. Together this is the longest single era in human development, the so-called "prime of life," including two distinct 20-year generational cohorts or **developmental eras in adulthood**—*young adulthood* (roughly ages 21 or 22–45) and *middle adulthood* or middle age (ages 45–65). According to Erikson (1963, 1968; see also Hayslip, Patrick, & Panek, 2011), the principal **normative developmental task in young adulthood** is to achieve **intimacy** (vs. the danger of isolation), while the *major task for development in middle adulthood* is **generativity** (vs. the danger of stagnation or self-absorption).

Despite notable differences, young and middle-aged adults share many issues arising from new family relationships, work roles, and an evolving set of death-related concerns. Among the special challenges the adults face is their role as *middle-escents or members of the sandwich generation*—individuals situated developmentally between their younger counterparts (children and adolescents), on one hand, and their predecessors (older adults), on the other. Still, it is wise to be cautious in making generalizations about these adults and their experiences because a large number of variables impact their lives and because many developmental aspects of adulthood have not been well or broadly studied.

In general, young and middle adulthood is a period of exploring and exploiting the identity established in earlier stages of development through choices about one's lifestyle, relationships, and work (Kail & Cavanaugh, 2015; Newman & Newman, 2014). Decisions made in the vitality of young adulthood chart much of the remaining course of human life in terms of relationships, vocation, and lifestyle, thereby enabling people to know themselves in much fuller ways than were possible during adolescence. In middle age, one typically conserves and draws on personal, social, and vocational resources that were established earlier. The transition in midlife from young to middle adulthood can focus on what is past and gone (youth and its distinctive opportunities), or it can lead to a renewed appreciation of life as one achieves a new understanding of one's self and decides how to live out the remainder of one's life. Once depicted as a tumultuous crisis, the **midlife transition** is now usually thought of as a more or less calm transition in which individual perceptions of responses to events are central (Hunter & Sundel, 1989).

Within the broad division between early and middle adulthood, Levinson (1978) distinguished several "seasons" or qualitatively distinct eras in human development with boundary zones, periods of transition, and characteristic issues. In *young adulthood*, there is an early transition from preadulthood, a novice phase in which one enters the adult world and is involved in "forming a dream," an internal transition at about age 30, and a period of "settling down." Similarly, *middle adulthood* involves another novice or introductory period, an internal transition at around age 50, and a concluding period, followed by a further transition into older adulthood. The boundary between young and middle adulthood for Levinson is the midlife transition, during which the individual reappraises the past and terminates young adulthood, modifies the life structure and initiates middle adulthood, and seeks to resolve four principal polarities: tensions between young/old, destruction/creation, masculine/feminine, and attachment/separateness.

It is only fair to note that much of the original research on adulthood was confined to male subjects. However, in a posthumously published study, Levinson (1996) reported results of detailed interviews with 45 women conducted from 1980 to 1982. This study examined three groups of young adult women: homemakers, women with careers in the corporate-financial world, and women with careers in academia. From this study, Levinson concluded that the "alternating sequence of structure build-ing-maintaining periods and transitional periods holds for both women and men" (p. 36). This is the schema of developmental seasons he identified in earlier studies of male adults.

Gilligan (1982/1993) was among the first prominent researchers to argue that the course of human development in females is likely to differ in significant ways from that of their male counterparts. For example, both male and female adults can find themselves caught between pressures from older and younger developmental cohorts (parents and/or children). Still, responses to issues facing the sandwich generation are likely to differ in important ways for males and females. For example, when an elderly relative or ill child needs care, adult males historically provided economic and logistical support, whereas responsibility for practical hands-on care and nurturing was assigned to adult females.

This traditional division of roles by gender may no longer be accurate for many in contemporary society, partly because many women have assumed new duties out-side the home in the workforce. Still, significant differences are likely to exist between men and women, largely because of the ongoing influence of gender splitting or dif-ferences in the social roles and responsibilities assigned to or taken on by males and females. Many women who work outside the home are expected to assume a "sec-ond shift" or double burden in which men may help out more but do not gener-ally assume domestic chores and caregiving. Thus, Levinson (1996) concluded that thorough descriptions of adult life need to take into account both developmental and gender factors. In short, common aspects in adult development may coexist with differences arising from gender, historical variables, and other factors.

ENCOUNTERS WITH DEATH DURING YOUNG AND MIDDLE ADULTHOOD

In this section, we explore numbers of deaths and death rates among young and mid-dle adults, leading causes of deaths in these eras, and two variables of gender and race.

Deaths and Death Rates among Young and Middle Adults

In 2014, adults between the ages of 25 and 64 made up 52.6% of the total popula-tion and they experienced just over 24% of the more than 2.6 million deaths in the United States (see Table 14.1).

Table 14.1 provides the *number of deaths* in 2014 from ages 25 to 64 in ten-year age groupings by gender, race, and Hispanic origin. Overall numbers of deaths rose rapidly throughout this 40-year period. Further, as shown in Table 14.2, an even steeper increase was found in death rates for young and middle adults, which rose by more than 8 times from *death rates* for those 25–34 years of age to rates for those 55–64 years of age. These patterns of rapid increase in numbers of deaths and death rates applied to male and female adults, as well as to all subgroups in the adult population.

Three principal comparisons highlight notable features of changing mortality patterns in the United States during adulthood. First, middle adults died in much larger numbers and at higher rates than did young adults. In 2014, more than four times as many Americans died in middle age as in young adulthood. This increase occurred in a middle-aged population that was significantly smaller than the popu-lation of young adults. Second, each successive ten-year cohort of adults experienced

Table 14.1 Number of Deaths during Young and Middle Adulthood, by Age, Race or Hispanic Origin,[a] and Gender: United States, 2014

	Ages 25 to 34			Ages 35 to 44		
	Both Sexes	Males	Females	Both Sexes	Males	Females
All origins[b]	47,177	32,697	14,480	70,996	43,693	27,303
Caucasian Americans, total	35,408	24,572	10,836	53,674	33,482	20,192
Non-Hispanic Caucasian Americans	28,969	19,845	9,124	44,565	27,413	17,152
African Americans	9,549	6,622	2,927	13,997	8,210	5,787
Hispanic Americans[c]	6,575	4,836	1,739	9,168	6,099	3,069
Asian and Pacific Island Americans	1,277	855	422	2,005	1,202	803
American Indians and Alaska Natives	943	648	295	1,320	799	521
	Ages 45–54			Ages 55–64		
	Both Sexes	Males	Females	Both Sexes	Males	Females
All origins[b]	175,917	106,377	69,540	348,808	212,198	136,601
Caucasian Americans, total	137,497	84,414	53,083	277,580	170,566	107,014
Non-Hispanic Caucasian Americans	120,679	73,411	47,268	252,298	154,680	97,618
African Americans	31,815	18,011	13,804	59,972	34,843	25,129
Hispanic Americans[c]	16,705	10,894	5,811	24,701	15,398	9,303
Asian or Pacific Island Americans	4,229	2,558	1,671	7,954	4,808	3,146
American Indians and Alaska Natives	2,376	1,394	982	3,302	1,981	1,321

[a]Data for specified groups other than Caucasian Americans and African Americans should be interpreted with caution because of inconsistencies between reporting race and/or Hispanic origin on death certificates and on censuses and surveys.

[b]Figures for origin not stated are included in "All origins" but not distributed among specified origins.

[c]Includes all persons of Hispanic origin of any race.

Source: Heron, 2016.

a larger number of deaths and a higher death rate. Third, the very high infant death rates for the population as a whole (594.7 per 100,000 discussed in Chapter 12) are not exceeded until the final ten-year cohort in middle adulthood (those 55–64 years of age) with death rates of 870.3 per 100,000.

Leading Causes of Death among Young and Middle Adults

Leading causes of death change during adulthood in ways that interact with developmental issues. For all young adults taken as a group (ages 25–44), accidents were by

Table 14.2   Death Rates (per 100,000) during Young and Middle Adulthood, by Age, Race or Hispanic Origin,[a] and Gender: United States, 2014

	Ages 25 to 34			Ages 35 to 44		
	Both Sexes	Males	Females	Both Sexes	Males	Females
All origins[b]	108.4	148.8	67.2	175.2	216.7	134.1
Caucasian Americans, total	106.9	145.3	66.9	172.1	212.6	130.7
Non-Hispanic Caucasian Americans	115.0	155.8	73.2	185.8	227.4	143.8
African Americans	148.6	212.1	88.6	247.9	308.5	193.9
Hispanic Americans[c]	74.0	103.6	41.3	114.7	149.4	78.5
Asian and Pacific Island Americans	38.9	54.1	24.8	65.0	83.0	49.1
American Indians and Alaska Natives	135.3	179.1	88.0	222.5	264.4	179.0

	Ages 45 to 54			Ages 55 to 64		
	Both Sexes	Males	Females	Both Sexes	Males	Females
All origins[b]	404.8	496.5	315.6	870.3	1,098.2	658.2
Caucasian Americans, total	397.1	488.9	305.8	844.2	1,063.8	635.1
Non-Hispanic Caucasian Americans	417.8	511.2	325.5	864.3	1,085.3	653.5
African Americans	557.2	671.8	455.8	1,265.2	1,611.5	974.8
Hispanic Americans[c]	263.9	341.0	185.3	609.4	787.7	443.3
Asian and Pacific Island Americans	164.5	212.3	122.3	390.7	519.9	283.2
American Indians and Alaska Natives	431.0	508.5	354.3	787.9	984.7	606.2

[a]Data for specified groups other than Caucasian Americans and African Americans should be interpreted with caution because of inconsistencies between reporting race and/or Hispanic origin on death certificates and on censuses and surveys.

[b]Figures for origin not stated are included in "All origins" but not distributed among specified origins.

[c]Includes all persons of Hispanic origin of any race.

Source: Heron, 2016.

far the leading cause of death in 2014 (Heron, 2016). Suicide and homicide were the next two leading causes of death among adults 25–34 years of age, but they declined in relative significance to third and fourth leading causes of deaths among adults 35–44 years of age, while cancer and heart disease became more prominent in this latter age group. This shift signals a decline during young adulthood in the relative significance of human-induced deaths and a parallel rise in the relative significance of degenerative diseases—trends that continue throughout the remainder of the human life course.

During middle adulthood (ages 45–65), cancer and heart disease accounted for more than 51% of all deaths in our society in 2014, followed at a great distance by accidents and a series of degenerative diseases like chronic lower respiratory diseases and diabetes. Among cancer deaths in adults, leading causes for both sexes were lung cancer, followed by prostate and colorectal cancer for males, and by breast and colorectal cancer for females.

Rates for accidental death during early and middle adulthood were lower than those in adolescence, but accidents other than those involving motor vehicles became increasingly more salient as causes of death. Homicide death rates declined during adulthood, while suicide death rates reached their highest point in the entire life course with a rate of 20.2 per 100,000 in adults between the ages of 45 and 54.

During the 1980s, a new factor appeared in encounters with death: human immunodeficiency virus (HIV) and acquired immune deficiency syndrome (AIDS). By 1994, HIV infection was the leading cause of death for young adults 25–44 years of age, accounting for 30,260 deaths (Singh, Mathews, Clarke, Yannicos, & Smith, 1995). Yet by 2014, young adult deaths from HIV had fallen to just 1,757 (Heron, 2016), a major decline in just 20 years because of better education about HIV/AIDS, more effective prevention measures, and better care for infected persons.

Beyond these present and former leading causes of death, Case and Deaton (2015, p. 15078) noted

> a marked increase in the all-cause mortality of middle-aged white non-Hispanic men and women in the United States between 1999 and 2013. This change reversed decades of progress in mortality and was unique to the United States ... This increase for whites was largely accounted for by increasing death rates from drug and alcohol poisonings, suicide, and chronic liver diseases and cirrhosis. Although all education groups saw increases in mortality from suicide and poisonings, and an overall increase in external cause mortality, those with less education saw the most marked increases. Rising midlife mortality rates of white non-Hispanics were paralleled by increases in midlife morbidity. Self-reported declines in health, mental health, and ability to conduct activities of daily living, and increases in chronic pain and inability to work, as well as clinically measured deteriorations in liver function, all point to growing distress in this population.

Two Variables in Deaths of Young and Middle Adults: Gender and Race

Tables 14.1 and 14.2 indicate gender and racial contrasts in numbers of deaths and death rates among American adults. The main gender difference is that adult males die far more frequently and at much higher rates than females. Both male and female young adults (ages 25–44) experience significant numbers of deaths from accidents, HIV infection, and homicide, but males are more prone to heart disease and suicide than females, whereas the influence of cancer as a cause of death appears much earlier among females than males. As these adults move into midlife (ages 45–64), degenerative diseases become more prominent as leading causes of death in both groups.

In both young and middle adults, there is a much larger *number* of deaths among Caucasian Americans than among other U.S. subgroups. However, African Americans (and, to a lesser extent, American Indians and Alaska Natives) experience much higher death *rates* than Caucasian Americans. In all of these groups, males greatly exceed females in both absolute numbers of deaths and death rates. HIV infection and homicide are more typical causes of death among African Americans, whereas suicide is more prevalent among Caucasian Americans.

ATTITUDES TOWARD DEATH AMONG YOUNG AND MIDDLE ADULTS

Some features of adult encounters with death are particularly significant in shaping attitudes toward death—especially during middle adulthood. For example, the years of the late 20s and early 30s are likely to be times of relative stability in self-understanding. As a result, anxiety about one's own death and defenses against that realization do not typically seem to be prominent among young adults. Of course, this may change if new or different encounters with death generate new threats and anxieties.

In general, patterns of death-related attitudes begin to alter for many as they move into middle adulthood. For example, typical encounters with death during adulthood tend to increase as the next-older generation begins to experience higher death rates. The death of the archbishop's mother described in the vignette near the beginning of this chapter is an example of events often confronting many middle-aged adults today. Together with issues arising from their developing children, this is what is meant by the **sandwich generation**, when this group feels caught by new and different pressures arising simultaneously from both the older and younger generations surrounding it on either developmental front.

For younger adults, death-related worries and concerns most likely relate to the deaths of others. However, as one advances developmentally and as one learns from one's own life experiences, one typically encounters a newly personalized awareness of mortality (Doka, 2014a). This recognition occurs mainly in two ways: through encounters with the deaths of parents, peers, siblings, and spouses, often for the first time in one's life and especially as a result of natural causes, and through one's own newly emerging realization of oneself as a mortal creature who could die at any time and who will die someday.

Peers, siblings, or a spouse can die at any time, but in adulthood, it is more likely that they will die of natural causes (such as heart attack, cancer, or stroke). When that happens, bereaved adults cannot easily dismiss such deaths as the result of ill fortune or external forces—both of which might, in principle, be avoided. Similarly, when adults begin to sense the limits of their bodily capacities or to recognize problems associated with aging or lifestyle, their personal sense of invulnerability diminishes. Thus, Neugarten (1974) noted a shift in perspective from time lived to time left to live. In making such a change, adults typically begin a retrospective assessment of their achievements, to realize that they have already passed through half or two-thirds of their average life expectancy, to appreciate that the future does not stretch endlessly ahead without any real possibility of a horizon or end point, and to entertain thoughts about retirement and eventual death. This can lead to a reappraisal of personal values and priorities, which may result in an enriched capacity for love and enjoyment, and a richer, more philosophical sense of meaning in one's life—or it may have less positive results such as a dissatisfaction with one's past and potential achievements in life (Jacques, 1965). In short, the implications of death play a prominent role in the reevaluation of life and self that characterizes middle age. As young and middle-aged adults turn to thoughts of their own death, they are likely to think of what that will mean for their children, family members, or significant others, as well as for the vocational and other creative projects that have occupied so much of their time and energy since becoming adults.

To all of this, terrorist attacks on 9/11 and in different forms around the world in recent years, along with conflicts in Afghanistan, Iraq, and Syria, have each had a special impact on many mature adults. Older members of the military reserve and National Guard who were called up for some of these conflicts because of their special skills were and are in a different situation from younger volunteers who were already serving on active duty. And the hundreds of firefighters and police officers who lost their lives or worked as rescuers at the World Trade Center were in large part adults in their active middle years.

In other words, in recent years a number of new death-related perils have been presented to young and middle adults. Some (such as issues related to nuclear threats or to the environment) are shared with all who inhabit the planet. Others (such as those involving war, alcoholism, or drug abuse) apply mainly to individuals in specific localities or roles. Still others (such as the deaths of significant age-mates from natural causes and the implications of an emerging sense of personal mortality) are particularly relevant to those in the long middle years of life. In general, however, death-related events often confront young adults with frustration and disappointment, even as they take on a very personal tone for middle adults with interpersonal implications for their loved ones.

YOUNG AND MIDDLE ADULTS WHO ARE COPING WITH LIFE-THREATENING ILLNESS AND DYING

If the basic developmental task in young adulthood is that of achieving intimacy, then life-threatening illness and dying challenge the needs of young adults to develop intimate relationships, express their sexuality, and obtain realistic support for their goals and future plans. "*Intimacy* involves the ability to be open, supportive, and close with another person, without fear of losing oneself in the process. The establishment of intimacy with a significant other implies the capacity for mutual empathy, the ability to help meet one another's needs, the acceptance of each other's limitations, and the commitment to care deeply for the other person" (Cook & Oltjenbruns, 1998, p. 329). In short, intimacy depends on a sense of one's own identity and trust in the other.

Coping as a Young Adult

To achieve quality in living, young adults who are seriously ill or dying still need to pursue and maintain intimacy. An inability to develop intimate relationships usually results in isolation. As we saw in Chapter 6, abandonment and isolation are often the principal concerns of individuals who are coping with dying. Thus, life-threatening illness and dying directly challenge the main developmental task of young adulthood. As a result, when there is difficulty in achieving or maintaining intimacy, all concerned should reexamine barriers (such as death-related fears or lack of information about the person's disease) and consider what may be gained by renewed efforts to risk sharing in a pressured and precious time.

Many couples express their intimacy most naturally through *sexuality*. Not confined to sexual intercourse, sexuality includes a broad range of thoughts, feelings, and behaviors. Such expressions of sexuality in the lives of seriously ill and dying adults should be fostered (Marzo, 2015). That may involve decisions about grooming or dressing, a gentle touch or caress, open discussion of physical and psychological needs, and other aspects of feeling positive about oneself. Nonjudgmental attitudes, privacy, and efforts to adapt to changes brought about by disease and treatment (e.g., mastectomy or colostomy) can all be helpful in this area.

For young adults, a life-threatening illness may threaten *goals and future plans* in many areas, such as getting married, having children, and pursuing educational or vocational aspirations. If so, young adults must reevaluate their plans and determine what may be appropriate in their new situation. They may appreciate assistance from healthcare providers, such as those in palliative care, who can clarify the realities of the situation while also supporting their autonomy and decision-making processes (Cook, Jack, Siden, Thabane, & Browne, 2016). This respects efforts to satisfy important personal and developmental needs while also recognizing constraints on former hopes and dreams.

Coping as a Middle-Aged Adult

If the principal developmental task for middle-aged adults is the pursuit of *generativity*, life-threatening illness and dying normally involve reevaluating one's life, continuing in one's roles, and putting one's affairs in order. Reassessment, conservation, and preparation are characteristic activities of all middle-aged adults. They involve "stock-taking" (Butler & Lewis, 1998), efforts to sustain generativity as an alternative to self-indulgence and stagnation, and a need to prepare for the future and to carry out one's responsibilities to others. Awareness of a life-threatening illness and challenges involved in coping with dying are likely to heighten, rather than to thwart, these developmental processes.

In middle adulthood, *reevaluation* relates to the meaning and direction of one's life. Such issues become more, not less, poignant and urgent under the dual stimuli of illness and maturation. One person might more vigorously pursue a creative, vocational, or personal project established in young adulthood in recognition of new threats to its completion. Another midlife adult might change earlier projects and strike out in new directions or relationships. In either case, the individual might experience grief over what he or she has not attained, along with some overshadowing awareness of other losses yet to come.

However they choose to look toward a future that may now be perceived as more clouded and less expansive than it was before, in coping with life-threatening illness or dying middle-aged adults can be expected to consider prospects for *continuation or enduring value* in the legacies they have been establishing for the future. They may strive more diligently to achieve such goals, alter their form in ways that appear more satisfying or more achievable, or choose to settle for what has already been achieved. Insofar as possible, it is desirable to support constructive processes of generativity in ill or dying midlife adults by enabling them to continue to take part in meaningful roles and relationships in suitable ways.

Looking to the future within a context of life-threatening illness or dying, and in light of developmental tasks of middle adulthood, typically leads midlife adults to strive to *put their affairs in order*. Most often, this involves an effort to continue to meet responsibilities to those whom they love and to ensure such obligations are met after the individual dies. Life-threatening illness and dying may challenge one's ability to meet such commitments but need not render them completely impossible. With support, one can strive to influence the future to the degree possible or to arrange for others to assume specific responsibilities on one's behalf. This can involve making a will, disposing of property, or conveying important wishes and messages. Activities like making one's own funeral and burial arrangements can reflect a healthy vitality in continuing to fulfill prized roles and an ability to minimize postdeath disruptions or burdens on others.

YOUNG AND MIDDLE ADULTS WHO ARE COPING WITH BEREAVEMENT AND GRIEF

Young and middle adults may find themselves confronted by many different types of losses that can involve bereavement, grief, and mourning (Harris, 2011). Two examples can be seen in loss of a valued job and infertility or involuntary childlessness, both of which can challenge a sense of who one is and bring about powerful psychological and social impacts (Froelker, 2015). Thus, one's vocation and skills may no longer be valued, there may be no more jobs like the one the person had, one may have to rethink and retrain, and one's sense of self-identity, purpose, and relationships may all be tested.

Beyond these, members of an aging, sandwich generation often find themselves beset with death-related losses on all sides. Young and middle-aged adults may suffer a full range of deaths, including those of their parents, grandparents, and other older relatives; their spouses or life partners, siblings, peers, and friends; and their children. This is distinctive in some respects: most adolescents do not experience the deaths of their own children and most elderly adults have already experienced the deaths of their parents some time ago. Young and middle adults may also encounter losses of celebrities whom they admire. What is most characteristic of bereavement in young and middle adults is the very real potential for so many kinds of death-related losses during this era of the life course.

Even the birth of a child who is somehow impaired may present adult parents with losses, challenges, and opportunities with which they must cope (see Personal Insights 14.1). Each loss is difficult in its own way, but research by Sanders (1980)

Adults can offer consolation and support to each other in difficult times.

Steve Skjold/Alamy Stock Photo

Welcome to Holland

I am often asked to describe the experience of raising a child with a disability—to try to help people who have not shared that unique experience to understand it, to imagine how it would feel. It's like this....

When you're going to have a baby, it's like planning a fabulous vacation trip—to Italy. You buy a bunch of guidebooks and make your wonderful plans. The Coliseum. The Michelangelo David. The gondolas in Venice. You may learn some handy phrases in Italian. It's all very exciting.

After months of eager anticipation, the day finally arrives. You pack your bags and off you go. Several hours later, the plane lands. The stewardess comes in and says, "Welcome to Holland."

"Holland?!?" you say. "What do you mean, Holland?? I signed up for Italy! I'm supposed to be in Italy. All my life I've dreamed of going to Italy."

But there's been a change in the flight plan. They've landed in Holland and there you must stay.

The important thing is that they haven't taken you to a horrible, disgusting, filthy place, full of pestilence, famine and disease. It's just a different place.

So you must go out and buy new guidebooks. And you must learn a whole new language. And you will meet a whole new group of people you would never have met.

It's just a different place. It's slower-paced than Italy, less flashy than Italy. But after you've been there for a while and you catch your breath, you look around ... and you begin to notice that Holland has windmills ... Holland has tulips. Holland even has Rembrandts.

But everyone you know is busy coming and going from Italy ... and they're all bragging about what a wonderful time they had there. And for the rest of your life, you will say, "Yes, that's where I was supposed to go. That's what I had planned."

The pain of that will never, ever, ever go away ... because the loss of that dream is a very, very significant loss.

But ... if you spend your life mourning the fact that you didn't get to Italy, you may never be free to enjoy the very special, the very lovely things ... about Holland.

Source: From "Welcome to Holland," by E. P. Kingsley.
Copyright © 1987 Emily Perl Kingsley. Reprinted by permission.

showed that bereavement in adults is usually impacted most significantly by the death of a child, a spouse, and a parent—in that order. This finding is consistent with what bereaved adults often say: "The death of my parent is the death of my past; the death of my spouse is the death of my present; the death of my child is the death of my future." What bereavement means to adults can be seen in the following analyses of different types of deaths encountered during adulthood and in what some bereaved adults have written about their experiences (see Focus On 14.1).

FOCUS ON 14.1

Selected Accounts of Bereavement Experiences during Young and Middle Adulthood

ABOUT THE DEATH OF CHILD:

Claypool, J. R. (2004). *Tracks of a Fellow Struggler: Living and Growing through Grief*

Daher, D. (2003). *And the Passenger Was Death: The Drama and Trauma of Losing a Child*

Didion, J. (2012). *Blue Nights*

Evans, R. P. (2012). *The Christmas Box*

Fleming, D. (2005). *Noah's Rainbow: A Father's Emotional Journey from the Death of His Son to the Birth of His Daughter*

Hirsch, E. (2014). *Gabriel: A Poem by Edward Hirsch*

Housden, M. (2002). *Hannah's Gift: Lessons from a Life Fully Lived*

Redfern, S., & Gilbert, S. K. (Eds.). (2008). *The Grieving Garden: Living with the Death of a Child*

R.N., & Schwiebert, P. (2012). *A Grandparent's Sorrow*

Rosenblatt, R. (2010). *Making Toast: A Family Story*

Schrauger, B. (2001). *Walking Taylor Home*

Simonds, W., & Rothman, B. K. (Eds.). (1992). *Centuries of Solace: Expressions of Maternal Grief in Popular Literature*

Smith, G. H. (2006). *Remembering Garrett*

Wagner, S. (1994). *The Andrew Poems*

ABOUT THE DEATH OF A SPOUSE, LIFE PARTNER, SIBLING, PEER, OR FRIEND:

Brothers, J. (1990). *Widowed*

Caine, L. (1975). *Widow*

Didion, J. (2007). *The Year of Magical Thinking*

Elmer, L. (1987). *Why Her, Why Now: A Man's Journey through Love and Death and Grief*

Graham, L. (1990). *Rebuilding the House*

Jamison, K. R. (2009). *Nothing Was the Same: A Memoir*

Kaimann, D. S. (2002). *Common Threads: Nine Widows' Journeys through Love, Loss and Healing*

Lewis, C. S. (1976). *A Grief Observed*

Oates, J. C. (2011). *A Widow's Story: A Memoir*

Rehm, D. (2016). *On My Own*

Rice, P. (2016). *Winter Sun: A Memoir of Love and Hospice*

Roberts, B. K. (2003). *Death without Denial, Grief without Apology: A Guide for Facing Death and Loss*

Sandberg, S., & Grant, A. (2017). *Option B: Facing Adversity, Building Resilience, and Finding Joy*

Sharp, N. (2014). *Both Sides Now: A True Story of Love, Loss and Bold Living*

Smith, H. I. (1996). *Grieving the Death of a Friend*

(continues)

FOCUS ON 14.1 *(continued)*

Selected Accounts of Bereavement Experiences during Young and Middle Adulthood

Smith, H. I. (2001). *Friendgrief: An Absence Called Presence*
Walter, C. A. (2003). *The Loss of a Life Partner: Narratives of the Bereaved*
Wray, T. J. (2003). *Surviving the Death of a Sibling: Living through Grief when an Adult Brother or Sister Dies*

ABOUT THE DEATH OF A PARENT:

Abrams, R. (2012). *When Parents Die: Learning to Live with the Loss of a Parent* (3rd ed.)
Jury, M., & Jury, D. (1978). *Gramps: A Man Ages and Dies*
March, A. (2007). *Dying into Grace: Mother and Daughter … a Dance of Healing*
Nouwen, H. (2005). *In Memoriam*
O'Rourke, M. (2012). *The Long Goodbye: A Memoir*
Safer, J. (2010). *Death Benefits: How Losing a Parent Can Change an Adult's Life—For the Better*
Smith, H. I. (1994). *On Grieving the Death of a Father*
Smith, H. I. (2003). *Grieving the Death of a Mother*

ABOUT ONE'S OWN STRUGGLES WITH LIFE-THREATENING ILLNESS:

Hanlan, A. (1979). *Autobiography of Dying*
Pausch, R., with Zaslow, J. (2008). *The Last Lecture*
Simmons, P. (2002). *Learning to Fall: The Blessings of an Imperfect Life*

As we think about many different types of losses detailed in this section, it may help to reflect on the many resources or strategies detailed in Chapters 10 and 11 that young and middle-aged adults might draw upon in coping with their losses and their grief. In particular, look again at Figure 11.1 and think about the many ways social media and the Internet might be helpful to many of these adults.

Death of a Child

Fetal Death   Along with some adolescent parents, many young adults experience the death of a child in the uterus or during the birthing process. These are **fetal deaths**, a category that is properly defined as a death "prior to delivery of a product of human conception, irrespective of the duration of pregnancy, and which is not an induced termination of pregnancy" (Gregory, MacDorman, & Martin, 2014). This category includes "stillbirth" or a "fetal death that occurs later in pregnancy" (i.e., at 20–28 weeks of gestation) and overlaps with "perinatal death," a phrase that applies to "infant deaths under age 7 days and fetal deaths at 28 weeks of gestation or more." Gregory and colleagues reported that, "the U.S. fetal mortality rate declined 8% from 2000 through 2006 (6.61–6.05 per 1,000 births and fetal deaths)" and remained "generally stable" thereafter through 2012.

Some think that fetal death experiences have minimal impact on the parents and do not generate a significant grief reaction. Parents have been offered false consolation: "Now you have a little angel in heaven" or "You can always have another child." Such easy dismissal of the losses in a fetal death reflects ignorance and frequently the discomfort of outsiders. It is often bolstered by an erroneous claim that there could not be much grief when there had not been real bonding with the infant. In fact, during pregnancy most parents begin to actively reshape their lives and self-concepts to accommodate the anticipated baby. Such parents observe the fetus moving in the womb with the aid of imaging techniques, explore potential names for the baby, plan accommodations, and develop dreams. When the death occurs in the uterus, it is often important to complete a process of bonding that is already under way in order to enhance opportunities for productive grief and mourning (Mehran, Simbar, Shams, Ramezani-Tehrani, & Nasiri, 2013). Parental grief associated with fetal or infant death is a reality that is related not to the length of a baby's life but to the nature of the attachment (Gamino & Cooney, 2002; Kohn, Moffit, & Wilkins, 2000). We must recognize the depth of the parents' grief and how they cope with their losses (Gray & Lassance, 2002; Ilse, 2013); otherwise, the grief is disenfranchised (see Chapter 10). Fetal death can be further complicated when one member of a set of twins dies.

Thus, programs have emerged in which parents and other family members are permitted (if they wish to do so) to see and hold their dead infant, name the child, take pictures (e.g., Hochberg, 2011), retain other mementos (such as a blanket, name tag, lock of hair, or cast of a hand or foot), obtain information from a postmortem examination, and take part in rituals that validate the life and the loss. Such practices provide opportunities to interact with the baby, share experiences, and strengthen a realistic foundation for mourning (Kuebelbeck & Davis, 2011). Implementing such practices requires attention to detail and sensitivity to individual preferences. The key is to understand the meaning of the loss for the parents and then to provide appropriate support. The website Stillbirthday affirms that the child and the abbreviated life were real and have value, as well as honoring the needs of those bereaved by the death.

In cases of elective abortion when the parent(s) feel(s) unable or unwilling to bring the baby to term or in cases of infant adoption when the child is given over shortly after birth to be raised by others, one often experiences a lingering sense of loss and grief (Peppers, 1988). When one chooses (deliberately or ambivalently) to abort, even if one believes that the fetus is not yet a human person, one often feels a sense of a loss that must be mourned. To opt for adoption, even when convinced that one is really not able to rear this child, may also leave one with feelings of pain or

The death of a child at the time of or shortly after birth is always very painful for family members.

To Celebrate the Life of

Riley Ann Dooley

The joy she has given shall forever etch her footprints on our hearts

Courtesy of Ann Fitzsimmons

Courtesy of Ann Fitzsimmons

regret. Neither elective abortion nor adoption need result in grief that incapacitates. It is wrong, however, to assume that these are easy, painless decisions and to dismiss out of hand the implications for parents of events and decisions that close off opportunities involving what is or would become their biological offspring.

Neonatal and Other Infant Deaths   After birth, the principal causes of death during infancy present contrasting scenarios for parents and significant others. On one hand, congenital malformations, disorders related to short gestation and low birth weight, newborns affected by maternal complications of pregnancy, and respiratory distress syndrome (RDS) may involve a struggle for life, the intervention of professionals and advanced technology prior to the death, and lingering implications of genetic origins or other feelings of parental responsibility. In such circumstances, the death of the infant is likely to occur in an institutional context, when the parents may not always be able to be present. On the other hand, sudden infant death syndrome (SIDS) will likely involve none of these factors, since it is the prototype of an encounter whose first symptom is death, as well as a death arising from an unknown cause that mostly occurs at home and for which parents often feel guilty in terms of what they did or did not do (see Focus On 12.1; Corr et al., 1991; Horchler & Morris, 2003).

When neonatal and other infant deaths are encountered, they most often have in common the untimely and perhaps unheralded death of a vulnerable individual. Even though pregnancy, the birthing process, and infancy are known to be risky times for the offspring, we commonly believe that tiny babies should not die. Thus, it is often said in the wake of such a death that "it's just not fair." Nevertheless, the hard fact is that "none of us is guaranteed long life, only a lifetime" (Showalter, 1983, p. x).

The specific impact of various types of infant deaths will depend on diverse factors that enter into the mode of death and the situation of the bereaved. For example, the death of an infant in a neonatal intensive care unit (NICU) can be an excruciating experience for professionals and parents alike. The experience may be even more difficult if there is conflict between professional care providers and family members (or between family members themselves) about care goals. Some bereaved mothers may prefer to remain on a maternity ward because of the staff's expertise in postpartum care, whereas others may wish to be relocated in order not to be around happy parents interacting with newborn babies.

In most cases associated with the death of an infant, a variety of issues arise for the parents and others involved. These issues include feelings of responsibility, loss of the idealized baby, loss of a part of oneself and one's future, lack of memories and rituals of mourning, and lack of social or professional support (Picard, 2002). Even when support is offered, it may not match the parents' needs or be available for as long as they require (Brabant, Forsyth, & McFarlain, 1995).

The death of an infant and the unique ways in which surviving parents experience and express their grief responses may create or add to existing strains on parental relationships (Rosenblatt, 2001; Schwab, 1990, 1996). In addition, single parents face special challenges when they must cope with an infant's death on their own (Wyler, 1989). Most of these bereaved parents display amazing resilience in finding ways to go on with productive living. Such parents deserve the best that can be offered in terms of information (e.g., about the nature of the infant's death and about parental loss and grief), professional support, and contact with those who have had similar experiences (Brabant, Forsyth, & McFarlain, 1995; Klass, 1988). In many cases, key areas of decision making involve whether (and, if so, when) to consider undertaking another pregnancy and how to help subsequent children relate to the older sibling who died before they were born (Schwiebert, 2003, 2007). It is always important to help bereaved parents identify their own needs and not to overburden them with criticisms or expectations of others.

Deaths of Children, Adolescents, or Other Young Adults   A child, adolescent, or young adult (who is often still viewed as a child by his or her parents) can die in many ways—for example, through some sort of accident (often involving a motor vehicle), as a result of homicide or suicide, from misuse of alcohol or illicit drugs, through natural causes, or even through social conflict, terrorism, or war. Typically, these deaths take place suddenly and without much warning or opportunity for preparation; often they involve trauma. In all cases, these deaths involve multiple dimensions for parents and other bereaved adults: loss of the life of the child, loss of what was or is a part of the self, loss of the hopes and dreams that the child represents, and a search for meaning (Feigelman, Jordan, McIntosh, & Feigelman, 2012; Klass, 1999).

Pain associated with the death of a child is often extraordinarily deep, pervasive, and enduring (Davies et al., 1998; Murphy, Johnson, & Lohan, 2003; Talbot, 2002). Charles Dickens (1848/1963, p. 274) recognized this fact in his novel *Dombey and Son* when he put the following exclamation into the mouth of a bereaved father: "And can it be that in a world so full and busy, the loss of one weak creature makes a void in any heart, so wide and deep that nothing but the width and depth of vast eternity can fill it up!" A few years earlier than Dickens, Ralph Waldo Emerson (1970, p. 165) made a similar point after the death of his son, when he wrote in his journal on January 28, 1842, "sorrow makes us all children again." Much the same is evident both in a novel centered on a long-past but not-forgotten experience of the death of a child, *The Christmas Box* (Evans, 2012), and in a prizewinning book of poems by a bereaved mother, *The Andrew Poems* (Wagner, 1994; see Personal Insights 14.2).

See! I will not forget you..I have carved you in the palm of my hand" (Isaiah 49:51)

Carol Kinghorn-Landry

PERSONAL INSIGHTS 14.2

Shelly Wagner: The Tie

At night, I imagine
lying on my side next to him,
my arm under his head,
whispering in his ear,
smoothing the child-sized red tie
that lies on his chest
like an upside-down
exclamation mark.
I put off buying him
men's clothing,
but for Easter he wanted a tie—
a red one
and a navy blue blazer.
Now, just under six years old,
he is buried wearing it forever—
as old a man
as he will ever be.
At night,
lying next to my husband,
I back into
the curved question mark
of his body
and ask,
"What is Andrew like now?"
He always whispers,
"His coat and tie are the same."

Source: From *The Andrew Poems*, by S. Wagner, p. 36.
Copyright © 1994 Shelley Wagner. Reprinted with permission from Texas Tech University.

Every resource an individual and a family can command is required to cope with such deep and intimate experiences, including for some efforts to create virtual online memorials to facilitate ongoing connections with the deceased child (Mitchell, Stephenson, Cadell, & Macdonald, 2012).

A special problem for parents who have experienced the death of a child arises from simple, everyday questions like "How many children do you have?" The difficulty is partly a matter of how the bereaved parent should view his or her own identity ("Am I still a parent?"; "What does this death mean for me?") and partly an issue of how much of one's personal life one might or should be willing to disclose to the person who posed the question. Above all, the challenge is how to be faithful to the deceased child and to his or her memory. Bereaved parents meet this challenge often and in different ways, but not so easily as it may seem to those who have not been bereaved (see Personal Insights 14.3).

How Many Children Do You Have?

It is early fall and I am standing in line at the grocery store. As I turn around to check the items in my cart, the woman behind me notices that I am very pregnant. "Is this your first child?" she asks innocently. Tears form in my eyes as I try to decide what to answer. If I say no, this will lead to the inevitable question: "How many children do you have?" Am I up for the possible reaction to my answer? Am I ready to bring up old feelings and memories? That day, I decide yes.

I turn to the woman and say, "This is my second child. My first child, my son, died in October of 1985 of Sudden Infant Death Syndrome." She puts her hand on my shoulder and tells me how sorry she is. She asks me some questions about our son and about SIDS. I appreciated so much the opportunity to talk about our son, Brendan, and SIDS, even to a complete stranger!

Unfortunately, that is not always the response I receive. Many times people will mumble something unintelligible and walk away. That is okay, too. I understand how difficult it is to hear about a baby dying—no one likes to hear about that.

Responses among bereaved parents will differ when they are asked how many children they have. In most cases, I will tell people I have a son who died, and two daughters.

There have been situations when I haven't mentioned Brendan. This is okay—it doesn't mean I don't love him or that I deny that he ever existed. It doesn't mean that I am a bad mother. What it does mean, is that, for the moment, I choose not to share Brendan. Early in my bereavement, I told everyone about Brendan's life and death. More than twelve years later, I have learned to cope with his absence and do not feel the need to mention him every time I meet someone new.

There are many ways in which my family and I keep his memory alive. As bereaved parents, we decide what is right for each of us. When we choose to mention our deceased children, we may make some people uncomfortable, but we may also have the opportunity to educate others. If we choose not to mention our deceased children, that does not mean that we deny them or that we should feel guilty. The only correct choice is what feels right to the bereaved parent.

Source: Maruyama, N. L. (1998). "How Many Children Do You Have?" *Bereavement Magazine, 12*(5), p. 16. Reprinted with permission from Bereavement Publishing, Inc., 4765 N. Carefree Circle, Colorado Springs, CO 80917; 888-604-4673.

When the child's death has come about by some form of more or less deliberate behavior (e.g., suicide or homicide), by inadvertence (e.g., accidents), by irresponsible behavior (such as drunken driving), or by war and terrorism, elements of responsibility, anger against the person or persons who are thought to be responsible, guilt or blame (by oneself or by others) may enter into the bereavement experience (Conrad, 1997; Stetson, 2002). Such elements can be expected to add to the burdens of parental grief and mourning (Bolton, 1995; Burroway, 2014; Chance, 1994; Matthews & Marwit, 2004). Despite all of the difficulties involved in parental bereavement, however, there are many things that professional care providers and others can do to be helpful, and bereaved parents have taken part in formulating guidelines for how professionals might help others in similar situations from the initial notification of a death through care of the body and the funeral (Janzen, Cadell, & Westhues, 2004).

Guilt in Parental Bereavement   Guilt is in part the conviction that one has done wrong by violating some principle or responsibility. Guilt may be realistic and well founded or unrealistic and unjustified. Typically associated with guilt are lowered self-esteem, heightened self-blame, and a feeling that one should make retribution for the supposed wrong. Guilt is by no means exclusive to parental bereavement, but it is almost always—at least initially—a prominent part of such bereavement.

Miles and Demi (1984, 1986) argued that guilt in parental bereavement arises from feelings of helplessness and responsibility. Such feelings lead parents to ask how their past and present actions might have contributed to the child's death. Inevitable discrepancies between ideal standards and actual performance can lead to guilt feelings. How individuals experience guilt depends on parental, situational, personal, and societal variables. At least six potential sources of guilt may apply to bereaved parents:

1. *Death causation guilt*, related to the belief that the parent either contributed to or failed to protect the child from the death
2. *Illness-related guilt*, related to perceived deficiencies in the parental role during the child's illness or at the time of death
3. *Parental role guilt*, related to the belief that the parent failed to live up to self-expectations or societal expectations in the overall parental role
4. *Moral guilt*, related to the belief that the child's death was punishment or retribution for violating a moral or religious standard
5. *Survival guilt*, related to violating the standard that a child should outlive his or her parents
6. *Grief guilt*, related to the behavioral and emotional reactions at the time of or following the child's death—that is, feeling guilty about how one acted at or after the time of the child's death

In the case of a bereaved parent, one must identify and address any of these elements of guilt that might appear in the overall bereavement experience. Each needs to be attended to in the mourning process.

Gender and Role Differences in Parental Bereavement   Fathers and mothers are different; married, unmarried, and divorced parents are different. Each bereaved individual is distinguished by his or her gender, role(s), and personal characteristics. Each of these distinguishing factors may and likely will influence the bereavement experience (Schwab, 1990, 1996). For example, according to traditional gender-based roles, expression of strong feelings was sanctioned for females but discouraged for males. Similarly, wives were expected to remain at home, while husbands went out to work. Although such gender-based roles do not apply in all relationships and are changing in many areas of society, factors like these may encourage different types of grief experiences for mothers and fathers (e.g., Davies et al., 1998, 2004). Even simply because they are two different individuals, at any given time spouses may be coping with loss and grief in different ways and may not be available to support each other as they otherwise do in healthy marital relationships (Simonds & Rothman, 1992). Moreover, research has shown that "although parents try to protect their partners through POSR [partner-oriented self-regulation], this effort has the opposite of the desired outcome" (Stroebe et al., 2013, p. 395). Thus, it is important for bereaved parents to share their grief, while being tolerant and patient with each other (Ilse & Nelson, 2008; Rosenblatt, 2000, 2016). Assistance from empathetic friends, other bereaved parents (e.g., through a support group like The Compassionate Friends), or an experienced counselor may be helpful.

Responses to parental bereavement are likely to be affected as gender expectations are altered, as social roles change, and as individual differences are permitted freer expression. A single parent and a surviving couple will be alone in different ways after the death of their child. Divorced or widowed parents whose child dies may face competing demands from grief and surviving children. A young parent and a grandparent may not always be able to help each other in mourning. We must appreciate the many factors that enter into individual experiences of parental bereavement during adulthood.

Death of a Spouse, Life Partner, Sibling, Peer, or Friend

Pair relationships can be very important in human life. Among adults, pair relationships may be established and carried over from childhood or adolescence or newly formed during the adult years. Such relationships may be of many types; those involving marital ties are not the only model. One may have special bonds with many other adults, such as a brother or sister, another relative, friend, coworker, lover, or life partner (heterosexual, gay, or lesbian). The relationship may be overt or hidden, continuous or intermittent, satisfying or complicated, healthy or abusive. There are perhaps as many variables in adult-to-adult relationships as there are in the individuals involved and in the ways they interact.

The dimensions of an adult's bereavement occasioned by the death of someone who is also an adult will depend, in the first place, on the intimacy and significance of the roles that the deceased person played in that individual's life. For example, the sibling relationship is typically the longest and most enduring familial relationship. Where that relationship is especially close, the death of one sibling may involve both his or her loss and the loss of an important part of the surviving sibling's identity (Marshall, 2013; Marshall & Winokuer, 2017; White, 2006; see also Personal Insights 14.4 and 14.5). Multiple siblings may react quite differently to the death of their brother or sister (Van Riper, 1997).

In spousal or other intimate friendships, two individuals are likely to have established a relationship that gradually becomes an important and enduring part of their identity (Romer, 2012, 2014; Smith, 1996, 2001). The deceased individual is no longer alive to receive love, his or her contributions to the relationship go unfulfilled, the comforting presence to which one formerly turned for love and solace is no longer available, and plans that the couple had made for the future may now go unrealized (Caine, 1990; Kaimann, 2002). Some of Al Joyner's experiences after the death of his wife, FloJo, reflect issues encountered by many bereaved adult spouses (see Personal Insights 14.6).

Another important factor in this type of bereavement has to do with the cause of the death and the circumstances in which it occurred. This is evident when an adult is confronted with the death of a significant other adult as a result of suicide or homicide. Such deaths are challenging and difficult (Johnsen & Dyregrov, 2016). Similar

PERSONAL INSIGHTS 14.4

Cokie Roberts on the Death of Her Sister

At some point during Barbara's illness I began preparing myself for a different vision of my old age. Without really thinking about it, I had always assumed we'd occupy adjacent rockers on some front porch, either literally or figuratively. Now one of those chairs would be empty. Intellectually I understood that. But every time some new thing happens that she's not here for, emotionally it hits me all over again—that sense of charting new territories without the map of my older sister.

And here's what I didn't expect at all—not only was I robbed of some part of my future, I was also deprived of my past. When a childhood memory needed checking, all my life I had simply run it by Barbara. Now there's no one to set me straight. My mother and brother can help some. My brother and I have, in fact, grown a good deal closer since our sister died; after all, without him, I would not only not have a sister, I would not be a sister. But Tommy didn't go to school with me, share a room with me, grow up female with me. Though I love him dearly, he is not my sister.

There it is. For all of the wonderful expressions of sisterhood from so many sources, for all of the support I both receive and provide, for all of the friendships I cherish, it's not the same. I only had one sister.

Source: C. Roberts (1998, pp. 16–17).

PERSONAL INSIGHTS 14.5

Jon Davis on the Death of His Brother

I had a brother and he died. I didn't cause it; I couldn't stop it. He got on his motorcycle and rode away. A car turned in front of him and that began his dying. How terrible for everyone involved. Do I sound bitter? I felt the usual guilts: Did I love him enough? Did I show it?

It happened eleven years ago and what I remember: Looking out at the lawn, September and a breeze; watching him ride—flash of red gas tank, brown leather jacket; the sound of the bike; what we said, which I recall as a kind of gesture, the sound of *what are you doing*, some dull rhythm and *see you later*.

The phone call. The drive to the hospital. I think I drove but I can't be sure. We drove the wrong way down a one-way street and I remember feeling responsible. I cried most of the time. I knew he was dying. My brother's girlfriend asked me *Why are you crying?* And I couldn't say or else I sobbed *It's bad I know it's bad*.

Then we were taken into a green room and told he was dead. I curled on a red plastic chair. My body disappeared or seemed to. I was looking for my brother; a nurse called me back: *Your family needs you.* I came back.

(continues)

PERSONAL INSIGHTS 14.5 *(continued)*

Jon Davis on the Death of His Brother

But why am I telling you this? Because I want you to love me? To pity me? To understand I've suffered and that excuses my deficiencies? To see how loss is loss and no elegy, no quiet talk late at night among loved ones who suddenly feel the inadequacy of their love and the expression of that love can take it away? Or give it back? Perhaps even loss is lost?

My brother is gone and the world, you, me, are not better for it. There was no goodness in his death. And there is none in this poem, eleven years later and still confused. An attempt, one might say, to come to terms with his death as if there were somewhere to come to, as if there were terms. But there is nowhere to come to; there are no terms. Just this spewing of words, this gesture neither therapy nor catharsis nor hopelessness nor consolation. Not elegy but a small crumb. An offering.

Source: Reprinted with the permission of the University of Akron Press, from *Scrimmage of Appetite*, pp. 12–13, by Jon Davis. Copyright © 1995 by Jon Davis.

PERSONAL INSIGHTS 14.6

The Death of Florence Griffith Joyner and Its Aftermath

Florence Griffith Joyner, known to friends and fans as "FloJo," died unexpectedly on September 21, 1998, at the age of 38 (Gregorian, 1998).

FloJo was known for her athletic abilities and flamboyant style. She set new world records in track while winning three gold medals and a silver medal at the Olympic Games in Seoul in 1988.

FloJo's husband, Al Joyner, and his sister, Jackie Joyner-Kersee, experienced the sudden death of their mother at the age of 37 as a result of cerebrospinal meningitis. But Al said that tragic event did not prepare them for FloJo's death.

On September 21, 1998, Al woke at 6:30 a.m. to the sounds of the bedroom alarm clock. When he went to wake his wife, in bed with their 7-year-old daughter, Mary, Al experienced what he later said was "the most hopeless moment of my life" (Brennan, 1998, p. 5E).

A postmortem examination determined that FloJo had died in her sleep of an epileptic seizure.

Several weeks after FloJo's death, Al was reported to have said: "If Mary were not here, I really think I would do something stupid. I feel like I have nothing to live for, until I think of her" (Brennan, 1998, p. 5E).

Al also said that he has not had his wife's mobile telephone service disconnected. In fact, from time to time he calls that number just to hear the voice of Florence on the answering tape saying, "This is Florence. I can't talk to you right now. Please leave a message."

difficulties in bereavement may be seen when members of the military die during war and other conflicts. The social context of the loss may be problematic because of questions about the military role in those situations. More importantly for many, their loss is hard because the deaths often occur in traumatic ways and frequently involve not just young adults in the regular military, but also older members of the military reserves and National Guard (both male and female), many of whom have spouses and children. Suicide and homicide in recent years after returning from these wars have also been difficult for many family members (Dreazen, 2014; LeardMann et al., 2013).

Death of a fellow adult—a spouse, life partner, sibling, peer, or friend—can change the world, the other, and the self for a bereaved adult (as well as for children and others who may also be involved) (Noel & Blair, 2008; Rodger, Sherwood, O'Connor, & Leslie, 2007). The death of only one person like this can entail many social, emotional, financial, spiritual, and other losses. It can also precipitate renewed struggles with personal identity (Golan, 1975). Much depends on how the death occurred, on the perspective of the survivor, and on social norms. For example, if it was an ex-spouse who died, is the bereaved individual to be thought of and recognized as a widow or widower (Campbell & Silverman, 1996; Stillion, 1985)? And will thoughts arise about the possibility of remarriage or other forms of new relationships (Bishop & Cain, 2003)?

Death of a Parent or Grandparent

Young and middle adults typically emancipate themselves in some measure from parental and family bonds. For example, they may move away from parental influences, either geographically or psychosocially. Usually, but not always, they reestablish new relationships with parents, grandparents, and other family members, revising the relationships that characterized their childhood. In any case, adults have unique relationships—simple, ambivalent, or complicated though they may be—with their own parents and grandparents throughout their adult lives. These members of an older generation often are sources of advice, support, and assistance to their adult children and grandchildren. Sometimes they become individuals who need to be cared for by their adult children (Comer, 2006).

In contemporary societies, most adults expect their parents and grandparents to precede them in death and this is the most common form of bereavement during adult life. But even when expected, such deaths often are difficult experiences for those left behind (Moss & Moss, 2007, 2013). They involve the loss of a lifelong relationship, full of shared (playful and sorrowful) experiences. The surviving adult may have devoted much time and energy to the care of the older person who has now died (e.g., Collier, 2003). An individual like this may also perceive the death as the removal of a "buffer" or source of generational "protection" against his or her own personal death (Akner & Whitney, 1993; Angel, 1987). Literature on experiences after the death of a mother or father (e.g., Gilbert, 1999; Lutovich, 2001; Smith, 1994, 2003), as well as specific situations involving motherless daughters (Edelman, 2014), fatherless daughters (Simon, 2001), and fatherless sons (Chethik, 2001; Veerman & Barton, 2006), describes special complications that may apply to each of these bereavement situations. Sometimes, the death may be perceived as the completion of a long, full life or as a release from suffering. However, it may involve lost opportunities or unfinished business and a failure to experience certain developmental or situational milestones by the deceased, the bereaved adult, or that person's children. For example, following the death of a parent or grandparent, the adult child no longer has an opportunity to renew or extend relationships with the deceased person on an adult-to-adult basis. Difficult and important issues may be left unresolved. In these and other ways, the death of a parent almost inevitably gives his or her adult children a "developmental push," which most often alters their sense of themselves and through which they may feel with added force their own finitude or the weight of their own responsibility as members of the now-oldest living generation (Umberson, 2003). Finally, the death of a parent of one partner has also been shown to have multiple impacts, not just on that individual, but also on various practical matters and shifting issues of closeness/intimacy versus distance in couple relationships (Rosenblatt & Barner, 2006).

For all of these reasons, it is worth noting that the Hospice Foundation of America (2015) has made available a free two-page handout on "Grieving the Loss of a Father—On Father's Day" addressing ways to remember the deceased individual and ways to support yourself or a friend experiencing a similar loss, a resource that can easily be adapted to other losses of an adult family member.

Summary

In this chapter, we explored many aspects of interactions between young and middle-aged adults and death. We noted how the distinctive developmental tasks of young adulthood and middle age have a direct bearing on how such adults relate to death. These tasks influence encounters with death among young and middle adults (we noted an accelerating increase in death rates involving diseases of the heart and cancer) and attitudes of these adults toward death (special concerns about the deaths of others in young adults and the appearance of a newly personalized sense of mortality in middle-aged adults). We also explored some of the main concerns that arise when young and middle adults are coping with life-threatening illness and dying or with many typical types of bereavement encounters.

Glossary

Developmental eras in adulthood: young adulthood and middle adulthood

Fetal death: death resulting from miscarriage, stillbirth, or spontaneous abortion

Generativity: maintaining productivity in one's life and projects; typically involves reassessing or reevaluating the meaning and direction of one's life, conserving or considering prospects for the continuation or enduring value in one's legacies, and preparatory efforts to put one's affairs in order

Intimacy: the ability to be open, supportive, and close with another person, without fear of losing oneself in the process

Midlife transition: the transition from young to middle adulthood

Normative developmental tasks in adulthood: to achieve intimacy (vs. the danger of isolation) in young adulthood; to pursue generativity (vs. the danger of stagnation or self-absorption) in middle adulthood

Sandwich generation: adults who experience pressures from both older and younger generations

Questions for Review and Discussion

1. Think back to the vignette near the beginning of this chapter. What types of losses were the archbishop and his mother coping with? If you were their friend, how would you try to help?
2. What types of death-related losses are most typical in adulthood, and what do such losses usually mean to adults?
3. Think about some of the losses you have experienced as an adult or you have witnessed in other adults. What were those losses like for you or the other person? How did you cope or help?
4. Have you ever drawn on social media or the Internet in efforts to learn about or cope with the situations described in this chapter? Did it help? Why or why not?

Suggested Readings

Concerning life-threatening illness in adulthood, consult:

Cousins, N. (1979). *Anatomy of an Illness as Perceived by the Patient: Reflections on Healing and Regeneration*
Charon, R. (2006). *Narrative Medicine: Honoring the Stories of Illness*
Frank, A. W. (2002). *At the Will of the Body: Reflections on Illness*
Frank, A. W. (2013). *The Wounded Storyteller: Body, Illness, and Ethics* (2nd ed.)
Mehl-Madrona, L. (2007). *Narrative Medicine: The Use of History and Story in the Healing Process*

Bereavement and grief in adulthood are explored in many ways from a broad developmental standpoint:

McCoyd, J.L.M., & Walter, C. A. (2016). *Grief and Loss across the Lifespan: A Biopsychosocial Perspective* (2nd ed.; especially Chapters 6 & 7)

In terms of the death of a child:

Buckle, J. L., & Fleming, S. J. (2011). *Parenting after the Death of a Child: A Practitioner's Guide*
Burroway, J. (2014). *Losing Tim: A Memoir*
Corr, C. A., Fuller, H., Barnickol, C. A., & Corr, D. M. (Eds.). (1991). *Sudden Infant Death Syndrome: Who Can Help and How*
Davis, D. L. (2016). *Empty Cradle, Broken Heart: Surviving the Death of Your Baby* (3rd ed.)
Feigelman, W., Jordan, J., McIntosh, J., & Feigelman, B. (2012). *Devastating Losses: How Parents Cope with the Death of a Child to Suicide or Drugs*
Gray, K., & Lassance, A. (2002). *Grieving Reproductive Loss: A Healing Process*
Horchler, J. N., & Morris, R. R. (2003). *The SIDS and Infant Death Survival Guide: Information and Comfort for Grieving Families and Friends and Professionals Who Seek to Help Them* (3rd ed.)
Ilse, S. (2013). *Empty Arms: Coping with Miscarriage, Stillbirth and Infant Death* (20th, rev. ed.)
Klass, D. (1988). *Parental Grief: Solace and Resolution*

Klass, D. (1999). *The Spiritual Lives of Bereaved Parents*

Kohn, I., Moffit, P-L., & Wilkins, I. A. (2000). *A Silent Sorrow: Pregnancy Loss— Guidance and Support for You and Your Family* (rev. 2nd ed.)

Lafser, C. (1998). *An Empty Cradle, a Full Heart: Reflections for Mothers and Fathers after Miscarriage, Stillbirth, or Infant Death*

Limbo, R. K., & Wheeler, S. R. (1998). *When a Baby Dies: A Handbook for Healing and Helping* (2nd ed.)

Mitchell, E. (2009). *Beyond Tears: Living after Losing a Child* (rev. & enlarged ed.)

Myers, M. F., & Fine, C. (2006). *Touched by Suicide: Hope and Healing after Loss*

Peckinpah, S. (2014). *How to Survive the Worst That Can Happen: A Parent's Step by Step Guide to Healing after the Loss of a Child*

Rando, T. A. (Ed.). (1986a). *Parental Loss of a Child*

Rosenblatt, P. C. (2000). *Help Your Marriage Survive the Death of a Child*

Rosenblatt, P. C. (2016). *Parent Grief: Narratives of Loss and Relationship*

Stetson, B. (2002). *Living Victims, Stolen Lives: Parents of Murdered Children Speak to America*

Talbot, K. (2002). *What Forever Means after the Death of a Child: Transcending the Trauma, Living with the Loss*

Tedeschi, R. G., & Calhoun, L. G. (2003). *Helping Bereaved Parents: A Clinician's Guide*

In terms of the death of a spouse, life partner, sibling, peer, or friend:

Campbell, S., & Silverman, P. R. (1996). Widower: *When Men Are Left Alone*

Lewis, C. S. (1976). *A Grief Observed*

Marshall, B. J., & Winokuer, H. R. (Eds.). (2017). *Sibling Loss across the Lifespan: Research, Practice and Personal Stories* (especially Parts III & IV)

Romer, J. (2012). *Widow: A Survival Guide for the First Year*

Romer, J. (2014). *The Widower's Guide to a New Life*

Stroebe, W., & Stroebe, M. S. (2003). *Bereavement and Health: The Psychological and Physical Consequences of Partner Loss*

White, P. G. (2006). *Sibling Grief: Healing after the Death of a Sister or Brother*

In terms of the death of the adult's parent or grandparent:

Akner, L. F., with C. V. Whitney. (1993). *How to Survive the Loss of a Parent: A Guide for Adults*

Chethik, N. (2001). *FatherLoss: How Sons of All Ages Come to Terms with the Deaths of Their Dads*

Edelman, H. (2006). *Motherless Daughters: The Legacy of Loss* (2nd ed.)

Edelman, H. (2007). *Motherless Mothers: How Losing a Mother Shapes the Parent You Become*

Gilbert, A., & Kline, C. B. (2006). *Always Too Soon, Voices of Support for Those Who Have Lost Both Parents*

Levy, A. (2000). *The Orphaned Adult: Understanding and Coping with Grief and Change after the Death of Our Parents*

Lutovich, D. S. (2001). *Nobody's Child: How Older Women Say Good-Bye to Their Mothers*

Simon, C. (2002). *Fatherless Women: How We Change after We Lose Our Dads*

Veerman, D., & Barton, B. B. (2006). *When Your Father Dies: How a Man Deals with the Loss of His Father*

Selected Web Resources

Some useful search terms include: ADULTS AND DEATH; CAUSES OF DEATH IN ADULTHOOD; DEVELOPMENTAL TASKS IN ADULTHOOD; "SANDWICH" GENERATION; YOUNG AND MIDDLE-AGED ADULTS.

You can also visit the following *organizational and other Internet sites*:

Bereaved Parents of the USA

The Compassionate Friends

National Widower's Organization

Partnership for Parents/Padres con padres

Pregnancy Loss and Infant Death Alliance (PLIDA)

Widow's Hope

Older Adults

Objectives of this **Chapter**

▸ To enhance our discussion of distinctive developmental tasks of older adults

▸ To describe typical encounters with death among older adults in the United States

▸ To explore death-related attitudes among older adults

▸ To identify key issues for older adults who are coping with life-threatening illness and dying

▸ To survey central issues for older adults who are coping with bereavement and grief

▸ To investigate issues related to suicide among older adults

LIVES CROWNED BY LOVE

He calls her Miss America. Sometimes she calls him John, the name of her deceased husband. ...Francis Eldridge is 92. Marie Franzen is 97. Both lived full and happy lives before they met nine years ago. Francis was married to his Edyth for 58 years. Marie was married to John for 64.

Neither was looking to begin again when they were introduced during lunch at the ... Senior Center. ... Instead they became soul mates. Francis remembers what happened later, at Marie's home. "She was having trouble lifting a window," he says. "I went by to fix it and never left."

They decided against marriage, but after a month Francis moved into Marie's ... bungalow. ...Francis loved Marie's cooking. Her beef stew, Hungarian goulash and stuffed cabbage pushed his weight up to a robust 175 pounds.

Then Marie was diagnosed with Alzheimer's. But as long as Francis was around, Marie eventually found the words she intended to say.

Everything changed in March of 1999 when Francis developed a severe case of pneumonia that landed him in the ... Medical Center for three weeks.

He was released from the hospital too weak to take care of himself and Marie. He moved in with his daughter, Sylvia Whitney ... Marie moved into [a nursing home].

"He was happy to be with me, but he missed her so much," says Whitney. "I would take him to visit her once or twice a week, but he kept losing weight. Marie is the only woman—besides my mother—that my dad ever cared about."

As Francis shriveled, Marie languished. "He dropped to 114 pounds; she was lost," says Whitney. Out of desperation, she moved Francis to Crystal Oaks to live with Marie.

Francis is back up to 137 pounds. No one expects Marie's Alzheimer's to go away, but she now has longer stretches of clarity.

"You don't know what your feelings can do to your body," says Francis as he and Marie soak up the sun on a green metal bench in front of Crystal Oaks. They come here each morning after breakfast to hold hands and say hello to all who pass....

The two are teasing each other about their dancing when Francis's black wrist watch begins to talk. "Ten forty-two," it says in a monotone. This is followed by a recording of a crowing rooster. Francis and Marie are both legally blind. They depend on the rooster to tell them when to go inside.

They shuffle along the polished floors until they come to the large water fountain they use as a landmark. "When we find the fountain, we've found our room," says Marie.

Inside, she has a collection of teddy bears. Friends bring them as gifts, and Marie keeps them for a while before passing them on to visitors and friends. But the small white bear dressed in blue never leaves the room. It was a gift from Francis.

When they melt into Marie's single bed for their daily noontime rest, the bear is there too. They will spend the next hour wrapped in each other's arms, Miss America and her darling John. (*SOURCE:* "Lives Crowned by Love" by Jamie Francis, p. 1D in the Floridian, *St. Petersburg Times*, March 9, 2001, Reprinted by permission.)

OLDER ADULTS, DEVELOPMENTAL TASKS, AND DEATH

In 2014, there were a little over 46 million *older adults*—those who are 65 years of age and older—in the United States, representing 14.5% of the total population.

The overall number of these older adults in the United States is projected to increase to 82.3 million by 2040 (more than double their number in 2000) and 98 million by 2060, while the population of those 85 years and older is projected to increase from 6.3 million in 2014 to 14.6 million in 2040 (see Administration on Aging, 2016). As a result, some have spoken of the **graying of America**. In many societies, these older adults would be thought of as the repository of social wisdom, but America's youth-oriented society does not typically take this view. Thus, the position of older adults is more ambiguous and less honored by much of our society.

With the emergence of a body of knowledge about **older adulthood**, much has been learned about the developmental tasks and other issues that distinguish them from other members of American society. In particular, it has been recognized that aging is not identical with pathology. Becoming an older adult is often marked by a variety of biological, psychological, and social changes—but the majority of older adults in the United States are living vigorous, productive, and satisfying lives (Cavanaugh & Blanchard-Fields, 2014; Hooyman & Kiyak, 2010). NBC news correspondent Tom Brokaw (1998) has called older adults in our society *The Greatest Generation*, and former President Jimmy Carter (1998) has written about *The Virtues of Aging*. One notable example of achievement by an older American occurred in 2010 when Betty White was named Entertainer of the Year by the Associated Press at the age of 88 years. Around the same time, the actress, perhaps best known for her role in the television sitcom *Golden Girls*, appeared on *Saturday Night Live* after a Facebook campaign for her to host the show. She won her seventh Emmy Award for that performance, did a top-rated Super Bowl commercial for Snickers candy bars, became a regular on the television series *Hot in Cleveland*, posed with hunky guys for a 2011 calendar, and published two new books (White, 2010, 2011). In 2013, the Guinness World Records recognized White as having the longest television career for a female entertainer and in 2017 she celebrated her 95th birthday.

Nevertheless, American society often gives evidence of what Butler (1969) called **ageism**, which he (1975, p. 12) defined as "a process of systematic stereotyping of and discrimination against people because they are old." In fact, it is wrong, unfair, and potentially harmful to older adults when they are casually lumped together, when their lives are devalued, and when appreciation is lacking for what they have in common with all other human beings. Against this stereotyping, it is desirable to acknowledge the shared humanity, the significant human values, the potential contributions they might still make, and the great diversity to be found in this portion of the population (Thomas, 2007; see also Issues for Critical Reflection #12). If it is true that "human beings are

Betty White at the "Dr. Seuss' The Lorax" Premiere, on February 19, 2012, at Universal Studios, Universal City, CA.

more alike at birth than they will ever be again" (Stillion, 1985, p. 56), then it should also be true that human beings are most unalike in older adulthood, in view of the many years in which each individual has had to work out his or her long story.

Research on *late adulthood* has demonstrated that it is not appropriate to speak of "old age" without qualification. In fact, older adults are neither a static nor a monolithic segment of the population (Erikson, Erikson, & Kivnick, 1986; Havighurst, 1972). As one researcher has reported, "old people do not perceive meaning in aging itself, so much as they perceive meaning in being themselves in old age. Thus … [the central issue is] how old people maintain a sense of continuity and meaning that helps them cope with change" (Kaufman, 1986, pp. 13–14).

In Erikson's (1959) original schema of human development, the last era in the human life course was called **senescence**. This term had been used earlier by Hall (1922) to designate the entire last half of human life. The word itself identifies the process of growing old, and thus by transference designates older adults themselves. Unfortunately, *senescence* is etymologically linked to the terms *senile* and *senility*, which now designate not merely the condition of being old but the presence of cognitive impairment often mistakenly associated with old age. This unqualified linkage between normative developmental eras and pathology is not accurate and thus undesirable (Madey & Chasteen, 2004). Perhaps to avoid such implications, Erikson later (1963, 1982) spoke about this period as the era of **maturity** or one in which human development is "completed."

ISSUES FOR CRITICAL REFLECTION
#12 Two Old Women: Do Older Adults Still Have Anything to Contribute?

It is sometimes assumed that old age necessarily leads to incapacity and increasing dependence on others. This belief is not limited to contemporary culture. In cultures living near the Arctic Circle, tribes sometimes abandoned elderly persons who were considered no longer able to contribute to the needs of the group. Velma Wallis (2004) in her book *Two Old Women* develops an Alaskan Athabaskan legend she learned from her mother.

Wallis's tale begins by describing a tribe in which there are two old women who are viewed by tribal members as complaining, demanding, and not contributing to the needs of the society. They are seen as a burden on the tribe's scarce resources. When the tribe faces starvation during a particularly harsh winter, the leader of the tribe decides to leave the two old women behind.

Wallis continues her tale:

> The two old women sat old and small before the campfire with their chins held up proudly, disguising their shock. …They stared ahead numbly as if they had not heard the chief condemn them to a certain death—to be left alone to fend for themselves in a land that understood only strength. Two weak old women stood no chance against such a rule. (p. 7)

But this is only the beginning of Wallis's story. The two old women do not simply descend into loneliness, despair, and death. Instead, their dire situation calls forth from them resources—psychological, physical, intellectual, and spiritual— they hardly knew they had, and they survive, even flourish. A year later, the tribe encounters the old women once more when the tribe's condition is again very precarious. The two old women offer some of the food from the stores they had accumulated through their own labor and resourcefulness. In the end, the tribe and the two old women realize that they are each able to help the other. Thus, the two women and the tribe come to recognize that old age need not always lead to incapacity and dependence, but rather can lead to a new level of *interdependence* from which *all* can benefit.

Different developmental theorists describe the principal **developmental task of older adulthood** in similar ways. Erikson (1963, 1982) described this task as involving *the achievement of* **ego integrity** *versus despair or disgust*, Maslow (1968) spoke of *self-actualization*, and Birren (1964) wrote about *reconciliation*. For each of these theorists, the principal developmental work of old age involves the attainment of an inner sense of wholeness. Successfully resolving earlier developmental tasks and coming to terms with one's past helps older adults achieve the balance and harmony in this wholeness (integrity means being whole or undivided) that emerges from a process of introspection, self-reflection, and reminiscence that Butler (1963) called a **life review**. Marshall (1980) suggested that older adults develop an *awareness of finitude*—recognizing that death may come at any time. This is often seen when older adults qualify comments on the future by saying things like, "*I hope I am alive when you marry*." Recognition of finitude leads to a life review process as older adults try to affirm that their lives mattered.

In pursuing heightened interiority, past experiences are spontaneously brought to consciousness, reviewed and assessed, and perhaps reinterpreted or reintegrated. The aim is to resolve old conflicts and to achieve a new sense of meaning, both to account to oneself for one's past life and to prepare for death. If this process is successful, it results in integrity and wisdom (Erikson & Erikson, 1981). If not, it yields a sense of despair because one is not satisfied with what one has done with one's life and does not feel that sufficient time or energy remains to alter directions and compensate for how one has lived.

Customarily, older adults have been thought of as those who are 65 years of age or older (perhaps in part because many faced a social marker of mandatory retirement at that age). In the 21st century, however, the situation is more complicated because mandatory retirement is less common nowadays. Also, persons reaching age 65 in the United States in 2014 had an estimated average life expectancy of an additional 23.3 years (24.7 years for females; 21.7 years for males) and such averages have been trending upward in recent years. In fact, the portion of those in the very oldest segment of our society, those aged 100 years or more (72,227 in 2014; more than double the 1980 figure) is projected to grow most rapidly of all during the first half of the 21st century (see Figure 15.1 and Issues for Critical Reflection #13).

Figure 15.1 **Actual and Projected Centenarian Populations by Gender, United States, 2000–2050**

Source: U.S. Bureau of the Census, National Population Projections, 2001.

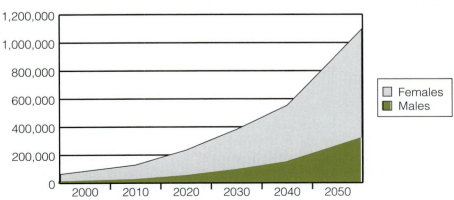

- Have a pool of "good" genes (choose your parents wisely!).
- Keep your blood pressure low; take an aspirin a day.
- Participate in regular exercise and maintain your weight.
- Avoid a diet high in protein and saturated fats; limit coffee drinking.
- Do not smoke cigarettes or use other tobacco products; avoid secondhand smoke.
- Limit your use of alcohol products to not more than two drinks per day.
- Avoid excessive exposure to the sun.
- Practice effective stress management techniques and maintain a good sense of humor.
- Engage in rewarding hobbies.
- Enjoy many friends (of all age groups) and share gratifying activities with them.

Consult the book *Living to 100: Lessons in Living to Your Maximum Potential at Any Age* (Perls, Silver, & Lauerman, 1999) and check the Life Expectancy Calculator at the website livingto100.com to see how you are doing in this regard.

If you could increase your life expectancy substantially (perhaps even reach age 100 or older):

- What would you want to do?
- What would be your goals?
- How would you plan to support yourself financially?
- What health problems would you anticipate?
- With whom would you want to live?
- Where would you choose to live?
- What living facilities would you desire?

In short, many older adults in our society—especially those in the 65- to 74-year-old age group—possess relatively good health, education, purchasing power, and free time—and are politically active. If so, we need to distinguish between the following **developmental eras in older adulthood**: the "young old" (those 65–74 years of age), the "old" or "old old" (those 75–84 years of age), and the "oldest old" or "very old" (those 85 years of age and older). Some speak of the very old as the "frail elderly," but that is a health category, not a developmental term. Older adults of any age (as well as younger persons) may or may not be frail. Still, there clearly are different social cohorts among older adults and distinctive developmental tasks in this evolving population. (For discussions about whether aging should be classified as a disease, see Bulterijis, Hull, Björk, & Roy, 2015; Faragher, 2015; and Zhavoronkov & Bhullar, 2015.)

ENCOUNTERS WITH DEATH DURING OLDER ADULTHOOD

In this section, we explore numbers of deaths and death rates among older adults, leading causes of these deaths, and the variables of gender and race.

Deaths and Death Rates among Older Adults

A total of just over 1.9 million deaths in 2014 among those who were 65 years of age or older represented a little over 73% of the total of more than 2.6 million deaths in that year. These deaths occurred among older adults who make up approximately 14.5% of the total U.S. population.

Table 15.1 provides an overview of the number of deaths in the United States in 2014 for three groups of older adults: individuals 65–74 years of age, 75–84 years of age, and 85 years and older. Comparing these data shows that the *number of deaths* increases significantly from among individuals 65–74 years of age to those 75–84 years of age, and

Table 15.1 **Number of Deaths, Ages 65 and Older, by Age, Race or Hispanic Origin,[a] and Gender, United States, 2014**

	Ages 65 to 74 Years			Ages 75 to 84 Years			Ages 85 & Older		
	Both Sexes	**Males**	**Females**	**Both Sexes**	**Males**	**Females**	**Both Sexes**	**Males**	**Females**
All origins[b]	471,541	268,648	202,893	624,504	316,430	308,074	826,226	308,785	517,441
Caucasian-Americans, total	396,428	227,249	169,179	545,948	279,177	266,771	749,222	282,424	466,798
Non-Hispanic Caucasian Americans	367,779	210,808	156,971	510,281	261,374	248,907	711,340	267,765	443,575
African Americans	60,955	33,499	27,456	60,428	28,161	32,267	56,327	18,100	38,227
Hispanic Americans[c]	28,036	15,948	12,088	35,342	17,544	17,798	37,292	14,395	22,897
Asian and Pacific Island Americans	10,728	6,037	4,691	14,979	7,563	7,416	18,319	7,370	10,949
American Indians and Alaska Natives	3,430	1,863	1,567	3,149	1,529	1,620	2,258	891	1,467

[a] Data for specified groups other than Caucasian Americans and African Americans should be interpreted with caution because of inconsistencies between reporting race and/or Hispanic origin on death certificates and on censuses and surveys.

[b] Figures for origin not stated are included in "All origins" but not distributed among specified origins.

[c] Includes all persons of Hispanic origin of any race.

Source: Heron, 2016.

then continues to increase among the much smaller population of those 85 years of age and older. This curve continues the general pattern of a continuous increase in the number of deaths throughout the whole of adulthood in the United States.

Similar patterns are true of *death rates* among older adults (see Table 15.2). In 2014, very high overall death rates among individuals who were 65–74 years of age rose to exceptional heights among persons who were 85 years of age or older. Similar increases in death rates appeared in all segments of the older adult population. All of these figures are greatly in excess of the overall mortality rate in the United States. In short, death is very much a part of the life of older adults. Since humans are mortal and cannot live indefinitely, the longer one lives, the closer one comes to the limit of the human life course.

Leading Causes of Death among Older Adults

All of the five leading causes of death in 2014 for the three age groupings among adults who were 65 years of age or older were chronic or degenerative diseases, led by heart disease and cancer. In the same year, human-induced deaths and communicable

Table 15.2 **Death Rates (per 100,000), Ages 65 and Older, by Age, Race or Hispanic Origin,[a] and Gender: United States, 2014**

	Ages 65–74 Years			Ages 75–84 Years			Ages 85 & Older		
	Both Sexes	Males	Females	Both Sexes	Males	Females	Both Sexes	Males	Females
All origins[b]	1,786.3	2,175.5	1,444.2	4,564.2	5,369.2	3,955.1	13,407.9	14,642.2	12,765.7
Caucasian Americans, total	1,769.2	2,143.3	1,433.1	4,619.3	5,419.1	4,001.3	13,742.6	15,000.3	13,079.1
Non-Hispanic Caucasian Americans	1,798.8	2,170.0	1,462.9	4,700.7	5,499.0	4,078.9	13,977.4	15,286.4	13,290.4
African Americans	2,381.5	3,047.4	1,880.2	5,049.0	6,172.6	4,356.8	12,136.5	13,291.7	11,656.8
Hispanic Americans[c]	1,316.5	1,655.1	1,036.7	3,415.6	4,103.3	2,931.3	9,635.1	10,318.0	9,250.2
Asian and Pacific Island Americans	883.0	1,107.1	700.5	2,584.4	3,047.8	2,237.5	8,427.6	9,263.1	7,945.3
American Indians and Alaska Natives	1,585.8	1,830.2	1,368.6	3,598.0	4,097.9	3,226.6	8,149.9	8,610.4	7,893.5

[a]Data for specified groups other than Caucasian Americans and African Americans should be interpreted with caution because of inconsistencies between reporting race and/or Hispanic origin on death certificates and on censuses and surveys.

[b]Figures for origin not stated are included in "All origins" but not distributed among specified origins.

[c]Includes all persons of Hispanic origin of any race.

Source: Heron, 2016.

diseases declined in relative significance as causes of death. For both male and female older adults, leading causes of death are essentially the same, with only minor differences in their relative significance. One important recent development has been the appearance of Alzheimer's disease among the five leading causes of death in the two oldest cohorts of older adults. In 2014, Alzheimer's disease was the cause of nearly 93,541 deaths among these older adults. (See Chapter 20 in this book for an analysis of Alzheimer's disease and related disorders.)

Nevertheless, other causes of death among older adults are also of interest. For example, accidental deaths are increasingly prominent as leading causes of deaths among older adults as they age and death rates caused by accidents also increase substantially during older adulthood. However, accidental deaths caused by motor vehicles are far less frequent among older adults than all other accidental deaths (Heron, 2016). Accidental falls are the leading cause of nonfatal injuries among older adults and thus are often the source of debilitation among such individuals (Tideiksaar, 2010). In terms of overall *numbers*, homicide, suicide, and HIV infection do not appear among the ten leading causes of death for older adults, although suicide rates among older adults (and especially among those age 85 and older) have been a matter of ongoing concern and are discussed later in this chapter.

Two Variables in Deaths of Older Adults: Gender and Race

Tables 15.1 and 15.2 show contrasts by gender in the number of deaths and death rates among older adults. At first, males die in larger numbers than females, but that changes as individuals reach 75 years of age and older. Because more American females than males live to a more advanced age, there are more of them to die among the "oldest old" in our society. Thus, in 2014, there were far more deaths in the oldest group of American females (those 85 years of age and older) than among females 75–84 years of age. Death rates for males remain constantly higher throughout older adulthood than those for females.

In terms of other subgroups among older adults, the number of deaths climbs sharply among "young old" and "old old" Caucasian-Americans before falling slightly among those 85 years of age and older. This trend reflects a crossover effect in which the population of the "oldest old" who remain alive in our society is less numerous than any other ten-year age group. Much smaller numbers of deaths among other principal subgroups among older adults rise only modestly at first in these age groups and then decline in relatively steeper fashion. In all these groups, death rates rise steadily throughout older adulthood, and males have higher death rates than their female counterparts.

ATTITUDES TOWARD DEATH AMONG OLDER ADULTS

There is general and long-standing agreement that older adults are significantly less fearful of death than younger persons (Catt et al., 2005; Cicirelli, 2002). Of course, "fear of death" is not an uncomplicated notion (as we saw in Chapter 3), and older adults may differ among themselves in this regard. Also, variables that reduce or threaten the quality of life in older adults, such as poor physical and mental health, being widowed, or being institutionalized, appear likely to be inversely associated with fear of death. Nevertheless, authors such as Matse (1975) and Saul and Saul (1973) have shown that older adults often talk about aging and death, even within fairly restrictive institutional environments that may not encourage such discussions.

Kalish (1985a) proposed three explanations for the relatively low level of fear of death among older adults: (1) they may accept death more easily than others because they have been able to live long, full lives; (2) they may have come to accept their own deaths as a result of a socialization process through which they repeatedly experience the deaths of others; and (3) they may have come to view their lives as having less value than the lives of younger persons and thus may not object so strenuously to giving them up. For any of these reasons, death may seem to an older adult to represent less of a threat than, for example, debility, isolation, or dependence. As a result, most older adults want to die at home, without pain, and without becoming a burden on their families.

OLDER ADULTS WHO ARE COPING WITH LIFE-THREATENING ILLNESS AND DYING

Older adults who are coping with life-threatening illness or dying have four basic needs: "maintaining a sense of self, participating in decisions regarding their lives, being reassured that their lives still have value, and receiving appropriate and adequate health care services" (Cook & Oltjenbruns, 1998, p. 346).

Maintaining a Sense of Self

Preserving and affirming the value in the identity established in one's developmental work throughout life is an important task for individuals involved in transitions and

reassessments like those that characterize developmental work in older adulthood. One's sense of integrity is founded on one's self-concept and self-esteem. As we have already noted, in older adults this reassessment is typically pursued through the processes of a *life review*—reflection, reminiscence, and reevaluation (Coleman, 2005).

For older adults who are coping with a life-threatening illness or dying, these processes need not be eliminated, although they may be curtailed by distress, lack of energy or inability to concentrate, absence of social support, and what often appear to be societal tendencies to devalue aging and older adults. Against these inhibiting factors, family and professional caregivers can encourage life review activities in a number of ways. For example, they can directly participate by listening and serving as sounding boards or by providing stimuli, such as photographs and prized mementos. Enabling older adults who are ill or dying to remain at home or to retain and express their individuality within an institution is another way of affirming the person's uniqueness and value. Hospice programs often encourage older adults who are ill or dying to identify achievable goals in craftwork or other ways of making tangible gifts to give to others. Passing on such gifts or valued personal items can be a cherished activity in itself and a way of leaving behind an enduring legacy. Accepting such gifts with warmth and appreciation is an act of affection, not an expression of a wish for the death of an older adult.

Participating in Decisions about Their Lives

In Western societies, autonomy or the ability to be in charge of one's own life is a prized value for many individuals. This may be particularly true for older adults, who may already have experienced a number of losses and who are often concerned with issues related to dependence. Older adults often want to continue to take part in decisions about their own lives, insofar as that is possible (Taylor, 2011). They may have a very broad and active role in such decision making or that role might be highly constrained and largely symbolic. Nevertheless, as former President Jimmy Carter has pointed out (see Personal Insights 15.1), older adults typically want to participate in decisions about their lives and their ability to do so should be sustained as much as possible.

Fostering autonomy may require delicate negotiations between a specific older adult, his or her family members, and professional care providers (Norlander &

PERSONAL INSIGHTS 15.1

Jimmy Carter, on Aging and Facing Death

We are not alone in our worry about both the physical aspects of aging and the prejudice that exists toward the elderly, which is similar to racism or sexism. What makes it different is that the prejudice also exists among those of us who are either within this group or rapidly approaching it. When I mentioned the title of this book to a few people, most of them responded, "Virtues? What could possibly be good about growing old?" The most obvious answer, of course, is to consider the alternative to aging. But there are plenty of other good answers—many based on our personal experiences and observations...

Perhaps the most troubling aspect of our later years is the need to face the inevitability of our own impending physical death. For some people, this fact becomes a cause of great distress, sometimes with attendant resentment against God or even those around us....

We can either face death with fear, anguish, and unnecessary distress among those around us or, through faith and courage, confront the inevitable with equanimity, good humor, and peace. When other members of my family realized that they had a terminal illness, the finest medical care was available to them. But each chose to forego elaborate artificial life-support systems and, with a few friends and family members at their bedside, they died peacefully. All of them retained their life-long character and their personal dignity. During the final days of their lives they continued to enjoy themselves as well as possible and to reduce the suffering and anguish of those who survived. My older sister Gloria was surrounded by her biker friends and talked about Harley-Davidsons and their shared pleasures on the road. Her funeral cortege, in fact, was a hearse preceded by thirty-seven Harley-Davidson motorcycles. Until the end, my brother Billy and my mother retained their superb sense of humor, and my youngest sister, Ruth, was stalwart in her faith as an evangelist.

Rosalynn and I hope to follow in their footsteps, and we have signed living wills that will preclude the artificial prolongation of our lives.

Source: Carter (1998, pp. 8–9, 82, 85–86).

McSteen, 2001). For example, many older adults desire to remain in their own homes at the end of their lives (Gott, Seymour, Bellamy, & Ahmedzai, 2004). For such individuals, the decision to enter a long-term care facility may become a matter of contention between older adults and other family members; in some cases, it may lead to a kind of learned helplessness when the older adult's wishes are not supported or validated.

As a culture, American society has long valued individualism and autonomy. However, it is only lately that our society has gradually come to realize—in theory, at least—the need that older adults in particular have for autonomy and the values that it represents. Thus, according to the Patient Self-Determination Act, which went into effect in 1991, individuals who are admitted to a health care facility must be informed of their rights to fill out a living will or health care proxy, grant someone their durable power of attorney in health care matters, or otherwise have their wishes about treatment recorded and respected (Annenberg Washington Program, 1993; Cate & Gill, 1991). While the act is not without its limitations, its effects can contribute to positive mental health and general satisfaction with life especially by encouraging older adults to participate in decision making about their own lives. This works against premature psychosocial and even physical decline and death, especially in older adults who may have felt beset by loss of control and other external or internal pressures that undermine autonomy and quality of life and that foster hopelessness, helplessness, and "giving up."

Being Reassured That Their Lives Still Have Value

As already noted, in a youth-oriented society, ageism can foster discrimination against and devaluation of the lives of older adults. Combined with losses that such older adults may have experienced, such as those involved in bodily functioning or in giving up one's vocational status in retirement, this attitude may encourage older persons to depreciate their own value and sense of worth. Life-threatening illness or dying may compound this process of devaluation by older adults and others. Reduced contacts with significant others may lead to isolation and justified or unjustified

Recording precious memories can be a valuable part of a lifetime legacies project.

Courtesy Suncoast Hospice

concerns about social death even when physical death is not imminent. At least for some older adults, a lasting dimension of quality of life involves the possibility of expressing one's sexuality and sexual needs. Sexuality may take the form of sexual intercourse, but often it involves no more than simple touching or hugging, as we saw in the vignette near the beginning of this chapter.

The hospice philosophy's emphasis on life and maximizing present quality in living suggests an antidote to this sort of devaluation of the lives of elderly persons. Conveying to older adults—even those who are coping with life-threatening illness and dying—that their lives are still valued and appreciated, that they are important and have much to teach others, and that they can still find satisfaction in living can enhance their sense of self-worth. One can foster self-esteem and dignity simply by not talking down to older adults and not assuming deafness or incompetence on their part. Showing family members how to be involved in constructive ways in the life and care of an older adult who is ill or dying can improve present quality in living and diminish feelings of guilt or frustration for all concerned.

Receiving Appropriate and Adequate Health Care

Studies conducted many years ago in both the United States (Sudnow, 1967) and Great Britain (Simpson, 1976) demonstrated that older adults who were brought to hospital emergency departments in critical condition were likely to receive care that was not as thorough or vigorous as that provided to younger persons. Recent research tends to confirm this type of discrimination in end-of-life care (Rietjens, Deschepper, Pasman, & Deliens, 2012). This finding raises questions of equity and issues of decision making that may often be difficult, particularly for those who are critically ill, dying, vulnerable, and perhaps alone or not fully competent. Constructive lessons drawn from the life-affirming orientation of hospice programs, as well as positive developments in geriatric medicine and in gerontological specializations in other fields, such as nursing, social work, and law, can do much to change this situation. Older adults who are coping with life-threatening illness or dying have helped to create and support societal health care and welfare systems. In return, such systems should address their health care needs appropriately. Through political action and organizations such as AARP, older adults are mobilizing to try to ensure that these needs are addressed. Also, among its many services, *ConsumerReports* offers "Advice for Those Caring for the Elderly" as part of its ConsumerHealthChoices series (http://consumerhealthchoices.org/caregiving/).

OLDER ADULTS WHO ARE COPING WITH BEREAVEMENT AND GRIEF

Most older adults encounter many occasions for bereavement (Hansson & Stroebe, 2006), some of which were illustrated in the vignette near the beginning of this chapter. Not all of these losses, such as the loss of a home the person has occupied and cherished over many years, are directly associated with death. However, death-related losses alone offer a broad array of challenges for many elderly persons in the form of the deaths of spouses, life partners, siblings, friends, and peers; the deaths of "very old" parents who may have lived to such advanced old age that their children have now reached "young old" status; the deaths of adult children; and the deaths of grandchildren or great-grandchildren. In addition, there is the special poignancy of the death of a pet or companion animal when its owner is an older adult, as well as the possible impact of physical disability or psychosocial impoverishment. In fact, as Kastenbaum

(1969) noted, older adults are likely to experience losses in greater number, variety, and rapidity than any other age group. Consequently, older adults are often exposed to **bereavement overload**, a situation in which they do not have the time or other resources they need to process their grief and mourn one significant loss effectively before another occurs. For such older persons, grief is a constant companion.

As we think about many different types of losses detailed in this section, it may help to reflect on the many resources or strategies detailed in Chapters 10 and 11 that older adults might draw upon in coping with their losses and their grief. In particular, look again at Figure 11.1 and think about the many ways social media and the Internet might be helpful to these older adults.

Illness, Disability, and Loss

Older adults may also be grieving as a result of the many "little deaths" they have experienced throughout life or in later adulthood. Among these are losses associated with illness of various sorts. Not every older adult experiences such losses, but many live with one or more illness-related burdens. For example, high blood pressure and constriction or obstruction in the arteries are common in many older adults, as are certain forms of cancer (lung and prostate cancer in males; lung and breast cancer in females). Even when these conditions are not fatal, they may restrict quality of life. Chronic health problems, such as those involved in arthritis, emphysema, and diabetes, have similar effects (Gorman, 2011b).

Some long-term degenerative diseases, such as Alzheimer's and Parkinson's diseases or ALS (amyotrophic lateral sclerosis; often called "Lou Gehrig's disease" in the United States), have special import for losses in older adults. These diseases may manifest themselves in ways that are physical (e.g., through pain or loss of muscle control), psychological (e.g., through confusion), social (e.g., through loss of mobility, institutionalization, and limited capacity for social exchanges), or spiritual (as in questions about the meaning of one's life and the nature of a universe in which these losses occur). They affect both the individual person—for example, an older adult with Alzheimer's disease who may be aware of his or her declining mental function—and those who love and must care for a person who may become unable to perform even the most basic activities of daily living (Bell & Troxel, 2012, 2016; Comer, 2006; Mace & Rabins, 2011; see Chapter 20 in this book). Often, these diseases generate the very special problems of complicated or "ambiguous" loss (Boss, 1999) and psychosocial death involved in what Toynbee (1968a, p. 266) termed "the premature death of the spirit in a human body that still remains physically alive." These issues can complicate difficult problems of decision making, choosing appropriate modes of care, and satisfying cost requirements.

Less dramatic, but still significant in terms of well-being, are the accumulated losses or deficits that older adults often experience in effective functioning. These can include sensory and cognitive impairments, oral and dental problems, loss of energy, reduced muscle strength, diminished sense of balance, and problems related to osteoporosis, arthritis, or sexual functioning. Specific losses like these and their combined effect on an individual older adult can reduce quality in living and generate regret for what has been lost on the part of that person, family members, and care providers.

The Death of a Spouse, Life Partner, Sibling, Friend, or Other Significant Peer

Surviving the death of a spouse, sibling, life partner, friend, or another significant peer is a common experience in older adulthood (Carr, Nesse, & Wortman, 2005).

The individual who has died may be a marriage partner, a brother or sister, an individual of the same or opposite sex with whom one has lived for some time and formed a stable relationship, or a special friend or peer. One problem for some older adults (particularly among the "very old" group) may be the loss through death or incapacitation of most or all of the members of one's family of origin. Survivors of losses of this type constitute a special group of "lonely oldies" whose particular form of loneliness and deprivation may not be assuaged even by the joy they find in the presence and attention of members of younger generations.

In general, sustaining roles and relationships is crucial for most older adults who are bereaved. Above all, this typically includes companionship, someone with whom one can talk, someone to share burdens, pleasures, and sexual gratification, and someone to offer presence and care in the future as one's own needs increase. When the relationship with the partner is such that their lives are closely interwoven, "the loss of one partner may cut across the very meaning of the other's existence" (Raphael, 1983, p. 177). Of course, most relationships with a partner are complicated in some ways and may not be without conflict. Still, every older adult experiences multiple losses in the death of a significant peer, and those who have experienced the death of a spouse or life partner may be at higher risk during the following years for increased morbidity and mortality (from illness or suicide, for example) (Stroebe & Stroebe, 2003).

The death of a spouse or close companion in late adulthood often generates bereavement experiences of separation and deprivation involving grief (including yearning, pain, and anger), isolation, and loneliness (D'Epinay, Cavalli, & Spini, 2003). In our society, the burdens of survival following the death of a spouse most often fall upon women (Hurd & Macdonald, 2001). This is partly because in our society, women outlive men on the average and women most often marry men who are their own age or older. In addition, widowers are more likely than widows to remarry, partly because of the relative availability of potential spouses for elderly males (and the opposite for elderly females). However, many older adults are resilient and it is not the case that all of the older adults who are widowed wish to marry again (Moore & Stratton, 2002). In any event, emotional ties to the deceased are likely to persist, and memories may be cherished by both sexes (Moss & Moss, 1985). Thus, it may not be so much the experience of bereavement as its expression that is influenced by gender roles.

Either in place of or as a supplement to other forms of social support, self-help groups (Hoy, 2016; Lund, Dimond, & Juretich, 1985) can be very helpful for older adults who are bereaved, as we saw in Chapter 11. Social interventions of this type typically serve the full range of bereaved persons who have experienced certain kinds of losses and do so on a foundation of shared experience. Through these interventions, individuals who have had similar experiences can share feelings and problems. They can also encourage each other to regain control in living by evaluating options and alternatives represented in the lives of the others, while obtaining helpful information about loss, grief, and living.

The Death of an Adult Child

To a parent, one's offspring always remains one's child in some important ways despite his or her age. As average life expectancy increases, it becomes more and more likely that middle-aged and elderly parents may experience the death of an **adult child**. For example, many young adults in their twenties and thirties who die in accidents or from communicable diseases and individuals in their forties, fifties, and sixties who die of degenerative diseases may leave behind a surviving parent (Rando, 1986b). In fact, one study (Moss, Lesher, & Moss, 1987) reported that as many as 10% of elderly persons with children had experienced the death of a child when the parent was 60 years of age or older.

For such a parent, the grief felt at this type of loss may be combined with special developmental complications (Blank, 1998; Moss et al., 1987). For example, surviving parents may feel that the death of an adult child is an untimely violation of the natural order of things, in which members of the older generation are expected to die before the younger. Such parents may experience survivor guilt and wish to have died in place of their child. In addition, there may be special hardships if the adult child had assumed certain responsibilities as helper or care provider for the parent. After the death, these needs will have to be met in some other way, and the parent may face an increased likelihood of diminished social contacts or institutionalization. How family legacies will be carried forward is now less certain. The parent may also join to his or her own sense of loss added regret and grief for the pain that the spouse or children of the adult child are experiencing. In all too many cases, the older survivor may be obliged to take over the care of surviving grandchildren (Hayslip & Goldberg-Glen, 2000).

The Death of a Grandchild or Great-Grandchild

If it is more likely that children and adolescents will have living grandparents and great-grandparents because of increased life expectancy among older adults, then it is also more likely that some of these older adults will experience the death of one of their grandchildren or great-grandchildren. It is important to attend to this type of bereavement because cross-generational relationships between grandchildren and grandparents can involve special bonds of intimacy (Wilcoxon, 1987).

Grandparents have been described as **forgotten grievers**, both connected to and distanced from events involving the fatal illness, death, or bereavement of a grandchild. The grief and mourning of such grandparents responds to their own losses, as well as to losses experienced by their son or daughter. Such grief may contain elements of hurt over such an "out of sequence" death, anger at parents who perhaps did not seem to take adequate care of the grandchild, guilt at their own presumed failure to prevent the loss or death, and resentment at God for letting such tragic events occur (Galinsky, 1999; Reed, 2000). All of these reactions may be complicated in situations in which there is unwillingness to acknowledge certain causes of death (such as those involving suicide, HIV infection, or misuse of alcohol or illicit drugs) or to discuss openly the circumstances of the death. Finally, there may be conflicts between grandparents and one or more surviving parent—for example, when members of the older or younger generation blame the others for a perceived failure to prevent the death or when grandparents are drawn into or otherwise affected by disputes between the surviving parents.

Loss of a Pet or Companion Animal

We discussed pet loss in Chapter 10, but it is important to note again that loss of a pet or companion animal can be of special importance in the lives of older adults (Peretti, 1990; Sable, 1995). Companion animals can be sources of unconditional love, as well as objects of care and affection in the lives of many older adults.

Some of these animals, such as service dogs, protect and aid handicapped elderly persons. In recent years, others have become welcome visitors in many long-term care facilities and other institutions. In these roles, companion animals can relieve loneliness, contribute to a sense of purpose, and enhance self-esteem (Rynearson, 1978).

When an older adult's companion animal dies, the key point is the relationship with that animal, rather than its intrinsic or monetary value (Lagoni, Butler, & Hetts, 1994). Such a loss can represent a major bereavement for an elderly person who may otherwise have only limited social contacts (Quackenbush, 1985; Shirley & Mercier, 1983; Toray, 2004) and thus should not be dismissed as insignificant. Similar losses and grief may occur when an older adult is no longer able to care for an animal, cannot pay for veterinary services it needs, cannot take it along when relocating to new living quarters or to an institution, or must have a sick or feeble animal euthanized (Kay et al., 1988). Older adults may also be concerned about what will happen to a prized pet if they should die.

SUICIDE AMONG OLDER ADULTS

Although suicide is no longer among the ten leading causes of death for older adults in our society, it caused the deaths of 7,912 individuals 65 years of age and older in the United States in 2015 (Drapeau & McIntosh, 2016). These deaths represented 17.9% of all deaths by suicide in the United States in that year, a year in which older adults made up only 14.9% of the total population. This high number of suicide deaths in this relatively small segment of the population means that very high rates of suicide in the United States were found among the oldest members of our society. In 2015, those rates were 17.9 per 100,000 among those aged 75–84 and 19.4 per 100,000 among those aged 85 years and older. The latter rate has increased since 2004, when it was 16.4 per 100,000 (see Table 17.1), and suicide rates for all older adults in our society are noticeably higher than the rate of 13.8 suicides per 100,000 for the U.S. population as a whole or the rate of 12.5 suicides per 100,000 among individuals ages 15–24 years. Among older adults, Caucasian-American males are by far the most likely to take their own lives. In general, older adults are less likely to attempt suicide than their younger counterparts, but far more deliberate once they have chosen their course. They are unlikely to ask for help that might interfere with or alter their decision, and they are unlikely to fail to complete their suicidal plan once they have initiated the attempt (McIntosh, 1985). Therefore, any indicators of suicidal tendencies on the part of older adults should be taken seriously and evaluated carefully (Conwell, Van Orden, & Caine, 2011).

It has long been known that the single most significant factor associated with suicidal behavior in older adults is *depression* (Leenaars, Maris, McIntosh, & Richman, 1992). Older adults may begin to contemplate suicide when the *life review* process results in a sense of despair about the meaning of their lives; when they experience physical or mental debility that limits their functioning or independence; when they experience the death of a spouse or another significant person (especially a person on whom they had been dependent for care and support); or when institutionalization in a long-term care facility seems to undermine control over their lives. In these circumstances, some may come to consider suicide an acceptable alternative to continued living under what appears to them to be unsatisfactory conditions (Osgood, 1992; Osgood, Brant, & Lipman, 1991; Segal, Mincic, Coolidge, & O'Riley, 2004).

Much higher rates (rising with age) of older adult male versus female suicides appear to result from other factors, such as an unwanted retirement by males whose identity had hitherto greatly depended on their vocational roles (a factor that is increasingly likely to impact women as they move into similar vocational roles), previous dependency on a now-deceased female caretaker, or social isolation (Conwell, 2001; Conwell & Duberstein, 2001).

There are a number of obstacles to interventions designed to minimize the likelihood of suicidal behavior among older adults, such as efforts to apply interventions that have been successful with younger persons in ways that are inappropriate to the developmental situation of older adults. For example, unhelpful approaches might include: claims that suicide is a permanent solution to a temporary problem (more relevant to impulsive decisions by adolescents); advice to concentrate on a promising future; or arguing that suicide terminates life prematurely thereby cutting short a full life. Some argue that efforts intended to thwart suicidal behavior in older adults are inappropriate assaults on the autonomy of older adults, although others make a vigorous case that too-ready tolerance of **suicide among older adults** may reflect a lack of interest in the lives of such individuals (Osgood, 1992).

More helpful approaches might include screening for depression; offering services designed to reduce disability and enhance independent functioning; and addressing social isolation and lack of access to social support (Erlangsen et al., 2011). In particular, one might use questions like the following to engage in constructive discussions with an at-risk older adult: "Have you ever attempted to harm yourself in the past?"; "Have you had thoughts about how you might actually hurt yourself?"; "How likely do you think it is that you will act on these thoughts about hurting yourself or ending your life sometime over the next month?"; "Is there anything that would prevent or keep you from harming yourself?" (Administration on Aging, 2012). These questions examine risk factors through brief explorations of suicide history, suicidal planning, perceived probability, and preventive factors.

In the end, suicidal behavior among older adults needs to be understood within the broad physical, psychosocial, and developmental situation of older adults in American society (Osgood, 2000). Particular attention must be paid to social attitudes associated with ageism, a devaluation of worth and meaning in the lives of older adults, and an unresponsiveness to the needs of older adults. Significant changes in these and other sociocultural factors will be required to alter suicidal behavior in older adults.

Summary

In this chapter, we explored many aspects of interactions between older adults and death in our society. We saw that the distinctive developmental tasks of older adulthood (striving to achieve ego integrity versus despair) have a direct bearing on how older adults relate to death. These tasks influence encounters with death among older adults (we noted high death rates mainly brought about by long-term degenerative diseases) and attitudes of older adults toward death (in general, manifesting less anxiety than younger persons). We explored the importance for older adults who are coping with life-threatening illness and dying to maintain a sense of self, participate in decisions regarding their lives, be reassured that their lives still have value, and receive appropriate and adequate health care services. We found that older adults may find themselves coping with bereavement and grief as a result of illness, disability, and loss; the death of a spouse, life partner, sibling, or another significant peer; the death of an adult child; the death of a grandchild or great-grandchild; or the loss of a pet or companion animal. We also observed that high rates of suicide among older adults are strongly associated with depression.

Glossary

Adult child: an individual who is an adult, but also the living child of an older parent

Ageism: Butler's term for systematic stereotyping and discrimination against people because they are old

Bereavement overload: Kastenbaum's phrase for a situation in which individuals (especially older adults) do not have the time or other resources needed to process their grief and mourn one significant loss effectively before another occurs

Developmental eras in older adulthood: the "young old" (those 65–74 years of age), the "old old" (those 75–84 years of age), and the "oldest old" or "very old" (those 85 years of age and older), although in fact these are chronological rather than developmental distinctions

Developmental tasks in older adulthood: Erikson's theory involves a tension between "ego integrity" versus "despair"; successfully resolving this polarity leads to the virtues of "renunciation and wisdom"

Ego integrity: Erikson's term to describe the attainment of an inner sense of wholeness; also described as "self-actualization" or "reconciliation"

Forgotten grievers: a term sometimes applied to grandparents who experience a double loss over the death of a grandchild and over the losses experienced by that child's parent(s) (their son or daughter)

Graying of America: a term pointing to the growing share of older adults in the population

Life review: a process of introspection, heightened interiority, self-reflection, and reminiscence, designed to resolve old conflicts and develop a new sense of meaning as means to achieve integrity, account to oneself for one's past life, and prepare for death (Butler)

Maturity: the term that Erikson substituted for "senescence" to designate the concluding period in the human life course; now more commonly replaced by "older adulthood" or "late adulthood"

Normative developmental task of older adulthood: the achievement of ego integrity (versus despair or disgust; according to Erikson); self-actualization (Maslow); reconciliation (Birren)

Older adulthood: an era in the human life course that follows "middle adulthood" or "middle age"; sometimes called "late adulthood"; includes those who are 65 years of age or older; encompasses distinctions within this era between the "young old," the "old old," and the "very old"

Senescence: Erikson's initial term for the last era in the human life course; replaced by the term *maturity*

Suicide among older adults: older adults in the United States have recently had the highest rates of suicide among all developmental groups; often involves deliberate behavior plus depression

Questions for Review and Discussion

1. Think about the elderly couple depicted in the vignette near the beginning of this chapter. What types of losses did they experience? How did those losses affect them? How did they help each other?
2. Do you know an older adult who has experienced significant death-related losses? What were those losses like for that person? How did you or could you help such a person?
3. Many older adults are now pretty savvy in involvements with social media and the Internet. Are you acquainted with such older adults? What have they told you about these involvements?

Suggested Readings

On aging and older adults, consult:

Butler, R. N. (2002). *Why Survive? Being Old in America*

Erikson, E. H., Erikson, J. M., & Kivnick, H. (1986). *Vital Involvements in Old Age*

Holstein, M. (2015). *Women in Later Life: Critical Perspectives on Gender and Age*

Moody, H. R., & Sasser, J. R. (2014). *Aging: Concepts and Controversies* (8th ed.)

Nouwen, H., & Gaffney, W. J. (1990). *Aging: The Fulfillment of Life*

Perls, T. T., Silver, M. H., & Lauerman, J. F. (1999). *Living to 100: Lessons in Living to Your Maximum Potential at Any Age*

Quadagno, J. (2014). *Aging and the Life Course: An Introduction to Social Gerontology* (6th ed.)

Stoller, E. P., & Gibson, R. C. (Eds.). (2000). *Worlds of Difference: Inequality in the Aging Experience* (3rd ed.)

On death, loss, and older adults, consult:

Campbell, S., & Silverman, P. R. (1996). *Widower: When Men Are Left Alone*

Carr, D., Nesse, R. M., & Wortman, C. B. (Eds.). (2005). *Spousal Bereavement in Late Life*

Doka, K. J. (Ed.). (2002b). *Living with Grief: Loss in Later Life*

Galinsky, N. (1999). *When a Grandchild Dies: What to Do, What to Say, How to Cope*

Hansson, R. O., & Stroebe, M. S. (2006). *Bereavement in Late Life: Coping, Adaptation and Developmental Influences*

Hurd, M., & Macdonald, M. (2001). *Beyond Coping: Widows Reinventing Their Lives*

Leenaars, A. A., Maris, R. W., McIntosh, J. L., & Richman, J. (Eds.). (1992). *Suicide and the Older Adult*

Marshall, B. J., & Winokuer, H. R. (Eds.). (2017). *Sibling Loss across the Lifespan: Research, Practice and Personal Stories* (especially Part V)

McCoyd, J.L.M., & Walter, C. A. (2016). *Grief and Loss across the Lifespan: A Biopsychosocial Perspective* (2nd ed.; especially Chapters 8 & 9)

Norlander, L., & McSteen, K. (2001). *Choices at the End of Life: Finding Out What Your Parents Want before It's Too Late*

Reed, M. L. (2000). *Grandparents Cry Twice: Help for Bereaved Grandparents*

Stroebe, W., & Stroebe, M. S. (2003). *Bereavement and Health: The Psychological and Physical Consequences of Partner Loss*

Troyer, J. M. (2014). *Counseling Widowers*

Walter, C. A. (2003). *The Loss of a Life Partner: Narratives of the Bereaved*

Selected Web Resources

Some useful search terms include: AGEISM; CAUSES OF DEATH IN OLDER ADULTS; DEVELOPMENTAL TASKS IN OLDER ADULTS; EGO INTEGRITY; GRAYING OF AMERICA; LATE ADULTHOOD; OLDER ADULTHOOD; PET LOSS; SENESCENCE; SUICIDE AND OLDER ADULTS; SURVIVOR GUILT.

You can also visit the following *organizational and other Internet sites:*

AARP (formerly American Association of Retired Persons)

Administration on Aging, U.S. Department of Health and Human Services

Aging Parents and Elder Care

The Center for Practical Bioethics

Eldercare Locator

Ethnic Elders Care

Leading Age (formerly American Association of Homes and Services for the Aging)

Living to 100

National Institute on Aging

National Widowers' Organization

SeniorNet

Widowed Persons Service (WPS)

Widow's Hope

PART Six

LEGAL, CONCEPTUAL, AND MORAL ISSUES

In Chapters 16 through 19, we address legal, conceptual, moral, religious, and philosophical issues that are directly related to dying, death, and bereavement. Issues related to the law, suicide, three principal forms of aided death (assisted suicide, euthanasia, and aid in dying), and questions of ultimate meaning are brought together here because they pose vital conceptual and moral challenges. In addressing these issues, we believe it is important to undertake two parallel tasks: first, to *understand* the facts and implications of the situation at hand, along with any options that might be available; second, to *choose* one's values and a particular course of action within the situation.

We begin with *legal issues* because the law is the most explicit framework of rules and procedures that every society establishes within its death system. In Chapter 16 we describe what the American legal system requires or permits before, at the time of, and after death. Topics covered include: conversations about end-of-life care and advance directives for health care; definition, determination, and certification of death; organ, tissue, and body donation; and disposition of one's body and property.

In Chapter 17, we seek to clarify the concept of *suicide*, provide data about some common patterns in suicidal and life-threatening behavior, describe some perspectives that seek to explain or understand this behavior better, discuss the impact of suicide on bereaved survivors, suggest constructive ways to intervene to minimize the likelihood of a completed suicide, introduce the concept of rational suicide, and identify selected religious views about suicide.

In Chapter 18, we explain the main forms of *aided death* (*assisted suicide*, *euthanasia*, and *aid in dying*), describe moral and religious arguments that have been advanced to favor or oppose such policies and activities, and illustrate what they might mean for society through examples taken from the state of Oregon, the Netherlands, and recent developments elsewhere.

In Chapter 19, we address questions of ultimate values by examining the *meaning and place of death in human life*. Many religious and philosophical perspectives seek answers to these questions and are frameworks within which both individuals and particular societies approach death-related experiences. We also explore in this chapter reports about near-death experiences and their interpretation.

Always in our hearts…

CHAPTER 16

Their gift lives

Legal Issues

Objectives of this Chapter

▸ To describe the origin and role of formal legal systems as they relate to death-related events

▸ To highlight the importance of conversations about end-of-life care and death-related matters

▸ To explain the nature and function of advance directives for health care

▸ To explore legal issues associated with definition, determination, and certification of death

▸ To examine topics related to organ and tissue donation and transplantation, and body donation

▸ To review subjects related to the disposition of one's body and one's property or estate

DONOR HUSBAND, DONOR FATHER

It was October 28, 1992, and Kenneth Moritsugu, M.D., M.P.H., was returning to his home in Silver Spring, Maryland, from Baltimore. He had taken his aunt and sister, visiting from Hawaii, on a day trip to visit art museums and the Inner Harbor—a mammoth shopping complex along the waterfront. His wife, Donna Lee, had elected to stay home.

As the three approached the end of their commute, traffic slowed. An accident had taken place, they thought. A long, tedious drive lay ahead as every car strained to advance.

As they approached the scene of the accident, Dr. Moritsugu looked out his window. He noticed the similarities in the wrecked vehicle and the car at home, the one Donna Lee drove. Panic set in as he realized the crushed vehicle on the road was in fact his wife's.

At the hospital, he learned Donna Lee was brain dead and would never recover.

"Several years before, we had talked about what we should do when the other died," Dr. Moritsugu recalled. "We had both said we wanted to donate. When the concept was brought up in that deepest, darkest moment, the memory of that conversation came back to me, and I had the privilege of carrying out her wishes. Because of her, many other individuals are surviving today."

A year later, Dr. Moritsugu, Assistant Surgeon General of the United States and Medical Director of the Federal Bureau of Prisons of the U.S. Department of Justice, began a personal crusade to encourage organ and tissue donation....

[Dr. Moritsugu] has suffered the bittersweet solace of donation not only once, but twice.

In 1996, Dr. Moritsugu's 22-year-old daughter, Vikki Lianne, was struck by an automobile while crossing the street. She, too, was declared brain dead and her organs donated.

It was only later that Dr. Moritsugu learned that Vikki Lianne and his older daughter, Erika Elizabeth, had made the commitment to donate their organs shortly after their mother's death. They had learned how much the donations had meant to others, and they had seen the comfort it had brought to their family.

"It makes me proud," Dr. Moritsugu said. "We talk about donation as affecting one person, but there are ripples. Each donation affects so many more people—family, friends, colleagues." Dr. Moritsugu is quick to point out that he should not be credited for the donations. "I didn't do anything," he noted. "I was just someone who happened to be there. They [Donna Lee and Vikki Lianne] are the ones who made the miracle."

Through Donna Lee:

- A marine biologist engaged in research on the effects of environmental pollution received a new heart.
- A 35-year-old diabetic hospital custodian received a kidney and pancreas.
- An 11-year-old child on dialysis, failing in school, received the other kidney. He is now making straight As and is on his way to college.
- A retired schoolteacher received a new liver.
- A young retarded woman who had lost her sight due to an accident received a cornea, while the other cornea provided new vision to a 49-year-old government worker.

Through Vikki Lianne:

- A mother of five received a new heart.
- A widow with four children received a lung.
- A 59-year-old man, an active volunteer with a local charitable organization, received a liver.
- A widower with one daughter received a kidney.
- A married, working father of several children received the other kidney.
- A 26-year-old man and a 60-year-old woman received her corneas.

Source: Benenson (1998). Donor husband, donor father: UNOS board member Kenneth Moritsugu looks beyond tragedy to serving others. *UNOS Update.* [Special edition, Spring], 26. Reprinted with permission.

AMERICAN SOCIETY AND ITS LAWS

Every society develops a more or less formal system of law to serve its interests as a community and to promote the welfare of its members. Such systems may include both written and unwritten rules and procedures that reflect values upheld by a society, as well as ways in which it organizes itself to implement those values.

Any such system of societal rules and procedures is likely to function most effectively when social values are well established and when it is responding to familiar events. It may be less effective when there is a lack of consensus about social values, when the values are in flux, or when social changes and progress pose new problems not easily addressed by existing legal frameworks. In recent years in the United States, challenges to the legal system have arisen from all three of these circumstances: there is disagreement in our heterogeneous population about some social values, other social values appear to be in transition, and new challenges have arisen from new circumstances and from new medical procedures and technology.

Our federal system assigns certain obligations (such as foreign relations and defense) to the national government and reserves most other responsibilities to the authority of the individual states and their subordinate entities. For most issues related to death, dying, and bereavement, state law governs what is to be done and how it is to be done. This results in different laws and procedures applying in different states. Some states might even have no legislation on a given subject. Thus, this chapter can only address legal issues and structures in a general way. Individuals should seek competent legal advice that is appropriate to their particular situations.

The establishment of *legislation* is often a slow and complicated process subject to political pressures, competing interests, and social circumstances. When values in society are changing or when there is no consensus on social values, the process of embodying and codifying those values in legislation may be arduous. Difficult cases may frustrate a society's process of determining how to implement its values. This is particularly true in cases that involve fast-moving advances in medical technology and procedures.

When no specific legislation covers a particular subject, decisions must still be made in individual cases. One way this is done is by drawing on precedents set by prior court decisions; these and other precedents constitute **case law**.

When neither the legislature nor the courts in their prior decisions have addressed a topic, the legal system turns to **common law**. Originally, this was a set of shared values and views drawn from English and early American legal and social history. In practice, it is typically represented in a more formal way by the definitions contained in standard legal dictionaries, such as *Black's Law Dictionary* (Garner, 2014).

It is important to be clear about which type(s) of legal rules and procedures apply to any given issue. The principles set forth here constitute the broad legal and social framework within which a large spectrum of moral, social, and human issues is addressed in American society. This legal framework is an important part of the contemporary American death system, but it is only one such component. Some death-related issues, such as cemetery regulations and cultural or religious rituals, are not directly addressed by the legal system. Other issues, such as different types of aided death (see Chapter 18), have challenged our legal system and remain wholly or partly outside its framework in different places.

CONVERSATIONS ABOUT DEATH-RELATED MATTERS AND ADVANCE DIRECTIVES

In this section, we explore thinking ahead about end-of-life care and other death-related matters through: conversations about these subjects; advance directives in the form of living wills, durable powers of attorney in health care matters, and the Five Wishes documents; and medical orders called physician orders for life-sustaining treatment (POLST).

Conversations about Death-Related Matters

Good advance care planning includes formulating **advance directives**. These are a wide range of instructions that in principal one might make orally but more typically would be set down in writing about actions one would or would not want to be taken if one were somehow incapacitated and unable to join in making decisions. A large body of literature is available to guide people in developing advance directives (e.g., Cebuhar, 2015; Fabiny & Sabatino, 2013; Fitzpatrick & Fitzpatrick, 2010; Rogne & McCune, 2013; Town & Kassel, 2014). Of course, any advance directive depends on the willingness of individuals to address ahead of time the implications of incapacitation and death for their lives and for their family members and friends. Nevertheless, Wright and colleagues (2016) learned from family members that advance care planning consistent with patients' preferences can lead to better end-of-life (EOL) care (see also Epstein et al., 2016; Mason, 2015). As well, McGreevy and colleagues (2016) showed that consultations concerning placement of gastrostomy tubes in seriously ill patients could provide important opportunities for establishing patient-centered goals of care. And research by Green and colleagues (2015, p. 1088) concluded that: "Engaging in ACP [advance care planning] … increases knowledge without diminishing hope, increasing hopelessness, or inducing anxiety in patients with advanced cancer. Physicians need not avoid ACP out of concern for adversely affecting patients' psychological well-being."

Unfortunately, other research has shown that many people, including both patients and physicians, are reluctant to consider issues like these, perhaps because they seem challenging and may involve contemplating the implications of one's own mortality (Rao et al., 2014; You et al., 2014, 2015). Still, as Narang and colleagues concluded (2015, p. 601): "Efforts that bolster communication of EOL care preferences and also incorporate surrogate decision makers are critically needed to ensure receipt of goal-concordant care."

In fact, many efforts have been made to try to motivate people to think about these subjects and to have conversations about end-of-life care and death-related matters with next of kin, family members, and their physicians (e.g., Landro, 2014). For example, since 1991 the Patient Self-Determination Act has required that individuals being admitted to a health care institution that receives federal Medicare or Medicaid funds be informed of their right to accept or refuse treatment and to execute an advance directive (Urich, 2001). Such individuals must also be told about the options available to them to implement those rights. Even so, many do not exercise their right to complete an advance directive—but that, too, is within their rights.

Going a step further, in 2016, the federal Medicare program, recognizing that approximately one-quarter of traditional Medicare spending for health care is for services provided to Medicare beneficiaries in their last year of life, authorized compensation for a new, separate, and billable service in the form of payments to physicians and other primary health care practitioners for engaging in *advance care planning* regarding end-of-life care and patient preferences. In addition, hospice programs have long undertaken similar discussions with the individuals and family members whom they serve and the National Hospice and Palliative Care Organization's CaringInfo program offers free resources to help people make decisions about end-of-life care and services before a crisis. As well, information about advance care planning in Canada is available on the Speak Up: Advance Care Planning website.

Furthermore, The Conversation Project (see also Volandes, 2016), a private, non-profit organization has undertaken to help people talk about their wishes for end-of-life care by developing free, downloadable "starter kits" that offer simple ways for family members and health care professionals to initiate such discussions. As of early 2017, these resources included:

- a general Starter Kit for adults (in English and several other languages).
- a Pediatric Starter Kid specifically designed to help parents of seriously ill children who want guidance about "having the conversation" with their children.
- a Starter Kit specifically designed to help families and loved ones of people with Alzheimer's disease or another form of dementia who want guidance about "having the conversation."
- a document on How to Choose a Health Care Proxy and How to Be a Health Care Proxy.
- a document on How to Talk to Your Doctor.

The Conversation Project does not envision that these starter kits will cover all possible topics that families might wish to include in their discussions. It also recognizes that a single discussion might not suffice. The important point is starting and facilitating such discussions. Our vignette near the beginning of this chapter makes clear that Donna Lee and Vikki Lianne Moritsugu had at least discussed organ donation with some family members before their untimely deaths.

Conversations about end-of-life care and other death-related matters among family members and their health care providers are valuable in themselves. Ultimately, they might be expected to lead to implementation in the form of written advance directives. Some such documents—such as directives on organ and tissue donation, the disposition of one's body, or the distribution of one's estate—are intended to come into force at the time of or after one's death. We discuss those directives later in this chapter. First, we consider advance directives directly concerned with decisions about health care before death, such as living wills, durable powers of attorney in health care matters, and the "Five Wishes" document, as well as Physician Orders for Life-Sustaining Treatment (POLST).

Living Wills

Living wills were originally developed in the early 1970s as a means whereby competent decision makers could express their wishes to professional care providers, family members, and friends about interventions they might desire or might not wish to permit in the event of a terminal illness. Because these early living wills had no legal standing, they could take any form. Common threads in these documents were: (1) concerns about the possibility or likelihood of finding oneself in a situation in which one would be unable to take part in making important decisions and (2) concerns about the context of dying in which one might be in an unfamiliar or alien environment, among strangers or others who might have their own individual or professional views of what should or should not be done, and who might not understand, appreciate, or agree with the wishes of the person who wrote the living will.

In response to such concerns, early living wills usually combined desires expressed by those who composed and signed them, a request that the desires be given serious consideration by those providing care to the signers, and an effort to share responsibility for certain decisions made in specified situations. In other words, living wills sought to promote individual autonomy in death-related matters by thinking ahead about issues of life and death, formulating one's views concerning important decisions, and communicating them to others. They also embodied an effort by their authors to protect health care providers from accusations of malpractice, civil liability, or criminal prosecution.

Early living wills typically focused on (1) a directive to withhold or withdraw treatments that merely prolong dying when one is in an incurable or irreversible condition with no reasonable expectation of recovery and (2) a directive to limit interventions in such circumstances to those designed to provide comfort and relieve pain. These living wills typically did not call for direct killing or active euthanasia. Most often, they explicitly stated: "I am not asking that my life be directly taken, but that my dying be not unreasonably prolonged." Most living wills were primarily intended to refuse certain kinds of cure-oriented interventions (**artificial means** and "heroic measures") when they were no longer relevant ("futile care," that is, care no longer expected to produce a cure), to request that dying be permitted to take its natural course, and to ask that suffering associated with life-threatening illness be eased with effective palliative care, even if such care should have a collateral or side effect of hastening the actual moment of death.

The broad legal context for living wills is the well-established **right to privacy** and the right of competent decision makers to give or withhold informed consent and to accept or refuse interventions even when that might affect the timing of the individual's death (Alderman & Kennedy, 1997; Annas, 2004; President's Commission, 1982, 1983a, 1983b; Rozovsky, 2015).

Following the enactment in 1976 in California of the first **natural death legislation**, similar legislation (sometimes with local variations) was passed in all 50 states and the District of Columbia. Typically, such legislation: (1) specifies the conditions under which a competent adult is authorized to sign a document of this type; (2) stipulates the form that such a document must take to have legal force; (3) defines what sorts of interventions can or cannot be refused—for example, interventions undertaken with a view toward cure, which may or may not include hydration or nutrition; (4) authorizes oral or written repudiation of the signed document by the signer at any time; (5) requires that professional care providers either cooperate with the document's directives or withdraw from the case and arrange for alternative care (consenting to do so is thus legally protected; failure to do so is theoretically subject not merely to potential malpractice liability but also to penalties that could extend in principle to loss of professional licensure); and (6) stipulates that death resulting from actions authorized by the legislation is not to be construed as suicide for insurance purposes.

A presidential commission (President's Commission, 1982) and other agencies proposed legislative models that (1) relate to all competent adults and mature minors—not only those who are dying; (2) apply to all medical interventions and do not limit the types of interventions that may be refused; (3) permit the designation of a **substitute or surrogate decision maker** in a manner similar to that described in the following section; (4) require health care providers to follow the directives of the individual and incorporate sanctions for those who fail to do so; and (5) stipulate that palliative care be continued for those who refuse other interventions. This model goes beyond the scope of early living wills and incorporates features now more typical of durable powers of attorney in health care matters.

Historically, living wills have not been without their limitations or potential difficulties (see Issues for Critical Reflection #14). Like any document written down in advance of a complex and life-threatening situation, living wills may not anticipate every relevant feature that might arise. Partly for this reason, their significance and force may be subject to interpretation or dispute among the very family members and professional care providers whom they seek to guide.

Durable Powers of Attorney in Health Care Matters

Because of limitations and potential difficulties associated with living wills, some prefer an alternative approach found in state legislation that authorizes a *durable power of attorney for making decisions in health care matters*. "Power of attorney" is a well-established legal doctrine whereby one individual authorizes another individual (or group of individuals) to make decisions and take actions on behalf of the first individual in specific circumstances or for a specified period of time. For example, a power of attorney might authorize someone to sign a contract on my behalf to close on the sale of a house at a time when I am not available to do so. Historically, such a power of attorney continued in force only while its author remained competent. A "durable" power of attorney is one that continues in force until it is revoked—even (or especially) when the individual who authorized it is no longer able to act as a competent decision maker. A durable power of attorney in health care matters is concerned with health care issues.

Advocates argue that a durable power of attorney has two significant advantages over other written or oral directives, such as a living will. First, it empowers someone else—a substitute decision maker often called a **health care proxy**—to make decisions on behalf of an individual in any and all circumstances that the document covers. Second, the substitute decision maker can be instructed to refuse all interventions, to insist on all interventions, or to approve some interventions and reject others. The first advantage attempts to minimize problems arising from changing circumstances

ISSUES FOR CRITICAL REFLECTION
#14 What Are Some Criticisms of Living Wills?

Although living wills are intended to preserve an individual's autonomy, some argue they fail to achieve this. Fagerlin and Schneider (2004) found seven problems with living will and argued these problems were so significant that public policy should not support their use. The problems they identified were:

- Most Americans do not have living wills, apparently for several reasons, such as, people do not know about them, doubt they are needed, believe they will not change the treatment they receive; or view them as incompatible with their cultural traditions (see Chapter 5 on this last point).
- People cannot be certain about what sorts of treatment they will want in the future and may change their mind when confronted with different circumstances.
- A living will is often not able to make clear just what a person's wishes are about the sorts of treatment he or she desires, often because those desires are stated in terms so general that they are of little help, or because desires become so specific that they overwhelm the ability of the person signing them to understand all the specifics.
- The living will may get "lost" and not be available when it is needed.

- The persons interpreting the living will often may not do so accurately in terms of the signer's actual wishes.
- Living wills cannot be shown actually to alter patient care.
- Living wills represent a significant cost to society without providing the desired benefit.

Although these are serious difficulties with living wills and at least some of them have been identified as such for some time, even Fagerlin and Schneider do not argue that living wills should be abolished nor do others who recognize the existence of some of these problems. Thus, Swartzberg (2004, p. 3) argued: "Do I still advise you to have one? Yes I do, simply on the chance that it might do some good. The act of writing the [living] will may help you to understand your own wishes now, as well as providing some guidance for your family." Also, most writers argue that difficulties with living wills make it even more important to appoint a health care agent or surrogate with durable power of attorney. If that is done and carried out with careful, updated communication between the individual and his or her proxy decision maker many of the problems associated with living wills should be alleviated.

and competing interpretations of written documents; the second allows the person authorizing the health care agent—and the agent—some degree of freedom in choosing which interventions to accept and which to refuse.

Durable powers of attorney in health care matters are now in force in all states and the District of Columbia. Sample documents and booklets explaining durable powers of attorney in health care matters are available from the American Bar Association, AARP, and many local sources, such as hospitals, long-term care facilities, and hospice programs. For example, the American Bar Association (2009) offers a free, how-to guide on *Making Medical Decisions for Someone Else* that is available online. Note that any durable power of attorney must satisfy the legislative requirements of the legal jurisdiction within which it is to be enforced. Competent legal advice should be sought to confirm this. Interested parties are usually advised (wherever possible) to complete both a state-authorized living will (providing general guidance to decision makers) and an appropriate durable power of attorney for health care (authorizing discretion within those guidelines on the part of a health care agent or substitute decision maker).

Five Wishes

The **Five Wishes** document combines many of the best elements of living wills and durable powers of attorney in health care in a way specially designed to be easy to understand, simple to use, personal in character, and thorough. Intended as "a gift to your family members and friends so that they won't have to guess what you want," "Five Wishes" asks the person filling out the document to express desires about the following issues and provides guidance on each: (1) the person I want to make health care decisions for me when I can't make them for myself; (2) the kind of medical treatment I want or don't want if I am close to death, in a coma, or have permanent and severe brain damage and am not expected to recover from that situation, or I am in another condition under which I do not wish to be kept alive; (3) how comfortable I want to be; (4) how I want people to treat me; and (5) what I want my loved ones to know.

The "Five Wishes" document is currently structured to meet the legal requirements of different jurisdictions and is said to be the most widely used advance directive in America. It meets the legal requirements of at least 42 states under their living will and durable power of attorney in health care matters regulations; in other states and countries, it can be used to help individuals offer guidance to their care providers. The "Five Wishes" document is available in versions for individuals and families, for organizations, for children ("My Wishes"), for adolescents ("Voicing My Choices"), and in bilingual versions in 28 different languages and Braille with side-by-side English translations for use with English-speaking care providers. These documents, companion guides, and supportive resources can be previewed and/or obtained at a nominal price from Aging with Dignity or ordered from its website.

POLST: Physician Orders for Life-Sustaining Treatment

In addition to advance directives described in this section, conversations between patients, loved ones, and their health care professionals might also lead to Physician Orders for Life-Sustaining Treatment (Bomba, Kemp, & Black, 2012; Fromme et al., 2014; Hickman et al., 2010, 2011). POLST are voluntary, actionable, portable documents designed to ensure that seriously ill or frail patients can choose the treatments they want or do not want and insure that their wishes are documented and will be honored. POLST are medical orders signed by a health care professional; they become part of an individual's medical file and can be modified at any time. In this way, POLST are similar to "Do Not Resuscitate" (DNR) or "allow natural death" orders. POLST are not an advance directive and do not substitute for a health care proxy, although they can be complementary. Because they are governed by state law, POLST may have different names (e.g., MOLST, MOST, POST), may or may not be available in different states, and may not necessarily be foolproof (Clemency et al., 2016). For additional information, contact The National POLST Paradigm.

DEFINITION, DETERMINATION, AND CERTIFICATION OF DEATH

The central issues that relate to death itself and the time at which it occurs are definition, determination, and certification of death.

Definition of Death

Definition of death reflects the fundamental human and social understanding of the difference between life and death. This distinction underlies all issues related to determination and certification of death, all of which involve approaches intended to identify whether the condition society has defined as death exists. Above all, determination of death must be based on a definition that discriminates between real and only apparent death. It is essential to be clear in this definition about who is to be included among those who are alive or dead. It would be just as wrong to treat the dead as if they were living as it would be to treat the living as if they were already dead. The dead are no longer alive; the living are not yet dead.

The difference between being alive and being dead is obviously a profoundly important one. Aristotle called death a kind of destruction or perishing involving a change from being to nonbeing (see *Physics*, bk. V, ch. 1; *Metaphysics*, bk. XI, ch. 11). He meant that death involves a change in the very substance of the being. When a human being dies, an important consequence follows: there is no longer a human being present—instead, there is only a dead body or a corpse. Because the dead body is still an object deserving honor and respect, it is not simply to be discarded in a cavalier or thoughtless manner. However, it is also critical not to confuse the bodily remains with a living human person. That is why we say two different things after the death of a loved one: "These are the hands that held and caressed me" and "Everything that was essential to the person whom I knew and loved is no longer here."

How can we define the condition that we call death, the condition that is the opposite of life? Here is one answer:

> An individual who has sustained either (1) irreversible cessation of circulatory and respiratory functions or (2) irreversible cessation of all functions of the entire brain, including the brain stem, is dead (President's Commission, 1981, p. 73).

That definition was codified in the Uniform Determination of Death Act (UDDA; reprinted in Iserson, 2001, p. 749) and has since been adopted (as such or in a closely modified form) by many state legislatures.

Several points in the UDDA are critical:

1. It speaks of "an individual," not "a person," because the issue is precisely whether a person is still present.
2. It requires *irreversible*—not merely temporary or reversible—cessation of the designated functions.
3. It recognizes the possibility of situations in which external interventions mask or hide the precise status of respiratory and circulatory functions—in which it may be unclear whether the individual is actually sustaining those functions spontaneously or is even capable of doing so.
4. In such circumstances, the UDDA requires evaluation of the capacities of the central nervous system—which is the body's command and control center—because the definition recognizes that under normal circumstances, the life of the central nervous system ends shortly (a matter of a few minutes) after respiratory and circulatory functions are brought to a halt.
5. Finally, and most important, in such circumstances, it concludes that irreversible cessation of all functions of the brain and brain stem (which controls autonomic activities, such as respiration and circulation) is the condition understood as death.

Some have proposed that the irreversible loss of the capacity for bodily integration and social interaction is sufficient to define the death of a human being (Veatch, 1975, 1989). If so, neocortical or upper brain activity (excluding lower brain or brain stem activity) would be definitive of the presence or absence of human life (Karakatsanis & Tsanakas, 2002). In this case, a human person could be considered to be dead even when bodily or vegetative functioning remained. In other words, this proposal would regard the presence of a "persistent vegetative state" as the equivalent of death (Gervais, 1987).

Critics have charged that this proposal could lead, in the extreme, to a situation in which society would be asked to bury a body that demonstrated no upper brain function but in which there was spontaneous respiratory and circulatory function (Ramsey, 1970; Ramsey et al., 2002; Walton, 1979, 1982). More realistically, this situation would call not for immediate burial but for the removal of artificial support, including artificial means of providing nutrition and hydration, on the grounds that the individual was no longer alive *as a human being*. These decisions depend on a concept or definition of death; if one conceded that the individual was alive and still proposed to remove artificial support, one would be advocating the withdrawal of an intervention that is no longer relevant to restoring the individual to a state of health; in other words, that might constitute some form of euthanasia (see Chapter 18).

Both the UDDA and the proposal from the President's Commission also include the following sentence: "A determination of death must be made in accordance with accepted medical standards."

Determination of Death

Determination of death has to do with deciding whether death has actually occurred, establishing the conditions under which it took place, evaluating the manner of the death, and confirming whether further investigation is required. This process is similar to the work of referees in organized sports. Those involved in the determination of death are expected to contribute expertise about the subject and good judgment in applying their expertise to individual cases. Like referees, those who determine that death has occurred do not make the rules. Their role is to apply tests or criteria in an expert manner to arrive at the best decisions possible. They may also help to develop new and better ways of determining death.

Traditional tests applied to determine whether someone has died are well known. In times past, one might hold a feather under an individual's nostrils to observe whether it moved when he or she exhaled or inhaled. Sometimes a mirror was used in a similar way to see whether moisture contained in exhalations from a warm body condensed on its cool surface. One could also place one's ear on the chest to listen for a heartbeat or touch the body at certain points to feel for arterial pulsation. Over time, more sensitive and discriminating tests have been developed. For example, stethoscopes make possible a more refined way of listening for internal body sounds.

In all cases, the tests used to determine death depend on established procedures and available technology. These tests vary from place to place and from time to time (Shrock, 1835). The complex testing procedures of a highly developed society are not likely to be available in the rudimentary health care system of an impoverished country, just as the advanced technology of a major urban medical center is not likely to be found in a sparsely populated rural area. Determination of death is closely related to the state-of-the-art or prevailing community practices in a particular setting. Although they can vary, procedures to determine death in modern societies are clearly adequate for the vast majority of deaths.

Still, as might be expected, determination of death is inevitably subject to human limitations and fallibility. In particular, modern medicine has in some ways made it more difficult to determine the meaning of *any* test used to determine whether or not death has occurred. We know that cells, tissues, and organs can be kept functioning in laboratory conditions (in Petri dishes, etc.) outside the body of a live human being. Advanced life-support systems can provide similar continuing support as well as for the functioning of bodily organs when it is uncertain whether or not that body is still a live human being in any meaningful sense.

Questions of this sort led a committee of the Harvard Medical School (Ad Hoc Committee, 1968; reprinted in Iserson, 2001, pp. 747–748) to develop the following criteria for irreversible coma as a basis for certifying that death has occurred:

1. *Unreceptivity and unresponsivity*. Neither externally applied stimuli nor inner need evokes awareness or response.
2. *No movements or breathing*. Observation over a period of at least one hour does not disclose spontaneous muscular movement, respiration, or response to stimuli. For individuals on respirators, one must turn off the machine for a specified period and observe for any effort to breathe spontaneously.
3. *No reflexes*. A number of reflexes that can normally be elicited are absent. For example, pupils of the eye will be fixed, dilated, and not responsive to a direct source of light. Similarly, ocular movement (which normally occurs when the head is turned or when ice water is poured into the ear) and blinking are absent.
4. *Flat electroencephalogram*. The electroencephalograph (EEG) is a machine that monitors minute electrical activity in the upper brain (cerebrum). A flat EEG reading suggests the absence of such activity. The Harvard Committee indicated that the EEG has its primary value in confirming the determination that follows from the previous three criteria.

The Harvard Committee added "all of the above tests shall be repeated at least 24 hours later with no change" (p. 338).

To apply the **Harvard criteria** properly, one must exclude two special conditions: hypothermia, in which the temperature of the body has fallen below 90 °F; and the presence of central nervous system depressants, such as barbiturates. In both of these special conditions, the ability of the body to function may be masked or suppressed in such a way as to yield a false negative on the Harvard Committee's tests.

The first three of the Harvard Committee's criteria are essentially sophisticated and modernized restatements of tests that have traditionally been employed in the determination of death. The fourth criterion adds an additional criterion in a confirmatory role—not as an independent test in its own right. Requiring that all four tests be repeated after a 24-hour interval indicates the committee's desire to proceed with great care in this important matter.

The committee was clear about the limits of its work: "We are concerned here only with those comatose individuals who have no discernible central nervous system activity" (p. 337). That is, these criteria are not intended to be applied to all determinations of death. Rather, they represent an effort to define "irreversible coma." A negative outcome resulting from a careful application of the Harvard criteria (two sets of four tests each, separated by a 24-hour period) is intended to demonstrate the presence of irreversible coma, and irreversible coma is to be understood as a new indicator that death has occurred.

The President's Commission (1981, p. 25) observed that the phrase "irreversible coma" may be misleading here since any coma is a condition of a living person, whereas "a body without any brain functions is dead and thus beyond any coma."

This observation reminds us of the need to be clear about language and concepts in matters of this sort, as well as the challenges in trying to do so.

There would have been no need for criteria of the kind proposed by the Harvard Committee if irreversible coma had not become an object of some puzzlement in modern society. In times past, individuals in irreversible coma would simply have begun to deteriorate. There would have been no way to sustain even the limited functioning they had or seemed to have. More recently, interventions resulting from advances in modern medical technology have made it possible to sustain the reality or the appearance of vital bodily functioning. The Harvard criteria are intended to identify situations in which life only appears to continue and to equate such situations with death.

Since the Harvard criteria first appeared, their implementation has been modified in some circumstances and additional or alternative tests, such as cerebral angiograms to test for blood flow in the brain, have sometimes been employed. Those changes are only to be expected as experts develop new tests and devise new ways to evaluate whether individuals are alive. In fact, various approaches to the determination of death might or might not all relate to the same definition of death. That is because determination of death is a separable matter from the more fundamental question of definition of death.

Certification of Death: Death Certificates, Coroners, and Medical Examiners

Most people in North America and in other developed countries die under the care of a physician—for example, while they are in health care institutions (such as hospitals or long-term care facilities) or in organized hospice or home care programs. In such circumstances, a physician or another authorized person usually determines the time and cause of death, together with other significant conditions. That information is recorded on a form called a **death certificate**, which is then signed or certified by the physician or other authorized person.

Death certificates are the basis for much of the record keeping and statistical data concerning mortality and health in modern societies. They serve a broad range of public and private functions, such as claiming life insurance and other death benefits, disposition of property rights, and investigating crime.

The U.S. Standard Certificate of Death (see Figure 16.1) and most state certificates of death are a single-page form containing the following categories of information: personal information about the deceased and the location of his or her death; the names of his or her parents, together with the name and address of the person who provided this and the previous information; causes and conditions of death; certification of death, along with the signature of and information about the certifier; and information about disposition of the body (whether by burial, cremation, removal, etc.), together with the signature of a funeral director. When completed, a death certificate is delivered to a local (usually county) registrar, who signs the form, records it, and provides a permit for disposition of the body.

Every death certificate classifies the *manner of death* in four basic categories: natural, accidental, suicide, or homicide. This system of classification is known as the **NASH system,** based on the first initials of these four terms. In addition, some deaths may be categorized as "undetermined" or "pending investigation." Deaths come under the jurisdiction of a coroner or medical examiner if the person who died was not under the care of a physician, if the death occurred suddenly, if there is reason to suspect foul

Figure 16.1 **U.S. Standard Certificate of Death.**

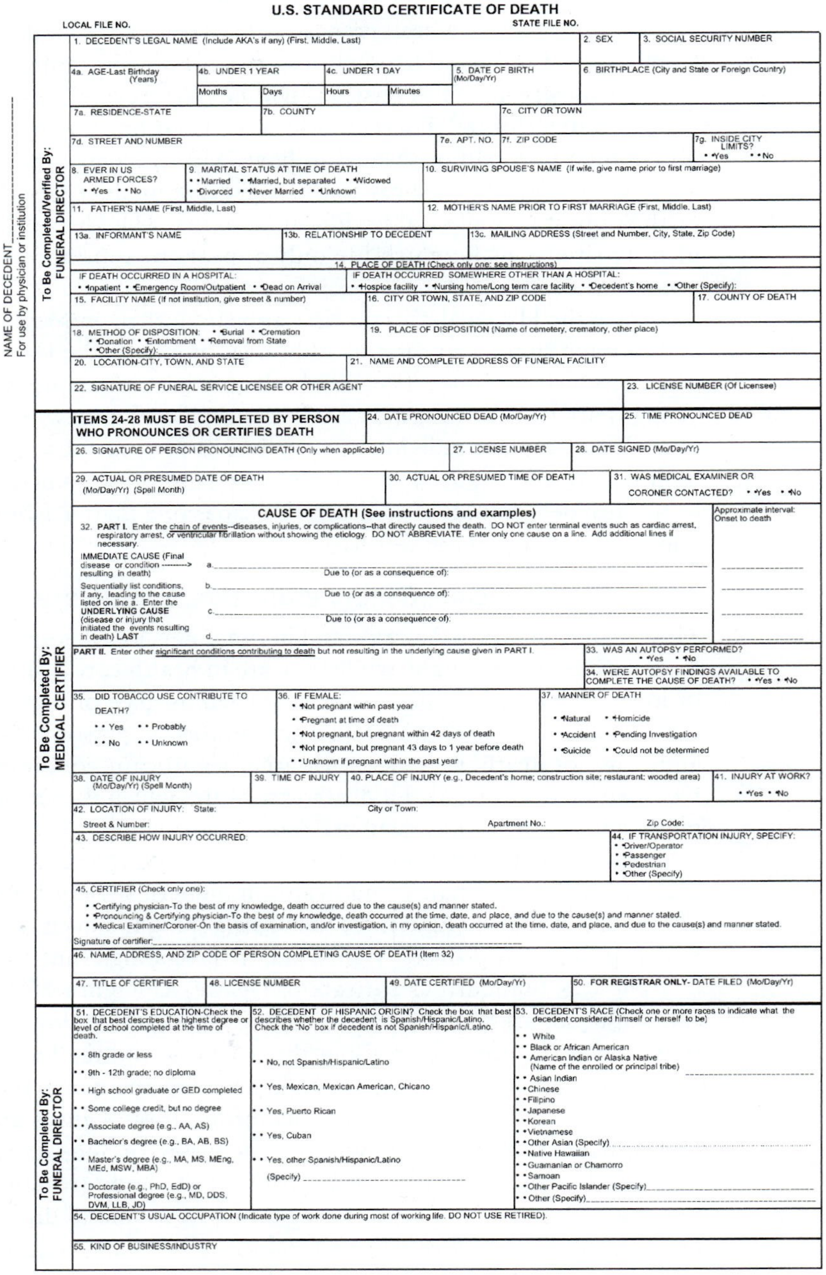

U.S. STANDARD CERTIFICATE OF DEATH

LOCAL FILE NO.
STATE FILE NO.

NAME OF DECEDENT_____________
For use by physician or institution

To Be Completed/Verified By: FUNERAL DIRECTOR

1. DECEDENT'S LEGAL NAME (Include AKA's if any) (First, Middle, Last)
2. SEX
3. SOCIAL SECURITY NUMBER
4a. AGE-Last Birthday (Years)
4b. UNDER 1 YEAR: Months, Days
4c. UNDER 1 DAY: Hours, Minutes
5. DATE OF BIRTH (Mo/Day/Yr)
6. BIRTHPLACE (City and State or Foreign Country)
7a. RESIDENCE-STATE
7b. COUNTY
7c. CITY OR TOWN
7d. STREET AND NUMBER
7e. APT. NO.
7f. ZIP CODE
7g. INSIDE CITY LIMITS? • Yes • No
8. EVER IN US ARMED FORCES? • Yes • No
9. MARITAL STATUS AT TIME OF DEATH • Married • Married, but separated • Widowed • Divorced • Never Married • Unknown
10. SURVIVING SPOUSE'S NAME (If wife, give name prior to first marriage)
11. FATHER'S NAME (First, Middle, Last)
12. MOTHER'S NAME PRIOR TO FIRST MARRIAGE (First, Middle, Last)
13a. INFORMANT'S NAME
13b. RELATIONSHIP TO DECEDENT
13c. MAILING ADDRESS (Street and Number, City, State, Zip Code)
14. PLACE OF DEATH (Check only one: see instructions)
IF DEATH OCCURRED IN A HOSPITAL: • Inpatient • Emergency Room/Outpatient • Dead on Arrival
IF DEATH OCCURRED SOMEWHERE OTHER THAN A HOSPITAL: • Hospice facility • Nursing home/Long term care facility • Decedent's home • Other (Specify):
15. FACILITY NAME (If not institution, give street & number)
16. CITY OR TOWN, STATE, AND ZIP CODE
17. COUNTY OF DEATH
18. METHOD OF DISPOSITION: • Burial • Cremation • Donation • Entombment • Removal from State • Other (Specify):____________
19. PLACE OF DISPOSITION (Name of cemetery, crematory, other place)
20. LOCATION-CITY, TOWN, AND STATE
21. NAME AND COMPLETE ADDRESS OF FUNERAL FACILITY
22. SIGNATURE OF FUNERAL SERVICE LICENSEE OR OTHER AGENT
23. LICENSE NUMBER (Of Licensee)

To Be Completed By: MEDICAL CERTIFIER

ITEMS 24-28 MUST BE COMPLETED BY PERSON WHO PRONOUNCES OR CERTIFIES DEATH
24. DATE PRONOUNCED DEAD (Mo/Day/Yr)
25. TIME PRONOUNCED DEAD
26. SIGNATURE OF PERSON PRONOUNCING DEATH (Only when applicable)
27. LICENSE NUMBER
28. DATE SIGNED (Mo/Day/Yr)
29. ACTUAL OR PRESUMED DATE OF DEATH (Mo/Day/Yr) (Spell Month)
30. ACTUAL OR PRESUMED TIME OF DEATH
31. WAS MEDICAL EXAMINER OR CORONER CONTACTED? • Yes • No

CAUSE OF DEATH (See instructions and examples)
Approximate interval: Onset to death
32. PART I. Enter the chain of events--diseases, injuries, or complications--that directly caused the death. DO NOT enter terminal events such as cardiac arrest, respiratory arrest, or ventricular fibrillation without showing the etiology. DO NOT ABBREVIATE. Enter only one cause on a line. Add additional lines if necessary.
IMMEDIATE CAUSE (Final disease or condition ---------> resulting in death) a.____________
Due to (or as a consequence of):
Sequentially list conditions, if any, leading to the cause listed on line a. Enter the UNDERLYING CAUSE (disease or injury that initiated the events resulting in death) LAST b.____________
Due to (or as a consequence of):
c.____________
Due to (or as a consequence of):
d.____________
PART II. Enter other significant conditions contributing to death but not resulting in the underlying cause given in PART I.
33. WAS AN AUTOPSY PERFORMED? • Yes • No
34. WERE AUTOPSY FINDINGS AVAILABLE TO COMPLETE THE CAUSE OF DEATH? • Yes • No
35. DID TOBACCO USE CONTRIBUTE TO DEATH? • Yes • Probably • No • Unknown
36. IF FEMALE: • Not pregnant within past year • Pregnant at time of death • Not pregnant, but pregnant within 42 days of death • Not pregnant, but pregnant 43 days to 1 year before death • Unknown if pregnant within the past year
37. MANNER OF DEATH • Natural • Homicide • Accident • Pending Investigation • Suicide • Could not be determined
38. DATE OF INJURY (Mo/Day/Yr) (Spell Month)
39. TIME OF INJURY
40. PLACE OF INJURY (e.g., Decedent's home; construction site; restaurant; wooded area)
41. INJURY AT WORK? • Yes • No
42. LOCATION OF INJURY: State: City or Town: Street & Number: Apartment No.: Zip Code:
43. DESCRIBE HOW INJURY OCCURRED:
44. IF TRANSPORTATION INJURY, SPECIFY: • Driver/Operator • Passenger • Pedestrian • Other (Specify)
45. CERTIFIER (Check only one):
• Certifying physician-To the best of my knowledge, death occurred due to the cause(s) and manner stated.
• Pronouncing & Certifying physician-To the best of my knowledge, death occurred at the time, date, and place, and due to the cause(s) and manner stated.
• Medical Examiner/Coroner-On the basis of examination, and/or investigation, in my opinion, death occurred at the time, date, and place, and due to the cause(s) and manner stated.
Signature of certifier:____________
46. NAME, ADDRESS, AND ZIP CODE OF PERSON COMPLETING CAUSE OF DEATH (Item 32)
47. TITLE OF CERTIFIER
48. LICENSE NUMBER
49. DATE CERTIFIED (Mo/Day/Yr)
50. **FOR REGISTRAR ONLY**- DATE FILED (Mo/Day/Yr)

To Be Completed By: FUNERAL DIRECTOR

51. DECEDENT'S EDUCATION-Check the box that best describes the highest degree or level of school completed at the time of death.
• 8th grade or less
• 9th - 12th grade; no diploma
• High school graduate or GED completed
• Some college credit, but no degree
• Associate degree (e.g., AA, AS)
• Bachelor's degree (e.g., BA, AB, BS)
• Master's degree (e.g., MA, MS, MEng, MEd, MSW, MBA)
• Doctorate (e.g., PhD, EdD) or Professional degree (e.g., MD, DDS, DVM, LLB, JD)
52. DECEDENT OF HISPANIC ORIGIN? Check the box that best describes whether the decedent is Spanish/Hispanic/Latino. Check the "No" box if decedent is not Spanish/Hispanic/Latino.
• No, not Spanish/Hispanic/Latino
• Yes, Mexican, Mexican American, Chicano
• Yes, Puerto Rican
• Yes, Cuban
• Yes, other Spanish/Hispanic/Latino (Specify) ____________
53. DECEDENT'S RACE (Check one or more races to indicate what the decedent considered himself or herself to be)
• White
• Black or African American
• American Indian or Alaska Native (Name of the enrolled or principal tribe) ____________
• Asian Indian
• Chinese
• Filipino
• Japanese
• Korean
• Vietnamese
• Other Asian (Specify)____________
• Native Hawaiian
• Guamanian or Chamorro
• Samoan
• Other Pacific Islander (Specify)____________
• Other (Specify)____________
54. DECEDENT'S USUAL OCCUPATION (Indicate type of work done during most of working life. DO NOT USE RETIRED).
55. KIND OF BUSINESS/INDUSTRY

Source: Retrieved 12/18/16, from https://www.cdc.gov/nchs/data/dvs/death11-03final-acc.pdf

play, and in all cases of accidents, suicide, or homicide. The function of a coroner or medical examiner is to investigate the circumstances and causes of such deaths.

Coroners and medical examiners are empowered to take possession of the body (or to release it to family members for donation or other forms of disposition), to arrange for various types of investigations (such as autopsies), and to hold an inquest or coroner's jury, which is a quasi-judicial proceeding designed to determine the cause of a death. The term **coroner** goes back to medieval times in England where it identified the representative of the crown (*corona* in Latin). Originally, the coroner's function was to determine whether the property of the crown—that is, the deceased—had been unlawfully appropriated or killed. In modern societies, coroners are usually individuals who have been elected to office. They are not normally required to have any special qualifications other than being adult citizens of their elective jurisdiction. Many—but not all—coroners or deputy coroners in the United States, especially in rural areas, are funeral directors. By contrast, **medical examiners** are appointed to their positions and are required to be qualified medical doctors (usually forensic pathologists). Some states have eliminated the office of coroner and have replaced that role with medical examiners. Other states continue to maintain a coroner system in rural areas, often with medical examiners in large, urban centers.

ORGAN, TISSUE, AND BODY DONATION

Death is the prerequisite for many forms of anatomical gifts that involve the donation of human organs, tissues, or an entire body, although living donors can donate kidneys and portions of their other organs, along with some tissues. Some background will help to clarify these complex subjects.

Background: Tissue Typing, Immunosuppression, and Organ Donation

The modern era of organ and **tissue donation** began in the 1950s when a combination of advances in knowledge, technology, pharmacology, and clinical practice made it possible for biomedical scientists and clinicians to transplant specific organs and tissues from one individual to another (Dowie, 1988; Fox & Swazey, 1974, 1992; Hamilton, 2012; Murray, 2004). One key advance involved learning how to classify or type and compare human tissues so as to achieve the greatest likelihood of success in matching the biological characteristics of donor and recipient. Another major breakthrough—which has been called "the most notable development in this area"—occurred when an immunosuppressant medication (cyclosporine) was developed in the mid-1970s and approved for commercial use in November 1983. Effective immunosuppression prevents the recipient's immune system from attacking and rejecting transplanted organs as foreign material. These advances made transplantation of human organs and tissues a real option for transplant recipients to save or enhance the quality of their lives.

Major organs that can currently be transplanted are listed in the top line of Table 16.1. They include individual kidneys and hearts; entire livers, pancreas, lungs, and intestines, or portions thereof; and joint transplants of a kidney/pancreas or heart/lung.

Tissue Donation

Human tissues are donated and transplanted for a wide variety of purposes. For example, skin grafts are used for burn and accident victims, heart valves and aortic patch grafts sustain heart functioning, veins from the legs are used in cardiac bypass surgery, eye components can restore or improve sight, and bone and connective tissue grafts make possible dental reconstructions, as well as orthopedic and neurosurgical

Table 16.1 Number of Candidates on the National Transplant Waiting List as of February 1, 2017, by Organ, Gender, Age, and Race or Ethnicity[a]

Number	Kidney	Liver	Pancreas	Kidney Pancreas	Heart	Lung	Heart Lung	Intestine	Total
Total[b]	98,324	14,387	945	1,747	4,014	1,386	46	275	118,457
By gender									
Males	59,789	8,868	455	949	3,004	552	22	144	72,236
Females	38,545	5,520	490	798	1,010	834	24	131	46,234
By age (years)									
<1	1	55	1	0	59	2	0	3	118
1–5	234	198	32	0	105	5	0	92	594
6–10	212	98	28	1	69	7	0	91	421
11–17	515	139	18	1	111	22	0	25	792
18–34	8,452	682	160	318	426	141	12	30	9,908
35–49	23,655	2,033	434	958	862	203	15	28	27,311
50–64	42,929	7,804	263	460	1,703	664	17	22	52,842
65+	22,327	3,378	9	9	679	342	2	4	26,473
By race or ethnicity									
White	35,875	9,781	674	953	2,439	1,074	24	149	49,517
Black	32,657	1,118	123	451	1,038	153	10	58	35,060
Hispanic	19,726	2,536	106	266	386	108	9	50	22,722
Asian	8,168	740	23	41	113	39	2	9	9,023
American Indian/Alaska Native	997	132	8	16	6	6	1	3	1,138
Pacific Islander	561	26	3	4	10	2	0	1	600
Multiracial	731	67	8	19	23	5	0	5	837

[a]Some patients are registered at more than one transplant center for the same organ. This table only counts individual transplant candidates.

[b]Totals may be less than the sums because of patients included in multiple categories.

Source: Based on data from the Organ Procurement and Transplantation Network (OPTN) as of February 1, 2017. Retrieved on February 2, 2017, from https://optn.transplant.hrsa.gov/data/view-data-reports/national-data/

procedures such as spinal fusions (see Personal Insights 16.1). Because blood and fat cells are removed during the processing of donated tissues, there is usually no problem of rejection after the transplantation. Also, many **transplantable human tissues** can be sterilized, frozen, and kept in storage for some time. It has been estimated that approximately 95% of all deaths in our society—mostly those that occur suddenly and unexpectedly as a result of cardiac death—could lead to tissue donation (versus only 5% leading to organ donation) and that each donation of human tissue could be life-enhancing for up to 50 individuals. Two distinctive forms of tissue transplantation are **xenotransplantation**, or transplantation from animals to humans, which has been successful in cases involving heart valves taken from pigs, and *skin donation from living donors after certain forms of weight-loss surgery*. Despite all this, tissue donation and transplantation is generally not well understood or appreciated by the general public (Youngner, Anderson, & Schapiro, 2003).

PERSONAL INSIGHTS 16.1

Donor Wife Holds Her Head High with Husband's Bone

By Douglas Harrell, Donor Husband

Growing up, Jean Reyes de Gonzalez had a low opinion of herself. Her father, a waiter on a Navy ship, was gone for months at a time, leaving Jean in the hands of abusive relatives. The sum of these experiences left her bitter and angry, but all of that changed when she met John Amato.

John was a happy-go-lucky guy who worked at the parts department of a local car dealership. He played the drums at his church and genuinely liked to help people when he could. They were married on October 30, 1997. "It wasn't until I met John that I found out what it was like to be loved. When I married John, God healed the psychological wounds of abandonment. John loved me unconditionally."

Jean's nightmarish past was behind her. John was an attentive and romantic husband, often bringing her small gifts of a perfect rose or a stuffed toy for no particular reason. She was truly happy for the first time in her life, but it was not to last. On May 31, 2000, John was unable to go to work due to severe back pain. A trip to the ER proved negative for a heart attack and he was given pain medication and sent home. Later that night, he collapsed and died from an undiscovered aortic aneurysm. When asked, Jean had no reservations about John being a donor. "John and I had spoken about donation and what we would do if the other died. I knew that John would not say no. He was all about helping others." Through her job with the Office of the Chief Medical Examiner in Farmington, Connecticut, Jean was already familiar with tissue donation. At one point, she had even been responsible for coordinating the recovery of cornea donations.

Only a month after John's death, the grief in Jean's heart was gradually accompanied by a severe pain in her left arm. She was told that she had a

(continues)

herniated disk in her neck and would need a cervical fusion with donated bone. "The surgeon told me I needed surgery and explained what needed to be done. Bone is used as scaffolding. Your own bone grows over it. I started wondering if I could use John's bone. I finally decided to call the Organ Procurement Organization (OPO) to see if any was available. When I finally asked, John's bone was at the point of being prepared for final use. A piece of it was prepared to suit my need."

In honor of John's gift, Jean spends a portion of her time volunteering to spread the word about donation. She is a frequent speaker for the Musculoskeletal Transplant Foundation (the tissue bank that handled John's bone), and she has spoken at the National Donor Recognition Ceremony in Washington, D.C. In addition, she served two years on the Executive Committee of the National Donor Family Council.

Jean is now healed and happily married to Eladio Gonzalez, a police officer she met at work. Eladio is supportive of her continued involvement with donation. "I think it is a great way for her to honor John. I know he is a very important part of who she is—perhaps the most important part," said Eladio. Jean adds, "Receiving John's bone made me not feel so alone. He was instrumental in healing my heart and mind, and, in death, he healed my body. Going through the experience has made me more compassionate of others. The physical pain of the surgery and the emotional pain of John's death have changed me forever. I feel more capable. If I could get through that, I can get through anything."

Source: Used by permission of National Kidney Foundation.

Body Donation

It is possible to donate entire bodies for medical education and research although there are some significant differences between organ or tissue donation and **body donation**, both as to the need for donated bodies and as to the ways in which they should (or should not) be prepared. Those who wish to make a gift of their bodies for these purposes after death should confirm arrangements in advance with intended recipients and follow required procedures (Iverson, 1990). These recipients might include the anatomy departments of medical or dental schools, state or regional agencies that serve this purpose, or organizations like the International Institute for the Advancement of Medicine or Science Care. Institutions receiving donated bodies typically have special procedures for disposing of their remains once such bodies have been used for educational or research purposes (e.g., Reece & Ziegler, 1990).

The Need for Organ Donation and Transplantation

The need for **transplantable human organs** arises from nonfunctioning or poorly functioning organs in potential recipients. Coupled with better screening practices and diagnostic techniques, this means that individuals who might benefit from transplantation are now being identified earlier and more effectively than they would have been previously. In addition, improved technical abilities for transplanting major organs at transplant centers contribute to a growing need for organ donation (Frist, 1989, 1995; Maier, 1991; Starzl, 2003).

Recognizing these developments, Congress enacted the National Organ Transplant Act (NOTA) in 1984. Among other things, **NOTA** established the national Organ Procurement and Transplantation Network (OPTN) to facilitate the procurement and distribution of scarce organs in a fair and equitable way by matching donated organs with potential recipients (Prottas, 1994). A private corporation, the United Network for Organ Sharing (**UNOS**), currently administers the **OPTN** under contract to the Division of Transplantation in the U.S. Department of Health and Human Services. NOTA also established the Scientific Registry of Transplant Recipients to measure the success of transplantation by tracing recipients from the time of transplant to the failure of the organ (graft) or patient death.

The need for organ transplantation is evident from Table 16.1, which provides data on the number of transplant candidates on the National Transplant Waiting List in the United States as of February 1, 2017, by organ, gender, age, and race or ethnicity. Among these candidates, most are waiting for kidneys and livers, 61% are males, 39% are females, the largest numbers by age are individuals 50–64 years of age followed by those 35–49 years old and 65 years or more older, and the largest numbers by race are Caucasian Americans and African Americans. The number of candidates on lists like these changes and tends to increase constantly. Even so, as many as 18 candidates on the National Transplant Waiting List die every day in the United States—a total of 6,452 such individuals died in 2016—because no suitable organs became available for transplantation.

Figure 16.2 shows that the need for organ donation and transplantation has grown substantially from 1989 through 2016. This figure reflects end-of-year data

Figure 16.2 Transplant Candidates, Organ Transplants, and Organ Donors, United States, 1988–2016

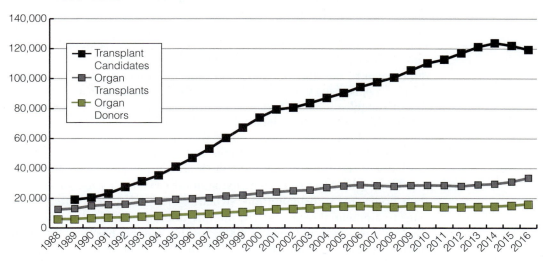

Source: Based on Organ Procurement and Transplantation Network (OPTN) data from United Network for Organ Sharing. Published data retrieved on February 2, 2017, from www.unos.org; unpublished data provided in personal communication on February 3, 2017. This work was supported in part by Health Resources and Services Administration contract 234-2005-37011C. The content is the responsibility of the authors alone and does not necessarily reflect the views or policies of the Department of Health and Human Services, nor does mention of trade names, commercial products, or organizations imply endorsement by the U.S. government.

for the number of candidates on the National Transplant Waiting List, the number of transplants accomplished in each year, and the number of donors from whom organs were recovered in each year. In brief, the number of candidates on the waiting list has increased dramatically during this 28-year period, while numbers of transplants and donors have grown at a significant but much slower rates. In other words, a notable increase in the need for transplantable organs has not been matched by their availability. As a result, *the single largest obstacle to organ transplantation today is the scarcity of transplantable organs*. Because there would be no organ transplantation if there were no organ donation, we look more closely at some facts about organ donation and at efforts to increase the number of donated organs.

Who Can Donate

Organ donation is only possible when: (1) the organ in question is not uniquely vital to the donor's health or (2) the donor is already dead when the organ is retrieved from his or her body. The former condition applies to living donors; the latter to nonliving or deceased donors. The Uniform Anatomical Gift Act (UAGA; reprinted in Iserson, 2001, pp. 751–756) was enacted in 1968, amended in 1987, and passed with only slight variations by all of the state legislatures in the United States. It allows persons to make known before their deaths their wishes about the donation of their organs. The act designates who may execute an anatomical gift; who may receive such donations and for what purposes; how such an anatomical gift may be authorized, amended, or revoked; and the rights and duties at death of an individual or organization to whom such a gift is made. Under the provisions of the **UAGA**, individuals who are of sound mind and 18 years of age or older can donate all or any part of their bodies, with the gift to take effect at the time of their deaths and to be donated for the purposes of health care education, research, therapy, or transplantation.

Living Donors   **Living donors** may be *directed donors* whose donation is made to help a *specific* transplant candidate they have chosen (Hamilton & Brown, 2002) or *nondirected donors* who donate for the benefit of *any* transplant candidate who might be in need of their gift. All living donors can offer replaceable materials (such as blood or blood products), one of a pair of twinned organs (such as a kidney), or a portion of certain organs (such as a liver, pancreas, lung, or intestine). (A very small number of living donors can be multiple-organ donors, as when someone donates a kidney and a segment of a pancreas.) Consent to donate is obtained directly from potential living donors after a suitable screening and evaluation process to determine that donors understand the procedure that will be undertaken, are consenting freely, are a good tissue match to the potential recipient, are likely to be able to withstand the donation process, and can be expected to cope effectively with the aftermath of the experience however that might work out (Authors for the Live Organ Donor Consensus Group, 2000).

Those who agree to become living donors exhibit a willingness to offer a part of their bodies for transplantation—whether or not they are related by blood or marriage to a potential recipient. The number of these individuals grew annually through the 1990s to a peak of 7,004 in 2004, but that number has been fluctuating ever since with a broad downward trend to 5,980 in 2016 when they represented about 37.5% of all donors and made possible 17.8% of all transplants.

Living donation has many advantages. The donor's medical history is known and can be investigated in advance of the donation, an extensive evaluation of the donor and the organ in question can be conducted prior to the donation, consent to donate is obtained directly from the potential donor rather than from a substitute decision maker, the organ is removed under elective conditions, and the donated organ is out of the body only a very short period, which is preferable because shorter time outside the body (ischemic time) maximizes the efficacy of the organ. Living donation has also made possible the development of imaginative strategies to facilitate organ donation and transplantation. For instance, it is now possible for a potential living donor who might desire to donate to a particular individual (transplant candidate A), but who is not biologically compatible with transplant candidate A, to arrange to donate to a second individual (transplant candidate B) with whom he or she is biologically compatible, in return for which a potential living donor who is incompatible with transplant candidate B will donate to transplant candidate A (with whom he or she is biologically compatible). Paired kidney exchanges like this demonstrate the flexibility made possible by living organ donors. They have also led to more complex arrangements, such as a living donor chain (Chain No. 95) described in a newspaper report on February 26, 2011, extending over 3 months, 9 states, 16 donors, and 16 recipients (Stein, 2011). Finally, a promise is typically made to potential living donors that, if at any time in the future their decision to donate might compromise their health status—for example, if they donated one kidney and then later discovered that their other kidney was failing—they would be put at the head of the list for an appropriate transplant.

Nonliving or Deceased Donors   In 2016, in the United States, there were 9,971 nonliving or deceased donors who represented approximately 62.5% of all donors that year and who made possible 27,630 organ transplants or 82.2% of all transplants that year. Most transplants come from deceased donors because each of them can donate six to eight major organs along with eye components and other tissues that can affect the lives of a large number of recipients (as we saw in the vignette near the beginning of this chapter), while most living donors can only donate one of a pair of organs or a portion of an organ to a single recipient. In the case of deceased donors, however, it is crucial that conditions preceding, at the time of, and immediately following the death do not damage the organs or otherwise render them unsuitable for transplantation. This means that organs must be recovered shortly after the death of an otherwise healthy donor and before they have begun to deteriorate (the time frame depends on the particular organ in question). Nonliving donors are also the source of almost all tissue donation.

There are two primary types of **nonliving or deceased donors**: those who have suffered brain death and those who have suffered cardiac death. In the vast majority of cases, a nonliving organ donor will have died suddenly and often traumatically of a cerebrovascular incident (e.g., a stroke or cerebral hemorrhage) or of an external blow to the head (e.g., as a result of an accident, homicide, or suicide). Typically, such individuals appear in an emergency department or another critical care situation where external support is initiated to stabilize their bodily functions and provide time for medical investigation and diagnosis. Later, these individuals will be pronounced dead, most often on the basis of clinical examinations including tests involving arterial blood flow, and will be said to have experienced *brain death* or *death by a neurological event*. This form of nonliving donation is called *donation after brain death*. At that point, external support will be continued, not to keep the dead individual "alive" (a contradiction in terms), but to sustain bodily functions for a limited period in order to determine whether or not donation has been authorized and, if so, to preserve the quality of organs that might eventually be transplanted. If donation is not authorized or after appropriate organs (and tissues) are recovered, external support will be removed and procedures for handling any dead body will apply.

A second group of nonliving donors is composed of individuals in persistent vegetative states or other conditions who have not experienced brain death and are not expected to do so. These individuals do display ventilatory and circulatory functioning, but it is not known whether such functioning is an artifact of the external support they are receiving (e.g., via respirators) or an ability they retain in their own right. To test which alternative applies in any given case, one must remove the external support to find out if a specific individual can continue such functioning on his or her own.

For many individuals in our society who are in this condition—quite apart from any issues of potential organ donation—competent decision makers (such as next of kin or other individuals who are authorized to act as substitute decision makers by such documents as durable powers of attorney in health care matters) may decide that continuing external support is futile care that serves no useful purpose.

With the permission of a competent decision maker in these circumstances, medical personnel may withdraw external support and things would be allowed, as is said, "to take their natural course." That is, the individual in question either will continue life-sustaining functioning on his or her own or will be allowed to die. If the individual does die, he or she will be said to have experienced *cardiac death* and, if a competent decision maker authorizes *donation after cardiac death*, specified organs would be removed (Steinbrook, 2007; Zamperetti, Bellomo, & Ronco, 2003; Truog, Miller, & Halpern, 2013). Interestingly, prior to the advent of brain-death legislation, a procedure much like this would have been the most common route to organ donation for nonliving donors. Since that time, donation involving what are called **non-heart beating donors** has been practiced in some, but not all, areas of the United States.

Authorizing Donation: Principles and Procedures

Living donors may decide to donate on their own, they may be asked to do so by a family member, friend, or some other person, or health care professionals may guide them in considering the relative advantages and disadvantages of their decision both for themselves and for a potential transplant recipient. Things are a bit more complicated in the case of nonliving donors.

Historically, the American death system has relied on altruism as the foundation for its organ donor programs. In particular, financial compensation (beyond out-of-pocket expenses) has not been offered to donors or their families, although arguments have been made against that restriction at least in part (e.g., Satel, 2009). In addition, America has not generally recognized a policy found in some other countries of "presumed consent" for donation of major organs (whereby organs can be retrieved unless there is a written directive to the contrary from the decedent or next of kin that specifically refuses donation). As a result, in our society, authorization for donation must be sought from an appropriate source in accordance with the requirements of the Uniform Anatomical Gift Act and state legislation (Wendler & Dickert, 2001). This can occur in one of two ways.

Donor Rights Legislation and First-Person Consent   Historically, in most jurisdictions in the United States, even a formal declaration of a desire to donate made by an individual prior to death and communicated in an appropriate way would not override a negative decision by next of kin or some other authorized decision maker. The reasoning behind this is: (1) the view that once a person has died, he or she no longer owns his or her body and (2) the practical reality that outsiders (such as hospitals and organ procurement organizations) would usually be unwilling to enter into conflicts involving family members on a matter of this degree of sensitivity when there is typically only a relatively short time for its resolution. More recently, many states have passed "donor rights" legislation establishing "first-person consent" registries open to enrollment by individuals aged 18 years or older. An individual giving *first-person consent* has made a legally binding decision that does not require additional witnesses or family consent to authorize organ and tissue donation in the event of death. Family members remain involved in various ways: donation is explained to them; their questions are answered and they are offered support; they provide a current medical/social history about the individual who died; and they are offered follow-up information and bereavement support.

Authorization for Donation by Next-of-Kin   When an individual has not satisfied the conditions required for first-person consent and has not given notice that he or she did not wish to donate, authorization for donation is normally sought from that person's next of kin. Under the UAGA, organ donation from a nonliving donor may be authorized by: a health care agent or surrogate; the donor's spouse; an adult son or daughter; either parent; an adult brother or sister; a legal guardian; or any other person authorized or under obligation to dispose of the body. In principle, the order of priority in this list of persons is important; an actual notice of opposition on the part of an individual of the same or a prior class would prevent a donation. Thus, a surviving spouse's decisions about donation would take precedence over those of the decedent's parents or adult children, whereas decisions authorized by a health care agent or surrogate would take precedence over those of any relative.

After a determination of death has been made by health care professionals who are not part of an organ recovery or transplant team, an effort will be made to inform family members of their loved one's death and give them time to absorb that fact before issues associated with donation are raised. Then, an approach will be made to family members to provide support, present information about donation and transplantation, offer the opportunity for donation, and permit the next of kin to consider decisions about donation (Albert, 1994). If the donation decision is favorable, external support will be continued while the donor is evaluated, a search for appropriate recipients is undertaken, arrangements are made for organ recovery and transportation, and a potential recipient is prepared to receive a transplant (Siebert, 2004).

In seeking authorization for donation from family members, the National Donor Family Council (NDFC) and others have recommended that this approach be framed as "offering the opportunity of donation," not as "requesting donation," since when one asks for or requests something from family members in these circumstances that may be perceived as asking to take one more thing away from them and as implying that if family members were to deny such a request, the requestor would have failed in his or her initiative. By contrast, it is thought that "offering the opportunity of donation" puts the family members back in charge of at least one aspect of a very difficult situation in which they have little else to control

(Corr, 2005). (The NDFC and many others have also recommended that talk about "harvesting" of organs is inappropriate and should be replaced with language about "recovering" organs and that the phrase "cadaver donors" or "cadaveric donors" should be replaced by talk of "nonliving donors" or "deceased donors" because the rejected language is offensive to donor family members.) Offering the opportunity of donation is meant to respect whatever decision a potential donor family might make; even a decision not to donate does not take away from the care embodied in this offer. In fact, the only failure would be not even to offer such an opportunity. Imagine the horror and sadness felt by family members who have reported that they had wanted to respect their loved one's wishes to donate but simply did not think of it in this time of great confusion, or family members who recognized too late that they would have wanted to make a decision to donate, but nobody mentioned it at the time!

Under a government regulation called the Medicare and Medicaid "Conditions of Participation for Organ, Tissue, and Eye Donation" that went into effect in 1998, all hospitals that receive Medicare or Medicaid funding must: (1) have a memorandum of agreement with their local or regional organ, tissue, and eye banks concerning organ donation; (2) report to their local or regional Organ Procurement Organization (**OPO**) all patients whose deaths are imminent or who have died in the hospital; (3) permit the OPO to determine the suitability or eligibility of such patients for donation; and (4) arrange for trained personnel (such as members of the OPO's staff or hospital personnel who have been trained by the OPO for this purpose) to offer the opportunity to donate (U.S. Department of Health and Human Services, 1998, 2000). As might be expected, trained procurement professionals (often working with ICU nurses) have been shown to be most effective in introducing the opportunity for donation (Evanisko, Beasley, & Brigham, 1998; Siminoff et al., 1995). Still, it is recognized that individuals cannot and should not be coerced to donate organs, either their own or those of a deceased relative, and that equal respect should be given both to decisions to donate and to decisions not to donate.

The **Conditions of Participation** regulation seeks to increase the number of donated organs, while also ensuring that family members are given an appropriate opportunity to know about and consider donation at a time when they have been victimized by the death of a loved one and when so little else is within their control. Many have reported that helping others by making a "gift of life" was the single most positive aspect in this difficult experience, a way of continuing the legacy of the donor's life and finding some measure of solace in their own bereavement (Personal Insights 16.2; Cowherd, 2004).

Conversations about the recovery of transplantable tissues from nonliving donors may be part of the overall discussion of organ donation. More often, they occur independently, frequently in the form of a telephone conversation rather than a face-to-face interaction. In the former instance, a procurement coordinator or donation advocate from an OPO might be the principal professional in the discussion; in the latter instance, a staff member from a specialized eye or tissue bank might fill that role.

CHAPTER 16 • Legal Issues 469

The Best Part of the Worst Day of My Life

I want to tell you about a woman who enriched the lives of everyone who knew her, and who, through her foresight, is even now enriching the lives of people she never even met. I want to tell you about my late wife Carolyn.

Carolyn was a cheerful person, and an optimist. She had boundless energy, and she loved life and all it had to offer. I was the cautious one who worried. Carolyn usually assumed that things would turn out all right, and they generally did.

That's why it took me by surprise about 7 years ago when she came home with a new driver's license and told me that she had registered as a donor. "If I die," she told me, "I want to help people."

Until that moment, I never had any problem with the idea of organ donation.

In my mind, it had always been something that happened to other people. Carolyn's statement forced me to think about the possibility of her death, and how I would feel about donating her organs.

I was uncomfortable, and I told her this. In fact, I asked her to change her mind. She smiled slyly, "It's my body, and this is what I want!" I was disturbed, and I said, "OK, if it's on your license, then that's fine, because I don't think I could make that decision."

Up to this point, everything on her side had been light and joking. Now she became serious. "Doug," she told me, "no matter what is on my license, if anything happened to me, you would have to give your consent. That's why I'm telling you."

I remember my reply very clearly. "Carolyn, do you realize what you're asking me? On what would be the worst day of my life, you're asking me to undergo that additional ordeal?" But, she was adamant. I was surprised how strongly she felt about it. I had initially thought it was a whim, but it was clearly something that she had given a lot of thought, and in the end, I had to promise.

That was 7 years ago, and in the meantime, I thought about it myself to the point where I realized that I agree with her. Having moved to Maryland, last January I went to get a new driver's license, and after a moment's hesitation, I, too, signed up to be a donor. Like a little boy, when I got home I proudly showed Carolyn my new license with the words DONOR/YES. It's strange to me now to remember how big her smile was, but that's the way Carolyn was with things that she cared deeply about.

Just two short months later, the worst day of my life arrived. On Friday, March 23rd, I was in Louisville, Kentucky, helping my mother make funeral arrangements for my grandmother who had died the day before. Just before noon, I got a call that Carolyn had collapsed at work and been rushed to the hospital with a massive heart attack. I was able to speak to her briefly, giving me hope, but ninety minutes later, after a brave struggle, she died.

(continues)

Shortly afterwards, talking to my father by phone, he relayed the question that I hoped I'd never have to answer. Did I want Carolyn to be a donor? At that moment I realized the great gift that Carolyn had given me with our conversation of 7 years ago. I didn't have to think. I knew. She wanted to help others, and I wanted that too. I gave my consent.

Then there were two things I had to do. One filled me with sorrow, but the other buoyed my spirit. I knew that I had to get myself back to Maryland to see Carolyn and spend some time with her, and, I knew that I had to hold myself together so that I could make the arrangements for her to be a tissue donor.

I think we've all heard it said that the body of a dead loved one doesn't really matter. The body is not the person; it's just an empty vessel. I can tell you that the time I spent with Carolyn there in the basement of the hospital, I felt very differently. It's true that it wasn't animated with her fabulous spirit, but this was the body of my wife, my soul-mate, my best friend. It's how I had known her all our life together. If this was just an empty vessel, then I wouldn't care what was done with it. But I did care—very much.

I still felt so much love for Carolyn, and I knew that I could express this to her through the loving and respectful disposition of her body. And it was so important to her that her body be used to improve the lives of others. Making the arrangements for her to be a tissue donor was an act done out of love: her love of life, our love for the unknown people who would be helped, and my love for her.

Most people are familiar with organ donation, such as a heart or a kidney. Before the day Carolyn died, I, like most people, had never heard of tissue donation. Carolyn told me, "If I die, I want to help people." Sadly, her death has come to pass, but the sorrow I feel over the loss of Carolyn is lightened by the knowledge that people have been helped. Already, two people have had their sight restored, and two others have received either life-saving or life-prolonging heart valve transplants.

If I could speak to these people, I would tell them two things. First, this gift you have received was given to you with great love by Carolyn and by me. Always know that wherever you are, there are two beings who love you profoundly. Second, please don't ever feel guilty about what you have received. Nothing could save Carolyn. You have given me a great gift by making it possible for something life-affirming to come out of her death.

On March 23rd [2001], my beloved Carolyn died. It has been a great source of comfort to me to know that through her compassion and her wisdom, two people are living richer lives, two people are leading longer lives, and, perhaps, somewhere, a family has been spared the anguish that nothing could spare mine. We must all take responsibility to spread the word about donation among our friends and colleagues so that people in need are helped, and so that families in grief can benefit from the comfort that donation brings. Perhaps for them, it will be like it was for me: the best part of the worst day of my life.

Source: Douglas Harrell.

Efforts to Increase Organ and Tissue Donation

In recent years, there have been many efforts to educate the public about organ and tissue donation and transplantation, to broaden the criteria for acceptable donors, to encourage more living donors, and to obtain more tissue donors from those who die suddenly and unexpectedly most often outside of hospitals. Above all, there have been efforts to try to obtain more organ donors from the estimated 10,500–13,800 potential donors among the approximately 1 million people who die in U.S. hospitals annually (Sheehy et al., 2003). (Similar efforts in Canada have shown wide variation across Canadian provinces in obtaining organ donors from among the more than 3,000 potential donors who die in Canadian hospitals annually; Canadian Institute for Health Information, 2014). For example, word of mouth and public education projects have sought to dispel myths about donation by emphasizing facts such as the following: "brain-dead" individuals cannot return to life; donor families incur no costs to donate; human organs and tissues cannot legally be bought or sold in the United States; organ and tissue donation usually have no substantive effect on desired funeral practices, other than the possibility of a brief delay; donation and transplantation are encouraged and supported (or at least not opposed) by nearly all religious communities in the United States; members of some minority groups whom research has shown to have lower rates of donation than the general population (Callender et al., 1991; Wheeler & Cheung, 1996) are most likely to find a close tissue match with other members of similar groups and gene pools; and a large and growing number of individuals on the National Transplant Waiting List are in desperate need of a transplanted organ. Public education efforts are reflected in efforts to counter media distortions (Morgan et al., 2007) and to convey messages like the following: "Don't take your organs to heaven … heaven knows we need them here!"; or "Jerry Orbach gave his heart and soul to acting, and the gift of sight to two New Yorkers." (The second quote is from The Eye Bank of New York and refers to the well-known Broadway and television actor ["Law and Order"] who made provisions for eye donation before his death in 2004.)

Other programs encourage individuals to sign up as potential donors either at state offices where automobile driver's licenses are obtained or renewed, or directly through state registries. Information about state registries can be obtained from the federal government's Division of Transplantation or organizations such as Donate Life America, UNOS, or the National Kidney Foundation. The goal of these systems is to sensitize the public to the need for transplantable organs and tissues, to encourage dialogue about donation among family members, and to have a readily accessible way to determine either intent or a prior decision to donate when death occurs. (Note that it is not appropriate to include wishes about donation in one's last will and testament, because wills are generally not officially read for some time after a death and thus are not a good vehicle for this time-sensitive purpose.)

Whatever one does to indicate an intention to be an organ or tissue donor, it is critically important to discuss this matter with one's next of kin. As the slogan says: "Share your life. Share your decision." The reason for this is to involve family members in one's decision, to prepare them in case a donation situation should arise, and to guide them when they need to follow one's wishes and authorize donation. *Historically, lack of discussion among family members about their wishes has been the most significant barrier to donation.* Therefore, for those who wish to donate: (1) report

A poster stresses the importance of making your wishes about organ and tissue donation known to your family members.

Is your family more likely to know how you like your coffee than how you feel about organ and tissue donation?

Signing an organ donor card is <u>not</u> enough.
Discuss organ and tissue donation with your family.

Northwest Donor Program *Share your life. Share your decision.*℠   For a free brochure call 1-800-355-SHARE
℠1996 NW Organ Procurement Agency

Courtesy LifeCenter Northwest

your decision to donate on a first-person consent registry and (2) convey your wishes in clear and unambiguous ways to your next of kin.

Research on factors that seem to influence family members in making decisions to donate organs (e.g., Irving et al., 2013; Siminoff et al., 2001; Sque, Long, & Payne, 2005) and tissue (e.g., Rodrigue, Scott, & Oppenheim, 2003) has suggested that family members who authorize a donation are more knowledgeable about brain death, more likely to have discussed donation previously, more likely to know the deceased's wishes about donation, and have more favorable attitudes and beliefs about donation compared with family members who did not consent to the donation. Family members who authorize a donation often reported that they were approached in a caring manner and were provided with both information and time to make their decision. Research on members of minority groups who have been less willing than the general population to donate organs found that African Americans generally expressed distrust of physicians and the health care system and had not previously had family discussions about organ donation (Minniefield, Yang, & Muti, 2001). Other research showed that culturally specific information about organ failure rates and organ donation could increase donations among Native Americans when presented by knowledgeable individuals from within the culture (Danielson et al., 1998). Still, some have suggested that there will never be enough organs available to provide transplants to all patients who need one (Sheehy et al., 2003).

In April 2003, the U.S. Department of Health and Human Services launched the first of two Organ Donation Breakthrough Collaboratives in an effort to increase access to transplantable organs (Shafer et al., 2006). Previous national data indicated that organs had been recovered from only about 46% of potential donors, although many large hospitals had average donation rates well above this figure (200 hospitals had provided 50% or more of eligible organ donors in the United States). The goal of the Collaboratives was to identify and share with other institutions practices that can be replicated from U.S. hospitals that had already achieved organ donation rates of 75% or greater. This and other initiatives led to a major increase of more than 24% in the "conversion rate" (the percentage of eligible donors who actually became donors) among nonliving donors from 2003 to 2006. Achieving an average donation rate of 75% in the 200 largest hospitals in the United States (and extending that effort to other hospitals) could save or enhance thousands of additional lives each year. The challenge is to continue this and other productive initiatives (Davis, Norton, & Jacobs, 2013; Ebadat et al., 2014).

Caring for Family Members at the Time of Donation and Afterwards

Caring for family members can help when "first-person consent" is explained to them as an expression of their loved one's desire to donate and they are then involved in the process. Alternatively, it can be important to empower family members of other deceased members by offering them the opportunity to authorize the donation of human organs and tissues from the body of their loved one (Jacoby, Breitkopf, & Pease, 2005). Many of these family members have reported that this opportunity enabled them to:

- Act in accordance with the previously expressed or perceived wishes and values of their loved one who has died.
- Give some meaning to the death of their loved one.
- Find some solace for themselves in a time of great difficulty.
- Help others in need by offering them something of benefit as a free gift of love.
- Act upon their generally favorable attitudes toward donation.

Offering the opportunity of donation should be accompanied by a comprehensive program of bereavement-centered care for potential donor families, donor family members who have authorized the donation, family members in "first-person consent" situations, and living donors—both before and after a death or donation (Holtkamp, 2002; Maloney & Wolfelt, 2001).

The National Kidney Foundation (NKF) founded the National Donor Family Council (NDFC) in 1992 to support donor families (Corr & the Members of the Executive Committee of the National Donor Family Council, 2001). Together they developed a series of publications to explain organ and tissue donation, including a "Bill of Rights for Donor Families"; a quarterly newsletter (*For Those Who Give and*

Grieve) and a booklet with the same name; and several other booklets and brochures on subjects such as brain death and the death of an adult child, spouse, or lifetime companion. The NDFC also developed a National Donor Family Quilt, "Patches of Love," consisting of individually designed, 8-inch quilt squares, that has become an effective way for donor families to commemorate their loved ones, participate in an international program of memorialization, and contribute to public awareness and education about organ and tissue donation (NKF, 2007).

NKF and NDFC also developed *National Communications Guidelines* concerning communications between all who are involved in donation and transplantation (NKF, 2004). These guidelines seek: to ensure that donor families and living, nondirected donors can obtain appropriate information about the consequences of their decisions to donate; to enable transplant recipients to express thanks for the gifts they have received; and to guide professionals in their roles in facilitating such communications. Albert (1998, 1999) has shown that (1) appropriate contacts between donor family members and transplant recipients can benefit all involved and (2) sound ethical considerations can facilitate such contacts.

In addition, from 1994 to 2011, the federal government's Division of Transplantation engaged the assistance of the NDFC in organizing the biennial National Donor Recognition Ceremony and Workshop, a special weekend of activities for living donors and donor family members, to pay tribute to America's donors. NKF also organized the biennial U.S. Transplant Games from 1990 to 2010, which included a recognition ceremony for deceased donors and their family members. These donor recognition ceremonies helped to recognize and validate the difficult decisions made by organ and tissue donors and their families (note the "Gift of Love, Gift of Life" inscription and medal on the photo of Karen Musto's gravestone; see also Musto, 1999). The Transplant Games demonstrated some of the successes of organ transplantation and the rich lives that many transplant recipients have achieved (e.g., Klug & Jackson, 2004).

As her memorial attests, Karen Musto was an organ donor.

DISPOSITION OF ONE'S BODY AND PROPERTY

Disposition of one's body and property are not uncomplicated matters. After a brief discussion of disposition of death bodies, we address: disposition of one's property through discussions of probate; wills and intestacy; trusts and other will substitutes; and estate and inheritance taxes.

Disposition of Dead Bodies

Apart from body donation for research or educational purposes (see Chapter 11), there are a number of issues that are concerned with disposition of dead bodies. State and local regulations provide a general framework for the disposition of bodies that is principally concerned with recording vital statistics, giving formal permission for burial or some other form of disposition, preventing bodies or institutions that handle bodies from becoming a source of contamination or a threat to the health of the living, protecting the uses of cemetery land, and governing processes of disinterment or exhumation. Beyond that, regulation of body disposition is essentially a matter of professional practice, social custom, and good taste.

For example, as we indicated in Chapter 11, there is no general legal requirement that bodies be embalmed following a death, although this is common practice among many groups in the United States. Embalming is legally required when bodies are to be transported via common carrier in interstate commerce. It may also be mandated when disposition of a body does not occur promptly and when refrigeration is not available. In other circumstances, the practice of embalming is mainly undertaken to permit viewing of the body prior to or as part of funeral ceremonies. Similarly, concrete grave liners and other forms of individual vaults that are used as the outer liners for caskets in the graves at many cemeteries are typically required not by law but by the cemeteries themselves to prevent settling of the ground and thus to minimize costs of grounds keeping and other maintenance activities in the cemetery.

Disposition of Property: Probate

After a death, it is necessary to distribute property owned by the deceased to others. In general, disposition of personal property is governed by the laws of the state where a person lived at the time of death, whereas disposition of real estate (land and the structures built on it) is governed by the laws of the state where the real estate is located. The process of administering and executing these functions is called **probate**, a term deriving from a Latin word (*probare*, "to prove") that has to do with proving or verifying the legitimacy of a will.

In the American death system, probate courts supervise the work of a decedent's personal representative who is charged to carry out necessary post-death duties (American Bar Association, 2012; Bove, 2005; Clifford, 2015a). That representative is called an *executor* if he or she has been named by the decedent in a will or an *administrator* if appointed by the court. Such a representative is responsible for: making an inventory and collecting the assets of the estate; notifying parties who may have claims against the estate of the decedent; paying debts, expenses, and taxes; winding up business affairs; arranging for the preparation of necessary documents; managing the estate during the process; distributing the decedent's remaining property to those entitled to receive it; and closing the estate (Dukeminier & Sitkoff, 2013). Charges levied against the estate may include a commission for the personal representative; fees charged by attorneys, accountants, or others who assist in administering the estate; and court costs. Many individuals seek to reduce these costs, along with the time consumed by the probate process, by arranging their affairs in ways that minimize involvements with or complexities for the probate process (Cullen & Irving, 2014; Hume, 2015; Smith & Castleman, 2013).

Wills and Intestacy

Individuals who die without a valid will are said to have died **intestate** or without a testament stating their wishes. In every state, there are laws governing how the estate of an intestate individual will be distributed. These rules vary from state to state but are generally based on assumptions made by state legislators as to how a typical person would wish to distribute his or her property (Silverman, 2011). For example, a surviving spouse and children are likely to be regarded as preferred heirs, and the decedent's descendants are likely to be given precedence over parents, other ancestors, or their descendants. In the case of an intestate individual with no one who qualifies as an heir under the intestacy statute, the estate *escheats* or passes to the state.

Individuals can gain some measure of control over the distribution of their property through estate planning and a formal statement of their wishes, commonly called a *will* (Clifford, 2014, 2015a). Each state has regulations on how a will must be prepared and submitted to the probate process. Such regulations are intended to communicate the importance the state attaches to the process of drawing up a will and to provide an evidentiary basis for proving during the probate process that the document really is the decedent's will and does actually represent his or her intentions. For example, wills are to be drawn up, signed, and dated by adults *(testators)* who are of "sound mind," who are not subject to undue influence, and whose action is witnessed by the requisite number (as provided by state law) of individuals who do not have a personal interest in the will whereby they would benefit from the disposition of the estate for which it provides. In general, through their wills, individuals are free to dispose of their property as they wish, subject to exceptions (such as community property laws relating to marriages) that have been enacted by most states to protect certain close family members from total disinheritance.

Holographic wills—those that are handwritten and unwitnessed—are acceptable in many states. However, state law varies greatly on this matter, and wills of this sort may be unreliable if they do not include specific, required language, or if the meaning of their language is ambiguous.

In general, professional legal assistance is usually recommended to draw up and execute a formal, written will in order to ensure that the document does convey its intended meaning and will have legal effect, notwithstanding changes in the testator's circumstances.

Wills can be changed at any time before the testator's death, assuming that the individual remains of sound mind and gives evidence of intent to make the change. This can be accomplished through a supplementary document called a *codicil*, which leaves the previous document intact while altering one or more of its provisions; through a new will that revokes the previous document either explicitly or implicitly; through a formal revocation process that does not establish a new will; or through some physical act, such as divorce, subsequent marriage, or marriage followed by the birth of a child. The most recent, valid will governs disposition of the decedent's estate. There are many published resources on these subjects, both for legal professionals and for lay readers (e.g., Clifford, 2014, 2015a; Esperti, Peterson, & Cahoone, 2012; Hughes & Klein, 2007; Silverman, 2011).

In addition, some (e.g., Baines, 2001, 2006; Cebuhar, 2010; Freed, 2013; Turnbull, 2012) have sought to renew an ancient tradition by advocating for *ethical wills*, moral statements that do not have legal force but through which individuals seek to record their values in order to pass them on to others.

Trusts and Other Will Substitutes

It is both possible and legal to seek to avoid the expense and delay of the probate process by *transferring assets during one's life*. For example, with the exception of certain limited circumstances in which death is imminent, one can simply make an irrevocable and unconditional *gift* of property in which full control of the gift is conveyed to the recipient at the time the gift is made. Such gifts can now be made by each individual in amounts as high as $14,000 per year per donee (the receiver of such a gift) without incurring any federal tax liability. Similarly, ownership of real estate (land and the structures built on it) can be directly and immediately transferred through a written *deed*. Both gifts and deeds surrender ownership of and benefit from the object of the gift or deed, although some states permit *revocable deeds* or other conditions under which the transfer is not absolute. Gifts and deeds may reduce the size of an estate that is presented for probate or considered for tax purposes.

Alternatively, one can make *transfers effective at death* that convey possession and complete ownership rights to another person upon the death of the current owner of the property, even though the current owner retains many benefits from and control over the property until his or her death. For example, *joint tenancy with right of survivorship* amounts to an arrangement for transfer of property at death through a form of co-ownership. Under this arrangement, two or more parties possess equal rights to the property during their mutual lifetimes. When one party dies, his or her rights dissolve, and the rights of the survivor(s) automatically expand to include that person's previous ownership rights. This process can continue until the last survivor acquires full and complete ownership of the entire property interest. At each stage in the process, nothing is left unowned by a living person, and nothing is therefore available to pass through the probate process. Joint tenancy with right of survivorship usually avoids delays in getting assets to survivors, but it does not necessarily reduce tax liability.

Life insurance policies are another familiar social vehicle through which assets are transferred from one person to another at the time of the first person's death. Such insurance policies depend on a contractual agreement in which premium payments made by the policyholder result in a payment of benefits to a specified beneficiary by an insurance company upon the death of the insured. Many life insurance policies provide considerable flexibility to the insured as to how the monetary value of the policy can be employed during his or her lifetime, including the power to change beneficiaries before death. Benefits from life insurance policies are not included as taxable assets in the estate of the insured, although they clearly add to the property or estate of the beneficiary.

A **trust** is one of the most adaptable and efficient ways of preserving one's assets from probate. One makes a trust by transferring property to a trustee (usually a third party, such as an officer of a corporation or a bank), with instructions on its management and distribution (Abts, 2002; Esperti & Peterson, 2014). Trustees are legally bound to use the trust property for the benefit of the beneficiaries according to the terms provided in the trust instrument or imposed by law. Typically, the maker of the trust retains extensive use and control over the property during his or her life.

Usually, upon the death of the person who established the trust (the *settlor*), the property is distributed to designated beneficiaries without becoming part of the estate in probate. However, a trust can be established that stipulates other circumstances for distribution of property. For example, a trust might stipulate that the settlor's surviving spouse receives a life estate in the income from the trust assets, with the principal to be distributed to children upon the death of the spouse. Rights to amend or revoke the trust can be retained by the person who established the trust. In addition to these *testamentary trusts*, one can also establish *living trusts*, which are essentially set up for the benefit of the trustor—for example, in case he or she is incapacitated and unable to act on his or her own behalf (Clifford, 2015b; Sharp, 2010). Couples often set up revocable living trusts in which they are both trustees for each other's trust to insure that property passes directly from one trust to the other upon a death and that one trustee can act for the other when that person is unable to do so. Living trusts are also useful for single adults with no dependents and minimal assets.

Estate and Inheritance Taxes

Two basic types of taxes follow upon a death: estate taxes and inheritance taxes. **Estate taxes** are imposed on and paid from the decedent's estate. They could be described as taxes not on property itself but on the transfer of property from a decedent to his or her beneficiaries. This occurs before all remaining assets in the estate are distributed to heirs or beneficiaries. By contrast, **inheritance taxes** are imposed on individuals who receive property through inheritance.

Federal estate tax law applies uniformly throughout the United States. As of 2017, estate tax legislation exempts from federal taxes an unlimited amount of property that is donated to charity, together with other property in an individual's estate valued at $5.49 million or twice that in the case of an estate of a couple. A tax rate of 40% applies to amounts exceeding these limitations. (There have been occasional attempts within Congress to increase the amounts exempted from federal estate tax or to do away with this tax altogether, even though the vast majority of estates—as many as 98%—are estimated to have already been exempt from its taxable burden.) Also, one can transfer to a surviving spouse an unlimited amount of property without estate taxes. However, such a transfer may only postpone or defer rather than avoid these taxes, since property transferred in this way that remains in the spouse's possession at the time of his or her death will become part of that individual's estate.

In addition, most states have estate and/or inheritance taxes. These taxes vary from state to state and may impose different rates on those who are more closely or more distantly related to the decedent. Thus, it is sound and prudent policy for those faced with potential estate and/or inheritance taxes to seek the advice of experts in order to minimize any tax burden that might arise.

Summary

In this chapter, we surveyed legal issues that arise before, at, and after the death of a human being in the United States. In particular, we first considered conversations about death-related matters and advance directives for health care (living wills, durable powers of attorney in health care matters, and "Five Wishes"). Next, we examined issues associated with definition, determination, and certification of death. We then explored organ, tissue, and body donation. Finally, we reviewed subjects related to the disposition of one's body and one's property or estate.

Glossary

Advance directives: instructions from an individual about actions that the individual would or would not want to be taken if he or she were somehow incapacitated and unable to join in making decisions

Artificial means: interventions or supports used to sustain life or bodily functioning

Case law: legal precedents arising from court decisions

Common law: shared values and views drawn from English and early American legal and social history; now, typically represented by definitions contained in standard legal dictionaries

Conditions of Participation: federal regulations under which hospitals that receive Medicare or Medicaid funding must cooperate in specified ways to facilitate organ donation

Coroner: originally, the representative of the crown in England; currently in the United States, an elected official authorized to investigate the deaths of individuals in specific circumstances

Death certificate: a legal document recording time and cause of death, and other significant information

Definition of death: a statement of the conditions under which an individual is understood to be dead

Determination of death: the process (or its result) by which competent authorities employ tests or criteria to decide whether death has actually occurred

Donation after brain death: applies to individuals who have experienced brain death and who then become organ and/or tissue donors; authorized by next-of-kin or their own expressed wishes

Donation after cardiac death: applies to individuals who have not experienced brain death, but who become organ and/or tissue donors after next-of-kin authorize removal of life-sustaining interventions and permit donation; formerly called "non-heart-beating donors"

Donor rights legislation: laws establishing registries allowing individuals 18 years of age or older to give "first-person consent," i.e., a legally binding authorization for organ and/or tissue donation

Durable powers of attorney in health care matters: advance directives through which an individual can authorize another individual to make decisions and take actions on his or her behalf under specific circumstances; both the directive and the individual appointed to act are sometimes called a "health care proxy"

Estate taxes: taxes levied on the assets of a person who has died

First-person consent: legislation allowing individuals 18 years of age or older to make a legally binding decision to authorize organ and tissue donation in the event of death

"Five Wishes": a type of advance directive that is intended to be easy to understand, simple to use, personal in character, and thorough

Harvard criteria: tests developed to determine the existence of irreversible coma

Health care proxy: see Durable powers of attorney in health care matters

Inheritance taxes: taxes levied by a government on the assets a beneficiary inherits from the estate of someone who has died

Intestate: the condition of an individual who dies without leaving a valid will or other legally qualified statement concerning the distribution of his or her estate or property

Living donor: a living individual who donates blood, one of a pair of twinned organs, a portion of certain organs, or certain bodily tissues for transplantation, research, or educational purposes

Living wills: advance directives intended to refuse certain cure-oriented interventions ("artificial means" or "heroic measures") not desired by an individual, ask that dying be permitted to take its natural course, and request that associated suffering be mitigated with effective palliative care

Medical examiner: a qualified medical doctor (usually a forensic pathologist) appointed to replace a coroner, especially in large, urban centers

NASH system: a fourfold classification system for identifying manner of death (natural, accidental, suicide, or homicide)

Natural death legislation: authorizes living wills or durable powers of attorney in health care matters

Non-heart beating donors: donors who have experienced cardiac death

Nonliving or deceased donors: individuals who have experienced brain death or cardiac death prior to donation and the subsequent recovery of one or more of their organs or tissues for transplantation, research, or educational purposes

NOTA: the National Organ Transplant Act, enacted by Congress in 1984 to regulate the procurement and transplantation of human organs

OPO: an organ procurement organization; an authorized local or regional agency that offers the opportunity of organ donation and recovers donated organs

OPTN: the Organ Procurement and Transplantation Network, established by NOTA to facilitate procurement and distribution of scarce human organs in a fair and equitable way by matching donated organs with potential transplant recipients

Organ, tissue, or body donation: making a gift of a human organ, tissue, or body for medical, research, or educational purposes

Probate: the legal system of administering and executing distribution of personal property and real estate after a death; proving or verifying the legitimacy of a will (where such exists) or carrying out estate law

Right to privacy: affirmed by the U.S. Supreme Court as an individual's right to be left alone

Substitute or surrogate decision maker: an individual authorized to act by a durable power of attorney in health care matters

Transplantable human organs: kidneys, hearts, livers, pancreas, intestines, and lungs in whole or part

Transplantable human tissues: skin, heart valves, leg veins, eye and eye components, bone, tendons, and ligaments

Trusts: legal arrangements to preserve one's assets from probate by transferring their ownership to a trustee with instructions for their management and distribution to a beneficiary; "living trusts" serve the interests of those who establish them; "testamentary trusts" control distribution of assets at death

UAGA: the Uniform Anatomical Gift Act, enacted by Congress in 1968 to establish criteria under which human organs can be donated; amended in 1987

UNOS: the United Network for Organ Sharing, a private corporation that administers the OPTN under contract to the Division of Transplantation in the U.S. Department of Health and Human Services

Will: a formal statement of one's wishes concerning the distribution of one's property after death

Xenotransplantation: transplantation across species, that is, from animals to humans, as in the transplantation of heart values obtained from pigs

Questions for Review and Discussion

1. Have you thought about or engaged in conversations about end-of-life care? Why or why not?
2. Which of the available advance directives for health care (living wills; durable powers of attorney; "Five Wishes") seems to you most desirable for situations in which you might be unable to participate in decision making about your medical treatment? Why?
3. Why is it difficult in some cases in contemporary American society to decide whether someone is dead? Why is it important to make such a decision?
4. What are your views about donating your body's organs or tissues for transplantation after your death? What about donating the organs or tissues of someone you love? What about living donation? What feelings, beliefs, and values led you to these views?
5. Have you thought about disposition of your body and/or property if you should die? What have you done about these matters, what do you think you should or might do, or why have you done nothing?
6. A vast amount of information about the subjects addressed in this chapter is available online. Have you ever searched for such information? If so, were your searches productive? Why or why not?

Suggested Readings

Three unusual resources on legal and other issues related to death and dead bodies are:

Iserson, K. V. (2001). *Death to Dust: What Happens to Dead Bodies?* (2nd ed.)
Roach, M. (2003). *Stiff: The Curious Lives of Human Cadavers*
Schechter, H. (2009). *The Whole Death Catalog: A Lively Guide to the Bitter End*

Concerning rights to privacy, informed consent, and advance directives, see:

Alderman, E., & Kennedy, C. (1997). *The Right to Privacy*
Cebuhar, J. K. (2015). *The Practical Guide to Health Care Advance Directives*
Doukas, D. J., & Reichel, W. (2007). *Planning for Uncertainty: Living Wills and Other Advance Directives for You and Your Family* (2nd ed.)
Fabiny, A., & Sabatino, C. P. (2013). *Living Wills: A Guide to Advance Directives, Health Care Power of Attorney, and Other Key Documents*
Fitzpatrick, J., & Fitzpatrick, E. M. (2010). *A Better Way of Dying: How to Make the Best Choices at the End of Life*
Rogne, L., & McCune, S. (Eds.). (2013). *Advance Care Planning: Communicating about Matters of Life and Death*
Rozovsky, F. A. (2015). *Consent to Treatment: A Practical Guide* (5th ed.)
Shenkman, M. M., & Klein, P. S. (2004). *Living Wills and Health Care Proxies: Assuring That Your End-of-Life Decisions Are Respected*
Urich, L. P. (2001). *The Patient Self-Determination Act: Meeting the Challenges in Patient Care*

Concerning organ and tissue donation and transplantation, consult:

Caplan, A. L., McCartney, J. J., & Reid, D. P. (Eds.). (2015). *Replacement Parts: The Ethics of Procuring and Replacing Organs in Humans*
Finn, R. (2000). *Organ Transplants: Making the Most of Your Gift of Life*
Foran, R. (2013). *Organ Transplants* [for teen readers]

Green, R. (Ed.). (2007). *The Gift that Heals: Stories of Hope, Renewal and Transformation through Organ and Tissue Donation*

Green, R. (2009). *The Nicholas Effect: A Boy's Gift to the World*

Hamilton, D. (2012). *A History of Organ Transplantation: Ancient Legends to Modern Practice*

Holtkamp, S. (2002). *Wrapped in Mourning: The Gift of Life and Organ Donor Family Trauma*

Jensen, S. J. (Ed.). (2011). *The Ethics of Organ Transplantation*

Kaserman, D. L., & Barrett, A. H. (2002). *The United States Organ Procurement System: A Prescription for Reform*

Kirk, A. D., Knechtle, S. J., Larsen, C. P., Madsen, J. C., Pearson, T. C., & Webber, S. A. (2014). *Textbook of Organ Transplantation*

Maloney, R., & Wolfelt, A. D. (2011). *Caring for Donor Families: Before, During and After* (2nd ed.)

Miller, F. G., & Truog, R. D. (2012). *Death, Dying, and Organ Transplantation: Reconstructing Medical Ethics at the End of Life*

Munson, R. (2004). *Raising the Dead: Organ Transplants, Ethics, and Society*

Parr, E., & Mize, J. (2001). *Coping with an Organ Transplant: A Practical Guide to Understanding, Preparing for, and Living with an Organ Transplant*

Satel, S. (Ed.). (2009). *When Altruism Isn't Enough: The Case for Compensating Kidney Donors*

Schwartz, T. P. (2005). *Organ Transplants: A Survival Guide for the Entire Family— The Ultimate Teen Guide*

Starzl, T. (2003). *The Puzzle People: Memoirs of a Transplant Surgeon* (rev. ed.)

Tilney, N. L. (2003). *Transplantation: From Myth to Reality*

Veatch, R. M., & Ross, L. F. (2015). *Transplantation Ethics* (2nd ed.)

Youngner, S. J., Anderson, M. W., & Schapiro, R. (Eds.). (2003). *Transplanting Human Tissue: Ethics, Policy, and Practice*

Concerning estate planning and disposition of property, consult:

The American Bar Association. (2012). *Guide to Wills and Estates* (4th ed.)

Bove, A. A. (2005). *Complete Book of Wills, Estates, and Trusts* (3rd ed.)

Brody, J. (2009). *Jane Brody's Guide to the Great Beyond: A Practical Primer to Help You and Your Loved Ones Prepare Medically, Legally, and Emotionally for the End of Life*

Chambers, J. S. (2005). *The Easy Will and Living Will Kit*

Clifford, D. (2014). *Plan Your Estate* (12th ed.)

Clifford, D. (2015a). *Estate Planning Basics* (8th ed.)

Clifford, D. (2015b). *Make Your Own Living Trust* (12th ed.)

Cullen, M., & Irving, S. (2014). *Get It Together: Organize Your Records so Your Family Won't Have To* (6th ed.)

Dukeminier, J., & Sitkoff, R. H. (2013). *Wills, Trusts, and Estates* (9th ed.).

Esperti, R. A., & Peterson, R. L. (2014). *21st Century Loving Trust: Revised and Expanded for the New Economy*

Esperti, R. A., Peterson, R. L., & Cahoone, D. K. (2012). *Protect and Enhance Your Estate: Definitive Strategies for Estate and Wealth Planning* (3rd ed.)

Hughes, T. E., & Klein, D. (2007). *A Family Guide to Wills, Funerals, and Probate: How to Protect Yourself and Your Survivors* (2nd ed.)

Hume, S. B. (2015). *ABA/AARP Checklist for My Family: A Guide to My History, Financial Plans and Final Wishes*

Pierce, M. (2008). *Your Wills, Trusts, and Estates Explained Simply: Important Information You Need to Know*

Sharp, R. F. (2010). *Living Trusts for Everyone: Why a Will Is Not the Way to Avoid Probate, Protect Heirs, and Settle Estates*

Silverman, R. A. (2011). *The Wall Street Journal Complete Estate Planning Guidebook*

Smith, S. T., & Castleman, M. (2013). *When Someone Dies: The Practical Guide to the Logistics of Death*

On ethical wills, see:

Baines, B. K. (2001). *The Ethical Will Writing Guide and Workbook: Preserving Your Legacy of Values for Your Family and Community*

Baines, B. K. (2006). *Ethical Wills: Putting Your Values on Paper* (2nd ed.)

Cebuhar, J. K. (2010). *So Grows the Tree: Creating an Ethical Will*

Freed, R. A. (2013). *Your Legacy Matters: A Multi-generational Guide for Writing Your Ethical Will*

Turnbull, S. B. (2012). *The Wealth of Your Life: A Step-by-Step Guide for Creating Your Ethical Will* (3rd ed.)

Selected Web Resources

Some useful search terms include: ADVANCE DIRECTIVES; CORONER; DECEASED DONORS; DEFINITION OF DEATH; DETERMINATION OF DEATH; DURABLE POWER OF ATTORNEY IN HEALTH CARE; ETHICAL WILLS; "FIVE WISHES"; HEALTH CARE PROXY; INHERITANCE TAXES; INTESTATE; LIVING DONORS; LIVING WILLS; MEDICAL EXAMINER; NONLIVING DONORS; ORGAN DONATION; POLST; PROBATE; TISSUE DONATION; TRANSPLANTATION; WILLS; XENOTRANSPLANTATION.

You can also visit the following *organizational and other Internet sites*:

Aging with Dignity

American Society of Law, Medicine, and Ethics (ASLME)

Division of Transplantation, U.S. Department of Health and Human Services

Donate Life America

Ethical Wills

National Donor Family Council (NDFC)

National Kidney Foundation (NKF)

United Network for Organ Sharing (UNOS)

@erics/Shutterstock.com

Suicide and Life-Threatening Behavior

Objectives of this Chapter

▶ To clarify the meaning of suicide and life-threatening behavior

▶ To describe some common patterns in suicidal behavior

▶ To identify psychological, biological, and sociological factors that might help to understand or explain suicidal behavior

▶ To explore the impact of suicide on those who are bereaved by such a death

▶ To describe warning signs for suicide and interventions that individuals or social groups can undertake to reduce the likelihood of a completed suicide or at least to minimize suicidal behavior

▶ To address the morality of suicide and briefly summarize several religions' views of suicide

TWO COMPLETED SUICIDES

When he died on July 1, 1961, Ernest Hemingway was 62 years old and a successful journalist and writer. Best known for his novels, such as *The Sun Also Rises* (1926), *A Farewell to Arms* (1929), and *For Whom the Bell Tolls* (1940), Hemingway won the Pulitzer Prize for his novella, *The Old Man and the Sea* (1952). Two years later he was awarded the Nobel Prize for literature. Hemingway's public image was that of a writer, hunter, and sportsman exemplifying courage and stoicism—the classic macho male—but in his private life, he was subject to severe depression and paranoia. In the end (like his father), he used a shotgun to complete his own suicide, a notoriously deliberate and effective means of ending one's life (Lynn, 1987). Perhaps it was foreshadowed in the words of a character in *For Whom the Bell Tolls* (1940, p. 468), who said, "Dying is only bad when it takes a long time and hurts so much that it humiliates you."

Sylvia Plath (1932–1963) was an American poet and novelist best known for her novel *The Bell Jar* (1971), first published in England under an assumed name in January 1963, only a month before her death. This book has an autobiographical quality in its description of a woman caught up in a severe crisis who attempts suicide. Like the author's poetry, *The Bell Jar* emphasizes conflicts that result from family tensions and rebellion against the constricting forces of society.

Bettmann/Getty Images

Ernest Hemingway:
1899–1961

The death of Plath's father when she was 8 years old was a major event in her life, as was what Alvarez (1970, p. 7) called her "desperately serious suicide attempt" in 1953 (in which she used stolen sleeping pills, left a misleading note to cover her tracks, and hid in a dark, unused corner of a cellar). Plath also survived a serious car wreck during the summer of 1962 when she apparently ran off the road deliberately. Plath seems to describe these events in a poem entitled "Lady Lazarus" (1964), in which she writes about being like a cat that has nine lives (and thus nine times to die) of which she has only used up three.

In December 1962, Plath separated from her husband—the British poet Ted Hughes, whom she had married in June 1956—and moved to London with her two children. Early on the morning of February 11, 1963, Plath died.

In the days before her death, Plath's friends and her doctor had been concerned about her mental state. Her doctor had prescribed sedatives and had tried to arrange an appointment for her with a psychotherapist. But Plath convinced them that she had improved and could return to her apartment to stay alone with her children. A new Australian *au pair* (an in-home child care provider) was due to arrive at 9 a.m. on the morning of Monday, February 11, to help with the children and housework.

When the *au pair* arrived, she received no response at the door of the building and went to search for a telephone to call her employer to confirm she had the right address. After returning, trying the door again, and then calling her employer a second time, she came back to the house at about 11 a.m. and was finally able to get into the building with the aid of some workmen. Smelling gas, they forced open the door of the apartment and found Plath's body, still warm, together with a note asking that her doctor be called and giving his telephone number. The children were

Sylvia Plath:
1932–1963

Bettmann/Getty Images

asleep in an upstairs room, wrapped snugly in blankets against the cold weather and furnished with a plate of bread and butter and mugs of milk in case they should wake up hungry before the *au pair* arrived—but their bedroom window was wide open, protecting them from the effects of the gas.

Apparently, at about 6 a.m., Plath had arranged the children and the note about calling her doctor, sealed herself in the kitchen with towels around the door and window, placed her head in the oven, and turned on the gas (Stevenson, 1989). A neighbor downstairs was knocked out by seeping gas and thus was not awake to let the *au pair* into the building when she arrived.

After Plath's death, Alvarez (1970, p. 34) wrote: "I am convinced by what I know of the facts that this time she did not intend to die." However that may be, interest in Plath's life, chronic suicidality, and death continues long after her death (e.g., Gerisch, 1998; Lester, 1998).

SUICIDE: INDIVIDUALITY AND PERPLEXITY

For many people, behavior that appears to involve a deliberate intention to end one's life is puzzling (Marcus, 2010; Torres, 2016). First, such behavior seems to challenge widely held values, including the value of human life. Second, the motivations or intentions behind suicidal behavior frequently appear to be enigmatic or incomprehensible to outside observers. Thus, when a death occurs by suicide, there is often a desperate search for a note, an explanation, or some elusive meaning that must have been involved in the act. Typically, however, there is no single explanation or meaning in all of the individuality and complexities that typify suicidal and life-threatening behavior. We see some of this perplexity in the ways Ernest Hemingway and Sylvia Plath chose to end their lives, lives that to outsiders seemed to have many positive features (see also the example of Robin Williams in Focus On 20.4 in Chapter 20 in this book). Thus, Jamison (1999, p. 73) wrote: "Each way to suicide is its own: intensely private, unknowable, and terrible. Suicide will have seemed to its perpetrator the last and best of bad possibilities, and any attempt by the living to chart this final terrain of a life can be only a sketch, maddeningly incomplete." That may be the most tantalizing aspect of it all.

Note that we have already considered some issues related to suicide, especially as related to adolescents and the elderly in Chapters 13 and 15. Also, we will discuss intentionally deciding to end a human life via assisted suicide, euthanasia, and aid in dying in Chapter 18.

WHAT IS SUICIDE?

I can become dead by killing myself. If so, I do something to cause my own death, or I do not do something to prevent my own death. No one else is directly involved in the actions that bring about my death. The deaths of Hemingway and Plath exemplify this. No one else was present and no one else acted to bring about these deaths. This is part of the meaning of **suicide**: an individual acts to cause his or her own death.

However, this is not enough by itself to make a death a suicide. Someone might engage in an action that accidentally causes his or her death. For example, a sky diver whose parachute does not open engages in an action that causes his or her own death, but that death is not a suicide. What is missing is the *intention* to die.

Thus, for death to be a suicide, the person carrying out the act must have the *intention* that the act results in death. But determining the intention of anyone—even of ourselves—is seldom easy, and suicidal behavior often turns out to be a particularly ambiguous and ambivalent sort of behavior. The intentions of those who engage in suicidal behavior are varied. They may include attempts to end some form of perceived suffering, to gain attention, to kill others (as perhaps in suicide bombers), or simply to end one's life—or, perhaps, some combination of one or more of these and other intentions.

Partly because of this ambiguity in intentions, it is not always clear whether a specific situation should be described as a suicide. We see that clearly in the case of Sylvia Plath and in Alvarez's comment that "this time she did not intend to die." Suppose someone has been warned about a diabetic condition and cautioned to monitor his or her diet. If that person fails to do so and dies in a diabetic coma, was the death caused intentionally? What if someone drove too rapidly for road conditions and died when his or her car crashed into a bridge abutment at high speed with no brake marks on a clear, dry day? Can one unconsciously act to end one's life (Do unconscious intentions even exist?) (Farberow, 1980)? **Suicidologists** struggle with questions like these and disagree about how to answer them.

Uncertainty about whether a particular act was a suicidal one has important consequences for anyone studying this subject. For example, it may have social significance if certain acts are not included among those classified as suicidal because one is uncertain about them. If so, then statistical data on the number of deaths resulting from suicidal behavior will at best be inaccurate.

Data on suicide may also be inaccurate because authorities are reluctant to call a death a suicide in order to give the person who died and his or her survivors the benefit of the doubt and to protect family members from guilt and the social stigma often attached to suicide. Family members themselves and those concerned with their welfare may resist labeling a death as a suicide. For reasons like these, it has long been suggested that the actual number of deaths due to suicide may be at least twice the number recorded. If so, the impact of suicide on individual lives and on society may be seriously misunderstood.

Further, difficulties in recognizing someone's actual intentions may contribute to our failing to recognize suicidal behavior when confronted by it. If we do not believe that someone's intention is to end up dead or if that person does not express or even denies such an intention, we may pay less attention to that person. Thus, certain forms of life-threatening behavior are sometimes discounted on the grounds that they are *only* a "cry for help" (Farberow & Shneidman, 1965). At a minimum, though, the case of Sylvia Plath shows that life-threatening acts are a desperate way to seek help, and even a cry for help can have lethal consequences, whether or not they were fully foreseen or intended. It is, therefore, important to try to get a clear understanding of suicidal and life-threatening behavior and to become familiar with common patterns of such behavior in our society.

SOME COMMON PATTERNS IN SUICIDAL BEHAVIOR

Suicide (designated as "intentional self-harm" in the international classification system) was the tenth leading cause of death in the United States in 2015, accounting for 44,193 deaths (approximately 121.1 per day) and a death rate of 13.8 per 100,000 (Drapeau & McIntosh, 2016; see Table 17.1). During the decade of the 1990s, suicide had been the eighth or ninth leading cause of death in the United States, overall numbers of suicide deaths had fluctuated between 30,000 and 31,000, and death rates from suicide had declined from 12.4 per 100,000 in 1990 to 10.7 in 1999. However, numbers of deaths, death rates, and its status as a leading cause of death increased during the years 2005–2015. Still, for some years the United States has had one of the lowest suicide rates (in the bottom third) in the world.

Drapeau and McIntosh (2016) identified the following patterns in **completed suicides** in 2015 in the United States: an average of 1 person killed himself or herself every 11.9

Table 17.1   Suicide Rates per 100,000 Population by Age: United States, 2005–2015

Age	2005	2006	2007	2008	2009	2010	2011	2012	2013	2014	2015
5–14	0.7	0.5	0.5	0.6	0.7	0.7	0.7	0.8	1.0	1.0	1.0
15–24	10.0	9.9	9.7	10.0	10.1	10.5	11.0	11.1	11.1	11.6	12.5
25–34	12.4	12.3	13.0	12.9	12.8	14.0	14.6	14.7	14.8	15.1	15.7
35–44	14.9	15.1	15.6	15.9	16.1	16.0	16.2	16.7	16.2	16.6	17.1
45–54	16.5	17.2	17.7	18.7	19.3	19.6	19.8	20.0	19.7	20.2	20.3
55–64	13.9	14.5	15.5	16.3	16.7	17.5	17.1	18.0	18.1	18.8	18.9
65–74	12.6	12.6	12.6	13.9	14.0	13.7	14.1	14.0	15.0	15.6	15.3
75–84	16.9	15.9	16.3	16.0	15.7	15.7	16.5	16.8	17.1	17.5	17.9
85+	16.9	15.9	15.6	15.6	15.6	17.6	16.9	17.8	18.6	19.3	19.4
65+	14.7	14.2	14.3	14.8	14.8	14.9	15.3	15.4	16.1	16.6	16.6
Total	11.0	11.1	11.5	11.8	12.0	12.4	12.7	12.9	13.0	13.4	13.8
Men	17.7	17.8	18.3	19.0	19.2	20.0	20.2	20.6	20.6	21.1	21.5
Women	4.5	4.6	4.8	4.9	5.0	5.2	5.4	5.5	5.7	6.0	6.3
Whites	12.3	12.4	12.9	13.3	13.5	14.1	14.5	14.8	14.9	15.4	15.8
Nonwhites	5.5	5.5	5.6	5.7	5.8	5.8	5.8	6.1	6.0	6.0	6.3
Blacks	5.1	4.9	4.9	5.2	5.1	5.1	5.3	5.5	5.4	5.5	5.6

Source: Drapeau, C. W., & McIntosh, J. L. (for the American Association of Suicidology). (2016). *U.S.A. suicide 2015: Official final data.* Washington, DC: American Association of Suicidology, dated December 23, 2016, downloaded from http://www.suicidology.org.

minutes; an average of 1 old person killed himself or herself about every 66 minutes; an average of 1 young person (15–24 years of age) killed himself or herself just over every 1 hour and 36 minutes. An estimated 25 attempts at suicide for every completed suicide would imply 1,104,825 suicide attempts or 1 every 29 seconds. There are vastly more suicide attempts for every completed suicide among young people than among the elderly. In general, suicide rates are highest among divorced, separated, and widowed persons; lowest among married persons. Further, Drapeau and McIntosh cited estimates that for each completed suicide 147 people are exposed and, among those 6 people experience a major life disruption, resulting in 250,000 suicide loss survivors each year.

The following data fill out some patterns of suicidal behavior in the United States in 2015.

- By gender: men carried out a completed suicide more frequently than did women, by a ratio of more than 3.3:1. However, women attempted suicide more frequently than did men, by an estimated ratio of approximately 3:1. The risk of attempted, but nonfatal, suicide is greatest among females and the young.
- By methods: firearms were the main means used by both men and women to carry out suicide, accounting for almost half of all suicides. Hanging (including strangulation and suffocation) led other lethal means for men; poisoning was the second most common means for women.

A woman who has completed a suicide.

StockPhotosArt/Shutterstock.com

- By age group:

  - Among young people aged 15–24 years, suicide was the second leading cause of death (following accidents), accounting for 5,491 deaths (see Chapter 13 for a fuller discussion of youth suicide). Also, suicide was the cause of 409 deaths among 10- to 14-year-olds (see Sheftall et al., 2016).

  - Among adults, suicide death rates peaked in middle adulthood and again in individuals 85 years of age or older. Among the elderly, high suicide rates were especially found among white males.

- By race, ethnicity, or culture:

  - Caucasian Americans completed approximately 90% of all suicides in the United States in 2015: 39,796 deaths (30,658 males and 9,138 females) and a death rate of 15.8 per 100,000.

  - African Americans experienced 2,504 suicide deaths overall in 2015 (2,023 males and 481 females) with a death rate of 5.6 per 100,000.

  - Hispanic Americans experienced 3,303 suicide deaths overall in 2015 with a death rate of 5.8 per 100,000. Still, as noted in Chapter 5, all reports on deaths by suicide are dependent on available data, and it has been suggested that among Hispanic Americans (and African Americans) many suicide deaths may be reported as accidents or homicides.

  - Asian and Pacific Island Americans experienced 1,316 deaths by suicide in 2015 for a death rate of 6.6 per 100,000. Again, there are many differences in this very diverse population and one must be cautious in comparisons between or within subgroups.

  - Native Americans experienced 577 deaths by suicide in 2015 for a death rate of 12.6 per 100,000. Although these are low numbers of deaths, this is a relatively high death rate among a minority group in American society, but it is lower than the overall rate for Caucasian-American suicides and does not justify the commonly heard claim that suicide rates among American Indians are extraordinarily high. See Chapter 5 for a discussion of criticisms of that claim, which note that it is often based on small numbers of suicides over short time spans and among small population bases. In fact, there is no single common American-Indian pattern for suicides, such rates vary markedly from area to area and tribe to tribe, and suicide rates in the various tribes seem most closely related to suicide rates in their surrounding populations. The only generalization about American Indians that appears to be valid is that suicide in this group is largely a phenomenon of young males, since suicide rates among the elderly are low in this cultural group.

    Still, the myth of extraordinarily high suicide rates among American Indians persists and even influences beliefs among some members of this group. Thus, Levy and Kunitz (1987, p. 932) reported that the Hopi have become concerned about suicide rates among themselves, even though "Hopi suicide rates are no higher than those of the neighboring counties." As well, no evidence was found that Hopi suicide rates are increasing. That does not suggest there should be no concern about suicide rates in any particular American Indian group, but only that such rates need to be understood in context if we are to appreciate them properly.

■ By region: although suicide is sometimes portrayed as an urban phenomenon, the highest rates of suicide in 2015 actually occurred in the Mountain region, with the lowest rates in the Middle Atlantic and New England areas. The largest number of suicides were in the South Atlantic region; the smallest number in the New England region. Among the states, Alaska, Wyoming, and Montana had the highest suicide rates (each over 26.0 per 100,000), while the District of Columbia, New York, and New Jersey had the lowest suicide rates (each under 9.0 per 100,000). Of course, annual fluctuations in state levels of suicide combined with some that have relatively small populations can result in highly variable data from year to year.

■ By season: suicides seem to peak during springtime in ways that are puzzling (Dobbs, 2013; Pappas, 2014).

With these data about common patterns in suicidal behavior in hand, we can now examine some of the leading interpretations of this behavior—psychological, biological, and sociological—that have been offered to help understand suicide. In each case, part of the work of these interpretations has been to try to elucidate the factors that contribute to suicidal behavior.

EFFORTS TO UNDERSTAND OR EXPLAIN SUICIDAL BEHAVIOR

As suggested, acts of suicide typically produce an intense urgency in survivors to find an explanation—a reason for or a way of understanding this unsettling behavior. Although this pressure to find a reason is understandable, it is not an easy one to respond to with clarity.

For instance, when terrorists flew airplanes into the World Trade Center or when individuals killed themselves in an act of suicide bombing, many wanted to know why anyone would do such things. At first glance, it appeared that these and other self-destructive and murderous acts were the product of distorted fanatical religious beliefs. However, this cannot be an adequate explanation of what such individuals have done. As Ariel Merari (who heads the Political Violence Research Center at Tel Aviv University and who has studied terrorist violence extensively) argues, there are many religious believers (from all religions) who hold distorted and fanatical beliefs but who do not engage in such behaviors (Martin, 2001).

Merari then looked for other reasons for these acts. First, he noticed that such behavior is not limited to religious believers. For example, Japanese pilots during World War II also performed suicidal acts that bore similarities to the 9/11 events. Second, Merari found that the common factor was that these people belonged to cultural groups that encouraged them to do these things. In particular, he claims groups that get members to engage in suicidal or murderous acts share three characteristics: (1) they build up motivation to overcome ambivalence and perform the act; (2) they provide group pressure to stick to the mission; and (3) they get a direct commitment from the individual to perform the act. This last element includes identifying the individual before the group as a "living martyr" and having the individual identify himself (until recently, these acts have nearly always been performed by males) this way, for instance, by writing letters to family members in which he proclaims this identity. Having publicly announced himself as having accepted this role, it is difficult to back out.

Whether or not this explanation is adequate, it demonstrates the difficulty and complexity of providing a single explanation of suicide. Perhaps that is why there are three general types of explanations and some subtypes within them that have been offered to help us understand suicide.

Psychological Explanations of Suicide

Leenaars (1990) identified three major forms that psychological explanations of suicide have taken. The first of these is based on Freud's psychoanalytic theory. Freud argued that suicide is *murder turned around 180 degrees* (Litman, 1967) and suggested that it is related to the loss of a desired person or object. Psychologically, the person at risk comes to identify himself or herself with the lost person. He or she feels anger toward this lost object of affection and wishes to punish (even to kill) the lost person. However, since the individual has identified him or her self with this object of affection, the anger and its correlated wish to punish become directed against the self. Thus, self-destructive behavior is the result.

A second psychological approach sees the problem as *essentially cognitive in nature*. In this view, clinical depression (suicide is highly correlated with depression) is believed to be an important contributing factor, especially when it is associated with hopelessness (see Gotlib & Hammen, 2002; Kessler et al., 2005). The central issue here is that negative evaluations are a pervasive feature of the suicidal person's worldview. The future, the self, the present situation, and the limited number of possible options envisioned by the individual are all viewed as undesirable. Along with these evaluations, impaired thinking is present: such thinking is "often automatic and involuntary ... characterized by a number of possible errors, some so gross as to constitute distortion" (Leenaars, 1990, p. 162). This way of looking at things may help to understand what has come to be called "suicide by cop" (Lindsay & Lester, 2004), that is, behavior in which a police officer is provoked by an individual to cause that person's death, or "suicide by train" (Wilson, 2012).

A third psychological theory claims that *suicidal behavior is learned*. This theory contends that as a child the suicidal individual learned not to express aggression outward but rather to turn it back on the self. Again, depression is noted as an important factor, now the result of negative reinforcement from the environment for a person's actions. Furthermore, this depression (and its associated suicidal or life-threatening behavior) may even be seen as being positively reinforced—that is, rewarded by those around the individual. It might be argued, for example, that Ernest Hemingway's depression, as mentioned earlier, was positively reinforced by the example of his father's own suicide (Slaby, 1992). In any event, this theory views the suicidal individual as poorly socialized and maintains that constructive cultural evaluations of life and death have not been learned.

Jamison (1999)—a psychiatrist who herself had once attempted suicide—argued that psychopathology is "the most common element in suicide" (p. 100). In particular, she focused on the relationships between "mood disorders, schizophrenia, borderline and antisocial personality disorders, alcoholism, and drug abuse." She believes that these mental illnesses play a (and perhaps *the*) significant role in accounting for suicidal acts. She also described genetic and brain chemistry abnormalities (discussed next) and related these to psychopathological factors. In that discussion, she reiterated her view that even when these other factors are taken into account, they are of most significance when associated with mental illness.

A middle-aged man contemplates suicide while dealing with seasonal depression.

Mark Hayes/Shutterstock.com

These psychological theories are not necessarily incompatible. Putting them together helps bring our overall understanding of suicide and suicidal behavior more sharply into focus. Since suicide is a complex behavior, it probably makes most sense to see it as arising (at least often) from a complex basis.

Biological Explanations of Suicide

Some studies have sought to discover whether there are biological explanations for suicidal behavior (e.g., Roy, 1990). These have typically focused on biological explanations relating to either neurochemical or genetic factors. Some theorists believe that there may be a disturbance in the levels of certain neurochemicals found in the brain, such as a reduction in the level of serotonin (a chemical related to aggressive behavior and the regulation of anxiety) in suicidal individuals. However, such studies have not made clear whether such a decrease is associated with depression, suicidal behavior, or the violent outward or inward expression of aggression.

Other studies (e.g., Egeland & Sussex, 1985; Roy, 1990) have suggested that some predispositions to suicidal behavior may be inherited. For example, a study of adopted children in Denmark looked at the biological families of adopted children diagnosed with "affective disorder" who had completed suicide (Wender et al., 1986). More of these persons who showed signs of "affective disorder" and had completed a suicide had relatives who showed the same signs and actions than was the case for a control group. However, it is uncertain from this study exactly what it is that may be inherited. Perhaps the inherited element is an inability to control impulsive behavior, not suicidal behavior in itself.

Thus, it has not yet been demonstrated that biological factors can be clearly related to suicidal behavior. Nevertheless, continued research into biological explanations of suicide may eventually yield helpful information to add to what is already known about other factors contributing to suicidal behavior.

Sociological Explanations of Suicide

The oldest and best-known attempt to offer an explanation of influential factors in suicide is the work of a French sociologist, Emile Durkheim (1951; Selkin, 1983), originally published at the end of the 19th century. Durkheim argued that no psychological condition *by itself* invariably produces suicidal behavior. Instead, he believed that suicide can be understood as an outcome of the relationship of the individual to his or her society, with special emphasis on ways in which individuals are or are not *integrated* and *regulated* in their relationships with society. Durkheim's analysis has been critically examined (e.g., Douglas, 1967; Lester, 2000; Maris, 1969), but his book remains a classic in the literature on suicide. In it, he identified three primary sorts of relationships between individuals and society as conducive to suicidal behavior, and he made brief reference to the possibility of a fourth basic type of suicide.

Egoistic Suicide   The first of these relationships may result in what Durkheim called **egoistic suicide**, or suicide involving more or less isolated individuals. The risk of suicide is diminished in the presence of a social group that provides some integration for the individual, especially in terms of meaning for his or her life. When such integration is absent, loses its force, or is somehow removed (especially abruptly), suicide becomes a more likely possibility.

Durkheim argued for this thesis in the case of three sorts of "societies"—religious society, domestic society, and political society. A *religious society* may provide integration (meaning) for its members in many ways—for example, by means of a unified, strong creed. A *domestic society* (e.g., marriage) also seems to be a factor that tends to reduce suicidal behavior by providing individuals with shared "sentiments and memories," thereby locating them in a kind of geography of meaning. In addition, a *political society* can be another vehicle that assists individuals in achieving social integration. When any of these societies—religious, domestic, or political—does not effectively help individuals to find meaning for their lives or when the society disintegrates or loses its influence, individuals may be thrown back on their own resources, may find them inadequate for their needs, and may become more at risk for suicidal or life-threatening behavior.

In short, Durkheim's thesis here is that whenever an individual experiences himself or herself in a situation wherein his or her society fails to assist that individual in finding his or her place in the world, suicidal behavior can result. Thus, egoistic suicide depends on an *under*involvement or *under*integration, a kind of disintegration and isolation of an individual from his or her society.

Altruistic Suicide   The second form of social relationship that is or may be related to suicide arises from an *over*involvement or *over*integration of the individual into his or her society. In this situation, the ties that produce the integration between the individual and the social group are so strong that they may result in **altruistic suicide** or suicide undertaken on behalf of the group. Personal identity may give way to identification with the welfare of the group, and the individual may find the meaning of his or her life (completely) outside of self. For example, in some strongly integrated societies, there are contexts in which suicide may be seen as a duty. In other words, the surrender of the individual's life may be demanded on behalf of what is perceived to be the welfare of the society.

Durkheim listed several examples found in various historical cultures that involve relationships of strong integration or involvement and that lead to suicidal behavior: persons who are aged or ill (the Eskimo); women whose husbands have died (the practice of *suttee* in India before the British came); servants of social chiefs who have died (many ancient societies). One might think also of persons who have failed in their civic or religious duties so as to bring shame on themselves, their families, or their societies—for example, the samurai warrior in Japanese society who commits ritual *seppuku*. Also, involvement in a religious cult led some Americans to altruistic suicide at the People's Temple in Georgetown in British Guyana (1978) and at the Heaven's Gate complex in California (1997), and there may be religious explanations that account in part for the events of 9/11 and similar acts since then.

Anomic Suicide   Durkheim described a third form of suicide, **anomic suicide**, not in terms of integration of the individual into society but rather in terms of how the society *regulates* its members. All human beings need to regulate their desires (for material goods, for sexual activity, etc.). To the extent that a society assists individuals in this regulation, it helps keep such desires under control. When a society is unable or unwilling to help its members in the regulation of their desires—for example, because the society is undergoing rapid change and its rules are in a state of flux—a condition of *anomie* is the result. (The term *anomie* comes from the Greek *anomia* = *a* [without] + *nomoi* [laws or norms] and means "lawlessness" or "normlessness.")

Anomie can be conducive to suicide, especially when it thrusts an individual suddenly into a situation perceived to be chaotic and intolerable. In contemporary American society, examples of this sort of suicide might involve adolescents who have been unexpectedly rejected by a peer group, some farmers forced into bankruptcy and loss of both their livelihood and their way of life as a result of economic and social forces outside their control, or middle-aged employees who have developed specialized work skills and have devoted themselves for years to their employer only to be suddenly thrown out of their jobs and are economically dislocated. For such individuals, *under*regulation or a sudden withdrawal of control may be intolerable because of the absence of (familiar) principles to guide them in living.

Fatalistic Suicide   Durkheim only mentions a fourth type of suicide, called fatalistic suicide, in a footnote in his book, where it is described as the opposite of anomic suicide. **Fatalistic suicide** derives from *excessive regulation* of individuals by society—for example, when one becomes a prisoner or a slave. These are the circumstances of "persons with futures pitilessly blocked and passions violently choked by oppressive discipline" (1951, p. 276). Durkheim did not think that this type of suicide was very common in his own society, but it may be useful as an illustration of social forces that lead an individual to seek to escape from an *overcontrolling* social context.

SUICIDE: AN ACT WITH MANY DETERMINANTS AND LEVELS OF MEANING

In a way similar to Durkheim's claim that suicidal behavior cannot be understood solely by studying the psychology of those who engage in such behavior, Menninger (1938, p. 23) wrote, "Suicide is a very complex act, and not a simple, incidental, isolated act of impulsion, either logical or inexplicable." Both of these theorists saw a completed suicide as an outcome of *many* causes, not only one. Shneidman (1980/1995), Douglas (1967), and others (such as Breed, 1972) also have suggested that a variety of elements may enter into suicidal behavior.

One common way to reflect the complexity of suicidal behavior is to think of it as involving three elements: **haplessness** (being ill fated or unlucky), **helplessness**, and **hopelessness**. Shneidman (1980/1995) took this understanding forward to a still more complex and precise account by thinking of the factors that lead to suicide in terms of three main components and a triggering process: (1) **inimicality**, or an unsettled life pattern in which one acts against one's own best interests; (2) **perturbation**, or an increased psychological disturbance in the person's life; (3) **constriction**, which appears in **tunnel vision** and **either/or thinking** and which represents a narrowing of the range of perceptions, opinions, and options that occur to the person's mind; and (4) the idea of **cessation**, of resolving the unbearable pain of disturbance and isolation by simply ending it or being out of it. Shneidman (1996) also formulated ten commonalities in suicidal behavior that can help to expand our understanding of this behavior (see Table 17.2).

These characterizations of suicide can lead to an important conclusion in the search for an understanding of suicidal behavior. As we have noted, there is often a natural impulse among students of suicidal behavior and bereaved family members to look for *the* cause of a suicide. This need can be illustrated in the efforts of many people to find a suicide note that they hope might explain what has happened. In fact, however, there usually is no such single cause. Suicide is most often an act with many determinants and levels of meaning. It may arise from a context of many sorts of causes, among which biological, psychological, and social factors are surely prominent (Lester, 1992, 2003; Maris, 1981, 1988; Maris, Berman, Maltsberger, & Yufit, 1992). In fact, one expert on suicide notes wrote that "in order to commit suicide, one cannot write a meaningful suicide note; conversely, if one could write a meaningful note, one would not have to commit suicide" (Shneidman, 1980/1995, p. 58).

Table 17.2   Ten Commonalities of Suicide

The common purpose of suicide is to seek a solution
The common goal of suicide is cessation of consciousness
The common stimulus of suicide is unbearable psychological pain
The common stressor in suicide is frustrated psychological needs
The common emotion in suicide is hopelessness-helplessness
The common cognitive state in suicide is ambivalence
The common perceptual state in suicide is constriction
The common action in suicide is escape
The common interpersonal act in suicide is communication of intention
The common pattern in suicide is consistency of lifelong styles

Source: Shneidman, 1996, p. 131.

THE IMPACT OF SUICIDE

In addition to the individual who dies or who puts his or her life in jeopardy, a suicidal act always affects other people. Reports in the literature from the 1970s and ongoing communications from counselors, therapists, and members of suicide support or bereavement self-help groups have indicated that *survivors of the person who has died from suicide* almost always have a difficult time dealing with that death (e.g., Cain, 1972; Wallace, 1973). The common theme here is the claim that the aftereffects of suicide intensify experiences of anger, sadness, guilt, physical complaints, and other dimensions of grief found in all loss and bereavement. Thus, Lindemann and Greer (1972, p. 67) wrote: "The survivors of a suicide are likely to get 'stuck' in their grieving and to go on for years in a state of cold isolation, unable to feel close to others and carrying always with them the feeling that they are set apart or under the threat of doom."

Other reports have questioned the adequacy of this account of bereavement following a suicide (e.g., Barrett & Scott, 1990; Clark & Goldney, 2002; Dunne, McIntosh, & Dunne-Maxim, 1987; Ellenbogen & Gratton, 2001; Jordan, 2001; Nelson & Frantz, 1996; Silverman, Range, & Overholser, 1994). In particular, it has been noted that most of the published studies on this subject have had significant methodological weaknesses (McIntosh, 1987). The size of the study groups has been small. Persons who participate in these studies have often come from clinical sources, from support groups, and from college students (and each of these groups may include people who are atypical in one way or another). For obvious reasons, participants in most studies have been volunteers. Thus, large numbers of survivors who are not members of these types of group or who have refused to participate (and who may in fact make up the largest group of survivors) have not been studied (Van Dongen, 1990). Also, there have been few comparison studies in which survivors of someone who completed suicide are compared to other bereaved persons (Hauser, 1987). Those studies that have made some comparison between different groups of survivors have yielded inconclusive results (Demi & Miles, 1988; McIntosh, 1987).

Most researchers (such as Barrett & Scott, 1990; Calhoun, Abernathy, & Selby, 1986; Demi & Miles, 1988; Hauser, 1987) themselves warn against making generalizations on the basis of their work. Still, actual empirical study is important to correct impressions that arise from "clinical observation, intellectual conjecture, and theoretical speculation" (Barrett & Scott, 1990, p. 2). Only such study can prevent us from making false generalizations or from stereotyping suicide survivors and thus increasing the difficulty of their mourning by placing expectations on them that they may or may not meet.

For these reasons, what can be said about the nature of the mourning process for **survivors of suicide**, and how it differs from that process for other survivors, is still somewhat tentative. Perhaps one of the clearest statements on this subject comes from Barrett and Scott (1990) who pointed out that suicide survivors at least have *more types of issues* to deal with than do other survivors. The survivors of someone's suicide must cope with: (1) the tasks anyone has *after the death of someone to whom one has been close*; (2) tasks related to a death that *arises from some cause other than a natural one* and is often therefore *perceived to have been a death that was avoidable*; (3) tasks associated with *a sudden death*; and finally (4) tasks due to *the suicidal nature of the death*, such as the repudiation of life-affirming values and abandonment issues that it seems to imply.

Some aspects of these tasks are present in the mourning process of suicide survivors more often than in the mourning of persons bereaved as a result of other types of death. Blame (of others or of oneself) and guilt (the response to a sense of being at fault), a sense of being rejected by the deceased, and, perhaps especially significant, a search for an explanation for why the person acted to end his or her life often play heightened roles in the lives of these mourners (Bailley, Kral, & Dunham, 1999; Lukas & Seiden, 2007; Pitman, Osborn, King, & Erlangsen, 2014; Reed & Greenwald, 1991; Silverman et al., 1994; Van Dongen, 1990, 1991).

Although some have claimed that suicide survivors are themselves subject to self-destructive and suicidal thoughts and actions, other studies have reported that these survivors found a strong deterrent to such actions in realizing how devastating another suicide in the family would be for fellow survivors (Dunn & Morrish-Vidners, 1988; Van Dongen, 1990).

Not all suicide survivors will have to deal with these tasks to the same extent. Some evidence indicates that it is the degree of emotional attachment to the deceased that matters most here (as with all mourning), as much as or even more than the formal nature (parent, sibling, friend) of the relationship or the type of death. Thus, Cerel, Maple, Aldrich, and van de Venne (2013, p. 413) reported that "perceived psychological closeness to the deceased showed a robust association with self-identified survivor status." A suicide that has been expected may also impact survivors differentially (Wojtkowiak, Wild, & Egger, 2012). Not surprisingly, however, children may face special problems in understanding and making sense of a parent's suicide (Requarth, 2006; see also Personal Insights 17.1).

PERSONAL INSIGHTS 17.1

Life with Dad, a True Story by Reyna Paez, Age 9

Seven years ago, there was a two-year-old girl. Her father had committed suicide. She had asked where he was a lot but her Mom lied and said, "He died in a car accident." Her Mom had cried a lot since that had happened....

When it was her birthday, they were in a car driving to her party. The little girl's Grandparents thought she was talking to herself. Her Grandma asked, "Who are you talking to?" The girl said, "My Daddy." They were confused. When they got to the party, they told her Mom what had happened. Her Mom thought that was weird. She asked her daughter if she was really talking to her Dad. The girl said straight up, "Yup, I was talking to him the whole time. He was sitting right next to me."

When she was four, she headed off to preschool. Every day she would bring a blanket that was given to her by her Dad. She called the blanket "KyKy," and she also would squeeze it tight all the time at school. At school they had nap time, and the girl didn't like nap time so she just thought about her Dad and cuddled with her blanket.

The next year her Mom was with another guy. The girl cried because she didn't know him. But after awhile she got to know him and later began to call him Dad.

(continues)

When she was six, her Mom and new Dad said, "You are going to have a baby sister!" The girl was so happy. Then one day her Mom had the baby. After the baby was born, the girl got to hold her. The girl kissed her new baby sister. Every night the girl would tell her about her Dad when nobody was there.

Then in the third grade, the girl told her class that her Dad had died. One day a classmate teased the girl about not having a Dad. The girl didn't say anything, and she just walked away. The boy said, "Sorry," but she said, "There is no way I can forgive you."

After school one day, when she was eight, the girl was told how her Dad died. The girl was a bit excited to hear how but she was mostly scared to know because her family was keeping it a secret for six years! "Well," her Mom said, "I'm going to tell you how your Dad died. He died by taking his own life. He grabbed an object and killed himself." The girl burst into tears.

The next day her Mother called the school counselor to talk with the girl. The counselor pulled her out of class and walked with her to her counseling room. The counselor gave her a bear just in case. They talked about what had happened and the girl felt much better. After that talk, the girl wasn't sad to talk about her Daddy ever again.

Although there are few longitudinal studies of survivors of another's suicide, one study of elderly survivors indicated that whereas many mourners of other sorts of death begin to experience a change in their mourning around six months, these survivors take longer to reach that first change. Even after two-and-a-half years, suicide survivors rated their mental health differently than did the survivors of natural deaths or other types of sudden death (Farberow, Gallagher-Thompson, Gilewski, & Thompson, 1992).

Barlow and Coleman (2003) studied the role of the family in the mourning process of suicide survivors. They found that families that were able to form a "healing alliance" were better able to cope with the aftereffects of a suicide, while the inability to form such an alliance made the grief process more difficult. Healing alliances included watching the responses of other family members to the suicide, normalizing the grief, easing the guilt, and respecting differences by allowing other family members to grieve in their own ways. Such watchful waiting was motivated by both a fear of another suicide and the emotional need to take care of each other.

This pattern was also reflected in how family members communicated with each other about the suicide. Some talked openly among themselves about it whereas others guarded what they said around each other. Some families simply did not talk about the suicide among themselves, often to protect emotionally vulnerable family members. However, Barlow and Coleman (2003) found that failing to communicate with each other, along with interactions when a family member assigned guilt or blame for the suicide to another member of the family, resulted in a breakdown or even severing of familial relationships. This complicated mourning processes. Thus, books for children and adolescents can help young readers and adults to become more sensitive to the potential implications of suicide (see Focus On 17.1).

FOCUS ON 17.1

Eight Books for Children and Adolescents about Suicide

For children, *Are You Like Me?: Helping Children Cope with Suicide* and *Someone I Love Died by Suicide: A Story for Child Survivors and Those Who Care for Them* both seek to explain death and suicide, validate reactions after a loved one dies from suicide, offer security, promote discussion with trusted adults, and guide conversations, while *After a Suicide: A Workbook for Grieving Kids* encourages children to write, draw, or decorate its pages as they learn about topics like: why people die this way; their reactions and common questions; how to talk about suicide; and ways to feel better.

Another book for children, *Bart Speaks Out: Breaking the Silence on Suicide*, is an interactive storybook in which a dog tells about his grief and other events following the death of his owner, Charlie. Bart then invites readers to write about or draw pictures of similar events in their lives before he turns to suicide and Charlie's depression. Suicide is described as "when someone chooses to make their body stop working" (p. v), and the book says it is a mistake because "there is always another way" (p. v).

For adolescents, *Living When a Young Friend Commits Suicide—Or Even Starts Talking about It* guides adolescents through typical reactions and questions after a friend's suicide. There are ideas for how to cope and how to help suicidal people, popular misconceptions about suicide, and getting on with one's life. *A Teenager's Book about Suicide: Helping Break the Silence and Preventing Death* offers brief text passages in boxes and spaces for readers to write or draw to open up discussion of suicide. Writings by teens describe thinking about suicide or being affected by someone else's suicide. Comments dispel myths, identify danger signals and warning signs, and suggest what a teen might do if he or she suspects a friend or family member is thinking about suicide. Finally, *Tunnel Vision* and *Tears of a Tiger* each describe a teen's suicide, as well as the hurt, sadness, bewilderment, and guilt among those left behind. They ask what they might have done to prevent these deaths. There were clues to what was going on, but they only become fully evident in hindsight and easy answers are not available. One mother asks, "Why did Anthony believe that death was the only kind of peace he could find?"

Another issue affecting the mourning of survivors of another's suicide is the interaction of survivors with persons outside of the family. Some studies indicate that these survivors find less helpful support than do other bereaved persons (Dunn & Morrish-Vidners, 1988). Rudestam (1987) noted that in one study, 84% of funeral directors who were interviewed said that people reacted differently to suicide survivors. Such studies imply that suicide survivors may be an example of persons experiencing disenfranchised grief (see Chapter 10).

Part of the difficulty for suicide survivors concerns the social rules governing how to behave in this situation. Not only are there fewer social rules to guide people but also the rules that do exist seem to constrain behavior more than those rules governing other mourning situations (Calhoun et al., 1986; Van Dongen, 1990). Another complicating factor is that the survivors themselves often seem to withdraw from others and do not reach out for or readily accept other people's support. Thus, survivors may experience the stigmatization associated with suicide intrapsychically as much as socially (Allen et al., 1994; Rudestam, 1987).

As we have noted, however, mourning is a process in which most people need a support system. If one is to cope adequately with mourning a suicide, then communication, or at least the nonjudgmental presence of others, can be helpful (Archibald, 2012; Bolton, 1995; Chance, 1994; Jordan & Baugher, 2016; Jordan & McIntosh, 2010; Jordan & McMenamy, 2004). For all survivors of suicide, the American Association of Suicidology offers a survivor's page on its website that makes available a great deal of information and resources, including *A Handbook for Survivors of Suicide* (Jackson, 2003). See also the website for Survivors of Suicide and the document, *Responding to Grief, Trauma, and Distress After a Suicide: National Guidelines*, published by the Survivors of Suicide Loss Task Force of the National Action Alliance for Suicide Prevention (2015).

Another issue of concern around suicide involves what have been called *cluster* or *copycat* suicides. There is no agreement about how to define such suicides (Davies, 1993; Gould, Wallenstein, Kleinman, O'Carroll, & Mercy, 1990). To the extent that a set of suicides can be seen as being formed by more than chance, such sets occur more frequently among 15- to 19- and 20- to 24-year-olds and perhaps among 45- to 64-year-olds (Gould et al., 1990). However, careful study of such events is still in development. Although it may be the case that some adolescents are influenced by the experience of an earlier suicide, either directly (by actually knowing someone who has committed suicide) or indirectly (by knowing of a suicide from the media or from other people's accounts), the adolescents who have committed suicide following earlier suicides and who have been carefully studied share other attributes that are at least as likely to account for their behavior as this contact (Davidson, Rosenberg, Mercy, & Franklin, 1989). Those attributes include substance abuse, mental illness, losing a girlfriend or boyfriend, witnessing or using violence themselves, damaging themselves physically, being more easily offended, attending more schools, moving more frequently, and having more than two adults who served as parents.

SUICIDE INTERVENTION

In this section we focus on **suicide prevention**. However, because one cannot really prevent very determined acts of suicide, it is better to speak here of **suicide intervention** *aimed at reducing the likelihood of a completed suicide* (Jobes, 2006; Shneidman, 1971). Many programs have been developed throughout the United States and in other countries to work toward this goal, often using the techniques of *crisis intervention* (consult local crisis intervention programs in your area or contact the American Association of Suicidology's National Suicide Prevention Lifeline, which is staffed 24 hours per day, seven days per week by trained counselors, at 1-800-273-TALK [8255] or www.suicidepreventionlifeline.org). This program ministers to the needs of persons who feel themselves to be in crisis or who sense an inclination toward suicide. By contrast, the Canadian Association for Suicide Prevention

(1-519-884-1470, ext. 2277) is not a crisis center, but does provide information and resources designed to reduce the suicide rate and minimize the harmful consequences of suicidal behavior, and it offers links to crisis centers. Over decades of work, much has been learned about how persons contemplating suicide behave. In turn, much has been learned about how others can assist such people—that is, about how to intervene constructively in cases of suicidal or life-threatening behavior (see, for example, ASIST: Applied Suicide Intervention Skills Training: https://www.livingworks.net/programs/asist/; tel. 1-888-733-5484).

First, mistaken impressions about suicidal behavior must be confronted (see Table 17.3). For instance, many people believe that suicidal persons do not talk about their intentions, that suicide is the result of a sudden impulse, and that mentioning suicide to someone who is emotionally upset may make a suggestion to that person that he or she had not previously entertained. It has long been recognized that these are all erroneous beliefs (Maris, 1981).

Table 17.3 Facts and Fables about Suicide

These Statements Are *Not* True	These Statements *Are* True
Fable: People who talk about suicide don't commit suicide.	**Fact:** Of any ten persons who kill themselves, eight have given definite warnings of their suicidal intentions. Suicide threats and attempts *must* be taken seriously.
Fable: Suicide happens without warning.	**Fact:** Studies reveal that the suicidal person gives many clues and warnings regarding his suicidal intentions. Alertness to these cries for help may prevent suicidal behavior.
Fable: Suicidal people are fully intent on dying.	**Fact:** Most suicidal people are undecided about living or dying, and they "gamble with death," leaving it to others to save them. Almost no one commits suicide without letting others know how he is feeling. Often this "cry for help" is given in "code." These distress signals can be used to save lives.
Fable: Once a person is suicidal, he is suicidal forever.	**Fact:** Happily, individuals who wish to kill themselves are "suicidal" only for a limited period of time. If they are saved from self-destruction, they can go on to lead useful lives.
Fable: Improvement following a suicidal crisis means that the suicidal risk is over.	**Fact:** Most suicides occur within about three months following the beginning of "improvement," when the individual has the energy to put his morbid thoughts and feelings into effect. Relatives and physicians should be especially vigilant during this period.

(continues)

Table 17.3 **Facts and Fables about Suicide** *(continued)*

These Statements Are *Not* True	These Statements *Are* True
Fable:	**Fact:**
Suicide strikes more often among the rich—or, conversely, it occurs more frequently among the poor.	Suicide is neither the rich man's disease nor the poor man's curse. Suicide is very "democratic" and is represented proportionately among all levels of society.
Fable:	**Fact:**
Suicide is inherited or "runs in a family."	Suicide does not run in families. It is an individual matter and can be prevented.
Fable:	**Fact:**
All suicidal individuals are mentally ill, and suicide is always the act of a psychotic person.	Studies of hundreds of genuine suicide notes indicate that although the suicidal person is extremely unhappy, he is not necessarily mentally ill. His overpowering unhappiness may result from a temporary emotional upset, a long and painful illness, or a complete loss of hope. It is circular reasoning to say that "suicide is an insane act," and therefore all suicidal people are psychotic.

Source: From Shneidman and Farberow (1961), for the U.S. Government Printing Office, PHS Publication No. 852.

People who are thinking about killing themselves most often *do* talk about this. One researcher claimed that 80% of persons who are inclined toward suicide communicate their plans to family members, friends, authority figures (such as physicians or clergy), or telephone intervention programs (Hewett, 1980). Thus, it has been said that most suicidal people desperately want to live or are at least ambivalent about choosing between life and death; they are simply unable to see alternatives to their problems.

Suicide rarely occurs without warning. It is seldom an action that erupts from nowhere. It is often thought-out well in advance and carefully planned. Frequently, suicidal persons give many clues about their intentions (see Focus On 17.2, which v the acronym "IS PATH WARM"). These clues may or may not be verbal. They might include giving away beloved objects, changing eating or sleeping habits, or even displaying a sense of calmness after a period of agitation (calmness because a *decision* has finally been made about what to do).

Asking someone if he or she is thinking about attempting suicide is *not* planting an idea that would otherwise not have occurred to the person. Individuals who are depressed or who are severely agitated most likely have already thought about killing themselves. Many suicidologists believe that almost all human beings think about the possibility of suicide at one time or another. Thus, suicide is not an infrequently encountered idea. If the person does not volunteer information about suicidal thoughts or plans, the simplest way to discover this is to ask.

Once suicidal intentions are noticed, intervention can take many forms (Pompili & Tatarelli, 2010; Rudd, Joiner, & Rajab, 2001; Westefeld et al., 2006; Worchel & Gearing, 2010; Yufit & Lester, 2005). Some practical ways to help suicidal people are summarized in Focus On 17.3. First, one should note that many suicidal

FOCUS ON 17.2

Warning Signs of Suicide

A person at risk for suicidal behavior most often will exhibit warning signs.

I	Ideation	Expressed or communicated ideation
		■ Threatening to hurt or kill him/herself, or talking of wanting to hurt or kill him/herself; and/or
		■ Looking for ways to kill him/herself by seeking access to firearms, available pills, or other means; and/or
		■ Talking or writing about death, dying, or suicide, when these actions are out of the ordinary
S	Substance abuse	Increased substance (alcohol or drug) use
P	Purposelessness	No reason for living; no sense of purpose in life
A	Anxiety	Anxiety, agitation, unable to sleep or sleeping all the time
T	Trapped	Feeling trapped (like there's no way out)
H	Hopelessness	Hopelessness
W	Withdrawal	Withdrawal from friends, family, and society
A	Anger	Rage, uncontrolled anger, seeking revenge
R	Recklessness	Acting reckless or engaging in risk activities, seemingly without thinking
M	Mood Change	Dramatic mood changes

Source: Based on American Association of Suicidology

intentions are not long lasting. A primary goal may be to help the person work through a relatively short-term crisis period. That is a basic strategy employed by all crisis intervention programs.

To help suicidal persons it is critical to listen actively to them. Paying attention to and being present for someone who is suffering is an essential step toward helping. Others really must hear the feelings being expressed to try to understand what this person needs. Part of the listening process is to hear suicidal remarks for what they are and to recognize the several levels or dimensions that each remark may contain. Crisis intervention workers insist that *every* suicidal remark must be taken seriously.

Once such a remark is heard, the actual intentions and plans should be evaluated. The more the person has thought about suicide and the more he or she has worked out actual plans for suicide, the more seriously must the remarks be taken. A remark like "Sometimes I just feel like killing myself" with no follow-up is less serious than remarks that indicate someone's having thought out when and how he or she intends

FOCUS ON 17.3

Some Practical Ways to Help Suicidal Persons

- Take the person seriously; be available to get involved and to listen.
- Allow the person to express his or her feelings and try to accept the person for what he or she is; be empathetic, calm, and nonjudgmental.
- Don't be afraid to speak openly about suicide; ask questions like "Have you ever thought about hurting or killing yourself?" You can also offer concrete examples of what leads you to believe the person is close to suicide.
- Express your concern for the person by listening attentively, maintaining eye contact, moving closer to the person, and touching the person or holding his or her hand, if that seems appropriate.
- Don't debate with the person whether suicide is right or wrong or whether the person's feelings are good or bad; an argumentative or lecturing posture will distance you from the person.
- Never challenge a potentially suicidal person to complete the act; don't dare him or her to do it.
- Find out if the person has a specific plan to carry out a suicidal action or has taken concrete steps to prepare to do so (such as gaining access to the means that might be used to end his or her life).
- Point out constructive alternatives that are available, but do not offer glib reassurance; stress that suicide is most often a permanent solution for temporary problems.
- Take action by removing the means (such as firearms or stockpiled pills) that the person might use to end his or her life.
- Remind the person that although he or she is ultimately responsible for his or her actions, help is available, people do care, and you will try to make connections with helping resources.
- Get help from people or agencies that are knowledgeable about intervening in crises and preventing suicide.
- Until you can get such help, try to stay with the person and not leave him or her alone; if you must leave, ask the person to make a contract with you or promise not to take any further steps to end his or her life until you can get help or can return to address the situation further.
- Do not allow yourself to promise confidentiality or to be sworn to unconditional secrecy; such commitments should be contingent on a contract that the person not act before certain conditions that you set (such as seeking professional help) are met.

Source: Based on guidelines from the American Association of Suicidology and the Depression and Bipolar Support Alliance.

to accomplish the act. The situation becomes even more serious when actual steps have been taken to implement the plan.

In general, changes in affect are significant. If someone has been depressed but now seems suddenly much lighter in emotional tone, this is not necessarily a time for reduced concern (Farberow, 1983). Suicidal actions actually increase when people are coming out of depression. In such situations, they may finally have the requisite energy to act. Similarly, a change toward agitation can signal a crisis.

In actively listening, attention must be paid to what the person says. This usually means that one should not engage in evaluating in a judgmental way (from one's own point of view) what the person believes or feels. What looks like a problem from the suicidal person's point of view *is* a problem for that person. Telling such individuals that their problems are insignificant is not likely to be of much help. More likely, it sounds as though we are not really hearing them or are unwilling to appreciate the magnitude of the problems they believe themselves to be facing. Not surprisingly, they may then turn away from us.

Many suicidal persons experience **tunnel vision**, a process in which the individual perceives only a very narrow range of possible solutions for resolving the crisis, among which suicide may seem to be the only available solution. One way to help is to point out other, constructive options for resolving the crisis, such as drawing on inner resources not previously recognized or turning to external resources available in the community that might help with the crisis (whether they might be emotional, physical, financial, spiritual, or other types).

Finally, specific action is necessary. Getting some particular agreement can be helpful, such as to the following questions: Will you agree *not* to do anything until I get there?; Will you go with me to talk to a counselor?; Will you promise not to harm yourself until after you next see your therapist? It is also usually important not to let the person be alone or to have access to the means intended to be used to commit suicide. In many cases, the involvement of a trained professional will be essential (Leenaars, Maltsberger, & Neimeyer, 1994). Contact 1-800-273-TALK (8255) or www.nationalsuicideprevention.org for assistance or a referral from the National Suicide Prevention Lifeline.

Note that those who work in this field of suicide or crisis intervention have often pointed out that in the end no one can really take responsibility for someone else's life. If a person is seriously determined to end his or her life, ordinarily someone else cannot prevent that event—short of essentially "jailing" the person. Although guilt is a frequently encountered response to suicide, suicide is, finally, an action over which others have little control. It is an option for human beings.

Most of the suggestions in this section concern what individuals can do to minimize the likelihood of suicidal behavior, although they also note the value of societal efforts as illustrated in crisis intervention programs. Because over half of all suicides in the United States involve firearms, it may also be useful to attend to the results of a study by Anestis and Anestis (2015) that examined the impact of four handgun laws (waiting periods, universal background checks, gun locks, and open carrying regulations) on suicide rates and concluded that

> each law was associated with significantly lower firearm suicide rates and the proportion of suicides resulting from firearms. ... indicating that the reduced overall suicide rate was attributable to fewer suicide attempts, fewer handguns in the home, suicide attempts

using less lethal means, or a combination of these factors. States that implemented any of these laws saw a decreased suicide rate in subsequent years, whereas the only state that repealed 1 of these laws saw an increased suicide rate.

We should add that several writers (e.g., Lester, 2006a, 2006b; Werth, 1996, 1999b) have argued that at least in some cases suicide can be a rational and morally acceptable action for some people, while others have disagreed (e.g., Feldman, 2006; Leenaars, 2006; see also Issues for Critical Reflection #15). For example, the philosopher, Seneca (1932, vol. 1, p. 239), offered the following views on this subject:

> But life, as you know, needn't always be held fast. It isn't in living, but in living well, that the good consists. Hence the philosopher-adept [i.e., the wise person] lives as long as he ought, and not as long as he can....The quality of life, not its length, is always his thought. If he encounters a throng of troubles fatal to peace of mind, he sets himself free.... It matters not a whit to him whether he procures his end or accepts it, whether it comes slowly or quickly.... To die soon or die late matters nothing: to die badly or die well is the important point. But to die well is to escape the risk of living badly.

ISSUES FOR CRITICAL REFLECTION
#15 Can Suicide Ever Be a Morally Appropriate Act?

One issue that has been discussed since ancient times is whether suicide can ever be a morally appropriate act. In part, the answer to this question hinges on whether one believes that suicide can ever be a "rational" act. As we have seen, depression, ambivalence, and other powerful emotions play central roles in much suicidal behavior. This leads some to argue that suicide is always or almost always an "irrational" act (Jamison, 1999). If this is actually the case, it would influence how we are to view the moral status of suicide.

However, others have argued that there may be lucid, rational, even morally appropriate motives for suicide (Lester, 2003; Werth, 1996, 1999b). Rollin (1985) agreed with this view, at least under some circumstances. She wrote, "The real question is, does a person have a right to depart from life when he or she is nearing the end and has nothing but horror ahead?" (Humphry, 2002, p. 14). Rollin views suicide as a legitimate form of "self-deliverance." This position is based on an assertion that the legitimate scope of an individual's autonomy should include a "right to die" or a right to end one's life (Hillyard & Dombrink, 2001; Humphry & Clement, 1998; Meisel & Cerminara, 2004;

Nitschke & Stewart, 2007; Wanzer & Glenmullen, 2007). Because it is not illegal to commit suicide in any jurisdiction in the United States, many people in our society believe suicide lies legitimately within the range of the individual's autonomy.

Other societies think of suicide only as appropriate under some types of conditions. Social, political, and moral contexts may be held to demand the suicide of an individual for the sake of the good of the society or the family (see the discussion of altruistic suicide in this chapter). However, most arguments supporting the moral appropriateness of suicide require at least that the person engaged in such an action be rational when the action is undertaken.

Arguments opposed to the morality of suicide assume that anyone engaged in such an action is not rational or that there are other overriding moral values that come into play. For instance, as discussed elsewhere in this chapter, almost all religions oppose taking one's own life. This may be because they believe that the individual's life does not belong to him or her alone (it belongs ultimately to God) or because a sacred writing forbids it.

As a result, Seneca and other writers argue that it is not universally appropriate to intervene to prevent a suicide and that it might equally be acceptable to assist a person who seeks to carry out a **rational suicide**. (We discuss various forms of aided death in Chapter 18.)

RELIGIOUS VIEWS OF THE MORAL APPROPRIATENESS OF SUICIDE

Although it is impossible to describe in any simple way a given religious tradition's view on suicide, the following statements offer a sampling of religious positions.

Judaism

"For Judaism, human life is 'created in the image of God'....The sanctity of human life prescribes that, in any situation short of self-defense or martyrdom, human life be treated as an end in itself....Even individual autonomy is secondary to the sanctity of human life and therefore, a patient is not permitted to end his or her life" (Feldman & Rosner, 1984, p. 106). Notice the exceptions given in this quotation.

Christianity

The *Declaration on Euthanasia* from the Roman Catholic tradition includes the following statement: "Intentionally causing one's own death, or suicide, is ... equally as wrong as murder; such an action on the part of a person is to be considered as a rejection of God's sovereignty and loving plan. Furthermore, suicide is also often a refusal of love for self, the denial of the natural instinct to live, a flight from the duties of justice and charity owed to one's neighbor, to various communities, or to the whole of society" (Sacred Congregation for the Doctrine of the Faith, 1982, p. 512). This last point is reinforced by Smith (1986, p. 64), arguing from the Anglican tradition: "In any context suicide is a social act ... because selfhood is so social, suicide cannot be simply a matter of private right.... As a child of God the Christian must relate all choices to that relationship." He also argues (in the context of suicide because of medical circumstances, but this argument might be extended to all suicidal contexts), "the great difficulty with supposed altruistic suicide, on medical grounds, is that it ignores the guilt felt by others and the desertion of them that is involved."

Islam

The *Qur'an* contains the following relevant passages: "Do not with your own hands cast yourselves into destruction" (2, 195) and "Do not destroy yourselves ... he that does that through wickedness and injustice shall be burned in fire" (4, 29). However, Rahman (1987, p. 126) reports, "The only way a Muslim can and is expected to freely give and take life is 'in the path of Allah,' as a martyr in jihad or holy war. According to a Hadith a person who dies defending self, family, and property (by extension also the country) against aggression is also a martyr."

Hinduism

"Hinduism condemns suicide as evil when it is a direct and deliberate act with the intention voluntarily to kill oneself for self-regarding motives. Subjectively, the evil resides in the act as the product of ignorance and passion; objectively, the evil encompasses the karmic consequences of the act which impede the progress of liberation." This view is modified, however, under some circumstances: "Hinduism permits selective recourse to suicide when it is religiously motivated.... The whole of Hindu discipline is an exercise in progressive renunciation, and continuous with that, *suicide is the supreme act of renunciation*. For the sage, it is the death of death" (Crawford, 1995, pp. 68, 71).

Buddhism

"The standard Buddhist attitude towards suicide is that it is a futile, misguided act motivated by the desire for annihilation ... the affirmation of nirvana cannot be a choice against life." Again, however, under some circumstances, suicide might be acceptable to Buddhists: "Bodhisattvas who sacrifice themselves are not choosing against life but displaying a readiness to lay down their lives in the service of their fellow man. They do not seek death for its own sake, but accept that death may come, so to speak, in the course of their duty" (Keown, 1995, pp. 58, 59).

Summary

In this chapter, we explored some of the many dimensions and implications of suicide and life-threatening behavior. We sought to clarify the concept of suicide and to emphasize the many elements that may enter into a completed suicide. We also described some common patterns in suicidal behavior, and we examined psychological, biological, and sociological efforts to understand or explain such behavior. We gave special attention to the impact on someone who survives the suicide of another person. In addition, we identified warning signs for suicide, along with interventions that individuals and society might initiate to minimize suicidal behavior. Finally, we reported statements from five major religious traditions as to whether suicide could ever be considered a morally appropriate action.

Glossary

Altruistic suicide: suicide undertaken on behalf of one's social group; a sociological category in which suicide arises from an overinvolvement or overintegration of an individual into his or her society

Anomic suicide: suicide undertaken when society is unable or unwilling to help its members in regulating their desires; a sociological category in which suicide arises from social underregulation or sudden withdrawal of social control

Cessation: the idea of resolving the unbearable pain of disturbance and isolation by simply ending it or being out of it

Completed suicide: professionals prefer this language to "committed suicide"

Constriction: a narrowing of the range of perceptions, opinions, and options that occur to a suicidal person's mind; seen in tunnel vision and either/or thinking

Egoistic suicide: suicide undertaken when society fails to help individuals find meaning in their lives so that they (often suddenly) find themselves alone or isolated; a sociological category in which suicide arises from underinvolvement or underintegration of an individual from his or her society

Either/or thinking: constricted thought processes in which one can only envision continuing in a painful condition or escaping that condition by ending one's life

Fatalistic suicide: suicide undertaken when an individual seeks to escape from an overcontrolling social context; a sociological category in which suicide arises from excessive regulation of individuals by society

Haplessness: describes persistently ill-fated or unlucky behavior

Helplessness: an inability to assist or take care of oneself

Hopelessness: a condition in which one has no positive expectations for his or her future

Inimicality: an unsettled life pattern in which one acts against one's own best interests

Life-threatening behavior: actions that put one's life at risk, whether or not they actually end it; a more general phrase than "suicidal behavior"

Perturbation: heightened psychological disturbance in a person's life

Rational suicide: the ending of one's life as a result of motives that are thought to be lucid, rational, and morally appropriate

Suicide: the deliberate or intentional ending of one's own life; sometimes called intentional self-harm

Suicide intervention: efforts made to reduce the likelihood of completed suicides or at least to minimize suicidal behavior; "intervention" is preferred to "prevention" since the latter is not always possible

Suicidology and suicidologists: the scientific study of suicide and suicidal behavior; individuals who study suicidal behavior, intervene to minimize such behavior, or treat its aftereffects

Survivors of suicide: in this context, a phrase referring to individuals who experience the aftereffects of the suicide of another; not ordinarily used to refer to individuals who attempt to end their lives but do not succeed in their attempts

Tunnel vision: a condition of constricted thinking in which one can only envision few or limited options; a narrowing of one's range of perceptions, opinions, and options

Questions for Review and Discussion

1. This chapter began with examples of two individuals who ended their own lives: Ernest Hemingway and Sylvia Plath. Using what you have learned about suicide, what similarities and differences do you see in these two examples? (See also the example of Robin Williams in Focus On 20.4 in Chapter 20 in this book.)

2. Have you ever thought about ending your life? Has anyone you know and care about reported to you thoughts about ending his or her life? What was going on in your life (or in the other person's life) that led to such thoughts or that helped you (or the other person) get past that point? What might you (or someone else) have done to help a person with such thoughts get past that point?

3. Have you ever known someone who ended his or her life by suicide? What was your response to that action? Think about how other people reacted to that action. How were these responses like what we learned about grief and mourning in Chapter 9? How were they different?

4. Social media and the Internet offer examples of suicidal behavior, information about such behavior, and guidance to help minimize such behavior. Have you ever searched online to learn about these subjects or obtain advice in helping someone who is suicidal? Did it help? Why or why not?

Suggested Readings

Archibald, L. (2012). *Finding Peace without All the Pieces: After a Loved One's Suicide*

Bertini, K. (2009). *Understanding and Preventing Suicide: The Development of Self-Destructive Patterns and Ways to Alter Them*

Cobain, B., & Larch, J. (2006). *Dying to Be Free: A Healing Guide for Families after a Suicide*

Colucci, E., & Lester, D. (Eds.). (2013). *Suicide and Culture: Understanding the Context*

Dunne, E. J., McIntosh, J. L., & Dunne-Maxim, K. (Eds.). (1987). *Suicide and Its Aftermath: Understanding and Counseling the Survivors*

Hawton, K., & Van Heeringen, K. (2000). *The International Handbook of Suicide and Attempted Suicide*

Humphry, D. (2002). *Final Exit: The Practicalities of Self-Deliverance and Assisted Suicide for the Dying* (3rd ed.)

Jacobs, D. G. (1999). *The Harvard Medical School Guide to Suicide Assessment and Intervention*

Jamison, K. R. (1999). *Night Falls Fast: Understanding Suicide*

Jobes, A. A. (2006). *Managing Suicidal Risk: A Collaborative Approach*

John's Sister. (2011). *The Forgotten Mourners: Sibling Survivors of Suicide*

Jordan, J., & Baugher, B. (Eds.). (2016). *After Suicide Loss: Coping with Your Grief* (2nd ed.)

Jordan, J. R., & McIntosh, J. L. (Eds.). (2010). *Grief after Suicide: Understanding the Consequences and Caring for the Survivors*

Leenaars, A. A., & Wenckstern, S. (Eds.). (1991). *Suicide Prevention in the Schools*

Leenaars, A. A., Maltsberger, J. T., & Neimeyer, R. A. (Eds.). (1994). *Treatment of Suicidal People*

Leenaars, A., Sakinofsky, I., Wenckstern, S., Dyck, R., Kral, M., & Bland, R. (Eds.). (1998). *Suicide in Canada*

Leong, F.T.L., & Leach, M. M. (Eds.). (2007). Ethnicity and Suicide in the United States. [Special issue]. *Death Studies, 31*(5)

Lukas, C., & Seiden, H. M. (2007). *Silent Grief: Living in the Wake of Suicide* (Rev. ed.)

Marcus, E. (2010). *Why Suicide? Questions and Answers about Suicide, Suicide Prevention, and Coping with the Suicide of Someone You Know*

Maris, R. W., Berman, A. L., & Silverman, M. M. (2000). *Comprehensive Textbook of Suicidology*

Miller, D. N. (2011). *Child and Adolescent Suicidal Behavior: School-based Prevention, Assessment, and Intervention*

Opalewski, D. A. (2008). *Answering the Cry for Help: A Suicide Prevention Manual*

Pompili, M., & Tatarelli, R. (Eds.). (2010). *Evidence-based Practice in Suicidology: A Source Book*

Rogers, J. R., & Lester, D. (2010). *Understanding Suicide: Why We Don't and How We Might*

Rudd, M. D., Joiner, T., & Rajab, M. H. (2001). *Treating Suicidal Behavior: An Effective, Time-Limited Approach*

Shneidman, E. S. (1980/1995). *Voices of Death*

Shneidman, E. S. (1985). *Definition of Suicide*

Smolin, A., & Guinan, J. (1993). *Healing after the Suicide of a Loved One*

Torres, O. B. (Ed.). (2016). *Encyclopedia of Suicide* (3 vols.)

Weaver, J. C. (2014). *Sorrows of a Century: Interpreting Suicide in New Zealand, 1900–2000*

Worchel, D., & Gearing, R. E. (2010). *Suicide Assessment and Treatment: Empirical and Evidence-Based Practices*

Yufit, R. I., & Lester, D. (Eds.). (2005). *Assessment, Treatment and Prevention of Suicidal Behavior*

Selected Web Resources

Some useful search terms include: ALTRUISTIC SUICIDE; ANOMIC SUICIDE; EGOISTIC SUICIDE; FATALISTIC SUICIDE; LIFE-THREATENING BEHAVIOR; RATIONAL SUICIDE; SUICIDE; SUICIDOLOGY; SURVIVORS OF SUICIDE.

You can also visit the following *organizational and other Internet sites:*

American Association of Suicidology

American Foundation for Suicide Prevention

Canadian Association for Suicide Prevention

Depression and Bipolar Support Alliance

International Association for Suicide Prevention (IASP)

Metanoia (counseling, especially related to suicide)

National Suicide Prevention Lifeline

Samaritans International

Suicide and Life-Threatening Behavior (journal published by Guilford Press)

Suicide and Mental Health Association International (SMHAI)

Survivors of Loved One's Suicides (SOLOS)

Survivors of Suicide

CHAPTER
18

Aided Death: Assisted Suicide, Euthanasia, and Aid in Dying

Objectives of this Chapter

▷ To examine conceptual and moral issues involving aided death

▷ To define *assisted suicide* and *euthanasia* and to distinguish them from other modes of aided death

▷ To differentiate assisted suicide and euthanasia by considering *agency* (who acts?) and *intent* (what goals guide decision making?)

▷ To identify differences between assisted suicide and aid in dying

▷ To describe social policies on aided death in the state of Oregon and in the Netherlands

▷ To explore the morality of aided death by examining philosophical arguments and the perspectives of several world religions on these topics

▷ To offer some examples of recent developments and what may happen with aided death in the future

TERRI SCHIAVO

On February 25, 1990, Terri Schiavo was 26 years old and had been married to Michael Schiavo for six years. She had not signed either a living will or a durable power of attorney. On that day, Terri's heart stopped (apparently as a consequence of an eating disorder) and her brain was deprived of oxygen. From that date forward, Terri was in a coma and some (including several physicians) believed that she was in a persistent vegetative state. The National Institute of Neurological Disorders and Stroke (2015) defines a persistent vegetative state as one in which individuals are in "a profound or deep state of unconsciousness.... Individuals in such a state have lost their thinking abilities and awareness of their surroundings, but retain non-cognitive function and normal sleep patterns.... Spontaneous movements may occur, and the eyes may open in response to external stimuli. Individuals may even occasionally grimace, cry, or laugh." Terry showed many of these symptoms; that fact eventually led to a legal battle between her husband (her court-appointed legal guardian) and her parents. On one hand, after several years of rehabilitative efforts, Michael Schiavo came to believe that Terri would never recover. He said she told him previously that she would not want to be kept alive by artificial means. On that basis, since 1998 he repeatedly asked a local circuit court to order the removal of a tube that had been surgically implanted in Terri's stomach to provide hydration, nutrition, and medications. On the other hand, Terri's parents and siblings (who believed that she still had some cognitive function and at least limited potential for improved quality of life) repeatedly blocked Michael's requests by various legal means.

In February 2000, a Florida circuit court judge ruled that the implanted tube (technically, a gastrostomy tube, but commonly called a "feeding tube") could be removed. That was done on April 24, 2001. However, on April 26, 2001, a different Florida circuit court judge ordered physicians to reinstate the stomach tube while Terri's parents pursued a lawsuit against Michael (Ulferts & Lindberg, 2003, p. 1A). In November 2002, the first judge again ordered the tube removed, but stayed

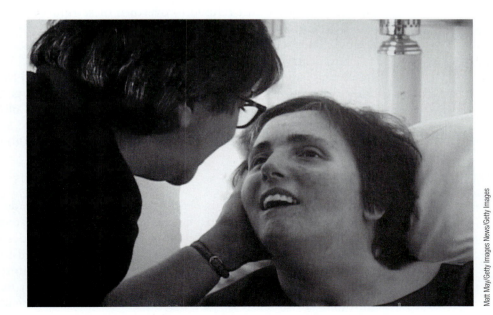

Terri Schiavo
(1963–2005).

implementation of his order until a state appeals court upheld it and the Florida Supreme Court declined to review the decision of the appeals court. The tube was then removed for a second time on October 15, 2003.

Some opponents of this action and supporters of the parents' view began a round-the-clock vigil outside the hospice facility where Terri was receiving care. Then, after receiving many calls and e-mails from around the country opposing the removal of Terri's stomach tube, the Florida legislature stepped in and very quickly (without holding the usual hearings or taking testimony from experts) passed "Terri's Law." This bill gave authority to the governor of Florida, Jeb Bush, to order the stomach tube to be reinserted; that was done on October 21, 2003. (A poll in December 2003 showed that 65% of Florida voters were opposed to this law [Smith, 2003, pp. 1A, 21A], although some disability rights groups and others supported the governor's action [*Times* Staff Writer, 2004, p. 3B].)

In May 2004, a Florida circuit court judge ruled Terri's Law to be a violation of the Florida constitution. The governor appealed, but the Florida appellate court passed the issue directly to the Florida Supreme Court. In August, 2004, arguments were heard by that court, which ruled unanimously in September that Terri's Law was an unconstitutional violation of the separation of powers. The same court then refused to reconsider that decision. In December 2004, the Florida governor asked the U.S. Supreme Court to review that decision, but his request was turned down without comment in January 2005.

On February 25, 2005, the original local judge gave permission to remove the stomach tube. That was done on March 18. Subsequently, the U.S. Congress passed and President George W. Bush signed a bill to allow a federal court to review the case. In response to a request from Terri Schiavo's parents for such a review, a federal district judge declined to order the stomach tube reinserted. That ruling was sustained by the Eleventh U.S. Circuit Court of Appeals and the U.S. Supreme Court again declined to hear the case. Additional local court rulings prohibited the state of Florida from reinserting the stomach tube or taking Terri into state custody. The Florida Supreme Court refused to overturn these rulings, and the federal district court, the Eleventh U.S. Circuit Court of Appeals, and the U.S. Supreme Court once again declined to intervene.

Terri Schiavo finally died on March 31, 2005, more than 15 years after the heart attack that had begun her long saga. Her death was followed by a flood of publications by her husband, her family of origin, lawyers, bioethicists, and other commentators (e.g., Caplan, McCartney, & Sisti, 2006; Clift, 2008; Colby, 2006; Eisenberg, 2005; Gibbs & DeMoss, 2006; Gostin, 2005; Lynne, 2005; Schiavo Case, 2005; Schiavo & Hirsh, 2006; Terri's Family et al., 2006; Werth, 2006).

SITUATING THE ISSUES

The issues addressed in this chapter concern decisions made in certain specific situations intentionally to end a human life. Broadly speaking, these decisions involve what is called "aided death." People in contemporary societies may be led to contemplate such decisions in part as a result of advances used to extend the length of human lives. Beginning in the second half of the 20th century, examples of such advances have been seen when modern technology kept many individuals alive who clearly would have died previously. Such persons include those unable to breathe on their own and persons with severe brain trauma or progressive debilitating diseases who would have died when respirators or nasogastric feeding tubes were unavailable. In addition, chemotherapy, radiation therapy, organ and tissue transplants, and many other techniques have extended the lives of many persons. This is a widely admired outcome of modern medicine.

However, these technologies not only have made possible the continuation of someone's living but sometimes have also increased the depth, length, and degree of that individual's suffering. In some instances, the life continued by these techniques has been felt by some to be demeaning and demoralizing as well as filled with suffering. When contemporary therapies are unable to effectively handle these aspects of people's situations, some have argued that death is to be preferred to continuing such a living/dying.

How often this issue needs to be confronted is a matter of dispute. Hospice philosophy (see Chapter 8) might argue that inadequate care is being provided when someone experiences a demeaning dying process filled with suffering. That is, hospice philosophy suggests it is seldom, if ever, necessary that anyone with a life-threatening illness should be faced with the question of whether his or her death is to be preferred to this present existence. That may be true. However, hospice care is not (yet) available to everyone who is dying, and there are a (perhaps small) number of situations when even hospice or palliative care is unable to successfully handle the suffering being experienced. In these situations, the question of the desirability of choosing to end a life may still arise.

The basic question examined in this chapter is: Is it ever appropriate to choose to end rather than to continue a human life? If this question is answered affirmatively, then other questions arise, including: Under what specific circumstances or in what ways is it appropriate to intentionally end a person's life? And who may properly be involved in that process? In addressing such questions, we look for some basis on which they might appropriately be answered, and we enter a path that compels us to think explicitly about the morality of intentionally ending a human life.

In the United States, Canada, and several other developed countries questions such as these have been most closely associated with discussions of assisted suicide or euthanasia and what has been termed aid in dying. We explore these issues here because they have become matters of intense social debate in recent years and because they are often associated with a degree of conceptual and moral confusion that hinders such debate. Our principal aim is to clarify the concepts of assisted suicide, euthanasia, and aid in dying. Our goal is to help sort out these concepts as various forms of aided death, along with arguments made on behalf of or against such ways of deciding to end a human life. We begin with assisted suicide and euthanasia.

DECIDING TO END A HUMAN LIFE: WHO ACTS?

One key issue in deciding to end a human life is the matter of *agency*. Put briefly, the question is: *Who acts?* In both assisted suicide and euthanasia, at least two individuals are always involved. The difference lies in the ways these individuals are said to take part in bringing about the ultimate outcome.

Assisted Suicide: Who Acts?

In all cases of assisted suicide, like all other instances of suicide, an individual ends his or her own life. The classic portrait of a suicidal act is one in which an individual obtains a lethal means and uses it to cause his or her own death. (We assume here that the person engaging in this act is under no coercion from someone else to engage in that act. Such coercion fundamentally alters the situation from the one being discussed here.) As a form of suicide, then, *assisted suicide* follows this same pattern. The difference is that now the suicide is deliberately assisted. That is, in assisted suicide, the means used to end the life of one person are obtained from and with the cooperation of a second individual who understands that the first person intends to use those means to end his or her life. In cases of assisted suicide, the first person performs the act that ends his or her own life. No other individual commits this act. If a gun is used to kill the person, the person pulls the trigger. If a lethal drug is ingested, the person ingests it himself or herself. No one else need even be present when this action takes place.

Euthanasia: Who Acts?

The situation is quite different when an individual is asked to act in some way to commit or forego an action in order to end the life of another person. Suppose a person is suffering physically or emotionally and would prefer to be dead. That person might call upon some other individual to act in such a way as to end the first person's life. The action of the second individual is critical to what is meant by the term **euthanasia**. Euthanasia occurs when at least two people are involved and one of those persons dies because some other individual intends that person to die and acts so as to bring about that outcome.

To be more precise, euthanasia properly refers to a situation in which the intention of the second individual who contributes to the death of the first person embodies an attempt to end the suffering of that first person. Whether that suffering must already be present (e.g., the person is in great suffering right now) or may be expected to be present in the future is, as we note later, a matter of some dispute. What is not in dispute in all cases of euthanasia is that the individual who does not die is the principal agent involved in bringing about the death.

Discussions of euthanasia frequently make use of *a distinction concerning whether the death is accomplished with or without the permission of the person who dies*. If the person who dies asked for or assented to his or her death, this is **voluntary euthanasia** (Gruman, 1973); the will of the person who dies is known. It is **nonvoluntary euthanasia** if the will of the person who dies remains unknown. For example, the person might be unconscious or unable to make plain his or her choice for some other reason (think of a person who has had a severe stroke). Or a person, such as a child or someone intellectually or emotionally disabled, might be incompetent to make such a decision. If a second individual somehow intentionally contributes to the death of this sort of person, it is nonvoluntary euthanasia.

A third possibility (in theory, at least) is one in which the wishes of the person are known—he or she wants to be kept alive—but someone else decides to end that life anyway. Perhaps this could be called "involuntary euthanasia." However, to act *against* someone's wishes is more like homicide than like a "good death" (see our discussion of the meaning of the term *euthanasia* next), so one might not want to associate this possibility with the term *euthanasia* in any way.

Some argue that a person who is acutely suffering, by the very fact of that suffering, has diminished capacity to make difficult decisions. If that were true, one might be uncomfortable following the directions of a person in severe physical or emotional pain. Choosing to cooperate in a person's death is an irreversible decision; in the face of that irrevocability, one would want to be as certain as possible that the person's own choice was clearly and competently presented.

So far, we have sought to distinguish between assisted suicide and euthanasia by indicating who the agent is who performs (or fails to perform) an act that results in the death. However, we acknowledge that there are situations in which the usefulness of this distinction is less obvious than our discussion indicates. Consider three possibilities. First, suppose you are able to carry out an act that results in your death. Now suppose you ask someone else to provide you with the means to carry out this act and that individual agrees to provide the means for you to kill yourself. That is **assisted suicide**. Second, now suppose you could perform such an action, but you ask someone else to perform it. Suppose what that individual does next is done out of compassion and results in your death. That is *euthanasia*. Third, now suppose you are unable to perform the action yourself (you are paralyzed, for instance). Then if someone else performs the action that produces your death, it can be less clear whether that action is an assisted suicide or an act of euthanasia. You would kill yourself if you could (but you cannot because of your paralysis); thus, the other individual acts in your place because of your inability to carry out the act.

As a result, we might describe assisted suicide and euthanasia as belonging on opposite ends of a continuum. At one end of the continuum, it is obvious that you (with means provided by another individual) end your life. At the other end of the continuum, someone else ends your life. In between these will be a variety of situations that lie closer to one end or the other of the continuum. However, these situations will be less easily assigned to the category of assisted suicide or euthanasia.

This lack of certainty matters most when we begin to think about the morality of certain sorts of acts. Also, this lack of certainty suggests that any attempt to reason adequately about the morality of these issues must be subtle enough to take note of relevant differences between these various sorts of cases.

DECIDING TO END A HUMAN LIFE: WHAT IS INTENDED?

Another key issue in discussions about deciding to end a human life is *the nature of the act itself*. One helpful element in characterizing the nature of the act is the *intention* that underlies it.

Assisted Suicide: What Is Intended?

The phrase *assisted suicide* applies to a wide range of actions in which one person intentionally acts to end his or her life and secures assistance from another individual to achieve that result. Assisted suicide occurs only when: (1) one person *intentionally* acts to obtain assistance in ending his or her life from a second individual; (2) the second individual *intentionally* acts to provide the necessary assistance to bring about the death of the first person *with full awareness of how that assistance is to be used*; and (3) the first person *intentionally* uses the assistance provided to carry out his or her own self-destruction. The role of intent is evident in all aspects of the assistance that defines assisted suicide.

The assistance provided in an assisted suicide could be the means used to produce the death (e.g., a gun or a drug), the environment or place in which the act occurs, emotional support, or some combination of these elements. Whether someone needs such forms of assistance is usually related to the person's ability to obtain the required means. Situations that are not instances of assisted suicide include ones in which a person is able on his or her own to buy a gun and use it to end his or her life or go to get a physician's prescription for a particular medication, then go to a pharmacist and get that prescription filled, and then use that medication to end his or her own life. Only if the person buying the gun or requesting the medication (explicitly or implicitly) informs the seller or the physician/pharmacist that he or she intends to use the gun or the medication to end his or her life, and the seller or health care provider *acts in concurrence with that intention*, could these situations be regarded as instances of *assisted* suicide.

When a person asks a physician to help end his or her life—for example, by prescribing medications that only physicians can order—this becomes a special kind of assisted suicide called **physician-assisted suicide** (Battin, Rhodes, & Silvers, 1998; Emanuel, 1998). In view of the special professional authority accorded to physicians and their access to certain means that can be used to end a human life, physician-assisted suicide is the type of assisted suicide that has received most public attention in recent years. However, the physician in this situation does nothing to the person when the action is taken that ends the life of the person. As we noted previously, this absence of participation in the lethal act in most situations clearly marks off physician-assisted suicide from cases of euthanasia. In physician-assisted suicide, the physician provides (indirectly, if giving the person a prescription) only the means (and perhaps emotional support)—as was typical in Dr. Kevorkian's early cases (see Focus On 18.1).

Other individuals may also provide such means. For example, a friend or relative might have access to medications or to weapons that could be used for suicidal acts and might provide them to help a person end his or her life. Whenever there is a mutual (explicit or implicit) understanding of a suicidal intention, the involvement of these other individuals in deciding to end a person's life constitutes an instance of assisted suicide but not physician-assisted suicide.

FOCUS ON 18.1

Dr. Jack Kevorkian

During the 1990s, Dr. Jack Kevorkian helped bring to public attention issues associated with assisted suicide and euthanasia. A retired pathologist, Kevorkian publicly announced in 1990 his willingness to assist individuals to end their own lives (Betzold, 1993; DeCesare, 2015). Later that year, he was involved in the assisted suicide of Janet Adkins, 54, of Portland, Oregon. Although he asked others to join him in these activities, Kevorkian insisted that he would do what he thought was right in what he viewed as matters of self-determination and choice, regardless of individual or community opposition.

(continues)

Dr. Jack Kevorkian

Dr. Jack Kevorkian burns a cease-and-desist order in April 1997 in Detroit.

Kevorkian initially provided a "suicide machine" that individuals could use to control the administration of a series of eventually lethal drugs. Later, he simply gave instructions to individuals who could then bring about their deaths in other ways. Kevorkian took pains to ensure he was not present or took no active role when an individual undertook the action resulting in death. For whatever reasons, prosecutors were unable to convict Kevorkian of assisted suicide or any other substantial legal wrongdoing. Later, one retrospective examination of autopsy reports (Roscoe, Melphurs, Dragovic, & Cohen, 2000) claimed that only 17 of the first 69 persons whom Kevorkian helped kill were actually terminally ill or had less than six months to live, though most had chronic, often painful life-threatening illnesses (5 seemed to have no major physical disease).

In 1998, after acknowledging being present at or involved in about 130 deaths, Kevorkian videotaped his own direct participation in bringing about the death of Thomas Youk, a 52-year-old man with advanced amyotrophic lateral sclerosis (ALS or Lou Gehrig's disease). A videotape from September 15, 1998, showed Youk agreeing to this act of euthanasia and signing what Kevorkian said was a consent form. Another videotape from September 17 showed Kevorkian injecting Youk with two chemicals that caused

(continues)

FOCUS ON 18.1 *(continued)*

Dr. Jack Kevorkian

his death (Werth, 2001). On Sunday, November 22, an edited version of these videotapes was shown on the CBS television show *60 Minutes*.

On November 25, the local prosecutor charged Kevorkian with first-degree murder and criminal assisted suicide. This occurred after Kevorkian challenged the prosecutor to charge him within a week. It also followed the defeat in early November by Michigan voters of a ballot referendum approving of assisted suicide. Although the prosecutor had been elected after a pledge not to waste more public funds in futile prosecutions of Kevorkian, he is reported to have regarded the public showing of the videotape as demonstrating an obvious violation of law that he could not ignore.

At trial in March 1999, Kevorkian acted as his own lawyer. After the charge of assisted suicide was withdrawn, the judge prohibited testimony by Thomas Youk's family members as irrelevant to the remaining charges of murder. Subsequently, Kevorkian rested his case without calling himself or any other witnesses for the defense. On March 26, the jury found Kevorkian guilty of second-degree murder and delivering a controlled substance (his medical license that allowed him to be in possession of controlled substances had been revoked by the State of Michigan in 1991).

On April 13, 1999, Kevorkian was sentenced to 10–25 years in prison for murder and 3–7 years for delivery of a controlled substance. In handing down these sentences, the judge is reported to have said to Kevorkian that, "This trial was not about the political or moral correctness of euthanasia. It was about you, sir. It was about lawlessness. It was about disrespect for a society that exists because of the strength of the legal system. No one, sir, is above the law. No one" (*St. Louis Post-Dispatch*, 1999, p. A1). The judge agreed to allow these sentences to run concurrently but refused to release Kevorkian on bail, and his subsequent appeals were rejected. Kevorkian did not fulfill a pledge he once made to starve himself to death. With time off for good behavior, he was granted a parole on June 1, 2007, conditioned in part on his pledge not to assist others in the future to end their lives. Subsequently, he was interviewed by Anderson Cooper in April of 2010 (www.youtube.com/watch?v=EQmyo6EvUY8).

Jack Kevorkian died of natural causes on June 3, 2011, at the age of 83.

Euthanasia: What Is Intended?

The intention to end a human life is also central in cases of euthanasia. Still, there is some confusion and disagreement about what is meant by "euthanasia" in many contemporary discussions. Etymologically, *euthanasia* comes from the Greek (*eu* = "good" + *thanatos* = "death") and literally means a "good death." Since few would oppose a good death for themselves or others, the real question is what might be involved in bringing about such a death, even when acting for benevolent motives (Gordon, 2016). Clearly, it would not be a good death if whatever is done or not done were not guided by a beneficent or well-meaning intention. A malevolent intention would define some form of homicide.

However, this description is incomplete. Euthanasia properly refers to a situation in which the individual who contributes to the death of another person *intends to end the suffering of that second person*. That suffering might already be present (the person is in great suffering right now), or it might be expected to be present in the future (think of someone in the early stages of Lou Gehrig's disease or Alzheimer's disease). Note that this understanding of euthanasia does not limit it to situations in which someone is close to death. Some people would further limit the use of the term *euthanasia* to these latter situations—that is, they hold that a person must be close to death for euthanasia to be at issue. In this view, if the person were not near death, we would be discussing some type of homicide, not euthanasia. This viewpoint led some to criticize the actions of Dr. Jack Kevorkian (see Focus On 18.1) on the grounds that some of those whom he helped end their lives had not previously been near death or actively dying.

Active versus Passive Euthanasia

Another distinction frequently encountered in discussions of the morality of euthanasia concerns the means by which the ending of a suffering person's life will occur. Here some draw a distinction between active and passive euthanasia. Actively doing something to end suffering by ending a human life is often called **active euthanasia**. In situations of this type, one deliberately commits an act (for benevolent motives) that in itself causes the death. This definition allows little room for ambiguity.

The case is a bit more complex when we turn to **passive euthanasia**. Two alternatives often come up in this discussion: the first alternatives refers to *withholding* (not supplying) some intervention necessary to sustain life; the second alternative involves *withdrawing* (taking away) some intervention that is currently in place and may be helping to sustain life. Those who see no moral difference between these two alternatives often speak of "foregoing" some intervention, which includes either withholding (not initiating some intervention) or withdrawing (taking away some intervention) that may be necessary to sustain life (Lynn, 1986). In practice, some individuals in our society and many health care providers have been concerned that the act of withdrawing is not passive (Miller & Truog, 2012). (In part, their concern may also be about their legal responsibilities that would be involved in stopping or removing some existing intervention.) Acting to withdraw an intervention seems to involve doing something to take away the existing intervention. This appears to be so even if the result does not in itself end the life but only removes an obstacle that is or may be blocking the natural processes of dying leading to death.

Because of the uncertainty we just noted, this distinction between active and passive euthanasia is not always as clear or helpful as we might like it to be. If the person who is ill is able to walk away from the care provider, that person can simply refuse any treatment offered, and in most jurisdictions is *legally* allowed to do so as an expression of what is now said to be a well-established *right of privacy* (Alderman & Kennedy, 1997; Annas, 2004). Also, such walking away is not typically described as *immoral*. If a care provider offers you an intervention he or she believes is necessary to sustain your life (e.g., hemodialysis or chemotherapy) and you refuse it and never return to receive it, this is not an example of an illegal (or to many minds, an immoral) act. Your personal autonomy includes the right to make such a choice.

This issue may appear to be more obscure when someone is unable to walk away (because he or she is too weak or is bedridden, paralyzed, etc.). For someone who has a life-threatening illness and who is in a medical care institution—willingly or not—to refuse apparently necessary treatment to sustain his or her life raises questions for many persons about the legitimacy of that refusal. In these circumstances, in many eyes, to refuse the chemotherapy, surgery, or other intervention carries a nuance of choosing to die that is not as clear in the situation described in the previous paragraph. That is, it may appear to be a request for someone else to help one to die and is thus an instance of active euthanasia.

To recognize what is really going on in these situations, however, once more we must understand the *intentions* of the person who refuses the treatment and those of the caregiver. The person who walks away may or may not intend to die; if he or she does have that intention, then walking away may be part of a *suicidal* act. The person who cannot walk away may or may not intend to die; if he or she does have this intention, the refusal of treatment may be a request for *passive euthanasia*. Simply refusing treatment, *in and of itself*, need be neither an instance of suicide nor a request for passive euthanasia. A person might refuse treatment simply because it has become too burdensome (physically, financially, psychologically, etc.). Everything hinges on the intentions of the persons involved. It is suicide or euthanasia only when the person who refuses some treatment does this *in order to die*, and, if another person is involved, only when that other person also *intends for death to occur*.

Ordinary versus Extraordinary Means

Another distinction often advanced in discussions about ending a human life is that between *ordinary and extraordinary means of treatment*. The point of this distinction is to argue that there is no moral obligation to provide extraordinary means of treatment. Many have made this claim; for instance, Roman Catholic ethicists (e.g., McCormick, 1974) have long argued that care providers have no such moral obligation.

Several criteria are offered to help implement this distinction. **Ordinary means of treatment** are those that: (1) have outcomes that are predictable and well known; (2) offer no unusual risk, suffering, or burden for either the person who is being treated or others; and (3) are effective. **Extraordinary means of treatment** fail to meet one or more of these criteria. Extraordinary means may have outcomes that are not predictable or well known, as in the case of some experimental procedures. Such procedures may not have been widely used or studied, so that one cannot be certain what will happen when one embarks on their use in particular cases. Or it may be that a procedure itself puts the patient at risk or imposes undue burdens on those who would assist the patient. That is, the procedure may have a broad range of outcomes, some of which make the person worse off than he or she was before. For example, the side effects of a treatment might produce more suffering than the person was undergoing before the treatment began. An extraordinary means of treatment might even produce effects that are worse than the disease. Since the outcome of using such means is unpredictable, one might have little confidence that they will in fact be helpful in dealing either with the person's symptoms or disease. That is, the actual effectiveness of an extraordinary means of treatment may be uncertain, too.

What counts as ordinary and extraordinary means cannot be determined independently of an individual person's context. What might be ordinary treatment in one situation could be extraordinary in another. There is no list of treatments that can—purely on their own—be determined to be ordinary in this moral sense and another list of treatments that can be determined to be extraordinary. Whether a specific treatment is ordinary or extraordinary must be decided in terms of a particular person's situation.

It is important not to confuse this *moral* distinction between ordinary and extraordinary means with an empirical distinction between that which is routine or familiar and that which is not. What is *medically* ordinary may not also be *morally* ordinary in the context of this discussion. For example, the use of ventilators and respirators is quite common in many hospitals and long-term care facilities, but that does not determine their moral status according to the ordinary/extraordinary distinction. Similarly, in recent years, various forms of artificial feeding have become common, especially for individuals in various forms of temporary coma or in the more serious condition described as a permanent or persistent vegetative state (PVS). Artificial nutrition and hydration for individuals in persistent vegetative states is a form of medical treatment commonly delivered as special liquid formulas through a feeding tube implanted directly into the stomach. Many bioethicists and moral theologians have suggested that such medical interventions may be or may become (after sufficient time has enabled specialists to confirm the diagnosis of PVS) examples of extraordinary means. If so, in this view their removal could become morally optional (see, however, Issues for Critical Reflection #15). But again, that would need to be assessed on an individual basis with full understanding of the particular situation.

ISSUES FOR CRITICAL REFLECTION
#15 Pope John Paul II on Artificial Nutrition and Hydration for Individuals in Permanent Vegetative States

On March 22, 2004, Pope John Paul II spoke to an international congress on life-sustaining treatments and the vegetative state. In that speech, the pope first spoke of the importance of arriving at a correct diagnosis of such a state in any individual case. Then, arguing that individuals in these states retain their "intrinsic value and personal dignity," he went on:

> This important congress ... is dealing with a very significant issue: the clinical condition called the *vegetative state*....
> The person in a vegetative state, in fact, shows no evident sign of self-awareness or of awareness of the environment, and seems unable to interact with others or to react to specific stimuli.... Moreover, not a few of these persons, with appropriate treatment and with specific rehabilitation programs, have been able to emerge from a vegetative state.

On the basis of these assertions, the pope went on to discuss the moral ramifications of treating persons in a permanent or persistent vegetative state. He asserted that "the administration of water and food, even when provided by artificial means, always represents a natural means of preserving life, not a medical act." As a result, the pope claimed that such administration is always morally required.

Two American bioethicists (Shannon & Walter, 2004) observed that this statement represents "a major reversal of the moral tradition of the Catholic church." Further, these commentators pointed out that the moral claim as to what is obligatory or required seems to be based on an unclear distinction between "natural" and "artificial" treatments. One of the most difficult issues in discussions of the morality of treating persons in these states lies in determining just what counts as natural versus clinical or medical treatment. This distinction in turn has been related—often in tenuous ways—to the moral distinction between ordinary and extraordinary treatments. As Shannon and Walter wrote:

> [T]he primary determinant of whether the intervention is morally ordinary or extraordinary is not how the intervention—whether a medical therapy or some other kind of intervention—is classified. Historically, the determinant has been the effect on the patient. Thus the fact that some intervention is considered a "natural means" ... does not determine the moral or obligatory status of the intervention. (pp. 9–10)

Some of these issues can be seen historically in three celebrated cases:

- In April of *1975*, Karen Ann Quinlan at the age of 21 slipped into a comatose state, apparently as a result of ingesting alcohol and some tranquilizers at a party. On May 22, 1976, Karen Ann's parents were permitted by the New Jersey Supreme Court to have a respirator (which they regarded as having become an extraordinary intervention that would not restore Karen to health) removed. However, they did continue intravenous feeding and regular visits with her. Karen did not die until June 11, 1985 (see Colen, 1976; Quinlan, Quinlan, & Battelle, 1977).
- In January of *1983*, Nancy Cruzan, at the age of 26, experienced severe brain damage from a lack of oxygen following an automobile accident. After a lengthy court battle that reached both the Missouri and the U.S. Supreme Courts, Nancy's parents and sister were permitted to act on her behalf to remove artificial nutrition and hydration delivered through a tube implanted directly into her stomach. She died in a matter of days on December 26, 1990 (Colby, 2002).
- In February of *1990*, Terri Schiavo at the age of 26 entered into the situation described in the vignette near the beginning of this chapter. She died on March 31, 2005, and it has been argued that her death shaped the "right to die" movement whose implications we explore in this chapter (Sanburn, 2015; see also Fine, 2005), even if that slogan may not always be appropriate or helpful.

Note that none of these young women had completed a written advance directive (a document not even available to Karen Ann Quinlan in 1975) to communicate her wishes about end-of-life care.

In general, then, if the therapy proposed for use or already in use is an extraordinary means of treatment according to the criteria listed here, then most moralists agree that there is no moral obligation to use it. Individuals may choose not to begin (withhold) the use of such a therapy, or they may choose to terminate (withdraw) its use with no moral culpability attached to that decision.

This brings the discussion back to issues associated with euthanasia. The distinction between extraordinary and ordinary means is often employed in the following way. Many would hold that not to begin to use or to stop using extraordinary means of treatment is tantamount to not being engaged in decisions about euthanasia. In this view, questions about euthanasia arise only when one is trying to decide whether to use ordinary means of treatment. Those who argue in favor of euthanasia will

Nancy Cruzan's grave marker.

Courtesy of the Center for Practical Bioethics

suggest that in some situations there is no moral requirement to use ordinary means of treatment. Those who argue against euthanasia will suggest that in this situation (or in all situations) morally one must use the ordinary means of treatment under discussion; otherwise, one would be intending to end a human life.

AID IN DYING

In recent years, some have argued that it is inappropriate to apply any form of the label "suicide" to individuals who have already been determined to be dying and have only a limited time to live. For example, individuals who act under the Oregon "Death with Dignity" legislation (see a discussion of that law and its implementation next in this chapter) to obtain from a physician a prescription for medications that, if taken, will end their lives, are said under the terms of the legislation not to be engaged in suicidal behavior. Consider the following comment from the Oregon Department of Human Services (2006, p. 7):

> The Death with Dignity Act allows terminally ill Oregon residents to obtain and use prescriptions from their physicians for self-administered, lethal medications. Under the Act, ending one's life in accordance with the law does not constitute suicide.

Instead of talking about suicide, proponents of the Oregon Death with Dignity Act (DWDA) insist that it only contemplates **aid in dying**. Consider the following comment from a representative of the Death with Dignity National Center (Melissa Barber, personal communication, 4/15/11) who observed:

> A terminally ill patient making a request under the Oregon or Washington law is doing so to hasten an already inevitable and imminent death; therefore, the act cannot properly be equated with suicide. None of the moral, existential, or religious connotations of "suicide" apply when the patient's primary objective is not to end an otherwise open-ended span of life but to find dignity in an already impending exit from this world. Individuals who use the law may be offended by the use of "assisted suicide," because they are participating in an act to shorten the agony of their final hours, not killing themselves. It's cancer (or other underlying condition) which is killing them.

In a policy statement dated October 28, 2008, The American Public Health Association (APHA) agreed with this view by stating that it:

- supports allowing a mentally competent, terminally ill adult to obtain a prescription for medication that the person could self-administer to control the time, place, and manner of his or her impending death, where safeguards equivalent to those in the Oregon DDA are in place....
- rejects the use of inaccurate terms such as "suicide" and "assisted suicide" to refer to the choice of a mentally competent terminally ill patient to seek medications to bring about a peaceful and dignified death.

The APHA also wrote that it "notes the importance of using accurate language to describe care options." Many would agree with the need to employ accurate concepts and language in discussing these matters, whether or not one agrees that "aid in dying" should be understood as a distinct category of aided death.

SOCIAL POLICY AND PRACTICES IN OREGON AND THE NETHERLANDS

We can illustrate social policy and practices related to the subjects of this chapter by exploring the Death with Dignity Act in the state of Oregon and euthanasia practices and legislation in the Netherlands.

The Death with Dignity Act in Oregon

In 1994, the citizens of the state of Oregon approved, by a margin of just 51%–49%, a **Death with Dignity Act** (DWDA). To request a prescription for lethal medications, the DWDA requires that an individual must be 18 years of age or older, a resident of Oregon, capable of making and communicating health care decisions, and diagnosed with a terminal illness that will lead to death within six months. Not surprisingly, the DWDA, which went into effect in October 1997, was (and is) controversial leading to various challenges to its legitimacy and implementation (see Issues for Critical Reflection #16).

To receive a prescription for lethal medications, the law requires that: (1) the patient must make two oral requests to his or her physician, separated by at least 15 days; (2) the patient must provide a written request to his or her physician, signed in the presence of two witnesses; (3) the prescribing physician and a consulting physician must confirm the patient's diagnosis and prognosis; (4) the prescribing physician and a consulting physician must determine whether the patient is capable of making and communicating health care decisions for him/herself; (5) if either physician believes the patient's judgment is impaired by a psychiatric or psychological disorder

---

ISSUES FOR CRITICAL REFLECTION
#16 What Have Been Some Legal Challenges to the Oregon "Death with Dignity Act"?

The Oregon "Death with Dignity Act," authorizing physician-assisted suicide, has been controversial among some Americans (Werth & Wineberg, 2005). Part of the controversy lies in the act's having raised questions about where the authority to legalize physician-assisted suicide (and perhaps implicitly other forms of aided death) lies—at the federal level or with the states. From the outset, several groups went to court to prevent the implementation of the act. In 1997, the U.S. Supreme Court ruled that although there is no "right to die" in the U.S. Constitution, states have the constitutional right to make laws that provide for physician-assisted suicide. Meanwhile, an attempt to repeal the law was placed on the ballot in Oregon in November of 1997, only to be rejected by a vote of 60%–40%.

On November 6, 2001, the Attorney General of the United States announced that Oregon's Death with Dignity Act violated federal drug laws. He then issued a directive authorizing cancelation of the federal license of physicians to prescribe what are called controlled substances or "scheduled drugs" if they are used to provide assistance in dying. The practical effect of that action would be to make it difficult, if not impossible, to

implement the DWDA. However, in November 2001 a federal district court judge issued a temporary injunction to halt that action, and in April 2002 the same judge made the injunction permanent, ruling that the Attorney General did not have the authority to interfere with state laws governing the practice of medicine.

In May of 2004, a three-judge panel of the Ninth U.S. Circuit Court of Appeals rejected the government's appeal of those decisions. The panel's ruling held that the so-called "Ashcroft Directive" cannot be enforced because it violates the clear language of the Controlled Substances Act, runs contrary to the legislative intent of Congress, and disregards the limits of the Attorney General's lawful authority. In August 2004 a majority of that federal appeals court's 25 full-time judges voted to refuse to reconsider that decision. Subsequently, the U.S. Supreme Court ruled 6–3 on January 17, 2006, that the Attorney General does not have the authority to regulate medical practice, a responsibility left to the states and that the Oregon DWDA does not violate the intent of Congress when it passed the 1970 Controlled Substances Act to regulate illicit drug dealing and trafficking.

(such as depression), the patient must be referred for a psychological examination; (6) the prescribing physician must inform the patient of feasible alternatives to the DWDA including comfort care, hospice care, and pain control; (7) the prescribing physician must request, but may not require, the patient to notify his or her next-of-kin of the prescription request. A patient can rescind a request at any time and in any manner. To comply with the law, physicians must report all prescriptions for lethal medications to the Oregon Health Authority. As of 1999, pharmacists must be informed of the prescribed medication's ultimate use.

It is important to be clear that the act only authorizes voluntary self-administration of lethal medications prescribed by a licensed Oregon physician for the purpose of ending one's life; euthanasia, or situations in which a physician or other person directly administers a medication to end another's life, is specifically prohibited. Although the DWDA makes clear that physicians and health care systems are under no obligation to participate in its implementation, those physicians and patients who adhere to the requirements of the act are protected from criminal prosecution, and the choice to end one's life in this way cannot affect the status of a patient's health or life insurance policies. The DWDA stipulates that a death under these conditions does not constitute suicide, mercy killing, or homicide under the law. The law also requires the collection of information and a published annual report on its implementation.

Those supporting the Oregon DWDA have argued that quality in living, personal choice or autonomy, and quality in medical decision making are the important values to be considered in this matter (e.g., Annas, 1994, 2004; Quill & Battin, 2004). Opponents generally describe such practices and policies as rife with danger and not possessing adequate safeguards, especially those to protect vulnerable patients from coercion of various sorts (e.g., Foley & Hendin, 2002; Hendin, 1998). Since the DWDA came into effect, only a limited number of persons in Oregon have requested and even fewer have carried out physician-assisted suicide (PAS), representing 37.2 of every 10,000 deaths in the state in 2016 (see Table 18.1).

Given the relatively small numbers of individuals involved, annual variations among those who have taken advantage of the DWDA in Oregon are unavoidable. Still, it is important to understand the typical characteristics of those who seek out this form of aided death (Blanke, LeBlanc, Hershman, Ellis, & Meyskens, 2017). For example, among those who ended their lives under the DWDA in 2016, the median age was 73, the vast majority were white, males and females were nearly equally likely, individuals with a higher level of education were more typical, and individuals with terminal cancer were most prominent. The vast majority of those implementing the DWDA were enrolled in hospice care, died at home, and had some form of health insurance. Similar to previous years, leading concerns of those who ended their lives in Oregon under the DWDA in 2016 included loss of autonomy, a decreasing ability to participate in activities that made life enjoyable, and loss of dignity. Fear of intractable physical pain has not seemed to be a central motivation. As Szabo (2016) has written: "the latest research shows that terminally ill patients who seek out aid-in-dying aren't primarily concerned about pain. Those who've actually used these laws thus far have been far more concerned about controlling the way they exit the world than controlling pain."

Beyond this, it has been suggested that the availability of death with dignity may have led to efforts to improve end-of-life care in Oregon through other modalities. For example, it has encouraged individuals to explore with medical providers their fears and wishes around end-of-life care (Tolle & Teno, 2017). Also, the DWDA has increased awareness on the part of both patients and physicians about other end-of-life care options such as hospice and palliative care (Gorman, 2015; Schencker,

Table 18.1   **Numbers of Prescriptions Written and Individuals Who Died under the Oregon Death with Dignity Act (DWDA), 1998–2016 (as of 1/23/17)**

	Number of Prescriptions Written under the DWDA	Number of Individuals Who Ingested Lethal Medications and Died
2016	204	133
2015	218	135
2014	155	105
2013	121	73
2012	116	85
2011	114	71
2010	97	65
2009	95	59
2008	88	60
2007	85	49
2006	65	46
2005	65	38
2004	60	37
2003	68	42
2002	58	38
2001	44	21
2000	39	27
1999	33	27
1998	24	16
Total	1749	1127

Note: Individuals who received prescriptions under the DWDA may have died of their illnesses before they could act on those prescriptions; some received a prescription in one year but did not act on it immediately to ingest lethal medications and thus died in a subsequent year.

Source: Oregon Department of Human Services, 2017

2015). In addition, a study of family members concluded that "pursuit of aid in dying does not have negative effects on surviving family members and may be associated with greater preparation and acceptance of death" (Ganzini, Goy, Dobscha, & Prigerson, 2009, p. 807). Finally, the DWDA seems to have helped physicians improve their knowledge about the use of pain medications in terminal illness and to better recognize psychiatric disorders such as depression.

Euthanasia Practices and Legislation in the Netherlands

In the Netherlands euthanasia is technically illegal, but for many years has also been familiar in practice (Cohen-Almagor, 2010; De Wachter, 1989, 1992; Thomasma,

Kimbrough-Kushner, Kimsma, & Ciesielski-Carlucci, 1998). Here, euthanasia is defined as "the administration of drugs with the explicit intention of ending the patient's life, at the patient's explicit request" (Van der Maas et al., 1996, p. 1700). In 1984, the Royal Dutch Medical Association issued guidelines for this practice that were later endorsed by a government-appointed commission on euthanasia. The guidelines are: "(1) the patient must be a mentally competent adult; (2) the patient must request euthanasia voluntarily, consistently, and repeatedly over a reasonable time, and the request must be documented; (3) the patient must be suffering intolerably, with no prospect of relief, although the disease need not be terminal; and (4) the doctor must consult with another physician not involved in the case" (Angell, 1996, p. 1676). Physicians in the Netherlands who practice euthanasia under these guidelines have not been subject to criminal sanctions for many years. Apparently, no moral or legal distinction is drawn in the Netherlands between this form of active euthanasia and assisted suicide (Swarte & Heintz, 1999).

In November 2001, new legislation—**The Dutch Termination of Life on Request and Assisted Suicide (Review Procedures) Act**—went into effect. According to an official "question and answer" pamphlet on the subject (Anonymous, 2001) and more recent documents of a similar nature, this legislation incorporated in the Dutch criminal code "a special ground for exemption from criminal liability," which provides that "doctors who terminate life on request or assist in a patient's suicide can no longer be prosecuted, provided they satisfy the statutory due care criteria and notify death by non-natural causes to the appropriate regional euthanasia review committee" (p. 4). In other words, under the new legislation, when a doctor carries out euthanasia or assisted suicide in accordance with the legislative criteria and has reported his or her actions correctly, and when a regional review committee (composed of at least one lawyer, one physician, and an ethicist) has decided on the basis of that report that the physician has acted with due care, the Public Prosecution Service will not be informed, and no further action will be taken. Only when a review committee finds that a doctor has failed to satisfy the statutory due care criteria will the case be referred to the public prosecutor for possible prosecution.

According to official documents, "the basic principle underlying the legislation is that patients have no absolute right to euthanasia and doctors no absolute duty to perform it" (Anonymous, 2001, p. 6). Thus, approximately two-thirds of all requests for euthanasia in the Netherlands are refused, and one hospice doctor could say that his attitude toward this legislation and the practices it sanctions was one of "peaceful coexistence and respectful nonparticipation" (Z. Zylicz, in a discussion at the meeting of the International Work Group on Death, Dying, and Bereavement, June 13, 2001).

Although official studies of euthanasia practices in the Netherlands had been conducted in 1990, 1995, and 2001 (Onwuteaka-Philipsen et al., 2003), implementation of the new Euthanasia Act called for additional research. As a result of their examination of deaths under this legislation, Van der Heide et al. (2007, p. 1957) reported:

> In 2005, of all deaths in the Netherlands, 1.7% were the result of euthanasia and 0.1% were the result of physician-assisted suicide. These percentages were significantly lower than those in 2001, when 2.6% of all deaths resulted from euthanasia and 0.2% from assisted suicide. Of all deaths, 0.4% were the result of the ending of life without an explicit request by the patient. Continuous deep sedation was used in conjunction with possible hastening of death in 7.1% of all deaths in 2005, significantly increased from 5.6% in 2001.

This study concluded that, "The Dutch Euthanasia Act was followed by a modest decrease in the rates of euthanasia and physician-assisted suicide. The decrease may have resulted from the increased application of other end-of-life care interventions, such as palliative sedation." A separate study (Rietjens et al., 2007, p. 220) reported that "ending life without an explicit request of the patient seems to be a part of medical end-of-life practices in the Netherlands as well as other countries," practices that are said mainly to apply to incompetent, terminally ill patients without opening the door to the acceptance of other forms of ending life. (An official question and answer document on these practices is available from the Netherlands Euthanasia Commission.)

Those who favor the Dutch policies and practices note that all citizens of the Netherlands enjoy a high standard of living, full health insurance, a home physician, and generous retirement and social services. Nevertheless, the population of the Netherlands is aging, and the government recognizes that dying patients may request euthanasia for reasons of pain, degradation, and the longing to die with dignity. Advocates also draw attention to the fact that euthanasia accounts for only a small fraction of all deaths in the Netherlands and that it is performed in less than one-third of cases when a request is made. It is further argued that this type of euthanasia is performed "almost entirely on those who were terminally ill; 87% of the patients were expected to die within a week, and another 12% in a month" (Angell, 1996, p. 1676). In addition, advocates note that in cases when there was no explicit request, factors such as a previous discussion of the subject, present lack of competency, or discussions with other physicians, nurses, or family members influenced the decision. Finally, advocates of euthanasia in the Netherlands observe that reporting of these cases increased from about 18% in 1990 to over 80% in 2005 (Van der Heide et al., 2007; Van der Wal et al., 1996). Thus, the authors of the 1995 studies contended, "in our view, these data do not support the idea that physicians in the Netherlands are moving down a slippery slope" (Van der Maas et al., 1996, p. 1705). They add, "A large majority of Dutch physicians consider euthanasia an exceptional but accepted part of medical practice." Family members involved in these practices also seem to find them acceptable (Georges et al., 2007; Swarte, van der Lee, van der Born, van den Bout, & Heintz, 2003).

Opponents of these practices and policies (such as Hendin, 1995, 1998, 2002; Hendin, Rutenfrans, & Zylicz, 1997) generally describe them as rife with danger and not possessing adequate safeguards. They seize on what they see as "the gradual extension of assisted suicide to widening groups of patients after it is legally permitted for patients designated as terminally ill" (Hendin et al., 1997, p. 1720), failures of the guidelines and problems of underreporting despite the implementation since 1991 of a notification procedure (see Van der Wal et al., 1996), and "the documentation of cases in which patients who have not given their consent have their lives ended by physicians" (p. 1721).

News reports concerning additional developments in the Netherlands state that total numbers of deaths under the country's euthanasia and assisted suicide policy rose by 13% in 2009 following a 10.5% increase in 2008 (Anonymous, 2010; Ertelt, 2010). The total of 2,636 cases represented 2% of all deaths in the country in 2009. Subsequently, in 2010 a group calling itself "Out of Free Will" circulated petitions proposing that "all Dutch people over 70 who feel tired of life should have the right to professional help in ending it" (Jensma, 2010a). This effort is distinctive in two ways: (1) It would expand the scope of euthanasia, which under current Dutch law is only legal in cases of "hopeless and unbearable" suffering and (2) It envisages establishing a new profession of specially trained and certified nurses, psychologists, or spiritual professionals who would verify the request for assisted suicide in a series of conversations with the patient and have the patient's death wish confirmed by a second health care professional before providing lethal drugs and supervising the process, by contrast with current Dutch law that limits this role to medical doctors and is illegal for others (Jensma, 2010b).

Because their populations, social services, and health care systems are so dissimilar, Angell (1996, p. 1677) noted that "it is virtually impossible to draw any meaningful comparisons" between the Dutch experience and practices in the United States. She added that, "until recently, physician-assisted dying has been considered in the United States to be quite different" from accepted practices in end-of-life care. However, "support for decriminalizing assisted suicide has been growing, whereas support for euthanasia remains weak," perhaps because "euthanasia can be involuntary, where suicide, by definition, must be voluntary," and assisted suicide may be considered to be less liable to abuse than euthanasia (see also Emanuel, Onwuteaka-Philipsen, Urwin, & Cohen, 2016, on public and physician-attitudes on these subjects).

DECIDING TO END A HUMAN LIFE: MORAL ARGUMENTS

We turn next to issues relating to the morality of intentionally ending a human life. Some have argued that intentionally doing something to end someone's life and intentionally not doing something to sustain that life ought to be distinguished morally. For instance, many people hold that active euthanasia is morally unacceptable. Their argument is that in active euthanasia the agent (the cause) of death is a person, the agent intends to bring about the death, and it is morally unacceptable for one person to deliberately kill another (in the circumstances under consideration in this chapter). However, many of these same people argue that passive euthanasia can, under some circumstances, be morally appropriate. Their argument is that in passive euthanasia the agent (the cause) of death is a disease process—no person directly causes the death of another or intends to do so—and thus this is morally acceptable.

Not everyone accepts these claims. Some argue that in either case, another human being is involved, and whether that person commits an act to cause the death or omits an action that could prevent the death is morally irrelevant. In either case, it is argued that the person is involved in the occurrence of the death and is aware that death may likely follow from the action or omission whatever he or she may be intending, so the two situations are morally equivalent. People who think this way believe that if passive euthanasia is morally acceptable, so too must active euthanasia be morally acceptable. They also believe that if active euthanasia is morally unacceptable, then passive euthanasia must be morally unacceptable.

Arguments in Support of Intentionally Ending a Human Life

Prevention of Suffering   An argument to support the moral acceptability of aided death of the types discussed in this chapter is that suffering is evil. Therefore, one function of caregivers is to prevent and, if possible, end suffering. Hence, to achieve such a goal, actions involving assisted suicide, euthanasia, and aid in dying would be permissible. Again, one could take this argument to its extreme and urge that *all* suffering is evil and therefore that one ought *always* to strive to end *any* suffering—but probably few would hold this view. From slogans supporting physical exercise as a means to health ("no pain, no gain") to the realization that success in most valued endeavors (such as intellectual growth, emotional maturity, artistic creativity) involves some suffering ("when the going gets tough, the tough get going"), the conclusion seems to follow that some suffering can have consequences that are good. Therefore, at least as a means to some desired good end, suffering cannot automatically be taken as something to be eliminated altogether. Thus, one is forced to evaluate particular instances of suffering rather than to issue blanket condemnations (Cassell, 1991; Nabe, 1999). This conclusion, of course, may leave us uncertain about what to do in a particular instance.

Enhancement of Liberty   Another argument sometimes used to support aided death is based on the value placed on human liberty. Most Americans and many others believe that liberty is good. That is, they value being free from external coercion when making decisions about themselves and their lives. In other words, many people value autonomy—a word that literally means being able to make law *(nomos)* for oneself *(auto)* (Childress, 1990). Such individuals disvalue interference from others in matters they believe to be their own affair. This position supports the rights of individuals to decide what to do about their own suffering. In this view, if someone so disvalues the suffering he or she is experiencing and that individual prefers that his or her life end, that decision ought to be supported. In short, those who value autonomy must seriously consider the view that it is the suffering person's right as an autonomous agent to make that decision, and others ought not to interfere with it (see Kaplan, 1999; Werth, 1999b). This is the view that Dr. Kevorkian—correctly or incorrectly—consistently stressed.

There are two difficulties with accepting this argument as definitive. One is that it presupposes that one can tell when someone is acting autonomously. However, someone who is experiencing severe pain or emotional trauma may not be completely free of coercion. The pain or emotional suffering itself may be so affecting the person that any decision made under its influence is *not*, in fact, autonomous. It is not always easy to decide about this. However, one position to guard against is the belief that such pain or trauma is *always* a coercive factor in someone's ability to make rational decisions. Even with severe suffering, it may be possible that the person is still an autonomous agent. Individuals involved in the lives of people who are experiencing severe suffering must find ways—actively listening to such a person is a step in this direction—to decide what is happening in the particular person and the concrete situation.

Still, even if the person is autonomous, that does not automatically decide what *others* ought to do in the face of that person's autonomy. Difficult moral dilemmas often involve conflicts between autonomous persons. Individuals may decide autonomously that they want their lives to end, but that may come into conflict with the autonomous decisions of others. Remember that aided deaths of the types discussed in this chapter always involve (at least) two persons. One person's autonomous decision to have his or her life ended may conflict with another person's autonomous decision not to participate in that sort of event. Further, a decision to engage in aided death seldom involves only the persons who are directly associated with the particular event of this one death. Typically, these decisions have broader social effects or repercussions. So even if someone's decision to end his or her life is autonomous, the acting out of that decision will inevitably affect others and that, too, should be taken into account.

Quality of Life   Another argument relevant to this discussion depends on *the value assigned to quality of life*. This argument holds that it is not *life as such* that is good, but rather *a certain form of life*. Most people do not concern themselves with life as such on a purely biological level; for example, they are perfectly willing to kill bacteria, viruses, pesky mosquitoes, and so forth. Rather, this argument maintains that we are properly concerned primarily with specific forms of life. In particular, some urge that we ought to be concerned specifically with what we understand to be *human* forms of life.

This argument compels its supporters to clarify what counts as human life. Some people hold that life in certain forms, such as those that involve high levels of suffering or a lack of individual autonomy (e.g., life in a persistent vegetative state) are inhuman or undignified and therefore not worth living. If such situations are intolerable, then when individuals say, "I wouldn't want to live like that," the argument is that death or ending a life is to be preferred to those situations.

This argument depends on asserting that some form of life is so disvalued that it is less valuable than death. Widespread agreement about this is unlikely. For example, a powerful videotape (*Please Let Me Die*, 1974; compare Kliever, 1989; Platt, 1975; White & Engelhardt, 1975) depicts a young man who was burned over 67% of his body and was subjected to excruciatingly painful baths each day to prevent infection. The young man requested that his treatments be discontinued and that he be allowed to die. It has been argued that the young man and those around him could learn from his suffering; others have insisted that he was clearly competent and should have had the right to reject unwanted and painful interventions. Clearly, what one person counts as unbearable suffering someone else may not. However, there are also moral questions focused around someone's deciding that someone else's suffering is bearable or unbearable. It could be argued (though not everyone would agree even on this point) that each of us is in the best position to decide what is for us unbearable suffering and therefore no one else is in a position (and certainly not a better position than we are) to make such a judgment.

Arguments against Intentionally Ending a Human Life

Preservation of Life   One argument used to show that intentionally ending a human life is morally inappropriate is that it violates the caregiver's (and society's) *commitment to the preservation of life*. According to this argument, it is part of the caregiver's role as a provider of care to preserve life. Thus, if a caregiver deliberately behaves in such a way that the death of the person for whom he or she has been caring will result, then that caregiver has behaved immorally. That is, the person has not fulfilled in an appropriate manner his or her role as a provider of care.

This argument holds that life is good, that there is a *sanctity* to life. If so, we ought to preserve and support life whenever we can. A qualified form of this view might contend that life is valuable, but it is not the *preeminent* value. That is, it does not take precedence over *all* other values in *all* instances. As has been said, human life is sacred but not absolute in its value. If this is the view one holds, it will not be possible to decide whether aided deaths are morally acceptable (or even desirable) in some instances merely by appealing to the sanctity of life.

Slippery Slope Arguments   Another argument used against the morality of aided death is a *slippery slope argument*. It contends that once a decision is made to end someone's life for whatever reason, then one will have moved onto a slippery slope where it is all too easy to slide toward ending other people's lives for other reasons (e.g., Doughart, 2014; Smith, 2006). If it is too difficult to stop once one has begun to act in these ways, this argument contends that it is better not to begin at all—at least until some way of knowing where to stop has been established. However, it is not clear that the slide down this slope is inevitable. In many parts of our lives, we are able to make careful distinctions between one sort of situation and another. Why not here?

Additional Arguments   Others argue against aided death for the following reasons: medicine is at best an uncertain science. Wrong diagnoses and prognoses are made. Also, medicine moves quickly sometimes and nearly always with some degree of unpredictability. New therapies and new cures are discovered at unknown moments. So when one contemplates ending a person's life, there is always the possibility of a misdiagnosis or of the appearance of a new cure or therapy that might ease or even end that person's suffering. Furthermore, some suggest that aided deaths may undermine the trust that is essential to the physician/patient relationship or that they may detract from the role of the physician as healer and preserver of life.

These arguments have some weight. If that were not so, probably no one would ever have thought to advance them. Whether these arguments are persuasive in showing that one ought never to engage in aided death depends on *how much* weight one gives to them. Human wisdom is always imperfect; if one waits for complete certainty in any moral matter, one will seldom act at all. But not to decide is to decide. If one chooses not to engage in aided deaths, one might simply allow suffering to continue. Doing so involves its own danger. If a person's suffering is allowed to continue because of moral uncertainty or lack of clarity, there is a risk of becoming inured or hardened to suffering.

Further, although it is true that a new therapy or cure may come along at any time, it is not certain that such a discovery will help all persons with the particular disease or condition at issue. They may have progressed too far in the course of the disease, or their condition may involve other problems that the new therapy or cure can do nothing about. Thus, these issues are relevant but not necessarily decisive.

DECIDING TO END A HUMAN LIFE: SOME RELIGIOUS PERSPECTIVES

For many persons, religious teachings are important sources of beliefs about the morality of intentionally ending a human life. Therefore, it may help to review some religious teachings related to these issues. At the same time, we must note that most religious traditions are themselves complex. For example, it is not possible to state *the* Christian view of intentionally ending a human life because Christians disagree among themselves about this issue. Such disagreements can be found in almost all religious traditions. Because there is a danger of stereotyping persons and beliefs when only brief summaries of religious traditions are given, the following discussions should be understood as no more than abbreviated introductions to some of the unique beliefs in each tradition. These are some (not all) of the beliefs that might have an impact on how believers in that tradition think about the morality of aided death.

Judaism

Jewish teachings come from the Hebrew scriptures (what most Christians call the Old Testament), from oral traditions (the *Mishnah*), from commentaries on these earlier sources (the *Talmuds*), and from the decisions of rabbis throughout the centuries on specific situations. Important Jewish beliefs related to the morality of decisions to end a human life include the following: many Jews believe that God created and thus owns a person's body (Bleich, 1979). Thus, a person is caretaker of his or her body but has no right to do with it whatever he or she chooses. A second belief held by many Jews is that life is of infinite value, independent of its quality (Davis, 1994). Based on this view, the duty to preserve life is held to take precedence over almost all other human duties. Orthodox and Conservative Jews often find these to be the most significant teachings related to aided death, thus judging these acts to be morally unacceptable.

However, many Reform Jews (who are often more oriented toward secular Western moral views) hold that autonomy and self-determination are also values of primary importance. On this basis, these Jews often assert that it is individuals who have ultimate control over their bodies. Insofar as that is so, Reform Jews may be less critical of some forms of aided death.

Active euthanasia seems to be universally condemned by all Jewish groups (Rosner, 1979). Support for this condemnation is often traced to a teaching from the *Mishnah* (Shabbat, 23:5):

> They do not close the eyes of a corpse on the Sabbath, nor on an ordinary day at the moment the soul goes forth. And he who closes the eyes of a corpse at the moment the soul goes forth, lo, this one sheds blood. (Neusner, 1988, p. 207)

Using this statement from the *Mishnah* as its basis, the *Babylonian Talmud* (Tract Sabbath, p. 353) argued that one must not hasten death:

> The rabbis taught: Who closes the eyes of a dying man is like a murderer, for it is the same as a candle which is about to go out. If a man lays a finger on the dying flame, it immediately becomes extinguished, but if left alone would still burn for a little time. The same can be applied to the case of an expiring man; if his eyes were not closed, he would live a little longer, and hence it is like murder. (Rodkinson, 1896, p. 353)

Moses Maimonides (1949), a 12th-century Jewish physician/philosopher regarded by many Jews as a significant voice on moral issues, used a similar image:

> One who is in a dying condition is regarded as a living person in all respects.... He who touches him is guilty of shedding blood. To what may he be compared? To a flickering flame, which is extinguished as soon as one touches it. Whoever closes the eyes of the dying while the soul is about to depart is shedding blood. One should wait a while; perhaps he is only in a swoon. (*The Code of Maimonides*, Book 14, The Book of Judges, chapter 4, paragraph 5)

Thus, most Jews find only passive euthanasia to be morally acceptable, if they accept it at all.

Christianity

Christianity has three major branches: the Orthodox churches, Roman Catholicism, and Protestantism. These three branches are themselves complex. For example, there is no Protestant church as such, but rather dozens of Protestant denominations, all independent of each other. Although this complexity should always be kept in mind, Christians do share some basic beliefs, values, and practices.

Christians also share several beliefs with Judaism and Islam. Among these is the belief that since human life comes from God, it is inherently valuable, indeed sacred. However, Christians are also likely to emphasize that only God has absolute, ultimate value; human life does not. Christians identify the sacredness of this life in its bearing and manifesting the image and purpose of the Creator (Breck, 1995; Sacred Congregation for the Doctrine of the Faith, 1982). Christians also locate human dignity in considering each person to be an image of God (Cohen, 1996).

Uniquely Christian features arise from several other notions. As a Trinitarian faith, ultimate reality is understood by Christianity to be irreducibly relational (Harakas, 1993). Human beings are made for community with God and with each other; as Cicely Saunders (1970, p. 116) put it: "We belong with all other men (and) we belong with God also."

This essential interpersonal component of our humanness is also said to be revealed in the life of Jesus. Compassion and love for God and for his fellow human beings were central characteristics of Jesus' way of life. Much of his ministry involved healing, reducing the suffering of others. Since Christians are called to be an image of Christ, they too are to heal and, where that is not possible, to suffer with (be compassionate toward) others.

Some Christians hold that suffering is part of God's plan for all humans, whereas others find this belief difficult to fit with Jesus' emphasis on healing others (Breck, 1995). Suffering may be redemptive (bring individuals closer to each other and to God), but Christians are not required merely to accept it. One Christian document said of physical suffering that "human and Christian prudence suggest for the majority of sick people the use of medicines capable of alleviating or suppressing pain" (Sacred Congregation for the Doctrine of the Faith, 1982, p. 514). Christianity also teaches that we need not see ourselves as alone in our suffering; "in Jesus God was identified with (our) brokenness and suffering.... God in Christ ... has owned suffering for himself by undergoing it ... thus the sufferer is not alone" (Smith, 1986, p. 7).

Christianity also has an eschatological emphasis. This means that human life's "ultimate value and meaning lie outside itself, beyond the limits of earthly existence" (Breck, 1995, p. 325). Harakas (1993, p. 540) echoes this point: Christianity "does not see any of the strivings of this world as ultimate."

What this means for the issues under discussion in this chapter is that many Christians oppose any intentional killing of the types described in this chapter, whether of oneself or of others. Staying with, providing the necessary care to alleviate suffering, being compassionate toward each other: these are the desired goals for Christians faced with their own or someone else's death.

Islam

"Islam" means submission (to the will of Allah). Important Muslim beliefs include the following: Allah alone is God, and since Allah creates everything that exists, He is therefore the owner of every life. Thus, Muslims share with many Jews and Christians the belief that God alone may decide when a person's life is to end. Since suffering is used by Allah to remind human beings of their misdeeds and to lead them closer to Allah, to interfere with a person's suffering may also interfere with Allah's plan for that person (Hamel, 1991; Larue, 1985).

A Muslim's whole (public and private) life is ideally to be governed by Islamic law *(Shari'a)*. All Muslims accept the *Qur'an* and the *sunna* (practices and teachings) of Mohammed as sources of this law (Kelsay, 1994). Although there is no clearly stated position by Islamic leaders on aided death (Islam has no definitive hierarchy to issue such a statement), the general impression is that they would be disapproved. A *sura* (chapter) in the *Qur'an* (4:29) reads: "Do not destroy yourselves." Many commentators take this to refer not only to suicide but also to one Muslim killing another.

A statement from a 1981 conference in Kuwait is also relevant here:

> The doctor is well advised to realize his limit and not transgress it. If it is scientifically certain that life cannot be restored, then it is futile to diligently [maintain] the vegetative state of the patient by heroic means.... It is the process of life that the doctor aims to maintain and not the process of dying. In any case, the doctor shall not take positive measures to terminate the patient's life. (*Islamic Code of Medical Ethics*, First International Conference on Islamic Medicine, 1981, p. 10)

Hinduism

Hinduism is more like a cluster of various religious traditions than a single religion. As a group of various traditions, Hinduism has no central teaching authority or hierarchy. What most Hindus share is respect for the *Vedas* (scriptures, some of which may have been written as much as 3,500 years ago). Hindus may believe in creator gods, or they may believe that all reality is founded on Brahman, an impersonal, featureless entity from which rises all that is as waves rise from the ocean.

Many Hindus believe that most individuals will be reincarnated again and again, passing through death and rebirth through many lifetimes. The cause of these rebirths lies in one's *karma*, the actions one performs. One reaps inevitably and inexorably what one sows in one's actions. Thus, some Hindus believe that illness (life-threatening illness, in particular) is an effect of one's karma and must be suffered through to pay one's karmic debt (Crawford, 1995). If so, to end life before it has run its natural course may interfere with the process of working off this debt. Aided death would interfere with the karmic process and is thus undesirable.

However, other Hindus argue that this is a misunderstanding of karma (Crawford, 1995). If ending a human life interferes with the karmic process, then extending a human life through medical intervention interferes with that process, too. However, Hindus have developed a rich medical tradition (Ayurvedic medicine), and people who follow that tradition do not believe it is inappropriate to alleviate someone's suffering and to heal life-threatening diseases. In this view, one is not interfering with the effects of karma if one seeks or provides treatment or even perhaps ends a life.

Hinduism also emphasizes that one ought to avoid violence whenever possible. The Hindu term for this practice is *ahimsa*. *Ahimsa* is grounded in the view that life is sacred. Mohandas Gandhi taught that ahimsa is a central feature of a Hindu view of life. He explained what is meant by this term as follows: "*Ahimsa* does not simply mean non-killing. *Himsa* means causing pain to or killing any life out of anger, or from a selfish purpose, or with the intention of injuring it. Refraining from so doing is *ahimsa*" (quoted in Crawford, 1995, p. 115).

At first glance, the teaching on ahimsa seems to argue against aided death. But the intention in active euthanasia, for example, is to end suffering, not produce it. Gandhi (1980) himself used an example suggesting that intentionally ending a life might be compatible with the doctrine of ahimsa: "Should my child be attacked with rabies and there was no helpful remedy to relieve his agony, I should consider it my duty to take his life" (p. 84).

Thus, Hindu attitudes toward the intentional ending of human life are likely to be as diverse as Hinduism itself. One can locate teachings arguing against such actions and teachings supporting their use in some circumstances.

Buddhism

Buddhism differs from theistic religions in holding that there is no god who is creator of all that is. Its core doctrines include the beliefs that every action performed has consequences for the individual who performs it (karma), that one of the effects of one's actions (one's karma) is to cause one to be reincarnated again and again, and that life as we know it here is filled with suffering, so salvation lies ultimately in ending the cycle of rebirths. The Buddha also taught an eightfold path that helps one along the way to salvation. One of the precepts in this path is the rule never to kill a living creature. It is largely from this rule that Buddhist teaching on the intentional ending of human life is derived.

Because Buddhism holds that life is a basic good (in part because it is only in life—especially in a human life—that one may reach salvation), intentionally ending such a life is unacceptable (Keown, 1995). Some of the earliest scriptures of Buddhism offer teachings as to how Buddhist monks ought to live their lives. Some commentators use these teachings as a basis for Buddhist ethics in general (not only for monks). In the *Vinaya-Pitaka* (Book of Discipline), the Buddha is reported to have said:

> Whatever monk should intentionally deprive a human being of life or should look about so as to be his knife-bringer, or should praise the beauty of death, or should incite (anyone) to death, saying, 'Hullo there, my man, of what use to you is this evil, difficult life? Death is better for you than life,' or who should deliberately and purposefully in various ways praise the beauty of death or incite (anyone) to death: he also is one who is defeated, he is not in communion. (Horner, 1949, vol. 1, pp. 125–126)

The reference to being someone's "knife-bringer" could be understood as referring to either assisted suicide or active euthanasia. A monk who engages in such activity has failed in his religious/moral responsibilities (is defeated) and is to be excommunicated.

Although individual autonomy is also an important value in Buddhist thought (Becker, 1990), it cannot override the principle that life is a basic good. Preferring death to life is never morally acceptable (Keown, 1995).

Compassion *(karuna)* is a central virtue in Buddhism (Lecso, 1986), and thus to ease the suffering of someone is appropriate. This means that when someone is near death, one may use drugs that may have the effect of suppressing respiration and even lead to death. Also, one may legitimately not start or may remove therapies that simply prolong someone's dying. These are acts of compassion. However, one must not do this intending to cause death. What is forbidden is the intentional killing of someone.

SOME RECENT DEVELOPMENTS AND PROSPECTS FOR THE FUTURE

The issues discussed in this chapter are longstanding as shown by a detailed "History of the End-of-Life Choice Movement" (Compassion and Choices, 2016). Nor are these issues likely to disappear or be easily resolved in the future. For example, see the *Journal of the American Medical Association*, (2016, Vol. 315, No. 3, pp. 245–260) for an active debate in the form of several Viewpoint articles by physicians on aided death. In terms of formal social policy in the United States, a ballot initiative similar to the Oregon DWDA passed in November of 2008 in Washington State and the legislature approved a similar law in 2013 in Vermont. In addition, in December 2009, Montana's Supreme Court ruled nothing in the state's law prohibited a physician from honoring a terminally-ill, mentally competent patient's request by prescribing medication to hasten the patient's death and in January 2014 a New Mexico district court judge ruled terminally-ill, mentally competent residents have a constitutional right to request prescribed medication to shorten their suffering. In May 2015, the California Medical Association became the first state medical association to drop its opposition to aid in dying and legislation to authorize aided dying was signed into law in October of that year. In November 2016 voters in Colorado approved a ballot initiative authorizing aided death. However, many other states in the United States still have in force explicit bans against assisted suicide. Moreover, even in states where aided death has been legalized, some hospitals, hospices, and health care systems have opted out and some have forbidden affiliated physicians to write such prescriptions even if acting privately. Also, Medicare and the Department of Veterans Affairs do not allow assisted suicide.

Meanwhile, on February 6, 2015, the Supreme Court of Canada in a unanimous ruling struck down a 21-year-old ban on assisted suicide (Attaran, 2015; MacCharles, 2015; see also Downie, 2004). The Court declared that assisted suicide is constitutional in Canada for consenting adults under a physician's care who determine they cannot tolerate the physical or psychological suffering brought on by a severe, incurable illness, disease, or disability. The ruling is not limited to disabled individuals who are unable to kill themselves unaided, nor to cases of terminal illness or people near death. Instead, the ruling applies broadly in cases of a major illness, disease, or disability that inflict intolerable physical or psychological suffering on a patient (Kim & Lemmens, 2016). Specifically, the court declared the right to life enshrined in Canada's constitution does not mean individuals "cannot 'waive' their right to life." The court said nothing in its ruling would compel a physician to act against his or her conscience or religious beliefs. In June 2016, the federal legislature in Canada passed a bill authorizing assisted suicide for those who: are eligible for government-funded health care (thus limiting assisted suicide to Canadians and permanent residents); are mentally component adults age 18 or older; have a serious and incurable disease, illness, or disability; and are in an advanced state of irreversible decline with enduring and intolerable suffering (An example of what was involved in establishing a hospital-based program of medical assistance in dying in Toronto is provided by Li et al., 2017).

Elsewhere, the Belgian parliament legalized euthanasia in May of 2002 for individuals with both a terminal and a non-terminal illness (Chambere, Vander Stichele, Mortier, Cohen, & Deliens, 2015). Although the law requires consent on the part of the patient, in practice it has been extended to individuals unable to give explicit voluntary consent (Aviv, 2015). In December 2013, the Parliament passed an amendment to the Belgium Act on Euthanasia that authorizes euthanasia for terminally-ill children who are experiencing "constant and unbearable suffering" (Dan, Fonteyne, & Clément de Cléty, 2014; Siegel, Sisti, & Caplan, 2014). With the support of a majority of Belgians and having been signed into law by the King in February 2014, the amendment requires both parental consent and the child's explicit and voluntary consent. There is no age limit specified, but the law requires that a multidisciplinary team examine the child's "capacity for discernment," that is his or her understanding of the consequences of euthanasia. Children with intellectual disability or mental illness are excluded. Some offer alternatives or describe these changes in Belgium as classic examples of sliding down a slippery slope (e.g., Carter, 2016; Hain, 2014).

In fact, as medical technology advances and individual and social attitudes change, more people may find themselves in situations wherein they seriously question the quality of life offered by continued medical interventions and wish to take control of end-of-life decisions, either for themselves or for others about whom they care. For example, Brittany Maynard, a 29-year-old woman with a diagnosis of glioblastoma, a deadly form of brain cancer, moved from her home in California to Oregon in order to take advantage of the provisions of the DWDA. Fearing a particularly painful way to die, Maynard ended her life on November 1, 2014.

From the standpoint of health care providers, many may find themselves in situations in which those for whom they are caring ask for assistance in ending their lives. It is already clear that especially difficult challenges appear in cases involving: (1) individuals who are not regarded as competent to make any formal decision on these or other matters (such as infants, children, or the mentally ill); (2) those who once were thought to be competent but who did not then make known their wishes about conditions under which they might want to continue or end their lives (such as those now in an irreversible coma or persistent vegetative state); and (3) when the issues involve assisted suicide, active euthanasia, aid in dying, or the removal not only of external support (e.g., a respirator) but also of artificially assisted nutrition and hydration (Lynn, 1986; Tomlinson, Spector, Nurock, & Stott, 2015).

Finally, it is likely that more efforts will be made to legitimize and seek social approval for various forms of aided death in some form of public policy. In this process, individual citizens, their elected representatives, and the court systems in their societies will be called upon to make decisions concerning policies and practices like those described in this chapter. Meanwhile, decisions about these matters will continue to be made in individual circumstances. That is, situations will arise in which individuals cannot avoid deciding whether to (help) end the life of another and, if so, how. In short, whether as a matter of public policy or in individual cases, *someone will decide*. Many are most concerned about this latter point—who will or ought to decide whether assistance of these types can, should, or will be provided. However, although the question of identifying appropriate decision makers is significant, the grounds for making moral decisions are the most fundamental matter. In addition, questions of who will carry out these decisions (physicians, family members, etc.)—whatever the grounds and whoever the decision maker may be—will need to be addressed, as will what kind of psychological or social impact such actions might create on others (Werth, 1999a; Werth & Blevins, 2009).

Summary

In this chapter, we examined issues related to aided death, that is, intentionally ending a human life. We began by giving special attention to assisted suicide and euthanasia. We sought to define these two concepts and the central ideas to which they are linked. In this process, we focused on two key issues: the agent who takes the decisive action and the intention behind whatever action is taken. In addition, we explored the distinction between voluntariness and nonvoluntariness, contrasts between ending a life actively or passively, and the difference between ordinary and extraordinary means of treatment. During this discussion, we also considered the concept of "aid in dying" and we asked readers to ponder whether this is a separate category in end-of-life situations. In order to clarify the real-life implications of these issues, we explored two examples from social policy and practices in Oregon and the Netherlands.

Then our focus shifted to arguments for and against intentionally ending a human life, arguments drawn from general moral or philosophical premises, as well as from perspectives arising from five of the world's great religions. In presenting these arguments and perspectives, we recognized that none of them was without potential objection and that easy answers to the issues addressed were unlikely for most people. However, this does not mean that no answers of any sort are available. Obviously, many people have different positions on various aspects of this subject. Thoughtful positions in this complex conceptual and moral arena of human life require careful and sustained reflection.

Finally, we suggested that these topics are likely in the future to grow in importance for individual decision makers and for social policy. We illustrated such possibilities by noting developments in other states in the United States, decisions by the Supreme Court and the federal legislature in Canada, and new legislation in Belgium that authorizes voluntary euthanasia for terminally-ill children

Our primary concern throughout this discussion has been to help individuals think about this subject as clearly as possible before they are forced to confront it in their own lives and to suggest some possible options in these aspects of end-of-life care.

Glossary

Active euthanasia: taking direct action to end suffering by ending the life of a suffering person

Aid in dying: actions in which an individual who has already been determined to be dying and to have only a limited time to live obtains from a physician a prescription for lethal medications and uses those medications to end his or her life

Assisted suicide: actions in which one person intentionally acts to end his or her life and secures assistance from another individual who intends to help the first person achieve that result

The Dutch Termination of Life on Request and Assisted Suicide (Review Procedures) Act: legislation that exempts from criminal liability physicians who terminate life on request or assist in a patient's suicide in accordance with the due care and notification criteria set forth in the law

Euthanasia: literally, "a good death"; now mainly refers to situations in which one individual contributes to the death of another person in order to end the suffering of that second person

Extraordinary means of treatment: interventions to sustain life that do not have predictable and well-recognized outcomes; offer unusual risks, suffering, or burdens for the person being treated or for others; and may not be effective

Nonvoluntary euthanasia: euthanasia performed when the wishes of the person who dies are unknown

Ordinary means of treatment: interventions to support life that have predictable and well-recognized outcomes; offer no unusual risk, suffering, or burden for the person being treated or for others; and are effective

Oregon "Death with Dignity Act": legislation specifying the conditions under which a terminally ill, adult resident of Oregon is permitted to request that a physician provide a prescription for lethal medication that the individual can use to end his or her life

Passive euthanasia: allowing someone to die by either not doing (withholding) or omitting (withdrawing) some action that is necessary to sustain life

Physician-assisted suicide: a form of assisted suicide in which it is a physician who intentionally provides the assistance that a person needs and uses to end his or her life

Voluntary euthanasia: euthanasia performed at the request of the person who dies

Questions for Review and Discussion

1. In this chapter, we suggested that humans value such things as freedom, privacy, persons, religious traditions, life, self-respect, justice, and a good life. Which of these are most important to you? Why? Which, if any, of these would you be sacrifice to preserve some other more important value(s)? Why? Relate your responses to the issue of deciding whether to assist someone who is incurably ill to die.

2. Would you be willing to assist someone to end his or her life if that person: (1) was not dying (i.e., any disease condition the person had would not cause his or her death); (2) was suffering great emotional distress; or (3) was suffering great physical distress that could not be relieved? What values led to your responses to these questions?

3. In this chapter, we described arguments to support the moral appropriateness of various forms of aided death, as well as arguments against their moral appropriateness. Which of these arguments do you find most compelling? Which are least persuasive to you? Why?

4. Would you support a law allowing physicians to undertake actions involving some type of aided death? Why or why not?

5. Have you ever turned to social media or the Internet to learn more about the subjects discussed in this chapter? Were your searches helpful? Why or why not?

Suggested Readings

Battin, M. P. (Ed.). (1994). *The Least Worst Death: Essays in Bioethics on the End of Life*

Battin, M. P. (1996). *The Death Debate: Ethical Issues in Suicide*

Battin, M. P. (2005). *Ending Life: Ethics and the Way We Die*

Battin, M. P., Rhodes, R., & Silvers, A. (Eds.). (1998). *Physician Assisted Suicide: Expanding the Debate*

Beauchamp, T. L. (Ed.). (1996). *Intending Death: The Ethics of Assisted Suicide and Euthanasia*

Beauchamp, T. L., & Childress, J. F. (2001). *Principles of Biomedical Ethics*

Berlinger, N., Jennings, B., & Wolf, S. M. (2013). *The Hastings Center Guidelines for Decisions on Life-Sustaining Treatment and Care near the End of Life* (2nd ed.)

Camenisch, P. F. (Ed.). (1994). *Religious Methods and Resources in Bioethics*

Cohen-Almagor, R. (2010). *Euthanasia in the Netherlands: The Policy and Practice of Mercy Killing*

Colby, W. H. (2002). *Long Goodbye: The Deaths of Nancy Cruzan*

Colby, W. H. (2006). *Unplugged: Reclaiming Our Right to Die in America*

Doka, K. J., Jennings, B., & Corr, C. A. (Eds.). (2005). *Living with Grief: Ethical Dilemmas at the End of Life*

Emanuel, L. L. (1998). *Regulating How We Die: The Ethical, Medical, and Legal Issues Surrounding Physician Assisted Suicide*

Foley, K. M., & Hendin, H. (Eds.). (2002). *The Case against Assisted Suicide: For the Right to End-of-Life Care*

Gordon, P. S. (2016). *Psychosocial Interventions in End-of-Life Care: The Hope for a "Good Death"*

Gorsuch, N. M. (2009). *The Future of Assisted Suicide and Euthanasia*

Hamel, R. (Ed.). (1991). *Choosing Death: Active Euthanasia, Religion, and the Public Debate*

Jamison, S. (1995). *Final Acts of Love: Families, Friends, and Assisted Dying*

Lewy, G. (2011). *Assisted Death in Europe and America: Four Regimes and Their Lessons*

McKhann, C. F. (1999). *A Time to Die: The Place for Physician Assistance*

Post, S. (Ed.). (2004). *Encyclopedia of Bioethics* (3rd ed.)

Randall, F., & Downie, R. (2010). *End of Life Choices: Consensus and Controversy*

Rehmann-Sutter, C., Gudat, H., & Ohnsorge, K. (Eds.). (2015). *The Patient's Wish to Die: Research, Ethics, and Palliative Care*

Schotsmans, P., & Meulenbergs, T. (Eds.). (2005). *Euthanasia and Palliative Care in the Low Countries*

Smith, W. J. (2006). *Forced Exit: Euthanasia, Assisted Suicide and the New Duty to Die*

Weir, R. F. (Ed.). (1997). *Physician-Assisted Suicide*

Werth, J. L. (Ed.). (1999b). *Contemporary Perspectives on Rational Suicide*

Werth, J. L., & Blevins, D. (Eds.). (2009). *Decision Making Near the End of Life: Issues, Developments, and Future Directions*

Selected Web Resources

Some useful search terms include: ACTIVE EUTHANASIA; AIDED DEATH; AID IN DYING; ARTIFICAL NUTRITION AND HYDRATION; ASSISTED SUICIDE; DEATH WITH DIGNITY; EUTHANASIA; NONVOLUNTARY EUTHANASIA; PASSIVE EUTHANASIA; PERSISTENT (OR PERMANENT) VEGETATIVE STATE; PHYSICIAN-ASSISTED SUICIDE; VOLUNTARY EUTHANASIA.

You can also visit the following *organizational and other Internet sites:*

American Journal of Bioethics (published by Taylor and Francis, Ltd.)

American Society for Bioethics and Humanities (ASBH)

American Society of Law, Medicine, and Ethics (ASLME)

The Center for Bioethics and Culture (CBC)

Center for Ethics in Health Care, Oregon Health and Sciences University

The Center for Practical Bioethics

Compassion and Choices

Death with Dignity National Center

Dying with Dignity Canada

The Hastings Center

Kennedy Institute of Ethics, Georgetown University

Cengage Learning, Inc.

The Meaning and Place of Death in Life

Objectives of this **Chapter**

▷ To explore issues related to the meaning of death

▷ To examine selected religious and philosophical ideas about the afterlife and the meaning of death

▷ To examine the content and interpretation of near-death experiences

▷ To consider the place of death in human life

THE BUDDHA ON THE PLACE OF DEATH IN HUMAN EXPERIENCE

The following tale is drawn from Buddhist scriptures. It occurs in various forms; the one presented here draws on several sources.

> A young woman named Gotami had a son. But when he had barely begun to walk, he died. Overcome by grief, she carried the dead boy from one house to another, begging people if they had some medicine for her son. At one house, an old man told her that there was one person who could give her medicine, Gautama (the Buddha).
>
> Gotami went to the Buddha and asked him for medicine for her dead child. He told her that he did know of such a medicine. She was to gather a little mustard seed from each house in the village that had not been touched by death. She went from house to house, but all in vain: nowhere did she find a family that had not known death.
>
> She now began to reflect: "I thought that my son alone had been overtaken by this thing which people call death. But I was wrong. This happens to everyone" (paraphrased from Burtt, 1955, pp. 45–46). She now understood that everything that exists is impermanent and eventually passes away.
>
> After giving her son over to the funeral rites, Gotami returned to the Buddha. He asked her if she had brought the medicine he required. She told him no, that she knew now that all people die. The Buddha said to her: "All living beings resemble the flame of these lamps, one moment lighted, the next extinguished." (Ballou, 1944, p. 143)

THE MEANING OF DEATH

Almost all human beings eventually come up against an inescapable fact about themselves and the persons they love: they are mortal. For many persons, as for Gotami in our vignette, this fact raises questions of meaning: Why are we born? What is the meaning of our having lived? What is the impact of our death on the value and significance of our life? In short, what is the relationship between life and death? Are they simply opposites so that where there is death, there can be no life (Terkel, 2001)? Or is their relationship more complex than this?

These questions form part of our human reality. As the Buddha told Gotami, the fact of eventual death is common to all forms of life. But human beings can think about or reflect on this fact and its implications beforehand. The ability to know in advance that one will die is perhaps unique to human beings. Awareness of death is especially sharpened when our security is threatened, for example, when we are confronted by mass homicides (see Chapter 4 and Issues for Critical Reflection #17).

In fact, issues related to the meaning of death and its place in human life have been claimed to underlie almost all human activity. For instance, Socrates said that "those who really apply themselves in the right way to philosophy are directly and of their own accord preparing themselves for dying and death" (Plato, 1961, p. 46; *Phaedo*, 64a), and he argued this meant that everything human beings do in life is finally to be evaluated by testing it against the fact of their mortality. If he was right, then everything we have considered in this book (e.g., how to treat dying and bereaved persons, suicide, or aided death, in fact all reflective actions related to death and dying) originates from more basic questions about the meaning of mortality. For instance, to say that people should care for dying persons in one way rather than in another way finds part of its justification in beliefs about death. If one believes that

ISSUES FOR CRITICAL REFLECTION
#17 Violent Incidents and Our Security

Numerous examples of mass murders in the United States are set forth in Issues for Critical Reflection #6 in Chapter 4 in this book, although this is by no means a complete list of such events in recent years. Analysis of these and similar events often focuses on how society can prevent such deadly events. This directs attention to what some have claimed is an inevitable component of being a human person: anxiety about death. As some have said: "We would like to think that violence and tragedy are avoidable so we can feel less anxious about life." But this is always to some degree an illusion. Total security from violence and tragedy—including death—cannot be achieved.

Our desire for security from threats to our very existence arises on several levels. On the surface, there are questions about what society can do to protect its citizens from violence and "meaningless" death. To the extent that society can, with reasonable means, achieve such protection, those means should be pursued and encouraged. They will always, however, be limited in their effectiveness; no society can protect *every* citizen in *every* situation from *every* threat of death.

But at a deeper level, our insecurity in the face of violence reveals what philosophers and religious teachers have often described as an inescapable condition of being human: we are, as Martin Heidegger (1962) put it, beings onto death. In most of our everyday lives, we are able to keep this condition below the surface of our awareness. However, when we are forcibly confronted with that inevitability (as in the incidents cited here), almost everyone experiences some anxiety facing that very inescapability. And there is nothing civil society can do to alleviate this *essential* insecurity about our being. To cope with this anxiety, we need something other than civil laws or civic responses: here philosophy and religion must go to work, if anything is to help.

Confronted by this essential truth about ourselves, we often respond in one of two ways. We may experience an anxiety that almost overwhelms us. Or we may take notice of the reality that our lives will one day come to an end and recognize that this makes every moment of our lives precious. In other words, when we face the inevitability of our death authentically, in that same moment the preciousness of our lives is also realized in a profound way. Thus, as we have suggested throughout this book, our death and the preciousness of our life are wholly intertwined.

death is always and everywhere to be disvalued and if one holds that death is the greatest evil known, this belief is likely to affect how one faces and deals with dying persons. If one believes there can be something worse than death, that too will influence how one acts in these situations.

Possible Responses to These Questions

As human beings have reflected on questions raised by death, they have responded in many different ways (e.g., Becker, 1973; Grof & Halifax, 1978). The ancient Chinese Yin/Yang symbol at the beginning of this chapter provides one response to these questions. It suggests that life (represented by the light portion of the symbol—the Yang) and death (represented by the dark portion of the symbol—the Yin) interpenetrate each other; the Yin overlaps and intrudes into the space of the Yang and vice versa. More than this, at the very *center* of the Yin is the Yang, and again, vice versa. Thus, this symbol suggests that wherever there is life, there is death, and wherever there is death, there is life.

Another response to these questions has involved the attempt to understand just what happens after death (Adams, 2004; Toynbee et al., 1976). Art, popular culture (Bertman, 1991; Bolton, 2007), folk tales (Gignoux, 1998), anthropology (Reynolds & Waugh, 1977), literature (Enright, 1983; Koppelman, 2011; Weir, 1980), philosophy (Carse, 1980; Choron, 1963, 1964), religion (Johnson & McGee, 1998; Obayashi, 1992), and theology (Gatch, 1969; Mills, 1969; Rahner, 1973) have all provided suggestions related to this question. Indeed, some of the best thinking ever done by humans has focused on such issues. In the works of such thinkers as Socrates and Albert Camus, Paul of Tarsus and Muhammad, the writer of *Ecclesiastes* and the writer of the *Bhagavad Gita* can be found examples of attempts to address the disturbing implications of death in human life.

DEATH: A DOOR OR A WALL?

Feifel (1977b) simplified (perhaps overly so) how humans are likely to think about death when he wrote that death can be portrayed as either a door or a wall. He meant that when one looks at death, one can ask oneself what one sees. Is death simply the cessation of life? Is it the case that where death intrudes, life is irrevocably lost? If so, death is something we all will come up against, and it will mean the end of everything one does or can know. It is a wall into which one crashes and through which one cannot pass.

However, some people believe that death is a stage along life's way. It is a river to cross, a stair to climb, a door through which to pass. If this is one's view, then death may be seen not as the irrevocable opposite to life but rather as a passage from one sort (or stage) of life to another.

Most people hold one or the other of these beliefs. Of course, these ideas and beliefs may be unconscious or not thought through clearly. But if one is (for example) afraid of death, that fear is based on some notion of the meaning of death, such as "I will never see loved ones again," or "I will never experience a sunset like that again," or "I will be punished for my sins," or "I may be reborn into a life of poverty." Since most of us have some sort of reaction to the fact of death—happiness or sadness, fear or anticipation—we also have some beliefs about its meaning, whether they are overt or unstated.

Note that the evaluation one makes of death is not tied in any obvious way to whether one sees it as a door or as a wall. One can think of death as a wall and evaluate that as good: for example, at least all suffering is over. One can see death as a door and evaluate that as evil: for example, it may bring eternal torment or a shadowy, shallow form of life. And, of course, some would see death as a wall as something evil (e.g., all that I value is over) or death as a door as something good (e.g, as an entryway to a different, better form of life). The point is that how one thinks of death is tied in important ways to how one values it.

ALTERNATIVE IMAGES OF AN AFTERLIFE

Exploring some of the principal alternative religious or philosophical images that human beings have employed to try to understand how death and life are related enriches our own thinking about these questions. Here we examine several of these images and their intended responses to questions like: Is *this life* all there is? Is death the irrevocable loss of any sort of life? It soon becomes clear that human beings have tried to respond to these questions in quite an astonishing array of ways (Toynbee, 1968b). Thus, we can only briefly consider here several of the best known of these ways.

Greek Concepts of the Afterlife

More than 400 years before the birth of Christ, the philosopher Socrates lived in the city-state of Athens. When he was 70 years old, some of his critics brought charges against him for not believing in the official state gods and for corrupting the youth by teaching them to challenge the beliefs of their elders. Socrates was found guilty of these charges and condemned to death.

After these actions by the jury, Socrates described what death meant to him. He said he believed that humans cannot *know* what death means in terms of our continued existence. Instead, he maintained that all people are left with *beliefs* on this point. On this most pressing question, Socrates contended that we can only make a choice to believe on less than demonstrative proof.

Socrates finally was content not to decide just what death means for our continued existence. Perhaps that was in part due to the options he presented for what death might involve. (Look at what he said about this, in Personal Insights 19.1.) If death is either a permanent sleep (unconsciousness) or a form of life in which one meets old friends and can make new ones, then death need not appear to be frightening or threatening.

But these scenarios do not exhaust the possibilities. Another ancient Greek, Homer, provided a different, less happy description of the afterlife. At one point in Homer's *Odyssey*, Odysseus calls up another Greek hero (Achilles) from his afterlife in **Hades**. Achilles says about that life, "No winning words about death to me.... By god, I'd rather slave on earth for another man—some dirt-poor tenant farmer who scrapes to keep alive—than rule down here over all the breathless dead" (Homer, 1996, p. 265). Achilles says this because Hades is described as an unhappy place; the dead have no sense or feeling and are mere "phantoms."

A third view found in ancient Greek sources is that of the **immortality of the soul**. This view appears in the writings of Plato, who sometimes represented human

---

PERSONAL INSIGHTS 19.1

Socrates' Thoughts about the Meaning of Death

This thing that has come upon me must be a good; and those of us who think that death is an evil must needs be mistaken.... For the state of death is one of two things: either the dead man wholly ceases to be and loses all consciousness or ... it is a change and a migration of the soul to another place. And if death is the absence of all consciousness, and like the sleep of one whose slumbers are unbroken by any dreams, it will be a wonderful gain.... For it appears that all time is nothing more than a single night. But if death is a journey to another place, and what we are told is true—that all who have died are there—what good could be greater than this? ... What would you not give to converse with Orpheus and Musaeus and Hesiod and Homer? ... It would be an inexpressible happiness to converse with [heroes such as these] and to live with them and to examine them.

Source: Plato (1948, pp. 47–48), *Apology,* 40b–41a.

beings as made up of two parts, a body (earthly, mortal) and a soul (immortal). Plato offered arguments intended to prove the inherent immortality of the soul. For Plato, souls are essentially immortal, deathless by their very nature. Nothing can cause a soul not to be; thus it must exist forever. Because humans (and all bodies that move "of themselves"—i.e., animals) are in part souls, death must mean only the separation of the body and the soul. It does not mean the end of the soul.

Greek thought provided one major strand of Western beliefs about the relationship of life and death. Another major strand came from the Judeo-Christian tradition and its biblical scriptures.

Some Western Religious Beliefs

Many different beliefs about an afterlife are expressed in the Hebrew and Christian scriptures. Bailey (1978) found the following notions associated with an afterlife in those texts:

1. "Immortality" is sometimes associated only with divine beings (1 Timothy 6:16).
2. Sometimes "deathlessness" is seen as being given by the gods to specific human beings (e.g., Enoch in Genesis 5:24 and Elijah in 2 Kings 2:1–12).
3. An afterlife might be related to a phantom-like existence, a sort of "diminished life." (Compare Achilles' description of Hades noted earlier.) Some people have found this view present in Saul's consultations with a witch, who calls up Samuel from the afterworld (see 1 Samuel 28).
4. Ongoing life after death is often linked to what is left behind at one's death, for example, one's children.

Actually, the notion of the individual surviving death is only rarely encountered in the Hebrew scriptures. If there is a notion of ongoing life after death, it is found in the community and in one's own descendants: I may die, but my community will go on. I may die, but my children and their children will go on. It is the community's life that is important and the ongoing life of the familial line that is significant (Bowker, 1991).

In fact, it is even uncertain whether the Greek notion of a soul discussed earlier is found in the Hebrew scriptures. The Hebrew word often translated as "soul" *(nepesh)* means most simply "life." It is necessarily tied up with a body. Thus, at death, the **nepesh** ceases to exist because it is no longer bound up with a particular body. Eichrodt (1967) reports that various images are used: at death, the *nepesh* "dies; at the same time it is ... feasible to think of it leaving a man at death, though this does not mean that one can ask where it has gone! ... It is described as having been taken or swept away" (p. 135). He added: "In no instance does there underlie the use of *nepes* [a] conception of an immortal *alter ego*.... Equally remote from the concept ... is the signification of a numinous substance in Man who survives death" (p. 140). If this is correct, then the notion of an immortal soul is not part of the original Judaic tradition. In fact, Eichrodt holds that this idea entered Judaic thought much later, under the influence of Hellenic (Greek) culture.

The Hebrew scriptures provided another image of an afterlife—the image of resurrection. This image grows out of the Judaic belief that the human being is not a combination of two different sorts of entities, a body and a soul; each of us is rather an integrated whole. To be a human being is not to be a soul entombed in a body as Plato claimed in some of his dialogues; it is to be a living body. Life in this view cannot be understood *except* as embodied. (Islam sometimes teaches this precept, too; see Muwahidi, 1989, pp. 40–41). Thus, if there is to be a life after death, it must be an embodied life. That is what *resurrection* means: it refers to the "raising up" of a human being as a living body. This raising up would require a new action by God—namely, a recreation of the human being.

Western religion has also often associated an afterlife with the concepts of **heaven and hell**. These concepts are well developed in Islam. According to Islam, at a last judgment each individual's behavior while living in this world will be judged. If a person submits to Allah ("Islam" means "to submit"), rewards will be waiting after death. If a person rebels against Allah, punishments will be waiting. These rewards or punishments are often described vividly:

> For those that fear the majesty of their lord there are two gardens … planted with shady trees.… Each is watered by a flowering spring.… Each bears every kind of fruit.… They shall recline on couches lined with thick brocade … there shall wait on them immortal youths with bowls and ewers and a cup of purest wine.… And theirs shall be the dark-eyed houris, chaste as hidden pearls … those [who are cursed] shall dwell amongst scorching winds and seething water: in the shade of pitch-black smoke. (*Qur'an*, 1993, 55:35–56:55)

Similar concepts can be identified in Christianity, in Hinduism, and in some forms of Buddhism.

Islam has other beliefs that are of interest here. Sakr (1995) and Smith and Haddad (2002) reported that for Islam there is a form of life in the grave. The soul of the person who has died is believed to visit the grave regularly to receive reward or punishment. The "grave is a center of transformation, a center of molding, a center of reshaping, a center of preparation, and a place of resynthesis" (Sakr, 1995, p. 59).

Other cultures, however, have quite different beliefs.

A casket containing the body of Muhammad Ali, who died on June 3, 2016, at the age of 74, arrives in Louisville for an Islamic prayer service.

John Moore/Getty Images News/Getty Images

Some African Beliefs

The continent of Africa contains many cultures, and the philosophical and theological beliefs of the people in these various cultures have not been extensively described or studied. However, some preliminary generalizations have been made (Mbiti, 1970).

In general, for many of these people, the power that makes life possible is everywhere the same—in plants, in animals, and in human beings (Opoku, 1978, 1987). So human life is part of nature, and it is a constant cyclic process of becoming (as is nature). This process has certain distinguishing moments or turning points in it: birth, adolescence, marriage, and death. But each of these crises only marks a particular point in the process of becoming. Those in the community who are alive are in one stage; those who are the **living-dead** (i.e., those who are not living as we are here) are simply in a further stage. The community contains both the living and the living-dead. The living-dead are not thought of as being in another world; they are only in a different part of this world. The transition to this other part of the world is sometimes symbolized as a land journey, often including the crossing of a river, perhaps because rivers form natural boundaries between one part of the natural world and another part. This view typically does not include a notion of a heaven (a life of bliss) or of a hell (a life of torment).

The living-dead, in this view, are quasi-material beings. As ancestors, they are prized and respected. Their lives are those of serenity and dignity, given over to concern for the well-being of the living members of their families and clans. Thus, the family extends into this other world.

These are images drawn from a people living in close contact with nature. There is no notion of a pale, empty afterlife, as seen in Homer. Nor is there a notion of resurrection or of heaven or hell. The afterlife portrayed here is a simple, natural continuation of the life we know. There *are* differences, just as living in the desert on this side of the river is different from living in the forest on the other side of the river. However, the life of the living-dead is not a wholly foreign existence. It is not a threatening one, quite different from fear of the dead said to be found in some "primitive" religions (Frazer, 1977).

Some African Americans share this sort of belief. Sullivan (1995) reported that for such persons the dead and the living have reciprocal functions that create a unified whole. For these persons, to "pass on" is to be involved in "movement," a change in form whereby one moves on to the world of the ancestors.

Hindu and Buddhist Beliefs

When Westerners think about the philosophical and theological beliefs of the people of the Indian subcontinent, perhaps the notion that most often springs to mind is **reincarnation.** (A variety of terms are associated with this idea: *transmigration of souls, metempsychosis, rebirth;* we treat these terms here as if they are interchangeable.) This is a very ancient idea, one that can sometimes be found in Western thought, too. For example, ideas like this are found in some of Plato's dialogues. However, the idea of reincarnation is certainly older than Plato's writings (from the fourth century BCE).

The first writings that discuss the idea of reincarnation go back at least to the seventh century BCE. One Hindu scripture (the *Katha Upanishad*) contains the following passage (Radhakrishnan & Moore, 1957, pp. 45–46):

A Hindu funeral pyre in Calcutta, India, on February 19, 2012.

WIN-Initiative/Photolibrary/Getty Images

> The wise one … is not born, nor dies.
> This one has not come from anywhere, has not become anyone.
> Unborn, constant, eternal, primeval, this one
> Is not slain when the body is slain.
> If the slayer think to slay,
> If the slain think himself slain,
> Both these understand not.
> Know thou the self *(atman)* as riding in a chariot,
> The body as the chariot…
> He … who has not understanding,
> Who is unmindful and ever impure,
> Reaches not the goal,
> But goes on to transmigration.…
> He … who has understanding,
> Who is mindful and ever pure,
> Reaches the goal
> From which he is born no more…

This passage expresses several important characteristics of a Hindu view of the human being. Humans are essentially an unborn, undying soul (**atman**). This soul is repeatedly incarnated in bodies (and not necessarily always in human bodies, but also in "lower" forms). What body the soul is incarnated into depends on what one has done in previous lives. "Unmindfulness," "impurity," and a lack of understanding about the nature of reality will lead to transmigration of the soul from one body or one sort of body to another. But transmigration necessarily brings with it suffering, so the goal is to end transmigration, or rebirth. Perhaps one of the clearest statements of this view is found in the *Bhagavad Gita*. It contains the teachings of the lord Krishna (a god) to a human being (Arjuna). Arjuna is agonized about the killing that occurs in war, but Krishna tells him:

> Wise men do not grieve for the dead or for the living.… Never was there a time when I was not, nor thou … nor will there ever be a time hereafter when we shall cease to be.… Just as a person casts off worn-out garments and puts on others that are new, even so does the embodied soul cast off worn-out bodies and take on others that are new. (Radhakrishnan, 1948, pp. 102–108)

If this is so, then what does it tell people about how to live their lives here? Krishna answers:

> Endowed with a pure understanding, firmly restraining oneself, turning away from sound and other objects of sense and casting aside attraction, and aversion.… Dwelling in solitude, eating but little, controlling speech, body, and mind … taking refuge in dispassion … casting aside self-sense, force, arrogance, desire, anger, possession, egoless, and tranquil in mind, he becomes worthy of becoming one with *Brahman*. (Radhakrishnan, 1948, p. 370)

That is, right living can lead to an end of the rebirths and to complete peace or union with a transcendent reality.

After death, three possibilities exist: (1) the *atman* may be in one of the heavens, awaiting rebirth; (2) the *atman* is immediately reborn; or (3) the *atman* is in a state of eternal bliss with Brahman (the transcendent reality), having achieved liberation from the cycle of rebirths.

The founder of Buddhism (Siddhartha Gautama) was raised as a Hindu but eventually found its practices and beliefs unacceptable. After years of spiritual struggle, he experienced an awakening (thus becoming the Buddha—the enlightened one). As the Buddha, he taught that all is impermanence; nothing (not even a soul) exists in some eternal, unchanging condition (see Focus On 19.1 for an expression of this viewpoint in a death-related book for children). This fact produces suffering for everything that is aware of it. For human beings, "birth is suffering; sickness is suffering; death is suffering; sorrow and lamentation, pain, grief, and despair are suffering; association with the unpleasant is suffering; dissociation from the pleasant is suffering; not to get what one wants is suffering" (Rahula, 1974, p. 93). As long as

---

FOCUS ON 19.1

A Buddhist Perspective in a Book for Children

First Snow (Coutant, 1974) is a book about a young girl named Liên who has recently come with her family from Vietnam to live in a small town in New England. Liên is impatiently waiting to experience snow for the first time when she overhears her parents say, "Grandmother is dying." No one really answers Liên when she asks, "What does it mean that Grandmother is dying?" Finally, one day her grandmother tells Liên to go out into the garden and hold her hand up to heaven to discover for herself what dying means. When a snowflake lands on her finger, Liên appreciates it as a tiny, fleeting thing that is both beautiful and delicate. Then when the sun causes the edges of the snowflake to burst into a thousand tiny rainbows, it changes to a drop of water and falls on the ground where it nourishes a tiny pine tree. All of this affirms Liên's Buddhist beliefs that life and death are but two parts of the same thing.

one fails to recognize this fact—and to confront and transcend it—one will live again and again, reincarnated into one suffering body after another. In this condition of ignorance about the true, impermanent nature of all reality, death is an evil because it only leads to rebirth into another life of suffering. Ideally, by transcending desire, one can escape the wheel of rebirths, achieving **nirvana**, a state beyond desire and thus beyond suffering, a state serene and peaceful (Radhakrishnan & Moore, 1957).

A Common Concern in Images of an Afterlife

The various concepts we have described about what happens after death range from a permanent sleep (unconsciousness) through recreation in an embodied form (resurrection) and on to a "blowing out" or a condition of absolute stillness. Some of these pictures seem threatening: a hell involving punishment or a Hades as it is described in Homer. Some seem attractive: meeting old companions or eternal joy in a heavenly state. Some provide a sense of peace: a surcease from a constant round of suffering. Each concept is likely to affect how one lives one's life here and now and how one evaluates death.

In our "developed" societies in the 21st century, many persons no longer hold the typical religious beliefs of earlier times. The modern, scientific worldview has convinced many people that they are simply natural bodies. On that basis, it seems to many that when our bodies no longer function, then we simply are no more. Death means extinction.

How this view might affect one's evaluation of death is not obvious. In part, it is an unthreatening view because there is no suffering after death, although of course, death means the loss of everything one has valued and loved. If this life is seen as basically good, then its loss is likely to be viewed as an unhappy event. Death may then only be feared and hated—and denied. This may be one source of death denial.

In the face of uncertainty, people seek evidence. They would like to know what death means in terms of ongoing existence. Yet Socrates seems to have been correct; we cannot *know*. We must choose some idea of what death means and make do with it. For all of us, religious and nonreligious alike, faith is the only possible route here.

NEAR-DEATH EXPERIENCES

Or is faith the only possible route? Moody's (1975) book *Life after Life* drew attention to a set of phenomena reported by many people. Often, the phenomena were interpreted as providing evidence that there is a life after death and what that life might be like. However, these interpretations are controversial. To understand the issues involved, we look first at the general pattern of these phenomena and then at some of the competing interpretations.

What Are Near-Death Experiences?

Those whom Moody interviewed provided similar reports of their experiences. Typically, these persons reported out-of-body experiences in which they felt themselves to be in a peaceful and quiet state. During these experiences, they frequently reported they were aware of their surroundings and heard themselves being pronounced clinically dead. They also often had unusual sensory encounters: hearing loud noises or other auditory sensations, being in a dark tunnel, coming into contact with others, meeting a being of light, reviewing their own lives, and approaching a border or limit of some type. Often, people who had these experiences were hesitant to share them with others for fear of being disbelieved or ridiculed. When encouraged to share, however, they noted difficulties in communicating what appeared to them to be overwhelming, beyond words, and indescribable. They also typically reported that their experiences had changed their lives, leaving them content, joyful, and no longer afraid of death.

Moody pointed out that these reports were not all identical, although he judged there were sufficient similarities on the main points that it was worth paying attention to the phenomena being reported. Other writers recorded similar phenomena and attempted to describe what they considered the key components of the **near-death experience (NDE)**. For example, Ring (1980) examined 102 cases, in which 60% reported a feeling of peace and a sense of well-being. Some also reported "a sense of detachment from one's physical body" (p. 45) and a sense of "entering the darkness" (p. 53). A few described an appearance of light, with 10% telling of "entering the light" (p. 60). Similarly, Sabom (1982) concluded that the most common features in the cases he examined were a sense of calm and peace, bodily separation, being dead, and "returning" to life. Other writers (e.g., Greyson, 1999, 2005; see also Suggested Readings at the end of this chapter) provided further portraits of NDEs or made efforts to define their essential features.

In order to bolster the so-called archetypal NDE and control for cultural bias, others tried to widen the field of investigation. Some looked for reports from persons who had experienced some type of trauma but who were not near death (Owens, Cook, & Stevenson, 1990; Stevenson, Cook, & McClean-Rice, 1990). Others recorded interviews with individuals who were dying, underwent an NDE experience, recovered to communicate it to others, and then died (Osis & Haraldsson, 1997). Still others sought NDE reports from cardiac arrest survivors (French, 2005) or from people outside North America (Van Lommel, van Wees, Meyers, & Elfferich, 2001). Atwater (1992) and Greyson and Bush (1992) also reported near-death experiences that were distressing or frightening. Palmieri and colleagues (2014) employed a hypnosis-based protocol and neurological testing in their study. Many of these efforts have been summed up by Holden, Grayson, and James (2009), Lichfield (2015), and Sleutjes, Moreira-Almeida, and Greyson (2014).

Interpreting the Meaning of Near-Death Experiences

The most common interpretative claim made by those who report having had an NDE is the assertion that they had been dead and then had returned to life. Supporters of this claim believe that NDEs provide conclusive evidence of the existence of an afterlife—into which the NDE is thought to have offered a brief glimpse. This is the view of Elisabeth Kübler-Ross in the foreword to Moody's (1975) book.

By contrast, some people argued with Socrates that beliefs about the afterlife are in principle restricted to the realm of faith and are not issues on which empirical evidence can be demonstrative. As Kelly (2001, p. 230) reported, "most scientific investigators of NDEs have virtually ignored this question [of whether human consciousness survives the death of the physical body], concentrating instead on less controversial activities such as describing the aftereffects of NDEs or speculating about the physiological mechanisms that might underlie them." These scientists seem to hold such views as: survival after death is nonsensical; interpretations favoring post-death survival on grounds of NDEs are unsound and incapable of controlled replication; and NDEs most likely are artifacts of the unusual situations in which they occur, for example, arising physiologically from anoxia (being without oxygen for a time) or chemical imbalances associated with anesthesia and surgical procedures (Nuland, 1994). In short, NDEs are essentially hallucinations (Mobbs & Watt, 2011).

In fact, the claim that some persons were at one time dead and are now alive to report an NDE is awkward. If what it means to be dead is to be *irreversibly* without biological life, then such persons were not dead. Perhaps they were almost dead, or near dead, or their experiences occurred during a set of processes that often lead to death. For example, they might have been *clinically dead* where that phrase means they met some criteria used to decide when death has occurred. However, the connection between meeting such medical criteria and actually being dead is unclear; the two need not be identical. For instance, because someone shows no external signs of consciousness does not mean that person is having no experiences. *Unconscious* in this context means little more than "not showing signs of consciousness"; it does not mean no consciousness is present.

Kelly, Greyson, and Stevenson (2000) drew attention to three particular features of NDEs: "enhanced mental processes at a time when physiological functioning is seriously impaired; the experience of being out of the body and viewing events going on around it as from a position above; and the awareness of remote events not accessible to the person's ordinary senses" (p. 513). None of these features on its own is conclusive in settling the dispute as to whether NDEs can offer an expectation of an afterlife or are merely hallucinations. However, Kelly (2001) concluded that their convergence suggests the survival hypothesis "may be worthy of closer, more serious consideration—both as a framework for generating empirical research and as a candidate explanation for phenomena observed—than it has so far received from researchers" (p. 246). But note this qualification: "We emphasize, however, that near-death experiences can provide only *indirect* evidence of the continuation of consciousness after death: because the persons having these experiences have lived to report them, they were therefore not dead, however close they may have been to that condition" (Kelly et al. , 2000, p. 518). And Moody has said: "I am a complete skeptic regarding the possibility that science as we know it or any sort of conventionally established methodological procedures will be able to get evidence of life after death or to come to some sort of rational determination of this question" (Kastenbaum, 1995, p. 95).

None of this rules out other lines of evidence that might support beliefs about an afterlife. However, they have not been studied extensively, and when they have been studied, the evidence is at best ambiguous. Socrates' dictum seems to stand: we do not, and perhaps cannot, know what happens after death. We must take a stand—even those who are agnostic are under the same practical compulsion—on less than complete proof. This central fact of our humanness—our mortality—remains a mystery.

THE PLACE OF DEATH IN HUMAN LIFE

Now that we have considered several concepts or images of what happens after death, it is useful to ask: What conclusions can we draw from these viewpoints for the meanings of our lives as we live them in this temporal, physical world?

Afterlife Images and Life Here and Now

One might argue that what we do in this life influences what will happen to us after death. That becomes an argument meant to persuade us to behave in one way rather than another in order to reap benefits in an afterlife. Certain forms of Christianity,

Islam, Hinduism, and Buddhism offer proposals like this. They contend that what we do here and now has desirable or undesirable consequences (for us) after death.

But even if one holds no such ideas, one can still make ties between what happens after death and life in this world now. For instance, if death is permanent extinction, then perhaps humans ought to live life to the fullest and seek to get as much experience as they can. Or, again, if death means extinction, one might hold that this eliminates the value of everything we know and do in our lives: all is vanity. Also, death can mean an end to suffering, as Hindus and Buddhists claim; it eliminates "the heartache and the thousand natural shocks that flesh is heir to" (*Hamlet*, III, i: 62). In this sense, death might be courted, even welcomed, as in those seem to do who seek some form of aided death as described in Chapter 18.

Some have gone beyond this to maintain the "conviction that in the last analysis all human behavior of consequence is a response to the problem of death" (Feifel, 1977b, xiii) or that concerns about immortality drive civilizations (Cave, 2014). If those claims seem too bold or too broad, then at least it can be said that we humans are able to make of death an important steering force in the way we interpret its place in our lives. If so, "appreciation of finiteness can serve not only to enrich self-knowledge but to provide the impulse to propel us forward toward achievement and creativity" (Feifel, 1977b, p. 11).

Efforts to Circumvent or Transcend Death

Many people have tried to circumvent death and have gone about it in a variety of ways. In other words, some people have sought to find a way to continue after they die what they have found valuable in their lives. Lifton (1979) pointed to several such forms of what he called **symbolic immortality**. The main varieties that he described are biological, social, natural, and theological immortality. That is, one's life (and the values one finds in life) might be continued through one's *biological* descendants. Or it could be continued *socially* in what one has created—a painting, a garden, a book—or perhaps in the lives of others one has touched—students, patients, clients, friends. Some people have sought a continuation of their lives after their own deaths in the *natural* world around them. In this view, one's body returns to the ground (dust to dust), wherein its components dissolve and are reorganized into new life. And as we have seen earlier, other people have looked for immortality *theologically* in the form of an afterlife and reunion with or absorption into the divine. Furthermore, some have favored a program of **cryonics** in which one's entire body or perhaps just one's head would be frozen at the moment of death and maintained in that state until a time comes (or so they hope) when they could be thawed out and the cause of their death cured by future generations.

Attempts to circumvent death reveal a meaning for that unavoidable moment: it produces suffering. If anything is valued in this life, death threatens that value. It means the loss (at least for now) of persons we have loved, places we have enjoyed, music, a stunning sunrise, or the feeling of material (soil, paper, and ink, the bow on the strings) coming into form through our labor.

If this is the meaning we find for death, inevitably it will influence how we live and how we treat each other. It teaches us that life is precious. So we entitled this book *Death & Dying, Life & Living*. It seems that whatever meaning we find for death, to look at death leads us to realize the fragility and the value of life. Indeed, perhaps death makes possible the value of life. A life (as we know life here) that went on indefinitely might become unbearable. Why do anything today, when there are endless tomorrows in which to do it?

Ultimately, the meaning any individual finds for death will be his or her own. In this sense, each individual is alone in facing his or her own death. But there is a history—thousands of years long—and a cultural diversity among persons with whom one can enter into dialogue. Each person can enter into this dialogue to gain help in choosing how to live his or her own life, as well as how to make sense of his or her own death and the deaths of those for and about whom he or she cares. Each individual can also contribute to the history of human debate about the meaning and place of death in human life. This book is but one voice in that ongoing dialogue.

Summary

In this chapter, we engaged in a reflection on the meaning and place of death in human life. We considered questions that human beings have raised about death and responses offered, on one hand, by religious and philosophical perspectives and, on the other, by those who have examined reports of near-death experiences. The lesson we drew is that each person is both free and responsible to determine for himself or herself the stand that he or she will take in the face of death.

Glossary

Atman: the unborn, undying self (in Hindu writings)

Cryonics: a practice in which one's body (or sometimes just the head) is frozen at the time of death and held in that state until a time comes when, it is hoped, it could be thawed and the cause of death cured by future generations

Hades: the kingdom of the dead in Homer's *Odyssey;* the place where one goes after death according to some ancient Greek thought; a dreary place

Heaven and hell: places of reward or punishment, respectively, after death, according to some Western religions

Immortality of the soul: a view originating in ancient Greek thought according to which an essential element in living beings cannot die

Living-dead: a view found in some African thought according to which the human community consists of both the living and the living-dead or those individuals who are no longer living here, but are living in some different part of the world

Near-death experiences (NDEs): phenomena reported by individuals who have experiences they and/or others claim demonstrate the existence of an afterlife

Nepesh: a Hebrew word for "soul," implying an inextricable involvement with a body, such that when the body dies, the *nepesh* also ceases to exist

Nirvana: a goal in Buddhism; a serene and peaceful state, beyond desire and suffering (which lead to rebirth)

Reincarnation: literally, to be reborn or reinserted in a body; an ancient concept found both in Greek thought and Hindu writings; allied notions include *transmigration* of souls and *metempsychosis*, which imply movement of souls from body to body

Resurrection of the body: "raising up" by God of a human being as a "living body"

Symbolic immortality: Lifton's term for efforts made to transcend or circumvent death through biological, social, natural, or theological accounts of continuity

Questions for Review and Discussion

1. This chapter reviewed several notions of what happens after death. These included: (1) immortality of the soul; (2) resurrection of the body; (3) life continued in a place of bliss (heaven) or torture (hell) or exceeding boredom (the Greek Hades); (4) rebirth (transmigration or reincarnation of the soul); (5) a life much like this one only somewhere else; and (6) permanent peace and stillness (nirvana, extinction). To which of these views are you inclined? How might your response to this question affect how you live your life? How might it influence how you treat someone who is dying or bereaved?

2. This chapter discussed near-death experiences. What is your assessment of what such experiences can or do tell us about what happens to us after we die?

3. Have you ever turned to social media or the Internet to learn more about the subjects discussed in this chapter? Did that help you? Why or why not?

Suggested Readings

For religious, philosophical, spiritual, and other perspectives on death-related issues, see:

Badham, P., & Badham, L. (Eds.). (1987). *Death and Immortality in the Religions of the World*

Berger, A., Badham, P., Kutscher, A. H., Berger, J., Perry, M., & Beloff, J. (Eds.). (1989). *Perspectives on Death and Dying: Cross-Cultural and Multi-Disciplinary Views*

Cave, S. (2014). *Immortality: The Quest to Live Forever and How It Drives Civilization*

Chidester, D. (2002). *Patterns of Transcendence: Religion, Death, and Dying* (2nd ed.)

Coward, H. (2005). *Life after Death in World Religions*

Cox, G. R., & Fundis, R. J. (Eds.). (1992). *Spiritual, Ethical and Pastoral Aspects of Death and Bereavement*

Edwards, P. (Ed.). (1997). *Immortality*

Gignoux, J. H. (1998). *Some Folk Say: Stories of Life, Death, and Beyond*

Goss, R. J., & Klass, D. (2005). *Dead but Not Lost: Grief Narratives in Religious Traditions*

Johnson, C. J., & McGee, M. G. (Eds.). (1998). *How Different Religions View Death and Afterlife*. (2nd ed.)

Kauffman, J. (Ed.). (1995). *Awareness of Mortality*

Klass, D. (Ed.). (2006). Death, grief, religion, and spirituality [special issue]. *OMEGA—Journal of Death and Dying, 53*(1–2)

Morgan, J. D., & Laungani, P. (Eds.). (2002). *Death and Bereavement around the World: Vol. 1, Major Religious Traditions*

Obayashi, H. (Ed.). (1992). *Death and Afterlife: Perspectives of World Religions*

Reynolds, F. E., & Waugh, E. H. (Eds.). (1977). *Religious Encounters with Death: Insights from the History and Anthropology of Religion*

Steffen, L., & Cooley, D. R. (2014). *The Ethics of Death: Religious and Philosophical Perspectives*

Descriptions and analyses of near-death experiences are offered in:

Alexander, E. (2012). *Proof of Heaven: A Neurosurgeon's Journey into the Afterlife*

Atwater, P. M. H. (2007). *The Big Book of Near-Death Experiences; The Ultimate Guide to What Happens When We Die* (2nd ed.)

Engmann, B. (2014). *Near-Death Experiences. Heavenly Insight or Human Illusion?*

Fenwick, P., & Fenwick, E. (1995). *The Truth in the Light: An Investigation of over 300 Near-Death Experiences*

Fenwick, P., & Fenwick, E. (2008). *The Art of Dying*

Holden, J. M., Grayson, B., & James, D. (Eds.). (2009). *The Handbook of Near-Death Experiences: Thirty Years of Investigation*

Kellehear, A. (1996). *Experiences near Death: Beyond Medicine and Religion*

Long, J., & Perry P. (2010). *Evidence of the Afterlife: The Science of Near-Death Experiences*

Moody, R. A. (1975). *Life after Life*

Neal, M. C. (2012). *To Heaven and Back: A Doctor's Extraordinary Account of Her Death, Heaven, Angels, and Life Again: A True Story*

Osis, K., & Haraldsson, E. (1997). *At the Hour of Death* (3rd ed.)

Perera, M., Jagadheesan, K., & Peake, A. (Eds.). (2011). *Making Sense of Near-Death Experiences: A Handbook for Clinicians*

Ring, K. (1980). *Life at Death: A Scientific Investigation of the Near-Death Experience*

Ring, K. (1984). *Heading toward Omega: In Search of the Meaning of the Near-Death Experience*

Ring, K., & Valarino, E. E. (1998). *Lessons from the Light: What We Can Learn from the Near-Death Experience*

Sabom, M. B. (1982). *Recollections of Death: A Medical Investigation*

Van Lommel, P. (2010). *Consciousness beyond Life: The Science of the Near-Death Experience*

Selected Web Resources

Some useful search terms include: AFTERLIFE; ATMAN; CRYONICS; HADES; IMMORTALITY OF THE SOUL; LIVING-DEAD; METEMPSYCHOSIS; NEAR-DEATH EXPERIENCES; NEPESH; NIRVANA; REINCARNATION; RESURRECTION OF THE BODY; SYMBOLIC IMMORTALITY; TRANSMIGRATION OF SOULS; YIN AND YANG SYMBOL.

You can also visit the following *organizational and other Internet sites:*

American Cryonics Society

Association for Clinical Pastoral Education

Association for Professional Chaplains

BELIEVE: Religious Information Source (multiple topics)

International Association for Near-Death Studies (IANDS) and its *Journal of Near-Death Studies*

Near-Death Experiences and the Afterlife

PART Seven

AN EXAMPLE OF A SPECIFIC DISEASE CONTEXT

In this book, we examined numerous death-related subjects, while focusing on several central themes:

- Three components of **death-related experiences**: death-related (a) *encounters,* (b) *attitudes,* and (c) *practices*
- *Death systems* in our society and in other parts of the world
- *Gender, racial, and cultural patterns* in death-related experiences
- *Efforts to cope* with life-threatening illness, dying, and bereavement
- *Ways to help* others and ourselves in coping with life-threatening illness, dying, and bereavement
- *Developmental* influences on death-related experiences
- *Legal, conceptual, moral, religious, and spiritual* topics
- Some important *lessons about life and living*

Previously, we addressed these issues in general ways. In so doing, we mentioned a wide variety of causes of death, disease entities, and contexts in which life-threatening illness, dying, death, and bereavement are encountered. We now offer an extended portrait of one specific disease context to help us integrate as many of these issues as we can. The disease context chosen for this purpose must provide both an example of as many of our central themes as possible and a test case of their power to illuminate human interactions with death.

Several life-threatening diseases might serve this purpose as long as they have enough complexity in their realization and sufficiently lengthy dying trajectories to allow these issues to emerge. A sudden dying (e.g., from an accident, suicide, or heart attack) would not serve well as the model to achieve our goals here.

For Chapter 20, we chose one particular disease context. Some readers might prefer to choose some other disease context. We encourage such efforts and would be interested to learn what the portrait would look like for diseases such as influenza, lung or breast cancer, Lou Gehrig's disease (amyotrophic lateral sclerosis), or Parkinson's disease.

In the meantime, in Chapter 20, we explore how the issues raised throughout this book are realized in the particular framework of one specific disease context: Alzheimer's disease and related disorders.

Illustrating the Themes of this Book: Alzheimer's Disease and Related Disorders

PROLOGUE

As explained in the Introduction to Part Seven, this chapter differs in important ways from other chapters in this book. In other chapters, we examined how dying, death, and bereavement are experienced in a wide variety of contexts. In so doing, we emphasized a number of central themes and addressed them individually, most often in separate discussions. In this chapter, we show how these themes come together and get played out in *one specific context*. That is, instead of studying these themes individually, here we examine many of these central themes in relationship to one specific disease context: Alzheimer's disease and related disorders. Our primary goal in this chapter is to provide an illustration of how the central themes of this book reveal themselves in this particular context so that the framework of the entire book becomes the explicit structure for this final chapter.

We selected the example of Alzheimer's disease (AD) and related disorders for three primary reasons: (1) Alzheimer's disease is a progressive, degenerative brain disease that has no known cure and leads inevitably to death; (2) AD is increasingly prevalent in both the United States and around the world, its mortality rates are climbing, and it is now at least the sixth leading cause of death in high-income countries like the United States; and (3) AD imposes substantial physical, psychological, social, spiritual, and economic burdens on affected individuals, family members and friends, professional caregivers, and social systems.

Objectives of this **Chapter**

The principal objectives of this chapter are:

▶ To provide an extended example of how the central themes of this book come together in the experience of one specific disease context

▶ To offer an overview of experiences with Alzheimer's disease and related disorders in the United States and around the world

SANDRA DAY O'CONNOR AND ALZHEIMER'S DISEASE

Sandra Day O'Connor became the first female member of the Supreme Court of the United States in 1981. In 2005, she announced her intention to retire from the Court effective upon the confirmation of a successor, citing her age and the need to spend more time with her ailing husband and her family. Her husband, John, had been diagnosed with Alzheimer's disease in 1989 at the age of 60.

According to one contemporary report, "O'Connor, who is still physically and mentally fit, said it was her plan to follow the tradition of previous justices who enjoy lifetime appointments, to work until they die or are virtually incapacitated. 'Most of them get ill and are really in bad shape, which I would've done at the end of the day myself, I suppose, except my husband was ill and I needed to take action there,' O'Connor said" (Anonymous, 2007).

After her retirement, the situation became more difficult because her husband's loss of memory soon rendered him unable to recognize members of his family. A year later, John's condition had deteriorated, and it was decided to put him in a care center near their home in Phoenix. At that time, Justice O'Connor is reported to have said: "It's such a miserable disease. It's so sad. It's so hard. I did the best I could. He wants me there all the time" (Stritof & Stritof, 2009).

U.S. Supreme Court Justice Sandra Day O'Connor dances with her husband, John, at a ball in Washington D.C. on October 17, 1998.

Karin Cooper/Liaison/Hulton Archive/Getty Images

In the institution where he was living, the desire for love and companionship that often continues to be felt by individuals with dementia soon led John O'Connor to form a new personal attachment with a female resident. The two individuals were reported to spend time together and hold hands, even in the presence of Justice O'Connor.

Some spouses of persons with advanced dementia interpret the development of new relationships like this as a rejection of them, but commentators have noted that when a person with dementia can no longer recognize his or her family members and constantly finds his or her surroundings to be strange or scary, there is no question of rejection. "Imagine if all the people you know and loved disappeared," said Dr. Richard Powers, chairman of the medical advisory board of the Alzheimer's Foundation of America. "Wouldn't you want to find someone who was your friend, who would hold your hand and watch old television shows with you? The person with Alzheimer's still searches for joy" (Parker-Pope, 2007).

Justice O'Connor and her family were relieved to see her husband of 55 years so content. She and her family did not hide the newfound romance he had found at his assisted living facility. As one of their sons is reported to have said: "Mom was thrilled that Dad was relaxed and happy and comfortable living here and wasn't complaining" (Associated Press, 2007).

John O'Connor died on November 11, 2009, at the age of 79 of complications arising from his Alzheimer's disease (Nelson, 2009).

DEMENTIA, ALZHEIMER'S DISEASE, AND RELATED DISORDERS

In this section, we provide an overview of dementia, Alzheimer's disease, and related disorders.

Dementia

According to the Alzheimer's Association (2015, p. 5), **dementia** is "characterized by a decline in memory, language, problem-solving and other cognitive skills that affects a person's ability to perform everyday activities. This decline occurs because nerve cells (neurons) in parts of the brain involved in cognitive function have been damaged and no longer function normally."

The fifth edition of the *Diagnostic and Statistical Manual of Mental Disorders (DSM 5; American Psychiatric Association, 2013)* incorporates dementia into the diagnostic categories of major and mild neurocognitive disorders, which are explained by the Alzheimer's Association (2015, p. 5) in this way:

> To meet *DSM-5* criteria for *major neurocognitive disorder*, an individual must have evidence of significant cognitive decline, and the decline must interfere with independence in everyday activities (for example, assistance may be needed with complex activities such as paying bills or managing medications). To meet *DSM-5* criteria for *mild neurocognitive disorder*, an individual must have evidence of modest cognitive decline, but the decline does not interfere with everyday activities (individuals can still perform complex activities such as paying bills or managing medications, but the activities require greater mental effort).

In both cases, the underlying cause must be specified, for example, Alzheimer's disease or some other condition.

In other words, *dementia* is a general term for a wide range of symptoms involved in a decline in mental ability severe enough to interfere with daily life. Some *other chronic disorders*, like Parkinson's disease or amyotrophic lateral sclerosis (Lou Gehrig's disease) involve progressive loss of control over bodily functioning not usually accompanied by cognitive impairment, although dementia can develop in their late stages.

Alzheimer's Disease

A sketch of the history of our understanding of Alzheimer's disease appears in Focus On 20.1 (see also Ballenger, 2006; Shenk, 2003). AD is the most common cause of dementia: a chronic and progressive brain disorder primarily affecting memory, thinking, behavior, and the ability to perform everyday activities. Typically beginning with mild cognitive impairment (MCI), AD advances more or less gradually and inexorably until affected individuals can no longer function or care for themselves and inevitably die. It is important to note, however, that AD and dementias of all types are not a part of normal aging and only about 15% of individuals with mild cognitive impairment go on to develop AD. An estimated 15–20% of people aged 65 and older have MCI, but "MCI can develop for reasons other than Alzheimer's, and MCI does not always lead to dementia" (Alzheimer's Association, 2017, p. 10).

"Late onset" Alzheimer's disease occurs in individuals 65 years of age or older. By contrast, some people in their 40s and 50s experience "early onset" AD, comprising up to 5% of people with AD. Both forms of AD involve the development of

---

FOCUS ON 20.1

History and Evolution of Knowledge about Alzheimer's Disease

- Alois Alzheimer is credited with discovering a yet unnamed disease. After observing the constellation of symptoms now associated with dementia in one of his patients while she was alive, he performed an autopsy when she died in 1907. In addition to reduced brain volume, he noted lesions around the neurons.

- The disease remained without an accepted name until 1910, when a former colleague of Alzheimer published a book in which he labeled the condition "Alzheimer's disease."

- Progress was relatively slow until the late 1960s, when validation of the first cognitive assessment tool enabled researchers to relate decline in cognitive function to changes in the brain at the cellular level.

- In 1976 Robert Katzman, cofounder of the Alzheimer's Association, in an editorial in the *Archives of Neurology* proposed that Alzheimer's disease and what was then called "senile dementia" were one and the same, making it a leading—but unrecognized—cause of death in the United States.

- The Alzheimer's Association, a national nonprofit organization devoted to care, support, and research, was founded in 1980 and funded its first grant in 1982.

- A series of scientific breakthroughs occurred in the late 1980s. First, the protein tau was identified in 1986 as the major component of neurofibrillary tangles associated with neuronal degeneration. The first gene associated with some rare forms of Alzheimer's disease was discovered in 1987. Also in 1987, the first drug trial began with a drug targeted toward treating the symptoms of AD.

(continues)

FOCUS ON 20.1 *(continued)*

History and Evolution of Knowledge about Alzheimer's Disease

- Research continued throughout the 1990s. Several drug treatments were developed and approved by the Food and Drug Administration, a genetic risk factor (APOE-e4) was identified, and a vaccine was found to be effective in preventing brain changes associated with AD in mice.
- Research related to treatment, causes, diagnosis, and prevention of Alzheimer's disease has continued to expand in the early 21st century, leading to much of what is known today and the identification in 2011 of three stages of AD and the potential use of biomarker tests to guide researchers (as explained further in this section).

Source: Adapted from the Alzheimer's Association website, www.alz.org.

---

beta-amyloid plaques (deposits of the protein fragment beta-amyloid that build up between, that is, *outside*, neurons or nerve cells in the brain), and **tangles** (twisted strands of the protein **tau** that form *inside* dying cells). Most people develop some plaques and tangles as they age, but those with AD develop far more of them and they form in areas affecting learning and memory, block communication among nerve cells in the brain that increasingly disrupts its functioning, and upset activities those cells need to survive. As AD progresses, the brain shrinks dramatically in size.

At present, there is no known cure for AD, although for many years researchers have been actively seeking to identify causes of this disease and interventions to slow its progress or improve quality of life (e.g., Snowdon, 2002). Strictly speaking, AD can only be definitively diagnosed on autopsy, although several tests have been developed to predict the likelihood of AD with a reasonable degree of certitude, and many efforts have been devoted to early detection and diagnosis.

In April 2011, the National Institute on Aging and the Alzheimer's Association jointly announced what has been called "a major milestone in the field" that: (1) identifies three stages of AD, with the first occurring perhaps as much as 20 years before symptoms, such as memory loss, develop and (2) incorporates the potential use of biomarker tests to guide researchers in their understanding and study of progression of this disease (Albert et al., 2011; Jack et al., 2011; McKhann et al., 2011; Sperling et al., 2011). The three stages of AD proposed by the 2011 criteria and guidelines are preclinical Alzheimer's disease, mild cognitive impairment (MCI) due to Alzheimer's disease, and dementia due to Alzheimer's disease. More specifically,

> under the proposed revised guidelines of 2011, Alzheimer's disease encompasses an entire continuum from the initial pathologic changes in the brain before symptoms appear through the dementia caused by the accumulation of brain changes. This means that Alzheimer's disease includes not only those with dementia due to the disease, but also those with mild cognitive impairment due to Alzheimer's and asymptomatic individuals who have verified biomarkers of Alzheimer's (2017, p. 1).

Currently, the Alzheimer's Association has noted that "there is no single test for Alzheimer's" (p. 8). Instead, physicians use a combination of the individual's medical and family history, family reports of changes in thinking skills and behavior, cognitive tests and physical and neurological examinations, and blood tests and brain imaging to rule out other potential causes of dementia symptoms (e.g., tumors or certain vitamin deficiencies). If reliable and valid biomarker tests could be developed, it is thought that potential disease-modifying treatments could be administered during the preclinical and MCI stages of disease to slow or stop the progression of AD and preserve brain function.

Related Disorders

Several disorders closely related or similar to AD are listed in Focus On 20.2. Each of these related disorders appears to have its own underlying factors, many of which are akin to AD. They differ primarily in the ways they manifest themselves and in the speed of their progression. However recent research has suggested that distinctions between these various types of dementia may not be as clear cut as formerly

---

FOCUS ON 20.2

Types of Dementia and Associated Characteristics*

Alzheimer's disease (AD) is the most common type of dementia, accounting for an estimated 60–80% of cases. Memory impairment is often the first symptom in persons with AD, commonly followed by visual, spatial, and language problems. Symptoms may not be severe enough to interfere with daily life in early stages, but usually gradually worsen over a period of years to include impaired communication, disorientation, confusion, and, ultimately, difficulty speaking, swallowing, and walking. *Early-onset AD* typically occurs between 30 and 60 years of age, causes more rapid decline than late-onset, and has a strong genetic component. *Late-onset AD* is usually diagnosed after age 60, is by far the more common form, and has a more ambiguous genetic association than that in early-onset AD.

Vascular dementia, previously known as multi-infarct dementia or post-stroke dementia, is thought to account for about 10% of dementia cases and to increase in incidence with age. Vascular dementia is caused by decreased blood flow to the brain due to a stroke or series of "mini strokes" (infarcts). Diminished blood flow deprives the brain of nutrients, leading to structural damage and functional impairment. Symptoms vary depending on affected location(s) in the brain. Onset of symptoms may occur gradually or all of a sudden, with intermittent intervals of rapid deterioration amid periods of maintenance or steady decline. Persons with vascular dementia often experience initial symptoms of impaired judgment or difficulties in making decisions, planning, or organizing versus the memory loss more typical of early AD. Physical symptoms commonly associated with stroke can sometimes occur, such as sudden weakness, difficulty speaking, or confusion. Reducing modifiable cardiovascular risk factors may prevent or delay the onset of vascular dementia, but it is not reversible once it develops. Brain changes typical of Alzheimer's dementia and vascular dementia may coexist.

(continues)

> ### FOCUS ON 20.2 *(continued)*
>
> ## Types of Dementia and Associated Characteristics*
>
> **Lewy body dementia** or dementia with Lewy Bodies (DLB) is a disease in which deposits of the protein alpha-synuclein form inside neurons in the cortex of the brain. Symptoms mimic some aspects of AD and Parkinson's disease, thus making diagnosis difficult. Early symptoms of DLB may include visual/spatial impairment without significant memory impairment, plus sleep disturbances, visual hallucinations, and movement disorders often associated with Parkinson's disease, such as slowness, gait imbalance, and tremors. Persons with DLB commonly have coexisting Alzheimer's or vascular dementia pathology.
>
> **Frontotemporal dementia** (FTD) is a clinical syndrome characterized by loss of tissue in the frontal and temporal lobes of the cortex. FTD comprises multiple disorders, including Pick's disease, that present quite differently from other types of dementia. In early stages, memory typically remains intact while marked changes in personality and behavior appear, as well as difficulty in producing or comprehending language. Rapid onset of symptoms contrasts with AD, following either behavioral or language changes.
>
> **Mixed dementia** refers to the co-morbid presence of more than one cause of dementia, such as Alzheimer's and vascular dementia. It is now thought that this condition may be more prevalent than previously realized, becomes more common with advancing age, and may characterize about half of all persons with dementia. Symptoms and disease progression may be similar to AD or some combination of dementias.
>
> *More information about these and other types of dementia can be found on the Alzheimer's Association website.

thought; some individuals may have multiple or mixed forms of dementia and/or other diseases. For that reason, in the remainder of this chapter when we wish to identify Alzheimer's disease alone, we speak of AD; when we describe more broadly **Alzheimer's disease and related disorders,** we speak of ADRD.

RECENT ENCOUNTERS WITH ALZHEIMER'S DISEASE AND DEATH

In this section, we describe recent encounters with Alzheimer's disease as a cause of death and some projections concerning numbers of individuals who are expected to be living with AD in the near future, as well as how deaths related to AD differ among specified groups.

Prevalence of Disease and Death

As noted above, Alzheimer's disease is now the sixth leading cause of death in the United States and the fifth leading cause of death for individuals age 65 or older. In 2014, AD was the cause of 93,541 deaths in the United States with a crude death rate of 29.3 per 100,000 (Kochanek, Murphy, Xu, & Tejada-Vera, 2016). Whereas most other leading causes of death have shown a gradual decrease in numbers in recent years, between 2000 and 2014, deaths attributed to AD increased by 89%. AD is a particularly challenging cause of death because at present it is the only one of the ten leading causes of death in the United States that cannot be prevented, cured, or slowed in any appreciable degree. Numbers of deaths from AD have risen rapidly in recent years, partly as a result of improved identification and awareness of this condition, partly because of changes in the way diseases are classified in the international coding system, and partly because of increases in the population of older adults (especially older females) who are most likely to experience AD.

Nevertheless, because AD is a leading cause of disability and poor health (morbidity) that may have lasted for many years prior to death, AD deaths may be under-reported when the immediate cause of death is ascribed to complications arising from dementia, such as aspiration pneumonia from being bed-bound at the end of life or falls associated with wandering (James et al., 2014). If so, actual numbers of AD deaths may be much higher than those reported on death certificates. In addition, many persons with AD also have unrelated health problems that can lead to debilitation and death. Thus, Ganguli and Rodriguez (1999) noted that there may be a fuzzy distinction between dying *from* AD and dying *with* AD.

The Alzheimer's Association (2017) has estimated that there were 5.5 million persons living with AD in the United States in 2015, of which some 5.3 million were age 65 or older. This means approximately one in ten older Americans are estimated to have AD. Unfortunately, it is thought that fewer than half of those people have been told of their diagnosis of AD by their physicians and are unaware of their dementia. The total number of people age 65 and older with AD in the United States is estimated to increase to 7.1 million (an increase of 35%) by 2025 and to approximately 13.8 million by 2050, barring the development of medical breakthroughs to prevent or cure this disease. From a global standpoint, Alzheimer's Disease International (2016; the worldwide federation of Alzheimer's associations) has estimated there were 47 million people living with Alzheimer's disease and other dementias worldwide in 2016. Projections indicate that this population will increase to 131.5 million by 2050. These projections are higher than earlier reported, although Langa and colleagues (2017) have reported that "the prevalence of dementia in the United States declined significantly between 2000 and 2012" (p. 51). What remains worrisome is that populations in both the United States and many other countries are rapidly aging, and AD and related disorders primarily affect individuals over the age of 65.

Differential Encounters with Alzheimer's Disease and Death

In terms of *age*, AD is primarily found among older adults and causes many deaths in that age group. In 2014, all but 937 of the 93,541 deaths ascribed to AD in the United States were of individuals over 65 years of age (Kochanek et al., 2016). After age 65 the likelihood of developing AD or other dementias doubles every five years.

In terms of *gender*, almost two-thirds of people with AD are women and females accounted for nearly 70% of AD deaths in the United States in 2014. Historically, it has been thought that the higher incidence of AD in females occurs primarily because females tend to live longer on average than males in our society and living longer increases the time during which persons are likely to get AD. However, the Alzheimer's Association (2015, p. 17) has reported that "limited new research suggests that risk could be higher for women, potentially due to biological or genetic variations or even different life experiences (e.g., type and amount of education, or occupational choices)."

In terms of the *racial and cultural groups* highlighted in Chapter 5 in this book, the largest numbers of deaths and the highest death rates from AD are found among Caucasian Americans. Nevertheless, the Alzheimer's Association reported in 2017 that,

> A review of many studies by an expert panel concluded that older African-Americans are about twice as likely to have Alzheimer's or other dementias as older whites, and Hispanics are about one and one-half times as likely to have Alzheimer's or other dementias as older whites.... Variations in health, lifestyle and socioeconomic risk factors across racial groups likely account for most of the differences in risk of Alzheimer's disease and other dementias by race" (p. 20).

In terms of *income and education levels*, recent research has indicated that the prevalence of AD is higher in individuals with low levels of education and low income by contrast with those who have advantages of better education and higher economic status.

ATTITUDES COMMONLY ASSOCIATED WITH ALZHEIMER'S DISEASE AND RELATED DISORDERS

Because ADRD vary in many ways and fluctuate in specific individuals, we can only describe here examples of attitudes associated with some of the most common difficulties or challenges that arise.

Initial Difficulties

In their initial manifestations, Alzheimer's disease and related disorders are most likely to show up as minor lapses in memory and what appear to be trivial problems with uncertainty, misunderstandings, and/or bewilderment. These faults are often viewed as inconsequential or petty eccentricities. They may be written off as insignificant or typical accompaniments of aging. However, the Alzheimer's Association has identified 10 warning signs of this disease and has distinguished them from typical, age-related behaviors (see Focus On 20.3). As AD progresses, however, sporadic forgetfulness is likely to become more persistent, especially in relationship to recent events. As it does, both the person affected and those in contact with that individual are apt to become frustrated and puzzled about what is happening. They will ask questions like: "Why can't I remember things like I used to?"; "Why doesn't she recall what we were just talking about?"; or "Why is he repeating the same question, remark, or story all over again?" Valiant efforts by persons with these diseases (and perhaps also others) to cover over or compensate for difficulties may be insufficient to disguise a gradually increasing, but real need for help.

Individual experiences occur in quite different ways. One person we know asked, "What is that golden thing hanging in the sky this evening?" It was the moon. On another occasion, he wanted to know what the tool was that he was holding in his hand. It was a screwdriver. Later, he wanted to go outside to smoke a cigarette—following a past pattern in which he tried not to smoke inside the house—but he no longer knew how to open the door. Nevertheless, he could still carry on plausible conversations and recall many events from the more distant past. Around this time or perhaps a bit earlier our beloved "Uncle Jim" (and we) realized that things were not going well, but did not know exactly what was happening or what to do about the situation (Corr & Corr, 2015).

FOCUS ON 20.3

10 Warning Signs of Alzheimer's Disease—by Contrast with Typical Age-Related Changes

1. **Memory loss that disrupts daily life.** One of the most common signs of Alzheimer's disease is memory loss, especially forgetting recently learned information. Other signs include forgetting important dates or events; asking for the same information over and over; relying on memory aides (e.g., reminder notes or electronic devices) or family members for things one used to handle on one's own. *What's a typical age-related change? Sometimes forgetting names or appointments, but remembering them later.*

2. **Challenges in planning or solving problems.** Some people may experience changes in their ability to develop and follow a plan or work with numbers. They may have trouble following a familiar recipe or keeping track of monthly bills. They may have difficulty concentrating and take much longer to do things than they did before. *What's a typical age-related change? Making occasional errors when balancing a checkbook.*

3. **Difficulty completing familiar tasks at home, at work, or at leisure.** People with Alzheimer's disease often find it hard to complete daily tasks. Sometimes, they may have trouble driving to a familiar location, managing a budget at work, or remembering the rules of a favorite game. *What's a typical age-related change? Occasionally needing help to use the settings on a microwave or to record a television show.*

4. **Confusion with time or place.** People with Alzheimer's can lose track of dates, seasons, and the passage of time. They may have trouble understanding something if it is not happening immediately. Sometimes they may forget where they are or how they got there. *What's a typical age-related change? Getting confused about the day of the week but figuring it out later.*

5. **Trouble understanding visual images and spatial relationships.** For some people, having vision problems is a sign of Alzheimer's. They may have difficulty reading, judging distance, and determining color or contrast. In terms of perception, they may pass a mirror and think someone else is in the room. They may not realize they are the person in the mirror. *What's a typical age-related change? Vision changes related to cataracts.*

6. **New problems with words in speaking or writing.** People with Alzheimer's may have trouble following or joining a conversation. They may stop in the middle of a conversation and have no idea how to continue, or they may repeat themselves. They may struggle with vocabulary, have problems finding the right word, or call things by the wrong name (e.g., calling a watch a "hand-clock"). *What's a typical age-related change? Sometimes having trouble finding the right word.*

7. **Misplacing things and losing the ability to retrace steps.** Persons with Alzheimer's disease may put things in unusual places. They may lose things and be unable to go back over their steps to find them again. Sometimes, they may accuse others of stealing. This may occur more frequently over

(continues)

10 Warning Signs of Alzheimer's Disease—by Contrast with Typical Age-Related Changes

time. *What's a typical age-related change? Misplacing things from time to time, such as a pair of glasses or the remote control.*

8. **Decreased or poor judgment.** People with Alzheimer's may experience changes in judgment or decision making. For example, they may use poor judgment when dealing with money or giving large amounts of money to telemarketers. They may pay less attention to grooming or keeping themselves clean. *What's a typical age-related change? Making a bad decision once in a while.*

9. **Withdrawal from work or social activities.** Persons with Alzheimer's may start to remove themselves from hobbies, social activities, work projects, or sports. They may have trouble keeping up with a favorite sports team or remembering how to complete a favorite hobby. They may also avoid being social because of the changes they have experienced. *What's a typical age-related change? Sometimes feeling weary of work, family, and social obligations.*

10. **Changes in mood and personality.** The mood and personalities of people with Alzheimer's can change. They can become confused, suspicious, depressed, fearful, or anxious. They may be easily upset at home, at work, with friends, or in places where they are out of their comfort zone. *What's a typical age-related change? Developing very specific ways of doing things and becoming irritable when a routine is disrupted.*

Source: Based on "10 warning Signs of Alzheimer's Disease" from Alzheimer's Association, www.alz.org/10signs. Used by permission.

Events like these are often described as the early signs of ADRD. In fact, as they become more prominent and more persistent, they may simply be the first noticeable manifestations of brain disorders leading to dementia in general and AD in particular that are now thought to have begun and had been occurring for many years before expressing themselves in the form of recognizable symptoms. A pattern emerges from behaviors that are otherwise merely puzzling in isolation or in passing. In addition, external stressors like changes in routines or the death of a spouse may reveal an underlying decline in abilities.

Much of this is fairly benign until the affected individual begins to have problems driving, getting lost while out walking, abandoning food cooking on a stove, failing to take needed medications, or wandering off at night or when not properly dressed for harsh weather. Now the individual can become a danger to himself or herself and to others. Family members can no longer deny that problems are real and are becoming increasingly severe. Much more is involved than mere absentmindedness even though a lot of what is described here can change from day to day or moment to moment. (See Personal Insights 20.1 for one wife's description of her experiences with her husband who had Lewy body dementia.)

A Wife's Experiences with Her Husband's Lewy Body Dementia

Among the first things I noticed about my husband that seemed unusual were some forgetfulness and small changes in behavior. For example, he was a man who read constantly, even during TV commercials, but now he stopped reading completely. And his excellent handwriting suddenly became tiny and cramped. But he was still working and playing racquetball three times a week as he had been for 47 years.

He was then initially diagnosed with Parkinson's disease, partly on the basis of an essential tremor in one hand (a feature he had experienced for 20 years and shared with his mother and sister). Unfortunately, the medication used for that diagnosis led to delusions and hallucinations.

A few weeks later, as was our habit after his morning racquetball game, we were to meet at a restaurant for Sunday lunch. A man who was always very punctual, he arrived 30 minutes late wearing a hat! He whispered to me that he had not been able to remember how to comb his hair. More hallucinations and strange behavior followed quickly, along with a rapid decline to needing total care.

I am a nurse, so I thought "I know how to provide his care" and "I can do this." Within a few weeks, I began saying to myself, "I hate this." In addition to caring for my husband there were unexpected legal, business, and other burdens just when I was least able to cope. Then I woke one morning and couldn't move with pain in my hip and leg. The pain, difficulties in walking, and loss of weight continued for many months. In retrospect, I think I was experiencing a conversion reaction that legitimized turning over my husband's care to our children and hired aides.

When I returned to my own work seeing clients in counseling, I felt no pain. Others noted that at those times I would be smiling and walking unaided. But when people told me "At least you still have your husband," I knew this wasn't the man I had been married to for 58 years. I was widowed but not yet a widow, a person engaged in a difficult process of grief learning. Then when a psychiatrist told me I would be finished grieving when my husband died, I knew from my professional work with bereaved people that he was wrong. My grief before my husband's death was worse than after he died, but I still had lots of later grief reactions to experience.

I kept my husband at home as long as I could, but eventually I had to place him in an assisted living facility and move myself into an apartment in a nearby senior citizens complex. When he learned we were going to sell our home of 49 years, my husband had two lucid moments. First, he teared up and said "Where will we go?" Then, after a visit from a realtor, he asked, "How much can we get for the house?"

Lewy body disease is a strange malady even by comparison with other dementias. It varies from person to person and doesn't usually involve a constant, steady decline. My husband's mental condition fluctuated wildly. One day, one hour, he could be lucid, and his eyes would sparkle. It was easy for me at those times to get caught up in a fantasy of improvement, even though

(continues)

A Wife's Experiences with Her Husband's Lewy Body Dementia

I knew that was impossible. There always were moments when he could act very deliberately, offer a big hug or wink, or plainly say good-bye. I often wondered if there was more going on inside his head than was showing in his behavior. But those flashes of clarity didn't mean he could take care of himself or that his disease had gone away.

One day, four-and-a-half years after his diagnosis, my husband announced, "I've had it!" and he stopped eating and drinking. During the two-and-a-half weeks it took before he died, we created opportunities for him to talk to each of our children and grandchildren. After he died, my son and I sat at his bedside for several hours just talking. For me, this was a very comforting leave taking. We didn't call the funeral home right away. So I always remind others that they are in charge at these times and should do whatever they need and want.

For myself, I learned along the way that I had to get out of the house and live my own life. I always loved my husband, and I was blessed that our children (some of whom lived many miles away) arranged a shared rotation to be with me and help out. We were also fortunate to have sufficient resources to hire aides and pay for the assisted living facility. But even in difficult times, I couldn't let him be my whole life. I don't have to grieve forever; I can go on living and that doesn't dishonor my husband. My best coping mechanism was an ability to compartmentalize during this very difficult time.

Source: Edie Stark. Used by permission.

Increasing Difficulties

Concern increases in conjunction with diminished drive or lack of initiative and especially with outbursts of irritation or anger and rapid mood swings or personality changes. Affected individuals are likely to become self-centered and insensitive or impulsive and uninhibited in their speech and behavior. Foul language and aggression toward others is likely to cause dismay in those others when it occurs. Irrational delusions and accusations of stealing or extramarital affairs will generate astonishment. People who are frightened or hurt by these behaviors often withdraw from the person with the disease.

The inability to recognize family members or a tendency to mistake them for long-dead relatives can be experienced as especially hurtful by loved ones. A medical consultation can be in order if not previously sought, and a provisional diagnosis of AD or some related disorder is likely to result.

It is important to keep in mind that these are just a few of the ways in which AD and other related disorders may manifest themselves. Changes caused by these diseases in the brain, the seat of a person's mental life and the controller of bodily functioning, can express themselves in many different ways and often in fluctuating patterns of behavior. Likewise, the attitudes of affected individuals (insofar as they can be divined from the outside) and of others around such individuals can vary widely.

Advanced Difficulties

A sign of the advanced difficulties that eventually appear in AD was seen in Ronald Reagan's celebrated announcement on November 5, 1994 (after completing his second term as president in January 1989), in a handwritten letter to the American people:

> I have recently been told that I am one of the millions of Americans who will be afflicted with Alzheimer's disease....
>
> At the moment, I feel just fine. I intend to live the remainder of the years God gives me on this earth doing the things I have always done. I will continue to share life's journey with my beloved Nancy and my family. I plan to enjoy the great outdoors and stay in touch with my friends and supporters.
>
> Unfortunately, as Alzheimer's disease progresses, the family often bears a heavy burden....
>
> I now begin the journey that will lead me into the sunset of my life. I know that for America there will always be a bright dawn ahead.

In fact, Mr. Reagan did not die until June 5, 2004, and during at least part of that time he did remain active in various ways. Still, Mr. Reagan's letter points quite clearly to the advanced difficulties that confront or are about to confront many in connection with AD. For example, most people in advanced stages of AD eventually lose the ability to communicate and care for themselves, become bed-bound, and require round-the-clock care. We will examine those burdens and the attitudes associated with them in discussions of coping with dying and coping with bereavement that follow. In the meantime, we look to some practices associated with AD.

PRACTICES ASSOCIATED WITH ALZHEIMER'S DISEASE AND RELATED DISORDERS

There are a broad range of practices associated with ADRD. In this section we explore practices related to communicating diagnoses, family caring, and community caring.

Communicating Diagnoses

There is some evidence that many physicians have not been very open in communicating diagnoses of Alzheimer's disease and other related disorders. For example, the Alzheimer's Association (2017, p. 18) has reported that "fewer than half of those who have a diagnosis of Alzheimer's or another dementia in their Medicare records (or their caregiver, if the person was too impaired to respond to the survey) report being told of the diagnosis." This is especially important in the early stages of disease when they would have been in the best position to make informed decisions. Thus, the Alzheimer's Association notes that many professional organizations in brain health have issued guidelines that "uniformly advocate revealing the diagnosis to the person who has been diagnosed and doing so in clear language" (2015, p. 59), even while respecting diagnostic difficulties, individual preferences, and situations in which such communication is neither possible nor practicable. There are obvious risks, such as fears of causing emotional distress, stigma, or even adverse behavior. Still, it is thought that communicating diagnoses in a caring and supportive manner can outweigh such concerns. The goal here is to support individual autonomy, informed decision making and planning for the future, constructive coping, and better access to services and social support, while facilitating truth telling, trust, and cooperation among all involved. Two examples of how well-known celebrities responded to their diagnoses are given in Focus On 20.4.

FOCUS ON 20.4

Robin Williams and Glen Campbell

Robin Williams hung himself on August 11, 2014, at the age of 63. His death shocked fans who had known him as a stand-up comedian, through the TV series, *Mork & Mindy*, and in motion pictures ranging from *The World According to Garp*, *Good Morning, Vietnam*, and *Mrs. Doubtfire*, to *Dead Poets Society*, *Awakenings*, and *Good Will Hunting* (for which he won an Academy Award as Best Supporting Actor). His death was initially thought to have resulted from depression, Parkinson's disease, and paranoia, but a study of his brain tissue later showed that Williams suffered from "diffuse Lewy body dementia." After his death, his widow, Susan Schneider Williams, said, "It was not depression that killed Robin... Depression was one of let's call it 50 symptoms, and it was a small one" (Itzkoff & Carey, 2015). She added that her husband had had "this endless parade of symptoms" since fall 2013, "and not all of them would raise their head at once." Unfortunately, Lewy body dementia is often mistaken for Alzheimer's disease or Parkinson's disease because it combines deficits in memory and thinking often found in Alzheimer's, with stiffness and movement problems seen in Parkinson's disease. Williams would likely have been aware of the distinctive signs of his dementia—including chronic sleep problems, fluctuations in thinking, and visual hallucinations—and of the fact that it is not curable. If so, he likely took action to avoid his fate.

Glen Campbell is famous for his renditions of songs like "Gentle on My Mind," "By the Time I Get to Phoenix," "Wichita Lineman," "Galveston," "Rhinestone Cowboy," and "Southern Nights." In 2011 at the age of 75 he revealed his diagnosis

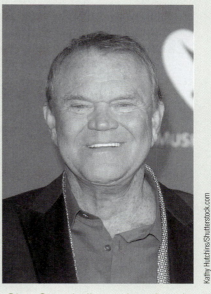

Robin Williams at a Los Angeles party, 7/29/13

Glen Campbell at a Los Angeles celebration, 2/10/12

(continues)

FOCUS ON 20.4 *(continued)*

Robin Williams and Glen Campbell

of Alzheimer's disease. Glen then began a two-and-a-half year, 151-city tour with family members joining in his backup band. A documentary film of the tour entitled, "I'll Be Me," was highlighted by duos involving Glen and his daughter, Ashley. Later, his final recording, "I'm Not Gonna Miss You," received an Oscar nomination for best original song. Trevor Albert, the film's producer, said, "The amazing thing about Glen was that he was the first public figure to come and say, 'I have Alzheimer's, and I'm going to continue to show people that I can still live a full life and perform and be creative'" (Burtt, 2015). Albert added, "This is a story about how we choose to live our lives when faced with adversity.... [His family] chose to embrace life and Glen wasn't defined by the disease and they laughed and hugged through it all." In March 2016, Glen Campbell was reported to be in the final stages of his disease and living in a Nashville memory care facility. He died on August 8, 2017, at the age of 81.

Family Caring

Families are usually the first and primary providers of support to persons with Alzheimer's disease and related disorders. Although they may find it difficult to recognize the initial signs of disease, when things become clearer family members often come together to care for and keep the person in their home. Latent strengths of informal networks may be mobilized to help. Efforts will be made to draw upon assistance from any family members and friends who are available and willing to lend a hand. Books for children can explain to young readers what is happening and dispel fears (see Focus On 20.5). And age-appropriate roles can be found for youngsters to contribute to the care of their loved one. As long as safety and security can be assured and family care providers can bear up under what is required of them, the home provides a familiar surrounding and a comforting routine for the person with ADRD.

Things are less satisfactory when a safe and secure home does not exist, when there is no family or other natural network to rally to support an isolated person, when there are preexisting difficulties or strains in family relationships, or when family members are overburdened by health and other challenges of their own. In these cases, a sense of desperation may set in, and it may be necessary to call upon community resources at an early stage in the disease process.

Community Caring

The founding of the Alzheimer's Association in 1980 helped lead to increased public and professional recognition of the prevalence and the challenges of AD and related disorders. The National Institute on Aging supports the Alzheimer's Disease Education and Referral Center (ADEAR) while also funding a consortium of centers devoted to research and clinical drug trials. Other helpful resources include: the Alzheimer's Foundation of America; more specialized organizations like the Lewy Body Dementia

Children's Books about Alzheimer's Disease and Other Dementias

Here is a sampler of the many books intended to aid young readers in understanding and helping people with dementia. Most of these books tell similar stories about memory problems, confusion, behavioral changes, and children's concerns. They differ mainly in their intended audiences, the metaphors they use to explain the disease, and the particular issues or messages they emphasize.

Several books emphasize understanding what is happening. In *What's Wrong with Grandma?: A Family's Experience with Alzheimer's* (Margaret Shawver; Amherst, NY: Prometheus, 2003; Grade 3–6) a girl describes changes in her Grandma's behavior. After Grandma is diagnosed, the girl concludes, "Now that we know what's happening to Grandma, it's a little easier to be around her" (p. 61). In *Always My Grandpa: A Story for Children About Alzheimer's Disease* (Linda Scacco; Washington, DC: Magination Press, 2006; Gr ≥K) a mother tells a boy that Grandpa's mind is like a seashell they found, once full of life and memories, but now they are leaving him like the sea creature left the shell. Grandpa adds, "I want you to know that when I don't seem like myself, or when I'm acting in a way that seems strange or confusing to you, I still love you" (p.17). *Grandpa Has Changed* (Jennifer Moore-Mallinos; Hauppage, NY: Barron's Educational Series, 2009; ≥K), describes two children who are sad and puzzled as they recognize their beloved grandfather has changed. He often forgets things and sometimes even forgets where he is. After Mom explains that Grandpa is suffering from AD, the children realize that Grandpa loves them as much now as he always has, and they can still enjoy happy times together. *Remember, Grandma?* (Laura Langston; New York: Viking Juvenile, 2004; K–3), is a similar story in which Margaret's mother tells her "She still loves you, even if she can't remember your name."

In some books, as children begin to understand what is happening, they express their love by trying to see how they can help. *Striped Shirts and Flowered Pants: A Story about Alzheimer's Disease for Young Children* (Barbara Schnurbush; Washington, DC: Magination Press, 2007; Pre–3) describes a little girl who notices Nana's clothes don't always match, she forgets things, and she has trouble saying some words in a book they are reading together. Libby's parents explain that Nana's brain isn't working right because she has a disease that kids can't get. Libby talks to her parents when she feels sad or worried about Nana, but mostly the two of them share activities and their love.

Hugging Grandma: Loving Those with Memory Disorders (Zina Kramer; Northville, MI: Ferne Press, 2009; Pre–3) starts with questions like: What happens when your grandma doesn't know it's your birthday or can't remember things? Because they had shared wonderful times before Grandma developed AD, the child seeks ways to help Grandma still feel useful and needed.

Two Canadian books include *Really and Truly* (Émilie Rivard; Toronto: Owlkids Books, 2012; ≥Pre), which describes a time when grandpa no longer

(continues)

Children's Books about Alzheimer's Disease and Other Dementias

tells the stories that Charlie so loved and sometimes doesn't even recognize Charlie, so the boy develops a plan to tell those stories back to grandpa to make him laugh, while *Weeds in Nana's Garden: A Heartfelt Story of Love that Helps Explain Alzheimer's Disease and Other Dementias* (Kathryn Harrison; Toronto: Flipturn Publishing, 2016; K–4) uses the metaphor of tangled weeks in Nana's magical garden to explain what is happening to Nana and to describe how a young girl recognizes those changes and determines to become the garden's caregiver.

Two books focus on specific things children can do to help a grandparent in the early stages of AD. In *The Memory Box* (Mary Bahr; Morton Grove, IL: Albert Whitman & Co., 1992; Gr1–4) a boy and his grandfather work together to make a box to store memories, photos, souvenirs, and family tales so that no matter what happens to Gramps, the memories are saved forever. *What's Happening to Grandpa?* (Maria Shriver; Boston & New York: Little, Brown, 2004; Pre–Gr 3) describes a girl who gradually notices Grandpa is repeating stories and questions over and over, has become forgetful, and even got angry at Grandma one day. Kate involves Grandpa in making a scrapbook of his life by collecting his "olden-day photos" while he tells about the stories behind them, his memories, and the joy he still finds in each new day. He adds, "The important memories of my life will forever be in my heart." Kate's mother adds some important advice: "Honey, what we do now is support Grandma and just keep on loving and respecting Grandpa the way we always have."

Finding a new, safer environment is important for some people with dementia. *Singing with Momma Lou* (Linda J. Altman; New York: Lee & Low Books, 2015; Gr1–4) depicts a 9-year-old African-American girl who is initially resentful when she has to visit her grandmother in a nursing home. But when her father shows her pictures of Momma Lou singing in jail after a civil rights demonstration, Tamika recalls how much they had shared and times when they were best friends. Tamika plans to give Momma Lou back some of her memories with photographs, newspaper stories, other mementos, and songs like "We Shall Overcome." *Still My Grandma* (Véronique Van den Abeele; Grand Rapids, MI: Eerdmans, 2007; Pre–5) portrays fun activities and special traditions shared by a young girl and her Grandma. In weekly visits to the nursing home, Camille brings cupcakes and prized treasures to share and tells stories to Grandma. Even though Grandma has changed, Camille says "she's still my Grandma and I love her very much. She loves me too. I can tell because she still remembers our special kiss." Similarly, when her grandmother begins showing signs of AD in *Forget Me Not* (Nancy Van Laan; New York: Schwartz & Wade, 2014; Pre–3), Julia and her parents must face the illness and get Grandma the care she needs. Grandma gradually forgets names and things they had done together, but when

(continues)

Children's Books about Alzheimer's Disease and Other Dementias

she is found outside in the snow in her nightie digging for forget-me-nots, they make the difficult decision to move her to a facility. Julia is upset by this change, but soon realizes that Grandma is happier in her new environment. Julia misses the old, sweet grandma, but still loves her and greets her with a big hug each time she visits. Even if Grandma can't remember, Julia will never forget. In *My New Granny* (Elisabeth Steinkellner; New York: Sky Pony Press, 2012; Pre–3), Fini's Granny has changed from the person with whom she used to share many fun things and even tries to eat bread crumbs meant for the ducks in the park. In time, Granny comes to live with Fini and her family because she needs to be watched, almost like a little child. She needs help dressing and washing, falls asleep underneath the kitchen table, and has a woman named Agatha who comes to care for her. Fini is unsure what to think of this "new" Granny—she looks the same but she acts like a completely different person. At first, Fini is upset that she has to help take care of Granny, but ultimately proclaims that she loves her new Granny as much as the old one.

Two books show music's deep roots for people with dementia and children. *Faraway Grandpa* (Roberta Karim; New York: Henry Holt, 2004; K–4) gets lost in the house, makes trouble with neighbors, and even forgets Kathleen's name, but he still remembers things from long ago. Kathleen knows her grandfather is still "in there," and, on his "shadowy" days she can sometimes pull his head out of the clouds as they sing "Danny Boy" together. *Grandpa's Music: A Story about Alzheimer's* (Alison Acheson; Morton Grove, IL: Albert Whitman, 2009; Gr3–5) addresses the delicate transitions from independent living to moving into the home of younger relatives to being admitted to a long-term care facility. When Grandpa moves into their home, the family arranges a routine to provide him security. A young girl accompanies Grandpa in the garden and when he plays the piano his fingers remember the old-time music, even if they have to make up words to sing. When it is time to take Grandpa to live in a nursing home, he is pleased to find a piano there.

For older children, *An Early Winter* (Marion Dane Bauer; New York: Dell Yearling, 2001; Gr4–7) depicts an 11-year-old boy, who idolizes his grandfather and refuses to believe Granddad has AD. Tim thinks Granddad is simply sad because they have been separated. Tim is sure his presence during a visit will make things right and convince the adults that they should be together. Ignoring warning signs, he takes Granddad on a calamitous fishing trip. Ultimately, Grandma says the two of them are moving to live in the senior apartments near Tim and his mother. In *The Graduation of Jake Moon* (Barbara Park; New York: Alladin, 2002; Gr4–7), as his grandfather's AD progresses and a boy advances from third grade to his eighth grade graduation, Jake increasingly takes on a caregiver role for Skelly.

Association; and AD centers and memory disorder clinics at many academic medical centers. There are bulletin boards, chat rooms, and discussion groups devoted to ADRD on the Internet, as well as numerous websites on helpful organizations and topics associated with various types of dementia and related issues. Also, the Alzheimer's Association has local chapters that seek to advance public awareness of ADRD and that provide community education through books, pamphlets, and videos.

Local chapters devoted to ADRD are perhaps the most useful resource for affected individuals and families. Their educational offerings can provide the first window into dementia for those who find themselves in a new and bewildering life situation. In addition, support groups can bring together individuals with shared experiences so as to give vent to their reactions and learn about how others have coped with these challenges.

COPING WITH ALZHEIMER'S DISEASE AND RELATED DISORDERS

In Chapter 6 in this book, we discussed coping with dying. Here we address coping in relationship to Alzheimer's disease and related disorders when the disease and dying trajectories typically extend over years, not merely weeks or months. Especially in the early stages of ADRD, there may be fluctuations in an individual's abilities and even moments of lucidity. While these brief moments are certainly welcome, they may lead to the false impression that broader recovery is possible.

It is challenging to attempt to discuss coping with ADRD for several reasons:

1. As with any life-threatening situation, there are two groups of persons who are drawn into coping with ADRD: *persons who have the disease themselves* and *other individuals who are affected because someone they know or love has the disease*. This reinforces what we learned earlier in this book: life-limiting and life-threatening diseases have an impact on many individuals, not only those who are directly suffering from a disease.
2. Persons with ADRD, as well as family care providers, are unique individuals with their own personalities, backgrounds, and lifestyles. Their individuality needs to be taken into account in order to understand how they are coping with these diseases.
3. Persons impacted by ADRD see their lives changed dramatically in many ways: physically, cognitively, emotionally, socially, economically, behaviorally, and spiritually.
4. ADRD express themselves in a very wide range of manifestations, they progress irregularly, and they usually do so over an extended period of time.

For these reasons, we can only here sketch out some common themes in coping with ADRD, while also mentioning additional useful resources that provide detailed guidance for care providers.

Individual Coping

In the early stages of AD and other related disorders, more or less urgent, short-term challenges involving memory problems and confusion can be frustrating and frightening especially when they occur in unexpected ways and at unanticipated times. As the disease progresses, the ordinary course of the lives of both the person with ADRD and others around that person must often be modified. "New normals" will need to be developed and often modified repeatedly in order to take into account changes in the person's abilities and requirements for assistance. Because themes of loneliness, isolation, and fear are often found in persons in the early stages of ADRD, it is important to reassure them that they will not be abandoned and that they are still valued by those who love them. Because "awareness of decline in mental abilities is often coupled with appreciation of the remaining gifts in one's life" (Kuhn, 2013, p. 86), it is equally important to continue to share valued activities and to offer the gift of one's presence.

Issues like this have been the focus of individuals who have sought to communicate to others what it is like to experience ADRD, as it were, "from the inside" (see the personal stories in the Suggested Readings at the end of this chapter). These autobiographical accounts often observe that life can still be good and that it is the simple pleasures in life that are most prized, such as the company of cherished persons, places, and things. Many individuals at this point in their disease trajectory report how important it is for them to continue to be appreciated as persons and to be assisted in finding activities that provide them with satisfaction. Recall the motto, "Make Today Count," mentioned in Chapter 1 of this book. Here it means that individuals with ADRD should be helped to focus not merely on what they have lost, but on what they retain and on the benefits of advance warnings of mortality that may not be available to others in different life-threatening situations.

In the longer term it is desirable for individuals with early-stage dementia to plan ahead as much as possible for what can be anticipated, preferably in conjunction with assistance from a close family member or trusted advisor. It makes sense, for example, to consider what the disease will mean for one's various responsibilities, to try to put one's affairs in order, to write down advance directives and appoint a health care surrogate, to make a will and perhaps to develop and/or fund a revocable living trust with some responsible person(s) as trustee(s) (for legal matters, see Chapter 16 in this book). To facilitate such planning, The Conversation Project, a private, non-profit organization has undertaken to help people talk about their wishes for end-of-life care by developing a free, downloadable "starter kit" specifically designed to help families and loved ones of people with ADRD who want guidance about "having the conversation." Failing to plan ahead when one can condemns oneself (and others) to a time when one will no longer be able to make and execute plans.

Planning ahead inevitably involves others who can anticipate a time when there will be a need to mobilize resources in order to enable the person with dementia to stay in the familiar surroundings of his or her home, if that is at all possible. Familiar surroundings support a sense of safety and security, as well as a degree of control and dignity. In addition, advance planning can also take into account what to do when an individual can no longer perform activities of daily living, becomes bedbound, and needs round-the-clock care. Much of this may require professional in-home care, adult day care, and/or respite care, as well as hospital, long-term care, or hospice services. Advance planning also does well to take into account issues that are all too often neglected, such as how to respond in the event of natural disasters, for example, how to transport a wheelchair-bound individual if it becomes necessary to leave one's home and where to go since crowded emergency shelters are often challenging for confused individuals.

Families Coping

In addition to those who themselves have ADRD, *people who are coping with dementia in others* will also see their lives change in dramatic ways. Children, spouses, partners, and others will be challenged as they live with and try to care for those with these diseases. The Alzheimer's Association (2017) has estimated that in 2016 some 15 million family members and friends were providing unpaid care to a person with AD or another dementia. Two-thirds of these informal caregivers were women, one-third were aged 65 or older, and many had health problems of their own. Such informal caregivers often face increased burdens as the disease progresses. This can lead to high levels of physical and psychological stress, increased out-of-pocket expenses, and problems arising from living at a distance from the impaired person or from the need to take time off from work, care for children, or meet other obligations.

From the outset, the most immediate challenge often is to enable the person with ADRD to remain in the familiar surroundings of his or her home. That can soon become a round-the-clock predicament. As Sandra Day O'Connor remarked in the vignette near the beginning of this chapter: "He wants me there all the time." The constant call for the presence of family caregivers is wholly understandable as the person with dementia becomes less confident and less sure of his or her surroundings. It is, however, a difficult burden to carry over the long term.

Families that have internal resources or that can call upon friends, hired aides, or adult day care and respite programs may be able to work out arrangements to care for the person with ADRD in the home for some time. Still, most can expect to face a need to turn to community resources when care requirements increase as the disease progresses.

Communities Coping

Diseases like ADRD that have powerful impacts on the lives of individuals and families also have dramatic impacts on communities. *Local communities coping with these diseases* have responded in a variety of ways. Often, the first priority has

Care providers often play an important role in helping individuals cope with Alzheimer's disease.

Lisa F. Young/Shutterstock.com

been to provide health care and social services for sick people. Typically, this has involved the development of medical, nursing, and social work expertise and services to address the challenges and complexities of these diseases. As these disorders became better understood and new responses were developed, requirements for care and costs increased greatly, as well as the need for effective coordination between various types of health care and social service agencies. For example, in Chapter 8 in this book we learned that approximately 15% of people admitted to U.S. hospice programs in 2013 involved persons with a primary diagnosis of AD or another cause of dementia, representing a growing challenge to those services (see Tarter, Demiris, Pike, Washington, & Oliver, 2016, for an example).

Without a cure for ADRD, communities quickly realized the importance of education about, minimizing the likelihood of, and treating these diseases. Many communities undertook campaigns to increase awareness, knowledge, and sensitivity about ADRD among the general public, professionals, and groups deemed to be at high risk for the development of dementia. Other communities sent informed persons into schools, churches, health care facilities, and businesses to provide accurate information about ADRD. Many communities developed "Silver Alert" systems to notify professionals and members of the public when an individual with dementia wanders away from his or her living quarters.

Because ADRD often strain the financial resources of individuals and families, many have needed to turn to local communities for assistance. For example, if individuals become unable to work or to pay for health insurance or other services, they may need financial assistance from a variety of public and private agencies. Some community programs help pay for health insurance or for the deductible amounts associated with that insurance. A good place to begin to explore helpful resources and services is one of the local Area Agencies on Aging (see "Aging" or "Social Services" under city or county government listings in local telephone or Internet directories), which administer the National Family Caregiver Support Program under the Administration on Aging of the U.S. Department of Health and Human Services. Another good source of information is Eldercare Locator.

Persons with ADRD are high users of health and social services. For example, the Alzheimer's Association (2017) has estimated that total payments for such services in 2017 reached $259 billion, including $131 billion from Medicare and $44 billion from Medicaid, along with out-of-pocket spending. Such expenditures are projected to increase to more than $1.1 trillion in 2050 (in 2016 dollars), which is a five-fold increase in Medicare/Medicaid spending and a nearly five-fold increase in out-of-pocket spending (see also Kelley, McGarry, Gorges, & Skinner, 2015). Similarly, the total estimated worldwide costs of dementia have been estimated by Alzheimer's Disease International (2016) to amount to $818 billion in 2015, with projected increases to $1 trillion in 2018 and $2 trillion by 2030. Alzheimer's Disease International has noted that the 2016 figure means that if global dementia care were a country it would be the 18th largest economy in the world, exceeding the market values of companies such as Apple, Google, and Exxon!

Another area in which community assistance is often needed is housing for persons with ADRD, especially for those who live alone or who can no longer be maintained in a private residence. People living with dementia need safe, dependable, and affordable housing. Suitable housing for such persons improves their quality of life, encourages compliance with complicated medical regimens, increases access to critically needed health care services, and can help family members stay together.

Funding for community programs can come from many sources. Federal grants, private donations, and grants from state and local governments all play a role. Medicare and Medicaid programs provide some funds for these community activities. However, fund-raising is a continuous, ongoing necessity for any community agency seeking to provide programs for those affected by ADRD. Such fund-raising is difficult when economic times are hard or when other worthwhile causes seem more pressing.

We also see here, once again, a *death system* at work (see Chapter 4). Although dementia does not represent an instantaneous death sentence in most instances, it is still a life-affecting and eventually life-threatening disease. Because increasingly large numbers of persons are being diagnosed and because such persons typically require continuous and expensive care, ADRD will continue to strain community resources. These diseases demand creative, compassionate responses, and they do this in a social and political environment in which there are many barriers and competing demands.

HELPING PERSONS WITH ALZHEIMER'S DISEASE AND RELATED DISORDERS

In Chapters 7 and 8 in this book, we discussed helping persons who are coping with dying. Here we need to step back from a focus on imminent death to consider helping with the long trajectory of ADRD and their specific requirements.

Helping Individuals

Because each person with dementia is a unique individual, we must try to look at the world from their point of view in order to help them. However, many of these individuals may not be able to describe how the world looks to them. For that reason, Ferman, Smith, and Melom (2008) offered the following advice:

> Persons with dementia often lose their ability to express themselves before they lose their ability to understand. Behavior becomes a means of communication. Ask yourself why your loved one is behaving this way. Then you can take steps to manage the behavior.

This approach is far more likely to be helpful than trying to reason with individuals who can no longer think clearly or challenging them to do things that are beyond their current capacities. We cannot force individuals with dementia to be the persons they once were but no longer are nor can we fit them into external agendas they can no longer uphold. It may take great tact to find ways to help those who forget that they are forgetful or are unaware that their deficiencies are becoming more obvious to others.

Kuhn (2013, pp. 95–98) observed that in order to be happy, people with dementia have three central needs that go beyond the physical requirements of food, clothing, and shelter:

1. *Intimacy* or closeness to and familiarity with other people, places, and things; this counters real or imagined fears and loneliness by providing a sense of safety and connectedness
2. *Community*, a sense of belonging to a group with whom one shares a common bond, of being accepted for who they are not for what they can do; this counters feelings of being cut off, unwelcome, out of place, or rejected

3. *Meaningful activities*, whatever those activities are and whether one can do them alone or only with the help of others

Detailed suggestions on how to address what can seem to be an overwhelming number of problems encountered in helping individuals with ADRD are available from a variety of sources. Book-length guides for care providers can be found in the list in the Suggested Readings at the end of this chapter. Also, Focus On 20.6 provides a list of activity books that can be used by or with persons with dementia.

Examples of helpful booklets that can be read online or downloaded from the Internet include: *Caring for a Person with Alzheimer's Disease: Your Easy-to-Use Guide from the National Institute on Aging* and *End of Life: Helping with Coping and Care*; *Understanding Behavioral Changes in Dementia* and *Lewy Body Dementia: Information for Patients, Families, and Professionals* (both available from the

---

FOCUS ON 20.6

Activity Books for People with Dementia

In addition to the Suggested Readings for caregivers listed at the end of this chapter, here are selected examples of many activity books describing ideas for use by or with persons with dementia.

Bell, V., Troxel, D., Cox, T. M., & Hamon, R. (2004/2008). *The Best Friends Book of Alzheimer's Activities, Vol. 1 & Vol. 2*

Brackey, J. (2008). *Creating Moments of Joy for the Person with Alzheimer's or Dementia: A Journal for Caregivers* (4th ed.)

Burdick, L. (2006). *Happy New Year to You!: A Read-Aloud Book for Memory-Challenged Adults*

Burdick, L. (2009). *Wishing on a Star: A Read-Aloud Book for Memory-Challenged Adults*

Burdick, L. (2015). *The Sunshine on My Face: A Read-Aloud Book for Memory-Challenged Adults (2nd ed.)*

Dowling, J. R. (1995). *Keeping Busy: A Handbook of Activities for Persons with Dementia*

Gitlin, L. N., & Piersol, C. V. (2014). *A Caregiver's Guide to Dementia: Using Activities and Other Strategies to Prevent, Reduce and Manage Behavioral Symptoms*

Green, C. R., & Beloff, J. (2008). *Through the Seasons: An Activity Book for Memory-Challenged Adults and Caregivers*

Jones, M. M. (2013). *Bring Back the Fun: Activity Ideas for Caregivers and People with Dementia*

Levy, J. A. (2014). *Activities to do with Your Parent Who Has Alzheimer's Dementia*

MacLachlan, B. S. (2016). *Connecting Memories, Book 3: Coloring and Activities Book for People with Dementia, Alzheimer's, Brain Injuries, Stroke and Other Cognitive Conditions.*

Sobel, E. (2012). *Blue Sky, White Clouds: A Book for Memory-Challenged Adults*

Lewy Body Dementia Association); and *Dementia: Hope through Research* (available from the National Institute of Neurological Disorders and Stroke). In addition, A *Caregiver Notebook: A Guide to Caring for People with Alzheimer's and Related Dementias* can be purchased from the Alzheimer's Association.

Typically, booklets like these address topics like changes in communication skills (including memory loss, difficulties in finding words to articulate thoughts, and forgetting steps in common activities); changes in personality and behavior (including a wide range of feelings, wandering and agitation, hiding things, aggression, sleep problems, hallucinations, and paranoia); changes in intimacy and sexuality; health, legal, and financial issues; safety issues at home and in driving; exercise and eating; daily activities and personal care; self care and getting help; institutional placements; and end-of-life care.

Helping Family Caregivers

One of the most important things family members and professionals who are providing care for a person with ADRD can do is to *take good care of themselves*. That's why commercial airlines advise passengers that if oxygen masks suddenly become needed and fall from the ceiling, they should put their own mask on first before trying to help a child or someone else seated next to them. Sadly, many family members who are providing this type of care believe there is so much they need to do for the person with the disease that they can neglect to care for themselves or that they simply do not have time for self care. That belief is false and dangerous simply because any caregiver is likely to quickly wear out under the multiple demands of ADRD. If that happens, the caregiver will no longer be able to provide care for the person with disease, and everyone will be worse off. Also, becoming absorbed in caring for the person with disease often leads family caregivers to withdraw from friends and community resources that could otherwise help in these tasks. *The critical need for and value of self care cannot be overemphasized.* Advice for caregivers is provided in Personal Insights 20.2 by a woman who cared for her husband with AD until his death.

PERSONAL INSIGHTS 20.2

A Wife's Advice after Caring for Her Husband with Alzheimer's Disease

My husband was a brilliant man who completed college at age 16 and finished his doctorate at age 21. Subsequently, he went on to earn wide renown in his chosen professional field. He was a charming person and a gifted communicator who enjoyed a number of hobbies, from vegetable gardening to photography, excelling at them all. Unfortunately, both his mother and his first wife died of complications of Alzheimer's disease. Perhaps that is why it was difficult both for him and his adult children to recognize the early signs of this terrible disease, and, except for one son, it continued to prove difficult to acknowledge until the last few weeks of his life. I want here to describe some of our experiences and to offer some advice for others who find themselves in similar situations.

(continues)

A Wife's Advice after Caring for Her Husband with Alzheimer's Disease

1. **This disease sneaks up on you.** We didn't really see it starting. And it was a slow and uneven process stretching over nearly a decade. Or perhaps we didn't want to acknowledge what was happening. For much too long, I tried to interact with my husband as if he were rational because that fostered my denial, but I should have known by his reactions that he was not. In any event, we disregarded early indications of disease. A man who previously had an eidetic memory now kept calling wrong numbers because he could not believe he had to look up the correct ones. It's heartbreaking when a mind begins to go. The lesson is that it is invaluable to act quickly to have a complete medical examination to determine what is going on.

2. Finding **a competent physician is critical.** Preferably this should be a geriatrician with experience in diagnosing and treating dementias. Unfortunately, our primary physician (a longtime family friend) had not acted appropriately when my husband's first wife began to drive erratically, had several accidents, and eventually needed institutional placement. In the case of my husband, this physician listened to my husband (not to me) who said he was fine, even though by then, as on one occasion, he stayed in his study, did not eat, and became incoherent. When I pleaded with his nurse to have the physician call my husband and ask him to come in for a visit, he could barely get into the car and was immediately hospitalized with dehydration and blood poisoning. While this physician was saying all is well, my husband was falling out of bed, having hallucinations, experiencing temper tantrums, and engaging in behaviors that previously would have been unthinkable. In the end, I no longer found it possible to stay with this physician, and my husband's son agreed to take over the doctor visits. At one point I set up an urgent appointment when I realized there was something terribly wrong. During this visit his physician told my husband he was fine, but I knew he was in trouble. That's when I asked my new geriatrician for help. Persuading my husband to come with me to see my new doctor and preparing this doctor to treat him (for free, as he thought!) with great cordiality and deference led to a diagnosis of active kidney failure and immediate hospitalization. This intervention wasn't a magic solution, but it did solve some problems. I still needed a doctor who was skilled in treating dementia or who would refer me to one who was.

3. **Don't keep IT a secret; secrecy helps no one, especially not the patient.** For a long time, my husband hid some of his problems from me and I was complicit perhaps because I felt protective of him. I thought: "How do you tell a brilliant man he has dementia?" But then I realized he was putting bourbon into his morning coffee, and I found porno magazines covered by scientific books when he fell asleep. Later episodes involved inappropriate sexual behavior in front of a large picture window and with a female hired helper. My husband tried very hard to keep his many

(continues)

A Wife's Advice after Caring for Her Husband with Alzheimer's Disease

colleagues from knowing about his condition to the point he no longer wanted to see them. Had we been open and faced this disease from the beginning, together with a knowledgeable geriatrician we might have mobilized some resources for delaying the progression of this disease, modifying symptoms, or at least planning together.

4. **Confide in family members and friends who are able and willing to be helpful.** Early on, my husband and I didn't want to admit to ourselves or others that he had Alzheimer's. Perhaps subconsciously we thought our situation was somehow shameful, even though this disease is the product of unknown causes and did not somehow arise from improper behavior. When we did share this information with family members and friends, not surprisingly, some withdrew. Even the word "Alzheimer's" scares some people. At the same time, I realized it was unrealistic to depend heavily on support from children since they often live at great distances and typically have their own career obligations and caring responsibilities for their own families. Thankfully, a few people found the courage and time to offer help we desperately needed. Eventually, my husband's erratic driving frightened our neighbors and, on one occasion, required the police to bring him back home. Shortly thereafter, with the help of one of members from our church's adult Sunday School classes, my husband was persuaded to offer himself as an example of an older person (in his 80s) who willingly gave up his driving license.

5. **Seek out an appropriate support group.** These are the people who know what it is really like to struggle with dementia and who can identify with your experiences. They can help you give vent to what you are experiencing and show you how to cope better with this situation. When I was caring for my husband alone with little respite, I knew there were resources on the Web, but by the time he finally slept, I was too exhausted to research those resources. For me, it was particularly difficult when my husband thought I was his mother whom he loved very much. I didn't know whether to correct him or go along with the pretense. Perhaps I could have gotten helpful advice on this point. At an earlier time, my husband experienced great anxiety when he realized that he could no longer remember the names of his distant family, including cousins, nieces, second cousins, uncles, and aunts. When we created an extended family tree, added photos, and put everything together in a special album, we learned that his brain remained very strong on visualizing/imaging. A support group might have guided us about losing and retaining different abilities in the course of Alzheimer's disease.

6. **Everything is exponentially more difficult when complicated by age and health problems.** I had five surgeries during the five years before my husband's death and after the last one I needed two additional weeks in a rehabilitation facility. One surgery for renal carcinoma was so

(continues)

A Wife's Advice after Caring for Her Husband with Alzheimer's Disease

anxiety-provoking that my husband convinced himself it wasn't cancer even after part of one of my kidneys had been removed. Although I had arranged for full-time help for my husband while I was in the hospital, he called several times every day asking if I was well now and pleading with me to come home. By the time my husband died I was physically, mentally, and emotionally exhausted.

7. **Time away from responsibilities as a care provider is essential.** My husband followed me around almost everywhere in the house while he was awake. The strain was intense. In fact, there were times when I ran out the door screaming because I could not deal with my situation. But when he ran after me, I managed to come to my senses. In order to find some time for myself, I hired comfort keepers to spend two hours three afternoons a week with my husband and drive him around, take him out for lunch or to a park. Typically my husband chose to stay home. In most cases, these people were not to my husband's liking, and I found I needed to be present to supervise and intervene. After more than a year, one young man arrived who showed great respect for my husband, treated him as his college advisor, and developed a deep affection for him, thus becoming part of the family. This young man showed that care for persons with dementia must be not only instrumentally effective, but also calming and comforting, without depleting the caregiver emotionally and spiritually.

8. **You inevitably find yourself grieving—long before your husband dies—the person and intimate life partner he used to be.** This is a natural response to the many losses you are experiencing both before and after the death of the person you love. As an old person I had grieved the death of most family members and some close friends, but I was completely unprepared for the depth of the pain and the sorrow and shattering loneliness I experienced. At that time a support group or a close friend could be invaluable for sharing your burden. If such help is not sought or found, it may help to try to set aside your own need for comfort and focus instead with renewed determination on your husband's needs, as best you can, no matter what.

9. **Cherish the good times.** My husband had numerous lucid times, especially in the earlier years when he was physically well. They occurred mostly in the mornings, when he loved to be the orator of famous speeches, including the Sermon on the Mount, or he enjoyed belting out some of his favorite hymns. We recited poems, made up silly limericks, and did crossword puzzles with both of us cheating a bit. Or he told one of his lengthy jokes with or without the punch lines. Like most old people we loved to reminisce. We looked at albums of old photos and carousels of the many slides he had produced. My advice is to consciously enjoy these times. They are precious and go a long way to sustain us when the going gets rough.

Source: Anonymous. Used by permission.

In fact, good self care is actually not all that difficult in principle if one simply steps back to consider what it involves. Self care begins with a frank assessment of the stressors one is facing. People need to ask themselves questions like: What is causing me the most stress? What tasks or behaviors are most frustrating or difficult for me? What am I most anxious about? Most people who are providing care for a person with ADRD find it easy to answer questions like this when they take time to consider them.

The next step is to consider what the caregiver can do about these stressful factors. Here is where difficulties arise in practice for many caregivers. Most find that a good place to begin—indeed, perhaps an indispensable place from which to start—is to educate themselves about dementia. Educating oneself is critical to understanding this disease better, to learning about the effects it has on persons with dementia, and to recognizing the burdens it imposes on caregivers. "Forewarned is forearmed," as the saying goes. Caregivers who are baffled by a situation will likely not know how to cope with it. If they understand the situation better, they may be able to identify alternative ways of coping and to evaluate which of those alternatives might work best for them.

Writing down feelings or thoughts in a journal has helped many caregivers give vent to strong emotions and to put their situations into better perspective. On that basis, caregivers can set realistic goals concerning how much they can do for the person with dementia. Realistic goals are important because unrealistic goals are the ones that most often overwhelm caregivers.

Once caregivers have established clear goals in their minds, they can decide whether they need help to provide this type of care and how or from whom to seek the help they need. There is no shame in seeking assistance when one is caring for a person with dementia. None of us is omnipotent. None of us can do everything by ourselves. These situations are difficult for everyone who finds himself or herself providing this care. Everyone needs help from time to time, even though many care providers find it hard to ask for assistance. Few people will help if they are never asked—it's a self-fulfilling prophecy. Those who offer to help without being asked are the true angels in life. Still, many people will help if they are invited to do specific things like making a meal, visiting or staying with the person for a little while, or taking the person out for a short walk or drive.

One can also seek help from a local home health care agency or adult day care service. If such assistance does nothing else, it can bring some relief to a care provider. Finding some relief from burdens is important to keep up one's spirits, to make it possible to run errands outside the home, and to keep the caregiver from getting ill or depressed. Screening the individuals and programs that provide such services and asking for recommendations from those who have used them is essential.

Caregivers for persons with dementia can also benefit from support groups that address their specific needs. Sharing one's situation and one's reactions to that situation with others in similar situations has been repeatedly shown to be of great benefit, as noted in our discussion of bereavement support groups in Chapter 11. People in AD or dementia support groups who are having or have had similar experiences know that caregivers deserve repeated praise and rewards for their patience and endurance. They recognize the need for a little time off on occasion, legitimate uses of humor to relieve stress, and other ways to find some happiness even in difficult times. Caregivers who try to understand and appreciate their emotional and spiritual needs often can find ways to improve their situations at least a little bit. In the midst of sometimes feeling powerless, hopeless, and sad, caregivers can reaffirm their own values and motivations for choosing to take care of the person with dementia.

Lastly, it is important for caregivers to eat and drink in healthy ways, to get adequate rest and exercise whenever possible, and to take little breaks every day. Good self care is often about many small things; it rarely is about moving mountains. Living with a person with dementia means one is in for the long haul. Most people want to be there for those whom they love even if the person gets angry with them, no longer recognizes them, forgets who they are, or cannot acknowledge and thank them for the care they are providing. Caregivers who forge on in situations like this can often find moments of comfort and satisfaction they can cherish, secure in the knowledge they are doing the best they can do.

Additional guidance about self care is available in the many books for caregivers listed in the Suggested Readings near the end of this chapter and in the booklets mentioned in the previous section.

ALZHEIMER'S DISEASE, RELATED DISORDERS, AND BEREAVEMENT

Many persons with dementia, especially those in the early stages of disease, along with their family members, have identified good times and lucid moments in which there was much they could share and appreciate. In addition, as they look back on their efforts in caring for a person with ADRD, many family members have been able to recognize some positive aspects of those experiences. Thus, the oldest daughter in the family described in Personal Insights 20.1 commented that, "Through this experience, the bond that the four of us (three adult children and their mother) created is so strong, full of love and forever." Nevertheless, we now turn to many encounters with loss and grief associated with ADRD.

In Chapter 8 we learned that hospice programs say that good bereavement care for a family begins with the admission of a member to the program, not with that member's death. In this chapter, we learn that bereavement begins with the diagnosis of dementia—or perhaps even earlier when the first significant losses are noticed. Many losses are encountered during a journey with dementia. For the person with the disease, as long as that person's cognitive abilities remain intact many losses may be recognized. In addition, even when a person is no longer able to think clearly or to understand why his or her feelings and behaviors have changed, the person can often still be aware that something is different or wrong. The sense that one can no longer do the things one was once able to do and still wants to do can be distressing. Commonly, there is a strong urge to remain connected to the world the person once knew so well and to the people and things the person valued. All the feelings and other reactions we have noted previously, such as frustration, anger, sadness, isolation, and loneliness, are really part of this long journey in bereavement, a journey that only ends for the person with dementia when he or she is no longer aware of what is happening.

Care providers and others around the person with dementia will also have experienced many losses. They are challenged to cope with changes in the person they love, to bear the burdens of caring, and to grieve the loss of the person they have previously known. Many speak of being divorced by this disease, separated from a spouse or loved one while still remaining married or otherwise connected. Some speak of a "long good-bye" as they are forced to face the premature death of the person before the death of the individual's body. There can be so many "little deaths" before a final physical death that many experience bereavement overload.

At almost any point during the typically lengthy course of this disease, there will be losses that have already occurred, those that are currently taking place, and those that can be expected to take place. This is the classic pattern of pre-death losses, grief reactions, and mourning processes that we described in Chapter 9 in connection with our discussion of anticipatory grief and mourning. It ends in one sense with the physical death of the person with dementia, but in another sense it continues in a new form as a more traditional post-death bereavement. Note, however, that bereavement after the death of a person with dementia may be complicated by a mixture of grief reactions, some sense of relief from burdens long borne, and confusion about one's identity when the role of long-term care provider has been removed.

LESSONS AND VALUES

Several constructive lessons and positive values have been implicit in our explorations of death-related experiences with Alzheimer's disease and related disorders (and actually throughout this entire book). These lessons and values can help to highlight things to keep in mind as we look to the future.

As we indicated in Chapter 1, because life and death, living and dying, are inexorably intertwined, learning about death, dying, and bereavement is also a way of learning about life and living. This chapter has demonstrated that lesson well. Consider, for example, the four themes we identified in Chapter 1: control/limitation, individual persons/community, vulnerability/resilience, and quality in living/the search for meaning. In introducing these four themes, we suggested they would underlie many of the subjects addressed throughout this book, and we have seen them explicitly at work in this chapter.

For instance, the identification of AD early in the last century and the renewed appreciation of its significance as a distinct disease entity since the 1960s remind us that we human beings are finite and limited creatures. It took a long time for this disease entity to become recognized for the wide impact it has on the quality and length of human lives. Even now, well into the 21st century, there is much we still do not know about this disease, its causes, and its relationship to other dementing disorders. All of this prompts us again to confront our *limitations,* even as we appreciate that there are many things about living with ADRD that we can influence and some we can at least partly *control.*

In this chapter, we also learned how powerful an impact ADRD have upon the lives of *individuals* (both individuals directly affected by these disease entities and other persons around them) and *communities* in the United States and around the world. Individuals, families, societies, nations, and the global village have all been forced to face and try to cope with the challenges of ADRD, even as many have reached out to help those most affected.

Our *vulnerability* to the suffering, caregiver burdens, losses, and deaths wrought by dementia has been all too apparent, while at the same time there have been many fine examples of often unsung courage and *resilience* in the ways people have responded to ADRD and lived with the scourge of these complex and sometimes interrelated diseases.

In the end, encounters with AD and related disorders have shown the importance of *quality in living*, of trying to enable as many persons as possible to live as well as they can in the shadow of these disease entities and to join with them as we all engage in the existential and spiritual *human search for meaning*.

Alzheimer's disease and related disorders challenge us as individuals, as family members and friends, as members of society, and as participants in a global community to look again at our beliefs, feelings, values, and behaviors associated with life-limiting and life-threatening disease, dying, death, and bereavement. As we do so, information must replace ignorance and reasoned judgment must replace irrational decisions in all aspects of individual behavior, interpersonal relations, public policy, and the provision of care, education, and research. The reason for this is that each person who is living with dementia is, in the end, like all of the rest of us: most fundamentally, he or she is a person. And he or she is a person living with suffering.

In the last sentence of his novel, *The Bridge of San Luis Rey*, Thornton Wilder (1927/2003 p. 148) wrote: "There is a land of the living and a land of the dead and the bridge is love, the only survival, the only meaning." As health care providers, as spiritual guides, as members of social communities, as friends, as family members, and finally, simply as fellow human beings, we must care about and for persons with dementia and their family members, just as we must do so for all of those who are coping with dying, death, and bereavement. Not to do so is to risk the loss of our own best selves, our humanness. In caring for others, we care for ourselves—as individuals, as members of our own societies, and as people in the worldwide community—and we become fully who we are—human beings.

Summary

In this chapter, we used one specific disease context as an example to illustrate the central themes in this book. We examined death-related encounters, attitudes, and practices related to Alzheimer's disease and related disorders in the United States and around the world. In terms of *death-related encounters*, we explored how AD came to be identified and understood. We also examined recent data concerning individuals in our society who are living with or have died from ADRD. That led us to effects this disease has had on different age cohorts, as well as gender, racial, and cultural groups in the United States.

In terms of *death-related attitudes*, we explored early confusion, frustration, and fear. In relationship to *death-related practices*, we noted how many family members and friends have taken on great burdens in caring for individuals with ADRD and how organizations and communities have sought to educate people about these disorders, fund research into causes and treatments, and support those affected.

We next considered *coping and helping*, by individuals, families, and communities. This also involved societal death systems as they recognized and responded to the threat of ADRD. We described the increasingly harmful effects of these diseases both within our own society and around the world, and also because of the growing threats they pose for the future.

In conclusion, we noted lessons learned from the recent history of involvements with ADRD and some of the positive values that have shown through their difficult history. And we saw again that Alzheimer's disease and related disorders provide a living model that simultaneously illustrates and reflects many of the central themes and patterns we have discussed throughout this book.

Glossary

Alzheimer's disease (AD): a chronic and progressive brain disorder primarily affecting memory, thinking, behavior, and the ability to perform everyday activities; it leads inexorably to death

Alzheimer's disease and related disorders (ADRD): a group of dementing diseases similar to and sometimes confused with Alzheimer's disease (see Focus On 20.2 for some examples)

Beta-amyloid plaques: an extracellular protein buildup found in the brains of persons with AD

Dementia: an incurable condition produced by several neurodegenerative diseases involving irreversible cognitive impairment and eventual death

Frontotemporal dementia: a clinical syndrome comprising multiple disorders characterized by loss of tissue in the frontal and temporal lobes of the cortex

Lewy Body dementia: a disease in which deposits of the protein alpha-synuclein form inside neurons

Mixed dementia: the co-morbid presence of both Alzheimer's disease and vascular dementia

Tangles: twisted strands of the protein tau in the brains of persons with AD

Tau: the major component of neurofibrillary tangles associated with neuronal degeneration

Vascular dementia (multi-infarct dementia or vascular cognitive impairment): a dementia caused by decreased blood flow to the brain due to a stroke or a series of "mini strokes" (infarcts)

Questions for Review and Discussion

1. Read once again the vignette near the beginning of this chapter. Has AD or any other dementia affected your family? If so, how? If not, what might you have to cope with if ADRD appeared?
2. In your judgment, what should individuals and communities do to help those persons and families already challenged by ADRD? Are you or your community doing such things? Why or why not?
3. Have you ever drawn on social media or the Internet to help you understand or cope better with AD or other related disorders? Did you get useful assistance? Why or why not?

Suggested Readings

Personal descriptions of living with Alzheimer's disease and/or other forms of dementia include:

Bryden, C. (2005). *Dancing with Dementia: My Story of Living Positively with Alzheimer's*

Bryden, C. (2012). *Who Will I Be When I Die?*

Comer, M. (2014). *Slow Dancing with a Stranger: Lost and Found in the Age of Alzheimer's*

DeBaggio, T. (2003). *Losing My Mind: An Intimate Look at Life with Alzheimer's*

DeBaggio, T. (2007). *When It Gets Dark: An Enlightened Reflection on Life with Alzheimer's*

Fox, J. (2009). *I Still Do: Loving and Living with Alzheimer's*

Genova, L. (2007). *Still Alice*

Henderson, C. S. (1998). *Partial View: An Alzheimer's Journal*

Marley, M. (2011). *Come Back Early Today: A Memoir of Love, Alzheimer's and Joy*

McGowin, D. F. (1993). *Living in the Labrynith: A Personal Journey through the Maze of Alzheimer's*

O'Brien, G. (2014). *On Pluto: Inside the Mind of Alzheimer's*

Petersen, B. (2010). *Jan's Story: Love Lost to the Long Goodbye of Alzheimer's*

Phelps, R. (2012). *While I Still Can... One Man's Journey through Early Onset Alzheimer's Disease*

Rauschi, T. M. (2001). *A View from Within: Living with Early Onset Alzheimer's*

Rose, L. (1995). *Show Me the Way to Go Home*

Saunders, G. (2017). *Memory's Last Breath: Field Notes on My Dementia*

Taylor, R. (2007). *Alzheimer's from the Inside Out*

Thelwell, D. G. (2014). *The Dance: Our Journey through Frontotemporal Degeneration*

Some of the many resources for caregivers include:

Ali, N. (2012). *Understanding Alzheimer's: An Introduction for Patients and Caregivers*

Alzheimer's Association. (2017). *2017 Alzheimer's Disease Facts and Figures*

Bell, V., & Troxel, D. (2002). *The Best Friends Approach to Alzheimer's Care*

Bell, V., & Troxel, D. (2012). *A Dignified Life: The Best Friends Approach to Alzheimer's Care—A Guide for Care Partners* (rev. ed.)

Bell, V., & Troxel, D. (2016). *The Best Friends Approach to Dementia Care* (2nd ed.)

Boss, P. (2011). *Loving Someone Who Has Dementia: How to Find Hope while Coping with Stress and Grief*

Botonis, M. (2016). *When Caring Takes Courage: A Compassionate, Interactive Guide for Alzheimer's and Dementia Caregivers*

Calistoga Press. (2013). *Understand Alzheimer's: A First-Time Caregiver's Plan to Understand & Prepare for Alzheimer's & Dementia*

Callone, P. R., Kudlacek, C., Vasiloff, B. C., Mantemach, J., & Brumback, R. A. (2006). *A Caregiver's Guide to Alzheimer's Disease: 300 Tips for Making Life Easier*

Comer, J. (2006). *When Roles Reverse: A Guide to Parenting Your Parents*

Coste, J. K. (2003). *Learning to Speak Alzheimer's: A Groundbreaking Approach for Everyone Dealing with the Disease*

Cummings, T. (2013). *Untangling Alzheimer's: The Guide for Families and Professionals* (2nd ed.).

Kuhn, D. (2013). *Alzheimer's Early Stages: First Steps for Family, Friends, and Caregivers* (3rd ed.)

Mace, N. L., & Rabins, P. V. (2011). *The 36-Hour Day: A Family Guide for People Who Have Alzheimer Disease, Related Dementias, and Memory Loss* (5th ed.)

Mayo Clinic. (2009). *Mayo Clinic Guide to Alzheimer's Disease*

Pearce, N. (2011). *Inside Alzheimer's: How to Hear and Honor Connections with a Person Who Has Dementia* (rev. ed.)

Rabins, P. V., Lyketsos, C. G., & Steele, C. D. (2016). *Practical Dementia Care* (3rd ed.)

Rabins, P. V., & Morrison, A. S. (2013). *Caring for a Loved One with Alzheimer's Disease: A Guide for the Home Caregiver*

Radin, G., & Radin, L. (Eds.). (2014). *What If It's Not Alzheimer's?: A Caregiver's Guide To Dementia* (3rd ed.)

Scott, P. S. (2014). *Surviving Alzheimer's: Practical Tips and Soul-Saving Wisdom for Caregivers*

Shagam, J. Y. (2013). *An Unintended Journey: A Caregiver's Guide to Dementia*

Shriver, M. (2001). *Alzheimer's in America: The Shriver Report on Women and Alzheimer's*

Small, N., Froggat, K., & Downs, M. (2007). *Living and Dying with Dementia: Dialogues about Palliative Care*

Zeisel, J. (2009). *I'm Still Here: A New Philosophy of Alzheimer's Care*

Selected Web Resources

Some useful search terms include: ALZHEIMER'S DISEASE (EARLY/LATE ONSET); BETA-AMYLOID PLAQUES; DEMENTIA; FRONTOTEMPORAL DEMENTIA; LEWY BODY DIMENTIA; MIXED DEMENTIA; MULTI-INFARCT DEMENTIA NEUROFIBULARY TANGLES; PROTEIN TAU; VASCULAR DEMENTIA.

You can also visit the following *organizational and other Internet sites:*

Alzheimer's Association

Alzheimer's Disease Education and Referral Center (ADEAR)

Alzheimer's Disease International

Alzheimer's Foundation of America

Eldercare Locator

Ethnic Elders Care

Lewy Body Dementia Association

National Institute of Neurological Disorders and Stroke

National Institute on Aging

Calendar Date Gives Mom Reason to Contemplate Life
by Elizabeth Vega-Fowler

I used to think life's defining moments were dramatic, like a speeding train that hits you head on and throws you forward.

This week, however, I changed my mind.

I decided that progress in life can more often be measured in inches, not miles. All those heavenly epiphanies are really the accumulation of everyday wisdom breaking through the surface.

All this was prompted by a date on my calendar.

Somewhere in my mind, June 9 registered as familiar. It took a few moments for me to realize the significance. It was the four-year anniversary of my daughter's death.

Gabrielle was born with a malignant brain tumor. In truth, she was terminally ill before birth.

She was 16 days old when she died in her father's arms.

Even today I marvel at the brevity of her life.

Her father, brothers, 8-year-old Christopher and 6-year-old Joey, and I decided that if we couldn't give her longevity, we could give her quality.

So in 16 days, she smelled flowers and tasted cotton candy. She felt the sun on her face and heard countless lullabies. Even though we knew it was only a matter of time before we had to let her go, we opened ourselves up to knowing her.

Despite her medical condition—a condition doctors said left her with only one-fourth of her brain—my daughter responded in kind.

She would look into our eyes and without a word would communicate volumes of love.

Once she took every ounce of her strength and lifted a tiny wavering hand to touch my face.

When Gabrielle died quietly at home, I thought that my life had changed forever.

Time has taught me otherwise.

My daughter's death didn't place me on a new path but rather allowed me to experience things I had missed before. In fact, everything looked the same. It just felt different.

It was this journey—continuing along every day without her—that changed me and is still changing me.

The beginning was the most arduous.

For a time, I was enraged at God. Like a town crier I shouted "Unfair" through the streets.

I cried gallons of tears. Tears I never even knew I had.

I learned grieving was not just an emotional experience. It was a physical one.

My arms throbbed with the need to hold her.

My heart really hurt from the emptiness.

I had a perpetual lump in my throat for years.

Seeing the date brought another simple realization.

Instead of the torrential sorrow of years past, this June 9 brought a gentle melancholy. There is a definite sadness of what will never be—birthday parties, frilly dresses, first dates and prom.

I know that loss will always be there.

But there in the midst of it is something else—memories of a sweet little girl whose death taught me everything that was important about life.

Like the power of magnolia blossoms and unconditional love, and how the joy of knowing another human being far outweighs the void that is left when they're gone.

There is also the new knowledge that this state called grief is not a final destination but rather a continuous journey that changes me in a thousand small ways— slowly and mysteriously.

I don't know exactly where I will end up. I just know that somehow without even realizing it I found peace along the way.

Source: Elizabeth Vega-Fowler, 1998.
Reprinted by permission.

Appendix A

Selected Literature for Children: Annotated Descriptions

Picture Books for Preschoolers and Beginning Readers

Badger's Parting Gifts. S. Varley. New York: Mulberry Books, 1992. Although Badger is old and knows he will soon be "going down the Long Tunnel," he is not afraid. He worries about his woodland friends and tries to prepare them. They are sad when he dies but are consoled by the special memories he left with each of them and in sharing those memories with others.

Blow Me a Kiss, Miss Lilly. N. W. Carlstrom. New York: Harper & Row, 1990. An old lady who lives across the street with her cat is Sara's best friend. They share lots of interesting activities. When Miss Lilly is suddenly taken to the hospital and dies, Sara cries, looks for the light in her house, and is lonely. Later, Sara finds happiness in Miss Lilly's garden and in her belief that Miss Lilly is blowing her a kiss.

Cat Heaven. C. Rylant. New York: Blue Sky Press/Scholastic, 1997. Vivid acrylic images and a charming story line describe the delights cats might hope to find in their own special heaven: trees to climb, kitty toys, catnip, and soft angel laps. See also *Dog Heaven*.

Davey McGravy. D. Mason. Philadelphia: Paul Dry Books, 2015. A series of poems and etchings tell the story of a boy who lives in the tall-treed forest with his father and brothers, but who is mired in mourning for his mother. Davey wanders through his grief and the mysteries of life and death.

The Dead Bird. M. W. Brown. Reading, MA: Addison-Wesley, 1958. This story tells about some children who find a dead wild bird, touch its cold, stiff body, bury it in the woods in a simple ceremony, and return to the site each day to mourn ("until they forgot").

Sadness need not last forever; life can go on again. An early classic for our youngest readers.

Dog Heaven. C. Rylant. New York: Blue Sky Press/Scholastic, 1995. Bright colored illustrations and a delightful story line depict a special canine heaven where dogs can run, play with angel children, chew on dog biscuits, and rest on fluffy clouds. See also *Cat Heaven*.

Ethan's Butterflies. C. Jonas-Simpson. Victoria, BC: Trafford Publishing, 2006. When her third child was stillborn, the author sought ways to find spiritual comfort and respond to his two young brothers' questions. Here, Emma the elephant describes a similar situation and Momma explains that "sometimes babies live a very short life on Earth and then go back to our home with the Great Loving Spirit." It's still not easy, but Emma says "we learned that love and life exist forever" and "now we know he is not lost to us anymore."

The Fall of Freddie the Leaf: A Story of Life for All Ages. L. Buscaglia. Thorofare, NJ: Slack, 1982. Photographs of leaves on a park tree accompany a text in which one leaf (Freddie) asks another to explain how the first frost signals their change of colors and their expected fall from the tree. Fear of dying is compared to fear of the unknown and to natural changes in the seasons. Life itself is its own purpose; death is a kind of comfortable sleep (a metaphor that can easily mislead children and should be approached cautiously) and the beginning of a new cycle.

The Goodbye Boat. M. Joslin. Grand Rapids, MI: Eerdmans, 1998. Austere pictures and few words describe friendships, laughing and loving, loss and grief, and the view that when a boat is gone from view it is surely sailing somewhere new.

Goodbye, Brecken: A Story about the Death of a Pet. D. Lupton. Washington, DC: Magination Press, 2012. After her big, shaggy dog died, Isabelle was sad and angry. That night when she fell asleep, she dreamed of a long journey to find Brecken. She was lonely and afraid, but when she woke she knew she would always love Brecken and he would forever be close in her heart.

Goodbye Mousie. R. H. Harris. New York: Simon & Schuster, 2001. One morning a boy finds that his pet won't wake up. Daddy says Mousie is dead, but the boy refuses to accept that. Over time, the boy comes to understand that Mousie has died and will not be coming back. He shares his grief with his father and mother and they prepare a shoebox to bury Mousie.

Grandma's Scrapbook. J. Nobisso. Westhampton Beach, NY: Gingerbread House, rev. ed., 2000. An older girl remembers how her grandma kept a scrapbook with pictures and mementos of times they shared as the girl grew up. Grandma's gone now, but memories of her remain in the book and in the girl's heart. A companion to *Grandpa Loved.*

Grandpa Loved. J. Nobisso. Westhampton Beach, NY: Gingerbread House, rev. ed., 2000. An older boy recalls how his grandpa shared his love for the beach, the woods, the city, and family and friends. Grandpa is dead now, but his love lives on in their hearts. A companion to *Grandma's Scrapbook.*

The Heart and the Bottle. O. Jeffers. New York: Philomel, 2010. A little girl enjoys discovering wonders of the world with her grandfather. But when his chair is empty, she copes by putting her heart in a bottle. Not until she grows older and meets another young girl does she find a way to free her heart again.

The Hurt. T. Doleski. Mahwah, NJ: Paulist Press, 1983. Justin is hurt by his friend's angry insult. Without saying anything, Justin takes The Hurt into his room, like a big, round, cold, hard stone. When he doesn't share his feelings with anyone, The Hurt just gets bigger and bigger and bigger. It is ruining everything until he finally tells Daddy. As he gradually lets it go, The Hurt gets smaller and smaller until at last it goes away.

I Heard Your Daddy Died. M. Scrivani. Omaha, NE: Centering Corporation, 1996. This slim booklet offers an empathic approach for a child about two to six years of age whose father has died. The child's feelings and needs are recognized and affirmed. Suggestions are offered for expressing strong reactions in constructive ways and for things a child can do for self help. Permission is given to go on with living and loving, even while remembering the deceased parent. See also *I Heard Your Mommy Died.*

I Heard Your Mommy Died. M. Scrivani. Omaha, NE: Centering Corporation, 1994. A second booklet offers an empathic approach for a preschool child whose mother has died. The child's feelings and needs are recognized and affirmed. Suggestions are offered for expressing strong feelings in constructive ways and for things a child can do for self help. Permission is given to go on with living and loving, even while remembering the deceased parent. See also *I Heard Your Daddy Died.*

I'll Always Love You. H. Wilhelm. New York: Crown, 1985. A boy and his dog grow up and play together as best friends, but Elfie grows old and dies while the boy is still young. Afterward, family members regret not telling Elfie they loved her. But the boy did so every night and he realizes his love for her will continue even after her death. He doesn't want a new puppy right away, even though he knows Elfie will not come back and a time will come when he will be ready for a new pet.

Little Tree. K. Komagata. Otaku Tokyo, Japan: One Stroke, 2009. This pop-up book traces the life-cycle of a single tree as it explores deeper themes of impermanence and the cycle of all life. The story is told in Japanese, French, and English, but it centers on the images of a tiny seedling poking out of the snow and then on through growth and different seasons until it sparks a new cycle of life

Love Is Forever. C. Rislov. Wyoming: Casey Rislov Books, 2013. A young owl misses his deceased grandfather, but learns to keep his love alive forever. He is comforted by this advice: "Remember as you share, laugh, and learn, my love will always be right there beside you." The book includes advice from experts about how to talk children about death and whether they should attend funerals.

Jungle Journey: Grieving and Remembering Eleanor the Elephant. B. B. McIntyre. Traverse City, MI: Traverse Publishing, 2000. Each animal reacts in his or her own way to the death of their beloved Eleanor the Elephant who had protected them while they slept. As they mourn, they bury Eleanor and work together to continue their jungle journey. Sharing fears and bad dreams makes them less scary.

Lifetimes: A Beautiful Way to Explain Death to Children. B. Mellonie & R. Ingpen. New York: Bantam, 1983. Pictures of things that are or once were alive and concise text on facing pages affirm that "there is a beginning and an ending for everything that is alive. In between is living.... So, no matter how long they are, or how short, lifetimes are really all the same. They have beginnings, and endings, and there is living in between."

Lost and Found: Remembering a Sister. E. Yeomans. Omaha, NE: Centering Corporation, 2000. A young girl describes confusing experiences she and her parents have after her sister dies, but she also realizes many ways in which she still feels her sister's love. So Paige isn't "lost" forever; she is right there in their hearts and "I know where to find her."

Meggie's Magic. A. Dean. New York: Viking Penguin, 1992. After eight-year-old Meggie's illness and death, her parents and sister feel very sad and lonely. But one day when Meggie's sister goes to their special place, she finds it still filled with the magical qualities of games they used to play and she realizes that Meggie's magic remains inside each of them.

My Father's Arms Are a Boat. S. E. Lunde. Brooklyn, NY: Enchanted Lion Books, 2013. One night, a boy who is grieving and unable to sleep, climbs into his father's arms and asks questions about various losses, including will his mother ever wake up. His father offers warmth and reassurance.

My Grandpa Died Today. J. Fassler. New York: Human Sciences, 1971. Although David's grandfather has tried to prepare the boy for his impending death, when it actually does happen David still must mourn his loss. He finds comfort in many good memories from his relationship with his grandfather and in the knowledge that his grandfather does not want him to be afraid to live and enjoy life.

My Grandson Lew. C. Zolotow. New York: Harper & Row, 1974. When six-year-old Lewis asks why his grandfather has not visited lately and says "I miss Grandpa" (p. 6), Mother says they didn't tell Lewis his grandfather died when he was two because he never asked. The boy says he never needed to ask; Grandpa just appeared. When his parents were away, Lewis says Grandpa would come in the night, pick the boy up in his strong arms, and give him "eye hugs." Mother says Grandpa was so proud and happy when Lewis was born. After sharing warm memories of someone they both miss, Mother concludes, "Now we will remember him together and neither of us will be so lonely as we would be if we had to remember him alone" (p.32).

My Turtle Died Today. E. G. Stull. New York: Holt, Rinehart & Winston, 1964. When a pet turtle dies, a boy cries and cries and asks "Why?" The boy and his friends bury Boxer and talk about this event: Does Boxer need food? Is he in heaven? The children decide that life can go on in another way through their cat Patty's newborn kittens. Much of this is sound, but the book also poses two questions that need to be addressed with care: Can you get a new pet in the way that one child has a new mother? And do you have to live first—a long time—before you die?

Nana Upstairs and Nana Downstairs. T. De Paola. New York: Putnam's, rev. ed., 1998. Tommy loves visiting his grandmother and great-grandmother. When he visits Nana Upstairs (his great-grandmother) in her bedroom, they share candy and talk about the "Little People" while they are both tied in their chairs so they don't fall out. When Tommy is told that Nana Upstairs has died, he does not believe it until he sees her empty bed. Later when he sees a falling star, Tommy's mother suggests that it may represent a kiss from Nana who is now "upstairs" in a new way. Later, an older Tommy has a similar experience after the death of Nana Downstairs and thinks "now you are both Nana Upstairs."

Never Say Goodbye. L. G. Gant. Nashville, TN: Tommy Nelson, 2003. An older rabbit tells a beloved younger rabbit that she has to "go away." That evokes a flood of questions from Hannah. Netta calmly replies to each question, displaying her conviction that "God has made me a new home" and that even in death they will always be connected.

No New Baby: For Siblings Who Have a Brother or Sister Die before Birth. M. Gryte. Omaha, NE: Centering Corporation, 1988. Also available in Spanish as *No Tenremos Un Nuevo Bebé*. A young child describes her reactions when the anticipated birth of a new sibling does not happen. Grandma picks up a young bud off the ground and uses it to explain that while most buds keep growing and become flowers, some don't—like this one. Something like this happened to their baby, no one is to blame, and we do not always have answers.

Psalm Twenty-Three. Illustrated by T. Ladwig. Grand Rapids, MI: Eerdmans, 1997. The familiar text of this psalm, comparing God to a loving shepherd, is here accompanied by forceful artwork depicting the world of love and fear faced by an urban, African-American family.

Ragtail Remembers: A Story That Helps Children Understand Feelings of Grief. L. Duckworth. Omaha, NE: Centering Corporation, 2003. A mouse named Ragtail is sad, lonely, and angry when he learns that his friend, Old Tim the cat, is dead. Ragtail wishes Old Tim would come back, but as he learns what dead means he begins to come to terms with his loss and he makes a new friend.

Someone Came before You. P. Schwiebert. Portland, OR: Grief Watch, 2007. This book describes a mommy and a daddy who love each other very much but really want to share their love with a child. They are excited during the pregnancy but heartbroken when the baby dies. In time, their hearts are able to stretch enough to enable them to have a new baby—YOU! Through this book and in other ways, they share the memory of that prior baby with you.

A Story for Hippo: A Book about Loss. S. Puttock. New York: Scholastic Press, 2001. Hippo and Monkey share a warm friendship. Hippo is the oldest animal in the jungle who tells the best stories; Monkey is the funniest. Together they eat cabbages, play games, and tell stories. One day, Hippo tells Monkey it is time for her to die. Monkey is sad: who will tell great stories, play games, and laugh at his jokes? When Monkey promises not to forget her, Hippo says "that will be part of my happily ever after." When Hippo does die, Monkey is very sad, but finally Little Chameleon persuades him that Hippo's stories still need to be told—and a new friendship begins.

Sweet, Sweet Memory. J. Woodson. New York: Hyperion Books for Children, 2000. When Grandpa dies, a young African-American girl named Sarah and her grandmother are consoled by stories and sweet memories of him. They recall that he always said, "The earth changes.... Like us it lives, it grows. Like us ... a part of it never dies. Everything and everyone goes on and on."

Tell Me, Papa: A Gentle Explanation for Children about Death and the Funeral (rev. ed.). J. Johnson & M. Johnson. Omaha, NE: Centering Corporation, 2001. Through a discussion between children and a grandparent, this slim book provides an explanation of death, funerals, and saying good-bye.

The Tenth Good Thing about Barney. J. Viorst. New York: Atheneum, 1971. When a pet cat dies, a boy's mother suggests that he try to think of ten good things about Barney to say at the funeral. At first, he can only think of nine: Barney was brave and smart and funny and clean; he was cuddly and handsome and he only once ate a bird; it was sweet to hear him purr in my ear; and sometimes he slept on my belly and kept it warm. Out in the garden, he realizes the tenth good thing: "Barney is in the ground and he's helping grow flowers.... That's a pretty nice job for a cat" (p. 24).

A Terrible Thing Happened. M. M. Holmes. Washington, DC: Magination Press, 2000. Sherman Smith is a raccoon who saw a terrible thing happen. He is afraid and tries not to think about it, but keeping it inside bothers him. He has stomachaches and headaches, feels sad and nervous, isn't hungry, can't sleep, and has bad dreams. Often he is angry and gets into trouble at school. Ms. Maple listens to Sherman and helps him understand and find ways to vent his feelings.

There's No Such Thing as a Dragon. J. Kent. New York: Golden Books, 1975. One morning, Billy Bixbee finds a small dragon in his room. But when Billy tells his mother, she says, "There's no such thing as a dragon!" Even so, the dragon gradually gets bigger while Billy dresses. At breakfast, the dragon sits on the table and eats Billy's pancakes, but his mother couldn't object because she had already said dragons don't exist. During the day, the dragon naps while it gets larger and larger. After it wakes it is hungry and chases after a bakery truck, carrying the house on its back like a

shell on a snail. Finally, when Mr. Bixbee came home and Billy tries to explain what the dragon had done, his mother still wanted to insist that there is no such thing as a dragon. But Billy says, "There IS a dragon" and he patted it on its head. That makes the dragon happy and it immediately starts getting smaller. When it is kitten-size again, Mother says, "I don't mind dragons THIS size. ...Why did it have to grow so BIG?" Billy answers, I'm not sure ... but I think it just wanted to be noticed."

This Book Is for All Kids, but Especially My Sister Libby. Libby Died. J. Simon. Austin, TX: Idea University Press, 2001. Five-year-old Jack struggled to understand the death of his young sister who had been born with a rare disorder. This book reproduces his questions and comments, along with his mother's dramatic, colorful illustrations.

Timothy Duck: The Story of the Death of a Friend. L. B. Blackburn. Omaha, NE: Centering Corporation, rev. ed., 1999. Timothy Duck had never thought about how he might feel if someone he loved died. When his friend John got sick and dies, Timothy struggles to understand his feelings. It seemed so unfair and he felt empty inside. Sharing concerns with his mother and a duck friend helps Timothy.

Tough Boris. M. Fox. New York: Harcourt Brace, 1994. Boris von der Borch is a tough, massive, scruffy, greedy, fearless, and scary pirate—just like all pirates. But when his parrot died, Boris cried and cried—just like all pirates, and everyone else. A simple story and pictures give children permission to experience and express their grief.

We Were Gonna Have a Baby, but We Had an Angel Instead. P. Schwiebert. Portland, OR: Grief Watch, 2003. A young boy tells how he excited he was as he anticipated the birth of the new baby. But something happened; the baby died and everyone is sad. Grandy says the baby can always live in our hearts, but the boy knows having the baby would have been more fun than missing him.

What's Heaven? M. Shriver. New York: Golden Books, 1999. This story about a little girl's talks with her mother arose from the author's discussions with her children, nieces, and nephews when their great-grandmother, Rose Fitzgerald Kennedy, died. It says heaven is a place we believe in, where there are no hurts, "where you go when you die," and "where God will love [those who died] forever."

When a Pet Dies. F. Rogers. New York: Puffin Books, 1998. Here, the star of *Mr. Rogers Neighborhood* helps children share feelings following the loss of a pet while reassuring them that grieving is a natural and healing thing to do. Pain will ease and fond memories of shared happiness will prevail.

When Dinosaurs Die: A Guide to Understanding Death. L. Krasny Brown & M. Brown. Boston: Little, Brown, 1996. A distinctive cartoon format offers a unique way to introduce young children to issues like: what it means to be alive; why someone dies; what "dead" means; feelings about death; how life might change after a death; saying good-bye; mourning customs; beliefs about what comes after death; and ways to remember someone.

When I Die, Will I Get Better? J. Breebaart & P. Breebaart. New York: Peter Bedrick Books, 1993. Fred and Joe are rabbit brothers who live in the woods. When Joe doesn't get out of bed one morning, Doctor Owl says he has a high fever and will get better. But Joe dies and the neighbors help prepare things: the Mole family digs the grave, Beaver makes the coffin, and Fred talks to Hedgehog about his feelings. At the burial, Fred reads a letter to Joe, puts Joe's favorite things in the coffin, and promises to play in a nearby field every day. Afterwards, Fred wants to be alone and is very angry, but gradually he and his parents begin to feel better with the support of their friends.

When I Feel Sad. C. M. Spelman. Chicago: Albert Whitman, 2002. A young guinea pig describes many situations that make her sad, how it feels to be sad, and how she can feel better.

When Someone Dies. S. Greenlee. Atlanta: Peachtree Publishers, 1992. This book explores what people typically experience when someone close to them dies. It acknowledges that many changes occur, but encourages sharing tears with someone you love, writing a letter to the person who died, and keeping a special part of that person in our hearts.

When Violet Died. M. Kantrowitz. New York: Parents' Magazine Press, 1973. After the death of their pet bird, Amy, Eva, and their friends have a funeral with poems, songs, punch, and even humor. It is sad to think that nothing lasts forever, but then Eva recognizes that life can go on in another way through an ever-changing chain of life involving the family cat, Blanche, who is pregnant, and her kittens. So Eva decides that "maybe nothing lasts forever, but she knew a way to make it last a long, long time!"

Where's Jess? J. Johnson & M. Johnson. Omaha, NE: Centering Corporation, rev. ed., 2004. Simple drawings and text help young children cope with infant sibling death by exploring topics like what "death" means, remembering the dead child, and the value of tears.

You Hold Me and I'll Hold You. J. Carson. New York: Orchard Books, 1992. When her Daddy's Aunt Ann dies, a little girl thinks about her parents' divorce, the death of a hamster, and other losses she has experienced. During the memorial ceremony, the girl watches all the people and everything that happens. She wonders how sorry she will have to get. Being held and holding others is comforting.

Storybooks and Other Texts for Primary School Readers

Aarvy Aardvark Finds Hope: A Read Aloud Story for People of All Ages about Loving and Losing, Friendship and Hope. D. O'Toole. Burnsville, NC: Compassion Books, 1988. Aarvy Aardvark struggles to come to terms with the loss of his mother and brother who had been taken to a zoo. Many animals try to cheer Aarvy up, but their advice is not helpful. Only one friend, Ralphy Rabbit, really listens to Aarvy as the two of them explore their losses. Sharing and remembering help Aarvy learn to say good-bye and to cope with encountering a dead bird.

The Accident. C. Carrick. New York: Seabury Press, 1976. When Christopher calls his dog as they walk along a road, Bodger runs in front of a truck and is killed. Christopher is angry at the driver, at his father for not being mad at the driver, and at himself for not paying attention and letting Bodger wander across the road. Christopher's parents quickly bury Bodger the next morning before he can take part, but anger dissolves into tears when he and his father erect a marker at Bodger's grave.

Alex, the Kid with AIDS. L. W. Girard. Morton Grove, IL: Albert Whitman, 1991. The new boy in fourth grade gets special treatment and is left out of some activities because everyone knows he has AIDS. Alex misbehaves, but he has a weird sense of humor and gradually becomes Michael's best friend. The best thing is when Alex is included in activities and treated just like one of the other kids.

Animal Crackers: A Tender Book about Death and Funerals and Love. B. Marshall. Omaha, NE: Centering Corporation, 1998. A young girl describes her Nanny, who had a secret candy bowl full of M&Ms and who hid animal crackers all over her house for her grandchildren. After Nanny became increasingly forgetful, she went to live in a nursing home, became gradually more feeble, and eventually died. At the funeral, the children remember Nanny fondly through the good times they shared with her and through her "Nanny Crackers" that everyone shared.

Anna's Corn. B. Santucci. Grand Rapids, MI: Eerdmans, 2002. Grandpa taught Anna to hear the raspy music of the wind breathing through the dry corn stalks and he gave her a few kernels of corn to keep for her own. After his death, Anna is reluctant to keep her promise to Grandpa to plant her seeds next spring because she fears they will then be gone forever. Mama explains that the seeds won't be gone; they'll just be different. So Anna finally plants the seeds and after the corn has grown, she once again hears the song she had shared with Grandpa and she takes some new seeds to plant next spring.

Annie and the Old One. M. Miles. Boston: Little, Brown, 1971. A ten-year-old Navajo girl is told it will be time for her grandmother to "go to Mother Earth" when her mother finishes weaving a rug. Annie tries to delay the weaving by misbehaving in school, hoping her parents will be summoned to talk about her conduct. At night, she lets the goat and sheep out of their pen and unravels the wool from the loom. Eventually, the adults realize what is going on and grandmother explains that we are all part of a natural cycle. When Annie realizes she cannot hold back time, she is ready to join in the weaving.

Are You Like Me?: Helping Children Cope with Suicide. M. Tesh & E. Schleich. Clearwater, FL: The Hospice of the Florida Suncoast (now Suncoast Hospice), 2009. This brightly colored book responds to difficult questions children might have about the meaning and causes of suicide. It seeks to explain suicide, validate reactions after a loved one dies from suicide, offer security, encourage discussion with trusted adults, and guide conversations.

Babka's Serenade. M. Zebrowski. Omaha, NE: Centering Corporation, 2002. Babka shared magical stories with her granddaughter in her garden, stories that Babka had told Mama when she was a girl. But one day Babka dies. Pipchin cannot imagine not seeing Babka anymore and finds it hard when Mama and Daddy sell her house. In spring, the girl decides to build Babka's garden in their backyard. Her parents help so Pipchin can visit that special place any time she wishes where she smells the flowers and thinks of Babka and her stories.

Bear's Last Journey. U. Weigelt. New York: North-South Books, 2003. All the forest animals are anxious when they learn that Bear is sick. Bear explains he will have to say good-bye to his friends because he is "going on a very special journey, one that every bear and every animal makes at the end of his life." He says he is dying and adds that no one really knows what it means to be dead. The little fox is frustrated: he wants to know right now what will happen and is upset when Bear dies. Sharing memories and gifts from Bear helps the little fox and the other animals.

Because the Sky Is Everywhere. N. Sharp. Denver, CO: Eleven Eleven Press, 2017. When young Liam is told that his father has died, he searches everywhere to understand what that means and to find comfort. Eventually, he finds a deep inner connection to his father through the vastness of the sky and the endlessness of love.

Ben's Flying Flowers. I. Maier. Washington, DC: Magination Press, 2012. Emily introduces her younger brother, Ben, to butterflies, which he calls "flying flowers." She draws him pictures when his illness makes him too weak to go see them. But after his death, she doesn't want to draw happy things, at least until she finds ways to make her sadness go away and she can remember happy times with Ben.

The Best Gift for Mom. L. Klein. New York: Paulist Press, 1995. A boy can't remember his dad who died when he was a baby. So Jonathan is uncomfortable when his classmates talk about both of their parents and he can only mention his Mom. After Mom shares stories about his Dad, including the only two songs Dad knew how to sing when he put Jonathan to bed ("Taps" and "Silent Night"), Jonathan joins a glee club at school and plans a special gift for Mom. At the Christmas concert, Jonathan sings a solo rendition of "Silent Night" as a surprise present for Mom and then writes a letter to his father.

Beyond the Ridge. P. Goble. New York: Aladdin/Simon & Schuster, 1993. At her death, while her family members prepare her body according to their customs, an elderly Plains Indian woman experiences the afterlife in which her people believe. She makes the long climb up a difficult slope to see the Spirit World beyond the ridge.

Bluebird Summer. D. Hopkinson. New York: Greenwillow Books, 2001. Every summer, Meg and her little brother Cody visit Grandpa's farm. But now Grandma has died. They miss her especially the way she puttered around in her wonderful garden of flowers and vegetables, as well as the bluebirds who used to visit regularly to enjoy their favorite plants. Then the children have an inspiration: they will pull out the tangle of weeds and grass that have sprung up, and replace them with a new garden in memory of Grandma. Above all, they will install a new birdhouse to encourage the bluebirds to return.

The Brightest Star. K. M. Hemery. Omaha, NE: Centering Corporation, 1998. Before Mommy got sick and died, Molly and her parents used to go to the beach, wait until it was very dark, and look at the stars. Afterwards, Molly is troubled when Ms. Baylor asks the children to draw a picture of their families for the school open house. Molly doesn't want to make a picture without Mommy in it. Daddy takes Molly to the beach again and points out the brightest star, which helps remind her of her mother's love.

The Butterfly Bush: A Story about Love. D. M. Evarts. Omaha, NE: Centering Corporation, 1998. For her birthday, Grandma gave Lindsay a pot of sticks that turned out to be a butterfly bush they planted in a clearing by the woods. But nothing happened and

Lindsay forgot the butterfly bush. Then each year, Grandma would give Lindsay beautiful, expensive birthday gifts. Lindsay would always thank Grandma, but then would run off to open other presents or be with friends while Grandma went out to visit the butterfly bush. One year Grandma died, but not before mailing Lindsay a small package for her birthday. It contained a lovely locket with two pictures inside; one of Grandma holding Lindsay as a small child, the other of a mass of beautiful purple flowers. Lindsay ran out to the woods where she found the butterfly bush was now over 15 feet tall and covered all over with beautiful flowers and butterflies. Years later, Grandma Lindsay gave her granddaughter a pot of sticks on her birthday.

The Cherry Blossom Tree: A Grandfather Talks about Life and Death. J. Godfrey. Minneapolis: Augsburg Fortress, 1996. Grandpa and five-year-old Harriet plant a cherry tree that is covered with pink blossoms each year on his birthday. Later, they find the tree has fallen down and Grandpa says, "It was very, very old, and time for it to die." He explains, "Everything that is born has to die sometime.... that makes us sad. But death is a new beginning, like waking up after a long sleep." He adds: everyone who loves God can go and be with him when they die in a new and different place called heaven.

The Christmas Cactus. E. Wrenn. Omaha, NE: Centering Corporation, 2001. As Christmas nears, Nana is hospitalized and Megan is sad. When they prepare to visit, Megan asks her father if Nana is dying. He says, "We never know for sure when someone will die.... So what we need to do is tell the people we love just how much we love them, every chance we get." As a present for Nana, Megan brings a Christmas cactus and Nana explains that this plant waits all year for the one season when it blooms. "I think our lives are like that. We live and grow for a whole lifetime. And then, at the end of our lives, we bloom. We become something very different and wonderful." Nana asks Megan to take care of the plant and when it blooms to think of her. She did and that made Christmas good.

The Class in Room 44: When a Classmate Dies. Lynn B. Blackburn. Omaha, NE: Centering Corporation, rev. ed., 1999. When a boy dies in an auto accident, his classmates experience reactions like disbelief, anger, regret for things not done, and guilt. After their teacher says that "each person needed to do the things that helped them with Tony's death" (p. 4), they agree to make a "Tony museum" in the corner of their schoolroom. At the end of the school year, they invite Tony's family to visit, give them a scrapbook they had made, and share memories.

A Complete Book about Death for Kids. E. Grollman & J. Johnson. Omaha, NE: Centering Corporation, 2006. The three parts of this book discuss death and feelings, funerals and cemeteries, and cremation, respectively. Most pages have two photos and a few simple sentences directed to child readers and adults who might interact with those children. The authors are well-known experts in this field who are sensitive to the needs of children and insightful in how to address those needs.

Cry, Heart, But Never Break. G. Ringtved. Brooklyn, NY: Enchanted Lion Books, 2016. Four siblings are aware that their grandmother is gravely ill. They make an agreement to keep death from taking her, but death does arrive as it must. Death comes gently and naturally, and with time to share a story that helps the children realize the value of loss to life and the importance of being able to say good-bye.

Daddy's Chair. S. Lanton. Rockville, MD: Kar-Ben Copies, Inc., 1991. After his father's death, Michael doesn't want anyone to sit in Daddy's chair so it will be ready for him when he comes back. Mommy explains what it means to be sick and die, as well as Jewish customs involved in sitting shiva. Sharing memories of Daddy gradually enables Michael to sit in the chair and to allow others to use it again.

The Dragonfly Door. J. Adams. Maple Plain, MN: Feather Rock Books, 2007. Lea and Nym are two water nymph friends who play together in the marsh. One day, Nym can't find Lea; she has gone to climb up a reed. As Nym searches, she discovers Lea had turned into a beautiful dragonfly. Nym looks forward to their eventual reunion.

Dusty Was My Friend: Coming to Terms with Loss. A. F. Clardy. New York: Human Sciences, 1984. Benjamin is eight when his friend Dusty is killed in an automobile accident. As Benjamin struggles to understand his reactions to this tragic event, his parents allow him to express his thoughts and feelings, mourn his loss, remember the good times shared with Dusty, and go on with his own life. As Benjamin says, "Dusty was my friend and I am glad that he was."

Emily's Sadhappy Season: The Story of a Young Girl's Feelings after the Death of Her Father. S. G. Lowden. Omaha, NE: Centering Corporation, 1993. Before he died, Emily's Daddy helped her become a good baseball player. After he died, Emily and Mom are alone. Emily's grief is confusing and complicated. She is afraid that playing baseball might have caused Daddy's death, she worries that now Mom might die, too, and she is really angry that Daddy is dead. In time, Mom encourages Emily to teach her to play baseball. Mom says they will feel "sadhappy": happy remembering the fun times they had with Daddy, but sad because he is not with them.

Finding Grandpa Everywhere: A Young Child Discovers Memories of a Grandparent. J. Hodge. Omaha, NE: Centering Corporation, 1999. A little boy realizes that Grandpa is dead, not "lost" as the adults keep saying. He consoles himself and his Grandma with this thought: Grandpa always said "to do something for someone you have to put a little of yourself into it." So memories of Grandpa and his love live on everywhere the boy looks.

First Snow. H. Coutant. New York: Knopf, 1974. A young girl who has recently come to the United States with her family from Vietnam is eager to experience snow for the first time, but puzzled to hear her parents say "Grandmother is dying." No one explains to Liên what it means to be dying until Grandmother tells her to go outside and hold her hand up to heaven. When Liên catches a snowflake on her finger she finds it to be "a tiny, fleeting thing, beautiful and delicate" (p. 22). Then when the sun causes the edges of the snowflake to burst into a thousand tiny rainbows, it changes to a drop of water and falls on the ground where it nourishes a tiny pine tree. This affirms Liên's Buddhist beliefs that life and death are but two parts of the same thing.

The Flat Rabbit. B. Oskarsson. Toronto, Canada: Owlkids Books, 2014. When a dog and a rat come upon a rabbit flattened on the roadway, they wonder what they should do to help her. Should they move her, but how and to where? Their solution may surprise readers.

The Garden Angel: A Young Child Discovers a Grandparent's Love Grows Even after Death. J. Czech. Omaha, NE: Centering Corporation, 2000. After her grandpa died, eight-year-old Camilla remembers many things about him and especially how he loved gardening. This year she plants the new garden herself, dresses a scarecrow with his old clothes, and spreads his old quilt behind it like angel wings.

Gentle Willow: A Story for Children about Dying. J. C. Mills. Washington, DC: Magination Press, 1993; 2nd ed., 2004. A squirrel becomes upset when she learns her tree-friend, Gentle Willow, is dying. The Tree Wizards explain they can give Gentle Willow their love and some medicines to help her feel stronger and more comfortable, but they cannot make her all better. Still, they point out the many gifts Gentle Willow has given to Amanda over the years—which are now memories in her mind. One day, Gentle Willow begins to cry and tells Amanda she is afraid to face this change. Amanda just listens, stays close, and tells Gentle Willow the comforting story of a caterpillar that changed into Yellow Butterfly. See also *Little Tree: A Story for Children with Serious Medical Problems.*

Geranium Morning. E. S. Powell. Minneapolis, MN: CarolRhoda Books, 1990. Two children—one, whose father died in an accident, the other, whose mother is dying—struggle with strong feelings, memories, guilt ("if onlys"), and unhelpful adult actions. The children help each other by sharing their losses. Frannie's father and her mother (before she dies) also help. Finally, Timothy revives a tradition he shared with his father of buying geraniums to plant.

The Giant. C. Ewart. New York: Walker & Co., 2003. Before she died, a young girl's mother said that a giant would look after her. As the seasons pass on the family farm, the girl misses her mother and searches for the giant. Her hardworking Pa says there is no such thing as a giant, but the girl keeps searching everywhere until she finally realizes that her tall, strong Pa is the giant looking after her.

Goodbye, Mitch. R. Wallace-Brodeur. Morton Grove, IL: Albert Whitman, 1995. When Michael's 15-year-old cat, stops eating, his Mom explains that the veterinarian believes Mitch has an inoperable tumor. They agree to try to keep Mitch comfortable and let him find his own way. It isn't easy for Michael, but being with Mitch, crying, and finally just holding him in a blanket as he dies somehow feels good, too.

Grandfather Hurant Lives Forever. S. Pitzer. Omaha, NE: Centering Corporation, 2001. Grigor loves to spend time with his grandfather who teaches him about their Armenian history and how to weave a rug. Their warm relationship is disturbed when grandfather becomes sick and enters a hospital. When Grigor visits, grandfather says, "I will always be with you." But grandfather dies and Grigor feels betrayed, angry, and unable to cry. Not until Grigor returns to the rug shop does he realize that grandfather lives on in him and in this special place.

Grandfather's Shirt. B. Morning. Omaha, NE: Centering Corporation, 1994. Grandfather loved working in his garden and teaching his buddy, Peter, to help him. After Grandfather's death, Peter and his parents share special memories. Dad says the two of them "are the seeds Grandfather left behind when he died. Grandfather lives forever through us and our memory of him." Peter finds comfort in Grandfather's old baseball cap and his musty old gardening shirt, which he wears to tend the garden.

Grandpa Abe. M. Russo. New York: Greenwillow Books, 1996. Soon after Sarah's first birthday, her grandmother married Abe and she got a new grandfather. Sarah describes special times shared with Abe on her birthdays. Abe died when Sarah is nine, but she knows he enriched her life in many ways.

Grandpa's Soup. E. Kadono. Grand Rapids, MI: Eerdmans, 1999. After his wife's death, an old man slowly realizes that making her meatball soup and sharing it with friends eases his loneliness. While singing the song his wife used to guide her soup making, the old man gradually adds more ingredients as he progresses from smaller to larger pots and better and better tasting soup to share with his newfound friends (three mice, a cat, a dog, and some children).

The Great Change. G. Horn (White Deer of Autumn). Hillsboro, OR: Beyond Words Publishing, Inc., 1992. A Native American woman uses a caterpillar that will change into a butterfly to explain to her nine-year-old granddaughter, Wanba, that death is not the end, but the Great Change—part of the unbreakable Circle of Life in which our bodies become one with Mother Earth while our souls or spirits endure.

Green Mittens From Grandma: A Gentle Story about a Child's Grief. B. H. Hanks. Omaha, NE: Centering Corporation, 1996. While Grandma made green mittens for a young girl, she told stories about when she was a little girl and the girl's mother was small. After Grandma died and during the funeral, the girl missed her Grandma, recalled things she had said and done, and held tight to her green mittens. The girl knew her memories of Grandma and the green mittens would stay with her always.

Growing Time. S. S. Warburg. Boston: Houghton Mifflin, 1969. Jamie grew up with a collie dog, but now King is old and tired. When King dies, Uncle John says, "Death is not a going away. It's a going back to the earth, which is our home" (p. 9). Granny adds, "The spirit of something you really love can never die. It lives in your heart. It belongs to you always, it is your treasure" (p. 24). Still, Jamie misses King and wants him back. So at first when Jamie's father gets him a new puppy, Jamie is not ready for the new dog, but after he expresses his grief he finds it possible to accept the new relationship.

Grunt. S. S. Tamberrino. Omaha, NE: Centering Corporation, 2001. At the age of 16, Grunt is an old dog, now blind, in pain, and sick with both cancer and arthritis. A boy and his Dad agree that it will be best for Grunt to be euthanized. Still, it isn't easy to carry out that decision, to take Grunt in the car to the veterinarian's office and hold him on the table while the shot takes effect. They bury Grunt in a box in the back yard under a big oak tree, and then just sit together for a long time while they talk about happy times with Grunt and many memories of a good dog.

The Happy Funeral. E. Bunting. New York: Harper & Row, 1982. Two young Chinese-American girls are puzzled when their mother says they will have a "happy funeral" for their grandfather. "Those words don't fit together," the girls think, "It doesn't make sense." At the funeral, there are flowers everywhere, food is provided for the journey to the other side, play money and pictures of a beloved dog are burned, Grandmother puts half a comb into the coffin, people cry and give speeches, a woman gives them a small candy after the ceremony to "sweeten your sorrow," and there is a grand procession to the cemetery with a marching band. In the end, Laura and May-May realize the truth of what their mother says: "When someone is very old and has lived a good life, he is happy to go." But they also think, "She never said it was happy for us to have him go."

The Healing Tree. K. M. Hemery. Omaha, NE: Centering Corporation, 2001. One day Baba Marta tells Sammy a story about the backyard oak tree with a long bare strip on its trunk where there is no bark. Baba says when she was a little girl her mamma became very sick and died. Baba just wanted to be alone, so she went to the swing under the tree where she had shared many good times with her mother. When a storm came up, Baba didn't want to leave that special place. Her Papa rushed out, grabbed Baba, and ran to the porch with her just before lightning struck the tree and tore off one of its huge branches. Then, Papa explained that they were all like the tree: in pain from losing a big part of their family. Like the tree, he said, we will heal and go on living, but life will be different and forever changed. After telling her story, Baba explains that Sammy's was right; she did have a wonderful life.

Her Mother's Face. R. Doyle. New York: Scholastic, 2008. Siobhán's mother died when she was three. Now Siobhán is ten, but there is a big, empty space in her life because she can't remember her mother's face. Her pain grows when she sees other children with their mothers, but she can't talk about it with her very sad father. One day Siobhán meets a beautiful woman who recognizes her sadness and says, "You should look in the mirror.... Because then you'll see your mother. You'll see the way she looked when she was your age." Siobhán does and it works! Then, on her 30th birthday she looked in the mirror again and saw the beautiful woman: it was her mother whom she now looked exactly like.

I Am My Grandpa's Enkelin. W. Wangerin. Brewster, MA: Paraclete Press, 2007. A little girl describes the many activities she shares with her grandfather on a farm. Much later, when she is in college and after grandpa died, the girl knows that she is still his Enkelin (granddaughter) and that while there is pain, he is still in her heart—like the German song he always used to sing.

I Had a Friend Named Peter: Talking to Children about the Death of a Friend. J. Cohn. New York: William Morrow, 1987. This book describes Betsy's reactions when a car kills her friend, along with helpful ways her parents and teacher respond to Betsy, her classmates, and Peter's parents.

I Know I Made It Happen: A Gentle Book about Feelings. L.B. Blackburn. Omaha, NE: Centering Corporation, 1991. Many young children believe they must somehow be responsible when bad things happen. Here, adults explain that bad things don't happen because of a child's words or wishes. It helps to share bad feelings and to know you're not at fault.

It Isn't Easy. M. Connolly. New York: Oxford University Press, 1997. When his nine-year-old brother is killed in a car accident, a little boy is sad, lonely, and angry. As he ponders memories of good times (and some bad times) with Ross, the boy gradually gets used to being an only child—but it isn't easy.

Jasper's Day. M. B. Parker. Toronto: Kids Can Press, 2002. On Jasper's day, Riley and his parents let their dog sleep late, feed him his favorite foods, take him for a ride, get him ice cream, and bring him to visit Grandma. But this isn't Jasper's birthday. He sleeps a lot, is stiff with arthritis, and has cancer. This is the day for Jasper to go to the clinic before his pain pills wear off. There the veterinarian gives him a shot and his death is quick and gentle. Afterwards, the family buries Jasper's body in the backyard and Riley plans a memory book of Jasper's life.

Kate, the Ghost Dog: Coping with the Death of a Pet. W. L. Wilson. Washington, DC: Magination Press, 2010. When an African-American girl finds her dog has died, she is angry and tries to claim that Kate has come back as a ghost. With the help of family and friends, Aleta is eventually able to remember Kate as "a memory worth cherishing."

King Emmett the Second. M. Stolz. New York: Greenwillow, 1991. Emmett lives in an apartment in New York City, with a collection of lots of images of pigs and objects shaped like pigs and his very own live pig (King Emmett) who lives upstate on a farm. One day, Emmett's parents tell him they are moving to a new job and a house in a small town in Ohio and they admit his pig had been slaughtered. Emmett is very angry about these events. He is sure he will never like Ohio or anything else about the new home and he will not want a new pet. But gradually he adapts, makes friends, and ultimately agrees to accept from the animal shelter a dog named King who will now be called King Emmett the Second.

Lessons from Lions: Using Children's Media to Teach about Grief and Mourning + CD. G. Adams. Little Rock, AR: Center for Good Mourning, 2006. This booklet explains how to use ten slides from the Disney film, *The Lion King* (1994), with children in classrooms or support groups to encourage discussions about grief and mourning. The text and slides illustrate three unhelpful reactions following a loss: (1) running away from the problem, the pain, and those who know and love you best; (2) pretending the bad thing never happened—living as if the past doesn't matter; and (3) treating your feelings, experiences, and story as a big secret—never telling anyone about them. The positive grief lesson is: By not making any of these three mistakes, we can keep the person with us in our hearts.

Lilacs for Grandma. M. W. Hucek. Omaha, NE: Centering Corporation, 2002. Megan has a special hiding place under a giant lilac bush in her grandmother's yard. Both Grandmother (when she was a child) and Megan enjoy that special place. So when Grandmother becomes sick and is getting ready to die she asks Megan to bring her a bouquet each morning when the lilacs bloom and promises she will enjoy them even when she is no longer able to talk. After Grandmother dies, Megan brings a big bouquet of lilacs to put on her grave as "a kiss for you Grandma, to send you on your way" (p. 20).

A Little Bit of Rob. B. J. Turner. Morton Grove, IL: Albert Whitman, 1996. After the death of her big brother, Rob, Lena and her parents are unable to mention his name and try not to cry. As Lena says, "we were all trying to be strong. We were all trying to pretend nothing had changed." Several weeks later, they take their boat out crabbing again in an effort to resume some activities they had shared with Rob. In doing so and by sharing Rob's old sweatshirt, they are finally able to speak about Rob and to realize they would always have their memories of him to comfort them.

Little Tree: A Story for Children with Serious Medical Problems. J. C. Mills. Washington, DC: Magination Press, 2nd ed., 2003. Little Tree and her squirrel friend lived happily in the forest until a storm caused her to lose some of her branches and made them sad. Two tree wizards removed some dead branches and pointed out that Little Tree still had a strong trunk, deep roots, and a beautiful heart. Wizardly care helped Little Tree cope with her fears and discover that she still had special strengths and abilities. See also a companion book: *Gentle Willow: A Story for Children about Dying*.

Losing Uncle Tim. M. K. Jordan. Morton Grove, IL: Albert Whitman, 1989. Uncle Tim was Daniel's best friend. They spent lots of good time together. When Tim became infected with HIV, developed AIDS, and died, Daniel found solace in an idea they had once discussed: "Maybe Uncle Tim is like the sun, just shining somewhere else."

Mama's Going to Heaven Soon. K. M. Copeland. Minneapolis, MN: Augsburg Fortress, 2005. This book describes two children's reactions when their Mama becomes ill and Daddy says she will soon go to heaven to live with God and the angels. Mama will be gone forever but will always love her children.

Remembering her love and talking with Daddy and other caring adults about feelings can help.

The Memory String. E. Bunting. New York: Clarion, 2000. Laura's grief after her mother's death three years earlier is still vivid and she has trouble accepting her new stepmother, Jane. Laura consoles herself with a string of buttons given to her by her mother that goes back three generations in her family. Each button has special significance, especially the buttons from Mom's prom and wedding dresses and from the nightgown she was wearing when she died. When the string breaks, the buttons are scattered all over the yard. Laura, Dad, and Jane find all but one button. Dad proposes that they substitute a twin for the missing button, but Jane wisely says, "It's like a mother. No substitute allowed" (p. 25). When Jane finds the missing button, Laura asks her to help restring her buttons.

Molly's Rosebush. J. Cohn. Morton Grove, IL: Albert Whitman, 1994. Molly eagerly awaited the birth of the new baby, but her mother had a miscarriage. Her father explains that not all babies are strong enough to be born. Mommy says, "It's sort of like when a flower bud doesn't get to blossom into a flower." Grandma helps by planting a rosebush with Molly for Mommy.

A Mural for Mamita/Un Mural Para Mamita. A. K. Alexander. Omaha, NE: Centering Corporation, 2002. A young girl, her family, and their neighborhood plan a fiesta to celebrate the life of her grandmother who recently died after a long illness. Mamita was well known and greatly loved in her community. The girl tells about her Mexican-American family, her love for her grandmother, and her abuela's activities as proprietor of the local bodega. The girl's special contribution to the celebration is a brilliant mural painted on the side of Mamita's store. The text of this book appears in both English and Spanish.

Mustard. C. Graeber. New York: Bantam Skylark, 1983. Mustard is an elderly cat with a heart condition who needs to avoid stress. But one day Mustard runs outside and gets into a fight with another animal, leading to a heart attack and his death. After Father buries Mustard, Alex donates Mustard's dishes and some money to the animal shelter. Because he is preoccupied with sadness, Alex declines (for now) a well-meaning offer of a new pet.

My Grandmother's Cookie Jar. M. Miller. Los Angeles: Price Stern Sloan, 1987. Grandma's cookie jar is shaped like an Indian head and is a little scary to her granddaughter, but not when she removes its headdress and takes out a cookie. As they share cookies each evening, Grandma tells stories of her Indian people of long ago. The stories make Indian ways, Indian pride, and Indian honor come alive for the little girl. After Grandma's death, Grandfather gives the jar to the girl and tells her it is full, not of cookies but of Grandma's love and her Indian spirit heritage. He says someday the girl will have children of her own and will put cookies in the jar. When she tells Grandma's stories with each cookie, the girl knows she will be keeping alive Grandma's spirit and the spirit of those who went before her.

My Mom Is Dying: A Child's Diary. J. W. McNamara. Minneapolis, MN: Augsburg Fortress, 1994. This book's format looks like a child's illustrated diary. Its contents record Kristine's imaginary conversations with God and her concerns while her mother is dying and after her mom's death. Several pages of author's notes identify Kristine's reactions and suggest how adults could use them as a basis for talking with children.

Nadia the Willful. S. Alexander. New York: Pantheon Books, 1983. After Nadia's eldest brother disappears into the desert and is never found, her father, the leader of his Bedouin clan, in his grief decrees that no one may speak Hamed's name. He promises to punish anyone who reminds him of what he has lost. But Nadia cannot contain her memories of Hamed and speaking about him helps ease her grief. In the end, Nadia helps all of the clan and particularly her father cope with their grief by willfully talking about her brother and keeping his memory alive.

The New King. D. Rappaport. New York: Dial Books for Young Readers, 1995. Young Prince Rakoto cannot accept his father's death. He commands court officials to bring his father back to life. When they cannot do that, a Wise Woman shares an old Malagasy tale. She explains that when the earth was new God gave the first human couple a choice. God said, "One day you must die. When it is your turn, do you want to die like the moon or like a banana tree?" The moon starts out like a sliver, grows bigger and bigger until it is full, then gets smaller and smaller until at last it disappears, only later to begin to grow all over again. By contrast, the banana tree grows and sends forth shoots. When the tree dies, the shoots keep growing until they are big enough and strong enough to send out their own shoots. At first, the man wanted to die like the moon so as to come back to life and live forever, but the woman persuaded him that it would be better to live, love, and die, while one's children carry on—and thus to find a way of living forever by giving life to others. Realizing all that he had been given by his father, Prince Rakoto "ruled with love and justice as his father had taught him, and he passed his father's lessons on to his children."

Nonna. J. Bartoli. New York: Harvey House, 1975. A boy and his younger sister, with good memories of their grandmother, are allowed to take part in her funeral, burial, and the division of her property among family members so that each receives some memento of her life. At Christmas, the children make Nonna's cookies in her memory.

Not Just a Fish. K. M. Hemery. Omaha, NE: Centering Corporation, 2000. Marybeth thinks Puffer is the best goldfish in the world; he always listens to her and watching him makes her feel calm and peaceful. It shocks Marybeth to find Puffer floating upside down in his bowl. Although people tell Marybeth they are sorry Puffer died, they also say he was "just a fish" and that makes her angry. Then her father flushes Puffer down the toilet before Marybeth can bury him! Only Aunt Lizzie understands Marybeth's loss and helps by arranging a memorial service with music, a few words from Marybeth about Puffer, and a heart-shaped pin with a fish painted on it.

Ocho Loved Flowers. A. Fontaine. Seattle, WA: Stoneleigh Press, 2007. Annie's good friend is a cat who is crazy about flowers. When Annie finds Ocho hiding under the bed and making strange sounds, she knows he isn't well. After the vet confirms that Ocho will not get better and is going to die soon, Annie is very sad. Mom says they will give Ocho medicine so he will not be in pain and can stay at home even though he might start eating less. Annie buys flowers for Ocho and he dies peacefully.

The Purple Balloon. C. Raschka. New York: Schwartz & Wade (Random House), 2007. The author explains that when they become aware of their impending death children often draw a blue or purple balloon, released and floating free. Here the balloon images first depict the death of an elderly person before turning to a dying youngster. The text says, "Good help makes leaving easier" and offers suggestions for those who want to help make dying not so hard.

A Quilt for Elizabeth. B. W. Tiffault. Omaha, NE: Centering Corporation, 1992. When Elizabeth was eight, her Daddy got sick, had to be hospitalized, and eventually died. Elizabeth got angrier and angrier. One day, Grandma suggests that together they sew a patchwork quilt out of swatches of material from their old clothes. Each square of fabric has a story to tell and memories to recall as it binds the quilt and their lives together.

Rachel and the Upside Down Heart: A True Story. E. Douglas. Los Angeles: Price Stern Sloan, 1990. After Rachel's daddy died when she was four years old, she is sad and has to move from a house with a yard, green grass, and two dogs in Kentucky to a noisy apartment in New York City. Mommy says Daddy would always be in Rachel's heart, so she begins to draw hearts but can only make them upside down. Later, Rachel finds some new friends and some of her hearts are upside

up. Finally, when his father dies, Rachel is able to talk to a new friend and help him with his loss.

The Rag Coat. L. Mills. Boston: Little, Brown, 1991. After Papa died, Minna couldn't start school because she had to stay home and help Mama make quilts to support the family. When she was eight Minna wanted to go to school, but she didn't have a winter coat. So she was happy when the Quilting Mothers volunteered to piece together a coat for her out of scraps of their old materials and had it ready for Sharing Day. At first, the children teased her about her rag coat, but not after she explained the stories behind each scrap that she had selected.

Remembering Oakley. C. J. Schutt. Inkus Imagination, 2009. Young Jacob's emotions range from anger and hurt to fear and denial as he learns the difficulty of saying good-bye to his dog, who is dying from cancer. Jacob gradually takes comfort in Oakley's freedom from pain and suffering, and ultimately opts to celebrate the love they shared. The pain does get easier to deal with and he will heal. You can learn to love yourself through loving another creature.

Rosalie. J. Hewett. New York: Lothrop, Lee & Shepard, 1987. This story describes an aging dog who plays an important role in the life of a child. When Rosalie is 16 years old, Cindy's veterinarian tells her Rosalie would be nearly 100 years old if she was a person! Rosalie is now in poor health, deaf, and less active than she used to be, but Cindy, her relatives, and her friends still enjoy visiting and playing with Rosalie. Rosalie continues to give love to Cindy and all of those around her, and is cared for and loved in return by everyone.

Rudi's Pond. E. Bunting. New York: Clarion, 1999. Rudi is a young girl's best friend. When he becomes sick as a result of a congenital heart defect, the girl visits him until he is taken to the hospital and Mom says he is "sinking." The girl and her classmates send cards and make a big "GET WELL RUDI" banner for his hospital room. After Rudi dies, the children write poems and make a memorial pond in the schoolyard that attracts a beautiful hummingbird.

Sadako. E. Coerr. New York: Putnam's, 1993. This book retells the story of *Sadako and the Thousand Paper Cranes* (see next entry), with new text and attractive new pastel images.

Sadako and the Thousand Paper Cranes. E. Coerr. New York: Putnam's, 1977. Sadako was a Japanese girl who died of leukemia in 1955 as one of the long-term results of the atomic bombing of Hiroshima that happened when she was just a baby. In the hospital, a friend reminds Sadako of the legend that the crane is supposed to live for a thousand years and the gods will grant her wish and good health to a person who folds 1,000 origami paper cranes. With family members and friends, they begin folding. After Sadako's death her classmates continued the work and children all over Japan have since contributed money to erect a statue in her memory.

Samantha Jane's Missing Smile: A Story about Coping with the Loss of a Parent. J. Kaplow & D. Pincus. Washington, DC: Magination Press, 2007. After her dad's death, Sammy Jane worries that sadness will overwhelm her and her mother. If she starts crying, she fears she won't be able to stop. Later she worries that if she smiles too much and has fun, people will think she didn't love her dad. Eventually, a wise neighbor shows her that trying to push bad feelings away won't work; they will always return just like a twig will pop back up when pushed under water. Together they seek reminders of happy times with dad and Sammy Jane realizes that dad wouldn't want her always to be sad.

Saying Goodbye to Daddy. J. Vigna. Morton Grove, IL: Albert Whitman, 1991. Clare is scared, lonely, and angry after her father is killed in a car accident. To help Clare understand death, her mother and grandparents ask her to recall Sam, the hamster who died earlier. They also help her cope with her grief and anger, get through the funeral and burial, and recall good memories.

A Season for Mangoes. R. Hanson. New York: Clarion, 2005. In Jamaica, a girl named Sareen is concerned about participating in her first sit-up, a ritual in which villagers share food, tell stories, and engage in activities to celebrate the life of her recently deceased grandmother. Sareen discovers that sharing her stories of Nana's passion for mangoes helps ease her sadness.

Since My Brother Died/Desde Que Murió Mi Hermano. M. Muñoz-Kiehne. Omaha, NE: Centering Corporation, 2000. With parallel texts in English and Spanish, a child wonders if a brother's death is only a dream or if something could have kept him from dying. The child reports family sadness as well as his (her?) own physical reactions like headaches and stomachaches. Afraid of forgetting this brother, the child begins to paint; colorful illustrations gradually turn into rainbows and the trust that life can go forward.

The Snowman. R. H. Vogel. Omaha, NE: Centering Corporation, rev. ed., 2002. Two brothers are building their first snowman since their Dad died eight months ago. Talking about their father's illness and how he died helps answer some of eight-year-old Buddy's questions. It also lets 12-year-old Tommy vent some of his anger for the first time. Using Dad's old pipe, hat, and favorite scarf, the two boys finish the snowman and share good memories of Dad.

Someone I Love Died by Suicide: A Story for Child Survivors and Those Who Care for Them. D. Cammarata. Palm Beach Gardens, FL: Grief Guidance, Inc., 2000.

This book seeks to explain some factors that might lead to suicide, normal grief reactions to that experience, how to get help for yourself, and ways of saying good-bye and still remembering the person.

Stacy Had a Little Sister. W. C. Old. Morton Grove, IL: Albert Whitman, 1995. Stacy liked her baby sister sometimes, but not always. Ashley took up a lot of her parents' time and Stacy was jealous until one night she woke up to find that the baby had died from Sudden Infant Death Syndrome. Stacy wonders if she caused the baby to die and if she will get SIDS. She also has trouble sleeping until she talks about her concerns with her parents.

Sunflowers and Rainbows for Tia: Saying Goodbye to Daddy. A. Alexander-Greene. Omaha, NE: Centering Corporation, 1999. A ten-year-old African-American girl describes what it is like when her Daddy dies suddenly. Tia tells about her sadness, grief, and fears that Mama might also die and leave the children alone. She relates how people came to the house to share their love for Daddy, offer support, and bring food. Being involved in the preparations and taking part in the funeral itself helps Tia, especially when she is allowed to bring Daddy's favorite sunflowers to the ceremony and a big rainbow shines through the clouds.

Tear Soup: A Recipe for Healing after Loss. P. Schwiebert & C. DeKlyen. Portland, OR: Grief Watch, 1999; 2nd ed., 2001. Grandy is "an old and somewhat wise woman" who has just suffered a big loss in her life. She fills a soup pot over and over again with her tears, feelings, memories, and misgivings. Making tear soup is a lonely and difficult task everyone must do alone. Many people avoid this work, although it can be helped by a good friend who listens and by special soup gatherings. Rejecting foolish advice, *Tear Soup* affirms all of the reactions that bereaved people experience, while encouraging them as they cope with loss and grief. Five pages offer Grandy's cooking tips and two new pages in the second edition offer an expanded list of helpful resources.

Tell Me about Death, Tell Me about Funerals. E. A. Corley. Santa Clara, CA: Grammatical Sciences, 1973. While avoiding euphemisms, a young girl whose grandfather recently died rather suddenly and her father talk about guilt and other feelings, birth and death, and choices about embalming, funerals, burial, cemeteries, and cremation. At one point, we are treated to a child's delightful misunderstanding about the "polarbears" who carry the casket.

Thank You, Grandpa. L. Plourde. New York: Dutton Children's Books, 2003. Over the years, a girl and her grandfather enjoy walking in the woods together. They share discoveries of many different animals and insects. One day when they find a dead grasshopper, the girl asks, "What can we do?" Grandpa says: "We can say thank you and good-bye." In time, Grandpa becomes too old to walk and one day the girl finds herself walking alone. When she finds a dandelion, she says to herself: "Thank you, Grandpa, for our walks. You kept me steady when I wasn't so steady. You let me run ahead when I was ready to run ahead. Thank you for sharing spiderweb tears and firefly flashes. But most of all, thank you for teaching me the words I need to say.... Grandpa, I love you and I'll miss you. But I will never forget you. Thank you and good-bye."

Too Far Away to Touch. L. Newman. New York: Clarion, 1995. Uncle Leonard is Zoe's favorite relative. He takes her to special places, tells her jokes, and makes her laugh, but now he is sick and has less energy (gradually, we learn he has AIDS). One day he takes Zoe to a planetarium and later explains that if he dies he will be like the stars, "too far away to touch, but close enough to see." The lesson is confirmed one evening at the seashore where they watch the night sky and witness a shooting star.

The Very Beautiful Dragon. J. Johnson. Omaha, NE: Centering Corporation, 2001. Two young boys are scared when they first encounter a dragon with scary teeth and claws; they become even more frightened when they see it again on other occasions. It isn't enough for them to be shown that there is actually no dragon present. What really helps is a neighbor who teaches the boys that they have to face their fears and get to know what scares them. That's the way to face down one's dragons and recognize one's own strengths and power. This book is accompanied by *Beautiful Dragons and Other Fears: A Workbook for Children* (see Appendix C in this book).

Water Bugs and Dragonflies: Explaining Death to Young Children. D. Stickney. New York: Pilgrim Press, 1982. This short story uses transformations within life as a metaphor for transformations between life and death. A colony of water bugs wonders why none of its members ever returns when they climb up a lily stalk and disappear from sight. They promise each other the next one will come back to explain where he or she went. But the next water bug to go discovers he has been transformed into a dragonfly and cannot return to the underwater colony to explain what happened.

We Are All in the Dumps with Jack and Guy: Two Nursery Rhymes with Pictures. M. Sendak. New York: HarperCollins, 1993. Two wicked rats capture a poor, homeless, Black child and some kittens, but Jack and Guy, with the help of the Moon and a giant white cat, chase them off only to return those they have rescued to the uncertainties of the street.

We Remember Philip. N. Simon. Chicago: Albert Whitman, 1979. When the children are told that the adult son of their elementary school teacher died in a mountain climbing accident, Sam and other members of his class observe how Mr. Hall is affected by his grief. Sam talks to his mother about death and grief, including the death of his dog, Skye. Then the children write condolence letters to Mr. Hall. In time, the children persuade Mr. Hall to share with them a scrapbook and other memories of his son, and they plant a tree as a class memorial to Philip.

What about Me? When Brothers and Sisters Get Sick. A. Peterkin. Washington, DC: Magination Press, 1992. Laura is two years older than her brother and likes helping to care for him. They play together every day but often quarrel. When Aunt Ann tells Laura that Tom is sick and in the hospital, Laura misses him, feels responsible for his illness because she yelled at him, and worries that he might die. Sadly, their parents and other adults seem to focus only on Tom while ignoring Laura's needs. Finally, Laura's parents and the doctor tell Laura about Tom's illness, explain that it is not catching, predict that he should be able to come home soon, let them play together, and take her out for a special treat.

Where Is Grandpa? T. A. Barron. New York: Philomel Books, 2000. After Grandpa dies, family members share memories of him. When a young boy wants to know where Grandpa is now, they decide that Grandpa is in heaven and that "heaven is any place where people who love each other have shared some time together." The thought that Grandpa is way off in the Never Summer range of the Rockies that they used to look at together "as far as we can possibly see" from the tree house they built comforts the boy.

Where the Balloons Go. P. Coleman. Omaha, NE: Centering Corporation, 1996. When Corey asks where balloons go as they fly up into the sky, Grandma suggests that perhaps their destination is a lovely Balloon Forest. Later, after Grandma becomes sick and dies, Corey wishes that his balloons could carry him up to the Balloon Forest to see Grandma. He and his father settle for attaching messages of love to their balloons and releasing them.

Zach and His Dog: A Story of Bonding, Love, and Loss for Children and Adults to Share Together. D. K. Meagher. Bloomington, IN: AuthorHouse, 2009. Printed on colored paper and with lively illustrations facing each of its ten short chapters, this is the story of a boy who gets a puppy for his fifth birthday. The two become best friends. But one day when Freckles dashes into the street he is hit by a car, runs away to hide, and is found dead. The book then turns to Zach's grief, a memorial service, making a memory box for Freckles, and Zach's deep sense of loss. Each chapter offers questions to stimulate discussion between a child and an adult about bonding with a pet and coping with crisis and loss.

For additional information about death-related literature for children, contact the **Centering Corporation**.

Selected Literature for Adolescents: Annotated Descriptions

Literature for Middle School Readers

After. K. Harmel. New York: Delacorte Books, 2009. The death of Lacey Mann's father precipitates negative grief responses in her family members. A year later, she still feels guilty thinking that her actions might have unwittingly contributed to his death. She finds a way forward by helping others and starting a support group for students who have lost a parent.

Annie and the Sand Dobbies: A Story about Death for Children and Their Parents. J. B. Coburn. New York: Seabury Press, 1964. Before 11-year-old Danny encounters the deaths of his toddler sister (from a respiratory infection) and his dog (after it ran away from home and is found frozen to death), a neighbor introduced him to some imaginary characters called "sand dobbies" who are a little like fairies or elves. Now, the sand dobbies are used to suggest that the deceased are safe with God.

Autobiography of My Dead Brother. W. D. Myers. New York: HarperCollins, 2005. In this sketchbook, a 15-year-old boy tells a complex story of life and death in Harlem, including his blood-brother bond with a slightly older friend, who gradually drifts away from him into a violent and wasted life.

Be a Friend: Children Who Live with HIV Speak. L. S. Wiener, A. Best, & P. A. Pizzo (Comps.). Morton Grove, IL: Albert Whitman, 1994. This book allows children living with HIV infection to speak in their own voices in ways that are poignant, charming, and compelling. Three examples include: an 11-year-old who writes: "I often wonder how other children without AIDS learn to appreciate life. That's the best part about having AIDS" (p. 13); a 12-year-old girl adds: "Thinking about dying is hard, but it is good to do because you think about it anyway. Most people don't want to talk about this because it makes them sad, but once you do, you can talk about it more easily next time. Then you can go on LIVING!" (p. 24); and an 8-year-old girl pleads: "The worst thing about having AIDS is not knowing if people will be your friends. So please be our friends. We need you to be our friends" (p. 39).

Bridge to Terabithia. K. Paterson. New York: HarperCollins, 1977. Jess and Leslie have a special, secret meeting place in the woods, called Terabithia. But when Leslie is killed in an accidental fall, the magic of their play and friendship is disrupted. Jess mourns the loss of this special relationship, is supported by his family, and at last can initiate new relationships to share friendship in a similar way with others.

Charlotte's Web. E. B. White. New York: Harper, 1952. This is a story of friendship on two levels: a young girl named Fern who lives on a farm and saves Wilbur, the runt of the pig litter; and Charlotte A. Caravatica, the spider, who spins fabulous webs to save an older and fatter Wilbur from the butcher's knife. In the end, Charlotte dies of natural causes, but her accomplishments and her offspring live on.

Daddy's Climbing Tree. C. S. Adler. New York: Clarion, 1993. After her cat, Mimsy, is accidentally killed and the family moves from the only home 11-year-old Jessica had ever known, her father is killed in a road accident. Jessica refuses to believe he is really dead, but there is no safe place for her to turn to avoid people's expressions of sympathy. So she takes her 6-year-old brother and sets out to walk through the state park to their old home where she thinks Daddy must be hiding in his favorite climbing tree. The journey is more difficult than Jessica had imagined. Only when she is high up in the tree does she finally accept that Daddy is dead and Mom truly does love her.

The Diary of a Young Girl. A. Frank. New York: Bantam, 1993. A young girl's classic record of her thoughts about events when she and her family had to hide from the Nazis in Amsterdam during World War II because they were Jewish.

Did Someone You Love Die? T. A. Phillips. Berkeley Heights, NJ: Enslow Publishers, 2016. This book explores the emotions involved when a teen's family member or friend dies. It also tries to show how to learn to get through the experience and to support someone living through a loss.

The Eagle Kite. P. Fox. New York: Bantam, 1996. A boy doesn't understand when his father gets sick, moves out of their home to a rented cabin, and eventually dies. Liam is confused, puzzled by the half-truths he is told, and unable to understand his mother and aunt's different reactions. Eventually, Liam recalls a day when he was flying his eagle kite and came upon his father embracing another man. He realizes his father is gay and has AIDS. Sharing this realization with his father and later telling his mother what he had seen help Liam come to terms with his experiences.

The Fault in Our Stars. J. Green. New York: Dutton/Penguin, 2012. Three teenagers meet in a cancer support group as they each struggle with the disease and its side effects. They find common ground in their irreverent use of humor and sarcasm to cope, even as those around them often misunderstand their behaviors, desires, and individual needs. The teens bond in complex ways as they grapple with large existential questions of meaning and the realities of life, love, and death.

Flowers for the Ones You've Known: Unedited Letters from Bereaved Teens. E. S. Traisman & J. Sieff (Comps.). Omaha, NE: Centering Corporation, 1995. These letters and poems by teens who have experienced the death of an important person in their lives are reproduced in various handwritten and print formats. There is also some artwork and writing guides from experienced group leaders.

Grover. V. Cleaver & B. Cleaver. Philadelphia: Lippincott, 1970. When Grover was 11, his mother became terminally ill. She took her own life, thinking to "spare" herself and her family the ravages of her illness. His father cannot face the facts of this death or the depth of his grief, so he tries to hold his feelings inside and convince his son it was an accident. Issues posed include: whether one's chief duty is to endure life no matter what suffering it holds; whether religion is a comfort; and how one should deal with grief.

Hate List. J. Brown. New York: Little, Brown, 2009. Valerie and her boyfriend compiled a "hate list" to ease the pain of being bullied and cope with her parents' constant fighting. But when Nick pulls a gun in the Commons and uses their list to kill six students and a teacher, while wounding many others including Valerie, she struggles with guilt feelings and others' erroneous views that she had something to do with the actual shootings. A therapist helps her face these challenges and return to school in fall.

How It Feels to Fight for Your Life. J. Krementz. New York: Simon & Schuster, 1991. Fourteen children and adolescents (7–16 years old) describe their struggles with life-threatening or life-limiting conditions. Photos of the authors accompany each essay.

How It Feels When a Parent Dies. J. Krementz. New York: Knopf, 1981, 2004. Eighteen children and adolescents (7–16 years old) describe their reactions to the death of a parent and subsequent events. Photos of the authors accompany each essay.

If I Die and When I Do: Exploring Death with Young People. F. Sternberg & B. Sternberg. Englewood Cliffs, NJ: Prentice-Hall, 1980. This book comes from a nine-week middle school course on death and dying taught by the first author. The text mainly consists of drawings, poems, and statements by the students on various death-related topics, with introductory and linking materials by the Sternbergs plus a closing chapter of 25 suggested activities.

If You Come Softly. J. Woodson. New York: Speak/Penguin, 2010. A black boy and a Jewish girl meet at a fancy prep school in Manhattan. Each struggles with difficult family relationships and as a mixed-race couple they must deal with more or less subtle bigotry. The tragic climax is stunning.

The Kids' Book about Death and Dying, by and for Kids. E. E. Rofes (ed.) and the Unit at Fayerweather Street School. Boston: Little, Brown, 1985. The result of a class project, this book reports what its 11- to 14-year-old authors learned about a wide range of death-related topics. They explain what children want to know about these subjects and how they want adults to talk to them. One lesson is that "a lot of the mystery and fear surrounding death has been brought about by ignorance and avoidance" (p. 111). Another is the hope "that children can lead the way in dealing with death and dying with a healthier and happier approach" (p. 114).

The Last Dance. C. A. Deedy. Atlanta, GA: Peachtree, 1995. Two children share a close friendship extending from childhood, throughout their lives, and even after Ninny's death. As children, Ninny and Bessie would sneak out at night to visit the graveyard where Ninny's grandparents were buried. Before his death, they would visit the graveyard with Ninny's grandfather, Oppa, who taught them to tell stories, to sing, and to dance. Oppa said, "Those we love are never really gone as long as their stories are told." After Oppa's death, Ninny and Bessie pledge to each other that when one of them dies, the other will come to the graveyard and dance on the grave. They share a rich life together and their love endures even after death.

Learning to Say Good-By: When a Parent Dies. E. LeShan. New York: Macmillan, 1976. This book offers advice to bereaved youngsters and the adults around them on a range of topics, including: what grief is like; the importance of honesty, trust, sharing, and funerals; fear of abandonment and guilt; accepting the loss of the deceased, maintaining a capacity for love, and meeting future changes. The basic conviction is that "a child can live through anything, so long as he or she is told the truth and is allowed to share with loved ones the natural feelings people have when they are suffering" (p. 3).

Losing Someone You Love: Dealing with Death and Dying. T. A. Phillips. Berkeley Heights, NJ: Enslow Publishers, 2009. This book examines grief and the grieving process along with variables in losing a parent, sibling, grandparent, friend, or pet. Then it explores events that typically occur before and after a death, and how to support one another. There is a glossary and short lists of resources.

Losing Someone You Love: When a Brother or Sister Dies. E. Richter. New York: Putnam's, 1986. In their own words, 16 adolescents and young adults describe their reactions to a wide variety of experiences of sibling death. Photos of the authors accompany most of the essays.

The Magic Moth. V. Lee. New York: Seabury, 1972. Things are difficult for six-year-old Mark-O and his family because his sister, Maryanne, is dying from an incurable heart disease. When Maryanne dies people come to the house and there is a funeral and burial. Mark-O is helped to make sense of this death by thinking about a seed that has to crumble so that the plant inside it can grow and by the metaphor of a moth as it experiences a transition from one mode of life to another.

Mama's Going to Buy You a Mockingbird. J. Little. New York: Viking Kestrel, 1984. Jeremy and his younger sister, Sarah, only learn their father is dying from cancer by overhearing people talk about it. They experience many losses, large and small, accompanying his dying and death, often compounded by lack of information and control over their situation. Their need for support is clear.

Mick Harte Was Here. B. Park. New York: Knopf, 1995 (Random House & Scholastic, 1996). Thirteen-year-old Phoebe recalls her younger brother and his death when he was hit by a truck while riding his bicycle without a helmet. Phoebe had argued with Mick that morning and later refused when he asked her to ride his bike home for him after school. She describes memories of her relationship with Mick and her profound grief after his death. Phoebe wants very much to know where Mick is now; eventually she decides that if Mick is with God (as people keep saying) and God is everywhere, then Mick is everywhere, too. Mick's body is cremated, there is a memorial service with funny stories about Mick, Phoebe speaks about bike safety at a school assembly, and in the fresh concrete at the new soccer field bleachers she prints: "M-I-C-K-H-A-R-T-E-W-A-S-H-E-R-E."

Missing May. C. Rylant. New York: Scholastic, 2003. After six-year-old Summer's mother dies, no one wants her until Uncle Ob and Aunt May take her into their rusty old trailer in Deep Water, West Virginia, and truly love her. But when Summer is 12 May dies suddenly, and Summer and Ob have a hard time coping. Summer worries about Ob and is irritated at the support he is getting from a strange neighboring boy. Summer wishes she could fix Ob's grief and they try to connect with May in the afterlife. Finally, a memory of May opens the floodgates and Summer cries her heart out. That catharsis and Ob's love reminds them that May will always be with them.

Never Blame the Umpire. G. Fehler. Grand Rapids, MI: Zonderkidz, 2010. Kate is 11 when she learns her mother has an incurable form of cancer. Mama's illness and anticipated death overshadow everything. Kate struggles with her faith in God until Mama compares God to an umpire. Mama says we need umpires to control our games, so we shouldn't blame them even when they make mistakes. But Mama says God doesn't make mistakes, so we need to accept his decisions even when we don't understand or disagree with them. "We can't see the future, so maybe what we think is bad might really be something God lets happen so that something even worse won't happen in the future" (p. 147). Kate finds consolation in her faith and Mama's love.

Nicolas. P. Girard. Montreal: Drawn and Quarterly, 2016. Simple black-and-white drawings explore the author's life and grief after the death of his younger brother at age five. A sparse tale for long-term mourners in which humor and raw grief combine.

November Blues. S. M. Draper. New York: Simon Pulse, 2009. Shortly after her boyfriend dies in a hazing accident, high school senior November discovers she's pregnant. She faces physical and emotional difficulties, along with legal and social problems associated with this unplanned event in her life.

Olive's Ocean. K. Henkes. New York: Greenwillow, 2003; HarperTrophy, 2005. Weeks after a girl is killed by a car while riding her bicycle, her mother delivers a page from her journal to 12-year-old Martha Boyle in which Olive had written about her three hopes: to become a writer, to see a real ocean, and to become friends with Martha, "the nicest person in my whole entire class" (p. 5). Martha is puzzled because she hardly knew Olive. Coincidentally, the next day her family is off to visit her grandmother who lives near the Atlantic Ocean. Martha spends the vacation thinking about many things: Olive; her aging grandmother (who calmly said, "Who knows, this might be our last summer together."); her relations with her parents and siblings; her plans to be a writer; and her emerging feelings for boys. Then Martha decides to bring a small jar of seawater—Olive's ocean—back to Olive's mother. That leads to a near-drowning experience (death can happen to anyone at any time). And back home Mrs. Barstow has moved away, so Martha uses the water to write Olive's name on the steps of her old house as a way of saying goodbye.

One Thousand Paper Cranes: The Story of Sadako and the Children's Peace Statue. I. Takayuki. New York: Dell Laurel Leaf, 2001. This book retells the story of *Sadako and the Thousand Paper Cranes* (see entry in Appendix A), supplemented by photographs, drawings, and narrative background to the atomic bombing that ultimately led to Sadako's death and to the memorial erected in her memory.

Sky Memories. P. Brisson. New York: Delacorte, 1999. While her mother struggles with her cancer and its treatments, 10-year-old Emily and Mom develop a ritual to celebrate their relationship. Together they gather "sky memories," mental pictures of the ever-changing sky in all its variety and wonder. The sky seems to reflect the phases of Mom's illness and the vitality of her soul.

So Long, Grandpa. Elfie Donnelly. New York: Crown, 1981. Ten-year-old Michael's close relationship with his Grandpa is threatened because Grandpa has cancer and knows he only has a few weeks to live. In this book, Michael describes his grandfather's deterioration and eventual death, along with his own reactions to these events. He also tells about the way in which his grandfather had helped to prepare Michael by taking him to an elderly friend's funeral.

Some Folk Say: Stories of Life, Death, and Beyond. J. H. Gignoux. New York: FoulkeTale Publishing, 1998. Here are 38 legends, retold in prose and poetry, that different cultures use to come to terms with the reality of death and hopes for life beyond the grave. The stories fall under five headings: origins of death; balancing life and death; lessons for life; after death; and reconciliation with death. Brief comments introduce each section and follow each story. The book also has eight full-page colorful illustrations. A treasury of global culture to stimulate discussions with young readers.

Sounder. W. Armstrong. New York: Harper & Row, 1969 (often reprinted in paperback). Only the dog has a proper name in this tale of an African-American sharecropper family in the late 19th century told from the point of view of the oldest son. After the father is arrested for stealing a ham to feed his family, their coon hound is shot and disappears. Angry and grieving, the son searches relentlessly for the dog and then for his father who is sent to hard labor in a prison camp. The boy grows, takes on the farm work, and is taught to read by a white teacher. Eventually, the dog returns (but is too injured to hunt); later the father comes back (hurt by an explosion in a prison quarry), only to die sometime thereafter. A harsh life in hard times for people "born to lose," as the devout mother says.

Sun and Spoon. K. Henkes. New York: Puffin, 1998. After his grandmother dies, 10-year-old Spoon searches for a keepsake to remember her. When he finds the deck of cards they had used, each card with a unique image of the sun, he takes it without asking. Later, he learns they also are a consolation to Pa, who thinks he misplaced them. When Spoon confesses, Pa understands, gives Spoon the cards to keep, and shows him a drawing of her hand that Gram made when she was Spoon's age. On the drawing, she inscribed a large capital letter "M" and smaller lowercase letters "a-r-t-h-a" with the legend "M is always for Martha" (her name). Spoon finds that the lines on the palm of his hand also make a large "M," which he takes as a special sign from Gram.

The Sunday Doll. M. F. Shura. New York: Dodd, Mead, 1988. Just as she turns 13, a girl must cope with family events, her own complex feelings, and the gift of an Amish doll with no face. Emily's parents exclude her from something terrible involving her older sister (the suicide of a boyfriend) by sending her off to visit Aunt Harriet. Emily loves this elderly aunt, but is frightened by one of Harriet's life-threatening "spells" (transient ischemic attacks). Through these challenges, Emily gradually learns she has strengths of her own and, like the doll, can choose which face to present to the world.

Sunflower Promise. K. M. Hemery. Omaha, NE: Centering Corporation, 2005. Willomina May Tyler and Davy are best friends in a small town in Ohio in 1948. One day as they are teasing, Davy accidentally tears the big, floppy, cloth sunflower off Willow's lovely new hat. She is furious and won't play with Davy any more even though he promises he will make it up to her some day. After Willow punches Davy on the arm, she is regretful when his bruises don't go away and he is hospitalized for testing. Will he never get better? Did she cause it? In the end, Davy dies, but not before he arranges a surprise for Willow: a gorgeous crop of sunflowers in the field where they used to play.

A Taste of Blackberries. D. B. Smith. New York: Harper-Trophy, 1988. Jamie loves playing tricks like stealing an apple from a farmer's yard or running on a forbidden lawn. One day he pokes a stick into a bee hive, provoking the bees to swarm and sting, and causing his death from an allergic reaction. Afterwards, his best friend (the book's unnamed narrator) reflects on this event: Did it really happen, or is it just another of Jamie's pranks? Could it have been prevented? Is it disloyal to go on living when Jamie is dead? The boy shares some of his concerns with a kind neighbor who says, "Honey, one of the hardest things we have to learn is that some questions do not have answers" (pp. 61–62). The boy nods and thinks: "This made more sense than if she tried to tell me some junk about God needing angels." In the end, he picks blackberries and gives them to Jamie's mom.

Teenagers Face to Face with Bereavement. Karen Gravelle & Charles Haskins. New York: Julian Messner, 1989. This book explores the unique qualities of adolescent grief by drawing on the experiences of 17 teens who have experienced the deaths of parents, siblings, and friends. Topics include what happens at the time of death, feelings after the numbness wears off, putting the family back together, and moving on.

There Are Two Kinds of Terrible. P. Mann. New York: Doubleday/Avon, 1977. Robbie's broken arm is one kind of terrible—but it ends. His mother's death leaves Robbie and his "cold fish" father without an ending. Each grieves alone until they find ways to share their suffering and their memories.

Tiger Eyes. J. Blume. Scarsdale, NY: Bradbury, 1981. After her father is killed during a holdup of his 7-Eleven store in Atlantic City, Davey (age 15), her mother, and her younger brother all react differently and are unable to help each other in their grief. Hoping it will help, they decide to live temporarily with Davey's aunt in Los Alamos ("the Bomb City"). Only when Davey and her mother, first separately and then together, finally face the horrors of the night her father was killed are they able to make a decision to move back to New Jersey to go ahead with rebuilding their lives.

Tunnel Vision. F. Arrick. New York: Dell, 1981. After 15-year-old Anthony hangs himself, his parents, sister, best friends, and teacher feel bewildered and guilty. They each ask what they might have done to prevent this awful event. Clues are evident in hindsight, but easy answers are not available. Anthony's suicide hurts everyone he loved. His mother asks, "Why did Anthony believe that death was the only kind of peace he could find" (p. 173)?

What Does That Mean? A Dictionary of Death, Dying and Grief Terms for Grieving Children and Those Who Love Them. H. I. Smith & J. Johnson. Omaha, NE: Centering Corporation, 2006. It is important to find the right words to use in talking with young people, especially so when the subjects involve loss and death. This book identifies 71 key terms, explains how to pronounce them and what they mean, and offers guidance about how to use these terms and discuss these subjects with children.

Winter Holding Spring. C. Dragonwagon. New York: Atheneum/Simon & Schuster, 1990. At first, nothing is the same for 11-year-old Sarah and her father after her mother dies. Each is in great pain, but gradually they begin to share their experiences and their memories of Sarah's mother. Eventually, they realize together that "nothing just *ends* without beginning the next thing at the same time" (p. 11). Each season somehow contains its successor; life and love and grief can continue together, for winter always holds spring. And Sarah knows that "love is alive in me and always will be" (p. 31).

Writing to Richie. P. Calvert. New York: Charles Scribner's Sons, 1994. David and his brother hope their new foster home will be a good one. Still, David worries about their new school and Richie's allergies. Sadly, Richie dies unexpectedly from a reaction to a food additive in the school lunch. Confused and angry, David refuses to go to Richie's funeral. To make matters worse, the foster parents now take in a strange, tough girl named Olivia. Gradually, David and Ollie develop a friendship and eventually she helps him confront his brother's death by writing letters to Richie and taking them to his grave.

Literature for High School Readers

34 Pieces of You. C. Rodrigues. New York: Simon Pulse, 2013. After a teen dies of a drug overdose, her brother and friends explore their grief and try to understand why she died.

Adios, Nirvana. C. Wesselhoeft. New York: Houghton-Mifflin, 2012. Following the accidental death of his twin brother, Jonathan is deeply affected and may have to repeat 11th grade. He is helped by some friends and a challenge to help a blind WWII veteran write about his losses and survivor's guilt.

Anne Frank: The Biography. M. Müller. New York: Metropolitan Books/Henry Holt, 1998. This biography is meant to supplement *The Diary of a Young Girl* (see the entry earlier in this Appendix) by offering an authentic picture of Anne's brief life.

Before I Die. J. Downham. New York: Random House, 2009. A teenage girl has just months to live. As she struggles with the many challenges she faces, she compiles a "To Do Before I Die" list.

The Dead Don't Dance: A Novel of Awakening. C. Martin. Nashville: WestBow Press, 2004. The expectations of Dylan Styles and his wife for the birth of their first child turn into tragedy when the baby dies at birth and Maggie is left comatose for many months. Eventually she recovers and there is a happy ending, but the real strength of this novel is how it conveys the pall that hangs over lives affected by grief, guilt, frustration, and anger. Dylan would end his life if it weren't for the seemingly unlikely possibility that Maggie might recover. Only after a terrible automobile accident is Dylan's faith restored and he can see a way forward.

Death Be Not Proud: A Memoir. J. Gunther. New York: Harper, 1949. Johnny Gunther was 15 when he was diagnosed with a brain tumor; he died 15 months later. His father describes Johnny's courageous struggle—alongside his parents and physicians—to maintain as much of a normal life as possible in the face of an incurable disease.

A Death in the Family. J. Agee. New York: Bantam, 1969. This Pulitzer Prize-winning novel unerringly depicts the point of view of two children in Knoxville, Tennessee, in 1915 when they are told of the accidental death of their father. Agee skillfully portrays ways in which the children experience unusual events, sense strange tensions within the family, struggle to understand what has happened, and strive to work out their implications with or without the help of the adults around them.

Death Is Hard to Live With: Teenagers and How They Cope with Death. J. Bode. New York: Delacorte, 1993. Based on interviews with teenagers and others, this book shows how teens experience death and how they can cope with their loss and their grief. The book mixes statements by teens, factual information from experts, cartoons, and pop art.

The Death of Ivan Ilych and Other Stories. L. Tolstoy. New York: New American Library, 1960. The title story is a literary classic in which a magistrate in the prime of life is afflicted with a grave illness that becomes steadily more serious. As his health deteriorates, Ivan realizes that glib talk in college about mortality does not apply only to other people or to humanity in general; now it is about him. While others withdraw, only one servant and his young son treat him with real compassion and candor.

Everything You Need to Know When Someone You Know Has Been Killed. J. Schleiter. New York: Rosen Publishing Group, 1998. This book describes real-life death as a taboo topic in our society, explores common fears and feelings when death happens, and suggests strategies to help yourself or to help a friend when coping with these reactions.

Facing Change: Falling Apart and Coming Together Again in the Teen Years. D. O'Toole. Burnsville, NC: Compassion Press, 1995. This book is intended to help teens understand the emotional, social, physical, cognitive, and spiritual impact of change and loss, and to think about ways to cope with their grief and do constructive things to help themselves.

Gone, Gone, Gone. H. Moskowitz. New York: Simon Pulse, 2012. In the context of the 2002 Beltway Sniper shootings in the D.C. area, two 15-year-old boys form a romantic relationship even as they each struggle with random tragedies in their own lives.

A Grief Observed. C. S. Lewis. New York: Bantam, 1976. The author, a celebrated British writer, is well known for books like *Out of the Silent Planet* and *The Lion, the Witch, and the Wardrobe*. When his wife died, Lewis recorded his grief on notebooks lying around the house. The published result is an unusual and extraordinary document, a direct and honest expression of one man's grief that has helped innumerable readers by normalizing their own experiences in bereavement.

Hunter in the Dark. M. Hughes. New York: Atheneum, 1984. A boy with overprotective parents sets out to face life and death on his own by confronting threats at different levels: his leukemia and the challenge of going hunting in the Canadian woods for the first time.

Living When a Young Friend Commits Suicide—Or Even Starts Talking about It. E. Grollman & M. Malikow. Boston: Beacon Press, 1999. This book is intended to guide adolescents through typical reactions and questions after a friend completes a suicide. It offers suggestions for how to cope and how to help suicidal people. Also addressed are religious questions, popular misconceptions about suicide, and getting on with one's life.

Looking for Alaska. J. Green. New York: Speak/Penguin, 2006. Miles Halter is 16 and in a new boarding school in Alabama. He enjoys great pranks with his new friends, especially Alaska Young, a smart, sexy, and sometimes self-destructive girl. But they all must search for answers about life and death after a fatal car crash.

Old Yeller. F. Gipson. New York: Harper & Brothers, 1956 (reissued by HarperTrophy, 1990). An ugly, yellow stray dog becomes a close companion of 14-year-old

Travis in Texas in the late 1800s and saves some members of his family from various dangers. But when the dog is bitten by a rabid wolf, Travis must kill him.

Ordinary People. J. Guest. New York: Viking, 1976 (Penguin, 1982). This impressive novel gradually reveals a 17-year-old boy's many problems after his older brother drowns in a boating accident. Conrad's grief is compounded by the guilt he feels for not saving the life of his sibling. An overprotective father and a cold mother are little help, but a therapist eventually helps Conrad realize that he is not to blame for his brother's death just because he lived through the accident.

Straight Talk about Death for Teenagers: How to Cope with Losing Someone You Love. E. A. Grollman. Boston: Beacon Press, 1993. Just a few sentences on each page address feelings and other reactions following soon after a death, special relationships and circumstances, facing one's immediate future (e.g., attending a funeral, returning to school), learning to cope, and rebuilding one's life. Uncomplicated reflections and sound advice from a well-known expert in this field.

Tears of a Tiger. S. M. Draper. New York: Atheneum, 1994. Without any narrative, this book uses excerpts from official statements, newspaper articles, letters, diaries, homework, phone calls and conversations to describe the aftermath of the death of a boy in a fiery automobile accident. The car's driver, Andrew Jackson, cannot get over Rob's death and his feelings of guilt. Two other friends in the car do well, but Andy sinks slowly into a deeper and more desperate depression. Smiling on the surface, he offers many clues about his inner trauma, but his parents, friends, teachers, and even a psychologist do not realize what is happening until he eventually takes his own life.

A Teenager's Book about Suicide: Helping Break the Silence and Preventing Death. E. Grollman & J. Johnson. Omaha, NE: Centering Corporation, 2001. See entry in Appendix C in this book.

Thirteen Reasons Why. J. Asher. New York: Razorbill/Penguin, 2011. Shortly after his classmate ended her life, Clay receives a package containing 13 cassettes explaining why she suicided. He spends a night listening to Hannah's pain and learning why he is one of the reasons she died.

Too Young to Die: Youth and Suicide. F. Klagsbrun. New York: Houghton Mifflin, 1976 (paperback edition by Pocket Books, 1977). An older, but still clear, informed, and readable introduction to myths and realities surrounding youth suicide, with useful advice for helpers.

With You and without You. A. M. Martin. New York: Holiday House, 1986 (paperback by Scholastic). The parents and their four children struggle to cope when the father is told that he will soon die as a result of an inoperable heart condition. Before his death, each member of the family tries to make the father's remaining time as good as possible; afterward, each strives to cope with his or her losses. No one is ever completely prepared for a death; each individual must cope in his or her own way.

The Yearling. M. K. Rawlings. New York: Charles Scribner's Sons, 1939 (50th anniversary ed.; New York: Simon Pulse, 1988). This Pulitzer Prize–winning novel describes a family eking out a subsistence living in rural Florida in the early 20th century where the struggle to survive overrides everything else. Young Jody's desire for a pet, something of his very own, is fulfilled in an orphaned fawn that he names Flag. Jody encounters many death-related events: all of his siblings die; a bear kills their brood sow and is later killed by Pa; Pa is bit by a rattler and almost dies, only later to become ill and frail; Jody's friend dies and is buried; wild animals are hunted and killed; a plague causes other animal deaths; and a pack of wolves kills their heifer calf. Finally, as Flag becomes a yearling, he gets into the family's garden and eats their precious crops. When Pa orders Jody to kill the deer because they cannot survive the loss of their food, Jody tries to refuse but ultimately must do so after Ma wounds the deer.

For additional information about death-related literature for children, contact the **Centering Corporation**.

Activity Books and Memory Books for Young Readers

This Appendix describes three types of workbooks that address death-related issues for young readers. Choose the ones best suited to the particular child or adolescent with whom you intend to use them.

- **Activity books** allow youngsters to color, draw, or write on pages with specific themes associated with death, loss, grief, and mourning. Many of these books are aimed at younger children with limited verbal and reading abilities who can benefit from a focus on art and pictures. Typically, these activity books seek to help children vent strong feelings and process reactions to death-related events in safe and constructive ways. Activity books also provide opportunities for adults to engage in constructive interactions with those children. Examples of activity books include the *Barklay and Eve Activity and Coloring Book Series, Beautiful Dragons and Other Fears*, and *Kids Can Cope*.

- **Memory books** include both journaling books and workbooks focused on memory boxes.

    - **Journals** provide opportunities for youngsters to make a record of their reactions to a death-related loss, to reflect on their relationship with the deceased, and to construct memorials to keep with them and revisit as needed. Examples of journaling books include *A Child Remembers* for children and *Fire in My Heart, Ice in My Veins* for teenagers.

    - **Books about memory boxes** seek to help youngsters create tangible collections of objects that reflect their relationship with the deceased. They show how to assemble collections of such objects, make collages, or put together scrapbooks. Creating memory boxes can help reinforce a continuing bond with the deceased. Examples include *Sweet*

Memories and *The Memory Box* (although the latter is more like the hybrid type mentioned in the next section).

- **Hybrid books** begin with a story that explicitly turns into a workbook with pages devoted to stimulating activities, creating a journal, or making a memory box. Examples of this type include *Anna's Scrapbook, A Bunch of Balloons*, and *Quilly's Sideways Grief*.

Almost all of the books described here provide some type of topical or thematic structure to guide the child or adolescent who is using the book and to focus his or her energies on some desired goals.

After a Death: An Activity Book for Children. The Dougy Center. Portland, OR: Author, 2007. A resource for grieving children from the leading U.S. support center in the field; with creative activities like drawing and writing exercises to help in remembering the person who died and learning new ways to live with the loss. Includes tips for coping with changes at school, home, and with friends.

After a Suicide: A Workbook for Grieving Kids. The Dougy Center. Portland, OR: Author, 2001. Here children are encouraged to write, draw, or decorate brightly colored pages so as to help them cope with the aftermath of a suicide. Topics covered include: what is suicide; finding out about a suicide; why people die this way; feelings, dreams, and nightmares; questions kids often ask; talking about suicide; going back to school; ways to honor and remember the person who died; advice about feeling better; and writing one's own story.

Anna's Scrapbook: Journal of a Sister's Love. S. Aiken. Omaha, NE: Centering Corporation, 2001. The first six pages of this book describe Anna and her sister. Anna loved Amelia; even though they were eight years apart, they shared many good times together. But one day, when she was a preschooler, Amelia had an accidental fall and died. Anna's grief was profound, as was the grief of the adults in her family. After the funeral, Anna kept a diary, which fills the next 18 pages of this book and in which she writes about her grief and describes a scrapbook she made of memories and photos of Amelia. Eighteen blank pages at the end of the book encourage readers to make their own similar scrapbooks.

Barklay and Eve Activity and Coloring Book Series. Karen L. Carney. Dragonfly Publishing Co., Wethersfield, CT, 1997–2001. The eight titles in this series are: Book 1, *Together, We'll Get through This! Learning to Cope with Loss and Transition*; Book 2, *Honoring Our Loved Ones: Going to a Funeral*; Book 3, *What Is the Meaning of Shiva? Jewish Mourning Rituals* (original ed., 1995; revised ed., 2001); Book 4, *Our Special Garden: Understanding Cremation*; Book 5, *What Is Cancer, Anyway? Explaining Cancer to Children of All Ages*; Book 6, *Everything Changes, But Love Endures. Explaining Hospice to Children*; Book 7, *Precious Gifts: Katie Coolican's Story. Barklay and Eve Explain Organ and Tissue Donation*; Book 8, *They're Part of the Family: Barklay and Eve Talk to Children about Pet Loss*. Each book tells a story and offers drawings to color or blank spaces to draw pictures about a loss-related topic that adults may find difficult to discuss with children. In each book, two curious Portuguese water dogs learn lessons like: loss and sadness do happen; those events are not their fault; it is OK to have strong feelings as long as they are expressed in constructive ways; and the enduring theme "we can get through anything with the love and support of family and friends."

Bart Speaks Out: Breaking the Silence on Suicide. L. Goldman. Los Angeles: Western Psychological Services, 1998. In this interactive storybook, a dog tells about his grief following the death of his owner, Charlie. Bart then invites readers to describe similar events related to the death of their loved one and to draw pictures of that person. Eventually, the focus turns to suicide, Charlie's depression, and the view that he wasn't thinking straight. Suicide is described as "when someone chooses to make their body stop working" (p. v). The book emphasizes that suicide is a mistake because "there is always another way" (p. v). Knowing the truth and understanding things better helps Bart.

Beautiful Dragons and Other Fears: A Workbook for Children. J. Johnson. Omaha, NE: Centering Corporation, 2003. This workbook offers pictures to color, pages on which to draw or write, and prompts for other activities designed to help children who are afraid so that they can "learn to express their fears and feelings and, over time, learn ways to meet those fears and recognize and cope with their feelings" (p. 2). Engaging in these activities at their own pace is thought to help children externalize their fears, gain power over them, and share them with adults. This workbook is correlated with *The Very Beautiful Dragon* (see Appendix A in this book).

A Bunch of Balloons. D. Ferguson. Omaha, NE: Centering Corporation, 1992. Here is a story about a child who loves to play with balloons. One day, the string slips out of his hand and the balloon flies away. Then the book shifts to ask readers if they also have encountered an important loss and may have experienced their own grief. Finally, the book contains an activity section of two pages with blank balloons in which readers can write about or draw pictures of what has been lost and what is still left.

A Child Remembers: A Write-in Memory Book for Grieving Children. E. Samuel-Traisman. Omaha, NE: Centering Corporation, rev. ed., 2003. This journal invites its owner to describe in detail a special person who has died, their relationship, the death and getting the news, the funeral or memorial service, going back to school, coping with feelings, addressing unfinished business, and ways to honor the life of the person who died.

Children Also Grieve: Talking about Death and Healing. L. Goldman. Philadelphia, PA: Jessica Kingsley Publishers, 2006. This book contains four main parts: a story told by a dog named Henry and his questions to readers; a section to be used to make a memory book; a two-page glossary of grief words; and advice for caring adults. Henry's story uses photos and text to tell about the sadness and other feelings that followed the death of Grandfather. He explains what death means, what grief is like, things to do when you are sad, angry, or scared, and ways to feel a bit better, all the while offering blank spaces in which readers can respond to questions.

Chill + Spill: A Place to Put It Down and Work It Out. S. Lorig & J. Jacobs. Seattle, WA: Art with Heart, 2005. This book is a guided, therapeutic journal for tweens and teens. Colorful pages introduce 20 activities each followed by blank pages to provide youngsters ways to express themselves in a creative (yet structured), comfortable (yet challenging) manner. Goals are to foster meaningful connections with caregivers, increase self-awareness and self-expression, enhance ability to manage emotions and stress, and make healthy, positive choices.

Deconstruction/Reconstruction: A Grief Journal for Teens. The Dougy Center. Portland, OR: Author,

2017. The engaging design in this journal offers grieving teens an advice-free place where they can go at their own pace and choose among prompts to draw, write, paint, and transform whatever they're thinking and feeling.

Finding Your Own Way to Grieve: A Creative Activity Workbook for Kids and Teens on the Autism Spectrum. K. Helbert. Philadelphia, PA: Jessica Kingsley, 2012. The subtitle clearly indicates this book's goals.

Fire in My Heart, Ice in My Veins: A Journal for Teenagers Experiencing a Loss. E. S. Traisman. Omaha, NE: Centering Corporation, 1992. A line or two of text on each page and many small drawings offer age-appropriate prompts to help a teen who has experienced the death of someone he or she loved.

Healing Activities for Children in Grief: Activities Suitable for Support Groups with Grieving Children, Preteens and Teens. G. McWhorter. Roanoke, TX: Author, 2003. This book comes from The WARM Place, a Fort Worth, Texas, support center for grieving children and adolescents. It offers activities for children ages 5–8, 9–12, and 13–18. Although designed for support groups, these activities could be used in other ways and contexts.

In My World: A Journal for Young People Facing Life-Threatening Illness. B. B. Crawford & L. Lazar. Omaha, NE: Centering Corporation, 1999. This 32-page journal seeks to help teenagers coping with a life-threatening illness to make a record of their lives and express thoughts, feelings, and worries they may find difficult to share with family members and friends.

Isabelle's Dream: A Story and Activity Book for a Child's Grief Journey. B. B. Arenella. Naples, FL: Quality of Life Publishing Co., 2007. This story tells Isabelle's dream of visiting her deceased sister in heaven. It's a wonderful place, but the visit is short and Isabelle cannot stay. As Sophia says, "You still have a lot of things to do on Earth." But Sophia adds they'll be sisters forever and Isabelle can always find Sophia in her dreams. The book includes activity pages and seven tips for parents of bereaved children.

Kids Can Cope: An Activity Book for Children from Children Who Are Living with Change and Loss. E. Parga. Omaha, NE: Centering Corporation, 2009. Over 60 pages of text offer numerous opportunities and cues for children to address changes and reactions they experience related to life-threatening illnesses—their own or those of loved ones. Children can write down questions, draw pictures, identify sources of help, and engage in other activities to help them cope. In addition, a four-page Glossary explains terms that may be puzzling to children.

The Last Goodbye I. J. Boulden & J. Boulden. Weaverville, CA: Boulden Publishing, 1994. Exercises for children at about grade level 5–8 to help process death-related feelings and issues. Also available in a Spanish version.

The Last Goodbye II. J. Boulden & J. Boulden. Weaverville, CA: Boulden Publishing, 1994. Exercises for youngsters at about grade levels 9–12 to help process death-related feelings and issues. Similar to *The Last Goodbye I,* but including topics appropriate to these older readers like suicide and not acting in a destructive manner.

Magnificent Marvelous Me! S. Lorig. Seattle, WA: Art with Heart, 2008. More than 50 dramatically colored pages offer engaging drawing and coloring activities with age-appropriate short questions and answers all designed to foster creative coping and stress-reduction strategies for children (especially siblings) who are going through difficult times.

Memories Matter: Activities for Grieving Children and Teens. Portland, OR: The Dougy Center, 2012. This collection of 85 activities aims to help children and teens process their unique grief using writing, drawing, talking, and movement. Sharing of feelings is encouraged to normalize these experiences. Can be used in peer support groups or by parents and teachers with their children.

The Memory Box. K. McLaughlin. Omaha, NE: Centering Corporation, 2001. This storybook models what a child can do to memorialize a loved one. When a young boy is first told his Grandpa has died, he is mad because now he and Grandpa won't be able to go fishing, play ball, and have root beer floats. Mommy acknowledges these feelings and the value of talking about them, but she urges the boy to hold onto good memories of all he had shared with Grandpa. The boy gathers some items linked with Grandpa and a picture of them to make a memory box out of Grandpa's old tackle box. He ends by saying, "I sometimes get a little sad looking at my memory box because I miss Grandpa. But my box also makes me smile because it reminds me of all the special times Grandpa and I shared."

My Always Sister Coloring Book. Anonymous. St. Paul, MN: A Place to Remember, 2004. After Callie the bunny learns that his new baby sister is sick and must stay in the hospital, Daddy tells him his sister has died and they have a funeral with music. Callie experiences many emotions and draws a picture of how he feels.

Oodles of Doodles: A Children's Hospital Activity Book. S. Lorig. Seattle, WA: Art with Heart, rev. ed. 2006; also in Spanish. This book is specially designed to encourage hospitalized children to explore, imagine, and create through writing, drawing, and doodling so as to express their feelings on pages.

Out of the Blue: Making Memories Last When Someone Has Died. J. Stokes & P. Oxley. Cheltenham, UK:

Winston's Wish, 2006. This small booklet from the leading English support program for grieving children and their families is filled with good ideas for honoring the life of a deceased loved one.

Quilly's Sideways Grief: A Story-Based Curriculum about Love and Loss. K. Rhoades-Dumler. Warminster, PA: Mar-Co Products, 2009. The story in this book tells about a porcupine who has been acting strangely since his grandpa died. Quilly only begins to feel better when a friend shares experiences after her grandma died and they each talk about what they are missing. After Quilly tells Barby that his mad and sad feelings are all tangled together so that they seem to come out sideways through his quills, she says, "When you keep your feelings bottled up inside, they'll overflow like a soft drink does when you shake it." Then the book offers suggestions for adults to help grieving children and a set of activity pages for children to use to help cope with their grief reactions.

Reactions: A Workbook to Help Young People Who Are Experiencing Trauma and Grief. A. Salloum. Omaha, NE: Centering Corporation, 1998. This workbook allows grieving youngsters to describe their experiences and their implications at their own pace. The text offers prompts for writing, drawing, and answering questions intended to legitimize different reactions people may have to loss and to lead eventually to a reflection on what has been learned from these exercises.

Remembering Our Baby: A Workbook for Children Whose Brother or Sister Dies before Birth. P. Keough. Omaha, NE: Centering Corporation, 2001. Intended for young children whose sibling dies before birth, this workbook encourages writing and drawing to help share thoughts and feelings. The book starts with finding out about the new baby who is to join the family and then learning about the death. Included are questions about these events and suggestions for things to do to remember the baby.

Remember Rafferty: A Book about the Death of a Pet ... for Children of All Ages. J. Johnson. Omaha, NE: Centering Corporation, rev. ed., 1998. When a sheepdog becomes ill and must be euthanized, a neighbor who lives with Rafferty's friend, a cat named Four-Eyes, helps by sharing stories of the deaths of other pets and validating the importance of such losses. Mom encourages the child to make a memory book about Rafferty. The moral: pet loss is important and children need to mourn such losses. There also are two pages of suggestions for adults and eight pages for a memorial scrapbook.

Saying Goodbye. J. Boulden. Santa Rosa, CA: Boulden Publishing, 1989. This book interweaves a story about death as a natural part of life, feelings that are involved in saying goodbye, and the conviction that "love is forever," while also allowing a child to draw, color, or insert thoughts on its pages.

Saying Goodbye to Your Pet: Children Can Learn to Cope with Grief. M. Heegaard. Minneapolis: Fairview Press, 2001. This activity book has checklists and pages on which to draw or color all designed to help 5- to 12-year-old children learn to express their feelings and cope with the loss or death of a pet.

Sweet Memories. E. Stillwell. Omaha, NE: Centering Corporation, 1998. Here are a dozen different, hands-on, craft activities through which children can preserve memories of loved ones who have died.

A Teenager's Book about Suicide: Helping Break the Silence and Preventing Death. E. Grollman & J. Johnson. Omaha, NE: Centering Corporation, 2001. Brief text boxes and spaces for readers to write or draw open up the topic of suicide. There are writings by teens who have contemplated suicide or been affected by the suicide of someone else, as well as the authors' comments designed to dispel myths and throw light on the subject. The authors identify danger signals and warning signs, and offer advice as to what a teen might do who suspects a friend or family member is thinking about suicide.

Uncle Jerry Has AIDS. J. Boulden & B. Boulden. Weaverville, CA: Boulden Publishing, 1992. This 32-page activity book allows children at about grade level 3–4 to gain information about HIV and its effects and to explore attitudes and emotions that might arise when a loved one has AIDS.

What's a Virus, Anyway? The Kids' Book about AIDS. D. Fassler & K. McQueen. Burlington, VT: Waterfront Books, 1990. Just a few words or pictures on each page leave room for coloring, drawing, and shared discussion about AIDS so that parents and teachers can begin to talk about this subject with children in about grades 1–5.

Why Did You Die? Activities to Help Children Cope with Grief and Loss. E. Leeuwenburgh & E. Goldring. Oakland, CA: Instant Help Books/New Harbinger Publications, 2008. Here are 40 simple activities to teach kids to express difficult feelings, separate myths from fact, and thrive despite their losses.

For additional information about death-related literature for children, contact the **Centering Corporation**.

References

Abrahamson, H. (1977). *The origin of death: Studies in African mythology.* New York: Arno Press.

Abrahm, J. L. (2014). *A physician's guide to pain and symptom management in cancer patients* (3rd ed.). Baltimore: Johns Hopkins University Press.

Abrams, R. (2012). *When parents die: Learning to live with the loss of a parent* (3rd ed.). New York: Routledge.

Accomando, B., & McVicker, N. (2014, November 26). Death café: Tea and cake make death more palatable. KPBS radio. Retrieved December 12, 2014, from http://www.kpbs.org/news/2014/nov/26/death-cafe-tea-and-cake-make-death-more-palatable/

Achté, K., Fagerström, R., Pentikäinen, J., & Farberow, N. L. (1990). Themes of death and violence in lullabies of different countries. *Omega, Journal of Death and Dying, 20,* 193–204. doi:10.2190/A7YP-TJ3C-M9C1-JY45

Ad Hoc Committee of the Harvard Medical School to Examine the Definition of Brain Death. (1968). A definition of irreversible coma. *Journal of the American Medical Association, 205,* 337–340. doi:10.1001/jama.1968.03140320031009

Adams, C. A. (2003). *ABC's of grief: A handbook for survivors.* Amityville, NY: Baywood.

Adams, D. W., & Deveau, E. J. (Eds.). (1993). *Coping with childhood cancer: Where do we go from here?* (New rev. ed.). Hamilton, Ontario: Kinbridge.

Adams, D. W., & Deveau, E. J. (Eds.). (1995). *Beyond the innocence of childhood* (3 vols.). Amityville, NY: Baywood.

Adams, G. (2006). *Lessons from lions: Using children's media to teach about grief and mourning* + CD. Little Rock, AR: Center for Good Mourning, Arkansas Children's Hospital.

Adams, J. R. (2004). *Prospects for immortality: A sensible search for life after death.* Amityville, NY: Baywood.

Adler, B. (1979, March). You don't have to do homework in heaven! *Good Housekeeping,* 46.

Administration on Aging, Administration for Community Living, U.S. Department of Health and Human Services. (2015). A profile of older Americans: 2015. Retrieved October 31, 2016, from http://www.aoa.acl.gov/Aging_Statistics/Profile/2015/docs/2015-Profile.pdf

Administration on Aging & Substance Abuse and Mental Health Services Administration. (2012). *Older Americans behavioral health issue brief 4: Preventing suicide in older adults.* Retrieved September 26, 2016, from http://www.aoa.gov/AoA_Programs/HPW/Behavioral/docs2/Issue%20Brief%204%20Preventing%20Suicide.pdf

Agee, J. (1969). *A death in the family.* New York: Bantam.

Ahronheim, J., & Weber, D. (1992). *Final passages: Positive choices for the dying and their loved ones.* New York: Simon & Schuster.

Ajemian, I., & Mount, B. M. (Eds.). (1980). *The R.V.H. manual on palliative/hospice care.* New York: Arno Press.

Akner, L. F. (with C. V. Whitney). (1993). *How to survive the loss of a parent: A guide for adults.* New York: Morrow.

Albert, M. S., DeKosky, S. T., Dickson, D., et al. (2011). The diagnosis of mild cognitive impairment due to Alzheimer's disease: Recommendations from the National Institute on Aging and Alzheimer's Association workgroup. *Alzheimer's and Dementia: The Journal of the Alzheimer's Association, 7*(3), 270–279. doi:10.1016/j.jalz.2011.03.008

Albert, P. L. (1994). Overview of the organ donation process. *Critical Care Nursing Clinics of North America, 6,* 553–556.

Albert, P. L. (1998). Direct contact between donor families and recipients: Crisis or consolation? *Journal of Transplant Coordination, 8,* 139–144. doi:10.7182/prtr.1.8.3.076j751573j23868

Albert, P. L. (1999). Clinical decision making and ethics in communications between donor families and recipients: How much should they know? *Journal of Transplant Coordination, 9,* 219–224. doi:10.7182/prtr.1.9.4.75r22071pv3l1p06

Albom, M. (1997). *Tuesdays with Morrie: An old man, a young man, and life's greatest lesson.* New York: Doubleday.

Alcántara, C., & Gone, J. P. (2007). Reviewing suicide in Native American communities: Situating risk and protective factors within a transactional-ecological framework. *Death Studies, 31,* 457–477. doi:10.1080/07481180701244587

Alcántara, C., & Gone, J. P. (2008). Suicide in Native American communities: A transcultural-ecological formation of the problem. In F. T. L. Leong & M. M. Leach (Eds.), *Suicide among racial and ethnic groups: Theory, research, and practice* (pp. 173–200). New York: Routledge.

Alderman, E., & Kennedy C. (1997). *The right to privacy.* New York: Vintage.

Alexander, A. K. (2002). *A mural for Mamita/Un mural para Mamita.* Omaha, NE: Centering Corporation.

Alexander, E. (2012). *Proof of heaven: A neurosurgeon's journey into the afterlife.* New York: Simon & Schuster.

Alexander, I. E., & Adlerstein, A. M. (1958). Affective responses to the concept of death in a population of children and early adolescents. *Journal of Genetic Psychology, 93,* 167–177. doi:10.1080/00221325.1958.10532416

Alexander-Greene, A. (1999). *Sunflowers and rainbows for Tia: Saying goodbye to Daddy.* Omaha, NE: Centering Corporation.

Allen, A. (2007). *Vaccine: The controversial story of medicine's greatest lifesaver.* New York: Norton.

Allen, B. G., Calhoun, L. G., Cann, A., & Tedeschi, R. G. (1994). The effect of cause of death on responses to the bereaved: Suicide compared to accident and natural causes. *Omega, Journal of Death and Dying, 28,* 39–48. doi:10.2190/T44K-L7UK-TB19-T9UV

Allison, G. (2004). *Nuclear terrorism: The ultimate preventable catastrophe.* New York: Times Books.

Allumbaugh, D. L., & Hoyt, W. T. (1999). Effectiveness of grief counseling: A meta-analysis. *Journal of Counseling Psychology*, 46, 370–380. doi:10.1037/0022-0167.46.3.370

Alperovitz, G. (1995). *The decision to use the atomic bomb and the architecture of an American myth*. New York: Knopf.

Alvarez, A. (1970). *The savage god: A study of suicide*. New York: Random House.

Alzheimer's Association. (2015). *2015 Alzheimer's disease facts and figures*. Chicago: Author. (Also published as *Alzheimer's & Dementia*, vol. 11, issue 3.)

Alzheimer's Association. (2016, March). *Factsheet: Costs of Alzheimer's to medicare and medicaid*. Chicago: Author. Retrieved November 21, 2016 from http://act.alz.org/site/DocServer/2012_Costs_Fact_Sheet_version_2.pdf?docID=7161

Alzheimer's Association. (2017). *2017 Alzheimer's disease facts and figures*. Chicago: Author. (Also published as *Alzheimer's & Dementia*, 13, 325–373.)

Alzheimer's Disease International. (2015). *World Alzheimer Report 2015: The global economic impact of dementia: An analysis of prevalence, incidence, costs and trends*. London: Author.

Alzheimer's Disease International. (2016). *World Alzheimer Report 2016: Improving healthcare for people living with dementia: Coverage, quality and costs now and in the future*. London: Author.

American Academy of Pediatrics (AAP), Committee on Bioethics and Committee on Hospital Care. (2000b). Palliative care for children. *Pediatrics*, 106(2), 351–357.

American Academy of Pediatrics (AAP), Committee on Communications. (1995). Media violence. *Pediatrics*, 95(6), 949–951.

American Academy of Pediatrics (AAP), Committee on Psychosocial Aspects of Child and Family Health. (2000a). The pediatrician and childhood bereavement. *Pediatrics*, 105(2), 445–447. doi:10.1542/peds.105.2.445

American Academy of Pediatrics (AAP), Hymel, K. P., & the Committee on Child Abuse and Neglect, National Association of Medical Examiners. (2006). Distinguishing sudden infant death syndrome from child abuse fatalities. *Pediatrics*, 118(1), 421–427. doi:10.1542/peds.2006-1245

American Academy of Pediatrics (AAP), Task Force on Infant Positioning and SIDS. (1992). Positioning and SIDS. *Pediatrics*, 89(6), 1120–1126.

American Academy of Pediatrics (AAP), Task Force on Sudden Infant Death Syndrome. (2005). The changing concept of sudden infant death syndrome: Diagnostic coding shifts, controversies regarding the sleeping environment, and new variables to consider in reducing risk. *Pediatrics*, 116(5), 1245–1255. doi:10.1542/peds.2005-1499

American Academy of Pediatrics, Section on Hospice and Palliative Medicine and Committee on Hospital Care. (2013). Pediatric palliative care and hospice care: Commitments, guidelines and recommendations. *Pediatrics*, 132, 966–972. doi:10.1542/peds.2013-2731

American Academy of Pediatrics, Task Force on Sudden Infant Death Syndrome. (2011). SIDS and other sleep-related infant deaths: Expansion of recommendations for a safe infant sleeping environment. *Pediatrics*, 128(5), e1341–e1367. doi:10.1542/peds.2011-2284

American Bar Association. (2009). *Making medical decisions for someone else: A how-to guide*. Chicago: Author.

American Bar Association. (2012). *Guide to wills and estates* (4th ed.). New York: Random House.

American Press Institute. (2014). The personal news cycle: How Americans choose to get their news. Retrieved July 8, 2016, from https://www.americanpressinstitute.org/publications/reports/survey-research/personal-news-cycle/

American Psychiatric Association. (2013). *Diagnostic and statistical manual of mental disorders (DSM-5)*. Arlington, VA: Author.

American Public Health Association. (2008). *Patients' rights to self-determination at the end of life* (Policy #20086). Washington, DC: Author. Retrieved October 10, 2016, from https://www.apha.org/policies-and-advocacy/public-health-policy-statements/policy-database/2014/07/29/13/28/patients-rights-to-self-determination-at-the-end-of-life

Anderson, M. L., & Taylor, H. F. (2007). *Sociology: Understanding a diverse society*. Belmont, CA: Wadsworth.

Anderson, R. (1968). *I never sang for my father*. New York: Dramatists Play Service.

Andrews, M. M., & Boyle, J. S. (Eds.). (2016). *Transcultural concepts in nursing care* (7th ed.). Philadelphia: Wolters Kluwer.

And We Were Sad, Remember? [Videotape]. (1979). Northern Virginia Educational Telecommunications Association. (Available from the National Audiovisual Center, Reference Department, National Archives and Records Service, Washington, DC 20409.)

Anestis, M. D., & Anestis, J. C. (2015). Suicide rates and state laws regulating access and exposure to handguns. *American Journal of Public Health*. doi:10.2105/AJPH.2015.302753

Angel, M. D. (1987). *The orphaned adult*. New York: Human Sciences.

Angell, M. (1996). Euthanasia in the Netherlands—Good news or bad? *New England Journal of Medicine*, 335, 1676–1678. doi:10.1056/NEJM199611283352209

Annas, G. J. (1994). Death by prescription: The Oregon initiative. *New England Journal of Medicine*, 331, 1240–1243. doi:10.1056/NEJM199411033311822

Annas, G. J. (2004). *The rights of patients: The authoritative ACLU guide to the rights of patients* (3rd ed.). New York: NYU Press.

Annenberg Washington Program. (1993). *Communications and the Patient Self-Determination Act: Strategies for meeting the educational mandate*. Washington, DC: Author.

Anonymous. (1957). *Read-aloud nursery tales*. New York: Wonder.

Anonymous. (1963). Medical ethics, narcotics, and addiction [Editorial]. (1963). *Journal of the American Medical Association*, 185, 962–963. doi:10.1001/jama.1963.03060120072027

Anonymous. (2001). *Q & A euthanasia 2001: A guide to the Dutch Termination of Life on Request and Assisted Suicide (Review Procedures) Act* (debated in the Senate of the States General on 10 April 2001). The Hague: Author.

Anonymous. (2007, February 5). Former Justice O'Connor: "I would have stayed longer". *Newsmax.com*. Retrieved December 27, 2010, from http://archive.newsmax.com/archives/articles/2007/2/5/92619.shtml

Anonymous. (2010, June 16). Sharp growth in euthanasia deaths. *DutchNews.nl*. Retrieved January 15, 2011, from http://www.dutchnews.nl/news/archives/2010/06/sharp_growth_in_euthanasia_dea.php

Anonymous. (2013). Little Red Riding Hood. In *My little treasury: Fairy tales* (pp. 28–37). Lincolnwood, IL; Publications International.

Anthony, S. (1939). A study of the development of the concept of death [abstract]. *British Journal of Educational Psychology*, 9, 276–277.

Anthony, S. (1940). *The child's discovery of death*. New York: Harcourt Brace.

Anthony, S. (1972). *The discovery of death in childhood and after.* New York: Basic Books (Revised edition of *The child's discovery of death*).

Archibald, L. (2012). *Finding peace without all the pieces: After a loved one's suicide.* Colorado Springs, CO: Larch Publishing.

Ariès, P. (1962). *Centuries of childhood: A social history of family life* (R. Baldick, Trans.). New York: Random House.

Ariès, P. (1974a). The reversal of death: Changes in attitudes toward death in Western societies (V. M. 10.2307/2711889, Trans.). *American Quarterly, 26,* 535–560. doi:10.2307/2711889

Ariès, P. (1974b). *Western attitudes toward death: From the middle ages to the present* (P. M. Ranum, Trans.). Baltimore: Johns Hopkins University Press.

Ariès, P. (1981). *The hour of our death* (H. Weaver, Trans.). New York: Knopf.

Ariès, P. (1985). *Images of man and death* (J. Lloyd, Trans.). Cambridge, MA: Harvard University Press.

Arkin, W., & Fieldhouse, R. (1985). *Nuclear battlefields.* Cambridge, MA: Ballinger.

Armstrong-Dailey, A., & Zarbock, S. (Eds.). (2009). *Hospice care for children* (3rd ed.). New York: Oxford University Press.

Arnett, J. (2000). Emerging adulthood: A theory of development from the late teens through the twenties. *American Psychologist, 55*(5), 469–480. doi:10.1037//0003-066X.55.5.469

Arnett, J. (2007). Emerging adulthood: What is it, and what is it good for. *Society for Research in Child Development, 1*(2), 68–73.

Arnett, J., & Tanner, L. (Eds.). (2006). *Emerging adults in America: Coming of age in the 21st century.* Washington, DC: American Psychological Association.

Arrick, F. (1980). *Tunnel vision.* Scarsdale, NY: Bradbury; Dell, 1981.

Arruda-Colli, M. N. F., Weaver, M. S., & Wiener, L. (2017). Communication about dying, death, and bereavement: A systematic review of children's literature. *Journal of Palliative Medicine, 20*(5), 548–559. doi: 10.1089/jpm.2016.0494

Arvio, R. P. (1974). *The cost of dying and what you can do about it.* New York: Harper & Row.

Ashenburg, K. (2003). *The mourner's dance: What we do when people die.* New York: North Point Press.

Associated Press. (2007, November 11). Arizona: A romance for O'Connor's husband. *New York Times.* Retrieved December 9, 2010, from http://query.nytimes.com/gst/fullpage.html?res=9E01E0DA1631F937A25752C1A9619C8B63&ref=sandra_day_oconnor

Associated Press. (2011, February 6). Buried with a best friend. *St. Petersburg Times,* p. 15A.

Associated Press. (2015, July 22). In mild memory issues, women worsen faster. *Tampa Bay Times,* p. 7A.

Attaran, A. (2015). Unanimity on death with dignity: Legalizing physician-assisted dying in Canada. *New England Journal of Medicine, 372,* 2080–2082. doi:10.1056/NEJMp1502442

Attig, T. (1991). The importance of conceiving of grief as an active process. *Death Studies, 15,* 385–393. doi:10.1080/07481189108252443

Attig, T. (1996). Beyond pain: The existential suffering of children. *Journal of Palliative Care, 12*(3), 20–23.

Attig, T. (2000). *The heart of grief: Death and the search for lasting love.* New York: Oxford University Press.

Attig, T. (2001). Relearning the world: Making and finding meanings. In R. A. Neimeyer (Ed.), *Meaning reconstruction and the experience of loss* (pp. 33–53). Washington, DC: American Psychological Association.

Attig, T. (2011). *How we grieve: Relearning the world* (rev. ed.). New York: Oxford University Press.

Attig, T. (2012). *Catching your breath in grief…and grace will lead you home.* Victoria, BC: Breath of Life Publishing (www.griefsheart.com).

Attig, T., Corless, I. B., Gilbert, K. R., et al. (2013). When does a broken heart become a mental disorder? Retrieved December 4, 2016, from http://www.dougy.org/news-events/news/when-does-a-broken-heart-become-a-mental-disorder/1487

Atwater, P. M. H. (1992). Is there a hell? Surprising observations about the near-death experience. *Journal of Near-Death Studies, 10,* 149–160.

Atwater, P. M. H. (2007). *The big book of near-death experiences: The ultimate guide to what happens when we die* (2nd ed.). Charlottesville, VA: Hampton Roads Publishing.

Auden, W. H. (1940). *Collected poems* (E. Mendelson, Ed.). New York: Random House.

Aungst, H. (2009, July 30). An integrated model for palliative care. *Contemporary Pediatrics.* Retrieved December 24, 2010, from www.modernmedicine.com

Authors for the Live Organ Donor Consensus Group. (2000). Consensus statement on the live organ donor. *Journal of the American Medical Association, 284,* 2919–2926. doi:10.1001/jama.284.22.2919

Aviv, R. (2015, June 22). The death treatment: When should people with a non-terminal illness be helped to die? *The New Yorker.* Retrieved June 20, 2015, from http://www.newyorker.com/magazine/2015/06/22/the-death-treatment

Bachelor, P. (2004). *Sorrow and solace: The social world of the cemetery.* Amityville, NY: Baywood.

Bachman, R. (1992). *Death and violence on the reservation: Homicide, family violence, and suicide in American Indian populations.* New York: Auburn House.

Bacon, F. (1962). Of marriage and single life. In *Francis Bacon's Essays.* New York: Dutton (Original work published 1625).

Badham, P., & Badham, L. (Eds.). (1987). *Death and immortality in the religions of the world.* New York: Paragon House.

Bailey, L. (1978). *Biblical perspectives on death.* Philadelphia: Fortress Press.

Bailley, S. E., Kral, M. J., & Dunham, K. (1999). Survivors of suicide do grieve differently: Empirical support for a common sense proposition. *Suicide and Life-Threatening Behavior, 29*(3), 256–271. doi:10.1111/j.1943-278X.1999.tb00301.x

Baines, B. K. (2001). *The ethical will writing guide and workbook: Preserving your legacy of values for your family and community.* Minneapolis: Josaba Ltd.

Baines, B. K. (2006). *Ethical wills: Putting your values on paper* (2nd ed.). Cambridge, MA: Perseus.

Balk, D. E. (1984). How teenagers cope with sibling death: Some implications for school counselors. *School Counselor, 32,* 150–158.

Balk, D. E. (1990). The self-concepts of bereaved adolescents: Sibling death and its aftermath. *Journal of Adolescent Research, 5,* 112–132. doi:10.1177/074355489051010

Balk, D. E. (Ed.). (1991a). Death and adolescent bereavement [Special issue]. *Journal of Adolescent Research, 6*(1).

Balk, D. E. (1991b). Death and adolescent bereavement: Current research and future directions. *Journal of Adolescent Research, 6,* 7–27. doi:10.1177/074355489161002

Balk, D. E. (1991c). Sibling death, adolescent bereavement, and religion. *Death Studies, 15,* 1–20. doi:10.1080/07481189108252406

Balk, D. E. (1997). Death, bereavement and college students: A descriptive analysis. *Mortality, 2*(3), 207–220. doi:10.1080/713685866

Balk, D. E. (2001). College student bereavement, scholarship, and the university: A call for university engagement. *Death Studies, 25,* 67–84. doi:10.1080/07481180126146

Balk, D. E. (2004). Recovery following bereavement: An examination of the concept. *Death Studies, 28,* 361–374. doi:10.1080/07481180490432351

Balk, D. E. (2008). Grieving: 22 to 30 percent of all college students. *New Directions for Student Services, 121,* 5–14. doi:10.1002/ss.262

Balk, D. E. (2011). *Helping the bereaved college student.* New York: Springer.

Balk, D. E. (2014). *Dealing with dying, death, and grief during adolescence.* New York: Routledge.

Balk, D. E., & Corr, C. A. (2001). Bereavement during adolescence: A review of research. In M. S. Stroebe, R. O. Hansson, W. Stroebe, & H. Schut (Eds.), *Handbook of bereavement research: Consequences, coping, and care* (pp. 199–218). Washington, DC: American Psychological Association.

Balk, D. E., & Corr, C. A. (Eds.). (2009). *Adolescent encounters with death, bereavement, and coping.* New York: Springer.

Balk, D. E., & Hogan, N. S. (1995). Religion, spirituality, and bereaved adolescents. In D. W. Adams & E. J. Deveau (Eds.), *Beyond the innocence of childhood: Helping children and adolescents cope with death and bereavement* (Vol. 3, pp. 61–88). Amityville, NY: Baywood.

Ballenger, J. F. (2006). *Self, senility, and Alzheimer's disease in modern America: A history.* Baltimore, MD: Johns Hopkins University Press.

Ballou, R. O. (Ed.). (1944). *The Viking portable world library bible.* New York: The Viking Press.

Balmer, L. E. (1992). *Adolescent sibling bereavement: Mediating effects of family environment and personality* (Unpublished doctoral dissertation). York University, Toronto.

Bandura, A. (1980). The stormy decade: Fact or fiction? In R. E. Muuss (Ed.), *Adolescent behavior and society: A book of readings* (3rd ed., pp. 22–31). New York: Random House.

Banks, M. R., & Banks, W. A. (2002). The effects of animal-assisted therapy on loneliness in an elderly population in long-term care facilities. *The Journals of Gerontology, Series A., 57*(7), M428–M432. doi:10.1093/gerona/57.7.M428

Banks, R. (1991). *The sweet hereafter.* New York: HarperCollins.

Barber, E. (2003). *Letters from a friend: A sibling's guide for coping and grief.* Amityville, NY: Baywood.

Barlow, C. A., & Coleman, H. (2003). The healing alliance: How families use social support after a suicide. *Omega, Journal of Death and Dying, 47,* 187–201. doi:10.2190/8N00-477Q-KUN1-5ACN

Barnard, D., Towers, A., Boston, P., & Lambrinidou, Y. (2000). *Crossing over: Narratives of palliative care.* Oxford: Oxford University Press.

Barnickol, C. A., Fuller, H., & Shinners, B. (1986). Helping bereaved adolescent parents. In C. A. Corr & J. N. McNeil (Eds.), *Adolescence and death* (pp. 132–147). New York: Springer.

Barr, D. A. (2014). *Health disparities in the United States: Social class, race, ethnicity, and health* (2nd ed.). Baltimore: Johns Hopkins University Press.

Barrett, H. C., & Behne, T. (2005). Children's understanding of death as the cessation of agency: A test using sleep versus death. *Cognition, 96,* 93–108. doi:10.1016/j.cognition.2004.05.004

Barrett, R. K. (1996). Adolescents, homicidal violence, and death. In C. A. Corr & D. E. Balk (Eds.), *Handbook of adolescent death and bereavement* (pp. 42–64). New York: Springer.

Barrett, R. K. (2006). Dialogues in diversity: An invited series of papers, advance directives, DNRs, and end-of-life care for African Americans. *Omega, Journal of Death and Dying, 52,* 249–261. doi:10.2190/8C1Y-CPWA-132N-UWXY

Barrett, T. W., & Scott, T. B. (1990). Suicide bereavement and recovery patterns compared with nonsuicide bereavement patterns. *Suicide and Life-Threatening Behavior, 20,* 1–15. doi:10.1111/j.1943-278X.1990.tb00650.x

Battin, M. P. (1996). *The death debate: Ethical issues in suicide.* Upper Saddle River, NJ: Prentice Hall.

Battin, M. P. (2005). *Ending life: Ethics and the way we die.* New York: Oxford University Press.

Battin, M. P. (Ed.). (1994). *The least worst death: Essays in bioethics on the end of life.* New York: Oxford University Press.

Battin, M. P., Rhodes, R., & Silvers, A. (Eds.). (1998). *Physician assisted suicide: Expanding the debate.* New York: Routledge.

Bauer, Y. (1982). *A history of the Holocaust.* New York: Franklin Watts.

Bauer, Y. (1986). Introduction. In E. Kulka, *Escape from Auschwitz* (pp. xiii–xvii). South Hadley, MA: Bergin & Garvey.

Baugher, B. (2013). *A guide for the bereaved survivor: A list of reactions, suggestions and steps for coping with grief.* Newcastle, WA: Caring People Press.

Beale, E. A., Baile, W. F., & Aaron, J. (2005). Silence is not golden: Communicating with children dying from cancer. *Journal of Clinical Oncology, 23,* 3629–3631. doi:10.1200/JCO.2005.11.015

Beamer, L. (with K. Abraham). (2002). *Let's roll!: Ordinary people, extraordinary courage.* Wheaton, IL: Tyndale House.

Beauchamp, T. L. (Ed.). (1996). *Intending death: The ethics of assisted suicide and euthanasia.* Upper Saddle River, NJ: Prentice Hall.

Beauchamp, T. L., & Childress, J. F. (2001). *Principles of biomedical ethics.* New York: Oxford University Press.

Becker, C. B. (1990). Buddhist views of suicide and euthanasia. *Philosophy East and West, 40,* 543–556. doi:10.2307/1399357

Becker, E. (1973). *The denial of death.* New York: Free Press.

Becvar, D. S. (2003). *In the presence of grief: Helping family members resolve death, dying, and bereavement issues.* New York: Guilford Press.

Beder, J. (2005). Loss of the assumptive world: How we deal with death and loss. *Omega, Journal of Death and Dying, 50,* 255–265. doi:10.2190/GXH6-8VY6-BQ0R-GC04

Bell, V., & Troxel, D. (2002). *The Best Friends approach to Alzheimer's care.* Deerfield Beach, FL: Health Communications Inc.

Bell, V., & Troxel, D. (2012). *A dignified life: The Best Friends approach to Alzheimer's care—A guide for care partners* (Rev. & expanded ed.). Baltimore: Health Professions Press.

Bell, V., & Troxel, D. (2016). *The Best Friends approach to dementia care* (2nd ed.). Baltimore: Health Professions Press.

Bell, V., Troxel, D., Cox, T. M., & Hamon, R. (2004/2008). *The Best Friends book of Alzheimer's activities, Vol. 1 & Vol. 2.* Baltimore: Health Professions Press.

Bell-Fialkoff, A. (1993). A brief history of ethnic cleansing. *Foreign Affairs, 72*(3), 110–112. doi:10.2307/20045626

Bendann, E. (1930). *Death customs: An analytical study of burial rites.* New York: Knopf.

Benenson, E. (1998). Donor husband, donor father: UNOS board member Kenneth Moritsugu looks beyond tragedy to serving others. *UNOS Update* [Special edition, Spring], 26.

Bennett, C. (1980). *Nursing home life: What it is and what it could be.* New York: Tiresias Press.

Berger, A., Badham, P., Kutscher, A. H., et al. (Eds.). (1989). *Perspectives on death and dying: Cross-cultural and multi-disciplinary views.* Philadelphia: Charles Press.

Berlinger, N., Jennings, B., & Wolf, S. M. (2013). *The Hastings Center guidelines for decisions on life-sustaining treatment and care near the end of life* (2nd ed.). New York: Oxford University Press.

Berman, A. L. (1988). Fictional depiction of suicide in television film and imitation effects. *American Journal of Psychiatry*, *145*, 982–986. doi:10.1176/ajp.145.8.982

Berman, A. L., Jobes, D. A., & Silverman, M. M. (2006). *Adolescent suicide: Assessment and intervention* (2nd ed.). Washington, DC: American Psychological Association.

Berman, J. (2011). *Death education in the writing classroom*. Amityville, NY: Baywood.

Bern-Klug, M., DeViney, S., & Ekerdt, D. J. (2000). Variations in funeral-related costs of older adults and the role of pre-need funeral contracts and type of disposition. *Omega, Journal of Death and Dying, 41*, 23–38. doi:10.2190/0Y0E-11G7-CXUX-MCQB

Berns, N. (2011). *Closure: The rush to end grief and what it costs us*. Philadelphia: Temple University Press.

Bertini, K. (2009). *Understanding and preventing suicide: The development of self-destructive patterns and ways to alter them*. Westport, CT: Praeger.

Bertman, S. L. (1991). *Facing death: Images, insights, and interventions*. Washington, DC: Hemisphere.

Bertman, S. L. (Ed.). (1999). *Grief and the healing arts: Creativity as therapy*. Amityville, NY: Baywood.

Berzoff, J., & Silverman, P. (Eds.). (2004). *Living with dying: A comprehensive resource for health care professionals*. New York: Columbia University Press.

Bettelheim, B. (1977). *The uses of enchantment—The meaning and importance of fairy tales*. New York: Vintage Books.

Betzold, M. (1993). *Appointment with Doctor Death*. Troy, MI: Momentum Books.

Binkewicz, M. P. (2005). *Peaceful journey: A hospice chaplain's guide to end of life*. Ithaca, NY: Paramont Market Publishing.

Birren, J. E. (1964). *The psychology of aging*. Englewood Cliffs, NJ: Prentice Hall.

Bishop, S. L., & Cain, A. C. (2003). Widowed young parents: Changing perspectives on remarriage and cohabitation rates and their determinants. *Omega, Journal of Death and Dying, 47*, 299–312. doi:10.2190/N50W-AGNC-0MXA-EP9B

Blackhall, L. J., Murphy, S. T., Frank, G., Michel, V., & Azen, S. (1995). Ethnicity and attitudes toward patient autonomy. *Journal of the American Medical Association, 274*, 820–825. doi:10.1001/jama.1995.03530100060035

Blais, J. J., Craig, W. M., Pepler, D., & Connolly, J. (2008). Adolescents online: The importance of internet activity choices to salient relationships. *Journal of Youth and Adolescence, 37*(5), 522–536. doi:10.1007/s10964-007-9262-7

Blakemore, E. (2016, February 1). Could the funeral of the future help heal the environment? *Smithsonian Magazine*. Retrieved December 24, 2016, from http://www.smithsonianmag.com/science-nature/could-funeral-future-help-heal-environment-180957953/#egitur3Z670S9Lwy.99

Blank, J. W. (1998). *The death of an adult child: A book for and about bereaved parents*. Amityville, NY: Baywood.

Blanke, C., LeBlanc, M., Hershman, D., Ellis, L., & Meyskens, F. (2017, April 6). Characterizing 18 years of the Death with Dignity Act in Oregon. *JAMA Oncology*. doi:10.1001/jamaoncol.2017.0243

Blauner, R. (1966). Death and social structure. *Psychiatry, 29*, 378–394. doi:10.1080/00332747.1966.11023480

Bleich, J. D. (1979). The obligation to heal in the Judaic tradition: A comparative analysis. In F. Rosner & J. D. Bleich (Eds.), *Jewish bioethics* (pp. 1–44). New York: Sanhedrin Press.

Blinderman, C. D., & Billings, J. A. (2015). Comfort care for patients dying in the hospital. *New England Journal of Medicine, 373*, 2549–2561. doi:10.1056/NEJMra1411746

Block, E. M., Casarett, D. J., Spence, C., et al. (2010). Got volunteers? Association of hospice use of volunteers with bereaved family members' overall rating of the quality of end-of-life care. *Journal of Pain and Symptom Management, 39*, 502–506. doi:10.1016/j.jpainsymman.2009.11.310

Bloom, A. (Metropolitan of Sourozh). (1999). Death and bereavement. In A. Walker & C. Carras (Eds.), *Living orthodoxy in the modern world: Orthodox Christianity and society* (pp. 85–107). Crestwood, NY: St. Vladimir's Seminary Press.

Blos, P. (1941). *The adolescent personality: A study of individual behavior*. New York: D. Appleton-Century-Crofts.

Blos, P. (1979). *The adolescent passage: Developmental issues*. New York: International Universities Press.

Bluebond-Langner, M. (1977). Meanings of death to children. In H. Feifel (Ed.), *New meanings of death* (pp. 47–66). New York: McGraw-Hill.

Bluebond-Langner, M. (1978). *The private worlds of dying children*. Princeton, NJ: Princeton University Press.

Bluebond-Langner, M. (1996). *In the shadow of illness: Parents and siblings of the chronically ill child*. Princeton, NJ: Princeton University Press.

Bluebond-Langner, M., Lask, B., & Angst, D. B. (Eds.). (2001). *Psychosocial aspects of cystic fibrosis*. London: Arnold.

Blume, J. (1981). *Tiger eyes*. Scarsdale, NY: Bradbury.

Blumenthal, D., & Collins, S. R. (2014, July 17). Health care coverage under the Affordable Care Act: A progress report. *New England Journal of Medicine, 371*, 275–281. doi:10.1056/NEJMhpr1405667

Bolton, C., & Camp, D. J. (1987). Funeral rituals and the facilitation of grief work. *Omega, Journal of Death and Dying, 17*, 343–352. doi:10.2190/VDHT-MFRC-LY7L-EMN7

Bolton, G. (Ed.). (2007). *Dying, bereavement and the healing arts*. Philadelphia: Jessica Kingsley.

Bolton, I. (1995). *My son, my son: A guide to healing after a suicide in the family* (Rev. ed.). Atlanta, GA: Bolton Press.

Bomba, P. A., Kemp, M., & Black, J. (2012, July). POLST: An improvement over traditional advance directives. *Cleveland Clinic Journal of Medicine, 79*(7), 457–464. doi:10.3949/ccjm.79a.11098

Bonanno, G., Wortman, C., & Nesse, R. (2004). Prospective patterns of resilience and maladjustment during widowhood. *Psychology and Aging, 19*(2), 260–271. doi:10.1037/0882-7974.19.2.260

Bonanno, G. A. (2004). Loss, trauma and human resilience: Have we underestimated the human capacity to thrive after extremely aversive events? *American Psychologist, 59*, 20–28. doi:10.1037/0003-066X.59.1.20

Bonanno, G. A. (2006). Is complicated grief a valid construct? *Clinical Psychology: Science and Practice, 13*, 129–134. doi:10.1111/j.1468-2850.2006.00014.x

Bonanno, G. A. (2009). *The other side of sadness: What the new science of bereavement tells us about life after loss*. New York: Basic Books.

Bonanno, G. A., Wortman, C. B., Lehman, D. R., et al. (2002). Resilience to loss and chronic grief: A prospective study from preloss to 18-months postloss. *Journal of Personality and Social Psychology, 83*, 1150–1164. doi:10.1037/0022-3514.83.5.1150

Bone, R. C. (1997). *A dying person's guide to dying*. Retrieved October 13, 2016, from http://www.hospicenet.org/html/dying_guide.html

Bonoti, F., Leondari, A., & Mastora, A. (2013). Exploring children's understanding of death: Through drawings and the death concept questionnaire. *Death Studies, 37*, 47–60. doi:10.1080/07481187.2011.623216

Bordere, T. C. (2009a). Culturally conscientious thanatology. *The Forum, 35*(2), 1–4.

Bordere, T. C. (2009b). "To look at death another way": Black teenage males' perspectives on second-lines and regular funerals in New Orleans. *Omega, Journal of Death and Dying, 58*, 213–232. doi:10.2190/OM.58.3.d

Borkman, T. (1976). Experiential knowledge: A new concept for the analysis of self-help groups. *Social Service Review, 50*, 445–456. doi:10.1086/643401

Borowsky, I. W., Resnick, M. D., Ireland, M., & Blum, R. W. (1999). Suicide attempts among American Indian and Alaska Native youth: Risk and protective factors. *Archives of Pediatric and Adolescent Medicine, 153*, 573–580. doi:10.1016/S1054-139X(97)83226-0

Boss, P. (1999). *Ambiguous loss: Learning to live with unresolved grief*. Cambridge, MA: Harvard University Press.

Boss, P. (2000). *Ambiguous loss: Learning to live with unresolved grief*. Cambridge, MA: Harvard University Press.

Boss, P. (2006). *Loss, trauma, and resilience: Therapeutic work with ambiguous loss*. New York: W. W. Norton.

Boss, P. (2011). *Loving someone who has dementia: How to find hope while coping with stress and grief*. San Francisco: Jossey-Bass.

Boss, P., & Carnes, D. (2012). The myth of closure. *Family Process, 51*(4), 456–460. doi:10.1111/famp.12005

Bosticco, C., & Thompson, T. L. (2005). Narratives and story telling in coping with grief and bereavement. *Omega, Journal of Death and Dying, 51*, 1–16. doi:10.2190/8TNX-LEBY-5EJY-B0H6

Botonis, M. (2014). *When caring takes courage: A compassionate, interactive guide for Alzheimer's and dementia caregivers*. Parker, CO: Outskirts Press.

Bottrell, M. M., O'Sullivan, J. E., Robbins, M. A., Mitty, E. L., & Mezey, M. D. (2001). Transferring dying nursing home residents to the hospital: DON perspectives on the nurse's role in transfer decisions. *Geriatric Nursing, 22*, 313–317. doi:10.1067/mgn.2001.120994

Bove, A. A. (2005). *Complete book of wills, estates, and trusts* (3rd ed.). New York: Owl Books.

Bowering, G., & Baird, J. (Eds.). (2011). *The heart does break: Canadian writers on grief and mourning*. Toronto: Vintage Canada.

Bowker, J. (1991). *The meanings of death*. Cambridge, England: Cambridge University Press.

Bowlby, J. (1961). Processes of mourning. *International Journal of Psychoanalysis, 42*, 317–340.

Bowlby, J. (1969–80). *Attachment and loss* (3 vols.). New York: Basic Books.

Bowman, L. E. (1959). *The American funeral: A study in guilt, extravagance and sublimity*. Washington, DC: Public Affairs Press.

Brabant, S. (1996). *Mending the torn fabric: For those who grieve and those who want to help them*. Amityville, NY: Baywood.

Brabant, S., Forsyth, C., & McFarlain, G. (1995). Life after the death of a child: Initial and long term support from others. *Omega, Journal of Death and Dying, 31*, 67–85. doi:10.2190/LHKX-QYH0-2J42-MNC2

Brackey, J. (2008). *Creating moments of joy for the person with Alzheimer's or dementia: A journal for caregivers* (4th ed.). West Lafayette, IN: Purdue University Press.

Brady, E. M. (1979). Telling the story: Ethics and dying. *Hospital Progress, 60*, 57–62.

Brandes, S. (2006). *Skulls to the living, bread to the dead: The Day of the Dead in Mexico and beyond*. Malden, MA: Blackwell.

Braun, K. L., Pietsch, J., & Blanchette, P. (Eds.). (2004). *Cultural issues in end-of-life decision making*. Thousand Oaks, CA: Sage.

Braun, K. L., Tanji, V. M., & Heck, R. (2001). Support for physician-assisted suicide: Exploring the impact of ethnicity and attitudes toward planning for death. *Gerontology, 41*(1), 51–60.

Braun, M. L., & Berg, D. H. (1994). Meaning reconstruction in the experience of bereavement. *Death Studies, 18*, 105–129. doi:10.1080/07481189408252647

Breck, J. (1995). Euthanasia and the quality of life debate. *Christian Bioethics, 1*, 322–337. doi:10.1093/cb/1.3.322

Breed, W. (1972). Five components of a basic suicide syndrome. *Life-Threatening Behavior, 2*, 3–18. doi:10.1111/j.1943-278X.1972.tb00451.x

Breitbart, W. S., & Alici, Y. (2014). *Psychosocial palliative care*. New York: Oxford University Press.

Breitman, R., & Goda, N. J. W. (2010, December 10). *Hitler's shadow: Nazi war criminals, U.S. intelligence, and the cold war*. Washington, DC: National Archives. Retrieved December 12, 2010, from http://www.archives.gov/iwg/reports/hitlers-shadow.pdf

Brennan, C. (1998, November 5). Al Joyner can't escape memories of FloJo. *USA Today*, p. 5E.

Brent, S. (1978). Puns, metaphors, and misunderstandings in a two-year-old's conception of death. *Omega, Journal of Death and Dying, 8*, 285–294. doi:10.2190/PCHX-PK2K-YREG-0TB6

Brent, S. B., & Speece, M. W. (1993). "Adult" conceptualization of irreversibility: Implications for the development of the concept of death. *Death Studies, 17*, 203–224. doi:10.1080/07481189308252618

Bristowe, K., Marshall, S., & Harding, R. (2016). The bereavement experiences of lesbian, gay, bisexual and/or trans people who have lost a partner: A systematic review, thematic synthesis and modelling of the literature. *Palliative Medicine, 30*, 730–744. doi:10.1177/0269216316634601

Brodman, B. (2011). *The Mexican cult of death in myth, art and literature*. Bloomington, IN: iUniverse.

Brody, J. (2009). *Jane Brody's guide to the great beyond: A practical primer to help you and your loved ones prepare medically, legally, and emotionally for the end of life*. New York: Random House.

Brokaw, T. (1998). *The greatest generation*. New York: Random House.

Brokaw, T. (2015). *A lucky life interrupted: A memoir of hope*. New York: Random House.

Brothers, J. (1992). *Widowed*. New York: Ballantine.

Brown, E., with B. Warr. (2007). *Supporting the child and the family in paediatric palliative care*. Philadelphia: Jessica Kingsley.

Brown, J. E. (1987). *The spiritual legacy of the American Indian*. New York: Crossroad.

Brown, J. H., Henteleff, P., Barakat, S., & Rowe, C. J. (1986). Is it normal for terminally ill patients to desire death? *American Journal of Psychiatry, 143*, 208–211. doi:10.1176/ajp.143.2.208

Browning, C. R. (2004). *The origins of the final solution: The evolution of Nazi Jewish policy, September 1939–March 1942*. Lincoln: University of Nebraska Press.

Bruera, E., Higginson, I., von Gunten, C. F., & Morita, T. (Eds.). (2016). *Textbook of palliative medicine and supportive care* (2nd ed.). Boca Raton, FL: CRC Press/Taylor & Francis.

Bruner, J. S. (1962). *The process of education*. Cambridge: Harvard University Press.

Bryden, C. (2005). *Dancing with dementia: My story of living positively with Alzheimer's*. Philadelphia: Jessica Kingsley.

Bryden, C. (2012). *Who will I be when I die?* Philadelphia: Jessica Kingsley.

Bryant, C. D. (Ed.). (2003). *Handbook of death and dying* (2 vols.). Thousand Oaks, CA: Sage.

Bryant, C. D., & Peck, D. L. (Eds.). (2009). *Encyclopedia of death and the human experience* (2 vols.). Thousand Oaks, CA: Sage.

Bryer, K. B. (1979). The Amish way of death: A study of family support systems. *American Psychologist, 34,* 255–261. doi:10.1037/0003-066X.34.3.255

Bucholz, J. A. (2002). *Homicide survivors: Misunderstood grievers.* Amityville, NY: Baywood.

Buchwald, A. (2006). *Too soon to say goodbye.* New York: Random House.

Buckle, J. L., & Fleming, S. J. (2011). *Parenting after the death of a child: A practitioner's guide.* New York: Routledge.

Bucklea, J. L. (2013). University students' perspectives on a psychology of death and dying course: Exploring motivation to enroll, goals, and impact. *Death Studies, 37,* 866–882. doi:10.1080/07481187.2012.699911

Buckley, S. (2001, Sept 2). Slow change of heart. *St. Petersburg Times,* pp. 1A, 8A–9A.

Buckman, R. (1992a). *How to break bad news: A guide for health care professionals.* Baltimore: Johns Hopkins University Press.

Buckman, R. (1992b). *I don't know what to say: How to help and support someone who is dying.* New York: Vintage Books.

Buckman, R. (2001). Communication skills in palliative care: A practical guide. *Neurologic Clinics, 19*(4), 989–1004. doi:10.1016/S0733-8619(05)70057-8

Buckman, R. (2010). *Practical plans for difficult conversations in medicine: Strategies that work in breaking bad news.* Baltimore: The Johns Hopkins University Press.

Buettner, D. (2012). *The Blue Zones: 9 lessons for living longer from people who've lived the longest* (2nd ed.). Washington, DC: National Geographic Press.

Buettner, D. (2015). *The Blue Zones solution: Eating and living like the world's healthiest people.* Washington, DC: National Geographic Press.

Bühler, C. (1968). The general structure of the human life cycle. In C. Bühler & F. Massarik (Eds.), *The course of human life: A study of goals in the humanistic perspective* (pp. 12–26). New York: Springer.

Bulterijs, S., Hull, R. S., Björk, V.C.E., & Roy, A. G. (2015). It is time to classify biological aging as a disease. *Frontiers in Genetics, 6,* 205. doi:10.3389/fgene.2015.00205

Bunting, E. (1982). *The happy funeral.* New York: Harper & Row.

Burdick, L. (2004). *The sunshine on my face: A read-aloud book for memory-challenged adults.* Baltimore: Health Professions Press.

Burdick, L. (2006). *Happy new year to you!: A read-aloud book for memory-challenged adults.* Baltimore: Health Professions Press.

Burdick, L. (2009). *Wishing on a star: A read-aloud book for memory-challenged adults.* Baltimore: Health Professions Press.

Burns, D. M. (2014). *When kids are grieving: Addressing grief and loss in school.* Thousand Oaks, CA: Corwin Press.

Burns, S. B. (1990). *Sleeping beauty: Memorial photography in America.* Altadena, CA: Twelvetrees Press.

Burroway, J. (2014). *Losing Tim: A memoir.* Minneapolis: Think Piece Publishing.

Burtt, E. A. (1955). *The teachings of the compassionate Buddha.* New York: New American Library.

Burtt, K. (2015, October 22). Glen Campbell reveals his life with Alzheimer's: 'I'll Be Me' film documents his love for music, life and fans. Retrieved November 10, 2015, from http://www.lifescript.com/health/centers/alzheimers/articles/glen_campbell_as_he_is_with_alzheimers.aspx?utm_source=aol&utm_medium=syn&utm_campaign=health&icid=maing-grid7|main5|dl33|sec1_lnk3%26pLid%3D-161258746

Busch, K. G., Zagar, R., Hughes, J. R., Arbit, J., & Bussell, R. E. (1990). Adolescents who kill. *Journal of Clinical Psychology, 46,* 472–485. doi:10.1002/1097-4679(199007)46:4<472

Butler, C. L., & Lagoni, L. S. (1996). Children and pet loss. In C. A. Corr & D. M. Corr (Eds.), *Handbook of childhood death and bereavement* (pp. 179–200). New York: Springer.

Butler, R. N. (1963). The life review: An interpretation of reminiscence in the aged. *Psychiatry, 26,* 65–76.

Butler, R. N. (1969). Age-ism: Another form of bigotry. *The Gerontologist, 9,* 243–246. doi:10.1093/geront/9.4_Part_1.243

Butler, R. N. (2002). *Why survive? Being old in America.* Baltimore: Johns Hopkins University Press.

Butler, R. N., & Lewis, M. I. (1998). *Aging and mental health* (5th ed.). St. Louis, MO: Mosby.

Byock, I. (1996). The nature of suffering and the nature of opportunity at the end of life. *Clinics in Geriatric Medicine, 12,* 237–252.

Byock, I. (1997). *Dying well: The prospect for growth at the end of life.* New York: Putnam.

Byock, I. (2004). *The four things that matter most: A book about living.* New York: Free Press.

Byock, I. (2012). *The best care possible: A physician's quest to transform care through the end of life.* New York: Avery.

Cade, S. (1963). Cancer: The patient's viewpoint and the clinician's problems. *Proceedings of the Royal Society of Medicine, 56,* 1–8.

Cagle, J. G., Van Dussen, D. J., Culler, K. L., et al. (2016). Knowledge about hospice: Exploring misconceptions, attitudes, and preferences for care. *American Journal of Hospice and Palliative Care, 33,* 27–33. doi:10.1177/1049909114546885.

Cain, A. (Ed.). (1972). *Survivors of suicide.* Springfield, IL: Bannerstone House.

Caine, L. (1975). *Widow.* New York: Bantam Books.

Caine, L. (1990). *Being a widow.* New York: Penguin Books.

Calhoun, L. G., & Tedeschi, R. G. (Eds.). (1999). *Facilitating posttraumatic growth: A clinician's guide.* Mahwah, NJ: Lawrence Erlbaum Associates.

Calhoun, L. G., & Tedeschi, R. G. (Eds.). (2006). *The handbook of posttraumatic growth: Research and practice.* Mahwah, NJ: Lawrence Erlbaum Associates.

Calhoun, L. G., Abernathy, C. B., & Selby, J. W. (1986). The rules of bereavement: Are suicidal deaths different? *Journal of Community Psychology, 14,* 213–218. doi:10.1002/1520-6629(198604)14:2<213

Calistoga Press. (2013). *Understand Alzheimer's: A first-time caregiver's plan to understand & prepare for Alzheimer's & dementia.* Berkeley, CA: Calisto Media.

Callanan, M. (2009). *Final journeys: A practical guide for bringing care and comfort at the end of life.* New York: Bantam.

Callanan, M., & Kelley, P. (2012). *Final gifts: Understanding the special awareness, needs, and communications of the dying.* New York: Simon & Schuster.

Callender, C. O., Hall, L. E., Yeager, C. L., et al. (1991). Organ donation and blacks: A critical frontier. *New England Journal of Medicine, 325,* 442–444. doi:10.1056/NEJM199108083250631

Callone, P. R., Kudlacek, C., Vasiloff, B. C., Mantemach, J., & Brumback, R. A. (2006). *A caregiver's guide to Alzheimer's disease: 300 tips for making life easier.* New York: Demos Medical Publishing.

Calvin, S., & Smith, I. M. (1986). Counseling adolescents in death-related situations. In C. A. Corr & J. N. McNeil (Eds.), *Adolescence and death* (pp. 215–230). New York: Springer.

Camenisch, P. F. (Ed.). (1994). *Religious methods and resources in bioethics.* Boston: Kluwer.

Campbell, J. (2016, January 21). A matter of life and death. *Mindful.* Retrieved January 29, 2016, from http://www.mindful.org/a-matter-of-death-and-life/

Campbell, S., & Silverman, P. R. (1996). *Widower: When men are left alone.* Amityville, NY: Baywood.

Canadian Hospice Palliative Care Association. (2015, October). *Fact sheet: Hospice palliative care in Canada.* Ottawa, Canada: Author. Retrieved July 17, 2016, from http://www.chpca.net/media/466867/Fact_Sheet_HPC_in_Canada%20Fall%202015%20Final.pdf

Canadian Institute for Health Information. (2014). *Deceased organ donor potential in Canada.* Ottawa, Canada: Author.

Canine, J. D. (1999). *What am I going to do with myself when I die?* Stamford, CT: Appleton & Lange.

Cantor, R. C. (1978). *And a time to live: Toward emotional well-being during the crisis of cancer.* New York: Harper & Row.

Caplan, A. L., McCartney, J. J., & Reid, D. P. (Eds.). (2015). *Replacement parts: The ethics of procuring and replacing organs in humans.* Washington, DC: Georgetown University Press.

Caplan, A. L., McCartney, J. J., & Sisti, D. A. (Eds.). (2006). *The case of Terri Schiavo: Ethics at the end of life.* Buffalo, NY: Prometheus.

Carlson, M., Herrin, J., Du, Q., et al. (2010). Impact of hospice disenrollment on health care use and Medicare expenditures for patients with cancer. *Journal of Clinical Oncology, 28,* 4371–4375. doi:10.1200/JCO.2009.26.1818

Carmack, B. J. (2003). *Grieving the death of a pet.* Minneapolis, MN: Augsburg Fortress.

Carney, C., McGehee, D., Harland, K., Weiss, M., & Raby, M. (2015). *Using naturalistic driving data to assess the prevalence of environmental factors and driver behaviors in teen driver crashes.* Washington, DC: AAA Foundation for Traffic Safety.

Carr, B. A., & Lee, E. S. (1978). Navajo tribal mortality: A life table analysis of the leading causes of death. *Social Biology, 25,* 279–287. doi:10.1080/19485565.1978.9988349

Carr, D., Nesse, R. M., & Wortman, C. B. (Eds.). (2005). *Spousal bereavement in late life.* New York: Springer.

Carrick, C. (1976). *The accident.* New York: Seabury Press.

Carse, J. P. (1980). *Death and existence: A conceptual history of mortality.* New York: Wiley.

Carson, U. (1984). Teachable moments occasioned by "small deaths". In H. Wass & C. A. Corr (Eds.), *Childhood and death* (pp. 315–343). Washington, DC: Hemisphere.

Carter, B. D., Abnet, C. C., Feskanich, D., et al. (2015), Smoking and mortality: Beyond established causes. *New England Journal of Medicine, 372,* 631–640. doi:10.1056/NEJMsa1407211

Carter, B. S. (2016). Why palliative care for children is preferable to euthanasia. *American Journal of Hospice and Palliative Medicine, 33,* 5–7. doi:10.1177/1049909114542648

Carter, B. S., Levetown, M., & Friebert, S. E. (Eds.). (2011). *Palliative care for infants, children, and adolescents: A practical handbook* (2nd ed.). Baltimore: Johns Hopkins University Press.

Carter, B., & McGoldrick, M. (Eds.). (1988). *The changing family life cycle: A framework for family therapy* (2nd ed.). New York: Gardner Press.

Carter, J. (1998). *The virtues of aging.* New York: Library of Contemporary Thought/Ballantine.

Case, A., & Deaton, A. (2015). Rising morbidity and mortality in midlife among white non-Hispanic Americans in the 21st century. *Proceedings of the National Academy of Sciences of the United States of America, 112*(49), 15078–15083. doi:10.1073/pnas.1518393112

Caserta, M. S., Lund, D. A., Utz, R. L., & Tabler, J. L. (2016). "One size doesn't fit all"—Partners in Hospice Care, an individualized approach to bereavement intervention. *Omega, Journal of Death and Dying, 73,* 107–125. doi:10.1177/0030222815575895

Cassell, E. J. (1985). *Talking with patients: Vol. 1, The theory of doctor-patient communication; Vol. 2, Clinical technique.* Cambridge, MA: MIT Press.

Cassell, E. J. (1991). *The nature of suffering and the goals of medicine.* New York: Oxford University Press.

Cate, F. H., & Gill, B. A. (1991). *The Patient Self-Determination Act: Implementation issues and opportunities.* Washington, DC: The Annenberg Washington Program.

Catt, S., Blanchard, M., Addington-Hall, J., et al. (2005). Older adults' attitudes to death, palliative treatment and hospice care. *Palliative Medicine, 19,* 402–410. doi:10.1191/0269216305pm1037oa

Cavanaugh, J. C., & Blanchard-Fields, F. (2014). *Adult development and aging* (7th ed.). Belmont, CA: Wadsworth.

Cave, S. (2014). *Immortality: The quest to live forever and how it drives civilization.* New York: Crown.

Cebuhar, J. K. (2010). *So grows the tree: Creating an ethical will.* West Des Moines, IA: Murphy Publishing.

Cebuhar, J. K. (2015). *The practical guide to health care advance directives.* Seattle, WA: Amazon Digital Services (Kindle ed.)

Center for the Advancement of Health. (2004). Report on bereavement and grief research [Special Issue]. *Death Studies, 28*(6).

Center to Advance Palliative Care. (2017). *Pediatric palliative care field guide: A catalog of resources, tools and training to promote innovation, development and growth.* Author. Retrieved February 28, 2017, from https://media.capc.org/filer_public/58/70/587067d2-ba65-4263-a29e-25dca6b2e0df/peds_pc_field_guide_111116.pdf

Centers for Disease Control (CDC). (1981a). Pneumocystis pneumonia—Los Angeles. *Morbidity and Mortality Weekly Report, 30,* 250–252.

Centers for Disease Control (CDC). (1981b). Kaposi's sarcoma and *Pneumocystis* pneumonia among homosexual men—New York City and California. *Morbidity and Mortality Weekly Report, 30,* 305–308.

Centers for Disease Control (CDC). (1981c). Follow-up on Kaposi's sarcoma and *Pneumocystis* pneumonia. *Morbidity and Mortality Weekly Report, 30,* 409–410.

Centers for Disease Control (CDC). (1992a). 1993 revised classification system for HIV infection and expanded surveillance case definition for AIDS among adolescents and adults. *Morbidity and Mortality Weekly Report, 41,* No. RR-17.

Centers for Disease Control and Prevention (CDC). (1992b). *HIV/AIDS Surveillance Report, 4*(1). Atlanta: U.S. Department of Health and Human Services, Centers for Disease Control and Prevention.

Centers for Disease Control and Prevention (CDC). (2006). Twenty-five years of HIV/AIDS—United States, 1981–2006. *Morbidity and Mortality Weekly Report, 55*(21), 585–589.

Centers for Disease Control and Prevention. (2008). Revised surveillance case definitions for HIV infection among adults, adolescents, and children aged <18 months and for HIV infection and AIDS among children aged 18 months to <13 years—United States, 2008. *Morbidity and Mortality Weekly Report; 57*(RR-10), 1–12.

Centers for Disease Control and Prevention. (2016). HIV in the United States: At a glance. Retrieved September 18, 2016, from http://www.cdc.gov/hiv/statistics/overview/ataglance.html

Central Intelligence Agency. (2016). *The World Factbook*. Retrieved January, 22, 2016, from https://www.cia.gov/library/publications/the-world-factbook/rankorder/2091rank.html

Cerel, J., Maple, M., Aldrich, R., & van de Venne, J. (2013). Exposure to suicide and identification as survivor: Results from a random-digit dial survey. *Crisis: The Journal of Crisis Intervention and Suicide Prevention, 34*(6), 413–419. doi:10.1027/0227-5910/a000220

Chambere, K., Vander Stichele, R., Mortier, F., Cohen, J., & Deliens, L. (2015, March 17). Recent trends in euthanasia and other end-of-life practices in Belgium. *New England Journal of Medicine, 372*, 1179–1181. doi:10.1056/NEJMc1414527

Chambers, J. S. (2005). *The easy will and living will kit* (+ CD-ROM). Naperville, IL: Sphinx Publishing.

Chance, S. (1994). *Stronger than death: When suicide touches your life—A mother's story*. New York: Avon.

Chandler, M. J., & Lalonde, C. E. (1998). Continuity as a hedge against suicide in Canada's First Nations. *Transcultural Psychiatry, 35*, 191–219. doi:10.1177/136346159803500202

Chandler, M. J., Lalonde, C. E., Sokol, B. W., & Hallet, D. (2003). Personal persistence, identity development, and suicide: A study of Native and non-Native North American adolescents. *Monographs of the Society for Research in Child Development, 68*(2), 50–76. doi:10.1111/j.1540-5834.2003.00251.x

Chappell, B. J. (2001). My journey to the Dougy Center. In O. D. Weeks & C. Johnson (Eds.), *When all the friends have gone: A guide for aftercare providers* (pp. 141–154). Amityville, NY: Baywood.

Chappell, B. J. (2008). *Children helping children with grief: My path to founding The Dougy Center for Grieving Children and Their Families*. Troutdale, OR: NewSage Press.

Chapple, H. S. (2010). *No place for dying: Hospitals and the ideology of rescue*. Walnut Creek, CA: Left Coast Press.

Charon, R. (2006). *Narrative medicine: Honoring the stories of illness*. New York: Oxford University Press.

Chase, S. (2012). *Surviving HIV/AIDS in the inner city: How resourceful Latinas beat the odds*. Piscataway, NJ: Rutgers University Press.

Chaudhuri, J. (2001). Some notes on political theory and American Indian values: The case of the Muscogee Creeks. *American Indian Culture and Research Journal, 25*, 129–135. doi:10.17953/aicr.25.2.n57340673021760n

Cheatham, C. (2014). *Hospice whispers: Stories of life*. Newark, DE: SCIE Publishing.

Cherny, N., Fallon, M., Kaasa, S., Portenoy, R. K., & Currow, D. C. (Eds.). (2015). *Oxford textbook of palliative medicine* (5th ed.). New York: Oxford University Press.

Chethik, N. (2001). *FatherLoss: How sons of all ages come to terms with the deaths of their dads*. New York: Hyperion Books.

Chidester, D. (2002). *Patterns of transcendence: Religion, death, and dying* (2nd ed.). Belmont, CA: Wadsworth.

Childers, P., & Wimmer, M. (1971). The concept of death in early childhood. *Child Development, 42*, 1299–1301. doi:10.2307/1127816

Childress, J. F. (1990). The place of autonomy in bioethics. *Hastings Center Report, 20*(1), 12–17. doi:10.2307/3562967

Chochinov, H. M. (2011). *Dignity therapy: Final words for final days*. New York: Oxford University Press.

Choron, J. (1963). *Death and Western thought*. New York: Collier Books.

Choron, J. (1964). *Death and modern man*. New York: Collier Books.

Christ, G. H. (2000). *Healing children's grief: Surviving a parent's death from cancer*. New York: Oxford University Press.

Christ, G. H., Siegel, K., & Christ, A. E. (2002). Adolescent grief: "It never really hit me … until it actually happened". *Journal of the American Medical Association, 288*, 1269–1278. doi:10.1001/jama.288.10.1269

Christakis, N., & Iwashyna, T. (2003). The health impact of hospice care on families: A matched cohort study of hospice use by decedents and mortality outcomes in surviving, widowed spouses. *Social Science and Medicine, 57*(3), 465–475. doi:10.1016/S0277-9536(02)00370-2

Churn, A. (2003). *The end is just the beginning: Lessons in grieving for African Americans*. New York: Broadway Books.

Cicirelli, V. G. (2002). *Older adults' views on death*. New York: Springer.

Clark, D. (2007). End-of-life care around the world: Achievements to date and challenges remaining. In C. M. Parkes (Ed.), "Hospice heritage": In memory of Dame Cicely Saunders [Special issue]. *Omega, Journal of Death and Dying, 56*, 101–110. doi:10.2190/OM.56.1.i

Clark, D. (Ed.). (2002). *Cicely Saunders – founder of the hospice movement. Selected letters 1959–1999*. Oxford, UK: Oxford University Press.

Clark, D., Small, N., Wright, M., Winslow, M., & Hughes, N. (2005). *A bit of heaven for the few?: An oral history of the modern hospice movement in the United Kingdom*. Lancaster, United Kingdom: Observatory Publications.

Clark, J., & Cheshire, A. (2004). RIP by the roadside: A comparative study of roadside memorials in New South Wales, Australia, and Texas, United States. *Omega, Journal of Death and Dying, 48*, 203–222. doi:10.2190/3RED-6H7D-PNNC-URT7

Clark, J., & Franzmann, M. (2006). Authority from grief, presence and place in the making of roadside memorials. *Death Studies, 30*, 579–599. doi:10.1080/07481180600742574

Clark, S. E., & Goldney, R. D. (2002). The impact of suicide on relatives and friends. In K. Hawton & K. van Heeringen (Eds.), *The international handbook of suicide and attempted suicide* (pp. 467–484). New York: Wiley.

Claypool, J. R. (2004). *Tracks of a fellow struggler: Living and growing through grief*. Harrisburg, PA: Morehouse.

Clayton, P. J. (1973). The clinical morbidity of the first year of bereavement: A review. *Comprehensive Psychiatry, 14*, 151–157. doi:10.1016/0010-440X(73)90007-2

Clayton, P. J. (1974). Mortality and morbidity in the first year of widowhood. *Archives of General Psychiatry, 30*, 747–750. doi:10.1001/archpsyc.1974.01760120013002

Clayton, P. J., Herjanic, M., Murphy, G. E., & Woodruff, R. A. (1974). Mourning and depression: Their similarities and differences. *Canadian Psychiatric Association Journal, 19*, 309–312.

Cleckley, M., Estes, E., & Norton, P. (Eds.). (1992). *We need not walk alone: After the death of a child* (2nd ed.). Oak Brook, IL: The Compassionate Friends.

Clemency, G., Cordes, C. C., Lindstrom, H. A., Basior, J. M., & Waldrop, D. P. (2016). Decisions by default: Incomplete and contradictory MOLST in emergency care. *Journal of the American Medical Directors Association*. doi:10.1016/j.jamda.2016.07.032

Clement, L. D., & Jamali, L. (Eds.). (2015). *Global perspectives on death in children's literature*. New York: Routledge.

Clements, P. T., & Weisser, S. M. (2003), Cries from the morgue. *Journal of Child and Adolescent Psychiatric Nursing, 16*, 153–161. doi:10.1111/j.1744-6171.2003.00153.x

Clements, P. T., Vigil, G. J., Manno, M. S., et al. (2003). Cultural perspectives of death, grief, and bereavement. *Journal of Psychosocial Nursing*, 41(7), 18–26. doi:10.3928/0279-3695-20030701-12

Clifford, D. (2014). Plan your estate (12th ed.). Berkeley, CA: Nolo.

Clifford, D. (2015a). *Estate planning basics* (8th ed.). Berkeley, CA: Nolo.

Clifford, D. (2015b). *Make your own living trust* (12th ed.). Berkeley, CA: Nolo.

Clift, E. (2008). *Two weeks of life: A memoir of love, death and politics*. New York: Basic Books.

Cobain, B. (2007). *When nothing matters anymore: A survival guide for depressed teens* (rev. & updated ed.). Minneapolis: Free Spirit Publishing.

Cobain, B., & Larch, J. (2006). *Dying to be free: A healing guide for families after a suicide*. Center City, MN: Hazelden.

Coffin, M. M. (1976). *Death in early America: The history and folklore of customs and superstitions of early medicine, burial and mourning*. Nashville, TN: Thomas Nelson.

Cohen, C. B. (1996). Christian perspectives on assisted suicide and euthanasia: The Anglican tradition. *Journal of Law, Medicine and Ethics*, 24, 369–379. doi:10.1111/j.1748-720X.1996.tb01881.x

Cohen, J. A., Mannarino, A. P., & Deblinger, E. (2006). *Treating trauma and traumatic grief in children and adolescents*. New York: Guilford.

Cohen-Almagor, R. (2010). *Euthanasia in the Netherlands: The policy and practice of mercy killing*. Dordrecht, Netherlands: Kluwer Academic Publishers.

Cohen-Almagor, R. (2015, June 3). First do no harm: Intentionally shortening lives of patients without their explicit request in Belgium. *Journal of Medical Ethics*. doi:10.1136/medethics-2014-102387

Colby, W. H. (2002). *Long goodbye: The deaths of Nancy Cruzan*. Carlsbad, CA: Hay House.

Colby, W. H. (2006). *Unplugged: Reclaiming our right to die in America*. New York: American Management Association.

Coleman, J. C. (1978). Current contradictions in adolescent theory. *Journal of Youth and Adolescence*, 7, 1–11. doi:10.1007/BF01538683

Coleman, P. G. (2005). Uses of reminiscence: Functions and benefits. *Aging and Mental Health*, 9(4), 291–294. doi:10.1080/13607860500169641

Colen, B. D. (1976). *Karen Ann Quinlan: Dying in the age of eternal life*. New York: Nash.

Collier, A. K. (2003). *Still with me: A daughter's journey of love and loss*. New York: Simon & Schuster.

Collins, C. O., & Rhine, C. D. (2003). Roadside memorials. *Omega, Journal of Death and Dying*, 47, 221–244. doi:10.2190/1654-01N2-2A3C-GQ9C

Colorado Collaboration on End-of-Life Care. (n.d.). *Five themes for caring: Spiritual care giving guide*. Denver, CO: Author.

Colucci, E., & Lester, D. (Eds.). (2013). *Suicide and culture: Understanding the context*. Ashland, OH: Hogrefe Publishing.

Combs, C. C., & Slann, M. (2002). *Encyclopedia of terrorism*. New York: Facts on File.

Comer, J. (2006). *When roles reverse: A guide to parenting your parents*. Charlottesville, VA: Hampton Roads Publishing Co.

Comer, M. (2014). *Slow dancing with a stranger: Lost and found in the age of Alzheimer's*. New York: HarperOne.

Compassion and Choices. (2016, February 2). *History of the end-of-life choice movement*. Denver, CO. Retrieved April 28, 2017, from https://www.compassionandchoices.org/wp-content/uploads/2016/02/FS-History-of-the-End-of-Life-Choice-Movement-FINAL-2.2.16-Approved-for-Public-Distribution.pdf

Comstock, G. A., & Paik, H. (1991). *Television and the American child*. San Diego, CA: Academic Press.

Conger, J. J., & Peterson, A. C. (1984). *Adolescence and youth: Psychological development in a changing world* (3rd ed.). New York: Harper & Row.

Connor, S. R. (2009). *Hospice and palliative care: The essential guide* (2nd ed.). New York: Routledge.

Connor, S. R., Elwert, F., Spence, C., & Christakis, N. A. (2007). Geographic variation in hospice use in the United States in 2002. *Journal of Pain and Symptom Management*, 34, 277–285. doi:10.1016/j.jpainsymman.2007.03.007

Connor, S. R., Elwert, F., Spence, C., & Christakis, N. A., (2008). Racial disparity in hospice use in the United States in 2002. *Palliative Medicine*, 22, 205–213. doi:10.1177/0269216308089305

Connor, S. R., Pyenson, B., Fitch, K., Spence, C., & Iwasaki, K. (2007). Comparing hospice and nonhospice patient survival among patients who die within a three-year window. *Journal of Pain and Symptom Management*, 33, 238–246. doi:10.1016/j.jpainsymman.2006.10.010

Conrad, B. H. (1997). *When a child has been murdered: Ways you can help the grieving parents*. Amityville, NY: Baywood.

Conwell, Y. (2001). Suicide in later life: A review and recommendations for prevention. *Suicide and Life-Threatening Behavior*, 31, 32–47. doi:10.1521/suli.31.1.5.32.24221

Conwell, Y., & Duberstein, P. R. (2001). *Suicide in elders*. Annals of the New York Academy of Sciences, 932, 132–150. doi:10.1111/j.1749-6632.2001.tb05802.x

Conwell, Y., Van Orden, K., & Caine, E. D. (2011). Suicide and older adults. *Psychiatric Clinics of North America*, 34(2), 451–468. doi:10.1016/j.psc.2011.02.002

Cook, A. S., & Dworkin, D. S. (1992). *Helping the bereaved: Therapeutic interventions for children, adolescents, and adults*. New York: Basic Books.

Cook, A. S., & Oltjenbruns, K. A. (1998). *Dying and grieving: Lifespan and family perspectives* (2nd ed.). Fort Worth, TX: Harcourt Brace.

Cook, K. A., Jack, S. M., Siden, H., Thabane, L., & Browne, G. (2016). Investing in uncertainty: Young adults with life-limiting conditions achieving their developmental goals. *Journal of Palliative Medicine*, 19, 1-6. doi:10.1089/jpm.2015.0241

Corace, B. (2001). End-of-life care: A personal reflection. In M. Z. Solomon, A. L. Romer, K. S. Heller, & D. E. Weissman (Eds.), *Innovations in end-of-life care: Practical strategies and international perspectives* (Vol. 2, pp. 81–82). Larchmont, NY: Mary Ann Liebert Publishers.

Cordaro, M. (2012). Pet loss and disenfranchised grief: Implications for mental health counseling practice. *Journal of Mental Health Counseling*, 34(4), 283–294. doi:10.17744/mehc.34.4.41q0248450t98072

Cordesman, A. H. (2005). *The challenge of biological terrorism*. Washington, DC: Center for Strategies and International Studies.

Corless, I. B., & Foster, Z. (Eds.). (1999). The hospice heritage: Celebrating our future [Special issue]. *Hospice Journal*, 14(3/4).

Corley, E. A. (1973). *Tell me about death, tell me about funerals*. Santa Clara, CA: Grammatical Sciences.

Corr, C. A. (1978). A model syllabus for death and dying courses. *Death Education*, 1, 433–457. doi:10.1080/07481187808252916

Corr, C. A. (1981). Hospices, dying persons, and hope. In R. A. Pacholski & C. A. Corr (Eds.), *New directions in death education and counseling: Enhancing the quality of life in the nuclear age* (pp. 14–20). Arlington, VA: Forum for Death Education and Counseling.

Corr, C. A. (1984a). Helping with death education. In H. Wass & C. A. Corr (Eds.), *Helping children cope with death: Guidelines and resources* (2nd ed., pp. 49–73). Washington, DC: Hemisphere.

Corr, C. A. (1984b). A model syllabus for children and death courses. *Death Education, 8*, 11–28. doi:10.1080/07481188408251379

Corr, C. A. (1992a). A task-based approach to coping with dying. *Omega, Journal of Death and Dying, 24*, 81–94. doi:10.2190/CNNF-CX1P-BFXU-GGN4

Corr, C. A. (1992b). Teaching a college course on children and death: A 13-year report. *Death Studies, 16*, 343–356. doi:10.1080/07481189208252582

Corr, C. A. (1993a). Coping with dying: Lessons that we should and should not learn from the work of Elisabeth Kübler-Ross. *Death Studies, 17*, 69–83. doi:10.1080/07481189308252605

Corr, C. A. (1993b). The day we went to Auschwitz. *Omega, Journal of Death and Dying, 27*, 105–113. doi:10.2190/KJC6-2C7L-LL7U-WL6C

Corr, C. A. (1996). Children and questions about death. In S. Strack (Ed.), *Death and the quest for meaning: Essays in honor of Herman Feifel* (pp. 317–338). Northvale, NJ: Jason Aronson.

Corr, C. A. (1998a). Developmental perspectives on grief and mourning. In K. J. Doka & J. D. Davidson (Eds.), *Living with grief: Who we are, how we grieve* (pp. 143–159). Washington, DC: Hospice Foundation of America.

Corr, C. A. (1998b). Enhancing the concept of disenfranchised grief. *Omega, Journal of Death and Dying, 38*, 1–20. doi:10.2190/LD26-42A6-1EAV-3MDN

Corr, C. A. (2000).What do we know about grieving children and adolescents? In K. J. Doka (Ed.), *Living with grief: Children, adolescents, and loss* (pp. 21–32). Washington, DC: Hospice Foundation of America.

Corr, C. A. (2001, July). Restructuring relationships: Four examples. *Journeys: A Newsletter to Help in Bereavement, 1*, 3.

Corr, C. A. (2002a). Revisiting the concept of disenfranchised grief. In K. J. Doka (Ed.), *Disenfranchised grief: New directions, challenges, and strategies for practice* (pp. 39–60). Champaign, IL: Research Press.

Corr, C. A. (2002b). Coping with challenges to assumptive worlds. In J. Kauffman (Ed.), *Loss of the assumptive world: A theory of traumatic loss* (pp. 127–138). New York: Brunner-Routledge.

Corr, C. A. (2002c). Teaching a college course on children and death for 22 years: A supplemental report. *Death Studies, 26*, 595–606. doi:10.1080/074811802760191726

Corr, C. A. (2003). Loss, grief, and trauma in public tragedy. In M. Lattanzi-Licht & K. J. Doka (Eds.), *Living with grief: Coping with public tragedy* (pp. 63–76). Washington, DC: Hospice Foundation of America.

Corr, C. A. (Ed.). (2004a). Death-related literature for children [Special issue]. *Omega, Journal of Death and Dying, 48*(4).

Corr, C. A. (2004b). Pet loss in death-related literature for children. *Omega, Journal of Death and Dying, 48*, 399–414. doi:10.2190/HXQY-DU5D-YC39-XKJ9

Corr, C. A. (2005). Organ donation: Ethical issues and issues of loss and grief. In K. J. Doka, B. Jennings, & C. A. Corr (Eds.). (2005). *Living with grief: Ethical dilemmas at the end of life* (pp. 251–266). Washington, DC: Hospice Foundation of America.

Corr, C. A. (2007). Anticipatory grief and mourning: An overview. In K. J. Doka (Ed.), *Living with grief: Before and after a death* (pp. 5–20). Washington, DC: Hospice Foundation of America.

Corr, C. A. (2010). Cancer, anticipatory grief, and anticipatory mourning. In K. J. Doka & A. S. Tucci (Eds.), *Living with grief: Cancer and end-of-life care* (pp. 169–180). Washington, DC: Hospice Foundation of America.

Corr, C. A. (2011). Strengths and limitations of the stage theory proposed by Elisabeth Kübler-Ross. In K. J. Doka &

A. S. Tucci (Eds.), *Beyond Kübler-Ross: New perspectives on dying, death, and grief* (pp. 3–16). Washington, DC: Hospice Foundation of America.

Corr, C. A. (2014). The death system according to Robert Kastenbaum, *Omega, Journal of Death and Dying, 70*, 13–25. doi:10.2190/OM.70.1.c

Corr, C. A. (2015a). Death education at the college and university level in North America. In J. M. Stillion & T. Attig (Eds.), *Death, dying, and bereavement: Contemporary perspectives, institutions, and practice* (pp. 207–219). New York: Springer.

Corr, C. A. (2015b). Let's stop "staging" persons who are coping with loss. *Illness, Crisis and Loss, 23*(3), 226–241. doi:10.1177/1054137315585423

Corr, C. A. (2015c). Teaching about life and living in courses on death and dying. *Omega, Journal of Death and Dying, 73*, 174–187. doi:10.1177/0030222815575902

Corr, C. A. (2015d). Four lessons from "The Horse on the Dining-Room Table". *Omega, Journal of Death and Dying, 73*, 250–262. doi:10.1177/0030222815576125

Corr, C. A., & Balk, D. E. (Eds.). (1996). *Handbook of adolescent death and bereavement*. New York: Springer.

Corr, C. A., & Balk, D. E. (Eds.). (2010). *Children's encounters with death, bereavement, and coping*. New York: Springer.

Corr, C. A., & Corr, D. M. (Eds.). (1983). *Hospice care: Principles and practice*. New York: Springer.

Corr, C. A., & Corr, D. M. (Eds.). (1985a). *Hospice approaches to pediatric care*. New York: Springer.

Corr, C. A., & Corr, D. M. (1985b). Situations involving children: A challenge for the hospice movement. *Hospice Journal, 1*, 63–77.

Corr, C. A., & Corr, D. M. (1985c). Pediatric hospice care. *Pediatrics, 76*(5), 774–780.

Corr, C. A., & Corr, D. M. (1988). What is pediatric hospice care? *Children's Health Care, 17*, 4–11.

Corr, C. A., & Corr, D. M. (1992a). Adult hospice day care. *Death Studies, 16*, 155–171. doi:10.1080/07481189208252565

Corr, C. A., & Corr, D. M. (1992b). Children's hospice care. *Death Studies, 16*, 431–449. doi:10.1080/07481189208252590

Corr, C. A., & Corr, D. M. (Eds.). (1996). *Handbook of childhood death and bereavement*. New York: Springer.

Corr, C. A., & Corr, D. M. (1998). Key elements in a framework for helping grieving children and adolescents. *Illness, Crisis and Loss, 6*(2), 142–160. doi:10.2190/IL6.2.c

Corr, C. A., & Corr, D. M. (2000). Anticipatory mourning and coping with dying: Similarities, differences, and suggested guidelines for helpers. In T. A. Rando (Ed.), *Clinical dimensions of anticipatory mourning: Theory and practice in working with the dying, their loved ones, and their caregivers* (pp. 223–251). Champaign, IL: Research Press.

Corr, C. A., & Corr, D. M. (2003a). Sudden infant death syndrome. In C. D. Bryant (Ed.), *Handbook of death and dying* (Vol. 1, pp. 275–283). Thousand Oaks, CA: Sage.

Corr, C. A., & Corr, D. M. (2003b). Death education. In C. D. Bryant (Ed.), *Handbook of death and dying* (Vol. 1, pp. 292–301). Thousand Oaks, CA: Sage.

Corr, C. A., & Corr, D. M. (2007a). Culture, socialization, and dying. In D. E. Balk, C. Wogrin, G. Thornton, & D. Meagher (Eds.), *ADEC handbook of thanatology* (pp. 3–9). Northbrook, IL: Association for Death Education and Counseling.

Corr, C. A., & Corr, D. M. (2007b). Historical and contemporary perspectives on loss, grief, and mourning. In D. E. Balk, C. Wogrin, G. Thornton, & D. Meagher (Eds.), *ADEC handbook of thanatology* (pp. 131–142). Northbrook, IL: Association for Death Education and Counseling.

Corr, C. A., & Corr, D. M. (2015). One family's encounters with dementia. In K. J. Doka & A. S. Tucci (Eds.). *The Longest Loss: Alzheimer's disease and dementia* (pp. 43–55). Washington, DC: Hospice Foundation of America.

Corr, C. A., & McNeil, J. N. (Eds.). (1986). *Adolescence and death*. New York: Springer.

Corr, C. A., Corr, K. M., & Ramsey, S. M. (2004). Alzheimer's disease and the challenge for hospice. In K. J. Doka (Ed.), *Living with grief: Alzheimer's disease* (pp. 227–243). Washington, DC: Hospice Foundation of America.

Corr, C. A., Doka, K. J., & Kastenbaum, R. (1999). Dying and its interpreters: A review of selected literature and some comments on the state of the field. *Omega, Journal of Death and Dying, 39*, 239–259. doi:10.2190/3KGF-52BV-QTNT-UBMX

Corr, C. A., Fuller, H., Barnickol, C. A., & Corr, D. M. (Eds.). (1991). *Sudden infant death syndrome: Who can help and how*. New York: Springer.

Corr, C. A., Nabe, C. M., & Corr, D. M. (1994). A task-based approach for understanding and evaluating funeral practices. *Thanatos, 19*(2), 10–15.

Corr, C. A., & the Members of the Executive Committee of the National Donor Family Council. (2001). The National Donor Family Council and its Giving, Grieving, Growing™ program. *Progress in Transplantation, 11*, 255–260. doi:10.1177/152692480101100406

Corr, C. A., & the Staff of the Dougy Center. (1991). Support for grieving children: The Dougy Center and the hospice philosophy. *American Journal of Hospice and Palliative Care, 8*(4), 23–27. doi:10.1177/104990919100800402

Coste, J. K. (2003). *Learning to speak Alzheimer's: A groundbreaking approach for everyone dealing with the disease*. Boston: Houghton Mifflin.

Counts, D. R., & Counts, D. A. (Eds.). (1991). *Coping with the final tragedy: Cultural variation in dying and grieving*. Amityville, NY: Baywood.

Cousins, N. (1979). *Anatomy of an illness as perceived by the patient: Reflections on healing and regeneration*. New York: Norton.

Cousins, N. (1989). *Head first: The biology of hope*. New York: E. P. Dutton.

Coutant, H. (1974). *First snow*. New York: Knopf.

Coward, H. (2005). *Life after death in world religions*. Maryknoll, NY: Orbis Books.

Cowell, A. (2007, February 4). Deadly bird flu confirmed in British turkeys. *New York Times*, p. 10.

Cowherd, R. (2004). *Healing the spirit: Inspirational stories of organ and tissue donors and their families*. Virginia Beach, VA: LifeNet Donor Memorial Foundation.

Cox, C., & Monk, A. (1993). Hispanic culture and family care of Alzheimer's patients. *Health and Social Work, 18*(2), 92–100. doi:10.1093/hsw/18.2.92

Cox, G. (2010). *Death and the American Indian*. Omaha, NE: Grief Illustrated Press, Omaha, Nebraska.

Cox, G. R., & Fundis, R. J. (Eds.). (1992). *Spiritual, ethical and pastoral aspects of death and bereavement*. Amityville, NY: Baywood.

Cox, G. R., & Stevenson, R. G. (Eds.). (2013). *Final acts: The end of life, hospice and palliative care*. Amityville, NY: Baywood.

Cox, G. R., Bendiksen, R. A., & Stevenson, R. G. (Eds.). (2004a). *Complicated grieving and bereavement: Understanding and treating people experiencing loss*. Amityville, NY: Baywood.

Cox, G. R., Bendiksen, R. A., & Stevenson, R. G. (Eds.). (2004b). *Making sense of death: Spiritual, personal, and pastoral aspects of dying and bereavement*. Amityville, NY: Baywood.

Crase, D. R., & Crase, D. (1976). Helping children understand death. *Young Children, 32*(1), 21–25.

Crase, D. R., & Crase, D. (1984). Death education in the schools for older children. In H. Wass & C. A. Corr (Eds.), *Childhood and death* (pp. 345–363). Washington, DC: Hemisphere.

Craven, J., & Wald, F. S. (1975). Hospice care for dying patients. *American Journal of Nursing, 75*, 1816–1822.

Crawford, S. C. (1995). *Dilemmas of life and death: Hindu ethics in a North American context*. Albany, NY: State University of New York Press.

Cremation Association of North America. (2016, October 10). Annual report. Chicago, IL: Author.

Crenshaw, D. A. (2002). *Bereavement: Counseling the grieving throughout the life cycle*. Eugene, OR: Wipf & Stock Publisher.

Crenshaw, D. A. (Ed.). (2010). Child and adolescent psychotherapy: Wounded spirits and healing paths. Lanham, MD: Lexington Books.

Crettaz, B. (2010). *Cafés mortels*. Genève, Switzerland: Labor et Fides.

Crissman, J. K. (1994). *Death and dying in central Appalachia: Changing attitudes and practices*. Urbana: University of Illinois Press.

Crowder, L. (2000). Chinese funerals in San Francisco Chinatown: American Chinese expressions in mortuary ritual performance. *Journal of American Folklore, 113*(450), 451–463. doi:10.2307/542042

Crowe, D. M. (2004). *Oskar Schindler: The untold account of his life, wartime activities and the true story behind the list*. Boulder, CO: Westview Press.

Cullen, D. (2009). *Columbine*. New York: Twelve/Hachette Book Group.

Cullen, M., & Irving, S. (2014). *Get it together: Organize your records so your family won't have to* (6th ed.). Berkeley, CA: Nolo.

Cummings, T. (2013). *Untangling Alzheimer's: The guide for families and professionals* (2nd ed.). North Charleston, SC: The Dementia Association.

Currier, J. M., Holland, J. M., & Neimeyer, R. A. (2007). The effectiveness of bereavement interventions with children: A meta-analytic review of controlled outcome research. *Journal of Clinical Child & Adolescent Psychology, 36*, 253–259. doi:10.1080/15374410701279669

Curtis, J. R., Nielsen, E. L., Treece, P. D., et al. (2011). Effect of a quality-improvement intervention on end-of-life care in the intensive care unit: A randomized trial. *American Journal of Respiratory and Critical Care Medicine, 183*, 348–355. doi:10.1164/rccm.201006-1004OC

Czarnecki, J. P. (1989). *Last traces: The lost art of Auschwitz*. New York: Atheneum.

Czech, D. (1990). *Auschwitz chronicle, 1939–1945*. New York: Holt.

Dadrian, V. N. (2003). *The history of the Armenian genocide: Ethnic conflict from the Balkans to Anatolia to the Caucasus* (6th rev. ed.). New York: Berghahn Books.

Daher, D. (2003). *And the passenger was death: The drama and trauma of losing a child*. Amityville, NY: Baywood.

Dain, A. S., Bradley, E. H., Hurzeler, R., & Aldridge, M. D. (2015). Massage, music, and art therapy in hospice: Results of a national survey. *Journal of Pain and Symptom Management, 49*, 1035–1041. doi:10.1016/j.jpainsymman.2014.11.295

Dallas, R. H., Kimmel, A., Wilkins, M. L., et al. (2016). Acceptability of family-centered advanced care planning for adolescents with HIV. *Pediatrics, 138*(6), 1–10. doi:10.1542/peds.2016-1854

Dan, B., Fonteyne, C., & Clément de Cléty, S. (2014). Self-requested euthanasia for children in Belgium. *Lancet, 383,* 671–672. doi:10.1016/S0140-6736(14)60110-0

Danforth, L. M. (1982). *The death rituals of rural Greece.* Princeton, NJ: Princeton University Press.

Danielson, B. L., LaPree, A. J., Odland, M. D., & Steffens, E. K. (1998). Attitudes and beliefs concerning organ donation among Native Americans in the upper Midwest. *Journal of Transplant Coordination, 8,* 153–156. doi:10.7182/prtr.1.8.3.f89854842113un43

Davidson, A. (2015). *Social determinants of health: A comparative approach.* New York: Oxford University Press.

Davidson, G. W. (1975). *Living with dying.* Minneapolis, MN: Augsburg Fortress.

Davidson, G. W. (1984). *Understanding mourning: A guide for those who grieve.* Minneapolis, MN: Augsburg Fortress.

Davidson, L. E., Rosenberg, M. L., Mercy, J., & Franklin, J. (1989). An epidemiologic study of risk factors in two teenage suicide clusters. *Journal of the American Medical Association, 262,* 2687–2692. doi:10.1001/jama.1989.03430190071034

Davidson, L., & Gould, M. S. (1989). Contagion as a risk factor for youth suicide. In *Alcohol, Drug Abuse, and Mental Health Administration, Report of the secretary's task force on youth suicide* (Vol. 2, pp. 88–109). Washington, DC: U.S. Government Printing Office.

Davies, B. (1999). *Shadows in the sun: The experiences of sibling bereavement in childhood.* Washington, DC: Taylor & Francis.

Davies, B., & Howell, D. (1998). Special services for children. In D. Doyle, G. W. C. Hanks, & N. MacDonald (Eds.), *Oxford textbook of palliative medicine* (2nd ed., pp. 1077–1084). New York: Oxford University Press.

Davies, B., Brenner, P., Orloff, S., Sumner, L., & Worden, J. W. (2002). Addressing spirituality in pediatric hospice and palliative care. *Journal of Palliative Care, 18*(1), 59–67.

Davies, B., Deveau, E., deVeber, B., et al. (1998). Experiences of mothers in five countries whose child died of cancer. *Cancer Nursing, 21*(5), 301–311.

Davies, B., Gudmundsdottir, M., Worden, J. W., et al. (2004). "Living in the dragon's shadow": Fathers' experiences of a child's life-limiting illness. *Death Studies, 28,* 111–135. doi:10.1080/07481180490254501

Davies, B., Reimer, J. C., Brown, P., & Martens, N. (1995). *Fading away: The experience of transition in families with terminal illness.* Amityville, NY: Baywood.

Davies, B., Sehring, S. A., Partridge, J. C., et al. (2008). Barriers to palliative care for children: Perceptions of pediatric health care providers. *Pediatrics, 121*(2), 282–288. doi:10.1542/peds.2006-3153

Davies, D. (1993). Cluster suicide in rural western Canada. *Canadian Journal of Psychiatry, 38,* 515–519.

Davies, R. E. (1999). The Diana community nursing team and paediatric palliative care. *British Journal of Nursing, 8,* 506–511. doi:10.12968/bjon.1999.8.8.6629

Davis, B. D., Norton, H. J., & Jacobs, D. G. (2013). The Organ Donation Breakthrough Collaborative: Has it made a difference? *American Journal of Surgery, 205,* 381–386. doi:10.1016/j.amjsurg.2012.11.004

Davis, C. G., & Nolen-Hoeksema, S. (2001). Loss and meaning: How do people make sense of loss? *American Behavioral Scientist, 44,* 726–741. doi:10.1177/0002764201044005003

Davis, C. G., Wortman, C. B., Lehman, D. R., & Silver, R. C. (2000). Searching for meaning in loss: Are clinical assumptions correct? *Death Studies, 24,* 497–540. doi:10.1080/07481180050121471

Davis, D. L. (2016). *Empty cradle, broken heart: Surviving the death of your baby* (3rd ed.). Golden, CO: Fulcrum.

Davis, D. S. (1994). Method in Jewish bioethics. In P. F. Camenisch (Ed.), *Religious methods and resources in bioethics* (pp. 109–126). Dordrecht, Germany: Kluwer.

Davis, J. (1995). The bait. In J. Davis, *Scrimmage of appetite* (pp. 12–13). Akron, OH: University of Akron Press.

Davis, K., Stremikis, K., Squires, D., & Schoen, C. (2014, June). *Mirror, mirror on the wall, 2014 update: How the U.S. health care system compares internationally.* New York: The Commonwealth Fund.

Davison, A., & Evans, S. (2014). *Care for the dying: A practical and pastoral guide.* Eugene, OR: Cascade Books.

Dawidowicz, L. S. (1975). *The war against the Jews 1933–1945.* New York: Holt, Rinehart & Winston.

De Leo, D., Cimitan, A., Dyregrov, K., Grad, O., & Andriessen, K. (Eds.). (2014). *Bereavement after traumatic death: Helping the survivors.* Ashland, OH: Hogrefe Publishing.

D'Epinay, C. J. L., Cavalli, S., & Spini, D. (2003). The death of a loved one: Impact on health and relationships in very old age. *Omega, Journal of Death and Dying, 47,* 265–284. doi:10.2190/3GMV-PGL9-UD68-NEKW

De Vries, B., & Roberts, P. (Eds.). (2004). Expressions of grief on the World Wide Web [Special issue]. *Omega, Journal of Death and Dying, 49*(1).

De Vries, B., & Rutherford, J. (2004). Memorializing loved ones on the World Wide Web. *Omega, Journal of Death and Dying, 49,* 5–26. doi:10.2190/DR46-RU57-UY6P-NEWM

De Wachter, M. A. M. (1989). Active euthanasia in the Netherlands. *Journal of the American Medical Association, 262,* 3315–3319. doi:10.1001/jama.1989.03430230101034

De Wachter, M. A. M. (1992). Euthanasia in the Netherlands. *Hastings Center Report, 22*(2), 23–30. doi:10.2307/3562561

Deaton, R. L., & Berkan, W. A. (1995). *Planning and managing death issues in the schools: A handbook.* Westport, CT: Greenwood Press.

DeBaggio, T. (2003). *Losing my mind: An intimate look at life with Alzheimer's.* New York: Free Press.

DeBaggio, T. (2007). *When it gets dark: An enlightened reflection on life with Alzheimer's.* New York: Free Press.

DeCesare, M. (2015). *Death on demand: Jack Kevorkian and the right-to-die movement.* Lanham, MD: Roman & Littlefield.

DeFede, J. (2002). *The day the world came to town: 9/11 in Gander, Newfoundland.* New York: ReganBooks/Harper Collins.

DeFord, B., & Gilbert, R. B. (Eds.). (2013). *Living, loving and loss: The interplay of intimacy, sexuality and grief.* Amityville, NY: Baywood.

DeGroot, J. M. (2012). Maintaining relational continuity with the deceased on Facebook. *Omega, Journal of Death and Dying, 65*(3), 195–212. doi:10.2190/OM.65.3.c

Delgado, M., & Tennstedt, S. (1997a). Making the case for culturally appropriate community services: Puerto Rican elders and their caregivers. *Health and Social Work, 22*(4), 246–255. doi:10.1093/hsw/22.4.246

Delgado, M., & Tennstedt, S. (1997b). Puerto Rican sons as primary caregivers of elderly parents. *Social Work, 42*(2), 125–134. doi:10.1093/sw/42.2.125

Demi, A. S., & Miles, M. S. (1987). Parameters of normal grief: A Delphi study. *Death Studies, 11,* 397–412. doi:10.1080/07481188708252206

Demi, A. S., & Miles, M. S. (1988). Suicide bereaved parents: Emotional distress and physical health problems. *Death Studies, 12,* 297–307.

Denny, T. (2016). *Being with the dying. Memories of a grateful hospice volunteer.* Mahomet, IL: Mayhaven Publishing.

Des Pres, T. (1976). *The survivor: An anatomy of life in the death camps.* New York: Oxford University Press.

Desserich, K., & Desserich, B. (2009). *Notes left behind*. New York: HarperCollins.

Detmer, C. M., & Lamberti, J. W. (1991). Family grief. *Death Studies, 15*, 363–374. doi:10.1080/07481189108252441

Deutsch, H. (1937). Absence of grief. *Psychoanalytic Quarterly, 6*, 12–22.

DeVita-Raeburn, E. (2004). *The empty room: Understanding sibling loss*. New York: Scribners.

Diamant, A. (1994, October). Special report: Media violence. *Parents Magazine*, 40–41, 45.

Diamond, R. (1992). *Making gray gold: Narratives of nursing home care*. Chicago: University of Chicago Press.

Dickens, C. (1963). *Dombey and son* (E. Johnson, Ed.). New York: Dell. (Original work published 1848)

Dickinson, G. E. (2012). Twenty-first century end-of-life issues in selected U.S. professional schools. *Illness, Crisis & Loss, 20*, 19–32. doi:10.2190/IL.20.1.c

Didion, J. (2007). *The year of magical thinking*. New York: Vintage.

Didion, J. (2012). *Blue nights*. New York: Vintage.

Disaster Mortuary Operational Response Team (DMORT). (1998). *Team member handbook*. Washington, DC: U.S. Department of Health and Human Services.

Dobbs, D. (2013, June 24). Clues in the cycle of suicide. *New York Times*. Retrieved March 16, 2015, from http://well.blogs.nytimes.com/2013/06/24/clues-in-the-cycle-of-suicide/?_r=1

Doka, K. J. (1989). Disenfranchised grief. In K. J. Doka (Ed.), *Disenfranchised grief: Recognizing hidden sorrow* (pp. 3–11). Lexington, MA: Lexington Books.

Doka, K. J. (1993a). *Living with life-threatening illness: A guide for patients, families, and caregivers*. Lexington, MA: Lexington Books.

Doka, K. J. (1993b). The spiritual needs of the dying. In K. J. Doka & J. D. Morgan (Eds.), *Death and spirituality* (pp. 143–150). Amityville, NY: Baywood.

Doka, K. J. (Ed.). (1995). *Children mourning, mourning children*. Washington, DC: Hospice Foundation of America.

Doka, K. J. (1996a). The cruel paradox: Children who are living with life-threatening illnesses. In C. A. Corr & D. M. Corr (Eds.), *Handbook of childhood death and bereavement* (pp. 89–105). New York: Springer.

Doka, K. J. (Ed.). (1996b). *Living with grief after sudden loss: Suicide, homicide, accident, heart attack, stroke*. Washington, DC: Hospice Foundation of America.

Doka, K. J. (Ed.). (2000). *Living with grief: Children, adolescents, and loss*. Washington, DC: Hospice Foundation of America.

Doka, K. J. (Ed.). (2002a). *Disenfranchised grief: New directions, challenges, and strategies for practice*. Champaign, IL: Research Press.

Doka, K. J. (Ed.). (2002b). *Living with grief: Loss in later life*. Washington, DC: Hospice Foundation of America.

Doka, K. J. (2003). The death awareness movement: Description, history, and analysis. In C. D. Bryant (Ed.), *Handbook of death and dying* (Vol. 1, pp. 50–56). Thousand Oaks, CA: Sage.

Doka, K. J. (2006). Fulfillment as Sanders' sixth phase of bereavement: The unfinished work of Catherine Sanders. *Omega, Journal of Death and Dying, 52*, 141–149. doi:10.2190/5BC9-035Q-HG1H-PALG

Doka, K. J. (Ed.). (2007a). *Living with grief: Before and after the death*. Washington, DC: Hospice Foundation of America.

Doka, K. J. (2007b). Challenging the paradigm: New understandings of grief. In K. J. Doka (Ed.), *Living with grief: Before and after the death* (pp. 87–102). Washington, DC: Hospice Foundation of America.

Doka, K. J. (Ed.). (2007c). *Death, dying and bereavement* (4 vols.). New York: Routledge. [Vol. 1, The human encounter with death; Vol. 2, Developmental perspectives; Vol. 3, Illness, dying and death; Vol. 4, Loss and grief.]

Doka, K. J. (2008). *Caring for someone who is dying*. Washington, DC: Hospice Foundation of America.

Doka, K. J. (2011). Introduction: Beyond Kübler-Ross: New perspectives on death, dying and grief. In K. J. Doka & A. S. Tucci (Eds.), *Beyond Kübler-Ross: New perspectives on dying, death, and grief* (pp. iii–xvii). Washington, DC: Hospice Foundation of America.

Doka, K. J. (2014a). The awareness of mortality: Continuing Kastenbaum's developmental legacy. *Omega, Journal of Death and Dying, 70*, 51–66. doi:10.2190/OM.70.1.g

Doka, K. J. (2014b). *Counseling individuals with life-threatening illness* (2nd ed.). New York: Springer.

Doka, K. J. (2016). *Grief is a journey: Finding your path through loss*. New York: Atria Books.

Doka, K. J. (2017). Complicated grief in the DSM-5: A brief review. In K. J. Doka & Tucci, A. S. (Eds.), *When Grief Is Complicated* (pp. 5–16). Washington, DC: Hospice Foundation of America.

Doka, K. J., & Martin, T. L. (2010). *Grieving beyond gender: Understanding the ways men and women mourn* (Rev. ed.). New York: Routledge.

Doka, K. J., & Tucci, A. S. (Eds.). (2009). *Diversity and end-of-life care*. Washington, DC: Hospice Foundation of America.

Doka, K. J., & Tucci, A. S. (Eds.). (2011). *Beyond Kübler-Ross: New perspectives on dying, death, and grief*. Washington, DC: Hospice Foundation of America.

Doka, K. J., & Tucci, A. S. (Eds.). (2014). *Living with grief: Helping adolescents cope with loss*. Washington, DC: Hospice Foundation of America.

Doka, K. J., & Tucci, A. S. (Eds.). (2017). *When grief is complicated*. Washington, DC: Hospice Foundation of America.

Doka, K. J., Jennings, B., & Corr, C. A. (Eds.). (2005). *Living with grief: Ethical dilemmas at the end of life*. Washington, DC: Hospice Foundation of America.

Dong, X., Milholland, B., & Vijg, J. (2016, October 5). Evidence for a limit to human lifespan. *Nature*. Published online; doi:10.1038/nature19793

Donnelley, N. H. (1987). *I never know what to say*. New York: Ballantine.

Doran, G., & Hansen, N. D. (2006). Constructions of Mexican American family grief after the death of a child: An exploratory study. *Cultural Diversity & Ethnic Minority Psychology, 12*(2), 199–211. doi:10.1037/1099-9809.12.2.199

Dorney, P. (2016). The empty desk: The sudden death of a nursing classmate. *Omega, Journal of Death and Dying, 74*, 164–192. doi:10.1177/0030222815598688

Doss, E. L. (2010). *Memorial mania: Public feeling in America*. Chicago: University of Chicago Press.

Doughart, J. (2014). The path from physician assisted suicide to involuntary euthanasia. *National Post*. Retrieved September 4, 2014, from http://fullcomment.nationalpost.com/2014/08/22/jackson-doughart-the-path-from-physician-assisted-suicide-to-involuntary-euthanasia/

Doughty, C. (2014). *Smoke gets in your eyes: And other lessons from the crematory*. New York: W.W. Norton.

Douglas, J. D. (1967). *The social meanings of suicide*. Princeton, NJ: Princeton University Press.

Douglas, M. (1970). *Natural symbols*. New York: Random House.

Dougy Center. (1998). *Helping the grieving student: A guide for teachers*. Portland, OR: Author.

Dougy Center. (2003). *When death impacts your school: A guide for school administrators*. Portland, OR: Author.

Doukas, D. J., & Reichel, W. (2007). *Planning for uncertainty: Living wills and other advance directives for you and your family* (2nd ed.). Baltimore: Johns Hopkins University Press.

Dowie, M. (1988). *"We have a donor": The bold new world of organ transplanting.* New York: St. Martin's Press.

Dowling, J. R. (1995). *Keeping busy: A handbook of activities for persons with dementia.* Baltimore: Johns Hopkins University Press.

Downie, J. (2004). *Dying justice: A case for decriminalizing euthanasia and assisted suicide in Canada.* Toronto: University of Toronto Press.

Drapeau, C. W., & McIntosh, J. L. (for the American Association of Suicidology). (2016, December 23). *U.S.A. suicide 2015: Official final data.* Washington, DC: American Association of Suicidology. Retrieved from http://www.suicidology.org

Dreazen, Y. (2014). *The invisible front: Love and loss in an era of endless war.* New York: Random House.

Duarté-Vélez, Y. M., & Bernal, G. (2007). Suicide behavior among Latino and Latina adolescents: Conceptual and methodological issues. *Death Studies, 31*(5), 435–455. doi:10.1080/07481180701244579

DuBoulay, S. (1984). *Cicely Saunders: The founder of the modern hospice movement.* London: Hodder & Stoughton.

Dukeminier, J., & Sitkoff, R. H. (2013). *Wills, trusts, and estates* (9th ed.). Rockville, MD: Aspen Systems Corp.

Dumanovsky, T., Augustin, R., Rogers, M., et al. (2015). The growth of palliative care in U.S. hospitals: A status report. *Journal of Palliative Medicine, 19*, 8–15. doi:10.1089/jpm.2015.0351

Dumont, R., & Foss, D. (1972). *The American view of death: Acceptance or denial?* Cambridge, MA: Schenkman.

Duncan, I. (1927). *My life.* Garden City, NY: Garden City Publishing Co.

Dunlop, R. J., & Hockley, J. M. (1998). *Hospital based palliative care teams: The hospital-hospice interface* (2nd ed.). Oxford: Oxford University Press.

Dunn, R. G., & Morrish-Vidners, D. (1988). The psychological and social experience of suicide survivors. *Omega, Journal of Death and Dying, 18*, 175–215. doi:10.2190/6K91-GN16-0DF6-5FUE

Dunne, E. J., McIntosh, J. L., & Dunne-Maxim, K. (Eds.). (1987). *Suicide and its aftermath: Understanding and counseling the survivors.* New York: Norton.

Dunsmore, J. C., & Quine, S. (1995). Information support and decision making needs and preferences of adolescents with cancer: Implications for health professionals. *Journal of Psychosocial Oncology, 13*(4), 39–56. doi:10.1300/J077V13N04_03

Durkheim, E. (1951). *Suicide: A study in sociology* (J. A. Spaulding & G. Simpson, Trans.). Glencoe, IL: Free Press. (Original work published 1897)

Durkheim, E. (1954). *The elementary forms of religious life* (J. W. Swaine, Trans.). London: Allen & Unwin. (Original work published 1915)

Dutton, Y. C., & Zisook, S. (2005). Adaptation to bereavement. *Death Studies, 29*, 877–903. doi:10.1080/07481180500298826

Dwyer, T., Ponsonby, A.-L., Blizzard, L., Newman, N. M., & Cochrane, J. A. (1995). The contribution of changes in the prevalence of prone sleeping position to the decline in sudden infant death syndrome in Tasmania. *Journal of the American Medical Association, 273*, 783–789. doi:10.1001/jama.1995.03520340039033

Dyregrov, K., Dyregrov, A., & Johnsen, I. (2013). Positive and negative experiences from grief group participation: A qualitative study. *Omega, Journal of Death and Dying, 68*, 45–62. doi:10.2190/OM.68.1.c

Dyregrov, K., Dyregrov, A., & Kristensen, P. (2016). In what ways do bereaved parents after terror go on with their lives, and what seems to inhibit or promote adaptation during their grieving process? A qualitative study. *Omega, Journal of Death and Dying, 73*, 374–399. doi:10.1177/0030222816653851

Ebadat, A., Brown, C. V., Ali, S., et al. (2014). Improving organ donation rates by modifying the family approach process. *Journal of Trauma and Acute Care Surgery, 76*(6), 1473–1475. doi:10.1097/TA.0b013e318265cdb9.

Eckert, P. (2007, January 15). Experts see bird flu challenge to US health system. *Reuters Health Information.* Retrieved from http://www.nlm.nih.gov/medlineplus/news/fullstory_43839.htm

Edelman, H. (2007). *Motherless mothers: How losing a mother shapes the parent you become.* New York: Harper Perennial.

Edelman, H. (2014). *Motherless daughters: The legacy of loss.* Cambridge, MA: Da Capo Press.

Education Development Center. (2003). *The initiative for pediatric palliative care curriculum.* Newton, MA: Author.

Edwards, P. (Ed.). (1997). *Immortality.* Amherst, NY: Prometheus Books.

Egan, K. (2016). *On living.* New York: Riverhead Books.

Egeland, J., & Sussex, J. (1985). Suicide and family loading for affective disorders. *Journal of the American Medical Association, 254*, 915–918. doi:10.1001/jama.1985.03360070053022

Egnoto, M. J., Sirianni, J. M., Ortega, C. R., & Stefanone, M. (2014). Death on the digital landscape: A preliminary investigation into the grief process and motivations behind participation in the online memoriam. *Omega, Journal of Death and Dying, 69*(3), 283–304. doi:10.2190/OM.69.3.d

Ehlers, A. (2006). Understanding and treating complicated grief: What can we learn from posttraumatic stress disorder? *Clinical Psychology: Science and Practice, 13*, 135–140. doi:10.1111/j.1468-2850.2006.00015.x

eHospice. (2015). Calculating the global need for children's palliative care. Retrieved June 3, 2015, from http://www.ehospice.com/usa/articleview/tabid/10708/articleid/15335/language/en-gb/calculating-the-global-need-for-children-s-palliative-care.aspx?utm_campaign=website&utm_source=sendgrid.com&utm_medium=email

Eichrodt, W. (1967). *Theology of the old testament*, Vol. 2. (J. A. Baker, Trans.). Philadelphia: Westminster.

Eisen, G. (1988). *Children and play in the Holocaust: Games among the shadows.* Amherst, MA: University of Massachusetts Press.

Eisenberg, J. B. (2005). *Using Terri: The religious right's conspiracy to take away our rights.* San Francisco: HarperSanFrancisco.

Eisenbruch, M. (1984). Cross-cultural aspects of bereavement. II: Ethnic and cultural variations in the development of bereavement practices. *Culture, Medicine and Psychiatry, 8*, 315–347. doi:10.1007/BF00114661

Elias, N. (1991). On human beings and their emotions: A process-sociological essay. In M. Featherstone, M. Hepworth, & B. S. Turner (Eds.), *The body: Social process and cultural theory* (pp. 103–125). London: Sage.

Elison, J. (2007, January 29). The stage of grief no one admits to: Relief. *Newsweek*, p. 18.

Elison, J., & McGonigle, C. (2004). *Liberating losses: When death brings relief.* Cambridge, MA: Perseus.

El-Jawahri, A., Jackson, V. A., Greer, J. A., et al. (2016). Effect of early integrated palliative care on family caregivers (FC) outcomes for patients with gastrointestinal and lung cancer. *Journal of Clinical Oncology, 24*(26, Suppl.), 234–234. doi:10.1200/jco.2016

Elk, R., (2016). Special issue: Palliative and end-of-life care for African Americans. *Journal of Palliative Medicine, 19*(2).

Elkind, D. (1967). Egocentrism in adolescence. *Child Development, 38,* 1025–1034. doi:10.2307/1127100

Ellenbogen, S., & Gratton, F. (2001). Do they suffer more? Reflections on research comparing suicide survivors to other survivors. *Suicide and Life-Threatening Behavior, 31,* 83–90. doi:10.1521/suli.31.1.83.21315

Ellershaw, J., & Wilkinson, S. (Eds.). (2011). *Care of the dying: A pathway to excellence* (2nd ed.). New York: Oxford University Press.

Elliot, G. (1972). *The twentieth century book of the dead.* New York: Random House.

Elmer, L. (1990). *Why her, why now: A man's journey through love and death and grief.* New York: Bantam.

Emanuel, E. J., Onwuteaka-Philipsen, B. D., Urwin, J. W., & Cohen, J. (2016). Attitudes and practices of euthanasia and physician-assisted suicide in the United States, Canada, and Europe. *Journal of the American Medical Association, 316*(1), 79–90. doi:10.1001/jama.2016.8499

Emanuel, L. L. (1998). *Regulating how we die: The ethical, medical, and legal issues surrounding physician assisted suicide.* Cambridge, MA: Harvard University Press.

Emerson, R. W. (1970). *The journals and miscellaneous notebooks of Ralph Waldo Emerson* (Vol. 8, 1841–1843). (W. H. Gilman & J. E. Parsons, Eds.). Cambridge, MA: Belknap Press of Harvard University Press.

Emswiler, M. A., & Emswiler, J. P. (2000). *Guiding your child through grief.* New York: Bantam.

End-of-Life Nursing Education Consortium (ELNEC). (2003). *Advancing palliative care in pediatric nursing: ELNEC— Pediatric palliative care.* Duarte, CA: American Association of Colleges of Nursing and City of Hope National Medical Center.

Engel, G. L. (1961). Is grief a disease? A challenge for medical research. *Psychosomatic Medicine, 23,* 18–22.

Englebrecht, C. M., Mason, D. T., & Adams, P. J. (2016). Responding to homicide: An exploration of the ways in which family members react to and cope with the death of a loved one. *Omega, Journal of Death and Dying, 73,* 355–373. doi:10.1177/003022815590708

Engmann, B. (2014). *Near-death experiences. Heavenly insight or human illusion?* New York: Springer International Publishing.

Enright, D. J. (Ed.). (1983). *The Oxford book of death.* New York: Oxford University Press.

Epstein, A. S., Prigerson, H. G., O'Reilly, E. M., & Maciejewski, P. K. (2016). Discussions of life expectancy and changes in illness understanding in patients with advanced cancer. *Journal of Clinical Oncology, 34*(20), 2398–2403. doi:10.1200/JCO.2015.63.6696

Erickson, K. A. (2013). *How we die now: Intimacy and the work of dying.* Philadelphia: Temple University Press.

Erikson, E. H. (1959). Identity and the life cycle: Selected papers. *Psychological Issues, 1,* 1–171.

Erikson, E. H. (1963). *Childhood and society* (2nd ed.). New York: Norton. (Original edition published 1950)

Erikson, E. H. (1968). *Identity: Youth and crisis.* London: Faber & Faber.

Erikson, E. H. (1982). *The life cycle completed: A review.* New York: Norton.

Erikson, E. H., & Erikson, J. M. (1981). On generativity and identity: From a conversation with Erik and Joan Erikson. *Harvard Educational Review, 51,* 249–269. doi:10.1007/BF00114661

Erikson, E. H., Erikson, J. M., & Kivnick, H. Q. (1986). *Vital involvements in old age.* New York: Norton.

Erlangsen, A., Nordentoft, M., Conwell, Y., et al. (2011). Key considerations for preventing suicide in older adults: Consensus opinions of an expert panel. *Crisis, The Journal of Crisis Intervention and Suicide Prevention, 32*(2): 106–109. doi:10.1027/0227-5910/a000053

Eron, L. D. (1993). *The problem of media violence and children's behavior.* New York: Guggenheim Foundation.

Ertelt, S. (2010, August 12). Dutch government: Euthanasia cases rose 13 percent in 2009, now 2% of all deaths. *LifeNews .com.* Retrieved January 15, 2011, from http://www.lifenews .com/2010/08/12/bio-3142/

Esperti, R. A., & Peterson, R. L. (2014). *21st century loving trust: Revised and expanded for the new economy.* Costa Mesa, CA: Quantum Press.

Esperti, R. A., Peterson, R. L., & Cahoone, D. K. (2012). *Protect and enhance your estate: Definitive strategies for estate and wealth planning* (3rd ed.). New York: McGraw-Hill.

Evanisko, M. J., Beasley, C. L., & Brigham, L. E. (1998). Readiness of critical care physicians and nurses to handle requests for organ donation. *American Journal of Critical Care, 7,* 4–12.

Evans, J. (1971). *Living with a man who is dying: A personal memoir.* New York: Taplinger.

Evans, R. P. (2012). *The Christmas box.* New York: Simon & Schuster.

Everett, H. (2002). *Roadside crosses in contemporary memorial culture.* Denton: University of North Texas Press.

Ewalt, P. L., & Perkins, L. (1979). The real experience of death among adolescents: An empirical study. *Social Casework, 60,* 547–551.

Fabiny, A., & Sabatino, C. P. (2013). *Living wills: A guide to advance directives, health care power of attorney, and other key documents.* Cambridge, MA: Harvard Health Publications.

Fadiman, A. (1997). *The spirit catches you and you fall down: A Hmong child, her American doctors, and the collision of two cultures.* New York: Farrar, Straus & Giroux.

Fagerlin, A., & Schneider, C. E. (2004). Enough: The failure of the living will. *Hastings Center Report, 34*(2), 30–42. doi:10.2307/3527683

Falconer, K., Sachsenweger, M., Gibson, K., & Norman, H. (2011). Grieving in the Internet age. *New Zealand Journal of Psychology, 40*(3), 79–88.

Fallowfield, L. J., Jenkins, V. A., & Beveridge, H. A. (2002). Truth may hurt but deceit hurts more: Communication in palliative care. *Palliative Medicine, 16,* 297–303. doi:10.1191/0269216302pm575oa

Family Caregiver Alliance. (2015). Selected long-term care statistics. Retrieved July16, 2016, from https://www.caregiver.org /selected-long-term-care-statistics

Fanestil, J. (2006). *Mrs. Hunter's happy death: Lessons on living from people preparing to die.* New York: Doubleday.

Faragher, R. G. A. (2015). Should we treat aging as a disease? The consequences and dangers of miscategorisation. *Frontiers in Genetics, 6,* 171. doi:10.3389/fgene.2015.00171

Farber, L. Z., & Sabatino, C. A. (2007). A therapeutic summer weekend camp for grieving children: Supporting clinical practice through empirical evaluation. *Journal of Child and Adolescent Social Work, 24,* 385–402. doi:10.1007/s10560-007-0090-0

Farberow, N. L. (1983). Relationships between suicide and depression: An overview. *Psychiatria Fennica Supplementum, 14,* 9–19.

Farberow, N. L. (Ed.). (1980). *The many faces of suicide: Indirect self-destructive behavior.* New York: McGraw-Hill.

Farberow, N. L., & Shneidman, E. S. (Eds.). (1965). *The cry for help.* New York: McGraw-Hill.

Farberow, N. L., Gallagher-Thompson, D., Gilewski, M., & Thompson, L. (1992). Changes in grief and mental health of bereaved spouses of older suicides. *Journal of Gerontology*, *47*(6), 357–366. doi:10.1093/geronj/47.6.P357

Farrell, J. J. (1980). *Inventing the American way of death: 1830–1920*. Philadelphia: Temple University Press.

Fauci, A. S., & Marston, H. D. (2015). Ending the HIV/AIDS pandemic: Follow the science. *New England Journal of Medicine*, *373*, 2197–2199. doi:10.1056/NEJMp1502020

Faulkner, W. (1930). *As I lay dying*. New York: Random House.

Fazakerley, J., Butlin-Battler, H., & Bradish, G. (2012). *Just stay: A couple's last journey together*. Toronto: Words Indeed Publishing.

Feifel, H. (Ed.). (1959). *The meaning of death*. New York: McGraw-Hill.

Feifel, H. (1963a). The taboo on death. *American Behavioral Scientist*, *6*(9), 66–67. doi:10.1177/000276426300600919

Feifel, H. (1963b). Death. In N. L. Farberow (Ed.), *Taboo topics* (pp. 8–21). New York: Atherton.

Feifel, H. (1977a). Preface and introduction: Death in contemporary America. In H. Feifel (Ed.), *New meanings of death* (pp. xiii–xiv, 4–12). New York: McGraw-Hill.

Feifel, H. (Ed.). (1977b). *New meanings of death*. New York: McGraw-Hill.

Feigelman, W., Jordan, J. R., McIntosh, J. L., & Feigelman, B. (2012). *Devastating losses: How parents cope with the death of a child to suicide or drugs*. New York: Springer.

Feldman, D. B. (2006). Can suicide be ethical? A utilitarian perspective on the appropriateness of choosing to die. *Death Studies*, *30*, 529–538. doi:10.1080/07481180600742517

Feldman, D. M., & Rosner, F. (Eds.). (1984). *Compendium on medical ethics* (6th ed.). New York: Federation of Jewish Philanthropies of New York.

Fenwick, P., & Fenwick, E. (1995). *The truth in the light: An investigation of over 300 near-death experiences*. New York: Berkley Books.

Fenwick, P., & Fenwick, E. (2008). *The art of dying*. New York: Continuum.

Ferman, T. J., Smith, G. E., & Melom, B. (2008). *Understanding behavioral changes in dementia*. Lilburn, GA: Lewy Body Dementia Association. Retrieved February 23, 2011, from www.lbda.org/feature/1898/understanding-behavioral-changes-in-dementia.htm

Ferrell, B. R., Coyle, N., & Paice, J. (Eds.). (2015). *Oxford textbook of palliative nursing* (4th ed.). New York: Oxford University Press.

Ferris, F. D., Balfour, H. M., Bowen, K., et al. (2002). *A model to guide hospice palliative care*. Ottawa, Canada: Canadian Hospice Palliative Care Association.

Ferszt, G. G., & Leveillee, M. (2009, May/June). Telling the difference between grief and depression. *LippincottNursingCenter.com*, pp. 12–13.

Feudtner, C., Kang, T. I., Hexem, K. R., et al. (2011). Pediatric palliative care patients: A prospective multicenter cohort study. *Pediatrics*, *127*, 1094–1101. doi:10.1542/peds.2010-3225

Feudtner, C., & Morrison, W. (2012). The darkening veil of "do everything". *Archives of Pediatric and Adolescent Medicine*, *166*, 694–695. doi:10.1001/archpediatrics.2012.175

Feudtner, C., Womer, J., Augustin, R., et al. (2013). Pediatric palliative care programs in children's hospitals: A cross-sectional national survey. *Pediatrics*, *132*, 1063–1070. doi:10.1542/peds.2013-1286

Field, D., Hockey, J., & Small, N. (Eds.). (1997). *Death, gender and ethnicity*. New York: Routledge.

Field, M. J., & Berhman, R. E. (Eds.). (2003). *When children die: Improving palliative and end-of-life care for children and their families*. Washington, DC: National Academies Press.

Field, M. J., & Cassel, C. K. (Eds.). (1997). *Approaching death: Improving care at the end of life*. Washington, DC: National Academies Press.

Field, N. P. (Ed.). (2006). Continuing bonds in adaptation to bereavement: I. Theoretical and empirical foundations; II. Clinical and cultural considerations. [Special Series.] *Death Studies*, *30*(8, 9).

Figley, C. R. (1999). *Traumatology of grieving*. New York: Brunner/Mazel.

Figley, C. R. (Ed.). (2015). *Compassion fatigue: Coping with secondary traumatic stress disorder in those who treat the traumatized*. New York: Bruner/Mazel.

Fine, P., & Kestenbaum, M. (Eds.). (2012). *The hospice companion: Best practices for interdisciplinary assessment and care of common problems during the last phase of life* (2nd ed.). New York: Oxford University Press.

Fine, R. L. (2005). From Quinlan to Schiavo: Medical, ethical, and legal issues in severe brain injury. *Baylor University Medical Center Proceedings*, *18*(4), 303–310.

Fineberg, H. V. (2014). Pandemic preparedness and response: Lessons from the H1N1 influenza of 2009. *New England Journal of Medicine*, *370*, 1335–1342. doi:10.1056/NEJMra1208802

Fingerhut, L. A., & Kleinman, J. C. (1989). Mortality among children and youth. *American Journal of Public Health*, *79*, 899–901. doi:10.2105/AJPH.79.7.899

Fingerhut, L. A., Kleinman, J. C., Godfrey, E., & Rosenberg, H. (1991). Firearm mortality among children, youth, and young adults 1–34 years of age, trends and current status: United States, 1979–88. *Monthly Vital Statistics Report*, *39*(11), Suppl. Hyattsville, MD: National Center for Health Statistics.

Finn, R. (2000). *Organ transplants: Making the most of your gift of life*. Sebastopol, CA: O'Reilly Media/Patient-Centered Guides.

Fiore, M. C. (2016). Tobacco control in the Obama era: Substantial progress, remaining challenges. *New England Journal of Medicine*, *375*, 1410–1412. doi:10.1056/NEJMp1607850.

Fiorini, J. J., & Mullen, J. A. (2006). *Counseling children and adolescents through grief and loss*. Champaign, IL: Research Press.

First International Conference on Islamic Medicine. (1981). Islamic Code of Medical Ethics. (Reprinted in *Choosing death; Active euthanasia, religion, and the public debate*, p. 62, by R. Hamel, Ed., 1991, Philadelphia: Trinity Press International)

Fitts, J. (2015, March 23). Silent treatment. From the author's *Grace Drops* essays. [gracedrops=gmail.com@mail75.atl11.rsgsv.net]

Fitzgerald, H. (1995). *The mourning handbook: A complete guide for the bereaved*. New York: Fireside.

Fitzgerald, H. (1999). *Grief at work: A manual of policies and practices*. Washington, DC: American Hospice Foundation.

Fitzgerald, H. (2000). *The grieving teen: A guide for teenagers and their friends*. New York: Simon & Schuster.

Fitzgerald, H. (2003). *Grief at school: A training guide*. Washington, DC: American Hospice Foundation.

Fitzpatrick, J., & Fitzpatrick, E. M. (2010). *A better way of dying: How to make the best choices at the end of life*. New York: Penguin.

Fleming, D. (2005). *Noah's rainbow: A father's emotional journey from the death of his son to the birth of his daughter*. Amityville, NY: Baywood.

Fleming, S. J. (1985). Children's grief: Individual and family dynamics. In C. A. Corr & D. M. Corr (Eds.), *Hospice approaches to pediatric care* (pp. 197–218). New York: Springer.

Fleming, S. J., & Adolph, R. (1986). Helping bereaved adolescents: Needs and responses. In C. A. Corr & J. N. McNeil (Eds.), *Adolescence and death* (pp. 97–118). New York: Springer.

Fleming, S., & Balmer, L. (1996). Bereavement in adolescence. In C. A. Corr & D. E. Balk (Eds.), *Handbook of adolescent death and bereavement* (pp. 139–154). New York: Springer.

Fogarty, J. A. (2000). *The magical thoughts of grieving children: Treating children with complicated mourning and advice for parents.* Amityville, NY: Baywood.

Foley, K. M., & Hendin, H. (Eds.). (2002). *The case against assisted suicide: For the right to end-of-life care.* Baltimore: Johns Hopkins University Press.

Folkman, S. (2001). Revised coping theory and the process of bereavement. In M. Stroebe, R.O. Hansson, W. Stroebe, & H. Schut, (Eds.). *Handbook of bereavement research: Consequences, coping, and care* (pp. 563–584). Washington, D.C.: American Psychological Association Press.

Folta, J. R., & Deck, E. S. (1976). Grief, the funeral, and the friend. In V. R. Pine, A. H. Kutscher, D. Peretz, et al. (Eds.), *Acute grief and the funeral* (pp. 231–240). Springfield, IL: Charles C Thomas.

Foran, R. (2013). *Organ transplants.* Edina, MN: Abdo Publishing.

Ford, G. (1979). Terminal care from the viewpoint of the National Health Service. In J. J. Bonica & V. Ventafridda (Eds.), *International symposium on pain of advanced cancer: Advances in pain research and therapy* (Vol. 2, pp. 653–661). New York: Raven Press.

Forte, A. L., Hill, M., Pazder, R., & Feudtner, C. (2004, July 26). Bereavement care interventions: A systematic review. *BMC Palliative Care, 3.* doi:10.1186/1472-684X-3-3

Foster, Z., Wald, F. S., & Wald, H. J. (1978). The hospice movement: A backward glance at its first two decades. *New Physician, 27,* 21–24.

Fox, J. (2009). *I still do: Loving and living with Alzheimer's.* New York: PowerHouse Books.

Fox, J. A. (2007). Why they kill. Retrieved May 17, 2007, from latimes.com/news/opinion/la-oe-fox17apr17,0,6739883 .story?coll5la-opinion-rightrail

Fox, J. A., & Levin, J. (2005). *Extreme killing: Understanding serial and mass murder.* Thousand Oaks, CA: Sage.

Fox, J. A., & Levin, J. (2006). *The will to kill: Explaining senseless murder.* Boston: Pearson/Allyn and Bacon.

Fox, R. C., & Swazey, J. P. (1974). *The courage to fail: A social view of organ transplants and dialysis.* Chicago: University of Chicago Press.

Fox, R. C., & Swazey, J. P. (1992). *Spare parts: Organ replacement in American society.* New York: Oxford University Press.

Francis, J. (2001, March 9). Lives crowned by love. *St. Petersburg Times,* p. 1D.

Francis, V. M. (1859). *A thesis on hospital hygiene.* New York: J. F. Trow.

Frank, A. W. (2002). *At the will of the body: Reflections on illness* (new Afterword). Boston: Houghton Mifflin.

Frank, A. W. (2010). *Letting stories breathe: A socio-narratology.* Chicago: University of Chicago Press.

Frank, A. W. (2013). *The wounded storyteller: Body, illness, and ethics* (2nd ed.). Chicago: University of Chicago Press.

Frankl, V. (1984). *Man's search for meaning.* New York: Simon & Schuster.

Frazer, J. G. (1977). *The fear of the dead in primitive religion.* New York: Arno Press.

Frean, M., Gruber, J., & Sommers, B. D. (2016). Disentangling the ACA's coverage effects: Lessons for policymakers. *New England Journal of Medicine, 375,* 1605–1608. doi:10.1056/ NEJMp1609016

Freed, R. A. (2013). *Your legacy matters: A multi-generational guide for writing your ethical will.* Minneapolis, MN: MinervaPress.

Freeman, H. P., & Payne, R. (2000). Racial injustice in health care. *New England Journal of Medicine, 342,* 1045–1047. doi:10.1056/NEJM200004063421411

Freeman, S. J. (2005). *Grief and loss: Understanding the journey.* Belmont, CA: Wadsworth.

French, C. C. (2005). Near-death experiences in cardiac arrest survivors. *Progress in Brain Research, 150,* 351–367.

Freud, A. (1958). Adolescence. *Psychoanalytic Study of the Child, 13,* 255–268.

Freud, S. (1959a). Mourning and melancholia. In J. Strachey (Ed. & Trans.), *The standard edition of the complete psychological works of Sigmund Freud* (Vol. 14, pp. 237–258). London: Hogarth Press. (Original work published 1917)

Freud, S. (1959b). *New introductory lectures on psycho-analysis.* In J. Strachey (Ed. & Trans.), *The standard edition of the complete psychological works of Sigmund Freud* (Vol. 22, pp. 1–182). London: Hogarth Press. (Original work published 1933)

Freud, S. (1959c). Thoughts for the time on war and death. In J. Strachey (Ed. & Trans.), *The standard edition of the complete psychological works of Sigmund Freud* (Vol. 14, pp. 273–300). London: Hogarth Press. (Original work published 1915)

Freud, S. (1960). *Letters of Sigmund Freud.* Edited by E. L. Freud. New York: Basic Books.

Freyer, D. R. (2004). Care of the dying adolescent: Special considerations. *Pediatrics, 113*(2), 381–388. doi:10.1542/ peds.113.2.381

Frieden, T. R., Foti, K. E., & Mermin, J. (2015). Applying public health principles to the HIV epidemic: How are we doing? *New England Journal of Medicine, 373,* 2281–2287. doi:10.1056/NEJMms1513641

Friedlander, H. (1995). *The origins of Nazi genocide: From euthanasia to the final solution.* Chapel Hill, NC: University of North Carolina Press.

Friedländer, S. (2007). *The years of extermination: Nazi Germany and the Jews, 1939–1945.* New York: HarperCollins.

Friedrich, M. J. (1999). Hospice care in the United States: A conversation with Florence Wald. *Journal of the American Medical Association, 281,* 1683–1685. doi:10.1001/ jama.281.18.1683

Friel, M., & Tehan, C. B. (1980). Counteracting burn-out for the hospice care-giver. *Cancer Nursing, 3,* 285–293.

Frist, W. H. (1989). *Transplant: A heart surgeon's account of the life and death dramas of the new medicine.* New York: Atlantic Monthly Press.

Frist, W. H. (1995). *Grand rounds and transplantation.* New York: Chapman & Hall.

Fristad, M. A., Cerel, J., Goldman, M., Weller, E. B., & Weller, R. A. (2001). The role of ritual in children's bereavement. *Omega, Journal of Death and Dying, 42,* 321–339. doi:10.2190/MC87-GQMC-VCDV-UL3U

Froelker, J. B. (2015). *Ever upward: Overcoming the life-long losses of infertility to define your own happy ending.* New York: Morgan James Publishing.

Fromme, E. K., Zive, D, Schmidt, T. A., Cook, J.N.B., & Tolle, S. W. (2014). Association between physician orders for life-sustaining treatment for scope of treatment and in-hospital death in Oregon. *Journal of the American Geriatrics Society, 62*(7), 1246–1251. doi:10.1111/jgs.12889

Frost, M. (2014). The grief grapevine: Facebook memorial pages and adolescent bereavement. *Australian Journal of Guidance and Counselling, 24*(2), 256–265. doi:10.1017/jgc.2013.30

Fulton, R. (1961). The clergyman and the funeral director: A study in role conflict. *Social Forces, 39,* 317–323. doi:10.2307/2573428

Fulton, R. (1978). The sacred and the secular: Attitudes of the American public toward death, funerals, and funeral directors. In R. Fulton & R. Bendiksen (Eds.), *Death and identity* (Rev. ed., pp. 158–172). Bowie, MD: Charles Press.

Fulton, R. (1995). The contemporary funeral: Functional or dysfunctional? In H. Wass & R. A. Neimeyer (Eds.), *Dying: Facing the facts* (pp. 185–209). Washington, DC: Taylor & Francis.

Fulton, R. (2003). Anticipatory mourning: A critique of the concept. *Mortality, 8,* 342–351. doi:10.1080/13576270310001613392

Fulton, R., & Fulton, J. (1971). A psychosocial aspect of terminal care: Anticipatory grief. *Omega, Journal of Death and Dying, 2,* 91–100. doi:10.2190/WE4J-9CJG-GJH5-R3VA

Fulton, R., & Gottesman, D. J. (1980). Anticipatory grief: A psychosocial concept reconsidered. *British Journal of Psychiatry, 137,* 45–54. doi:10.1192/bjp.139.1.79b

Funk, L. M., Waskiewich, S., & Stajduhar, K. I. (2013). Meaning-making and managing difficult feelings: Providing frontline end-of-life care. *Omega, Journal of Death and Dying, 68,* 23–43. doi:10.2190/OM.68.1.b

Furman, E. (Ed.). (1974). *A child's parent dies: Studies in childhood bereavement.* New Haven, CT: Yale University Press.

Furman, R. A. (1973). The child's capacity for mourning. In E. J. Anthony & C. Koupernik (Eds.), *The child in his family: Vol. 2, The impact of disease and death* (pp. 225–231). New York: Wiley.

Furth, G. M. (1988). *The secret world of drawings: Healing through art.* Boston: Sigo Press.

Gabb, E. M., Owens, G. R., & MacLeod, R. D. (2013). Caregivers' estimations of their children's perceptions of death as a biological concept. *Death Studies, 37,* 693–703. doi:10.1080/07481187.2012.692454

Gaes, J. (1987). *My book for kids with cansur: A child's autobiography of hope.* Aberdeen, SD: Melius & Peterson.

Galinsky, N. (1999). *When a grandchild dies: What to do, what to say, how to cope.* Houston, TX: Gal In Sky Publishing (P.O. Box 70976, Houston, TX 77270).

Gallagher-Allred, C., & Amenta, M. (Eds.). (1993). Nutrition and hydration in hospice care: Needs, strategies, ethics. [Special issue] *Hospice Journal, 9*(2/3).

Gambetta, D. (Ed.). (2006). *Making sense of suicide missions* (Rev. ed.). Oxford, UK: Oxford University Press.

Gamino, L. A., & Cooney, A. J. (2002). *When your baby dies through miscarriage or stillbirth.* Minneapolis: Augsburg Fortress.

Gandhi, M. (1980). *All men are brothers: Autobiographical reflections.* New York: Continuum.

Ganguli, M., & Rodriguez, E. G. (1999). Reporting of dementia on death certificates: A community study. *Journal of the American Geriatrics Society, 47,* 842–849. doi:10.1111/j.1532-5415.1999.tb03842.x

Gans, D., Hadler, M. W., Chen, X., et al. (2015). Impact of a pediatric palliative care program on the caregiver experience. *Journal of Hospice & Palliative Nursing, 17,* 559–565. doi:10.1097/NJH.0000000000000203

Gans, J. E. (1990). *America's adolescents: How healthy are they?* American Medical Association, Profiles of Adolescent Health Series. Chicago: American Medical Association.

Ganzini, L., Goy, E. R., Dobscha, S. K., & Prigerson, H. (2009). Mental health outcomes of family members of Oregonians who request physician aid in dying. *Journal of Pain and Symptom Management, 38*(6), 807–815. doi:10.1016/j.jpainsymman.2009.04.026.

Garber, M. (2016, January 20). Enter the grief police. *The Atlantic.* Retrieved July 26, 2016, from http://www.theatlantic.com/entertainment/archive/2016/01/enter-the-grief-police/424746/

Garciagodoy, J. (2000). *Digging the days of the dead: A reading of Mexico's Dias de muertos.* Boulder: University Press of Colorado.

Garfield, C. A. (1976). Foundations of psychosocial oncology: The terminal phase. In J. M. Vaeth (Ed.), *Breast cancer: Its impact on the patient, family, and community* (pp. 180–212). Basel, Switzerland: Karger.

Garner, B. A. (2014). *Black's law dictionary* (10th ed.). Eagan, MN: Thompson West.

Garrett, L. (1995). *The coming plague: Newly emerging diseases in a world out of balance.* New York: Penguin.

Gartley, W., & Bernasconi, M. (1967). The concept of death in children. *Journal of Genetic Psychology, 110,* 71–85. doi:10.1080/00221325.1967.10533718

Garvie, P. A., He, J., Wang, J., D'Angelo, L. J., & Lyon, M. E. (2012). An exploratory survey of end-of-life attitudes, beliefs and experiences of adolescents with HIV/AIDS and their families. *Journal of Pain and Symptom Management, 44*(3), 373–386.e 29. doi:10.1016/j.jpainsymman.2011.09.022

Gatch, M. McC. (1969). *Death: Meaning and mortality in Christian thought and contemporary culture.* New York: Seabury Press.

Gates, B. (2015, March 18). The next epidemic: Lessons from Ebola. *New England Journal of Medicine.* doi:10.1056/NEJMp1502918

Gawande, A. (2010, August 2). Letting go: What should medicine do when it can't save your life? *New Yorker, 86*(25), 36–49.

Gawande, A. (2014). *Being mortal: Medicine and what matters in the end.* New York: Metropolitan Books.

Gaylin, W., & Jennings, B. (2003). *The perversion of autonomy: The uses of coercion and constraints in a liberal society* (2nd ed.). Washington, DC: Georgetown University Press.

Geddes, G. E. (1981). *Welcome joy: Death in Puritan New England.* Ann Arbor, MI: UMI Research Press.

Geiger, G. (2002). Racial and ethnic disparities in diagnosis and treatment: A review of the evidence and a consideration of causes. In B. D. Smedley, A. Y. Stith, & A. R. Nelson (Eds.), *Unequal treatment: Confronting racial and ethnic disparities in healthcare* (pp. 417–454). Washington, DC: National Academies Press.

Gelfand, D. E., Balcazar, H., Parzuchowski, J., & Lenox, S. (2001). Mexicans and care for the terminally ill: Family, hospice, and the church. *American Journal of Hospice and Palliative Care, 18,* 391–396. doi:10.1177/104990910101800608

Gelfand, D. E., Raspa, R., Briller, S. H., & Schim, S. M. (Eds.). (2005). *End-of-life stores: Crossing disciplinary boundaries.* New York: Springer.

Genova, L. (2009). *Still Alice.* New York: Gallery Books.

Georges, J.-J., Onwuteaka-Philipsen, B. D., Muller, M. T., et al. (2007). Relatives' perspective on the terminally ill patients who died after euthanasia or physician-assisted suicide: A retrospective cross-sectional interview study in the Netherlands. *Death Studies, 31,* 1–15. doi:10.1080/07481180600985041

Gerisch, B. (1998). "This is not death, it is something safer": A psychodynamic approach to Sylvia Plath. *Death Studies, 22,* 735–761. doi:10.1080/074811898201245

Gervais, K. G. (1987). *Redefining death.* New Haven, CT: Yale University Press.

Gibbs, D. C., & DeMoss, B. (2006). *Fighting for dear life: The untold story of Terri Schiavo and what it means for all of us.* Minneapolis: Bethany House.

Gibson, P. (1994). Gay male and lesbian youth suicide. In G. Remafedi (Ed.), *Death by denial: Studies of suicide in gay and lesbian teenagers* (pp. 15–68). Boston: Alyson.

Giger, J. N. (2017). *Transcultural nursing: Assessment and intervention* (7th ed.). St. Louis, MO: Mosby.

Gignoux, J. H. (1998). *Some folk say: Stories of life, death, and beyond.* New York: FoulkeTale Publishing.

Gilbert, A., & Kline, C. B. (2006). *Always too soon: Voices of support for those who have lost both parents.* Emeryville, CA: Seal Press.

Gilbert, K. R. (1996). "We've had the same loss, why don't we have the same grief?" Loss and differential grief in families. *Death Studies, 20,* 269–283. doi:10.1080/07481189608252781

Gilbert, K. R. (2002). Taking a narrative approach to grief research: Finding meaning in stories. *Death Studies, 26,* 223–239. doi:10.1080/07481180211274

Gilbert, K. R., & Murray, C. I. (2007). The family, larger systems, and death education. In D. E. Balk, C. Wogrin, G. Thornton, & D. Meagher (Eds.), *ADEC handbook of thanatology* (pp. 345–353). Northbrook, IL: Association for Death Education and Counseling.

Gilbert, M. (1993). *Atlas of the Holocaust* (2nd rev. printing). New York: William Morrow.

Gilbert, R. B. (1999). *Finding your way after your parent dies: Help for grieving adults.* Notre Dame, IN: Ave Maria Press.

Gill, D. L. (1980). *Quest: The life of Elisabeth Kübler-Ross.* New York: Harper & Row.

Gill, T. M., Gahbauer, E. A., Han, L., & Allore, H. G. (2010). Trajectories of disability in the last year of life. *New England Journal of Medicine, 362,* 1173–1180. doi:10.1056/NEJMoa0909087

Gilligan, C. (1982/1993). *In a different voice: Psychological theory and women's development* (with a new "Letter to Readers, 1993"). Cambridge, MA: Harvard University Press.

Ginsburg, G. D. (2004). *Widow to widow: Thoughtful, practical ideas for rebuilding your life* (rev. ed.). Boston: Da Capo Press.

Gitlin, L. N., & Piersol, C. V. (2014). *A caregiver's guide to dementia: Using activities and other strategies to prevent, reduce and manage behavioral symptoms.* Philadelphia: Camino Books.

Glaser, B., & Strauss, A. (1965). *Awareness of dying.* Chicago: Aldine.

Glaser, B., & Strauss, A. (1968). *Time for dying.* Chicago: Aldine.

Glick, I., Weiss, R., & Parkes, C. (1974). *The first year of bereavement.* New York: Wiley.

Global Burden of Disease Study 2013. (2014, December 17). Global, regional, and national age–sex specific all-cause and cause-specific mortality for 240 causes of death, 1990–2013: A systematic analysis for the Global Burden of Disease Study 2013. *Lancet.* Published Online: 17 December 2014. doi:10.1016/S0140-6736(14)61682-2.

Goble, P. (1993). *Beyond the ridge.* New York: Aladdin/Simon & Schuster.

Golan, N. (1975). Wife to widow to woman. *Social Work, 20,* 369–374. doi:10.1093/sw/20.5.369

Golden, T. (2013). *The way men heal.* Gaithersburg, MD: G. H. Publishing.

Golden, T. R. (1996). *Swallowed by a snake: The gift of the masculine side of healing.* Kensington, MD: Golden Healing Publishing.

Goldman, A., Hain, R., & Liben, S. (2012). *Oxford textbook of palliative care for children* (2nd ed.). New York: Oxford University Press.

Goldman, C. (2002). *The gifts of caregiving: Stories of hardship, hope and healing.* Minneapolis, MN: Fairview Press.

Goldman, L. (2001). *Breaking the silence: A guide to helping children with complicated grief—suicide, homicide, AIDS, violence and abuse* (2nd ed.). New York: Brunner-Routledge.

Goldman, L. (2004). *Raising our children to be resilient: A guide to helping children cope with trauma in today's world.* New York: Routledge.

Goldman, L. (2006). *Children also grieve: Talking about death and healing.* Philadelphia: Jessica Kingsley.

Goldman, L. (2009). *Great answers to difficult questions: What children need to know.* Philadelphia: Jessica Kingsley.

Goldman, L. (2014). *Life and loss: A guide to help grieving children* (3rd ed.). New York: Routledge.

Goldscheider, F., & Goldscheider, C. (1999). *The changing transition to adulthood: Leaving and returning home.* Thousand Oaks, CA: Sage.

Golubow, M. (2001). *For the living: Coping, caring and communicating with the terminally ill.* Amityville, NY: Baywood.

Goodman, R. F., & Fahnestock, A. H. (Eds.). (2002). *The day our world changed: Children's art of 9/11.* New York: Harry N. Abrams.

Goody, J. (1962). *Death, property, and the ancestors: A study of the mortuary customs of the LoDagaa of West Africa.* Stanford, CA: Stanford University Press.

Gootman, M. E. (2005). *When a friend dies: A book for teens about grieving & healing.* Minneapolis: Free Spirit Publishing.

Gordon, A. K. (1974). The psychological wisdom of the law. In J. Riemer (Ed.), *Jewish reflections on death* (pp. 95–104). New York: Schocken.

Gordon, A. K. (1986). The tattered cloak of immortality. In C. A. Corr & J. N. McNeil (Eds.), *Adolescence and death* (pp. 16–31). New York: Springer.

Gordon, A. K., & Klass, D. (1979). *They need to know: How to teach children about death.* Englewood Cliffs, NJ: Prentice Hall.

Gordon, P. S. (2016). *Psychosocial interventions in end-of-life care: The hope for a "Good Death."* New York, NY: Routledge.

Gorer, G. (1965a). The pornography of death. In G. Gorer (Ed.), *Death, grief, and mourning* (pp. 192–199). Garden City, NY: Doubleday.

Gorer, G. (1965b). *Death, grief, and mourning.* Garden City, NY: Doubleday.

Gorman, A. (2015, December 2). Aid-in-dying laws only accentuate need for palliative care, providers say. Retrieved December 4, 2015, from https://www.ehospice.com/usa/ArticleView/tabid/10708/ArticleId/17681/language/en-GB/View.aspx

Gorman, E. (2011a). Adaptation, resilience, and growth after loss. In D. L. Harris (Ed.), *Counting our losses: Reflecting on change, loss, and transition in everyday life* (pp. 225–237). New York: Routledge.

Gorman, E. (2011b). Chronic degenerative conditions, disability, and loss. In D. L. Harris (Ed.), *Counting our losses: Reflecting on change, loss, and transition in everyday life* (pp. 195–208). New York: Routledge.

Gorsuch, N. M. (2009). *The future of assisted suicide and euthanasia.* Princeton, NJ: Princeton University Press.

Goss, R. J., & Klass, D. (2005). *Dead but not lost: Grief narratives in religious traditions.* Walnut Creek, CA: AltaMira Press.

Gostin, L. O. (2005). Ethics, the constitution, and the dying process: The case of Theresa Marie Schiavo. *Journal of the American Medical Association, 293,* 2403–2407. doi:10.1001/jama.293.19.2403

Gostin, L. O. (2016). 4 simple reforms to address mass shootings and other firearm violence. *Journal of the American Medical Association, 315,* 453–454. doi:10.1001/jama.2015.19497

Gotlib, I. H., & Hammen, C. L. (Eds.). (2002). *Handbook of depression*. New York: Guilford Press.

Gott, M., Seymour, J., Bellamy, G., Clark, D., & Ahmedzai, S. (2004). Older people's views about home as a place of care at the end of life. *Palliative Medicine, 18*, 460–467. doi:10.1191/0269216304pm889oa

Gottfried, R. S. (1983). *The black death: Natural and human disaster in medieval Europe*. New York: Free Press.

Gould, M. S., Kleinman, M. H., Lake, A. M., Forman, J., & Midle, J. B. (2014). Newspaper coverage of suicide and initiation of suicide clusters in teenagers in the USA, 1988–96: A retrospective, population-based, case-control study. *The Lancet Psychiatry, 1*(1), 34–43. doi:10.1016/S2215-0366(14)70225-1

Gould, M. S., Wallenstein, S., Kleinman, M. H., O'Carroll, P., & Mercy, J. (1990). Suicide clusters: An examination of age-specific effects. *American Journal of Public Health, 80*, 211–212. doi:10.2105/AJPH.80.2.211

Gourevitch, P. (1998). *We wish to inform you that tomorrow we will be killed with our families: Stories from Rwanda*. New York: Farrar Straus & Giroux.

Gozalo, P., Plotzke, M., Mor, V., Miller, S. C., & Teno, J. M. (2015). Changes in Medicare costs with the growth of hospice care in nursing homes. *New England Journal of Medicine 372*, 1823–1831. doi:10.1056/NEJMsa1408705

Grabowski, J. A., & Frantz, T. (1993). Latinos and Anglos: Cultural experiences of grief intensity. *Omega, Journal of Death and Dying, 26*, 273–285. doi:10.2190/7MG3-KXKH-NMV8-BY90

Graeber, C. (1982). *Mustard*. New York: Macmillan.

Graham, B. (with J. Nussbaum). (2004). *Intelligence matters: The CIA, the FBI, Saudi Arabia, and the failure of America's war on terror*. New York: Random House.

Graham, L. (1991). *Rebuilding the house*. New York: Viking Penguin.

Granek, L. (2010). Grief as pathology: The evolution of grief theory in psychology from Freud to the present. *History of Psychology, 13*(1), 46–73. doi:10.1037/a0016991

Grass, G. (1990). *Two states—one nation?* Trans. K. Winston & A. S. Wensinger. San Diego: Harcourt Brace Jovanovich.

Gray, K., & Lassance, A. (2002). *Grieving reproductive loss: A healing process*. Amityville, NY: Baywood.

Gray, R. E. (1987). Adolescent response to the death of a parent. *Journal of Youth and Adolescence, 16*, 511–525. doi:10.1007/BF02138818

Grayling, A. C. (2006). *Among the dead cities: The history and moral legacy of the WWII bombing of civilians in Germany and Japan*. New York: Walker.

Green, C. R., & Beloff, J. (2008). *Through the seasons: An activity book for memory-challenged adults and caregivers*. Baltimore: Johns Hopkins University Press.

Green, M. J., Schubart, J. R., Whitehead, M. M., et al. (2015). Advance care planning does not adversely affect hope or anxiety among patients with advanced cancer. *Journal of Pain and Symptom Management, 49*, 1088–1096. doi:10.1016/j.jpainsymman.2014.11.293

Green, R. (2009). *The Nicholas effect: A boy's gift to the world*. Sebastopol, CA: AuthorHouse.

Green, R. (Ed.). (2007). *The gift that heals: Stories of hope, renewal and transformation through organ and tissue donation*. Bloomington, IN: AuthorHouse.

Greenberg, J., Pyszczynski, T., & Solomon, S. (1986). The causes and consequence of a need for self-esteem: A terror management theory. In R. F. Baumeister (Ed.), *Public self and private self* (pp. 189–212). New York: Springer-Verlag.

Gregorian, V. (1998, September 22). Track superstar Flo-Jo is found dead at 38. *St. Louis Post-Dispatch*, p. A1.

Gregory, E. C. W., MacDorman, M. F., & Martin, J. A. (2014). Trends in fetal and perinatal mortality in the United States, 2006–2012. NCHS data brief, no 169. Hyattsville, MD: National Center for Health Statistics. Retrieved June 15, 2015, from http://www.cdc.gov/nchs/data/databriefs/db169.htm

Greiner, K. A., Perera, S., & Ahluwalia, J. S. (2003). Hospice usage by minorities in the last year of life: Results from the National Mortality Followback Survey. *Journal of the American Geriatrics Society, 51*, 970–978. doi:10.1046/j.1365-2389.2003.51310.x

Greitens, E. (2015). *Resilience: Hard-won wisdom for living a better life*. Boston: Houghton-Mifflin-Harcourt.

Greyson, B. (1999). Defining near-death experiences. *Mortality, 4*, 7–22. doi:10.1080/713685958

Greyson, B. (2005). "False positive" claims of near-death experiences and "false negative" denials of near-death experiences. *Death Studies, 29*, 145–155. doi:10.1080/07481180590906156

Greyson, B., & Bush, N. E. (1992). Distressing near-death experiences. *Psychiatry, 55*, 95–110.

Grinyer, A. (2012). *Palliative and end of life care for children and young people: Home, hospice, hospital*. Chichester, England: Wiley-Blackwell.

Grmek, M. D. (1990). *History of AIDS: Emergence and origin of a modern pandemic* (R. C. Maulitz & J. Duffin, Trans.). Princeton, NJ: Princeton University Press.

Grof, S., & Halifax, J. (1978). *The human encounter with death*. New York: Dutton.

Groff, A. C., Colla, C. H., & Lee, T. H. (2016). Days spent at home—A patient-centered goal and outcome. *New England Journal of Medicine, 375*, 1610–1612. doi:10.1056/NEJMp1607206

Grollman, E. A. (1967). Prologue: Explaining death to children. In E. A. Grollman (Ed.), *Explaining death to children* (pp. 3–27). Boston: Beacon Press.

Grollman, E. A. (1977). *Living when a loved one has died*. Boston: Beacon Press.

Grollman, E. A. (Ed.). (1981). *What helped me when my loved one died*. Boston: Beacon Press.

Grollman, E. A. (1993). *Straight talk about death for teenagers: How to cope with losing someone you love*. Boston: Beacon Press.

Grollman, E. A. (1995). *Caring and coping when your loved one is seriously ill*. Boston: Beacon Press.

Grollman, E. A. (2011). *Talking about death: A dialogue between parent and child* (4th ed.). Boston: Beacon Press.

Grollman, E., & Johnson, J. (2001). *A teenager's book about suicide: Helping break the silence and preventing death*. Omaha, NE: Centering Corporation.

Grollman, E., & Malikow, M. (1999). *Living when a young friend commits suicide—Or even starts talking about it*. Boston: Beacon Press.

Groopman, J. (2004). *The anatomy of hope: How people prevail in the face of illness*. New York: Random House.

Grove, S. (1978). I am a yellow ship. *American Journal of Nursing, 78*, 414.

Groves, B. M., Zuckerman, B., Marans, S., & Cohen, D. J. (1993). Silent victims: Children who witness violence. *Journal of the American Medical Association, 269*, 262–264. doi:10.1001/jama.1993.03500020096039

Gruman, G. J. (1973). An historical introduction to ideas about voluntary euthanasia, with a bibliographic survey and guide for interdisciplinary studies. *Omega, Journal of Death and Dying, 4*, 87–138. doi:10.2190/A7WG-A6EQ-0XFP-9T4J

Gubrium, J. F. (1997). *Living and dying at Murray Manor*. Charlottesville, VA: University of Virginia Press. [Originally, St. Martin's Press, 1975.]

Guest, J. (1976). *Ordinary people*. New York: Viking.

Gunther, J. (1949). *Death be not proud*. New York: Harper.

Gutierrez, I. & Park, C. (2015). Emerging adulthood, evolving worldviews: How life events impact college students' developing belief systems. *Emerging Adulthood, 3*(2), 85–97. doi:10.1177/2167696814544501

Gutman, I., & Berenbaum, M. (Eds.). (1994). *Anatomy of the Auschwitz death camp*. Bloomington: Indiana University Press.

Habenstein, R. W., & Lamers, W. M. (1962). *The history of American funeral directing* (Rev. ed.). Milwaukee, WI: Bulfin.

Habenstein, R. W., & Lamers, W. M. (1974). *Funeral customs the world over* (Rev. ed.). Milwaukee, WI: Bulfin.

Hain, R. D. W. (2014, July 12). Euthanasia: 10 myths. *Archive of Disease in Childhood, 99*, 798–799. doi:10.1136/archdischild-2014-306218

Haley, J. D. (2001). *How to write comforting letters to the bereaved: A simple guide for a delicate task*. Amityville, NY: Baywood.

Halifax, J. (2011). The precious necessity of compassion. *Journal of Pain and Symptom Management, 41*(1), 146–153. doi:10.1016/j.jpainsymman.2010.08.010

Hall, C. (2014). Bereavement theory: Recent developments in our understanding of grief and bereavement. *Bereavement Care, 33*(1), 7–12. doi:org/10.1080/02682621.2014.902610

Hall, C., & Reid, R. A. (2009). Adolescent bereavement over the deaths of celebrities. In Balk, D. E., & Corr, C. A. (Eds.), *Adolescent encounters with death, bereavement, and coping* (pp. 237–252). New York: Springer.

Hall, G. S. (1904). *Adolescence: Its psychology and its relationship to physiology, anthropology, sociology, sex, crime, religion and education* (2 vols.). New York: D. Appleton.

Hall, G. S. (1922). *Senescence: The last half of life*. New York: D. Appleton.

Hamano, J., Yamaguchi, T., Maeda, I., et al. (2016). Multicenter cohort study on the survival time of cancer patients dying at home or in a hospital: Does place matter? *Cancer, 122*(9), 1453–1460. doi:10.1002/cncr.29844

Hamel, R. (Ed.). (1991). *Choosing death: Active euthanasia, religion, and the public debate*. Philadelphia: Trinity Press International.

Hamilton, D. (2012). *A history of organ transplantation: Ancient legends to modern practice*. Pittsburgh: University of Pittsburgh Press.

Hamilton, M. M., & Brown, W. (2002). *Black and white and red all over: The story of a friendship*. New York: Public Affairs.

Hammes, B. J. (Ed.). (2012). *Having your own say: Getting the right care when it matters most*. LaCrosse, WI: Gundersen Health System.

Hampson, R. (2006, October 5). Amish community unites to mourn slain schoolgirls. *USA Today*, p. 3A.

Haney, C. A., Leimer, C., & Lowery, J. (1997). Spontaneous memorialization: Violent death and emerging mourning ritual. *Omega, Journal of Death and Dying, 35*, 159–171. doi:10.2190/7U8W-540L-QWX9-1VL6

Hanlan, A. (1979). *Autobiography of dying*. Garden City, NY: Doubleday.

Hanson, J. C., & Frantz, T. T. (Eds.). (1984). *Death and grief in the family*. Rockville, MD: Aspen Systems Corp.

Hanson, W. (1978). Grief counseling with Native Americans. *White Cloud Journal of American Indian/Alaska Native Mental Health, 1*(2), 19–21.

Hansson, R. O., & Stroebe, M. S. (2006). *Bereavement in late life: Coping, adaptation and developmental influences*. Washington, DC: American Psychological Association.

Harakas, S. S. (1993). An Eastern Orthodox approach to bioethics. *Journal of Medicine and Philosophy, 18*, 531–548. doi:10.1093/jmp/18.6.531

Harmer, R. M. (1963). *The high cost of dying*. New York: Collier Books.

Harmer, R. M. (1971). Funerals, fantasy and flight. *Omega, Journal of Death and Dying, 2*, 127–135. doi:10.2190/G03G-RWTN-QGC8-R48J

Harper, B. C. (1994). *Death: The coping mechanism of the health professional* (Rev. ed.). Greenville, SC: Swiger Associates.

Harper, S., Rushani, D., & Kaufman, J. S. (2012). Trends in the Black-White life expectancy gap, 2003–2008. *Journal of the American Medical Association, 307*, 2257–2259. doi:10.1001/jama.2012.5059

Harran, M. J., & Roth, J. (2000). *The Holocaust chronicle: A history in words and pictures*. Lincolnwood, IL: Publications International.

Harrell, D. (2009, Summer). Donor wife holds her head high with husband's bone. *For Those Who Give and Grieve, 18*(1), 7.

Harris, D. (2010). Oppression of the bereaved: A critical analysis of grief in Western society. *Omega, Journal of Death and Dying, 60*, 241–253. doi:10.2190/OM.60.3.c

Harris, D. L. (Ed.). (2011). *Counting our losses: Reflecting on change, loss, and transition in everyday life*. New York: Routledge.

Harris, D. L., & Bordere, R. C. (Eds.). (2016). *Handbook of social justice in loss and grief: Exploring diversity, equity, and inclusion*. New York: Routledge.

Harris, D. L., & Gorman, E. (2011). Grief from a broader perspective: Nonfinite loss, ambiguous loss, and chronic sorrow. In D. L. Harris (Ed.), *Counting our losses: Reflecting on change, loss, and transition in everyday life* (pp. 1–13). New York: Routledge.

Harris, D. L., & Winokuer, H. R. (2016). *Principles and practice of grief counseling* (2nd ed.). New York: Springer.

Harris, M. (2008). *Grave matters: A journey through the modern funeral industry to a natural way of burial*. New York: Scribner.

Harris-Kojetin, L., Sengupta, M., Park-Lee, E., et al. (2016). Long-term care providers and services users in the United States: Data from the National Study of Long-Term Care Providers, 2013–2014. *Vital Health Statistics, 3*(38). Hyattsville, MD: National Center for Health Statistics.

Hartig, J., & Viola, J. (2016). Online grief support communities: Therapeutic benefits of membership. *Omega, Journal of Death and Dying, 73*(1), 29–41. doi:10.1177/0030222815575698

Hatton, C. L., & Valente, S. M. (Eds.). (1984). *Suicide: Assessment and intervention* (2nd ed.). Norwalk, CT: Appleton-Century-Crofts.

Hauser, M. J. (1987). Special aspects of grief after a suicide. In Dunne, E. J., McIntosh, J. L., & Dunne-Maxim, K. (Eds.), *Suicide and its aftermath: Understanding and counseling the survivors* (pp. 57–70). New York: Norton.

Havighurst, R. J. (1953). *Human development and education*. New York: Longmans, Green.

Havighurst, R. J. (1972). *Developmental tasks and education* (3rd ed.). New York: McKay.

Hawkins, B. (2011). *Transitions: A nurse's education about life & death* (2nd ed.). Pryor, OK: Lady Hawk Publishing.

Hawton, K., & Van Heeringen, K. (2000). *The international handbook of suicide and attempted suicide*. New York: Wiley.

Hayasaki, E. (2014). *The death class: A true story about life*. New York: Simon & Schuster.

Hayslip, B., & Goldberg-Glen, R. (2000). *Grandparents raising grandchildren: Theoretical, empirical, and clinical perspectives*. New York: Springer.

Hayslip, B., & Preveto, C. A. (2005). *Cultural changes in attitudes toward death, dying, and bereavement.* New York: Springer.

Hayslip, B., Patrick, J. H., & Panek, P. E. (2011). *Adult development and aging* (5th ed.). Malabar FL: Krieger Publishing Company.

Hazell, L. V. (2001). Disaster mortuary operational response teams (DMORT). *Forum, 27*(6), 5, 8.

HealthCare Chaplaincy Network. (2016). *Spiritual care: What it means, why it matters in health care.* New York: Author.

Heberer, P. (2011). *Children during the Holocaust.* Lanham, MD: AltaMira Press.

Heidegger, M. (1962). *Being and time* (Rev. ed.) (J. Macquarrie & E. S. Robinson, Trans.). San Francisco: HarperSanFrancisco.

Helm, S. (2014). *Ravensbrück: Life and death in Hitler's concentration camp for women.* New York: Doubleday.

Hemingway, E. (1926). *The sun also rises.* New York: Scribner.

Hemingway, E. (1929). *A farewell to arms.* New York: Scribner.

Hemingway, E. (1940). *For whom the bell tolls.* New York: Scribner.

Hemingway, E. (1952). *The old man and the sea.* New York: Scribner.

Henderson, C. S. (1998). *Partial view: An Alzheimer's journal.* Dallas, TX: Southern Methodist University Press.

Henderson, D. X., Bond, G. D., Alderson, C. J., & Walker, W. R. (2015). This too shall pass: Evidence of coping and fading emotion in African Americans' memories of violent and nonviolent death. *Omega, Journal of Death and Dying, 71,* 291–311. doi:10.1177/0030222815572601

Hendin, H. (1995). Selling death and dignity. *Hastings Center Report, 25*(3), 19–23. doi:10.2307/3562109

Hendin, H. (1998). *Seduced by death: Doctors, patients and assisted suicide* (rev. ed.). New York: Norton.

Hendin, H. (2002). The Dutch experience. *Issues in Law & Medicine, 17,* 223–246.

Hendin, H., Rutenfrans, C., & Zylicz, Z. (1997). Physician-assisted suicide and euthanasia in the Netherlands: Lessons from the Dutch. *Journal of the American Medical Association, 277,* 1720–1722. doi:10.1001/jama.1997.03540450076039

Henke, E. (1972). The purpose of life. *Omega, Journal of Death and Dying, 3,* 163. Reprinted in C. A. Corr & D. M. Corr (Eds.), *Hospice care: Principles and practice* (pp. 354–355). New York: Springer, 1983.

Heron, M. (2016). Deaths: Leading causes for 2013. *National Vital Statistics Reports, 65*(2). Hyattsville, MD: National Center for Health Statistics.

Heron, M. (2016). Deaths: Leading causes for 2014. *National Vital Statistics Reports, 65*(5). Hyattsville, MD: National Center for Health Statistics.

Hersey, J. (1948). *Hiroshima.* New York: Bantam.

Hewett, J. (1980). *After suicide.* Philadelphia: Westminster Press.

Hickey, M. (2006). *Planning a celebration of life: A simple guide for turning a memorial service into a celebration of life.* San Francisco, CA: Renaissance Urn Company.

Hickman, S. E., Nelson, C. A., Moss, A. H., et al. (2011). Consistency between treatment provided to nursing facility residents and orders on the Physician Orders for Life-Sustaining Treatment form. *Journal of the American Geriatrics Society, 59*(11), 2091–2099. doi:10.1111/j.1532-5415.2011.03656.x

Hickman, S. E., Nelson, C. A., Perrin, N. A., et al. (2010). A comparison of methods to communicate treatment preferences in nursing facilities: Traditional practices versus the Physician Orders for Life-Sustaining Treatment program. *Journal*

of the American Geriatrics Society, 58(7), 1241–1248. doi:10.1111/j.1532-5415.2010.02955.x

Hilberg, R. (2003). *The destruction of the European Jews.* New Haven, CT: Yale University Press.

Hill, D. C., & Foster, Y. M. (1996). Postvention with early and middle adolescents. In C. A. Corr & D. E. Balk (Eds.), *Handbook of adolescent death and bereavement* (pp. 250–272). New York: Springer.

Hillyard, D., & Dombrink, J. (2001). *Dying right: The death with dignity movement.* New York: Routledge.

Himelstein, B. P., Hilden, J. M., Boldt, A. M., & Weissman, D. (2004). Pediatric palliative care. *New England Journal of Medicine, 350,* 1752–1762. doi:10.1056/NEJMra030334

Hinds, P. S., Drew, D., Oakes, L. L., et al. (2005). End-of-life care preferences of pediatric patients with cancer. *Journal of Clinical Oncology, 23,* 9146–9154. doi:10.1200/JCO.2005.10.538

Hinton, J. (1963). The physical and mental distress of the dying. *Quarterly Journal of Medicine,* New Series, *32,* 1–21. doi:

Hinton, J. (1984). Coping with terminal illness. In R. Fitzpatrick, J. Hinton, S. Newman, G. Scambler, & J. Thompson (Eds.), *The experience of illness* (pp. 227–245). London: Tavistock Publications.

Hirayama, K. K. (1990). Death and dying in Japanese culture. In J. K. Parry (Ed.), *Social work practice with the terminally ill: A transcultural perspective* (pp. 159–174). Springfield, IL: Charles C Thomas.

Hirsch, E. (2014). *Gabriel: A poem by Edward Hirsch.* New York: Knopf.

Hochberg, T. (2011). The art of medicine: Moments held—photographing perinatal loss. *The Lancet, 377,* 1310–1311. doi:10.1016/S0140-6736(11)60528-X

Hockey, J., Katz, J., & Small, N. (Eds.). (2001). *Grief, mourning and death ritual.* Philadelphia: Open University Press.

Hodgson, H. (2008). *Writing to recover: The journey from loss and grief to a new life.* Omaha, NE: Centering Corporation.

Hoess, R. (1959). *Commandant of Auschwitz: The autobiography of Rudolf Hoess* (C. FitzGibbon, Trans.). Cleveland, OH: World.

Hoff, B. (1983). *The Tao of Pooh.* New York: Penguin.

Hoffman, B. (2006). *Inside terrorism* (2nd ed.). New York: Columbia University Press.

Hogan, N. S., & Balk, D. E. (1990). Adolescent reactions to sibling death: Perceptions of mothers, fathers, and teenagers. *Nursing Research, 39,* 103–106.

Hogan, N. S., & DeSantis, L. (1992). Adolescent sibling bereavement: An ongoing attachment. *Qualitative Health Research, 2,* 159–177. doi:10.1177/104973239200200204

Hogan, N. S., & DeSantis, L. (1994). Things that help and hinder adolescent sibling bereavement. *Western Journal of Nursing Research, 16,* 132–153.

Hogan, N. S., & Greenfield, D. B. (1991). Adolescent sibling bereavement symptomatology in a large community sample. *Journal of Adolescent Research, 6,* 97–112. doi:10.1177/074355489161008

Holden, J. M., Grayson, B., & James D. (Eds.). (2009). *The handbook of near-death experiences: Thirty years of investigation.* Santa Barbara, CA: Praeger Publishers/ABC-CLIO.

Holinger, P. C., Offer, D., Barter, J. T., & Bell, C. C. (1994). *Suicide and homicide among adolescents.* New York: Guilford.

Holland, J. M., & Neimeyer, R. A. (2010). An examination of stage theory of grief among individuals bereaved by natural and violent causes: A meaning-oriented contribution. *Omega, Journal of Death and Dying, 61,* 103–120. doi:10.2190/OM.61.2.b

Holland, J. M., Currier, J. M., & Neimeyer, R. A. (2006). Meaning reconstruction in the first two years of bereavement: The role of sense-making and benefit-finding. *Omega, Journal of Death and Dying, 53,* 175–191. doi:10.2190/FKM2-YJTY-F9VV-9XWY

Holloway, K. F. C. (2003). *Passed on: African American mourning stories, a memorial.* Durham, NC: Duke University Press.

Holstein, M. (2015). *Women in later life: Critical perspectives on gender and age.* London: Rowman & Littlefield.

Holtkamp, S. (2002). *Wrapped in mourning: The gift of life and organ donor family trauma.* New York: Taylor & Francis.

Homer. (1996). *The Odyssey* (R. Fagles, Trans.). New York: Penguin.

Hooyman, N. R., & Kramer, B. J. (2006). *Living through loss: Interventions across the life span.* New York: Columbia University Press.

Hooyman, N., & Kiyak, H. A. (2010). *Social gerontology: A multidisciplinary perspective* (9th ed.). New York: Pearson.

Horchler, J. N., & Morris, R. R. (2003). *The SIDS and infant death survival guide: Information and comfort for grieving families and friends and professionals who seek to help them* (3rd ed.). Hyattsville, MD: SIDS Educational Services, Inc.

Horn, G. (White Deer of Autumn). (1992). *The great change.* Hillsboro, OR: Beyond Words.

Horner, I. B. (Trans.). (1949). *The book of discipline (Vinaya-Pitaka),* Vol. 1. London: Luzac.

Hospice Foundation of America. (2007). *The dying process: A guide for caregivers.* Washington, DC: Author.

Hospice Foundation of America. (2015). *Grieving the loss of a father—On father's day.* Washington, DC: Author.

Hostetler, J. A. (1993). *Amish society* (4th ed.). Baltimore: Johns Hopkins University Press.

Hostetler, J. A. (2013). *The Amish* (3rd ed., revised by Steven M. Nolt & Ann E. Hostetler). Harrisonburg, VA: Herald Press.

Housden, M. (2002). *Hannah's gift: Lessons from a life fully lived.* New York: Bantam.

Howarth, G. (1996). *Last rites: The work of the modern funeral director.* Amityville, NY: Baywood.

Howarth, G., & Leaman, O. (Eds.). (2001). *Encyclopedia of death and dying.* New York: Routledge.

Hoy, W. G. (2007). *Guiding people through grief: How to start and lead bereavement support groups.* Dallas, TX: Compass.

Hoy, W. G. (2013). *Do funerals matter? The purposes and practices of death rituals in global perspective.* New York: Routledge.

Hoy, W. G. (2016). *Bereavement groups and the role of social support: Integrating theory, research, and practice.* New York: Routledge.

Hughes, M. (1995). *Bereavement and support: Healing in a group environment.* Washington, DC: Taylor & Francis.

Hughes, T. E., & Klein, O. (2007). *A family guide to wills, funerals, and probate: How to protect yourself and your survivors* (2nd ed.). New York: Facts on File/Checkmark Books.

Hume, S. B. (2015). *ABA/AARP checklist for my family: A guide to my history, financial plans and final wishes.* Chicago: American Bar Association.

Humphry, D. (2002). *Final exit: The practicalities of self-deliverance and assisted suicide for the dying* (3rd ed.). New York: Dell.

Humphry, D., & Clement, M. (1998). *Freedom to die: People, politics, and the right-to-die movement.* New York: St. Martin's Press.

Hunter, D. J., Reddy, K. S. (2013). Noncommunicable diseases. *New England Journal of Medicine, 369,* 1336–1343. doi:10.1056/NEJMra1109345

Hunter, S. B., & Smith, D. E. (2008). Predictors of children's understanding of death: Age, cognitive ability, experience and maternal communicative competence. *Omega, Journal of Death and Dying, 57*(2), 143–162. doi:10.2190/OM.57.2.b

Hunter, S., & Sundel, M. (Eds.). (1989). *Midlife myths: Issues, findings, and practice implications.* Newbury Park, CA: Sage.

Hurd, M., & Macdonald, M. (2001). *Beyond coping: Widows reinventing their lives.* Halifax, Nova Scotia: Pear Press.

Hurwitz, C. A., Duncan, J., & Wolfe, J. (2004). Caring for the child with cancer at the close of life: "There are people who make it, and I'm hoping I'm one of them". *Journal of the American Medical Association, 292,* 2141–2149. doi:10.1001/jama.292.17.2141

Huston, A. C., Donnerstein, E., Fairchild, H., et al. (1992). *Big world, small screen: The role of television in American society.* Lincoln: University of Nebraska Press.

Huxley, A. (1939). *After many a summer dies the swan.* New York: Harper & Brothers.

Hyatt, E. G. (2015). *Grieving for the sibling you lost: A teen's guide to coping with grief and finding meaning after loss.* Oakland, CA: New Harbinger Publications.

Hyland, L., & Morse, J. M. (1995). Orchestrating comfort: The role of funeral directors. *Death Studies, 19,* 453–474. doi:10.1080/07481189508253393

Ilse, S. (1989). *Miscarriage: A shattered dream.* Long Lake, MN: Wintergreen Press.

Ilse, S. (2013). *Empty arms: Coping with miscarriage, stillbirth and infant death* (20th, rev. & enlarged ed.). Maple Plains, MN: Wintergreen Press.

Ilse, S., & Nelson, T. (2008). *Couple communication after a baby dies: Differing perspectives.* Maple Plains, MN: Wintergreen Press.

Ingles, T. (1974). St. Christopher's Hospice. *Nursing Outlook, 22,* 759–763.

Ingram, P. (1992). The tragedy of Tibet. *Contemporary Review, 261,* 122–125.

Inoue-Choi, M., Liao, L. M., Reyes-Guzman, C., et al. (2016). Association of long-term, low-intensity smoking with all-cause and cause-specific mortality in the National Institutes of Health–AARP Diet and Health Study. *JAMA Internal Medicine.* Published online December 5, 2016. doi:10.1001/jamainternmed.2016.7511

Institute of Medicine. (2011). *Relieving pain in America: A blueprint for transforming prevention, care, education, and research.* Washington, DC: National Academies Press.

Institute of Medicine. (2012). *Accelerating progress in obesity prevention: Solving the weight of the nation.* Washington, DC: National Academies Press.

Institute of Medicine. (2014). *Dying in America: Improving quality and honoring individual preferences near the end of life.* Washington, DC: The National Academies Press.

International Work Group on Death, Dying, and Bereavement. (1993). Palliative care for children: Position statement. *Death Studies, 17,* 277–280. doi:10.1080/07481189308252623 (Reprinted in *Statements about death, dying, and bereavement by the International Work Group on Death, Dying, and Bereavement,* pp. 17–19, by C. A. Corr, J. D. Morgan, & H. Wass, Eds., 1994, London: King's College).

International Work Group on Death, Dying, and Bereavement. (2006). Caregivers in death, dying, and bereavement situations. *Death Studies, 30,* 649–663. doi:10.1080/07481180600776036

Irish, D. P., Lundquist, K. F., & Nelson, V. J. (Eds.). (1993). *Ethnic variations in dying, death, and grief: Diversity in universality.* Washington, DC: Taylor & Francis.

Irving, J. (1989). *A prayer for Owen Meany*. New York: William Morrow & Co.

Irving, M. J., Tong, A., Jan, S., et al. (2013). Factors that influence the decision to be an organ donor: A systematic review of the qualitative literature. *Nephrology Dialysis Transplantation, 27*(6), 2526–2533. doi:10.1093/ndt/gfr683

Irwin, M. D. (2015). Mourning 2.0—Continuing bonds between the living and the dead on Facebook. *Omega, Journal of Death and Dying, 72*, 119–150. doi:10.1177/0030222815574830

Isenberg, N., & Burstein, A. (Eds.). (2003). *Mortal remains: Death in early America*. Philadelphia: University of Pennsylvania Press.

Iserson, K. V. (2001). *Death to dust: What happens to dead bodies?* (2nd ed.). Tucson, AZ: Galen Press.

Iserson, K. V., & Iserson, K. Y. (1999). *Grave words: Notifying survivors about sudden, unexpected death*. Tucson, AZ: Galen Press.

Itzkoff, D., & Carey, B. (2015, November 3). Robin Williams's widow points to dementia as a suicide cause. *The New York Times*. Retrieved November 4, 2015, from http://www.nytimes.com/2015/11/04/health/robin-williams-lewy-body-dementia.html?_r=0 [Nov. 4, 2015, p. C1 in print.]

Iverson, B. A. (1990). Bodies for science. *Death Studies, 14*, 577–587. doi:10.1080/07481189008252395

Iwashyna, T., & Chang, V. (2002). Racial and ethnic differences in place of death: United States. 1993. *Journal of American Geriatrics Society, 50*, 1113–1117. doi:10.1046/j.1532-5415.2002.50269.x

Jack, C. R., Albert, M. S., Knopman, D. S., et al. (2011). Introduction to the recommendations from the National Institute on Aging and the Alzheimer's Association workgroup on diagnostic guidelines for Alzheimer's disease. *Alzheimer's and Dementia: The Journal of the Alzheimer's Association, 7*(3), 257–262. doi:10.1016/j.jalz.2011.03.004

Jackson, C. O. (Ed.). (1977). *Passing: The vision of death in America*. Westport, CT: Greenwood Press.

Jackson, E. N. (1963). *For the living*. Des Moines, IA: Channel Press.

Jackson, E. N. (1984). The pastoral counselor and the child encountering death. In H. Wass & C. A. Corr (Eds.), *Helping children cope with death: Guidelines and resources* (2nd ed., pp. 33–47). Washington, DC: Hemisphere.

Jackson, J. (2003). *A handbook for survivors of suicide*. Washington, DC: American Association of Suicidology.

Jacobs, D. G. (1999). *The Harvard Medical School guide to suicide assessment and intervention*. San Francisco: Jossey-Bass.

Jacobs, L. G., Bonuck, K., Burton, W., & Mulvihill, M. (2002). Hospital care at the end of life: An institutional assessment. *Journal of Pain and Symptom Management, 24*, 291–298. doi:10.1016/S0885-3924(02)00494-3

Jacobs, S. (1999). *Traumatic grief: Diagnosis, treatment, and prevention*. Washington, DC: Taylor & Francis.

Jacoby, L. H., Breitkopf, C. R., & Pease, E. A. (2005). A qualitative examination of the needs of families faced with the option of organ donation. *Dimensions of Critical Care Nursing, 24*, 183–189.

Jacques, E. (1965). Death and the mid-life crisis. *International Journal of Psychoanalysis, 46*, 502–514.

James, B. D., Leurgans, S. E., Hebert, L. E., et al. (2014). Contribution of Alzheimer disease to mortality in the United States. *Neurology, 82*(12), 1045–1050. doi:10.1212/WNL.240

Jamison, K. R. (1999). *Night falls fast: Understanding suicide*. New York: Knopf.

Jamison, K. R. (2011). *Nothing was the same: A memoir*. New York: Vintage.

Jamison, S. (1995). *Final acts of love: Families, friends, and assisted dying*. New York: Tarcher/Putman.

JanMohamed, A. B. (2004). *The death-bound-subject: Richard Wright's archaeology of death*. Durham, NC: Duke University Press.

Janoff-Bulman, R. (1992). *Shattered assumptions: Towards a new psychology of trauma*. New York: Free Press.

Janzen, L., Cadell, S., & Westhues, A. (2004). From death notification through the funeral: Bereaved parents' experiences and their advice to professionals. *Omega, Journal of Death and Dying, 48*, 149–164. doi:10.2190/6XUW-4PYD-H88Q-RQ08

Jay, C., & Thomas, J. (2012). *What does dead mean?: A book for young children to help explain death and dying*. Philadelphia: Jessica Kingsley Publishers.

Jeffreys, J. S. (2011). *Helping grieving people—When tears are not enough: A handbook for care providers* (2nd ed.). New York: Routledge.

Jenkins, C., Lapelle, N., Zapka, J., Kurent, J. (2005). End-of-life care and African Americans: Voices from the community. *Journal of Palliative Medicine, 8*, 585–592. doi:10.1089/jpm.2005.8.585

Jennings, B., Kaebnick, G. E., & Murray, T. H. (Eds.). (2005). *Improving end of life care: Why has it been so difficult?* Garrison, NY: Hastings Center.

Jensen, F. E., & Nutt, A. E. (2015). *The teenage brain: A neuroscientist's survival guide to raising adolescents and young adults*. New York: Harper.

Jensen, S. J. (Ed.). (2011). *The ethics of organ transplantation*. Washington, DC: The Catholic University of America Press.

Jensma, F. (2010a, February 8). Citizens group argues "right to die". *NRC handelsblad*. Retrieved January 15, 2011, from http://vorige.nrc.nl/international/Features/article2478619.ece/Citizens_group_argues_right_to_die

Jensma, F. (2010b, February 9). "Right to die" for elderly back at center of Dutch debate. *Radio Netherlands Worldwide*. Retrieved January 15, 2011, from http://www.rnw.nl/english/article/right-die-elderly-back-centre-dutch-debate

Jha, P., Ramasundarahettige, C., Landsman, V., et al. (2013). 21st-century hazards of smoking and benefits of cessation in the United States. *New England Journal of Medicine, 368*, 341–350. doi:10.1056/NEJMsa1211128

Jin, J. (2016). Death in the United States: Changes from 1969 to 2013. *Journal of the American Medical Association, 315*(3), 318. doi:10.1001/jama.2015.17432

Jobes, A. A. (2006). *Managing suicidal risk: A collaborative approach*. New York: Guilford.

John Paul II, Pope. (2004). Care for patients in a "permanent" vegetative state. *Origins, 33*(43), 737, 739–740.

Johnsen, I., & Dyregrov, K. (2016). "Only a friend": The bereavement process of young adults after the loss of a close friend in an extreme terror incident—A qualitative approach. *Omega, Journal of Death and Dying, 74*, 16–34. doi:10.1177/0030222815622956

Johnson, C. J., & McGee, M. G. (Eds.). (1998). *How different religions view death and afterlife* (2nd ed.). Philadelphia: Charles Press.

John's Sister. (2011). *The forgotten mourners: Sibling survivors of suicide*. Parker, CO: Outskirts Press.

Johnson, C., & Weeks, O. D. (2001). How to develop a successful aftercare program. In O. D. Weeks & C. Johnson (Eds.), *When all the friends have gone: A guide for aftercare providers* (pp. 5–23). Amityville, NY: Baywood.

Johnson, J. (2006). *Keys: To helping children deal with death and grief*. Omaha: Centering Corporation.

Johnson, M. (2006). *The dead beat: Lost souls, lucky stiffs, and the perverse pleasures of obituaries*. New York: HarperCollins.

Jonah, B. A. (1986). Accident risk and risk-taking behaviour among young drivers. *Accident Analysis and Prevention, 18*, 255–271. doi:10.1016/0001-4575(86)90041-2

Jonas, D. F., & Bogetz, J. F. (2016). Identifying the deliberate prevention and intervention strategies of pediatric palliative care teams supporting providers during times of staff distress. *Journal of Palliative Medicine, 19*, 679–683. doi:10.1089/jpm.2015.0425

Jones, B. (1967). *Design for death*. Indianapolis, IN: Bobbs-Merrill.

Jones, D. S., Podolsky, S. H., & Greene, J. A. (2012). The burden of disease and the changing task of medicine. *New England Journal of Medicine, 366*(25), 2333–2338. doi:10.1056/NEJMp1113569

Jones, E. O. (1948). *Little Red Riding Hood*. New York: Golden Press.

Jones, J. H. (1992). *Bad blood: The Tuskegee syphilis experiment*. New York: Simon & Schuster.

Jones, M. M. (2013). *Bring back the fun: Activity ideas for caregivers and people with dementia*. Amazon.com: CreateSpace.

Jonker, G. (1997). The many facets of Islam: Death, dying and disposal between orthodox and historical convention. In C. M. Parkes, P. Laungani, & B. Young (Eds.), *Death and bereavement across cultures* (pp. 147–165). London: Routledge.

Jordan, J. R. (2001). Is suicide bereavement different? A reassessment of the literature. *Suicide and Life-Threatening Behavior, 31*, 91–102. doi:10.1521/suli.31.1.91.21310

Jordan, J. R., & McIntosh, J. L. (Eds.). (2010). *Grief after suicide: Understanding the consequences and caring for the survivors*. New York: Routledge.

Jordan, J. R., & Neimeyer, R. A. (2003). Does grief counseling work? *Death Studies, 27*, 765–786. doi:10.1080/713842360

Jordan, J. R., & Neimeyer, R. A. (2007). Historical and contemporary perspectives on assessment and intervention. In D. E. Balk, C. Wogrin, G. Thornton, & D. Meagher (Eds.), *ADEC handbook of thanatology* (pp. 213–225). Northbrook, IL: Association for Death Education and Counseling.

Jordan, J., & Baugher, B. (Eds.). (2016). *After suicide loss: Coping with your grief* (2nd ed.). Brandon, MO: Caring People Press.

Jordan, J., & McMenamy, J. (2004). Interventions for suicide survivors: A review of the literature. *Suicide and Life-Threatening Behavior, 34*, 337–339. doi:10.1521/suli.34.4.337.53742

Jung, C. (1954). *The development of personality*. In H. Read, M. Fordham, & G. Adler (Eds.), *The collected works of Carl G. Jung* (2nd ed., Vol. 17, p. 7). Princeton, NJ: Princeton University Press.

Jung, C. G. (1970). The stages of life. In H. Read, M. Fordham, & G. Adler (Eds.), *The collected works of Carl G. Jung* (2nd ed., Vol. 8). Princeton, NJ: Princeton University Press. (Original work published 1933)

Jupp, P. C. (2006). *From ashes to dust: The history of cremation in Britain*. London: Palgrave Press.

Jury, M., & Jury, D. (1978). *Gramps: A man ages and dies*. Baltimore: Penguin.

Kagawa-Singer, M., & Blackhall, L. (2001). Negotiating cross-cultural issues at the end of life: "You've got to go where he lives". *Journal of the American Medical Association, 286*, 2993–3001. doi:10.1001/jama.286.23.2993

Kail, R. V., & Cavanaugh, J. C. (2015). *Human development: A lifespan view* (7th ed.). Belmont, CA: Cengage Learning.

Kaimann, D. S. (2002). *Common threads: Nine widows' journeys through love, loss and healing*. Amityville, NY: Baywood.

Kalesan, B., Mobily, M. R., Keiser, O., Fagan, J. A., & Galea, S. (2016, March 10). Firearm legislation and firearm mortality in the USA: a cross-sectional, state-level study. *The Lancet*, published online. doi:10.1016/S0140-6736(15)01026-0

Kalish, R. A. (1985a). Death and dying in a social context. In R. H. Binstock & E. Shanas (Eds.), *Handbook of aging and the social sciences* (2nd ed., pp. 149–170). New York: Van Nostrand.

Kalish, R. A. (1985b). The horse on the dining-room table. In *Death, grief, and caring relationships* (2nd ed., pp. 2–4). Pacific Grove, CA: Brooks/Cole.

Kalish, R. A. (Ed.). (1980). *Death and dying: Views from many cultures*. Farmingdale, NY: Baywood.

Kalish, R. A., & Goldberg, H. (1978). Clergy attitudes toward funeral directors. *Death Education, 2*, 247–260. doi:10.1080/07481187808253311

Kalish, R. A., & Goldberg, H. (1980). Community attitudes toward funeral directors. *Omega, Journal of Death and Dying, 10*, 335–346. doi:10.2190/W7H8-4GMC-UYYC-9A6U

Kalish, R. A., & Reynolds, D. K. (1981). *Death and ethnicity: A psychocultural study*. Farmingdale, NY: Baywood. (Originally published, Los Angeles: Andrus Gerontology Center, 1976)

Kane, B. (1979). Children's concepts of death. *Journal of Genetic Psychology, 134*, 141–153. doi:10.1080/00221325.1979.10533406

Kaplan, K. B. (2014). *Encountering the edge: What people told me before they died*. Fayetteville, AR: Pen-L Publishing.

Kaplan, K. J. (1999). Right to die versus sacredness of life [Special issue]. *Omega, Journal of Death and Dying, 40*(1).

Karakatsanis, K. G., & Tsanakas, J. N. (2002). A critique on the concept of brain death. *Issues in Law and Medicine, 18*(2), 127–141.

Kaserman, D. L., & Barrett, A. H. (2002). *The United States organ procurement system: A prescription for reform*. Washington, DC: AEI Press.

Kashurba, G. J. (2006). *Quiet courage: The definitive account of Flight 93 and its aftermath*. Somerset, PA: SAJ Publishing.

Kass, J. (2014). *Columbine: A true crime story* (2nd ed.). Golden, CO: Conundrum Press.

Kassebaum, N. J., Barber, R. M., Bhutta, Z. A., et al. (2016). Global, regional, and national levels of maternal mortality, 1990–2015: A systematic analysis for the Global Burden of Disease Study 2015. *The Lancet, 388*(10053), 1775–1812. doi:10.1016/S0140-6736(16)31470-2

Kassis, H. (1997). Islam. In H. Coward (Ed.), *Life after death in world religions* (pp. 48–65). Maryknoll, NY: Orbis Books.

Kastenbaum, R. (1969). Death and bereavement in later life. In A. H. Kutscher (Ed.), *Death and bereavement* (pp. 28–54). Springfield, IL: Charles C Thomas.

Kastenbaum, R. (1972, December 23). The kingdom where nobody dies. *Saturday Review, 56*, 33–38.

Kastenbaum, R. (1973). On the future of death: Some images and options. *Omega, Journal of Death and Dying, 3*, 306–318. doi:10.2190/3AUQ-906Q-6LWH-JK5E

Kastenbaum, R. (1977). Death and development through the lifespan. In H. Feifel (Ed.), *New meanings of death* (pp. 17–45). New York: McGraw-Hill.

Kastenbaum, R. (1989). Ars moriendi. In R. Kastenbaum & B. Kastenbaum (Eds.), *Encyclopedia of death* (pp. 17–19). Phoenix, AZ: Oryx Press.

Kastenbaum, R. (1995). Raymond A. Moody, Jr.: An *Omega* interview. *Omega, Journal of Death and Dying, 31*, 87–98.

Kastenbaum, R. (2000). *The psychology of death* (3rd ed.). New York: Springer.

Kastenbaum, R. (2009). Should we manage terror—if we could? *Omega, Journal of Death and Dying, 59,* 271–304. doi:10.2190/OM.59.4.a

Kastenbaum, R. (Ed.). (2003). *Macmillan encyclopedia of death and dying* (2 vols.). New York: Macmillan.

Kastenbaum, R. J. (2004). Death writ large. *Death Studies, 28,* 375–392. doi:10.1080/07481180490432360

Kastenbaum, R. J. (2012). *Death, society, and human experience* (11th ed.). New York: Pearson.

Kastenbaum, R., & Aisenberg, R. (1972). *The psychology of death.* New York: Springer.

Kastenbaum, R., & Thuell, S. (1995). Cookies baking, coffee brewing: Toward a contextual theory of dying. *Omega, Journal of Death and Dying, 31,* 175–187. doi:10.2190/LQPX-71DE-V5AA-EPFT

Kasza, K. A., Ambrose, B. K., Conway, K. P., et al. (2017), Tobacco-product use by adults and youths in the United States in 2013 and 2014. *New England Journal of Medicine, 376,* 342–353. doi:10.1056/NEJMsa1607538

Katz, J. (2011). *Going home: Finding peace when pets die.* New York: Villard/Random House.

Katz, R. S., & Johnson, T. A. (Eds.). (2016). *When professionals weep: Emotional and countertransference responses in palliative and end-of-life care* (2nd ed.). New York: Routledge.

Katzenbach, J. (1986). *The traveler.* New York: Putnam's.

Kaufert, J. M., & O'Neil, J. D. (1991). Cultural mediation of dying and grieving among Native Canadian patients in urban hospitals. In D. R. Counts & D. A. Counts (Eds.), *Coping with the final tragedy: Cultural variation in dying and grieving* (pp. 231–251). Amityville, NY: Baywood.

Kauffman, J. (2004). *Guidebook on helping persons with mental retardation mourn.* Amityville, NY: Baywood.

Kauffman, J. (Ed.). (1995). *Awareness of mortality.* Amityville, NY: Baywood.

Kauffman, J. (Ed.). (2002). *Loss of the assumptive world: A theory of traumatic loss.* New York: Brunner-Routledge.

Kauffmann, J. C., & Jordan, M. (2013). *The essential guide to life after bereavement: Beyond tomorrow.* Philadelphia, PA: Jessica Kingsley.

Kaufman, K. R., & Kaufman, N. D. (2006). And then the dog died. *Death Studies, 30,* 61–76. doi:10.1080/07481180500348811

Kaufman, S. R. (1986). *The ageless self: Sources of meaning in late life.* Madison: University of Wisconsin Press.

Kaufman, S. R. (2006). *And a time to die: How American hospitals shape the end of life.* Chicago: University of Chicago Press.

Kavanaugh, R. E. (1972). *Facing death.* Los Angeles: Nash.

Kay, W. J., Cohen, S. P., Nieburg, H. A., et al. (Eds.). (1988). *Euthanasia of the companion animal: The impact on pet owners, veterinarians, and society.* Philadelphia: Charles Press.

Kaye, E. C., Friebert, S., & Baker, J. N. (2016). Early integration of palliative care for children with high-risk cancer and their families. *Pediatric Blood Cancer, 63,* 593–597. doi:10.1002/pbc.25848

Kean, T. H., & Hamilton, L. H. (2006). *Without precedent: The inside story of the 9/11 Commission.* New York: Knopf.

Keegan, L., & Drick, C. A. (2011). *End of life: Nursing solutions for death with dignity.* New York: Springer.

Keister, D. (2004). *Stories in stone: A field guide to cemetery symbolism and iconography.* Layton, UT: Gibbs Smith.

Kellehear, A. (1996). *Experiences near death: Beyond medicine and religion.* New York: Oxford University Press.

Kellehear, A. (2007). *A social history of dying.* New York: Columbia University Press.

Kellehear, A. (Ed.). (2009). *The study of dying: From autonomy to transformation.* New York: Cambridge University Press.

Kellehear, A. (2014). *The inner life of the dying person.* New York: Columbia University Press.

Kelley, A. S., & Meier, D. E. (2010). Palliative care—A shifting paradigm. *New England Journal of Medicine, 363,* 781–782. doi:10.1056/NEJMe1004139

Kelley, A. S., & Morrison, R. S. (2015). Palliative care for the seriously ill. *New England Journal of Medicine, 373,* 747–755. doi:10.1056/NEJMra1404684

Kelley, A. S., Deb, P., Du, Q., Aldridge Carlson, M. D., & Morrison, R. S. (2013). Hospice enrollment saves money for Medicare and improves care quality across a number of different lengths-of-stay. *Health Affairs, 32,* 552–561. doi:10.1377/hlthaff.2012.0851

Kelley, A. S., McGarry, K., Gorges, R., & Skinner, J. S. (2015). The burden of health care costs for patients with dementia in the last 5 years of life. *Annals of Internal Medicine, 163*(10).729–736. doi:10.7326/M15-0381

Kelly, E. W. (2001). Near-death experiences with reports of meeting deceased people. *Death Studies, 25,* 229–249. doi:10.1080/07481180125967

Kelly, E. W., Greyson, B., & Stevenson, I. (2000). Can experiences near death furnish evidence of life after death? *Omega, Journal of Death and Dying, 40,* 513–519. doi:10.2190/KNTM-6R07-LTVT-MC6K

Kelly, O. E. (1975). *Make today count.* New York: Delacorte Press.

Kelly, O. E. (1977). Make today count. In H. Feifel (Ed.), *New meanings of death* (pp. 182–193). New York: McGraw-Hill.

Kelly, S. (2015). *Greening death: Reclaiming burial practices and restoring our tie to the earth.* Lanham, MD: Roman & Littlefield.

Kelsay, J. (1994). Islam and medical ethics. In P. F. Camenisch (Ed.), *Religious methods and resources in bioethics* (pp. 93–107). Dordrecht, Germany: Kluwer.

Kemp, C. E. (1999). *Terminal illness: A guide to nursing care.* Philadelphia: Lippincott Williams & Wilkins.

Keneally, T. (1982). *Schindler's list.* New York: Simon & Schuster.

Kenyon, B. L. (2001). Current research in children's conceptions of death: A critical review. *Omega, Journal of Death and Dying, 43,* 63–91. doi:10.2190/0X2B-B1N9-A579-DVK1

Keown, D. (1995). *Buddhism and bioethics.* New York: St. Martin's Press.

Kerbel, M. R. (2000). *If it bleeds, it leads: An anatomy of television news.* Boulder, CO: Westview Press.

Kessler, D. (2000). *The needs of the dying: A guide for bringing hope, comfort, and love to life's final chapter.* New York: Perennial Currents.

Kessler, D. (2004). The extraordinary ordinary death of Elisabeth Kübler-Ross. *American Journal of Hospice and Palliative Medicine, 21,* 415–416. doi:10.1177/104990910402100605

Kessler, D. (2007). *The needs of the dying: A guide for bringing hope, comfort, and love to life's final chapter.* New York: HarperCollins.

Kessler, D. A. (2009). *The end of overeating: Taking control of the insatiable American appetite.* New York: Rodale Books.

Kessler, R. C., Berglund, P., Demler, O., et al. (2005). Lifetime prevalence and age-of-onset distributions of DSM-IV disorders in the national comorbidity survey replication. *Archives of General Psychiatry, 62,* 593–602, 188, 14 E337-E339. doi:10.1503/cmaj.160365

Keyes, R. (2010). *Euphemania: Our love affair with euphemisms.* New York: Little, Brown.

Kim, S., & Lemmens, T. (2016). Should assisted dying for psychiatric disorders be legalized in Canada? *Canadian Medical Association Journal, 188*, 14 E337–E339. doi:10.1503/cmaj.160365

King, A. (1990). A Samoan perspective: Funeral practices, death and dying. In J. K. Parry (Ed.), *Social work practice with the terminally ill: A transcultural perspective* (pp. 175–189). Springfield, IL: Charles C Thomas.

King, C. A., Foster, C. E., & Rogalski, K. M. (2013). *Teen suicide risk: A practitioner guide to screening, assessment, and management.* New York: Guilford.

Kirk, A. D., Knechtle, S. J., Larsen, C. P., et al. (2014). *Textbook of organ transplantation.* New York: Wiley-Blackwell.

Kirk, T. W., & Jennings, B. (Eds.). (2014). *Hospice ethics: Policy and practice in palliative care.* New York: Oxford University Press.

Kissane, D. W., & Bloch, S. (2002). *Family focused grief therapy: A model of family-centered care during palliative care and bereavement.* Philadelphia: Open University Press.

Klagsbrun, F. (1985). *Too young to die: Youth and suicide.* New York: Pocket.

Klass, D. (1982). Elisabeth Kübler-Ross and the tradition of the private sphere: An analysis of symbols. *Omega, Journal of Death and Dying, 12*, 241–261. doi:10.2190/0DGA-BQP5-LNTB-A93G

Klass, D. (1985a). Bereaved parents and the Compassionate Friends: Affiliation and healing. *Omega, Journal of Death and Dying, 15*, 353–373. doi:10.2190/K88L-6EAG-11QL-7PFG

Klass, D. (1985b). Self-help groups: Grieving parents and community resources. In C. A. Corr & D. M. Corr (Eds.), *Hospice approaches to pediatric care* (pp. 241–260). New York: Springer.

Klass, D. (1988). *Parental grief: Solace and resolution.* New York: Springer.

Klass, D. (1999). *The spiritual lives of bereaved parents.* Philadelphia: Taylor & Francis.

Klass, D. (2006). Continuing conversation about continuing bonds. *Death Studies, 30*, 843–858. doi:10.1080/07481180600886959

Klass, D. (Ed.). (2006). Death, grief, religion, and spirituality [Special issue]. *Omega, Journal of Death and Dying, 53*(1–2).

Klass, D., & Hutch, R. A. (1986). Elisabeth Kübler-Ross as a religious leader. *Omega, Journal of Death and Dying, 16*, 89–109. doi:10.2190/BVDJ-68WQ-D2XK-51DW

Klass, D., & Shinners, B. (1983). Professional roles in a self-help group for the bereaved. *Omega, Journal of Death and Dying, 13*, 361–375. doi:10.2190/VE7L-7ULX-CR86-50U2

Klass, D., Silverman, P. R., & Nickman, S. L. (Eds.). (1996). *Continuing bonds: New understandings of grief.* Washington, DC: Taylor & Francis.

Klebold, S. (2016). *A mother's reckoning: Living in the aftermath of tragedy.* New York: Crown.

Klevins, R. M., Morrison, M. A., Nadle, J., et al. (2007). Invasive methicillin-resistant *staphylococcus aureus* infections in the United States. *Journal of the American Medical Association, 298*, 1763–1771. doi:10.1001/jama.298.15.1763

Klicker, R. L. (2000). *A student dies, a school mourns: Dealing with death and loss in the school community.* New York: Taylor & Francis.

Kliever, L. D. (Ed.). (1989). *Dax's case: Essays in medical ethics and human meaning.* Dallas, TX: Southern Methodist University.

Klug, C., & Jackson, S. (2004). *To the edge and back: My story from organ transplant survivor to Olympic snowboarder.* New York: Carroll & Graf.

Kochanek, K. D., Murphy, S. L., Xu, J. Q., & Tejada-Vera, B. (2016). Deaths: Final data for 2014. *National Vital Statistics Reports, 65*(4). Hyattsville, Md.: National Center for Health Statistics.

Kohn, I., Moffit, P.-L., & Wilkins, I. A. (2000). *A silent sorrow: Pregnancy loss—Guidance and support for you and your family* (Rev. 2nd ed.). New York: Brunner-Routledge.

Kolb, P. (Ed.). (2014). *Understanding aging and diversity: Theories and concepts.* New York: Routledge.

Konigsberg, R. E. (2011). *The truth about grief: The myth of its five stages and the new science of loss.* New York: Simon & Schuster.

Koocher, G. (1973). Childhood, death, and cognitive development. *Developmental Psychology, 9*, 369–375.

Koocher, G. P. (1974). Talking with children about death. *American Journal of Orthopsychiatry, 44*, 404–411. doi:10.1111/j.1939-0025.1974.tb00893.x

Koocher, G. P., & O'Malley, J. E. (1981). *The Damocles syndrome: Psychosocial consequences of surviving childhood cancer.* New York: McGraw-Hill.

Koocher, G. P., O'Malley, J. E., Foster, D., & Gogan, J. L. (1976). Death anxiety in normal children and adolescents. *Psychiatria clinica, 9*, 220–229.

Koppelman, K. L. (2011). *Wrestling with the angel: Literary writings and reflections on death, dying and bereavement.* Amityville, NY: Baywood.

Kosminsky, P. S., & Jordan, J. R. (2016). *Attachment-informed grief therapy: The clinician's guide to foundations and applications.* New York: Routledge.

Kramer, K. (2005). You cannot die alone: Dr. Elisabeth Kübler-Ross (July 8, 1926–August 24, 2004). *Omega, Journal of Death and Dying, 50*, 83–101. doi:10.2190/K42X-F5MA-A2CP-3XBV

Kraybill, D. B. (2001). *The riddle of Amish culture* (Rev. ed.). Baltimore: Johns Hopkins University Press.

Kraybill, D. B., Johnson-Weiner, K. M., & Nolt, S. M. (2013). *The Amish.* Baltimore: Johns Hopkins University Press.

Kraybill, D. B., Nolt, S. M., & Weaver-Zercher, D. L. (2007). *Amish grace: How forgiveness transcended tragedy.* San Francisco: John Wiley & Sons.

Kraybill, D. B., Nolt, S. M., & Weaver-Zercher, D. L. (2010). *The Amish way: Patient faith in a perilous world.* San Francisco: Jossey-Bass.

Kraybill, R. B. (2003). *Who are the Anabaptists?: Amish, Brethren, Hutterites, and Mennonites.* Scottdale, PA: Herald Press.

Kreicbergs, U., Valdimarsdóttir, U., Onelöv, E., Henter, J.-I., & Steineck, G. (2004). Talking about death with children who have severe malignant disease. *New England Journal of Medicine, 351*, 1175–1186. doi:10.1056/NEJMoa040366

Krementz, J. (1989). *How it feels to fight for your life.* Boston: Little, Brown.

Krizek, B. (1992). Goodbye old friend: A son's farewell to Comiskey Park. *Omega, Journal of Death and Dying, 25*, 87–93. doi:10.2190/P5RF-G50T-MEYY-P8KU

Krueger, A. B. (2007). *What makes a terrorist: Economics and the roots of terrorism.* Princeton, NJ: Princeton University Press.

Krugman, P. (2001, February 24). Fowl play badmouthing the economy. *St. Petersburg Times*, p. 16A.

Krumholz, H. M., Phillips, R. S., Hamel, M. B., et al. (1998). Resuscitation preferences among patients with severe congestive heart failure: Results from the SUPPORT Project. *Circulation, 98*(7), 648–655. doi:10.1161/01.CIR.98.7.648

Kübler-Ross, E. (1969). *On death and dying.* New York: Macmillan.

Kübler-Ross, E. (1983). *On children and death.* New York: Macmillan.

Kübler-Ross, E. (1997). *The wheel of life: A memoir of living and dying.* New York: Scribner.

Kübler-Ross, E., & Kessler, D. (2005). *On grief and grieving: Finding the meaning of grief through the five stages of loss.* New York: Scribner.

Kuebelbeck, A., & Davis, D. L. (2011). *A gift of time: Continuing your pregnancy when your baby's life is expected to be brief.* Baltimore, MD: Johns Hopkins University Press.

Kuhl, D. (2002). *What dying people want: Practical wisdom for the end of life.* New York: Public Affairs.

Kuhl, D. (2006). *Facing death, embracing life: Understanding what dying people want.* Toronto: Doubleday Canada.

Kuhn, D. (2013). *Alzheimer's early stages: First steps for family, friends, and caregivers* (3rd ed.). Alameda, CA: Hunter House Publishers.

Kulka, E. (1986). *Escape from Auschwitz.* South Hadley, MA: Bergin & Garvey.

Kurzman, C. (2011). *The missing martyrs: Why there are so few Muslim terrorists.* New York: Oxford University Press.

Kushner, H. S. (1981). *When bad things happen to good people.* New York: Avon.

Lack, S. A., & Buckingham, R. W. (1978). *First American hospice: Three years of home care.* New Haven, CT: Hospice.

Laderman, G. (2005). *Rest in peace: A cultural history of death and the funeral home in twentieth century America.* New York: Oxford University Press.

Ladwig, T. (1997). *Psalm twenty-three.* Grand Rapids, MI: Eerdmans.

Lagoni, L., Butler, C., & Hetts, S. (1994). *The human-animal bond and grief.* Philadelphia: W. B. Saunders.

LaGrand, L. E. (1980). Reducing burnout in the hospice and the death education movement. *Death Education, 4,* 61–76. doi:10.1080/07481188008253349

LaGrand, L. E. (1981). Loss reactions of college students: A descriptive analysis. *Death Studies, 5,* 235–247. doi:10.1080/07481188108252096

LaGrand, L. E. (1986). *Coping with separation and loss as a young adult: Theoretical and practical realities.* Springfield, IL: Charles C Thomas.

LaGrand, L. E. (1988). *Changing patterns of human existence: Assumptions, beliefs, and coping with the stress of change.* Springfield, IL: Charles C Thomas.

LaGrand, L. E. (1997). *After-death communication: Final farewells.* St. Paul, MN: Llewellyn.

LaGrand, L. E. (1999). *Messages and miracles: Extraordinary experiences of the bereaved.* St. Paul, MN: Llewellyn.

LaGrand, L. E. (2001). *Gifts from the unknown: Using extraordinary experiences to cope with loss and change.* St. Paul, MN: Llewellyn.

LaGrand, L. E. (2006). *Love lives on: Learnings from the extraordinary encounters of the bereaved.* New York: Berkley Books.

Lamberti, J. W., & Detmer, C. M. (1993). Model of family grief assessment and treatment. *Death Studies, 17,* 55–67. doi:10.1080/07481189308252604

Lamers, E. P. (1986). Books for adolescents. In C. A. Corr & J. N. McNeil (Eds.), *Adolescence and death* (pp. 233–242). New York: Springer.

Lamers, E. P. (1995). Children, death, and fairy tales. *Omega, Journal of Death and Dying, 31,* 151–167. doi:10.2190/HXV5-WWE4-N1HH-4JEG

Lamm, M. (2000). *The Jewish way in death and mourning* (Rev. ed.). Middle Village, NY: Jonathan David.

Lamm, M. (2004). *Consolation: The spiritual journey beyond grief.* Philadelphia: Jewish Publication Society.

Landay, D. S. (1998). *Be prepared: The complete financial, legal, and practical guide for living with a life-challenging condition.* New York: St. Martin's Press.

Landro, L. (2014, November 30). How to make your wishes for end-of-life care clear: New concerns arise about how well patients and doctors understand advance directives. *Wall Street Journal.* Retrieved December 12, 2014, from http://www.wsj.com/articles/how-to-make-your-wishes-for-end-of-life-care-clear-1417408059

Landry, S. (1999a, June 15). He wanted you to know. *St. Petersburg Times,* p. 1D.

Landry, S. (1999b, June 22). His message transcends death. *St. Petersburg Times,* p. 3D.

Lang, A. (Ed.). (1904). *The blue fairy book.* New York: Longman's Green.

Lang, L. T. (1990). Aspects of the Cambodian death and dying process. In J. K. Parry (Ed.), *Social work practice with the terminally ill: A transcultural perspective* (pp. 205–211). Springfield, IL: Charles C Thomas.

Langa, K. M., Larson, E. B., Crimmins, E. M., et al. (2017). A comparison of the prevalence of dementia in the United States in 2000 and 2012. *JAMA Internal Medicine, 177,* 51–58. doi:10.1001/jamainternmed.2016.6807

Langbein, H. (1994). *Against all hope: Resistance in the Nazi concentration camps 1938–1945* (H. Zohn, Trans.). New York: Paragon House.

Langman, P. (2010). *Why kids kill: Inside the minds of school shooters.* New York: St. Martins Griffin.

Lankford, A. (2013). *The myth of martyrdom: What really drives suicide bombers, rampage shooters, and other self-destructive killers.* New York: Palgrave Macmillan.

Lareca, A. M., Silberman, W. K., Vernberg, E. M., & Roberts, M. C. (Eds.). (2002). *Helping children cope with disasters and terrorism.* Washington, DC: American Psychological Association.

Largo, M. (2006). *Final exits: The illustrated encyclopaedia of how we die.* New York: Harper.

Larson, D. G. (1993). *The helper's journey: Working with people facing grief, loss, and life-threatening illness.* Champaign, IL: Research Press.

Larson, D. G., & Hoyt, W. T. (2007a). The bright side of grief counseling: Deconstructing the new pessimism. In K. J. Doka (Ed.), *Living with grief: Before and after the death* (pp. 157–174). Washington, DC: Hospice Foundation of America.

Larson, D. G., & Hoyt, W. T. (2007b). What has become of grief counseling? An evaluation of the empirical foundations of the new pessimism. *Professional Psychology: Research and Practice, 38,* 347–355. doi:10.1037/0735-7028.38.4.347

Larson, D. G., & Tobin, D. R. (2000). End-of-life conversations: Evolving practice and theory. *Journal of the American Medical Association, 284,* 1573–1578. doi:10.1001/jama.284.12.1573

Larue, G. A. (1985). *Euthanasia and religion: A survey of the attitudes of world religions to the right to die.* Los Angeles: Hemlock Society.

Lattanzi, M. E. (1983). Professional stress: Adaptation, coping, and meaning. In J. C. Hanson & T. T. Frantz (Eds.), *Death and grief in the family* (pp. 95–106). Rockville, MD: Aspen Systems Corp.

Lattanzi, M. E. (1985). An approach to caring: Caregiving concerns. In C. A. Corr & D. M. Corr (Eds.), *Hospice approaches to pediatric care* (pp. 261–277). New York: Springer.

Lattanzi, M. E., & Hale, M. E. (1985). Giving grief words: Writing during bereavement. *Omega, Journal of Death and Dying, 15,* 45–52. doi:10.2190/TT15-WAPL-LLMT-X2WD

Lattanzi-Licht, M. E. (1996). Helping families with adolescents cope with loss. In C. A. Corr & D. E. Balk (Eds.), *Handbook of adolescent death and bereavement* (pp. 219–234). New York: Springer.

Lattanzi-Licht, M. E. (2007). Religion, spirituality, and dying. In D. E. Balk, C. Wogrin, G. Thornton, & D. Meagher (Eds.), *ADEC handbook of thanatology* (pp. 11–17). Northbrook, IL: Association for Death Education and Counseling.

Lauderdale, D. S., & Kestenbaum, B. (2002). Mortality rates of elderly Asian American populations based on Medicare and Social Security data. *Demography, 39*(3), 529–540. doi:10.1353/dem.2002.0028

LaVeist, T. A., & Isaac, L. A. (Eds.). (2012). *Race, ethnicity, and health: A public health reader* (2nd ed.). San Francisco, CA: Jossey-Bass.

Lazar, A., & Torney-Purta, J. (1991). The development of the subconcepts of death in young children: A short-term longitudinal study. *Child Development, 62*, 1321–1333. doi:10.2307/1130809

Lazarus, R. S., & Folkman, S. (1984). *Stress, appraisal, and coping.* New York: Springer.

Leach, M. M. (2006). *Cultural diversity and suicide: Ethnic, religious, gender, and sexual orientation perspectives.* New York: Routledge.

LeardMann, C. A., Powell, T. M., Smith, T. C., et al. (2013). Risk factors associated with suicide in current and former US military personnel. *Journal of the American Medical Association, 310*(5), 496–506. doi:10.1001/jama.2013.65164

Lecso, P. A. (1986). Euthanasia: A Buddhist perspective. *Journal of Religion and Health, 25*, 51–57. doi:10.1007/BF01533053

Lee, C. C. (Ed.). (2013). *Multicultural issues in counseling: New approaches to diversity* (4th ed.). Alexandria, VA: American Association for Counseling and Development.

Lee, P. W. H., Lieh-Mak, F., Hung, B. K. M., & Luk, S. L. (1984). Death anxiety in leukemic Chinese children. *International Journal of Psychiatry in Medicine, 13*, 281–290. doi:10.2190/5MFW-D1PM-KKGN-1W7R

Leenaars, A. A. (1990). Psychological perspectives on suicide. In D. Lester (Ed.), *Current concepts of suicide* (pp. 159–167). Philadelphia: Charles Press.

Leenaars, A. A. (2006). People who have committed a certain sin ought to be dead. *Death Studies, 30*, 539–553. doi:10.1080/07481180600742525

Leenaars, A. A., & Wenckstern, S. (1996). Postvention with elementary school children. In C. A. Corr & D. M. Corr (Eds.), *Handbook of childhood death and bereavement* (pp. 265–283). New York: Springer.

Leenaars, A. A., & Wenckstern, S. (Eds.). (1991). *Suicide prevention in the schools.* Washington, DC: Hemisphere.

Leenaars, A. A., Maltsberger, J. T., & Neimeyer, R. A. (Eds.). (1994). *Treatment of suicidal people.* Washington, DC: Taylor & Francis.

Leenaars, A. A., Maris, R. W., McIntosh, J. L., et al. *Suicide and the older adult.* New York: Guilford.

Leenaars, A., Sakinofsky, I., Wenckstern, S., et al. (Eds.). (1998). *Suicide in Canada.* Toronto: University of Toronto Press.

Leong, F. T. L., & Leach, M. M. (Eds.). (2007). Ethnicity and suicide in the United States. [Special issue]. *Death Studies, 31*(5).

Leong, F. T. L., & Leach, M. M. (Eds.). (2008). *Suicide among racial and ethnic groups: Theory, research, and practice.* New York: Routledge.

Leong, F. T. L., Leach, M. M., & Gupta, A. (2008). Suicide among Asian Americans: A critical review with research recommendations. In F. T. L. Leong & M. M. Leach (Eds.), *Suicide among racial and ethnic groups: Theory, research, and practice* (pp. 117–142). New York: Routledge.

Lerner, M. (1970). When, why, and where people die. In O. Brim, H. Freeman, S. Levine, & N. Scotch (Eds.), *The dying patient* (pp. 5–29). New York: Russell Sage Foundation.

Lerner, M. D., Volpe, J. S., & Lindell, B. (2003). *A practical guide for crisis response in our schools: A comprehensive school crisis response plan* (5th ed.). Commack, NY: American Academy of Experts in Traumatic Stress.

Lerner, M. D., Volpe, J. S., & Lindell, B. (2004). *A practical guide for university crisis response: A comprehensive crisis response plan for colleges and universities.* Commack, NY: American Academy of Experts in Traumatic Stress.

LeShan, E. (1976). *Learning to say good-by: When a parent dies.* New York: Macmillan.

LeShan, L. (1964). The world of the patient in severe pain of long duration. *Journal of Chronic Diseases, 17*, 119–126. doi:10.1016/0021-9681(64)90050-5

Lester, D. (1992). *Why people kill themselves* (3rd ed.). Springfield, IL: Charles C Thomas.

Lester, D. (1993). *The cruelest death: The enigma of adolescent suicide.* Philadelphia: Charles Press.

Lester, D. (1998). The suicide of Sylvia Plath: Current perspectives. [Special issue] *Death Studies, 22*(7).

Lester, D. (2000). The social causes of suicide: A look at Durkheim's *Le Suicide* one hundred years later. *Omega, Journal of Death and Dying, 40*, 307–321. doi:10.2190/JPYQ-LF4U-4UT8-YJRB

Lester, D. (2003). *Fixin' to die: A compassionate guide to committing suicide or staying alive.* Amityville, NY: Baywood.

Lester, D. (2006a). Can suicide be a good death? *Death Studies, 30*, 511–527. doi:10.1080/07481180600742509

Lester, D. (2006b). Can suicide be a good death? A reply. *Death Studies, 30*, 555–560. doi:10.1080/07481180600742541

Lester, D., Templer, D. I., & Abdel-Khalek, A. (2006). A cross-cultural comparison of death anxiety: A brief note. *Omega, Journal of Death and Dying, 54*, 255–260. doi:10.2190/W644-8645-6685-358V

Lesy, M. (1973). *Wisconsin death trip.* New York: Pantheon.

Levi, P. (1986). *Survival in Auschwitz and the reawakening: Two memoirs* (S. Woolf, Trans.). New York: Simon & Schuster.

Levin, A. (2006, October 6). Grief travels through Amish country. *USA Today*, p. 4A.

Levin, A., & Hall, M. (2006, October 5). Shooter's relatives: No recall of being molested. *USA Today*, p. 3A.

Levinson, D. J. (1978). *The seasons of a man's life.* New York: Knopf.

Levinson, D. J. (1996). *The seasons of a woman's life.* New York: Knopf.

Leviton, D. (Ed.). (1991a). *Horrendous death, health, and well-being.* Washington, DC: Hemisphere.

Leviton, D. (Ed.). (1991b). *Horrendous death and health: Toward action.* Washington, DC: Hemisphere.

Levy, A. (2000). *The orphaned adult: Understanding and coping with grief and change after the death of our parents.* New York: Perseus.

Levy, J. A. (2014). *Activities to do with your parent who has Alzheimer's dementia.* Amazon.com: CreateSpace.

Levy, J. E., & Kunitz, S. J. (1987). A suicide prevention program for Hopi youth. *Social Science and Medicine, 25*, 931–940. doi:10.1016/0277-9536(87)90264-4

Lewis, C. S. (1960). *The four loves.* New York: Harcourt, Brace & World.

Lewis, C. S. (1976). *A grief observed.* New York: Bantam Books.

Lewis, O. (1972). *A death in the Sanchez family.* New York: Penguin.

Lewy, G. (2011). *Assisted death in Europe and America: Four regimes and their lessons.* New York: Oxford University Press.

Ley, D. C. H., & Corless, I. B. (1988). Spirituality and hospice care. *Death Studies, 12*, 101–110. doi:10.1080/07481188808252227

Li, M., Watt, S., Escaf, M., et al. (2017). Medical assistance in dying: Implementing a hospital-based program in Canada. *New England Journal of Medicine, 376*, 2082–2088. doi:10.1056/NEJMms1700606

Lichfield, G. (2015, April). The science of near-death experiences: Empirically investigating brushes with the afterlife. *The Atlantic*. Retrieved March 19, 2015, from http://www.theatlantic.com/features/archive/2015/03/the-science-of-near-death-experiences/386231/

Lieberman, A. F., Compton, N. C., Van Horn, P., & Ippen, C. G. (2003). *Losing a parent to death in the early years: Guidelines for the treatment of traumatic bereavement in infancy and early childhood*. Washington, DC: Zero To Three Press.

Liegner, L. M. (1975). St. Christopher's Hospice, 1974: Care of the dying patient. *Journal of the American Medical Association, 234*, 1047–1048. doi:10.1001/jama.1975.03260230047022 (Reprinted in 2000 in Vol. 284, p. 2426. doi:10.1001/jama.284.19.2426)

Lifton, R. J. (1964). On death and death symbolism: The Hiroshima disaster. *Psychiatry, 27*, 191–210.

Lifton, R. J. (1967). *Death in life: Survivors of Hiroshima*. New York: Random House.

Lifton, R. J. (1979). *The broken connection*. New York: Simon & Schuster.

Lifton, R. J. (1982). *Indefensible weapons: The political and psychological case against nuclearism*. New York: Basic Books.

Lifton, R. J. (1986). *The Nazi doctors: Medical killing and the psychology of genocide*. New York: Basic Books.

Lifton, R. J., & Mitchell, G. (1995). *Hiroshima in America: Fifty years of denial*. New York: Putnam's.

Limbo, R. K., & Wheeler, S. R. (1998). *When a baby dies: A handbook for healing and helping* (2nd ed.). La Crosse, WI: Lutheran Hospital—La Crosse, Inc.

Lindemann, E. (1944). Symptomatology and management of acute grief. *American Journal of Psychiatry, 101*, 141–148. doi:10.1176/ajp.101.2.141

Lindemann, E., & Greer, I. M. (1972). A study of grief: Emotional responses to suicide. In A. C. Cain (Ed.), *Survivors of suicide* (pp. 63–69). Springfield, IL: Charles C Thomas. (Reprinted from *Pastoral Psychology*, 1953, 4, 9–13. doi:10.1007/BF01838832)

Linder, E. (2013). *Hospice voices: Lessons for living at the end of life*. Lanham, MD: Rowman & Littlefield.

Lindsay, M., & Lester, D. (2004). *Suicide by cop: Committing suicide by provoking police to shoot you*. Amityville, NY: Baywood.

Lindstrom, T. (2002). "It ain't necessarily so" … Challenging mainstream thinking about bereavement. *Family and Community Health, 25*(1), 11–21.

Linenthal, E. T. (2001). *The unfinished bombing: Oklahoma City in American memory*. New York: Oxford University Press.

Linn, E. (1986). *I know just how you feel … Avoiding the clichés of grief*. Incline Village, NV: Publisher's Mark.

Lipman, A. G., Jackson, K. C., & Tyler, L. S. (Eds.). (2000). *Evidence-based symptom control in palliative care: Systemic reviews and validated clinical practice guidelines for 15 common problems in patients with life-limiting disease*. Binghamton, NY: Haworth Press.

Lipman, A. R. (Ed.). (2004). *Pain management for primary care clinicians*. Bethesda, MD: American Society of Health-System Pharmacists.

Lipsky, D. (2013). *How people with autism grieve, and how to help: An insider handbook*. Philadelphia, PA: Jessica Kingsley.

Lipsky, L., with C. Burk. (2009). *Trauma stewardship: An everyday guide to caring for self while caring for others*. San Francisco: Berrett-Koehler Publishers.

Lipstadt, D. (1993). *Denying the Holocaust: The growing assault on truth and memory*. New York: Free Press.

Litman, R. E. (1967). Sigmund Freud on suicide. In E. S. Shneidman (Ed.), *Essays in self-destruction* (pp. 324–344). New York: Science House.

Liu, Y., Canada, K., Shi, K., & Corrigan, P. (2012). HIV-related stigma acting as predictors of unemployment of people living with HIV/AIDS. *AIDS Care, 24*(1), 129–135. doi:10.1080/09540121.2011.596512

Lloyd-Williams, M. (Ed.). (2008). *Psychosocial issues in palliative care* (2nd ed.). New York: Oxford University Press.

Loerzel, V. W., & Conner, N. (2016). Advances and challenges: Student reflections from an online death and dying course. *American Journal of Hospice and Palliative Care, 33*, 8–15. doi:10.1177/1049909114549182

Loftin, C., McDowall, D., Wiersema, B., & Cottey, T. J. (1991). Effects of restrictive licensing of handguns on homicide and suicide in the District of Columbia. *New England Journal of Medicine, 325*, 1615–1620. doi:10.1056/NEJM199112053252305

Loggers, E.T., Starks, H., Shannon-Dudley, M., et al. (2013). Implementing a Death with Dignity program at a comprehensive cancer center. *New England Journal of Medicine, 368*, 1417–1424. doi:10.1056/NEJMsa1213398

Lonetto, R. (1980). *Children's conceptions of death*. New York: Springer.

Lonetto, R., & Templer, D. I. (1986). *Death anxiety*. Washington, DC: Hemisphere.

Long, J., & Perry P. (2010). *Evidence of the afterlife: The science of near-death experiences*. New York: HarperOne.

Long, K. A. (1983). The experience of repeated and traumatic loss among Crow Indian children: Response patterns and intervention strategies. *American Journal of Orthopsychiatry, 53*, 116–126. doi:10.1111/j.1939-0025.1983.tb03356.x

Long, T. G. (2013). *Accompany them with singing: The Christian funeral*. Louisville, KY: Westminster John Knox Press.

Long, T. G., & Lynch, T. (2013). *The good funeral: Death, grief, and the community of care*. Louisville, KY: Westminster John Knox Press.

Longaker, C. (1998). *Facing death and finding hope: A guide to the emotional and spiritual care of the dying*. New York: Doubleday.

Losey, B. (2011). *Bullying, suicide, and homicide: Understanding, assessing, and preventing threats to self and others for victims of bullying*. New York: Routledge.

Lowenstein, L. (2006). *Creative interventions for bereaved children*. Toronto: Champion Press.

Lukas, C., & Seiden, H. M. (2007). *Silent grief: Living in the wake of suicide* (Rev. ed.). Philadelphia: Jessica Kingsley.

Lund, D. A. (2000). *Men coping with grief*. Amityville, NY: Baywood.

Lund, D. A., Dimond, M., & Juretich, M. (1985). Bereavement support groups for the elderly: Characteristics of potential participants. *Death Studies, 9*, 309–321. doi:10.1080/07481188508252526

Lustbader, D., Mudra, M., Romano, C., et al. (2016, August). The impact of a home-based palliative care program in an accountable care organization. *Journal of Palliative Medicine*. doi:10.1089/jpm.2016.0265

Lustig, A. (1977). *Darkness casts no shadow*. New York: Inscape.

Lutovich, D. S. (2001). *Nobody's child: How older women say good-bye to their mothers*. Amityville, NY: Baywood.

Luxmoore, N. (2012). *Young people, death and the unfairness of everything*. London: Jessica Kingsley.

Lynch, T. (2009). *The undertaking: Life studies from the dismal trade*. New York: Penguin.

Lynn, J. (Ed.). (1986). *By no extraordinary means: The choice to forgo life-sustaining food and water*. Bloomington: Indiana University Press.

Lynn, J., Harrold, J., & Schuster, J. L. (2011). *Handbook for mortals: Guidance for people facing serious illness* (2nd ed.). New York: Oxford University Press.

Lynn, K. S. (1987). *Hemingway.* New York: Simon & Schuster.

Lynne, D. (2005). *Terri's story: The court-ordered death of an American woman.* Medford, OR: WND Books.

Lyon, M. E., Jacobs, S., Briggs, L., Yi, B., & Wang, J. (2013). Family-centered advance care planning for teens with cancer. *JAMA Pediatrics, 167*(5), 460–467. doi:10.1001/jamapediatrics.2013.943

Lysiak, M. (2014). *Newtown: An American tragedy.* New York: Gallery Books.

Ma, J., Ward, E. M., Siegel, R. L., & Jemal, A. (2015). Temporal trends in mortality in the United States, 1969–2013. *Journal of the American Medical Association, 314*(16), 1731–1739. doi:10.1001/jama.2015.12319

MacCharles, R. (2015, February 6). Supreme Court strikes down assisted suicide ban: Canada's highest court has struck down the law against assisted suicide and in a unanimous ruling. Retrieved May 14, 2015, from http://www.thestar.com/news/canada/2015/02/06/supreme-court-rules-strikes-down-assisted-suicide-ban.html

Mace, N. L., & Rabins, P. V. (2011). *The 36-Hour day: A family guide to caring for people with Alzheimer disease, other dementias, and memory loss* (5th ed.). Baltimore: Johns Hopkins University Press.

Maciejewski, P. K., Zhang, B., Block, S. D., & Prigerson, H. G. (2007). An empirical examination of the stage theory of grief. *Journal of the American Medical Association, 297*, 716–723. doi:10.1001/jama.297.7.716

Mack, A. (Ed.). (1974). *Death in American experience.* New York: Schocken.

MacLachlan, B. S. (2016). *Connecting memories, Book 3: Coloring and activities book for people with dementia, Alzheimer's, brain injuries, stroke and other cognitive conditions.* Griswold, CT: Art Z Illustrations.

MacMillan, I. (1991). *Orbit of darkness.* San Diego, CA: Harcourt Brace Jovanovich.

MacPherson, M. (1999). *She came to live out loud: An inspiring family journey through illness, loss, and grief.* New York: Scribner.

Maddox, R. J. (1995). *Weapons for victory: The Hiroshima decision fifty years later.* Columbia, MO: University of Missouri Press.

Madey, S. F., & Chasteen, A. L. (2004). Age-related health stereotypes and illusory correlation. *International Journal of Aging and Human Development, 58*, 109–126. doi:10.2190/81XB-QPYN-9ADU-5L11

Mahoney, M. C. (1991). Fatal motor vehicle traffic accidents among Native Americans. *American Journal of Preventive Medicine, 7*, 112–116.

Maier, F. (1991). *Sweet reprieve: One couple's journey to the frontiers of medicine.* New York: Crown.

Maimonides, M. (1949). *The code of Maimonides (Mishneh Torah): Book Fourteen, The Book of Judges* (A. M. Hershman, Trans.). New Haven, CT: Yale University Press.

Makary, M. A., & Daniel, M. (2016, May 3). Medical error—the third leading cause of death in the US. *BMJ, 353*, 2139. doi:10.1136/bmj.i2139

Malinowski, B. (1954). *Magic, science, and religion and other essays.* New York: Doubleday.

Malone, P. A. (2016). *Counseling adolescents through loss, grief, and trauma.* New York: Routledge.

Maloney, R., & Wolfelt, A. D. (2011). *Caring for donor families: Before, during and after* (2nd ed.). Fort Collins, CO: Companion Press.

Mandelbaum, D. G. (1959). Social uses of funeral rites. In H. Feifel (Ed.), *The meaning of death* (pp. 189–217). New York: McGraw-Hill.

Mandell, H., & Spiro, H. (Eds.). (1987). *When doctors get sick.* New York: Plenum.

Mann, T. C., & Greene, J. (1962). *Over their dead bodies: Yankee epitaphs and history.* Brattleboro, VT: Stephen Greene Press.

Mann, T. C., & Greene, J. (1968). *Sudden and awful: American epitaphs and the finger of God.* Brattleboro, VT: Stephen Greene.

Manning, D. (1979). *Don't take my grief away from me: How to walk through grief and learn to live again.* Hereford, TX: In-Sight Books.

Manning, D. (2001). *The funeral: A chance to teach, a chance to serve, a chance to heal.* Oklahoma City, OK: In-Sight Books.

March, A. (2007). *Dying into grace: Mother and daughter … A dance of healing.* Cambridge, MA: Quantum Lens Press.

Marcus, E. (2010). *Why suicide? Questions and answers about suicide, suicide prevention, and coping with the suicide of someone you know.* New York: HarperOne.

Marczak, L., O'Rourke, K., & Shepard, D. (2016). When and why people die in the United States, 1990–2013. *Journal of the American Medical Association, 315*, 241. doi:10.1001/jama.2015.17599

Maris, R. W. (1969). *Social forces in urban suicide.* Homewood, IL: Dorsey Press.

Maris, R. W. (1981). *Pathways to suicide: A survey of self-destructive behaviors.* Baltimore: Johns Hopkins University Press.

Maris, R. W. (1985). The adolescent suicide problem. *Suicide and Life-Threatening Behavior, 15*, 91–109. doi:10.1111/j.1943-278X.1985.tb00644.x

Maris, R. W. (Ed.). (1988). *Understanding and preventing suicide.* New York: Guilford.

Maris, R. W., Berman, A. L., & Silverman, M. M. (2000). *Comprehensive textbook of suicidology.* New York: Guilford.

Maris, R. W., Berman, A. L., Maltsberger, J. T., & Yufit, R. I. (Eds.). (1992). *Assessment and prediction of suicide.* New York: Guilford.

Marks, A. S., & Calder, B. J. (1982). *Attitudes toward death and funerals.* Evansville, IL: Northwestern University, Center for Marketing Sciences.

Marks, R., & Sachar, E. (1973). Undertreatment of medical inpatients with narcotic analgesics. *Annals of Internal Medicine, 78*, 173–181. doi:10.7326/0003-4819-78-2-173

Marley, M. (2011). *Come back early today: A memoir of love, Alzheimer's and Joy.* Olathe, KS: Joseph Peterson Books.

Marmot, M. (2015). *The health gap: The challenge of an unequal world.* London: Bloomsbury Press.

Marshall, B. J. (2013). *Adult sibling loss: Stories, reflections and ripples.* Amityville, NY: Baywood.

Marshall, B. J., & Winokuer, H. R. (Eds.). (2017). *Sibling loss across the lifespan: Research, practice and personal stories.* New York: Routledge.

Marshall, V. (1980) *Last chapters: A sociology of aging and dying.* Monterrey, CA: Brooks/Cole.

Marta, S. Y. (2003). *Healing the hurt, restoring the hope: How to guide children and teens through times of divorce, death, and crisis with the RAINBOWS approach.* Emmaus, PA: Rodale Books.

Martin, G. (2003). *Understanding terrorism: Challenges, perspectives, and issues.* Thousand Oaks, CA: Sage.

Martin, S. T. (2001, November 29). Willing to kill and die, but why? *St. Petersburg Times*, pp. 1D, 3D.

Martinson, I. M. (Ed.). (1976). *Home care for the dying child.* New York: Appleton-Century-Crofts.

Martinson, I. M., Davies, E. B., & McClowry, S. G. (1987). The long-term effects of sibling death on self-concept. *Journal of Pediatric Nursing, 2,* 227–235.

Martorell, G., Papalia, D. E., & Feldman, R. E. (2014). *A child's world: Infancy through adolescence* (13th ed.). New York: McGraw-Hill.

Maruyama, N. L. (1998). How many children do you have? *Bereavement Magazine, 12*(5), 16.

Marzo, M. (2015). Sexuality. In B. R. Ferrell, N. Coyle, & J. Paice, (Eds.). (2015). *Oxford textbook of palliative nursing* (4th ed., pp. 420–421). New York: Oxford University Press.

Masera, G., Spinetta, J. J., Jankovic, M., et al. (1999). Guidelines for assistance to terminally ill children with cancer: A report of the SIOP working committee on psychosocial issues in pediatric oncology. *Medical and Pediatric Oncology, 32,* 44–48.

Maslow, A. (1968). *Toward a psychology of being* (2nd ed.). Princeton, NJ: Van Nostrand.

Maslow, A. (1971). *The farther reaches of human nature.* New York: Viking Penguin.

Mason, D. J. (2015). Conversations about how we die. *Journal of the American Medical Association, 313,* 1895–1896. doi:10.1001/jama.2015.3654

Mathews, L. L., & Servaty-Seib, H. L. (2007). Hardiness and grief in a sample of bereaved college students. *Death Studies, 31,* 183–204. doi:10.1080/07481180601152328

Mathieu, F. (2011). *The compassion fatigue workbook: Creative tools for transforming compassion fatigue and vicarious traumatization.* New York: Routledge.

Matse, J. (1975). Reactions to death in residential homes for the aged. *Omega, Journal of Death and Dying, 6,* 21–32. doi:10.2190/02XX-FHCY-8BG0-9KH2

Matthews, J. L. (2016). *Long-term care; How to plan and pay for it* (11th ed.). Berkeley, CA: Nolo.

Matthews, L. T., & Marwit, S. J. (2004). Examining the assumptive world views of parents bereaved by accident, murder, and illness. *Omega, Journal of Death and Dying, 48,* 115–136. doi:10.2190/KCB0-NNVB-UGY6-NPYR

Matthews, W. (1897). Navaho legends. *Memoirs of the American Folk-Lore Society* (Vol. 5). New York: G. E. Stechert.

Matzo, M., & Sherman, D. W. (Eds.). (2014). *Palliative care nursing: Quality care to the end of life* (4th ed.). New York: Springer.

Mauk, G. W., & Weber, C. (1991). Peer survivors of adolescent suicide: Perspectives on grieving and postvention. *Journal of Adolescent Research, 6,* 113–131. doi:10.1177/074355489161009

Maurer, A. (1964). Adolescent attitudes toward death. *Journal of Genetic Psychology, 105,* 75–90. doi:10.1080/00221325.1964.10533647

Maurer, A. (1966). Maturation of the conception of death. *Journal of Medical Psychology, 39,* 35–41.

May, G. (1992). For they shall be comforted. *Shalem News, 16*(2), 3.

Mayer, R. G. (2011). *Embalming: History, theory, and practice* (5th ed.). Norwalk, CT: Appleton & Lange.

Mayo Clinic. (2009). *Mayo Clinic guide to Alzheimer's disease.* Rochester, MN: Mayo Store.

Mazanec, P., & Tyler, M. K. (2003). Cultural considerations in end-of-life care. *American Journal of Nursing, 103*(3), 50–58.

Mbiti, J. S. (1970). *African religion and philosophy.* Garden City, NY: Doubleday Anchor.

McCabe, M. (1994). Patient Self-Determination Act: A Native American (Navajo) perspective. *Cambridge Quarterly of Healthcare Ethics, 3,* 419–421.

McCaffery, M., & Beebe, A. (1989). *Pain: Clinical manual for nursing practice.* St. Louis, MO: Mosby.

McCallum, D. E., Byrne, P., & Bruera, E. (2000). How children die in hospital. *Journal of Pain and Symptom Management, 20,* 417–423. doi:10.1016/S0885-3924(00)00212-8

McCartney, M. (2014). *Living with dying: Finding care and compassion at the end of life.* London: Pinter & Martin.

McCord, C., & Freeman, H. P. (1990). Excess mortality in Harlem. *New England Journal of Medicine, 322,* 173–177. doi:10.1056/NEJM199001183220306

McCormick, R. (1974). To save or let die: The dilemma of modern medicine. *Journal of the American Medical Association, 229,* 172–176. doi:10.1001/jama.1974.03230400034027

McCown, D. E., & Davies, B. (1995). Patterns of grief in young children following the death of a sibling. *Death Studies, 19,* 41–53. doi:10.1080/07481189508252712

McCoyd, J. L. M., & Walter, C. A. (2016). *Grief and loss across the lifespan: A biopsychosocial perspective* (2nd ed.). New York: Springer.

McCue, K., & Bonn, R. (1996). *How to help children through a parent's serious illness.* New York: St. Martin's Press.

McEwen, R. N., & Scheaffer, K. (2013). Virtual mourning and memory construction on Facebook: Here are the terms of use. *Bulletin of Science, Technology & Society, 33,* 64–75. doi:10.1177/0270467613516753

McFerran, K., Roberts, M., & O'Grady, L. (2010). Music therapy with bereaved teenagers: A mixed methods perspective. *Death Studies, 34,* 541–565. doi:10.1080/07481181003765428

McGinnis, J. M., & Foege, W. H. (1993). Actual causes of death in the United States. *Journal of the American Medical Association, 270,* 2207–2212. doi:10.1001/jama.1993.03510180077038

McGoldrick, M. (1988). Women and the family life cycle. In B. Carter & M. McGoldrick (Eds.), *The changing family life cycle: A framework for family therapy* (2nd ed., pp. 29–68). New York: Gardner Press.

McGoldrick, M., Carter, B., & Garcia-Preto, N. (2010). *The expanded family life cycle: Individual, family, and social perspectives* (4th ed.). Upper Saddle River, NJ: Prentice Hall.

McGoldrick, M., Giordano, J., & Garcia-Preto, N. (Eds.). (2005). *Ethnicity and family therapy* (3rd ed.). New York: Guilford.

McGoldrick, M., & Walsh, F. (2004). A time to mourn: Death and the family life cycle. In F. Walsh & M. McGoldrick (Eds.), *Living beyond loss: Death in the family* (2nd ed., pp. 27–46). New York: Norton.

McGowin, D. F. (1993). *Living in the labyrinth: A personal journey through the maze of Alzheimer's.* New York: Delacorte.

McGreevy, C. M., Pentakota, S. R., Mohamed, O., Sigler, K., Mosenthal, A. C., & Berlin, A. (2016). Gastrostomy tube placement: An opportunity for establishing patient-centered goals of care. *Surgery, 161*(4), 1100–1107. doi:10.1016/j.surg.2016.10.034

McGuffey, W. H. (1866). *McGuffey's new fourth eclectic reader: Instructive lessons for the young* (Enlarged ed.). Cincinnati, OH: Wilson, Hinkle.

McIntosh, J. L. (1985). Suicide among the elderly: Levels and trends. *American Journal of Orthopsychiatry, 55,* 288–293. doi:10.1111/j.1939-0025.1985.tb03443.x

McIntosh, J. L. (1987). Research, therapy, and educational needs. In E. J. Dunne, J. L. McIntosh, & K. Dunne-Maxim (Eds.), *Suicide and its aftermath: Understanding and counseling the survivors* (pp. 263–277). New York: Norton.

McKenzie, K. M., & Harra, T. (2014). *Over our dead bodies: Undertakers lift the lid.* New York: Citadel.

McKhann, C. F. (1999). *A time to die: The place for physician assistance*. New Haven, CT: Yale University Press.

McKhann, G. M., Knopman, D. S., Chertkow, H., et al. (2011). The diagnosis of dementia due to Alzheimer's disease: Recommendations from the National Institute on Aging and the Alzheimer's Association workgroup. *Alzheimer's and Dementia: The Journal of the Alzheimer's Association, 7*(3), 263–269. doi:10.1016/j.jalz.2011.03.005

McNeil, J. N. (1986). Talking about death: Adolescents, parents, and peers. In C. A. Corr & J. N. McNeil (Eds.), *Adolescence and death* (pp. 185–201). New York: Springer.

McNurlen, M. (1991). Guidelines for group work. In C. A. Corr, H. Fuller, C. A. Barnickol, & D. M. Corr (Eds.), *Sudden infant death syndrome: Who can help and how* (pp. 180–202). New York: Springer.

McQuay, J. (1995). Cross-cultural customs and beliefs related to health crises, death, and organ donation/transplantation: A guide to assist health care professionals understand different responses and provide cross-cultural assistance. *Critical Care Nursing Clinics of North America, 7*(3), 581–594.

Mead, M. (1973). Ritual and social crisis. In J. D. Shaughnessy (Ed.), *The roots of ritual* (pp. 87–101). Grand Rapids, MI: Eerdmans.

Mehl-Madrona, L. (2007). *Narrative medicine: The use of history and story in the healing process*. Rochester, VT: Bear and Company.

Mehran, P., Simbar, M., Shams, J., Ramezani-Tehrani, F., & Nasiri, N. (2013). History of perinatal loss and maternal–fetal attachment behaviors. *Women & Birth, 26*(3), 185–189. doi:10.1016/j.wombi.2013.04.005

Meier, D. E., Isaacs, S. L., & Hughes, R. (Eds.). (2010). *Palliative care: Transforming the care of serious illness*. San Francisco: Jossey-Bass.

Meisel, A., & Cerminara, K. L. (2004). *The right to die: The law of end-of-life decision-making*. New York: Aspen.

Mello, M. M., Studdert, D. M., & Parmet, W. E. (2015). Shifting vaccination politics: The end of personal-belief exemptions in California. *New England Journal of Medicine, 373*, 785–787. doi:10.1056/NEJMp1508701

Meltzer, M. I., Cox, N. J., & Fukuda, K. (1999). Modeling the impact of pandemic influenza in the United States: Implications for setting priorities for intervention/Background paper. Emerging infectious diseases. Retrieved from http://www.cdc.gov/ncidod/eid/vof5no5/meltzer.htm

Melzack, R. (1990, February). The tragedy of needless pain. *Scientific American*, pp. 27–33.

Melzack, R., Mount, B. M., & Gordon, J. M. (1979). The Brompton mixture versus morphine solution given orally: Effects on pain. *Canadian Medical Association Journal, 120*, 435–438.

Melzack, R., Ofiesh, J. G., & Mount, B. M. (1976). The Brompton mixture: Effects on pain in cancer patients. *Canadian Medical Association Journal, 115*, 125–129.

Melzack, R., & Wall, P. D. (1991). *The challenge of pain* (3rd ed.). New York: Penguin.

Menninger, K. (1938). *Man against himself*. New York: Harcourt, Brace & World.

Metzgar, M. M., & Zick, B. C. (1996). Building the foundation: Preparation before a trauma. In C. A. Corr & D. M. Corr (Eds.), *Handbook of childhood death and bereavement* (pp. 245–264). New York: Springer.

Metzger, A. M. (1980). A Q-methodological study of the Kübler-Ross stage theory. *Omega, Journal of Death and Dying, 10*, 291–302. doi:10.2190/LJR7-D5FG-6NF6-DWTL

Meyer, R. E. (Ed.). (1992). *Cemeteries and gravemarkers: Voices of American culture*. Logan, UT: Utah State University Press.

Michaelson, J. (2010). *Step into our lives at the funeral home*. Amityville, NY: Baywood.

Michalczyk, J. J. (Ed.). (1994). *Medicine, ethics, and the Third Reich: Historical and contemporary issues*. Kansas City, MO: Sheed & Ward.

Michel, L., & Herbeck, D. (2001). *American terrorist: Timothy McVeigh and the Oklahoma City bombing*. New York: Regan Books.

Miles, L. (2013, July). Death Cafés: Talking about the taboo. *ADEC Forum: The quarterly publication of the Association for Death Education and Counseling, 39*(3), 23.

Miles, L., & Corr, C. A. (2017). Death Cafe: What is it and what we can learn from it. *Omega, Journal of Death and Dying, 75*, 151–165. doi:10.1177/0030222815612602

Miles, M. (1971). *Annie and the old one*. Boston: Little, Brown.

Miles, M. S., & Demi, A. S. (1984). Toward the development of a theory of bereavement guilt: Sources of guilt in bereaved parents. *Omega, Journal of Death and Dying, 14*, 299–314. doi:10.2190/F8PG-PUN4-8VW6-REWQ

Miles, M. S., & Demi, A. S. (1986). Guilt in bereaved parents. In T. A. Rando (Ed.), *Parental loss of a child* (pp. 97–118). Champaign, IL: Research Press.

Milevsky, A. (2015). *Understanding adolescents for helping professions*. New York: Springer.

Miller, D. N. (2011). *Child and adolescent suicidal behavior: School-based prevention, assessment, and intervention*. New York: Guilford.

Miller, F. G., & Truog, R. D. (2012). *Death, dying, and organ transplantation: Reconstructing medical ethics at the end of life*. New York: Oxford University Press.

Miller, J., Engelberg, S., & Broad, W. (2001). *Germs: Biological weapons and America's secret war*. New York: Simon & Schuster.

Miller, M. (1987). *My grandmother's cookie jar*. Los Angeles: Price Stern Sloan.

Miller, S. C., Lima, J., Gozalo, P. L., & Mor, V. (2010). The growth of hospice care in U.S. nursing homes. *Journal of the American Geriatrics Society, 58*, 1481–1488. doi:10.1111/j.1532-5415.2010.02968.x

Mills, L. O. (Ed.). (1969). *Perspectives on death*. Nashville, TN: Abingdon.

Minnich, H. C. (1936a). *Old favorites from the McGuffey readers*. New York: American Book Company.

Minnich, H. C. (1936b). *William Holmes McGuffey and his readers*. New York: American Book Company.

Minniefield, W. J., Yang, J., & Muti, P. (2001). Differences in attitudes toward organ donation among African Americans and whites in the United States. *Journal of the National Medical Association, 93*, 372–379.

Minow, N. N., & LaMay, C. L. (1995). *Abandoned in the wasteland: Children, television and the First Amendment*. New York: Hill & Wang.

Mitchell, E. (2009). *Beyond tears: Living after losing a child* (rev. & enlarged ed.). New York: St. Martin's Griffin.

Mitchell, L. (1977). *The meaning of ritual*. New York: Paulist Press.

Mitchell, L. M., Stephenson, P. H., Cadell, S., & Macdonald, M. E. (2012). Death and grief on-line: Virtual memorialization and changing concepts of childhood death and parental bereavement on the Internet. *Health Sociology Review, 21*(4), 413–431. doi:10.5172/hesr.2012.21.4.413

Mitford, J. (1963). *The American way of death*. New York: Simon & Schuster.

Mitford, J. (1998). *The American way of death revisited*. New York: Knopf.

Mobbs, D., & Watt, C. (2011). There is nothing paranormal about near-death experiences: How neuroscience can explain seeing bright lights, meeting the dead, or being convinced you are one of them. *Trends in Cognitive Sciences*, 15(10), 447–449. doi:10.1016/j.tics.2011.07.010

Moffat, M. J. (1992). *In the midst of winter: Selections from the literature of mourning*. New York: Vintage.

Mokdad, A. H., Marks, J. S., Stroup, D. F., & Gerberding, J. L. (2004). Actual causes of death in the United States, 2000. *Journal of the American Medical Association*, 291, 1238–1245. doi:10.1001/jama.291.10.1238

Moller, D. W. (2012). *Dancing with broken bones: Poverty, race, and spirit-filled dying in the inner city* (rev. & expanded ed.). New York: Oxford University Press.

Monat, A., & Lazarus, R. S. (Eds.). (1991). *Stress and coping: An anthology* (3rd ed.). New York: Columbia University Press.

Monroe, B., & Kraus, F. (Eds.). (2010). *Brief interventions with bereaved children* (2nd ed.). Oxford, UK: Oxford University Press.

Montgomery, J., & Fewer, W. (1988). *Family systems and beyond*. New York: Human Sciences Press.

Moody, H. R., & Sasser, J. R. (2014). *Aging: Concepts and controversies* (8th ed.). Thousand Oaks, CA: Sage.

Moody, R. A. (1975). *Life after life*. Covington, GA: Mockingbird Books. (Reprinted New York: Bantam, 1976).

Moon, R. Y., & Hauck, F. R. (2015). Hazardous bedding in infants' sleep environment is still common and a cause for concern. *Pediatrics*, 135(1), 1–2. doi:10.1542/peds.2014-3218

Moore, A. J., & Stratton, D. C. (2002). *Resilient widowers: Older men speak for themselves*. New York: Springer.

Moore, F. (2009). *Celebrating a life: Planning memorial services and other creative remembrances*. New York: Stewart, Tabori, and Chang.

Moos, R. H., & Schaefer, J. A. (1986). Life transitions and crises: A conceptual overview. In R. H. Moos & J. A. Schaefer (Eds.), *Coping with life crises: An integrated approach* (pp. 3–28). New York: Plenum.

Morgan, E. (2010). *Dealing creatively with death: A manual of death education and simple burial* (14th rev. ed.). Hinesburg, VT: Upper Access.

Morgan, J. D., & Laungani, P. (Eds.). (2002). *Death and bereavement around the world: Vol. 1, Major religious traditions*. Amityville, NY: Baywood.

Morgan, J. D., Laungani, P., & Palmer, S. (Eds.). (2003–2009). *Death and bereavement around the world* (5 vols.). Amityville, NY: Baywood.

Morgan, R. (2006). *Flight 93 revealed: What really happened on the 9/11 "Let's Roll" flight*. New York: Carroll & Graf.

Morgan, S. E., Harrison, T. R., Chewning, L., Davis, L., & DiCorcia, M. (2007). Entertainment (mis)education: The framing of organ donation in entertainment television. *Health Communication*, 22(2), 143–151. doi:10.1080/10410230701454114

Morhaim, D. (2011). *The better end: Surviving (and dying) on your own terms in today's modern medical world*. Baltimore: Johns Hopkins University Press.

Morley, J., Tolson, D., Ouslander, J., & Vellas, B. (2013). *Nursing home care*. New York: McGraw-Hill.

Moroney, R. M., & Kurtz, N. R. (1975). The evolution of long-term care institutions. In S. Sherwood (Ed.), *Long-term care: A handbook for researchers, planners, and providers* (pp. 81–121). New York: Spectrum.

Morris, S. E., & Block, S. D. (2015). Adding value to palliative care services: The development of an institutional bereavement program. *Journal of Palliative Medicine*, 18, 915–922. doi:10.1089/jpm.2015.0080

Mortimer, J. T., & Larson, R. W. (Eds.). (2002). *The changing adolescent experience: Societal trends and the transition to adulthood*. Cambridge, England: Cambridge University Press.

Mosby, I. (2013). Administering colonial science: Nutrition research and human biomedical experimentation in Aboriginal communities and residential schools, 1942–1952. *Histoire sociale/Social history*, 46(91), 145–172. doi:10.1353/his.2013.0015

Moss, J. (2010). *The Day of the Dead: A pictorial archive of Dia de los Muertos*. Mineola, NY: Dover Publications.

Moss, M. S., & Moss, S. Z. (1985). Some aspects of the elderly widow(er)'s persistent tie with the deceased spouse. *Omega, Journal of Death and Dying*, 15, 195–206. doi:10.2190/BT34-JWW5-K6XA-JFEA

Moss, M. S., & Moss, S. Z. (2007). Death of a parent of an adult child. In K. J. Doka (Ed.), *Living with grief: Before and after a death* (pp. 255–269). Washington, DC: Hospice Foundation of America.

Moss, M. S., & Moss, S. Z. (2013). Meaning of the death of an elderly father: Two sisters' perspectives. *Omega, Journal of Death and Dying*, 66, 195–213. doi:10.2190/OM.66.3.a

Moss, M. S., Lesher, E. L., & Moss, S. Z. (1987). Impact of the death of an adult child on elderly parents: Some observations. *Omega, Journal of Death and Dying*, 17, 209–218. doi:10.2190/2QCM-UXYV-8NR2-1CYF

Mount, B. M., Jones, A., & Patterson, A. (1974). Death and dying: Attitudes in a teaching hospital. *Urology*, 4, 741–747. doi:10.1016/0090-4295(74)90264-7

Mueller, J. (2006). *Overblown: How politicians and the terrorism industry inflate national security threats, and why we believe them*. New York: Free Press.

Mukherjee, S. (2010). *The emperor of all maladies: A biography of cancer*. New York: Scribner.

Mullan, Z. (2015, July 8). The cost of Ebola. *The Lancet Global Health*, 3(8), e423. doi:10.1016/S2214-109X(15)00092-3

Munet-Vilaró, F. (1998). Grieving and death rituals of Latinos. *Oncology Nursing Forum*, 25(10), 1761–1763.

Muñoz-Kiehne, M. (2000). *Since my brother died/Desde que murió mi hermano*. Omaha, NE: Centering Corporation.

Munson, R. (1993). *Fan mail*. New York: Dutton.

Munson, R. (2004). *Raising the dead: Organ transplants, ethics, and society*. New York: Oxford University Press.

Murphy, S. A., Johnson, L. C., & Lohan, J. (2003). Challenging the myths about parents' adjustment after the sudden, violent death of a child. *Journal of Nursing Scholarship*, 35(4), 359–364. doi:10.1111/j.1547-5069.2003.00359.x

Murphy, S. L., Kochanek, K. D., Xu, J. Q., & Heron, M. (2015). Deaths: Final data for 2012. *National Vital Statistics Reports*, 63(9). Hyattsville, MD: National Center for Health Statistics.

Murray, J. E. (2004). *Surgery of the soul*. Sagamore Beach, MA: Science History Publications/USA.

Musto, B. (1999, January 19). Karen's gift. *Women's World*, 39.

Muwahidi, A. A. (1989). Islamic perspectives on death and dying. In A. Berger, P. Badham, A. H. Kutscher, J. Berger, M. Perry, & J. Beloff (Eds.), *Perspectives on death and dying: Cross-cultural and multi-disciplinary views* (pp. 38–54). Philadelphia: Charles Press.

Myers, M. F., & Fine, C. (2006). *Touched by suicide: Hope and healing after loss*. New York: Penguin.

Nabe, C. M. (1987). Fragmentation and spiritual care. In C. A. Corr & R. A. Pacholski (Eds.), *Death: Completion and discovery* (pp. 281–286). Lakewood, OH: Association for Death Education and Counseling.

Nabe, C. M. (1999). A caregiver's quandary: How am I to evaluate and respond to the other's suffering? *Omega, Journal of Death and Dying*, 39, 71–91. doi:10.2190/RYV1-BR6K-QJ5L-XU14

Nadeau, J. (1998). *Families make sense of death*. Thousand Oaks, CA: Sage.

Nader, K. (Ed.). (2011). *School rampage shootings and other youth disturbances: Early preventative interventions*. New York: Routledge.

Nagy, M. A. (1948). The child's theories concerning death. *Journal of Genetic Psychology, 73*, 3–27. doi:10.1080/08856559.1948.10533458 (Reprinted with some editorial changes as "The child's view of death." In H. Feifel (Ed.), *The meaning of death*, 1959, (pp. 79–98). New York: McGraw-Hill)

Naparstek, B. (2005). *Invisible heroes: Survivors of trauma and how they heal*. New York: Bantam.

Narang, A. K., Wright, A. A., & Nicholas, L. H. (2015, July 9), Trends in advance care planning in patients with cancer: Results from a national longitudinal survey. *JAMA Oncology, 1*, 601–608. doi:10.1001/jamaoncol.2015.1976

National Action Alliance for Suicide Prevention: Survivors of Suicide Loss Task Force. (2015). Responding to grief, trauma, and distress after a suicide: National Guidelines. Washington, DC: Author. Retrieved April 28, 2017, from http://actionallianceforsuicideprevention.org/sites/actionallianceforsuicideprevention.org/files/NationalGuidelines.pdf

National Alliance for Caregiving (NAC) & AARP Public Policy Institute. (2015). *Caregiving in the U.S. 2015*. Bethesda, MD: Authors.

National Commission on Terrorist Attacks. (2004). *The 9/11 Commission report: Final report of the National Commission on Terrorist Attacks upon the United States*. New York: Norton.

National Ethics Committee, Veterans Health Administration. (2007). The ethics of palliative sedation as a therapy of last resort. *American Journal of Hospice and Palliative Medicine, 23*, 483–491. doi:10.1177/1049909106294883

National Gang Intelligence Center. (2013). *2013 National Gang Report*. Washington, DC: Author. Retrieved September 21, 2015, from https://www.fbi.gov/stats-services/publications/national-gang-report-2013

National Hospice and Palliative Care Organization (NHPCO). (2003). *Education and training curriculum for pediatric palliative care*. Alexandria, VA: Author.

National Hospice and Palliative Care Organization (NHPCO). (2004). *Caring for kids: How to develop a home-based support program for children and adolescents with life-threatening conditions*. Alexandra, VA: Author.

National Hospice and Palliative Care Organization (NHPCO). (2010). *Standards of practice for hospice programs*. Alexandria, VA: Author. Retrieved June 18, 2011, from http://www.nhpco.org/files/public/quality/Standards/NHPCO_STANDARDS_2011CD.pdf

National Hospice and Palliative Care Organization (NHPCO). (2014). *NHPCO facts and figures: Pediatric palliative and hospice care in America*. Alexandria, VA: Author.

National Hospice and Palliative Care Organization (NHPCO). (2015). *NHPCO facts and figures: Hospice care in America, 2015*. Alexandria, VA: Author.

National Institute of Allergy and Infectious Diseases (NIAID). (2005, April 5). Focus on TB. Tuberculosis in history. A killer returns: The face of the epidemic. Retrieved January 28, 2007, from http://www3.niaid.nih.gov/news/focuson/tb/research/history/historical_killer.htm

National Institute of Neurological Disorders and Stroke. (2015, September 11). *NINDS coma information page*. Bethesda, MD: Author. Retrieved September 30, 2016, from http://www.ninds.nih.gov/disorders/coma/coma.htm

National Institute of Nursing Research. (2015). *Palliative care for children: Support for the whole family when your child is living with a serious illness*. Bethesda, MD: Author. (Also available in Spanish.)

National Institute on Aging. (2015). *Talking with your older patient: A clinician's handbook*. Bethesda. MD: Author. NIH publication 16-7105. Retrieved July 15, 2016, from https://www.nia.nih.gov/health/publication/talking-your-older-patient/including-families-and-caregivers

National Kidney Foundation. (2004). *National communications guidelines regarding communication among donor families, transplant candidates/recipients, non-directed living donors, and health care professionals* (2nd ed.). New York: Author.

National Kidney Foundation. (2007). *Patches of love: The National donor family quilt*. New York: Author.

National Safety Council. (2016). *Injury facts: 2016 edition*. Itaska, IL: Author.

Neal, M. C. (2012). *To heaven and back: A doctor's extraordinary account of her death, heaven, angels, and life again: A true story*. Colorado Springs, CO: WaterBrook Press.

Neaman, J. S., & Silver, C. G. (1983). *Kind words: A thesaurus of euphemisms*. New York: Facts on File.

Neimeyer, R. A. (1998). *Lessons of loss: A guide to coping*. New York: McGraw-Hill.

Neimeyer, R. A. (2000). Searching for the meaning of meaning: Grief therapy and the process of reconstruction. *Death Studies, 24*, 541–558. doi:10.1080/07481180050121480

Neimeyer, R. A. (2007). Meaning breaking, meaning making: Rewriting stories of loss. In K. J. Doka (Ed.), *Living with grief: Before and after a death* (pp. 193–208). Washington, DC: Hospice Foundation of America.

Neimeyer, R. A. (2009). Death anxiety. In C. D. Bryant & D. L. Peck (Eds.), *Encyclopedia of death and the human experience* (2 vols., I, pp. 296–300). Thousand Oaks, CA: Sage.

Neimeyer, R. A. (Ed.). (1994). *Death anxiety handbook: Research, instrumentation, and application*. Washington, DC: Taylor & Francis.

Neimeyer, R. A. (Ed.). (2001). *Meaning reconstruction and the experience of loss*. Washington, DC: American Psychological Association.

Neimeyer, R. A. (Ed.). (2012). *Techniques of grief therapy: Creative practices for counseling the bereaved*. New York: Routledge.

Neimeyer, R. A. (Ed.). (2016). *Techniques of grief therapy: Assessment and intervention*. New York: Routledge.

Neimeyer, R. A., & Van Brunt, D. (1995). Death anxiety. In H. Wass & R. A. Neimeyer (Eds.), *Dying: Facing the facts* (3rd ed., pp. 49–88). Washington, DC: Taylor & Francis.

Neimeyer, R. A., Wittkowski, J., & Moser, R. P. (2004). Psychological research on death attitudes: An overview and evaluation. *Death Studies, 28*, 309–340. doi:10.1080/07481180490432324

Nelson, B. J., & Frantz, T. T. (1996). Family interactions of suicide survivors and survivors of non-suicidal death. *Omega, Journal of Death and Dying, 33*, 131–146. doi:10.2190/3AQ4-KUQE-KJ4R-8Q89

Nelson, V. J. (2009, November 12). Obituary: John J. O'Connor III dies at 79; attorney and husband of former Supreme Court Justice Sandra Day O'Connor. *Los Angeles Times*. Retrieved December 29, 2010, from http://www.latimes.com/news/obituaries/la-me-john-oconnor12-2009nov12,0,7012487.story

Netherlands Euthanasia Commission. (n.d.). *Euthanasia: Q and A. The Termination of Life on Request and Assisted Suicide (Review Procedures) Act in practice*. Author. Retrieved March 26, 2013, from http://www.euthanasiecommissie.nl

Neugarten, B. L. (1974). Age groups in American society and the rise of the young-old. *Annals of the American Academy of Political and Social Science, 415*, 187–198. doi:10.1177/000271627441500114

Neugarten, B. L., & Datan, N. (1973). Sociological perspectives on the life cycle. In P. B. Baltes & K. W. Schaie (Eds.), *Lifespan developmental psychology: Personality and socialization* (pp. 53–69). New York: Academic Press.

Neusner, J. (Trans.). (1988). *The Mishnah: A new translation.* New Haven, CT: Yale University Press.

New England Primer. (1962). New York: Columbia University Press. (Original work published 1727)

Newcomb, A. (2014, June 13). Dead people get life-like poses at their funerals. *ABC News.* Retrieved July 24, 2016, from http://abcnews.go.com/US/dead-people-life-poses-funerals/story?id=23456853

Newman, B. M., & Newman, P. R. (2014). *Development through life: A psychosocial approach* (12th ed.). Belmont, CA: Cengage Learning.

Newman, K. S. (2004). *Rampage: The social roots of school shootings.* New York: Basic Books.

Newman, K. S. (2012). *The accordion family: Boomerang kids, anxious parents, and the private toll of global competition.* Boston: Beacon Press.

Nichols, M. P. (1995). *The lost art of listening.* New York: Guilford.

Nitschke, P., & Stewart, F. (2007). *The peaceful pill handbook* (Rev. international ed.). Waterford, MI: Exit International U.S., Ltd.

Noack, D. (1999). Controversial photo draws support from readers. *Editor and Publisher, 132*(26), 8.

Noel, B., & Blair, P. (2008). *I wasn't ready to say goodbye: Surviving, coping and healing after the sudden death of a loved one.* Naperville, IL: Sourcebooks.

Nolt, S. M. (2003). *A history of the Amish* (2nd ed.). Intercourse, PA: Good Books.

Nolt, S. M., & Meyers, T. J. (2007). *Plain diversity: Amish cultures and identities.* Baltimore: Johns Hopkins University Press.

Noppe, I. C. (2007). Historical and contemporary perspectives on death education. In D. E. Balk, C. Wogrin, G. Thornton, & D. Meagher (Eds.), *ADEC handbook of thanatology* (pp. 329–343). Northbrook, IL: Association for Death Education and Counseling.

Noppe, I. C., & Noppe, L. D. (1997). Evolving meanings of death during early, middle and later adolescence. *Death Studies, 21,* 253–275. doi:10.1080/074811897201967

Noppe, I. C., & Noppe, L. D. (2004). Adolescent experiences with death: Letting go of immortality. *Journal of Mental Health Counseling, 26,* 146–167. doi:10.1177/000271627441500114

Noppe, I. C., Noppe, L. D., & Bartell, D. (2006). Terrorism and resilience: Adolescents' and teachers' responses to September 11, 2001. *Death Studies, 30,* 41–60. doi:10.1080/07481180500348761

Noppe, L. D., & Noppe, I. C. (1991). Dialectical themes in adolescent conceptions of death. *Journal of Adolescent Research, 6,* 28–42. doi:10.1177/074355489161003

Noppe, L. D., & Noppe, I. C. (1996). Ambiguity in adolescent understandings of death. In C. A. Corr & D. E. Balk (Eds.), *Handbook of adolescent death and bereavement* (pp. 25–41). New York: Springer.

Norlander, L., & McSteen, K. (2001). *Choices at the end of life: Finding out what your parents want before it's too late.* Minneapolis, MN: Fairview Press.

Northcott, H. E., & Wilson, D. M. (2017). *Dying and death in Canada* (3rd ed.). Toronto: University of Toronto Press.

Nouwen, H. (1972). *The wounded healer: Ministry in contemporary society.* Garden City, NY: Doubleday.

Nouwen, H. (1994). *Our greatest gift: A meditation on dying and caring.* New York: HarperCollins.

Nouwen, H. (2005). *In memoriam.* Notre Dame, IN: Ave Maria Press.

Nouwen, H., & Gaffney, W. J. (1990). *Aging: The fulfillment of life.* New York: Doubleday.

Nouwen, N. J. M. (1986). *Out of solitude: Three meditations on the Christian life.* New York: Walker & Co.

Novack, D. H., Plumer, R., Smith, R. L., et al. (1979). Changes in physicians' attitudes toward telling the cancer patient. *Journal of the American Medical Association, 241,* 897–900. doi:10.1001/jama.1979.03290350017012

Novick, P. (1999). *The Holocaust in American life.* Boston: Houghton Mifflin.

Noyes, R., & Clancy, J. (1977). The dying role: Its relevance to improved patient care. *Psychiatry, 40,* 41–47.

Nuland, S. B. (1994). *How we die: Reflections on life's final chapter.* New York: Knopf.

Oates, J. C. (2011). *A widow's story: A memoir.* New York: Vintage.

Obayashi, H. (Ed.). (1992). *Death and afterlife: Perspectives of world religions.* Westport, CT: Praeger.

Öberg, M., Jaakkola, M. S., Woodward, A., Peruga, A., & Prüss-Ustün. (2011). Worldwide burden of disease from exposure to second-hand smoke: A retrospective analysis of data from 192 countries. *The Lancet, 377*(9760), 139–146. doi:10.1016/S0140-6736(10)61388-8

Obermeyer, Z., Makar, M., Abujaber, S., et al. (2014). Association between the Medicare hospice benefit and health care utilization and costs for patients with poor-prognosis cancer. *Journal of the American Medical Association, 312*(18), 1888–1896. doi:10.1001/jama.2014.14950

Obermeyer, Z., Powers, B. W., Makar, M., Keating, N. L., & Cutler, D. M. (2015). Physician characteristics strongly predict patient enrollment in hospice. *Health Affairs, 34*(6), 993–1000. doi:10.1377/hlthaff.2014.1055

O'Brien, G. (2014). *On Pluto: Inside the mind of Alzheimer's.* Brewster, MA: Codfish Press.

Offer, D. (1969). *The psychological worlds of the teenager.* New York: Basic Books.

Offer, D., & Offer, J. B. (1975). *From teenage to young manhood: A psychological study.* New York: Basic Books.

Offer, D., Ostrov, E., & Howard, K. I. (1981). *The adolescent: A psychological self-portrait.* New York: Basic Books.

Offer, D., Ostrov, E., Howard, K. I., & Atkinson, R. (1988). *The teenage world: Adolescents' self-image in ten countries.* New York: Plenum.

Offer, D., & Sabshin, M. (1984). Adolescence: Empirical perspectives. In D. Offer & M. Sabshin (Eds.), *Normality and the life cycle: A critical integration* (pp. 76–107). New York: Basic Books.

Ogden, C. L., Carroll, M. D., Kit, B. K., & Flegal, K. M. (2014). Prevalence of childhood and adult obesity in the United States, 2011–2012. *Journal of the American Medical Association, 311,* 806–814. doi:10.1001/jama.2014.732

O'Hara, K. (2006). *A grief like no other: Surviving the violent death of someone you love.* New York: Marlowe & Company.

Oken, D. (1961). What to tell cancer patients: A study of medical attitudes. *Journal of the American Medical Association, 175,* 1120–1128. doi:10.1001/jama.1961.03040130004002

Okun, B., & Nowinski, J. (2011). *Saying goodbye: How families can find renewal through loss.* New York: Berkley.

Oliver, D. P., Washington, K., Kruse, R. L., et al. (2014). Hospice family members' perceptions of and experiences with end-of-life care in the nursing home. *Journal of the American Medical Directors Association, 15,* 744–750. doi:10.1016/j.jamda.2014.05.014

Oliviere, D., Monroe, B., & Payne, S. (Eds.). (2012). *Death, dying, and social differences* (2nd ed.). New York: Oxford University Press.

Olson, L. M., & Wahab, S. (2006). American Indians and suicide: A neglected area of research. *Trauma, Violence, and Abuse, 7,* 19–33. doi:10.1177/1524838005283005

Oltjenbruns, K. A. (1991). Positive outcomes of adolescents' experience with grief. *Journal of Adolescent Research, 6,* 43–53. doi:10.1177/074355489161004

Oltjenbruns, K. A. (1996). Death of a friend during adolescence: Issues and impacts. In C. A. Corr & D. E. Balk (Eds.), *Handbook of adolescent death and bereavement* (pp. 196–215). New York: Springer.

Olusoga, D., & Erichsen, C. W. (2010). *The Kaiser's holocaust: Germany's forgotten genocide and the colonial roots of Nazism.* London: Faber & Faber.

O'Neill, J. F., Selwyn, P. A., & Schietinger, H. (2012). *A clinical guide to supportive & palliative care for HIV/AIDS.* Washington, DC: U.S. Department of Health and Human Services, Health Resources and Services Administration, HIV/AIDS Bureau.

Onwuteaka-Philipsen, B. D., van der Heide, A., Koper, D., et al. (2003). Euthanasia and other end-of-life decisions in the Netherlands in 1990, 1995, and 2001. *The Lancet, 362,* 395–399. doi:10.1016/S0140-6736(03)14029-9

Opalewski, D. A. (2008). *Answering the cry for help: A suicide prevention manual.* Chattanooga, TN: National Center for Youth Issues.

Opie, I., & Opie, P. (1969). *Children's games in street and playground: Chasing, catching, seeking, hunting, racing, dueling, exerting, daring, guessing, acting, and pretending.* Oxford, UK: Oxford University Press.

Opoku, K. A. (1978). *West African traditional religion.* Singapore: Far Eastern.

Opoku, K. A. (1987). Death and immortality in the African religious heritage. In P. Badham & L. Badham (Eds.), *Death and immortality in the religions of the world* (pp. 9–21). New York: Paragon House.

Oregon Department of Human Services. (2006). *Eighth annual report on Oregon's Death with Dignity Act.* Retrieved from http://egov.oregon.gov/DHS/ph/pas

Oregon Department of Human Services. (2017, February 10). *Oregon death with dignity act: 2016 data summary.* Retrieved April 28, 2017, from https://public.health.oregon.gov/ProviderPartnerResources/EvaluationResearch/DeathwithDignityAct/Documents/year19.pdf

O'Rourke, M. (2012). *The long goodbye: A memoir.* New York: Riverhead Books.

Osgood, N. J. (1992). *Suicide in later life: Recognizing the warning signs.* New York: Lexington.

Osgood, N. J. (2000). Elderly suicide [Special issue]. *Omega, Journal of Death and Dying, 42*(1).

Osgood, N. J., Brant, B. A., & Lipman, A. (1991). *Suicide among the elderly in long-term care facilities.* New York: Greenwood Press.

Osis, K., & Haraldsson, E. (1997). *At the hour of death* (3rd ed.). Norwalk, CT: Hastings House.

Osofsky, J. D. (Ed.). (2004). *Young children and trauma.* New York: Guilford.

Osterman, M. J. K., Kochanek, K. D., MacDorman, M. F., Strobino, D. M., & Guyer, B. (2015). Annual summary of vital statistics: 2012–2013. *Pediatrics, 135*(6), 1115–1125. doi:10.1542/peds.2015-0434

Osterweis, M., Solomon, F., & Green, M. (Eds.). (1984). *Bereavement: Reactions, consequences, and care.* Washington, DC: National Academies Press.

Owen, J. E., Goode, K. T., & Haley, W. E. (2001). End of life care and reactions to death in African-American and white family

caregivers of relatives with Alzheimer's disease. *Omega, Journal of Death and Dying, 43*(4), 349–361. doi:10.2190/YH2B-8VVE-LA5A-02R2

Owens, J. E., Cook, E. W., & Stevenson, I. (1990). Features of "near-death experience" in relation to whether or not patients were near death. *The Lancet, 336,* 1175–1177. doi:10.1016/0140-6736(90)92780-L

Oxford English Dictionary. (1989). (2nd ed.; 20 vols.) (J. A. Simpson & E.S.C. Weiner, Eds.). Oxford, England: Clarendon Press.

Packman, W., Carmack, B. J. & Ronen, R. (2012) Therapeutic implications of continuing bonds expressions following the death of a pet. *Omega, Journal of Death and Dying, 64,* 335–356. doi:10.2190/OM.64.4.d

Packman, W., Carmack, B. J., Katz, R., et al. (2014). Online survey as empathetic bridging for the disenfranchised grief of pet loss. *Omega, Journal of Death and Dying, 69,* 333–356. doi:10.2190/OM.64.4.d

Palmieri, A., Calvo, V., Kleinbub, J. R., et al. (2014). "Reality" of near-death-experience memories: Evidence from a psychodynamic and electrophysiological integrated study. *Frontiers in Human Neuroscience, 8,* 1–16. doi:10.3389/fnhum.2014.00429

Papadatou, D. (1989). Caring for dying adolescents. *Nursing Times, 85,* 28–31.

Papadatou, D. (2000). A proposed model of health professionals' grieving process. *Omega, Journal of Death and Dying, 41,* 59–77. doi:10.2190/TV6M-8YNA-5DYW-3C1E

Papadatou, D. (2009). *In the face of death: Professionals who care for the dying and the bereaved.* New York: Springer.

Papalia, D. E., & Martorell, G. (2014). *Experience human development* (13th ed.). New York: McGraw-Hill.

Pape, R. A. (2005). *Dying to win: The strategic logic of suicide terrorism.* New York: Random House.

Pappas, S. (2014, March 24). Springtime suicide peak still puzzles scientists. *LiveScience.* Retrieved March 13, 2015, from http://www.livescience.com/44290-suicides-peak-spring.html

Parker-Pope, T. (2007, November 14). Seized by Alzheimer's, then love. *New York Times.* Retrieved December 9, 2010, from http://well.blogs.nytimes.com/2007/11/14/seized-by-alzheimers-then-love/?ref=weekinreview

Parkes, C. M. (1970a). The first year of bereavement: A longitudinal study of the reaction of London widows to the death of their husbands. *Psychiatry, 33,* 444–467.

Parkes, C. M. (1970b). "Seeking" and "finding" a lost object: Evidence from recent studies of reaction to bereavement. *Social Science and Medicine, 4,* 187–201.

Parkes, C. M. (1975). What becomes of redundant world models? A contribution to the study of adaptation to change. *British Journal of Medical Psychology, 48,* 131–137. doi:10.1111/j.2044-8341.1975.tb02315.x

Parkes, C. M. (1976). Determinants of outcome following bereavement. *Omega, Journal of Death and Dying, 6,* 303–323. doi:10.2190/PR0R-GLPD-5FPB-422L

Parkes, C. M. (1987). Models of bereavement care. *Death Studies, 11,* 257–261.

Parkes, C. M. (1996). *Bereavement: Studies of grief in adult life* (3rd ed.). New York: Routledge.

Parkes, C. M. (Ed.). (2006a). Symposium on complicated grief. [Special issue] *Omega, Journal of Death and Dying, 52*(1).

Parkes, C. M. (2006b). Part I. Introduction to a symposium. *Omega, Journal of Death and Dying, 52,* 1–7. doi:10.2190/FQMX-QHJV-138X-NV6C

Parkes, C. M. (2006c). *Love and loss: The roots of grief and its complications.* New York: Routledge.

Parkes, C. M. (2007a). Complicated grief: The debate over a new DSM-V diagnostic category. In K. J. Doka (Ed.), *Living with grief: Before and after a death* (pp. 139–151). Washington, DC: Hospice Foundation of America.

Parkes, C. M. (Ed.). (2007b). "Hospice heritage": In memory of Dame Cicely Saunders [Special issue]. *Omega, Journal of Death and Dying, 56*(1).

Parkes, C. M., & Prigerson, H. G. (2010). *Bereavement: Studies of grief in adult life* (4th ed.). New York: Routledge.

Parkes, C. M., & Weiss, R. (1983). *Recovery from bereavement.* New York: Basic Books.

Parkes, C. M., Laungani, P., & Young, W. (2015). *Death and bereavement across cultures* (2nd ed.). New York: Routledge.

Parkes, C. M., Relf, M., & Couldrick, A. (1996). *Counseling in terminal care and bereavement.* Leicester, England: BPS Books.

Parkes, C. M., Stevenson-Hinde, J., & Marris, P. (Eds.). (1993). *Attachment across the life cycle.* New York: Routledge.

Parks, G. (1971). *Gordon Parks: Whispers of intimate things.* New York: Viking.

Parr, E., & Mize, J. (2001). *Coping with an organ transplant: A practical guide to understanding, preparing for, and living with an organ transplant.* New York: Avery/Penguin Putnam.

Parry, J. K. (Ed.). (2001). *Social work theory and practice with the terminally ill* (2nd ed.). New York: Routledge.

Parry, J. K., & Ryan, A. S. (Eds.). (2003). *A cross-cultural look at death, dying, and religion.* Belmont, CA: Wadsworth.

Parsons, T. (1951). *The social system.* New York: Free Press.

Parsons, T. (1963, May). Death in American society: A brief working paper. *The American Behavioral Scientist, 6*(9), 61–65. doi:10.1177/00027642630060091

Partridge, E. (1966). *A dictionary of slang and unconventional English.* New York: Macmillan.

Pastan, L. (1978). *The five stages of grief.* New York: Norton.

Pattison, E. M. (1977). *The experience of dying.* Englewood Cliffs, NJ: Prentice Hall.

Paulus, T. M. & Varga, M. A. (2015). "Please know that you are not alone with your pain": Responses to newcomer posts in an online grief support forum. *Death Studies, 39,* 633–640. doi:10.1080/07481187.2015.1047060

Pausch, R., with J. Zaslow. (2008). *The last lecture.* New York: Hyperion.

Pawelczynska, A. (1979). *Values and violence in Auschwitz: A sociological analysis* (C. S. Leach, Trans.). Berkeley: University of California Press.

Payne, R., Medina, E., & Hampton, J. W. (2003). Quality of life concerns in patients with breast cancer: Evidence for disparity of outcomes and experiences in pain management and palliative care among African-American women. *Cancer, 97*(1 Supp.), 311–317. doi:10.1002/cncr.11017

Peabody, F. W. (1927). The care of the patient. *Journal of the American Medical Association, 88,* 877–882. doi:10.1001/jama.1927.02680380001001

Pearce, N. (2011). *Inside Alzheimer's: How to hear and honor connections with a person who has dementia* (rev. ed.). Taylors, SC: Forrason Press.

Peck, M. L., Farberow, N. L., & Litman, R. E. (Eds.). (1985). *Youth suicide.* New York: Springer.

Peckinpah, S. (2014). *How to survive the worst that can happen: A parent's step by step guide to healing after the loss of a child.* Bloomington, IN: Balboa Press.

Pedersen, P. B., Lonner, W. J., Draguns, J. G., Trimble, J. E., & Scharron-del Rio, M. R. (Eds.). (2016). *Counseling across cultures* (7th ed.). Thousand Oaks, CA: Sage.

Pelaez, M., & Rothman, P. (1994). *A guide for recalling and telling your life story.* Washington, DC: Hospice Foundation of America.

Pendleton, E. (Comp.). (1980). *Too old to cry, too young to die.* Nashville, TN: Thomas Nelson.

Pennington, N. (2013). You don't de-friend the dead: An analysis of grief communication by college students through Facebook profiles. *Death Studies, 37,* 617–635. doi:10.1080/07481187.2012.673536

Peppers, L. G. (1988). Grief and elective abortion: Breaking the emotional bond. *Omega, Journal of Death and Dying, 18,* 1–12. doi:10.2190/PJET-58E4-E8E2-40TY

Perera, M., Jagadheesan, K., & Peake, A. (Eds.). (2011). *Making sense of near-death experiences: A handbook for clinicians.* Philadelphia: Jessica Kingsley.

Peretti, P. O. (1990). Elderly-animal friendship bonds. *Social Behavior and Personality, 18,* 151–156.

Perls, T. T., Silver, M. H., & Lauerman, J. F. (1999). *Living to 100: Lessons in living to your maximum potential at any age.* New York: Basic Books.

Petersen, B. (2010). *Jan's story: Love lost to the long goodbye of Alzheimer's.* Lake Forest, CA: Behler Publications.

Petersson. A. (2009). Swedish Offerkast and recent roadside memorials. *Folklore, 120,* 75–91. doi:10.1080/00155870802647841

Pew Research Center. (2015, June 11). *Multiracial in America: Proud, diverse and growing in numbers.* Washington, DC: Author. Retrieved December 1, 2016, from http://www.pewsocialtrends.org/2015/06/11/multiracial-in-america/

Phelps, R. (2012). *While I still can.... One man's journey through early onset Alzheimer's disease.* Bloomington, IN: Xlibris.

Piaget, J. (1998). *The equilibration of cognitive structures: The central problem of intellectual development* (T. A. Brown & K. J. Thampy, Trans.). Chicago: University of Chicago Press.

Piaget, J., & Inhelder, B. (1958). *The growth of logical thinking from childhood to adolescence* (A. Parsons & S. Milgram, Trans.). New York: Basic Books.

Picard, C. (2002). Family reflections on living through sudden death of a child. *Nursing Science Quarterly, 25,* 242–250. doi:10.1177/08918402015003011

Pierce, M. (2008). *Your wills, trusts, and estates explained simply: Important information you need to know.* Ocala, FL: Atlantic Publishing Group.

Piper, F. (1994). The number of victims. In I. Gutman & M. Berenbaum (Eds.), *Anatomy of the Auschwitz death camp* (pp. 61–76). Bloomington: Indiana University Press.

Pitman, A., Osborn, D., King, M., & Erlangsen, A. (2014). Effects of suicide bereavement on mental health and suicide risk. *The Lancet Psychiatry, 1*(1), 86–94. doi:10.1016/S2215-0366(14)70224-X

Planchon, L. A., Templer, D. I., Stokes, S., & Keller, J. (2002). Death of a companion cat or dog and human bereavement: Psychosocial variables. *Society & Animals, 10,* 93–105. doi:10.1163/156853002760030897

Plath, S. (1964). *Ariel.* New York: Harper & Row.

Plath, S. (1971). *The bell jar.* New York: Harper & Row.

Plato. (1948). *Euthyphro, Apology, Crito* (F. J. Church, Trans.). New York: Macmillan.

Plato. (1961). *The collected dialogues of Plato including the letters* (E. Hamilton & H. Cairns, Eds.). New York: Bollingen Foundation.

Platt, M. (1975). Commentary: On asking to die. *Hastings Center Report, 5*(6), 9–12.

Please Let Me Die. [Videotape]. (1974). Galveston: University of Texas Medical Branch.

Plepys, C., & Klein, R. (1995). *Health status indicators: Differentials by race and Hispanic origin* (10). Washington, DC: National Center for Health Statistics.

Poe, E. A. (1948). *The letters of Edgar Allan Poe* (2 vols.). (J. W. Ostrom, Ed.). Cambridge, MA: Harvard University Press.

Poland, S. (1989). *Suicide intervention in the schools*. New York: Guilford.

Pomeroy, E. C., & Garcia, R. B. (2011). *Children and loss: A practical handbook for professionals*. Chicago, IL: Lyceum.

Pompili, M., & Tatarelli, R. (Eds.). (2010). *Evidence-based practice in suicidology: A source book*. Ashland, OH: Hogrefe Publishing.

Portenoy, R. K., & Payne, R. (1992). Acute and chronic pain. In J. H. Lowinson, P. Ruiz, & R. B. Millman (Eds.), *Substance abuse: A comprehensive textbook* (2nd ed., pp. 691–721). Baltimore: Williams & Wilkins.

Post, M. A. (2017). How to say "It" when no one can: Death notification of children, teens, and adults: Grief after sudden or traumatic death. In N. Thompson, G. Cox, & R. G. Stevenson (Eds.), *Handbook of traumatic loss* (pp. 165-177). New York: Routledge.

Post, S. (Ed.). (2004). *Encyclopedia of bioethics* (3rd ed.). New York: Macmillan Reference USA.

Pound, L. (1936). American euphemisms for dying, death, and burial: An anthology. *American Speech*, *11*, 195–202. doi:10.2307/452239

Powell-Griner, E. (1988). Differences in infant mortality among Texas Anglos, Hispanics, and Blacks. *Social Science Quarterly*, *69*, 452–467.

Prensky, M. (2001). Digital natives, digital immigrants. *On the Horizon*, *9*(5), 1–6. Retrieved February 7, 2011, from http://www.marcprensky.com/writing/Prensky%20-%20Digital%20Natives,%20Digital%20Immigrants%20-%20Part1.pdf

President's Commission for the Study of Ethical Problems in Medicine and Biomedical and Behavioral Research. (1981). *Defining death: A report on the medical, legal, and ethical issues in the determination of death*. Washington, DC: U.S. Government Printing Office.

President's Commission for the Study of Ethical Problems in Medicine and Biomedical and Behavioral Research. (1982). *Making health care decisions: A report on the ethical and legal implications of informed consent in the patient-practitioner relationship. Vol. 1, Report; Vol. 3, Studies on the foundation of informed consent*. Washington, DC: U.S. Government Printing Office.

President's Commission for the Study of Ethical Problems in Medicine and Biomedical and Behavioral Research. (1983a). *Deciding to forego life-sustaining treatment: A report on the ethical, medical, and legal issues in treatment decisions*. Washington, DC: U.S. Government Printing Office.

President's Commission for the Study of Ethical Problems in Medicine and Biomedical and Behavioral Research. (1983b). *Summing up: Final report on studies of the ethical and legal problems in medicine and biomedical and behavioral research*. Washington, DC: U.S. Government Printing Office.

Preston, R. J., & Preston, S. C. (1991). Death and grieving among northern forest hunters: An East Cree example. In D. R. Counts & D. A. Counts (Eds.), *Coping with the final tragedy: Cultural variation in dying and grieving* (pp. 135–155). Amityville, NY: Baywood.

Prigerson, H. G., & Maciejewski, P. K. (2006). A call for sound empirical testing and evaluation of criteria for complicated grief proposed for DSM-V. *Omega, Journal of Death and Dying*, *52*, 9–19. doi:10.2190/ANKH-BB2H-D52N-X99Y

Prigerson, H. G., Bao, Y., Shah, M. A., et al. (2015). Chemotherapy use, performance status, and quality of life at the end of life. *JAMA Oncology*. doi:10.1001/jamaoncol.2015.2378

Prigerson, H. G., Vanderwerker, L. C., & Maciejewski, P. K. (2008). A case for inclusion of prolonged grief disorder DSM-V. In M. S. Stroebe, R. O. Hansson, H. A. Schut, &

W. Stroebe (Eds.), *Handbook of bereavement research and practice: Advances in theory and intervention* (pp. 165–186). Washington, DC: American Psychological Association.

Prothero, S. (2001). *Purified by fire: A history of cremation in America*. Berkeley: University of California Press.

Prothrow-Stith, D., & Spivak, H. R. (2004). *Murder is no accident: Understanding and preventing youth violence in America*. San Francisco: Jossey-Bass.

Prottas, J. (1994). *The most useful gift: Altruism and the public policy of organ transplants*. San Francisco: Jossey-Bass.

Puckle, B. S. (1926). *Funeral customs: Their origin and development*. London: Laurie.

Purnell, L. D. (2014). *Guide to culturally competent health care* (3rd ed.). Philadelphia: F. A. Davis.

Purnell, L. D. (Ed.). (2013). *Transcultural health care: A culturally competent approach* (4th ed.). Philadelphia: F. A. Davis.

Purtillo, R. B. (1976). Similarities in patient response to chronic and terminal illness. *Physical Therapy*, *56*, 279–284.

Quackenbush, J. (1985). The death of a pet: How it can affect pet owners. *Veterinary Clinics of North America: Small Animal Practice*, *15*, 305–402.

Quadagno, J. (2014). *Aging and the life course: An introduction to social gerontology* (6th ed.). New York: McGraw-Hill.

Quill, T. E. (1996). *A midwife through the dying process: Stories of healing and hard choices at the end of life*. Baltimore: Johns Hopkins University Press.

Quill, T. E. (2007). Legal regulation of physician-assisted death—The latest report cards. *New England Journal of Medicine*, *356*, 1911–1913. doi:10.1056/NEJMp078061

Quill, T. E., & Abernethy, A. P. (2013). Generalist plus specialist palliative care: Creating a more sustainable model. *New England Journal of Medicine*, *368*, 1173–1175. doi:10.1056/NEJMp1215620

Quill, T. E., & Battin, M. P. (2004). *Physician-assisted dying: The case for palliative care and patient choice*. Baltimore: Johns Hopkins University Press.

Quill, T. E., & Miller, F. G. (Eds.). (2014). *Palliative care and ethics*. New York: Oxford University Press.

Quill, T. E., Bower, K. A., Holloway, R. G., et al. (2014). *Primer of palliative care* (6th ed.). Chicago: American Academy of Hospice and Palliative Medicine.

Quill, T. E., Lo, B., & Brock, D. W. (1997). Palliative options of last resort: A comparison of voluntarily stopping eating and drinking, terminal sedation, physician-assisted suicide, and voluntary active euthanasia. *Journal of the American Medical Association*, *278*(23), 2099–2104. doi:10.1001/jama.1997.03550230075041

Quindlen, A. (1994). *One true thing*. New York: Random House.

Quinlan, J., Quinlan, J., & Battelle, P. (1977). *Karen Ann: The Quinlans tell their story*. Garden City, NY: Doubleday.

[*Qur'an.*] *Koran*. (1993). (N. J. Dawood, Trans.). London: Penguin.

Rabins, P. V., & Morrison, A. S. (2013). *Caring for a loved one with Alzheimer's disease: A guide for the home caregiver*. Baltimore: Johns Hopkins University Press.

Rabins, P. V., Lyketsos, C. G., & Steele, C. D. (2006). *Practical dementia care* (2nd ed.). New York: Oxford University Press.

Radhakrishnan, S. (1948). *The Bhagavadgita: With an introductory essay, Sanskrit text, English translation and notes*. New York: Harper & Brothers.

Radhakrishnan, S., & Moore, C. (1957). *A sourcebook in Indian philosophy*. Princeton, NJ: Princeton University Press.

Radin, G., & Radin, L. (Eds.). (2014). *What if it's not Alzheimer's?: A caregiver's guide to dementia* (3rd ed.). Amherst, NY: Prometheus Books.

Raether, H. C. (Ed.). (1989). *The funeral director's practice management handbook*. Englewood Cliffs, NJ: Prentice Hall.

Rahman, F. (1987). *Health and medicine in the Islamic tradition: Change and identity.* New York: Crossroad.

Rahner, K. (1973). *On the theology of death* (C. H. Henkey, Trans.). New York: Seabury Press.

Rahula, W. (1974). *What the Buddha taught.* New York: Grove Press.

Ramsey, P. (1970). *The patient as person: Explorations in medical ethics.* New Haven, CT: Yale University Press.

Ramsey, P., Farley, M., Jonsen, A. R., Wood, M. R., & May, W. F. (2002). *The patient as person: Explorations in medical ethics* (2nd ed.). New Haven, CT: Yale University Press.

Randall, F., & Downie, R. (2010). *End of life choices: Consensus and controversy.* New York: Oxford University Press.

Rando, T. A. (1984). *Grief, dying, and death: Clinical interventions for caregivers.* Champaign, IL: Research Press.

Rando, T. A. (Ed.). (1986a). *Parental loss of a child.* Champaign, IL: Research Press.

Rando, T. A. (1986b). Death of the adult child. In T. A. Rando (Ed.), *Parental loss of a child* (pp. 221–238). Champaign, IL: Research Press.

Rando, T. A. (Ed.). (1986c). *Loss and anticipatory grief.* Lexington, MA: Lexington Books.

Rando, T. A. (1988). Anticipatory grief: The term is a misnomer but the phenomenon exists. *Journal of Palliative Care, 4*(1/2), 70–73.

Rando, T. A. (1993). *Treatment of complicated mourning.* Champaign, IL: Research Press.

Rando, T. A. (1994). *How to go on living when someone you love dies.* New York: Bantam.

Rando, T. A. (1996). Complications in mourning traumatic death. In K. J. Doka (Ed.), *Living with grief after sudden loss: Suicide, homicide, accident, heart attack, stroke* (pp. 139–159). Washington, DC: Hospice Foundation of America.

Rando, T. A. (Ed.). (2000). *Clinical dimensions of anticipatory mourning: Theory and practice in working with the dying, their loved ones, and their caregivers.* Champaign, IL: Research Press.

Rando, T. A., Doka, K. J., Fleming, S., et al. (2012). A call to the field: Complicated grief in the DSM-5. *Omega, Journal of Death and Dying 65,* 251–256. doi:10.2190/OM.65.4.a

Rao, J. K., Anderson, L. A., Lin, F.-C., & Laux, J. P. (2014). Completion of advance directives among U.S. consumers. *American Journal of Preventive Medicine, 46,* 65–70. doi:10.1016/j.amepre.2013.09.008

Raphael, B. (1983). *The anatomy of bereavement.* New York: Basic Books.

Rathus, S. A. (2013). *Childhood and adolescence: Voyages in development* (5th ed.). Belmont, CA: Wadsworth.

Rauschi, T. M. (2001). *A view from within: Living with early onset Alzheimer's.* Albany, NY: Northeastern New York Chapter of the Alzheimer's Disease and Related Disorders Association.

Rawson, H. (1981). *A dictionary of euphemisms and other doubletalk.* New York: Crown.

Reagan, R. (1994, November 5). Alzheimer's letter. Retrieved February 17, 2011, from http://www.pbs.org/wgbh/americanexperience/features/primary-resources/reagan-alzheimers/

Reder, P. (1969). *Epitaphs.* London: Michael Joseph.

Redfern, S., & Gilbert, S. K. (Eds.). (2008). *The grieving garden: Living with the death of a child.* Charlottesville, VA: Hampton Roads Publishing Co.

Reece, R. D., & Ziegler, J. H. (1990). How a medical school (Wright State University) takes leave of human remains. *Death Studies, 14,* 589–600. doi:10.1080/07481189008252396

Reed, M. D., & Greenwald, J. Y. (1991). Survivor-victim status, attachment, and sudden death bereavement. *Suicide and Life-Threatening Behavior, 21,* 385–401. doi:10.1111/j.1943-278X.1991.tb00576.x

Reed, M. L. (2000). *Grandparents cry twice: Help for bereaved grandparents.* Amityville, NY: Baywood.

Rees, W. D. (1972). The distress of dying. *British Medical Journal, 3,* 105–107. doi:10.1136/bmj.3.5818.105

Reese, D. J. (2013). *Hospice social work.* New York: Columbia University Press.

Rehm, Diane. (2016). *On my own.* New York: Knopf.

Rehmann-Sutter, C., Gudat, H., & Ohnsorge, K. (Eds.). (2015). *The patient's wish to die: Research, ethics, and palliative care.* New York: Oxford University Press.

Reid, J. K., & Reid, C. L. (2001). A cross marks the spot: A study of roadside death memorials in Texas and Oklahoma. *Death Studies, 25,* 341–356. doi:10.1080/07481180125931

Reisbig, A. M. J., Hafen, M., Drake, A. A. S., Girard, D., & Breunig, Z. B. (2017). Companion animal death: A qualitative analysis of relationship quality, loss, and coping. *Omega, Journal of Death & Dying, 75,* 124–150.

Reith, M., & Payne, M. (2009). *Social work in end-of-life and palliative care.* New York: Lyceum Books.

Reitlinger, G. (1968). *The final solution: The attempt to exterminate the Jews of Europe 1939–1945* (2nd rev. ed.). London: Vallentine, Mitchell.

Renzenbrink, I. (2004). Relentless self-care. In P. Silverman & J. Berzoff (Eds.), *Living with dying: A handbook for end-of-life care practitioners* (pp. 848–868). New York: Columbia University Press.

Renzenbrink, I. (Ed.). (2011). *Caregiver stress and staff support in illness, dying, and bereavement.* New York: Oxford University Press.

Requarth, J. (2006). *After a parent's suicide: Helping children heal.* Sebastopol, CA: Healing Hearts Press.

Reynolds, F. E., & Waugh, E. H. (Eds.). (1977). *Religious encounters with death: Insights from the history and anthropology of religion.* State College: Pennsylvania State University Press.

Rhodes, R. L., Teno, J. M., & Connor, S. R. (2007). African American bereaved family members' perceptions of the quality of hospice care: Lessened disparities, but opportunities. *Journal of Pain and Symptom Management, 34,* 472–479. doi:10.1016/j.jpainsymman.2007.06.004

Rice, P. (2016). *Winter sun: A memoir of love and hospice.* Woodstock, IL: Canopic Publishing.

Richardson, A. (2007). *Life in a hospice: Reflections on caring for the dying.* Oxford, UK: Radcliffe Publishing.

Richardson, L. (2006). *What terrorists want: Understanding the enemy, containing the threat.* New York: Random House.

Richardson, V. (2010). The Dual Process Model of coping with bereavement: A decade later. *Omega, Journal of Death and Dying, 61,* 269–271. doi:10.2190/OM.61.4.a

Rickgarn, R. L. V. (1994). *Perspectives on college student suicide.* Amityville, NY: Baywood.

Rickgarn, R. L. V. (1996). The need for postvention on college campuses: A rationale and case study findings. In C. A. Corr & D. E. Balk (Eds.), *Handbook of adolescent death and bereavement* (pp. 273–292). New York: Springer.

Ridley, J. (2015, October 8). It's good for kids to tweet their grief. *New York Post.* Retrieved October 15, 2015, from http://nypost.com/2015/10/08/its-good-for-kids-to-tweet-their-grief/

Riedel, S. (2005). Edward Jenner and the history of smallpox and vaccination. *Baylor University Medical Center Proceedings, 18*(1), 21–25.

Rietjens, J. A. C., Bilsen, J., Fischer, S., et al. (2007). Using drugs to end life without an explicit request of the patient. *Death Studies, 31,* 205–221. doi:10.1080/07481180601152443

Rietjens, J. A., Deschepper, R., Pasman, R., & Deliens, L. (2012). Medical end-of-life decisions: Does its use differ in vulnerable patient groups? A systematic review and meta-analysis. *Social Science and Medicine, 74,* 1282–1287. doi:10.1016/j.socscimed.2011.12.046

Ring, K. (1980). *Life at death: A scientific investigation of the near-death experience.* New York: Coward, McCann & Geoghegan.

Ring, K. (1984). *Heading toward Omega, In search of the meaning of the near-death experience.* New York: Morrow.

Ring, K., & Valarino, E. E. (1998). *Lessons from the light: What we can learn from the near-death experience.* New York: Insight Press.

R. N., & Schwiebert, P. (2012). A grandparent's sorrow. Portland, OR: Grief Watch.

Roach, M. (2003). *Stiff: The curious lives of human cadavers.* New York: Norton.

Robben, A. (Ed.). (2005). *Death, mourning, and burial: A cross-cultural reader.* Hoboken, NJ: Wiley-Blackwell.

Robben, A. C. (Ed.). (2004). *Death, mourning, and burial: A cross-cultural reader.* Malden, MA: Blackwell.

Robers, S., Zhang, A., Morgan, R. E., & Musu-Gillette, L. (2015). *Indicators of school crime and safety: 2014* (NCES 2015-072/NCJ 248036). Washington, DC: National Center for Education Statistics, U.S. Department of Education, & Bureau of Justice Statistics, Office of Justice Programs, U.S. Department of Justice. Retrieved July 18, 2015, from http://nces.ed.gov; also available at http://bjs.ojp.usdoj.gov.

Roberts, B. K. (2003). *Death without denial, grief without apology: A guide for facing death and loss.* Troutdale, OR: NewSage Press.

Roberts, C. (1998). *We are our mothers' daughters.* New York: William Morrow.

Roberts, P. (2012). '2 people *like* this': Mourning according to format. *Bereavement Care, 31*(2), 55–61. doi:10.1080/02682621.2012.710492

Robertson, J. (2014, March 15). The changing face of death in video games. Retrieved January 27, 2016, from http://www.videogamer.com/features/article/the_changing_face_of_death_in_video_games.html

Rochlin, G. (1967). How younger children view death and themselves. In E. A. Grollman (Ed.), *Explaining death to children* (pp. 51–85). Boston: Beacon Press.

Rodger, M. L., Sherwood, P., O'Connor, M., & Leslie, G. (2007). Living beyond the unanticipated sudden death of a partner: A phenomenological study. *Omega, Journal of Death and Dying, 54,* 107–133. doi:10.2190/W423-0132-R010-14J7

Rodgers, L. S. (2004). Meaning of bereavement among older African American widows. *Geriatric Nursing, 25*(1), 10–16.

Rodkinson, M. L. (Trans.). (1896). *New edition of the Babylonian Talmud* (Vol. 2). New York: Talmud Publishing.

Rodrigue, J. R., Scott, M. P., & Oppenheim, A. R. (2003). The tissue donation experience: A comparison of donor and nondonor families. *Progress in Transplantation, 13*(4), 1–7. doi:10.1177/152692480301300404

Rogers, J. R., & Lester, D. (2010). *Understanding suicide: Why we don't and how we might.* Ashland, OH: Hogrefe Publishing.

Rogers, R. G., Hummer, R. A., & Nam, C. B. (1999). *Living and dying in the USA: Behavioral, health, and social differentials of adult mortality.* New York: Academic Press.

Rogne, L., & McCune, S. (Eds.). (2013). *Advance care planning: Communicating about matters of life and death.* New York: Springer.

Rollin, B. (1985). *Last wish.* New York: Warner Books.

Romanoff, B. D., & Thompson, B. E. (2006). Meaning construction in palliative care: The use of narrative, ritual, and the expressive arts. *American Journal of Hospice and Palliative Medicine, 23,* 309–316. doi:10.1177/1049909106290246

Romer, J. (2012). *Widow: A survival guide for the first year.* Hollister, CA: MSI Press.

Romer, J. (2014). *The widower's guide to a new life.* Hollister, CA: MSI Press.

Romm, R. (2009). *The mercy papers: A memoir of three weeks.* New York: Scribner.

Ropp, L., Visintainer, P., Uman, J., & Treloar, D. (1992). Death in the city: An American childhood tragedy. *Journal of the American Medical Association, 267,* 2905–2910. doi:10.1001/jama.1992.03480210067034

Roscoe, L. A., Melphurs, J. E., Dragovic, L. J., & Cohen, D. (2000). Dr. Jack Kevorkian and cases of euthanasia in Oakland County, Michigan, 1990–1998. *New England Journal of Medicine, 343,* 1735–1736. doi:10.1056/NEJM200012073432315

Rose, L. (1996). *Show me the way to go home.* Forest Knolls, CA: Elder Books.

Roseman, M. (2002). *The Wannsee conference and the final solution: A reconsideration.* New York: Metropolitan Books.

Rosen, E. J. (1998). *Families facing death: A guide for health care professionals and volunteers* (Rev ed.). San Francisco: Jossey-Bass.

Rosenbaum, L. (2015). Being like Mike—Fear, trust, and the tragic death of Michael Davidson. *New England Journal of Medicine, 372,* 798–799. doi:10.1056/NEJMp1501253

Rosenberg, A. R., Wolfe, J., Wiener, L., Lyon, M., & Feudtner, C. (2016, October 17). Ethics, emotions, and the skills of talking about progressing disease with terminally ill adolescents: A review. *JAMA Pediatrics,* published online. doi:10.1001/jamapediatrics.2016.2142

Rosenberg, C. E. (1987). *The care of strangers: The rise of America's hospital system.* New York: Basic Books.

Rosenblatt, P. C. (1983). *Bitter, bitter tears: Nineteenth-century diarists and twentieth-century grief theories.* Minneapolis: University of Minnesota Press.

Rosenblatt, P. C. (2001). *Help your marriage survive the death of a child.* Philadelphia: Temple University Press.

Rosenblatt, P. C. (2016). *Parent grief: Narratives of loss and relationship.* New York: Routledge.

Rosenblatt, P. C., & Barner, J. R. (2006). The dance of closeness-distance in couple relationships after the death of a parent. *Omega, Journal of Death and Dying, 53,* 277–293. doi:10.2190/X1W4-M210-6522-1034

Rosenblatt, P. C., & Wallace, B. R. (2005a). Narratives of grieving African-Americans about racism in the lives of deceased family members. *Death Studies, 29,* 217–235. doi:10.1080/07481180590916353

Rosenblatt, P. C., & Wallace, B. R. (2005b). *African American grief.* New York: Brunner-Routledge.

Rosenblatt, P. C., Walsh, P. R., & Jackson, D. A. (1976). *Grief and mourning in cross-cultural perspective.* Washington, DC: Human Relations Area Files.

Rosenblatt, R. (2010). *Making toast: A family story.* New York: Ecco/HarperCollins.

Rosengren, S., Miller, P. J., Gutierrez, I. T., et al. (2014). *Children's understanding of death: Toward a contextualized and integrated account.* New York: Wiley.

Rosenthal, N. R. (1986). Death education: Developing a course of study for adolescents. In C. A. Corr & J. N. McNeil (Eds.), *Adolescence and death* (pp. 202–214). New York: Springer.

Rosenthal, T. (1973). *How could I not be among you?* New York: George Braziller.

Rosner, F. (1979). The Jewish attitude toward euthanasia. In F. Rosner & J. D. Bleich (Eds.), *Jewish bioethics* (pp. 253–265). New York: Sanhedrin Press.

Ross, C. B., & Baron-Sorenson, J. (2007). *Pet loss and human emotion: A guide to recovery.* Philadelphia: Brunner-Routledge.

Ross, E. S. (1967). Children's books relating to death: A discussion. In E. A. Grollman (Ed.), *Explaining death to children* (pp. 249–271). Boston: Beacon Press.

Rowles, G. D., & Teaster, P. B. (Eds.). (2016). *Long-term care in an aging society: Theory and practice.* New York: Springer.

Rowling, L. (2003). *Grief in school communities: Effective support strategies.* Philadelphia: Open University Press.

Roy, A. (1990). Possible biologic determinants of suicide. In D. Lester (Ed.), *Current concepts of suicide* (pp. 40–56). Philadelphia: Charles Press.

Rozovsky, F. A. (2015). *Consent to treatment: A practical guide* (5th ed.). Philadelphia: Wolters Kluwer.

Rubin, B., Carlton, R., & Rubin, A. (1979). *L.A. in installments: Forest Lawn.* Santa Monica, CA: Hennessey & Ingalls.

Rubin, R. (2015). Improving the quality of life at the end of life. *Journal of the American Medical Association, 313,* 2110–2112. doi:10.1001/jama.2015.4234

Rubin, S. S. (1999). The two-track model of bereavement: Overview, retrospect, and prospect. *Death Studies, 23,* 681–714. doi:10.1080/074811899200731

Rubin, S. S., Malkinson, R., & Witztum, E. (2003). Trauma and bereavement: Conceptual and clinical issues revolving around relationships. *Death Studies, 27,* 667–690. doi:10.1080/713842342

Rubin, S. S., Malkinson, R., & Witztum, E. (2012). *Working with the bereaved: Multiple lenses on loss and mourning.* New York: Routledge.

Ruby, J. (1995). *Secure the shadow: Death and photography in America.* Cambridge, MA: MIT Press.

Ruccione, K. S. (1994). Issues in survivorship. In C. L. Schwartz, W. L. Hobbie, L. S. Constine, & K. S. Ruccione (Eds.), *Survivors of childhood cancer: Assessment and management* (pp. 329–337). St. Louis, MO: Mosby.

Rudd, M. D., Joiner, T., & Rajab, M. H. (2001). *Treating suicidal behavior: An effective, time-limited approach.* New York: Guilford.

Rudestam, K. E. (1987). Public perceptions of suicide survivors. In E. J. Dunne, J. L. McIntosh, & K. Dunne-Maxim (Eds.), *Suicide and its aftermath: Understanding and counseling the survivors* (pp. 31–44). New York: Norton.

Russac, R. J., Gotliff, C., Reece, M., & Spottswood, D. (2007). Death anxiety across the adult years: An examination of age and gender effects. *Death Studies, 31,* 549–561. doi:10.1080/07481180701356936

Ruth, J. L. (2011). *Forgiveness: A legacy of the West Nickel Mines Amish School* (rev. ed.). Harrisonburg, VA: Herald Press.

Rynearson, E. K. (1978). Humans and pets and attachment. *British Journal of Psychiatry, 133,* 550–555. doi:10.1192/bjp.133.6.550

Rynearson, E. K. (2001). *Retelling violent death.* New York: Brunner-Routledge.

Rynearson, E. K. (Ed.). (2006). *Violent death: Resilience and intervention beyond the crisis.* New York: Routledge/Tayor & Francis.

Sabatini, P., & Kastenbaum, R. (1973). The do-it-yourself death certificate as a research technique. *Suicide and Life-Threatening Behavior, 3,* 20–32. doi:10.1111/j.1943-278X.1973.tb00114.x

Sable, P. (1995). Pets, attachment and well-being across the life cycle. *Social Work, 40,* 334–341. doi:10.1093/sw/40.3.334

Sabom, M. B. (1982). *Recollections of death: A medical investigation.* New York: Harper & Row.

Sacred Congregation for the Doctrine of the Faith. (1982). Declaration on euthanasia. In A. Flannery (Ed.), *Vatican Council II: More postconciliar documents* (pp. 510–517). Grand Rapids, MI: Eerdmans.

Safer, J. (2010). *Death benefits: How losing a parent can change an adult's life—for the better.* New York: Basic Books.

Sageman, M. (2004). *Understanding terror networks.* Philadelphia: University of Pennsylvania Press.

Sakr, A. H. (1995). Death and dying: An Islamic perspective. In J. K. Parry & A. S. Ryan (Eds.), *A cross-cultural look at death, dying, and religion* (pp. 47–73). Chicago: Nelson-Hall.

Sampson, Z. T., & Mettler, K. (2015, February 3). Slip on skateboard leads to tragedy. *Tampa Bay Times,* pp. 1B & 7B.

Sanburn, J. (2015, March 31). How Terri Schiavo shaped the right-to-die movement. *Time.* Retrieved April 2, 2015, from http://time.com/3763521/terri-schiavo-right-to-die-brittany-maynard/#3763521/terri-schiavo-right-to-die-brittany-maynard/

Sandberg, S., & Grant, A. (2017). *Option B: Facing adversity, building resilience, and finding joy.* New York: Knopf.

Sanders, C. M. (1980). A comparison of adult bereavement in the death of a spouse, child and parent. *Omega, Journal of Death and Dying, 10,* 303–322. doi:10.2190/X565-HW49-CHR0-FYB4

Sanders, C. M. (1989). *Grief: The mourning after.* New York: Wiley.

Sanders, C. M. (1992). *Surviving grief ... and learning to live again.* New York: Wiley.

Sanders, M. A. (Ed.). (2007). *Nearing death awareness: A guide to the language, visions, and dreams of the dying.* Philadelphia: Jessica Kingsley.

Sapphire, P. (Ed.). (2012). *The disenfranchised: Stories of life and grief when an ex-spouse dies.* Amityville, NY: Baywood.

Satel, S. (Ed.). (2009). *When altruism isn't enough: The case for compensating kidney donors.* Washington, DC: AEI Press.

Saul, S. R., & Saul, S. (1973). Old people talk about death. *Omega, Journal of Death and Dying, 4,* 27–35. doi:10.2190/6X3T-T6AB-XJF4-734L

Saunders, C. M. (1967). *The management of terminal illness.* London: Hospital Medicine Publications.

Saunders, C. M. (1970). Dimensions of death. In M. A. H. Melinsky (Ed.), *Religion and medicine: A discussion* (pp. 113–116). London: Student Christian Movement Press.

Saunders, C. M. (1976). The challenge of terminal care. In T. Symington & R. L. Carter (Eds.), *Scientific foundations of oncology* (pp. 673–679). London: William Heinemann.

Saunders, C. M. (2003). *Watch with me: Inspiration for a life in hospice care.* Sheffield, England: Mortal Press.

Saunders, C. M. (Ed.). (1990). *Hospice and palliative care: An interdisciplinary approach.* London: Edward Arnold.

Saunders, C. M., & Kastenbaum, R. (1997). *Hospice care on the international scene.* New York: Springer.

Saunders, C. M., & Sykes, N. (Eds.). (1993). *The management of terminal malignant disease* (3rd ed.). London: Edward Arnold.

Saunders, C. M., Baines, M., & Dunlop, R. (1995). *Living with dying: A guide to palliative care* (3rd ed.). New York: Oxford University Press.

Saunders, G. 2017. *Memory's last breath: Field notes on my dementia.* New York: Hachette.

Schaefer, D., & Lyons, C. (2010). *How do we tell the children? A step-by-step guide for helping children two to teen cope when someone dies* (4th ed.). New York: Newmarket.

Schechter, D. S., Coates, S. W., & First, E. (2002). Observations of acute reactions of young children and their families to the World Trade Center attacks. *Zero to Three, 22*, 9–13.

Schechter, H. (2009). *The whole death catalog: A lively guide to the bitter end*. New York: Ballantine.

Schencker, L. (2015, May 16). Assisted-suicide debate focuses attention on palliative, hospice care. *Modern Health Care*. Retrieved October 13, 2016, from http://www.modernhealthcare.com /article/20150516/magazine/305169982/assisted-suicide-debate -focuses-attention-on-palliative-hospice-care

Scheper-Hughes, N. (1992). *Death without weeping: The violence of everyday life in Brazil*. Berkeley: University of California Press.

Schiavo Case. (2005). *Hastings Center Report, 35*(3), 16–27. doi:10.1353/hcr.2005.0071

Schiavo, M., & Hirsh, M. (2006). *Terri: The truth*. New York: Dutton.

Schilder, P., & Wechsler, D. (1934). The attitudes of children toward death. *Journal of Genetic Psychology, 45*, 406–451. doi:10.1080/08856559.1934.10533137

Schmid, A. P. (Ed.). (2011). *The Routledge handbook of terrorism research*. New York: Routledge.

Schneider, J. M. (1980). Clinically significant differences between grief, pathological grief, and depression. *Patient Counseling and Health Education, 2*, 161–169. doi:10.1016/ S0738-3991(80)80097-8

Schneider, J. M. (2012). *Finding my way: From trauma to transformation: The journey through loss and grief*. Traverse City, MI: Seasons Press.

Schonfeld, D. J., & Quackenbush, M. (2010). *The grieving student: A teacher's guide*. Baltimore, MD: Brookes Publishing.

Schonfeld, D. J., Demaria, T., & Committee on Psychosocial Aspects of Child and Family Health, Disaster Preparedness Advisory Council (2016, August 29). Supporting the grieving child and family. *Pediatrics, 138*(3), e20162147. doi:10.1542/ peds.2016-2147

Schotsmans, P., & Meulenbergs, T. (Eds.). (2005). *Euthanasia and palliative care in the Low Countries*. Leuven, Belgium: Peeters.

Schrauger, B. (2001). *Walking Taylor home*. Nashville, TN: Thomas Nelson.

Schultz, N. W., & Huet, L. M. (2000). Sensational! Violent! Popular! Death in American movies. *Omega, Journal of Death and Dying, 42*, 137–149. doi:10.2190/6GDX-4W40-5B94-MX0G

Schulz, R., & Aderman, D. (1974). Clinical research and the stages of dying. *Omega, Journal of Death and Dying, 5*, 137–144. doi:10.2190/HYRB-7VQK-VU9Y-7L5D

Schuurman, D. (2003). *Never the same: Coming to terms with the death of a parent*. New York: St. Martin's Press.

Schwab, R. (1990). Paternal and maternal coping with the death of a child. *Death Studies, 14*, 407–422. doi:10.1080/07481189008252381

Schwab, R. (1996). Gender differences in parental grief. *Death Studies, 20*, 103–113. doi:10.1080/07481189608252744

Schwartz, A. (2013, June 14). The difference between grief and depression, the DSM V. MentalHelp.net. Retrieved December 4, 2016, from https://www.mentalhelp.net/blogs /the-difference-between-grief-and-depression-the-dsm-v/

Schwartz, C. L., Hobbie, W. L., Constine, L. S., & Ruccione, K. S. (Eds.). (1994). *Survivors of childhood cancer: Assessment and management*. St. Louis, MO: Mosby.

Schwartz, M. (1999). *Morrie: In his own words*. New York: Walker. (Originally published in 1996 by the same publisher as *Letting go: Morrie's reflections on living while dying*.)

Schwartz, T. P. (2005). *Organ transplants: A survival guide for the entire family—The ultimate teen guide*. Lanham, MD: Scarecrow Press.

Schwiebert, P. (2003). *We were gonna have a baby, but we had an angel instead*. Portland, OR: Grief Watch (2116 NE 18th Avenue, Portland, OR 97212; 503-284-7426; www .griefwatch.com).

Schwiebert, P. (2007). *Someone came before you*. Portland, OR: Grief Watch.

Schwiebert, P., & DeKlyen, C. (1999). *Tear soup: A recipe for healing after loss*. Portland, OR: Grief Watch.

Scott, P. S. (2014). *Surviving Alzheimer's: Practical tips and soul-saving wisdom for caregivers*. San Francisco: Eva Birch Media.

Scott, S. (2000). Grief reactions to the death of a divorced spouse revisited. *Omega, Journal of Death and Dying, 41*, 207–219. doi:10.2190/KKML-1RGK-105U-L9PE

Seale, C. (2000). Changing patterns in death and dying. *Social Science and Medicine, 51*(6), 917–930. doi:10.1016/ S0277-9536(00)00071-X

Segal, D. L., Mincic, M. S., Coolidge, F. L., & O'Riley, A. (2004). Attitudes toward suicide and suicidal risk among younger and older persons. *Death Studies, 28*, 671–678.

Selkin, J. (1983). The legacy of Emile Durkheim. *Suicide and Life-Threatening Behavior, 13*, 3–14. doi:10.1111/j.1943-278X.1983.tb00001.x

Selye, H. (1978a, October). On the real benefits of eustress. *Psychology Today*, 60–61, 63–64, 69–70.

Selye, H. (1978b). *The stress of life* (Rev. ed.). New York: McGraw-Hill.

Seneca, L. A. (1932). *Seneca's letters to Lucilius* (2 vols.) (E. P. Barker, Trans.). Oxford: Clarendon Press.

Servaty-Seib, H. L. (2009). Death of a friend during adolescence. In Balk, D. E., & Corr, C. A. (Eds.), *Adolescent encounters with death, bereavement, and coping* (pp. 217–235). New York: Springer.

Servaty-Seib, H. L., & Fajgenbaum, D. G. (2015). *We get it: Voices of grieving college students and young adults (with contributions by 33 inspirational young adults)*. Philadelphia: Jessica Kingsley.

Servaty-Seib, H. L., & Hamilton, L. A. (2006). Educational performance and persistence of bereaved college students. *Journal of College Student Development, 47*, 225–234. doi:10.1353/csd.2006.0024

Servaty-Seib, H. L., Peterson, J. S., & Spang, D. (2003). Notifying individual students of a death loss: Practical recommendations for schools and school counselors. *Death Studies, 27*, 167–186. doi:10.1080/07481180302891

Servaty-Seib, H. L., & Pistole, M. C. (2007). Adolescent grief: Relationship category and emotional closeness. *Omega, Journal of Death and Dying, 54*, 147–167. doi:10.2190/ M002-1541-JP28-4673

Servaty-Seib, H. L., & Taub, D. J. (Eds.). (2008). *Assisting bereaved college students*. San Francisco, CA: Jossey-Bass.

Settersten, R., & Ray, B. E. (2010). *Not quite adults: Why 20-somethings are choosing a slower path to adulthood*. New York: Bantam.

Shachtman, T. (2006). *Rumspringa: To be or not to be Amish*. New York: North Point Press.

Shafer, T. J., Wagner, D., Chessare, J., et al. (2006). Organ Donation Breakthrough Collaborative: Increasing organ donation through system redesign. *Critical Care Nurse, 26*(2), 33–48.

Shagam, J. Y. (2013). *An unintended journey: A caregiver's guide to dementia.* Amherst, NY: Prometheus Books.

Shannon, T. A., & Walter, J. J. (2004, April 16). Artificial nutrition, hydration: Assessing papal statement. *National Catholic Reporter, 40*(24), 9–10. Retrieved from http://natcath.org /NCR_Online/archives2/2004b/041604/041604i.php

Shapiro, E. (1995). Grief in family and cultural context: Learning from Latino families. *Cultural Diversity and Mental Health, 1*(2), 159–176. doi:10.1037//1099-9809.1.2.159

Shapiro, E. R. (1994). *Grief as a family process: A developmental approach to clinical practice.* New York: Guilford.

Shapiro-Mendoza, C. K., Colson, E. R., Willinger, M., et al. (2014). Trends in infant bedding use: National Infant Sleep Position Study, 1993–2010. *Pediatrics, 134*(6). doi:10.1542/ peds.2014-1793

Sharp, N. (2014). *Both sides now: A true story of love, loss and bold living.* Denver: Books and Books Press.

Sharp, R. F. (2010). *Living trusts for everyone: Why a will is not the way to avoid probate, protect heirs, and settle estates.* New York: Allworth Press.

Shear, M. K. (2015). Complicated grief. *New England Journal of Medicine, 372,* 153–160. doi:10.1056/NEJMcp1315618

Shear, M. K., Boelen, P. A., & Neimeyer, R. A. (2011). Treating complicated grief: Converging approaches. In R. A. Neimeyer, D. L. Harris, H. R. Winokuer, & G. F. Thornton (Eds.), *Grief and bereavement in contemporary society: Bridging research and practice* (pp. 139–162). New York: Routledge.

Shear, M. K., Simon, N., Wall, M., et al. (2011). Complicated grief and related bereavement issues for DSM-5. *Depression and Anxiety, 28,* 103–117. doi:10.1002/da.20780

Sheehy, E., Conrad, S. L., Brigham, L. E., et al. (2003). Estimating the number of potential organ donors in the United States. *New England Journal of Medicine, 349,* 667–674. doi:10.1056/NEJMsa021271

Sheeler, J. (2008). *Final salute: A story of unfinished lives.* New York: Penguin.

Sheftall, A. H., Asti, L., Horowitz, L. M., et al. (2016, Sept 19). Suicide in elementary school-aged children and early adolescents. *Pediatrics, 138*(4), e20160436. doi:10.1542/ peds.2016-0436

Shenk, D. (2003). *The forgetting: Alzheimer's: Portrait of an epidemic.* New York: Anchor.

Shenkman, M. M., & Klein, P. S. (2004). *Living wills and health care proxies: Assuring that your end-of-life decisions are respected.* Teaneck, NJ: Law Made Easy Press.

Shephard, D. A. E. (1977). Principles and practice of palliative care. *Canadian Medical Association Journal, 116,* 522–526.

Shield, R. R. (1988). *Uneasy endings: Daily life in an American nursing home.* Ithaca, NY: Cornell University Press.

Shiels, M. S., Chernyavskiy, P., Anderson, W. F., et al. (2017). Trends in premature mortality in the USA by sex, race, and ethnicity from 1999 to 2014: An analysis of death certificate data. *The Lancet, 389,* 1043–1054. doi:10.1016/ S0140-6736(17)30187-3

Shilts, R. (1987). *And the band played on: Politics, people, and the AIDS epidemic.* New York: St. Martin's Press.

Shirley, V., & Mercier, J. (1983). Bereavement of older persons: Death of a pet. *The Gerontologist, 23,* 276.

Shneidman, E. (1996). *The suicidal mind.* New York: Oxford University Press.

Shneidman, E. S. (1971). Prevention, intervention, and postvention of suicide. *Annals of Internal Medicine, 75,* 453–458.

Shneidman, E. S. (1973a). *Deaths of man.* New York: Quadrangle.

Shneidman, E. S. (1973b). Suicide. *Encyclopedia Britannica* (14th ed.; Vol. 21, pp. 383–385). Chicago: William Benton.

Shneidman, E. S. (1980/1995). *Voices of death.* New York: Harper & Row/Kodansha International.

Shneidman, E. S. (1981). *Suicide thoughts and reflections, 1960–1980.* New York: Human Sciences Press.

Shneidman, E. S. (1983). Reflections on contemporary death. In C. A. Corr, J. M. Stillion, & M. C. Ribar (Eds.), *Creativity in death education and counseling* (pp. 27–34). Lakewood, OH: Forum for Death Education and Counseling.

Shneidman, E. S. (1985). *Definition of suicide.* New York: Wiley.

Shneidman, E. S., & Farberow, N. L. (1961). *Some facts about suicide* (PHS Publication No. 852). Washington, DC: U.S. Government Printing Office.

Showalter, J. E. (1983). Foreword. In J. H. Arnold & P. B. Gemma (Eds.), *A child dies: A portrait of family grief* (pp. ix–x). Rockville, MD: Aspen Systems Corp.

Shriver, M. (2011). *Alzheimer's in America: The Shriver report on women and Alzheimer's.* New York: Free Press.

Shrock, N. M. (1835). On the signs that distinguish real from apparent death. *Transylvanian Journal of Medicine, 13,* 210–220.

Siebert, C. (2004). *A man after his own heart: A true story.* New York: Crown.

Siegel, A. M., Sisti, D. A., & Caplan, A. L. (2014). Pediatric euthanasia in Belgium: Disturbing developments. *Journal of the American Medical Association, 311*(19), 1963–1964. doi:10.1001/jama.2014.4257

Siegel, D. J. (2014). *Brainstorm: The power and purpose of the teenager.* New York: Tarcher.

Siegel, K., & Weinstein, L. (1983). Anticipatory grief reconsidered. *Journal of Psychosocial Oncology, 1*(2), 61–73. doi:10.1300/J077v01n02_04

Siegel, M. (Ed.). (1997). *The last word: The New York Times book of obituaries and farewells—A celebration of unusual lives.* New York: William Morrow.

Siegel, M., Ross, C. S., & King, C. (2013). The relationship between gun ownership and firearm homicide rates in the United States, 1981–2010. *American Journal of Public Health, 103,* 2098–2105. doi:10.2105/AJPH.2013 .301409

Siegel, R. (1982). A family-centered program of neonatal intensive care. *Health and Social Work, 7,* 50–58. doi:10.1093/ hsw/7.1.50

Siegel, R., Rudd, S. H., Cleveland, C., et al. (1985). A hospice approach to neonatal care. In C. A. Corr & D. M. Corr (Eds.), *Hospice approaches to pediatric care* (pp. 127–152). New York: Springer.

Siegel, R. L., Jacobs, E. J., Newton, C. C., et al. (2015). Deaths due to cigarette smoking for 12 smoking-related cancers in the United States. *JAMA Internal Medicine, 175*(9), 1574–1576. doi:10.1001/jamainternmed.2015.2398

Sife, W. (2014). *The loss of a pet: A guide to coping with the grieving process when a pet dies* (4th ed.). New York: Howell Book House.

Sifton, E. (2003). *The serenity prayer: Faith and politics in time of peace and war.* New York: Norton.

Siggins, L. (1966). Mourning: A critical survey of the literature. *International Journal of Psychoanalysis, 47,* 14–25.

Silver, R. C., & Wortman, C. B. (1980). Coping with undesirable life events. In J. Garber & M. E. P. Seligman (Eds.), *Human helplessness: Theory and applications* (pp. 279–340). New York: Academic Press.

Silverman, E., Range, L., & Overholser, J. (1994). Bereavement from suicide as compared to other forms of bereavement.

Omega, Journal of Death and Dying, 30, 41–51. doi:10.2190/BPLN-DAG8-7F07-0BKP

Silverman, P. R. (1978). *Mutual help groups: A guide for mental health workers.* Rockville, MD: National Institute of Mental Health.

Silverman, P. R. (1980). *Mutual help groups: Organization and development.* Newbury Park, CA: Sage.

Silverman, P. R. (1986). *Widow to widow.* New York: Springer.

Silverman, P. R. (2000). *Never too young to know: Death in children's lives.* New York: Oxford University Press.

Silverman, P. R. (2004). *Widow to widow: How the bereaved help one another* (2nd ed.). New York: Routledge.

Silverman, P. R., & Kelly, M. (2009). *A parent's guide to raising grieving children: Rebuilding your family after the death of a loved one.* New York: Oxford University Press.

Silverman, P. R., & Worden, J. W. (1992a). Children and parental death. *American Journal of Orthopsychiatry, 62,* 93–104. doi:10.1037/h0079304

Silverman, P. R., & Worden, J. W. (1992b). Children's understanding of funeral ritual. *Omega, Journal of Death and Dying, 25,* 319–331. doi:10.2190/0QMH-FR98-R7XW -18VY

Silverman, P. R., Nickman, S., & Worden, J. W. (1992). Detachment revisited: The child's reconstruction of a dead parent. *American Journal of Orthopsychiatry, 62,* 494–503. doi:10.1037/h0079366

Silverman, R. A. (2011). *The Wall Street Journal complete estate planning guidebook.* New York: Crown Business.

Simeone, W. E. (1991). The Northern Athabaskan potlatch: The objectification of grief. In D. R. Counts & D. A. Counts (Eds.), *Coping with the final tragedy: Cultural variation in dying and grieving* (pp. 157–167). Amityville, NY: Baywood.

Siminoff, L. A., Arnold, R. M., Caplan, A. L., Virnig, B. A., & Seltzer, D. L. (1995). Public policy governing organ and tissue procurement in the United States. *Annals of Internal Medicine, 123,* 10–17. doi:10.7326/0003-4819-123-1-199507010-00037

Siminoff, L. A., Gordon, N., Hewlett, J., & Arnold, R. M. (2001). Factors influencing families' consent for donation of solid organs for transplantation. *Journal of the American Medical Association, 286,* 71–77. doi:10.1001/jama.286.1.71

Simmons, P. (2002). *Learning to fall: The blessings of an imperfect life.* New York: Bantam.

Simon, C. (2001). *Fatherless women: How we change after we lose our dads.* New York: Wiley.

Simon, N. (1979). *We remember Philip.* Chicago: Whitman.

Simonds, W., & Rothman, B. K. (Eds.). (1992). *Centuries of solace: Expressions of maternal grief in popular literature.* Philadelphia: Temple University Press.

Simone, P. M., & Dooley, S. W. (1994). Multidrug-resistant tuberculosis, 1994. CDC, Division of Tuberculosis Elimination. Retrieved from http://www.cdc.gov/nchstp/tb/pubs /mdrtb.htm

Simpson, M. A. (1976). Brought in dead. *Omega, Journal of Death and Dying, 7,* 243–248. doi:10.2190/PXW3-RLQG-Y61V-U5LY

Singer, A. E., Meeker, D., Teno, J. M., et al. (2015). Symptom trends in the last year of life from 1998 to 2010: A cohort study. *Annals of Internal Medicine, 162*(3), 175–183. doi:10.7326/M13-1609

Singh, G. K., Mathews, T. J., Clarke, S. C., Yannicos, T., & Smith, B. L. (1995). Annual summary of births, marriages, divorces, and deaths: United States, 1994. *Monthly Vital Statistics Report, 43*(13). Hyattsville, MD: National Center for Health Statistics.

Sjöqvist, S. (Ed.). (2007). *Still here with me: Teenagers and children on losing a parent* (M. Myers, Trans.). Philadelphia: Jessica Kingsley.

Skidelsky, R. (2004). The killing fields. *New Statesman, 26,* pp. 18–21.

Slaby, A. (1992). Creativity, depression, and suicide. *Suicide and Life-Threatening Behavior, 22,* 157–166. doi:10.1111/ j.1943-278X.1992.tb00226.x

Slaughter, V., & Griffiths, M. (2007). Death understanding and fear of death in young children. *Clinical Child Psychology and Psychiatry, 12,* 525–535. doi:10.1177/1359104507080980

Slaughter, V., & Lyons, M. (2003). Learning about life and death in early childhood. *Cognitive Psychology, 46,* 1–30. doi:10.1016/S0010-0285(02)00504-2

Sleutjes, A., Moreira-Almeida, A., & Greyson, B. (2014). Almost 40 years investigating near-death experiences: An overview of mainstream scientific journals. *The Journal of Nervous and Mental Disease, 202,* 833–836. doi:10.1097/ NMD.0000000000000205

Sloane, D. C. (1991). *The last great necessity: Cemeteries in American history.* Baltimore: Johns Hopkins University Press.

Slocum, J., & Carlson, L. (2011). *Final rights: Reclaiming the American way of death.* Hinesburg, VT: Upper Access.

Small, N., Froggat, K., & Downs, M. (2007). *Living and dying with dementia: Dialogues about palliative care.* New York: Oxford University Press.

Smedley, B. D., Stith, A. Y., & Nelson, A. R. (Eds.). (2004). *Unequal treatment: Confronting racial and ethnic disparities in healthcare.* Washington, DC: National Academies Press.

Smith, A. A. (1974). *Rachel.* Wilton, CT: Morehouse-Barlow.

Smith, A. C. (2003, December 7). Voters: Schiavo law was bad move. *St. Petersburg Times,* pp. 1A, 21A.

Smith, A. K., Cenzer, I. S., Knight, S. J., et al. (2010). The epidemiology of pain during the last 2 years of life. *Annals of Internal Medicine, 153,* 563–569. doi:10.7326/0003-4819-153-9-201011020-00005

Smith, D. H. (1986). *Health and medicine in the Anglican tradition: Conscience, community, and compromise.* New York: Crossroad.

Smith, F., & Himmel, S. (2013). *Changing the way we die: Compassionate end of life care and the hospice movement.* Berkeley, CA: Viva Editions.

Smith, G. H. (2007). *Remembering Garrett: One family's battle with a child's depression.* New York: Basic Books.

Smith, H. I. (1994). *On grieving the death of a father.* Minneapolis, MN: Augsburg Fortress.

Smith, H. I. (1996). *Grieving the death of a friend.* Minneapolis, MN: Augsburg Fortress.

Smith, H. I. (1999). *A decembered grief: Living with loss when others are celebrating.* Kansas City, MO: Beacon Hill Press of Kansas City.

Smith, H. I. (2001). *Friendgrief: An absence called presence.* Amityville, NY: Baywood.

Smith, H. I. (2003). *Grieving the death of a mother.* Minneapolis, MN: Augsburg Fortress.

Smith, H. I. (2004a). *Grievers ask: Answers to questions about death and loss.* Minneapolis, MN: Augsburg Fortress.

Smith, H. I. (2004b). *GriefKeeping: Learning how long grief lasts.* New York: Crossroads.

Smith, H. I. (2012). *When a child you love is grieving* (2nd ed.). Kansas City, MO: Beacon Hill Press of Kansas City.

Smith, H. I., & Jeffers, S. L. (2001). *ABC's of healthy grieving: Light for a dark journey.* Shawnee Mission, KS: Shawnee Mission Medical Center Foundation.

Smith, H. I., & Johnson, J. (2006). *What does that mean? A dictionary of death, dying and grief terms for grieving children and those who love them.* Omaha, NE: Centering Corporation.

Smith, H. I., & Johnson, J. (2008). *Partnered grief: When gay and lesbian partners grieve.* Omaha: NE: Centering Corporation.

Smith, I. (1991). Preschool children "play" out their grief. *Death Studies, 15,* 169–176. doi:10.1080/074811891082524

Smith, I. (2000). *A tiny boat at sea.* Portland, OR: Author (3254 SE Salmon, Portland, OR 97214).

Smith, J. C., & Medalia, C. (2015). *U.S. Census Bureau, Current Population Reports, P60-253, Health Insurance Coverage in the United States: 2014.* Washington, DC: U.S. Government Printing Office.

Smith, J. I., & Haddad, Y. Y. (2002). *The Islamic understanding of death and resurrection.* New York: Oxford University Press.

Smith, R., & Kelly, N. (2012, August 16). Global attempts to avoid talking directly about death and dying. Retrieved October 13, 2016, from http://blogs.bmj.com/bmj/2012/08/16/richard-smith-and-nataly-kelly-global-attempts-to-avoid-talking-directly-about-death-and-dying/

Smith, S. T., & Castleman, M. (2013). *When someone dies: The practical guide to the logistics of death.* New York: Scribner.

Smith, W. J. (2006). *Forced exit: Euthanasia, assisted suicide and the new duty to die.* New York: Encounter Books.

Smolin, A., & Guinan, J. (1993). *Healing after the suicide of a loved one.* New York: Simon & Schuster.

Snowdon, D. (2002). *Aging with grace: What the Nun Study teaches us about leading longer, healthier, and more meaningful lives.* New York: Bantam.

Sobel, E. (2012). *Blue sky, white clouds: A book for memory-challenged adults.* Faber, VA: Rainbow Ridge.

Sofka, C. J. (1997). Social support "Internetworks," caskets for sale, and more: Thanatology and the information superhighway. *Death Studies, 21*(6), 553–574. doi:10.1080/074811897201778

Sofka, C. J. (2009). Adolescents, technology and the Internet: Coping with loss in the digital world. In D. E. Balk & C. A. Corr (Eds.), *Adolescent encounters with death, bereavement, and coping* (pp. 155–173). New York: Springer.

Sofka, C., Cupit, I. N., & Gilbert, K. (2012). *Dying, death, and grief in an online universe.* New York: Springer.

Søfting. G. H., Dyregrov, A., & Dyregrov, K. (2016). Because I'm also part of the family. Children's participation in rituals after the loss of a parent or sibling: A qualitative study from the children's perspective. *Omega, Journal of Death and Dying, 73,* 141–158. doi:10.1177/0030222815575898

Solomon, A. (2013). *A stone boat.* New York: Scribner.

Solomon, M. Z., Sellers, D. E., Heller, K. S., et al. (2005). New and lingering controversies in pediatric end-of-life care. *Pediatrics, 116*(4), 872–883. doi:10.1542/peds.2004-0905

Solomon, S., Greenberg, J., & Pyszcynski, T. (2004). The cultural animal: Twenty years of terror management theory and research. In J. Greenberg, S. Koole & T. Pyszcynski (Eds.), *Handbook of experimental existential psychology* (pp. 13–34). New York: Guilford Press.

Sontag, S. (1978). *Illness as metaphor.* New York: Farrar, Straus & Giroux.

Sontag, S. (1989). *AIDS and its metaphors.* New York: Farrar, Straus & Giroux.

Sorlie, P. D., Backlund, E., & Keller, J. B. (1995). U.S. mortality by economic, demographic, and social characteristics: The National Longitudinal Mortality Study. *American Journal of Public Health, 85,* 949–956. doi:10.2105/AJPH.85.7.949

Sourkes, B. M. (1995). *Armfuls of time: The psychological experience of the child with a life-threatening illness.* Pittsburgh: University of Pittsburgh Press.

Sourkes, B. M. (1996). The broken heart: Anticipatory grief in the child facing death. *Journal of Palliative Care, 12*(3), 56–59.

Spector, R. E. (2012). *Cultural diversity in health and illness* (8th ed.). Upper Saddle River, NJ: Pearson.

Speece, M. W., & Brent, S. B. (1984). Children's understanding of death: A review of three components of a death concept. *Child Development, 55,* 1671–1686. doi:10.2307/1129915

Speece, M. W., & Brent, S. B. (1992). The acquisition of a mature understanding of three components of the concept of death. *Death Studies, 16,* 211–229. doi:10.1080/07481189208252571

Speece, M. W., & Brent, S. B. (1996). The development of children's understanding of death. In C. A. Corr & D. M. Corr (Eds.), *Handbook of childhood death and bereavement* (pp. 29–50). New York: Springer.

Sperling, R. A., Aisen, P. S., Beckett, L. A., et al. (2011). Toward defining the preclinical stages of Alzheimer's disease: Recommendations from the National Institute on Aging and the Alzheimer's Association workgroup. *Alzheimer's and Dementia: The Journal of the Alzheimer's Association, 7*(3), 280–292. doi:10.1016/j.jalz.2011.03.003

Spetz, J., Dudley, N., Trupin, L., et al. (2016). Few hospital palliative care programs meet national staffing recommendations. *Health Affairs, 35*(9), 1690–1697. doi:10.1377/hlthaff.2016.0113

Spinetta, J. J., & Deasy-Spinetta, P. (1981). *Living with childhood cancer.* St. Louis, MO: Mosby.

Spinetta, J. J., & Maloney, L. J. (1975). Death anxiety in the outpatient leukemic child. *Pediatrics, 56*(6), 1034–1037.

Spinetta, J. J., Rigler, D., & Karon, M. (1973). Anxiety in the dying child. *Pediatrics, 52*(6), 841–849.

Sprang, G., & McNeil, J. (1995). *The many faces of bereavement: The nature and treatment of natural, traumatic, and stigmatized grief.* New York: Bruner/Mazel.

Sque, M., Long, T., & Payne, S. (2005). Organ donation: Key factors influencing families' decision-making. *Transplantation Proceedings, 37,* 543–546. doi:10.1016/j.transproceed.2004.11.038

St. Louis Post-Dispatch. (1999, April 14). Judge assails "lawlessness" of Kevorkian, gives him 10–25 years, p. A1.

St. Petersburg Times. (2001, October 1). Brian Sweeney's last message, p. 10A.

Staff. (2014, October 23). Compassionate care benefits boost staff engagement. *Benefits Canada.* Retrieved November 14, 2014, from http://www.benefitscanada.com/benefits/other/compassionate-care-benefits-boost-staff-engagement-58488

Stahre, M., Roeber, J., Kanny, D., Brewer, R. D., & Zhang, X. (2014). Contribution of excessive alcohol consumption to deaths and years of potential life lost in the United States. *Preventing Chronic Disease, 11,* 1–12. doi:10.5888/pcd11.130293

Stambrook, M., & Parker, K. C. (1987). The development of the concept of death in childhood: A review of the literature. *Merrill Palmer Quarterly, 33,* 133–157. http://www.jstor.org/stable/23086325

Stannard, D. E. (1977). *The Puritan way of death: A study in religion, culture, and social change.* New York: Oxford University Press.

Stanworth, R. (2003). *Recognizing spiritual needs in people who are dying.* New York: Oxford University Press.

Staples, B. (1994). *Parallel time: Growing up in black and white.* New York: Pantheon.

Stargardt, N. (2006). *Witnesses of war: Children's lives under the Nazis*. New York: Alfred A. Knopf.

Starr, P. (1982). *The social transformation of American medicine*. New York: Basic Books.

Starzl, T. (2003). *The puzzle people: Memoirs of a transplant surgeon* (rev. ed.). Pittsburgh: University of Pittsburgh Press.

Staton, J., Shuy, R., & Byock, I. (2001). *A few months to live: Different paths to life's end*. Washington, DC: Georgetown University Press.

Staudacher, C. (1991). *Men and grief*. Oakland, CA: New Harbinger Publications.

Stearns, A. K. (1988). *Coming back: Rebuilding lives after crisis and loss*. New York: Random House.

Stedeford, A. (1978). Understanding confusional states. *British Journal of Hospital Medicine, 20*, 694–704.

Stedeford, A. (1979). Psychotherapy of the dying patient. *British Journal of Psychiatry, 135*, 7–14. doi:10.1192/bjp.135.1.7

Stedeford, A. (1984). *Facing death: Patients, families and professionals*. London: William Heinemann.

Stedeford, A. (1987). Hospice: A safe place to suffer? *Palliative Medicine, 1*, 73–74. doi:10.1177/026921638700100111

SteelFisher, G. K., Blendon, R. J., & Lasala-Blanco, N. (2015). Ebola in the United States: Public reactions and implications. *New England Journal of Medicine, 373*, 789–791. doi:10.1056/NEJMp1506290

Steffen, L., & Cooley, D. R. (2014). *The ethics of death: Religious and philosophical perspectives*. Minneapolis: Fortress Press.

Stein, L. (2011, February 26). A chain of compassion: The Tampa Bay area is part of a kidney donor chain including 16 recipients across nine states. *St. Petersburg Times*, pp. 1A & 10A.

Steinbrook, R. (2007). Organ donation after cardiac death. *New England Journal of Medicine, 357*, 209–213. doi:10.1056/NEJMp078066

Stern, J., & Berger, J. M. (2015). *ISIS: The state of terror*. New York: HarperCollins.

Stetson, B. (2002). *Living victims, stolen lives: Parents of murdered children speak to America*. Amityville, NY: Baywood.

Stevens, M. M. (1998). Psychological adaptation of the dying child. In D. Doyle, G. W. C. Hanks, & N. MacDonald (Eds.), *Oxford textbook of palliative medicine* (2nd ed., pp. 1046–1055). New York: Oxford University Press.

Stevens, M. M., & Dunsmore, J. C. (1996a). Adolescents who are living with a life-threatening issues. In C. A. Corr & D. E. Balk (Eds.), *Handbook of adolescent death and bereavement* (pp. 107–135). New York: Springer.

Stevens, M. M., & Dunsmore, J. C. (1996b). Helping adolescents who are coping with a life-threatening illness, along with their siblings, parents, and peers. In C. A. Corr & D. E. Balk (Eds.), *Handbook of adolescent death and bereavement* (pp. 329–353). New York: Springer.

Stevens, R. (1989). *In sickness and in wealth: American hospitals in the twentieth century*. New York: Basic Books.

Stevenson, A. (1989). *Bitter fame: A life of Sylvia Plath*. Boston: Houghton Mifflin.

Stevenson, D. G. (2012). Growing pains for the Medicare hospice benefit. *New England Journal of Medicine, 367*(18), 1683–1685. doi:10.1056/NEJMp1208465

Stevenson, I., Cook, E. W., & McClean-Rice, N. (1990). Are persons reporting "near-death experiences" really near death? A study of medical records. *Omega, Journal of Death and Dying, 20*, 45–54. doi:10.2190/D8Q9-HHKX-5JWC-FD3V

Stevenson, R. G. (2004). Where have we come from? Where do we go from here? Thirty years of death education in schools. *Illness, Crisis and Loss, 12*, 231–238. doi:10.1177/1054137304265756

Stevenson, R. G. (Ed.). (2002). *What will we do? Preparing a school community to cope with crises* (2nd ed.). Amityville, NY: Baywood.

Stevenson, R. G., & Stevenson, E. P. (1996a). Adolescents and education about death, dying, and bereavement. In C. A. Corr & D. E. Balk (Eds.), *Handbook of adolescent death and bereavement* (pp. 235–249). New York: Springer.

Stevenson, R. G., & Stevenson, E. P. (Eds.). (1996b). *Teaching students about death: A comprehensive resource for educators and parents*. Philadelphia: The Charles Press.

Stevick, R. A. (2007). *Growing up Amish: The teenage years*. Baltimore: Johns Hopkins University Press.

Stewart, M. F. (1999). *Companion animal death: A practical and comprehensive guide for veterinary practice*. Woburn, MA: Butterworth-Heinemann Medical.

Stiles, D. A., Moyer, J. M., Brewer, S., et al. (2015). Practising psychology in challenging times: Schools and the Ferguson crisis. *Educational and Child Psychology, 32*(4), 21–38.

Stillion, J. M. (1985). *Death and the sexes: An examination of differential longevity, attitudes, behaviors, and coping skills*. Washington, DC: Hemisphere.

Stillion, J. M., & McDowell, E. E. (1996). *Suicide across the life span: Premature exits* (2nd ed.).Washington, DC: Taylor & Francis.

Stillion, J. M., McDowell, E. E., & May, J. (1989). *Suicide across the life span: Premature exits*. Washington, DC: Hemisphere.

Stillion, J., & Attig, T. (Eds.). (2015). *Death, dying, and bereavement: Contemporary perspectives, institutions, and practices*. New York: Springer.

Stoddard, S. (1992). *The hospice movement: A better way of caring for the dying* (Rev. ed.). New York: Vintage.

Stokes, J., & Crossley, D. (1995). Camp Winston: A residential intervention for bereaved children. In S. C. Smith & M. Penells (Eds.), *Interventions with bereaved children* (pp. 172–192). London: Jessica Kingsley Publications.

Stokes, J. A. (2004). *Then, now and always—Supporting children as they journey through grief: A guide for practitioners*. Cheltenham, England: Winston's Wish.

Stoller, E. P., & Gibson, R. C. (Eds.). (2000). *Worlds of difference: Inequality in the aging experience* (3rd ed.). Thousand Oaks, CA: Sage.

Strasburger, V. C. (1993). Children, adolescents, and the media: Five crucial issues. *Adolescent Medicine: State of the Art Review, 4*, 479–493.

Strasburger, V. C., Jordan, A. B., & Donnerstein, E. (2012). Children, adolescents, and the media: Health effects. *Pediatric Clinics of North America, 59*, 533–587. doi:10.1016/j.pcl.2012.03.025

Strathdee, S. A., & Beyrer, C. (2015). Threading the needle: How to stop the HIV outbreak in rural Indiana. *New England Journal of Medicine, 373*, 397–399. doi:10.1056/NEJMp1507252

Straub, S. H. (2004). *Pet death*. Amityville, NY: Baywood.

Straub, S. H. (2015). *Death 101: A workbook for educating and healing* (2nd ed.). New York: Routledge.

Stritof, S., & Stritof, B. (2009, November 11). John and Sandra Day O'Connor marriage profile. *About.com*. Retrieved December 9, 2010, from http://marriage.about.com/od/politics/p/sandraoconnor.htm?rd=1

Stroebe, M. (2015). "Is Grief a Disease?" Why Engel posed the question. *Omega, Journal of Death and Dying, 71*, 272–279. doi:10.1177/0030222815575504

Stroebe, M., & Schut, H. (1999). The dual process model of coping with bereavement: Rationale and description. *Death Studies, 23*, 197–224. doi:10.1080/074811899201046

Stroebe, M., & Schut, H. (2005). To continue or relinquish bonds: A review of consequences for the bereaved. *Death Studies, 29*, 477–494. doi:10.1080/07481180590962659

Stroebe, M. & Schut, H. (2010). The Dual Process Model: A decade on. *Omega, Journal of Death & Dying, 61*, 273–291. doi:10.2190/OM.61.4.b

Stroebe, M., & Schut, H. (2016). Overload: A missing link in the Dual Process Model? *Omega, Journal of Death and Dying, 74*, 96–109. doi:10.1177/0030222816666540

Stroebe, M. S., Hansson, R. O., Schut, H. A., & Stroebe, W. (Eds.). (2008). *Handbook of bereavement research and practice: Advances in theory and intervention.* Washington, DC: American Psychological Association.

Stroebe, M. S., Hansson, R. O., Stroebe, W., & Schut, H. A. (Eds.). (2001). *Handbook of bereavement research: Consequences, coping, and care.* Washington, DC: American Psychological Association Press.

Stroebe, M., Finkenauer, C., Wijngaards-de-Meij, L., et al. (2013). Partner-oriented self-regulation among bereaved parents: The costs of holding in grief for the partner's sake. *Psychological Science, 24*, 395–402. doi:10.1177/0956797612457383

Stroebe, M., Schut, H., & Boerner, K. (2017). Cautioning healthcare professionals: Bereaved persons are misguided through the stages of grief. *Omega, Journal of Death & Dying, 74*, 455–473.

Stroebe, M., Schut, H., & van den Bout, J. (Eds.). (2013). *Complicated grief: Scientific foundations for health care professionals.* New York, NY: Routledge.

Stroebe, W., & Stroebe, M. S. (2003). *Bereavement and health: The psychological and physical consequences of partner loss.* Cambridge, UK: Cambridge University Press.

Suarez, R. (2013). *Latino Americans: The 500-year legacy that shaped a nation.* New York: Celebra Books.

Sudnow, D. (1967). *Passing on: The social organization of dying.* Englewood Cliffs, NJ: Prentice Hall.

Sue, D. W., & Sue, D. (2015). *Counseling the culturally diverse: Theory and practice* (7th ed.). New York: John Wiley.

Sugar, M. (1968). Normal adolescent mourning. *American Journal of Psychotherapy, 22*, 258–269.

Sullivan, D. (2005, August 8). Always go to the funeral. As heard on NPR's *All Things Considered.* Retrieved September 22, 2013, from http://thisibelieve.org/essay/8/

Sullivan, D. (2015, September 20). Gangs? *Tampa Bay Times*, pp. 1A & 14A.

Sullivan, M. A. (1995). May the circle be unbroken: The African-American experience of death, dying, and spirituality. In J. K. Parry & A. S. Ryan (Eds.), *A cross-cultural look at death, dying, and religion* (pp. 160–171). Chicago: Nelson-Hall.

Sumner, L. H., Kavanaugh, K., & Moro, T. (2006). Extending palliative care into pregnancy and the immediate newborn period: State of the practice of perinatal palliative care. *Journal of Perinatal and Neonatal Nursing, 20*, 113–116.

Supportive Care of the Dying: A Coalition for Compassionate Care. (1997). *Living and healing during life-threatening illness: Executive summary.* Portland, OR: Author.

Swanson, S. A., & Colman, I. (2013). Association between exposure to suicide and suicidality outcomes in youth. *Canadian Medical Association Journal, 185*, 870–877. doi:10.1503/cmaj.121377

Swarte, N., & Heintz, A. (1999). Euthanasia and physician-assisted suicide. *Annals of Medicine, 31*, 364–371. doi:10.3109/07853899908998793

Swarte, N., van der Lee, M., van der Born, J., van den Bout, J., & Heintz, A. (2003). Effects of euthanasia on the bereaved family and friends: A cross sectional study. *British Medical Journal, 327*, 189–192. doi:10.1136/bmj.327.7408.189

Swartzberg, J. (2004). Do living wills work? *UC Berkeley Wellness Letter, 20*(11), 3.

Szabo, L. (2016, October 26). Terminally ill patients don't use aid-in-dying laws to relieve pain. *Kaiser Health News.* Retrieved November 13, 2016, from http://khn.org/news/terminally-ill-patients-dont-use-aid-in-dying-laws-to-relieve-pain/

Talbot, K. (2002). *What forever means after the death of a child: Transcending the trauma, living with the loss.* New York: Brunner-Routledge.

Tangeman, J. C., Rudra, C. B., Kerr, C. W., & Grant, P. C. (2014). A hospice-hospital partnership: Reducing hospitalization costs and 30-day readmissions among seriously ill adults. *Journal of Palliative Medicine, 17*, 1005–1010. doi:10.1089/jpm.2013.0612

Tanner, J. G. (1995). Death, dying, and grief in the Chinese-American culture. In J. K. Parry & A. S. Ryan (Eds.), *A cross-cultural look at death, dying, and religion* (pp. 183–192). Chicago: Nelson-Hall.

Tarter, R., Demiris, G., Pike, K., Washington, K., & Oliver, D. P. (2016). Pain in hospice patients with dementia: The informal caregiver experience. *American Journal of Alzheimer's Disease and Other Dementias, 31*(6), 524–529. doi:10.1177/1533317516653825

Tatelbaum, J. (1980). *The courage to grieve.* New York: Lippincott & Crowell.

Taxis, J. C. (2006). Attitudes, values, and questions of African Americans regarding participation in hospice programs. *Journal of Hospice and Palliative Nursing, 8*(2), 77–85.

Taylor, D. H., Ostermann, J., Van Houtven, C. H., Tulsky, J. A., & Steinhauser, K. (2007). What length of hospice use maximizes reduction in medical expenditures near death in the US Medicare program? *Social Science and Medicine, 65*, 1466–1478. doi:10.1016/j.socscimed.2007.05.028

Taylor, J. C. (2011). Courageous conversations: Exploring matters of life and death in geriatric rehabilitation. *Topics In Geriatric Rehabilitation, 27*(1), 81–86. doi:10.1097/TGR.0b013e3181ff68b7

Taylor, R. (2007). *Alzheimer's from the inside out.* Baltimore: Health Professions Press.

Teater, M., & Ludgate, J. (2014). *Overcoming compassion fatigue: A practical resilience workbook.* Eau Claire, WI: PESI Publishing & Media.

Tedeschi, R. G. (1996). Support groups for bereaved adolescents. In C. A. Corr & D. E. Balk (Eds.), *Handbook of adolescent death and bereavement* (pp. 293–311). New York: Springer.

Tedeschi, R. G., & Calhoun, L. G. (1995). *Trauma and transformation: Growing in the aftermath of suffering.* Thousand Oaks, CA: Sage.

Tedeschi, R. G., & Calhoun, L. G. (2003). *Helping bereaved parents: A clinician's guide.* New York: Routledge.

Tedeschi, R. G., & Calhoun, L. G. (2007). Grief as a transformative struggle. In K. J. Doka (Ed.), *Living with grief: Before and after a death* (pp. 107–121). Washington, DC: Hospice Foundation of America.

Tedeschi, R. G., Park, C. L., & Calhoun, L. G. (Eds.). (1998). *Posttraumatic growth: Positive changes in the aftermath of crisis.* Mahwah, NJ: Lawrence Erlbaum Associates.

Tehan, M., & Thompson, N. (2013). Loss and grief in the workplace: The challenge of leadership. *Omega, Journal of Death and Dying, 66*, 265–280. doi:10.2190/OM.66.3.d

Temel, J. S., Greer, J. A., El-Jawahri, A., et al. (2017). Effects of early integrated palliative care in patients with lung and GI cancer: A randomized clinical trial. *Journal of Clinical Oncology, 35*(8), 834–841. doi:10.1200/JCO.2016.70.5046

Temel, J. S., Greer, J. A., Muzikansky, A., et al. (2010). Early palliative care for patients with metastatic non-small-cell lung cancer. *New England Journal of Medicine, 363,* 733–742. doi:10.1056/NEJMoa1000678

Templer, D. (1970). The construction and validation of a death anxiety scale. *Journal of General Psychology, 82,* 165–177. doi:10.1080/00221309.1970.9920634

Teno, J. M., & Connor, S. R. (2009). Referring a patient and family to high-quality palliative care at the close of life. *Journal of the American Medical Association, 301,* 651–659. doi:10.1001/jama.2009.109

Teno, J. M., Clarridge, B. R., Casey, V., et al. (2004). Family perspectives on end-of-life care at the last place of care. *Journal of the American Medical Association, 291,* 88–93. doi:10.1001/jama.291.1.88

Teno, J. M., Freedman, V. A., Kasper, J. D., Gozalo, P., & Mor, V. (2015). Is care for the dying improving in the United States? *Journal of Palliative Medicine, 18,* 622–666. doi:10.1089/jpm.2015.0039

Teno, J. M., Gozalo, P. L., Bynum, J. P. W., et al. (2013). Change in end-of-life care for Medicare beneficiaries: Site of death, place of care, and health care transitions in 2000, 2005, and 2009. *Journal of the American Medical Association, 309*(5), 470–477. doi:10.1001/jama.2012.207624

Teno, J. M., Plotzke, M., Gozalo, P., & Mor, V. (2014). A national study of live discharges from hospice. *Journal of Palliative Medicine, 17,* 1121–1127. doi:10.1089/jpm.2013.0595

Terkel, S. (2001). *Will the circle be unbroken?: Reflections on death, rebirth, and hunger for a faith.* New York: New Press.

Terri's Family, Schindler, M., Schindler, R., Vitadona, S. S., & Schindler, B. (2006). *A life that matters: The legacy of Terri Schiavo—A lessons for us all.* New York: Warner Books.

The Dougy Center and the American Foundation for Suicide Prevention. (n.d.). *Children, teens, and suicide loss.* Portland, OR: Authors.

The Economist Intelligence Unit. (2015). The 2015 Quality of Death Index: Ranking palliative care across the world. *The Economist.* Retrieved July 2, 2016, from http://www.economistinsights.com/healthcare/analysis/quality-death-index-2015

The GBD 2015 Obesity Collaborators. (2017, June 12). Health effects of overweight and obesity in 195 countries over 25 years. *The New England Journal of Medicine,* published online first. doi:10.1056/NEJMoa1614362

The SUPPORT Principal Investigators. (1995). A controlled trial to improve care for seriously ill hospitalized patients: The Study to Understand Prognoses and Preferences for Outcomes and Risks of Treatments (SUPPORT). *Journal of the American Medical Association, 274,* 1591–1598. doi:10.1001/jama.1995.03530200027032

Thelwell, D. G. (2014). *The dance: Our journey through frontotemporal degeneration.* Amazon.com: CreateSpace.

Thomas, N. (2001). The importance of culture throughout all of life and beyond. *Holistic Nursing Practice, 15*(2), 40–46.

Thomas, W. J. (2007). *What are old people for?: How elders will save the world.* Acton, MA: VanderWyk & Burnham.

Thomasma, D. C., Kimbrough-Kushner, T., Kimsma, G. K., & Ciesielski-Carlucci, C. (1998). *Asking to die: Inside the Dutch debate about euthanasia.* Boston: Kluwer Academic.

Thompson, B. E., Murphy, N. M., & Toms, M. E. (2009). Hospice care. In H. Mitsumoto (Ed.), *Amyotrophic lateral sclerosis: A guide for patients and families* (3rd ed., pp. 365–393). New York: Demos Medical Publishing.

Thompson, N. (Ed.). (2002). *Loss and grief: A guide for human service practitioners.* London: Palgrave Macmillan.

Thompson, N. (2012). *Grief and its challenges.* London: Palgrave Macmillan.

Thompson, N., Cox, G. R., & Stevenson, R. G. (Eds.). (2017). *Handbook of traumatic loss: A guide to theory and practice.* New York: Routledge.

Thorson, J. A. (1995). *Aging in a changing society.* Belmont, CA: Wadsworth.

Thorson, J. A., Powell, F. C., & Samuel, V. T. (1998). African and Euro-American samples differ little in scores on death anxiety. *Psychological Reports, 83,* 623–626. doi:10.2466/pr0.1998.83.2.623

Thun, M. J., Carter, B. D., Feskanich, D., et al. (2013). 50-year trends in smoking-related mortality in the United States. *New England Journal of Medicine, 368,* 351–364. doi:10.1056/NEJMsa1211127

Thurman, H. (1953). *Meditations of the heart.* New York: Harper & Row.

Tibbetts, E. (2001). Learning to value every moment. In M. Z. Solomon, A. L. Romer, K. S. Heller, & D. E. Weissman (Eds.), *Innovations in end-of-life care: Practical strategies and international perspectives* (Vol. 2, pp. 78–79). Larchmont, NY: Mary Ann Liebert Publishers.

Tideiksaar, R. (2010). *Falls in older people: Prevention and management* (4th ed.). Baltimore: Health Professions Press.

Tilney, N. L. (2003). *Transplantation: From myth to reality.* New Haven, CT: Yale University Press.

Times Staff Writer. (2004, July 14). Groups for disabled side with Schiavo. *St. Petersburg Times,* p. 3B.

Tobin, D. (1999). *Peaceful dying: The step-by-step guide to preserving your dignity, your choice, and your inner peace at the end of life.* Cambridge, MA: Perseus.

Todaro-Franceschi, V. (2012). *Compassion fatigue and burnout in nursing: Enhancing professional quality of life.* New York: Springer.

Tolle, S. W., & Teno, J. M. (2017). Lessons from Oregon in embracing complexity in end-of-life care. *New England Journal of Medicine, 376,* 1078–1082. doi:10.1056/NEJMsb1612511

Tolstoy, L. (1960). *The death of Ivan Ilych and other stories* (A. Maude, Trans.). New York: New American Library. (Original work published 1884)

Tomer, A., & Eliason, G. (1996). Toward a comprehensive model of death anxiety. *Death Studies, 20,* 343–366. doi:10.1080/07481189608252787

Tomer, A., Wong, P. T., & Eliason, G. T. (Eds.). (2007). *Existential and spiritual issues in death attitudes.* Mahwah, NJ: Lawrence Erlbaum.

Tomlinson, E., Spector, A., Nurock, S., & Stott, J. (2015). Euthanasia and physician assisted suicide in dementia: A qualitative study of the views of former dementia carers. *Palliative Medicine, 29,* 720–726. doi:10.1177/0269216315582143

Tong, K. L., & Spicer, B. J. (1994). The Chinese palliative patient and family in North America: A cultural perspective. *Journal of Palliative Care, 10*(1), 26–28.

Toray, T. (2004). The human-animal bond and loss: Providing support for grieving clients. *Journal of Mental Health Counseling, 26,* 244–259. doi:10.17744/mehc.26.3.udj040fw2gj75lqp

Toray, T., & Oltjenbruns, K. A. (1996). Children's friendships and the death of a friend. In C. A. Corr & D. M. Corr (Eds.), *Handbook of childhood death and bereavement* (pp. 165–178). New York: Springer.

Torres, O. B. (Ed.). (2016). *Encyclopedia of suicide* (3 vols.). Hauppauge, NY: Nova Sciences Publishers.

Town, L., & Kassel, K. (2014). *Advance directives, durable power of attorney, wills, and other legal considerations.* Seattle, WA: Amazon Digital Services (Kindle ed.).

Toynbee, A. (1968a). The relation between life and death, living and dying. In A. Toynbee, A. K. Mant, N. Smart, et al. (Eds.), *Man's concern with death* (pp. 259–271). New York: McGraw-Hill.

Toynbee, A. (1968b). Traditional attitudes towards death. In A. Toynbee, A. K. Mant, N. Smart, et al. (Eds.), *Man's concern with death* (pp. 59–94). New York: McGraw-Hill.

Toynbee, A., & Koestler, A. (1976). *Life after death*. New York: McGraw-Hill.

Trachtenberg, F. L., Haas, E. A., Kinney, H. C., Stanley, C., & Krous, H. F. (2012). Risk factor changes for Sudden Infant Death Syndrome after initiation of Back-to-Sleep campaign. *Pediatrics*, 129, 630–638; doi:10.1542/peds.2011-1419

Trask, B. S., & Hamon, R. R. (Eds.). (2007). *Cultural diversity and families: Expanding perspectives*. Thousand Oaks, CA: Sage.

Travis, S. S., Loving, G., McClanahan, L., & Bernard, M. (2001). Hospitalization patterns and palliation in the last year of life among residents in long-term care. *The Gerontologist*, 41(2), 153–160. doi:10.1093/geront/41.2.153

Troyer, J. M. (2014). *Counseling widowers*. New York: Routledge.

Trozzi, M., & Massimini, K. (1999). *Talking with children about loss: Words, strategies, and wisdom to help children cope with death, divorce, and other difficult times*. New York: Penguin Putnam.

Truog, R. D., Miller, F. G., & Halpern, S. D. (2013). The dead-donor rule and the future of organ donation. *New England Journal of Medicine*, 369, 1287–1289. doi:10.1056/NEJMp1307220

Tschann, J., Kaufmann, S., & Micco, G. (2003). Family involvement in end-of-life hospital care. *Journal of the American Geriatrics Society*, 51, 835–840. doi:10.1046/j.1365-2389.2003.51266.x

Tucker, J. B. (2001). *Scourge: The once and future threat of smallpox*. New York: Atlantic Monthly Press.

Turnbull, S. B. (2012). *The wealth of your life: A step-by-step guide for creating your ethical will* (3rd ed.). Wrenham, MA: Benedict Press.

Turner, M. (2006). *Talking with children and young people about death and dying* (2nd ed.). Philadelphia: Jessica Kingsley.

Tuzeo-Jarolmen, J. (2006). *When a family pet dies: A guide to dealing with children's loss*. Philadelphia: Jessica Kingsley.

Twomey, J. (2001, May 19). Youth crime: It's not what you think. *St. Petersburg Times*, p. 14A.

Twycross, R. (2011). *Introducing palliative care* (4th ed.). Oxford, England: Radcliffe Medical Press.

Twycross, R. G. (1976). Long-term use of diamorphine in advanced cancer. In J. J. Bonica & D. Albe-Fessard (Eds.), *Advances in pain research and therapy* (Vol. 1, pp. 653–661). New York: Raven Press.

Twycross, R. G. (1979a). The Brompton cocktail. In J. J. Bonica & V. Ventafridda (Eds.), *International symposium on pain of advanced cancer: Advances in pain research and therapy* (Vol. 2, pp. 291–300). New York: Raven Press.

Twycross, R. G. (1979b). Overview of analgesia. In J. J. Bonica & V. Ventafridda (Eds.), *International symposium on pain of advanced cancer: Advances in pain research and therapy* (Vol. 2, pp. 617–633). New York: Raven Press.

Twycross, R. G. (1982). Principles and practice of pain relief in terminal cancer. *Cancer Forum*, 6, 23–33.

Twycross, R. G. (1994). *Pain relief in advanced cancer*. New York: Churchill Livingstone.

Twycross, R. G., & Lack, S. A. (1997). *Oral morphine: Information for patients, families and friends* (3rd ed.). Beaconsfield, England: Beaconsfield Press.

Twycross, R. G., & Wilcock, A. (2002). *Symptom management in advanced cancer* (3rd ed.). Oxford, England: Radcliffe Medical Press.

Twycross, R., & Wilcock, A. (Eds.). (2008). *Hospice and palliative care formulary USA* (2nd ed.). Palliativedrugs.com Ltd.

U.S. Bureau of the Census. (1975). *Historical statistics of the United States, colonial times to 1970, bicentennial edition* (2 parts).Washington, DC: U.S. Government Printing Office.

U.S. Census Bureau, Population Division. (2016, June). *Annual estimates of the resident population by sex, single year of age, race, and Hispanic origin for the United States: April 1, 2010 to July 1, 2015*. Retrieved May 15, 2017 from https://factfinder.census.gov/faces/tableservices/jsf/pages/productview.xhtml?pid=PEP_2015_PEPALL6N&prodType=table

U.S. Department of Health and Human Services. (2001). *Youth violence: A report of the Surgeon General*. Washington, DC: U.S. Government Printing Office.

U.S. Department of Health and Human Services. (2010). *The Surgeon General's vision for a healthy and fit nation*. Rockville, MD: US Department of Health and Human Services, Office of the Surgeon General.

U.S. Department of Health and Human Services (2014). *The health consequences of smoking—50 years of progress: A report of the Surgeon General*. Atlanta, GA: U.S. Department of Health and Human Services, Centers for Disease Control and Prevention, National Center for Chronic Disease Prevention and Health Promotion, Office on Smoking and Health.

U.S. Department of Health and Human Services, Centers for Medicare & Medicaid Services. (2016, February). *Medicare hospice benefits*. CMS Product No. 02154. Baltimore: Author. Retrieved July 17, 2016, from https://www.medicare.gov/Pubs/pdf/02154.pdf

U.S. Department of Health and Human Services, Health Care Financing Administration. (1998). Medicare and Medicaid programs; hospital conditions of participation; identification of potential organ, tissue, and eye donors and transplant hospitals' provision of transplant-related data. *Federal Register*, 63, 33856–33874.

U.S. Department of Health and Human Services, Health Resources and Services Administration and Health Care Financing Administration. (2000). *Roles and training in the donation process: A resource guide*. Rockville, MD: Authors.

U.S. Department of Health and Human Services, Office of the Surgeon General. (2016, November). *Facing Addiction in America: The Surgeon General's Report on Alcohol, Drugs, and Health*. Washington, DC: Author.

U.S. Department of State, Bureau of Counterterrorism. (2015). *Country reports on terrorism 2014*. Washington, DC: Author. Retrieved June 20, 2015, from http://www.state.gov/documents/organization/239631.pdf

U.S. National Cancer Institute and World Health Organization. (2016). *The economics of tobacco and tobacco control*. National Cancer Institute Tobacco Control Monograph 21. NIH Publication No. 16-CA-8029A. Bethesda, MD: U.S. Department of Health and Human Services, National Institutes of Health, National Cancer Institute; and Geneva, CH: World Health Organization.

Ulferts, A. C., & Lindberg, A. (2003, October 15). Schiavo's family ends legal fight. *St. Petersburg Times*, pp. 1A, 5A.

Umaña-Taylor, A. J., & Yazedjian, A. (2006). Generational differences and similarities among Puerto Rican and Mexican mothers' experiences with familial ethnic socialization. *Journal of Social and Personal Relationships*, 23, 445–464. doi:10.1177/0265407506064214

Umberson, D. (2003). *Death of a parent: Transition to a new adult identity*. New York: Cambridge University Press.

Umberson, D., Olson, J. S., Crosnoe, R., et al. (2017). Death of family members as an overlooked source of racial disadvantage in the United States. *Proceedings of the National Academy of Sciences, 114,* 915–920. doi:10.1073/pnas.1605599114

UNAIDS. (2001). AIDS epidemic update: December 2000. Geneva, Switzerland: Author.

Ungerleider, S. (2015, October 19). I'm a doctor: Preparing you for death is as much a part of my job as saving lives. Retrieved October 20, 2015, from https://www.vox .com/2015/10/19/9554583/doctor-good-death

Unroe, K. T., Cagle, J. G., Dennis, M. E., et al. (2014). Hospice in the nursing home: Perspectives of front line nursing home staff. *Journal of the American Medical Directors Association, 15,* 881–884. doi:10.1016/j.jamda.2014.07.009

Unroe, K. T., Sachs, G. A., Dennis, M. E., et al. (2016). Effect of hospice use on costs of care for long-stay nursing home decedents. *Journal of the American Geriatrics Society, 64,* 723–730. doi:10.1111/jgs.14070

Urich, L. P. (2001). *The Patient Self-Determination Act: Meeting the challenges in patient care.* Washington, DC: Georgetown University Press.

Vachon, M. L. S. (1987). *Occupational stress in the care of the critically ill, the dying, and the bereaved.* Washington, DC: Hemisphere.

Vachon, M. L. S. (1997). Recent research into staff stress in palliative care. *European Journal of Palliative Care, 4,* 99–103.

Vachon, M. L. S. (2007). Caring for the professional caregivers: Before and after the death. In K. J. Doka (Ed.), *Living with grief: Before and after a death* (pp. 311–330). Washington, DC: Hospice Foundation of America.

Valdimarsdóttir, U., Kreicbergs, U., Hauksdóttir, A., et al. (2007). Parents' intellectual and emotional awareness of their child's impending death to cancer: A population-based long-term follow-up study. *Lancet Oncology, 8*(8), 706–714. doi:10.1016/S1470-2045(07)70209-7

Valente, S. M., & Saunders, J. M. (1987). High school suicide prevention programs. *Pediatric Nursing, 13*(2), 108–112, 137.

Valentine, D. (2011, September 2). St. Petersburg funeral home first in country with alkaline hydrolysis cremation option. *Tampa Bay Times.* Retrieved October 5, 2016, from http://www.tampabay.com/news/humaninterest /st-petersburg-funeral-home-first-in-country-with-alkaline -hydrolysis/1189232

Van der Heide, T., Onwuteaka-Philipsen, B. D., Rurup, M. L., et al. (2007). End-of-life practices in the Netherlands under the Euthanasia Act. *New England Journal of Medicine, 356,* 1957–1965. doi:10.1056/NEJMsa071143

Van der Maas, P. J., Van der Wal, G., Haverkate, I., et al. (1996). Euthanasia, physician-assisted suicide, and other medical practices involving the end of life in the Netherlands, 1990–1995. *New England Journal of Medicine, 335,* 1699–1705. doi:10.1056/NEJM199611283352227

Van der Wal, G., Van der Maas, P. J., Bosma, J. M., et al. (1996). Evaluation of the notification procedure for physician-assisted death in the Netherlands. *New England Journal of Medicine, 335,* 1706–1711. doi:10.1056/ NEJM199611283352228

Van der Zee, J., Dodson, O., & Billops, C. (1978). *The Harlem book of the dead.* Dobbs Ferry, NY: Morgan & Morgan.

Van Dongen, C. J. (1990). Agonizing questioning: Experiences of survivors of suicide victims. *Nursing Research, 39,* 224–229.

Van Dongen, C. J. (1991). Experiences of family members after a suicide. *Journal of Family Practice, 33,* 375–380.

Van Gennep, A. (1961). *The rites of passage* (M. B. Vizedom & G. L. Caffee, Trans.). Chicago: University of Chicago Press.

Van Lommel, P. (2010). *Consciousness beyond life: The science of the near-death experience.* New York: HarperOne.

Van Lommel, P., van Wees, R., Meyers, V., & Elfferich, I. (2001). Near-death experience in survivors of cardiac arrest: A prospective study in the Netherlands. *The Lancet, 358,* 2039–2045. doi:10.1016/S0140-6736(01)07100-8

Van Panhuis, W. G., Grefenstette, J., Jung, S. Y., et al. (2013). Contagious diseases in the United States from 1888 to the present. *New England Journal of Medicine, 369,* 2152–2158. doi:10.1056/NEJMms1215400

Van Riper, M. (1997). Death of a sibling: Five sisters, five stories. *Pediatric Nursing, 23,* 587–593.

Van Winkle, N. W. (2000). End-of-life decision making in American Indian and Alaska native cultures. In K. L. Braun, J. H. Pietsch, & P. L. Blanchette (Eds.), *Cultural issues in end-of-life decision making* (pp. 127–144). Thousand Oaks, CA: Sage.

Varga, M. A. & Paulus, T. M. (2014). Grieving online: Newcomers' constructions of grief in an online support group. *Death Studies, 38,* 443–449. doi:10.1080/07481187. 2013.780112

Varney, S. (2015, August 21). A racial gap in attitudes toward hospice care. *New York Times.* Retrieved September 10, 2015, from http://www.nytimes.com/2015/08/25/health /a-racial-gap-in-attitudes-toward-hospice-care.html?_r=0

Veatch, R. M. (1975). The whole-brain-oriented concept of death: An outmoded philosophical formulation. *Journal of Thanatology, 3*(1), 13–30.

Veatch, R. M. (1989). *Death, dying, and the biological revolution: Our last quest for responsibility* (rev. ed.). New Haven, CT: Yale University Press.

Veatch, R. M., & Ross, L. F. (2015). *Transplantation ethics* (2nd ed.). Washington, DC: Georgetown University Press.

Veerman, D., & Barton, B. B. (2006). *When your father dies: How a man deals with the loss of his father.* Nashville: Thomas Nelson.

Veninga, R. (1985). *A gift of hope: How we survive our trage-dies.* New York: Ballantine Books.

Vernick, J., & Karon, M. (1965). Who's afraid of death on a leukemia ward? *American Journal of Diseases of Children, 109,* 393–397. doi:10.1001/archpedi.1965.02090020395003

Viorst, J. (1986). *Necessary losses.* New York: Simon & Schuster.

Volandes, A. (2016). *The conversation: A revolutionary plan for end-of-life care.* New York: Bloomsbury USA.

Volavková, H. (Ed.). (1993). *I never saw another butterfly: Children's drawings and poems from Terezín concentration camp, 1942–1944* (2nd ed.). New York: Schocken.

Volkan, V. (1970). Typical findings in pathological grief. *Psychiatric Quarterly, 44,* 231–250. doi:10.1007/BF01562971

Voyich, J. M., Braughton, K. R., Sturdevant, D. E., et al. (2005). Insights into mechanisms used by *Staphylococcus aureus* to avoid destruction by human neutrophils. *The Journal of Immunology, 175*(6), 3907–3919. doi:10.4049/ jimmunol.175.6.3907

Wachterman, M. W., Marcantonio, E. R., Davis, R. B., & McCarthy, E. P. (2011). Association of hospice agency profit status with patient diagnosis, location of care, and length of stay. *Journal of the American Medical Association, 305,* 472–479. doi:10.1001/jama.2011.70

Waechter, E. H. (1971). Children's awareness of fatal illness. *American Journal of Nursing, 71,* 1168–1172.

Waechter, E. H. (1984). Dying children: Patterns of coping. In H. Wass & C. A. Corr (Eds.), *Childhood and death* (pp. 51–68). Washington, DC: Hemisphere.

Wagner, S. (1994). *The Andrew poems.* Lubbock: Texas Tech University Press.

Walker, A. C. (2008). Grieving in the Muscogee Creek tribe. *Death Studies, 32*, 123–141. doi:10.1080/07481180701801238

Walker, A. C., & Balk, D. E. (2007). Bereavement rituals in the Muscogee Creek tribe. *Death Studies, 31*, 633–652. doi:10.1080/07481180701405188

Walker, A. C., & Thompson, R. (2009). Muscogee Creek spirituality and meaning of death. *Omega, Journal of Death and Dying, 59*, 129–146. doi:10.2190/OM.59.2.c

Walker, J. S. (2004). *Three Mile Island: A nuclear crisis in historical perspective*. Berkeley: University of California Press.

Wall, P. (2002). *Pain: The science of suffering*. New York: Columbia University Press.

Wall, P. D., & Melzack, R. (Eds.). (1994). *Textbook of pain* (3rd ed.). New York: Churchill Livingstone.

Wallace, S. E. (1973). *After suicide*. New York: Wiley-Interscience.

Wallis, C. L. (1954). *Stories on stone: A book of American epitaphs*. New York: Oxford University Press.

Wallis, V. (2004). *Two old women: An Alaska legend of betrayal, courage and survival*. New York: Perennial/HarperCollins.

Walsh, F., & McGoldrick, M. (1988). Loss and the family life cycle. In C. J. Falicov (Ed.), *Family transitions: Continuity and change over the life cycle* (pp. 311–336). New York: Guilford.

Walsh, F., & McGoldrick, M. (2004b). Loss and the family: A systemic perspective. In F. Walsh & M. McGoldrick (Eds.), *Living beyond loss: Death in the family* (2nd ed., pp. 3–26). New York: Norton.

Walsh, F., & McGoldrick, M. (Eds.). (2004a). *Living beyond loss: Death in the family* (2nd ed.). New York: Norton.

Walsh, K. (2012). *Grief and loss: Theories and skills for the helping professions* (2nd ed.). Upper Saddle River, NJ: Pearson.

Walter, C. A. (2003). *The loss of a life partner: Narratives of the bereaved*. New York: Columbia University Press.

Walter, J. K., Rosenberg, A. R., & Feudtner, C. (2013). Tackling taboo topics: How to have effective advanced care planning discussions with adolescents and young adults with cancer. *JAMA Pediatrics, 167*(5), 489–490. doi:10.1001/jamapediatrics.2013.1323

Walter, T. (1999). *On bereavement: The culture of grief*. Buckingham, England: Open University Press.

Walton, D. N. (1979). *On defining death: An analytic study of the concept of death in philosophy and medical ethics*. Montreal, Quebec, Canada: McGill-Queen's University Press.

Walton, D. N. (1982). Neocortical versus wholebrain conceptions of personal death. *Omega, Journal of Death and Dying, 12*, 339–344. doi:10.2190/67M2-WFGY-9L9H-5RKK

Wanzer, S., & Glenmullen, J. (2007). *To die well: Your right to comfort, calm, and choice in the last days of life*. Philadelphia: Da Capo Press.

Ware, B. (2012). *The top five regrets of the dying: A life transformed by the dearly departing*. Carlsbad, CA: Hay House.

Warraich, H. (2017). *Modern death: How medicine changed the end of life*. New York: St. Martin's.

Warrick, J. (2015). *Black flags: The rise of ISIS*. New York: Doubleday.

Washington, H. A. (2006). *Medical apartheid: The dark history of medical experimentation on Black Americans from colonial times to the present*. New York: Doubleday.

Wass, H. (1984). Concepts of death: A developmental perspective. In H. Wass & C. A. Corr (Eds.), *Childhood and death* (pp. 3–24). Washington, DC: Hemisphere.

Wass, H. (2003). Children and media violence. In R. Kastenbaum (Ed.), *Macmillan encyclopedia of death and dying* (Vol. 1, pp. 133–139). New York: Macmillan.

Wass, H. (2004). A perspective on the current state of death education. *Death Studies, 28*, 289–308. doi:10.1080/07481180490432315

Wass, H., & Cason, L. (1984). Fears and anxieties about death. In H. Wass & C. A. Corr (Eds.), *Childhood and death* (pp. 25–45). Washington, DC: Hemisphere.

Wass, H., & Corr, C. A. (Eds.). (1984). *Childhood and death*. Washington, DC: Hemisphere.

Wasserman, H., & Danforth, H. E. (1988). *The human bond: Support groups and mutual aid*. New York: Springer.

Waters, C. M. (2001). Understanding and supporting African Americans' perspectives of end-of-life care planning and decision making. *Qualitative Health Research, 11*, 385–398. doi:10.1177/104973201129119172

Watson, M., Lucas, C., Hoy, A., & Wells, J. (2009). *The Oxford handbook of palliative care* (2nd ed.). New York: Oxford University Press.

Waugh, E. (1948). *The loved one*. Boston: Little, Brown.

Weaver, J. C. (2014). *Sorrows of a century: Interpreting suicide in New Zealand, 1900–2000*. Montreal, Canada: McGill-Queen's University Press.

Weaver, R. R., & Rivello, R. (2007). The distribution of mortality in the United States: The effects of income (inequality), social capital, and race. *Omega, Journal of Death and Dying, 54*, 19–39. doi:10.2190/C772-U444-8J65-2503

Weaver-Zercher, D. L. (2001). *The Amish in the American imagination*. Baltimore: Johns Hopkins University Press.

Webb, M. (1997). *The good death: The new American search to reshape the end of life*. New York: Bantam.

Webb, N. B. (Ed.). (2004). *Mass trauma and violence: Helping families and children cope*. New York: Guilford.

Webb, N. B. (Ed.). (2010). *Helping bereaved children: A handbook for practitioners* (3rd ed.). New York: Guilford.

Webb, N. B. (Ed.). (2015). *Play therapy with children in crisis: Individual, group, and family treatment* (4th ed.). New York: Guilford.

Weeks, O. D. (2001). Ritualistic downsizing and the need for aftercare. In O. D. Weeks & C. Johnson (Eds.), *When all the friends have gone: A guide for aftercare providers* (pp. 187–197). Amityville, NY: Baywood.

Weeks, O. D., & Johnson, C. (Eds.). (2001). *When all the friends have gone: A guide for aftercare providers*. New York: Routledge.

Wehr, J. (2015). *Peaceful passages: A hospice nurse's stories of dying well*. Wheaton, IL: Quest Books.

Wehrle, P. F., & Top, F. H. (1981). *Communicable and infectious diseases* (9th ed.). St. Louis, MO: Mosby.

Weir, R. F. (Ed.). (1980). *Death in literature*. New York: Columbia University Press.

Weir, R. F. (Ed.). (1997). *Physician-assisted suicide*. Bloomington: Indiana University Press.

Weisman, A. D. (1972). *On dying and denying: A psychiatric study of terminality*. New York: Behavioral Publications.

Weisman, A. D. (1977). The psychiatrist and the inexorable. In H. Feifel (Ed.), *New meanings of death* (pp. 107–122). New York: McGraw-Hill.

Weisman, A. D. (1984). *The coping capacity: On the nature of being mortal*. New York: Human Sciences Press.

Weizman, S. G. (2005). *About mourning: Support and guidance for the bereaved*. Beachwood, OH: Sunrise Publications.

Welch, F. S., Winters, R., & Ross, K. (Eds.). (2009). *Tea with Elisabeth: Tributes to hospice pioneer Dr. Elisabeth Kübler-Ross*. Naples, FL: Quality of Life Publishing.

Welch, K. J., & Bergen, M. B. (2000). Adolescent parent mourning reactions associated with stillbirth or neonatal death. *Omega, Journal of Death and Dying, 40*, 435–451. doi:10.2190/C4EJ-H1WR-75Q5-VTM8

Weller, E. B., Weller, R. A., Fristad, M. A., Cain, S. E., & Bowes, J. M. (1988). Should children attend their parent's funeral? *Journal of the American Academy of Child and Adolescent Psychiatry, 27,* 559–562. doi:10.1097/00004583-198809000-00007

Wender, P., Ketu, S., Rosenthal, D., Schulsinger, F., et al. (1986). Psychiatric disorders in the biological and adoptive families of adopted individuals with affective disorders. *Archives of General Psychiatry, 43,* 923–929. doi:10.1001/archpsyc.1986.01800100013003

Wendler, D., & Dickert, N. (2001). The consent process for cadaveric organ procurement: How does it work? How can it be improved? *Journal of the American Medical Association, 285,* 329–333. doi:10.1001/jama.285.3.329

Wentworth, H., & Flexner, S. B. (Eds.). (1967). *Dictionary of American slang* (with supplement). New York: Crowell.

Werth, J. L. (1996). *Rational suicide: Implications for mental health professionals.* Washington, DC: Taylor & Francis.

Werth, J. L. (1999a). The role of the mental health professional in helping significant others of persons who are assisted in death. *Death Studies, 23,* 239–255. doi:10.1080/074811899201064

Werth, J. L. (Ed.). (1999b). *Contemporary perspectives on rational suicide.* Philadelphia: Taylor & Francis.

Werth, J. L. (2001). Using the Youk-Kevorkian case to teach about euthanasia and other end-of-life issues. *Death Studies, 25,* 151–177.

Werth, J. L. (Ed.). (2006). Implications of the Theresa Schiavo case and end-of-life decisions [Special issue]. *Death Studies, 30*(2).

Werth, J. L., & Blevins, D. (Eds.). (2006). *Psychosocial issues near the end of life: A resource for professional care providers.* Washington, DC: American Psychological Association.

Werth, J. L., & Blevins, D. (Eds.). (2009). *Decision making near the end of life: Issues, developments, and future directions.* New York: Routledge.

Werth, J. L., & Wineberg, H. (2005). A critical analysis of criticisms of the Oregon Death with Dignity Act. *Death Studies, 29,* 1–27. doi:10.1080/07481180590519660

Weseen, M. H. (1934). *A dictionary of American slang.* New York: Crowell.

West, S. (2004). Culturally appropriate end-of-life care for the Black American. *Home Healthcare Nurse Journal, 22*(3), 164–168.

Westberg, G. E. (2010). *Good grief: 50th anniversary edition.* Minneapolis, MN: Augsburg Fortress.

Westefeld, J. S., Button, C., Haley, J. T., et al. (2006). College student suicide: A call to action. *Death Studies, 30,* 931–956. doi:10.1080/07481180600887130

Westerhoff, J. H. (1978). *McGuffey and his readers: Piety, morality, and education in nineteenth-century America.* Nashville, TN: Abingdon.

Wheeler, J. L. (2010). *Weird is normal when teenagers grieve.* Naples, FL: Quality of Life Publishing Co.

Wheeler, M. S., & Cheung, A. H. S. (1996). Minority attitudes toward organ donation. *Critical Care Nurse, 16,* 30–35.

Whipple, V. (2014). *Lesbian widows: Invisible grief.* New York: Routledge.

White, B. (2010). *Here we go again: My life in television.* New York: Scribner.

White, B. (2011). *If you ask me: (And of course you won't).* New York: Putnam.

White, P. G. (2006). *Sibling grief: Healing after the death of a sister or brother.* Lincoln, NE: iUniverse.

White, R., & Cuningham, A. M. (1991). *Ryan White: My own story.* New York: Dial Press.

White, R. B., & Engelhardt, H. T. (1975). A demand to die. *Hastings Center Report, 5*(3), 9–10, 47. doi:10.2307/3561115

Whitfield, J. M., Siegel, R. E., Glicken, A. D., et al. (1982). The application of hospice concepts to neonatal care. *American Journal of Diseases of Children, 136,* 421–424. doi:10.1001/archpedi.1982.03970410039009

Wiener, L. S., Best, A., & Pizzo, P. A. (Comps.). (1994). *Be a friend: Children who live with HIV speak.* Morton Grove, IL: Albert Whitman.

Wiesel, E. (1960). *Night* (S. Rodway, Trans.). New York: Avon.

Wilcoxon, S. A. (1987). Grandparents and grandchildren: An often neglected relationship between significant others. *Journal of Counseling and Development, 65,* 289–290. 10.1002/j.1556-6676.1987.tb01287.x

Wilhelm, H. (1985). *I'll always love you.* New York: Crown.

Wilkes, E. et al. (1980). *Report of the working group on terminal care of the standing subcommittee on cancer.* London: Her Majesty's Stationary Office.

Wilkes, E., Crowther, A. G. O., & Greaves, C. W. K. H. (1978). A different kind of day hospital—For patients with preterminal cancer and chronic disease. *British Medical Journal, 2,* 1053–1056. doi:10.1136/bmj.2.6144.1053

Willans, J. H. (1980). Nutrition: Appetite in the terminally ill patient. *Nursing Times, 76,* 875–876.

Williams, A. L. & Merten, M. J. (2009). Adolescents' online social networking following the death of a peer. *Journal of Adolescent Research, 24,* 67–90. doi:10.1177/0743558408328440

Willinger, M. (1995). Sleep position and sudden infant death syndrome [Editorial]. *Journal of the American Medical Association, 273,* 818–819. doi:10.1001/jama.1995.03520340074040

Willinger, M., James, L. S., & Catz, D. (1991). Defining the sudden infant death syndrome (SIDS): Deliberations of an expert panel convened by the National Institute of Child Health and Human Development. *Pediatric Pathology, 11,* 677–684.

Wilson, C. (2012, July 21). I put my brake on and blew the horn, but obviously there was nothing I could do –. *The Herald.* Retrieved March 17, 2017, from http://www.heraldscotland.com/news/13066260._I_put_my_brake_on_and_blew_the_horn__but_obviously_there_was_nothing_I_could_do___/

Wink, P., & Scott, J. (2005). Does religiousness buffer against the fear of death and dying in late adulthood? Findings from a longitudinal study. *The Journals of Gerontology, Series B, 60,* 207–214. doi:10.1093/geronb/60.4.P207

Winston, C., Leshner, P., Kramer, J., & Allen, G. (2005). Overcoming barriers to access and utilization of hospice and palliative care services in African American communities. *Omega, Journal of Death and Dying, 50*(2), 151–163. doi:10.2190/QQKG-EPFA-A2FN-GHVL

Wojtkowiak, J., Wild, V., & Egger, J. (2012). Grief experiences and expectance of suicide. *Suicide and Life-Threatening Behavior, 42*(1), 56–66. doi:10.1111/j.1943-278X.2011.00070.x

Wolf, S. M., Berlinger, N., & Jennings, B. (2015). Forty years of work on end-of-life care: From patients' rights to systemic reform. *New England Journal of Medicine, 372,* 678–682. doi:10.1056/NEJMms1410321

Wolfe, J., Hinds, P., & Sourkes, B. (Eds.). (2011). *Textbook of interdisciplinary pediatric palliative care.* Philadelphia: Saunders.

Wolfe, J., Klar, N., Grier, H. E., et al. (2000). Understanding of prognosis among parents of children who died of cancer: Impact on treatment goals and integration of palliative care. *Journal of the American Medical Association, 284,* 2469–2475. doi:10.1001/jama.284.19.2469

Wolfe, N. (2011). *The viral storm: The dawn of a new pandemic age.* New York: Times Books.

Wolfe, T. (1940). *You can't go home again.* New York: Harper & Brothers.

Wolfelt, A. (2004). *The understanding your grief support group guide: Starting and leading a bereavement support group.* Fort Collins, CO: Companion Press.

Wolfelt, A. (2005). *Companioning the bereaved: A soulful guide for counselors and caregivers.* Fort Collins, CO: Companion Press.

Wolfelt, A., & Yoder, G. (2005). *Companioning the dying: A soulful guide for counselors and caregivers.* Fort Collins, CO: Companion Press.

Wolfenstein, M. (1966). How is mourning possible? *Psychoanalytic Study of the Child, 21,* 93–123.

Woodson, J. (2000). *Sweet, sweet memory.* New York: Hyperion Books for Children.

Wooten-Green, R. (2001). *When the dying speak: How to listen to and learn from those facing death.* Chicago: Loyola Press.

Worchel, D., & Gearing, R. E. (2010). *Suicide assessment and treatment: Empirical and evidence-based practices.* New York: Springer.

Worden, J. W. (1982). *Grief counseling and grief therapy: A handbook for the mental health practitioner.* New York: Springer.

Worden, J. W. (1996). *Children and grief: When a parent dies.* New York: Guilford.

Worden, J. W. (2009). *Grief counseling and grief therapy: A handbook for the mental health practitioner* (4th ed.). New York: Springer.

World Health Organization. (1998). *Definition of palliative care for children.* Geneva, Switzerland: Author. Retrieved July 17, 2016, from http://www.who.int/cancer/palliative/definition/en/

World Health Organization. (2002). *Definition of palliative care for adults.* Geneva, Switzerland: Author. Retrieved July 17, 2016, from http://www.who.int/cancer/palliative/definition/en/

World Health Organization. (2014). *Global status report on violence prevention 2014.* Geneva, Switzerland: Author.

World Health Organization. (2015). *Trends in maternal mortality: 1990 to 2015: estimates by WHO, UNICEF, UNFPA, World Bank Group and the United Nations Population Division.* Geneva, Switzerland: Author. Retrieved July 2, 2016, from http://www.unfpa.org/sites/default/files/pub-pdf/Trends_in_Maternal_Mortality_1990-2015_eng.pdf

Worldwide Palliative Care Alliance. (2014). *Global atlas of palliative care at the end of life.* London: Author.

Worldwide Palliative Care Alliance. (2015). *Palliative care and the global goal for health.* London: Author.

Worobey, M., Watts, T. D., McKay, R. A., et al. (2016). 1970s and 'Patient 0' HIV-1. doi:10.1038/nature19827

Worswick, J. (2000). *A house called Helen: The development of hospice care for children* (2nd ed.). New York: Oxford University Press.

Wortman, C. B., & Silver, R. C. (1989). The myth of coping with loss. *Journal of Clinical Consulting Psychology, 57,* 349–357.

Wortman, C. B., & Silver, R. C. (2001). The myths of coping with loss revisited. In M. S. Stroebe, R. O. Hansson, W. Stroebe, & H. Schut (Eds.), *Handbook of bereavement research: Consequences, coping, and care* (pp. 405–429). Washington, DC: American Psychological Association.

Wray, T. J. (2003). *Surviving the death of a sibling: Living through grief when an adult brother or sister dies.* New York: Three Rivers Press.

Wright, A. A., Keating, N. L., Ayanian, J. Z., et al. (2016). Family perspectives on aggressive cancer care near the end of life. *Journal of the American Medical Association, 315,* 284–292. doi:10.1001/jama.2015.18604.

Wright, L. (2006). *The looming tower: Al-Qaeda and the road to 9/11.* New York: Knopf.

Wright, R. H., & Hughes, W. B. (1996). *Lay down body: Living history in African-American cemeteries.* Detroit: Visible Ink Press.

Wright, R. H., Mindel, C. H., Tran, T. V., & Habenstein, R. W. (2012). *Ethnic families in America: Patterns and variations* (5th ed.). Upper Saddle River, NJ: Pearson.

Wrobel, T. A., & Dye, A. L. (2003). Grieving pet death: Normative, gender, and attachment issues. *Omega, Journal of Death and Dying, 47,* 385–393. doi:10.2190/QYV5-LLJ1-T043-U0F9

Wyatt, K. M. (2011). *What really matters: 7 lessons for living from the stories of the dying.* New York: Selectbooks.

Wyler, J. (1989). Grieving alone: A single mother's loss. *Issues in Comprehensive Pediatric Nursing, 12,* 299–302. doi:10.3109/01460868909026837

Xu, J. Q., Murphy, S. L., Kochanek, K. D., & Bastian, B. A. (2016). Deaths: Final data for 2013. *National Vital Statistics Reports, 64*(2). Hyattsville, MD: National Center for Health Statistics.

Yalom, M. (2008). *The American resting place: 400 years of history through our cemeteries and burial grounds.* New York: Houghton Mifflin Harcourt.

Yancu, C., Farmer, D., & Leahman, D. (2010). Barriers to hospice use and palliative care service use by African American adults. *American Journal of Hospice and Palliative Medicine, 27,* 248–253. doi:10.1177/1049909109349942

Yang, Y. T., & Silverman, R. D. (2015). Social distancing and the unvaccinated. *New England Journal of Medicine, 372,* 1481–1483. doi:10.1056/NEJMp1501198

Yennurajalingam, S., & Bruera, E. (Eds.). (2016). *Oxford American handbook of hospice and palliative medicine and supportive care* (2nd ed.). New York: Oxford University Press.

Yeung, W. (1995). Buddhism, death, and dying. In J. K. Parry & A. S. Ryan (Eds.), *A cross-cultural look at death, dying, and religion* (pp. 74–83). Chicago: Nelson-Hall.

Yoder, H. (2007). *The happening: Nickel Mines school tragedy.* Berlin, OH: TGS International.

You, J. J., Downar, J., Fowler, R. A., et al. (2015). Barriers to goals of care discussions with seriously ill hospitalized patients and their families: A multicenter survey of clinicians. *JAMA Internal Medicine, 175*(4), 549–556. doi:10.1001/jamainternmed.2014.7732

You, J. J., Fowler, R. A., & Heyland, D. K., on behalf of the Canadian Researchers at the End of Life Network. (CARENET). (2014). Just ask: Discussing goals of care with patients in hospital with serious illness. *Canadian Medical Association Journal, 186,* 425–432. doi:10.1503/cmaj.121274

Youngner, S. J., Anderson, M. W., & Schapiro, R. (Eds.). (2003). *Transplanting human tissue: Ethics, policy, and practice.* New York: Oxford University Press.

Yufit, R. I., & Lester, D. (Eds.). (2005). *Assessment, treatment and prevention of suicidal behavior.* Hoboken, NJ: John Wiley & Sons.

Zaheer, K. (2007, January 8). Future flu pandemic could be "very scary." U. S. Reuters Health Information. Retrieved from http://www.nlm.nih.gov/medlineplus/news/fullstory_43531.html

Zamperetti, N., Bellomo, R., & Ronco, C. (2003). Defining death in non-heart beating organ donors. *Journal of Medical Ethics, 29*(3), 182–185. doi:10.1136/jme.29.3.182

Zeitlin, S. J., & Harlow, I. B. (2001). *Giving a voice to sorrow: Personal responses to death and mourning*. New York: Perigee (Penguin).

Zerwekh, J. V. (1983). The dehydration question. *Nursing 83, 13*, 47–51.

Zerwekh, J. V. (1994). The truth-tellers: How hospice nurses help patients confront death. *American Journal of Nursing, 94*, 31–34.

Zhang, B., Wright, A. A., Haiden, A., et al. (2009). Health care costs in the last week of life: associations with end-of-life conversations. *Archives of Internal Medicine, 169*(5), 480–488. doi:10.1001/archinternmed.2008.587

Zhavoronkov, A., & Bhullar, B. (2015). Classifying aging as a disease in the context of ICD-11. *Frontiers in Genetics, 6*, 326. Published online Nov 4; Retrieve September 27, 2016, from. doi:10.3389/fgene.2015.00326

Zielinski, J. M. (1997). *The Amish across America* (4th ed.). Kalona, IA: Amish Heritage Publications.

Zimmerman, J. (2005). *From the heart of a bear: True stories of the faith and courage of children facing life-threatening illness*. Des Moines, IA: Lazarus Publishing.

Zimmermann, C., Swami, N., Krzyzanowska, M., et al. (2014). Early palliative care for patients with advanced cancer: A cluster-randomised controlled trial. *The Lancet*. Early Online Publication, 19 February 2014. doi:10.1016/S0140-6736(13)62416-2

Zinner, E. S. (Ed.). (1985). *Coping with death on campus*. San Francisco: Jossey-Bass.

Zinner, E. S., & Williams, M. B. (1999). *When a community weeps: Case studies in group survivorship*. Philadelphia: Brunner/Mazel.

Zisook, S., & DeVaul, R. A. (1983). Grief, unresolved grief, and depression. *Psychosomatics, 24*, 247–256. doi:10.1016/S0033-3182(83)73227-5

Zitter, J. N. (2017). *Extreme measures: Finding a better path to the end of life*. New York: Avery.

Zucker, R. (2009). *The journey through grief and loss: Helping yourself and your child when grief is shared*. New York: St, Martins.

Name Index

AAP. *See* American Academy of Pediatrics
Aaron, J., 345
AARP (formerly American Association of
    Retired Persons), 168, 255, 282, 432, 441
Abernathy, C. B., 498
Abernethy, A. P., 204
Abdel-Khalek, A., 52
Abdulmutallab, U. F., 80
Abdulazeez, M. Y., 80
Abrahamson, H., 128
Abrahm, J. L., 179
Abrams, R., 406
Abts, H. W., 477
Accomando, B., 3
Acheson, A., 581
Achilles, 550, 551
Achté, K., 337
Ad Hoc Committee of the Harvard Medical
    School to Examine the Definition of
    Brain Death, 456
Adams, C. A., 280
Adams, D. W., 340, 356
Adams, G., 6, 236
Adams, J. R., 548
Aderman, D., 140
Adkins, J., 520
Adkins, T., 360, 372
Adler, B., 331
Adlerstein, A. M., 338, 373
Administration on Aging, U.S. Department of
    Health and Human Services, 422, 438,
    443, 587. *See also* U.S. Department of
    Health and Human Services
Adolph, R., 363
Agee, J., 346
Aging Parents and Elder Care (organization/
    website), 441
Aging with Dignity (organization), 453, 483
Ahluwalia, J. S., 114
Ahmedzai., S., 430
Ahronheim, J., 151
Aisenberg, R., 335
Ajemian, I., 196
Akner, L. F., 416, 419
al-Bashir, O., 82
Albert, P. L., 467, 474
Albert, M. S., 569
Albert, Prince, 235
Albert, T., 580
Albom, M., 136
Alcántara, C., 120
Alderman, E., 450, 481, 523
Aldrich, R., 499
Aldridge, M. D., 168
Aldridge Carlson, M. D., 200

Alexander, E., 562
Alexander, I. E., 338, 373
Ali, M., 552
Ali, N., 599
Alici, Y., 207
Allah, 538, 552
Allen, A., 39
Allen, B. G., 502
Allison, G., 87, 96
Allport, G., 17
Allumbaugh, D. L., 274
Alperovitz, G., 86
Al-Qaeda, 73
Alman, L. J., 580
Alvarez, A., 486, 487, 488
Alzheimer, A., 568c
Alzheimer's Association, 567, 568, 569, 570,
    571, 572, 573–575, 578, 580, 584, 586,
    587, 590, 599, 600
Alzheimer's Disease Education and Referral
    Center (ADEAR), 578, 600. *See also*
    National Institute on Aging
Alzheimer's Disease International, 572,
    587, 600
Alzheimer's Foundation of America, 578, 600
Amenta, M., 159
American Academy of Hospice and Palliative
    Medicine, 209
American Academy of Pediatrics (AAP),
    93, 201, 326–327, 339, 351,
    352, 358
American Anthropological Association, 64
American Association of Homes and Services
    for the Aging, 209. *See* Leading Age
American Association of Retired Persons. *See*
    AARP
American Association of Suicidology, 309, 489,
    502, 505, 506, 513
American Bar Association, 452, 475, 482
American Counseling Association, 282
American Cryonics Society, 317, 562
American Foundation for Suicide Prevention,
    391, 513
American Health Care Association, 209
American Hospice Foundation, 209
American Hospital Association, 209
American Press Institute, 94
American Psychiatric Association, 248, 567
American Psychological Association (APA),
    64, 152
American Public Health Association, 527
American School Counselors Association,
    358, 392
American Society for Bioethics and Humanities
    (ASBH), 545

American Society of Law, Medicine, and Ethics
    (ASLME), 483, 545
American Sociological Association, 64
Americans for Better Care of the Dying, 180
Amitabha Buddha. *See* Buddha
Ammann, J., 46
Anderson, K. N., 357
Anderson, M. L., 101
Anderson, M. W., 461, 482
Anderson, R., 243
Andrews, M. M., 126
Andriessen, K., 270, 281
Anestis, J. C., 507–508
Anestis, M. D., 507–508
Angel, M. D., 416
Angell, M., 531, 532, 533
Angst, D. B., 340
Annas, G. J., 171, 450, 523, 529
Annenberg Washington Program, 432
Anonymous, 8, 158, 531, 532, 566, 590–593
Anthony, S., 329
Antigone, 296
Applegate, B. 154, 155
Applegate, S., 154, 155
Arbit, J., 381
Archibald, L., 502, 512
Area Agencies on Aging, 587
Ariès, P., 58–59, 60, 190, 323, 360
Aristotle, 454
Arjuna, 554
Arkin, W., 86, 97
Armstrong-Dailey, A., 208, 351
Arnett, J., 361, 390
Arruda-Colli, M. N. F., 346
Artful Ashes, 291
Arvio, R. P., 299
Ashenburg, K., 286, 315
Associated Press, 265, 567
Association for Clinical Pastoral Education,
    180, 282, 562
Association for Death Education and
    Counseling (ADEC), 16
Association for Pet Loss and Bereavement, 265,
    282, 309
Association for Professional Chaplains, 180,
    282, 562
Association for the Care of Children's Health, 358
Association of Asian Pacific Community Health
    Organizations, 128
Association of Holocaust Organizations, 97
Atkinson, R., 361
Attaran, A., 541
Attig, T., 5, 16, 235, 241–242, 248, 254, 280,
    340
Atwater, P. M. H., 557, 562

Subject Index